Autodesk 3ds Max 2012: A Comprehensive Guide

CADCIM Technologies
525 St. Andrews Drive
Schererville, IN 46375
USA
(www.cadcim.com)

Contributing Author
Sham Tickoo
Professor
Purdue University Calumet
Hammond, Indiana, USA

CADCIM Technologies

Autodesk 3ds Max 2012: A Comprehensive Guide
Sham Tickoo

Published by CADCIM Technologies, 525 St Andrews Drive, Schererville, IN 46375 USA.

ISBN: 978-1-936646-01-2

www.cadcim.com

DEDICATION

To teachers, who make it possible to disseminate knowledge
to enlighten the young and curious minds
of our future generations

To students, who are dedicated to learning new technologies
and making the world a better place to live in

THANKS

To the faculty and students of the MET department of
Purdue University Calumet for their cooperation

To employees of CADCIM Technologies for their valuable help

Online Training Program Offered by CADCIM Technologies

CADCIM Technologies provides effective and affordable virtual online training on various software packages including Computer Aided Design and Manufacturing (CAD/CAM), computer programming languages, animation, architecture, and GIS. The training is delivered 'live' via Internet at any time, any place, and at any pace to individuals, students of colleges, universities, and CAD/CAM training centers. The main features of this program are:

Training for Students and Companies in a Class Room Setting

Highly experienced instructors and qualified Engineers at CADCIM Technologies conduct the classes under the guidance of Prof. Sham Tickoo of Purdue University Calumet, USA. This team has authored several textbooks that are rated "one of the best" in their categories and are used in various colleges, universities, and training centers in North America, Europe, and in other parts of the world.

Training for Individuals

The cost effective and time saving initiative of CADCIM Technologies strives to deliver the training in the comfort of your home or work place, thereby relieving you from the hassles of traveling to training centers.

Training Offered on Software Packages

We provide basic and advanced training on the following software packages:

***CAD/CAM/CAE**: CATIA, Pro/ENGINEER Wildfire, SolidWorks, Autodesk Inventor, Solid Edge, NX, AutoCAD, AutoCAD LT, Customizing AutoCAD, EdgeCAM, ANSYS*

***Computer Programming**: C++, VB.NET, Oracle, AJAX, and Java*

***Animation and Styling**: Autodesk 3ds Max, Autodesk 3ds Max Design, Autodesk Maya, and Autodesk Alias Design*

***Architecture, Civil, and GIS**: Autodesk Revit Architecture, Autodesk Revit Structure, AutoCAD Civil 3D, and AutoCAD Map 3D*

For more information, please visit the following link:

http://www.cadcim.com

Note

The free teaching and learning resources, mentioned in the cover page of this textbook, are available only for those who buy the textbook from our website **www.cadcim.com** or the university/college bookstores. We need proof of purchase when you request the technical support from us.

Table of Contents

Chapter 3: Extended Primitives

Chapter 5: Splines and Extended Splines

Chapter 6: Modifying 3D Mesh Objects

Chapter 7: Modifying Splines

Chapter 8: Materials and Maps

Chapter 9: Compound Objects

Chapter 10: Modifiers

Chapter 11: Lights and Cameras

Chapter 12: Animation Basics

Chapter 16: NURBS Modeling

Chapter 17: Rigid Body Dynamics and Helpers

Chapter 18: Graphite Modeling Technique

Preface

Autodesk 3ds Max 2012

Autodesk 3ds Max has been developed by Autodesk Inc. and it provides powerful tools for 3d modeling, animation, rendering, dynamics, and compositing that enables game developers, visual effects artists, architects, designers, engineers, and visualization specialists to create stunning artwork. Additionally, the intuitive user interface and workflow tools of 3ds Max 2012 have made the job of design visualization specialists easier.

Autodesk 3ds Max 2012: A Comprehensive Guide is a comprehensive textbook that aims at harnessing the power of Autodesk 3ds Max for modelers, animators, and designers. The textbook caters to the needs of both the novice and the advanced users of 3ds Max. Keeping in view the varied requirements of the users, the textbook first introduces the basic features of 3ds Max 2012 and then gradually progresses to cover the advanced 3D models and animations. Written with the tutorial point-of-view and the learn-by-doing theme, the textbook is ideally suited for learning at your convenience and at your pace.

This book will help you unleash your creativity, thus helping you create stunning 3D models and animations. The textbook will help the learners transform their imagination into reality with ease. Also, it takes the users across a wide spectrum of animations through progressive examples, comprehensive illustrations, and ample exercises.

The main features of this textbook are as follows:

- **Tutorial Approach**
  The author has adopted the tutorial point-of-view and the learn-by-doing theme throughout the textbook. About 35 real-world 3D animation and 3D modeling projects have been used as tutorials in the textbook. This enables the readers to relate these tutorials to the real-world models. In addition, there are about 50 exercises based on the real-world projects.

- **Tips and Notes**
  Additional information related to various topics is provided to the users in the form of tips and notes.

- **Learning Objectives**
  The first page of every chapter summarizes the topics that will be covered in that chapter. This will help the users to easily refer to a topic.

- **Tools Section**
  Each new topic begins with the tools section that provides a brief information of the 3ds Max tools.

- **Self-Evaluation Test, Review Questions, and Exercises**
  Every chapter ends with a Self-Evaluation test so that the users can assess their knowledge of the chapter. The answers to the Self-Evaluation Test are given at the end of the chapter. Also, the Review Questions and Exercises are given at the end of each chapter and they can be used by the Instructors as test questions and exercises.

- **Heavily Illustrated Text**
  The text in this book is heavily illustrated with about 1500 diagrams and screen captures.

Symbols Used in the Text

The author has provided additional information to the users about the topic being discussed in the form of notes.

Special information and techniques are provided in the form of tips that helps in increasing the efficiency of the users.

This symbol indicates that the command or tool being discussed is new.

This symbol indicates that the command or tool being discussed has been enhanced in Autodesk 3ds Max 2012.

Free Companion Website

It has been our constant endeavor to provide you the best textbooks and services at affordable price. In this endeavor, we have come out with a Free Companion Website that will facilitate the process of teaching and learning of Autodesk 3ds Max 2012. If you purchase this textbook from our website (***www.cadcimtech.com***), you will get access to the files on the Companion website.

To access the files, you need to register by visiting the **Resources** section at *www.cadcim.com.* The following resources are available for the faculty and students in this website:

Faculty Resources

- **Technical Support**
  You can get online technical support by contacting *techsupport@cadcim.com.*

- **Instructor Guide**
  Solutions to all review questions and exercises in the textbook are provided to help the faculty members test the skills of the students.

- **PowerPoint Presentations**
  The contents of the book are arranged in PowerPoint slides that can be used by the faculty for their lectures.

- **Part Files**
  The part files used in illustration, tutorials, and exercises are available for free download.

- **Rendered Images**
  If you do an exercise or tutorial, you can compare your rendered output with the one provided in the CADCIM website.

Student Resources

- **Technical Support**
  You can get online technical support by contacting *techsupport@cadcim.com.*

- **Part Files**
  The part files used in illustrations and tutorials are available for free download.

- **Rendered Images**
  If you do an exercise or tutorial, you can compare your rendered output with the one provided in the CADCIM website.

If you face any problem in accessing these files, please contact the publisher at *sales@cadcim.com* or the author at *stickoo@purduecal.edu* or *tickoo525@gmail.com.*

1

Introduction to Autodesk 3ds Max 2012

Learning Objectives

After completing this chapter, you will be able to:

- *Understand the project workflow in Autodesk 3ds Max*
- *Start a new project in Autodesk 3ds Max*
- *Understand the Autodesk 3ds Max screen components*
- *Use controls for creating or modifying the objects*
- *Use hotkeys in Autodesk 3ds Max*
- *Customize hotkeys*
- *Customize the colors of elements*

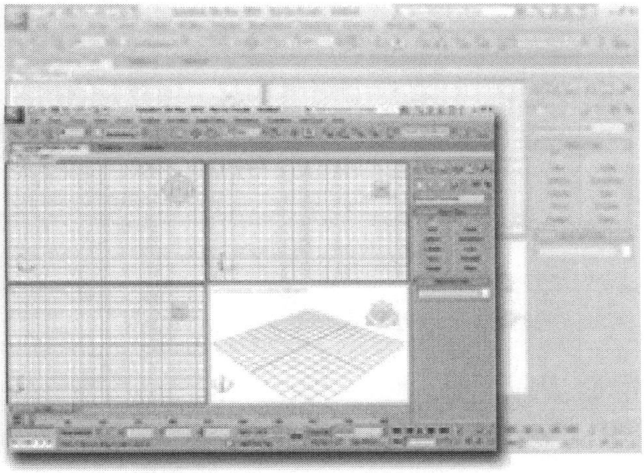

INTRODUCTION TO Autodesk 3ds Max 2012

Welcome to the world of Autodesk 3ds Max, an advanced application that is used to create still or animated 3D models and objects. With the help of this application, you can create realistic scenes by modifying objects, applying maps and materials to a scene, assigning environment to a scene, adding lights and cameras, and so on. Before working with Autodesk 3ds Max, you should have the basic knowledge of various tools and commands available in this software. In this chapter, you will learn the basic features of Autodesk 3ds Max.

PROJECT WORKFLOW

To start working in Autodesk 3ds Max, first you need to create models, apply maps and materials to them, assign lights and camera, animate objects in the scene, and then render the scene to view the final output.

GETTING STARTED WITH Autodesk 3ds Max

Enhanced

First, you need to install Autodesk 3ds Max on your system. On installing the software, the **Autodesk 3ds Max 2012** shortcut icon will automatically be created on the desktop. Double-click on this icon to start Autodesk 3ds Max. Alternatively, you can start Autodesk 3ds Max from the **Start** menu. To do so, choose **Start > All Programs > Autodesk > Autodesk 3ds Max 2012 > Autodesk 3ds Max 2012** from the **Start** menu, as shown in Figure 1-1.

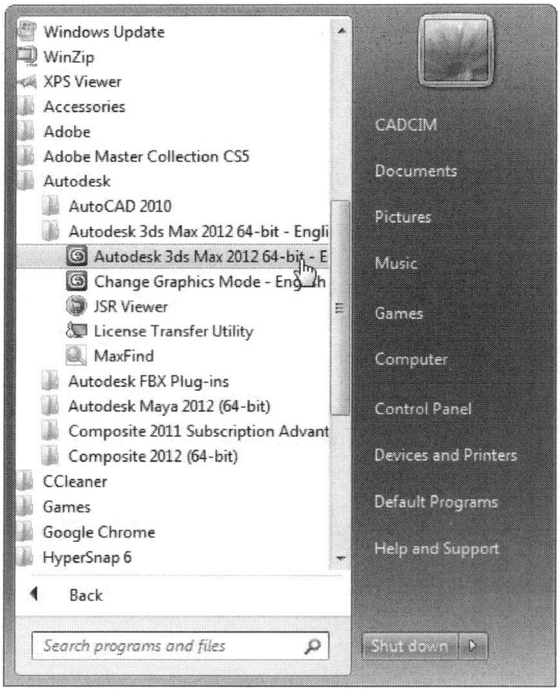

***Figure 1-1** Starting Autodesk 3ds Max 2012 using the **Start** menu*

The system will prepare to start Autodesk 3ds Max by loading all required files. If you are running Autodesk 3ds Max for the first time, the **Autodesk Customer Involvement Program** dialog box will be displayed, as shown in Figure 1-2, and you will be prompted to join the Customer Involvement Program (CIP). Select the **Yes, I would like to participate in CIP** radio button and then choose the **OK** button to join the CIP. Else, select the **No, thanks** radio button. On joining the CIP, Autodesk will gather product feature usage and system information every day from your system to analyze trends and patterns. This entire information helps Autodesk to improve its product. You can also invoke the **Autodesk Customer Involvement Program** dialog box by choosing **Help > Customer Involvement Program** from the menu bar.

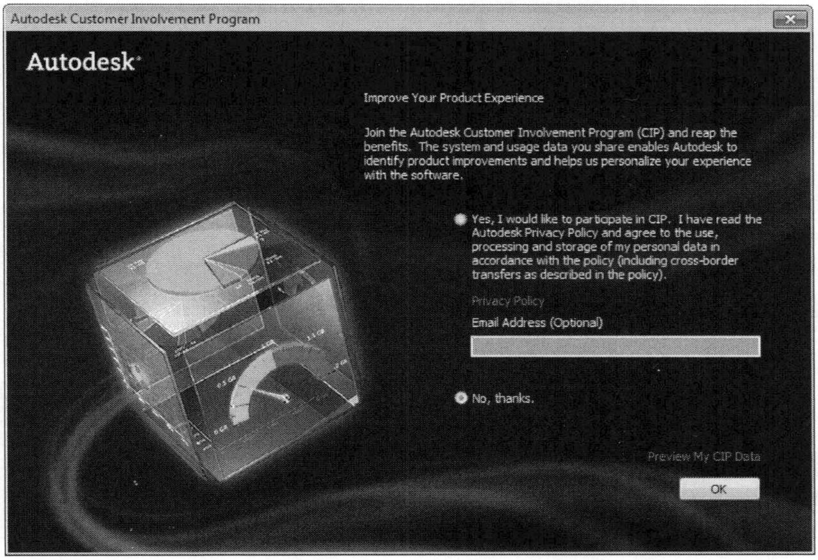

Figure 1-2 *The **Autodesk Customer Involvement Program** dialog box*

After all required files are loaded, the 3ds Max interface will be displayed along with the **Welcome to 3ds Max** dialog box, as shown in Figure 1-3. The **Welcome to 3ds Max** dialog box will display the video tutorials that help you to learn about the basic working environment of the software. To start a tutorial, choose one of the buttons available on the left in this dialog box; the corresponding tutorial will be displayed in separate window on the screen. Also, you can create a new file, open an existing file or any recently created files using this dialog box. Choose the **Close** button in the **Welcome to 3ds Max** dialog box to exit it.

Note

*It is necessary to install the **QuickTime** player on your computer to view the video tutorials.*

STARTING A NEW FILE IN Autodesk 3ds Max

To start a new file in Autodesk 3ds Max, choose the **Application** button at the top left corner of the interface; the **Application menu** will be displayed. Next, choose **New > New All** from the **Application menu**; a new file will be created in the 3ds Max interface. The new file will clear all contents of the current file. Alternatively, press the CTRL+N keys; the **New Scene** dialog box will be displayed, as shown in Figure 1-4. By default, the **New All** radio button is selected in this dialog box. It is used to clear all the contents in the current scene and open a new file. Choose the **OK** button; a new file will be displayed.

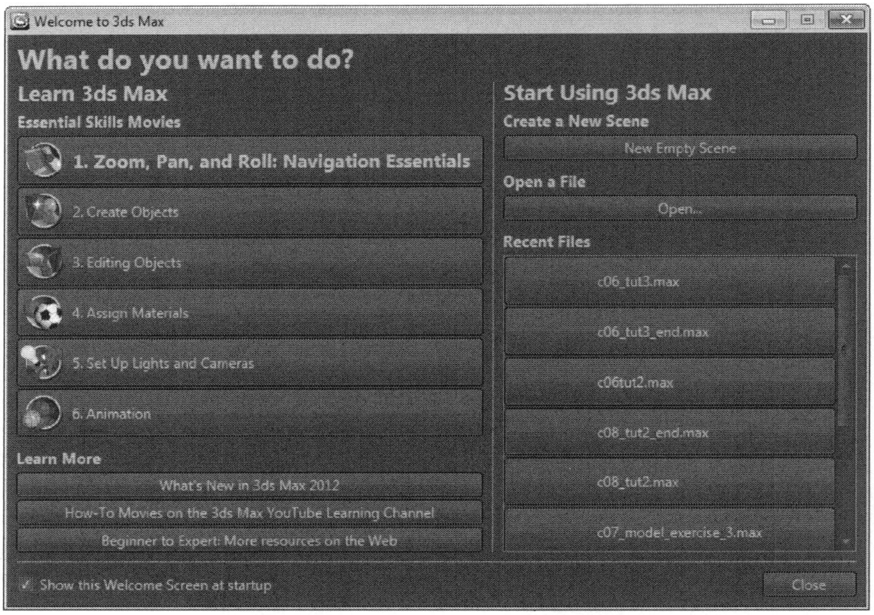

*Figure 1-3 The **Welcome to 3ds Max** dialog box*

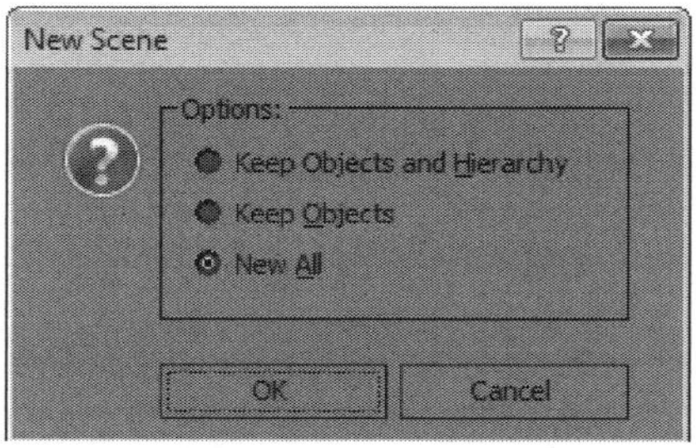

*Figure 1-4 The **New Scene** dialog box*

You can also reuse the objects from the current scene in the new file. Select the **Keep Objects** radio button in the **New Scene** dialog box to keep only the objects from the current scene for the new file. However, on selecting this radio button, all the animation keys and links between the objects will be cleared. To keep the objects and the links between them, select the **Keep Objects and Hierarchy** radio button. However, in this case, the animation keys will be deleted.

Before starting a new file in Autodesk 3ds Max, it is recommended to reset Autodesk 3ds Max and start afresh. By doing so, you will be able to reset all settings for the new file. To reset Autodesk 3ds Max, choose **Reset** from the **Application menu**; the **3ds Max** message box will be displayed, as shown in Figure 1-5. Also, you will be prompted to specify if you really want to reset 3ds Max. Choose the **Yes** button; the Autodesk 3ds Max will be reset.

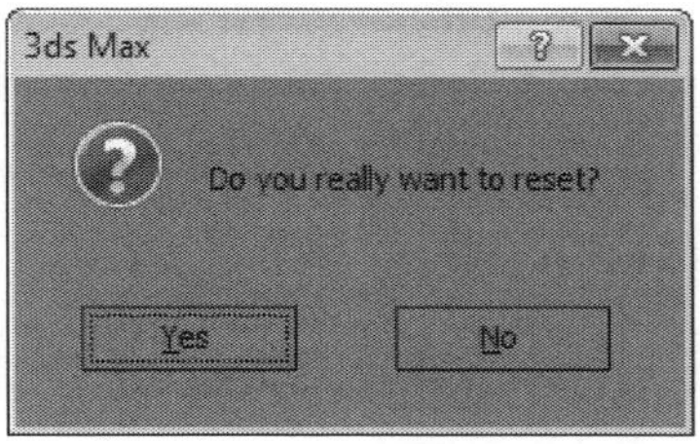

***Figure 1-5** The **3ds Max** message box*

Autodesk 3ds Max SCREEN COMPONENTS

The 3ds Max interface screen consists of different components, as shown in Figure 1-6. These components are discussed next.

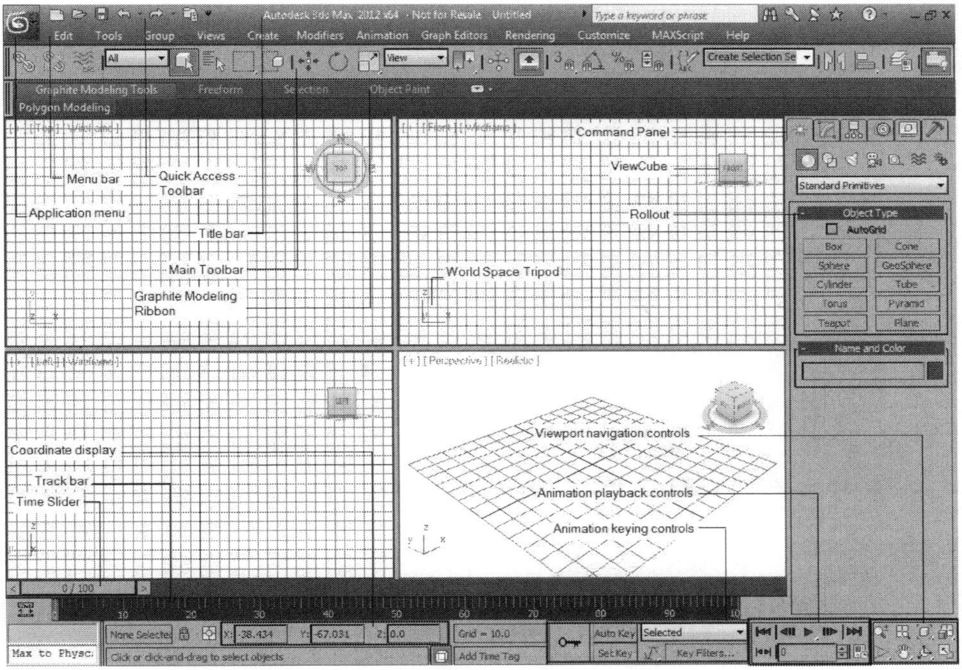

***Figure 1-6** Different screen components of Autodesk 3ds Max interface screen*

Menu Bar

The menu bar is located just below the title bar, as shown in Figure 1-6 and contains various pull-down menus. Some of the pull-down menus are standard window menus such as **Edit**, **Help**, and others are 3ds Max pull-down menus such as **Create**, **Modifiers**, **Animation**, **Graph Editors**, **Rendering**, **Customize**, and so on. The title of each pull-down menu indicates the purpose of commands in the menu. When you choose one of the menu titles, Autodesk 3ds Max displays the corresponding pull-down menu. Each menu consists of a collection of commands. In a pull-down menu, the dots after a command indicate that a dialog box will be displayed on choosing that command. An arrow next to a command indicates that a cascading menu will be displayed on placing the cursor on that command. For some of the commands in the pull-down menus, the keyboard shortcuts are available on their right side, as shown in Figure 1-7.

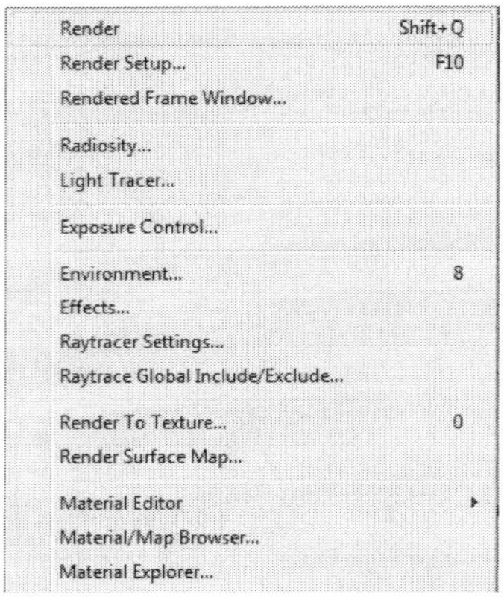

*Figure 1-7 The keyboard shortcuts for some commands in the **Rendering** pull-down menu*

Application Menu

The **Application menu** is used to manage the files created in 3ds Max. To display this menu, choose the **Application** button on the top left of the 3ds Max screen, as shown in Figure 1-8. This menu comprises the most commonly used file management options. In 3ds Max 2012, the **Send to** option is added which provides interoperability with Autodesk applications such as Softimage, MotionBuilder, and Mudbox. When you choose **Send to** from the **Application menu**, a cascading menu is displayed. It consists of options: **Send to Softimage**, **Send to MotionBuilder**, and **Send to Mudbox**. Choose the desired option from the cascading menu; a submenu will be displayed with the options **Send as New Scene**, **Update Current Scene**, **Add to Current Scene**, and **Select Previously Sent Objects**. You can choose the option from this menu as per your requirement.

On the right of the menu is the **Recent Documents** page that provides a complete information about the files that were previously saved in 3ds Max. You can change the size of the icons of the recent documents. To do so, choose the **Icon or Image Display** button from the **Application menu**, refer to Figure 1-8; a drop-down list will be displayed, as shown in Figure 1-9. Select the icon size from the drop-down list to change the size of the icons of the recent documents.

You can also use the keyboard shortcuts to work with the **Application menu**. To do so, press ALT+F; the **Application menu** will be displayed with all shortcuts, as shown in Figure 1-10. Next, press the shortcut key based on your requirement; the corresponding command will be executed. However, if you click again on the **Application menu** after pressing the ALT+F keys, the **Application menu** will not display the shortcuts. You can repeat the process to view the shortcuts again.

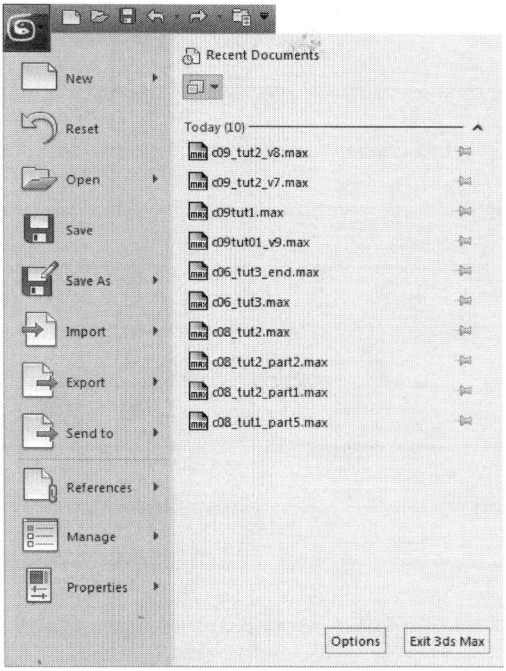

Figure 1-8** The **Application menu

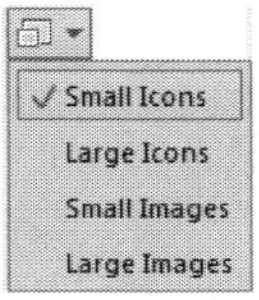

***Figure 1-9** The icon or image display drop-down list*

Quick Access Toolbar

The **Quick Access Toolbar** comprises of the most commonly used file management buttons, as shown in Figure 1-11. These buttons are also available in the **Application menu**. Apart from the commonly used buttons, the **Quick Access Toolbar** contains the **Redo Scene Operation** and **Undo Scene Operation** buttons.

Toolbars

In Autodesk 3ds Max, there are various commands available in toolbars as buttons or tools. By default, only the **Main Toolbar** will be displayed on Autodesk 3ds Max screen. However, you can display other toolbars such as **Snaps**, **Axis Constraints**, **Extras**, **MassFX Toolbar**, and so on in the 3ds Max screen. Also, you can move, resize, and undock them based on your requirements. To display these toolbars, right-click in the blank area on the **Main Toolbar**; a shortcut menu will be displayed with the names of all toolbars, as shown in Figure 1-12. Next, choose the name of the required toolbar; the chosen toolbar will be displayed on the screen. Also, you can hide any of the displayed toolbars by choosing its name from the shortcut menu.

The **Main Toolbar** provides quick access to many tools and dialog boxes such as **Select and Link**, **Unlink Selection**, **Select Object**, **Material Editor**, and so on. This toolbar is docked just below the menu bar. You will learn more about the tools available in various toolbars in the later chapters.

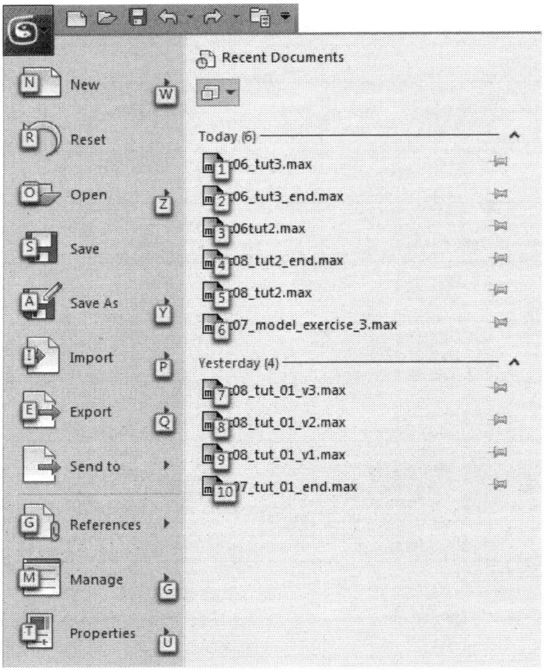

*Figure 1-10 The **Application menu** with the shortcuts*

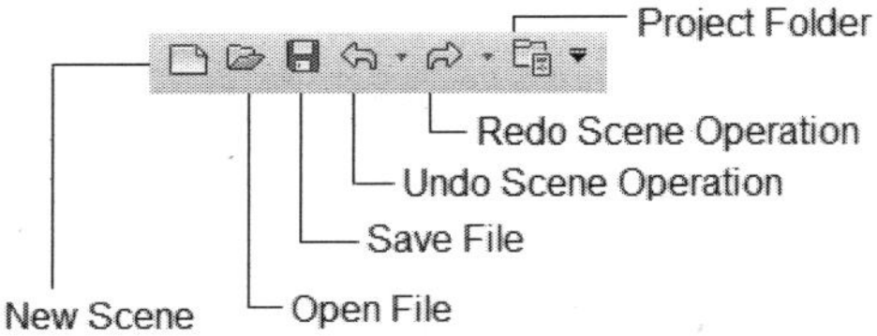

*Figure 1-11 The **Quick Access Toolbar***

Command Panel

By default, the **Command Panel** is docked on the right of the 3ds Max screen. There are six tabs in the **Command Panel**: **Create**, **Modify**, **Hierarchy**, **Motion**, **Display**, and **Utilities**, as shown in Figure 1-13. Most of the 3ds Max modeling and animation tools are placed in these tabs. The tools in the **Command Panel** are used to create, modify, and animate the objects. Each tab has several rollouts to create or modify the objects. You can collapse or expand these rollouts. The six tabs in the **Command Panel** are discussed next.

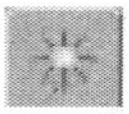

The **Create** tab is chosen by default. The tools in the **Create** tab are used to create objects, cameras, lights, and so on.

The **Modify** tab is used to modify the selected objects in the viewport by modifying the parameters, applying various modifiers, and editing the editable objects such as editable mesh or editable poly.

The **Hierarchy** tab is used to control the links in the hierarchy, joints, and inverse kinematics.

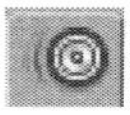

The **Motion** tab is used to control the animation controllers.

The **Display** tab is used to hide and unhide the objects in the viewport.

The **Utilities** tab is used to access various utility programs.

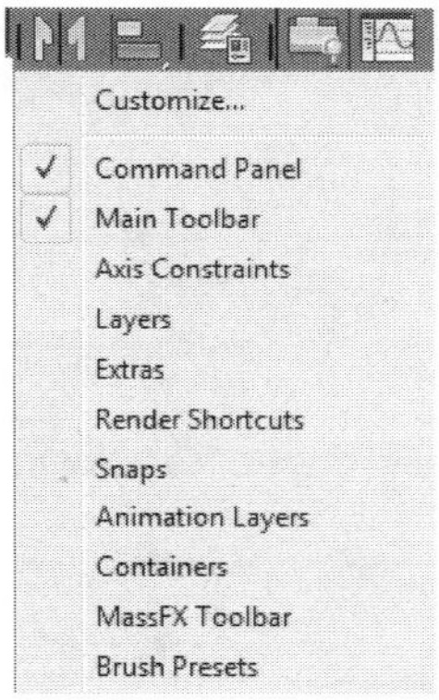

Figure 1-12 The shortcut menu displayed to view the hidden toolbars

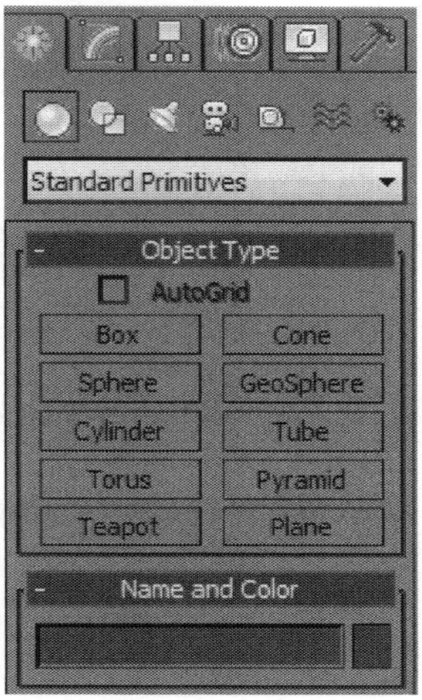

Figure 1-13** The **Command Panel

Note

*You can undock the **Command Panel** and **Main Toolbar** and place them anywhere on the screen. To do so, move the cursor on the top of the **Main Toolbar** that you want to relocate; the cursor will change into an arrow with two overlapping rectangles. Now, press and hold the left mouse button and drag the **Main Toolbar** to the desired location. Double-click on the **Main Toolbar** to dock it back to its default position.*

Viewports

When you start Autodesk 3ds Max, you are provided with a default interface. This interface consists of four equally sized viewports surrounded by tools and commands, refer to Figure 1-6. These viewports are labeled as Top, Front, Left, and Perspective. The viewports in Autodesk 3ds Max are used to create 3D scenes. Also, they enable you to view a scene from different angles. When you create an object in the viewport, the Top, Front, and Left viewports will display the top, front, and left orthographic views of the object, respectively.

You can modify the size of the viewports by dragging the intersection of the viewports. To restore the original size, right-click on the intersection of the dividing lines; a shortcut menu will be displayed, as shown in Figure 1-14. Choose the **Reset Layout** option from the shortcut menu; the default size of the viewports will be displayed.

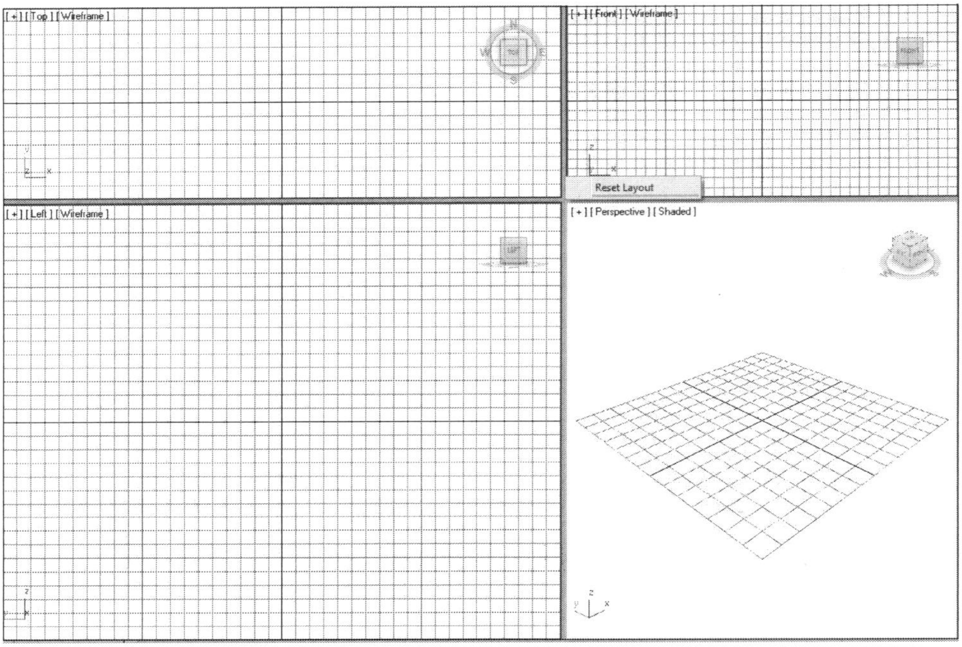

***Figure 1-14** The **Reset Layout** option displayed*

Among the four viewports, one will be highlighted in the yellow border. It is known as the active viewport. Note that only one viewport can be activated at a time. To activate another viewport, you need to click in it. You can also activate a viewport by right-clicking on it. On doing so, the selection state of the objects will be maintained.

On the bottom left corner of each viewport, there is a world-space tripod, as shown in Figure 1-15. The world-space tripod has three axes, X, Y, and Z, which are displayed in red, green, and blue colors, respectively. The tripod always refers to the world coordinate system, regardless of the local coordinate system. ViewCube is placed on the top right corner of the viewport, as shown in Figure 1-15. The ViewCube provides visual feedback of the current orientation of the viewport.

Note

The ViewCube will not be visible in the viewport for camera, light, or activeshade.

It is important to note that the local coordinate system defines an object's local position in a scene. Whereas, the world coordinate system uses fixed axes to define the position of all objects in the world space.

Each viewport has a grid placed in it, refer to Figure 1-15. It is like a graph paper in which all the lines intersect each other at right angles. You can modify the spacing in the grids. The grids in all viewports act as an aid to visualize the spacing and distance while creating objects. Also, they provide a construction plane to create and align the objects. You can also use the grids as a reference system while using the snap controls to align the objects. To hide the grid in the viewport, press the G key.

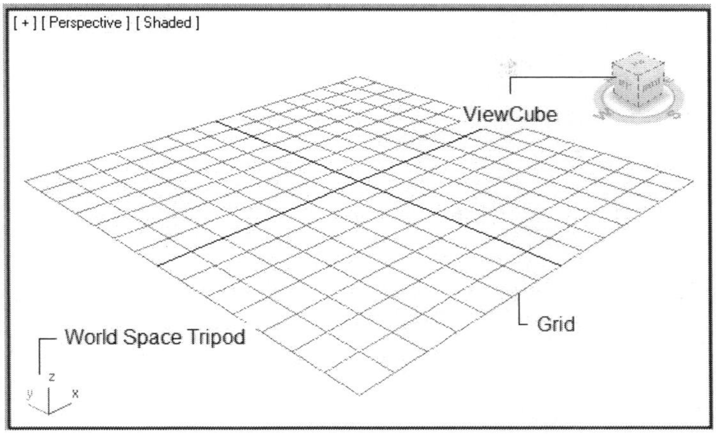

Figure 1-15 *The world space tripod and grids in the Perspective viewport*

On the top left corner of each viewport, there are three viewport labels: General viewport label, Point of view (POV) viewport label, and Shading viewport label, refer to Figure 1-16. When you click on any of the viewport labels, the corresponding shortcut menu will be displayed, as shown in Figure 1-17. The options in these shortcut menus are used to modify various aspects of the active viewport.

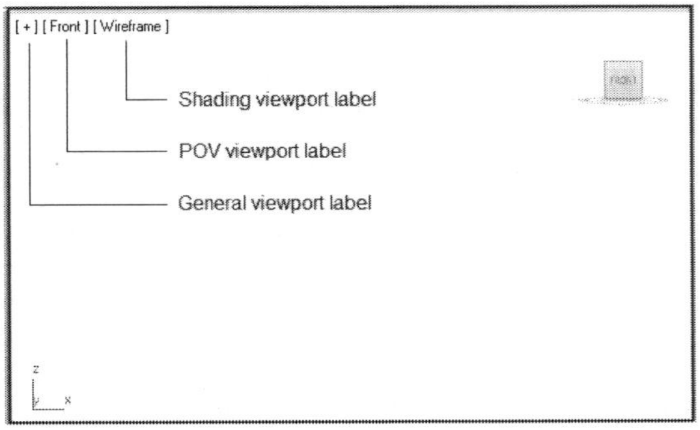

Figure 1-16 *The viewport labels in the Front viewport*

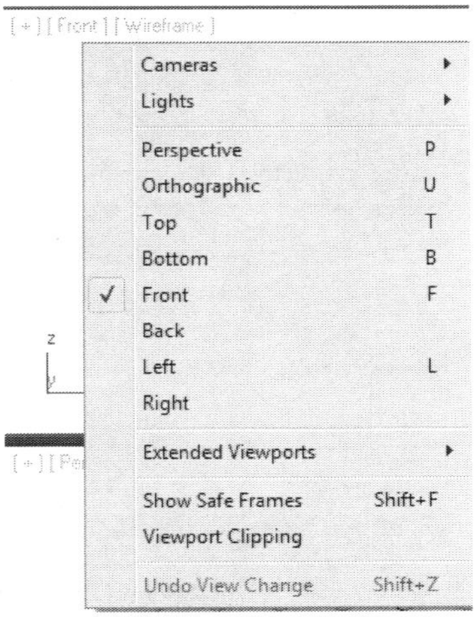

Figure 1-17 *The shortcut menu displayed on clicking the POV viewport label*

You can activate or disable the active viewport by using the options in the General viewport label menu. Choose the **Configure Viewports** option from this menu; the **Viewport Configuration** dialog box will be displayed. Various commands in this dialog box can be used to configure the viewports. You already know that four equally sized viewports are displayed on the screen. However, you can change the viewport configuration based on your requirement. To change the basic configuration of the viewports, choose the **Layout** tab in the **Viewport Configuration** dialog box, as shown in Figure 1-18. In the **Layout** tab, you can specify the division method of the viewports. There are 14 types of configurations displayed at the top in the dialog box. Select the required configuration and then choose the **OK** button; the viewports will be displayed according to the configuration that you have selected in the **Viewport Configuration** dialog box.

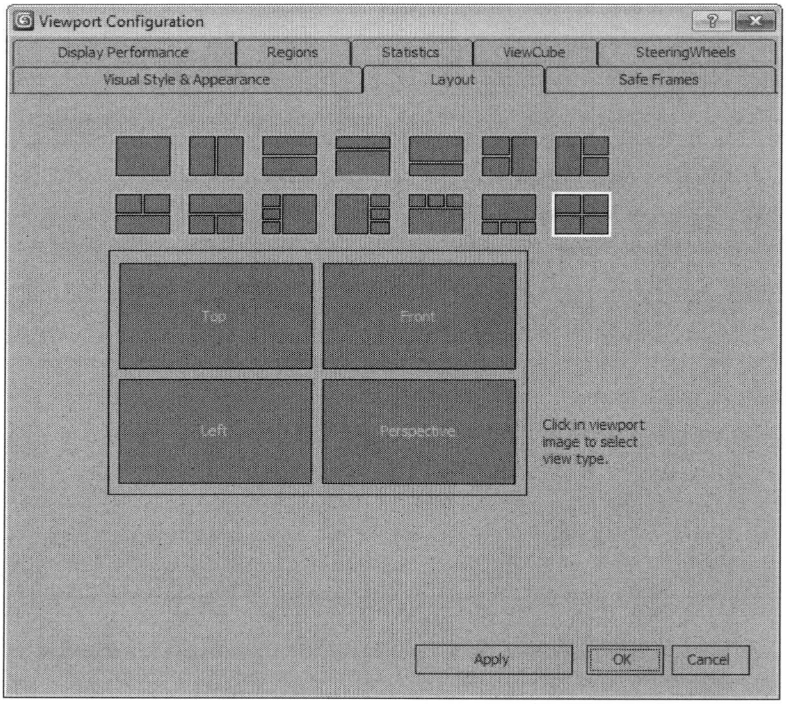

***Figure 1-18** The **Layout** tab of the **Viewport Configuration** dialog box*

Note

The viewport configuration specifies how the viewports or drawing areas will be arranged on the screen.

You can change the default viewport to any other viewport type available such as Bottom, Right, and so on, by using the options in the POV viewport label menu. To do so, click on the POV viewport label; a shortcut menu will be displayed. Choose the name of the viewport that you want to display.

You can also use the Shading viewport label menu for defining the type of shadings displayed in the viewport. The different types of shading types are: **Realistic**, **Shaded**, **Consistent Colors, Wireframe**, **Edged Faces**, **Bounding box**, **Hidden Line**, and so on. However, some of these shading types are available in the cascading menu of the **Stylized** option, refer to

Figure 1-19. These shading types are **Graphite**, **Color Pencil**, **Ink**, and so on. You will learn more about the shading types in the **Stylized** menu in the Chapter 2. You can choose any one of the options to change the shading.

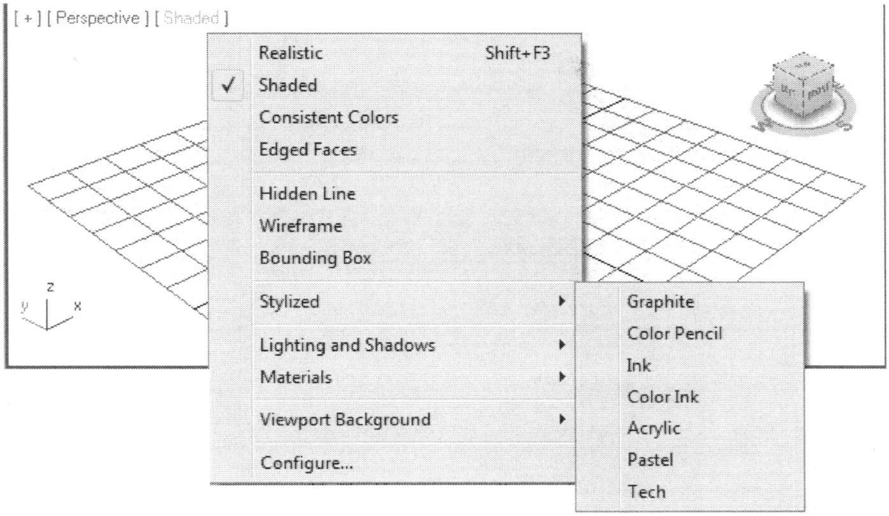

Figure 1-19 *Different shading types in the cascading menu of the **Stylized** option*

Viewport Navigation Controls

There are various tools available at the bottom right corner of the Autodesk 3ds Max screen, as shown in Figure 1-20. These tools are known as viewport navigation controls and they are used to control the display and navigation of the viewport. The tools displayed in the viewport navigation controls depend on the viewport selected. For example, if the Camera viewport is selected, its corresponding tools will be displayed in the viewport navigation control. These tools are discussed in detail in the later chapters.

Animation Playback Controls

The tools in the animation playback controls are displayed on the left side of the viewport navigation controls, as shown in Figure 1-21. These tools are used to control the animation in the active viewport. Also, you can set the total number of frames, animation length, and other settings of the animation using these tools.

Animation Keying Controls

The tools in the animation keying controls are displayed on the left side of the animation playback controls, as shown in Figure 1-22. These tools are used to enter or exit different animation modes.

Figure 1-20 *The viewport navigation controls*

Figure 1-21 *The animation playback controls*

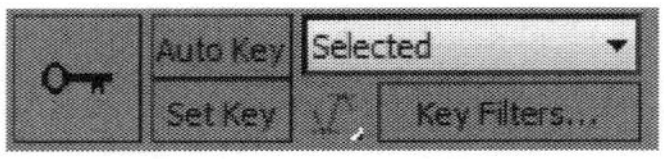

Figure 1-22 *The animation keying controls*

Track Bar

The track bar lies between the time slider and the status bar, refer to Figure 1-23. It displays a timeline along with the frame numbers.

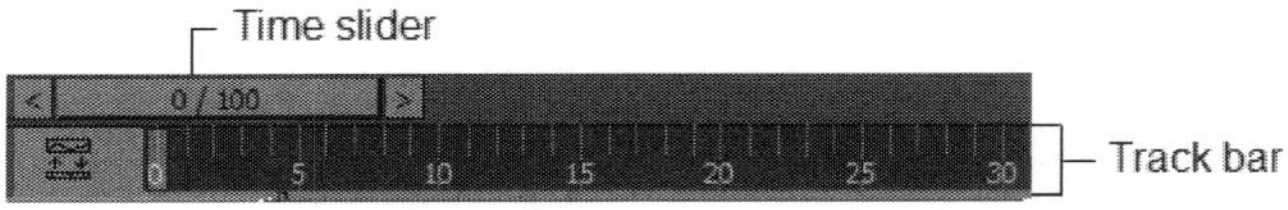

Figure 1-23 *Partial view of the track bar and the time slider*

Time Slider

The time slider displays the current frame and the total number of frames in the current time segment, refer to Figure 1-23. You can view the animation at each frame by dragging the time slider. The time segment is the total range of frames that you can access using the time slider. By default, it ranges from 0 to 100. You can set the range using the **Time Configuration** dialog box, about which you will learn in the later chapters.

Status Bar

There are various tools in the status bar that provide information about the scene and the active command, as shown in Figure 1-24. The prompt line, which is located at the bottom of the screen, displays information about the active command or tool. On top of the status bar, a text box known as the status line is available. This status line displays the number of currently selected objects (current selection set). The **Selection Lock Toggle** tool on the right side of the status bar is used to lock the selection set. The coordinate display/transform type-in area displays the X, Y, and Z coordinates of the cursor or the currently selected object. The coordinate display/transform type-in area can also be used to enter transform values while moving, scaling, or rotating the selected object(s).

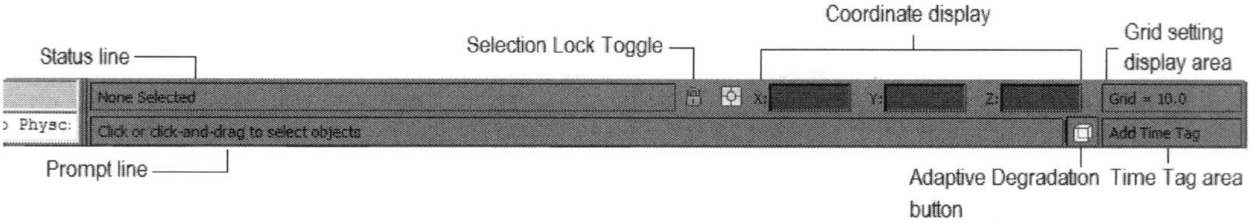

Figure 1-24 *The status bar*

The grid setting display area is placed on the right of the coordinate display area. It displays the size of the grid. The time tag area located below the grid setting display area is used to assign the text labels at any point of time in your animation. Click on the time tag area; the **Add**

Tag and **Edit Tag** options will be displayed. Use these options to add or edit the text labels at any point of time in your animation.

The **Progressive Display** button placed on the right of the prompt line is used to improve the viewport performance in a complex scene by decreasing the visual fidelity of some of the objects temporarily. This results in smoother viewport motions and object transformations in such scenes. It also improves viewport quality incrementally depending on the availability of processing time. To activate this feature, right-click on the **Progressive Display** button; the **Viewport Configuration** dialog box will be displayed. The **Display Performance** tab is chosen by default in this dialog box, as shown in Figure 1-25. Now, change the settings in the **Display Performance** tab based on your requirement and choose the **OK** button.

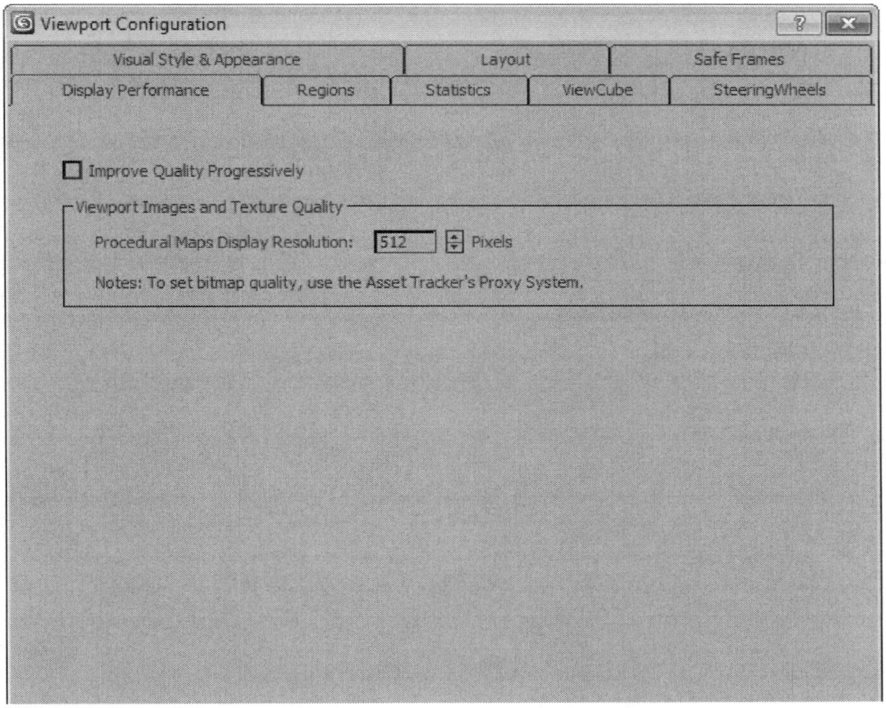

***Figure 1-25** The **Display Performance** tab chosen in the **Viewport Configuration** dialog box*

UNDERSTANDING CONTROLS

In Autodesk 3ds Max, there are some special controls that can be used for creating or modifying the objects in the viewports. These controls are discussed next.

Flyout

A flyout is an icon-based menu that contains the tools having similar type of functions. Figure 1-26 shows the **Snap Toggle** flyout. The buttons having a small triangle at their lower-right corner contain a flyout. Press and hold such a button; a flyout will be displayed, refer to Figure 1-26.

Right-click Menus

In Autodesk 3ds Max, the right-click menus provide quick access to the commonly used commands that are related to the current selection of an object. When you right-click on an object, a quad menu is displayed, as shown in Figure 1-27. Some of the options in the quad menu have an arrow on their right side. If you move the mouse on these options, a cascading menu will be displayed, refer to Figure 1-27. But, if you right-click in the viewport, a shortcut menu will be displayed, refer to Figure 1-28.

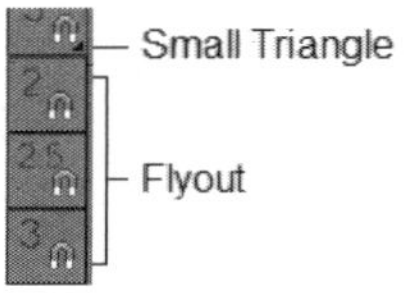

***Figure 1-26** The **Snap Toggle** flyout*

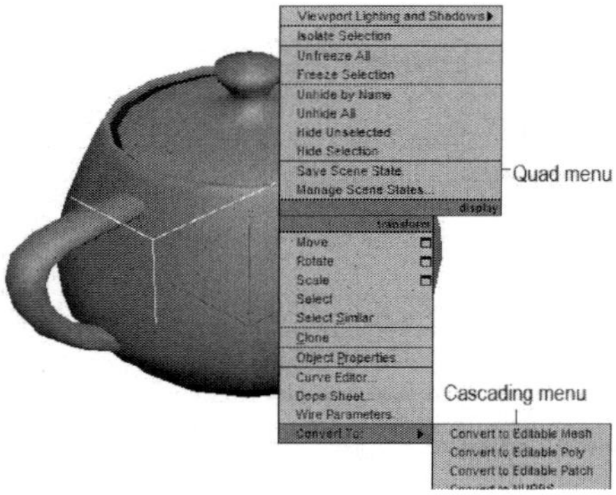

***Figure 1-27** The quad menu and the cascading menu*

Snaps Settings

Snaps restrict the movement of the cursor to a specific part of an object or grid. There are four buttons available for snap settings in the **Main Toolbar**: **Snaps Toggle**, **Angle Snap Toggle**, **Percent Snap Toggle**, and **Spinner Snap Toggle**. If you right-click on the **Snaps Toggle**, **Angle Snap Toggle**, or **Percent Snap Toggle** button, the **Grid and Snap Settings** dialog box will be displayed, as shown in Figure 1-29. In this dialog box, you can select different parts of the objects or grid where the cursor will snap to. You can turn the snap command on and off by pressing the S key or by selecting the **Snaps Toggle** button.

If you choose and hold the **Snaps Toggle** button, a flyout will be displayed. This flyout contains the **2D Snap**, **2.5 Snap**, and **3D Snap** tools, which can be invoked to snap the cursor.

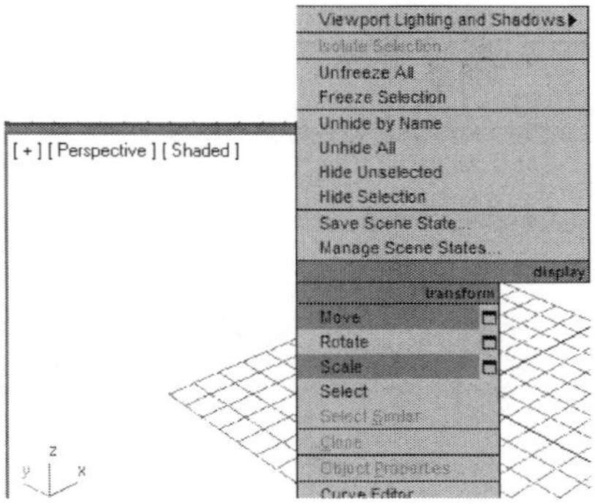

Figure 1-28 The shortcut menu displayed on right-clicking in the viewport

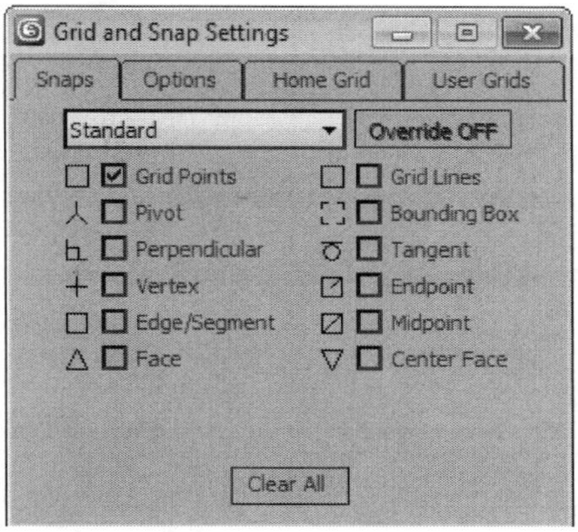

Figure 1-29 The ***Grid and Snap Settings*** *dialog box*

Units Setup

The units setup in Autodesk 3ds Max is used to specify the units that help in measuring the geometry in a scene. By default, the units in Autodesk 3ds Max are generic units, which are scaled in inches. You can change the settings for units by using the **Customize** pull-down menu. To do so, choose **Customize > Units Setup** from the menu bar; the **Units Setup** dialog box will be displayed, as shown in Figure 1-30. By default, the **Generic Units** radio button is selected in this dialog box. Select any other radio button as per the requirement from the **Display Unit Scale** area of this dialog box and then choose the **OK** button; the limits in all spinners in Autodesk 3ds Max will be modified accordingly.

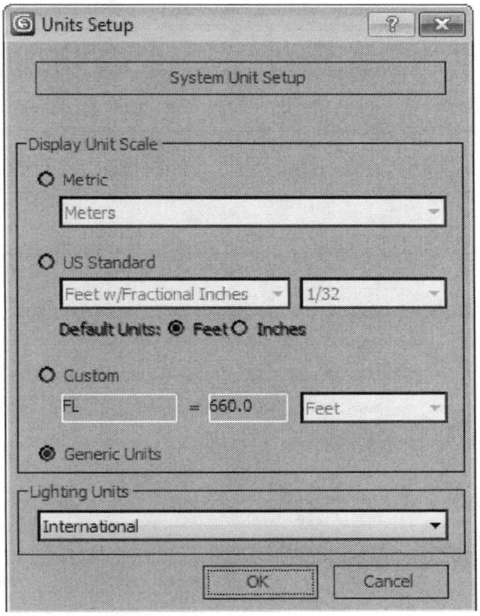

Figure 1-30 The ***Units Setup*** *dialog box*

Setting Grid Spacing

To set the spacing between the visible grids in the viewports, choose **Tools > Grids and Snaps > Grid and Snap Settings** from the menu bar; the **Grid and Snap Settings** dialog box will be displayed. Choose the **Home Grid** tab in this dialog box, as shown in Figure 1-31. In the **Grid Dimensions** area, set the value in the **Grid Spacing** spinner to specify the size of the smallest square of the grid. The value in the spinners will be measured in the units that you specify in the units setup. Set the value in the **Major Lines every Nth Grid Line** spinner to specify the number of squares between the major lines in the grid. Set the value in the **Perspective View Grid Extent** spinner to specify the size of the home grid in the Perspective viewport. Note that the default grid displayed in the viewports on starting Autodesk 3ds Max is known as the home grid.

In the **Dynamic Update** area, the **Active Viewport** radio button is selected by default. It is used to update the active viewport according to the new values of the **Grid and Snap Settings** dialog box. Select the **All Viewports** radio button to update all viewports simultaneously according to the new values that you set in the spinners of the **Grid and Snap Settings** dialog box.

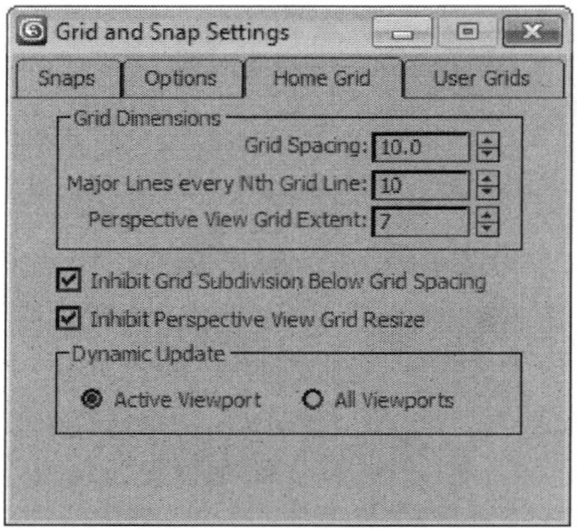

Figure 1-31 *The* ***Home Grid*** *tab chosen in the* ***Grid and Snap Settings*** *dialog box*

HOTKEYS

In Autodesk 3ds Max, you can use the keys on the keyboard to invoke some of the tools. These keys are known as the hotkeys. You can work faster and more efficiently using the hotkeys. The major hotkeys and their functions are listed next.

Main Toolbar

The hotkeys that can be used to invoke the tools from the **Main Toolbar** are given next.

H	Invokes the **Select by Name** tool
S	Invokes the tools from the **Snaps Toggle** button
A	Invokes the **Angle Snap Toggle** tool
CTRL+SHIFT+P	Invokes the **Percent Snap Toggle** tool
M	Invokes the **Material Editor** tool
SHIFT+Q	Invokes the **Quick Render** tool

Viewport Navigation Controls

The hot keys that can be used to invoke the tools in the viewport navigation controls are given next.

ALT+CTRL+Z	Performs the action of the **Zoom Extents** tool
ALT+W	Invokes the **Maximize Viewport Toggle** tool
ALT+Z	Invokes the **Zoom** tool
CTRL+W	Invokes the **Zoom Region** tool
CTRL+P	Invokes the **Pan** tool
Scroll the middle mouse button	Zooms in or out the active viewport
CTRL+R	Invokes the **Orbit** tool
SHIFT+Z	Used to undo the **Zoom** or **Pan** command actions
ALT+ press and hold the middle mouse button and move the mouse	Performs the actions of the **Orbit** tool

The following hot keys are used to change the POV viewport labels:

V	Invokes the viewport quad menu
T	Invokes the Top viewport
F	Invokes the Front viewport
L	Invokes the Left viewport
P	Invokes the Perspective viewport
B	Invokes the Bottom viewport
U	Invokes the Orthographic viewport

Animation Playback Controls

The hot keys that can be used to invoke the tools in the animation playback controls are given next.

N	Invokes the **Toggle Autokey Mode** tool
Home	Invokes the **Go To Start** button
End	Invokes the **Go To End** button
/ (backslash)	Invokes the **Play Animation** button
ESC	Invokes the **Stop Animation** button
, (comma)	Invokes the **Previous Frame** button
. (period)	Invokes the **Next Frame** button

CUSTOMIZING THE HOTKEYS

In Autodesk 3ds Max, you can create your own keyboard shortcuts. To do so, choose **Customize > Customize User Interface** from the menu bar; the **Customize User Interface** dialog box will be displayed, as shown in Figure 1-32. In this dialog box, the **Keyboard** tab is chosen by default. Next, select a command from the **Group** and **Category** drop-down lists; the list of the corresponding actions will be displayed just below the **Category** drop-down list. Now, select one of the actions from the list and then enter the key that you want to assign to the selected action in the **Hotkey** text box. Next, choose the **Assign** button; the key is assigned to the selected action.

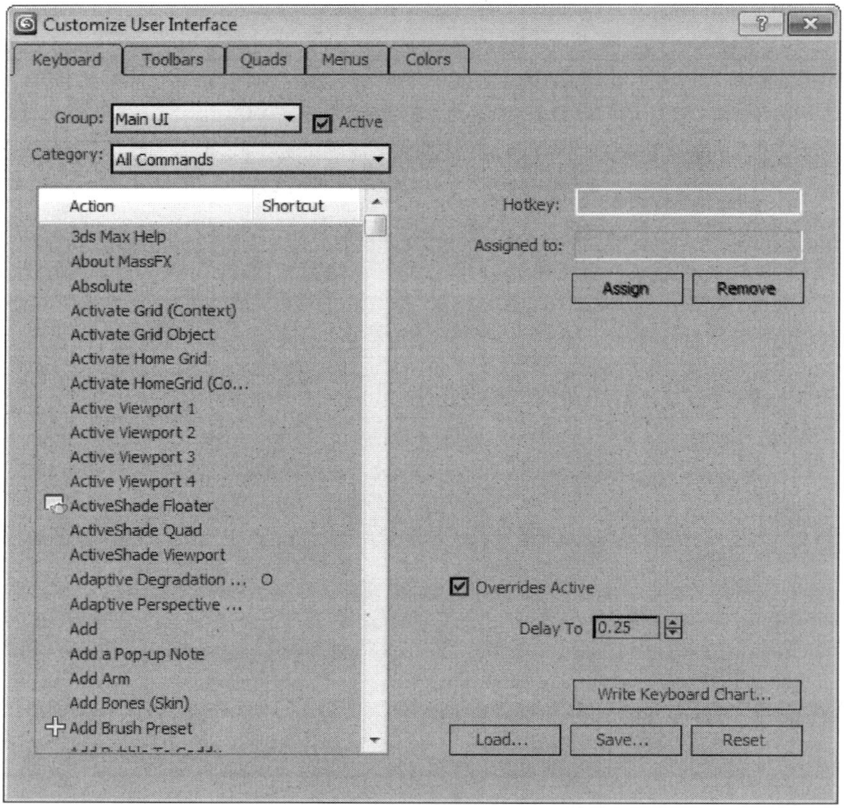

*Figure 1-32 The **Customize User Interface** dialog box*

CUSTOMIZING THE COLORS OF THE USER INTERFACE

Autodesk 3ds Max allows you to modify the colors of the software interface. You can modify the colors for almost every element in the interface. To modify the colors, choose **Customize > Customize User Interface** in the menu bar; the **Customize User Interface** dialog box will be displayed. Choose the **Colors** tab. Next, select the category of the interface element from the **Elements** drop-down list; the list of the corresponding elements will be displayed just below the **Elements** drop-down list. Now, select one of the elements from the list and choose the color swatch on the right of the **Elements** drop-down list; the **Color Selector** dialog box will be displayed. Select a new color and choose the **OK** button to close the **Color Selector** dialog box.

You can reset the new color to the default one. To do so, choose the **Reset** button at the bottom of the **Customize User Interface** dialog box; the **Revert Color File** message box will be displayed, as shown in Figure 1-33. Choose the **Yes** button; the default color will be displayed in the color swatch.

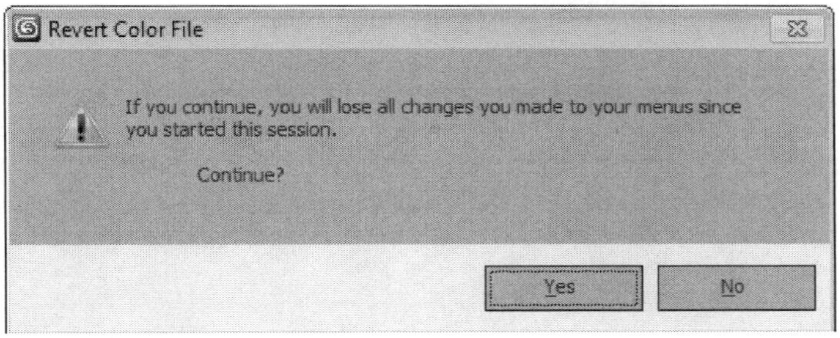

Figure 1-33 *The* ***Revert Color File*** *message box*

HELP PREFERENCES

When you choose **Help > Autodesk 3ds Max Help** from the menu bar; the 3ds Max help will be displayed from the Autodesk website. If you want to open the help from the local drive, you need to download it from *http://www.autodesk.com/3dsmax-helpdownload-enu* and then install it. Next, restart 3ds Max. Choose **Customize > Preferences** from the menu bar; the **Preference Settings** dialog box will be displayed. Choose the **Help** tab in this dialog box, refer to Figure 1-34. Select the **Local Computer/ Network** radio button from the **Help Location** area and then choose the **OK** button to exit the dialog box. Now, you can access the help from local drive.

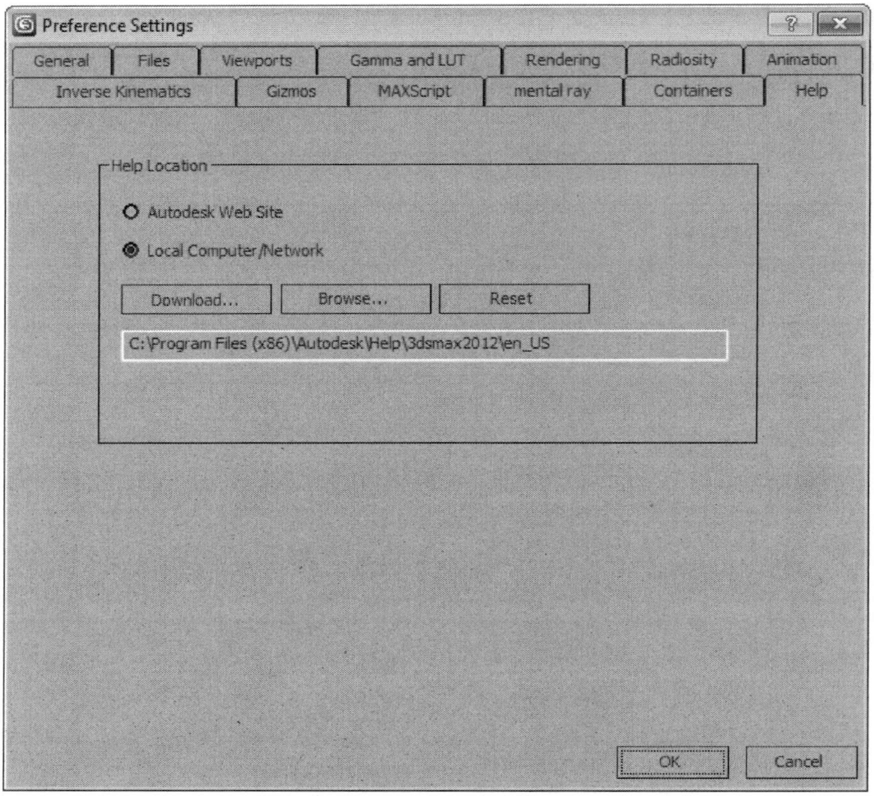

Figure 1-34 *The **Help tab** in the **Preference Settings** dialog box*

Note

For the printing purpose, this textbook will follow the white background. However, for a better understanding and a clear visualization at various places, this textbook will follow other color schemes as well.

Moreover, at some places in figures, grids will be hidden for better understanding and visualization. In some tutorials, you have been instructed to browse the images and max files from the CADCIM website. Therefore, before starting the tutorials, download the images and max files from http://www.cadcim.com. The path of the file is as follows:

Textbooks > Animation and Visual Effects > 3ds Max > Autodesk 3ds Max 2012: A Comprehensive Guide

Self-Evaluation Test

Answer the following questions and then compare them to those given at the end of this chapter:

1. Which of the following tools is used to improve the performance of a viewport in a complex scene by temporarily decreasing the visual fidelity of some of the objects?

   (a) **Progressive Display** (b) **Snaps Toggle** flyout
   (c) **Mirror** (d) All of these

2. Which of the following tabs should be chosen to control the animation controllers?

   (a) **Motion** (b) **Display**
   (c) **Hierarchy** (d) None of these

3. Which of the following dialog boxes is used to set the spacing in the grids displayed in the viewports?

   (a) **Customize User Interface** (b) **Grid and Snap Settings**
   (c) **Units Setup** (d) All of these

4. Which of the following combinations of keys is used to invoke the pan tool?

   (a) CTRL+P (b) SHIFT+Z
   (c) CTRL+A (d) CTRL+W

5. The __________ is located at the bottom of the screen and displays the information about the active command or tool.

6. The __________ dialog box displays video tutorials which help in learning the basic working environment of the software.

7. Most of the 3ds Max modeling and animation tools can be invoked from the tabs located in the **Command Panel**. (T/F)

8. The default interface of Autodesk 3ds Max consists of three equal viewports that are surrounded by tools and commands. (T/F)

9. In Autodesk 3ds Max, you can modify the colors of almost every element in the interface. (T/F)

10. The tools in the animation playback controls are used to control the display of a viewport. (T/F)

Review Questions

Answer the following questions:

1. The __________ provides visual feedback of the current orientation of the viewport.

2. The __________ is located between the time slider and the status bar.

3. The __________ tool located on the right of the status bar is used to lock a selection set.

4. Snapping restricts the movement of the cursor to a specific part of an object or grid. (T/F)

5. The options in the General viewport label menu are used for defining the type of shadings displayed in the viewport. (T/F)

Answers to Self-Evaluation Test

1. a, **2.** a, **3.** b, **4.** a, **5.** prompt line, **6. Welcome to 3ds Max**, **7.** T, **8.** F, **9.** T, **10.** F

2

Standard Primitives

Learning Objectives

After completing this chapter, you will be able to:

- ***Reset Autodesk 3ds Max***
- ***Understand viewport navigation controls***
- ***Understand selection techniques***
- ***Create standard primitives***
- ***Render a still image***
- ***Change the background color at rendering***

INTRODUCTION

In this chapter, you will learn to create the default 3D objects that are inbuilt in 3ds Max. Apart from that, you will learn how to scale, rotate, and move an object by using different tools.

VIEWPORT NAVIGATION CONTROLS

The tools at the lower right corner of the Autodesk 3ds Max screen are known as viewport navigation controls. These tools are used to control the display and navigation of the viewport.

To adjust the view of an object in a viewport, you need to be familiar with the tools in the viewport navigation controls. Note that some of the tools mentioned below are available in a flyout which will be displayed when you click on the arrow on the lower right corner of the tool icon. These tools are discussed next.

The **Zoom** tool is used to increase or decrease the magnification in the active viewport. You can zoom in by pressing the left mouse button and dragging the cursor up. Similarly, you can zoom out by pressing the left mouse button and then dragging the cursor down.

The **Zoom All** tool is the same as the **Zoom** tool with the only difference that this tool zooms the display in all four viewports simultaneously.

The **Zoom Extents** tool is used to view all objects in the active viewport.

The **Zoom Extents Selected** tool is used to view all selected objects in the active viewport.

The **Zoom Extents All** tool is the same as the **Zoom Extents** tool with the only difference that this tool is used to view all objects in all viewports.

The **Zoom Extents All Selected** tool is the same as the **Zoom Extents Selected** tool with the only difference that this tool is used to view all selected objects in all viewports.

The **Zoom Region** tool is used to define the area to be magnified and viewed in the current viewport. The area to be magnified is specified by a rectangle created by dragging the cursor. When you magnify an area that includes some dimensions, the dimensions will remain constant.

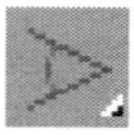

The **Field-of-View** tool is available only in the Perspective and Camera viewports. It is used to change the field of view of the scene in these viewports. More the **Field-of-View** of a camera, more will be the visibility of your scene, and vice-versa.

The **Pan View** tool is used to pan the scene in the viewport. This tool enables you to display the contents of the viewport that are outside the display area without changing the magnification of the current viewport.

The **Walk Through** tool is available in Perspective and Camera viewports only. It allows you to navigate through these viewports. On invoking this tool, the cursor changes into a circle with a dot at its center. Press and hold the left mouse button to navigate in the active viewport. Alternatively, invoke this tool and then press the arrow keys to navigate through the viewport. On pressing the arrow keys, the cursor shows a directional arrow indicating the navigation direction.

The **Orbit** tool is used to rotate the viewport around its view center. This enables you to see the three-dimensional (3D) view of the objects in the Perspective viewport. You can also rotate the Top, Front, and Left viewports. But in such cases, the respective viewport becomes the Orthographic viewport.

The **Orbit Selected** tool is the same as the **Orbit** tool with the only difference that it is used to rotate the viewport around the center of the current selection.

The **Orbit SubObject** tool is the same as the **Orbit** tool with the only difference that it is used to rotate the viewport around the center of the current sub-object selection.

The **Maximize Viewport Toggle** tool is used to maximize the active viewport so that you can view only the active viewport instead of all the four viewports.

SELECTION TECHNIQUES

In Autodesk 3ds Max, you can select objects using various tools such as **Select Object**, **Select by Name**, **Select and Move**, and so on. These tools are discussed next.

Select Object Tool

Quad Menu:	Select
Main Toolbar:	Select Object
Keyboard:	Q

The **Select Object** tool is used to select one or more objects in the viewport. To select an object, choose this tool and move the cursor over the object; the cursor will convert into a selection cursor. Next, press the left mouse button; the objects will be selected. To select more than one object at a time, hold the CTRL key and select the objects that you want to add to the selection. To remove an object from the selection set, hold the ALT key and select the object that you want to remove from the selection.

Select by Name Tool

Menu bar:	Edit > Select By > Name
Main Toolbar:	Select by Name
Keyboard:	H

The **Select by Name** tool is used to select an object from the list of objects in the scene. When you invoke the **Select by Name** tool from the **Main Toolbar**, the **Select From Scene** dialog box will be displayed. If there are some components in the scene, then those components will be displayed in this dialog box, as shown in Figure 2-1. Now, select an object in the list and choose the **OK** button. Alternatively, you can double-click on the object name in the list to select it. You can also select more than one object by holding the SHIFT or CTRL key. The buttons at the top of the dialog box are used to filter the objects in the list.

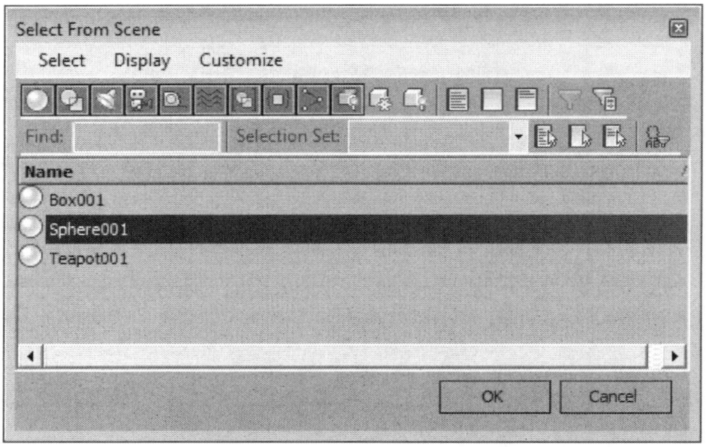

***Figure 2-1** The **Select From Scene** dialog box*

Select and Move Tool

Quad Menu: Move
Main Toolbar: Select and Move
Keyboard: W

The **Select and Move** tool is used to select and move the objects in the viewports. You can move an object by selecting it and then dragging the mouse along the X, Y, or Z axis. You can also move the selected object in the XY, YZ, or ZX plane. To move the selected object along one of the axes, invoke this tool and then select the object; all axes will be displayed. Move the cursor over the axis along which you want to move the object, press the left mouse button, and then drag the cursor. Similarly, to move the object in one of the planes, move the cursor over the plane displayed between the two axes; the plane will be highlighted in yellow. Next, press the left mouse button and drag the cursor.

Select and Rotate Tool

Quad Menu: Rotate
Main Toolbar: Select and Rotate
Keyboard: E

The **Select and Rotate** tool is used to rotate the objects in the viewport along the X, Y, or Z axis. To rotate the object along one of the axes, invoke the **Select and Rotate** tool, and then select the object; a rotate gizmo will be displayed along with the X, Y, and Z axes. Next, move the cursor over the axes along which you want to rotate the object, press the left mouse button, and then drag the cursor. When you rotate the object, a transparent slice will be displayed which will provide a visual representation of the direction and the degree of rotation, refer to Figure 2-2. Also, you can view the degree of rotation in the X, Y, and Z axes in the coordinates displayed at the bottom of the screen.

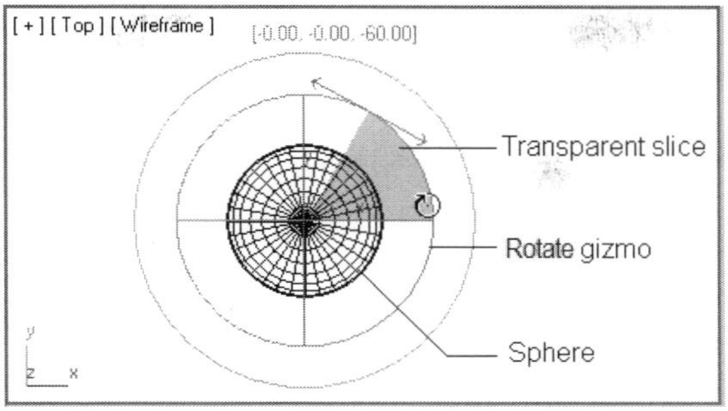

Figure 2-2 *The circular gizmo in the Top viewport while rotating the object*

Select and Scale Tools

Quad Menu: Scale
Main Toolbar: Select and Scale
Keyboard: R

There are three types of tools that are used to scale an object. These tools are available in the **Select and Scale** flyout and are discussed next.

Select and Uniform Scale

The **Select and Uniform Scale** tool is used to scale the objects proportionally along the three axes. To scale an object uniformly along all the three axes, invoke the **Select and Uniform Scale** tool from the **Main Toolbar** and select the object; the scale gizmo will be displayed, as shown in Figure 2-3. Move the cursor to the center of the gizmo and make sure its central portion is highlighted, refer to Figure 2-3. Next, drag the cursor up or down to scale the selected object. You can also perform non-uniform scaling using this tool. To do so, move the cursor over the axis along which you want to scale the object, as shown in Figure 2-4, and then drag the cursor. Similarly, you can perform non-uniform scaling along the XY, YZ, or ZX plane by selecting it and then dragging that particular plane, as shown in Figure 2-5.

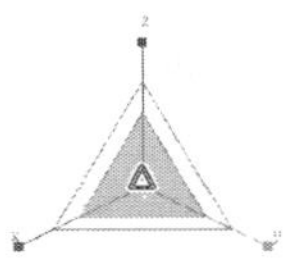

Figure 2-3 *The scale gizmo for uniform scaling*

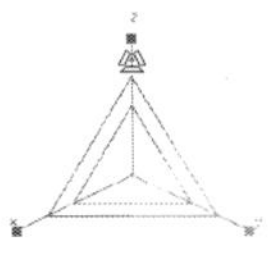

Figure 2-4 *Selecting the Z-axis for non-uniform scaling*

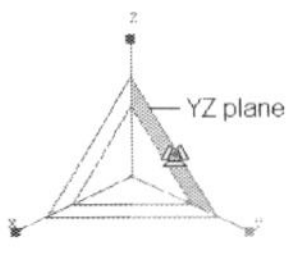

Figure 2-5 *Selecting the YZ plane for non-uniform scaling*

Select and Non-uniform Scale

The **Select and Non-uniform Scale** tool is used to scale an object along a particular axis or plane non-uniformly. To scale the object, invoke the **Select and Non-uniform Scale** tool from the **Select and Scale** flyout, and then select the object. Move the cursor over the X, Y, or Z axes along which you want to scale the object and drag the cursor to modify the shape of the object. Similarly, you can perform the non-uniform scaling along the XY, YZ, or ZX plane. You can also perform uniform scaling in the same manner, as described in the **Select and Uniform Scale** tool.

Select and Squash

The **Select and Squash** tool is used to stretch and squash the object along the selected axis. To squash the object along one of the axes, invoke the **Select and Squash** tool and select the object. Move the cursor over the axis along which you want to squash it. Next, drag the cursor. Similarly, you can squash the selected object along the XY, YZ, or ZX plane. To do so, move the cursor over the plane displayed between the two axes and drag the cursor to squash the object along that plane.

Note

By default, the X-axis, the Y-axis, and the Z-axis of the transform gizmos is red, green, and blue, respectively. When you move the cursor over any one of these axes, it gets activated and turns yellow. You can see the colors of these axes at the bottom left corner of each viewport or while selecting an object using the ***Select and Move****,* ***Select and Rotate****, or* ***Select and Scale*** *tool. Figures 2-6, 2-7, and 2-8 show the move gizmo, rotate gizmo, and the scale gizmo, respectively.*

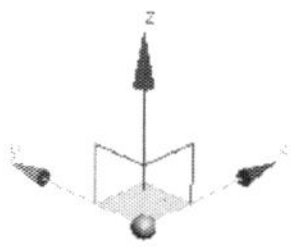

Figure 2-6 *The move gizmo*

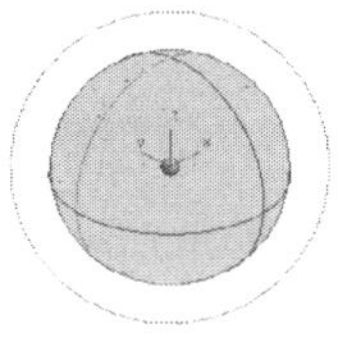

Figure 2-7 *The rotate gizmo*

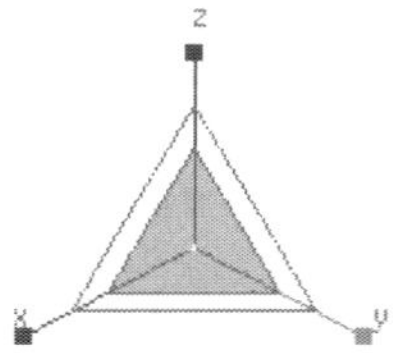

Figure 2-8 *The scale gizmo*

AXIS CONSTRAINTS TOOLBAR

The buttons in the **Axis Constraints** toolbar are used to specify the axis or plane along which the transformation would take place. The transformation includes movement, rotation, and scaling of an object. The **Axis Constraints** toolbar is not displayed by default on the interface.

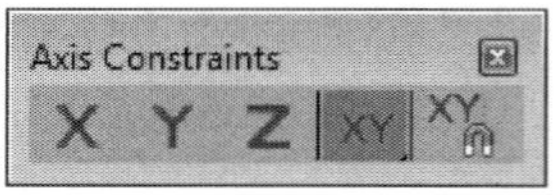

Figure 2-9 *The* ***Axis Constraints*** *toolbar*

To display it, right-click in the blank area on the **Main Toolbar**; a shortcut menu will be displayed. Choose **Axis Constraints** from the shortcut menu; the toolbar will be displayed on the screen, as shown in Figure 2-9. Now, choose one of the buttons available in the **Axis Constraints** toolbar to perform the transformation along the selected axis. You can use the F5, F6, and F7 function keys to invoke the **X**, **Y**, and **Z** constraints, respectively. To toggle between the **XY**, **YZ**, and **XZ** axes, you can use the F8 function key.

STANDARD PRIMITIVES

Autodesk 3ds Max has several basic three-dimensional geometric shapes which are known as standard primitives such as box, cone, sphere, cylinder, torus, tube, and so on. You can use these primitives to create simple 3D models such as a table, box, chair, and so on. All the standard primitives can be created dynamically using the mouse or by specifying the parameters in the Keyboard Entry rollout of the Command Panel.

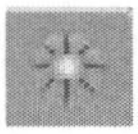

To create the standard primitives, choose **Create > Geometry** in the **Command Panel**. By default, the **Standard Primitives** option is selected in the drop-down list below the **Geometry** button. Now, activate the viewport in which you want to create the primitives by clicking in it. Next, invoke the corresponding tool from the **Object Type** rollout. In the following section, you will learn to create and modify the standard primitives using various tools available in the **Object Type** rollout.

Creating a Box

Menu bar:	Create > Standard Primitives > Box
Command Panel:	Create > Geometry > Standard Primitives> Object Type rollout > Box

To create a box, activate the viewport in which you want to create a box by clicking in it. Next, invoke the **Box** tool from the **Object Type** rollout; the **Name and Color**, **Creation Method**, **Keyboard Entry**, and **Parameters** rollouts will be displayed, as shown in Figure 2-10. Press and hold the left mouse button in the viewport to specify the first corner of the box and then drag the cursor to define the length and width of the box. Release the left mouse button to get the desired length and width. Now, move the cursor up or down to define the height of the box. Click after you get the desired height; the box will be created, as shown in Figure 2-11.

Various rollouts used to create and modify the box are discussed next.

Note

1. To view all rollouts, position the cursor over any rollout until you see the pan icon (hand). Then, press the left mouse button and drag the cursor in the rollout.

2. The plus sign (+) on the left side of the rollout head indicates that the rollout is collapsed and the minus sign (-) indicates that the rollout is expanded.

Name and Color Rollout

In Autodesk 3ds Max, a specific name and color is automatically assigned to the newly created box. To modify this name, expand the **Name and Color** rollout. Enter a new name in the **Name and Color** text box and press ENTER. To change the color of the box, choose the color swatch on the right side of the name text box; the **Object Color** dialog box will be displayed, as shown in Figure 2-12. Choose a new color from this dialog box; the selected color will be displayed in the **Current Color** color swatch. Now, choose the **OK** button; the new color will be assigned to the box.

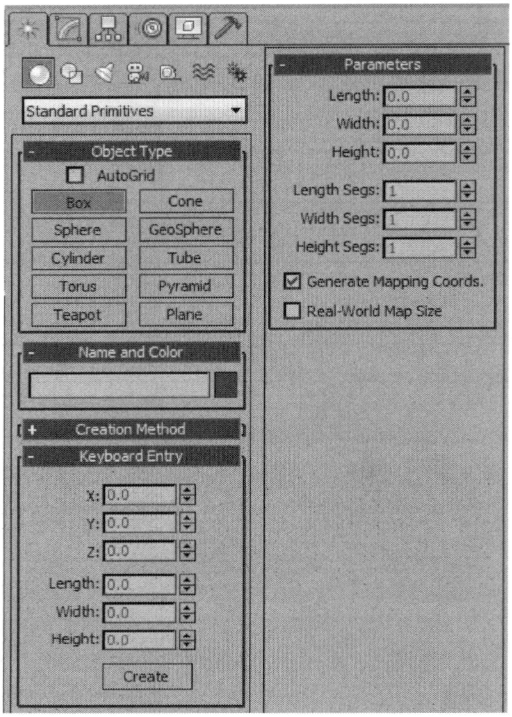

Figure 2-10 Various rollouts to create a box

Figure 2-11 A box

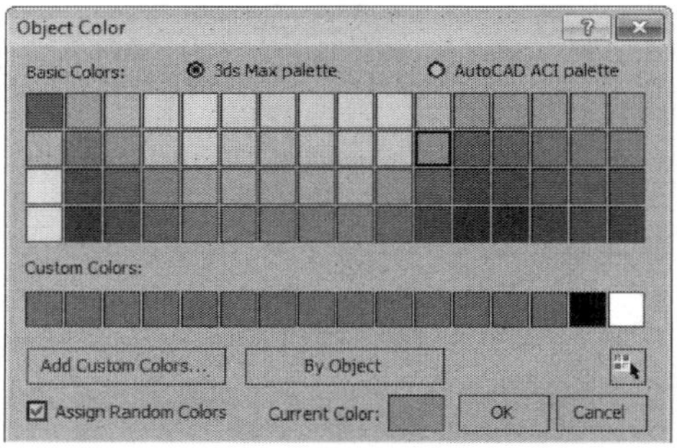

***Figure 2-12** The **Object Color** dialog box*

To customize the new color, choose the **Add Custom Colors** button in the **Object Color** dialog box; the **Color Selector: Add Color** dialog box will be displayed, as shown in Figure 2-13. Now, customize a new color in this dialog box and choose the **Add Color** button; the new color will be displayed in one of the color swatches in the **Custom Colors** area of the **Object Color** dialog box. Next, choose the **OK** button; the new color will be assigned to the box.

Note

*The options in the **Name and Color** rollout are the same for all standard primitives.*

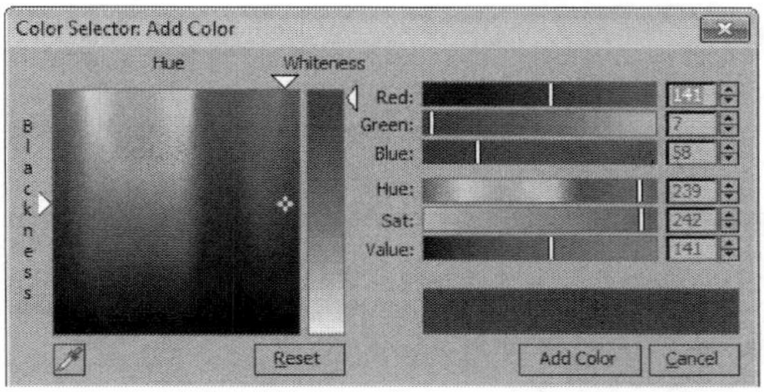

***Figure 2-13** The **Color Selector: Add Color** dialog box*

Creation Method Rollout

The options in this rollout are used for creating the box dynamically using the mouse. Select the **Cube** radio button to create a box of equal length, width, and height. Select the **Box** radio button to create a box having different length, width, and height.

Keyboard Entry Rollout

This rollout is used to create a box by entering the parameters in the **Keyboard Entry** rollout using the keyboard. To do so, expand the **Keyboard Entry** rollout and enter the values in the **Length**, **Width**, and **Height** spinners to specify the length, width, and height of the box, respectively. Also, enter the values in the **X**, **Y**, and **Z** spinners to specify the position of the box in the viewport along the axes of the home grid or a grid object. By default, the value in these spinners is 0, therefore, the object is created at the center of the home grid or a grid object in the viewport. Next, choose the **Create** button in the **Keyboard Entry** rollout; a box will be displayed with the specified dimensions in all viewports.

Note

The grid object is a type of helper object. It is a local grid other than the home grid that you can create yourself as per the requirement.

*The **Keyboard Entry** rollout in all standard primitives is used to create the corresponding primitive by entering the parameters in this rollout. The method of creating all primitives is the same as discussed. The only difference is in the type and number of parameters of various standard primitives.*

Parameters Rollout

After creating the box, you can modify its dimensions using the **Parameters** rollout. To do so, enter the new values of length, width, and height in the respective spinners in the **Parameters** rollout. Similarly, set the values in the **Length Segs**, **Width Segs**, and **Height Segs** spinners to define the number of divisions or segments along each axis of the object. Select the **Generate Mapping Coords.** check box to calculate the mapping of the box being created.

Note

*After creating a tool in the standard primitives list, if you right-click in the viewport to exit the tool, the **Parameters** rollout will disappear from the **Create** panel. In such a case, to modify the parameters of the tool, select the tool in the viewport and choose the **Modify** tab in the **Command Panel**; the **Parameters** rollout will appear again.*

Creating a Sphere

Menu bar: Create > Standard Primitives > Sphere
Command Panel: Create > Geometry > Standard Primitives > Object Type rollout > Sphere

To create a sphere, activate a viewport by clicking in it and invoke the **Sphere** tool from the **Object Type** rollout; the **Name and Color**, **Creation Method**, **Keyboard Entry**, and **Parameters** rollouts will be displayed, as shown in Figure 2-14. Press and hold the left mouse button to specify the center of the sphere and then drag the cursor to define the radius of the sphere. Release the left mouse button to get the desired radius; the sphere will be created, as shown in Figure 2-15. Note that the sphere will be displayed in all viewports.

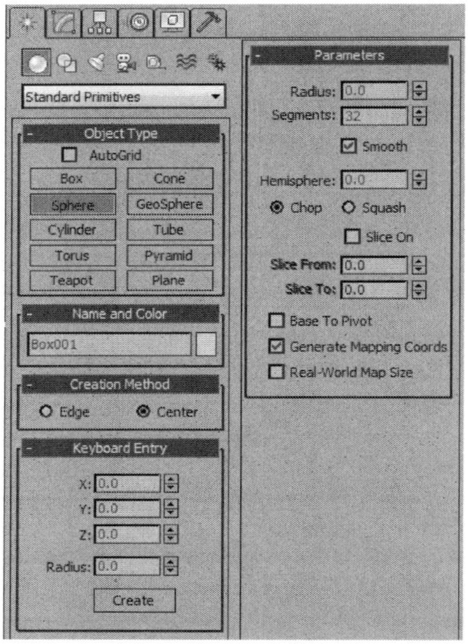

Figure 2-14 *Various rollouts to create a sphere*

Figure 2-15 *A sphere*

Various rollouts used to create and modify the sphere are discussed next.

Creation Method Rollout

The options in this rollout are used for creating a sphere dynamically. Select the **Edge** radio button to specify the first point on an edge at the surface of the sphere and then drag to specify its diameter. Select the **Center** radio button to specify the first point at the center of the sphere and then drag to specify the radius.

Parameters Rollout

The options in this rollout are used to modify the parameters of the sphere. To do so, enter a new value in the **Radius** spinner. By default, the **Smooth** check box is selected, therefore, the sphere appears smooth. If this check box is cleared, it will give a faceted appearance to the sphere. The **Hemisphere** spinner is used to create one-half of the sphere. To create a hemisphere, enter a value in the **Hemisphere** spinner. While creating a hemisphere, if you select the **Chop** radio button, then the number of vertices and faces in the hemisphere will be chopped or reduced. If you select the **Squash** radio button, the hemisphere will have the same number of vertices and faces as in the complete sphere. On selecting the **Slice On** check box, the **Slice From** and **Slice To** spinners will be enabled. Set the values in the **Slice From** and **Slice To** spinners to specify the start and end of the sphere around its local Z-axis. By default, the pivot point of the sphere is located at its center. If you select the **Base To Pivot** check box, then the pivot point of the sphere will shift toward its local Z-axis.

Note
The pivot point represents the local center and the local coordinate system of an object.

Creating a Geosphere

Menu bar:	Create > Standard Primitives > GeoSphere
Command Panel:	Create > Geometry > Standard Primitives > Object Type rollout > GeoSphere

To create a geosphere, activate the viewport by clicking in it and invoke the **GeoSphere** tool from the **Object Type** rollout; the **Name and Color**, **Creation Method**, **Keyboard Entry**, and **Parameters** rollouts will be displayed, as shown in Figure 2-16. Press and hold the left mouse button to specify the center of the geosphere and then drag the cursor to define the radius of the geosphere. Release the left mouse button to get the desired radius; a geosphere will be created, as shown in Figure 2-17. Notice that the geosphere will be displayed in all viewports.

Note
A geosphere generates a more regular surface than a sphere. Also, you can get three types of regular polyhedrons in a geosphere.

Various rollouts used to create and modify the geosphere are discussed next.

Creation Method Rollout

The options in this rollout are used for creating a geosphere dynamically. Select the **Diameter** radio button to specify the first point on an edge at the surface of the geosphere and then drag to specify the diameter. Select the **Center** radio button to specify the first point as the center of the geosphere and then drag to specify the radius.

Parameters Rollout

The options in this rollout are used to modify the geosphere. Set a new value in the **Radius** spinner. If you create a geosphere by selecting the **Tetra** radio button in the **Geodesic Base Type** area, the resulting surface will consist of tetrahedrons and triangular faces, as shown in Figure 2-18. Similarly, if you select the **Octa** radio button, you will get a surface consisting of octagons and triangular faces, as shown in Figure 2-19. Select the **Icosa** radio button to create a surface consisting of 20-sided polygons and equilateral triangles, as shown in Figure 2-20. Select the **Smooth** check box to make a smooth geosphere. On selecting the **Hemisphere** check box, one half of the geosphere will be created. If the **Base To Pivot** check box is selected, it will shift the pivot point of the geosphere toward the local Z-axis.

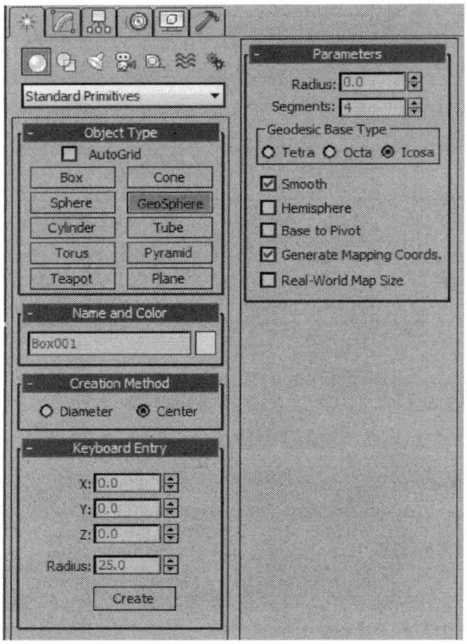

Figure 2-16 Various rollouts to create a geosphere

Figure 2-17 A geosphere

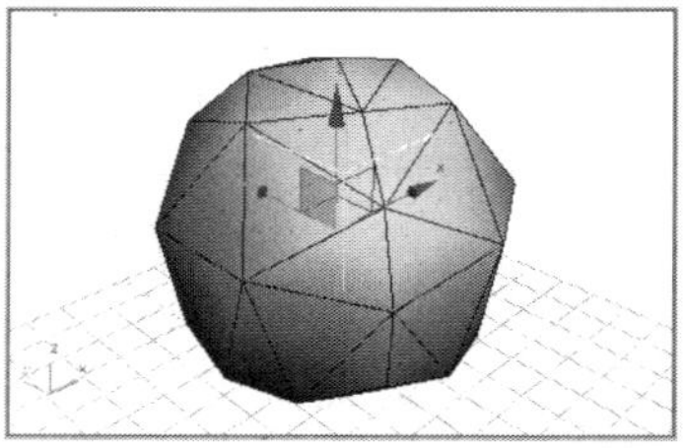

Figure 2-18 *The geosphere created on selecting the* ***Tetra*** *radio button*

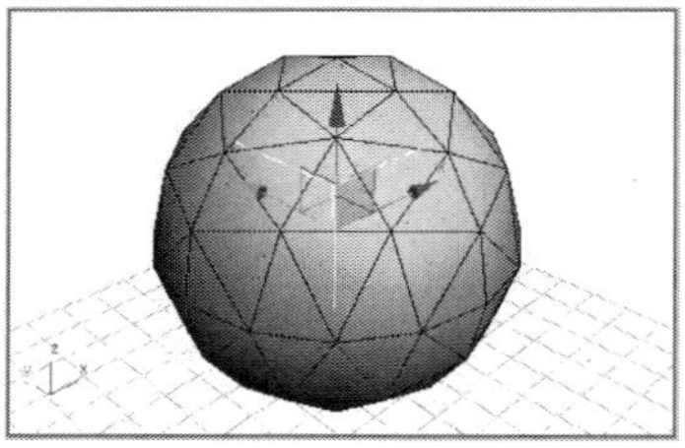

Figure 2-19 *The geosphere created on selecting the* ***Octa*** *radio button*

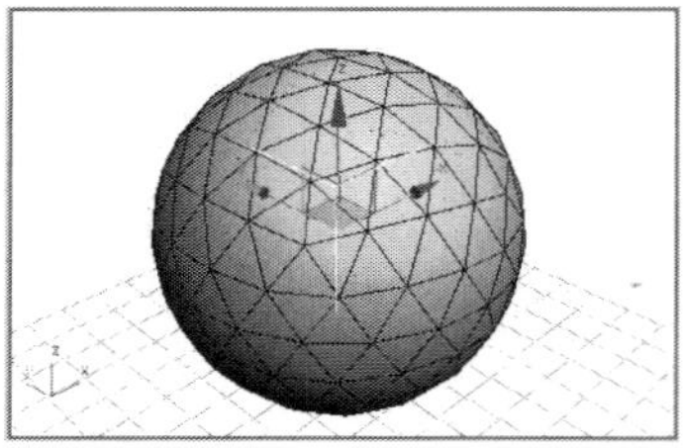

Figure 2-20 *The geosphere created on selecting the* ***Icosa*** *radio button*

Creating a Cylinder

Menu bar:	Create > Standard Primitives > Cylinder
Command Panel:	Create > Geometry > Standard Primitives > Object Type rollout > Cylinder

To create a cylinder, activate the viewport by clicking in it and invoke the **Cylinder** tool from the **Object Type** rollout; the **Name and Color**, **Creation Method**, **Keyboard Entry**, and **Parameters** rollouts will be displayed, as shown in Figure 2-21.

Press and hold the left mouse button to specify the center of the base of the cylinder and then drag the cursor to define the radius of the cylinder. Release the left mouse button. Next, move the cursor up or down to define the height of the cylinder. Click after you get the desired height; a cylinder will be created, as shown in Figure 2-22.

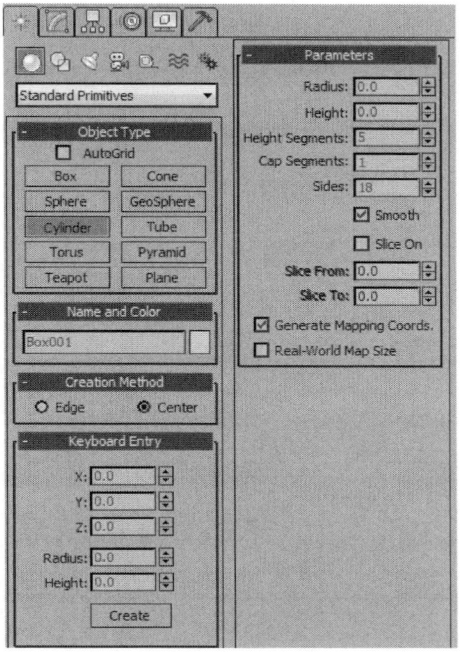

Figure 2-21 *Various rollouts to create a cylinder*

Figure 2-22 *A cylinder*

Various rollouts used to create and modify the cylinder are discussed next.

Creation Method Rollout

The options in this rollout are the same as those discussed in the **Sphere** tool.

Parameters Rollout

The options in this rollout are used to modify the cylinder. Enter a new value for the radius and height in the **Radius** and **Height** spinners, respectively. The value in the **Height Segments** spinner defines the number of segments along the height of the cylinder. The value in the **Cap Segments** spinner specifies the number of segments at the top and bottom of the cylinder. The value in the **Sides** spinner specifies the number of sides on the cylinder. Different shapes of the cylinder can be created by entering different values in the **Sides** spinner. By default, the **Smooth** check box is selected, therefore, the cylinder appears smoother. The **Slice On** check box is the same as described in the **Sphere** tool.

Creating a Cone

Menu:	Create > Standard Primitives > Cone
Command Panel:	Create > Geometry > Standard Primitives > Object Type rollout > Cone

To create a cone, activate the viewport and then invoke the **Cone** tool from the **Object Type** rollout; the **Name and Color**, **Creation Method**, **Keyboard Entry**, and **Parameters** rollouts will be displayed, as shown in Figure 2-23.

Press and hold the left mouse button to specify the center of the base of the cone and then, drag the cursor to define radius 1 of the cone. Release the left mouse button and move the cursor up or down to define the height of the cone. Next, click to get the desired height. Move the cursor up or down again and click to define radius 2 of the cone; a cone will be created, as shown in Figure 2-24.

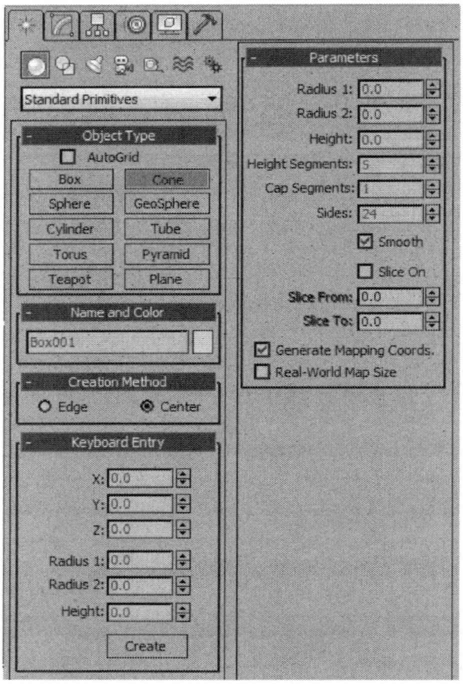

Figure 2-23 *Various rollouts to create a cone*

Figure 2-24 *A cone*

Various rollouts used to create and modify the cone are discussed next.

Creation Method Rollout

The options in this rollout are the same as those discussed in the **Sphere** tool.

Parameters Rollout

The options in this rollout are used to modify the cone. Enter the new values of first radius, second radius, and height in the **Radius 1**, **Radius 2**, and **Height** spinners, respectively. The other options in this rollout are the same as those described in the **Cylinder** tool.

Creating a Tube

Menu bar:	Create > Standard Primitives > Tube
Command Panel:	Create > Geometry > Standard Primitives > Object Type rollout > Tube

To create a tube, activate the viewport and invoke the **Tube** tool from the **Object Type** rollout; the **Name and Color**, **Creation Method**, **Keyboard Entry**, and **Parameters** rollouts will be displayed, as shown in Figure 2-25.

Press and hold the left mouse button to specify the center of the tube and then drag the cursor to define the first radius of the tube. It can be the inner or the outer radius of the tube. Next, release the left mouse button, move the cursor, and then click to define the second radius. Next, move the cursor up or down and click to get the desired height of the tube; a tube will be created, as shown in Figure 2-26.

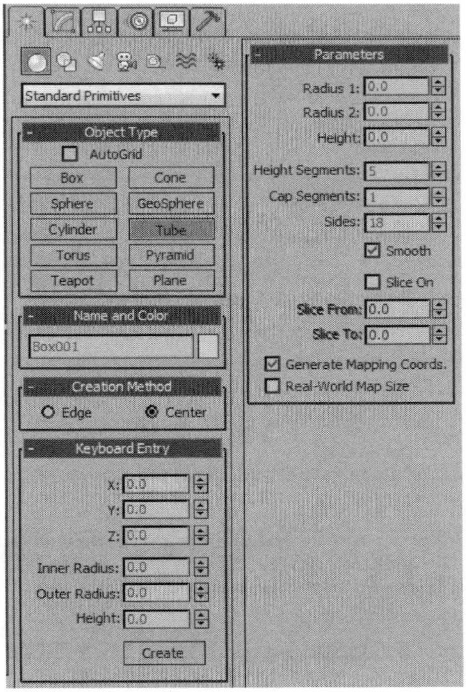

Figure 2-25 *Various rollouts to create a tube*

Figure 2-26 *A tube*

Various rollouts used to create and modify the tube are discussed next.

Creation Method Rollout

The options in this rollout are the same as those discussed in the **Sphere** tool.

Parameters Rollout

The options in this rollout are used to modify the tube. Enter new values in the **Radius 1**, **Radius 2**, and **Height** spinners. The other options in this rollout are the same as those described in the **Cylinder** tool.

Creating a Torus

Menu bar:	Create > Standard Primitives > Torus
Command Panel:	Create > Geometry > Standard Primitives > Object Type rollout > Torus

To create a torus, activate the viewport and invoke the **Torus** tool from the **Object Type** rollout; the **Name and Color**, **Creation Method**, **Keyboard Entry**, and **Parameters** rollouts will be displayed, as shown in Figure 2-27.

Press and hold the left mouse button to specify the center of the torus and then drag the cursor to define the radius of the torus. Release the left mouse button and then drag the cursor to adjust the radius of the circular cross-section of the torus. Click to get the desired radius; a torus will be created, as shown in Figure 2-28.

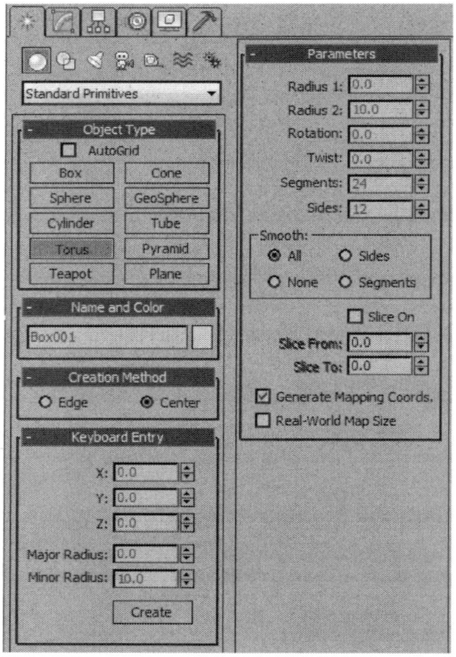

Figure 2-27 Various rollouts to create a torus

Figure 2-28 A torus

Various rollouts used to create and modify the torus are discussed next.

Creation Method Rollout

The options in this rollout are the same as those discussed in the **Sphere** tool.

Parameters Rollout

The options in this rollout are used to modify the torus. Enter new values in the respective spinners to modify the torus. The value in the **Rotation** spinner defines the degree of rotation of the circular cross-section of the torus. The value in the **Twist** spinner specifies how much the circular cross-section of the torus can be twisted. The **Segments** spinner defines the number of segments around the circumference of the torus. The **Sides** value specifies the number of sides in the circular cross-section of the torus. In the **Smooth** area of the **Parameters** rollout, there are four radio buttons. Select the **All** radio button to apply smoothness to all surfaces of the torus. Select the **Sides** radio button to apply smoothness between adjacent segments. Select the **Segments** radio button to apply smoothness to the segments individually. It results in the formation of ring-like segments along the torus. Select the **None** radio button, if you do not want to apply smoothness to the torus. The **Slice On** check box is the same as described in the **Sphere** tool.

Creating a Pyramid

Menu bar:	Create > Standard Primitives > Pyramid
Command Panel:	Create > Geometry > Standard Primitives > Object Type rollout > Pyramid

To create a pyramid, activate the viewport and invoke the **Pyramid** tool from the **Object Type** rollout; the **Name and Color**, **Creation Method**, **Keyboard Entry**, and **Parameters** rollouts will be displayed, as shown in Figure 2-29.

Press and hold the left mouse button to specify the first corner of the pyramid and then drag the cursor to define the width and depth of the pyramid. Release the left mouse button and drag the cursor upward. Click after you get the desired height; a pyramid will be created, as shown in Figure 2-30.

Various rollouts used to create and modify the pyramid are discussed next.

Creation Method Rollout

The options in this rollout are used for creating a pyramid dynamically. Select the **Base/Apex** radio button to specify the first point as the first corner of the base of the pyramid. Select the **Center** radio button to specify the first point as the center of the base of the pyramid.

Parameters Rollout

The options in this rollout are used to modify the pyramid. The values in the **Width Segs**, **Depth Segs**, and **Height Segs** spinners define the number of segments on the corresponding sides of the pyramid. Enter new values in the respective spinners to modify the pyramid.

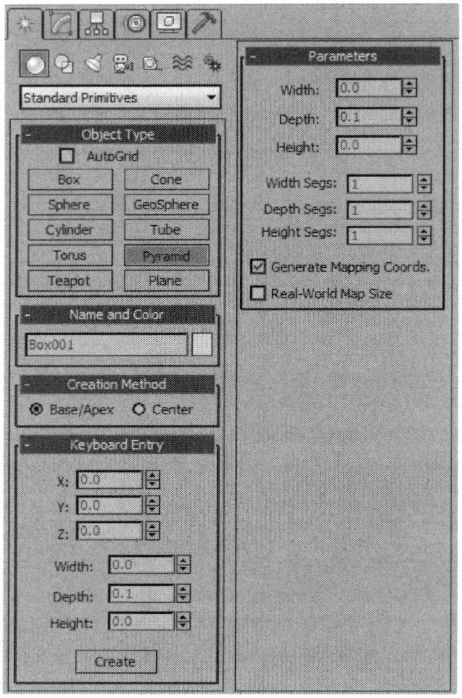

Figure 2-29 *Various rollouts to create a pyramid*

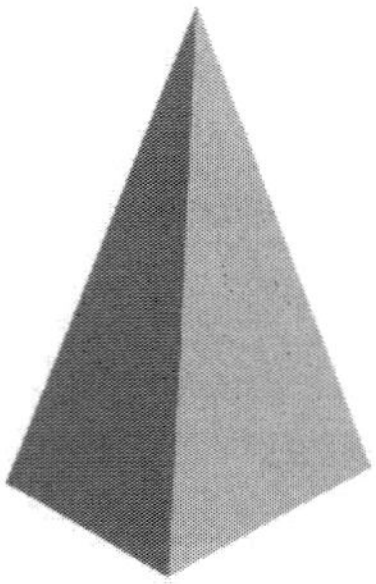

Figure 2-30 *A pyramid*

Creating a Plane

Menu bar:	Create > Standard Primitives > Plane
Command Panel:	Create > Geometry > Standard Primitives > Object Type rollout > Plane

To create a plane, activate the viewport by clicking in it and then invoke the **Plane** tool from the **Object Type** rollout; the **Name and Color**, **Creation Method**, **Keyboard Entry**, and **Parameters** rollouts will be displayed, as shown in Figure 2-31.

Press and hold the left mouse button to specify the first corner of the plane and then drag the cursor to define the length and width of the plane. Release the left mouse button; a plane will be created, as shown in Figure 2-32.

Various rollouts used to create and modify the plane are discussed next.

Creation Method Rollout

The options in this rollout are used for creating a plane dynamically. Select the **Rectangle** radio button to specify the first point as the corner of a rectangular plane. Select the **Square** radio button to specify the first point as the center of a square plane. Note that in the case of a square plane, the length and width of the plane will be equal.

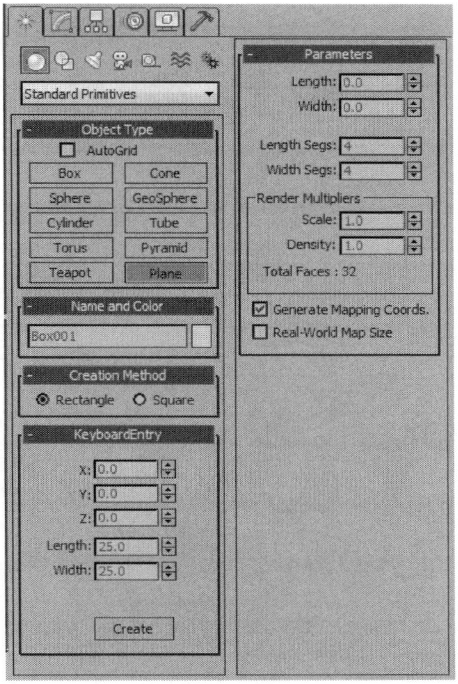

Figure 2-31 *Various rollouts to create a plane*

Figure 2-32 *A plane*

Parameters Rollout

The options in this rollout are used to modify the plane. Enter the new values in the **Length** and **Width** spinners to modify the plane. The values in the **Length Segs** and **Width Segs** spinners define the number of segments along the length and width of the plane, respectively. The **Render Multipliers** area is used to set the multipliers for rendering. The **Scale** spinner is used to specify the value by which the length and width will be multiplied at rendering. The **Density** spinner is used to specify the value by which the number of segments along the length and width will be multiplied at rendering.

Creating a Teapot

Menu bar:	Create > Standard Primitives > Teapot
Command Panel:	Create > Geometry > Standard Primitives > Object Type rollout > Teapot

To create a teapot, activate the viewport and invoke the **Teapot** tool from the **Object Type** rollout; the **Name and Color**, **Creation Method**, **Keyboard Entry**, and **Parameters** rollouts will be displayed, as shown in Figure 2-33.

Press and hold the left mouse button to define the center of the bottom face and then drag the cursor to define the radius of the teapot. Release the left mouse button after you get the desired radius; a teapot will be created, as shown in Figure 2-34.

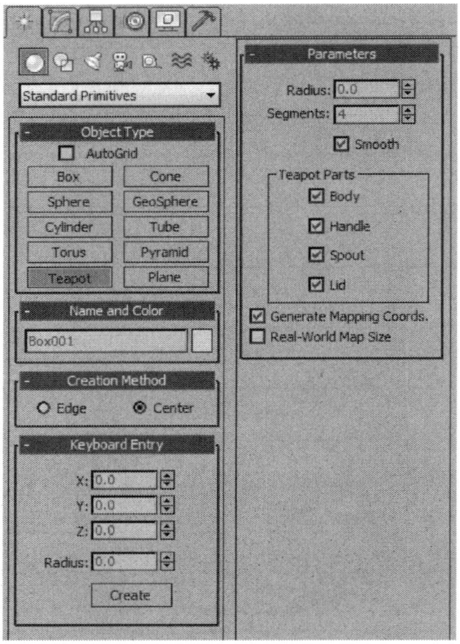

Figure 2-33 *Various rollouts to create a teapot*

Figure 2-34 *A teapot*

Various rollouts used to create and modify the teapot are discussed next.

Creation Method Rollout

The options in this rollout are the same as those discussed in the **Sphere** tool.

Parameters Rollout

The options in this rollout are used to modify the teapot. The value in the **Segments** spinner is used to specify the number of divisions in each quadrant of the body. By default, the **Smooth** check box is selected. Therefore, all parts of the teapot will be smoother. A teapot has four parts: body, handle, spout, and lid. If you want to remove any one of the parts, clear the check box corresponding to that part in the **Teapot Parts** area of the **Parameters** rollout. You can also use different parts of a teapot individually to make another object. For example, you can use the handle of the teapot for creating a coffee mug.

RENDERING A STILL IMAGE

Menu bar:	Rendering > Render
Toolbar:	Main Toolbar > Render Production
Keyboard:	SHIFT + Q

Rendering is a process of generating a 2-dimensional image from a 3-dimensional scene. It shows the lighting effects, materials applied, background, and other settings that you applied to the scene. The basic rendering for a still scene is discussed next, while the advance rendering for the animated scenes will be discussed in the later chapters.

To render a still image, activate the viewport and invoke the **Render Setup** tool from the **Main Toolbar**; the **Render Setup: Default Scanline Renderer** dialog box will be displayed. The **Common** tab is chosen by default in this dialog box. In the **Common Parameters** rollout, make sure that the **Single** radio button is selected in the **Time Output** area. This will enable you to render a single frame at a time. In the **Output Size** area, set the parameters or use the default ones and then choose the **Render** button at the lower right corner of the dialog box; the rendered image will be displayed in the **Perspective, frame 0, Display Gamma:2.2, RGBA Color16 Bits/Channel (1:1)** dialog box, as shown in Figure 2-35.

*Figure 2-35 The **Perspective, frame 0, RGBA Color16 Bits/Channel (1:1)** dialog box*

Here, **Perspective** refers to the name of the viewport that you have selected at rendering and **frame 0** refers to the number of frame that has been rendered.

Note

*To render a view quickly, choose the **Render Production** tool from the **Main Toolbar** or press the F9 key.*

To save the rendered image, choose the **Save Image** button in the **Perspective, frame 0, RGBA Color 16 Bits/Channel (1:1)** dialog box; the **Save Image** dialog box will be displayed. Now, select the type of image format from the **Save as type** drop-down list and enter the name of the image in the **File name** text box. Next, browse to the folder where you want to save the scene and choose the **Save** button; a dialog box will be displayed. You can adjust the settings for the file format you have chosen in this dialog box. Use the default settings and choose the **OK** button; the image file will be saved at the selected location.

Non-Photorealistic Style Rendering

New

By default, a 3ds Max scene is rendered using the scanline renderer. However, if you choose the quicksilver hardware renderer, you can achieve non-photorealistic rendering. To do so, you need to follow the steps given next.

1. Activate any of the viewport and invoke the **Render Setup** tool from the **Main Toolbar**; the **Render Setup: Default Scanline Renderer** dialog box will be displayed. The **Common** tab is chosen by default in this dialog box.

2. Collapse the **Common Parameters** rollout in this tab and expand the **Assign Renderer** rollout. In this rollout, choose the **Choose Renderer** button at the right of the **Production** text box; the **Choose Renderer** dialog box will be displayed. Select the **Quicksilver Hardware Renderer** option and choose the **OK** button to exit the **Choose Renderer** dialog box. Notice the change in the **Render Setup** dialog box, refer to Figure 2-36.

3. Choose the **Renderer** tab; various rollouts will be displayed, refer to Figure 2-36. In the **Visual Style** area of the **Visual Style & Appearance** rollout, various options are available in the **Rendering Level** drop-down list, as shown in Figure 2-37.

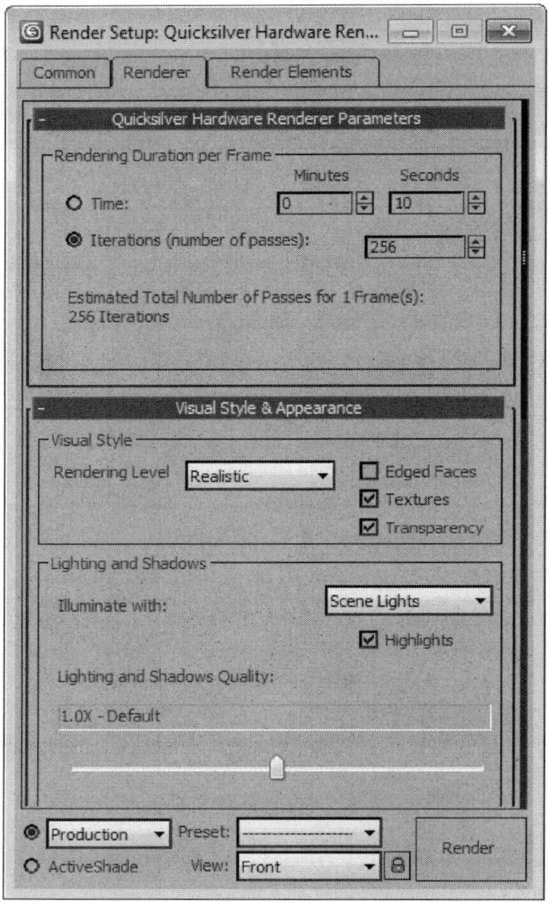

Figure 2-36 The ***Render Setup: Quicksilver Hardware Renderer*** *dialog box*

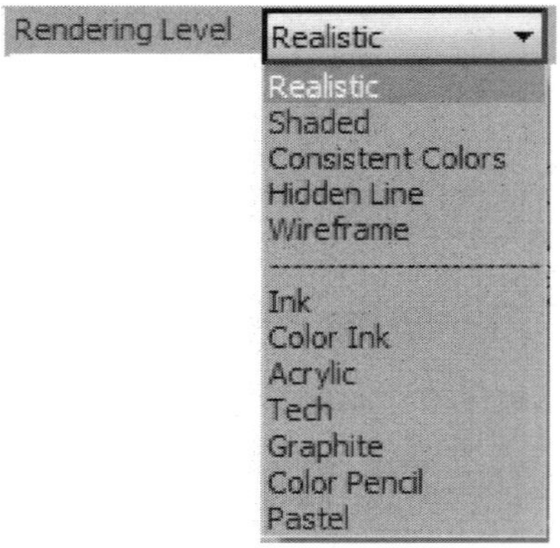

Figure 2-37 The ***Rendering Level*** *drop-down list*

4. To achieve non-photorealistic rendering, select the **Graphite**, **Ink**, **Color Ink**, **Pastel**, **Acrylic**, **Tech**, or **Color Pencil** option from the **Rendering Level** drop down list. Next, choose the Render button at the lower right corner of the dialog box; the rendered image will be displayed as per the option selected in the drop-down list.

iray Renderer

New

The iray renderer is a new renderer introduced in Autodesk 3ds Max 2012. In iray renderer, you can specify the length of time to render or number of iterations (passes) to compute. Alternatively, you can start the rendering for indefinite time and stop it when you are satisfied with the quality of rendering. When you change the current renderer to the iray renderer using the **Render Setup** dialog box, the **iray** and **Advanced**

Parameters rollouts will be displayed. The procedure to change the renderer has been explained in detail in the previous section. Figure 2-38 shows the **iray** rollout in the **Render Setup** dialog box. You can select the desired radio button in this rollout based on your requirement. The rendering done by the iray renderer appears more grainy in the first few passes. The graininess decreases as you increase the number of passes. The iray renderer renders glossy reflections and self illuminating objects with much more precision as compared to other renderers. However, this renderer supports only certain materials, maps, and shader types.

Changing the Background Color

Menu bar: Rendering > Environment
Keyboard: 8

By default, the background color of the final output is black at the time of rendering. To change the background color, choose **Rendering > Environment** from the menu bar; the **Environment and Effects** dialog box will be displayed, as shown in Figure 2-39. In this dialog box, the **Environment** tab is chosen by default. The **Common Parameters**, **Exposure Control**, and **Atmosphere** rollouts will be displayed under this tab. In the **Common Parameters** rollout, the **Background** area is used to change the background color of the scene at rendering. In the **Background** area, choose the color swatch; the **Color Selector: Background Color** dialog box will be displayed. Select a new color and choose the **OK** button. Next, close the **Environment and Effects** dialog box; the background will display the new color at rendering.

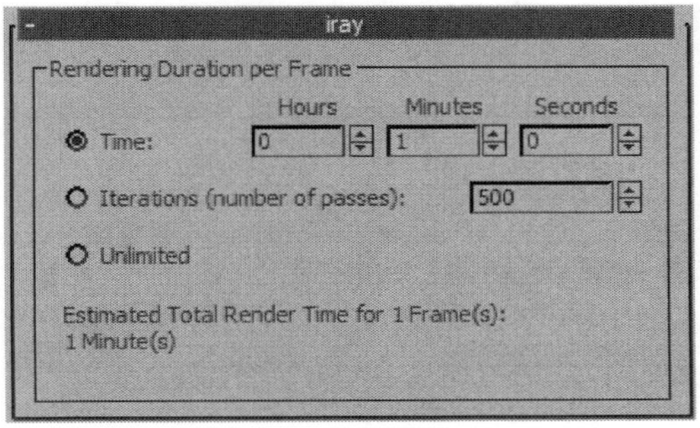

*Figure 2-38 The **iray** rollout in the **Render Setup** dialog box*

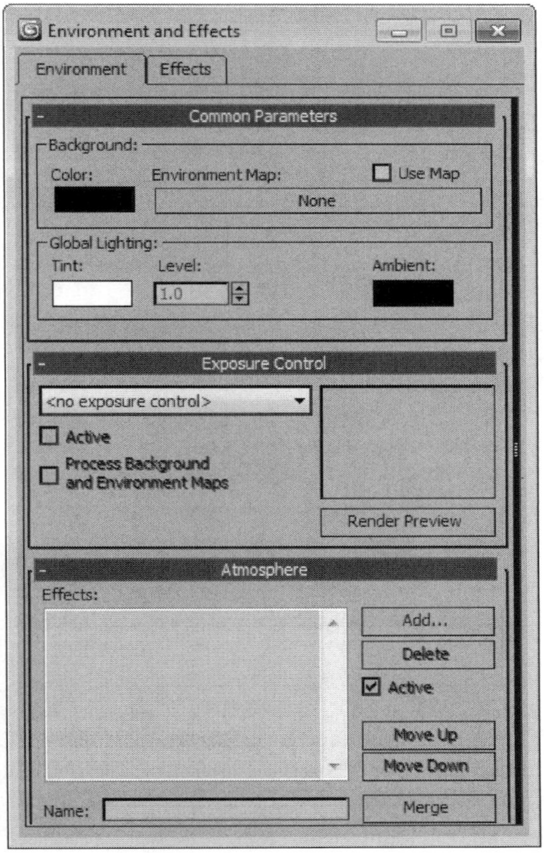

*Figure 2-39 The **Environment and Effects** dialog box*

Tutorial 1

In this tutorial, you will create the 3D model of a table with drawers, as shown in Figure 2-40, using the standard primitives. **(Expected time: 30 min)**

Figure 2-40 *The table model*

The following steps are required to complete this tutorial:

a. Set the project folder.
b. Create the left and right boxes of the table.
c. Create the drawers.
d. Create outer faces of the table.
e. Create the knobs for the drawers of the table.
f. Change the background color of the final output at rendering.
g. Render the scene for the final output.
h. Save the file.

Setting the Project Folder

Before starting a new file, it is recommended that you set the project folder at the beginning stage. Setting a project folder helps you keep all files of a project in an organized manner. You need to follow the steps given below to set the project folder.

1. Open the Windows File Browser and browse to the *Documents* folder. In this folder, create a new folder with the name *3dsmax*.

2. Start Autodesk 3ds Max 2012. If 3ds Max is already running, you need to reset it. To do so, choose **Reset** from the **Application menu**; the **3ds Max** message box is displayed. Choose the **Yes** button from the message box; a new screen is displayed with the original settings.

3. Choose the **Application** button; the **Application menu** is displayed. Next, choose **Manage > Set Project Folder** from it; the **Browse For Folder** dialog box is displayed.

4. In the **Browse For Folder** dialog box, navigate to *\Documents\3dsmax*. Next, choose the **Make New Folder** button to create a new folder with the name *c02_tut1*.

Creating the Left and Right Boxes

In this section, you need to create the basic shape of the table using the **Box** tool from **Standard Primitives**.

1. By default, the **Select Object** tool is invoked in the **Main Toolbar**. Choose **Create > Geometry** in the **Command Panel**; **Standard Primitives** is displayed in the drop-down list below the **Geometry** button. Also, the **Object Type** rollout is displayed in the **Command Panel**. Next, invoke the **Box** tool from the **Object Type** rollout.

2. Activate the Top viewport by clicking in it. Press and hold the left mouse button at the upper left corner of the viewport and then drag the cursor to the lower right corner. Release the left mouse button to set the length and width of the box. Next, move the mouse in the upward direction and click in the viewport to set the height of the box.

3. In the **Parameters** rollout, enter the values as given below:

   Length: **90** Width: **75** Height: **95**

4. Invoke the **Zoom Extents All** tool in the viewport navigation controls to view the box; the box is displayed in all viewports, as shown in Figure 2-41. Alternatively, press the Z key to invoke the **Zoom Extents All** tool.

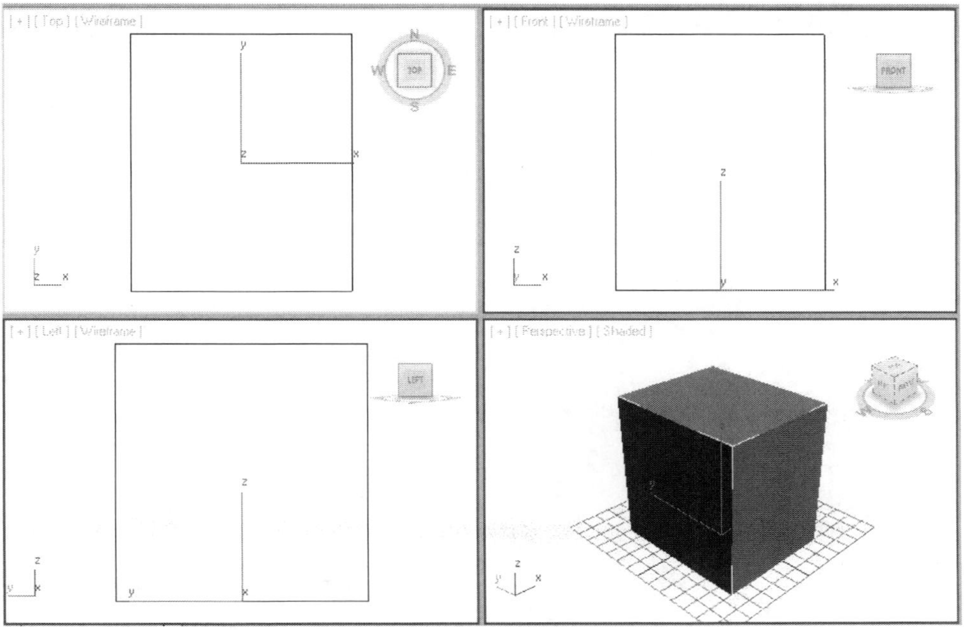

Figure 2-41 *The box displayed in all viewports*

5. In the **Name and Color** rollout, enter **left box** and press ENTER; the object is named as *left box*.

6. Choose the color swatch in the **Name and Color** rollout to change the color of the *left box*; the **Object Color** dialog box is displayed. Choose the **Add Custom Colors** button from this dialog box; the **Color Selector: Add Color** dialog box is displayed. Enter the values as given below:

   Red: **224** Green: **143** Blue: **87**

7. Choose the **Add Color** button in the **Color Selector: Add Color** dialog box to add the selected color; the color is displayed in one of the **Custom Colors** boxes in the **Object Color** dialog box. Choose the **OK** button to apply the color to the *left box*.

8. Create another box using the same method in the Top viewport. Enter the following values in the **Parameters** rollout:

   Length: **90** Width: **80** Height: **25**

9. In the **Name and Color** rollout, enter **right box** and press ENTER; the object is named as *right box*. Also, assign the same color to the right box that you assigned to the left box.

Aligning the Boxes

1. Invoke the **Select and Move** tool and make sure that the *right box* is selected. Move the *right box* along the X, Y, and Z axes in all viewports to align it with the *left box*, as shown in Figure 2-42. Click in the viewport and press the Z key to invoke the **Zoom Extents All** tool, refer to Figure 2-42.

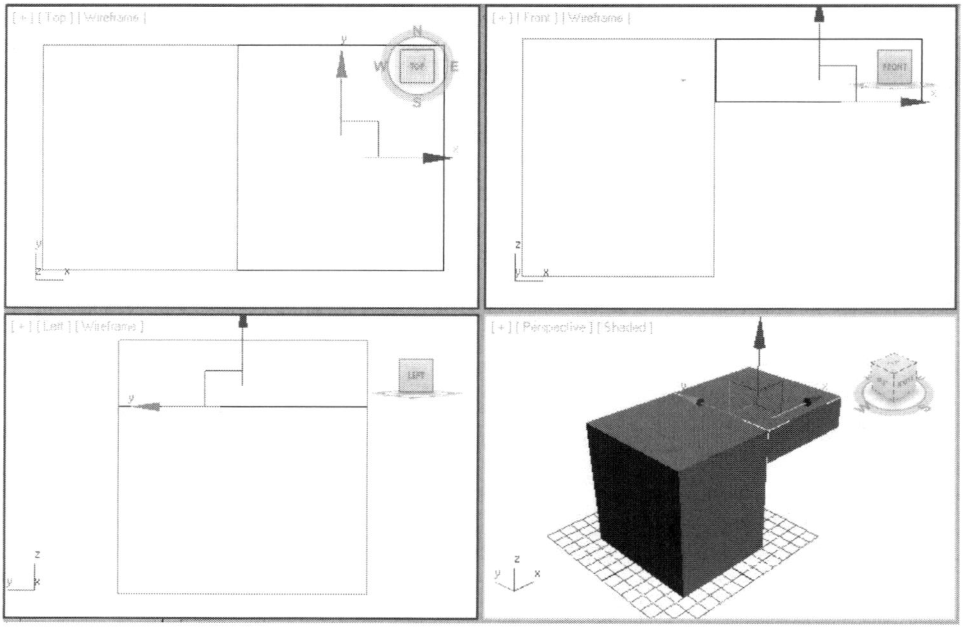

***Figure 2-42** Alignment of the left box with the right box in all viewports*

Note

While aligning the objects, you need to make sure that the objects are aligned properly in all viewports.

Creating the Drawer

1. Create another box in the Top viewport and enter the following values in the **Parameters** rollout:

   Length: **90** Width: **55** Height: **25**

2. In the **Name and Color** rollout, enter **drawer001** and press ENTER. Choose the color swatch to change the color of the *drawer001*; the **Object Color** dialog box is displayed. Choose the **Add Custom Colors** button; the **Color Selector: Add Color** dialog box is displayed. Enter the values as given below:

   Red: **177** Green: **88** Blue: **27**

3. Choose the **Add Color** button from the **Color Selector: Add Color** dialog box to add the selected color. The color is displayed in one of the **Custom Color** boxes in the **Object Color** dialog box. Choose the **OK** button; the new color is assigned to the *drawer001*.

4. Align the *drawer001* with the *left box* in all viewports using the **Select and Move** tool, as shown in Figure 2-43.

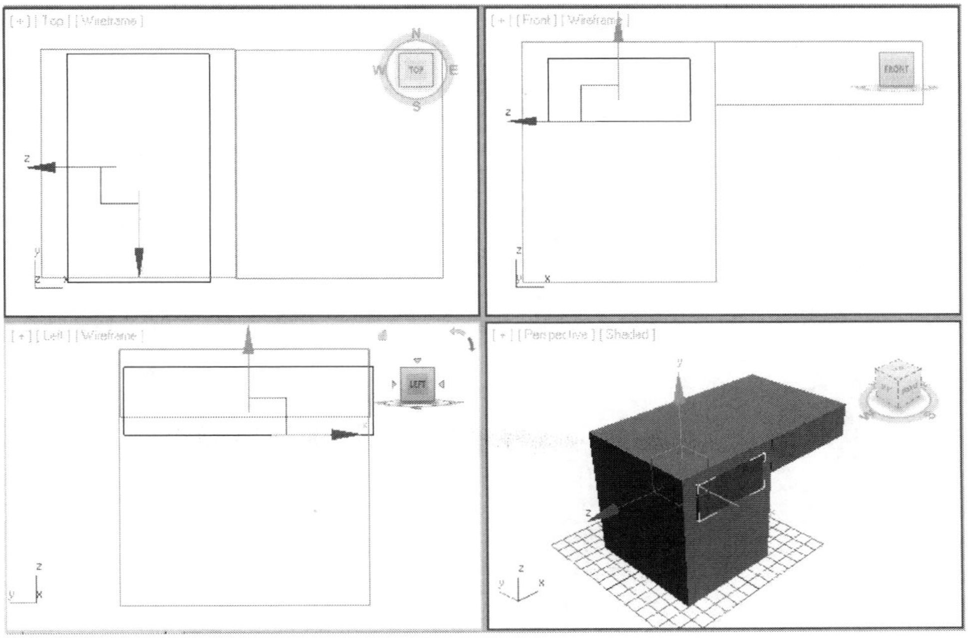

Figure 2-43 *Alignment of the drawer001 with the left box*

Copying the Drawer

1. To create copies of the *drawer001*, activate the Front viewport by right-clicking in it and make sure the *drawer001* is selected. Next, move the cursor over the Y axis, press and hold the SHIFT key, and drag the box downward until the value in the **Y** spinner of the coordinate display at the bottom of the screen becomes around **-29**. Release the left mouse button and the SHIFT key; the **Clone Options** dialog box is displayed, as shown in Figure 2-44.

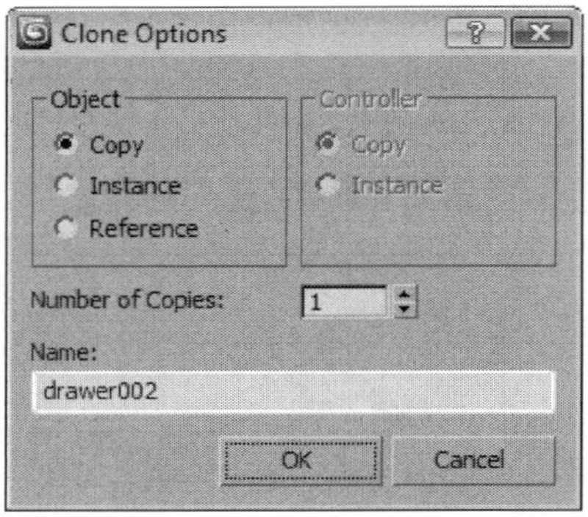

***Figure 2-44** The **Clone Options** dialog box*

2. Select the **Copy** radio button in the **Object** area of the **Clone Options** dialog box. In the **Number of Copies** spinner, enter **2** to create two copies of the *drawer001*. Then, choose the **OK** button; two drawers with same dimensions are created, as shown in Figure 2-45.

Note

The copied objects are automatically named sequentially as drawer002 and drawer003, based on the name of the original object. You can also copy an object by holding the SHIFT key while rotating or scaling it.

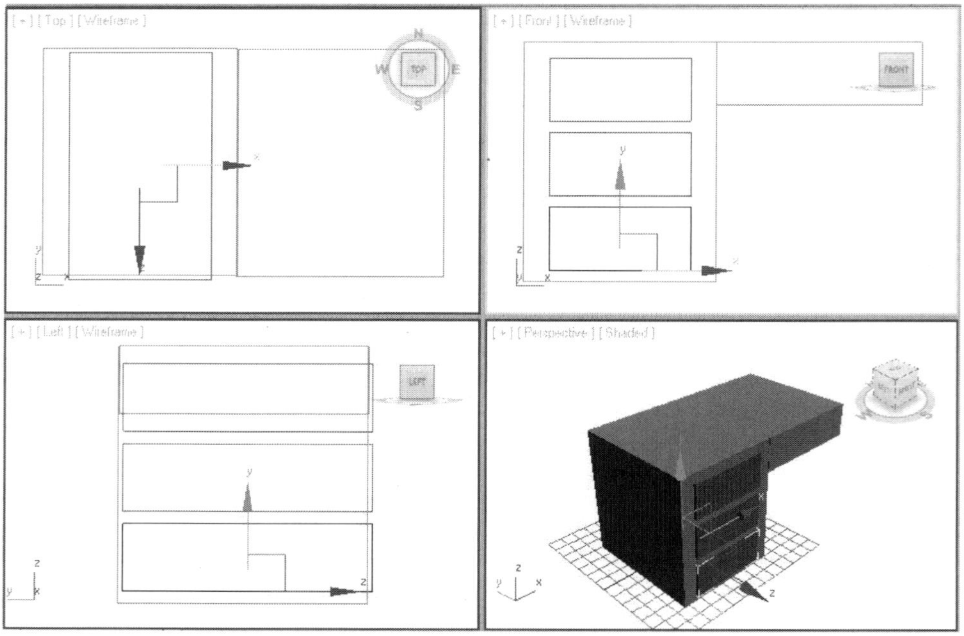

***Figure 2-45** The drawer002 and drawer003 created after copying the drawer001*

3. Create another box in the Top viewport using the values given below:

   Length: **90** Width: **70** Height: **17**

4. Name the newly created box as *drawer004* and change its color as you did for the drawers created previously.

5. Align the *drawer004* in all viewports, as shown in Figure 2-46.

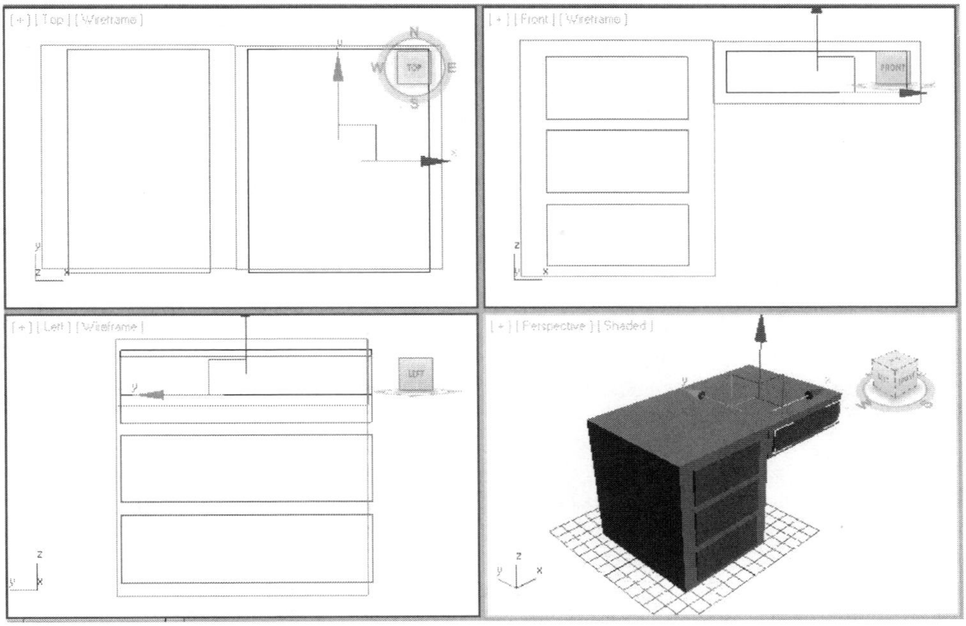

Figure 2-46 *The drawer004 aligned in all viewports*

Creating the Outer Faces of the Table

Next, you need to create the outer faces of the table to make it appear more realistic.

1. Create a box in the Left viewport using the values given below:

   Length: **95.5** Width: **90** Height: **1.5**

2. In the **Name and Color** rollout, enter **left face001** and press ENTER. Choose the color swatch to change the color of the box; the **Object Color** dialog box is displayed. Enter the values as given below:

   Red: **134** Green: **59** Blue: **8**

3. In all viewports, align the *left face001* with the left side of the *left box* using the **Select and Move** tool, as shown in Figure 2-47.

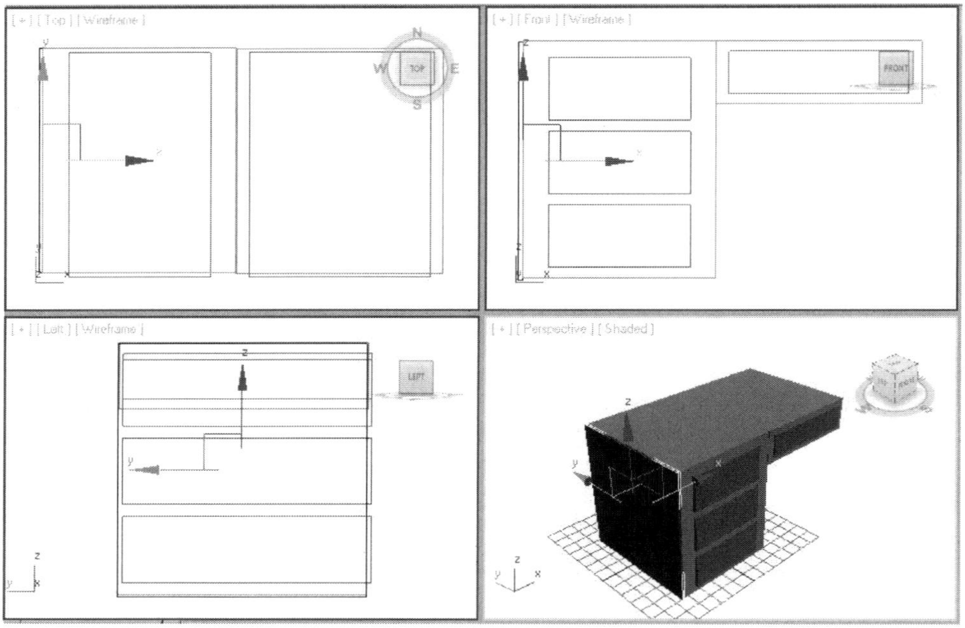

Figure 2-47 *Alignment of the left face001 with the left side of the left box*

4. In the Front viewport, copy the *left face001*; the new face is automatically named as *left face002*. Now, align it with the other side of the *left box*, as shown in Figure 2-48.

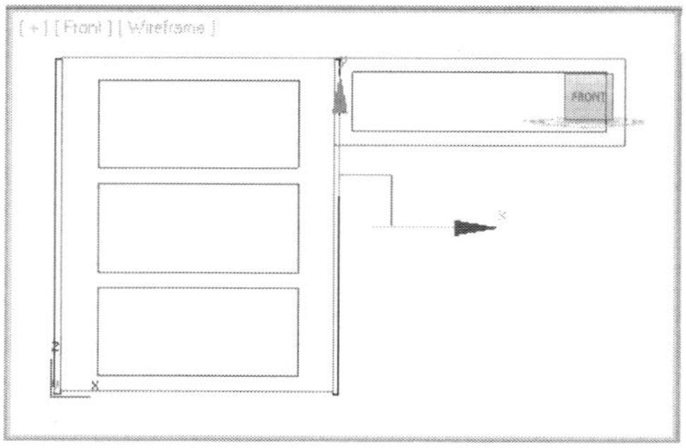

Figure 2-48 *Alignment of the left face002*

5. To create the upper face of the table, create another box in the Top viewport using the values given below:

   Length: **90.5** Width: **156.5** Height: **1.5**

6. Name the box as *upper face* and assign the same color to it as assigned to the other faces.

7. Align the *upper face* with the top of the table, as shown in Figure 2-49.

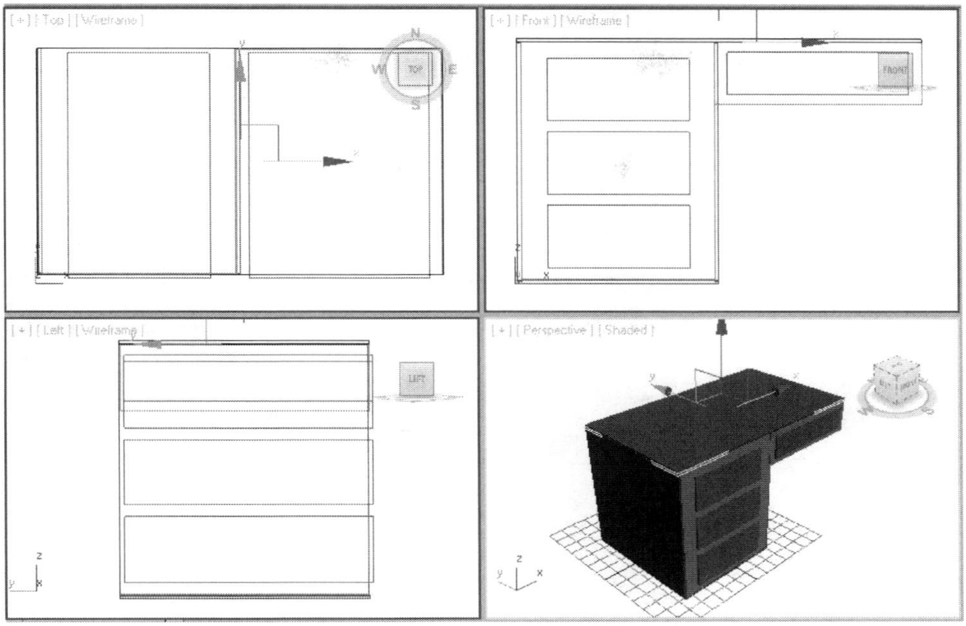

Figure 2-49 *Alignment of the upper face with the top of the table*

8. Create one more box in the Top viewport using the values given below:

   Length: **90.5** Width: **77.5** Height: **1.5**

9. Name the box as *lower face* and assign the same color to it as assigned to the other faces.

10. Align the *lower face* with the bottom of the *left box*, as shown in Figure 2-50.

11. Next, create a box for the lower face of the *right box* in the Top viewport using the following dimensions:

    Length: **90.5** Width: **79** Height: **1.5**

12. Name the box as the *right lower face* and assign the same color to it as assigned to the other faces.

13. Align the *right lower face* to the bottom of the *right box*, as shown in Figure 2-51.

14. Now, create a box for the right face of the *right box* in the Left viewport using the following dimensions:

    Length: **28.9** Width: **90** Height: **1.5**

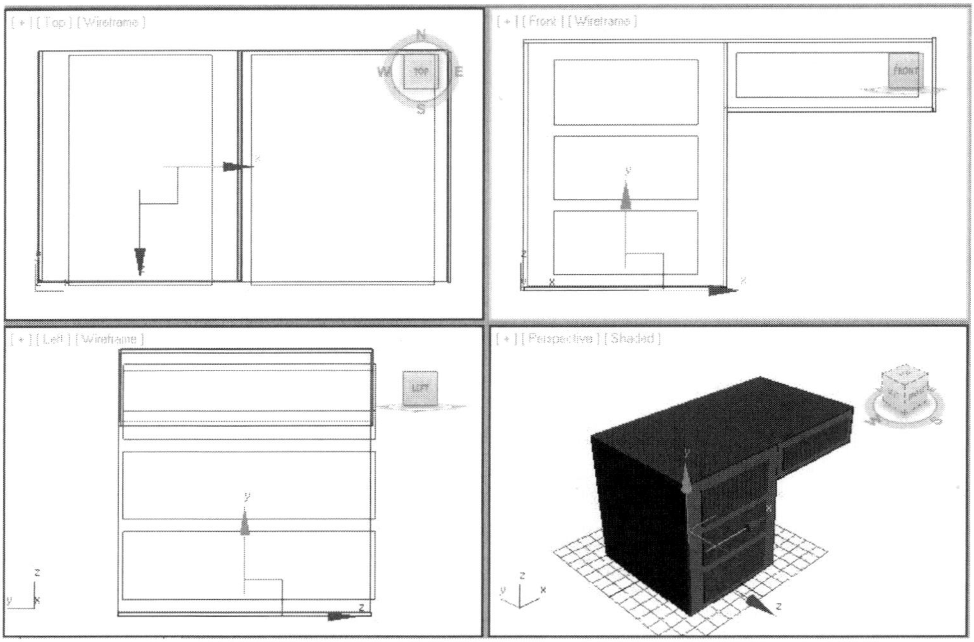

Figure 2-50 *Alignment of the lower face with the bottom of the left box*

15. Name the box as the *right face* and assign the same color to it as assigned to the other faces.

16. Align the *right face* with the right side of the *right box*, as shown in Figure 2-51.

Creating Knobs for the Drawers

In this section, you need to create a knob for one drawer. Then, you can copy the knob for the other drawers.

1. Invoke the **Sphere** tool from **Create > Geometry > Standard Primitives > Object Type** rollout of the **Command Panel**.

2. Now, create a sphere in the Front viewport and in the **Parameters** rollout, enter the following value:

   Radius: **2.3**

   Also, make sure the **Smooth** and **Generate Mapping Coords.** check boxes and the **Chop** radio button are selected in this rollout.

3. Name the sphere as *knob001* and use the color swatch to change its color to white.

4. Align *knob001* with *drawer001* in all viewports using the **Select and Move** tool, as shown in Figure 2-52.

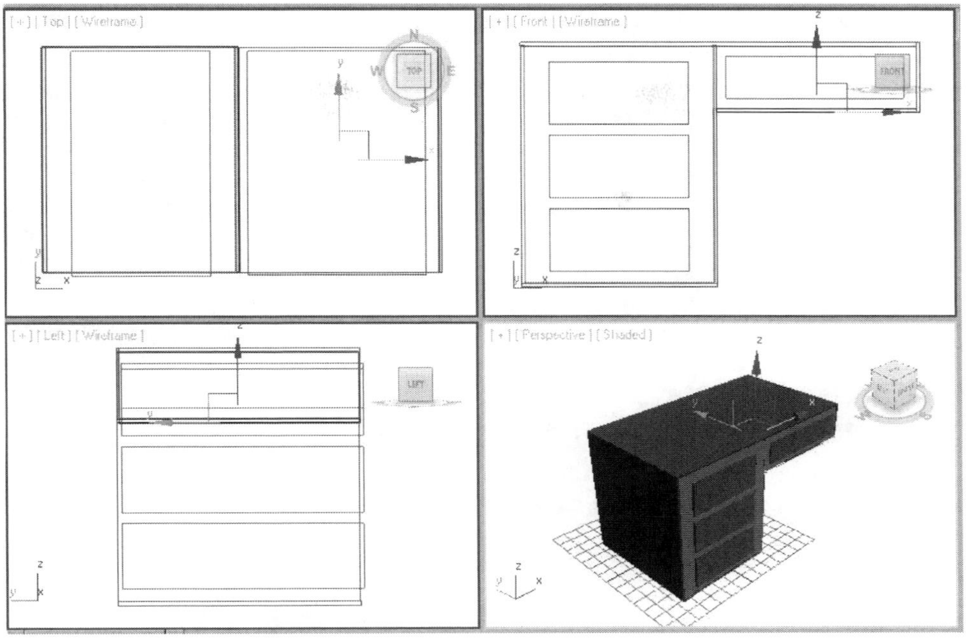

Figure 2-51 Alignment of the right lower face and the right face with the right box of the table

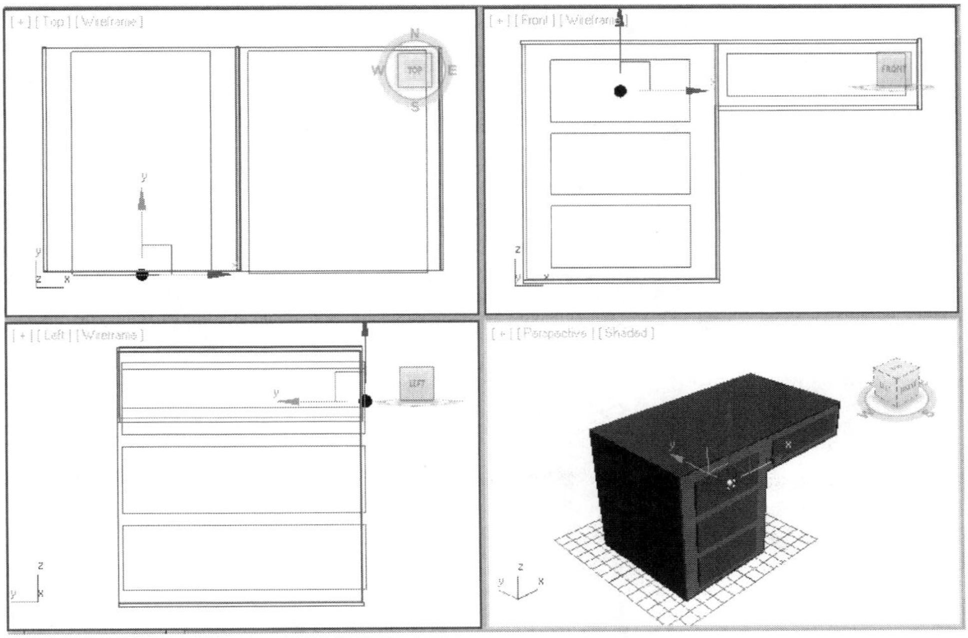

Figure 2-52 Alignment of knob001 with drawer001

5. Activate the Front viewport and create three copies of *knob001*; these are automatically named as *knob002*, *knob003*, and *knob004*. Next, align them in all viewports, as shown in Figure 2-53.

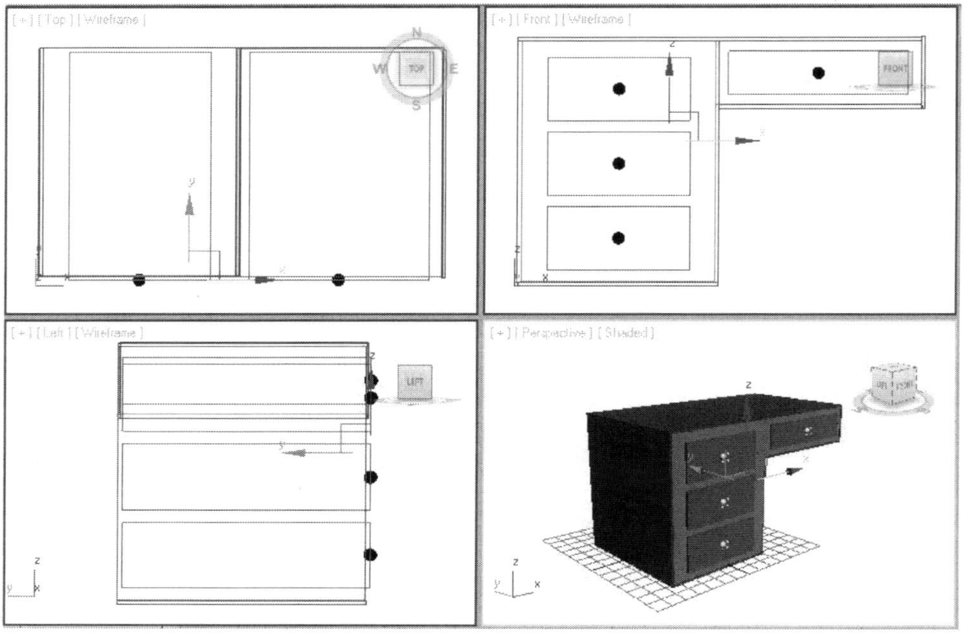

Figure 2-53 *Alignment of knobs in all viewports*

6. Set the view of the table in the Perspective viewport using the **Orbit** tool from the viewport navigation controls.

Changing the Background Color

The following steps are required to change the background color at rendering:

1. Choose **Rendering > Environment** from the menu bar; the **Environment and Effects** dialog box is displayed. The **Environment** tab is chosen by default in this dialog box.

2. Now, in the **Background** area of the **Common Parameters** rollout, choose the color swatch below the **Color** option; the **Color Selector: Background Color** dialog box is displayed. Select the white color and choose the **OK** button.

3. Close the **Environment and Effects** dialog box. Now, the background color will be displayed as white at rendering.

Rendering the Scene for the Final Output

Next, you need to render the scene for the final output.

1. Activate the Perspective viewport.

2. Invoke the **Render Production** tool from the **Main Toolbar**; the **Perspective, frame 0, Display Gamma 2.2, RGBA Color 16 Bits/Channel(1:1)** window is displayed with the final output of the table at one frame, refer to Figure 2-54.

Figure 2-54 *The final output after rendering*

3. Close this window.

   You can view the final rendered image of this model by downloading the *c02_3dsmax_2012_render.zip* file from *http://www.cadcim.com*. The path of the file is as follows:

   Textbooks > Animation and Visual Effects > 3ds Max > Autodesk 3ds Max 2012: A Comprehensive Guide

Saving the File

After completing the tutorial, you need to save the file using the steps given next:

1. Choose **Save** from the **Application menu**; the **Save File As** dialog box is displayed.

Note
*The 3D models created in 3ds Max are saved in the *.max format.*

   As the project folder is already set, the path *\Documents\3dsmax\c02_tut1\scenes* is displayed in the **Save in** text box of the **Save File As** dialog box.

2. Save the file with the name *c02tut1.max*.

Tutorial 2

In this tutorial, you will create the 3D model of a park bench, as shown in Figure 2-55, using the standard primitives. **(Expected time: 90 min)**

Figure 2-55 The bench model

The following steps are required to complete this tutorial:

a. Set the project folder.
b. Create the horizontal back supports.
c. Create the horizontal seat supports.
d. Create a vertical back support.
e. Create rivets for the horizontal back support.
f. Create leg supports.
g. Create the legs of the park bench.
h. Change the background color while rendering.
i. Render the final output.
j. Save the file.

Setting the Project Folder

Before starting a new file, it is recommended that you set the project folder.

1. Set the project folder with the name *c02_tut2* in the *3dsmax* folder as discussed in Tutorial 1.

Creating the Horizontal Back Supports

In this section, you need to invoke the **Box** tool to create the horizontal back supports of the park bench.

1. Activate the Top viewport. Choose **Create > Geometry** in the **Command Panel**; **Standard Primitives** is displayed in the drop-down list. Next, invoke the **Box** tool from the **Object Type** rollout; various rollouts are displayed in the **Command Panel**.

2. Expand the **Keyboard Entry** rollout and set the values as given below:

   Length: **1.5**   Width: **124**   Height: **6.03**

3. Choose the **Create** button from the **Keyboard Entry** rollout; a box is created in all viewports, as shown in Figure 2-56.

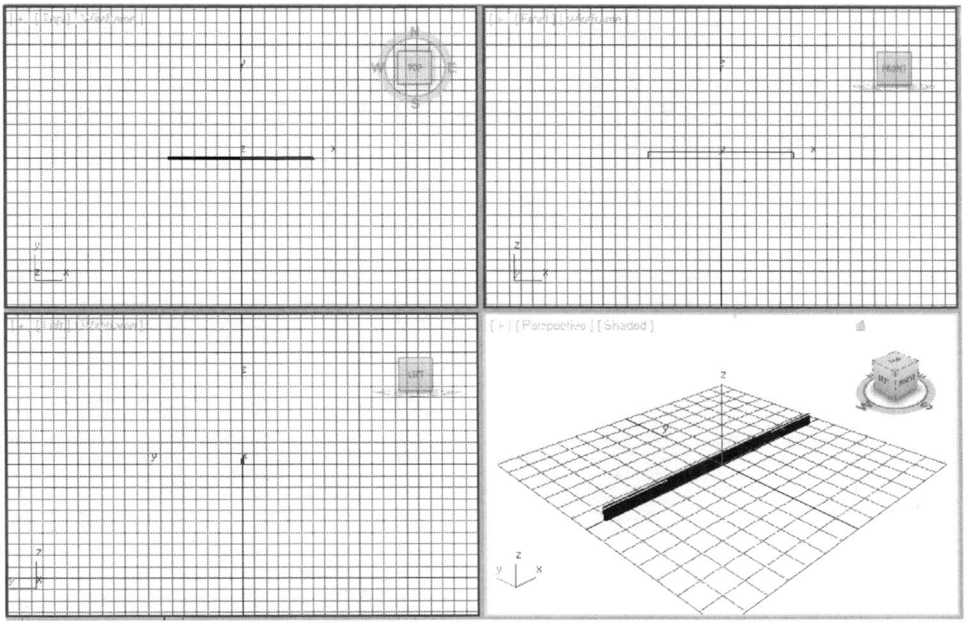

Figure 2-56 *A box created in all viewports*

4. In the **Name and Color** rollout, name the box as *horizontal back support001* and press the ENTER key.

5. Choose the color swatch from the **Name and Color** rollout; the **Object Color** dialog box is displayed. Now, using this dialog box, modify the color of the *horizontal back support001* to light brown. Choose the **OK** button to close the **Object Color** dialog box.

   Next, you need to create copies of the *horizontal back support001*.

6. Activate the Front viewport by right-clicking in it. Invoke the **Select and Move** tool from the **Main Toolbar** and make sure that the *horizontal back support001* is selected. Next, move the cursor over the Y axis. Press and hold the SHIFT key and the left mouse button. Now, drag the box upward until the value in the **Y** spinner in the coordinate display becomes around **8.0**. Release the left mouse button and the SHIFT key; the **Clone Options** dialog box is displayed.

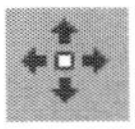

7. In the **Clone Options** dialog box, select the **Copy** radio button. Set the value in the **Number of Copies** spinner to **4**. Choose the **OK** button; four boxes with the same dimensions are displayed and they are automatically named as *horizontal back support002*, *horizontal back support003*, *horizontal back support004*, and *horizontal back support005*.

8. Invoke the **Zoom Extents All** tool from the viewport navigation controls; the horizontal back supports are displayed in all viewports, as shown in Figure 2-57.

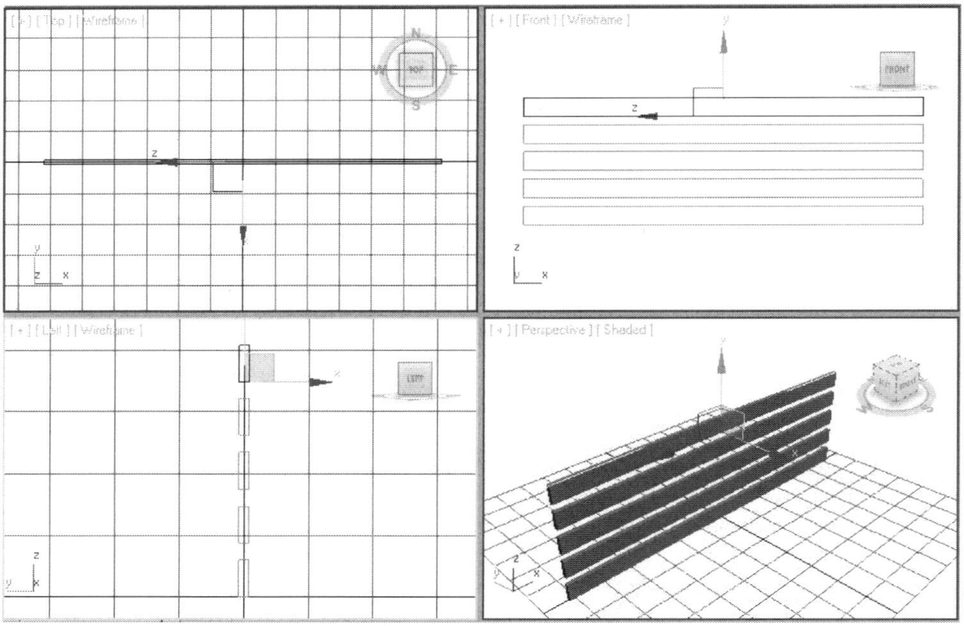

Figure 2-57 *Horizontal back supports in all viewports*

Next, you need to rotate the *horizontal back support005*.

9. Activate the Left viewport and select the *horizontal back support005*. Next, right-click on the **Select and Rotate** tool in the **Main Toolbar**; the **Rotate Transform Type-In** dialog box is displayed, as shown in Figure 2-58.

10. In the **Absolute:World** area, set the value **-15** in the **X** spinner and press the ENTER key; the *horizontal back support005* gets rotated, as shown in Figure 2-59. Now, close the **Rotate Transform Type-In** dialog box.

11. Next, click anywhere in the viewport to deselect the *horizontal back support005*.

Grouping All Horizontal Back Supports

1. Activate the Left viewport and invoke the **Select Object** tool. Now, select all horizontal back supports by dragging a selection box around them, as shown in Figure 2-60.

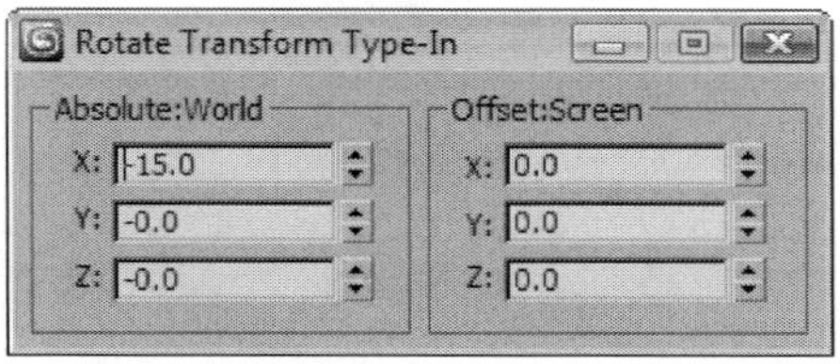

***Figure 2-58** The **Rotate Transform Type-In** dialog box*

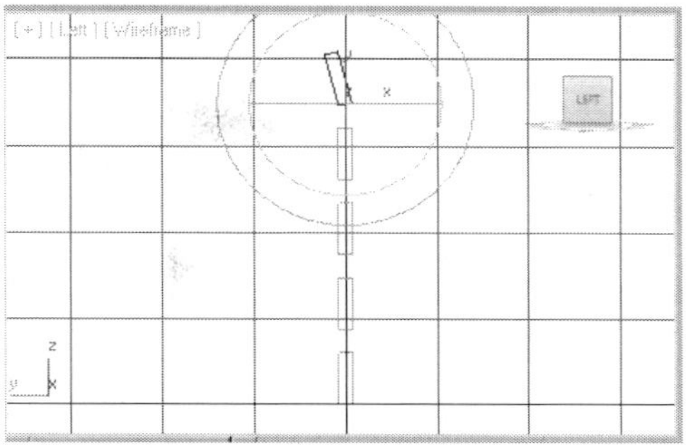

***Figure 2-59** The horizontal back support005 after rotating in the Left viewport*

2. Choose **Group > Group** from the menu bar; the **Group** dialog box is displayed.

3. In the **Group name** text box, enter **horizontal back support**, as shown in Figure 2-61 and then choose the **OK** button; all horizontal back supports are grouped together.

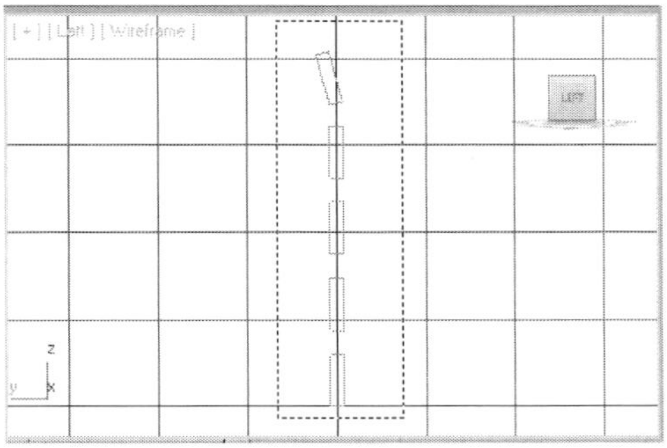

***Figure 2-60** All horizontal back supports selected simultaneously*

***Figure 2-61** The **Group** dialog box*

Creating the Horizontal Seat Supports

In this section, you need to create the horizontal seat supports using the following steps:

1. Activate the Top viewport and invoke the **Box** tool from the **Object Type** rollout.

2. Expand the **Keyboard Entry** rollout and set the values as given below:

   Length: **6.03** Width: **124** Height: **1.5**

3. Choose the **Create** button from the **Keyboard Entry** rollout; a box is created in all viewports.

4. In the **Name and Color** rollout, name the box as *horizontal seat support001*.

5. Use the color swatch to assign the same color to the *horizontal seat support001* that you assigned to the *horizontal back support*.

6. Invoke the **Select and Move** tool from the **Main Toolbar** and align the *horizontal seat support001* with the *horizontal back support* in all viewports, as shown in Figure 2-62.

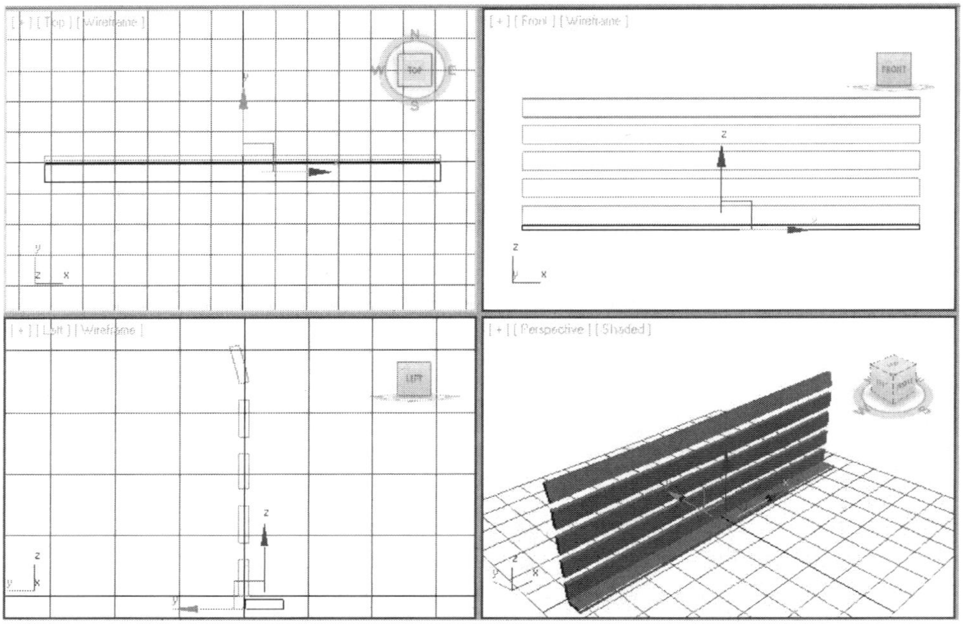

Figure 2-62 *Alignment of the horizontal seat support001 in all viewports*

Next, you need to create four copies of the *horizontal seat support001*.

7. Activate the Top viewport by right-clicking in it and make sure the *horizontal seat support001* is selected. Next, move the cursor over the vertical axis. Press and hold the SHIFT key and drag the box downward until the value in the **Y** spinner in the coordinate display becomes around **-7.5**. Release the left mouse button and the SHIFT key; the **Clone Options** dialog box is displayed.

8. In the **Clone Options** dialog box, select the **Copy** radio button. Set the value in the **Number of Copies** spinner to **4** and choose **OK**; four boxes with the same dimensions are displayed and they are automatically named as *horizontal seat support002*, *horizontal seat support003*, *horizontal seat support004*, and *horizontal seat support005*.

9. Invoke the **Zoom Extents All** tool; all objects are displayed in all viewports, as shown in Figure 2-63.

10. Click anywhere in the viewport to deselect the objects.

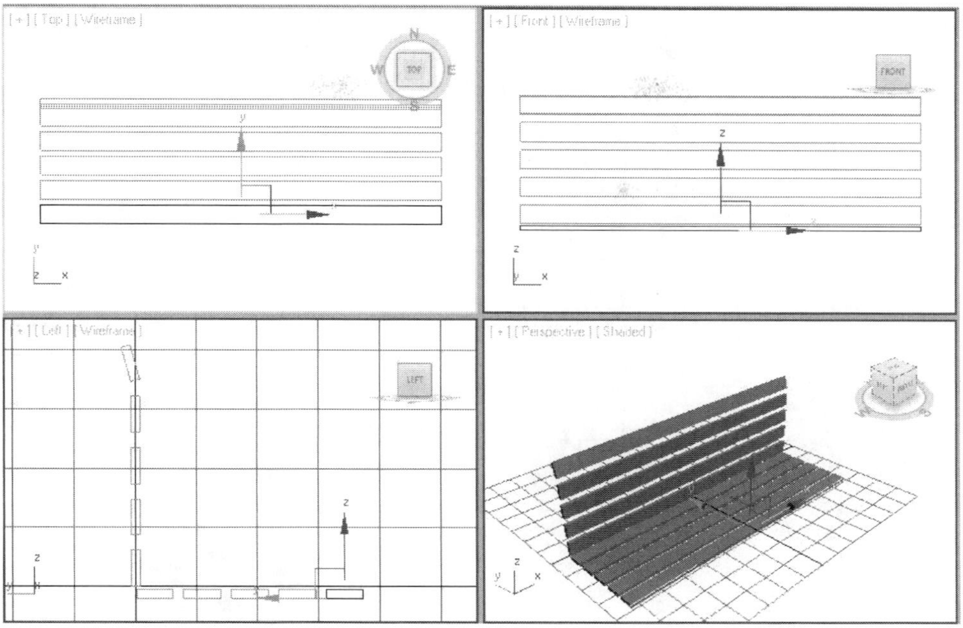

Figure 2-63 *Horizontal seat supports displayed in all viewports*

Grouping All Horizontal Seat Supports

In this section, you need to group all horizontal seat supports using the following steps:

1. Invoke the **Select Object** tool and select all horizontal seat supports by dragging a selection box around them in any viewport. 

2. Choose **Group > Group** from the menu bar; the **Group** dialog box is displayed.

3. In the **Group name** text box, enter **horizontal seat support** and then choose the **OK** button.

Creating the Vertical Back Supports

In this section, you need to create the vertical back supports of a park bench using the following steps.

1. Activate the Top viewport. Choose **Create > Geometry** in the **Command Panel**; **Standard Primitives** is displayed in the drop-down list. Next, invoke the **Cylinder** tool in the **Object Type** rollout.

2. In the **Keyboard Entry** rollout, set the values as given below:

X: **-60**	Y: **1.5**	Z: **0.0**
Radius: **1.0**	Height: **38.0**	

3. Now, choose the **Create** button in the **Keyboard Entry** rollout; a cylinder is created in all viewports, as shown in Figure 2-64.

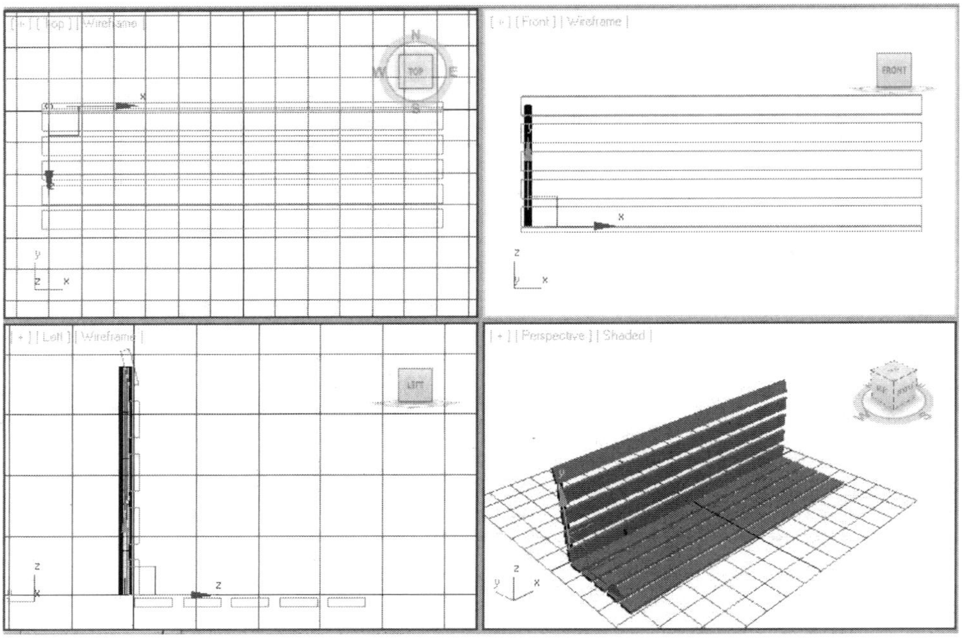

Figure 2-64 The vertical back support001 in all viewports

4. In the **Name and Color** rollout, name the cylinder as *vertical back support001* and press ENTER.

5. Change the color of the *vertical back support001* to black.

   Next, you need to create a copy of the *vertical back support001*.

6. Activate the Front viewport by right-clicking in it. Invoke the **Select and Move** tool and move the cursor over the horizontal axis. Press and hold the SHIFT key and the left mouse button, and then drag the *vertical back support001* to the right side to align it with the right side of the *horizontal back support*, as shown in Figure 2-65. Release the left mouse button and the SHIFT key; the **Clone Options** dialog box is displayed.

7. In the **Clone Options** dialog box, select the **Copy** radio button, if it is not already selected. Set the value **1** in the **Number of Copies** spinner and choose the **OK** button; the *vertical back support002* is created with the same dimensions as the *vertical back support001*, as shown in Figure 2-65.

8. Click anywhere in the viewport to deselect the objects.

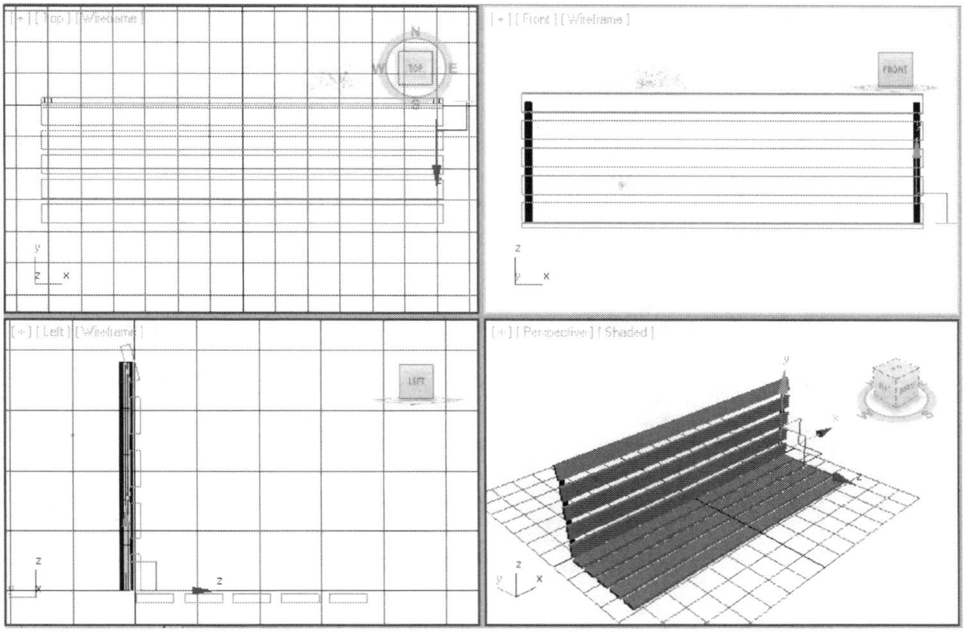

Figure 2-65 The vertical back support002 in all viewports

Creating Rivets for the Horizontal Back Support

In this section, you need to create a sphere and a cylinder to create the cap and the body of rivet, respectively.

1. Activate the Top viewport and choose **Create > Geometry** in the **Command Panel**; **Standard Primitives** is displayed in the drop-down list. Next, invoke the **Sphere** tool in the **Object Type** rollout.

2. In the **Keyboard Entry** rollout, set the value **0.8** in the **Radius** spinner and choose the **Create** button; a sphere is created.

3. In the **Parameters** rollout, make sure that the **Smooth** check box and the **Chop** radio button are selected. Also, in the **Hemisphere** spinner, enter the value **0.5**.

4. Name the sphere as *cap* and assign black color to it.

   Next, you need to create a cylinder for the body of the rivet.

5. From the **Command Panel**, choose **Create > Geometry > Standard Primitives > Object Type** rollout **> Cylinder**.

6. Next, in the **Keyboard Entry** rollout, set the values as given below:

X: **0**	Y: **0**	Z: **0**
Radius: **0.241**	Height: **3.5**	

7. Choose the **Create** button from the **Keyboard Entry** rollout; a cylinder is created.

8. Name the cylinder as *body* and assign black color to it.

9. Next, activate the Left viewport and invoke the **Select by Name** tool; the **Select From Scene** dialog box is displayed. Select the *cap* and the *body* simultaneously by holding the CTRL key. Choose the **OK** button; the *cap* and the *body* are selected in the viewports.

10. Invoke the **Zoom Extents All Selected** tool to increase the magnification of the selected objects in all viewports and click on the screen to deselect the objects.

11. Next, align the *cap* and the *body* of the rivet in the Left viewport using the **Select and Move** tool, as shown in Figure 2-66.

Note
*You may need to use the **Zoom** and **Pan View** tools to align the cap and the body of the rivet.*

Next, you need to group the *body* and the *cap* to create the rivet.

12. Select the *cap* and the *body* of the rivet in any viewport and group them as *rivet001*.

13. Invoke the **Zoom Extents All** tool and move the *rivet001* in the Left viewport to visualize it properly, as shown in Figure 2-67.

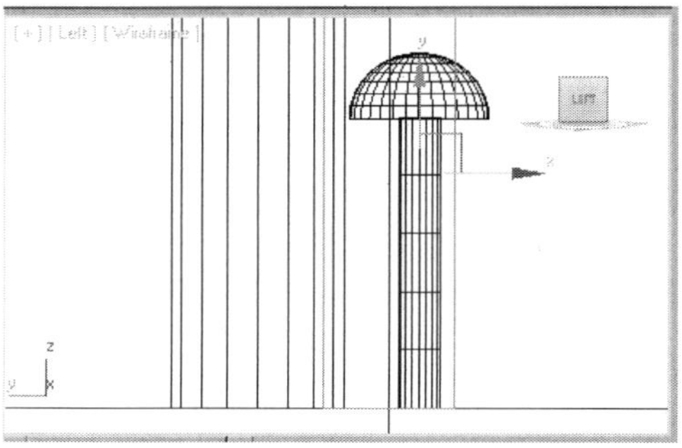

Figure 2-66 *Alignment of the cap and the body*

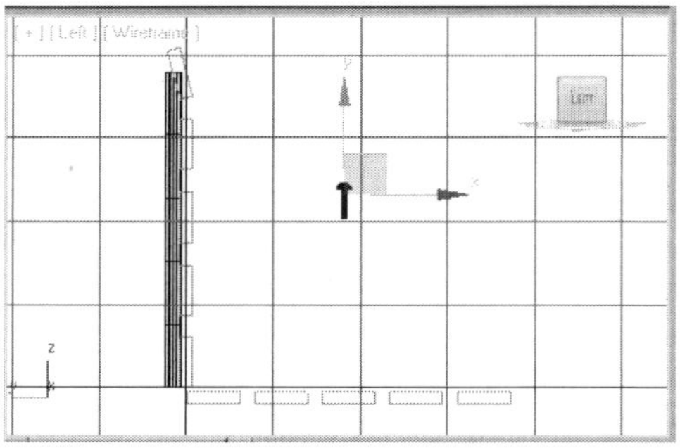

Figure 2-67 *The rivet001 in the Left viewport*

Aligning the Rivets

In this section, you need to align the rivets.

1. In the Left viewport, select *rivet001* and right-click on the **Select and Rotate** tool; the **Rotate Transform Type-In** dialog box is displayed. Also, a circular gizmo along with the X, Y, and Z axes is displayed.

2. In the **Offset:Screen** area of the **Rotate Transform Type-In** dialog box, enter **-90** in the **Z** spinner and press ENTER; the *rivet001* gets rotated, as shown in Figure 2-68. Now, close the **Rotate Transform Type-In** dialog box.

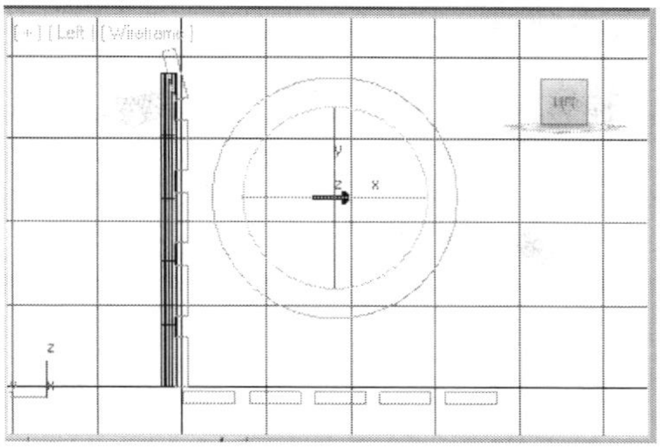

Figure 2-68 *Rotating rivet001 in the Left viewport*

3. Invoke the **Select and Move** tool and align *rivet001* with the *horizontal back support* in all viewports, as shown in Figure 2-69.

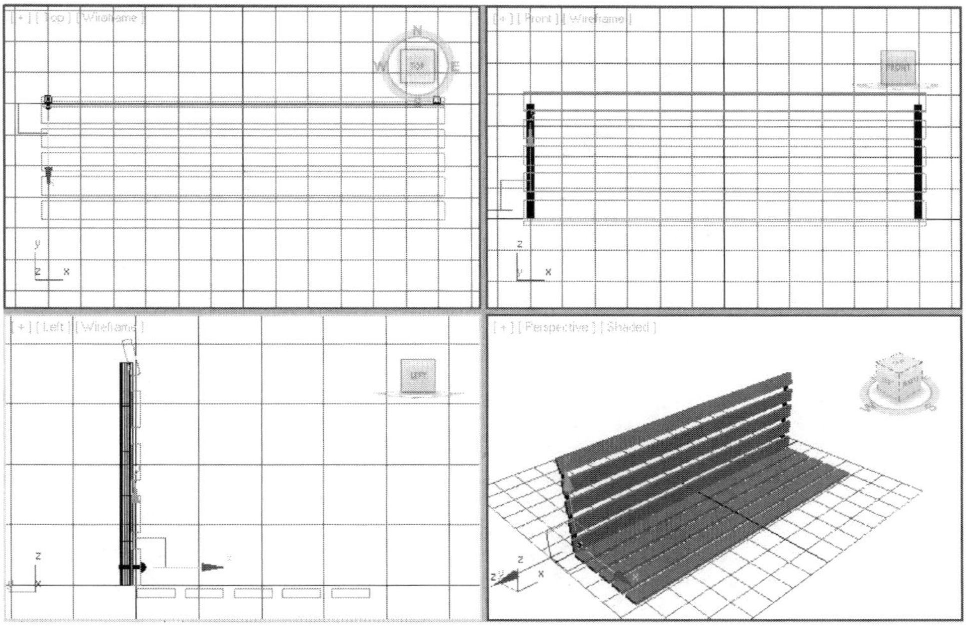

Figure 2-69 *Alignment of rivet001 with the horizontal back support*

4. Next, in the Left viewport, select *rivet001* using the **Select and Move** tool and move the cursor over the vertical axis. Now, create 4 copies of *rivet001*. These copies are automatically named as *rivet002*, *rivet003*, *rivet004*, and *rivet005*. Align them in the Left viewport, as shown in Figure 2-70.

5. Select the uppermost rivet and invoke the **Select and Rotate** tool. Now, rotate the uppermost rivet by using the outermost ring of the **Select and Rotate** tool in the

counterclockwise direction until the value in the **X** spinner in the coordinate display becomes **-20**, refer to Figure 2-71.

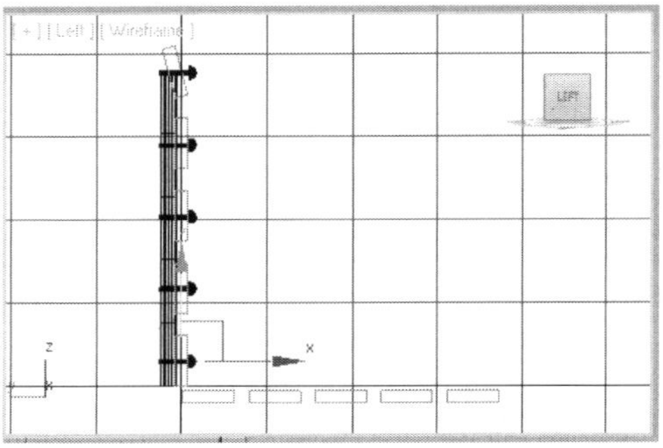

Figure 2-70 *Alignment of rivets in the Left viewport*

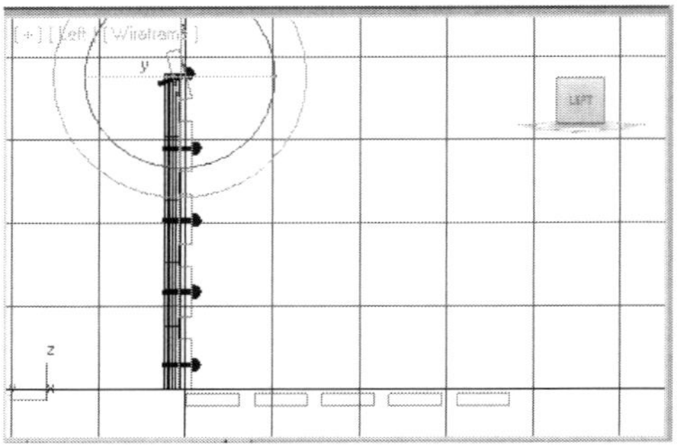

Figure 2-71 *Rotating the uppermost rivet*

6. Next, press and hold the CTRL key and select all rivets in the Left viewport and group them as the *left side rivets*. Click anywhere in the viewport to deselect the objects.

Note

To change the viewport without deselecting the objects, right-click in that viewport; the objects will remain selected.

Creating the Right Side Rivets

In this section, you need to copy the *left side rivets* for creating the right side rivets.

1. Select the *left side rivets* in the Front viewport using the **Select and Move** tool. Next, move the cursor over the horizontal axis, press and hold the SHIFT key and the left mouse button, and then drag the mouse toward the right side. Release the left mouse button and the SHIFT key exactly over the *vertical back support002* on the right side; the **Clone Options** dialog box is displayed.

2. In the **Clone Options** dialog box, select the **Copy** radio button. Set the value **1** in the **Number of Copies** spinner. In the **Name** spinner, enter **right side rivets** to modify the name of the group and choose **OK**; the *right side rivets* are displayed, as shown in Figure 2-72.

   Now, you need to select the *horizontal back support*, *vertical back support001*, *vertical back support002*, *left side rivets,* and *right side rivets*.

3. Invoke the **Select Object** tool and activate the Left viewport. Drag a selection box around the *horizontal back support*, *vertical back support001*, *vertical back support002*, *left side rivets*, and *right side rivets* to select them simultaneously, and then group them as *back support* as described earlier.

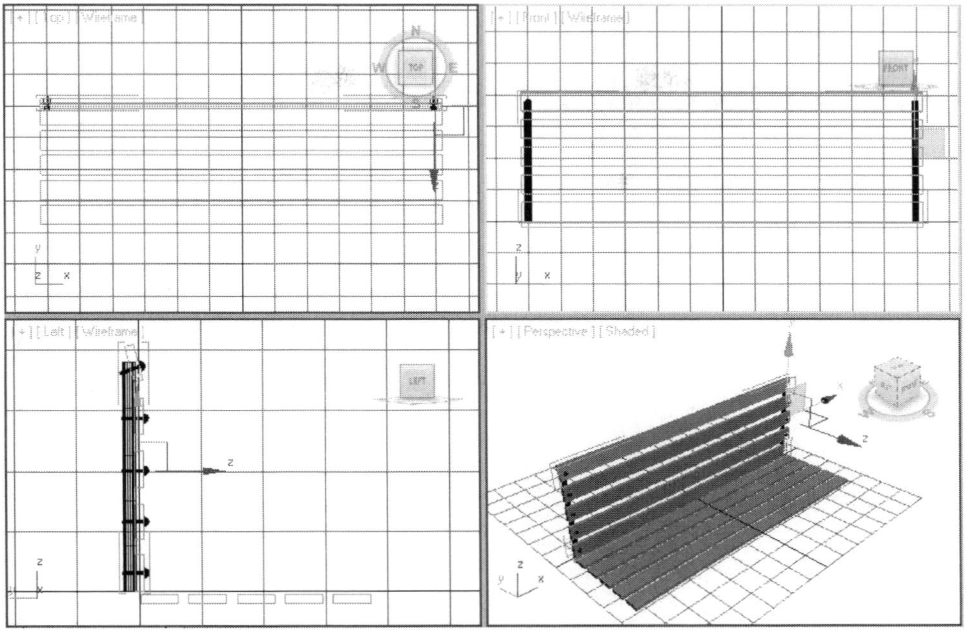

Figure 2-72 *The right side rivets displayed in all viewports*

Rotating the Back Support

1. Select the *back support* in the Left viewport and invoke the **Select and Rotate** tool; a circular gizmo is displayed.

2. Move the cursor over the Z-axis, which is blue in color; the Z-axis turns yellow and becomes active. Now, press the left mouse button and drag the cursor counterclockwise to rotate the back support until the value in the **Z** spinner in the coordinate display becomes **10**. Release the left mouse button. The *back support* is rotated, as shown in Figure 2-73.

3. Invoke the **Select and Move** tool and align the *back support* with the *horizontal seat support*, as shown in Figure 2-74.

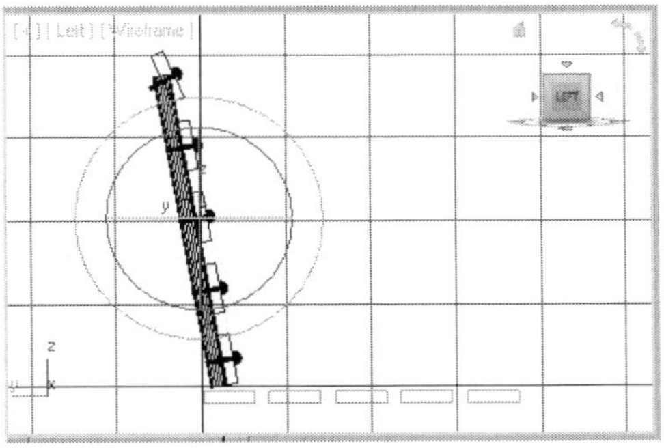

Figure 2-73 *Rotating the back support in the Left viewport*

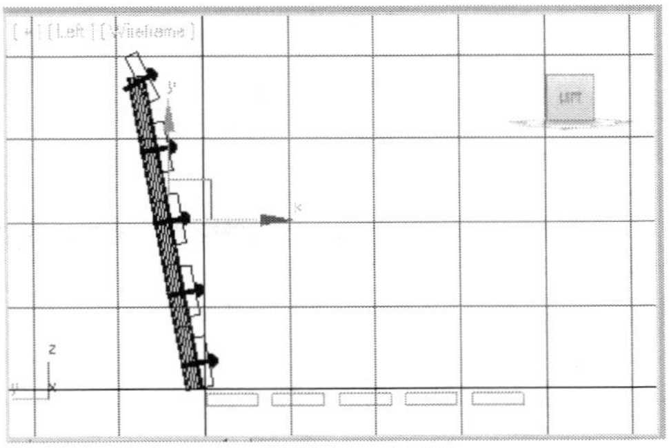

Figure 2-74 *Alignment of the back support in the Left viewport*

Creating the Leg Support

To create the leg support, you need to create a box.

1. Activate the Top viewport and choose **Create > Geometry** in the **Command Panel**; **Standard Primitives** is displayed in the drop-down list. Next, invoke the **Box** tool in the **Object Type** rollout.

2. In the **Keyboard Entry** rollout, set the parameters as given below:

   Length: **36.677** Width: **9.0** Height: **2.8**

3. Choose the **Create** button from the **Keyboard Entry** rollout; the box is created.

4. Name the box as *leg support001* and change its color to black.

5. Invoke the **Select and Move** tool and align the *leg support001* to the extreme left and below the *horizontal seat support* in all viewports, as shown in Figure 2-75.

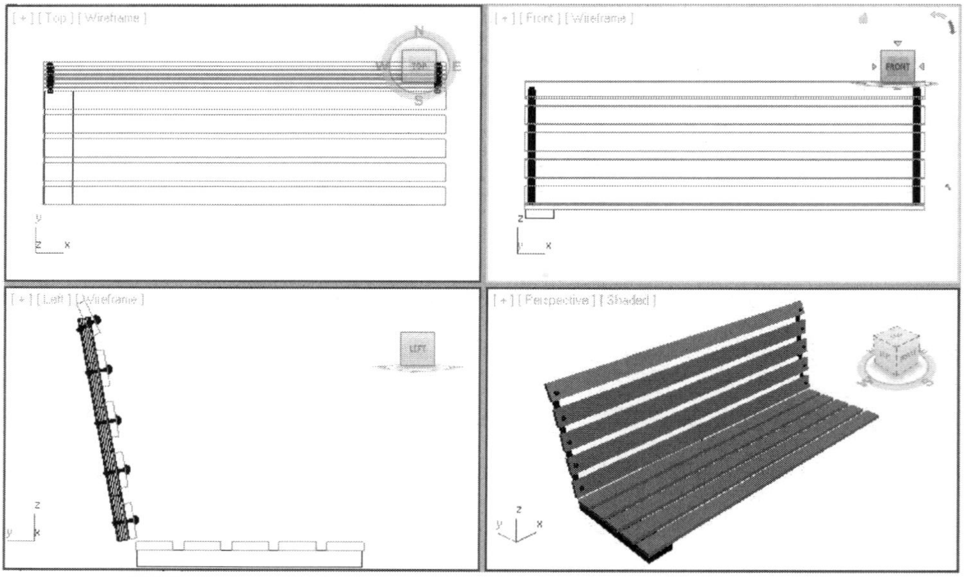

Figure 2-75 *Alignment of the leg support001 with the horizontal seat support*

Next, you need to copy the *leg support001* to create the leg support on the right side of the *horizontal seat support*.

6. Activate the Top viewport by clicking in it and create a copy of the *leg support001* as described earlier. It is automatically named as *leg support002*.

7. Invoke the **Select and Move** tool and align the *leg support002* to the *horizontal seat support* in all viewports, as shown in Figure 2-76.

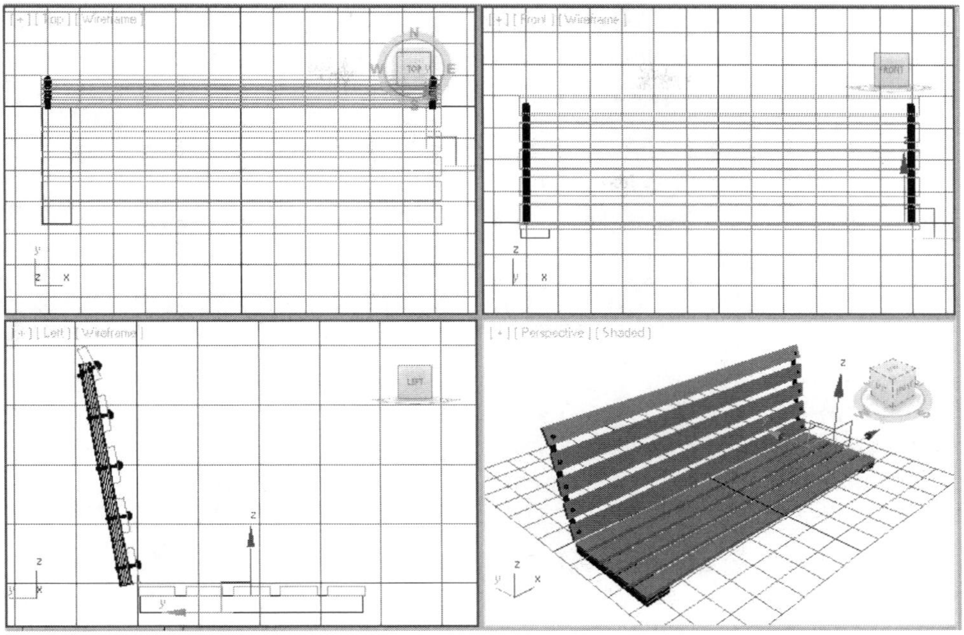

Figure 2-76 *Alignment of the leg support002 with the horizontal seat support*

Next, you need to create another box for other leg supports.

8. Activate the Top viewport and create a box using the values as given below:

   Length: **9.0**   Width: **124**   Height: **2.8**

9. In the **Name and Color** rollout, name the box as *leg support003* and change its color to black.

10. Invoke the **Select and Move** tool and align the *leg support003* with the *horizontal seat support* in all viewports, as shown in Figure 2-77.

Note

You need to use the ***Arc Rotate*** *tool to view the leg support003 properly in the Perspective viewport.*

11. Next, create a copy of the *leg support003* in the Top viewport; it is automatically named as *leg support004*.

12. Invoke the **Select and Move** tool and align the *leg support004* with the *horizontal seat support* in all viewports, as shown in Figure 2-78.

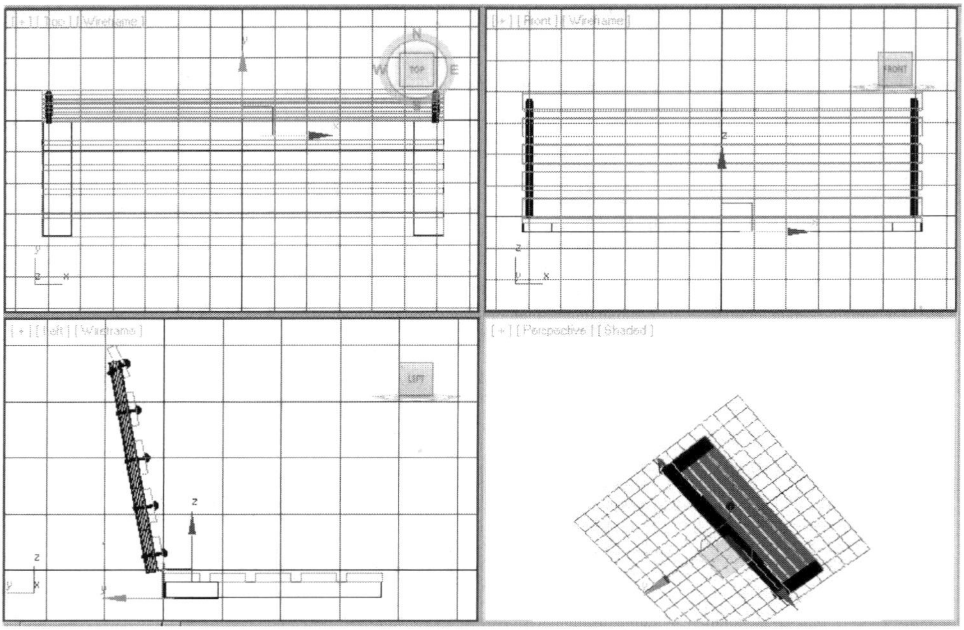

Figure 2-77 *Alignment of the leg support003 with the horizontal seat support in all viewports*

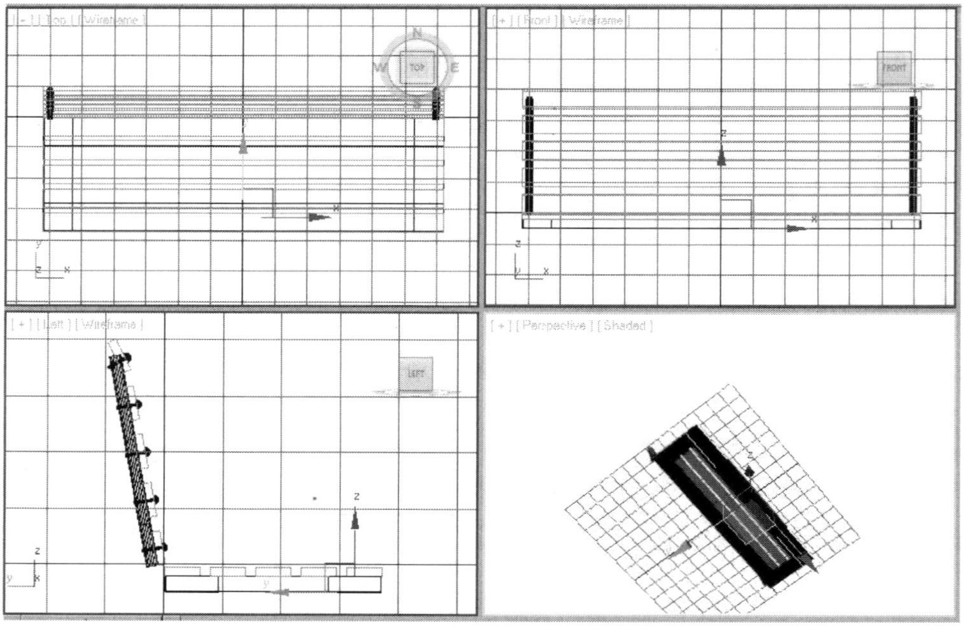

Figure 2-78 *Alignment of the leg support004 in all viewports*

Creating Rivets for the Seat Support

To create the rivets for the *horizontal seat support*, you need to copy the *right side rivets*. As you already know that the *right side rivets* are grouped under *back support,* therefore first you need to open this group to access them independently. After opening, the *back support* group will be ungrouped temporarily and you can transform the objects within it independently.

1. Activate the Left viewport and select the *back support*.

2. Choose **Group > Open** from the menu bar; the *back support* is now ungrouped temporarily. Also, a pink colored bounding box is displayed around the *back support*.

3. Now, invoke the **Select By Name** tool; the **Select From Scene** dialog box is displayed, as shown in Figure 2-79.

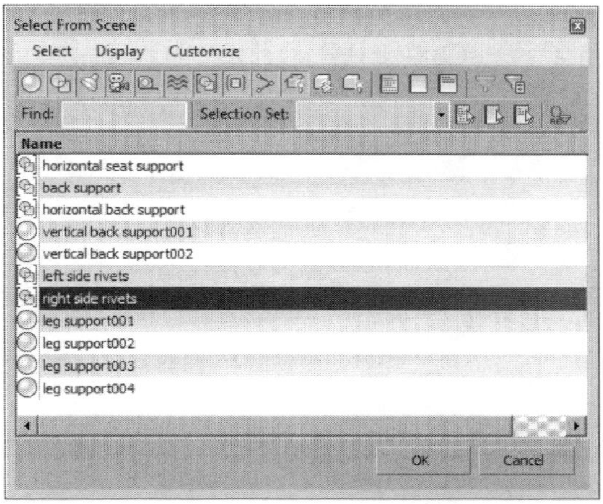

Figure 2-79 *The right side rivets selected in the* ***Select From Scene*** *dialog box*

4. In the **Select From Scene** dialog box, select the *right side rivets* and choose the **OK** button.

5. Activate the Left viewport by right-clicking in it. Make sure the *right side rivets* are still selected. Then, create a copy of the *right side rivets* and name them as *right side seat rivets*, as shown in Figure 2-80.

6. Make sure that the *right side seat rivets* are selected and choose **Group > Detach** from the menu bar; the *right side seat rivets* are detached from the *back support* group.

7. Select the pink colored gizmo of the *back support* group and choose **Group > Close** from the menu bar to group them again.

Next, you need to align the *right side seat rivets*.

8. Invoke the **Select and Rotate** tool and select the *right side seat rivets* in the Left viewport. Move the cursor over the Z-axis, which is blue in color; the gizmo for the Z-axis turns yellow and becomes active. Now, press the left mouse button and drag the cursor in the counterclockwise direction to rotate *rivet001* until the angle of rotation in the **Z** spinner becomes **80**, refer to Figure 2-81.

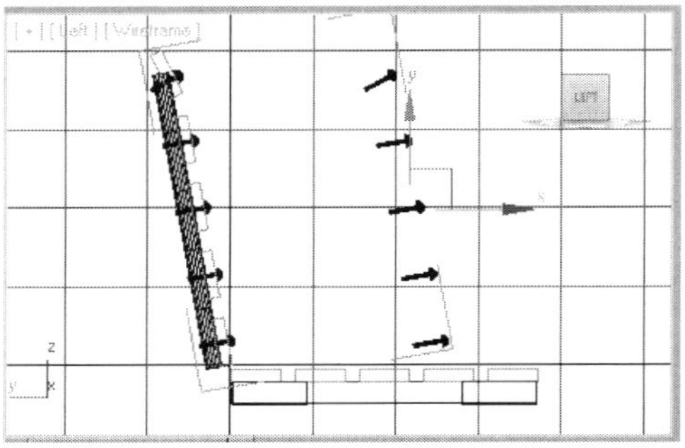

Figure 2-80 *The right side seat rivets in the Left viewport*

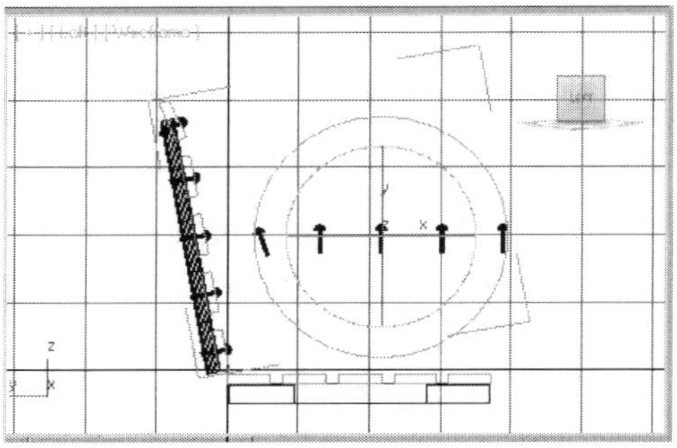

Figure 2-81 *Rotating the right side seat rivets in the Left viewport*

9. Invoke the **Select and Move** tool. Now, move the cursor over the vertical axis and then drag the mouse downward to align the *right side seat rivets* with the *horizontal seat support*, as shown in Figure 2-82.

   Next, you need to align the rivet (which is near the horizontal back support) to the horizontal seat support.

10. Make sure the *right side seat rivets* are selected and choose **Group > Open** from the menu bar to ungroup them temporarily.

11. Select the rivet which is near the *horizontal back support* and invoke the **Select and Rotate** tool. Move the cursor over the Z-axis, which is blue in color; the gizmo for the Z-axis turns yellow and becomes active. Now, press the left mouse button and drag the cursor in the clockwise direction to rotate it until the angle of rotation in the **Z** spinner in the coordinate display becomes **-20**, refer to Figure 2-83.

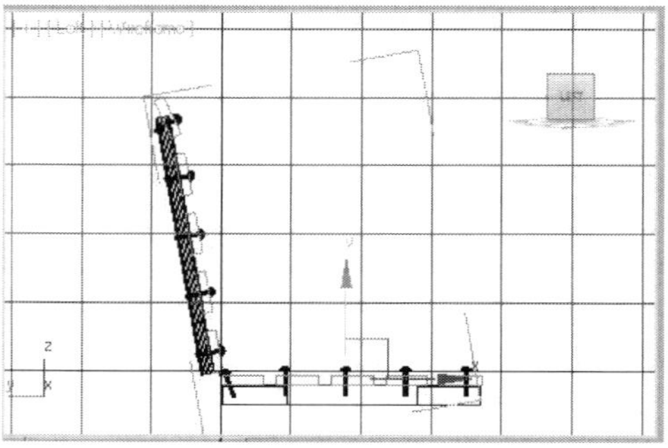

Figure 2-82 *Alignment of the right side seat rivets in the Left viewport*

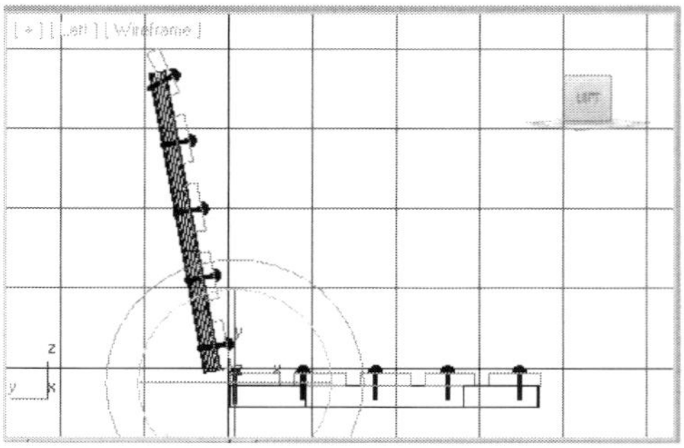

Figure 2-83 *Rotating the rivet in the Left viewport*

12. Invoke the **Select and Move** tool and align all rivets of the *right side seat rivets* group with the *horizontal seat support*, as shown in Figure 2-84.

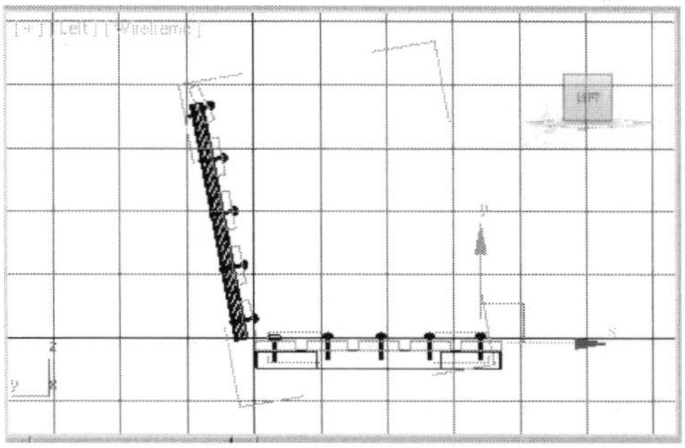

Figure 2-84 *Alignment of the right side of the rivets in the Left viewport*

13. Make sure that one of the rivets of the *right side seat rivets* group is selected and choose **Group > Close** from the menu bar to group them again.

    Next, you need to copy the *right side seat rivets* to create rivets on the left side of the *horizontal seat support*.

14. Activate the Top viewport and create a copy of the *right side seat rivets*. Name the new group as *left side seat rivets*.

15. Next, align the *left side seat rivets* using the **Select and Move** tool in all viewports, as shown in Figure 2-85.

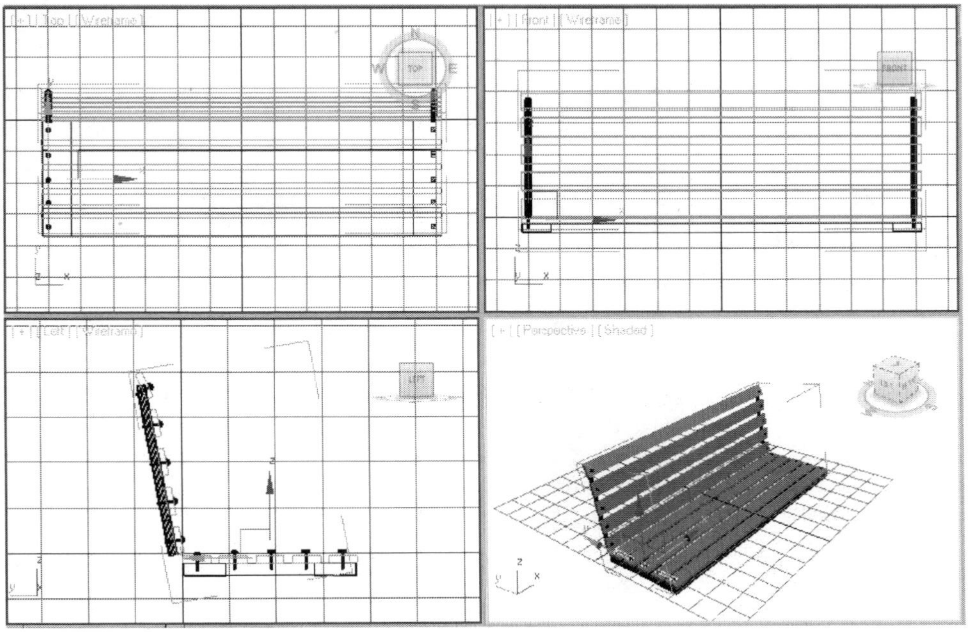

Figure 2-85 *Alignment of the left side seat rivets in all viewports*

Creating the Legs of the Park Bench

To create the legs of the park bench, you need to invoke the **Box** tool.

1. Activate the Top viewport and choose **Create > Geometry** in the **Command Panel**; **Standard Primitives** is displayed in the drop-down list. Next, invoke the **Box** tool in the **Object Type** rollout.

2. Next, in the **Keyboard Entry** rollout, set the values as given below:

   Length: **4.0** Width: **3.0** Height: **26.88**

3. Choose the **Create** button from the **Keyboard Entry** rollout; a box is created.

4. In the **Name and Color** rollout, name the box as *leg001*. Also, change its color to black.

5. Invoke the **Select and Move** tool and align the *leg001* with the *leg support001* in all viewports, as shown in Figure 2-86. You need to adjust the viewport to display all objects properly using the **Zoom** and **Pan View** tools.

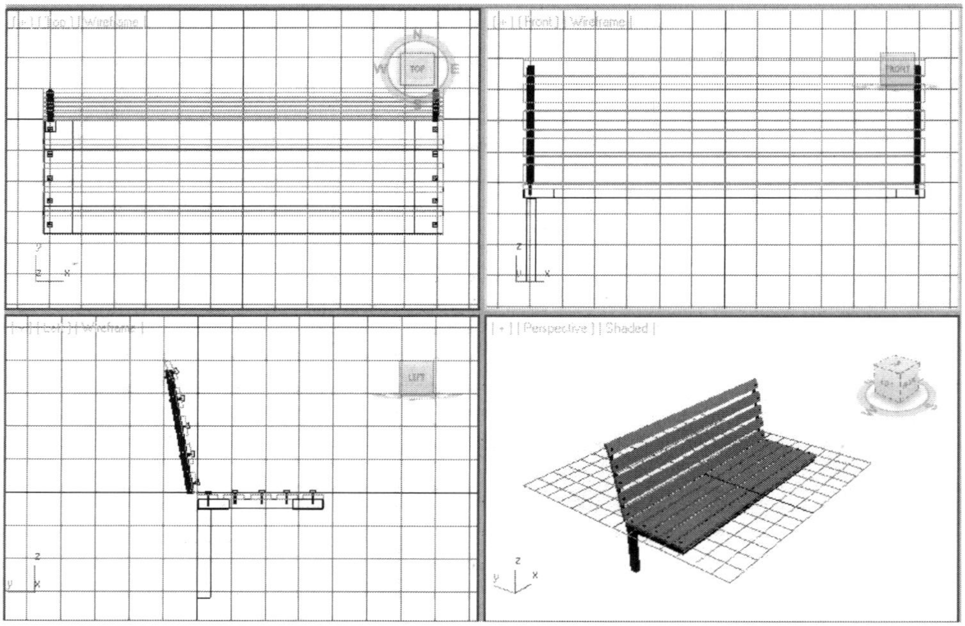

Figure 2-86 *Alignment of the leg001 in all viewports*

6. Next, create three copies of the *leg001* to create three more legs. These are automatically named as *leg002*, *leg003*, and *leg004*.

7. Invoke the **Select and Move** tool and align the *leg002*, *leg003*, and *leg004* at the corners of the *leg support002*, *003*, and *004*, respectively in all viewports, as shown in Figure 2-87.

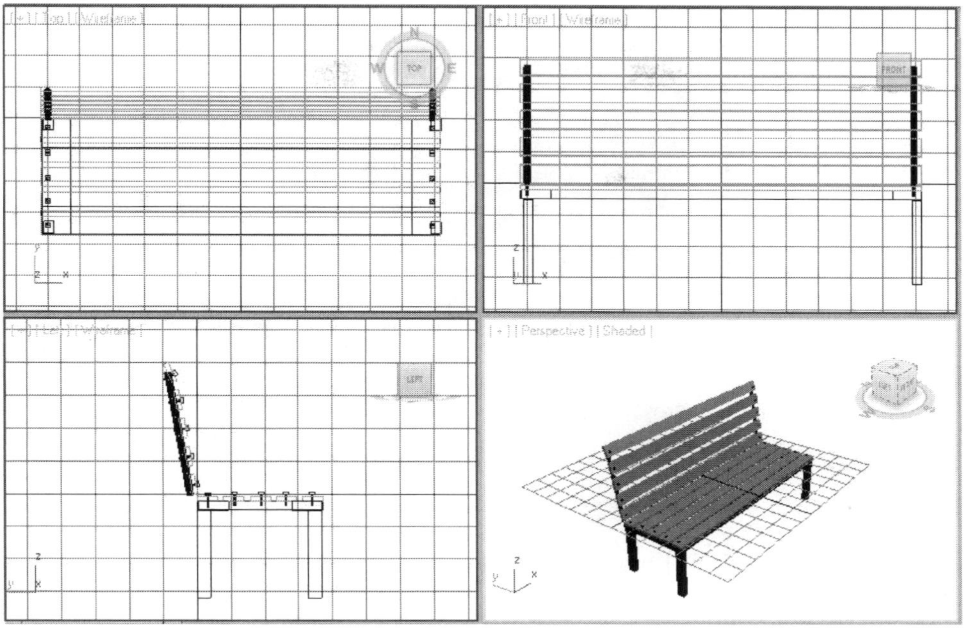

Figure 2-87 *Alignment of the legs in all viewports*

8. Invoke the **Zoom Extents All** tool and modify the view in the Perspective viewport using the **Orbit** tool.

Changing the Background Color

1. To change the background color of the scene to white in final output, follow the steps given in Tutorial 1.

Rendering the Final Output

1. Activate the Perspective viewport.

2. Invoke the **Render Production** tool in the **Main Toolbar**; the **Perspective, frame 0, Display Gamma 2.2, RGBA Color 16Bits/Channel (1:1)** window is displayed, showing the final output of the park bench at frame one, refer to Figure 2-88.

3. Close this window.

You can view the final rendered image of this model by downloading the *c02_3dsmax_2012_render.zip* file from *http://www.cadcim.com*. The path of the file is as follows:

Textbooks > Animation and Visual Effects > 3ds Max > Autodesk 3ds Max 2012: A Comprehensive Guide

Figure 2-88 *The final output at rendering*

Saving the File

Next, you need to save the file.

1. Choose **Save** from the **Application menu**; the **Save File As** dialog box is displayed.

   As the project folder is already set, the path *\Documents\3dsmax\c02_tut2\scenes* is displayed in the **Save in** text box of the **Save File As** dialog box.

2. Save the file with the name *c02tut2.max*.

Self-Evaluation Test

Answer the following questions and then compare them to those given at the end of this chapter:

1. Which of the following tools is used to rotate an object in the active viewport?

   (a) **Zoom Extents All** (b) **Orbit**
   (c) **Pan** (d) All of these

2. Which of the following tools is used to select an object by its name from the list of objects that are currently in the scene?

   (a) **Select Object** (b) **Select and Move**
   (c) **Select by Name** (d) **Select and Rotate**

3. Which of the following rollouts is available when you invoke the **Box** tool?

   (a) **Name and Color** (b) **Creation Method**
   (c) **Parameters** (d) All of these

4. Which of the following objects is not a standard primitive?

   (a) Pyramid (b) Geosphere
   (c) Torus Knot (d) Torus

5. On starting Autodesk 3ds Max, a screen with three viewports will be displayed. (T/F)

6. You can create any standard primitive dynamically as well as by entering the parameters in the **Keyboard Entry** rollout. (T/F)

7. The options in the **Creation Method** rollout are used only when you create an object using the keyboard. (T/F)

8. To stretch and squash an object, you need to invoke the __________ tool from the **Main Toolbar**.

9. To change the name and color of an object, use the __________ rollout.

10. To modify the dimensions of an object, you need to use the __________ rollout.

11. The ___________tool is used to move through the viewport.

Review Questions

Answer the following questions:

1. Which of the following tools is used to display all objects in all viewports?

   (a) **Zoom** (b) **Pan**
   (c) **Zoom Extents All** (d) **Orbit**

2. Which of the following tools is used to move an object along the X, Y, or Z axis?

   (a) **Select Object** (b) **Select and Move**
   (c) **Select by Name** (d) All of these

3. While creating the clone of an object, you need to hold the CTRL key and drag the object. (T/F)

4. To change the background color in the rendering, you need to choose **Rendering > Environment** from the menu bar. (T/F)

5. A geosphere is smoother than a sphere and has more regular surfaces. (T/F)

6. The **Zoom Region** tool is used to adjust the view of all objects in all viewports to display them properly. (T/F)

7. To render a view without using the dialog box, you need to invoke the **Render Production** tool from the **Main Toolbar**. (T/F)

8. You can use different parts of the teapot individually to make a new object. (T/F)

9. You need to choose **Reset** from the **Application menu** to reset all settings of Autodesk 3ds Max. (T/F)

10. To select more than one object simultaneously in a viewport, you need to invoke the __________ tool and press and hold the __________ key.

Exercises

Exercise 1

Start Autodesk 3ds Max 2012 and then perform the following operations:

1. Choose **Create > Geometry** in the **Command Panel**; **Standard Primitives** will be displayed in the drop-down list. Now, invoke different tools in the **Object Type** rollout and create the objects in the viewport dynamically or by entering the values in the **Keyboard Entry** rollout and notice the difference.

2. Create the objects dynamically using the options in the **Creation Method** rollout and notice the difference.

3. Change the name and color of the objects using the **Name and Color** rollout.

4. Modify the dimensions of the object using the **Parameters** rollout in the **Modify** tab.

5. Add more than one object to the scene and use different navigation controls to view their effects.

6. Select more than one object simultaneously by holding the CTRL key.

7. Use various tools in the **Main Toolbar** to modify the scene by moving, rotating, and scaling the objects.

8. Create a copy of any object.

9. Render the image to display its output and try to change the color of the background.

10. Reset Autodesk 3ds Max without saving the file.

Exercise 2

Create the model shown in Figure 2-89 using your own dimensions. You can view the final rendered image of this model by downloading the *c02_3dsmax_2012_render.zip* file from *http://www.cadcim.com*. The path of the file is as follows:

Textbooks > Animation and Visual Effects > 3ds Max > Autodesk 3ds Max 2012: A Comprehensive Guide

(Expected time: 15 min)

Figure 2-89 *Model for Exercise 2*

Exercise 3

Create the model shown in Figures 2-90 and 2-91 using your own dimensions. You can view the final rendered image of this model by downloading the *c02_3dsmax_2012_render.zip* file from *http://www.cadcim.com*. The path of the file is mentioned in Exercise 2.

(Expected time: 15 min)

Figure 2-90 *Model for Exercise 3 (view 1)*

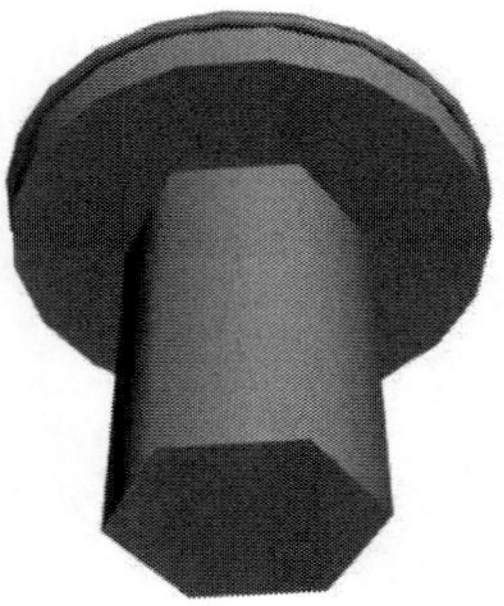

Figure 2-91 *Model for Exercise 3 (view 2)*

Exercise 4

Create the model shown in Figure 2-92 using your own dimensions. You can view the final rendered image of this model by downloading the *c02_3dsmax_2012_render.zip* file from *http://www.cadcim.com*. The path of the file is mentioned in Exercise 2.

(Expected time: 15 min)

Figure 2-92 *Model for Exercise 4*

Answers to Self-Evaluation Test

1. b, **2.** c, **3.** d, **4.** c, **5.** F, **6.** T, **7.** F, **8. Select and Squash**, **9. Name and Color**, **10. Parameters** **11. Walk Through**

3

Extended Primitives

Learning Objectives

After completing this chapter, you will be able to:

- *Use snap controls*
- *Understand Bend modifier*
- *Understand Taper modifier*
- *Create extended primitives*

INTRODUCTION

In this chapter, you will learn to create complex 3D shapes using extended primitives. Also, you will learn the usage of the **Bend** and **Taper** modifiers as well as different snap controls in detail.

SNAP CONTROLS

The snap controls in Autodesk 3ds Max enable you to control actions in a precise manner. If you use the snap controls, they automatically snap to the grid points in the viewport or to the specific parts of an object. The snap controls are discussed next.

Snaps Toggle

Main Toolbar: Snaps Toggle
Menu bar: Tools > Grids and Snaps > Snaps Toggle
Keyboard: S

The **Snaps Toggle** flyout has the following three tools that are used to snap the objects: **2D**, **2.5D**, and **3D** object snap tools, refer to Figure 3-1.

Figure 3-1 The Snaps Toggle flyout

2D Snap

If you choose the **2D Snap** tool from the **Snaps Toggle** flyout, then the cursor snaps to the active grid in two dimensions, X and Y. The Z-axis is not taken into consideration.

2.5D Snap

If you choose the **2.5D Snap** tool from the **Snaps Toggle** flyout, then the cursor snaps to the vertices and edges of the objects projected on the active grid.

3D Snap

If you choose the **3D Snap** tool from the **Snaps Toggle** flyout, then the cursor snaps to any object in 3D space using the **3D Snap** tool.

If you invoke any snap tool from the **Snaps Toggle** flyout, when **Select and Move** tools is active, the move gizmo will show a small circle at its center, as shown in Figure 3-2. On moving the gizmo or snap handle, this axis center will act as the start snap point. This feature will also help in increasing the accuracy of snaps.

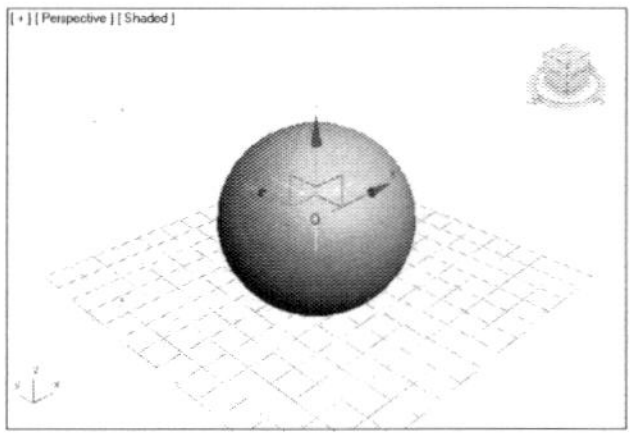

Figure 3-2 A small circle displayed at the center of the move gizmo

Angle Snap Toggle

Main Toolbar: Angle Snap Toggle
Menu bar: Tools > Grids and Snaps > Angle Snap Toggle
Keyboard: A

The **Angle Snap Toggle** tool enables you to rotate an object in the angular increments that are specified in the **Angle** spinner of the **Grid and Snap Settings** dialog box. You can change the value of angular increments using the **Grid and Snap Settings** dialog box. To invoke this dialog box, right-click on the **Angle Snap Toggle** tool; the **Grid and Snap Settings** dialog box will be displayed, as shown in Figure 3-3. By default, the **Options** tab is chosen and the value in the **Angle** spinner is set to 5.0.

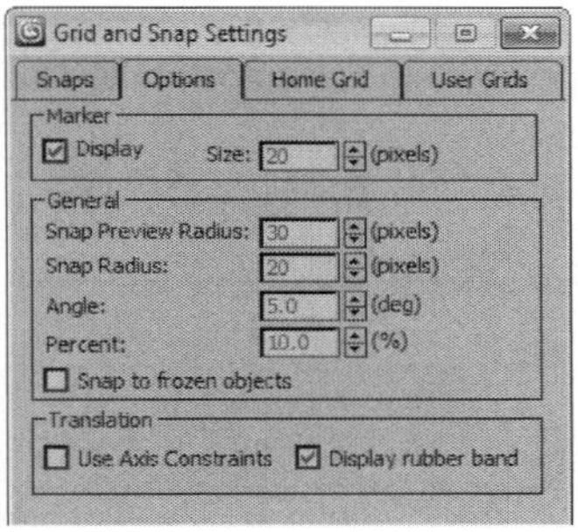

*Figure 3-3 The **Grid and Snap Settings** dialog box*

Percent Snap Toggle

Main Toolbar: Percent Snap Toggle
Menu bar: Tools > Grids and Snaps > Percent Snap Toggle
Keyboard: CTRL+SHIFT+P

The **Percent Snap Toggle** tool enables you to scale an object in the percent increments. These increments can be specified in the **Percent** spinner of the **Grid and Snap Settings** dialog box. You can also set another value for the percent increments. To do so, right-click on the **Percent Snap Toggle** tool; the **Grid and Snap Settings** dialog box will be displayed, refer to Figure 3-3. In the **Options** tab of the **Grid and Snaps Settings** dialog box, the default value set in the **Percent** spinner is 10.0.

Spinner Snap Toggle

Main Toolbar: Spinner Snap Toggle

The **Spinner Snap Toggle** tool is used to set the single increment or decrement value for all spinners in Autodesk 3ds Max. By default, the increment or decrement value is 1, but you can set another value also. To do so, right-click on the **Spinner Snap Toggle** tool; the **Preference Settings** dialog box will be displayed. In this dialog box, choose the **General** tab, if it is not already chosen. Now, in the **Spinners** area, set a value in the **Snap** spinner, refer to Figure 3-4.

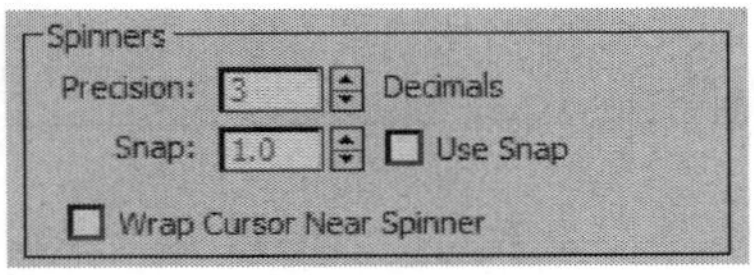

*Figure 3-4 The **Spinners** area in the **Preference Settings** dialog box*

Also, select the **Use Snap** check box and choose the **OK** button; the **Spinner Snap Toggle** tool in the **Main Toolbar** gets invoked. Now, when you use any spinner in Autodesk 3ds Max, the value will increase or decrease according to the value that you specified in the **Preference Settings** dialog box.

Keyboard Shortcut Override Toggle

Main Toolbar: Keyboard Shortcut Override Toggle

The **Keyboard Shortcut Override Toggle** tool is used to toggle between the use of the main user interface shortcut keys and the use of shortcut keys for groups such as Track View and editable mesh. When this toggle button is turned on, both the main user interface and the shortcut keys are recognized, whereas when this toggle button is off, only the main user interface shortcuts will work.

MODIFIERS

In Autodesk 3ds Max, modifiers are used to modify and apply various types of functions or effects on an object. There are different types of modifiers that perform different functions about which you will learn in the later chapters. In this section, you will learn about the **Bend** and **Taper** modifiers.

Bend Modifier

The **Bend** modifier is used to bend an object in the X, Y, or Z axis. To apply the **Bend** modifier on an object, select the object and choose **Modifiers > Parametric Deformers > Bend** from the menu bar. Alternatively, you can select the object in the viewport and choose the **Modify** tab in the **Command Panel**; the **Modifiers List** drop-down list will be displayed. Select **Object-Space Modifiers > Bend** from the **Modifier List** drop-down list; the **Bend** modifier will be displayed in the modifier stack, as shown in Figure 3-5. Also, the **Parameters** rollout will be displayed in the modify panel, as shown in Figure 3-6. The areas in the **Parameters** rollout are discussed next.

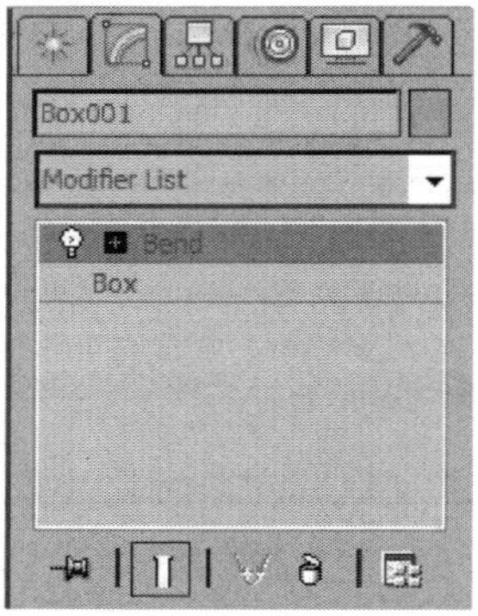

*Figure 3-5 The **Bend** modifier displayed in the modifier stack*

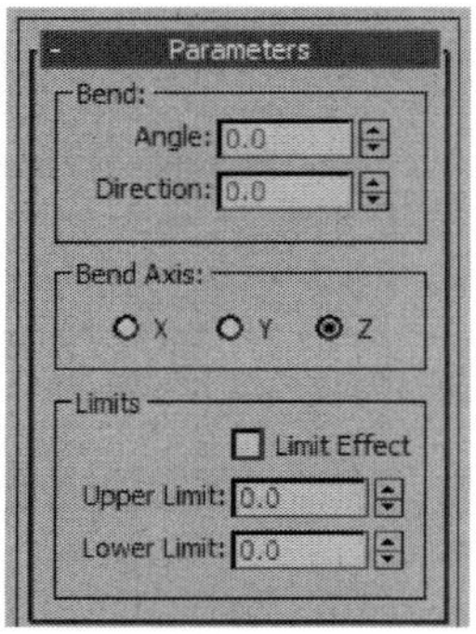

*Figure 3-6 The **Parameters** rollout of the **Bend** modifier*

Bend Area

The **Bend** area is used to set the parameters to bend an object. The value in the **Angle** spinner is used to define the angle of the bend along the X, Y, or Z axis. The value in the **Direction** spinner is used to define the direction of the bend.

Bend Axis Area

The **Bend Axis** area is used to define the axis, which needs to be bent. To do so, you need to select the **X**, **Y**, or **Z** radio button in this area.

Limits Area

The **Limits** area is used to define the upper and lower limits of the gizmo's axes to bend a part of an object. Select the **Limit Effect** check box to make the options in this area active. The default value in the **Upper Limit** spinner is zero or positive. Similarly, the default value in the **Lower Limit** spinner is zero or negative. The values in the **Lower Limit** and **Upper Limit** spinners are the distances from the modifier's center point, beyond which the modifier cannot affect the object.

Taper Modifier

The **Taper** modifier is used to taper an object by scaling it on both sides. On applying this modifier, one side of the object will be scaled up and another will be scaled down by an equal amount. To apply the **Taper** modifier on an object, choose **Modifiers > Parametric Deformers > Taper** from the menu bar; the **Taper** modifier will be displayed in the modifier stack, as shown in Figure 3-7. Also, the **Parameters** rollout will be displayed in the modify panel, as shown in Figure 3-8. The areas in this rollout are discussed next.

*Figure 3-7 The **Taper** modifier in the modifier stack*

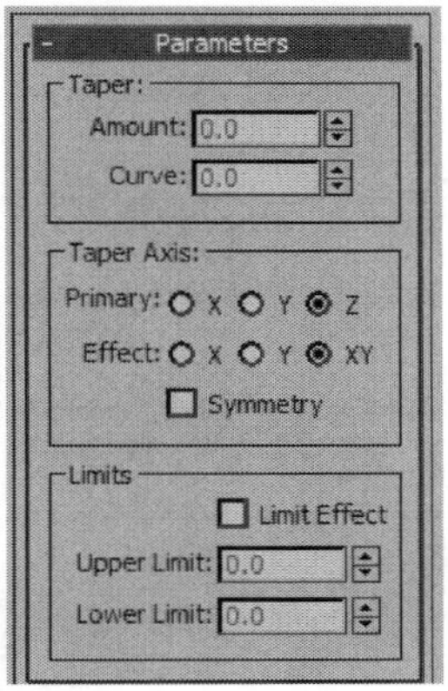

*Figure 3-8 The **Parameters** rollout of the **Taper** modifier*

Taper Area

The **Taper** area is used to set the parameters for scaling the shape of an object. The value in the **Amount** spinner in the **Taper** area is used to define the amount of taper. The value in the **Curve** spinner is used to define the curve applied to the gizmo, and it helps in creating different shapes of the taper. You can set the values of the **Amount** and **Curve** spinners from -10.0 to 10.0.

Taper Axis Area

You can define the central axis by selecting the **X**, **Y**, or **Z** radio button in the **Primary** group of this area. The **Effect** group is used to define the direction of the taper from the primary axis. The radio buttons under the **Effect** group get changed according to the selection of the primary axis. Select the **Symmetry** check box to create a symmetrical taper around the primary axis.

Limits Area

This area is the same as discussed in the **Bend** modifier.

EXTENDED PRIMITIVES

In Autodesk 3ds Max, there are some complex 3D geometric shapes, which can be used to create complex 3D objects. These shapes are known as extended primitives. The extended primitives are chamfer box, spindle, hedra, and so on. All extended primitives can be created dynamically using the mouse. Some of the extended primitives can also be created by entering the parameters in the **Keyboard Entry** rollout.

Note

*The hedra, ringwave, and hose extended primitives cannot be created using the keyboard, therefore, they do not have the **Keyboard Entry** rollout.*

To create the extended primitives, you need to choose **Create > Geometry** in the **Command Panel**; a drop-down list will be displayed with the **Standard Primitives** option selected by default in it. Now, select the **Extended Primitives** option from the drop-down list. Activate the viewport in which you want to create the primitives by clicking in it. Then, invoke the corresponding tool from the **Object Type** rollout. In this section, you will learn to create and modify the extended primitives using various tools available in the **Object Type** rollout.

Creating a Hedra

Menu bar:	Create > Extended Primitives > Hedra
Command Panel:	Create > Geometry > Extended Primitives > Object Type rollout > Hedra

To create a hedron, activate the viewport by clicking in it and make sure that the **Extended Primitives** option is selected from the drop-down list in the **Command Panel**. Now, invoke the **Hedra** tool from the **Object Type** rollout; the **Name and Color** and **Parameters** rollouts will be displayed, as shown in Figure 3-9. Now, press and hold the left mouse button in the viewport to define the center point of the hedron, and then drag the cursor to define its radius. Release the left mouse button to get the desired radius; a hedron will be created, as shown in Figure 3-10.

Various rollouts used to create and modify the hedron are discussed next.

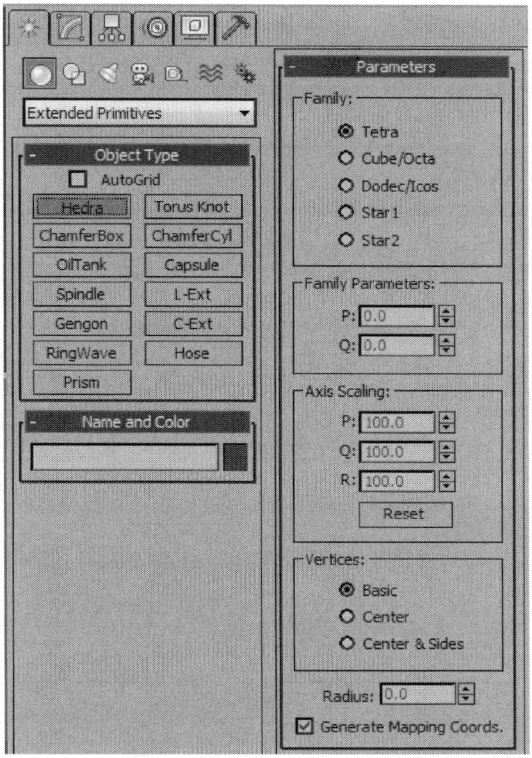

Figure 3-9 Various rollouts to create a hedron

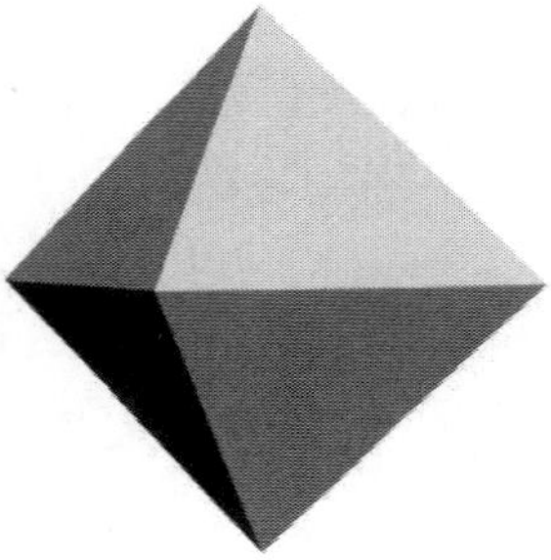

Figure 3-10 A hedron

Note

*The options in the **Name and Color** rollout of all the extended primitives are the same as those discussed in the **Box** tool of Chapter 2.*

*After creating a tool in the extended primitives list, if you right-click in the viewport to exit the tool, the **Parameters** rollout will disappear from the **Create** panel. In such a case, to modify the parameters of the tool, select the primitive in the viewport and choose the **Modify** tab in the **Command Panel**; the **Parameters** rollout will appear again.*

Parameters Rollout

The parameters in this rollout are discussed next.

Family Area

The **Family** area is used to define various types of hedra, refer to Figure 3-11. By default, the **Tetra** radio button is selected, which is used to create a tetrahedron. Select the **Cube/ Octa** radio button to create a cube or octahedron depending on the value you enter in the spinners in the **Family Parameters** area. Select the **Dodec/Icos** radio button to create a dodecahedron or icosahedron, which again depends on the value that you enter in the **Family Parameters** area. Select the **Star1** and **Star2** radio buttons to create two different star-like polyhedra.

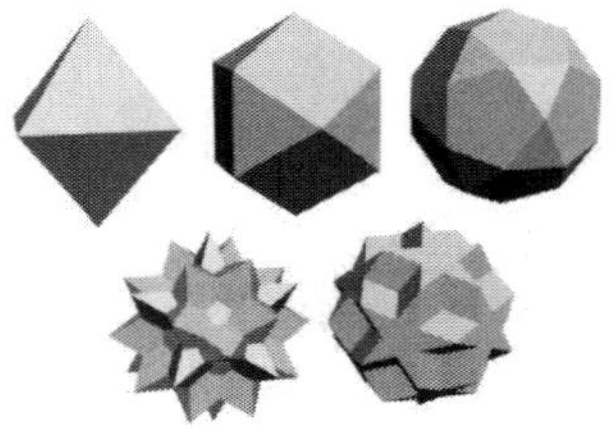

Figure 3-11 *Five basic shapes of hedra*

Family Parameters Area

The two spinners in this area, **P** and **Q**, are used to modify the vertices and facets of a polyhedron. They are related to each other and their combined value can be equal to or less than 1.0.

Axis Scaling Area

A polyhedron can have three shapes of polygonal facets, triangle, square, and pentagon. The **P**, **Q**, and **R** spinners in this area control the axis of reflection for one of the facets of a polyhedron. By default, the value in these spinners is 100.0. If you change the values in these spinners, they will push the facets in the object or out of the object. On choosing the **Reset** button, the values in these spinners will be reset to 100.0.

Vertices Area

The **Vertices** area determines the vertices and therefore, the facets of a polyhedron. By default, the **Basic** radio button is selected, which specifies the minimum vertices. Select the **Center** radio button to place an additional vertex at the center of each facet. Select the **Center & Sides** radio button to place an additional vertex at the center of each facet and at each edge. To view the vertices, you need to apply the **Edit Mesh** modifier to the polyhedron object, about which you will learn in the later chapters.

Radius

Set the value in the **Radius** spinner to modify the radius of a polyhedron.

Creating a Torus Knot

Menu bar:	Create > Extended Primitives > Torus Knot
Command Panel:	Create > Geometry > Extended Primitives > Object Type rollout > Torus Knot

To create a torus knot, activate a viewport by clicking in it and then invoke the **Torus Knot** tool from the **Object Type** rollout; the **Name and Color**, **Creation Method**, **Keyboard Entry**, and **Parameters** rollouts will be displayed, as shown in Figure 3-12. Now, press and hold the left mouse button in the viewport for defining the first point on the torus knot and drag the cursor to define its radius. Release the left mouse button and then move the cursor to define the radius of the cross-section. Click on the screen to get the desired radius; a torus knot will be created, as shown in Figure 3-13.

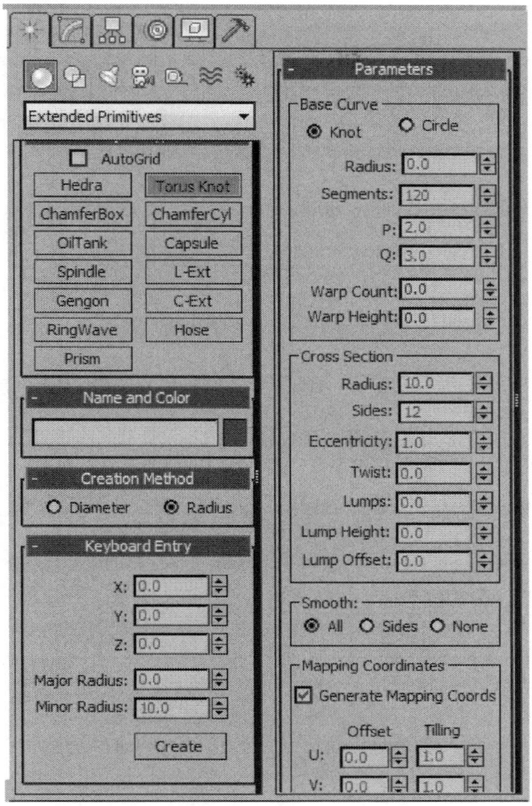

Figure 3-12 *Various rollouts to create a torus knot*

Figure 3-13 *A torus knot*

Various rollouts used to create and modify a torus knot are discussed next.

Creation Method Rollout

The options in this rollout are used for creating a torus knot dynamically. Select the **Diameter** radio button to specify the first point on an edge at the surface of the torus knot and then drag the mouse to specify its diameter. You can change the center point by moving the mouse. Select the **Radius** radio button to specify the first point on the center of the torus knot and then drag to specify its radius.

Keyboard Entry Rollout

To create a torus knot using the **Keyboard Entry** rollout, expand the **Keyboard Entry** rollout and set the values in the **Major Radius** and **Minor Radius** spinners. The major radius specifies the total size of the torus knot and the minor radius specifies the size of the circular cross-section. You can also set the values in the **X**, **Y**, and **Z** spinners to specify the position of the torus knot in the viewport along the axes of the home grid or a grid object. Next, choose the **Create** button in the **Keyboard Entry** rollout; a torus knot will be created with the given radii in all viewports.

Note

*The **Keyboard Entry** rollout in all extended primitives is used to create the corresponding primitive by entering the parameters using the keyboard. The method of creating all primitives is the same as discussed above. The only difference is in the type and number of parameters of various extended primitives.*

Parameters Rollout

The areas in this rollout are discussed next.

Base Curve Area

In the **Base Curve** area, select the **Knot** radio button to create a knot or select the **Circle** radio button to create a circle. The value in the **Radius** spinner specifies the major radius of the torus knot or the radius of the base curve. The value in the **Segments** spinner specifies the number of segments along the base curve. On selecting the **Knot** radio button, the **P** and **Q** spinners become active, while the **Warp Count** and **Warp Height** spinners remain inactive. The value in the **P** spinner defines the number of turns around the Z-axis. The value in the **Q** spinner defines the total ups and downs around the XY-plane. On selecting the **Circle** radio button, the **Warp Count** and **Warp Height** spinners become active, while the **P** and **Q** spinners remain inactive. The **Warp Count** spinner defines the number of curves around the circumference of the circle, while the **Warp Height** spinner defines the height of the curves, refer to Figure 3-14.

Note

*To view the segments or edged faces of an object, press the F4 key. Alternatively, move the mouse over the Shading viewport label in any viewport and click on it; a shortcut menu will be displayed. Choose the **Edged Faces** option; the segments of the object in the viewport will be displayed.*

Cross Section

In the **Cross Section** area, the **Radius** spinner defines the minor radius or the radius of the cross-section of the torus knot. The **Sides** spinner specifies the number of segments around the cross-section. The **Eccentricity** spinner specifies the shape of the torus knot. If you set the value **1** in this spinner, then a circular cross-section will be created, whereas on specifying a value other than 1, an elliptical cross-section of the torus knot will be created. The value in the **Twist** spinner specifies the number of twists on the cross-section. The **Lumps** spinner defines the number of bulges in the torus knot and the **Lump Height** spinner specifies the height of those lumps. The **Lump Offset** spinner is used to shift the lumps along a given length, refer to Figure 3-15.

Note

*To view lumps or bulges in a torus knot, you need to set a value in the **Lump Height** spinner.*

Smooth

In the **Smooth** area, select the **All** radio button to smoothen the whole knot. Select the **Sides** radio button to smoothen only the sides of the torus knot. Select the **None** radio button to create a faceted surface of the torus knot.

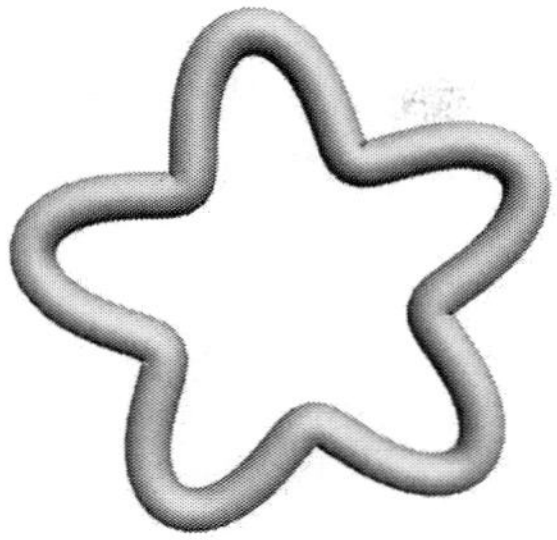

Figure 3-14 A torus knot with a circular base curve

Figure 3-15 A torus knot after defining lumps and lump height

Mapping Coordinates
Select the **Generate Mapping Coords** check box in the **Mapping Coordinates** area to calculate the mapping coordinates of the torus knot.

Creating a Chamfer Box

Menu bar:	Create > Extended Primitives > Chamfer Box
Command Panel:	Create > Geometry > Extended Primitives > Object Type rollout > ChamferBox

The chamfer box is similar to the box in the standard primitives. The only difference is that a chamfer box has beveled or rounded edges. To create a chamfer box, activate the viewport and invoke the **ChamferBox** tool from the **Object Type** rollout; the **Name and Color**, **Creation Method**, **Keyboard Entry**, and **Parameters** rollouts will be displayed, as shown in Figure 3-16.

Now, press and hold the left mouse button on a point in the viewport for defining the first corner of the chamfer box, and drag the cursor to define its length and width. Release the left mouse button to get the desired length and width. Next, move the cursor up or down to define its height, and click on the screen to get the desired height. Then, move the cursor to define the fillet and click on the screen to get the fillet or chamfer; a chamfer box will be created, as shown in Figure 3-17.

Various rollouts used to create and modify a chamfer box are discussed next.

Creation Method Rollout
The options in this rollout are used for creating a chamfer box dynamically. Select the **Cube** radio button to create a chamfer box of equal length, width, and height. Select the **Box** radio button to create a chamfer box having different length, width, and height.

Parameters Rollout
The options in this rollout are used to modify the chamfer box. Enter the new values in the **Length**, **Width**, **Height**, and **Fillet** spinners. The values in the **Length Segs**, **Width Segs**, and

Height Segs spinners are used to define the number of segments along the length, width, and height of the chamfer box, respectively. The value in the **Fillet Segs** spinner specifies the number of segments in the fillet of the chamfer box.

Select the **Smooth** check box, if it is not already selected, to create a chamfer box with rounded edges, as shown in Figure 3-17. If this check box is cleared, a chamfer box with beveled edges will be created, as shown in Figure 3-18.

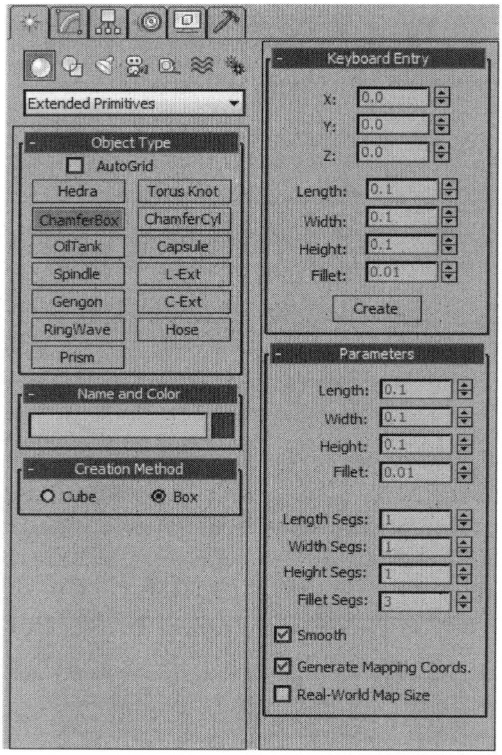

Figure 3-16 Various rollouts to create a chamfer box

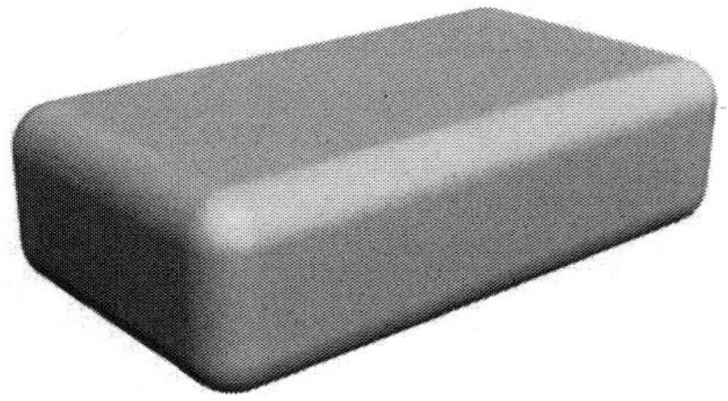

Figure 3-17 *A chamfer box with rounded edges*

Figure 3-18 *A chamfer box with beveled edges*

Creating a Chamfer Cylinder

Menu bar:	Create > Extended Primitives > Chamfer Cylinder
Command Panel:	Create > Geometry > Extended Primitives > Object Type rollout > ChamferCyl

The chamfer cylinder is similar to the cylinder in the standard primitives. The only difference is that the chamfer cylinder has beveled or rounded edges. To create a chamfer cylinder, activate the viewport and invoke the **ChamferCyl** tool from the **Object Type** rollout;

the **Name and Color**, **Creation Method**, **Keyboard Entry**, and **Parameters** rollouts will be displayed, as shown in Figure 3-19.

Next, press and hold the left mouse button on a point in the viewport for defining the center of the base of the cylinder, and drag the cursor to define its radius. Release the left mouse button and move the cursor up or down to define its height. Click on the screen to get the desired height and move the cursor to define the fillet. Again, click on the screen to get the desired fillet; a chamfer cylinder will be created, as shown in Figure 3-20.

Various rollouts used to create and modify a chamfer cylinder are discussed next.

Creation Method Rollout

The options in this rollout are the same as those discussed while creating the sphere in Chapter 2.

Parameters Rollout

The options in this rollout are used to modify the chamfer cylinder. Enter new values of the radius, height, and fillet in their respective spinners. The value in the **Height Segs** spinner is used to define the number of segments along the height of the chamfer cylinder. Similarly, the value in the **Fillet Segs** spinner is used to define the number of segments in the fillet area of the chamfer cylinder. The value in the **Sides** spinner specifies the number of sides of the chamfer cylinder. The **Cap Segs** spinner is used to define the number of segments on each end of the cylinder. Select the **Smooth** check box to create a chamfer cylinder with rounded edges, refer to Figure 3-20. If this check box is cleared, a chamfer cylinder with beveled edges will be created, as shown in Figure 3-21. The options available on selecting the **Slice On** check box are the same as those discussed in Chapter 2.

Creating an Oil Tank

Menu bar:	Create > Extended Primitives > Oil Tank
Command Panel:	Create > Geometry > Extended Primitives > Object Type rollout > OilTank

An oil tank is a type of cylinder with convex caps. To create an oil tank, activate the viewport and invoke the **OilTank** tool from the **Object Type** rollout; the **Name and Color**, **Creation Method**, **Keyboard Entry**, and **Parameters** rollouts will be displayed, as shown in Figure 3-22.

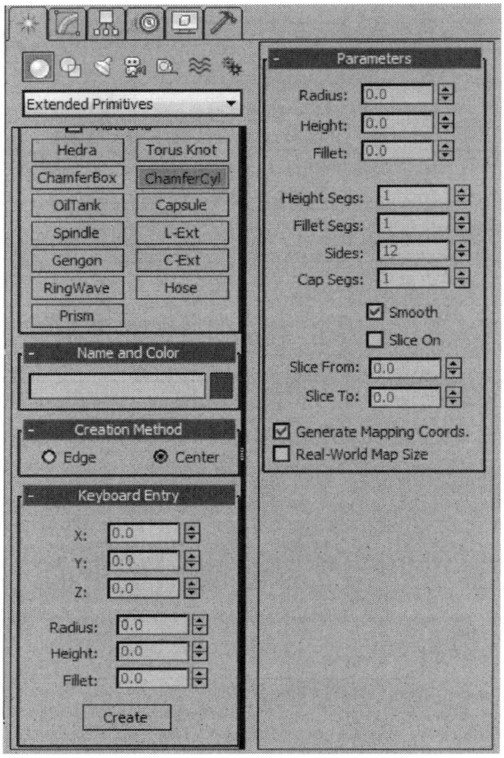

Figure 3-19 *Various rollouts to create a chamfer cylinder*

Figure 3-20 *A chamfer cylinder with rounded edges*

Figure 3-21 *A chamfer cylinder with beveled edges*

Now, press and hold the left mouse button in the viewport to specify the center of the first face and drag the cursor to define the radius of the oil tank. Release the left mouse button and move the cursor up or down to define the height of the oil tank. Click on the screen to get the desired height and move the cursor again to define the height of the convex caps. Click on the screen again to get the desired height; an oil tank will be created, as shown in Figure 3-23.

Various rollouts used to create and modify the oil tank are discussed next.

Creation Method Rollout

The options in this rollout are the same as discussed in the previous chapter.

Parameters Rollout

The options in this rollout are used to modify the dimensions of the oil tank. The values in the **Radius** and **Height** spinners specify the radius and height of the oil tank, respectively. The value in the **Cap Height** spinner defines the height of the convex cap of the oil tank. Select the **Overall** radio button to specify the overall height of the oil tank. Select the **Centers** radio button to specify the height of the cylinder excluding the height of the convex cap. Set the value in the **Blend** spinner to create a smooth bevel at the edge of the caps. The **Sides** spinner specifies the number of sides around the oil tank. The value in the **Height Segs** spinner defines the number of segments along the height of the oil tank. By default, the **Smooth** check box is selected; therefore the surface of the oil tank will be smooth. The options available on selecting the **Slice On** check box are the same as those discussed in the previous chapter.

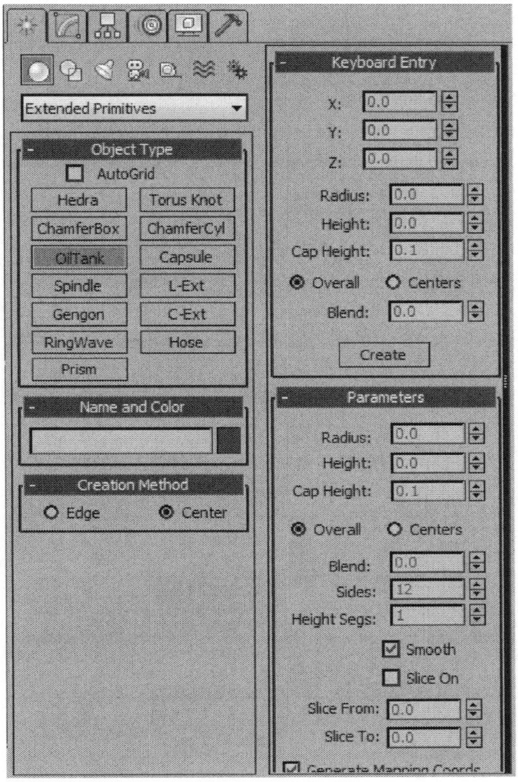

Figure 3-22 Various rollouts to create an oil tank

Figure 3-23 An oil tank

Creating a Capsule

Menu bar:	Create > Extended Primitives > Capsule
Command Panel:	Create > Geometry > Extended Primitives > Object Type rollout > Capsule

To create a capsule, activate the viewport and invoke the **Capsule** tool from the **Object Type** rollout; the **Name and Color**, **Creation Method**, **Keyboard Entry**, and **Parameters** rollouts will be displayed, as shown in Figure 3-24.

Now, press and hold the left mouse button in the viewport to specify the center of the first face and drag the cursor to define the radius of the capsule. Release the left mouse button and move the cursor up or down to define the height of the capsule. Click on the screen to get the desired height; a capsule will be created, as shown in Figure 3-25.

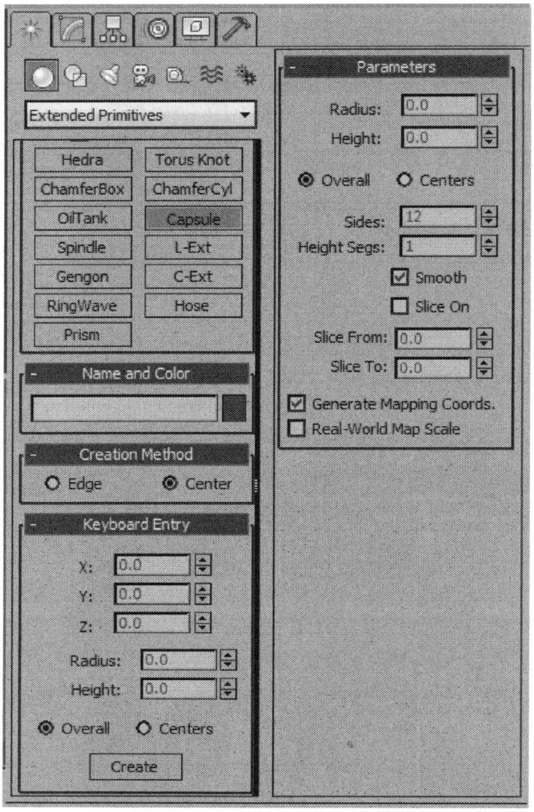

Figure 3-24 *Various rollouts to create a capsule*

Figure 3-25 *A capsule*

Various rollouts used to create and modify the capsule are discussed next.

Creation Method Rollout

The options in this rollout are the same as those discussed in the previous chapter.

Parameters Rollout

The options in this rollout are the same as discussed in the **Parameters** rollout of the oil tank extended primitive.

Creating a Spindle

Menu bar:	Create > Extended Primitives > Spindle
Command Panel:	Create > Geometry > Extended Primitives > Object Type rollout > Spindle

A spindle is a type of cylinder with conical caps. To create a spindle, activate the viewport and invoke the **Spindle** tool from the **Object Type** rollout; the **Name and Color**, **Creation Method**, **Keyboard Entry**, and **Parameters** rollouts will be displayed, as shown in Figure 3-26. Now, press and hold the left mouse button in the viewport to specify the center of the first face and drag the cursor to define the radius of the spindle. Release the left mouse button and move the cursor up or down to define the height of the spindle. Click on the screen to get the desired height and move the cursor again to define the height of the conical caps. Next, click on the screen again; a spindle will be created, as shown in Figure 3-27.

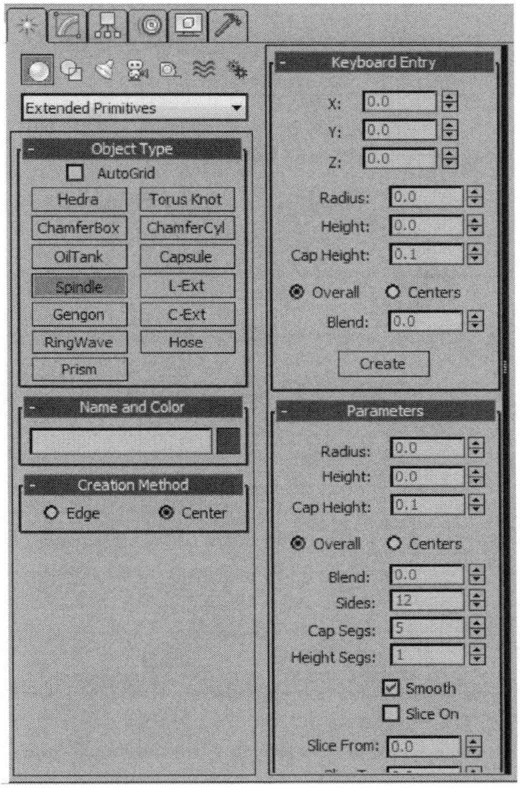

Figure 3-26 Various rollouts to create a spindle

Figure 3-27 A spindle

Various rollouts used to create and modify the spindle are discussed next.

Creation Method Rollout

The options in this rollout are the same as those discussed in the previous chapter.

Parameters Rollout

The options in this rollout are used to modify the spindle. To do so, select the spindle and choose the **Modify** tab in the **Command Panel**; the **Parameters** rollout will be displayed. Set the new values in the spinners to modify the spindle. The options in the **Parameters** rollout are the same as those described in the oil tank extended primitive.

Creating an L-Ext

Menu bar:	Create > Extended Primitives > L-Extrusion
Command Panel:	Create > Geometry > Extended Primitives > Object Type rollout > L-Ext

The L-Ext or L-Extrusion is an L-shaped object. To create an L-Ext, activate the viewport and invoke the **L-Ext** tool from the **Object Type** rollout; the **Name and Color**, **Creation Method**, **Keyboard Entry**, and **Parameters** rollouts will be displayed, as shown in Figure 3-28.

Now, press and hold the left mouse button in the viewport and drag the cursor to define the overall length and width of the object. Release the left mouse button and move the cursor up or down to define the height of the L-Ext. Click on the screen to get the desired height. Move the cursor again to define the thickness of the L-Ext and click on the screen; an L-Ext will be created, as shown in Figure 3-29.

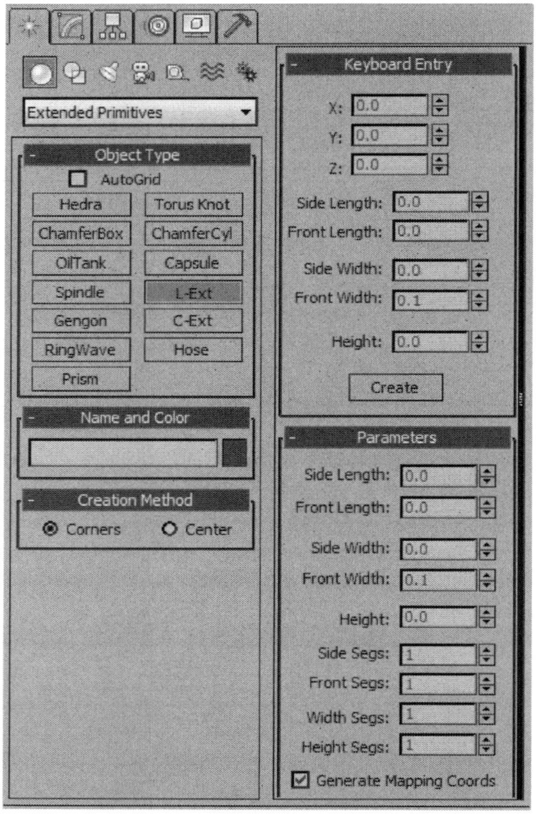

Figure 3-28 Various rollouts to create an L-Ext

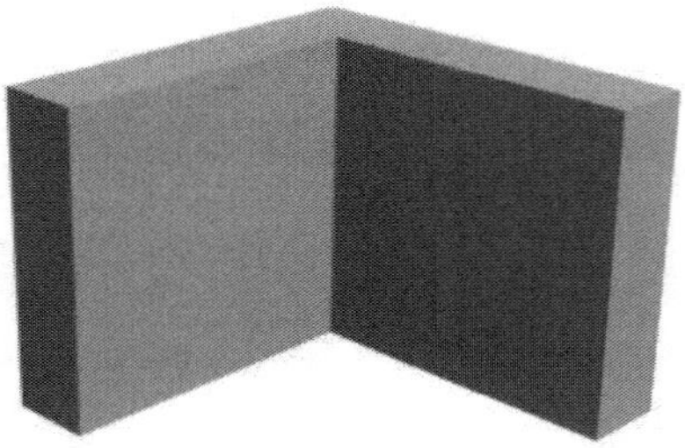

Figure 3-29 An L-Ext

Various rollouts used to create and modify the L-Ext are discussed next.

Creation Method Rollout

The options in this rollout are used for creating an L-Ext dynamically. Select the **Corners** radio button to create the L-Ext from one corner to another. Select the **Center** radio button to create the L-Ext from its center to the outward direction.

Parameters Rollout

The options in this rollout are used to modify the L-Ext. Set the new values in the spinners. The values in the **Side Length** and **Front Length** spinners are used to define the overall length of the L-Ext. Similarly, the values in the **Side Width** and **Front Width** spinners specify the overall width of the L-Ext. The value in the **Height** spinner is used to specify the height of the L-Ext. The values in the **Side Segs** and **Front Segs** spinners are used to define the number of vertical segments on the sides of the L-Ext. The value in the **Width Segs** spinner specifies the number of segments on the width or thickness of the L-Ext; whereas, the value in the **Height Segs** spinner specifies the number of segments along the height of the L-Ext.

Creating a Gengon

Menu bar:	Create > Extended Primitives > Gengon
Command Panel:	Create > Geometry > Extended Primitives > Object Type rollout > Gengon

To create a gengon, activate the viewport and invoke the **Gengon** tool from the **Object Type** rollout; the **Name and Color**, **Creation Method**, **Keyboard Entry**, and **Parameters** rollouts will be displayed, as shown in Figure 3-30. Now, press and hold the left mouse button in the viewport and drag the cursor to define the radius of the object. Release the left mouse button and move the cursor up or down to define the height of the gengon. Click on the screen to get the desired height and move the cursor again to define the size of the fillet of the gengon. Next, click on the screen; a gengon will be created, as shown in Figure 3-31.

Various rollouts used to create and modify the gengon are discussed next.

Creation Method Rollout

The options in this rollout are the same as those discussed in the **Sphere** tool of the previous chapter.

Parameters Rollout

The options in this rollout are used to modify the gengon. To do so, select the gengon and choose the **Modify** tab in the **Command Panel**; the **Parameters** rollout will be displayed. Enter new values of the sides, radius, fillet, and height in their respective spinners. Similarly, enter new values in the **Side Segs**, **Height Segs**, and **Fillet Segs** spinners to define the segments on the sides, height, and fillet of the gengon, respectively. Select the **Smooth** check box to smoothen the faces of the gengon.

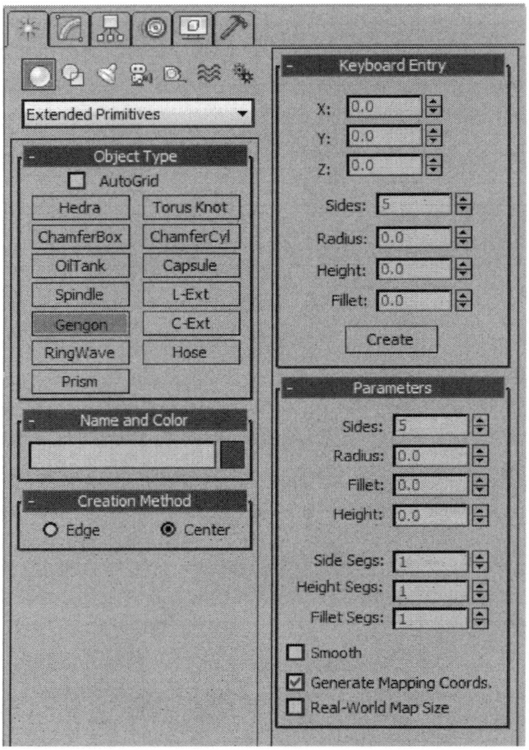

Figure 3-30 Various rollouts to create a gengon

Figure 3-31 A gengon

Creating a C-Ext

Menu bar:	Create > Extended Primitives > C-Extrusion
Command Panel:	Create > Geometry > Extended Primitives > Object Type rollout > C-Ext

The C-Ext or C-Extrusion is a C-shaped object. To create a C-Ext, activate the viewport and invoke the **C-Ext** tool from the **Object Type** rollout; the **Name and Color**, **Creation Method**, **Keyboard Entry**, and **Parameters** rollouts will be displayed, as shown in Figure 3-32. Now, press and hold the left mouse button in the viewport and drag the cursor to define the overall length and width of the object. Release the left mouse button and move the cursor up or down to define the height of the C-Ext. Click on the screen to get the desired height and move the cursor again to define the thickness of the C-Ext; a C-Ext will be created, as shown in Figure 3-33.

Various rollouts used to create and modify the C-Ext are discussed next.

Creation Method Rollout

The options in this rollout are the same as those discussed in the L-Ext primitive in this chapter.

Parameters Rollout

The options in this rollout are used to modify the C-Ext. Set the new values in the spinners. The **Back Length**, **Side Length**, and **Front Length** spinners specify the overall length of the C-Ext. Similarly, the **Back Width**, **Side Width**, and **Front Width** spinners specify the overall width of the C-Ext. The **Height** spinner specifies the height of the C-Ext. The values in the **Back Segs**, **Side Segs**, and **Front Segs** spinners define the number of vertical segments on the sides of the C-Ext. The value in the **Width Segs** spinner specifies the number of segments on the width or thickness of the C-Ext; whereas, the value in the **Height Segs** spinner specifies the number of segments along the height of the C-Ext.

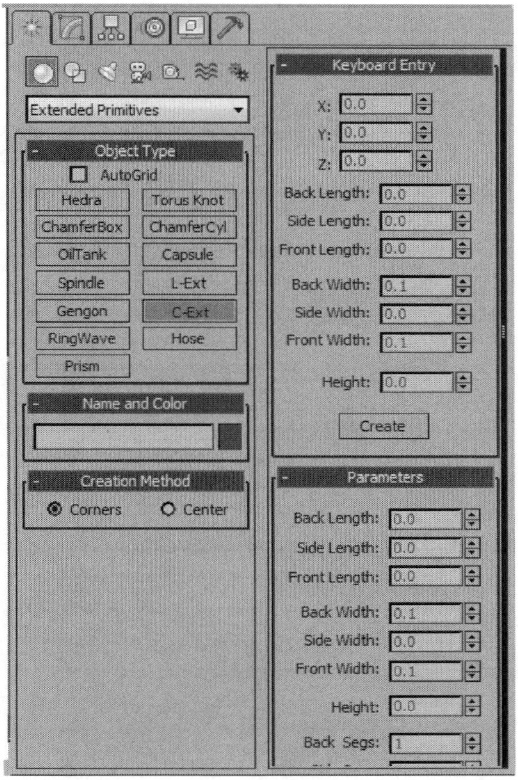

Figure 3-32 Various rollouts to create a C-Ext

Figure 3-33 A C-Ext

Creating a RingWave

Menu bar:	Create > Extended Primitives > RingWave
Command Panel:	Create > Geometry > Extended Primitives > Object Type rollout > RingWave

A ringwave is a ring-shaped object that can have irregular inner and outer edges that can be animated. To create a ringwave, activate the viewport and invoke the **RingWave** tool from the **Object Type** rollout; the **Name and Color** and **Parameters** rollouts will be displayed, as shown in Figures 3-34 and 3-35.

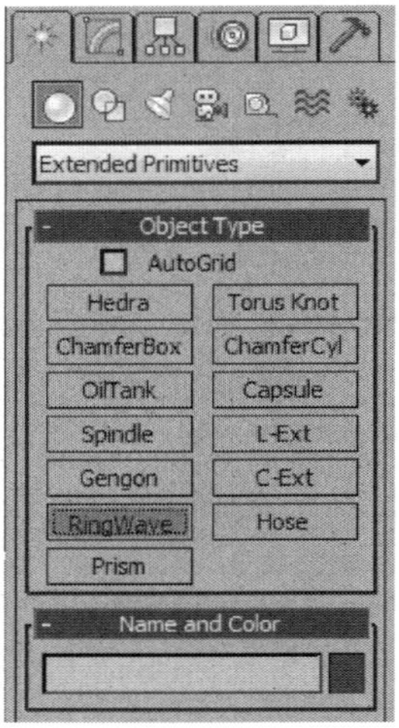

Figure 3-34 *The* ***Name and Color*** *rollout*

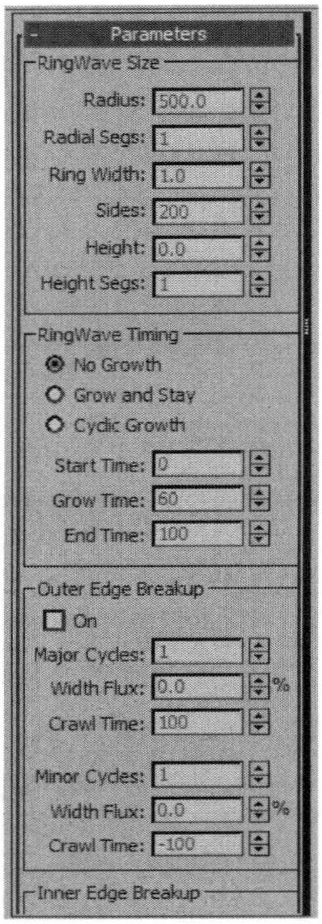

Figure 3-35 *Partial view of the* ***Parameters*** *rollout of the ringwave*

Now, press and hold the left mouse button on a point in the viewport to specify the center of the ringwave and drag the cursor to define its radius. Release the left mouse button and move the cursor to define the width of the ringwave. Click on the screen to get the desired radius of the object; a ringwave will be created, as shown in Figure 3-36.

Figure 3-36 *A ringwave*

> **Tip**. *After creating the ringwave, you can view its basic animation by dragging the time slider on the track bar or by choosing the* ***Play Animation*** *button from the animation playback controls.*

The rollouts used to create and modify the ringwave are discussed next.

Parameters Rollout

The options in this rollout are used to modify the ringwave. To do so, select the ringwave and choose the **Modify** tab in the **Command Panel**. Now, expand the **Parameters** rollout and enter the new values in the spinners. The areas in this rollout are discussed next.

RingWave Size Area

In the **RingWave Size** area, the **Radius** spinner is used to define the outer radius of the ringwave. The **Radial Segs** spinner specifies the number of segments between the inner and outer surfaces along the circumference of the ringwave. The **Ring Width** spinner specifies the ring width. The value in the **Sides** spinner specifies the number of sides around the circumference of the ringwave. The **Height** spinner specifies the height of the ringwave and the **Height Segs** spinner specifies the number of segments along its height.

RingWave Timing Area

The **RingWave Timing** area is used to animate the ringwave. The ringwave grows from the value 0 to the value specified in the **Radius** spinner of the **RingWave Size** area. Select the **No Growth**, **Grow and Stay**, or **Cyclic Growth** radio button to define the pattern of the ringwave growth. The values in the **Start Time**, **Grow Time**, and **End Time** spinners are used to specify the number of frames at which the ring wave starts appearing, reaches to its full size, and disappears, respectively.

On selecting the **No Growth** radio button, the ringwave will not grow over the time. It just appears at the frame number specified in the **Start Time** spinner and disappears after the frame number specified in the **End Time** spinner. Select the **Grow and Stay** radio button to animate a single growth cycle. In this case, the ringwave starts growing at the frame number specified in the **Start Time** spinner, grows up to its maximum radius in the number of frames specified in the **Grow Time** spinner, and disappears at the frame number specified in the **End Time** spinner. On selecting the **Cyclic Growth** radio button, the ringwave animates repeatedly. In this case, the ringwave starts growing in the frame number specified in the **Start Time** spinner, grows up to its maximum radius in the number of frames specified in the **Grow Time** spinner, and continues to grow up further up to the frame specified in the **End Time** spinner.

Outer Edge Breakup Area

The **Outer Edge Breakup** area is used to change the shape of the outer edge of the ringwave and define the breakup of the outer edge. To activate the options in this area, you need to select the **On** check box. The **Major Cycles** spinner specifies the number of major waves around the outer edge of the ringwave. The **Width Flux** spinner specifies the size of the major wave in percentage. The **Crawl Time** spinner specifies the number of frames in which a single major wave moves around the outer circumference of the ringwave.

The **Minor Cycles** spinner is used to define the number of small and random-sized waves in each major wave. The **Width Flux** spinner specifies the size of the smaller waves in percentage. The **Crawl Time** spinner specifies the number of frames in which a single minor wave moves around its respective major wave.

Inner Edge Breakup Area

The **Inner Edge Breakup** area is used to change the shape of the inner edge of the ringwave. Also, it defines the breakup of the inner edge. To activate the options in this area, you need to select the **On** check box. The **Inner Edge Breakup** area has the same options for defining the inner edge of the ringwave as those discussed in the **Outer Edge Breakup** area for defining the outer edge of the ringwave.

Surface Parameters Area

The **Texture Coordinates** and **Smooth** check boxes are selected by default in the **Surface Parameters** area. The **Texture Coordinates** check box is used to define the required coordinates for the mapped-material on the ringwave. The **Smooth** check box is used to smoothen the ringwave.

Creating a Hose

Menu bar:	Create > Extended Primitives > Hose
Command Panel:	Create > Geometry > Extended Primitives > Object Type rollout > Hose

A hose is an extended primitive that can link two objects. To create a hose, activate the viewport and invoke the **Hose** tool from the **Object Type** rollout; the **Name and Color** and **Hose Parameters** rollouts will be displayed, as shown in Figures 3-37 and 3-38. Now, press and hold the left mouse button in the viewport to specify the center of the hose and drag the cursor to define its radius. Release the left mouse button and move the cursor up or down to define the height of the hose. Click on the screen to get the desired height of the hose; a hose will be created, as shown in Figure 3-39.

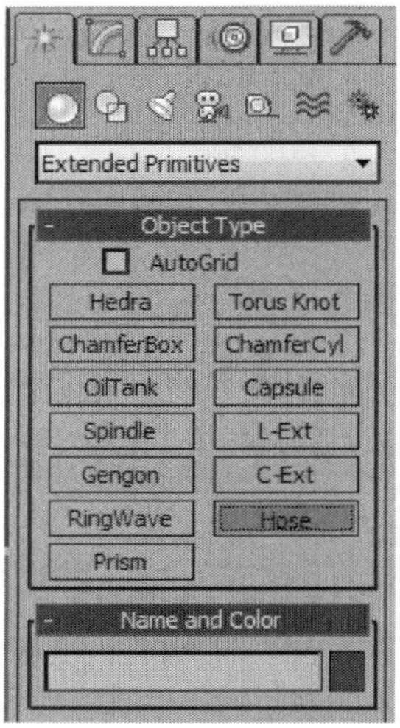

Figure 3-37 The ***Name and Color*** *rollout*

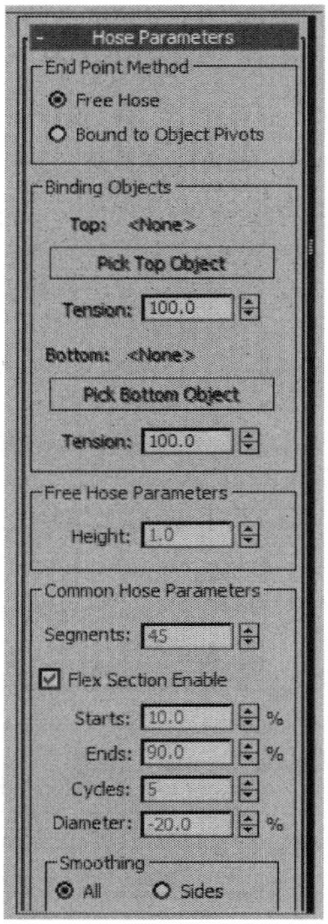

Figure 3-38 Partial view of the ***Hose Parameters*** *rollout*

The rollouts used to create and modify a hose are discussed next.

Figure 3-39 A hose

Hose Parameters Rollout

The options in this rollout are used to modify the hose. To do so, select the hose and choose the **Modify** tab in the **Command Panel**; the **Parameters** rollout will be displayed. Set the new values in the spinners in this rollout. The different areas in this rollout are discussed next.

End Point Method Area

In the **End Point Method** area, select the **Free Hose** radio button to create a free hose. You can modify the height of the free hose by setting the value in the **Height** spinner of the **Free Hose Parameters** area. If you want to bind the hose with two objects, then you need to select the **Bound to Object Pivots** radio button in the **End Point Method** area. On selecting this radio button, the options in the **Binding Objects** area will be enabled.

Binding Objects Area

The options in this area are used to bind two objects to the hose at the pivot point of these objects. To do so, choose the **Pick Top Object** button in the **Binding Objects** area and move the cursor over the object that you want to bind with the top of the hose; a selection cursor will be displayed. Select the object in the viewport to bind it at the top of the hose. Choose the **Pick Bottom Object** button in this area and move the cursor over another object that you want to bind with the bottom of the hose; a selection cursor will be displayed. Select the object in the viewport to bind it at the bottom of the hose. When you select the objects for the top and bottom of the hose, the name of these objects will be displayed in the **Top** and **Bottom** labels. The value in the **Tension** spinner is used to control the tension between the bend in the hose and the top or bottom objects.

Common Hose Parameters Area

In the **Common Hose Parameters** area, the **Segments** spinner specifies the number of segments along the length of the hose. By default, the **Flex Section Enable** check box is selected. As a result, the **Starts**, **Ends**, **Cycles**, and **Diameter** spinners will be enabled. The values in all these spinners are a percentage of the values of the main hose. The value in the **Starts** spinner specifies the point where the flex section starts along the hose. The value in the **Ends** spinner specifies the point where the flex section ends. The **Cycles** spinner is used to define the number of cycles in the flexible section. To display all cycles properly, the number of segments should be more. The **Diameter** spinner is used to specify the secondary diameter of the flexible section.

Smoothing Area

You need to select the **All** radio button in this area to add smoothness to the entire hose. Select the **Sides** radio button to smoothen only the sides of the hose. Select the **None** radio button to create a faceted surface of the hose. Select the **Segments** radio button to apply smoothness on the inner section of the hose.

By default, the **Renderable** and **Generate Mapping Coords** check boxes are selected in this area. The **Renderable** check box is used to view the hose at rendering. The **Generate Mapping Coords** check box is used to automatically assign the mapping coordinates to an object.

Hose Shape Area

The **Hose Shape** area is used to define the basic shape of the hose. Select the **Round Hose** radio button to create a circular cross-section; the **Diameter** and **Sides** spinners will be activated. The **Diameter** spinner specifies the diameter of the hose. The **Sides** spinner specifies the number of sides of the hose.

Select the **Rectangular Hose** radio button to create a rectangular hose; various spinners below this radio button will be activated. The **Width** and **Depth** spinners are used to define the width and depth of the hose, respectively. The **Fillet** spinner specifies the value by which the cross-section corners of the hose get rounded. The value in the **Fillet Segs** spinner should be higher in order to view the fillet. The value in the **Rotation** spinner rotates the hose around its local Z-axis.

Select the **D-Section Hose** radio button to create a D-shaped hose; various spinners below this radio button will be activated. The **Width** and **Depth** spinners in the **D-Section Hose** radio button are used to define the width and depth of the hose, respectively. The value in the **Round Sides** spinner specifies the total number of segments along the rounded side of the D-shaped hose. The **Fillet** spinner specifies the value by which the square corners of the cross-section get rounded. The value in the **Fillet Segs** spinner should be higher to view the fillet. The value in the **Rotation** spinner rotates the D-shaped hose around its local Z-axis.

Creating a Prism

Menu bar:	Create > Extended Primitives > Prism
Command Panel:	Create > Geometry > Extended Primitives > Object Type rollout > Prism

A prism is a three-sided object. To create a prism, activate the viewport and invoke the **Prism** tool from the **Object Type** rollout; the **Name and Color**, **Creation Method**, **Keyboard Entry**, and **Parameters** rollouts will be displayed, as shown in Figure 3-40.

You can create a prism dynamically using two methods. By default, the **Base/Apex** radio button is selected in the **Creation Method** rollout. In this case, a prism will be created with obtuse (more than 90 degrees) triangle at its base. Now, press and hold the left mouse button on a point to define the first corner of the triangle of the prism, drag the cursor horizontally to define the length of side 1 of the prism, and then drag the cursor again vertically to define the length of side 2 and side 3. Release the left mouse button and move the cursor to specify the apex of the triangle. Then, click again in the viewport to place it. Now, move the cursor up or down to define the height of the prism. Click on the screen to get the desired height; a prism will be created, as shown in Figure 3-41.

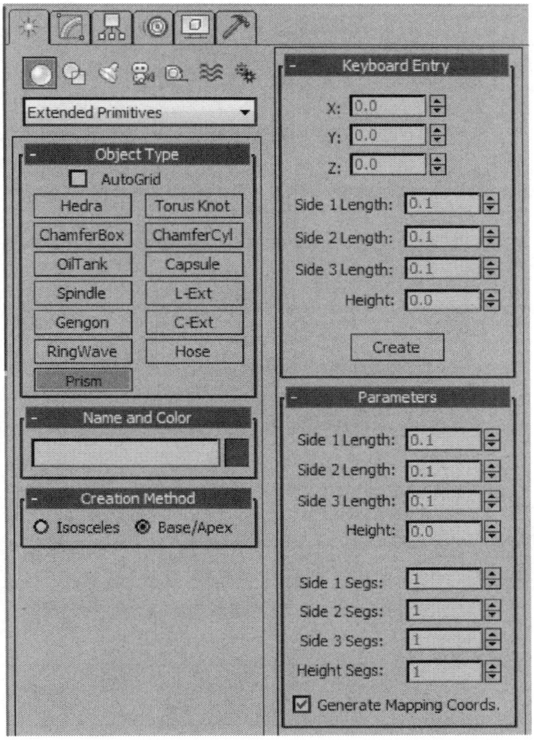

Figure 3-40 *Various rollouts to create a prism*

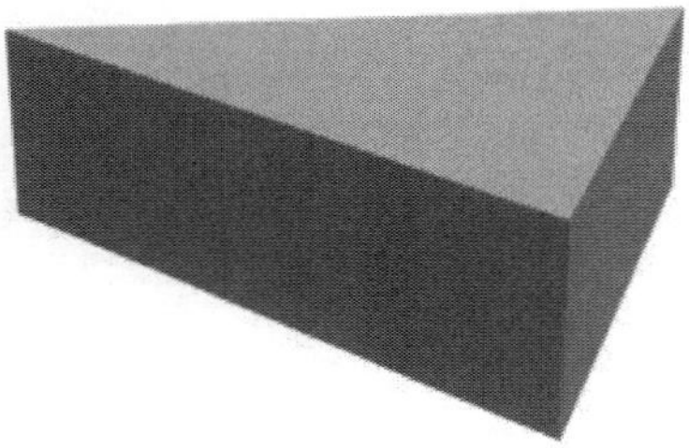

Figure 3-41 *A prism*

Select the **Isosceles** radio button in the **Creation Method** rollout. On doing so, a prism with isosceles triangle at its base will be created. Press and hold the left mouse button on a point to define the first corner of the triangle of the prism and drag the cursor horizontally to define the length of its side 1. Again, drag the cursor vertically to define the length of side 2 and side 3 and release the left mouse button. Now, move the cursor up or down to define the height of the object. Click on the screen after you get the desired height; a prism will be created.

Various rollouts used to create and modify the prism are discussed next.

Creation Method Rollout

The options in this rollout are used for creating a prism dynamically. Select the **Isosceles** radio button to create a prism with an isosceles triangle at its base. Select the **Base/Apex** radio button to create a prism with an obtuse triangle at its base.

Parameters Rollout

The options in this rollout are used to modify the prism. To do so, select the prism and choose the **Modify** tab in the **Command Panel**; the **Parameters** rollout will be displayed. Set the new values in the **Side 1 Length**, **Side 2 Length**, **Side 3 Length**, and **Height** spinners. The values in the **Side 1 Segs**, **Side 2 Segs**, **Side 3 Segs**, and **Height Segs** spinners are used to define the number of segments on each side of the prism.

Tutorial 1

In this tutorial, you will create a 3D model of a couch, as shown in Figure 3-42, using the extended primitives. **(Expected time: 30 min)**

Figure 3-42 *The couch model*

The following steps are required to complete this tutorial:

a. Set the project folder.
b. Create the seat support.
c. Create the back support.
d. Create the left side of the couch.
e. Create the right side of the couch.
f. Create the base of the couch.
g. Change the background color at rendering.
h. Render the scene for the final output.
i. Save the file.

Setting the Project Folder

Before starting a new file, it is recommended that you set the project folder.

1. Set the project folder with the name *c03_tut1* in the *3dsmax* folder, as discussed in Tutorial 1 of Chapter 2.

Creating the Seat Support

You need to use the **ChamferBox** tool from **Extended Primitives** to create the seat support of the couch.

1. Activate the Top viewport by clicking in it. Choose **Create > Geometry** in the **Command Pane**. By default, the **Standard Primitives** option is displayed in the drop-down list. Select

the **Extended Primitives** option from the drop-down list and invoke the **ChamferBox** tool from the **Object Type** rollout.

2. Expand the **Keyboard Entry** rollout and set the parameters in the respective spinners as given below:

   Length: **62.342** Width: **155.575** Height: **22.222** Fillet: **6.0**

3. Choose the **Create** button; a chamfer box is created, as shown in Figure 3-43.

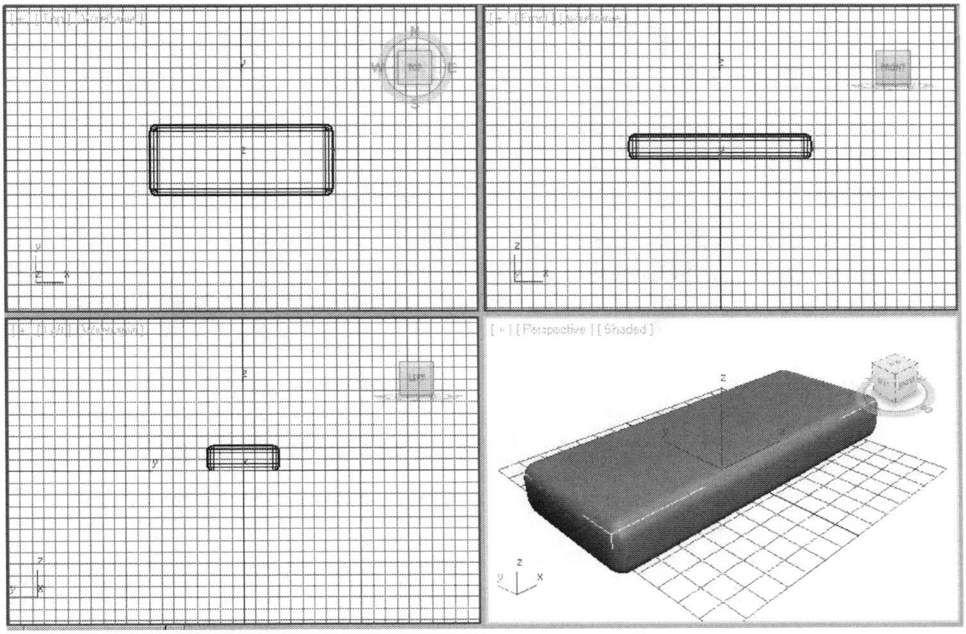

Figure 3-43 *A chamfer box created for the seat support*

4. In the **Parameters** rollout, enter the value **3.0** in the **Fillet Segs** spinner.

5. In the **Name and Color** rollout, enter **seat support** as the name of the chamfer box and press ENTER. Also, use the color swatch to modify the color of the *seat support* by entering the values as given below:

   Red: **225** Green: **143** Blue: **87**

Creating the Back Support

Again, you need to create a chamfer box primitive to create the back support of the couch.

1. Make sure that the Top viewport is activated and the **ChamferBox** tool is invoked.

2. In the **Keyboard Entry** rollout, set the values given below:

   Length: **15.413** Width: **155.575** Height: **48.089** Fillet: **6.0**

3. Choose the **Create** button; another chamfer box is created.

4. In the **Name and Color** rollout, enter **back support** as the name of the new chamfer box and press ENTER.

5. Assign the same color to the *back support* that was assigned to the *seat support*.

6. In the **Parameters** rollout, make sure the value in the **Fillet Segs** spinner is **3.0**.

7. Invoke the **Zoom Extents All** tool to display the objects to their extent in all viewports.

   Next, you need to align the *back support* with the *seat support*.

8. To do so, invoke the **Select and Move** tool, select the *back support* if it is not selected, and move it in all viewports to align it with the *seat support*, as shown in Figure 3-44.

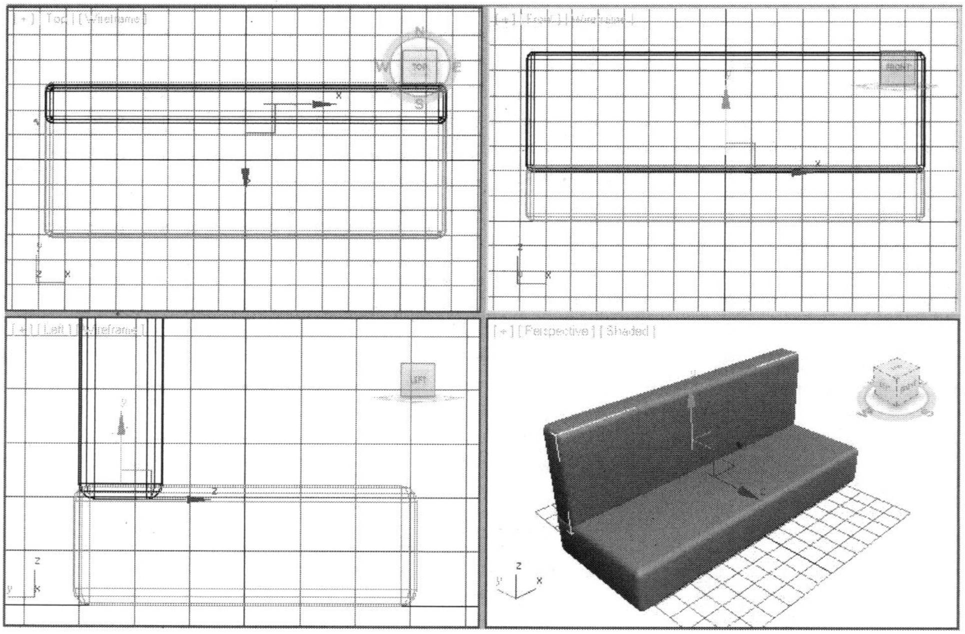

Figure 3-44 *Alignment of the back support with the seat support*

Creating the Left Side of the Couch

Next, you need to create a chamfer box for the left side of the couch.

1. Activate the Top viewport and invoke the **ChamferBox** tool. Now, in the **Keyboard Entry** rollout, set the values in the respective spinners as given next:

X: **-80.0** Length: **62.323** Width: **14.506**
Height: **48.895** Fillet: **6.0**

Use the default values for other parameters.

2. Choose the **Create** button; another chamfer box is created, as shown in Figure 3-45.

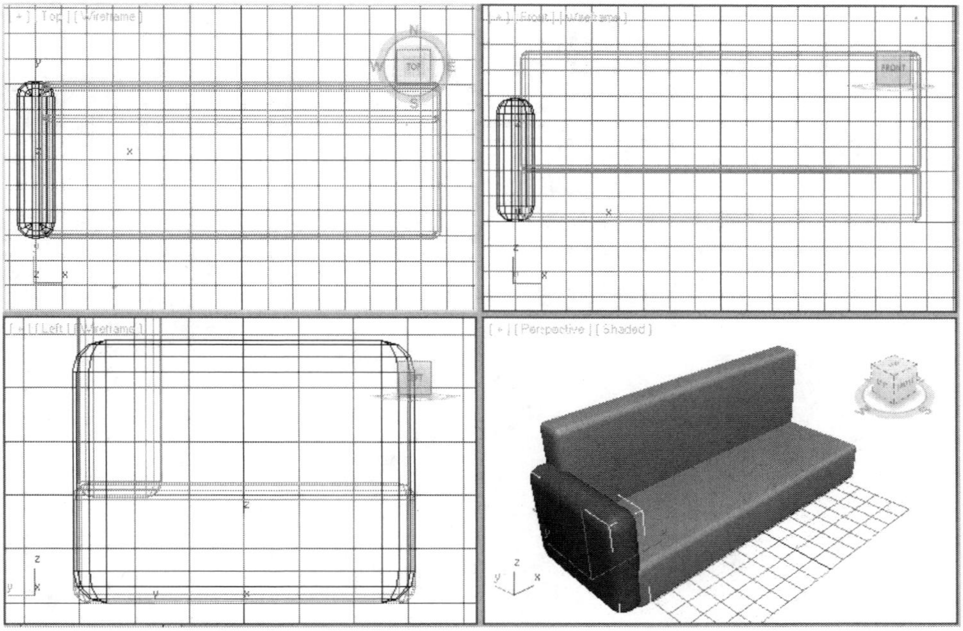

Figure 3-45 *The left side of the couch in all viewports*

3. In the **Parameters** rollout, make sure that the value in the **Fillet Segs** spinner is **3.0**.

4. In the **Name and Color** rollout, enter **left side** and press the ENTER key. Assign the same color to the *left side* that you assigned to the *seat support*.

Creating the Right Side of the Couch

To create the right side of the couch, you need to copy the *left side* of the couch.

1. Activate the Top viewport. Select the *left side* of the couch using the **Select and Move** tool.

2. Move the cursor over the horizontal axis; it turns yellow. Press and hold the SHIFT key and the left mouse button, and then drag the cursor toward the right side of the couch until the value in the **X** spinner in the coordinate display becomes about 159. Release the left mouse button and the SHIFT key; the **Clone Options** dialog box is displayed.

3. In the **Clone Options** dialog box, make sure that the **Copy** radio button is selected. In the **Number of Copies** spinner, set the value **1**. In the **Name** text box, enter **right side** and choose **OK**; the *right side* of the couch is displayed, as shown in Figure 3-46.

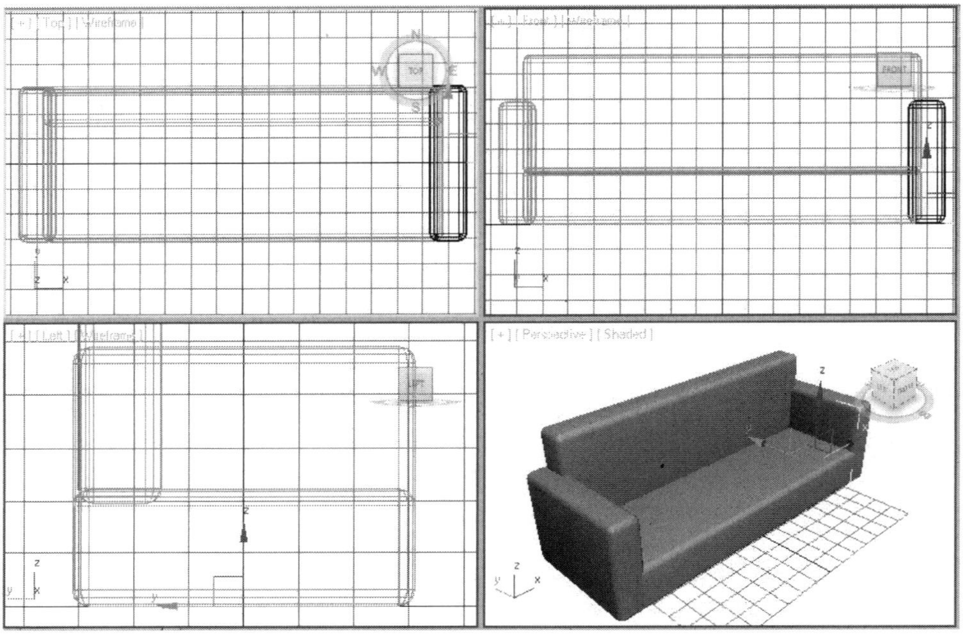

Figure 3-46 *The right side of the couch*

Creating the Base of the Couch

To create the base of the couch, you need to create another chamfer box.

1. Activate the Top viewport and invoke the **ChamferBox** tool. In the **Keyboard Entry** rollout, set the values as given below:

   Z: **-5.0** Length: **62.782** Width: **172.0** Height: **5.0**
   Fillet: **6.0**

   Make sure that the values entered in the **X** and **Y** spinners are set to **0**.

2. Choose the **Create** button; another chamfer box is created, as shown in Figure 3-47.

3. In the **Name and Color** rollout, enter **base** as the name of the chamfer box and press the ENTER key.

4. Assign the same color to the *base* that you assigned to the *seat support*.

Changing the Background Color in the Final Output

1. To change the background color of the scene to white in final output, follow the steps given in Tutorial 1 of Chapter 2 .

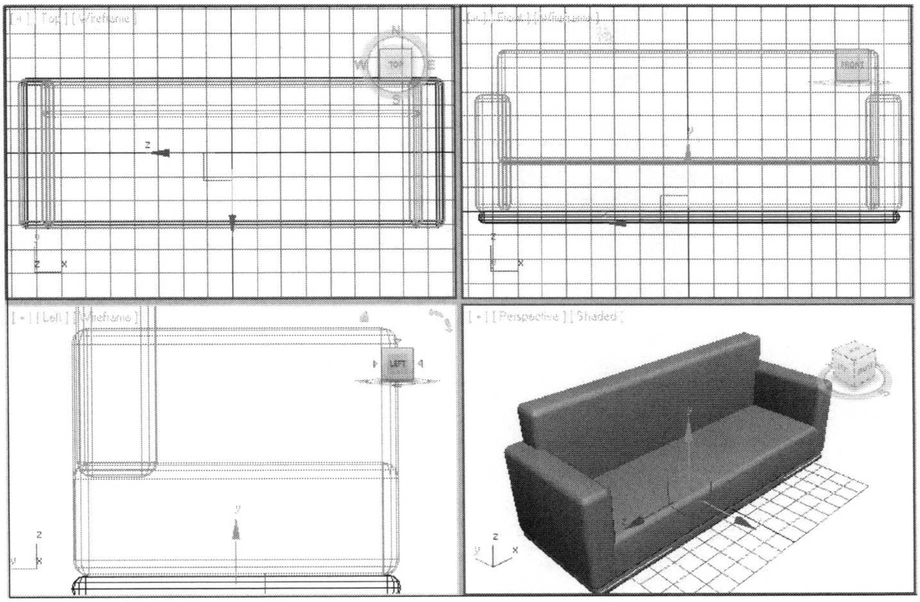

Figure 3-47 The base of the couch in all viewports

Rendering the Scene for the Final Output

1. Activate the Perspective viewport by clicking on it.

2. Invoke the **Render Production** tool in the **Main Toolbar**; the **Perspective, frame 0, Display Gamma:2.2, RGBA Color16 Bits/Channel (1:1)** window is displayed that shows the final output of the couch at one frame, refer to Figure 3-48.

3. Close this window.

Figure 3-48 The final output at rendering

You can view the final rendered image of this model by downloading the file *c03_3dsmax_2012_render.zip* from *http://www.cadcim.com*. The path of the file is as follows:

Textbooks > Animation and Visual Effects > 3ds Max > Autodesk 3ds Max 2012: A Comprehensive Guide

Next, you need to save the file.

Saving the File

1. Choose **Save** from the **Application menu**; the **Save File As** dialog box is displayed.

   As the project folder is already set, by default the path *\Documents\3dsmax\c03_tut1\scenes* is displayed in the **Save in** text box of the **Save File As** dialog box.

2. Save the file with the name *c03tut1.max*.

Tutorial 2

In this tutorial, you will create the model of a chair, as shown in Figure 3-49, using the extended primitives and modifiers. **(Expected time: 30 min)**

Figure 3-49 *The chair model*

The following steps are required to complete this tutorial:

a. Set the project folder.
b. Create the seat support.
c. Create the back support.
d. Create the spring support.
e. Create the leg support.
f. Create legs.
g. Create rollers for legs.
h. Create the right hand support.
i. Create the left hand support.
j. Change the background color at rendering.
k. Render the scene for the final output.
l. Save the file.

Setting the Project Folder

Before starting a new file, it is recommended that you set the project folder.

1. Set the project folder with the name *c03_tut2* in the *3dsmax* folder as discussed in Tutorial 1 of Chapter 2.

Creating the Seat Support

You need to create a chamfer box primitive to create the seat support of the chair.

1. Activate the Top viewport by clicking on it. Choose **Create > Geometry** in the **Command Panel**; the **Standard Primitives** option is displayed by default in the drop-down list. Select the **Extended Primitives** option from the list and then invoke the **ChamferBox** tool from the **Object Type** rollout.

2. Expand the **Keyboard Entry** rollout and set the values as given below:

   Length: **90.0** Width: **100.0** Height: **17.0**
   Fillet: **10.0**

3. Choose the **Create** button; a chamfer box is created.

4. Now, make sure that the chamfer box is selected. In the **Parameters** rollout, set the value **10** in the **Fillet Segs** spinner; the chamfer box is modified, as shown in Figure 3-50.

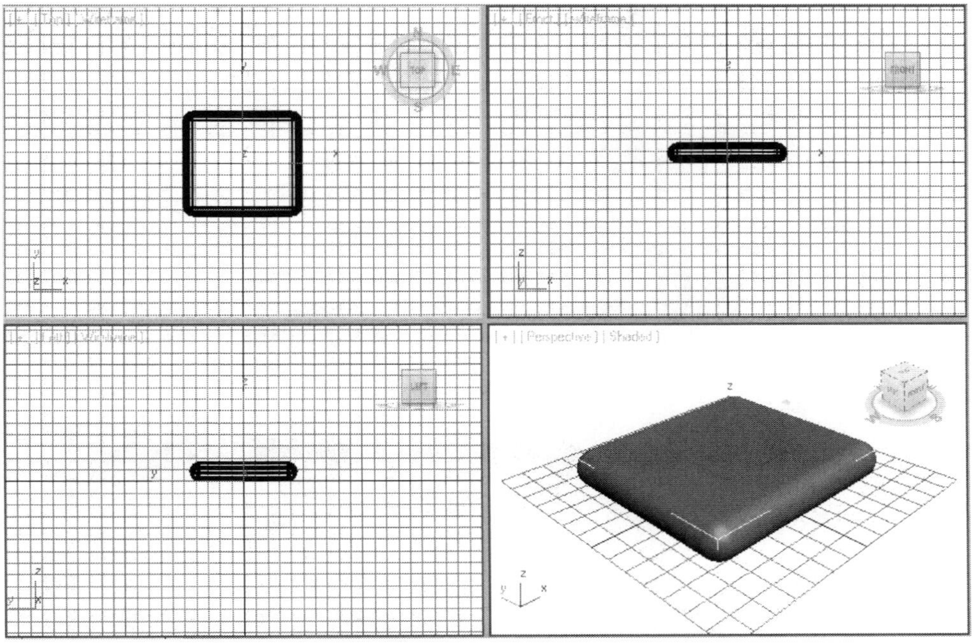

Figure 3-50 *The chamfer box created for the seat support of the chair*

5. In the **Name and Color** rollout, enter **seat support** as the name of the chamfer box and press ENTER.

6. Use the color swatch to modify the color of the *seat support* by entering the values as given below:

   Red: **88**　　Green: **199**　　Blue: **225**

Creating the Back Support

Again, you need to use the **ChamferBox** tool from the extended primitives to create the back support of the chair.

1. Activate the Front viewport and make sure that the **ChamferBox** tool is invoked.

2. Expand the **Keyboard Entry** rollout and set the values as given below:

   X: **0.0**　　Y: **65.0**　　Z: **-65.0**
   Length: **90.0**　　Width: **100.0**　　Height: **19.633**　　Fillet: **10.0**

3. Choose the **Create** button; a chamfer box is created.

4. Now, make sure that the chamfer box is selected. In the **Parameters** rollout, set the value **10** in the **Fillet Segs** spinner; the chamfer box is modified, as shown in Figure 3-51.

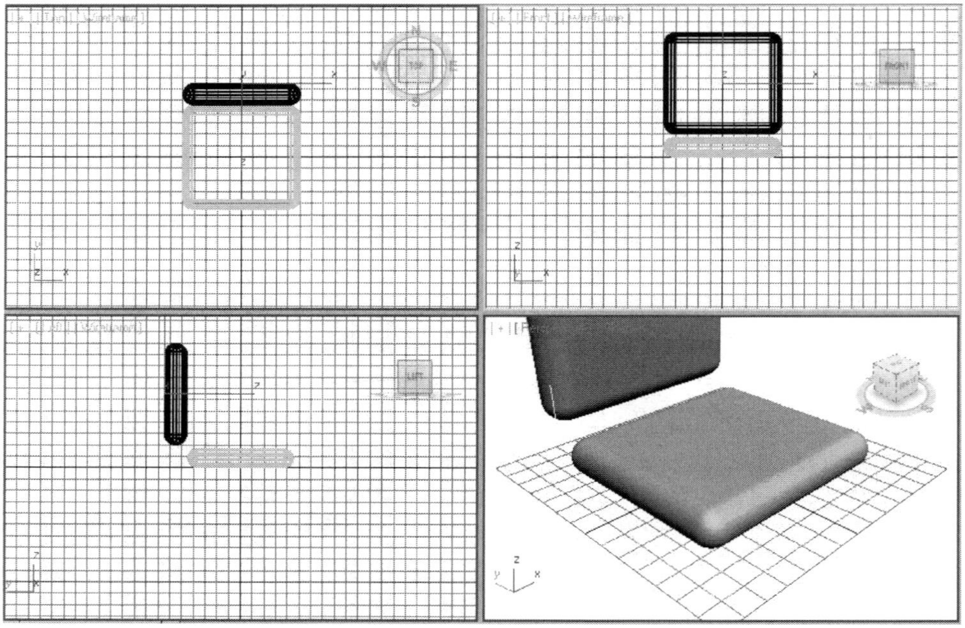

Figure 3-51 *The back support for the chair in all viewports*

5. In the **Name and Color** rollout, enter **back support** as the name of the chamfer box and press ENTER.

6. Choose the color swatch and assign the same color to the *back support* that you assigned to the *seat support*.

7. Invoke the **Zoom Extents All** tool to display the objects properly in all viewports.

   Next, you need to create the spring support to join the *seat* and the *back support*.

Creating the Spring Support

To create the spring support, you need to use the **Hose** tool from the extended primitives.

1. Activate the Top viewport by clicking on it. Choose **Create > Geometry** in the **Command Panel**. Make sure that the **Extended Primitives** option is selected in the drop-down list, Then, invoke the **Hose** tool from the **Object Type** rollout.

2. In the Top viewport, press and hold the left mouse button, drag the cursor to define the radius of the hose, and then release the left mouse button. Next, move the cursor up to define the height of the hose and click on the screen; a hose is created.

3. In the **Name and Color** rollout, enter **spring support** as the name of the hose and press ENTER. Then, modify the color of the *spring support* to black.

4. In the **Hose Parameters** rollout, set the values of the *spring support* as given below:

   End Point Method Area
   Make sure that the **Free Hose** radio button is selected.

   Free Hose Parameters Area
   Height: **25.815**

   Common Hose Parameters Area
   Cycles: **9**
   Use the default values for the other options in this area.

   Smoothing Area
   Select the **All** radio button.

   Hose Shape Area
   Select the **Round Hose** radio button.
   Diameter: **15.0** Sides: **8**

   After setting the values in the **Hose Parameters** rollout, align the *spring support* in all viewports, as shown in Figure 3-52.

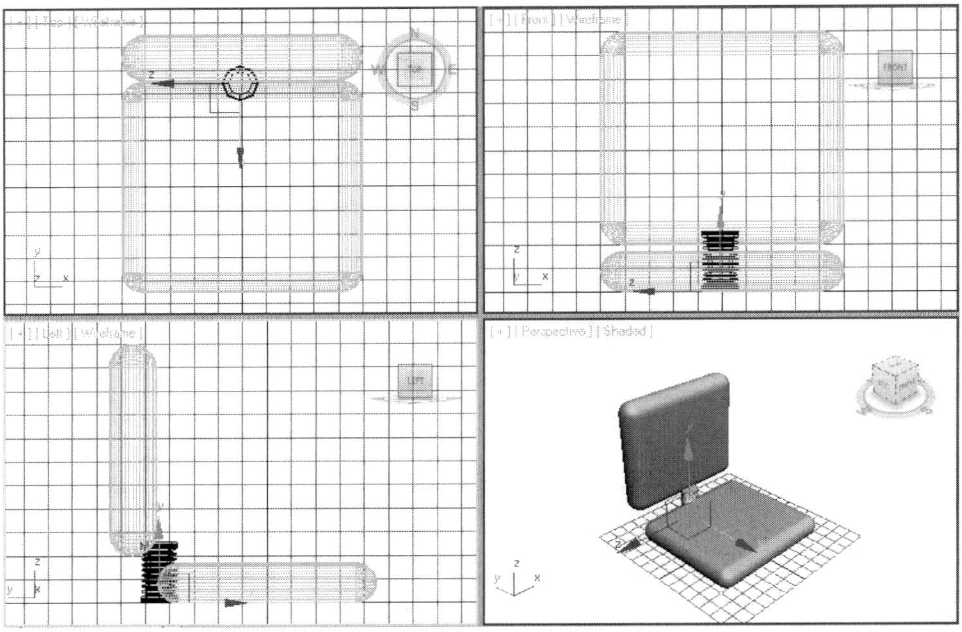

Figure 3-52 *The spring support in all viewports*

Next, you need to apply the **Bend** modifier to the *spring support* to join the *seat* and the *back support*.

Applying the Bend Modifier

1. First, make sure that the *spring support* is selected and then choose **Modifiers > Parametric Deformers > Bend** from the menu bar; the **Bend** modifier is displayed in the modifier stack. Also, the **Parameters** rollout is displayed in the modify panel.

2. In the **Parameters** rollout of the **Bend** modifier, set the values as given below:

   Bend Area
   Angle: **90.0** Direction: **90**

   Bend Axis area
   Make sure that the **Z** radio button is selected.

3. After entering the values, the *spring support* is displayed, as shown in Figure 3-53.

   Next, you need to align the *spring support*.

Aligning the Spring Support

1. Activate the Left viewport and make sure that the *spring support* is selected. Invoke the **Zoom Extents Selected** tool; the *spring support* is zoomed in the Left viewport, as shown in Figure 3-54.

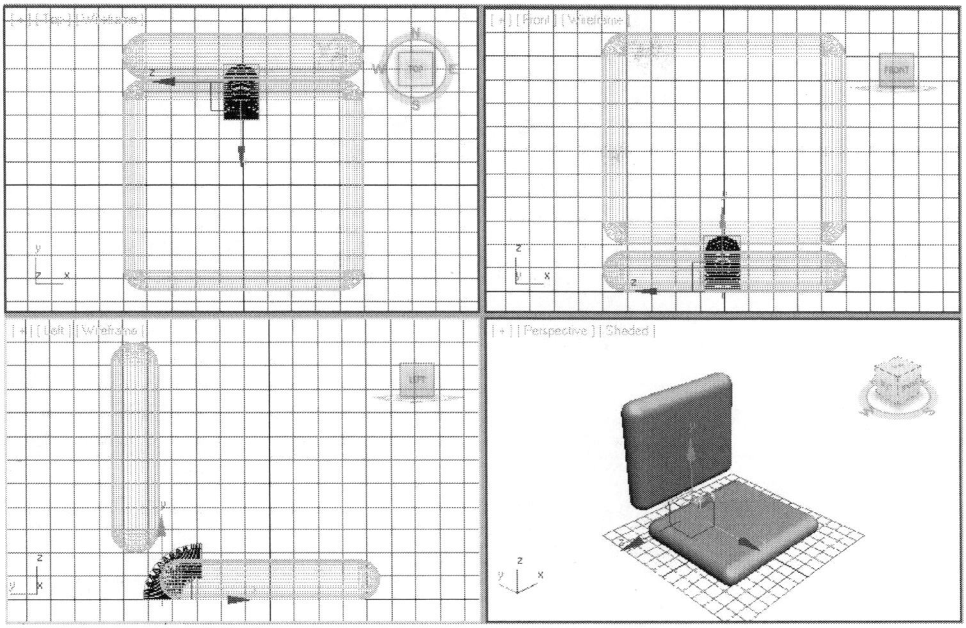

Figure 3-53 *The spring support after applying the* ***Bend*** *modifier*

2. Right-click on the **Select and Rotate** tool; the **Rotate Transform Type-In** dialog box is displayed. In the **Offset: Screen** area, set the value **90** in the **Z** spinner; the *spring support* is rotated, as shown in Figure 3-55. Now, close the **Rotate Transform Type-In** dialog box.

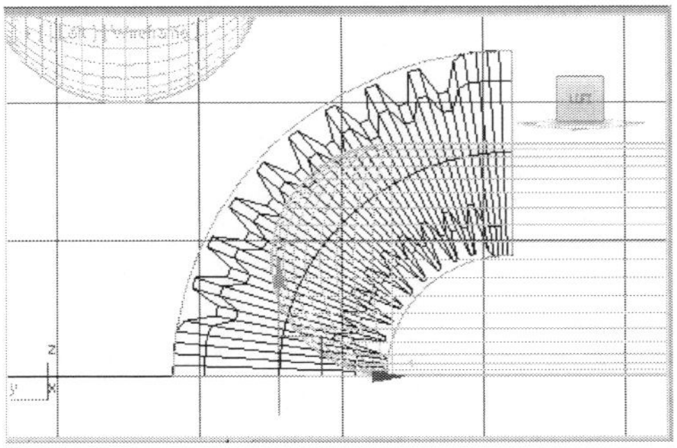

Figure 3-54 *The spring support zoomed in the Left viewport*

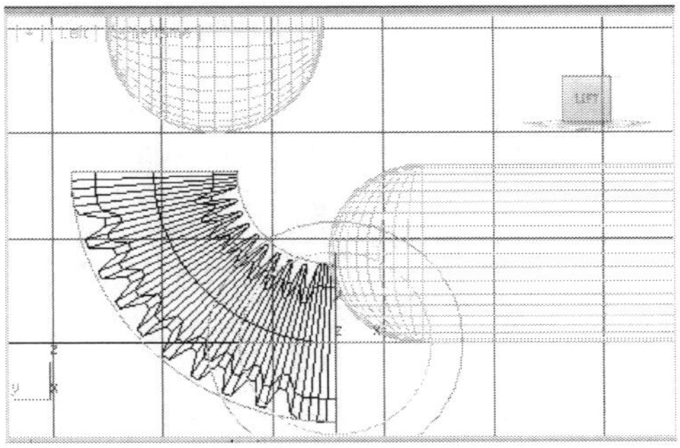

Figure 3-55 *The spring support rotated in the Left viewport*

3. Invoke the **Select and Move** tool and align the *spring support*, as shown in Figure 3-56.

4. Align the *spring support* in all viewports, refer to Figure 3-57. Invoke the **Zoom Extents All** tool to display all objects properly in all viewports.

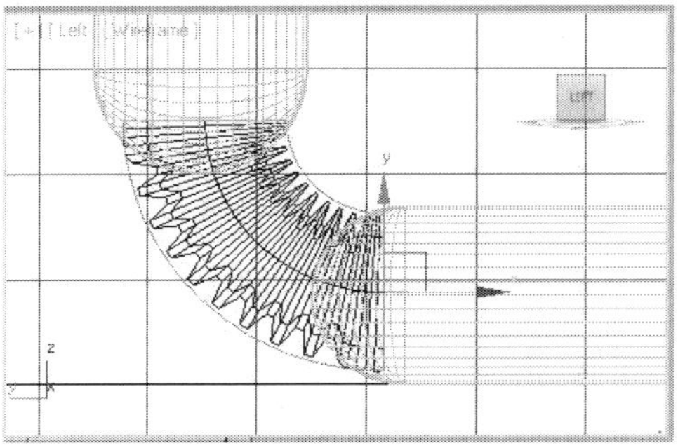

Figure 3-56 *Alignment of the spring support in the Left viewport*

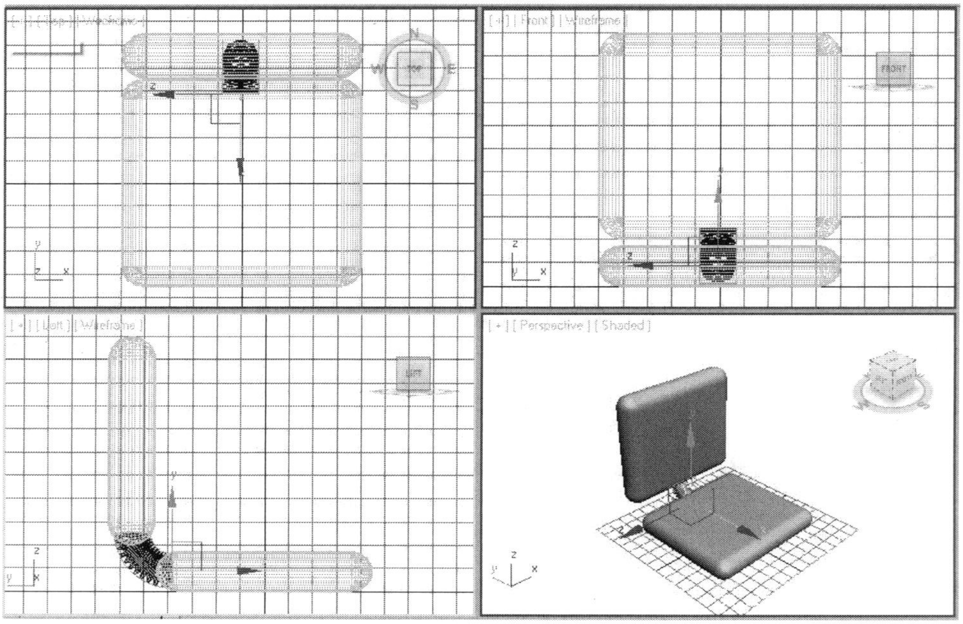

Figure 3-57 *Alignment of the spring support in all viewports*

Creating the Leg Support

To create the leg support, you need to use the **Hose** tool from the extended primitives.

1. Activate the Top viewport by clicking on it and then create a hose object as discussed earlier.

2. In the **Name and Color** rollout, enter **leg support** as the name of the hose and press ENTER. Also, modify the color of the *leg support* to black.

3. In the **Hose Parameters** rollout, set the values of the *leg support* as given next.

   End Point Method Area
   Make sure that the **Free Hose** radio button is selected.
   Free Hose Parameters Area
   Height: **42.0**

   Common Hose Parameters Area
   Make sure that the **Flex Section Enable** check box is selected.
   Starts: **22.0** Ends: **82.0**
   Cycles: **10** Diameter: **-20.0**

   Smoothing Area
   Select the **All** radio button.

   Hose Shape Area
   Select the **Round Hose** radio button.
   Diameter: **17.0**
   Sides: **8**

4. Invoke the **Select and Move** tool and align the *leg support* in all viewports, as shown in Figure 3-58.

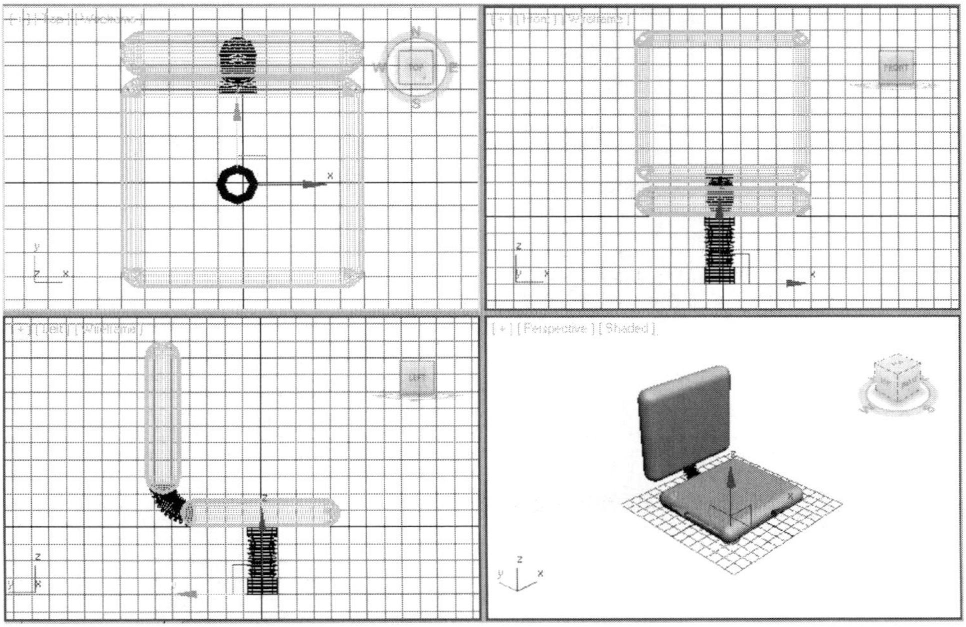

Figure 3-58 *Alignment of the leg support in all viewports*

Creating the Legs

In this section, you need to use the **ChamferBox** tool from **Extended Primitives** to create the legs of the chair.

1. Activate the Top viewport and invoke the **ChamferBox** tool.

2. Expand the **Keyboard Entry** rollout and set the values as given next.

   X: **-29** Y: **0.0** Z: **-42.0**
   Length: **5.748** Width: **44.0** Height: **7.0** Fillet: **2.0**

3. Choose the **Create** button; a chamfer box is created.

4. Now, make sure that the chamfer box is selected. In the **Parameters** rollout, set the values as given below:

   Length Segs: **10** Width Segs: **10** Height Segs: **10**
   Fillet Segs: **10**

   After entering the values, the chamfer box is modified.

5. In the **Name and Color** rollout, enter **leg01** as the name of the chamfer box and press ENTER. Also, modify its color to black.

6. Invoke the **Select and Move** tool and align the *leg01* with the *leg support* in all viewports, as shown in Figure 3-59.

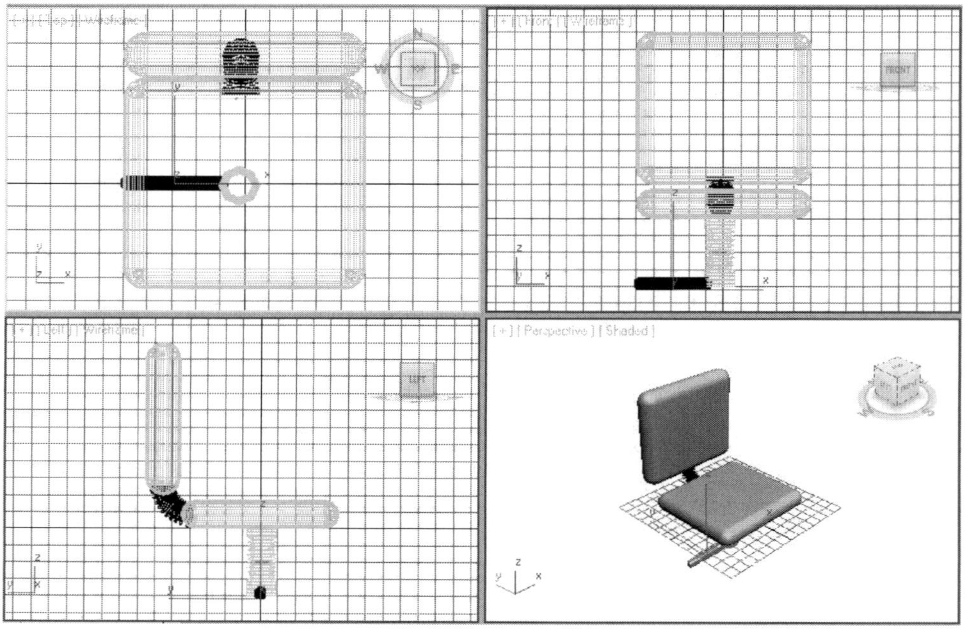

Figure 3-59 *Alignment of the leg01 in all viewports*

Next, you need apply the **Taper** modifier to the *leg01* to taper it.

Applying the Taper Modifier

1. First, make sure that the *leg01* is selected, and then invoke the **Zoom Extents All Selected** tool; the *leg01* is zoomed in all viewports, as shown in Figure 3-60.

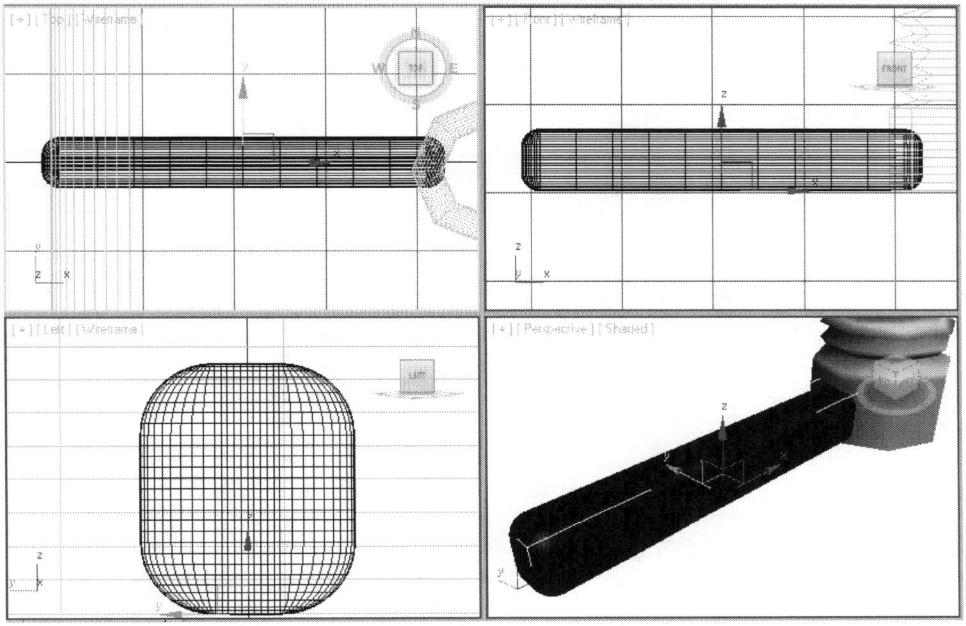

Figure 3-60 *The leg01 after invoking the* ***Zoom Extents All Selected*** *tool*

2. Choose **Modifiers > Parametric Deformers > Taper** from the menu bar; the **Taper** modifier is displayed in the modifier stack. Also, the **Parameters** rollout is displayed in the modify panel.

3. In the **Parameters** rollout of the **Taper** modifier, set the values as given next:

   Taper Area
   Amount: **0.53**

   Taper Axis Area
   Select the **X** radio button in the **Primary** group and the **ZY** radio button in the **Effect** group.

4. After entering the values, *leg01* is tapered, as shown in Figure 3-61.

   Next, you need to create rollers.

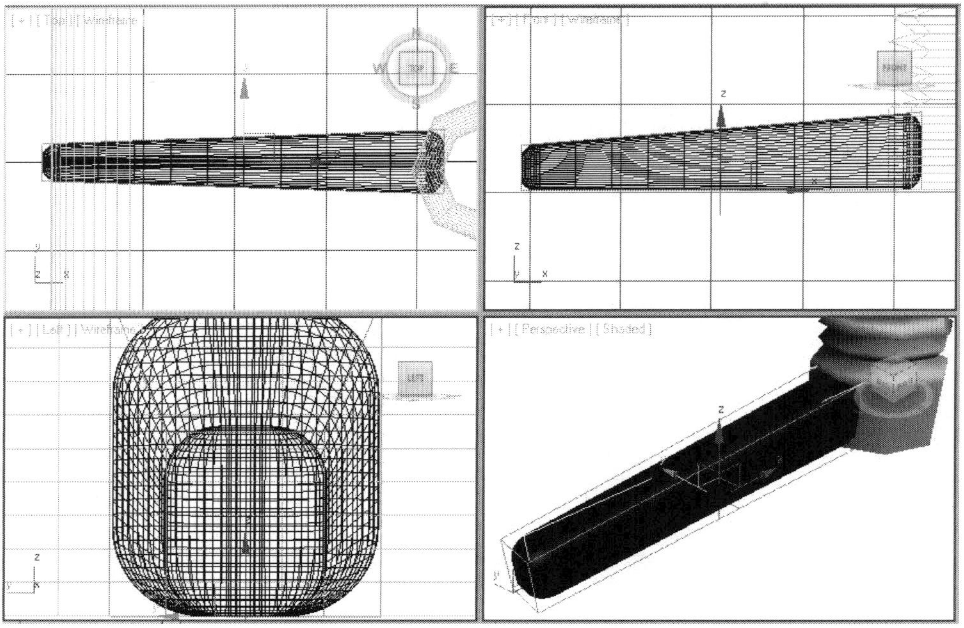

***Figure 3-61** The leg01 displayed in all viewports after applying the **Taper** modifier*

Creating Rollers for Legs

You need to use the chamfer box and chamfer cylinder primitives to create rollers.

1. Activate the Top viewport and invoke the **ChamferBox** tool.

2. Expand the **Keyboard Entry** rollout and set the values as given next:

   X: **-40** Y: **0.0** Z: **-20.0**
   Length: **7.032** Width: **14.816** Height: **1.799** Fillet: **1.0**

3. Choose the **Create** button; a chamfer box is created.

4. Make sure that the chamfer box is selected. In the **Parameters** rollout, set the values as given next:

   Length Segs: **10** Width Segs: **10** Height Segs: **10**
   Fillet Segs: **10**

5. In the **Name and Color** rollout, enter **box01** as the name of the chamfer box and press ENTER. Also, modify its color to black.

Note
*To view the box01 in all viewports, you need to adjust the view by invoking the **Zoom** and **Pan View** tools.*

Next, you need to apply the **Bend** modifier to the *box01*.

6. Choose **Modifiers > Parametric Deformers > Bend** from the menu bar; the **Bend** modifier is displayed in the modifier stack. Also, the **Parameters** rollout is displayed in the modify panel.

7. In the **Parameters** rollout of the **Bend** modifier, set the values as given below:

   Bend Area
   Angle: **173.5**

   Bend Axis Area
   Select the **X** radio button.

8. After applying the **Bend** modifier, the *box01* is displayed, as shown in Figure 3-62.

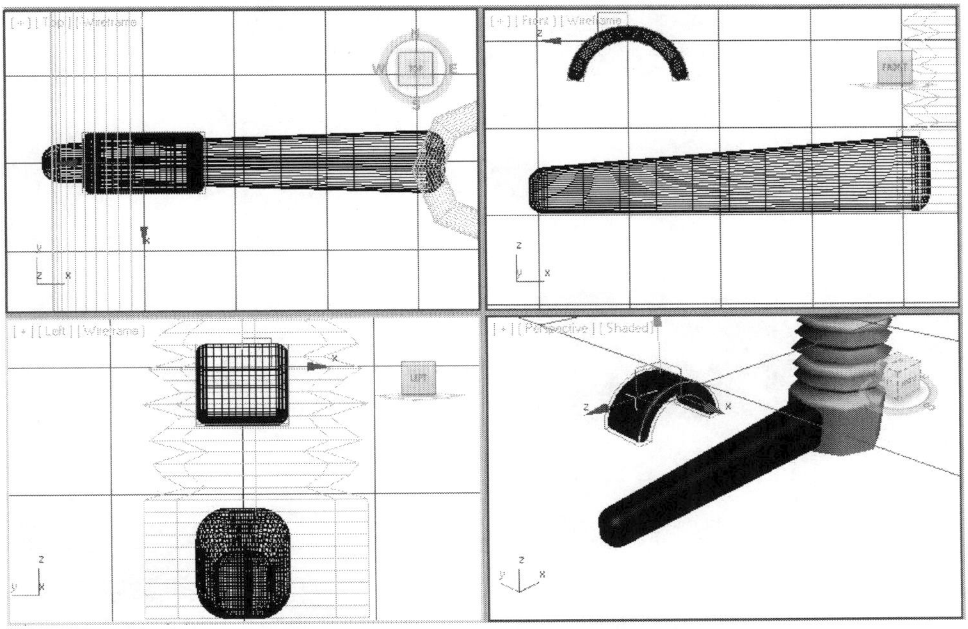

Figure 3-62 *The box01 displayed in all viewports after applying the* ***Bend*** *modifier*

Next, you need to create a chamfer cylinder.

9. Make sure that the **Extended Primitives** option is selected in the drop-down list of the **Command Panel**. Now, invoke the **ChamferCyl** tool in the **Object Type** rollout.

10. Activate the Top viewport and expand the **Keyboard Entry** rollout. Set the values as given next:

X: **-40**	Y: **0.0**	Z: **-20.0**
Radius: **5.0**	Height: **7.0**	Fillet: **1.0**

11. Choose the **Create** button; a chamfer cylinder is created.

12. Now, make sure that the chamfer cylinder is selected. In the **Parameters** rollout, set the values as given next.

Height Segs: **10**	Fillet Segs: **10**	Sides: **12**
Cap Segs: **11**		

Make sure that the **Smooth** check box is selected.

13. In the **Name and Color** rollout, enter **cylinder01** as the name of the chamfer box and press ENTER. Also, modify its color by entering the values given next:

Red: **151**	Green: **151**	Blue: **151**

14. Align the *cylinder01* with the *box01* in all viewports using the **Select and Rotate** and **Select and Move** tools, refer to Figure 3-63.

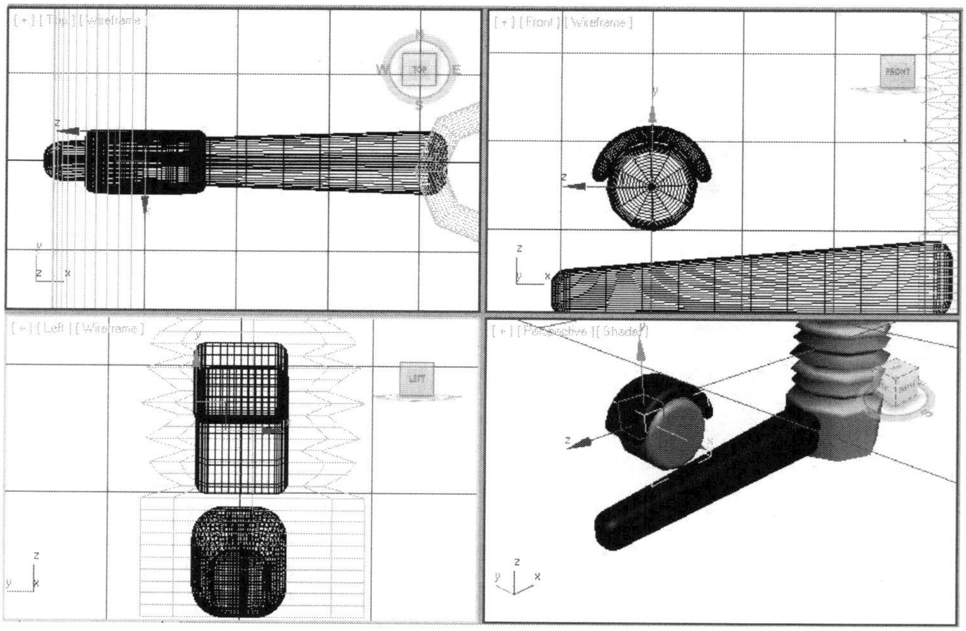

Figure 3-63 *Alignment of the cylinder01 with the box01 in all viewports*

Next, you need to group *cylinder01* and *box01*.

15. Invoke the **Select Object** tool from the **Main Toolbar** and select the *cylinder01* and *box01* by dragging a selection box around them.

16. Choose **Group > Group** from the menu bar; the **Group** dialog box is displayed.

17. Enter **roller01** in the **Group name** text box and choose **OK**; the group is named as *roller01*.

18. Using the **Select and Move** and **Select and Rotate** tools, align the *roller01* with the *leg01*, in all viewports, as shown in Figure 3-64.

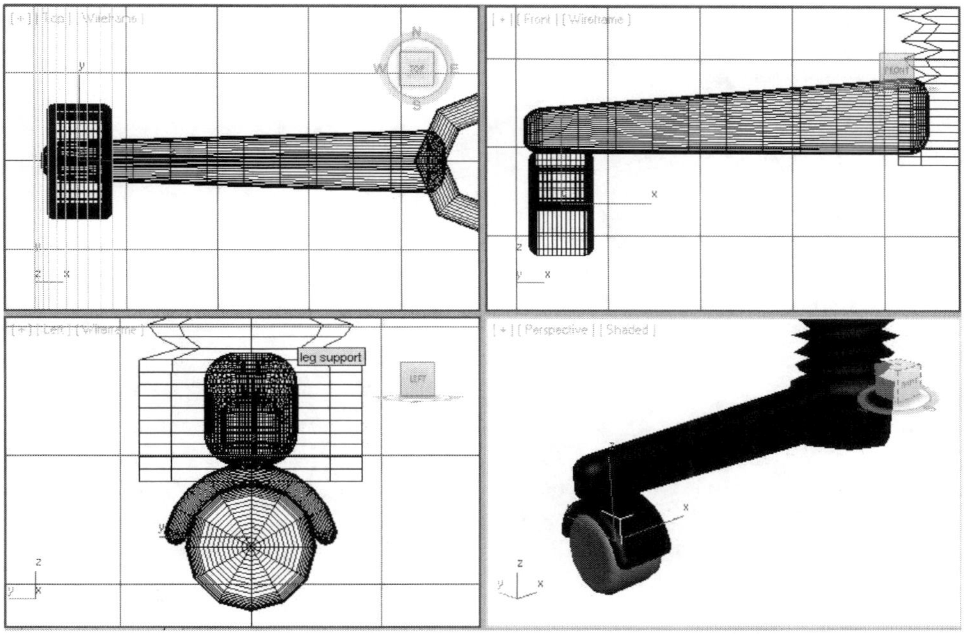

Figure 3-64 *Alignment of the roller01 with the leg01 in all viewports*

19. Next, group the *leg01* and the *roller01* as *f_leg01*.

20. Invoke the **Zoom Extents All** tool to view all objects in all viewports.

Next, you need to create other legs for the chair using the same dimensions. To do so, you need to copy *f_leg01*.

21. Activate the Top viewport and select the *f_leg01*. Now, choose the **Hierarchy** tab in the **Command Panel**; the **Pivot** tab is chosen by default in the hierarchy panel.

22. In the **Pivot** tab, choose the **Use Working Pivot** button in the **Working Pivot** rollout; the cursor is displayed at the center of the scene. Also, the **USE WP** text is displayed below the

viewport label in all viewports. The working pivot point enables you to rotate the *f_leg01* about an arbitrary and persistent point in the scene without affecting the original pivot point of the object.

23. In the Top viewport, invoke the **Select and Rotate** tool; a circular gizmo is displayed, as shown in Figure 3-65.

24. Next, move the cursor over the Z-axis that is blue in color; it is highlighted in yellow color. Now, press and hold the SHIFT key as well as the left mouse button, and drag the cursor until the value in the **Z** spinner in the coordinate display becomes about **-72**, as shown in Figure 3-66. Release the left mouse button; the **Clone Options** dialog box is displayed. Make sure that the **Copy** radio button is selected. Set the value **4** in the **Number of Copies** spinner. Choose the **OK** button; the *f_leg002*, *f_leg003*, *f_leg004*, and *f_leg005* are displayed in all viewports, as shown in Figure 3-67.

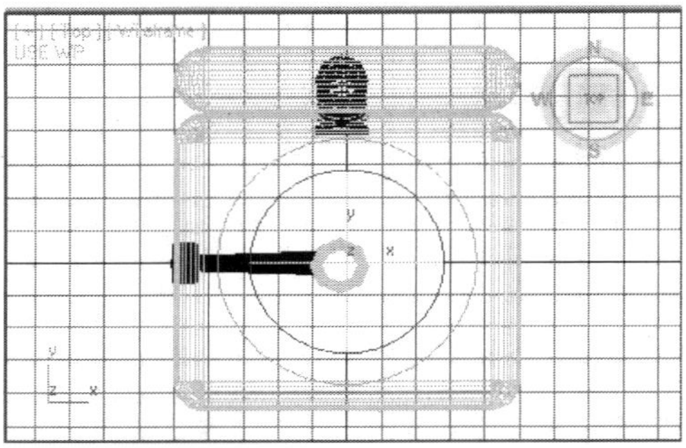

Figure 3-65 *A circular gizmo displayed at the location of the working pivot point*

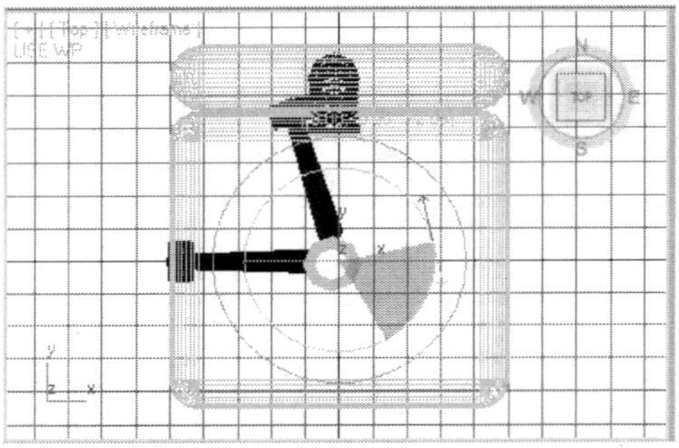

Figure 3-66 *The f_leg01 rotated about* ***-72*** *degrees according to the working pivot point*

25. Deactivate the **Use Working Pivot** button by choosing it again in the **Working Pivot** rollout; the cursor is moved to its original position. Also, the USE WP text disappears from the viewport label in all viewports.

Creating the Right Hand Support

Now, you need to use the **Box** tool from **Standard Primitives** to create the right hand support of the chair.

1. Activate the Top viewport and choose **Create > Geometry** in the **Command Panel**. Now, select the **Standard Primitives** option from the drop-down list. Invoke the **Box** tool in the **Object Type** rollout.

2. Expand the **Keyboard Entry** rollout and set the values as given below:

   Length: **5.515** Width: **9.0** Height: **55.0**

3. Choose the **Create** button; a box is created.

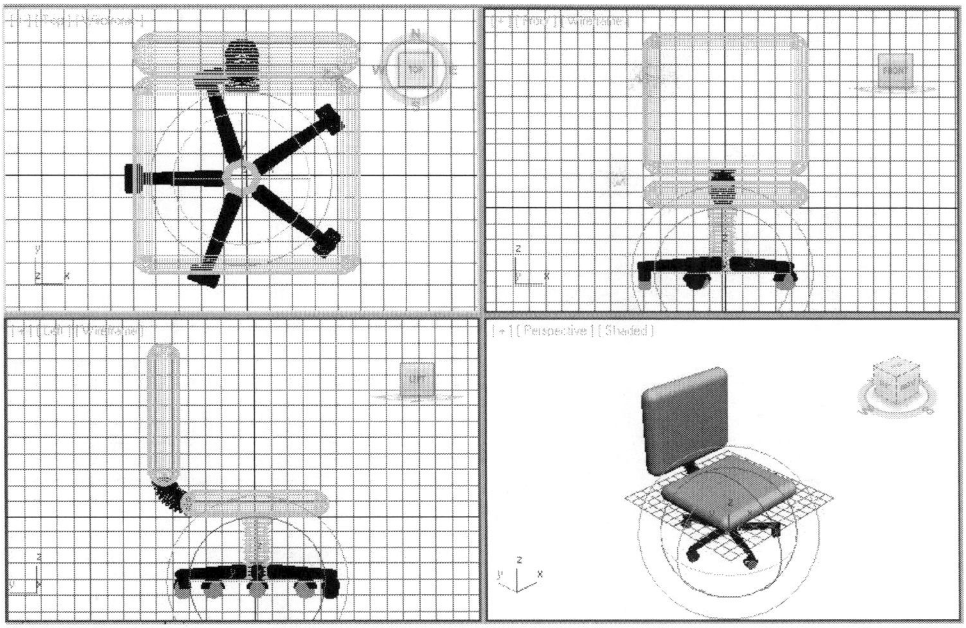

Figure 3-67 The f_leg002, f_leg003, f_leg004, and f_leg005 in all viewports

4. In the **Parameters** rollout, set the values as given below:

   Length Segs: **15** Width Segs: **15** Height Segs: **15**

Note

More the number of segments in an object, smoother will be its surface when you apply a modifier to it.

5. In the **Name and Color** rollout, enter **right hand support01** as the name of the box and press ENTER. Also, modify its color to black.

   Next, you need to apply the **Bend** modifier to the *right hand support01* to give it a shape.

6. Make sure that the *right hand support01* is selected and then apply the **Bend** modifier to it as discussed earlier.

7. In the **Parameters** rollout of the **Bend** modifier, set the parameters as given below:

   Bend Area
   Angle: **107.5** Direction: **270.0**

Bend Axis Area
Select the **Z** radio button.

8. Align the *right hand support01* in all viewports, as shown in Figure 3-68.

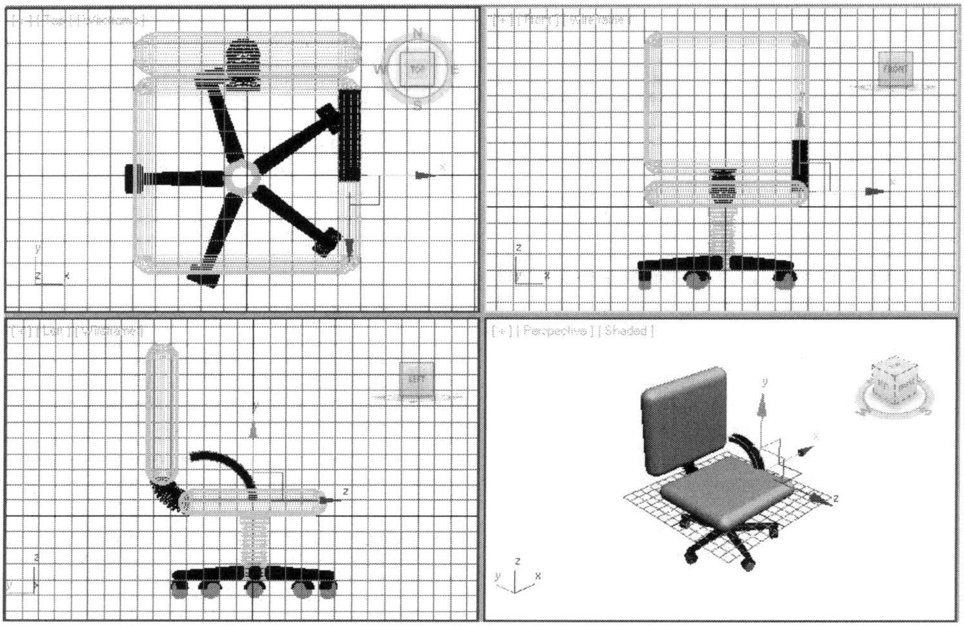

Figure 3-68 *Alignment of the right hand support01 in all viewports*

Next, you need to create the second part of the *right hand support01*. To do so, you need to copy the *right hand support01*.

9. Activate the Top viewport, select the *right hand support01,* and then create its copy; it is automatically named as the *right hand support002*.

10. In the **Parameters** rollout of the **Bend** modifier, set the values as given below:

Bend Area
Angle: **90** Direction: **180**
Bend Axis Area
Select the **Z** radio button.
Limits Area
Select the **Limit Effect** check box.
Upper Limit: **18.0**

11. After entering the values, the *right hand support002* is modified, as shown in Figure 3-69.

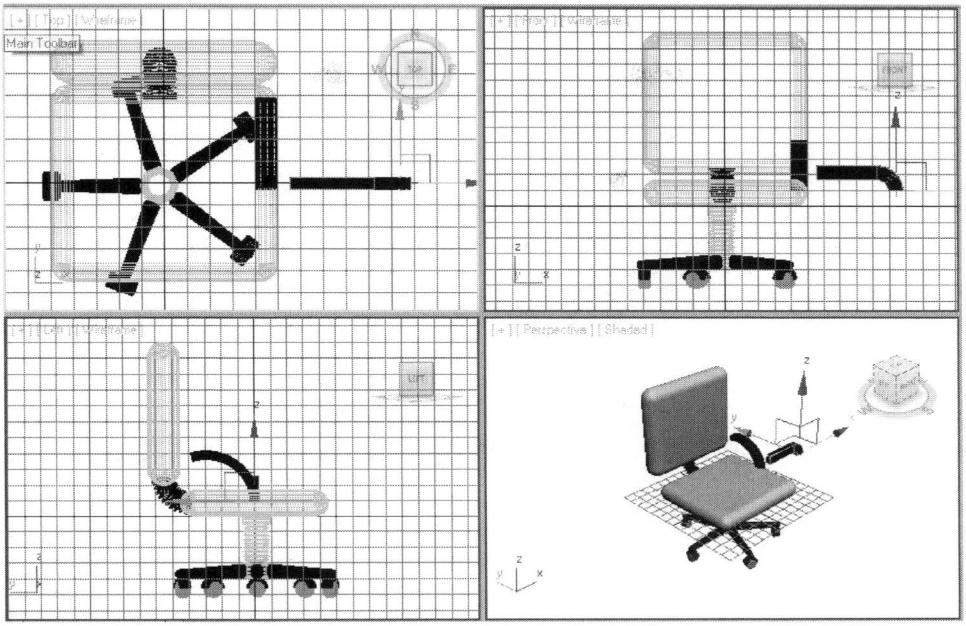

Figure 3-69 *The right hand support002 after modifying the values of the* ***Bend*** *modifier*

12. Align the *right hand support002* in all viewports using the **Select and Move** and **Select and Rotate** tools, as shown in Figure 3-70.

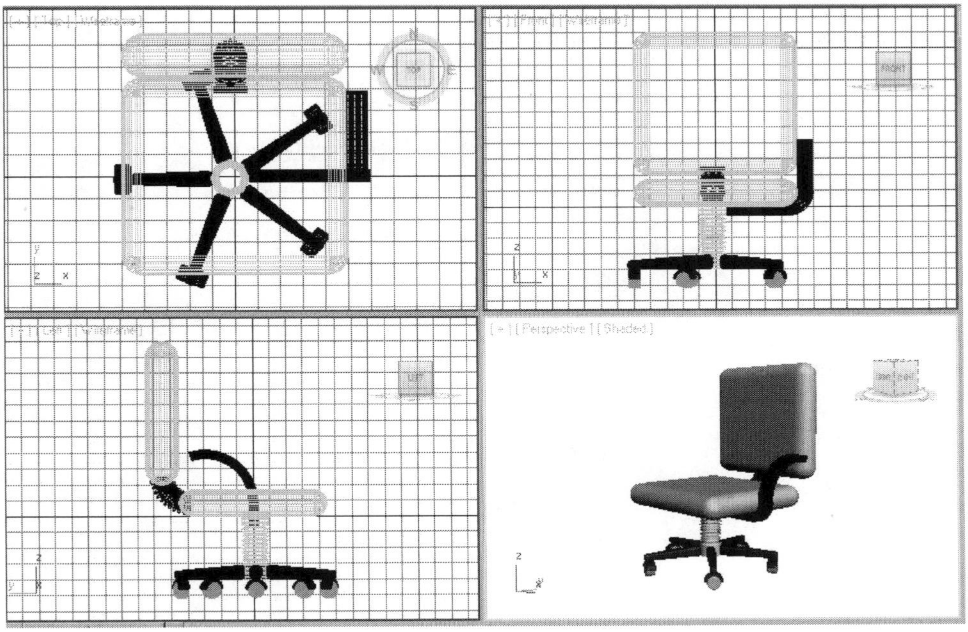

Figure 3-70 *Alignment of the right hand support002 in all viewports*

Note

*You can use the **Orbit** tool in the Perspective viewport to view the proper alignment of the right hand support002 in all viewports.*

13. Now, select the *right hand support01* and *right hand support002* and group them as the *right hand support*.

14. Invoke the **Zoom Extents All** tool to view all objects in all viewports.

Creating the Left Hand Support

To create the *left hand support*, you need to create a copy of the *right hand support*.

1. Activate the Top viewport, select the *right hand support*, and create its copy. Modify the name of the newly created copy to *left hand support*.

2. Invoke the **Mirror** tool from the **Main Toolbar**; the **Mirror: Screen Coordinates** dialog box is displayed, as shown in Figure 3-71.

3. In this dialog box, make sure that the **X** radio button is selected in the **Mirror Axis** area and the **No Clone** radio button is selected in the **Clone Selection** area. Then, choose the **OK** button.

4. Align the *left hand support* in all viewports, as shown in Figure 3-72.

Changing the Background Color in the Final Output

Change the background color to white as discussed earlier.

Rendering the Scene for the Final Output

1. Activate the Perspective viewport by clicking on it.

2. Invoke the **Render Production** tool from the **Main Toolbar**; the **Perspective, frame 0, Display Gamma:2.2, RGBA Color 16 Bits/Channel (1:1)** dialog box is displayed that shows the final output of the model at one frame, refer to Figure 3-73. Now, close this dialog box.

   Next, you need to save the file.

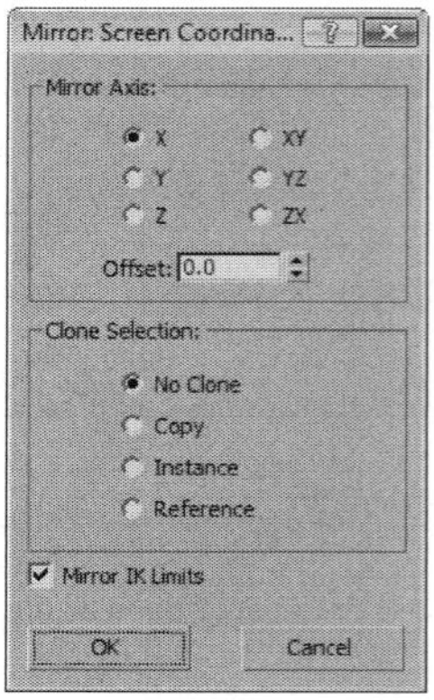

__Figure 3-71__ The __Mirror: Screen Coordinates__ dialog box

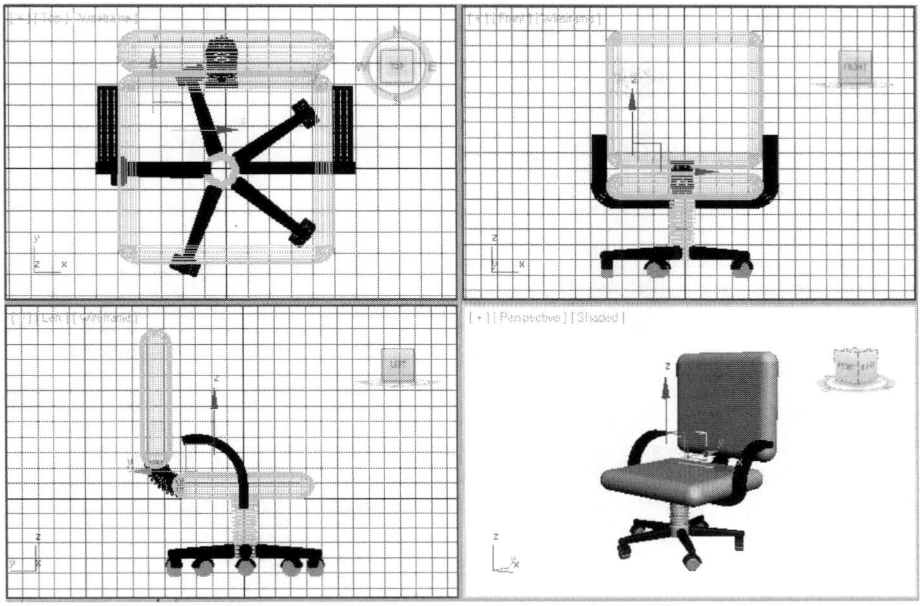

Figure 3-72 *Alignment of the left hand support in all viewports*

You can view the final rendered image of this model by downloading the file *c03_3dsmax_2012_render.zip* from *http://www.cadcim.com*. The path of the file is as follows:

Textbooks > Animation and Visual Effects > 3ds Max > Autodesk 3ds Max 2012: A Comprehensive Guide

Figure 3-73 *The final output after rendering*

Saving the File

1. Choose **Save** from the **Application menu**; the **Save File As** dialog box is displayed.

   As the project folder is already set, the path *\Documents\3dsmax\c03_tut2\scenes* is displayed in the **Save in** text box of the **Save File As** dialog box.

2. Save the file with the name *c03tut2.max*.

Self-Evaluation Test

Answer the following questions and then compare them to those given at the end of this chapter:

1. Which of the following tools is available in the **Snaps Toggle** flyout?

   (a) **Angle Snap Toggle** (b) **Percent Snap Toggle**
   (c) **Spinner Snap Toggle** (d) **2.5 Snap**

2. Which of the following modifiers is used to bend an object along its axis?

   (a) **Bend** (b) **Taper**
   (c) **Percent Snap Toggle** (d) None of these

3. Which of the following tools in the extended primitives does not have the **Creation Method** and **Keyboard Entry** rollouts?

   (a) **RingWave** (b) **Hedra**
   (c) **Hose** (d) All of these

4. Which of the following keys is used to view the number of segments or edged faces of an object?

   (a) F4 (b) F12
   (c) F5 (d) None of these

5. To create a star-like polyhedron, you need to invoke the __________ tool from the **Object Type** rollout in the extended primitives.

6. To view animation at each frame, you need to drag the __________ located below the four viewports.

7. To rotate an object in angular increments, you need to press the __________ key.

8. The time slider displays the current frame and the total number of frames in the current time segments. (T/F)

9. In the **Parameters** rollout of the torus knot, the **P** and **Q** spinners are active only when the **Circle** radio button is selected. (T/F)

10. In the **Family Parameters** area of the **Parameters** rollout of the hedra, the combined value of the **P** and **Q** spinners can be either equal to or less than 1.0. (T/F)

Review Questions

Answer the following questions:

1. Which of the following tools is used to snap the objects in 3D space?

   (a) **2.5D Snap** (b) **Angle Snap Toggle**
   (c) **3D Snap** (d) **Percent Snap**

2. Which of the following tools is used to define the increment or decrement value for all spinners in Autodesk 3ds Max?

   (a) **Percent Snap Toggle** (b) **Spinner Snap Toggle**
   (c) **2D Snap** (d) None of these

3. Which of the following animation playback buttons is used to set the time slider at the last frame of the active time segment?

   (a) **Play Animation** (b) **Go to End**
   (c) **Go to Start** (d) None of these

4. The **Percent Snap Toggle** in the **Main Toolbar** is used to scale an object in the percent increments set by you. (T/F)

5. In the time slider, you can change the total number of frames in the active time segment. (T/F)

6. In the **Parameters** rollout of the chamfer cylinder, the **Slice On** check box is used to create different portions of the chamfer cylinder in the viewport. (T/F)

7. The **Angle Snap Toggle** tool enables you to rotate an object in the angular increments. (T/F)

8. In the **Parameters** rollout of an oil tank, the__________ spinner creates a smooth level at the edge of the caps.

9. In the **Parameters** rollout of the **Taper** modifier, the **Primary** area is used to define the __________ axis and the **Effect** area is used to define the __________ from the primary axis.

10. In the **Limits** area of the **Parameters** rollout of the **Bend** modifier, the value in the **Upper Limit** spinner is zero or __________ and the value in the **Lower Limit** is zero or__________.

Exercises

Exercise 1

Start Autodesk 3ds Max 2012 and then perform the following operations:

1. Choose **Create > Geometry** in the **Command Panel**. Select the **Extended Primitives** option from the drop-down list below the **Geometry** button; various tools are displayed in the **Object Type** rollout.

1. Invoke the **Hedra** tool from the **Object Type** rollout and create a hedron in the viewport. In the **Family** area of the **Parameters** rollout, select different radio buttons and notice the difference in shapes. In the **Family Parameters** and **Axis Scaling** areas, change the values in the **P**, **Q**, and **R** spinners, and notice the difference in shapes.

2. Invoke the **ChamferBox** tool in the **Object Type** rollout and create a chamfer box. In the **Parameters** rollout, modify the value in the **Fillet** spinner and clear the **Smooth** check box to notice the difference.

3. Similarly, create different objects using the tools in the **Object Type** rollout. Choose the **Modify** tab in the **Command Panel**. Try various options in the **Parameters** rollout of each object.

4. Create an object using one of the tools in the **Object Type** rollout. Invoke the **Angle Snap Toggle** tool in the **Main Toolbar** and rotate the object using the **Select and Rotate** tool. Notice the difference in the values displayed in the **X**, **Y**, or **Z** spinner in the coordinate display.

5. Invoke the **Percent Snap Toggle** tool in the **Main Toolbar** and scale any object using the **Select and Scale** tool, and then notice the difference. The object will be scaled in the percent increments.

6. Invoke the **RingWave** tool and create a ringwave. Then, try different animation playback buttons. When playing the animation, observe the time slider to view the current and total number of frames on it.

Exercise 2

Create the model shown in Figure 3-74 using your own dimensions. You can view the final rendered image of this model by downloading the file *c03_3dsmax_2012_render.zip* from *http://www.cadcim.com*. The path of the file is as follows:

Textbooks > Animation and Visual Effects > 3ds Max > Autodesk 3ds Max 2012: A Comprehensive Guide
(Expected time: 30 min)

Figure 3-74 *The rotatable stool model*

Exercise 3

Create the models shown in Figures 3-75, 3-76, and 3-77 using your own dimensions. You can view the final rendered scene by downloading the file *c03_3dsmax_2012_render.zip* from *http://www.cadcim.com*. The path of the file is mentioned in Exercise 2.
(Expected time: 30 min)

Figure 3-75 *The table model*

Figure 3-76 *The chair model*

Figure 3-77 *The final scene for Exercise 3*

Answers to Self-Evaluation Test

1. d, **2.** a, **3.** d, **4.** a, **5. Hedra**, **6.** time slider, **7.** A, **8.** T, **9.** F, **10.** T

4

Default Objects and Patch Grids

Learning Objectives

After completing this chapter, you will be able to:

- *Use the Mirror tool*
- *Use the Align tool*
- *Create AEC extended objects*
- *Create doors*
- *Create windows*
- *Create patch grids*

INTRODUCTION

In this chapter, you will learn to create the default objects and patch grids in Autodesk 3ds Max. Also, you will learn to use the **Mirror** and **Align** tools while modeling the objects with the help of various primitives and default objects.

MIRROR TOOL

Menu bar: Tools > Mirror
Main Toolbar: Mirror

The **Mirror** tool is used to mirror or clone the selected object about the center of the current coordinate system. You can also move the object while mirroring its orientation. To mirror an object, select it and invoke the **Mirror** tool from the **Main Toolbar**; the **Mirror: Screen Coordinates** dialog box will be displayed, as shown in Figure 4-1. Set the parameters in this dialog box and choose the **OK** button to mirror the objects. The two areas in this dialog box are discussed next.

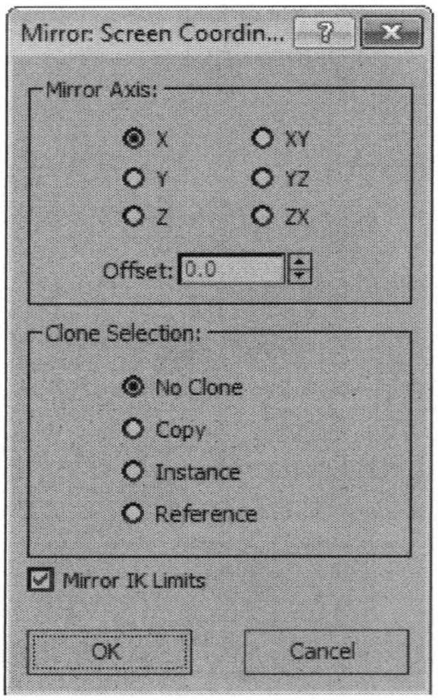

Figure 4-1 The ***Mirror: Screen Coordinates*** *dialog box*

Mirror Axis Area

Select the **X**, **Y**, **Z**, **XY**, **YZ**, or **ZX** radio button in the **Mirror Axis** area to define the direction of the object while mirroring. The value in the **Offset** spinner defines the distance of the mirrored object from the original one.

Clone Selection Area

The **Clone Selection** area is used to define the type of clone created by the **Mirror** tool. By default, the **No Clone** radio button is selected in this area. As a result, the selected object is mirrored but not retained. Select the **Copy** radio button to retain the selected object after mirroring. You can also change the position of the copied object by entering the required value in the **Offset** spinner in the **Mirror Axis** area. Select the **Instance** radio button to mirror the selected object as an instance. Select the **Reference** radio button to mirror the selected object as reference of the selected object.

An instance is a type of clone in which the changes are reflected when they are made in the original object. Also, if you make any change in the instanced object, then it will transfer to the original object.

A reference object is similar to an instance object with the only difference that the changes made in the reference object are not reflected in the original object.

ALIGN TOOL

Menu bar: Tools > Align > Align
Main Toolbar: Align
Keyboard: ALT+A

The **Align** tool enables you to align the current object with the target object. To align an object using the **Align** tool, select the current object and then invoke the **Align** tool from the **Main Toolbar**; the align cursor attached to a pair of crosshairs will be displayed, as shown in Figure 4-2. Move the cursor over the target object and click on it; the **Align Selection (X)** dialog box will be displayed, as shown in Figure 4-3. Here, **X** refers to the name of the target object. You need to use the options in the **Align Selection (X)** dialog box to align the objects. Various areas and options in this dialog box are discussed next.

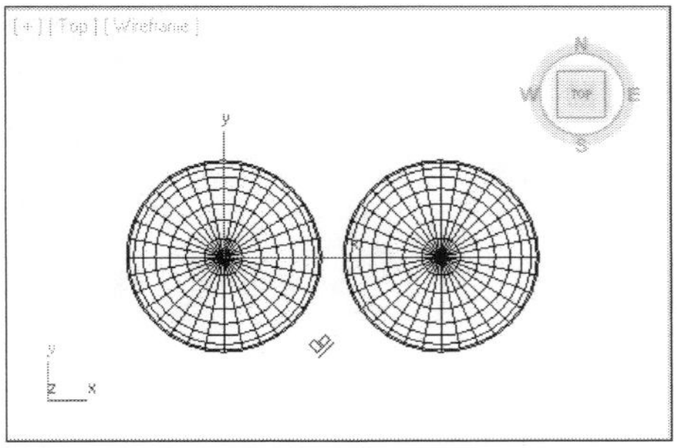

Figure 4-2 The align cursor in the Top viewport

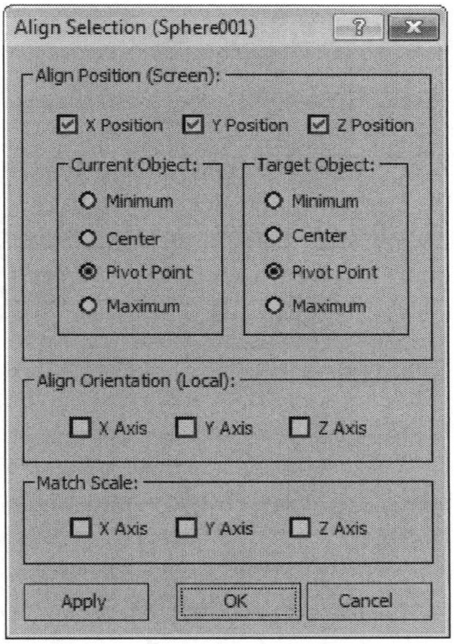

*Figure 4-3 The **Align Selection (Sphere001)** dialog box*

Align Position Area

You can select the check box(es) in this area to specify the axis along which you want to align the object. You can also select all the check boxes simultaneously. By default, all the check boxes are selected.

Current Object/Target Object Area

The **Minimum**, **Center**, **Pivot Point**, or **Maximum** radio button in the **Current Object** and **Target Object** areas can be selected to specify different points on the current and target objects to be used for alignment.

Note

*You should try different combinations of axes in the **Align Position** area. Also, try using different options in the **Current Object** and **Target Object** areas to notice the difference.*

AEC EXTENDED PRIMITIVES

In Autodesk 3ds Max, there are some default objects such as trees, railings, walls, and so on. These objects can be used to make a scene more realistic and are known as AEC extended objects. All AEC extended objects can be created dynamically using the mouse or by entering the parameters in the **Keyboard Entry** rollout.

To create an AEC extended object, you need to choose **Create > Geometry** in the **Command Panel**; the **Standard Primitives** option will be displayed by default in the drop-down list. Select the **AEC Extended** option from the drop-down list and activate the viewport in which you want to create the objects. Next, invoke the corresponding tool from the **Object Type** rollout. In this section, you will learn to create and modify the AEC extended objects using various tools available in the **Object Type** rollout.

Creating a Foliage

Menu:	Create > AEC Objects > Foliage
Command Panel:	Create > Geometry > AEC Extended > Object Type rollout > Foliage

To create a foliage or a tree, activate the viewport in which you want to create it. Then, invoke the **Foliage** tool from the **Object Type** rollout; the **Name and Color**, **Keyboard Entry**, **Favorite Plants**, and **Parameters** rollouts will be displayed, as shown in Figure 4-4.

In the **Favorite Plants** rollout, select one of the trees, and then double-click on it; the selected tree will be displayed in the viewports. One of the sample trees is shown in Figure 4-5. Alternatively, you can create a tree by dragging it from the **Favorite Plants** rollout to the desired location in the viewport. Also, you can select one of the trees from the **Favorite Plants** rollout and then click in the viewport at the desired location to place it. You need to invoke the **Zoom Extents All** tool to view the entire tree in the viewports.

Various rollouts used to create and modify the tree are discussed next.

***Figure 4-4** Various rollouts to create a tree*

Note

*The options in the **Name and Color** rollout are the same for all AEC extended objects.*

*The **Keyboard Entry** rollout is used to create various objects by entering the parameters using the keyboard. The method of creating these objects is the same as discussed earlier in Chapter 2. However, the railing object cannot be created using the keyboard, therefore, it does not have the **Keyboard Entry** rollout.*

Favorite Plants Rollout

The **Favorite Plants** rollout has a palette consisting of a list of default trees to create them in the viewport. By default, the **Automatic Materials** check box is selected. It is used to assign the default material to the trees. If you clear this check box and create a tree, then the tree created will not show any material. Also, the default color will be displayed in it. Choose the **Plant Library** button below the **Automatic Materials** check box; the **Configure Palette** dialog box will be displayed. This dialog box is used to give information such as **Name**, **Scientific Name**, **Type**, **Description**, and **Faces** about all the default trees in the **Favorite Plants** rollout. You can also use this dialog box to remove or add a particular plant from the palette in the **Favorite Plants** rollout. To do so, select the name of a plant from the **Configure Palette** dialog box and choose the **Remove from Palette** button; the **no** option will be displayed in the **Fav.** row, and the selected plant will not be displayed in the **Favorite Plants** rollout. Similarly, to display a plant in the **Favorite Plants** rollout, select the name of the plant from the **Configure Palette** dialog box, and then choose the **Add to Palette** button; the **no** option will be replaced by the **yes** option in the **Fav.** row. Next, choose the **OK** button to save the changes.

Note

*To modify the default material of the trees, you need to use the **Material Editor** tool, which will be discussed in detail in the later chapters.*

Parameters Rollout

The options in this rollout are used to modify the tree created using the **Foliage** tool. To do so, select the tree and choose the **Modify** tab in the **Command Panel**; the **Parameters** rollout will be displayed, as shown in Figure 4-6. Enter a new value in the **Height** spinner to modify the height of the tree. The value in the **Density** spinner varies from 0.0 to 1.0 and is used to set the amount of leaves and flowers in the tree. The value in the **Pruning** spinner varies from 0.0 to 1.0 and is used to remove the branches of the tree based on the value entered in this spinner, refer to Figures 4-7 and 4-8.

Figure 4-5 *A tree created using the **Foliage** tool*

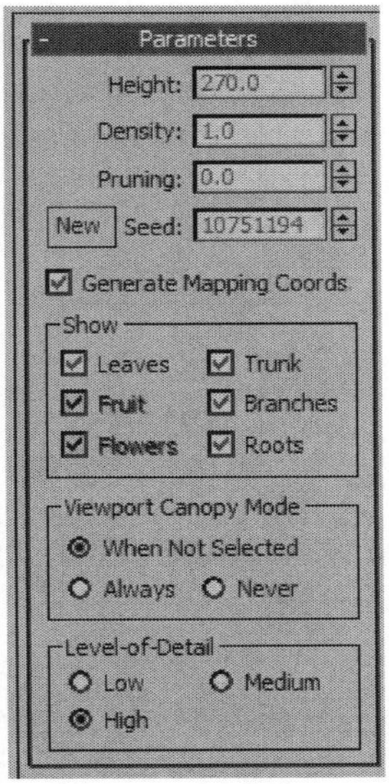

Figure 4-6 *The **Parameters** rollout*

Figure 4-7 *A tree with the **0** value in the **Pruning** spinner*

Figure 4-8 *A tree with the **0.5** value in the **Pruning** spinner*

Choose the **New** button to view the variation in the placement of leaves, branches, and the angle of trunk of the selected plant. When you choose the **New** button the value in the **Seed** spinner changes accordingly, showing the possible variation in the selected tree. The other areas in the **Parameters** rollout are discussed next.

Show Area

The options in this area are used to display leaves, trunk, fruits, branches, flowers, and roots. Select the check boxes to display the corresponding parts of a tree.

Note

*In the **Show** area, some options will not be available for some trees. For example, if you select a tree that does not have flowers, the **Flowers** check box will not be available.*

Viewport Canopy Mode Area

The options in this area are used to display the plant in the canopy mode in the viewports. The canopy of a plant is a type of covering area which covers the outermost parts of the tree such as leaves, branches, and trunk. Select the **When Not Selected** radio button to display the tree in the canopy mode in the viewport, if the tree is not selected. Select the **Always** radio button to display the tree always in the canopy mode, whether it is selected or not. Select the **Never** radio button to display the tree in a simple mode.

Level-of-Detail Area

This area is used to define how a tree will be displayed at the time of rendering. Select the **Low** radio button to display the lowest detail of a tree. It renders the tree in the canopy mode, as shown in Figure 4-9. Select the **Medium** radio button to render the tree with less number of faces in the branches and trunk, as shown in Figure 4-10. By default, the **High** radio button is selected. It is used to render the tree with all its faces in the branches and trunk. It will provide the highest detail of a tree, as shown in Figure 4-11.

Figure 4-9 The tree with low level of detail at rendering

Figure 4-10 The tree with medium level of detail at rendering

Figure 4-11 The tree with high level of detail at rendering

Creating a Railing

Menu bar:	Create > AEC Objects > Railing
Command Panel:	Create > Geometry > AEC Extended > Object Type rollout > Railing

To create a railing, activate the viewport in which you want to create it. Then, invoke the **Railing** tool from the **Object Type** rollout; the **Name and Color**, **Railing**, **Posts**, and **Fencing** rollouts will be displayed, as shown in Figure 4-12. Now, press and hold the left mouse button on the left side of the viewport and then drag the cursor to the right side to specify the length of the railing. Release the left mouse button to set the length. Now, move the cursor up to specify the height of the railing and click on the screen; the railing will be created in the viewports, as shown in Figure 4-13. You may need to use the **Zoom Extents All** tool from the **Main Toolbar** to view the entire railing.

Various rollouts used to modify the railing are discussed next.

Railing Rollout

The **Pick Railing Path** button is used to create railing paths using the splines. You can create the splines using the tools placed in **Create > Shapes** in the **Command Panel**. You will learn more about these tools in the later chapters. To create a railing according to the railing path or the spline, first create a spline and a railing in the viewport. Next, select the railing and choose the **Modify** tab in the **Command Panel**. Then, choose the **Pick Railing Path** button in the **Railing** rollout and move the cursor over the spline in the viewport; the pick cursor will be displayed and it will prompt you to pick the spline to create a railing according to the spline as path. Next, click on the spline; a railing will be created. Now, set a value in the **Segments** spinner to specify the number of segments in the railing. Select the **Respect Corners** check box to put the corners in the railing to match the corners of the railing path. The **Segments** spinner and the **Respect Corners** check box will be activated only if you create a railing using the railing path. The value in the **Length** spinner specifies the length of the railing. The areas in the **Railing** rollout are discussed next.

Top Rail Area

The top rail is the topmost part of the railing, refer to Figure 4-13, and the options in this area are used to modify the top rail. The **Profile** drop-down list is used to define the cross-section shape of the top rail. Select the **Round** or the **Square** option from the drop-down list to make the top rail round or square, respectively. Select the **none** option to remove the top rail from the railing. The values entered in the **Depth**, **Width**, and **Height** spinners specify the depth, width, and height of the top rail, respectively, refer to Figure 4-14.

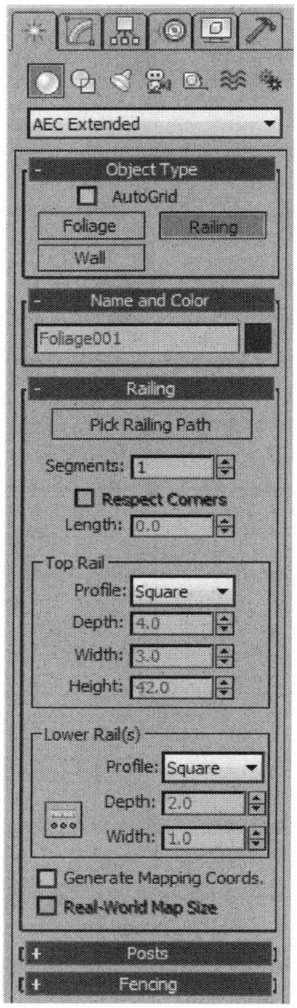

Figure 4-12 Partial view of various rollouts to create a railing

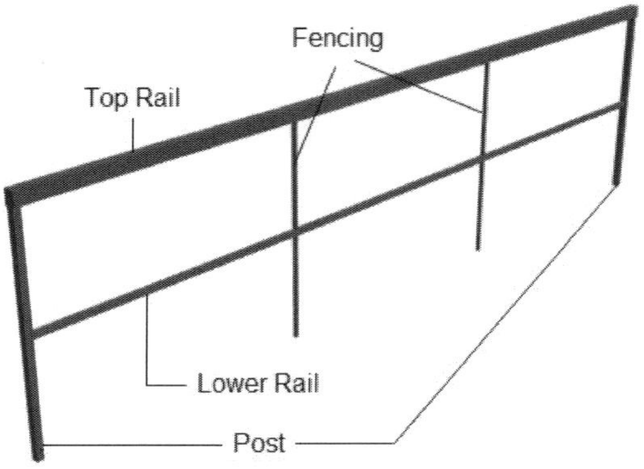

Figure 4-13 *The railing with different parts labeled*

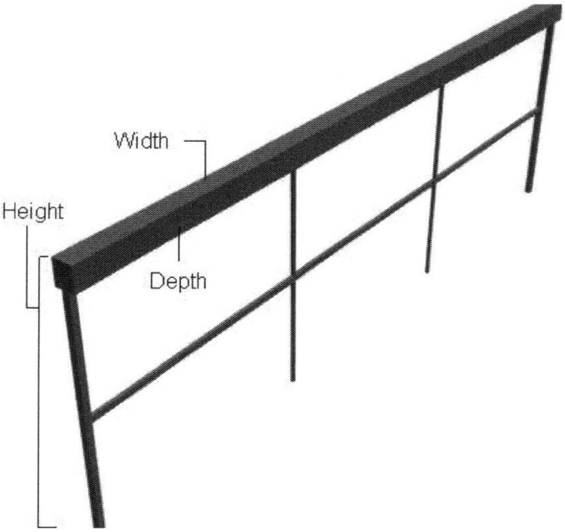

Figure 4-14 *The railing with different dimensions*

Lower Rail(s) Area

The lower rail is placed below the top railing, refer to Figure 4-13, and the options in this area are used to modify the lower rail of the railing. The **Profile** drop-down list is used to define the shape of the cross-section of the lower rail. The value in the **Depth** spinner specifies the depth of the rail, whereas the value in the **Width** spinner specifies the width of the lower rail. Choose the **Lower Rail Spacing** button on the left side of the **Lower Rail(s)** area; the **Lower Rail Spacing** dialog box will be displayed, as shown in Figure 4-15. In this dialog box, select the **Count** check box, if it is not already selected. The value in the spinner on the right of this check box specifies the number of lower rails in the railing. Choose the **Close** button to close the dialog box.

Posts Rollout

The posts are the left and right supports of the railing, refer to Figure 4-13, and the options in this rollout are used to modify them. Most of the options in this rollout are the same as those discussed in the **Lower Rail(s)** area of the **Railing** rollout, except the **Extension** spinner. The value in the **Extension** spinner is used to extend the posts of the railing from the bottom of the top rail, as shown in Figure 4-16.

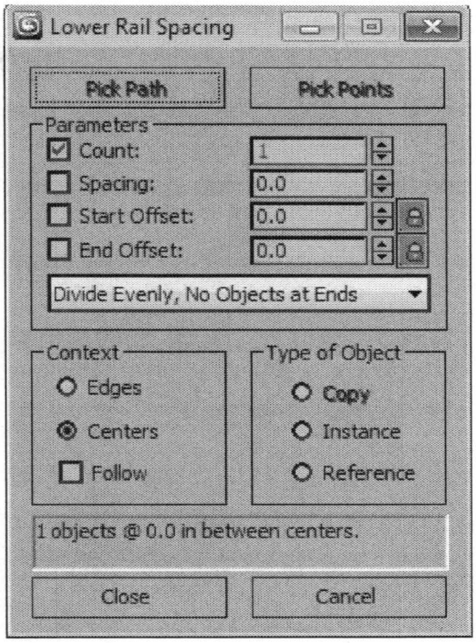

*Figure 4-15 The **Lower Rail Spacing** dialog box*

Fencing Rollout

The fencing is placed in between the posts of the railing, refer to Figure 4-13, and the options in this rollout are used to modify it. The options in the **Type** drop-down list define the type of fencing in the railing. If you select the **(none)** option in the **Type** drop-down list, the fence will not be displayed and the options in the **Picket** and **Solid Fill** areas will become inactive. If you select the **Pickets** option in the **Type** drop-down list, then the pickets will be displayed in between the posts, as shown in Figure 4-17. Also, the **Picket** area will be activated in this rollout. If you select the **Solid Fill** option in the **Type** drop-down list, then the solid box type shape will be displayed in between the posts, as shown in Figure 4-18. Also, the **Solid Fill** area will be activated. The areas in the **Fencing** rollout are discussed next.

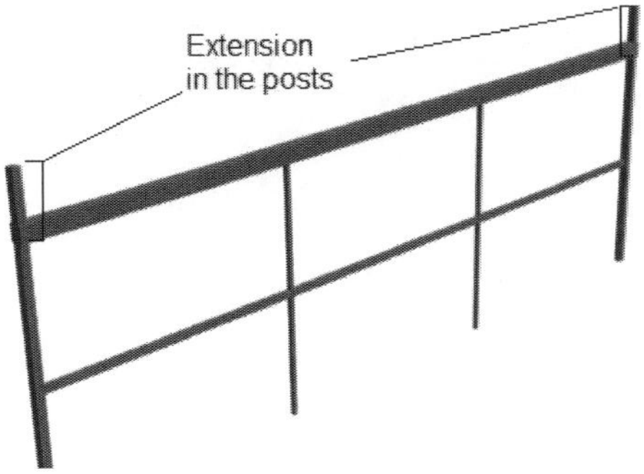

Figure 4-16 The railing with the extension in the posts

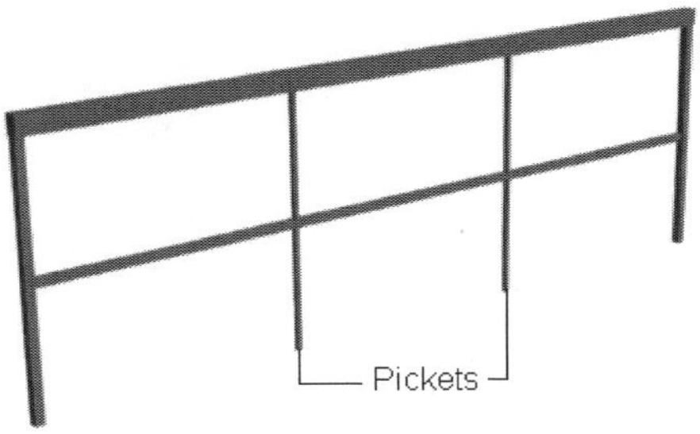

*Figure 4-17 The railing with the **Picket** type of fencing*

Picket Area

You need to select the **Pickets** option from the **Type** drop-down list to activate this area. The **Profile**, **Depth**, **Width**, and **Extension** options in this area are the same as those discussed in the **Posts** rollout. The value in the **Bottom Offset** spinner is used to set the height of the picket from the bottom of the railing, refer to Figure 4-19.

Solid Fill Area

Select the **Solid Fill** option from the **Type** drop-down list to activate this area. The value in the **Thickness** spinner is used to set the thickness of the solid fill. The value in the

Top Offset spinner is used to set the distance of the solid fill from the bottom of the top railing. The value in the **Bottom Offset** spinner is used to set the distance of the solid fill from the bottom of the railing. The value in the **Left Offset** spinner is used to set the distance of the solid fill from the left post. The value in the **Right Offset** spinner is used to set the distance of the solid fill from the right post, refer to Figure 4-20.

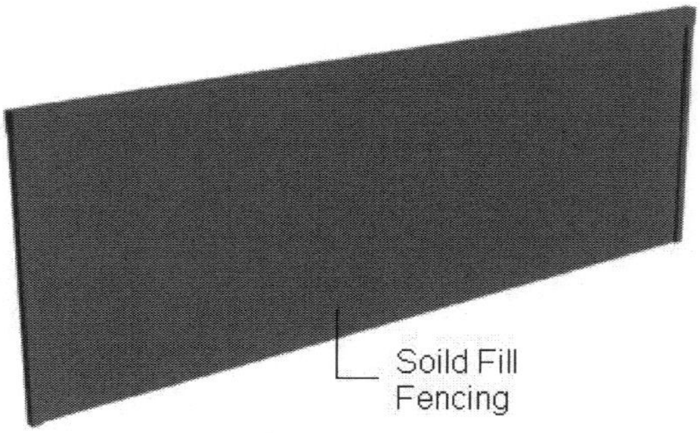

Figure 4-18 *The railing with the* ***Solid Fill*** *type of fencing*

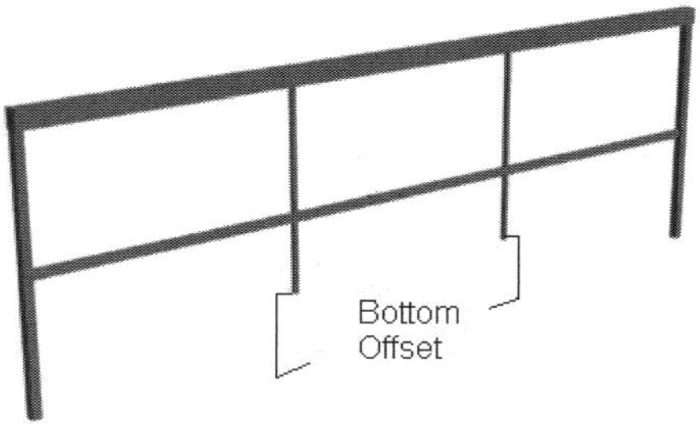

Figure 4-19 *The* ***Bottom Offset*** *in the* ***Picket*** *fencing*

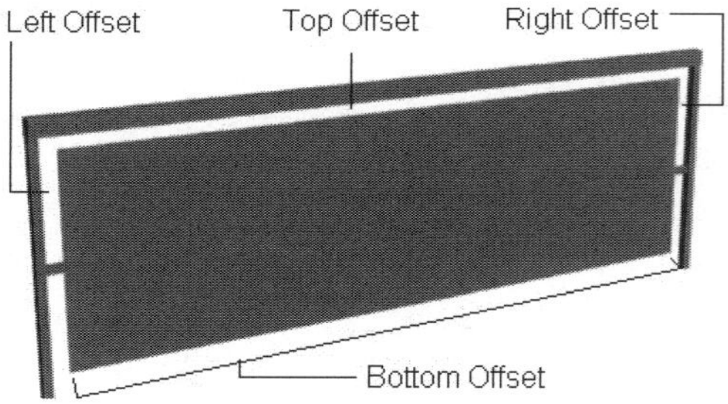

Figure 4-20 *Various offsets in the* ***Solid Fill*** *fencing*

Creating a Wall

Menu bar:	Create > AEC Objects > Wall
Command Panel:	Create > Geometry > AEC Extended > Object Type rollout > Wall

To create a wall, activate the Top viewport and then invoke the **Wall** tool from the **Object Type** rollout; the **Name and Color**, **Keyboard Entry**, and **Parameters** rollouts will be displayed, as shown in Figure 4-21. Now, in the **Parameters** rollout, set the width and height by entering values in the **Width** and **Height** spinners, respectively. Next, click on the left of the Top viewport to create the starting point of the wall. Drag the cursor to the right to define the length of the wall and then click on the screen. Now, right-click to exit the command; a wall segment will be created, as shown in Figure 4-22. If you want to create another segment of the wall in continuation, then you need to repeat the same procedure as followed for the first segment without right-clicking. Next, to create a closed wall, click on the starting point of the first wall segment; the **Weld Point?** dialog box will be displayed, as shown in Figure 4-23. Choose the **Yes** button in this dialog box; a closed wall will be displayed, as shown in Figure 4-24. Next, right-click to exit the command.

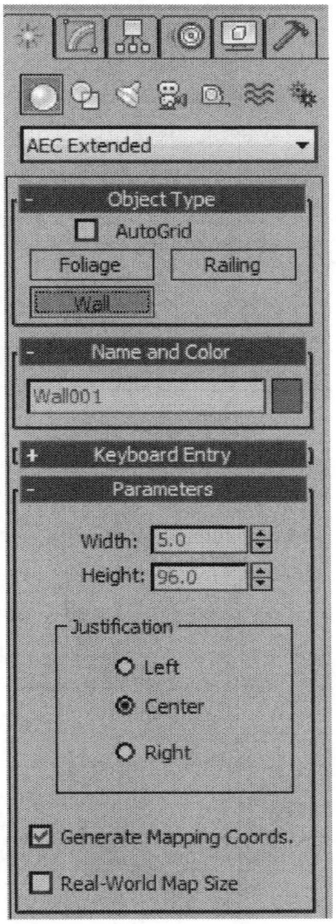

Figure 4-21 *Various rollouts to create a wall*

Figure 4-22 *A wall segment*

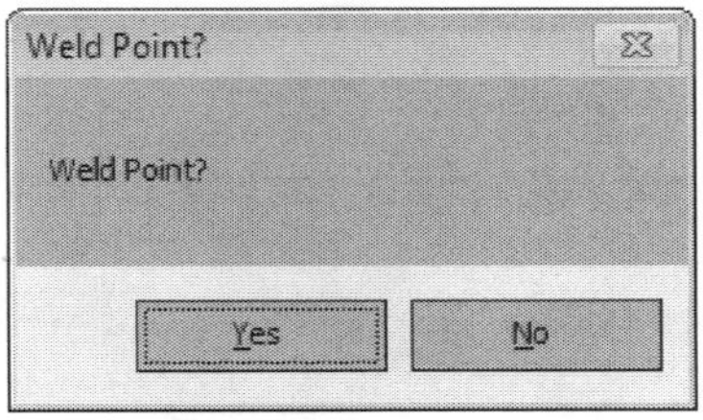

Figure 4-23 *The* ***Weld Point?*** *dialog box*

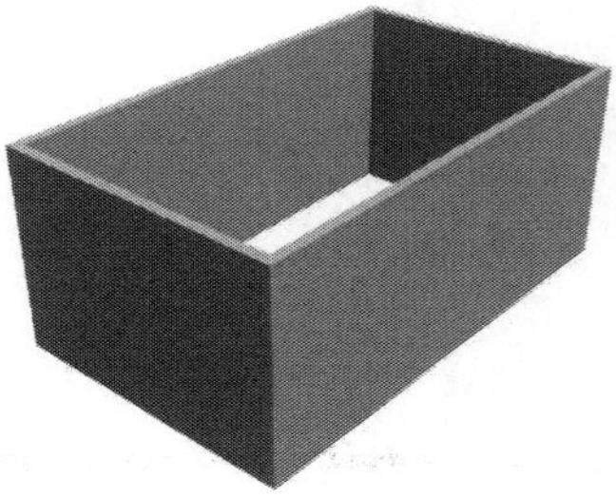

Figure 4-24 *A closed wall*

Various rollouts used to modify the wall are discussed next.

Keyboard Entry Rollout

This rollout is used to create a wall by entering the parameters in the **Keyboard Entry** rollout. To do so, expand the **Keyboard Entry** rollout. Enter the values in the **X**, **Y**, and **Z** spinners to specify the position of the starting point of the wall segment in the viewport along the axes of the home grid or a grid object. Now, choose the **Add Point** button to add a point. Repeat the same procedure to create another segment. Next, choose the **Close** button to create a closed wall. Choose the **Finish** button to end the creation of the wall. When you choose the **Pick Spline** button, you will be prompted to select a spline in the viewport to create a wall along with the spline as a path. You can create a spline using the tools given in **Create > Shapes > Splines** in the **Command Panel**. You will learn about these tools in the later chapters.

Parameters Rollout

In this rollout, enter the values in the **Width** and **Height** spinners to define the width and height of the wall, respectively. The **Justification** area in the **Parameters** rollout is discussed next.

Justification Area

The options in this area are used to align the wall at its baseline. The baseline is the line between the front and back sides of a wall and it is equal to the thickness of the wall. By default, the **Center** radio button is selected in this area and is used to align the wall at the center of its baseline. Select the **Left** radio button to align the wall at the left edge of its baseline. Select the **Right** radio button to align the wall at the right edge of its baseline.

Edit Object Rollout

Select the wall and choose the **Modify** tab in the **Command Panel**; the **Edit Object** rollout will be displayed, as shown in Figure 4-25. Choose the **Attach** button; it will become active and you will be prompted to select another wall in the viewport to attach it with the selected wall. When you select another wall, it will automatically take the same material as that of the selected wall. Choose the **Attach Multiple** button; the **Attach Multiple** dialog box will be displayed, containing the list of all walls in the viewport. Select the multiple walls that you want to attach from the list by holding the CTRL key and then choose the **Attach** button; multiple walls will be attached to the selected wall.

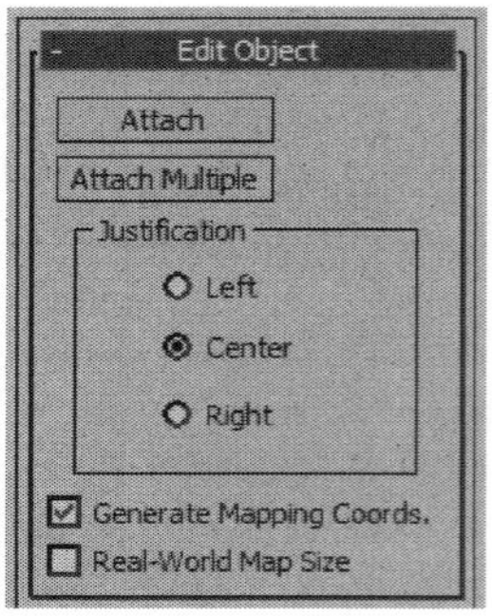

Figure 4-25 *The* ***Edit Object*** *rollout*

CREATING DOORS

In Autodesk 3ds Max, there are three tools to create the default doors. These tools are **Pivot**, **Sliding**, and **BiFold**. You can use these doors while creating houses, offices, rooms, and so on. To invoke the tools for creating doors, choose **Create > Geometry** in the **Command Panel**; the **Standard Primitives** option will be displayed in the drop-down list. Select the **Doors** option from the drop-down list and activate the viewport in which you want to create the doors. Next, invoke the corresponding tool from the **Object Type** rollout. In this section, you will learn to create and modify different types of doors using various tools available in the **Object Type** rollout.

Creating a Pivot Door

Menu bar:	Create > AEC Objects > Pivot Door
Command Panel:	Create > Geometry > Doors > Object Type rollout > Pivot

The pivot door is jointed or hinged only on one side and the door swings on this side. To create the pivot door, invoke the **Pivot** tool from the **Object Type** rollout; the **Name and Color**, **Creation Method**, **Parameters**, and **Leaf Parameters** rollouts will be displayed, as shown in Figure 4-26.

Activate the Top viewport and press and hold the left mouse button on the left of the viewport. Now, drag the cursor to the right of the viewport and release the left mouse button to define the width. Next, move the cursor up or down to define the depth of the door and click on the screen to set the depth. Now, again move the cursor up or down to define the height of the door. Click on the screen; the pivot door will be created in all viewports, refer to Figure 4-27.

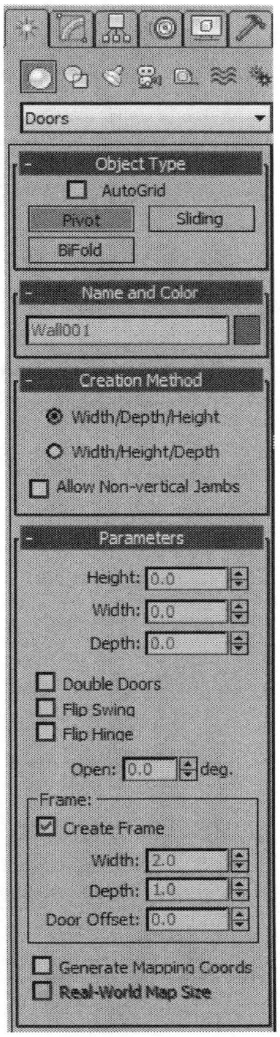

***Figure 4-26** Partial view of various rollouts to create a pivot door*

***Figure 4-27** A pivot door*

Various rollouts used to create and modify the pivot door are discussed next.

Creation Method Rollout

The options in this rollout are used to creating the pivot door dynamically. You can create the pivot door using any of the two methods discussed next.

Width/Depth/Height

To create the door using this method, make sure the **Width/Depth/Height** radio button is selected. Now, first you need to define the width and depth of the door, and then you need to move the cursor to define the height, as discussed earlier while creating the pivot door dynamically.

Width/Height/Depth

To create the door using this method, you need to select the **Width/Height/Depth** radio button. Now, first you need to specify the width and height of the door, and move the cursor to specify the depth. To do so, press and hold the left mouse button on the left side of the viewport, drag the cursor to the right of the viewport to specify the width of the pivot door, and release the left mouse button. Next, move the cursor up to define the height of the door and click on the screen to set the height. Next, move the cursor up or down to specify the depth of the door. Click on the screen; the pivot door will be created in all viewports.

Parameters Rollout

The options in this rollout are used to modify the pivot door. Select the pivot door and choose the **Modify** tab in the **Command Panel**; the **Parameters** and **Leaf Parameters** rollouts will be displayed. Enter the new values in the **Height**, **Width**, and **Depth** spinners to modify the height, width, and depth of the pivot door, respectively. Select the **Double Doors** check box to create two pivot doors, one on the left and other on the right, as shown in Figure 4-28. Select the **Flip Swing** check box to change the direction of swing of the door. Select the **Flip Hinge** check box to change the placement of the joint or the hinge of the pivot door on the opposite side. When you select the **Double Doors** check box, the **Flip Hinge** check box becomes inactive. The value in the **Open** spinner is used to specify the amount in degree to which the door will open, refer to Figure 4-29. The **Frame** area in the **Parameters** rollout is discussed next.

Frame Area

The options in this area are used to modify the frame of the pivot door. By default, the **Create Frame** check box is selected. If you clear the **Create Frame** check box, then the other options in this area will become inactive. Also, the frame will not be displayed in the door. Enter the values in the **Width** and **Depth** spinners to specify the width and depth of the frame of the pivot door. The value in the **Door Offset** spinner specifies the location of the door in reference to the frame.

Figure 4-28 A double pivot door

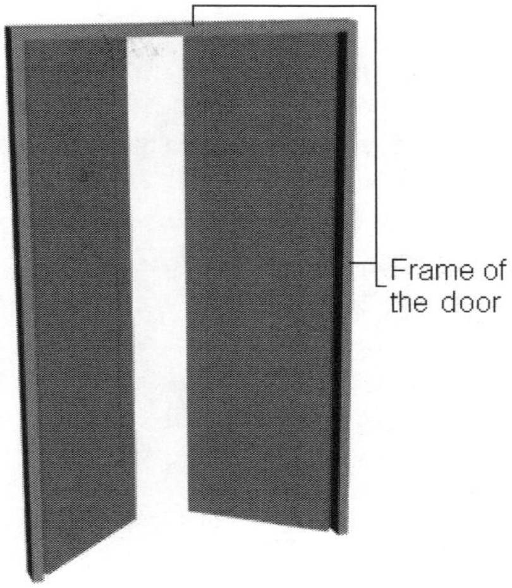

Figure 4-29 An opened double door

Leaf Parameters Rollout

This rollout is used to modify the leaf of a door. Set a new value in the **Thickness** spinner to modify the thickness of the leaf of the door. Enter a new value in the **Stiles/Top Rail** spinner to modify the frame of the door leaf on the top, left, and right side, as shown in Figure 4-30. Set a value in the **Bottom Rail** spinner to modify the frame at the bottom of the door leaf. The value in the **# Panels Horiz** spinner specifies the horizontal panels on the leaf of the door. The value in the **# Panels Vert** spinner specifies the vertical panels on the leaf of the door, refer to Figure 4-30. The value in the **Muntin** spinner is used to specify the width of the gap between the panels of the door leaf. The **Panels** area in the **Leaf Parameters** rollout is discussed next.

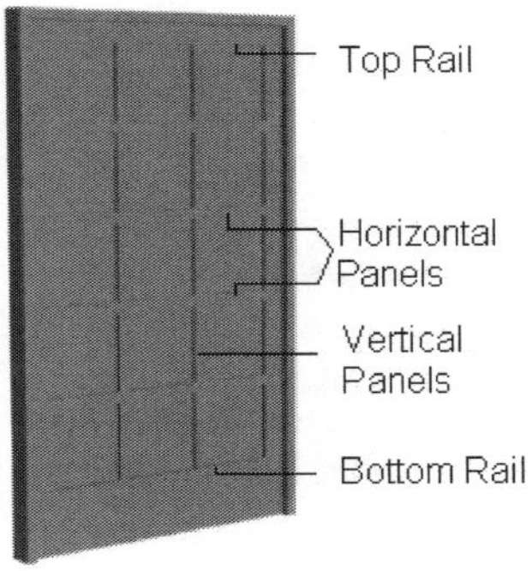

Figure 4-30 A door with the glass panels

Panels Area

The options in this area are used to modify the panels on the door leaf. The three radio buttons in this area are discussed next.

None

Select the **None** radio button; the panels will not be displayed in the door leaf.

Glass

Select the **Glass** radio button to create the glass panels, refer to Figure 4-30. Also, the **Thickness** spinner will be activated. It is used to set the thickness of the glass panel.

Beveled

Select the **Beveled** radio button to create the beveled panels, as shown in Figure 4-31. When you select the **Beveled** radio button, the options under this radio button will be activated. The **Bevel Angle** spinner is used to define the angle between the outer surface of the door and the panel surface. The **Thickness 1** spinner is used to define the outer thickness of the panel. The **Thickness 2** spinner is used to define the thickness of the starting point of the bevel. The **Middle Thick** spinner is used to define the inner thickness of the panel. The **Width 1** spinner is used to define the width of the starting point of the bevel and the **Width 2** spinner is used to define the inner width of the panel.

Figure 4-31 *A door with the beveled panels*

Creating a Sliding Door

Menu: Create > AEC Objects > Sliding Door
Command Panel: Create > Geometry > Doors > Object Type rollout > Sliding

A sliding door has two door components, one is fixed, whereas the other slides or moves over the fixed component to open. To create a sliding door, invoke the **Sliding** tool from the **Object Type** rollout; the **Name and Color**, **Creation Method**, **Parameters**, and **Leaf Parameters** rollouts will be displayed.

Now, to create the sliding door, follow the same procedure as you did for the pivot door; a sliding door will be created, as shown in Figure 4-32.

Figure 4-32 *A sliding door*

The options in the **Name and Color**, **Creation Method**, **Parameters**, and **Leaf Parameters** rollouts are the same as discussed in the pivot door. However, some options in the **Parameters** rollout are different and these are discussed next.

Select the **Flip Front Back** check box to choose the component that you want to place in the front. Select the **Flip Side** check box to change the fixed component to the sliding component.

Creating a BiFold Door

Menu: Create > AEC Objects > BiFold Door
Command Panel: Create > Geometry > Doors > Object Type rollout > BiFold

The bifold door has two door components and two joints in it. To create the bifold door, invoke the **BiFold** tool from the **Object Type** rollout; the **Name and Color**, **Creation Method**, **Parameters**, and **Leaf Parameters** rollouts will be displayed in the **Command Panel**. Now, create a bifold door dynamically using the same method as discussed for creating the pivot door; a bifold door will be created, as shown in Figure 4-33.

The options in the **Name and Color**, **Creation Method**, **Parameters**, and **Leaf Parameters** rollouts are the same as those discussed in the pivot door.

Figure 4-33 A bifold door

CREATING WINDOWS

In Autodesk 3ds Max, there are six tools to create different types of default windows such as **Awning**, **Casement**, and so on. You can use these windows at various places for architectural designs.

To invoke these tools for creating the windows, choose **Create > Geometry** in the **Command Panel**; the **Standard Primitives** option will be displayed in the drop-down list. Now, select the **Windows** option from this drop-down list; various tools will be displayed in the **Object Type** rollout. In this section, you will learn to create various types of windows using these tools.

Creating an Awning Window

Menu:	Create > AEC Objects > Awning Window
Command Panel:	Create > Geometry > Windows > Object Type rollout > Awning

An awning window has one or more cases that are jointed at its top. To create an awning window, invoke the **Awning** tool from the **Object Type** rollout; the **Name and Color**, **Creation Method**, and **Parameters** rollouts will be displayed, as shown in Figure 4-34.

Activate the Top viewport and press and hold the left mouse button on the left side of the viewport, drag the cursor to the right side to specify the width of the window, and release the left mouse button. Next, move the cursor up or down to define the depth of the window and click on the screen. Now, move the cursor up or down to specify the height of the window. Click on the screen; the awning window will be created in all viewports, refer to Figure 4-35. The options in the **Name and Color** and **Creation Method** rollouts are the same for all windows as those discussed in the pivot door.

Parameters Rollout

The options in this rollout are used to modify the awning window. To do so, select the awning window and choose the **Modify** tab in the **Command Panel**; the **Parameters** rollout will be displayed. Enter new values in the **Height**, **Width**, and **Depth** spinners to modify the height, width, and depth of the awning window, respectively. The areas in the **Parameters** rollout are used to modify the window. These areas are discussed next.

Frame

The options in this area are used to modify the frame of the window, refer to Figure 4-35. Enter a value in the **Horiz. Width** spinner to set the width of the horizontal (top and bottom) frames of the window. Enter a value in the **Vert. Width** spinner to set the width of the vertical (left and right) frames of the window. Similarly, enter a value in the **Thickness** spinner to set the overall thickness of the frame of the window.

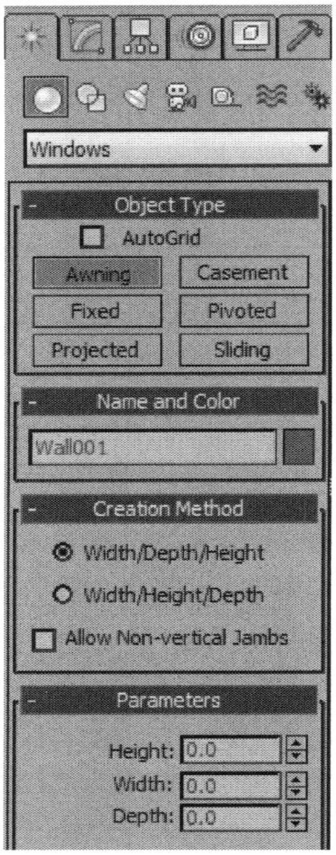

Figure 4-34 Partial view of various rollouts to create an awning window

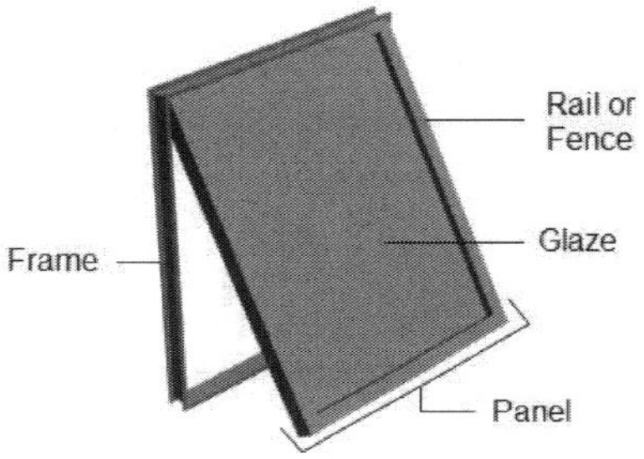

Figure 4-35 An awning window

Glazing

The **Thickness** spinner in this area is used to set the thickness of the glaze or the glass of the window, refer to Figure 4-35.

Rails and Panels

This area is used to modify the panel of the window. Enter a value in the **Width** spinner to set the width of the fence in the panel. Enter a value in the **Panel Count** spinner to set the number of panels in the window, as shown in Figure 4-36.

Figure 4-36 An awning window with two panels

Open Window

The **Open** spinner in this area is used to open the window. Its value will be in percentage.

Creating a Casement Window

Menu bar:	Create > AEC Objects > Casement Window
Command Panel:	Create > Geometry > Windows > Object Type rollout > Casement

A casement window has one or more cases that are jointed on the sides. To create the casement window, invoke the **Casement** tool from the **Object Type** rollout; the **Name and Color**, **Creation Method**, and **Parameters** rollouts will be displayed. Create a casement window dynamically using the same method as discussed for creating the awning window. A casement window is shown in Figure 4-37.

Parameters Rollout

The options in this rollout are the same as those discussed in the **Awning** tool, except the **Casement** and **Open Window** areas. These areas are discussed next.

Casements Area

This area is used to modify the panel of the window. Enter a value in the **Panel Width** spinner to set the width of the fence in the panel. By default, the **One** radio button is selected to create one panel in the window. If you want to create two panels in the window, as shown in Figure 4-38, you need to select the **Two** radio button.

Figure 4-37 *A casement window*

Figure 4-38 *A casement window with two panels*

Open Window Area

The **Open** spinner in this area is used to open the window. Its value will be in percentage. Select the **Flip Swing** check box to swap the swinging of the panel of the window.

Creating a Fixed Window

Menu bar:	Create > AEC Objects > Fixed Window
Command Panel:	Create > Geometry > Windows > Object Type rollout > Fixed

A fixed window cannot be opened. To create a fixed window, activate the viewport and invoke the **Fixed** tool from the **Object Type** rollout; the **Name and Color**, **Creation Method**, and **Parameters** rollouts will be displayed.
Now, activate the Top viewport and follow the same method as discussed for creating the awning window; a fixed window will be created, as shown in Figure 4-39.

Parameters Rollout

The options in this rollout are the same as those discussed in the **Awning** tool, except the **Rails and Panels** area. This area is discussed next.

Rails and Panels Area

This area is used to modify the panel of the window. Enter a value in the **Width** spinner to set the width of the fence in the panel. Set a value in the **#Panels Horiz** spinner to define the number of horizontal divisions in the panel. Similarly, set a value in the **#Panels Vert** spinner to define the number of vertical divisions in the panel, as shown in Figure 4-40.

Figure 4-39 *A fixed window*

Figure 4-40 *A fixed window with horizontal and vertical divisions*

Creating a Pivoted Window

Menu bar:	Create > AEC Objects > Pivoted Window
Command Panel:	Create > Geometry > Windows > Object Type rollout > Pivoted

A pivoted window has only one panel that is jointed in the middle of the frame. When you open this window, it will swing around the horizontal axis. To create a pivoted window, activate the viewport and invoke the **Pivoted** tool from the **Object Type** rollout; the **Name and Color**, **Creation Method**, and **Parameters** rollouts will be displayed. Now, follow the same method as discussed while creating the awning window; a pivoted window will be created, as shown in Figure 4-41.

Parameters Rollout

Most of the options in this rollout are the same as discussed in the **Awning** tool, except the **Rails** and **Pivots** areas. These areas are discussed next.

Rails Area

This area is used to modify the panel of the window. Enter a value in the **Width** spinner to set the width of the fence in the panel.

Pivots Area

When you open the window, by default it rotates about the horizontal axis. To rotate the window about the vertical axis, select the **Vertical Rotation** check box; it will be rotated, as shown in Figure 4-42.

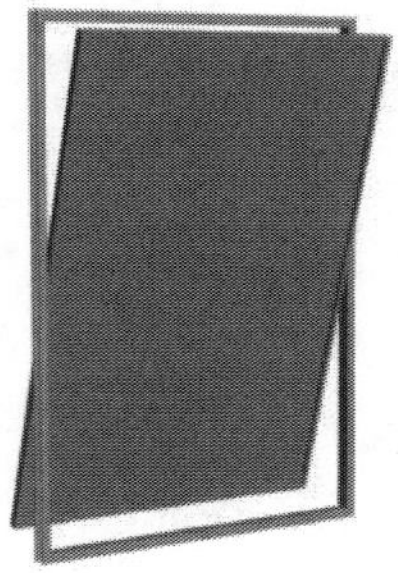

Figure 4-41 A pivoted window rotated around the horizontal axis

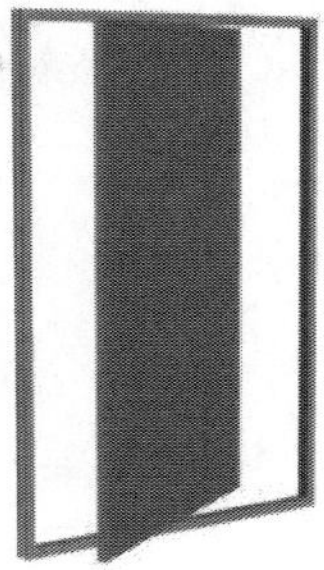

Figure 4-42 A pivoted window rotated around the vertical axis

Creating a Projected Window

Menu bar:	Create > AEC Objects > Projected Window
Command Panel:	Create > Geometry > Windows > Object Type rollout > Projected

A projected window has three panels in which the top one remains still, and the other two swing in the opposite direction. To create a projected window, activate the viewport and invoke the **Projected** tool from the **Object Type** rollout; the **Name and Color**, **Creation Method**, and **Parameters** rollouts will be displayed. Now, follow the same method as discussed while creating the awning window; a projected window will be created, as shown in Figure 4-43.

Figure 4-43 A projected window

Parameters Rollout

Most of the options in this rollout are the same as discussed in the **Awning** tool, except the **Rails and Panels** area. This area is discussed next.

Rails and Panels Area

This area is used to modify the panel of the window. Set the value in the **Width** spinner to specify the width of the fence in the panel. Set the value in the **Middle Height** spinner to define the height of the middle panel relative to the frame of the window. Similarly, set the value in the **Bottom Height** spinner to define the height of the bottom panel relative to the frame of the window.

Creating a Sliding Window

Menu bar:	Create > AEC Objects > Sliding Window
Command Panel:	Create > Geometry > Windows > Object Type rollout > Sliding

A sliding window has two panels in which one remains still and the other one slides to open. To create a sliding window, activate the viewport and invoke the **Sliding** tool from the **Object Type** rollout; the **Name and Color**, **Creation Method**, and **Parameters** rollouts will be displayed.

Now, create a sliding window dynamically using the same method as discussed while creating the awning window; a sliding window will be created, as shown in Figure 4-44.

Parameters Rollout

Most of the options in this rollout are the same as those discussed in the **Awning** tool, except the **Rails and Panels** and **Open Window** areas. These areas are discussed next.

Rails and Panels

This area is used to modify the panel of the window. Set the value in the **Rail Width** spinner to set the width of the fence in the panel. Set the value in the **#Panels Horiz** spinner to define the number of horizontal divisions in the panel. Set the value in the **#Panels Vert** spinner to define the number of vertical divisions in the panel. Select the **Chamfered Profile** check box to chamfer the fence between the panels, as shown in Figure 4-45.

Open Window

The **Open** spinner in this area is used to open the window and its value will be in percentage. By default, the **Hung** check box is selected. As a result, the panel slides in the vertical direction. Clear the **Hung** check box to slide the panel in the horizontal direction, refer to Figure 4-46.

Figure 4-44 *The sliding window*

Figure 4-45 *The sliding window with two horizontal and vertical chamfered divisions*

Figure 4-46 *The sliding window with the horizontal sliding*

CREATING STAIRS

In Autodesk 3ds Max, there are four tools to create different types of default stairs such as **LType Stair**, **Spiral Stair**, and so on. To invoke these tools, choose **Create > Geometry** in the **Command Panel**; the **Standard Primitives** option will be displayed in the drop-down list. Now, select the **Stairs** options from the drop-down list; various tools will be displayed in the **Object Type** rollout. In this section, you will learn to create various types of stairs using these tools.

Creating L-type Stairs

Menu bar:	Create > AEC Objects > L-Type Stair
Command Panel:	Create > Geometry > Stairs > Object Type rollout > LTypeStair

The L-type stairs have two stairways that are jointed at right angles to each other. To create the L-type stairs, invoke the **LType Stair** tool from the **Object Type** rollout; the **Name and Color**, **Parameters**, **Carriage**, **Railings**, and **Stringers** rollouts will be displayed, as shown in Figure 4-47.

Now, activate the Top viewport. Press and hold the left mouse button on the left side of the viewport, drag the cursor to the right side of the viewport to specify the length of the first stairway of the stair, and then release the left mouse button. Next, move the cursor up or down at right angle to define the length of the second stairway of the stair and then click on the screen. Now, move the cursor up to specify the overall height of the stair and then click on the screen; the L-type stairs will be created in all viewports, as shown in Figure 4-48.

Various rollouts used to create and modify the L-type stairs are discussed next.

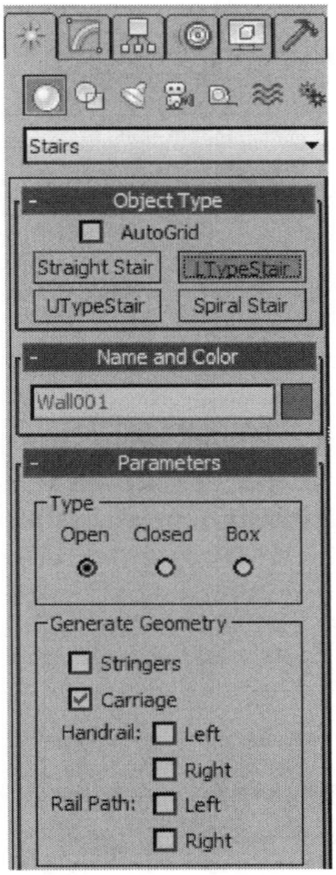

Figure 4-47 Partial view of various rollouts to create L-type stairs

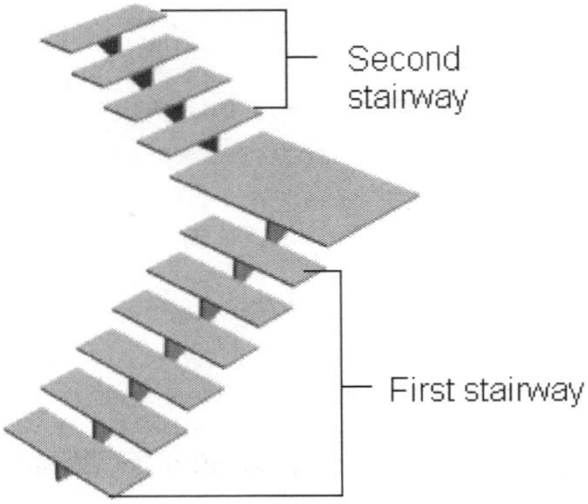

Figure 4-48 The L-type open stairs

Parameters Rollout

The options in this rollout are used to modify the L-type stairs. To do so, select the L-type stairs and choose the **Modify** tab in the **Command Panel**; the **Parameters**, **Carriage**, **Railings**, and

Stringers rollouts will be displayed. The **Parameters** rollout has a number of areas to modify the stairs. These are discussed next.

Type Area

The options in this area are used to define the type of stairs. By default, the **Open** radio button is selected, and therefore the stairs with open steps are created, as shown in Figure 4-48. Select the **Closed** radio button to create the stairs with closed steps, as shown in Figure 4-49. Select the **Box** radio button to create a support for the steps of the stairs, as shown in Figure 4-50.

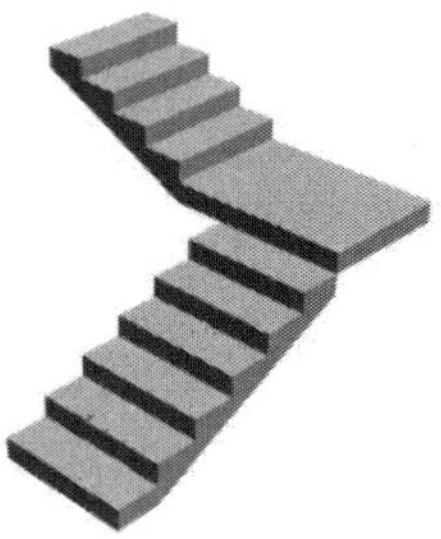

Figure 4-49 *The L-type closed stairs*

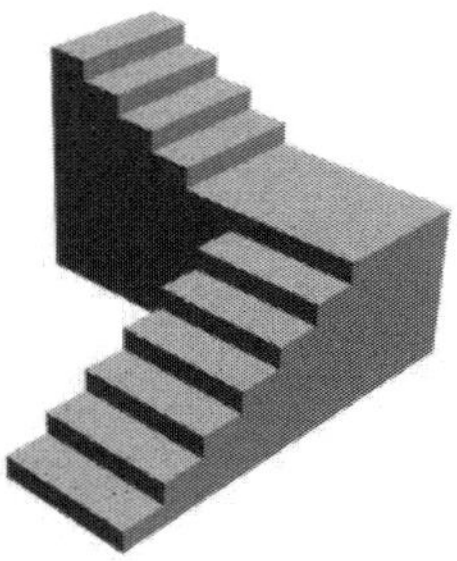

Figure 4-50 *The L-type box stairs*

Generate Geometry Area

The options in this area are used to modify the stairs by incorporating the geometry shapes. Select the **Stringers** check box to create the left and right support for the steps of the stairs. Select the **Carriage** check box to create support for the steps of the stairs. Select the **Left** and **Right** check boxes in the **Handrail** group to create the left and right handrails, as shown in Figure 4-51. On selecting the **Left** and **Right** check boxes in the **Rail Path** group, a path will be created on the left and right of the stairs, as shown in Figure 4-52. By using these paths, you can insert the default railings for stairs. To do so, invoke the **Railing** tool from **Create > Geometry > AEC Extended > Object Type** rollout. In the **Railing** rollout, choose the **Pick Railing Path** button and move the cursor over the path that is created while selecting the **Left** and **Right** check boxes in the **Rail Path** of the stairs; the cursor will get changed and prompts you to select the path. Select one of the rail paths in the viewport; the default railing will be displayed. Next, modify the default railings as discussed earlier in the **Railing** tool.

Layout Area

The options in this area are used to modify the dimensions of the stairs. Enter a value in the **Length 1** spinner to set the length of the first stairway. Similarly, enter a value in the **Length 2** spinner to set the length of the second stairway. The value in the **Width** spinner is used to set the width of the overall steps in the stairs. Enter a value in the **Angle** spinner to set the angle between the second stairway and the landing of the stairs. Enter a value in the **Offset** spinner to set the distance from the second stairway to the landing of the stairs.

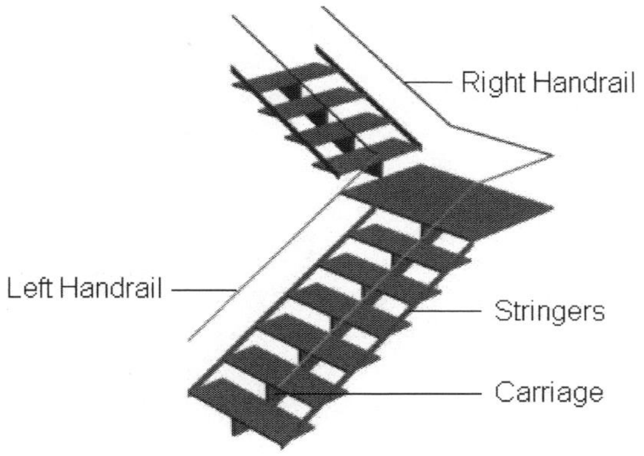

Figure 4-51 The L-Type stairs with handrails, carriage, and stringers

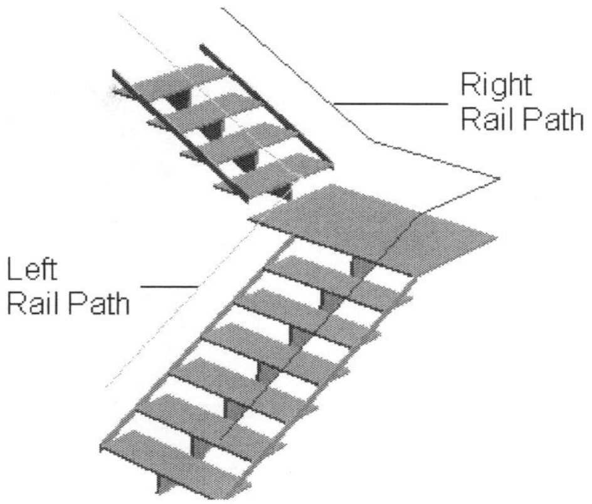

Figure 4-52 The L-Type stairs with rail paths

Rise Area

There are three spinners in this area. These spinners are controlled by choosing the buttons available on their left side. When you choose one of the buttons, the spinner on the right side of that button becomes inactive. You can modify only two spinners at a time. Enter a value in the **Overall** spinner to define the height of stairways. The **Riser Ht** spinner is used to set the height of the risers in the stairs. The **Riser Ct** spinner is used to set the number of risers in the stairs. The riser is the gap between the steps in a stairways.

Steps Area

Enter a value in the **Thickness** spinner to modify the thickness of the steps of the stairs. This spinner is activated only if the **Open** radio button is selected in the **Type** area. Select the check box on the left side of the **Depth** spinner; the **Depth** spinner will become active. Set a value in the **Depth** spinner to modify the depth of the steps of the stairs.

Carriage Rollout

To activate the options in this rollout, make sure the **Carriage** check box in the **Generate Geometry** area of the **Parameters** rollout is selected. In the **Parameters** area of the **Carriage** rollout, enter a value in the **Depth** spinner to set the depth of the carriage. Enter a value in the **Width** spinner to set the width of the carriage. Choose the **Carriage Spacing** button just below the **Width** spinner; the **Carriage Spacing** dialog box will be displayed. Select the **Count** check box, if it is not already selected. The value in the spinner on the right side of the **Count** check box specifies the number of carriages in the stairs. Set the required value and then choose the **Close** button to close the dialog box. The **Spring from Floor** check box in this rollout is used to control the starting point of the carriage from the floor.

Railings Rollout

To activate the options in this rollout, you need to select one of the **Handrail** check boxes in the **Generate Geometry** area of the **Parameters** rollout. Enter a value in the **Height** spinner to set the height of the railing from the steps of the stairs. The **Offset** spinner is used to set the offset of the railing from the ends of the steps. The value in the **Segments** spinner is used to set the number of segments in the railing. More the number of segments, smoother will be the railing. The value in the **Radius** spinner is used to set the radius of the railing.

Stringers Rollout

To activate the options in this rollout, you need to select the **Stringers** check box in the **Generate Geometry** area of the **Parameters** rollout. Enter a value in the **Depth** spinner to set the distance of the stringers from the floor. The value in the **Width** spinner is used to set the width of the stringers. The **Offset** spinner is used to set the distance of the stringers from the steps. The **Spring from Floor** check box is used to control the starting point of the stringers from the floor.

Creating Spiral Stairs

Menu bar:	Create > AEC Objects > Spiral Stair
Command Panel:	Create > Geometry > Stairs > Object Type rollout > Spiral Stair

The spiral stairs have a spiral shaped staircase. To create the spiral stairs, invoke the **Spiral Stair** tool from the **Object Type** rollout; the **Name and Color**, **Parameters**, **Carriage**, **Railings**, **Stringers**, and **Center Pole** rollouts will be displayed. To create the spiral stairs dynamically, activate the Top viewport. Next, click on a point in the viewport to specify the center of the spiral stair, hold the left mouse button, and drag downward to specify the radius and width. Release the left mouse button and move the cursor up or down to specify the overall rise in the height. Then, click on the screen; the spiral stairs will be created in all viewports. Different types of spiral stairs are shown in Figures 4-53, 4-54, and 4-55.

Figure 4-53 *The spiral stairs*

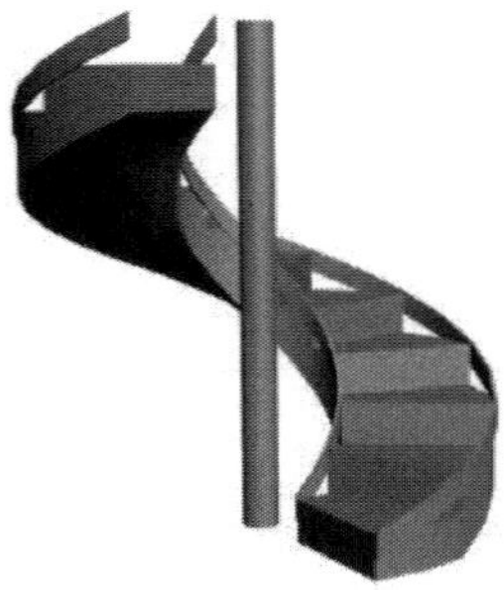

Figure 4-54 *The closed spiral stairs*

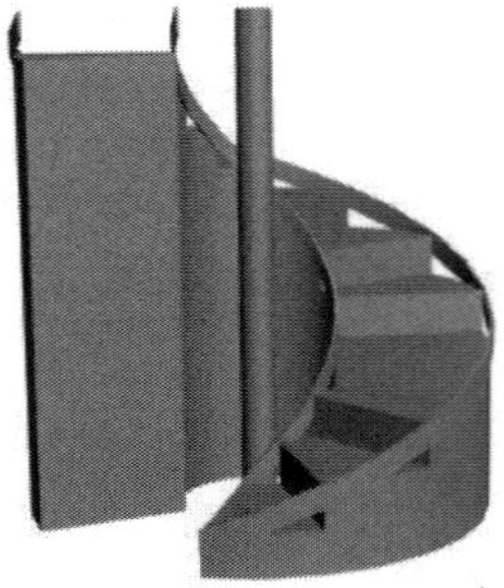

Figure 4-55 *The spiral box stairs*

Note

*The options in the **Carriage**, **Railings**, and **Stringers** rollouts are the same for the **Spiral**, **Straight**, and **UType** stairs as discussed in the L-type stairs.*

Parameters Rollout

In this rollout, the **Type**, **Rise**, and **Steps** areas are the same as discussed in the **LType Stair** tool. But, the **Generate Geometry** and **Layout** areas are different and these areas are discussed next.

Generate Geometry

The options in this area are used to modify the stairs by incorporating the geometry shapes. Select the **Stringers** check box to create the left and right supports for the steps of the stairs. Select the **Carriage** check box, if it is not already selected, to create support for the steps of the stairs. Select the **Center Pole** check box to create a pole at the center of the stairs, refer to Figure 4-53. Select the **Inside** and **Outside** check boxes in the **Handrail** area to create the handrails on both sides. The **Inside** and **Outside** check boxes in the **Rail Path** area are used to create a path on the left and right sides of the stairs.

Layout

The options in this area are used to modify the dimensions of the stairs. Select the **CCW** radio button, if it is not already selected, to rotate the stairs in the counterclockwise direction. Select the **CW** radio button to rotate the stairs in the clockwise direction. Enter a value in the **Radius** spinner to set the radius of the spiral stairs. Enter a value in the **Revs** spinner to set the number of revolutions of the stairs. The value in the **Width** spinner is used to set the width of the spiral stairs.

Center Pole Rollout

To activate the options in this rollout, you need to select the **Center Pole** check box in the **Generate Geometry** area of the **Parameters** rollout. In the **Parameters** area of the **Center Pole** rollout, set a value in the **Radius** spinner to set the radius of the center pole. Set the value in the **Segments** spinner to set the number of segments of the center pole. Select the check box on the left side of the **Height** spinner to activate it and set the value in this spinner to define the height of the pole.

Creating Straight Stairs

Menu bar:	Create > AEC Objects > Straight Stair
Command Panel:	Create > Geometry > Stairs > Object Type rollout > Straight Stair

The straight stairs have only one stairway. To create the straight stairs, activate the Top viewport and invoke the **Straight Stair** tool from the **Object Type** rollout; the **Name and Color**, **Parameters**, **Carriage**, **Railings**, and **Stringers** rollouts will be displayed.

Now, press and hold the left mouse button on the left side of the viewport, drag the cursor to the right side of the viewport to specify the length of the stairs, and release the left mouse button. Next, move the cursor up or down to define the width of the stairs and click on the screen to set the width. Next, move the cursor up or down to specify the height of the stairs. Click on the screen; the straight stairs will be created in all viewports, as shown in Figure 4-56. You can also create the closed and box straight stairs in the same way as described in the L-type stairs, refer to Figures 4-57 and 4-58.

Parameters Rollout

In this rollout, all areas are same as discussed in the **LType Stair** tool, except the **Layout** area and this area is discussed next.

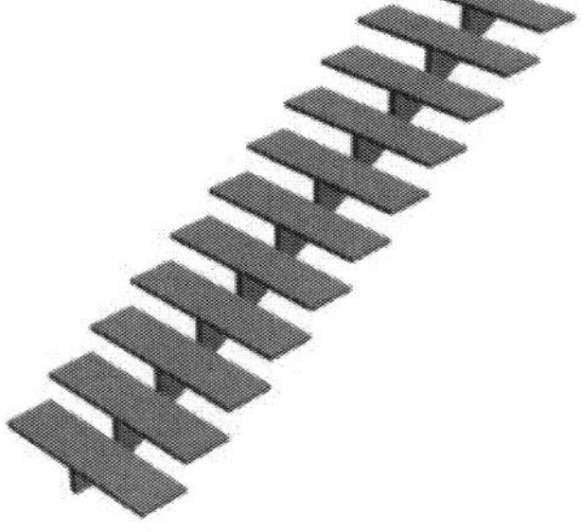

Figure 4-56 *The straight stairs*

Figure 4-57 *The straight closed stairs*

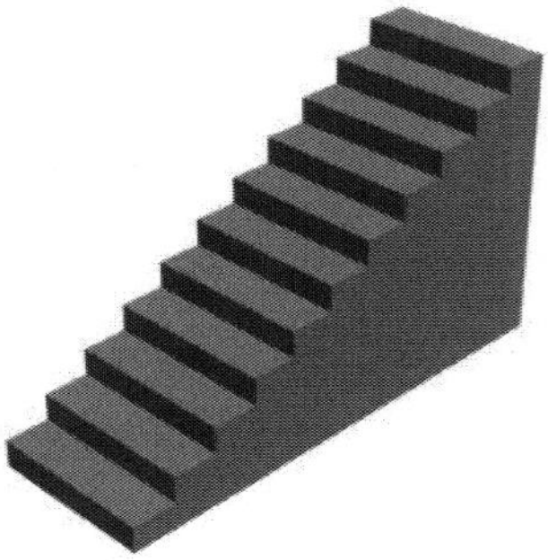

Figure 4-58 *The straight box stairs*

Layout Area

The options in this area are used to modify the dimensions of the stairs. The value in the **Length** spinner is used to set the length and the value in the **Width** spinner is used to set the width of the stairs.

Creating U-Type Stairs

Menu bar:	Create > AEC Objects > U-Type Stair
Command Panel:	Create > Geometry > Stairs > Object Type rollout > UTypeStair

The U-type stairs have two stairways parallel to each other in U shape. To create the U-type stairs, activate the Top viewport and invoke the **UType Stair** tool from the **Object Type** rollout; the **Name and Color**, **Parameters**, **Carriage**, **Railings**, and **Stringers** rollouts will be displayed.

Next, press and hold the left mouse button on the left side of the viewport, drag the cursor to the right side to specify the length of the stairs, and release the left mouse button. Now, move the cursor up to define the width of the stairs and the distance between the two stairways. Click on the screen to set the width. Next, move the cursor up or down to specify the rise of the stairs. Click on the screen; the U-type stairs will be created in all viewports. Different U-type stairs are shown in Figures 4-59, 4-60, and 4-61.

Figure 4-59 The U-type stairs

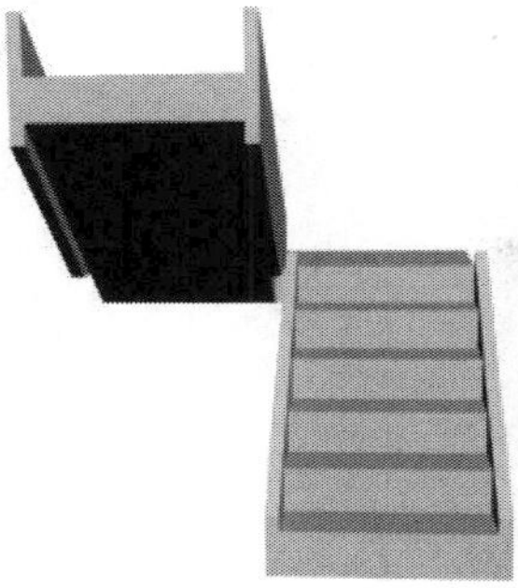

Figure 4-60 The U-type closed stairs

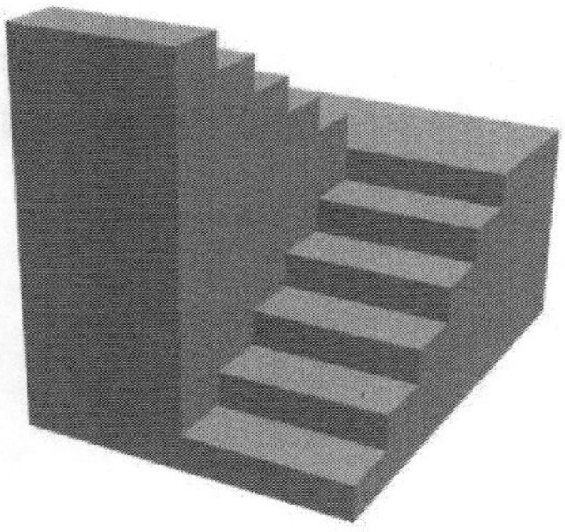

Figure 4-61 The U-type box stairs

CREATING PATCH GRIDS

The patch grids are 2D objects that are used to create 3D surfaces. To invoke the tools for creating the 3D surfaces, choose **Create > Geometry** in the **Command Panel**; the **Standard Primitives** option will be displayed in the drop-down list. Now, select the **Patch Grids** option from the drop-down list; the **Quad Patch** and **Tri Patch** tools will be displayed in the **Object Type** rollout. In this section, you will learn to create the path grids using these tools.

Creating a Quad Patch

Menu bar:	Create > Patch Grids > Quad Patch
Command Panel:	Create > Geometry > Patch Grids > Object Type rollout > Quad Patch

You can create a quad patch using the **Quad Patch** tool. It has 36 visible rectangular faces. Each rectangular face is divided into two triangular faces, therefore, in all it has 72 triangular faces. To create a quad patch, activate the Top viewport and invoke the **Quad Patch** tool from the **Object Type** rollout; the **Name and Color**, **Keyboard Entry**, and **Parameters** rollouts will be displayed, as shown in Figure 4-62.

Creating the Quad Patch Dynamically

To create the quad patch dynamically, press and hold the left mouse button on the upper left side of the Top viewport and drag the cursor to the lower right side of the viewport to specify the length and width of the patch. Release the left mouse button; the quad patch will be created in all viewports, refer to Figures 4-63 and 4-64.

Note

*The **Keyboard Entry** rollout is used to create the quad patch and tri patch by entering the parameters using the keyboard. The method of creating these patch grids using this rollout is the same as discussed earlier.*

To view the faces in the quad patch or the tri patch, you need to convert them into editable mesh about which you will learn in the later chapters.

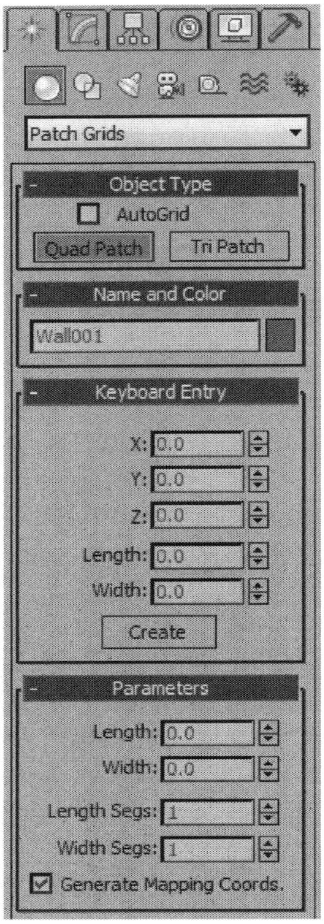

Figure 4-62 Various rollouts to create a quad patch

Figure 4-63 The quad patch

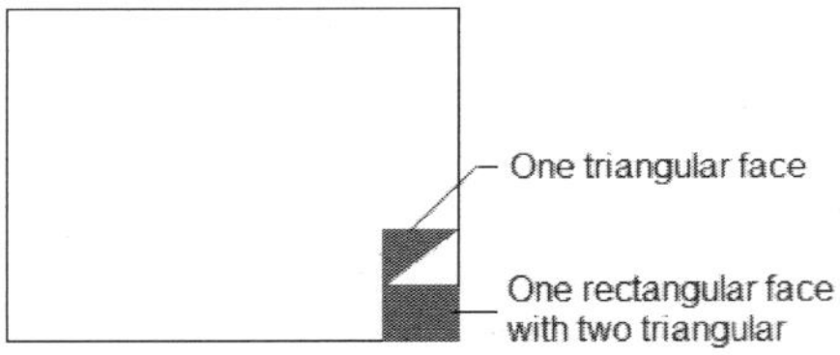

Figure 4-64 The quad patch with rectangular and triangular faces in the Top viewport

The **Parameters** rollout is used to modify the quad patch is discussed next.

Parameters Rollout

This rollout is used to modify the quad patch. To do so, select the quad patch and choose the **Modify** tab in the **Command Panel**; the **Parameters** rollout will be displayed. Set the new values in the **Length** and **Width** spinners to modify the length and width. Similarly, enter a value in the **Length Segs** spinner to specify the number of segments along the length of the patch. And, enter a value in the **Width Segs** spinner to specify the number of segments along the width of the patch.

Note

*The value 1 in the **Length Segs** and **Width Segs** spinners specifies 36 rectangular faces in a quad patch. If you increase the number of segments, then the number of faces will also be increased accordingly.*

Creating a Tri Patch

Menu bar:	Create > Patch Grids > Tri Patch
Command Panel:	Create > Geometry > Patch Grids > Object Type rollout > Tri Patch

The object created using the **Tri Patch** tool is very similar to the object created using the **Quad Patch** tool. It also has 72 visible triangular faces. To create a tri patch, activate the Top viewport and invoke the **Tri Patch** tool from the **Object Type** rollout; the **Name and Color**, **Keyboard Entry**, and **Parameters** rollouts will be displayed, as shown in Figure 4-65.

Next, press and hold the left mouse button on the upper left side of the viewport, drag the cursor to the lower right side of the viewport to specify the length and width of the patch, and release the left mouse button; the tri patch will be created in all viewports, refer to Figures 4-66 and 4-67.

The **Parameters** rollout is used to modify the tri patch is discussed next.

Parameters Rollout

This rollout is used to modify the tri patch. To do so, select the tri patch and choose the **Modify** tab in the **Command Panel**; the **Parameters** rollout will be displayed. Set the new values in the **Length** and **Width** spinners to modify the length and width of the tri patch, respectively.

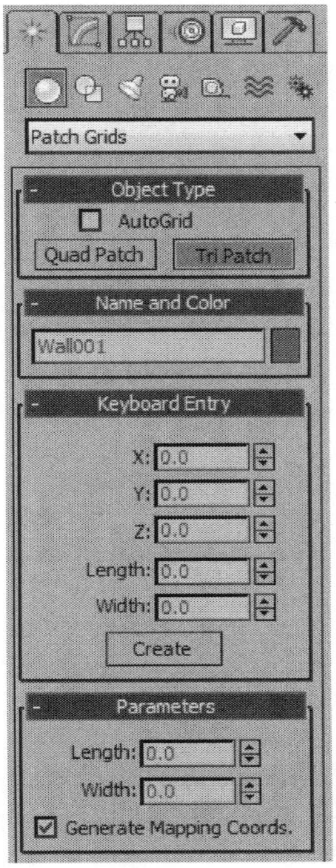

***Figure 4-65** Various rollouts to create a tri patch*

***Figure 4-66** The tri patch*

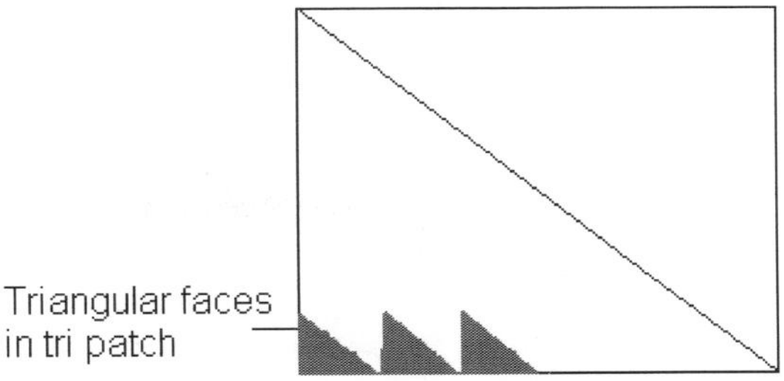

***Figure 4-67** The tri patch with triangular faces in the Top viewport*

Note

You cannot increase the number of segments in a tri patch.

Tutorial 1

In this tutorial, you will create a nature scene, as shown in Figure 4-68, using the AEC extended objects and the standard primitives. **(Expected time: 15 min)**

The following steps are required to complete this tutorial:

a. Set the project folder.
b. Create the floor.
c. Create railings.
d. Create trees.
e. Change the background color at rendering.
f. Render the scene for the final output.
g. Save the file.

Figure 4-68 *Model for Tutorial 1*

Setting the Project Folder

Before starting a new file, it is recommended that you set the project folder.

1. Set the project folder with the name *c04_tut1* in the *3dsmax* folder as discussed in Tutorial 1 of Chapter 2.

Creating the Floor

Start Autodesk 3ds Max and reset it as discussed in the earlier chapters; a new screen with default settings is displayed. Next, you need to use the **Plane** tool from **Standard Primitives** to create the floor of the scene.

1. Activate the Top viewport. Choose **Create > Geometry** in the **Command Panel**; the **Standard Primitives** option is displayed in the drop-down list. Invoke the **Plane** tool from the **Object Type** rollout.

2. In the **Keyboard Entry** rollout, set the values as given below:

   Length: **1485.0**   Width: **1605.15**

3. Choose the **Create** button in the **Keyboard Entry** rollout; a plane is displayed in all viewports. Now, invoke the **Zoom Extents All** tool or press the Z key to display the entire plane in the viewports.

4. In the **Name and Color** rollout, enter **floor** and press ENTER; the plane is named as *floor*.

5. Use the color swatch to modify the color of the *floor* to green.

6. Activate the Perspective viewport and set the view using the **Zoom** and **Orbit** tools, as shown in Figure 4-69.

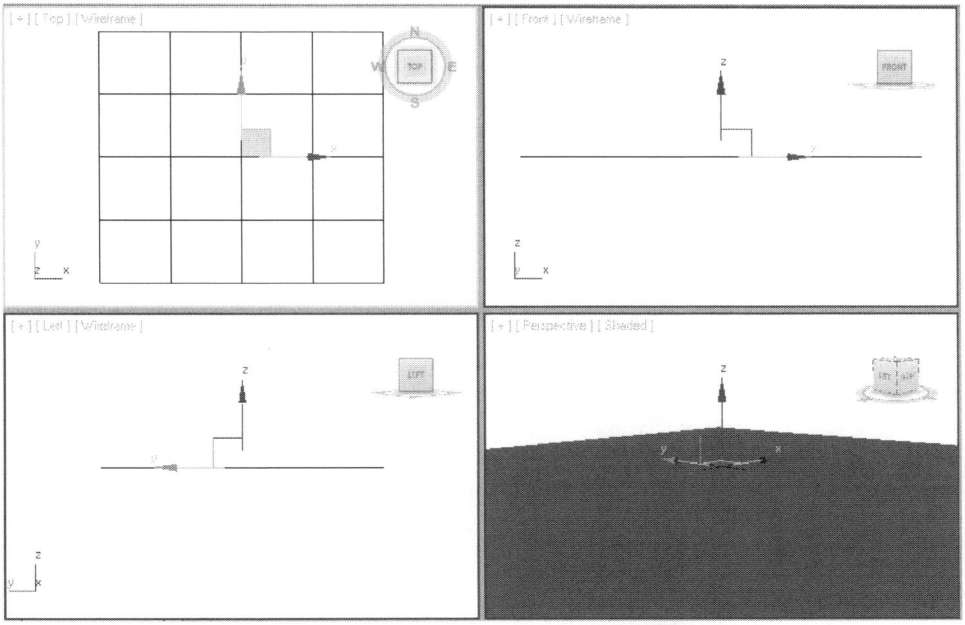

***Figure 4-69** The floor after using the **Zoom** and **Orbit** tools*

Creating Railings

You need to use the **Railing** tool from **AEC Extended** to create railings around the *floor*.

1. Choose **Create > Geometry** in the **Command Panel**; a drop-down list is displayed below the **Geometry** button. Select the **AEC Extended** option from the drop-down list and then invoke the **Railing** tool from the **Object Type** rollout.

2. Activate the Top viewport and invoke the **Maximize Viewport Toggle** tool or press the ALT+W keys to maximize the Top viewport.

3. Move the cursor to the upper left corner of the *floor*, press and hold the left mouse button, and drag the cursor to the upper right corner of the *floor* to specify the length of the railing. Release the left mouse button to set the length, and then move the cursor up to specify the height of the railing. Click on the screen; a railing is created. Next, invoke the **Maximize Viewport Toggle** tool; the railing is displayed in all viewports.

4. In the **Name and Color** rollout, enter **railing01** and press ENTER.

5. Use the color swatch to modify the color of the *railing01* and enter the values given below:

   Red: **177** Green: **88** Blue: **26**

6. Make sure the *railing01* is still selected. Choose the **Modify** tab in the **Command Panel**; the **Railing**, **Posts**, and **Fencing** rollouts are displayed.

7. In the **Railing** rollout, set the values as given below:

   Length: **1400.0**

   Top Rail area
   Profile: **Round** Depth: **10.0**
   Width: **3.0** Height: **100.0**

   Lower Rail(s) area
   Profile: **Round** Depth: **4.0**
   Width: **3.0**

8. Choose the **Lower Rail Spacing** button in the **Lower Rail(s)** area; the **Lower Rail Spacing** dialog box is displayed. Make sure the **Count** check box is selected. Next, set the value **3** in the spinner on the right side of the **Count** check box and choose the **Close** button; the railing is displayed in all viewports, as shown in Figure 4-70.

9. In the **Posts** rollout, set the values as given below:

   Profile: **Round** Depth: **7.0**
   Width: **5.0** Extension: **2.0**

10. Choose the **Post Spacing** button in the **Post** rollout; the **Post Spacing** dialog box is displayed. Make sure the **Count** check box is selected. Then, set the value **4** in the spinner on the right side of the **Count** check box and choose the **Close** button.

11. In the **Fencing** rollout, select **(none)** from the **Type** drop-down list.

Note
If you want to add fencing in the railing, then select the type of fencing from the ***Type*** *drop-down list and set the parameters in the respective area.*

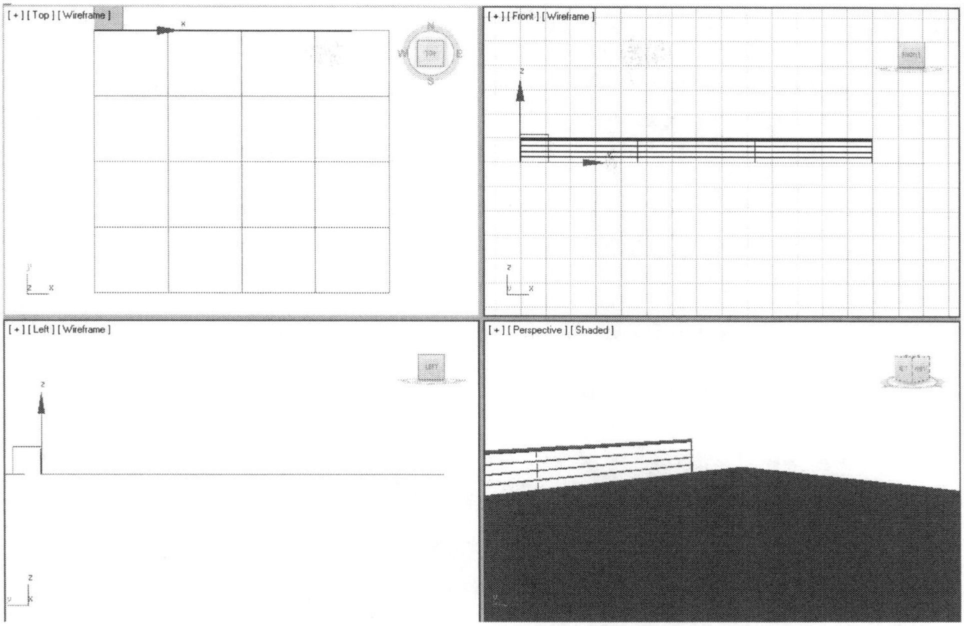

Figure 4-70 *The railing01 displayed in all viewports*

12. Make sure the *railing01* is selected in the Top viewport. Now, invoke the **Select and Move** tool from the **Main Toolbar** and align the railing manually, as shown in Figure 4-71.

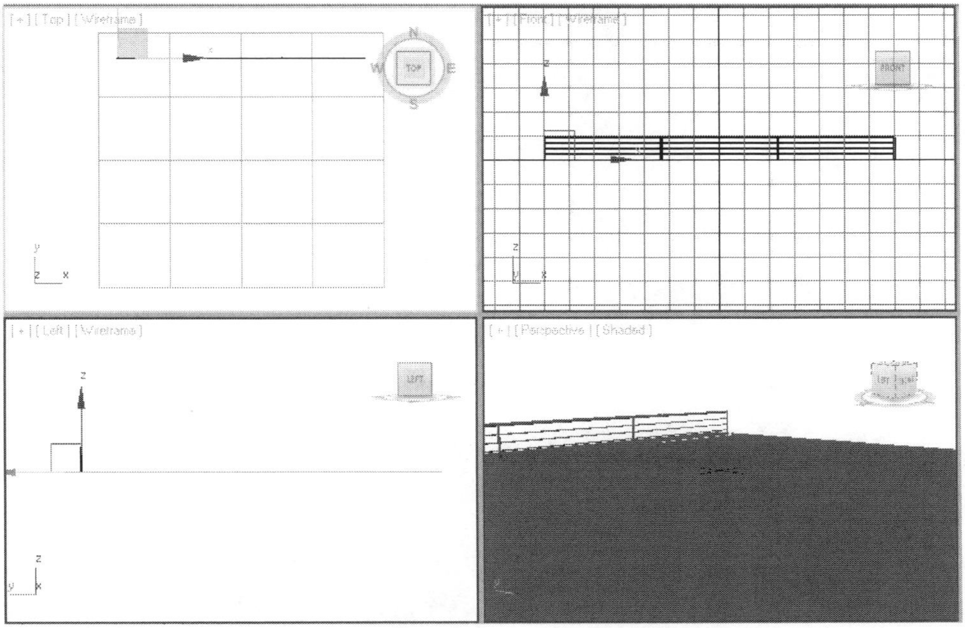

Figure 4-71 *The railing01 in all viewports after aligning it in the Top viewport*

Next, you need to create one more railing.

13. Activate the Top viewport and invoke the **Railing** tool. Create one more railing at the right angle of the *railing01* using the same method as discussed for creating the *railing01*, refer to Figure 4-72.

Note
*When you create another railing, all dimensions of the railing01, except the **Length** and **Height**, will be taken automatically.*

14. In the **Name and Color** rollout, enter **railing02** and press ENTER.

15. Assign the same color to the *railing02* as was assigned to the *railing01*.

16. Make sure the *railing02* is selected. Next, choose the **Modify** tab in the **Command Panel**; the **Railing**, **Post**, and **Fencing** rollouts are displayed.

17. In the **Railing** rollout, set the values as given next:

    Length: **600.0**

    Top Rail area
    Height: **100.0**

18. Invoke the **Select and Move** and **Select and Rotate** tools and align the *railing02* in all viewports, as shown in Figure 4-72.

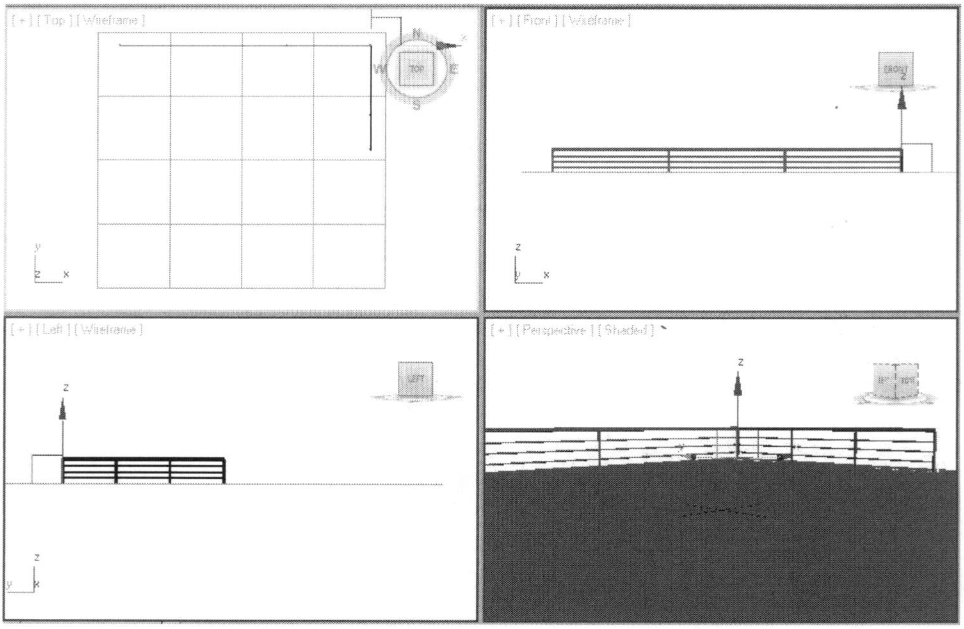

***Figure 4-72** The railing02 in all viewports after alignment*

Next, you need to create another railing.

19. Invoke the **Railing** tool and activate the Top viewport. Create another railing starting from the endpoint of *railing02* using the same method as discussed earlier.

20. In the **Name and Color** rollout, enter **railing03** and press ENTER; the railing is named as *railing03*.

21. Assign the same color to the *railing03* as was assigned to the *railing01*.

22. Make sure the *railing03* is selected. Choose the **Modify** tab in the **Command Panel**; the **Railing**, **Posts**, and **Fencing** rollouts are displayed.

23. In the **Railing** rollout, set the values as given below:

    Length: **600.0**
    Top Rail area
    Height: **100.0**

24. Invoke the **Select and Move** tool and make sure the *railing03* is aligned in all viewports, as shown in Figure 4-73.

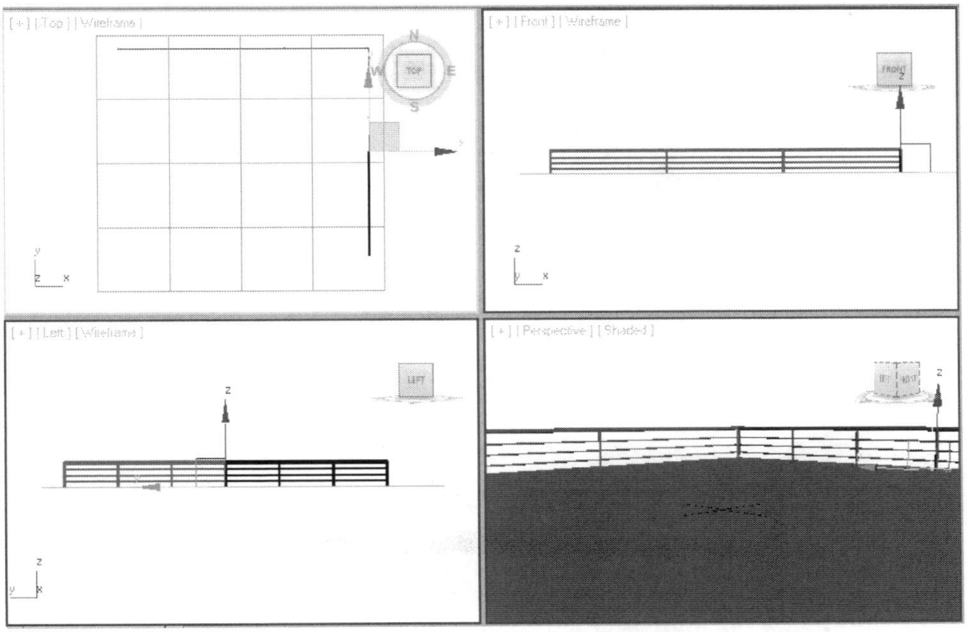

Figure 4-73 *The railing03 starting from the endpoint of railing02 after alignment*

25. Activate the Top viewport and select the *railing03*. Invoke the **Select and Rotate** tool, move the cursor over the Z-axis and rotate it to -45 degrees in the clockwise direction, as shown in Figure 4-74.

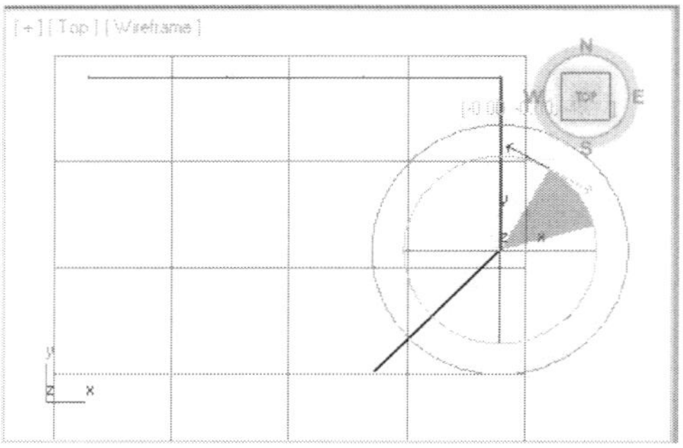

Figure 4-74 *The railing03 rotated in the Top viewport*

Note

While rotating the railing03, invoke the ***Angle Snap Toggle*** *tool from the* ***Main Toolbar*** *to measure the angle of rotation in increments.*

Now, you need to create the fourth railing.

26. Activate the Top viewport and create another railing starting from the endpoint of *railing03*.

27. In the **Name and Color** rollout, enter **railing04** and press ENTER.

28. Assign the same color to the *railing04* as was assigned to the *railing01*.

29. Make sure the *railing04* is selected. Choose the **Modify** tab in the **Command Panel**; the **Railing**, **Post**, and **Fencing** rollouts are displayed.

30. In the **Railing** rollout, set the values as given below:

    Length: **310.0**

    Top Rail area
    Height: **100.0**

31. Make sure the *railing04* is aligned in all viewports, as shown in Figure 4-75.

32. Next, invoke the **Select By Name** tool; the **Select From Scene** dialog box is displayed. Now, select the *railing02*, *railing03*, and *railing04* and choose the **OK** button; the railings are selected in the viewports.

33. Invoke the **Mirror** tool from the **Main Toolbar**; the **Mirror: Screen Coordinates** dialog box is displayed. In the **Mirror Axis** area of this dialog box, select the **X** radio button. In the **Offset** spinner, set the value **-990**. In the **Clone Selection** area, select the **Copy** radio button and choose the **OK** button; one copy of all railings created earlier is displayed and they are automatically named as *railing005*, *railing006*, and *railing007*, refer to Figure 4-76.

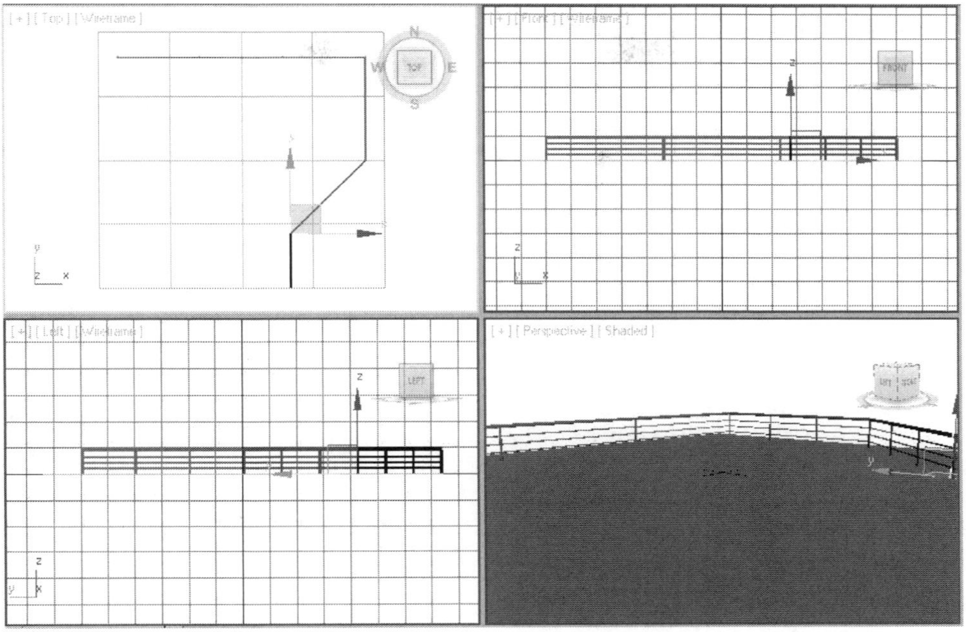

Figure 4-75 *The railing04 created from the endpoint of railing03 and aligned in all viewports*

34. Adjust the view in the Perspective viewport using the tools in the viewport navigation controls, refer to Figure 4-76.

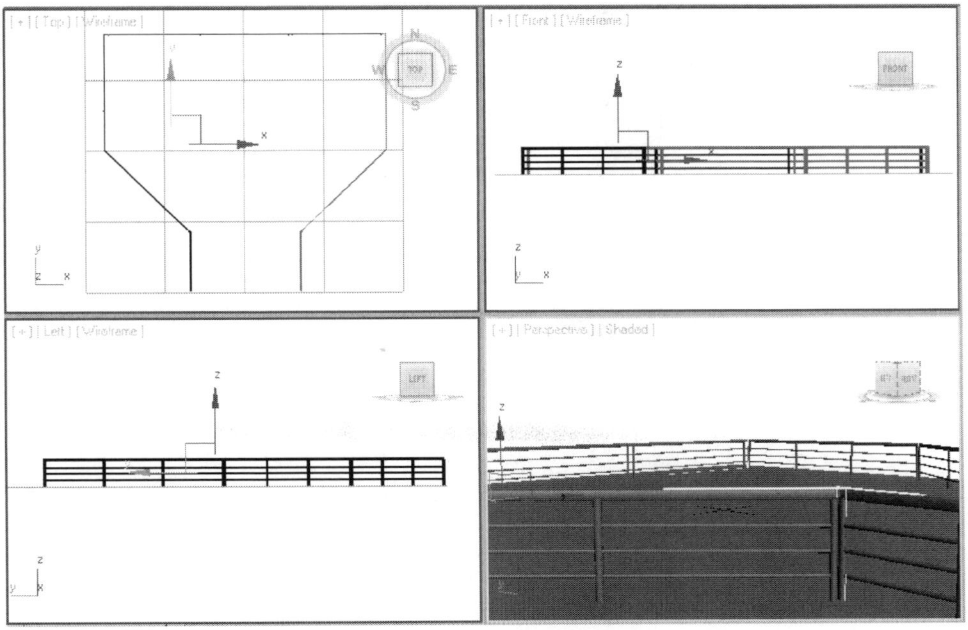

Figure 4-76 *The railings displayed in all viewports*

Creating Trees

Next, you need to use the **Foliage** tool from **AEC Extended** to create the trees.

1. Choose **Create > Geometry** in the **Command Panel**; a drop-down list is displayed below the **Geometry** button. Select the **AEC Extended** option from the drop-down list and then invoke the **Foliage** tool from the **Object Type** rollout.

2. Activate the Top viewport. In the **Favorite Plants** rollout, select the **Generic Palm** tree and double-click on it; the tree is created and displayed in all viewports.

Note

*If the **Generic Palm** tree is not displayed in the palette of the **Favorite Plants** rollout, then choose the **Plant Library** button on the bottom of the rollout; the **Configure Palette** dialog box is displayed. Select the **Generic Palm** tree and double-click on it; the **yes** option is displayed in the **Fav.** row indicating that the tree will be available in the palette. Next, choose the **OK** button.*

3. In the **Name and Color** rollout, enter **tree01** and press ENTER; the tree is named as *tree01*.

4. Make sure the *tree01* is still selected. Choose the **Modify** tab in the **Command Panel**; the **Parameters** rollout is displayed.

5. In the **Parameters** rollout, set the following parameters:

   Height: **300.0**

   Use the default values for other options.

6. In the Top viewport, invoke the **Select and Move** tool and move the *tree01* toward the *railing01* in all viewports, as shown in Figure 4-77.

7. Next, create multiple copies of the *tree01* in the Top viewport and align them using the **Select and Move** tool, as shown in Figure 4-78.

Changing the Background Color in the Final Output

1. Change the background color to light blue for the final output as discussed in Tutorial 1 of Chapter 2, using the following parameters:

   Red: **145** Green: **241** Blue: **244**

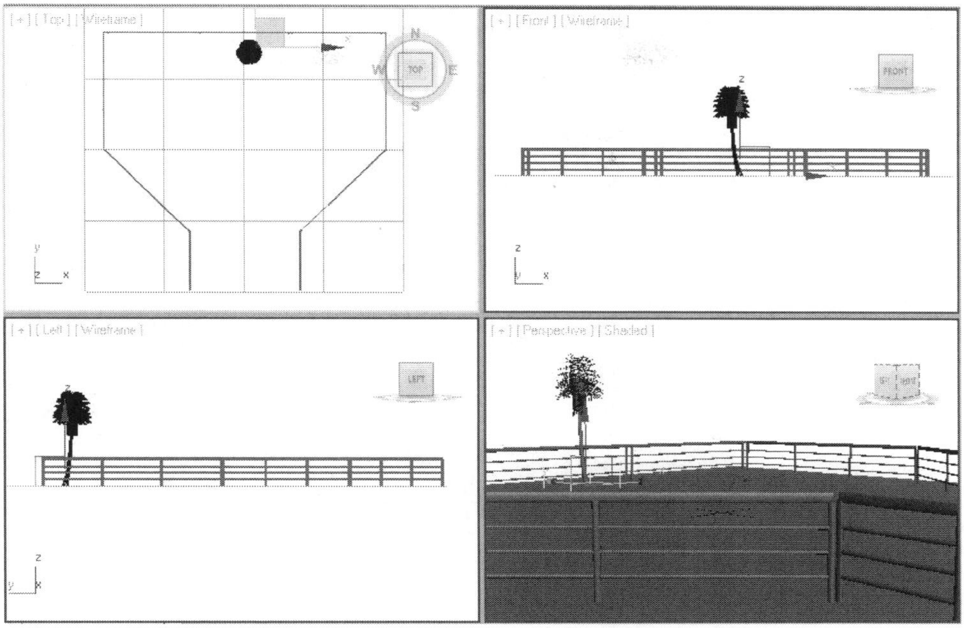

Figure 4-77 Alignment of the tree01 in all viewports

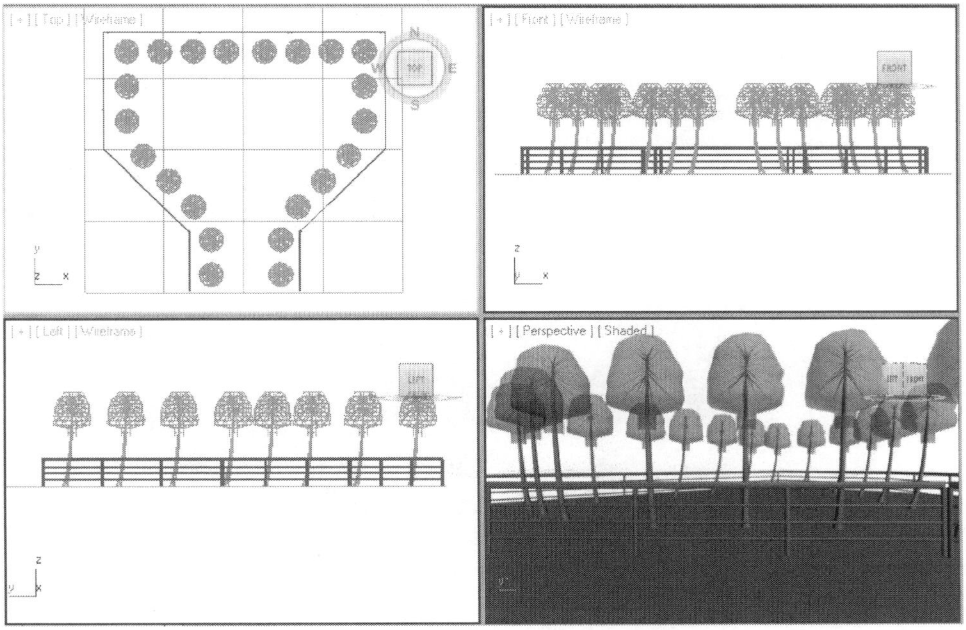

Figure 4-78 Multiple copies of tree01 created and aligned in all viewports

Rendering the Scene for the Final Output

1. Activate the Perspective viewport.

2. Invoke the **Render Production** tool from the **Main Toolbar**; the **Perspective, frame 0, Display Gamma:2.2, RGBA Color16 Bits/Channel (1:1)** dialog box is displayed, showing the final output of the scene at one frame, refer to Figure 4-79.

Figure 4-79 The final output at rendering

3. Close this window.

   You can view the final rendered image of this model by downloading the file *c04_3dsmax_2012_render.zip* from *http://www.cadcim.com*. The path of the file is as follows:

   Textbooks > Animation and Visual Effects > 3ds Max > Autodesk 3ds Max 2012: A Comprehensive Guide

Saving the File

1. Save the file with the name *c04tut1.max* as discussed in earlier chapters. The location of this file is given below:

   \Documents\3dsmax\c04_tut1\scenes

Tutorial 2

In this tutorial, you will create a scene, as shown in Figure 4-80, using the AEC extended objects and the standard primitives. **(Expected time: 15 min)**

Figure 4-80 Model for Tutorial 2

The following steps are required to complete this tutorial:

a. Set the project folder.
b. Create the floor.
c. Create railings.
d. Create the room.
e. Create the window.
f. Create the door.
g. Create trees.
h. Change the background color at rendering.
i. Render the scene for the final output.
j. Save the file.

Setting the Project Folder

Before starting a new file, it is recommended that you set the project folder.

1. Set the project folder with the name *c04_tut2* in the *3dsmax* folder as discussed in Tutorial 1 of Chapter 2.

Creating the Floor

Start Autodesk 3ds Max and reset it as described earlier; a new screen with default settings is displayed. Next, you need to use the **Plane** tool from **Standard Primitives** to create the floor of the scene.

1. Activate the Top viewport and choose **Create > Geometry** in the **Command Panel**; the **Standard Primitives** option is displayed in the drop-down list. Invoke the **Plane** tool from the **Object Type** rollout.

2. In the **Keyboard Entry** rollout, set the values as given below:

   Length: **1100.0** Width: **1200.0**

3. Choose the **Create** button from the **Keyboard Entry** rollout; a plane is created in all viewports. Invoke the **Zoom Extents All** tool to display the entire plane in all viewports.

4. In the **Name and Color** rollout, enter **floor** and press ENTER; the plane is named as *floor*.

5. Modify the color of the floor by entering the values as given below:

   Red: **61** Green: **135** Blue: **6**

6. Activate the Perspective viewport and press the G key to hide grids in it. Also, set the view using the **Zoom** and **Orbit** tools, as shown in Figure 4-81.

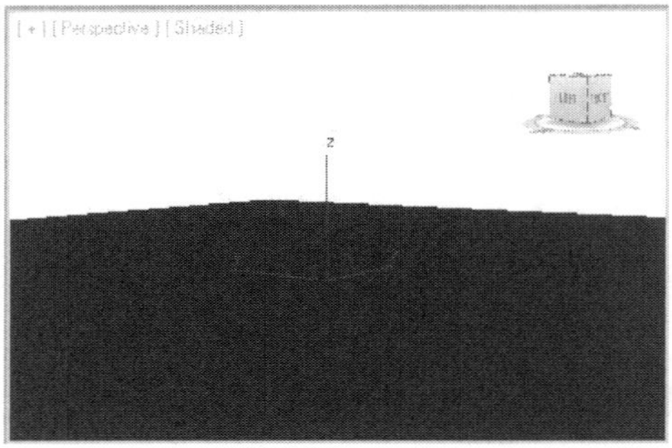

Figure 4-81 *The floor in the Perspective viewport*

Creating Railings

Next, you need to use the **Railing** tool from **AEC Extended** to create railings around the *floor*.

1. Activate the Top viewport and create a railing starting from the upper left corner of the *floor* to its upper right corner.

2. In the **Name and Color** rollout, enter **railing01** and press ENTER.

3. Use the color swatch and change the color of the *railing01* by entering the values as given below:

   Red: **177** Green: **88** Blue: **27**

4. Make sure the *railing01* is still selected. Choose the **Modify** tab in the **Command Panel**; the **Railing**, **Post**, and **Fencing** rollouts are displayed.

5. In the **Railing** rollout, set the values as given below:

   Length: **1200.0**

   Top Rail area
   Profile: **Round** Depth: **15.0**
   Width: **13.0** Height: **100.0**

   Lower Rail(s) area
   Profile: **Round** Depth: **7.0** Width: **7.0**

6. Choose the **Lower Rail Spacing** button in the **Lower Rail(s)** area; the **Lower Rail Spacing** dialog box is displayed. Select the **Count** check box and set the value **3** in the spinner on the right side of the **Count** check box and choose the **Close** button.

7. In the **Posts** rollout, set the values as follows:

   Profile: **Round** Depth: **10.0**
   Width: **5.0** Extension: **0.0**

   Choose the **Post Spacing** button in the **Post** rollout; the **Post Spacing** dialog box is displayed. Select the **Count** check box and set **5** in the spinner on the right of the **Count** check box and choose the **Close** button.

8. In the **Fencing** rollout, set the following parameter:

   Type: **(none)**

9. Invoke the **Select and Move** tool and align the *railing01* in all viewports, as shown in Figure 4-82.

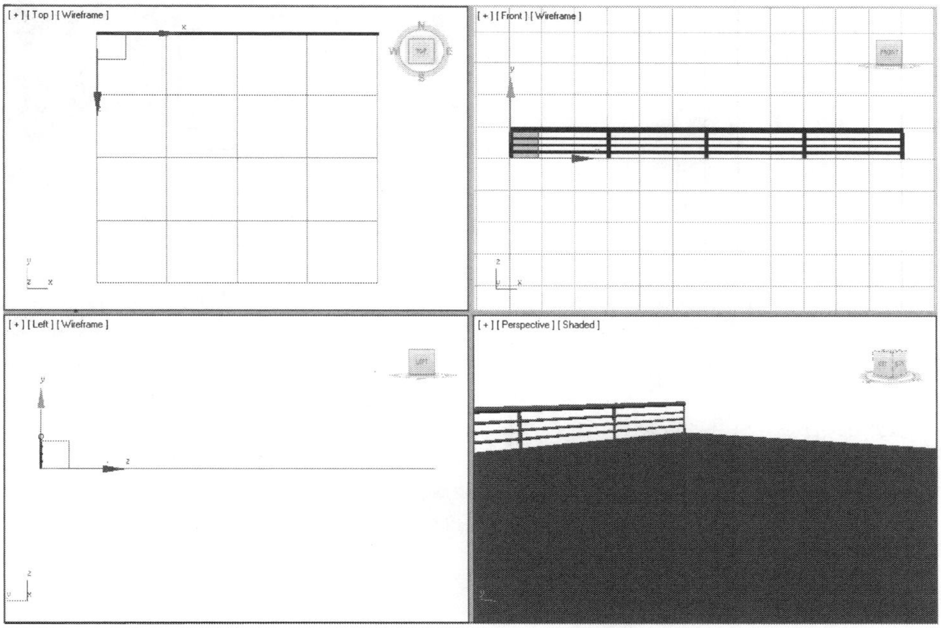

Figure 4-82 *The railing01 in all viewports after alignment*

10. Next, create the other railings to surround the *floor* using the same dimensions except for the length. Also, activate the Perspective viewport and set the view using the **Pan**, **Zoom**, and **Orbit** tools, as shown in Figure 4-83.

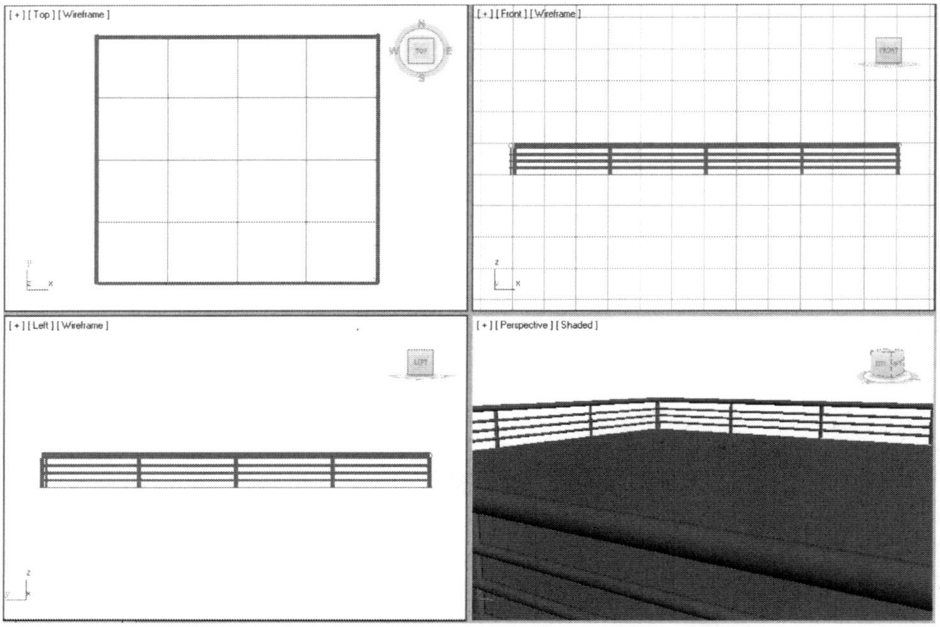

Figure 4-83 *The railings displayed in all viewports*

Creating the Room

You need to use the **Wall** tool from **AEC Extended** to create the walls of the room.

1. Activate the Top viewport. Choose **Create > Geometry** in the **Command Panel**; a drop-down list is displayed below the **Geometry** button. Select the **AEC Extended** option from the drop-down list and then invoke the **Wall** tool from the **Object Type** rollout.

2. In the **Parameters** rollout of the wall, set the values as given below:

   Width: **5.0** Height: **230.0**

3. Next, click on the upper left side of the Top viewport to specify the starting point of the wall, drag the cursor on the right side to define the length, and then click on the screen; a wall segment is created. Then, create another segment of the wall in continuation at the right angle of the first segment. Repeat the same procedure to create the wall in a rectangular shape, refer to Figure 4-84. Now, click on the starting point of the first wall segment; the **Weld Point?** message box is displayed. Choose the **Yes** button to weld the end points of the wall. Next, right-click to end the creation of the wall.

Note

*You can modify the wall using the tools in the **Select and Scale** flyout in the **Main Toolbar**.*

4. In the **Name and Color** rollout, enter **wall** and press the ENTER key.

5. Use the color swatch and change the color of the *wall* by entering the values given below:

   Red: **248** Green: **231** Blue: **120**

6. Invoke the **Select and Move** tool and align the *wall* in all viewports, as shown in Figure 4-84.

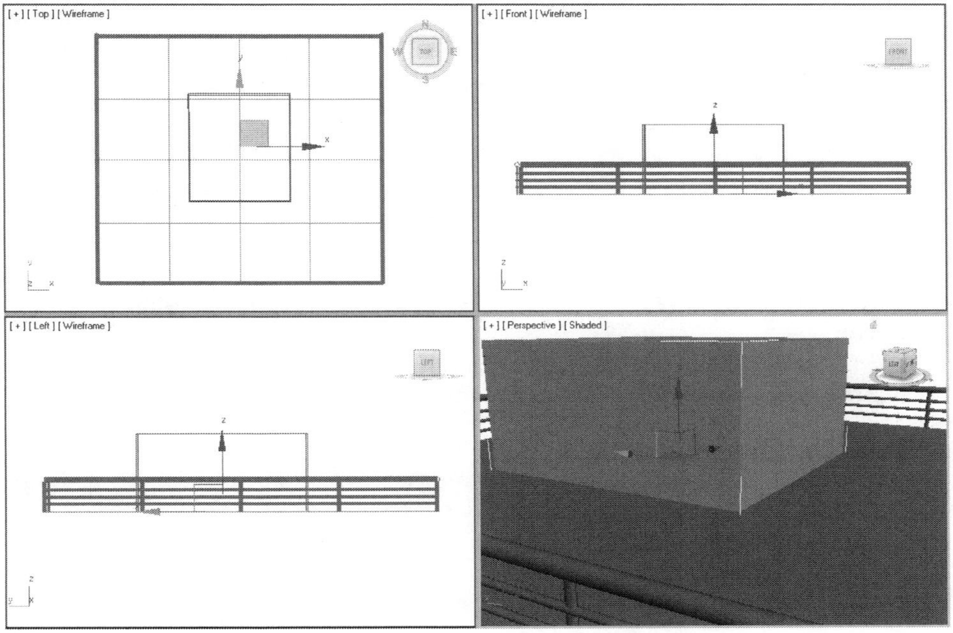

Figure 4-84 *The wall displayed in all viewports*

7. Next, select **Standard Primitives** from the drop-down list below the **Geometry** button. Invoke the **Box** tool from the **Object Type** rollout to create the roof of the *wall*.

8. Activate the Top viewport and create a box.

9. In the **Name and Color** rollout, enter **roof** and press the ENTER key.

10. Change the color of the *roof* by entering the values as given below:

    Red: **143** Green: **225** Blue: **87**

11. In the **Parameters** rollout, set the values in the **Length** and **Width** spinners to cover the upper portion of the wall, refer to Figure 4-85. Set the value **5.0** in the **Height** spinner.

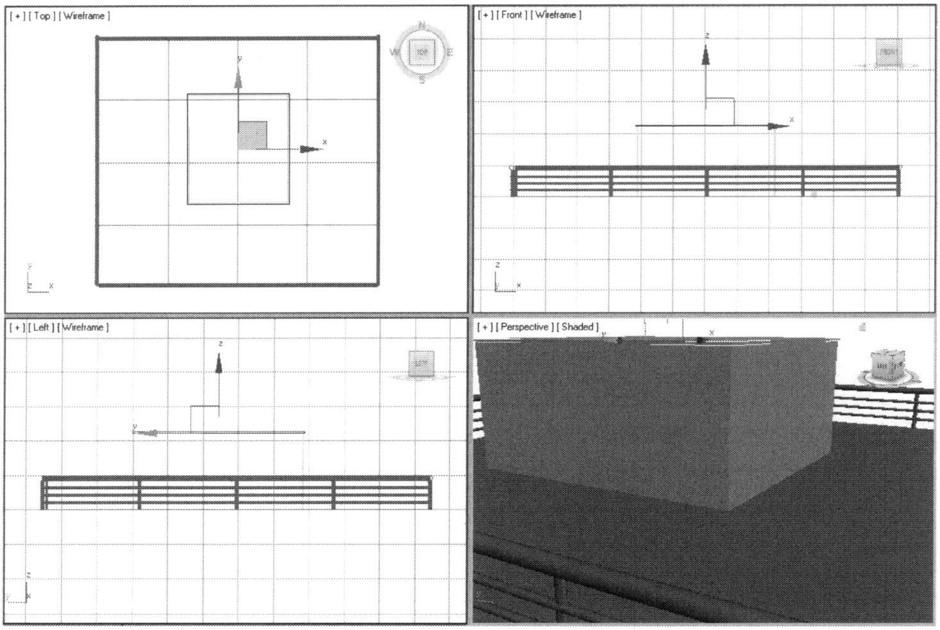

Figure 4-85 *The roof of the wall in all viewports after alignment*

12. Invoke the **Select and Move** tool and align the *roof* at the top of the wall in all viewports, refer to Figure 4-85.

13. Activate the Front viewport and make sure the *roof* is selected.

14. Invoke the **Mirror** tool from the **Main Toolbar**; the **Mirror: Screen Coordinates** dialog box is displayed. In the **Mirror Axis** area of this dialog box, select the **Y** radio button. In the **Offset** spinner, set the value **0**. In the **Clone Selection** area, select the **Copy** radio button and choose the **OK** button; the *roof001* is displayed at the top of the *roof*.

15. In the **Name and Color** rollout, modify the name as *roof fencing*.

16. Use the color swatch to change the color of the *roof fencing* by entering the values as given below:

    Red: **243** Green: **93** Blue: **47**

    Make sure the *roof fencing* is still selected.

17. Invoke the **Select and Uniform Scale** tool from the **Main Toolbar** and right-click on it; the **Scale Transform Type-In** dialog box is displayed. Now, in the **Offset: Screen** area, set the value **105** and press ENTER; the *roof fencing* is scaled, as shown in Figure 4-86. Close this dialog box.

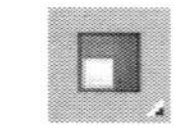

    Next, you need to create fencing for the corners of the *wall*.

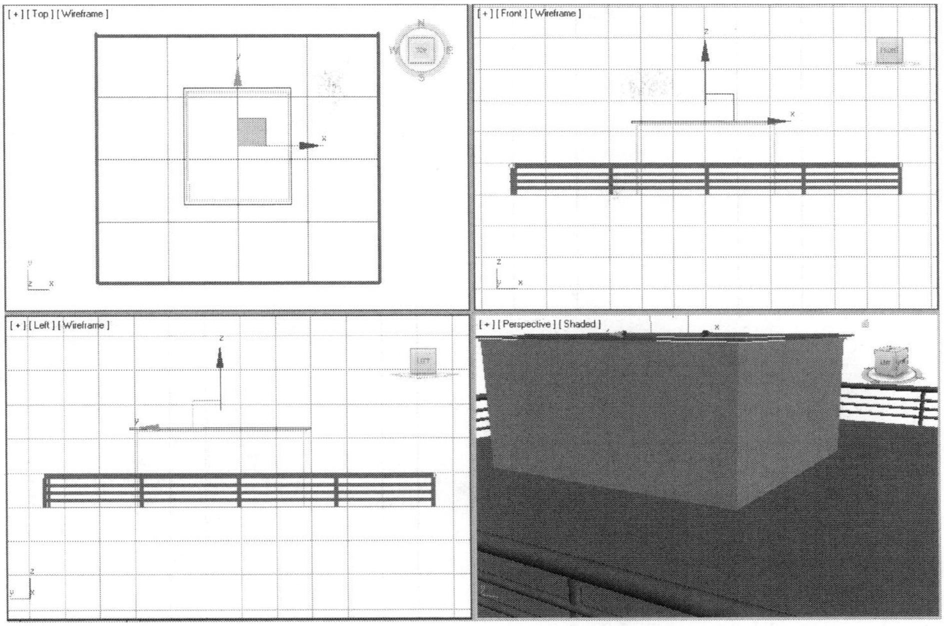

Figure 4-86 *The roof fencing after scaling in the Front viewport*

18. Activate the Top viewport and invoke the **Box** tool. In the **Keyboard Entry** rollout, set the values as given below:

X: **-300** Length: **6.0** Width: **1.0** Height: **290.207**

Note

You may need to adjust the height of the box, if you have modified the size of the wall earlier.

19. Next, choose the **Create** button; a box is displayed in all viewports.

20. In the **Name and Color** rollout, enter **fc01** and press ENTER; the box is named as *fc01*.

21. Assign the same color to the *fc01* that was assigned to the *roof fencing*.

22. Invoke the **Maximize Viewport Toggle** tool to maximize the Top viewport.

23. Invoke the **Zoom Region** tool and drag a selection box around the *roof fencing* and the lower left corner of the wall to zoom in the selected portion of the Top viewport. Next, invoke the **Select and Move** tool and align the *fc01* with the *wall*, as shown in Figure 4-87.

24. Next, make sure the *fc01* is selected in the Top viewport and invoke the **Select and Rotate** tool. Now, press and hold the SHIFT key, move the cursor over the Z-axis, and rotate it until the value in the **Z** spinner in the coordinate display becomes **90**; the copy of *fc01* gets rotated and it is automatically named as *fc002*.

25. Invoke the **Select and Move** tool and align the *fc002* with the *wall*, as shown in Figure 4-88.

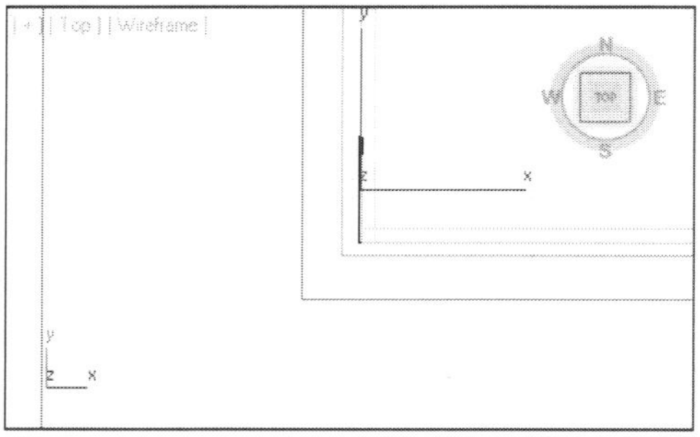

Figure 4-87 *The fc01 in the Top viewport after alignment*

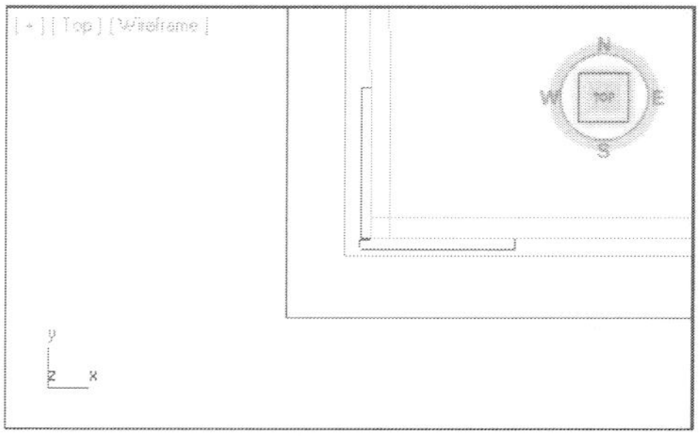

Figure 4-88 *The fc002 in the Top viewport after alignment*

26. Next, select *fc01* and *fc002* simultaneously by holding the CTRL key and group them as *fencing01*.

27. Select the *fencing01* and create three copies of it. The copies are automatically named as *fencing002*, *fencing003*, and *fencing004*. Now, align them at the corners of the *wall* using the **Select and Rotate** and **Select and Move** tools, refer to Figure 4-89. Also, you can use the **Zoom** tool to view the corners of the *wall*.

28. Next, invoke the **Maximize Viewport Toggle** tool to view the four viewports, as shown in Figure 4-89.

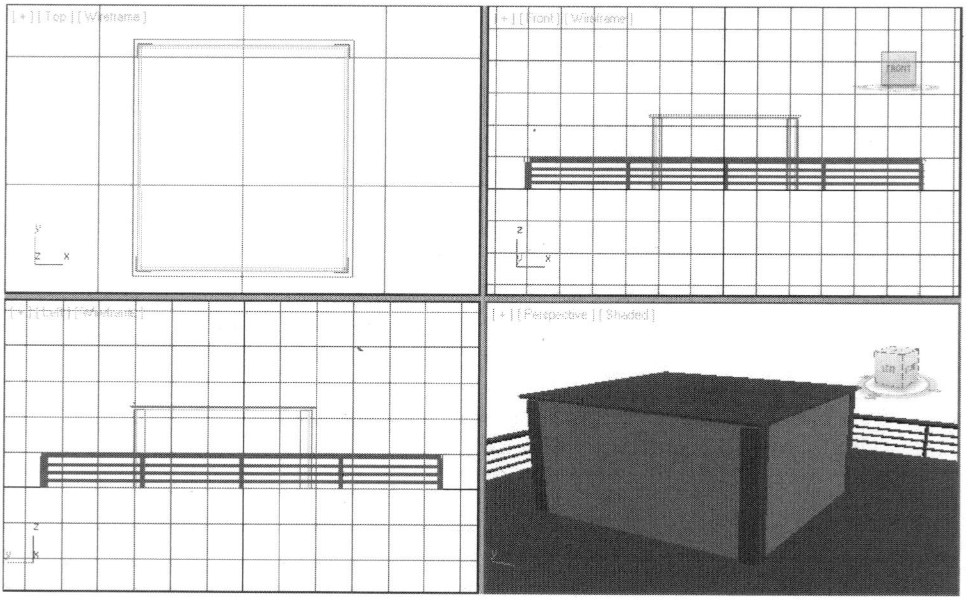

Figure 4-89 *The fencing at the four corners of the wall in all viewports*

Note
*You can also use the **Mirror** tool to create copies of fencing01.*

Creating the Window

You need to use the **Awning** tool to create a window.

1. Choose **Create > Geometry** in the **Command Panel**; a drop-down list is displayed. Select the **Windows** option from the drop-down list and then invoke the **Awning** tool from the **Object Type** rollout.

2. Activate the Top viewport. Press and hold the left mouse button on the left of the viewport, drag the cursor to the right to specify the width of the window, and then release the left mouse button. Next, move the cursor up to define the depth of the window, and then click on the screen. Now, move the cursor up to specify the height of the window and then click on the screen; an awning window is created in all viewports.

3. In the **Name and Color** rollout, enter **window** and press ENTER; the window is named as *window*.

4. Use the color swatch to change the color of the *window* by entering the following values:

   Red: **135** Green: **59** Blue: **8**

5. Make sure the *window* is still selected. Choose the **Modify** tab in the **Command Panel**; the **Parameters** rollout is displayed.

6. In the **Parameters** rollout, set the values as given below:

   Height: **148.826** Width: **106.116** Depth: **10.0**

   Frame area
   Horiz. Width: **8.94** Vert. Width: **8.94** Thickness: **0.5**

   Glazing area
   Thickness: **0.25**

   Rails and Panels area
   Width: **14.554** Panel Count: **3**

   Open Window area
   Open: **25**

   You may need to adjust the height, length, and width of the *window* according to the *wall* size in your scene.

7. Next, align the *window* on the left of the *wall* in all viewports, as shown in Figure 4-90.

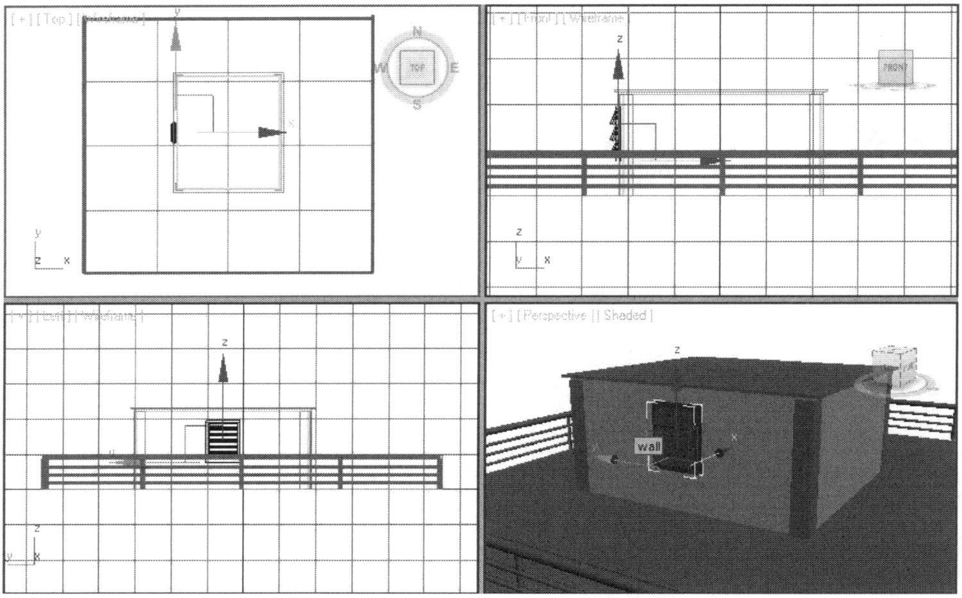

Figure 4-90 *The window in all viewports after alignment*

Creating the Foot Support

Next, you need to create a box primitive to create the foot support.

1. Activate the Top viewport and create a box.

2. In the **Parameters** rollout, set the values as given below:

   Length: **157.098** Width: **135.743** Height: **10.0**

3. In the **Name and Color** rollout, enter **foot support** and press ENTER.

4. Use the color swatch to change the color of the *foot support* by entering the following values:

   Red: **241** Green: **249** Blue: **200**

5. Align the *foot support* with the front side of the *wall* in all viewports, as shown in Figure 4-91.

Creating the Door

You need to use the **Pivot** tool from **Doors** to create a door.

1. Choose **Create > Geometry** in the **Command Panel**; a drop-down list is displayed below the **Geometry** button. Select the **Doors** option from the list and invoke the **Pivot** tool from the **Object Type** rollout.

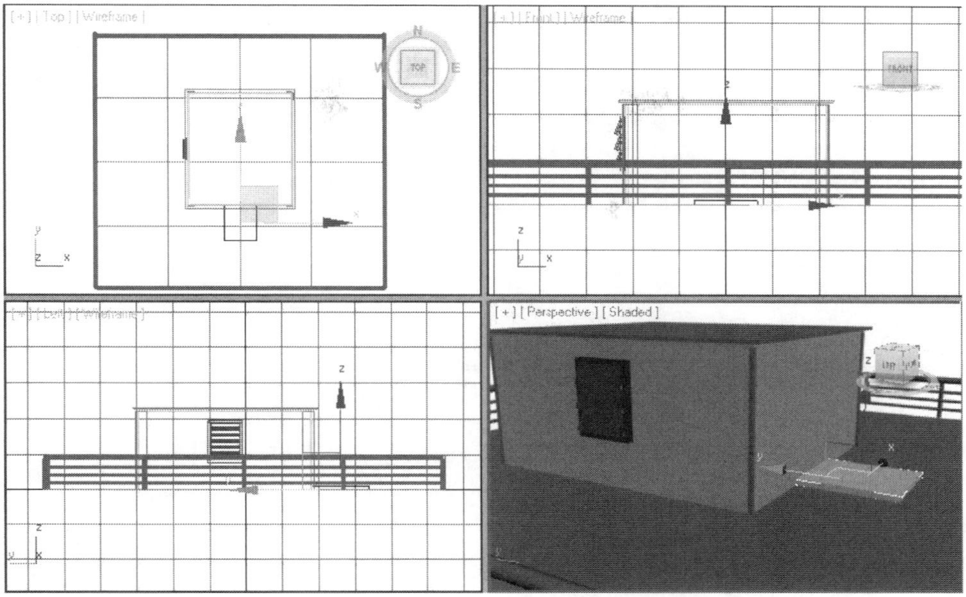

Figure 4-91 The foot support in all viewports after the alignment

2. Activate the Top viewport. Press and hold the left mouse button on the left of the viewport, drag the cursor to the right to specify the width of the door, and release the left mouse button. Next, move the cursor up to define the depth of the door, and then click on the screen. Next, move the cursor up again to specify the height of the door and click on the screen; the pivot door is created in all viewports.

3. In the **Name and Color** rollout, enter **door** as the name of the pivot door and assign it the same color that was assigned to the *window*.

4. Make sure the *door* is still selected. Choose the **Modify** tab in the **Command Panel**; the **Parameters** and **Leaf Parameters** rollouts are displayed.

5. In the **Parameters** rollout, set the values as given below:

   Height: **200.0** Width: **120.341** Depth: **12.0**
   Select the **Flip Swing** check box.
   Open: **30**

   Frame area
   Make sure the **Create Frame** check box is selected.
   Width: **2.0** Depth: **1.0** Door Offset: **0.0**

   You may need to set the height and width of the door according to the size of the *wall* in your scene.

6. In the **Leaf Parameters** rollout, set the values as given below:

   Thickness: **2.0** Stiles/Top Rail: **10.0** Bottom Rail: **20.0**
   # Panels Horiz: **3** # Panels Vert: **4** Muntin: **3.265**

   Panels area
   Select the **Beveled** radio button and set the values as given below:

   Bevel Angle: **45.0** Thickness 1: **9.46** Thickness 2: **10.0**
   Middle Thick: **3.0** Width 1: **3.0** Width 2: **3.0**

7. Next, align the *door* in all viewports, as shown in Figure 4-92.

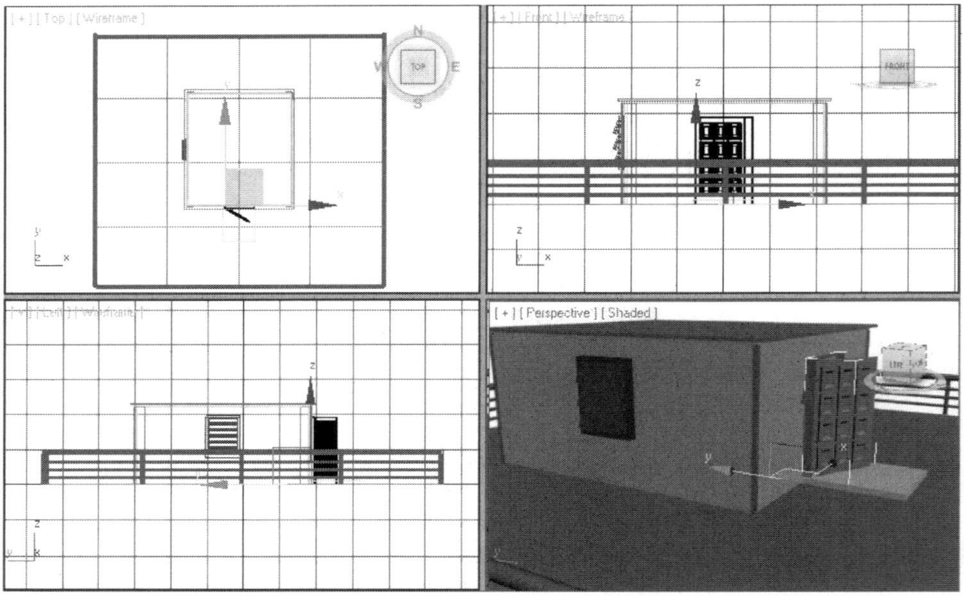

Figure 4-92 *The door in all viewports after alignment*

Note

You need to apply the boolean command on the wall to see inside the room through the window and the door. You will learn about this in the later chapters.

Creating the Trees

You need to use the **Foliage** tool from **AEC Extended** to create the trees.

1. Choose **Create > Geometry** in the **Command Panel**; a drop-down list is displayed. Select the **AEC Extended** option and invoke the **Foliage** tool from the **Object Type** rollout.

2. Activate the Top viewport. Select the **Banyan tree** from the **Favorite Plants** rollout and double-click on it; a tree is displayed in all viewports.

3. In the **Name and Color** rollout, enter **tree01** as the name of the tree.

4. Make sure the *tree01* is still selected. Choose the **Modify** tab in the **Command Panel**; the **Parameters** rollout is displayed.

5. In the **Parameters** rollout, set the values as given below:

   Height: **120.0**

   Level-of-Detail area
   Select the **Medium** radio button.

   Use the default values for other options.

6. Invoke the **Select and Move** tool and align the *tree01* in the Top viewport, as shown in Figure 4-93.

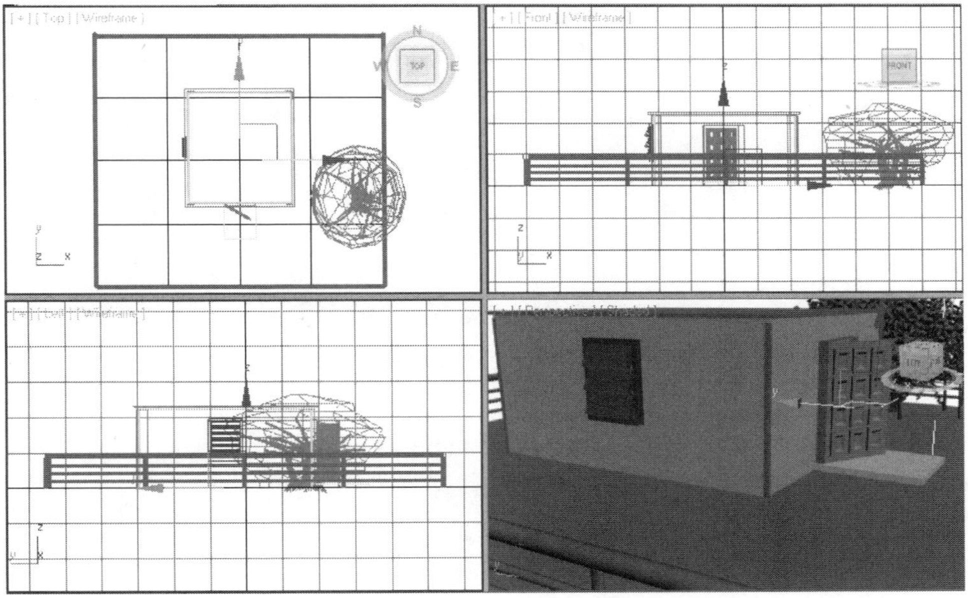

Figure 4-93 *The tree01 displayed in all viewports after alignment*

Now, you need to create another tree.

7. Activate the Top viewport. Choose the **Create** tab in the **Command Panel** and make sure the **Foliage** tool is invoked. Now, select the **American Elm** tree from the **Favorite Plants** rollout and double-click on it; the tree is displayed in all viewports.

8. In the **Name and Color** rollout, enter **tree02** as the name of the new tree created.

9. Choose the **Modify** tab in the **Command Panel**; the **Parameters** rollout is displayed.

10. In the **Parameters** rollout, set the values as given below:

    Height: **300.0**

    Use the default values for other options.

11. Invoke the **Select and Move** tool and align the *tree02* in all viewports, refer to Figure 4-94.

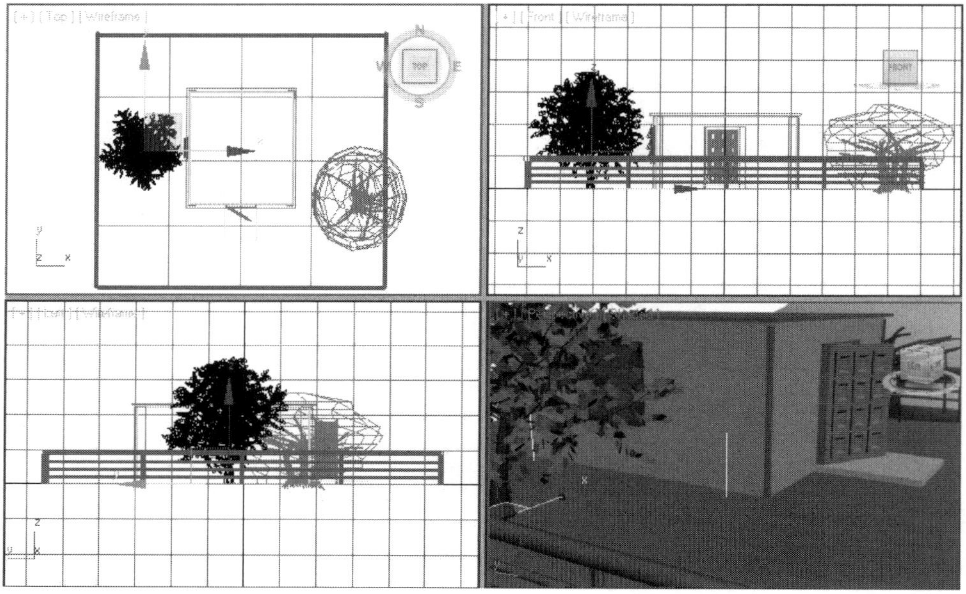

***Figure 4-94** The tree02 in all viewports after the alignment*

Changing the Background Color in the Final Output

1. Change the background color to light blue for the final output, as discussed in Tutorial 1 of Chapter 2, using the following parameters:

   Red: **145** Green: **241** Blue: **244**

Rendering the Scene for the Final Output

1. Activate the Perspective viewport.

2. Invoke the **Render Production** tool from the **Main Toolbar**; the **Perspective**, **frame 0, Display Gamma: 2.2, RGBA Color16 Bits/Channel (1:1)** window is displayed. This dialog box shows the final output of the scene at one frame, refer to Figure 4-95.

3. Close this window.

Figure 4-95 *The final output of the scene at rendering*

You can view the final rendered image of this model by downloading the file *c04_3dsmax_2012_render.zip* from *http://www.cadcim.com*. The path of the file is as follows:

Textbooks > Animation and Visual Effects > 3ds Max > Autodesk 3ds Max 2012: A Comprehensive Guide

Saving the File

1. Save the file with the name *c04tut2.max* as discussed in earlier chapters. The location of this file is given below:

   \Documents\3dsmax\c04_tut2\scenes

Self-Evaluation Test

Answer the following questions and then compare them to those given at the end of this chapter:

1. Which of the following tools is a part of the **AEC Extended** objects?

   (a) **Foliage** (b) **Railing**
   (c) **Wall** (d) All of these

2. Which of the following tools is used to create doors?

   (a) **Awning** (b) **Bifold**
   (c) **Projected** (d) **Fixed**

3. Which of the following tools is used to create windows?

    (a) **Pivot** (b) **Railing**
    (c) **Casement** (d) **Bifold**

4. Which of the following tools is used to create stairs?

    (a) **Straight Stair** (b) **UType Stair**
    (c) None of these (d) Both (a) and (b)

5. To activate the **Align** tool, you need to press the __________ keys.

6. The __________ button in the **Favorite Plants** rollout of the **Foliage** tool in **AEC Extended** is used to give information about all the default trees.

7. You can increase the number of lower rails in the railing by entering the value in the __________ spinner of the __________ dialog box.

8. The **Mirror** tool is used to clone an object about the center of the current coordinate system. (T/F)

9. You can change the default material of the plants that you create using the tools given in **Create > Geometry > AEC Extended > Foliage > Favorite Plants** rollout. (T/F)

10. The **Align** tool is used to align the current object with the target object. (T/F)

Review Questions

Answer the following questions:

1. Which of the following tools is used to create patch grids?

    (a) **Tri Patch** (b) **Tetra Patch**
    (c) Both (a) and (b) (d) None of these

2. Which of the following tools is used to create spiral stairs?

    (a) **LType Stair** (b) **Straight stair**
    (c) **UType Stair** (d) None of these

3. Which of the following rollouts is used to modify the panels of the doors?

    (a) **Name and Color** (b) **Parameters**
    (c) **Leaf Parameters** (d) **Creation Method**

4. An instance of an object is a clone in which the changes are reflected when they are made in the original object. (T/F)

5. To invoke the **Tri Patch** tool, you need to choose **Create > Geometry > AEC Extended** from the drop-down list in the **Command Panel**. (T/F)

6. You can create default trees in the viewports by invoking the **Foliage** tool from the **AEC Extended** drop-down list. (T/F)

7. You cannot increase the number of segments in a quad patch object. (T/F)

8. The object created using the **Quad Patch** tool has__________ rectangular and __________ triangular faces.

9. When you select the stair in the viewport and choose the **Modify** tab in the **Command Panel**, the __________, __________, __________, and __________ rollouts are displayed.

10. The object created using the **Tri Patch** tool has__________ triangular faces.

Exercises

Exercise 1

Start Autodesk 3ds Max 2012 and then perform the following operations:

1. Choose **Create > Geometry** in the **Command Panel**; a drop-down list will be displayed. Select the **AEC Extended** option from the drop-down list.

2. Invoke the **Foliage** tool from the **Object Type** rollout, create different default plants given in the **Favorite Plants** rollout, and then notice the difference. Also, try to modify the plants using different options given in the **Parameters** rollout.

3. Invoke the **Railing** tool and create a railing. In the **Railing**, **Posts**, and **Fencing** rollouts, try using different options and notice the difference.

4. Choose **Create > Geometry** in the **Command Panel**; a drop-down list will be displayed. Select **Doors** from the drop-down list. Create different type of doors using the **Pivot**, **Sliding**, and **BiFold** tools in the **Object Type** rollout. Choose the **Modify** tab in the **Command Panel**, and in the **Parameters** rollout of each door, set different values in the **Open** spinner to notice the difference.

5. Choose **Create > Geometry** in the **Command Panel**; a drop-down list will be displayed. Select **Windows** from the drop-down list. Create different type of windows using the tools in the **Object Type** rollout. Choose the **Modify** tab in the **Command Panel**, and in the **Parameters** rollout of window, set different values in the **Open** spinner to notice the difference.

6. Choose **Create > Geometry** in the **Command Panel**; a drop-down list will be displayed. Select **Stairs** from the drop-down list. Create different type of stairs using the tools in the **Object Type** rollout and notice the difference in the stairs.

7. Choose **Create > Geometry** in the **Command Panel**; a drop-down list will be displayed. Select **Patch Grids** from the drop-down list. Create different patches using the **Quad Patch** and **Tri Patch** tools in the **Object Type** rollout and notice the difference.

Exercise 2

Create the model shown in Figure 4-96 using the dimensions of your choice. You can view the final rendered image of this model by downloading the file *c04_3dsmax_2012_render.zip* from *http://www.cadcim.com*. The path of the file is as follows: **(Expected time: 15 min)**

Textbooks > Animation and Visual Effects > 3ds Max > Autodesk 3ds Max 2012: A Comprehensive Guide

Figure 4-96 *Model for Exercise 2*

Answers to Self-Evaluation Test

1. d, **2.** b, **3.** c, **4.** d, **5.** ALT+A, **6. Plant Library**, **7. Count**, **Lower Rail Spacing 8.** T, **9.** T, **10.** T

5

Splines and Extended Splines

Learning Objectives

After completing this chapter, you will be able to:

- *Use the Undo and Redo tools*
- *Use the Hold and Fetch tools*
- *Use the AutoGrid option*
- *Create splines*
- *Create extended splines*

INTRODUCTION

In this chapter, you will learn to create splines and extended splines in Autodesk 3ds Max. Also, you will learn to use the **Undo**, **Redo**, **Hold**, and **Fetch** tools while modeling the 3D objects.

UNDO AND REDO TOOLS

Menu bar :	Edit > Undo or Redo
Quick Access Toolbar:	Undo Scene Operation or Redo Scene Operation
Keyboard:	CTRL+Z (Undo) or CTRL+Y (Redo)

The **Undo** tool is used to revert the last actions performed while creating or modifying a model in Autodesk 3ds Max. To undo an action, invoke the **Undo Scene Operation** tool from the **Quick Access Toolbar** or press the CTRL+Z keys. You need to invoke the **Undo Scene Operation** tool repeatedly till you want to reverse the last actions. To reverse a number of actions at a time, click on the arrow of the **Undo Scene Operation** tool in the **Quick Access Toolbar**; a list of actions will be displayed, refer to Figure 5-1. Move the cursor over the number of actions that you want to reverse; the actions will be selected. Next, click on the list. By default, you can reverse your actions up to 20 times. If you want to change this number, choose **Customize > Preferences** in the menu bar; the **Preference Settings** dialog box will be displayed. By default, the **General** tab is chosen in this dialog box. In the **Scene Undo** area, set the new value in the **Levels** spinner, as shown in Figure 5-2.

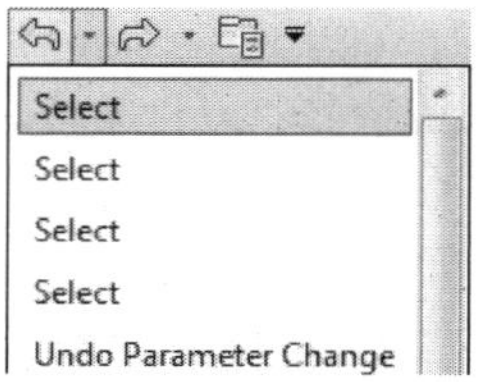

***Figure 5-1** The list of actions displayed after clicking on the **Undo Scene Operation** tool*

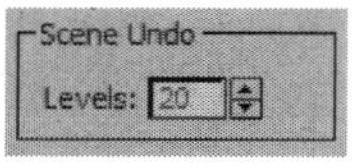

***Figure 5-2** The **Scene Undo** area in the **Preference Settings** dialog box*

The **Redo** tool is used to revert the last actions performed by the **Undo** tool. To redo an action, invoke the **Redo Scene Operation** tool from the **Quick Access Toolbar** or press the CTRL+Y keys. You need to invoke the **Redo Scene Operation** tool repeatedly till you want to reverse the actions. To reverse a number of actions at a time, click on the arrow of the **Redo Scene Operation** tool in the **Quick Access Toolbar**; a list of last actions will be displayed. Move the cursor over the number of actions that you want to reverse; the actions will be selected. Next, click on the list.

HOLD AND FETCH TOOLS

Menu bar :	Edit > Hold or Fetch
Keyboard:	CTRL+H (Hold) or ALT+CTRL+F (Fetch)

If you want to perform various experiments on a scene, then you need to hold the scene. The **Hold** tool is used to hold a scene and it saves the work in a temporary file with the name *maxhold.mx*.

The file is saved at the location *\Documents\3dsmax\autoback*. To perform an experiment on the new commands in a scene, invoke the **Hold** tool from the **Edit** menu or press the CTRL+H keys. Next, if you need to go back to the previous command, then choose the **Fetch** tool from the **Edit** menu or press ALT+CTRL+F; the **About to Fetch. OK?** dialog box will be displayed, as shown in Figure 5-3. Choose the **Yes** button; the scene with the previous command will be displayed. Therefore, you can go back to a series of commands using these tools.

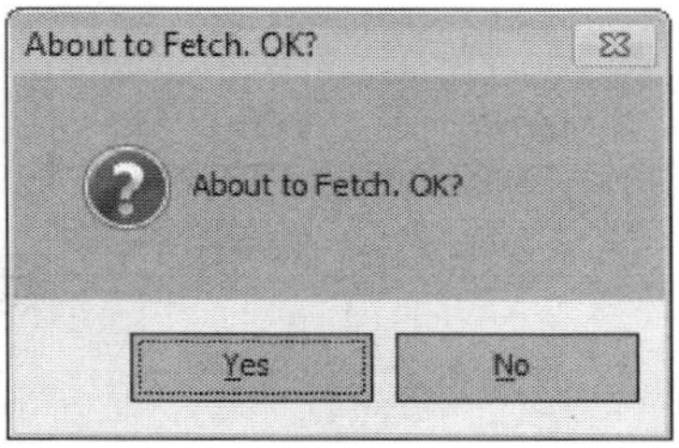

***Figure 5-3** The **About to Fetch. OK?** dialog box*

Note
*When you use the **Fetch** tool in a file, the history list of the actions performed so far will be deleted. As a result, you cannot undo or redo the actions performed before invoking this tool.*

AutoGrid

The **AutoGrid** option helps you to create an object on the surface of another object by generating a temporary grid on it. You can use this option by selecting the **AutoGrid** check box, which is available in the **Object Type** rollout of all object categories such as **Geometry**, **Shapes**, **Lights**, **Cameras**, and so on in the **Create** tab of the **Command Panel**. When you invoke a tool from the **Object Type** rollout, the **AutoGrid** check box becomes active. To understand the use of the **AutoGrid** check box, refer to the following example:

Choose **Create > Geometry** in the **Command Panel**; the **Standard Primitives** option will be displayed in the drop-down list. Now, invoke the **Sphere** tool and create a sphere in the Top viewport. Next, you need to create a torus on the surface of the sphere. Invoke the **Torus** tool and create a torus in the Top viewport; it will be displayed in the Perspective viewport, as shown in Figure 5-4. Now, align the torus on the surface of the sphere using the **Select and Move** tool.

In case you do not want to align the torus, then invoke the **Torus** tool; the **AutoGrid** check box, located at the top of the **Object Type** rollout, will be activated. Select this check box; the coordinate system will be displayed in the viewport along with the cursor to specify the position of the torus. Click on a point in the Top viewport; a temporary grid will be created in the Perspective viewport. Now, drag the cursor to create the torus; it will be created on the surface of the sphere, as shown in Figure 5-5.

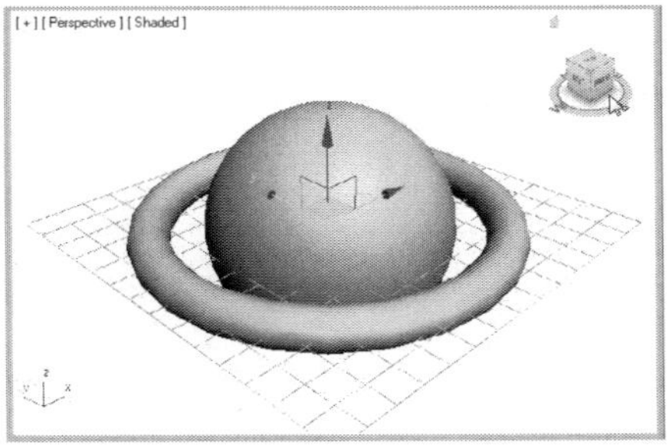

***Figure 5-4** The torus created without selecting the **AutoGrid** check box*

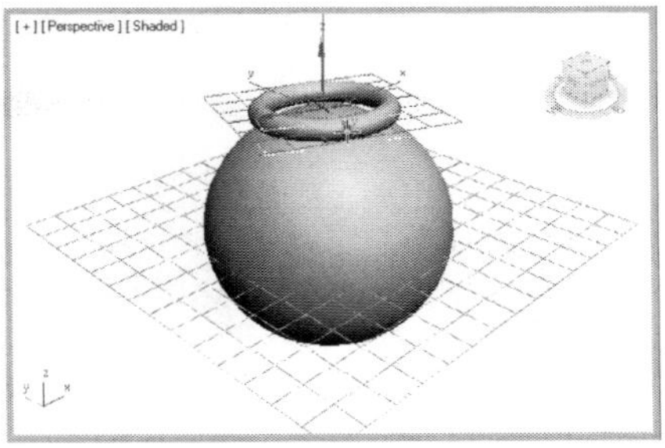

***Figure 5-5** The torus created after selecting the **AutoGrid** check box*

Note
The temporary grid will be visible only in the Perspective viewport.

SPLINES AND EXTENDED SPLINES

Autodesk 3ds Max has several basic 2D geometric shapes known as splines and extended splines. They are used to create 3D objects, 3D surfaces, and paths for lofting and animations. All splines and extended splines can be created dynamically by using the mouse or by entering the parameters in the **Keyboard Entry** rollout.

To create these splines, choose **Create > Shapes** in the **Command Panel**; the **Splines** option will be displayed in the drop-down list, as shown in Figure 5-6. Now, activate the viewport in which you want to create the primitives by clicking in it and then invoke the corresponding tool from the **Object Type** rollout. In this section, you will learn to create and modify the splines and extended splines using various tools available in the **Object Type** rollout.

Note
*By default, the **Start New Shape** check box is selected in the **Object Type** rollout. This check box enables you to create new shapes separately in the viewport using different tools such as **Line**, **Circle**, **Arc**, and so on available in the **Object Type** rollout. If you clear this check box and then create new shapes, they will be added to the current shape in the viewport. However, the **Section** shape is exceptions.*

Creating a Line Spline

Menu bar:	Create > Shapes > Line
Command Panel:	Create > Shapes > Splines > Object Type rollout > Line

To create a line, activate the viewport and then invoke the **Line** tool from the **Object Type** rollout; the **Name and Color**, **Rendering**, **Interpolation**, **Creation Method**, and **Keyboard Entry** rollouts will be displayed, as shown in Figure 5-6.

To create a line spline dynamically, click in the Top viewport to specify the first vertex or the start point of the line. Now, move the cursor to define the distance between the first and the second vertex, and click on the screen to create the second vertex. Again, move the cursor and click to create additional vertices. Next, right-click to end the command; an open line spline will be created, as shown in Figure 5-7. To create a closed line spline, instead of right-clicking at the end, move the cursor over the first vertex and click on it; the **Spline** dialog box will be displayed, as shown in Figure 5-8. Choose the **Yes** button; a closed line spline will be created, as shown in Figure 5-9.

You can also create a line spline using another method. To do so, click in the viewport to specify the first vertex and then move the cursor to define the distance between the first and the second vertex. Now, press and hold the left mouse button and drag the cursor to create additional vertices; a line spline with the bezier vertex and the smooth curve will be created. The bezier vertex is controlled by two points on both endpoints, which help in modifying the curve of the line.

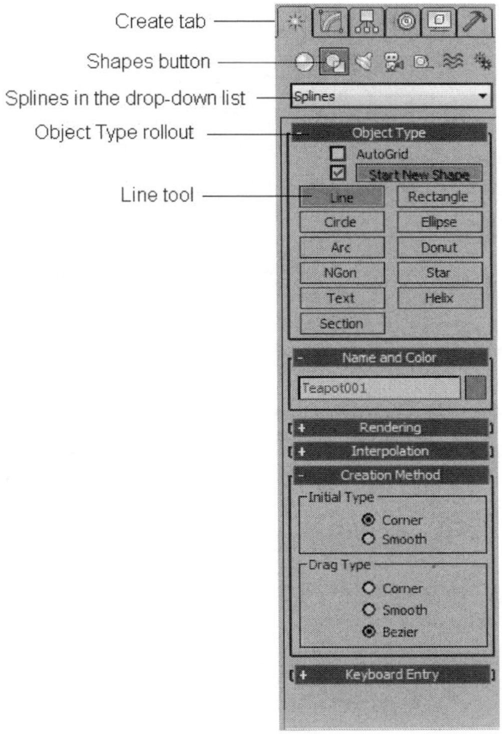

Figure 5-6 Various rollouts to create and modify a line spline

*Figure 5-7 An open line spline created using the **Line** tool*

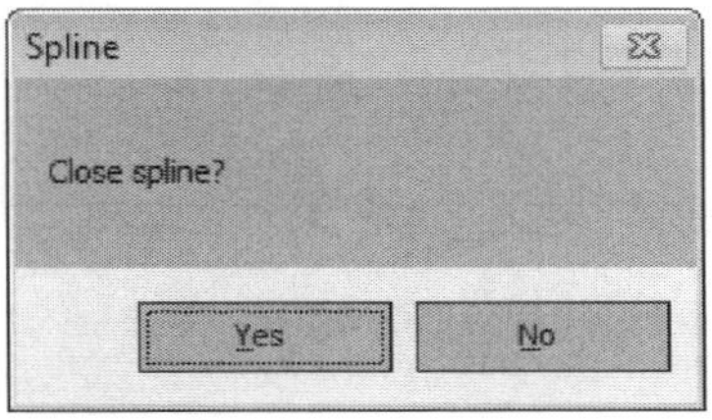

*Figure 5-8 The **Spline** dialog box*

*Figure 5-9 A closed line spline created using the **Line** tool*

While creating a line, if you click in the viewport to create additional vertices, they will become corner vertices, as shown in Figure 5-10. But, if you click and drag to create additional vertices, the curve between the vertices will be smooth and the vertices will be bezier, as shown in Figure 5-11, depending on the options you select in the **Drag Type** and **Initial Type** areas of the **Creation Method** rollout.

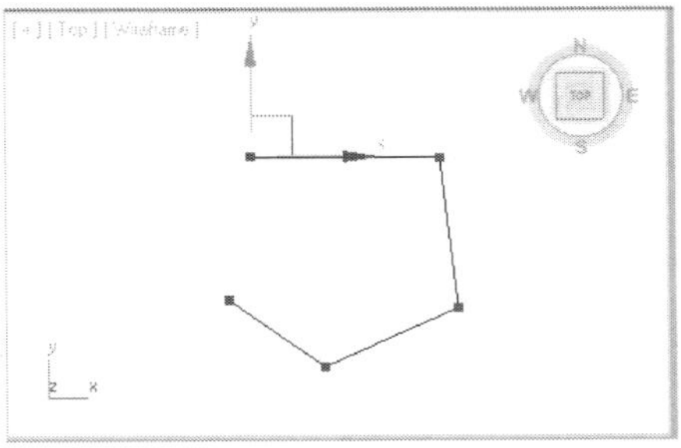

Figure 5-10 A line with corner vertices

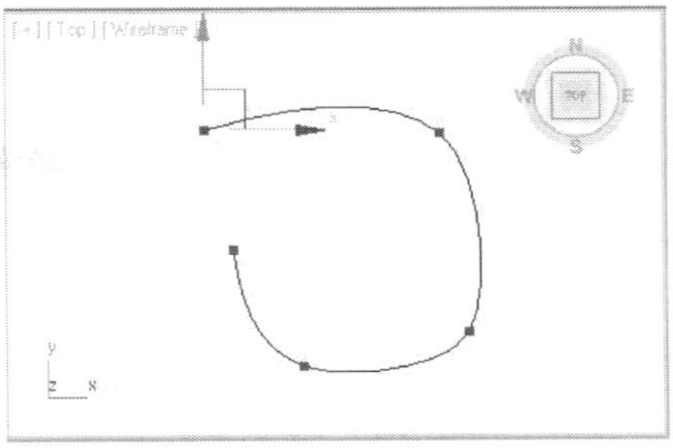

Figure 5-11 A line with bezier vertex and smooth curve

Various rollouts used to create and modify a line are discussed next.

Rendering Rollout

The options in this rollout are used to modify a line at rendering, refer to Figure 5-12. These options are discussed next.

Enable In Renderer

By default, the line created by you is not visible at the time of rendering. Select the **Enable In Renderer** check box to make the line visible as 3D mesh at rendering.

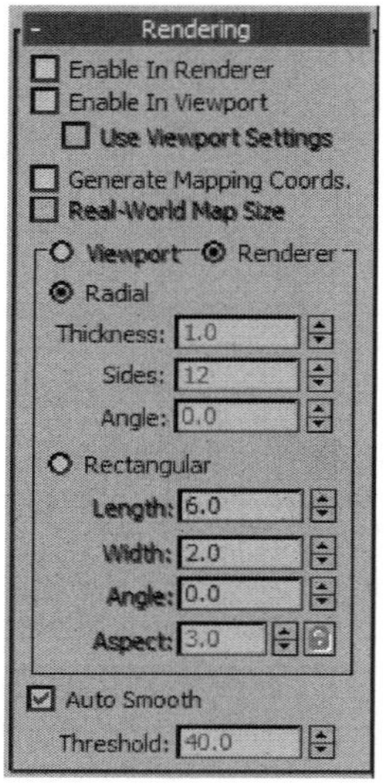

Figure 5-12 *The* ***Rendering*** *rollout*

Enable In Viewport

Select the **Enable In Viewport** check box to make the line visible as 3D mesh in the viewport.

Use Viewport Settings

By default, this check box is not active. When you select the **Enable In Viewport** check box, the **Use Viewport Settings** check box will be activated. Select this check box; the **Viewport** radio button will be activated. Select this radio button and modify the parameters such as thickness and sides in the respective spinners; the line will be displayed as a 3D mesh in the viewport according to the parameters you set.

Viewport

This radio button will be activated only if the **Use Viewport Settings** check box is selected. You can modify the dimensions of the line in the viewport using the **Radial** or the **Rectangular** radio button.

Renderer

This radio button is used to modify the dimensions of the line at rendering using the **Radial** or **Rectangular** radio button. Note that you can view the modifications in the line at rendering only if the **Enable In Renderer** check box is selected.

Radial

This radio button is used to display the cylindrical 3D mesh line. The **Thickness** spinner is used to set the thickness of the line. Similarly, the **Sides** spinner is used to set the number of faces along with the cross-section of the line. The value in the **Angle** spinner is used to set the position of the cross-section of the line by rotating it.

Note

*To view the faces of the line spline in the Perspective viewport, press the F4 key. Alternatively, click on the Shading viewport label in the viewport; a shortcut menu will be displayed. Now, choose **Edged Faces** from the shortcut menu.*

Rectangular

This radio button is used to display the rectangular 3D mesh line. You can set the length and width of the line in the **Length** and **Width** spinners, respectively. The **Angle** spinner is used to set the position of the cross-section of the line by rotating it. The **Aspect** spinner is used to set the constant ratio of width to length. Choose the lock icon on the right side of the **Aspect** spinner to lock the constant ratio of width to length. Now, if you set the value in the **Length** or the **Width** spinner, the values will be set in both the spinners simultaneously.

Auto Smooth

The **Auto Smooth** check box is used to smoothen the angle between the line segments depending upon the value set in the **Threshold** spinner. The value in the **Threshold** spinner is used to set the threshold angle in degrees.

Interpolation Rollout

The options in the **Interpolation** rollout are used to define how a line will be created, refer to Figure 5-13. The number of segments between each vertex on the line are called steps. The value in the **Steps** spinner defines the number of steps between each vertex on the line. Larger the value in the **Steps** spinner, smoother will be the line.

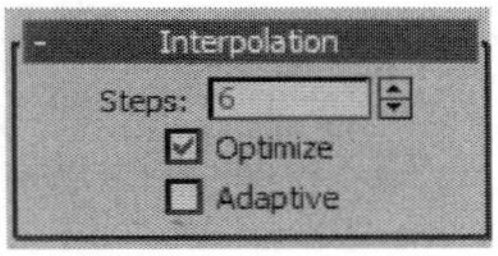

***Figure 5-13** The **Interpolation** rollout*

By default, the **Optimize** check box is selected, which helps you to remove the unwanted steps on the straight line, and you can set the number of steps by entering the value in the **Steps** spinner. If you select the **Adaptive** check box, then the **Optimize** check box and the **Steps** spinner will become inactive. Also, the number of steps will automatically be set to create a smooth line.

Note

*The options in the **Name and Color**, **Rendering**, and **Interpolation** rollouts are same for all splines and extended splines in Autodesk 3ds Max.*

Creation Method Rollout

The options in this rollout are used while creating a line dynamically. The two areas in this rollout are discussed next.

Initial Type Area

The options in this area are used to define the type of vertex when you click on the screen to create it. Select the **Corner** radio button to create a corner vertex; the line between the two corner vertices will be straight. Select the **Smooth** radio button to create a smooth curve in between the two vertices.

Drag Type Area

The options in this area are used to define the type of vertex when you click on the screen to create it and then drag the cursor by holding the left mouse button. The **Corner** and

Smooth radio buttons perform the same functions as described in the **Initial Type** area. Select the **Bezier** radio button to create a smooth curve with bezier vertices. You can modify the shape of the curve using the two control points of these bezier vertices.

Keyboard Entry Rollout

The options in this rollout are used to create a line by entering the parameters in the **Keyboard Entry** rollout, as shown in Figure 5-14. To do so, expand the **Keyboard Entry** rollout and enter the coordinates in the **X**, **Y**, and **Z** spinners to specify the position of the first vertex of the line along the axes of the home grid or a grid object.

Next, choose the **Add Point** button; a vertex will be created at the specified location. Again, enter the coordinates in the **X**, **Y**, and **Z** spinners to specify the position of the second vertex of the line and choose the **Add Point** button; the line with two vertices will be displayed in all viewports. Follow the same procedure as described above to create more vertices. Next, choose the **Close** button to create a closed line or choose the **Finish** button to create an open line.

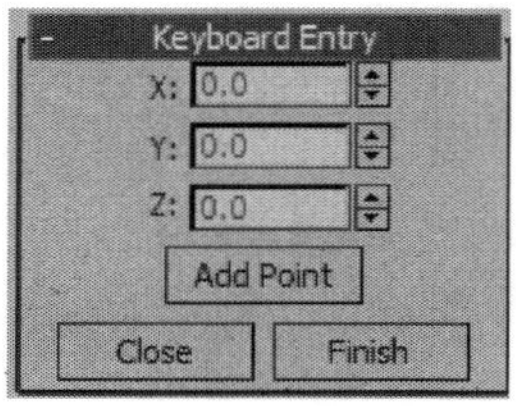

Figure 5-14 *The* ***Keyboard Entry*** *rollout*

Note

The ***Keyboard Entry*** *rollout in all splines and extended splines is used to create the corresponding spline by entering the parameters using the keyboard. The method of creating all splines is the same as discussed above with the only difference in the type and number of parameters entered for various splines and extended splines.*

Creating a Rectangular Spline

Menu bar: Create > Shapes > Rectangle
Command Panel: Create > Shapes > Splines > Object Type rollout > Rectangle

To create a rectangular spline, activate the viewport in which you want to create it and then invoke the **Rectangle** tool from the **Object Type** rollout; the **Name and Color**, **Rendering**, **Interpolation**, **Creation Method**, **Keyboard Entry**, and **Parameters** rollouts will be displayed, as shown in Figure 5-15. Click at the upper left corner of the viewport and hold the left mouse button and then drag the cursor to the lower right corner of the viewport. As you drag the cursor, the length and width values appear in their respective spinners in the **Parameters** rollout. Next, release the left mouse button to set the length and width values; a rectangular spline will be created in the viewport, as shown in Figure 5-16.

Note

You can also create a square spline, as shown in Figure 5-17, using the same method as described above. The only difference in this case is that you need to hold the CTRL key while dragging the cursor.

Various rollouts used to create and modify the rectangular spline are discussed next.

Creation Method Rollout

The options in this rollout are used while creating a rectangle dynamically. Select the **Edge** radio button to specify the first point at the corner of the shape and then drag the cursor to define the diagonal corner of the shape. This distance between the two corner points will be the diagonal of the rectangle. Select the **Center** radio button to specify the first point at the center of the rectangle and then drag the cursor to specify the distance between the center and its corner.

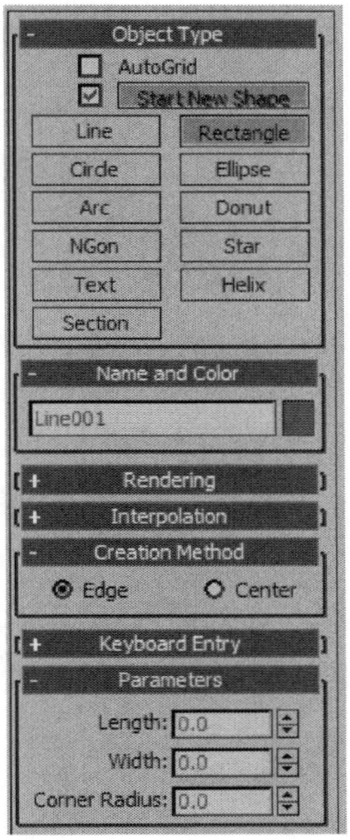

Figure 5-15 Various rollouts to create and modify a rectangular spline

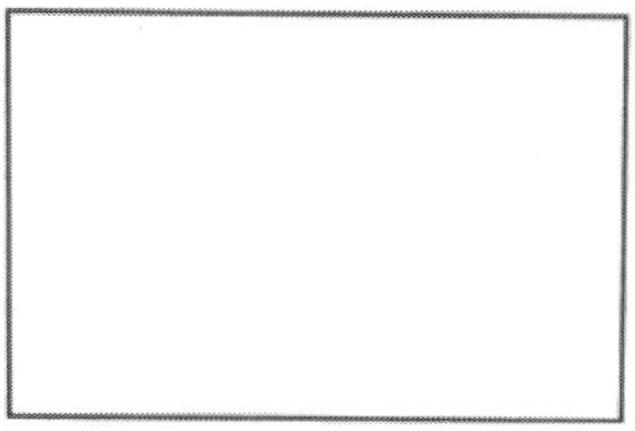

Figure 5-16 A rectangular spline

Figure 5-17 A square spline

Parameters Rollout

The options in this rollout are used to modify the rectangular spline. To do so, select the rectangle and choose the **Modify** tab in the **Command Panel**; the **Parameters** rollout will be displayed. In this rollout, set the new values in the **Length**, **Width**, and **Corner Radius** spinners to modify the rectangle, as shown in Figure 5-18.

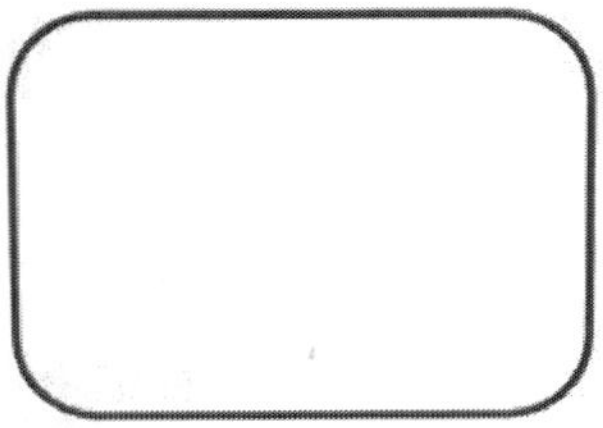

Figure 5-18 A rectangle with corner radius

Creating a Circular Spline

Menu bar:	Create > Shapes > Circle
Command Panel:	Create > Shapes > Splines > Object Type rollout > Circle

To create a closed circular spline, activate the viewport in which you want to create it and then invoke the **Circle** tool from the **Object Type** rollout; the **Name and Color**, **Rendering**, **Interpolation**, **Creation Method**, **Keyboard Entry**, and **Parameters** rollouts will be displayed, as shown in Figure 5-19. Next, press and hold the left mouse button and then drag the cursor. As you drag the cursor, the radius value will be displayed in the **Radius** spinner in the **Parameters** rollout. Next, release the left mouse button to set the radius of the circle; a circular spline will be created in the viewport, as shown in Figure 5-20.

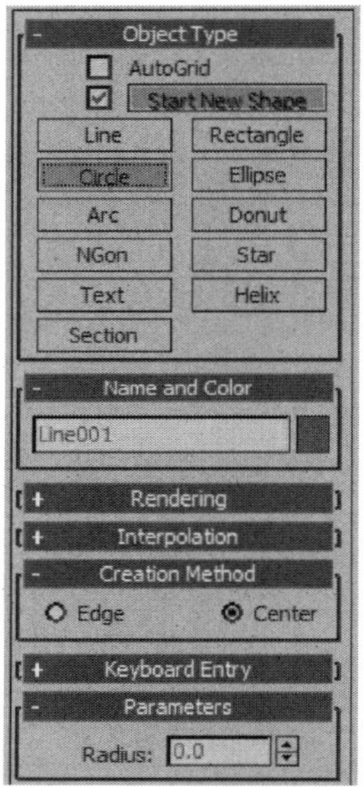

Figure 5-19 *Various rollouts to create and modify a circular spline*

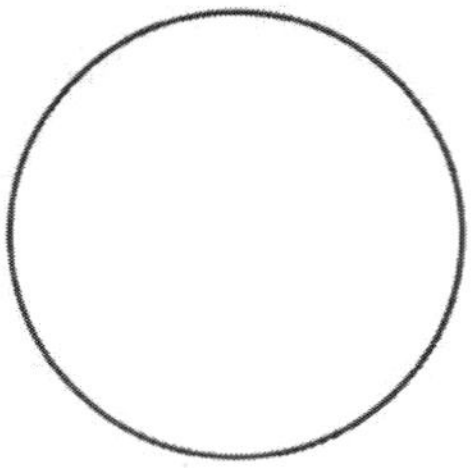

Figure 5-20 *A circular spline*

Various rollouts used to create and modify the circular spline are discussed next.

Creation Method Rollout

The options in this rollout are used while creating a circular spline dynamically. Select the **Edge** radio button to specify the first point on the circumference of the circle and then drag to specify its diameter. Select the **Center** radio button to specify the first point at the center of the circle and then drag to specify its radius.

Parameters Rollout

The options in this rollout are used to modify the circular spline. To do so, select the circle and choose the **Modify** tab in the **Command Panel**; the **Parameters** rollout will be displayed. Set the new value in the **Radius** spinner to modify the radius of the circular spline.

Creating an Elliptical Spline

Menu bar:	Create > Shapes > Ellipse
Command Panel:	Create > Shapes > Splines > Object Type rollout > Ellipse

To create an elliptical spline, activate the viewport in which you want to create it and then invoke the **Ellipse** tool from the **Object Type** rollout; the **Name and Color**, **Rendering**, **Interpolation**, **Creation Method**, **Keyboard Entry**, and **Parameters** rollouts will be displayed, as shown in Figure 5-21. Next, press and hold the left mouse button and then drag the cursor. As you drag the cursor, the length and width values will appear in the **Length** and **Width** spinners of the **Parameters** rollout. Release the left mouse button to set the length and width; an elliptical spline will be created in the viewport, as shown in Figure 5-22.

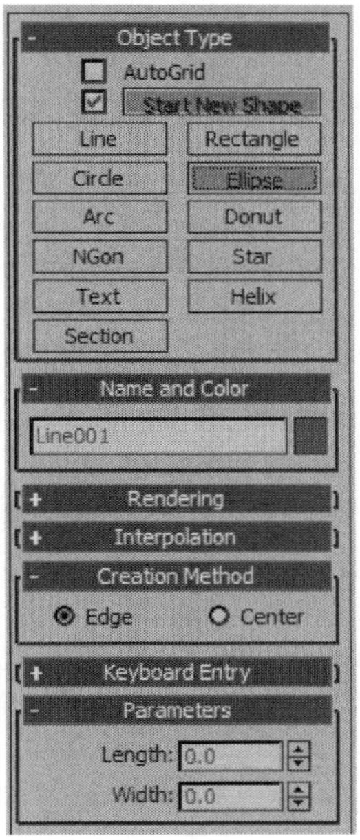

Figure 5-21 Various rollouts to create and modify an elliptical spline

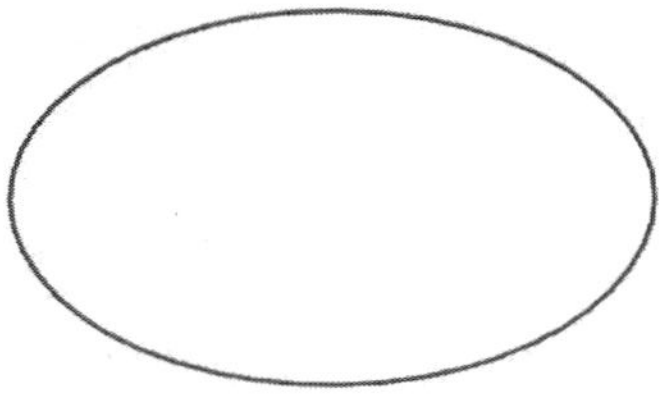

Figure 5-22 An elliptical spline

Note

You can also create a circular spline using the same method as discussed above. The only difference in this case is that you need to hold the CTRL key while dragging the cursor.

Various rollouts used to create and modify the ellipse are discussed next.

Creation Method Rollout

The options in this rollout are used while creating an elliptical spline dynamically. These options are the same as those discussed earlier.

Parameters Rollout

The options in this rollout are used to modify the elliptical spline. To do so, select the elliptical spline and choose the **Modify** tab in the **Command Panel**; the **Parameters** rollout will be displayed. Set the new values in the **Length** and **Width** spinners to modify the elliptical spline.

Creating an Arc Spline

Menu bar:	Create > Shapes > Arc
Command Panel:	Create > Shapes > Splines > Object Type rollout > Arc

To create an arc spline, activate the viewport in which you want to create it and then invoke the **Arc** tool from the **Object Type** rollout; the **Name and Color**, **Rendering**, **Interpolation**, **Creation Method**, **Keyboard Entry**, and **Parameters** rollouts will be displayed, as shown in Figure 5-23. Various rollouts used to create and modify an arc are discussed next.

Creation Method Rollout

You can create an arc using two methods, which depend on the selection of the radio button in the **Creation Method** rollout. Select the **End-End-Middle** radio button to specify the first two points as the two endpoints of an arc and then specify the third point between the two endpoints on the arc. Select the **Center-End-End** radio button to specify the first point as the center of the arc, and then the two points to specify the two endpoints of the arc. These methods are discussed next.

End-End-Middle Method

To create an arc using this method, activate the Top viewport and make sure that the **End-End-Middle** radio button is selected in the **Creation Method** rollout. Next, press and hold the left mouse button and drag the cursor to define the two endpoints of the arc. Release the left mouse button and move the mouse up or down to define the third point between the two endpoints on the arc, refer to Figures 5-24 and 5-25. Click on the screen; an arc spline will be created, as shown in Figure 5-26.

Center-End-End Method

To create an arc using this method, activate the Top viewport and select the **Center-End-End** radio button in the **Creation Method** rollout. Press and hold the left mouse button to specify the center point of an arc and drag the cursor to specify the first endpoint of the arc. Now, release the mouse button and move the cursor up or down to specify the second endpoint of the arc, refer to Figures 5-27 and 5-28. Click on the screen; an arc will be created.

Parameters Rollout

The options in this rollout are used to modify an arc. To do so, select the arc and choose the **Modify** tab in the **Command Panel**; the **Parameters** rollout will be displayed. Set the new values in the **Radius**, **From**, and **To** spinners to modify the arc. The **Pie Slice** check box is used to create a line from each endpoint to the center of the arc, as shown in Figure 5-29. The

Reverse check box is used to reverse the direction of the arc. To view the reversed direction, you need to convert it into an editable spline object about which you will learn in the later chapters.

Creating a Donut Spline

Menu bar:	Create > Shapes > Donut
Command Panel:	Create > Shapes > Splines > Object Type rollout > Donut

The **Donut** tool is used to create a closed spline with two concentric circles known as donut. To create a donut spline, activate the viewport in which you want to create it and then invoke the **Donut** tool from the **Object Type** rollout; the **Name and Color**, **Rendering**, **Interpolation**, **Creation Method**, **Keyboard Entry**, and **Parameters** rollouts will be displayed, as shown in Figure 5-30.

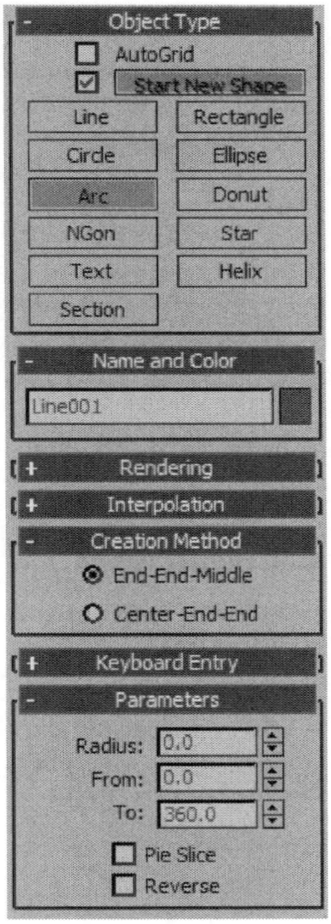

Figure 5-23 Various rollouts to create and modify an arc spline

Figure 5-24 Creating an arc using the end-end-middle method (step-1)

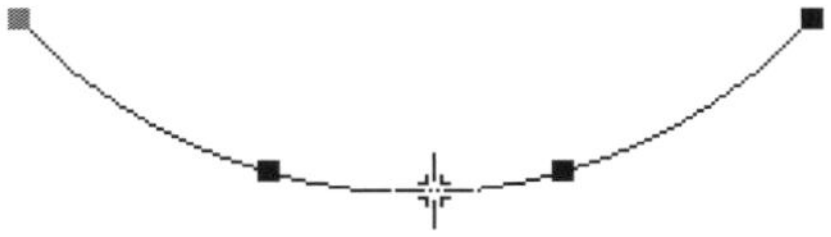

Figure 5-25 Creating an arc using the end-end-middle method (step-2)

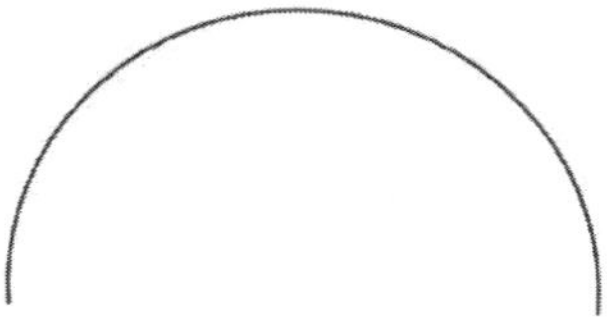

Figure 5-26 An arc spline

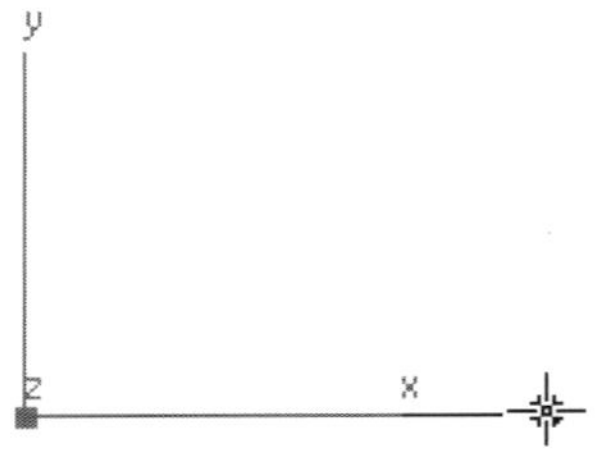

Figure 5-27 *Creating an arc using the center-end-end method (step-1)*

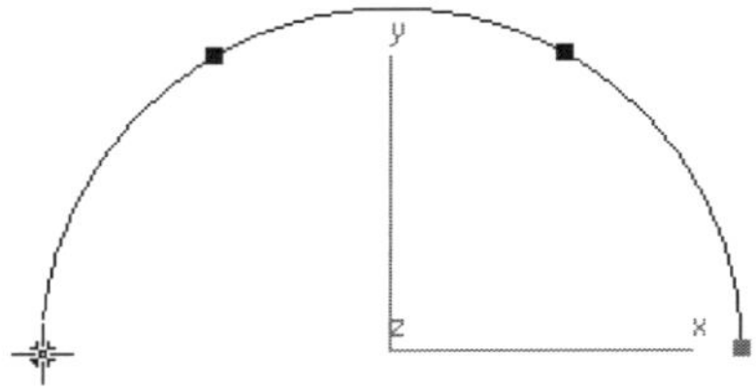

Figure 5-28 *Creating an arc using the center-end-end method (step-2)*

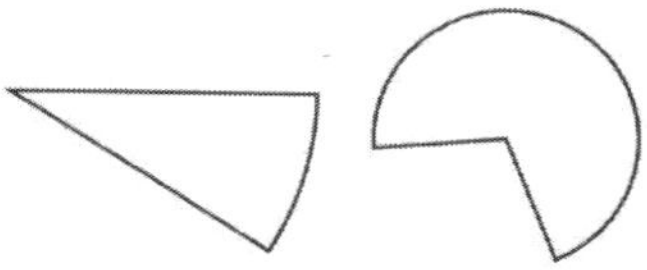

Figure 5-29 *The arcs created on using the* ***Pie Slice*** *check box*

Next, press and hold the left mouse button and drag the cursor. As you drag the cursor, the radius of the first circle will appear in the **Radius1** spinner of the **Parameters** rollout. Release the left mouse button to set the radius 1. Next, drag the cursor again to define the radius 2 of the second circle. Click on the screen; a donut spline will be created in the viewport, as shown in Figure 5-31.

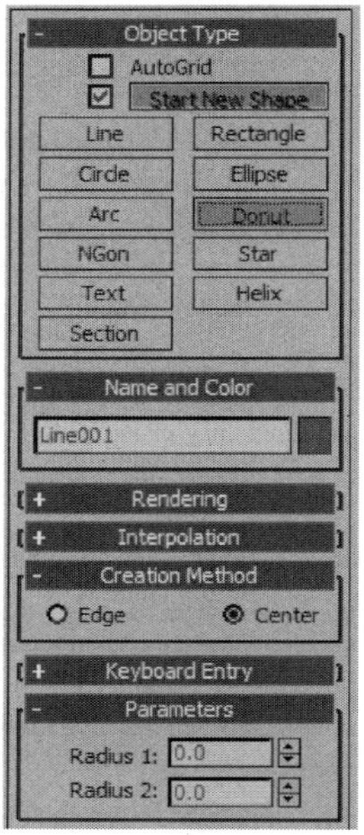

Figure 5-30 *Various rollouts to create and modify the donut spline*

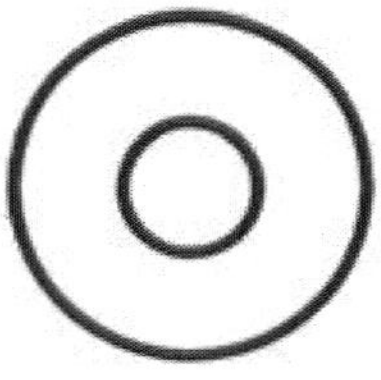

Figure 5-31 *A donut spline*

Various rollouts used to create and modify the donut spline are discussed next.

Creation Method Rollout

The options in this rollout are used while creating a donut spline dynamically. These are the same as discussed earlier while creating a rectangular spline.

Parameters Rollout

The options in this rollout are used to modify the donut. To do so, select the donut and choose the **Modify** tab in the **Command Panel**; the **Parameters** rollout will be displayed. Set the new values in the **Radius 1** and **Radius 2** spinners to modify the radius of the donut.

Creating an NGon Spline

Menu bar:	Create > Shapes > NGon
Command Panel:	Create > Shapes > Splines > Object Type rollout > NGon

The **NGon** tool is used to create a closed spline with three or more number of sides known as NGon. To create an NGon spline, activate the viewport in which you want to create it and then invoke the **NGon** tool from the **Object Type** rollout; the **Name and Color**, **Rendering**, **Interpolation**, **Creation Method**, **Keyboard Entry**, and **Parameters** rollouts will be displayed, as shown in Figure 5-32.

Next, press and hold the left mouse button and then drag the cursor. As you drag the cursor, the radius value of NGon will be displayed in the **Radius** spinner of the **Parameters** rollout. Release the left mouse button to set the radius of the NGon spline; an NGon spline will be created in the viewport, as shown in Figure 5-33.

Various rollouts used to create and modify the NGon spline are discussed next.

Creation Method Rollout

The options in this rollout are used while creating the NGon dynamically. These are the same as discussed earlier while creating a rectangular spline.

Parameters Rollout

The options in this rollout are used to modify the NGon spline. To do so, select the NGon from the viewport and choose the **Modify** tab in the **Command Panel**; the **Parameters** rollout will be displayed. In this rollout, enter a value in the **Radius** spinner to modify the radius of NGon. Select the **Inscribed** radio button to specify the radius of the NGon from its center to its corners. Select the **Circumscribed** radio button to specify the radius of the NGon from its center to the sides of the NGon. The **Sides** spinner specifies the number of sides of the NGon, as shown in Figure 5-34. The value in the **Corner Radius** spinner is used to round the corners of the NGon in degrees, as shown in Figure 5-35. Select the **Circular** check box to create a circular NGon.

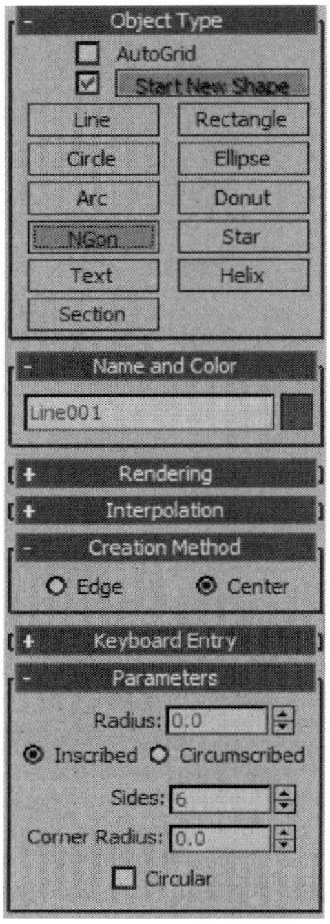

***Figure 5-32** Various rollouts to create and modify an NGon spline*

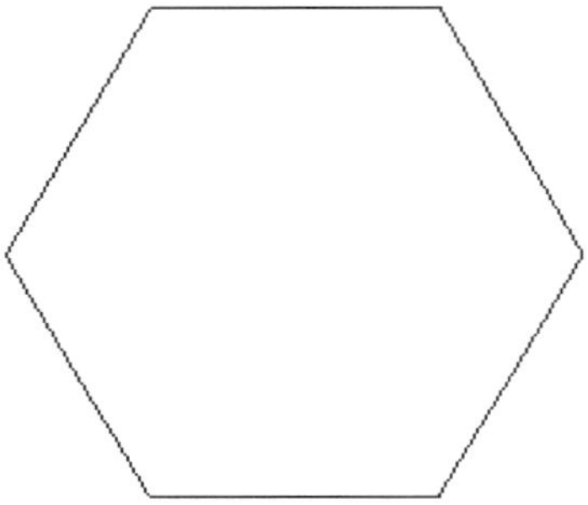

***Figure 5-33** An NGon spline*

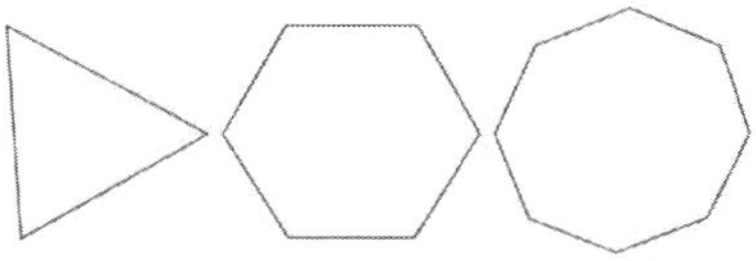

***Figure 5-34** The NGons with 3, 6, and 8 number of sides*

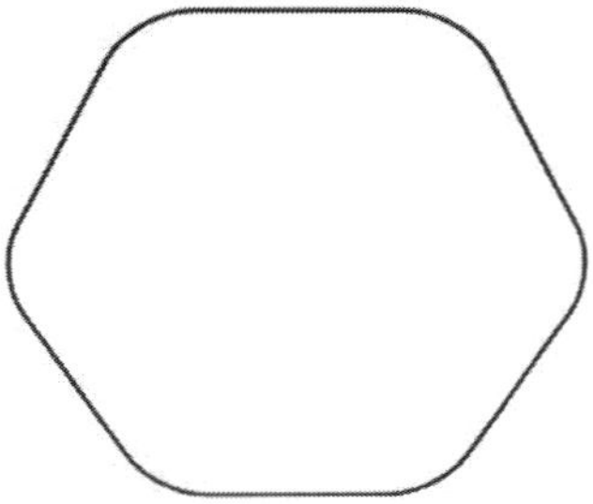

***Figure 5-35** The NGon with round corners*

Note

*Create a circle and an NGon with the same radius and place them in the viewport, as shown in Figure 5-36. Select the NGon and choose the **Modify** tab in the **Command Panel**. In the **Parameters** rollout, select the **Inscribed** and **Circumscribed** radio buttons one by one to notice the difference between them, refer to Figures 5-36 and 5-37.*

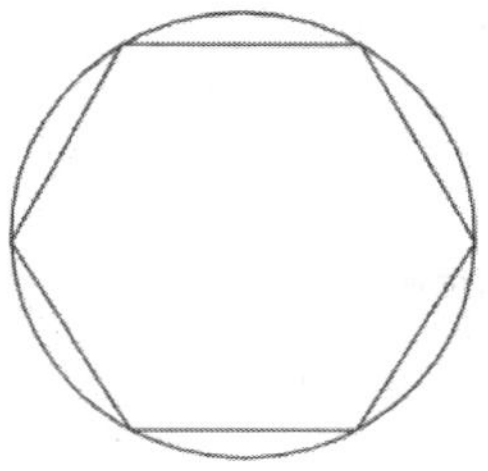

*Figure 5-36 An NGon after selecting the **Inscribed** radio button*

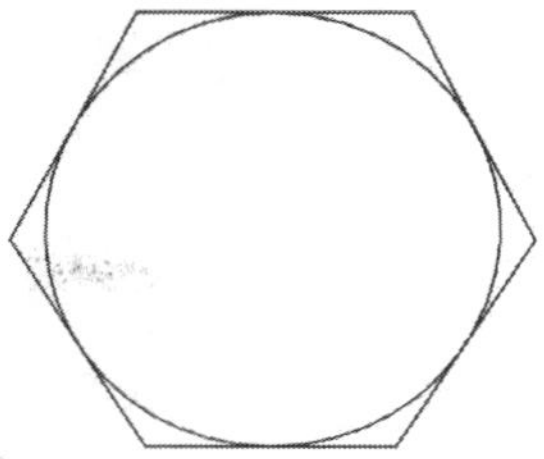

*Figure 5-37 An NGon after selecting the **Circumscribed** radio button*

Creating a Star Spline

Menu bar:	Create > Shapes > Star
Command Panel:	Create > Shapes > Splines > Object Type rollout > Star

The **Star** tool is used to create a star-shaped closed spline with three or more number of points. To create a star spline, activate the viewport in which you want to create it and then invoke the **Star** tool from the **Object Type** rollout; the **Name and Color**, **Rendering**, **Interpolation**, **Keyboard Entry**, and **Parameters** rollouts will be displayed, as shown in Figure 5-38.

Next, press and hold the left mouse button and then drag the cursor. As you drag the cursor, the radius value of the outer points and the inner points of the star will be displayed in the **Radius1** and **Radius2** spinners of the **Parameters** rollout, respectively. Release the left mouse button and then drag the cursor again inside or outside to define the radius of the inner points of the star. Now, click on the screen; a star spline will be created in all viewports, as shown in Figure 5-39.

Various rollouts used to create and modify the star are discussed next.

Parameters Rollout

The options in this rollout are used to modify a star. To do so, select the star and choose the **Modify** tab in the **Command Panel**; the **Parameters** rollout will be displayed. Set the new values of radius 1 and radius 2 in the respective spinners. Set the value in the **Points** spinner to specify the number of points in the star, refer to Figure 5-40. Set the value in the **Distortion** spinner to rotate the inner points around the center of the star, refer to Figure 5-41. Set the values in the **Fillet Radius 1** and **Fillet Radius 2** spinners to round the inner and outer points of the star, as shown in Figure 5-42.

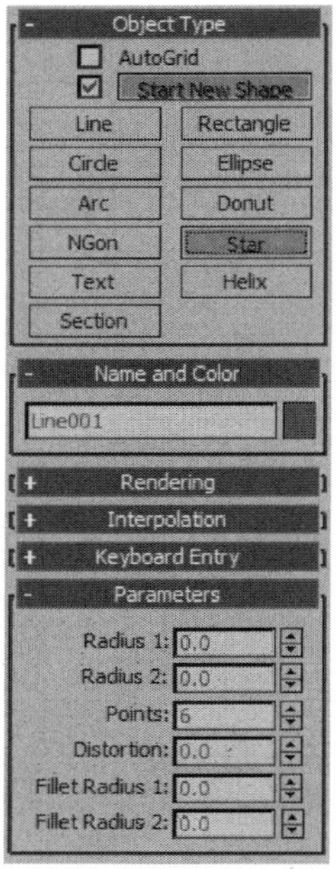

Figure 5-38 *Various rollouts to create and modify a star spline*

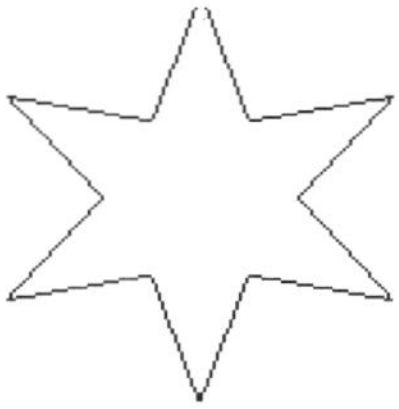

Figure 5-39 *A star spline*

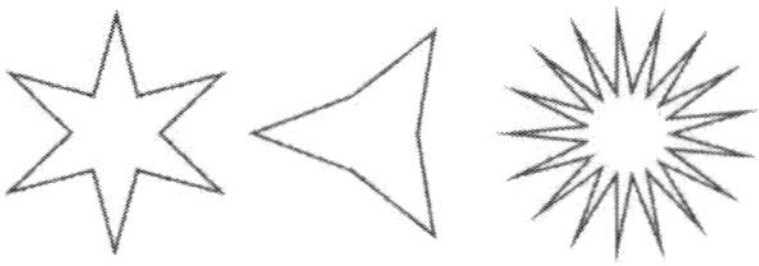

Figure 5-40 *The star splines with different number of points*

Figure 5-41 *A star after setting the value in the **Distortion** spinner*

Figure 5-42 *A star with fillet radius 1 and fillet radius 2*

Creating a Text Spline

Menu bar:	Create > Shapes > Text
Command Panel:	Create > Shapes > Splines > Object Type rollout > Text

The **Text** tool is used to create a spline in the text shape. To create a text spline, activate the viewport in which you want to create it and then invoke the **Text** tool from the **Object Type** rollout; the **Name and Color**, **Rendering**, **Interpolation**, and **Parameters** rollouts will be displayed, as shown in Figure 5-43.

To create the text dynamically, type the text in the text box of the **Text** area in the **Parameters** rollout. Then, activate the Front viewport and click on the screen; the text will be displayed in the viewport, as shown in Figure 5-44.

Various rollouts used to create and modify the text are discussed next.

Parameters Rollout

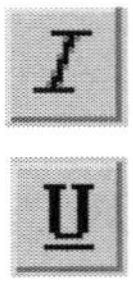

The options in this rollout are used to modify the text. To do so, select the text and choose the **Modify** tab in the **Command Panel**; the **Parameters** rollout will be displayed. At the top of this rollout, a drop-down list is displayed. You can modify the font type of the text in the viewport by selecting the font from this drop-down list. Choose the ***I*** and **U** buttons to italicize and underline the text, respectively. You can also choose the alignment buttons placed on the right of the **U** button for the proper alignment of the text, refer to Figure 5-45. Set the value in the **Size** spinner to modify the size of the text. The **Kerning** spinner is used to set the distance between the letters. If the text is written in two lines, then the **Leading** spinner is used to set the distance between these lines.

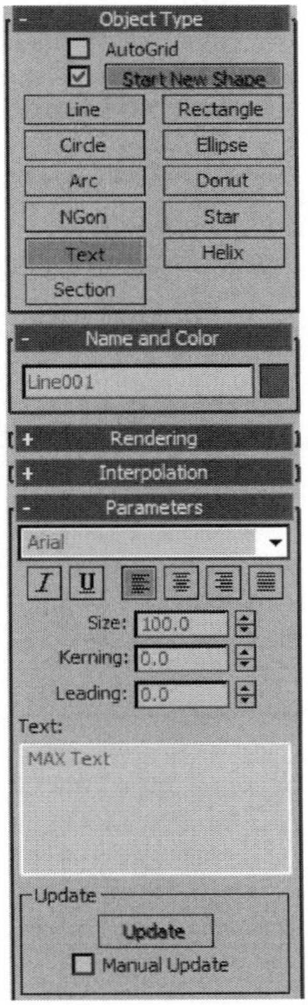

Figure 5-43 Various rollouts to create and modify a text spline

Figure 5-44 The text

Figure 5-45 Various align buttons to align the text

Text Area

The text box in the **Text** area is used to enter the text that you want to display in the viewport. By default, the text in the text box is MAX Text.

Update Area

If you make any modification in the text using various rollouts in the modify panel, then the text will automatically be updated in the viewport. But, if you select the **Manual Update** check box in this area and modify the text, then you need to choose the **Update** button to view the updated output in the viewports.

Creating a Helix Spline

Menu bar:	Create > Shapes > Helix
Command Panel:	Create > Shapes > Splines > Object Type rollout > Helix

The **Helix** tool is used to create a spline with spirals. To create a helix spline, activate the viewport in which you want to create it and then invoke the **Helix** tool from the **Object Type** rollout; the **Name and Color**, **Rendering**, **Creation Method**, **Keyboard Entry**, and **Parameters** rollouts will be displayed, as shown in Figure 5-46.

Next, press and hold the left mouse button and then drag the cursor. As you drag the cursor, the radius value of the start point and the endpoint of the helix will be displayed in the **Radius 1** and **Radius 2** spinners of the **Parameters** rollout, respectively. Release the left mouse button and then drag the cursor up or down to define the height of the helix. Now, click on the screen and move the cursor up or down to set the radius 2 of the endpoint. Again, click on the screen; a helix spline will be created in all viewports, as shown in Figure 5-47.

Various rollouts used to create and modify the helix are discussed next.

Creation Method Rollout

The options in this rollout are used while creating a helix dynamically. These are the same as discussed earlier.

Parameters Rollout

The options in this rollout are used to modify the helix. To do so, select the helix and choose the **Modify** tab in the **Command Panel**; the **Parameters** rollout will be displayed. In this rollout, set the new values of radius 1, radius 2, and height in the respective spinners. Set the value in the **Turns** spinner to specify the number of turns between the start point and endpoint of the helix. The value in the **Bias** spinner forces the turns of the helix to accumulate toward its start point or endpoint. By default, the value in the **Bias** spinner is 0, which evenly distributes the turns between the start point and endpoint. It varies from -1 to +1. The -1 value forces the turns to accumulate toward the start point of the helix and +1 value forces the turns to accumulate toward the endpoint of the helix, as shown in Figures 5-48, 5-49, and 5-50. Select the **CW** radio button to turn the helix in the clockwise direction. Select the **CCW** radio button to turn the helix in the counterclockwise direction.

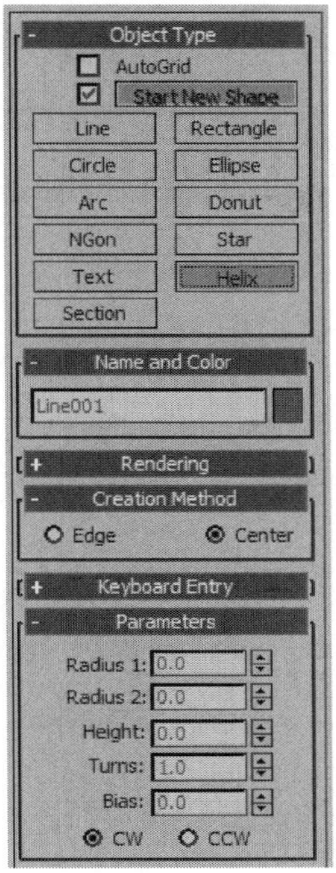

Figure 5-46 *Various rollouts to create and modify a helix spline*

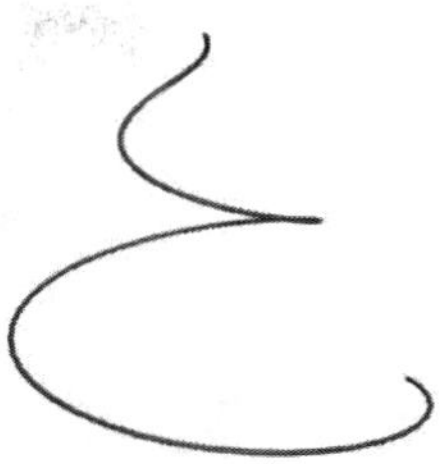

Figure 5-47 *A helix spline*

Figure 5-48 *The helix spline with three turns and zero value in the **Bias** spinner*

Figure 5-49 *The helix spline with three turns and +1 value in the **Bias** spinner*

Figure 5-50 *The helix spline with three turns and -1 value in the **Bias** spinner*

Creating a Section Spline

Menu bar:	Create > Shapes > Section
Command Panel:	Create > Shapes > Splines > Object Type rollout > Section

The **Section** tool is used to create a bisected rectangular spline, which generates other splines based on the cross-sectional slice of other objects. To create a section spline, activate the viewport in which you want to create it and then invoke the **Section** tool from the **Object Type** rollout; the **Name and Color**, **Section Parameters**, and **Section Size** rollouts will be displayed, as shown in Figure 5-51.

Next, press and hold the left mouse button and then drag the cursor. As you drag the cursor, the length and width values of the section will appear in the **Length** and **Width** spinners of the **Parameters** rollout, respectively. Release the left mouse button to set the length and width of the section spline; a section spline will be created in the viewport, as shown in Figure 5-52.

Various rollouts used to create and modify the section spline are discussed next.

Section Parameters Rollout

The options in this rollout are used to create a new shape, based on the cross-section where the section spline slices the objects, refer to Figure 5-53. To do so, select the section spline in the viewport and choose the **Modify** tab in the **Command Panel**; the **Section Parameters** and **Section Size** rollouts will be displayed. Now, move or rotate the section spline so that it intersects the mesh object in the viewport. When you move the section spline on the mesh object, the **Create Shape** button in the **Section Parameters** rollout will be activated. Choose this button; the **Name Section Shape** dialog box will be displayed, as shown in Figure 5-54. In the **Name** text box, enter the name of the new shape and choose the **OK** button; a new shape will be created. This new shape will be editable and will have vertex, segment, and splines sub-objects. You will learn to edit these types of splines in the later chapters. The areas in the **Section Parameters** rollout are discussed next.

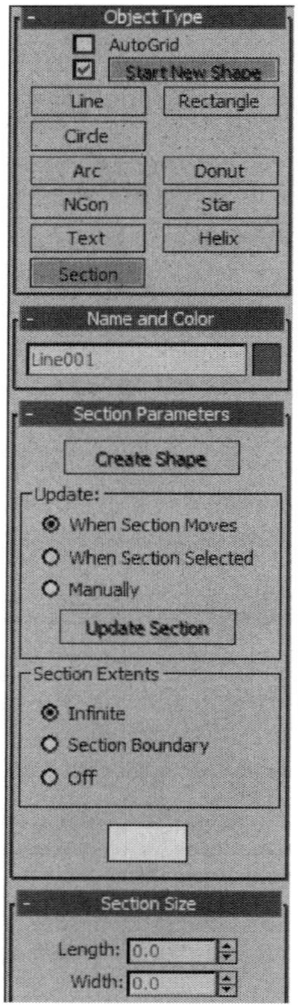

***Figure 5-51** Various rollouts to create and modify a section spline*

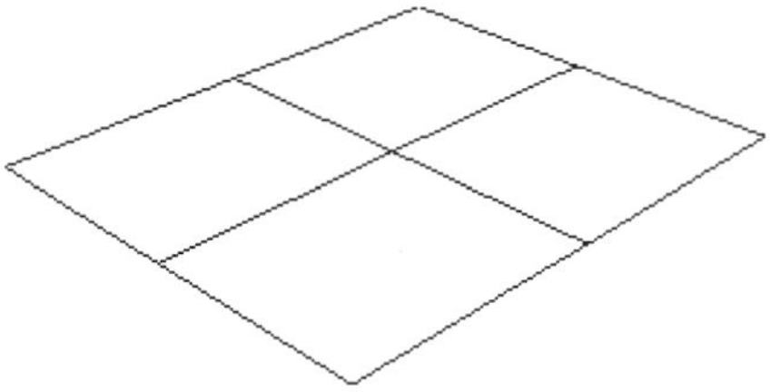

***Figure 5-52** A section spline*

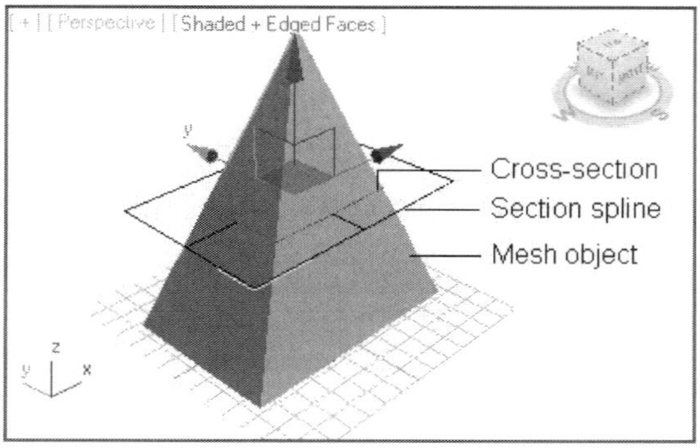

***Figure 5-53** The cross-section of the section spline according to the object*

Update Area

This area has three radio buttons to specify when the cross-section will be updated. Select the **When Section Moves** radio button to update the cross-section while moving the section spline. The **When Section Selected** radio button is used to update the cross-section when you select the section spline. Also, you need to choose the **Update Section** button to update it. The **Manually** radio button is used to update the cross-section manually by choosing the **Update Section** button.

Section Extents Area

The radio buttons in this area are used to define the extent of cross-section produced by the section spline. When you select the **Infinite** radio button, the section plane will be infinite in all directions. It generates the cross-section for all the objects that come in its plane, as shown in Figure 5-55. The **Section Boundary** radio button is used to generate the cross-section only for the objects that are touched by the boundary or are inside the section plane. When you select the **Off** radio button, the cross-section will not be displayed and the **Create Shape** button will be inactive.

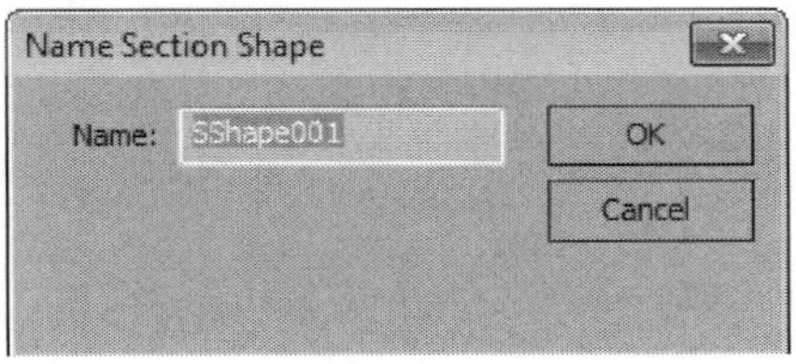

***Figure 5-54** The **Name Section Shape** dialog box*

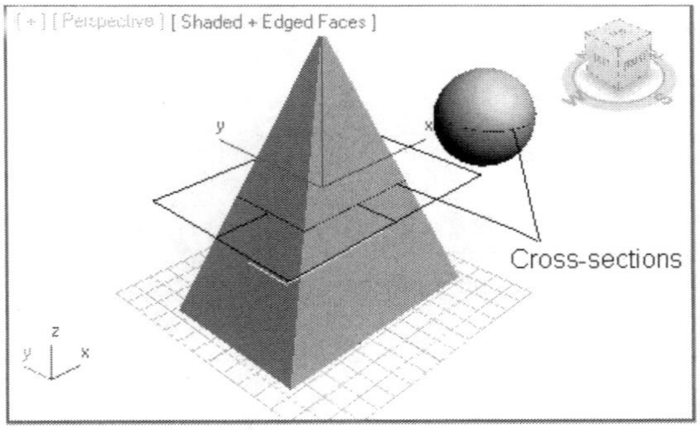

***Figure 5-55** The cross-sections generated in both the objects in their planes on selecting the **Infinite** radio button*

By default, the color of the cross-section in a section spline is yellow. If you want to change it, choose the color swatch at the bottom of the **Section Extents** area; the **Color Selector** dialog box will be displayed. Select the new color and choose the **OK** button; the new color will be displayed in the color swatch.

Section Size Rollout

The options in this rollout are used to modify the overall size of the rectangular section spline. Set the value in the **Length** and **Width** spinners to modify the size of the rectangular section spline.

CREATING EXTENDED SPLINES

To create the extended splines, choose **Create > Shapes** in the **Command Panel**; the **Splines** option will be displayed in the drop-down list. Select the **Extended Splines** option from the drop-down list, as shown in Figure 5-56; all tools to create extended splines will be displayed in the **Object Type** rollout. In this section, you will learn to create and modify extended splines using various tools available in the **Object Type** rollout.

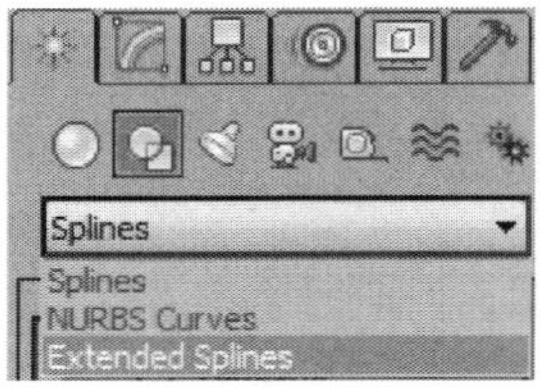

***Figure 5-56** Selecting the **Extended Splines** option from the drop-down list*

Creating a WRectangle Spline

Menu bar:	Create > Extended Shapes > WRectangle
Command Panel:	Create > Shapes > Extended Splines > Object Type rollout > WRectangle

The WRectangle spline is a closed spline with two concentric rectangles. To create a WRectangle spline, invoke the **WRectangle** tool from the **Object Type** rollout; the **Name and Color**, **Rendering**, **Interpolation**, **Creation Method**, **Keyboard Entry**, and **Parameters** rollouts will be displayed, as shown in Figure 5-57.

Next, press and hold the left mouse button and then drag the cursor. As you drag the cursor, the length and width values of the WRectangle will be displayed in the **Length** and **Width** spinners of the **Parameters** rollout, respectively. Release the left mouse button to set the length and width, and then move the cursor to define the thickness or the inner rectangle. Click on the screen; a WRectangle spline will be created in the viewport, as shown in Figures 5-58 and 5-59.

Various rollouts used to create and modify the WRectangle are discussed next.

Note

*The options in the **Creation Method** rollout for all extended splines are the same as described earlier in this chapter.*

Parameters Rollout

The options in this rollout are used to modify the WRectangle spline. To do so, select the WRectangle and choose the **Modify** tab in the **Command Panel**; the **Rendering**, **Interpolation**, and **Parameters** rollouts will be displayed. In the **Parameters** rollout, set the new values of length, width, and thickness in the respective spinners. The **Sync Corner Fillets** check box is used to control the radius of the corners of the outer rectangle using the **Corner Radius 1** spinner. By default, this check box is selected. If you clear this check box, it will control the radius of the corners of both the concentric rectangles through the **Corner Radius 1** and **Corner Radius 2** spinners.

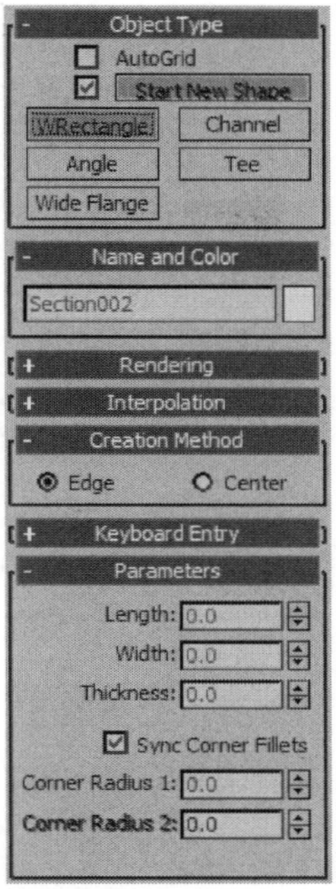

Figure 5-57 *Various rollouts to create and modify a WRectangle spline*

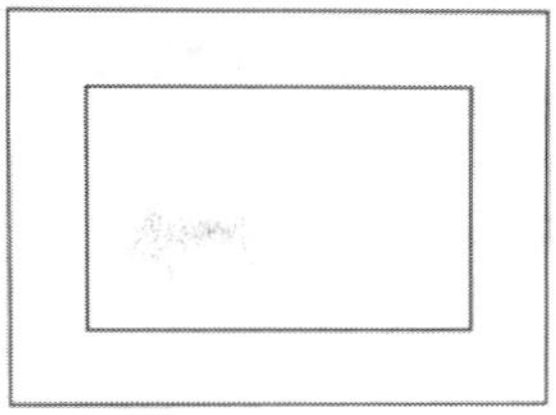

Figure 5-58 *A WRectangle spline*

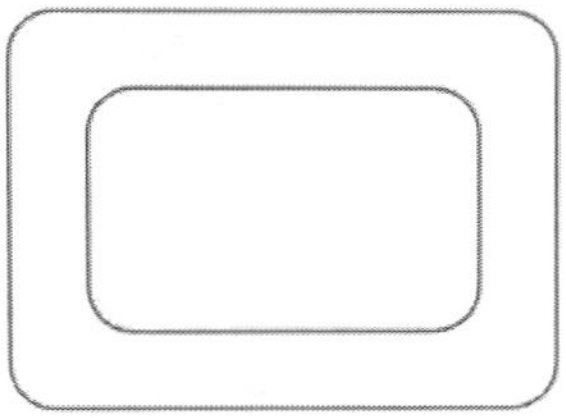

Figure 5-59 *The WRectangle spline with corner radius*

Creating a Channel Spline

Menu bar:	Create > Extended Shapes > Channel
Command Panel:	Create > Shapes > Extended Splines > Object Type rollout > Channel

The channel spline is a C-shaped closed spline. To create a channel spline, activate the viewport in which you want to create it and then invoke the **Channel** tool from the **Object Type** rollout; the **Name and Color**, **Rendering**, **Interpolation**, **Creation Method**, **Keyboard Entry**, and **Parameters** rollouts will be displayed, as shown in Figure 5-60.

Now, press and hold the left mouse button and drag the cursor to set the length and width of the channel. Next, release the left mouse button and move the cursor to define the thickness or the inner shape. Click on the screen; a channel spline will be created in the viewport, as shown in Figure 5-61.

Parameters Rollout

The options in this rollout are used while creating a channel dynamically. These options are the same as those discussed in the **WRectangle** tool. The channel spline with the corner radius is shown in Figure 5-62.

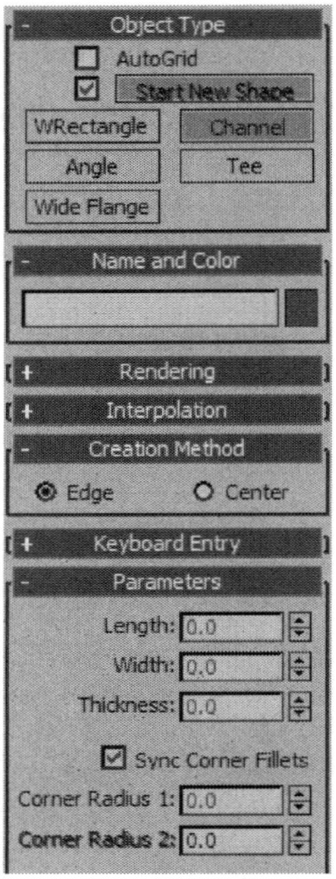

Figure 5-60 *Various rollouts to create and modify a channel spline*

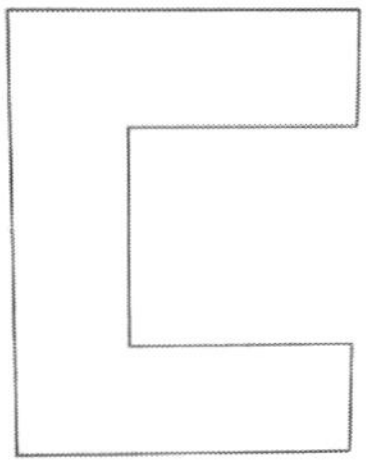

Figure 5-61 *A channel spline*

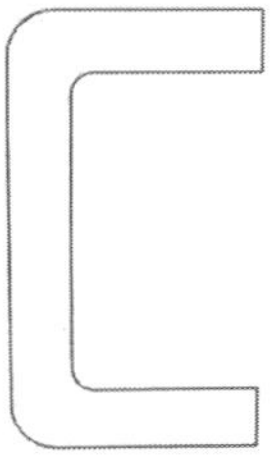

Figure 5-62 *The channel spline with corner radius*

Creating an Angle Spline

Menu bar:	Create > Extended Shapes > Angle
Command Panel:	Create > Shapes > Extended Splines > Object Type rollout > Angle

The angle spline is an L-shaped closed spline. To create an angle spline, activate the viewport in which you want to create it and then invoke the **Angle** tool from the **Object Type** rollout; the **Name and Color**, **Rendering**, **Interpolation**, **Creation Method**, **Keyboard Entry**, and **Parameters** rollouts will be displayed, as shown in Figure 5-63.

Next, press and hold the left mouse button and drag the cursor to set the length and width of the angle spline. Next, release the left mouse button and move the cursor inside to define the thickness or the inner shape. Click on the screen; an angle spline will be created in the viewport, as shown in Figure 5-64.

The **Parameters** rollout used to modify the angle spline is discussed next.

Parameters Rollout

The options in this rollout are used to modify an angle spline. To do so, select the angle spline and choose the **Modify** tab in the **Command Panel**; the **Rendering**, **Interpolation**, and **Parameters** rollouts will be displayed. In the **Parameters** rollout, set the new values of length, width, and thickness in the respective spinners. The **Sync Corner Fillets** check box is used to control the radius of the corners of the outer shape through the **Corner Radius 1** spinner.

By default, this check box is selected. If you clear this check box, it will control the radius of the corners of inner and outer shapes through the **Corner Radius 1** and **Corner Radius 2** spinners, as shown in Figure 5-65. The **Edge Radii** spinner is used to define the radius of the edges of the legs of the L-shaped spline, as shown in Figure 5-66.

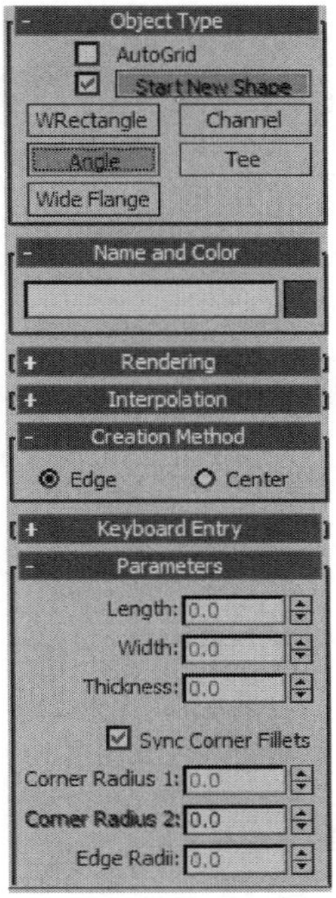

Figure 5-63 *Various rollouts to create and modify an angle spline*

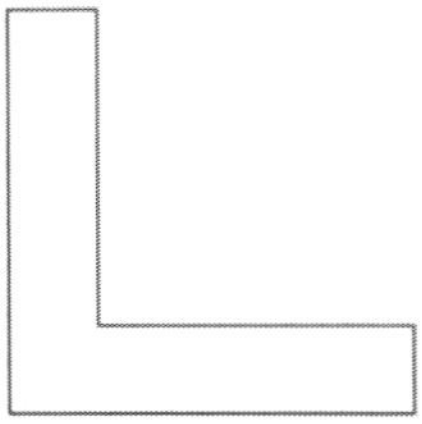

Figure 5-64 *An angle spline*

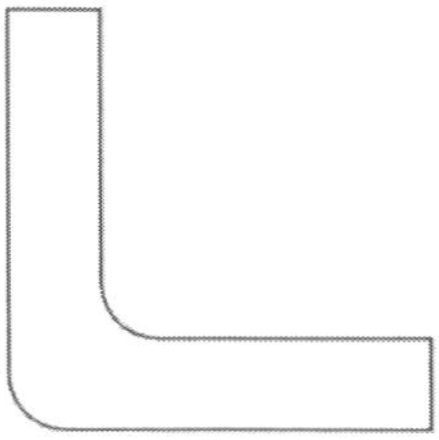

Figure 5-65 *The angle spline with corner radius*

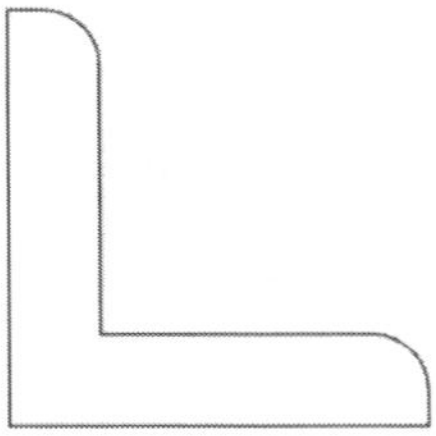

Figure 5-66 *An angle spline with edge radii*

Creating a Tee Spline

Menu bar:	Create > Extended Shapes > Tee
Command Panel:	Create > Shapes > Extended Splines > Object Type rollout > Tee

The tee spline is a T-shaped closed spline. To create a tee spline, activate the viewport in which you want to create it and then invoke the **Tee** tool from the **Object Type** rollout; the **Name and Color**, **Rendering**, **Interpolation**, **Creation Method**, **Keyboard Entry**, and **Parameters** rollouts will be displayed, as shown in Figure 5-67.

Next, press and hold the left mouse button and drag the cursor to set the length and width of the tee spline. Now, move the cursor to define the thickness and click on the screen; a T-shaped tee spline will be created in the viewport, as shown in Figure 5-68. The **Parameters** rollout used to modify the tee spline is discussed next.

Parameters Rollout

The options in this rollout are used to modify the tee spline. To do so, set the new length, width, and thickness values in the respective spinners. Set the value in the **Corner Radius** spinner to round the corners between the horizontal and vertical shapes, as shown in Figure 5-69.

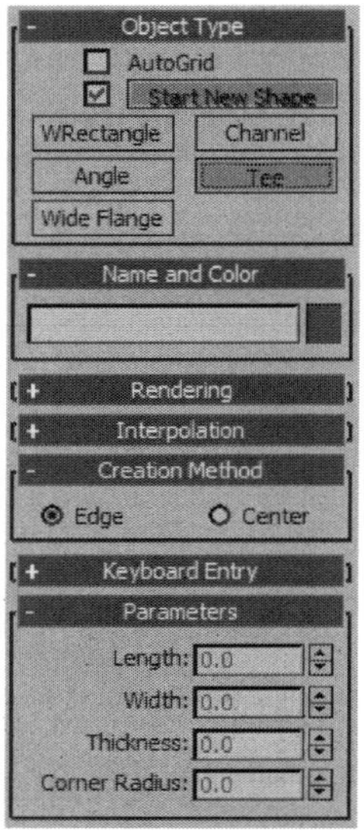

Figure 5-67 Various rollouts to create and modify a tee spline

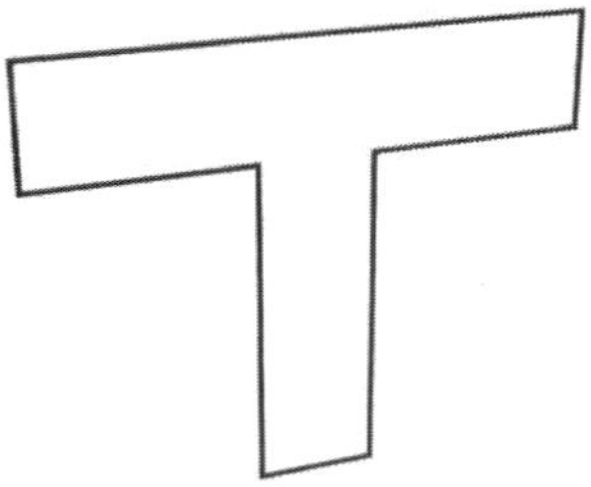

Figure 5-68 A T-shaped tee spline

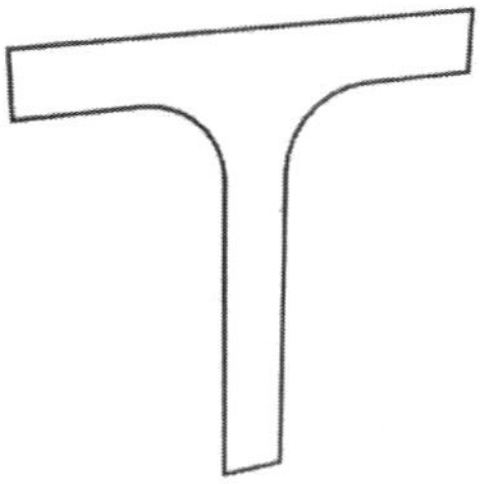

Figure 5-69 A tee spline with corner radius

Creating a Wide Flange Spline

Menu bar:	Create > Extended Shapes > Wide Flange
Command Panel:	Create > Shapes > Extended Splines > Object Type rollout > Wide Flange

The wide flange spline is an I-shaped closed spline. To create a wide flange spline, activate the viewport in which you want to create it and then invoke the **Wide Flange** tool from the **Object Type** rollout; the **Name and Color**, **Rendering**, **Interpolation**, **Creation Method**, **Keyboard Entry**, and **Parameters** rollouts will be displayed, as shown in Figure 5-70.

Next, press and hold the left mouse button and drag the cursor to set the length and width of the wide flange spline. Next, move the mouse to define the thickness and click on the screen; an I-shaped wide flange spline will be created in the viewport, as shown in Figure 5-71.

The **Parameters** rollout used to modify the wide flange spline is discussed next.

Parameters Rollout

The options in this rollout are used to modify the wide flange spline. To do so, select the wide flange spline and choose the **Modify** tab in the **Command Panel**; the **Rendering**, **Interpolation**, and **Parameters** rollouts will be displayed. In the **Parameters** rollout, set the new values of length, width, and thickness in the respective spinners. Set the value in the **Corner Radius** spinner to round the corners between the horizontal and vertical shapes of the wide flange spline, as shown in Figure 5-72.

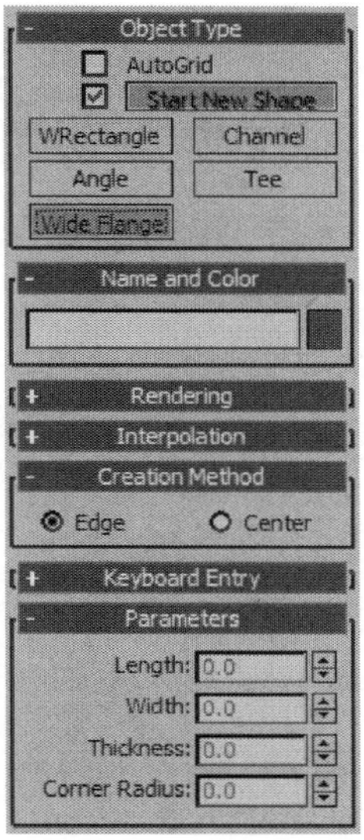

Figure 5-70 Various rollouts to create and modify a wide flange spline

Figure 5-71 An I-shaped wide flange spline

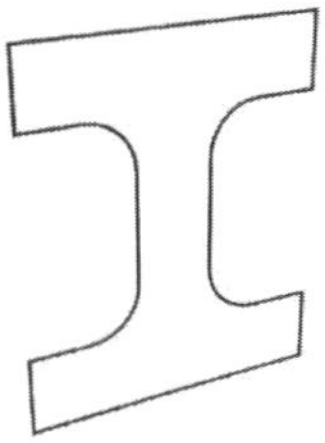

Figure 5-72 The wide flange spline with corner radius

Tutorial 1

In this tutorial, you will create a Christmas tree, as shown in Figure 5-73, using the AEC extended objects and then decorate it using different splines. **(Expected time: 45 min)**

Figure 5-73 A Christmas tree model

The following steps are required to complete this tutorial:

a. Set the project folder.
b. Create a Christmas tree using the AEC extended objects.
c. Create helix spline.
d. Create stars.
e. Create spiral coils.
f. Create balloons.
g. Create rings.
h. Change the background color for the final output.
i. Render the scene for the final output.
j. Save the file.

Setting the Project Folder

1. Set the project folder with the name *c05_tut1* in the *3dsmax* folder as discussed in Tutorial 1 of Chapter 2.

Creating a Christmas Tree

Reset Autodesk 3ds Max, if the program is already running. Now, you need to create a tree.

1. Activate the Top viewport. Choose **Create > Geometry** in the **Command Panel**; a drop-down list is displayed. Select **AEC Extended** from the drop-down list. Next, invoke the **Foliage** tool from the **Object Type** rollout; a number of default plants are displayed in the **Favorite Plants** rollout.

2. Select the **Scotch Pine** plant from the **Favorite Plants** rollout. Next, double-click on the **Scotch Pine** plant; the **Scotch Pine** plant is displayed in all viewports.

3. In the **Name and Color** rollout, modify the default name to *Christmas tree*.

4. Invoke the **Zoom Extents All** tool to view the entire tree in all viewports, as shown in Figure 5-74.

5. Change the view of the Perspective viewport using the **Orbit** and **Zoom** tools, as shown in Figure 5-75.

Note

If the default plant is not selected in the viewport, then it gets displayed in the canopy mode.

Creating the Helix Spline

Next, you need to create a spiral ring to cover the *Christmas tree*.

1. Activate the Top viewport. Choose **Create > Shapes** in the **Command Panel**; the **Splines** option is displayed in the drop-down list. Next, invoke the **Helix** tool from the **Object Type** rollout.

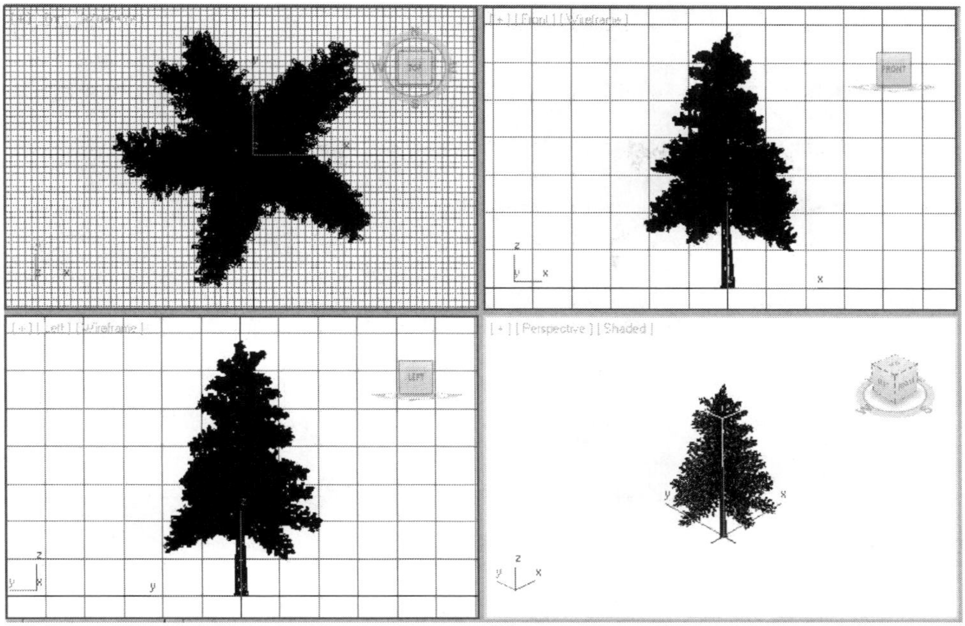

Figure 5-74 *The Christmas tree displayed in all viewports*

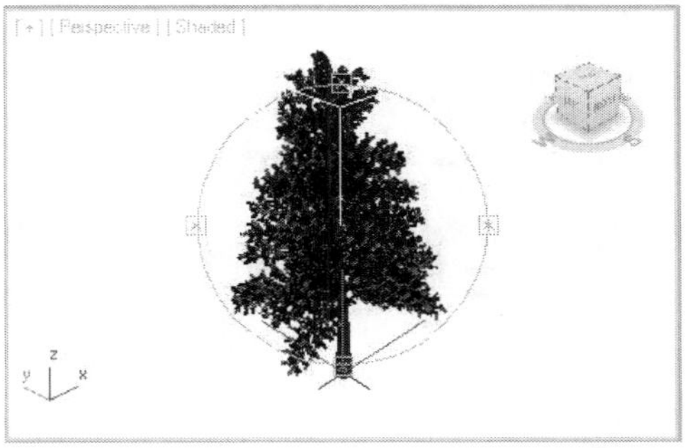

Figure 5-75 *The Christmas tree displayed in the Perspective viewport*

2. Expand the **Keyboard Entry** rollout and enter the values as given below:

   Radius 1: **212.449** Radius 2: **61.256** Height: **451.902**

3. Now, choose the **Create** button; the helix is displayed in all viewports.

4. Name the helix as *outer spiral ring* and use the color swatch to change the color of the helix using the values given below:

   Red: **248** Green: **58** Blue: **0**

5. Choose the **Modify** tab in the **Command Panel** and set the parameters of the *outer spiral ring* in various rollouts as given below:

   Rendering rollout
   Select the **Enable In Renderer** check box.
   Select the **Enable In Viewport** check box.
   Select the **Radial** radio button, if it is not already selected.
   Thickness: **6.0** Sides: **12**

   Parameters rollout
   Turns: **7.0**
   Make sure that the **CW** radio button is selected.

6. Next, invoke the **Select and Move** tool and align the *outer spiral ring* in all viewports, as shown in Figure 5-76.

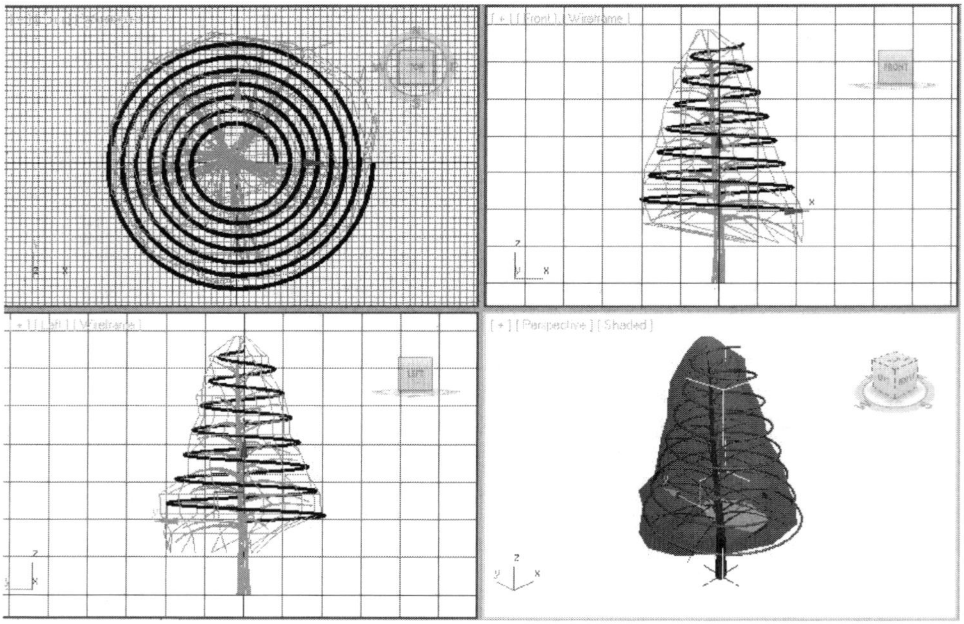

Figure 5-76 *Alignment of the outer spiral ring in all viewports*

Creating the Stars

1. To create stars, invoke the **Star** tool from **Create > Shapes > Splines > Object Type** rollout in the **Command Panel**.

2. Activate the Front viewport. Expand the **Keyboard Entry** rollout and enter the values as given below:

   Y: **400.0** Z: **100.0**
   Radius 1: **28.249** Radius 2: **14.04**

3. Now, choose the **Create** button; the star spline is displayed in all viewports.

4. Name the star spline as *star A01* and change its color using the color swatch by entering the values as given below:

   Red: **250** Green: **241** Blue: **0**

5. Choose the **Modify** tab in the **Command Panel** and set the parameters of the *star A01* in various rollouts as given below:

   Rendering rollout
   Select the **Enable In Renderer** check box.
   Select the **Enable In Viewport** check box.
   Select the **Radial** radio button.
   Thickness: **7.0**

   Use default parameters for other options.

   Use default parameters for the options in the **Interpolation** rollout.

   Parameters rollout
   Points: **12**

6. Now, align the *star A01* in all viewports using the **Select and Move** and **Select and Rotate** tools, as shown in Figure 5-77.

Note
While aligning objects, make sure that the objects are aligned properly in all viewports.

7. Create two copies of the *star A01*. Now, align the copied *star A002* and *star A003* in all viewports using the **Select and Rotate** and **Select and Move** tools, as shown in Figure 5-78.

   Next, you need to create another star spline with a different shape.

8. Activate the Front viewport and invoke the **Star** tool.

9. Expand the **Keyboard Entry** rollout and then enter the values as given below:

   Y: **400.0** Z: **100.0**
   Radius 1: **41.648** Radius 2: **1.896**

10. Choose the **Create** button; another star spline is created.

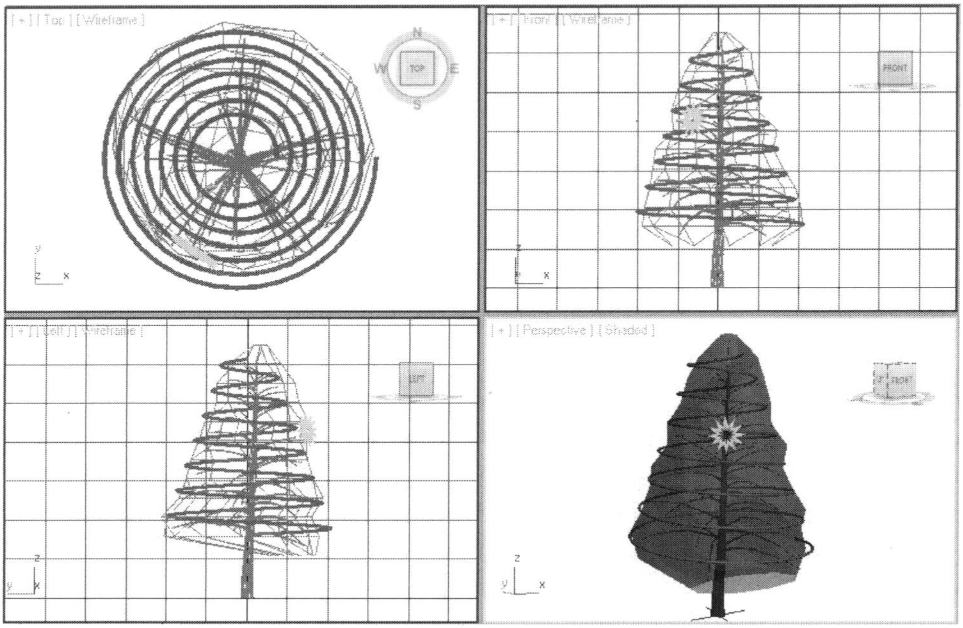

***Figure 5-77** The star A01 displayed in all viewports after the alignment*

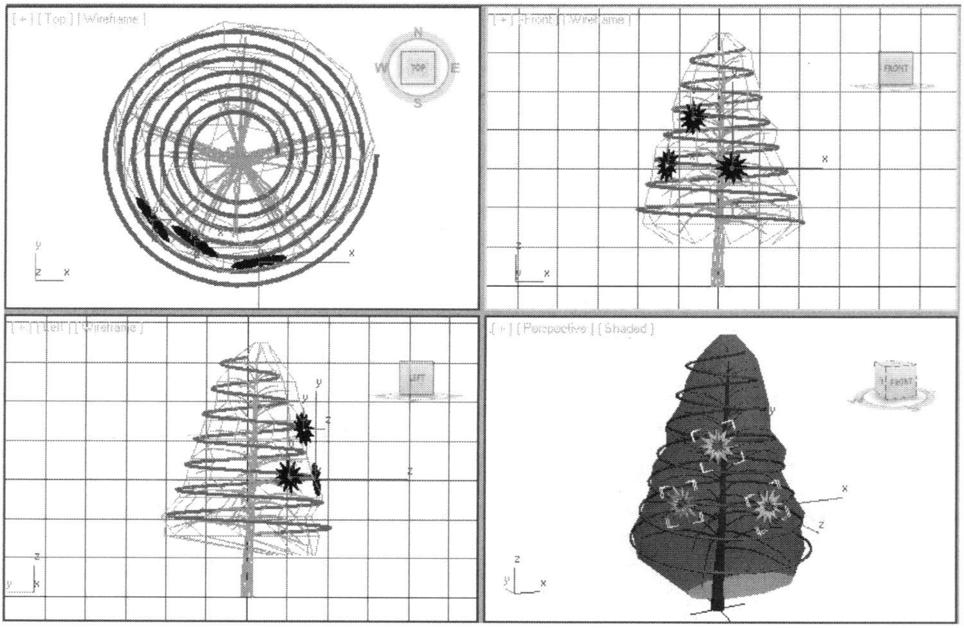

***Figure 5-78** The star A002 and star A003 displayed after the alignment*

11. Name it as *star B01* and then change its color by entering the values given below:

    Red: **248** Green: **58** Blue: **0**

12. Make sure that the *star B01* is selected and then choose the **Modify** tab in the **Command Panel**. Now, set the parameters of the *star B01* in various rollouts as given below:

    Rendering rollout
    Select the **Enable In Renderer** check box.
    Select the **Enable In Viewport** check box.
    Select the **Radial** radio button.
    Thickness: **7.0**
    Use default parameters for other options.

    Use default parameters for the options in the **Interpolation** rollout.

    Parameters rollout
    Points: **10**

13. Invoke the **Select and Move** and **Select and Rotate** tools and align the *star B01* at the top of the *outer spiral ring* in all viewports, as shown in Figure 5-79.

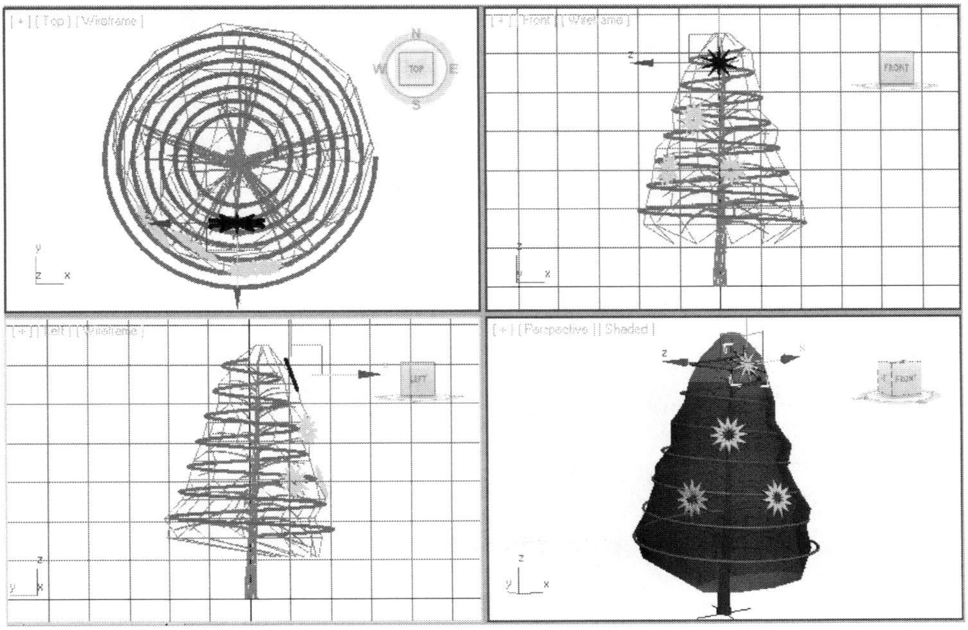

Figure 5-79 *Alignment of the star B01 in all viewports*

14. In the Front viewport, create three copies of the *star B01* and change the color of the copied stars, *star B002*, *star B003*, and *star B004* by entering the values as given below:

    Red: **247** Green: **0** Blue: **238**

15. Align the *star B002*, *star B003*, and *star B004* in all viewports using the **Select and Rotate** and **Select and Move** tools, as shown in Figure 5-80.

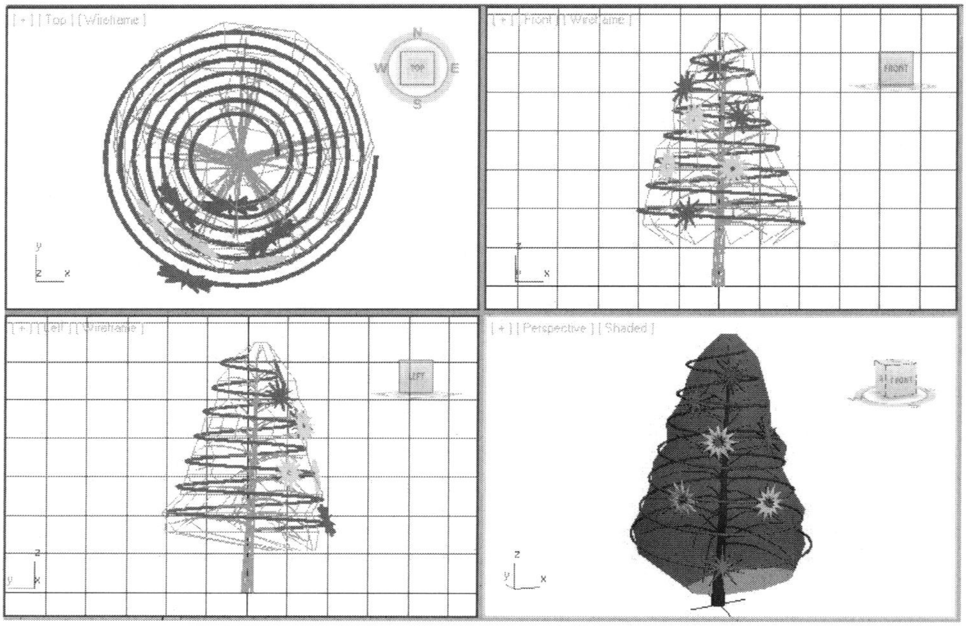

Figure 5-80 *Alignment of the star B002, star B003, and star B004 in all viewports*

Next, you need to create another star spline with a different shape.

16. Activate the Front viewport and invoke the **Star** tool.

17. Expand the **Keyboard Entry** rollout and enter the values as given next.

    Y: **400.0** Z: **100.0**
    Radius 1: **28.074** Radius 2: **10.686**

18. Choose the **Create** button; another star spline is created.

19. Name it as *star C01* and change its color by entering the values as given below:

    Red: **248** Green: **58** Blue: **0**

20. Make sure that the *star C01* is selected and choose the **Modify** tab in the **Command Panel**. Now, set the parameters of the *star C01* in various rollouts as given below:

    Rendering rollout
    Select the **Enable In Renderer** check box.
    Select the **Enable In Viewport** check box.
    Select the **Radial** radio button.
    Thickness: **7.0**
    Use default parameters for other options.
    Use default parameters for options in the **Interpolation** rollout.

    Parameters rollout
    Set the value **6.0** in the **Points** spinner.

21. Invoke the **Select and Move** and **Select and Rotate** tools and align the *star C01* in all viewports, as shown in Figure 5-81.

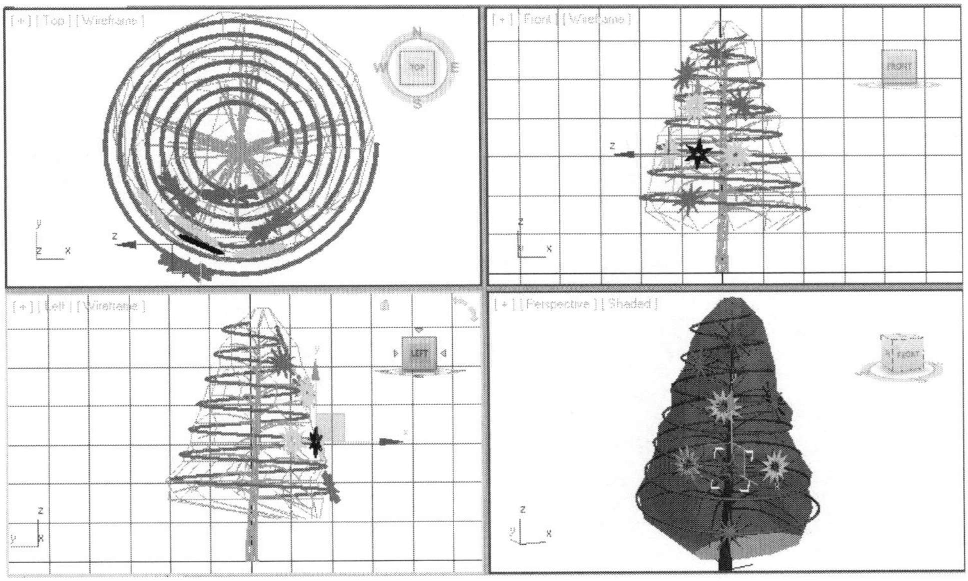

Figure 5-81 *Alignment of the star C01 in all viewports*

Creating the Spiral Coils

To create spiral coils, you need to use the helix spline.

1. Activate the Top viewport and invoke the **Helix** tool.

2. Expand the **Keyboard Entry** rollout and enter the values as given below:

   Radius 1: **17.904** Radius 2: **0.0** Height: **67.04**

3. Choose the **Create** button; the helix is created in all viewports.

4. Name the helix as *spiral coil01* and change its color by entering the values as given below:

   Red: **248** Green: **58** Blue: **0**

5. Choose the **Modify** tab in the **Command Panel** and set the parameters of the *spiral coil01* in various rollouts as given next.

   Rendering rollout
   Select the **Enable In Renderer** check box.
   Select the **Enable In Viewport** check box.
   Select the **Radial** radio button.
   Thickness: **7.0**

   Parameters rollout
   Set the value **4.0** in the **Turns** spinner.
   Make sure that the **CW** radio button is selected.

6. Next, align the *spiral coil01* in all viewports using the **Select and Move** and **Select and Rotate** tools, as shown in Figure 5-82.

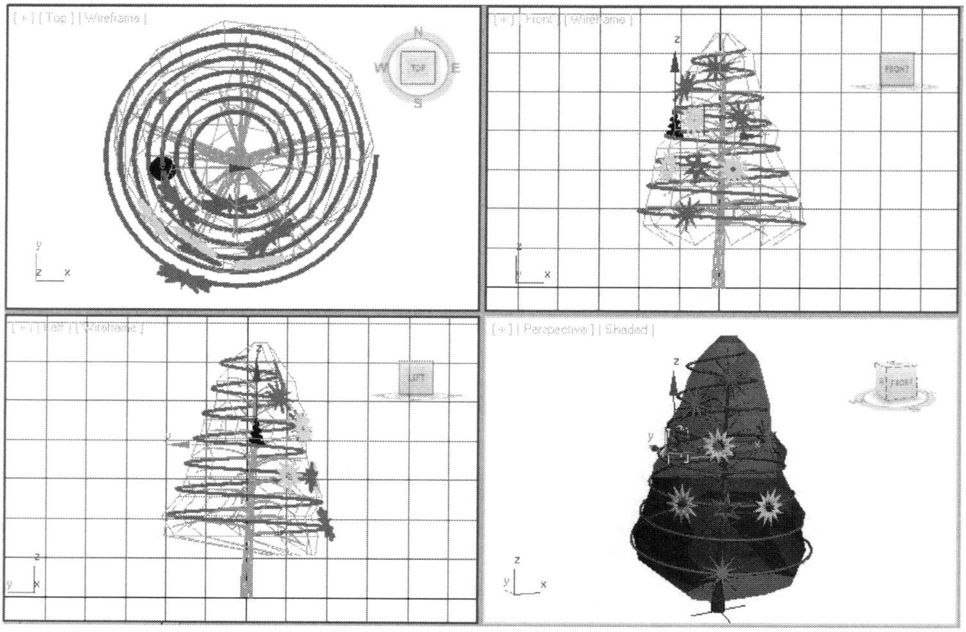

Figure 5-82 *Alignment of the spiral coil01 in all viewports*

7. Next, in the Front viewport, create two copies of the *spiral coil01*. Now, change the color of the copied *spiral coil002* by entering the values as given below:

   Red: **247** Green: **0** Blue: **238**

8. Change the color of the copied *spiral coil003* by entering the values as given below:

   Red: **241** Green: **250** Blue: **0**

9. Align the *spiral coil002* and the *spiral coil003* in all viewports using the **Select and Rotate** and **Select and Move** tools, as shown in Figure 5-83.

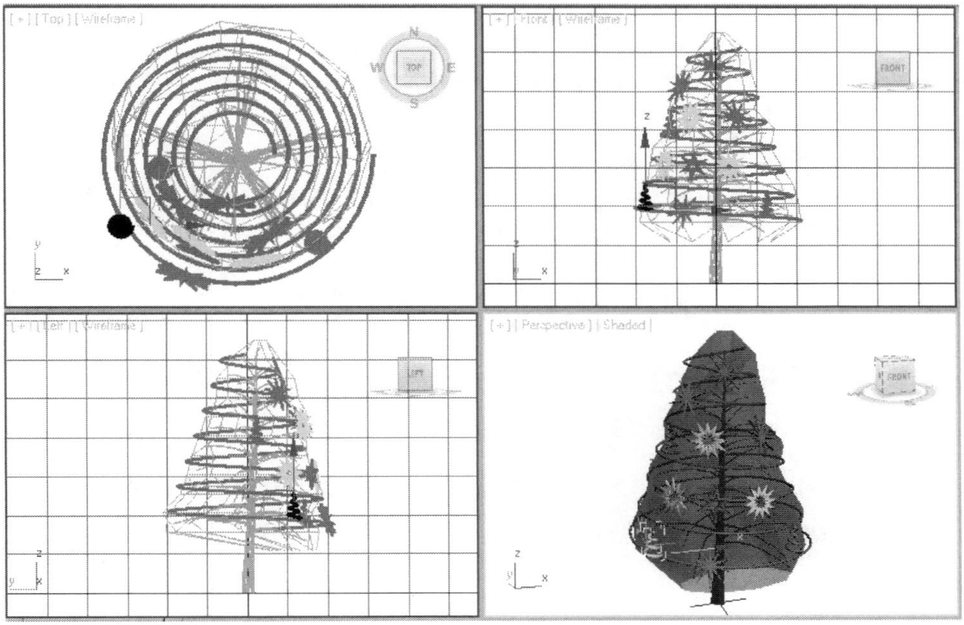

Figure 5-83 *Alignment of the spiral coil002 and the spiral coil003 in all viewports*

Creating the Balloons

To create balloons, you need to use the **Sphere** tool.

1. Activate the Top viewport and choose **Create > Geometry** in the **Command Panel**. Now, make sure that the **Standard Primitives** option is selected in the drop-down list.

2. Invoke the **Sphere** tool. In the **Keyboard Entry** rollout, set the value **24.0** in the **Radius** spinner. Choose the **Create** button; a sphere is displayed in all viewports.

3. Name the sphere as *balloon01* and change its color using the values given below:

   Red: **0** Green: **0** Blue: **255**

4. Next, activate the Front viewport by right-clicking in it.

5. Invoke the **Zoom Extents All Selected** tool from the viewport navigation controls; the *balloon01* is displayed to its maximum extent in the Front viewport, as shown in Figure 5-84.

6. In the Front viewport, click and hold on the **Select and Uniform Scale** tool; a flyout is displayed. Choose the **Select and Non-uniform Scale** tool from the flyout and then right-click on it; the **Scale Transform Type-In** dialog box is displayed. In the **Offset: Screen** area of this dialog box, set the value **130** in the **Y** spinner and press ENTER; the *balloon01* is scaled in the Y-axis, as shown in Figure 5-85.

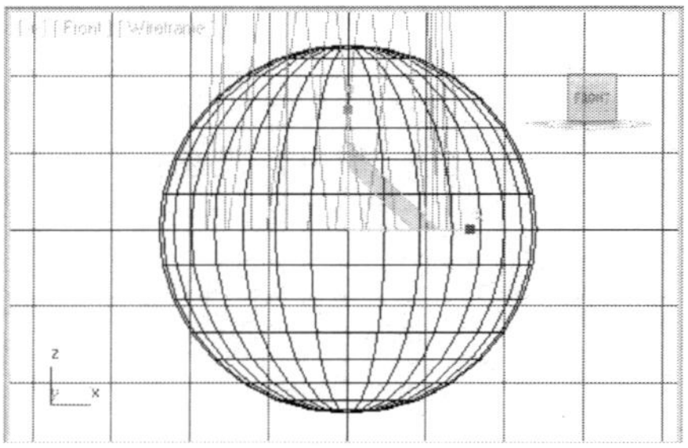

Figure 5-84 *The balloon01 in the Front viewport*

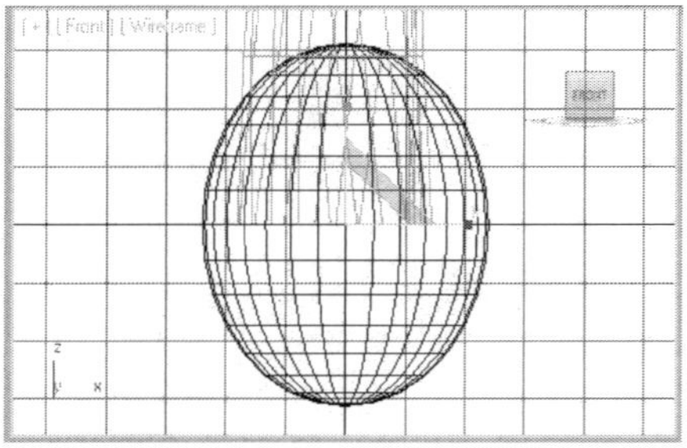

Figure 5-85 *The balloon01 in the Front viewport after scaling*

7. Close the **Scale Transform Type-In** dialog box.

8. Invoke the **Zoom Extents All** tool to view all objects in all viewports properly.

9. Align the *balloon01* in all viewports using the **Select and Move** tool, as shown in Figure 5-86.

10. In the Front viewport, create two copies of the *balloon01*, and then change the color of the copied *balloon002* using the values as given below:

    Red: **247** Green: **0** Blue: **238**

11. Change the color of the *balloon003* by entering the values as given below:

    Red: **241** Green: **250** Blue: **0**

12. Then, align the copied *balloon002* and *balloon003* in all viewports using the **Select and Rotate**, **Select and Move**, and **Zoom** tools, as shown in Figure 5-87.

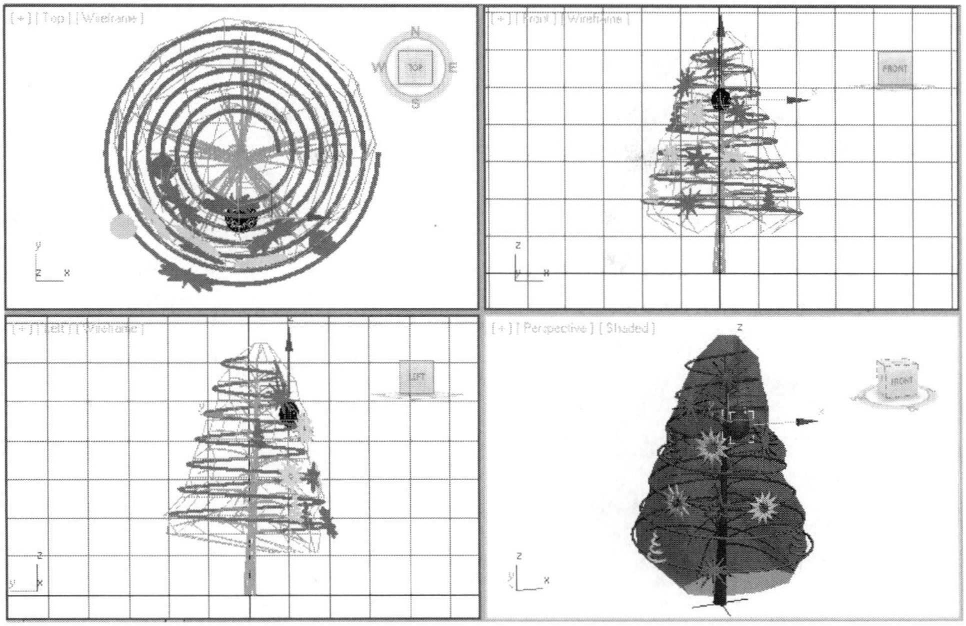

Figure 5-86 Alignment of the balloon01 in all viewports

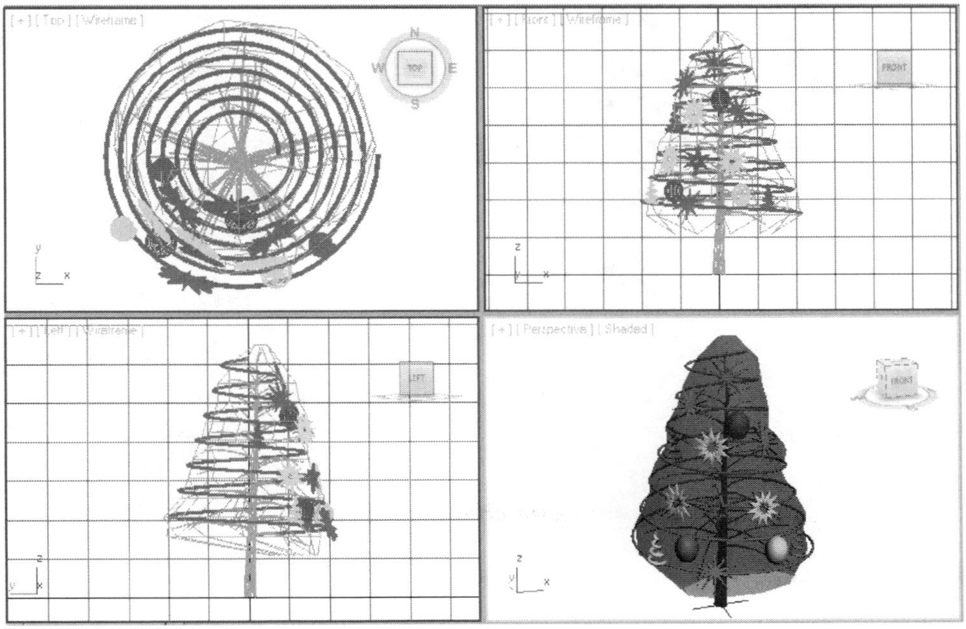

Figure 5-87 Alignment of the balloon002 and the balloon003 in all viewports

Creating the Rings

To create rings, you need to invoke the **Torus** tool from the **Object Type** rollout.

1. Activate the Front viewport and choose **Create > Geometry** in the **Command Panel**. Make sure that the **Standard Primitives** option is selected in the drop-down list.

2. Invoke the **Torus** tool. In the **Keyboard Entry** rollout, set the values as given below:

   Major Radius: **25.328** Minor Radius: **5.191**

3. Choose the **Create** button; a torus is displayed in all viewports.

4. Name the torus as *ring01* and change its color by entering the values as given below:

   Red: **255** Green: **0** Blue: **84**

5. Invoke the **Select and Move** tool and align the *ring01* in all viewports, as shown in Figure 5-88.

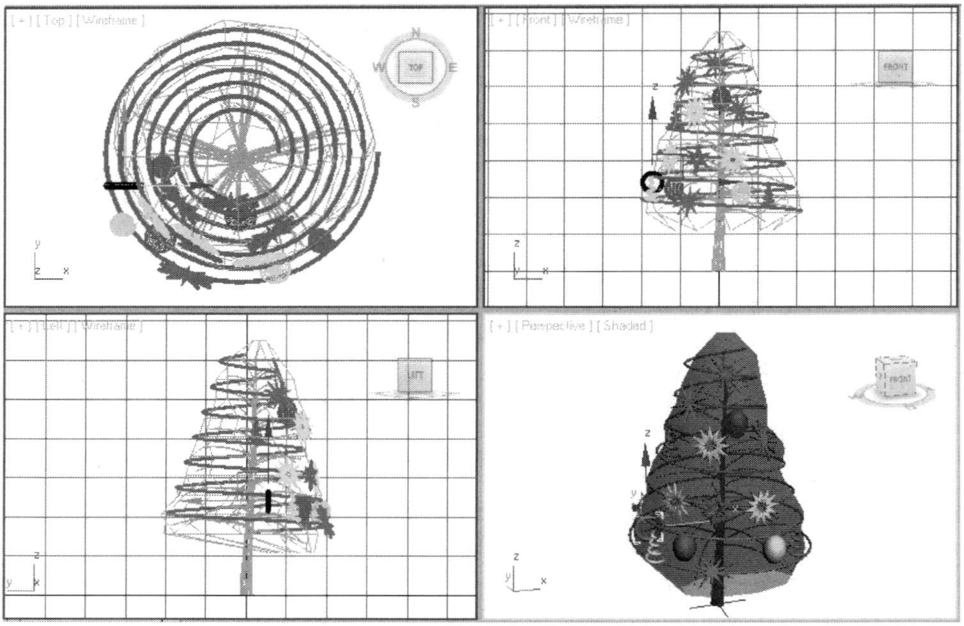

Figure 5-88 *Alignment of the ring01 in all viewports*

6. In the Front viewport, create two copies of the *ring01* and change the color of the copied *ring002* by entering the values as given below:

   Red: **247** Green: **0** Blue: **238**

7. Similarly, change the color of the copied *ring003* by entering the values as given below:

   Red: **245** Green: **29** Blue: **0**

8. Now, align *ring002* and *ring003* in all viewports using the **Select and Rotate**, **Select and Move**, and **Zoom** tools, as shown in Figure 5-89.

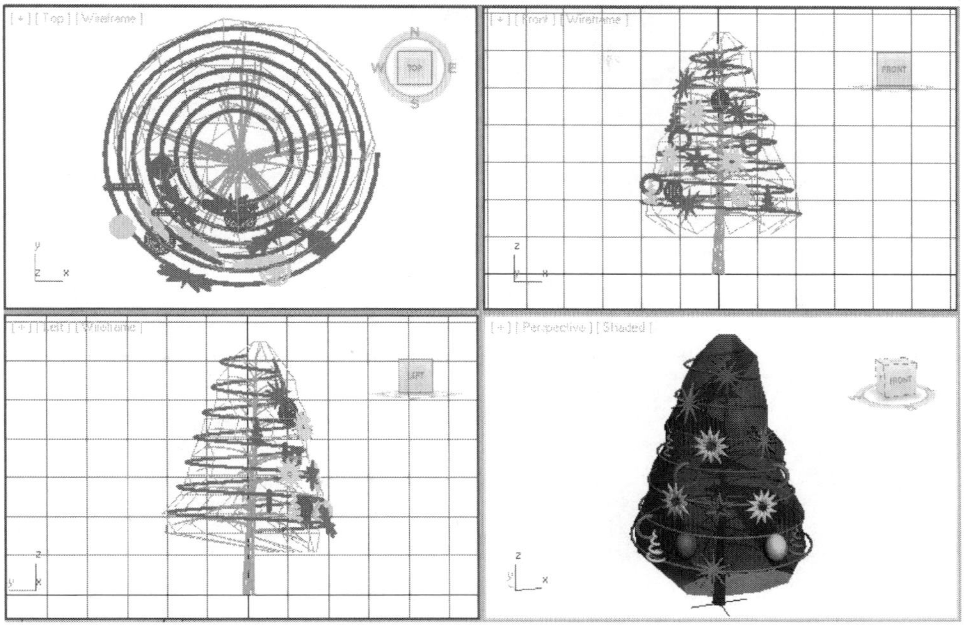

Figure 5-89 *Alignment of ring002 and ring003 in all viewports*

Note

In this tutorial, you have decorated only the front part of the Christmas tree. You can also decorate the whole tree using different splines and primitives by following the same procedure.

Changing the Background Color

1. To change the background color of the scene to white in the final output, follow the steps given in Tutorial 1 of Chapter 2.

Rendering the Scene for the Final Output

1. Activate the Perspective viewport.

2. Invoke the **Render Production** tool from the **Main Toolbar**; the **Perspective, frame 0, Display Gamma:2.2, RGBA Color16 Bits/Channel (1:1)** window is displayed, showing the final output of the *Christmas tree* at one frame, refer to Figure 5-90.

Figure 5-90 *The final output at rendering*

You can view the final rendered image of this model by downloading the *c05_3dsmax_2012_render.zip* file from *http://www.cadcim.com*.

Saving the File

1. Save the file with the name *c05tut1.max* as discussed in earlier chapters. The location of this file is given below:

   \Documents\3dsmax\c05_tut2\scenes

Tutorial 2

In this tutorial, you will create a book, as shown in Figure 5-91, using splines and extended primitives. **(Expected time: 15 min)**

Figure 5-91 *A book model*

The following steps are required to complete this tutorial:

a. Set the project folder.
b. Create a book.
c. Create the spiral binding for the book.

d. Create the text on the book.
e. Change the background color for the final output.
f. Render the scene for the final output.
g. Save the file.

Setting the Project Folder

1. Set the project folder with the name *c05_tut2* in the *3dsmax* folder as discussed in Tutorial 1 of Chapter 2.

Creating a Book

First, reset Autodesk 3ds Max, if the program is already running to start afresh. To create a book, you need to invoke the **Hose** tool from **Extended Primitives**.

1. Activate the Top viewport. Choose **Create > Geometry** in the **Command Panel** and then select **Extended Primitives** from the drop-down list displayed below the **Geometry** button. Now, invoke the **Hose** tool from the **Object Type** rollout.

2. In the Top viewport, press and hold the left mouse button and drag the cursor to define the radius of the hose. Next, release the left mouse button and move the cursor up to define the height of the hose. Now, click on the screen to get the desired height; a hose is created.

3. Name the hose as *book* and change its color by entering the values as given below:

   Red: **153** Green: **228** Blue: **214**

4. Choose the **Modify** tab in the **Command Panel** and set the parameters of the *book* in the **Hose Parameters** rollout as given below:

   Free Hose Parameters area
   Height: **29.798**

   Common Hose Parameters area
   Make sure that the **Flex Section Enable** check box is selected and use default values for other options.

   Hose Shape area
   Select the **Rectangular Hose** radio button.
   Width: **144.927** Depth: **210.827**

   Use the default values for other options.

5. Invoke the **Zoom Extents All** tool to view the entire *book* in all viewports, as shown in Figure 5-92.

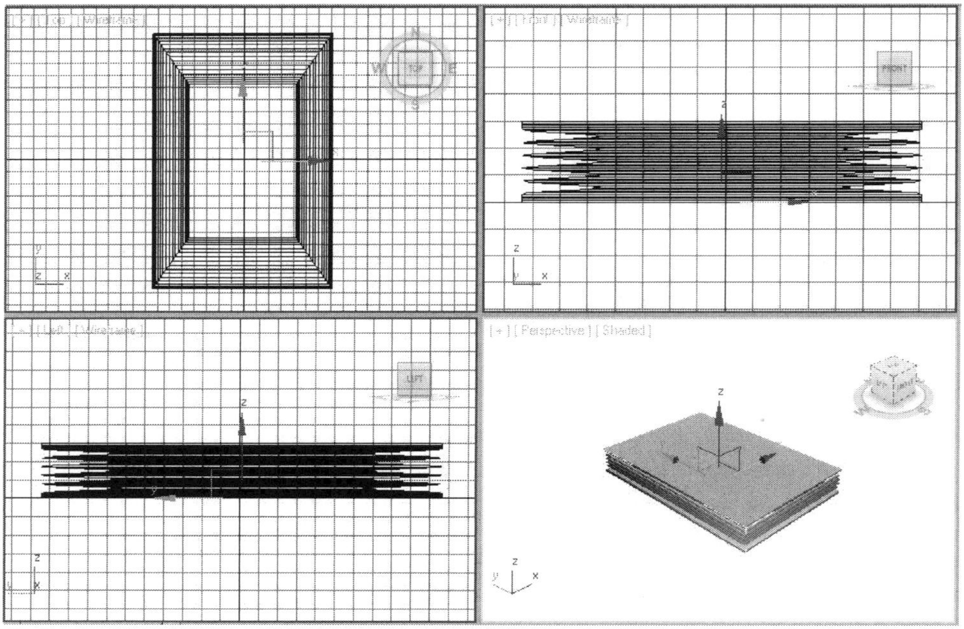

***Figure 5-92** The book after invoking the **Zoom Extents All** tool*

Creating the Spiral Binding

To create the spiral binding of the book, you need to create the helix spline.

1. Activate the Front viewport and choose **Create > Shapes** in the **Command Panel**. Make sure that **Splines** is selected in the drop-down list displayed below the **Shapes** button. Now, invoke the **Helix** tool from the **Object Type** rollout.

2. Expand the **Keyboard Entry** rollout and enter the values as given below:

   Radius 1: **17.0** Radius 2: **17.0** Height: **205.0**

3. Choose the **Create** button; a helix shape is created.

4. Name the helix as *spiral binding* and change its color by entering the values as given below:

   Red: **6** Green: **134** Blue: **6**

5. Choose the **Modify** tab in the **Command Panel** and set the parameters of the *spiral binding* in various rollouts as given below:

   Rendering rollout
   Select the **Enable In Renderer** check box.
   Select the **Enable In Viewport** check box.
   Select the **Radial** radio button.
   Thickness: **1.5**

Parameters rollout
Turns: **17.0**
Make sure that the **CW** radio button is selected.

6. Next, invoke the **Select and Move** tool and align the *spiral binding* with the *book* in all viewports, as shown in Figure 5-93.

Creating the Text on the Book

To create the text on the book, you need to use the **Text** tool.

1. Choose **Create > Shapes** from the **Command Panel**; the **Splines** option is selected in the drop-down list. Now, invoke the **Text** tool from the **Object Type** rollout. Also, select the **AutoGrid** check box in the **Object Type** rollout.

2. In the **Parameters** rollout of the **Text** tool, enter **CADCIM 3ds Max** in the text box of the **Text** area. Then, click on the screen in the Top viewport; the text is displayed in all viewports.

Note
To write the text in two lines, you need to arrange it in the text box of the **Text** *area by pressing the ENTER key.*

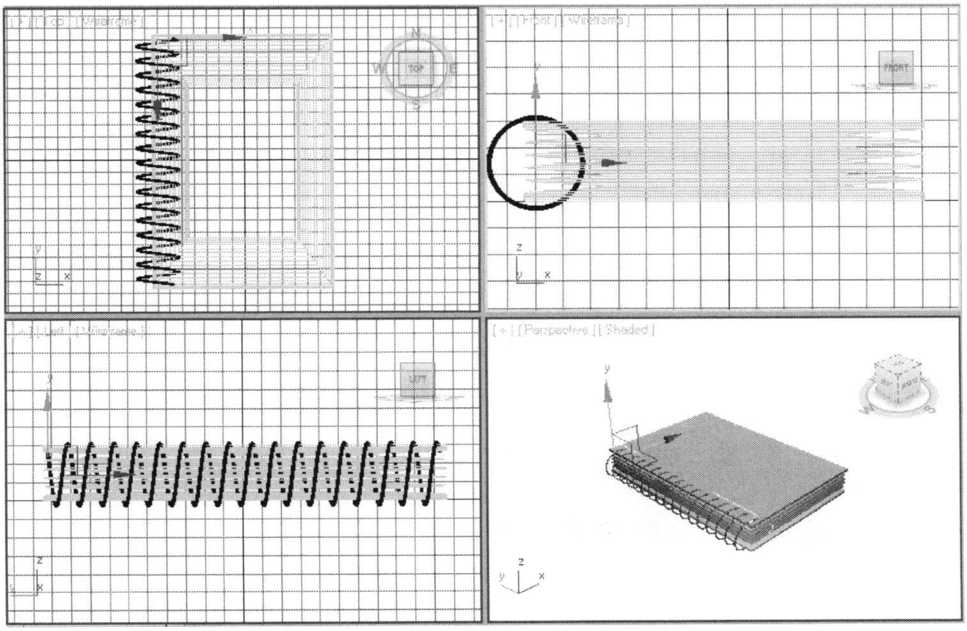

Figure 5-93 *Alignment of the spiral binding with the book in all viewports*

3. Name the text as *text01* and change its color by entering the values as given below:

Red: **6** Green: **134** Blue: **6**

4. Choose the **Modify** tab in the **Command Panel** and set the parameters of the *text01* in the **Parameters** rollout as given next.

   Select the **Monotype Corsiva** font type from the drop-down list.

   Choose the center align button and enter the values as given below:

   Size: **23** Kerning: **1.0** Leading: **1.0**

5. Invoke the **Select and Move** tool and align the *text01* in all viewports, as shown in Figure 5-94.

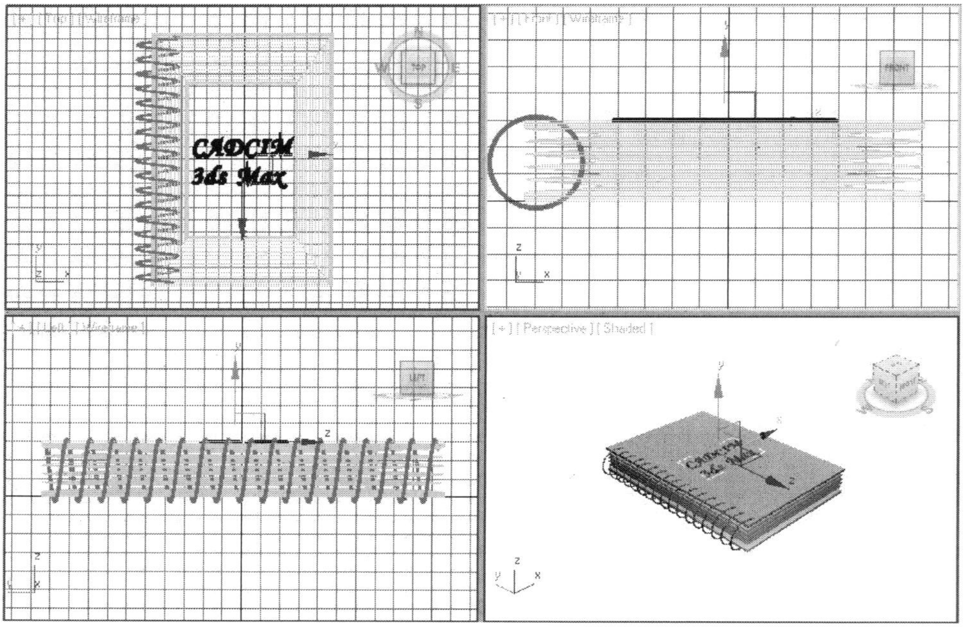

Figure 5-94 *Alignment of the text01 on the book in all viewports*

Now, you need to create a rectangular design over the text.

6. Invoke the **Rectangle** tool from the **Object Type** rollout. Make sure that the **AutoGrid** check box is still selected.

7. Activate the Top viewport. Click at the upper left corner of the *book*, hold the left mouse button, and then drag the cursor to the lower right corner of the *book*. Next, release the left mouse button to set the length and width; a rectangular spline is created in all viewports.

8. Name the rectangle as the *rectangular design* and change its color using the values as given below:

   Red: **6** Green: **134** Blue: **6**

9. Choose the **Modify** tab in the **Command Panel** and set the parameters of the *rectangular design* in various rollouts as given below:

   Rendering rollout
   Select the **Enable In Renderer** check box.
   Select the **Enable In Viewport** check box.
   Select the **Radial** radio button.
   Thickness: **1.0**

   Parameters rollout
   Length: **126.581** Width: **86.824**
   Corner Radius: **10.0**

10. Invoke the **Select and Move** tool and align the *rectangular design* in all viewports, as shown in Figure 5-95.

Changing the Background Color

1. To change the background color of the scene to white in the final output, follow the steps given in Tutorial 1 of Chapter 2 .

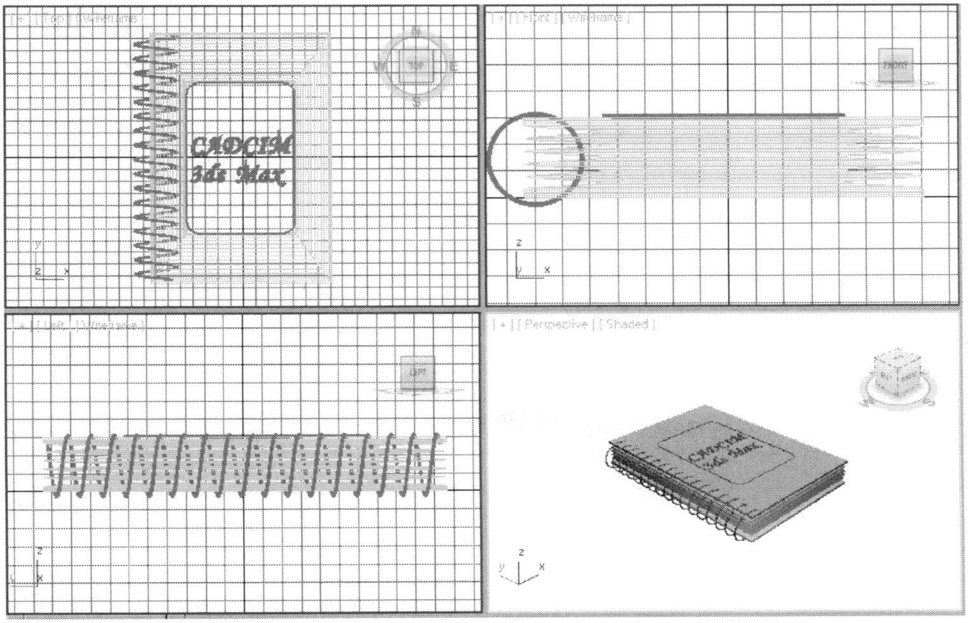

Figure 5-95 *Alignment of the rectangular design in all viewports*

Rendering the Scene for the Final Output

1. Activate the Perspective viewport.

2. Invoke the **Render Production** tool in the **Main Toolbar**; the **Perspective, frame 0, Display Gamma:2.2, RGBA Color16 Bits/ Channel (1:1)** dialog box is displayed, showing the final output of the *book* at one frame, refer to Figure 5-96.

3. Next, close this dialog box.

   You can view the final rendered image of this model by downloading the *c05_3dsmax_2012_render.zip* file from *http://www.cadcim.com*.

Figure 5-96 *The final output at rendering*

Saving the File

1. Save the file with the name *c05tut2.max* as discussed in earlier chapters. The location of this file is given below:

   \Documents\3dsmax\c05_tut2\scenes

Self-Evaluation Test

Answer the following questions and then compare them to those given at the end of this chapter:

1. By default, how may times can you reverse your actions using the **Undo** tool?

   (a) 5 (b) 20
   (c) 1 (d) 10

2. Which of the following keys are used to invoke the **Hold** tool?

   (a) CTRL+Z (b) CTRL+H
   (c) CTRL+ALT+F (d) None of the above

3. Which of the following rollouts is used to make the splines visible as 3D mesh in the viewport and at rendering?

   (a) **Rendering** (b) **Interpolation**
   (c) **Creation Method** (d) **Parameters**

4. Which of the following keys is used to create a square spline using the **Rectangle** tool?

(a) CTRL
(b) F10
(c) SHIFT
(d) None of these

5. The **AutoGrid** option in the **Create** tab helps you create an object on the __________ of another object by generating a __________ on it.

6. The __________ spinner in the **Parameters** rollout of the **Text** tool is used to set the distance between the letters of the text.

7. To view the faces of an object, you need to press the __________ key.

8. When you use the **Fetch** tool in a file, the history list of the actions performed so far will be deleted. (T/F)

9. On selecting the **Start New Shape** check box in the **Object Type** rollout of splines, you can add a new shape to the current shape in the viewport. (T/F)

10. The options in the **Rendering** and **Interpolation** rollouts are same for all splines in Autodesk 3ds Max. (T/F)

Review Questions

Answer the following questions:

1. Which of the following options is available in the drop-down list when you choose the **Shapes** button in the **Create** tab of the **Command Panel**?

(a) **Splines**
(b) **Extended Splines**
(c) **NURBS Curves**
(d) All of these

2. Which of the following tools is not a part of the **Extended Splines**?

(a) **Tee**
(b) **Channel**
(c) **Angle**
(d) **NGon**

3. Which of the following methods is used to create an arc dynamically?

(a) **End-End-Middle**
(b) **Center-End-End**
(c) both (a) and (b)
(d) None of these

4. The **Renderer** radio button in the **Rendering** rollout is used to modify a line at rendering. (T/F)

5. The **Pie Slice** check box in the **Parameters** rollout of the **Arc** tool is used to create a line from each endpoint to the center of an arc. (T/F)

6. You need to select the __________ check box in the __________ rollout to make the splines visible as 3D mesh in the viewport and at rendering.

7. The __________ radio button in the **Parameters** rollout of the **NGon** tool is used to specify the radius of the NGon from the center to corners and the __________ radio button is used to specify the radius of the NGon from the center to the sides of the NGon.

8. In the **Section Parameters** rollout of the **Section** tool, the __________ button is used to create a new section spline where the cross-section cuts the object.

9. The **Sync Corner Fillets** check box is available in the **Parameters** rollout of __________, __________, and __________ in the **Extended Splines**.

Exercises

Exercise 1

Start Autodesk 3ds Max 2012 and perform the following operations:

1. Select **Shapes > Splines** or **Extended Splines** from the drop-down list in the **Create** tab of the **Command Panel**. Then, invoke various tools such as **Line**, **Donut**, **Star**, **Tee**, **Angle**, and so on from the **Object Type** rollout.

2. Invoke the **Line** tool in **Splines**. In the **Creation Method** rollout, select different radio buttons in the **Initial Type** and **Drag Type** areas to create the line dynamically and notice the difference.

3. Create a sphere in the Top viewport using the **Sphere** tool in **Standard Primitives**. Invoke the **Star** tool and select the **AutoGrid** check box in the **Object Type** rollout of **Splines**. Create a star and notice the effect on selecting the **AutoGrid** check box.

4. Create any spline using various tools available in the **Object Type** rollout of **Splines**. Choose the **Modify** tab in the **Command Panel** and try various options available in the **Rendering** rollout.

5. Create different splines and extended splines using the tools available in the **Object Type** rollout. Choose the **Modify** tab in the **Command Panel** and try various options in the **Parameters** rollout of each object.

6. Create a scene using the splines, extended primitives, and standard primitives and use the **Hold** and **Fetch** options, as described in this chapter.

7. By default, you can reverse your actions up to 20 times using the **Undo** tool. To change this number, choose **Customize > Preferences** in the menu bar; the **Preference Settings** dialog box will be displayed. In this dialog box, choose the **General** tab and then in the **Scene Undo** area, enter a new value in the **Levels** spinner.

Exercise 2

Create the model shown in Figure 5-97 using your own dimensions.

(Expected time: 15 min)

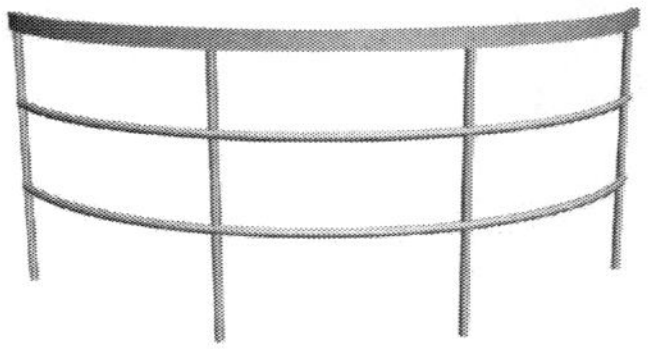

Figure 5-97 *Model for Exercise 2*

Exercise 3

Create the model shown in Figure 5-98 using your own dimensions.

(Expected time: 20 min)

Figure 5-98 *Model for Exercise 3*

Exercise 4

Create the scene shown in Figure 5-99 using your own dimensions.

(Expected time: 20 min)

Figure 5-99 *Model for Exercise 4*

Answers to Self-Evaluation Test

1. b, **2.** b, **3.** a, **4.** a, **5.** surface, temporary grid, **6. Leading**, **7.** F4, **8.** T, **9.** F, **10.** T

6

Modifying 3D Mesh Objects

Learning Objectives

After completing this chapter, you will be able to:

- *Understand editable mesh objects*
- *Understand sub-object levels*
- *Understand editable poly objects*
- *Understand editable patch objects*
- *Modify editable mesh, editable poly, and editable patch objects*

INTRODUCTION

In the previous chapters, you have learned to create different 3D mesh objects and shapes using the tools in the **Create** tab of the **Command Panel**. In this chapter, you will learn to modify the 3D mesh objects at advanced level using the **Modify** tab in the **Command Panel**, refer to Figure 6-1.

MODIFYING THE 3D MESH OBJECTS USING THE MODIFY TAB

To modify the 3D mesh objects, create any object using the tools from **Create > Geometry > Object Type** rollout in the **Command Panel**, as discussed in the previous chapters. Next, select the object and choose the **Modify** tab in the **Command Panel**; the modify panel will be displayed with various rollouts. In the modify panel, the default name and color of the object will be displayed at the top. Just below is the **Modifier List** drop-down list followed by the modifier stack, which consists of the name of the tool that you have used for creating the object, as shown in Figure 6-2 (in this case, the object is box).

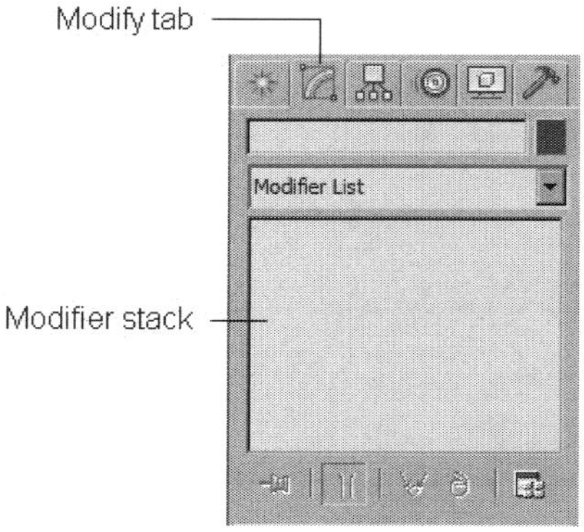

Figure 6-1 *The **Modify** tab in the **Command Panel***

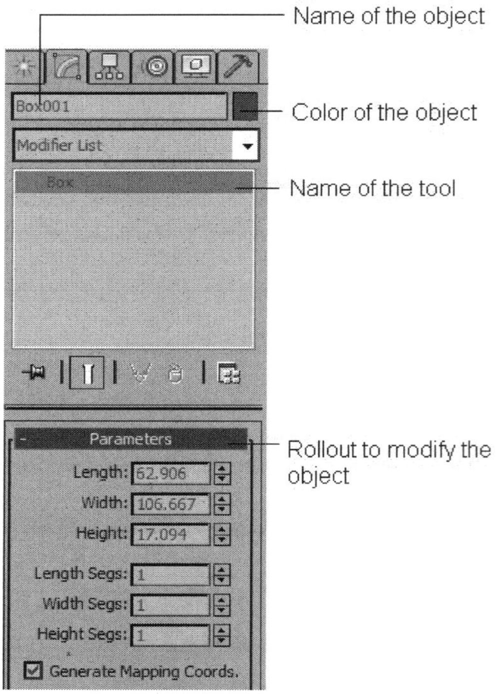

Figure 6-2 *The modify panel*

Note

The rollouts displayed at the bottom of the modify panel depend on the type of the object selected.

Next, you can modify the selected object using one of the following methods:

1. By entering new parameters in the rollouts displayed in the modify panel. This has been discussed in the previous chapters.

2. By applying a modifier from the **Modifier List** drop-down list. You will learn about applying modifiers in the later chapters.

3. By converting the object into editable mesh, editable poly, and editable patch. These methods are discussed next.

Converting Objects into Editable Mesh

You can modify most of the objects at advanced level by converting them into editable mesh. However, the open splines such as line, arc, and so on cannot be converted into editable mesh. The editable mesh provides you the sub-object levels of an object. These sub-object levels help you to select the sub-objects of an object in the viewport. You need to move, rotate, and scale these sub-objects to modify the shape of the object.

You can convert an object into editable mesh using one of the following methods:

1. Create an object and select it in the viewport. Next, right-click on the object; a quad menu will be displayed. Choose the **Convert To:** option; a cascading menu will be displayed, as shown in Figure 6-3. Choose **Convert to Editable Mesh**; the object will be converted into editable mesh.

2. Create an object and select it in the viewport. Choose the **Modify** tab in the **Command Panel**; the modifier stack will be displayed in the modify panel. In the modifier stack, right-click on the name of the tool which has been used to create the object; a shortcut menu will be displayed, as shown in Figure 6-4. Choose the **Editable Mesh** option from the shortcut menu; the object will be converted into editable mesh.

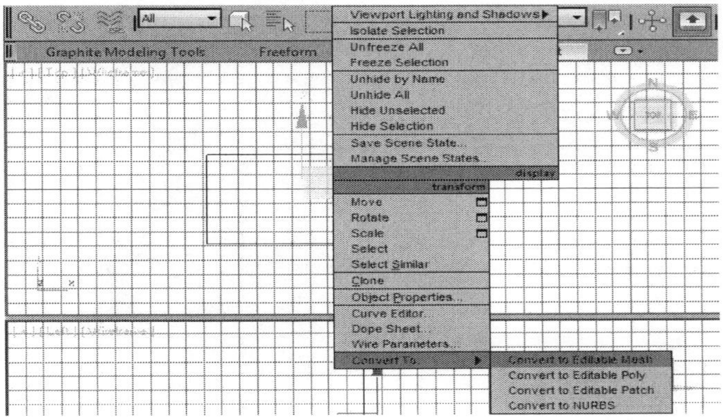

Figure 6-3 *The cascading menu after right-clicking on the object*

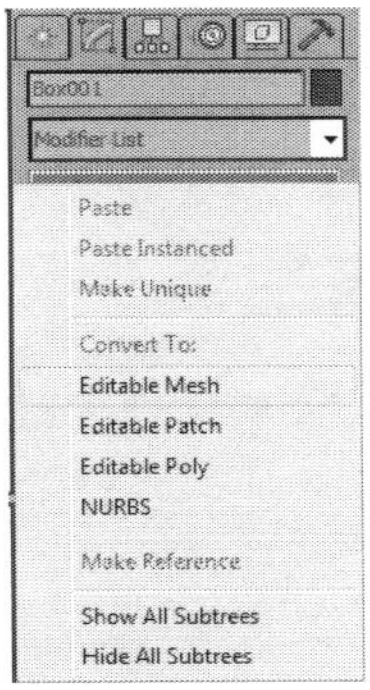

Figure 6-4 The shortcut menu in the modifier stack

3. Create an object and select it in the viewport. Choose the **Utilities** tab in the **Command Panel**; the **Utilities** rollout will be displayed, as shown in Figure 6-5. Choose the **Collapse** button in this rollout; the **Collapse** rollout will be displayed. Choose the **Collapse Selected** button in this rollout; the object will be converted into editable mesh.

Note

After converting an object into editable mesh, it cannot be modified using the creation parameters rollouts such as ***Parameters*** *rollout, and so on, as they become collapsed in the editable mesh objects. So, it is recommended to set the parameters of an object before converting it into editable mesh.*

Sub-object Levels in Editable Mesh

When you convert an object into editable mesh, the name of the tool in the modifier stack will be replaced with Editable Mesh, which is known as object level. By clicking on the plus sign (+) on the left side of the Editable Mesh, you can view the sub-object levels such as **Vertex**, **Edge**, **Face**, **Polygon**, and **Element**, as shown in Figure 6-6. Various rollouts will also be displayed at the bottom of the modifier stack such as **Selection**, **Soft Selection**, **Edit Geometry**, and **Surface Properties**. These sub-object levels and rollouts are discussed next.

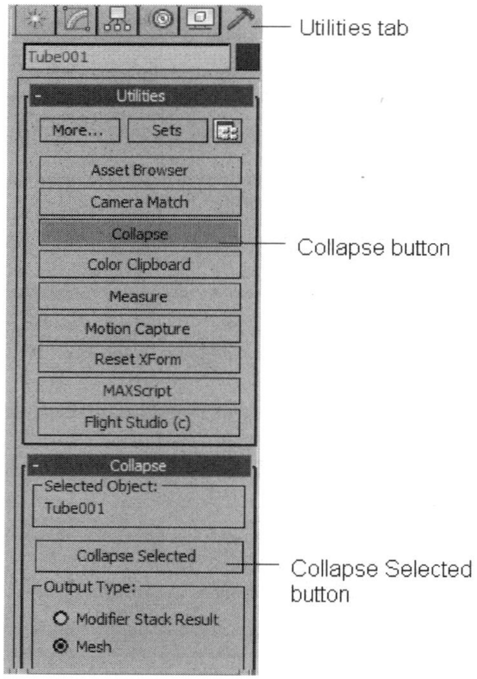

Figure 6-5 *The* ***Utilities*** *rollout displayed after choosing the* ***Utilities*** *tab*

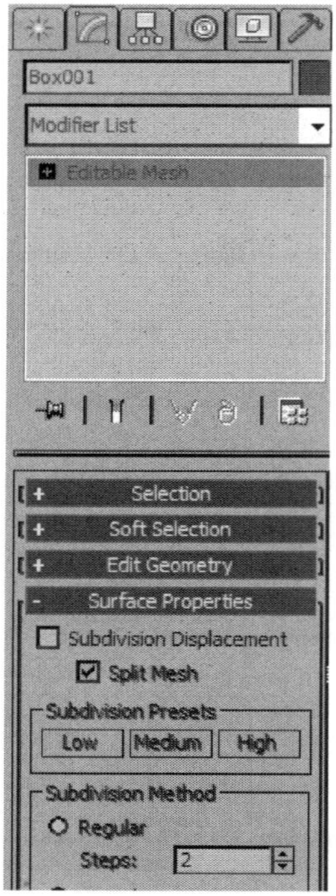

Figure 6-6 *The partial view of various rollouts and the sub-object levels after converting the object into editable mesh*

Sub-object Levels

The sub-object levels help you modify the object by moving, rotating, and scaling the sub-objects. To do so, select one of the sub-object levels in the modifier stack; it will be activated and turn yellow. Alternatively, you can select the **Vertex**, **Edge**, **Face**, **Polygon**, and **Element** sub-object levels by pressing the 1, 2, 3, 4, and 5 keys on the keyboard, respectively. When you select any sub-object level, it will prompt you to select the corresponding sub-objects in the viewport. These sub-objects are discussed next.

Vertex

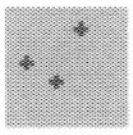

The vertex is a point on the object. To modify the object through vertex, you need to select the **Vertex** sub-object level; the vertices of the object will be displayed in the viewports, as shown in Figures 6-7 and 6-8. The number of vertices depends on the number of segments in the object. To view the segments of the object in the Perspective viewport, press the F4 key.

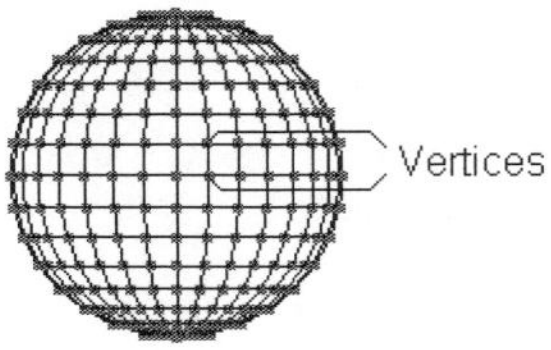

Figure 6-7 *A sphere with vertices*

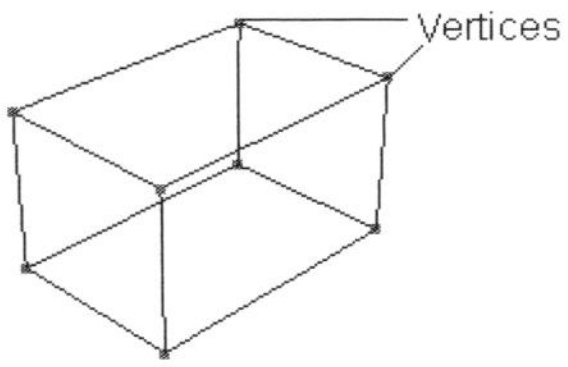

Figure 6-8 *A box with vertices*

Note

You need to set the number of segments in the object before converting it into editable mesh.

You cannot view the sub-objects such as **vertex**, **face**, *and so on at rendering.*

Edge

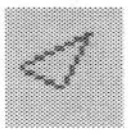

The edge is a line joining two vertices. To modify the object through edges, you need to select the **Edge** sub-object level, which will prompt you to select the edges of the object, refer to Figures 6-9 and 6-10.

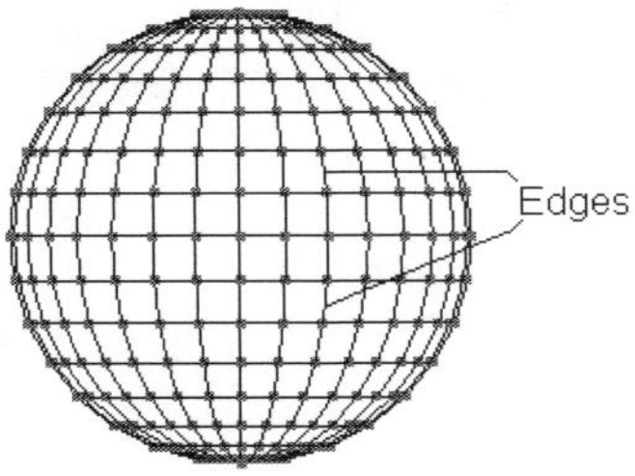

Figure 6-9 *A sphere with edges*

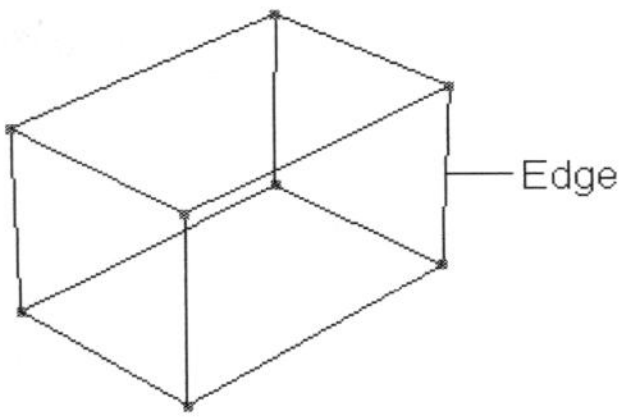

Figure 6-10 *A box with an edge*

Face

A face is a triangular shape sub-object jointed with three vertices and three edges, refer to Figures 6-11 and 6-12. To modify the object through faces, you need to select the **Face** sub-object level, which will prompt you to select the triangular faces of the object.

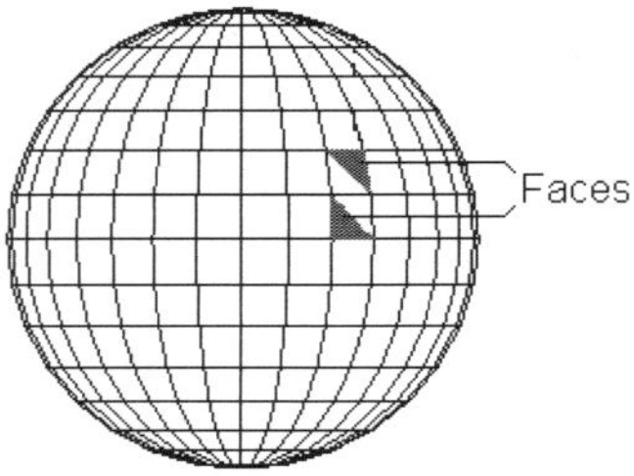

Figure 6-11 A sphere with the faces selected

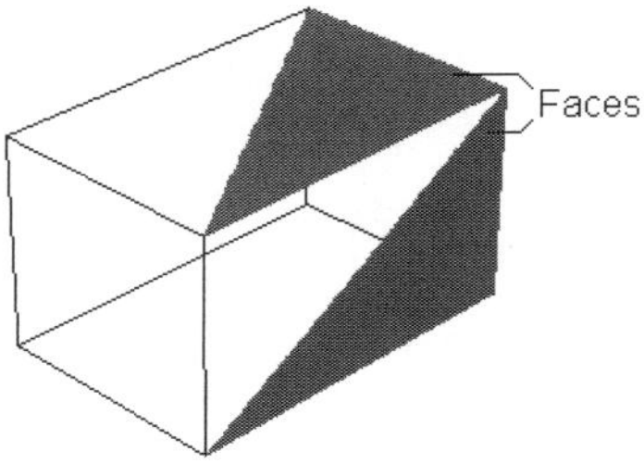

Figure 6-12 A box with the faces selected

Polygon

A polygon is a rectangular shape sub-object that consists of two triangular faces. To modify the object through polygons, you need to select the **Polygon** sub-object level, which will prompt you to select the polygons of the object, refer to Figures 6-13 and 6-14.

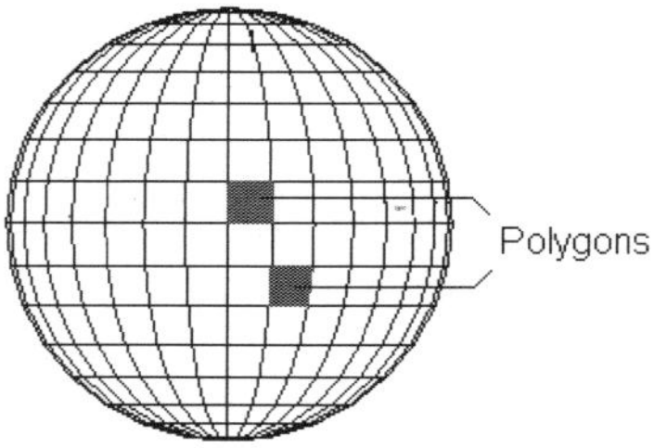

Figure 6-13 A sphere with the polygons selected

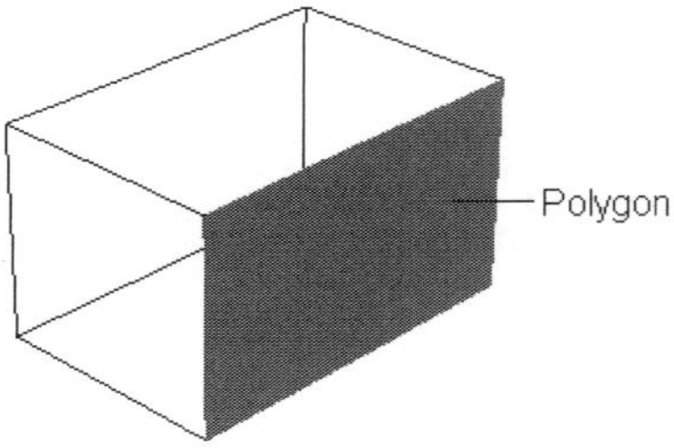

Figure 6-14 A box with the polygon selected

Element

To modify the object through elements, you need to select the **Element** sub-object level, which will prompt you to select all adjacent faces of the object, refer to Figures 6-15 and 6-16.

Rollouts

As mentioned earlier that when you convert an object into editable mesh, various rollouts will be displayed at the bottom of the modifier stack in the modify panel to modify the objects at sub-object levels. These rollouts are discussed next.

Figure 6-15 A sphere with the element selected

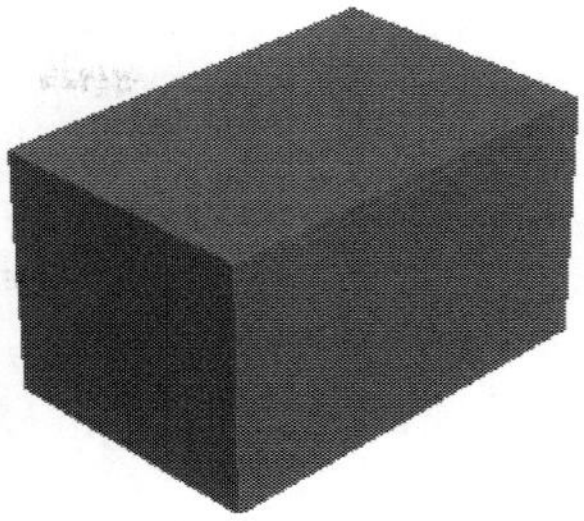

Figure 6-16 A box with the element selected

Selection Rollout

This rollout is used to toggle between various sub-object levels. At the top of the **Selection** rollout, there are five buttons, **Vertex**, **Edge**, **Face**, **Polygon**, and **Element**. These buttons are used to select the sub-objects of the object in the viewport and are same as discussed earlier in this chapter. Choose one of the buttons to make it active and it is same as selecting the sub-object level in the modifier stack. The **By Vertex** check box is available at the **Edge**, **Face**, **Polygon**, and **Element** sub-object levels. On selecting the **By Vertex** check box, you will be able to select all the sub-objects that use the vertices that you will select in the viewport. For example, if you select the **Polygon** sub-object level and click on a vertex of the object in the viewport, then all the polygons that are using the selected vertex will be selected. Select the **Ignore Backfacing** check box to select the sub-objects that are facing toward you in the viewports. Note that you cannot select backfacing sub-objects on selecting this check box.

Note

*After selecting the **By Vertex** check box, you can select the sub-objects only by clicking on a vertex or by selecting a portion of the object by dragging a selection box around it.*

Soft Selection Rollout

This rollout enables you to display a soft selection on an object. The options in this rollout are used to affect the action of move, rotate, and scale functions at sub-object level of the editable mesh object. To activate this rollout, you need to select a sub-object level. Then, select the **Use Soft Selection** check box to activate the other options in this rollout. When you select the sub-objects of an object in the viewport, it shows the falloff in different color combinations. The influence of the colored zone is determined by the value in the **Falloff** spinner. The shape of the falloff is controlled by the value in the **Pinch** and **Bubble** spinners.

Edit Geometry Rollout

The options in this rollout are used to edit the object at the object as well as the sub-object levels. These options are discussed next.

Create

The **Create** button is used to add the sub-objects to the selected object in the viewport. This button is available at the **Vertex**, **Face**, **Polygon**, and **Element** sub-object levels. To add the sub-objects, select the editable mesh object in the viewport, choose the **Modify** tab, and then select one of the sub-object levels in the modifier stack. Next, choose the **Create** button in the **Edit Geometry** rollout. Now, click anywhere in the viewport to add vertices in the selected object (if the **Vertex** sub-object level is selected), as shown in Figure 6-17. If you have selected the **Face** sub-object level, then click on the three vertices one by one to add a new face, as shown in Figure 6-18.

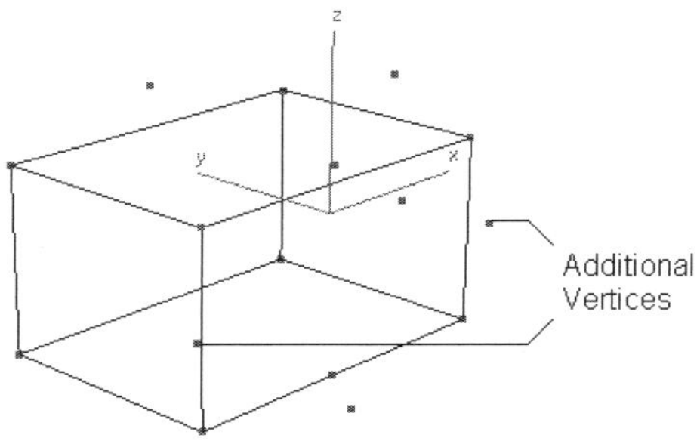

***Figure 6-17** Additional vertices created in a box using the **Create** button*

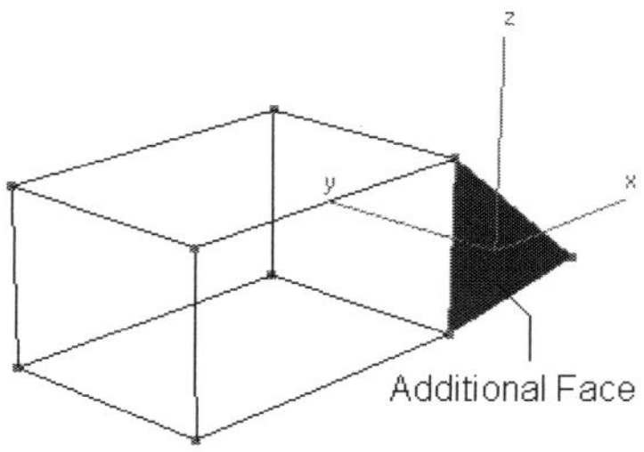

***Figure 6-18** Additional face created in a box using the **Create** button*

Delete

The **Delete** button is used to delete the sub-objects in the selected object. To delete a sub-object, select the editable mesh object in the viewport, choose the **Modify** tab, and then select one of the sub-objects levels in the modifier stack. Next, select the sub-object in the viewport that you want to delete and choose the **Delete** button; the selected sub-object will be deleted.

Attach

The **Attach** button is used to attach an object to the selected object in the viewport. To attach an object, select the editable mesh object in the viewport and choose the **Modify** tab. Next, choose the **Attach** button in the **Edit Geometry** rollout. Now, when you move the cursor over another object in the viewport, the attach cursor will be displayed, as shown in Figure 6-19, and you will be prompted to select the object. Click on the object; it will be attached to the selected object. Also, it will display the same color and properties as those of the selected object.

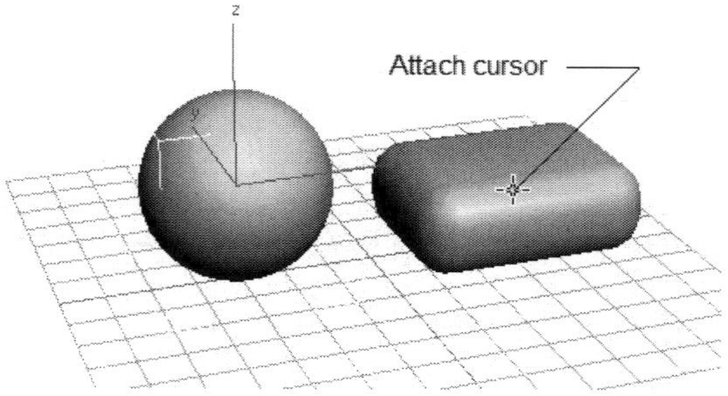

***Figure 6-19** The attach cursor after choosing the **Attach** button*

Attach List

The **Attach List** button is used to attach a number of objects simultaneously in the viewport to the selected object. To do so, select the editable mesh object in the viewport and choose the **Modify** tab in the **Command Panel**. Now, choose the **Attach List** button from the **Edit Geometry** rollout; the **Attach List** dialog box will be displayed, as shown in Figure 6-20. This dialog box displays a list of all objects in the viewports. From this list, select the name of the objects that need to be attached by holding the CTRL or SHIFT key, and then choose the **Attach** button; the selected objects will be attached to the object selected in the viewport. Note that these attached objects will display the same color and properties as that of the selected object.

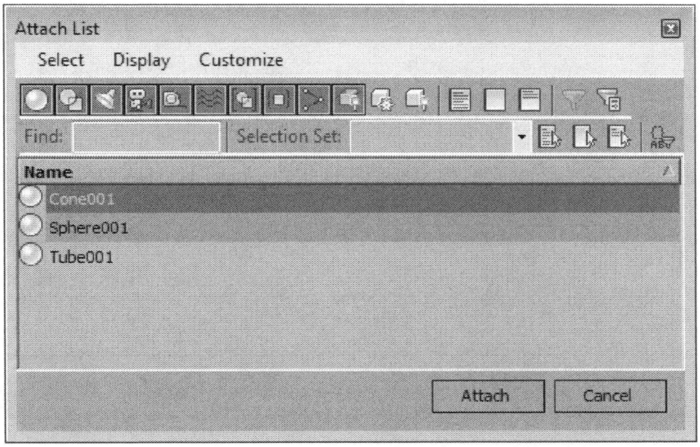

***Figure 6-20** The **Attach List** dialog box*

Detach

The **Detach** button is used to detach the sub-objects from the selected object to make them an individual object. This option is available for the **Vertex**, **Face**, **Polygon**, and **Element** sub-object levels. To detach a sub-object, select the editable mesh object in the viewport, choose the **Modify** tab, and then select one of the sub-object levels in the modifier stack. Next, select the sub-object in the viewport that you want to create as an individual object, and then choose the **Detach** button; the **Detach** dialog box will be displayed, as shown in Figure 6-21.

Enter the name of the new object in the **Detach as** text box and choose the **OK** button; the selected sub-object will be detached and treated as an individual object. Now, when you move this individual object at the object level, it will leave a hole in the original object. In the **Detach** dialog box, if you select the **Detach As Clone** check box, then the selected sub-object will be copied and treated as individual object. Also, the original object will not get modified.

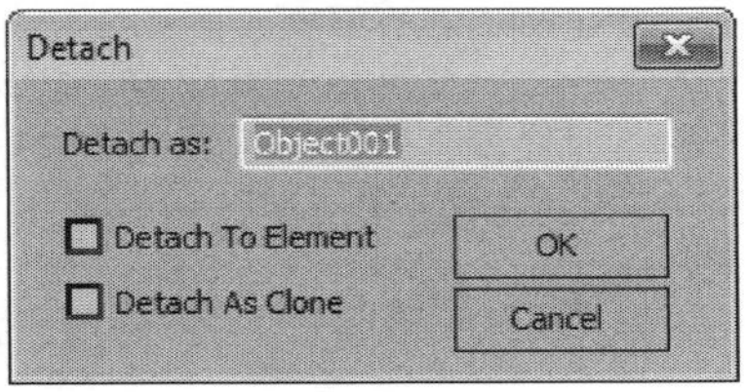

***Figure 6-21** The **Detach** dialog box*

Break

The **Break** button is available only for the **Vertex** sub-object level. It creates a new vertex for each face attached to the selected vertices. If a vertex is used only by one face, then it will be unaffected.

Turn

The **Turn** button is available only for the **Edge** sub-object level. It is used to rotate the edges of an object. To do so, select the editable mesh object in the viewport, choose the **Modify** tab, and then select the **Edge** sub-object level in the modifier stack. Now, choose the **Turn** button in the **Edit Geometry** rollout and select the edges of the object in the viewport one by one; the edges will be rotated, refer to Figures 6-22 and 6-23.

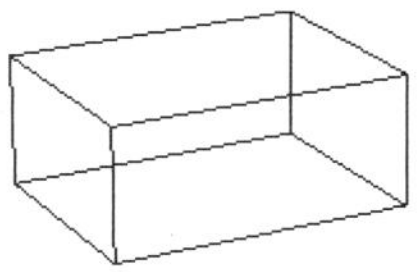

Figure 6-22 *The box before choosing the* ***Turn*** *button*

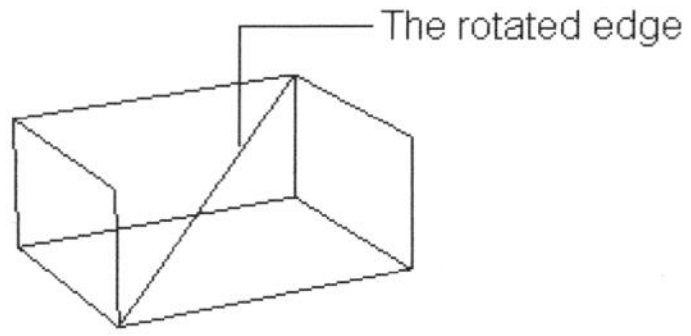

Figure 6-23 *The rotated edge in the box after choosing the* ***Turn*** *button*

Divide

The **Divide** button is available only for the **Face**, **Polygon**, and **Element** sub-object levels. It divides the faces into three smaller faces. If you divide the sub-object at the **Polygon** or **Element** sub-object level, then also it will be divided into three faces. To do so, select the editable mesh object in the viewport, choose the **Modify** tab, and then select one of the sub-object levels in the modifier stack, except Vertex and Edge. Next, choose the **Divide** button in the **Edit Geometry** rollout, and click on the sub-object in the viewport; the sub-object will be divided into three faces, refer to Figures 6-24 and 6-25.

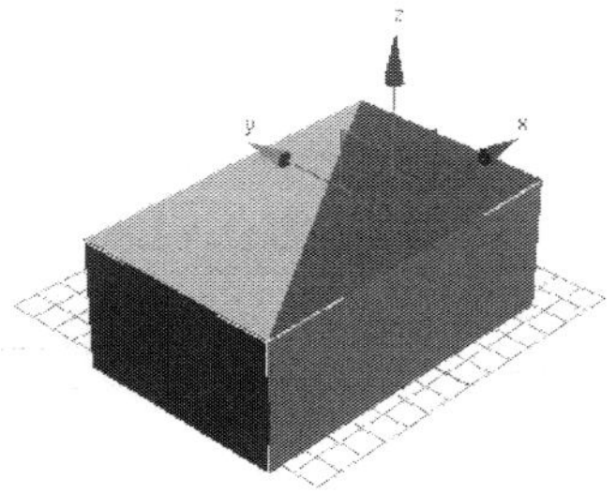

Figure 6-24 *A face selected to be divided*

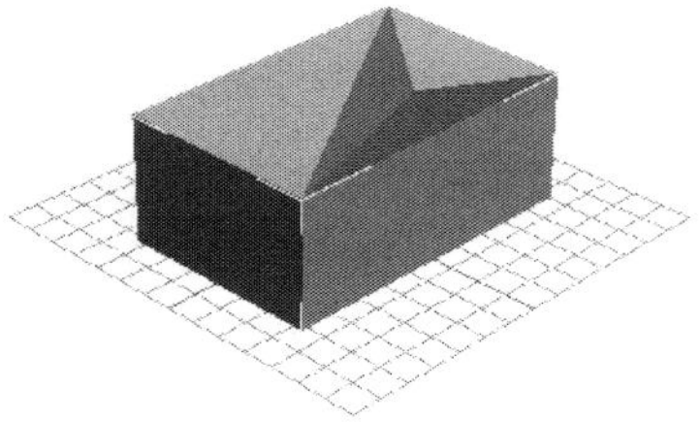

Figure 6-25 *The face divided into three smaller faces after using the* ***Divide*** *button*

Extrude

The **Extrude** button is available for the **Edge**, **Face**, **Polygon**, and **Element** sub-object levels. It is used to extrude the sub-objects either by dragging the cursor or by entering the value in the spinner. To do so, select the editable mesh object in the viewport, choose the **Modify** tab, and then select one of the sub-object levels in the modifier stack, except

Vertex. Next, select the sub-object in the viewport and choose the **Extrude** button to activate it. Now, move the cursor over the selected sub-object; the extrude cursor will be displayed, as shown in Figure 6-26. Next, press and hold the left mouse button and move the cursor up or down for the extrusion; the value for the extrusion will be displayed in the spinner on the right of the **Extrude** button. You can also enter the value directly in this spinner to extrude the selected sub-object, as shown in Figure 6-27.

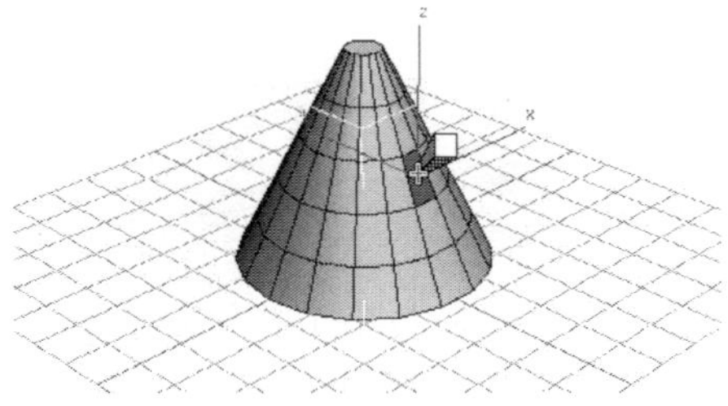

Figure 6-26 *The extrude cursor displayed over the selected polygon*

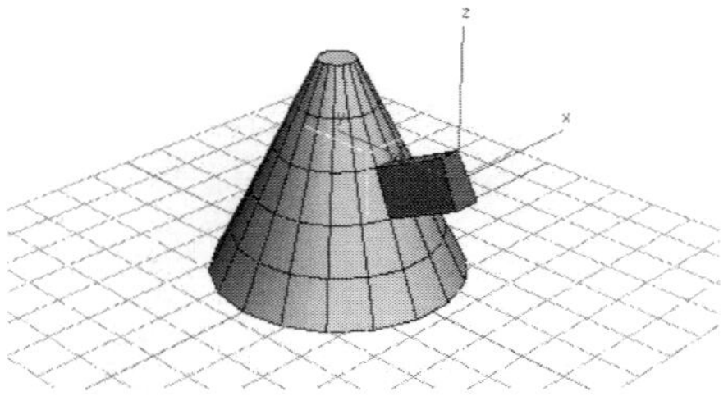

Figure 6-27 *The selected polygon sub-object after extrusion*

Note

To extrude more than one sub-object simultaneously for the same amount of extrusion, select them by holding the CTRL key, and then perform the extrude command.

You can also enter a negative value in the ***Extrude*** *spinner for negative extrusion, as shown in Figure 6-28.*

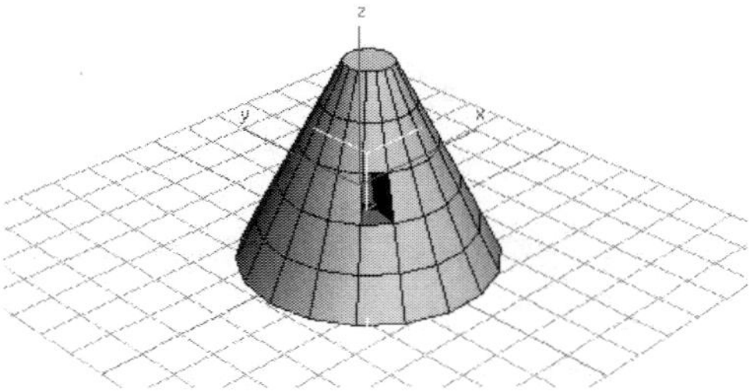

Figure 6-28 *The selected polygon after negative extrusion*

Bevel

The **Bevel** button is available only for the **Face**, **Polygon**, and **Element** sub-object levels. It is used to change the shape of the extruded object. This button can perform the extrude and bevel functions at the same time. You can bevel the sub-objects either by dragging the cursor or by entering the value in the spinner on the right side of the **Bevel** button. To do so, select the editable mesh object in the viewport, choose the **Modify** tab, and then select one of the sub-object levels in the modifier stack, except Vertex and Edge. Next, select the sub-object in the viewport, choose the **Bevel** button, and then move the cursor over the selected sub-object; the bevel cursor will be displayed, as shown in Figure 6-29. Now, press and hold the left mouse button and move the cursor up or down to extrude the sub-object, as shown in Figure 6-30. Release the left mouse button and then move the cursor up or down again to bevel or change the shape of the sub-object, as shown in Figures 6-31 and 6-32. You can also enter the value directly in the spinner on the right side of the **Bevel** button to bevel the selected sub-object.

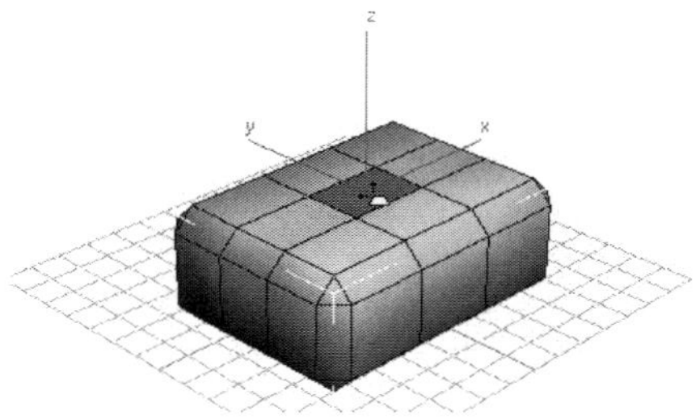

Figure 6-29 *The bevel cursor displayed over the selected polygon*

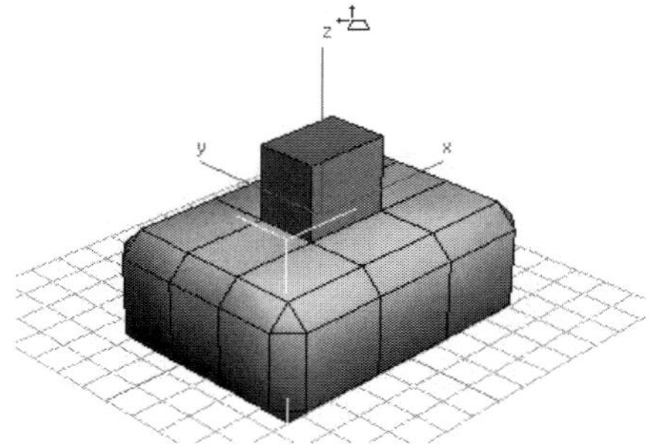

Figure 6-30 *The extruded polygon after using the **Bevel** button*

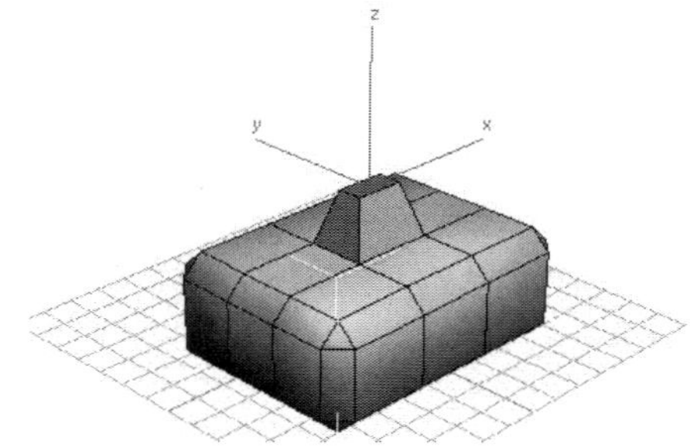

Figure 6-31 *The reduced size of the extruded polygon using the **Bevel** button*

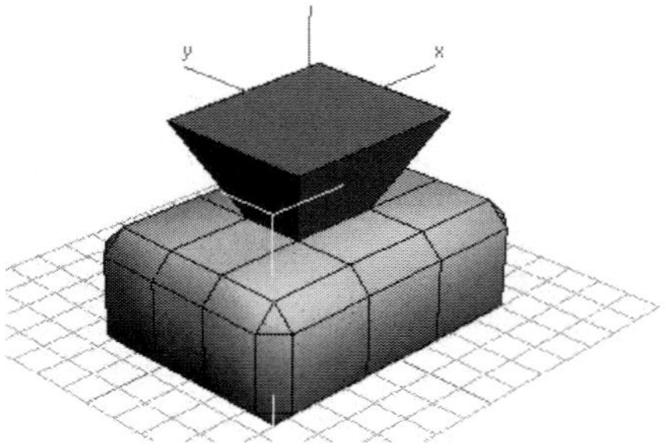

Figure 6-32 *The increased size of the extruded polygon using the **Bevel** button*

Chamfer

The **Chamfer** button is available only for the **Vertex** and **Edge** sub-object levels. It is used to cut the corners of the sub-object at an angle of 45-degree. You can chamfer the sub-objects either by dragging the cursor or by entering the value in the spinner on the right side of the **Chamfer** button. To do so, select the editable mesh object in the viewport, choose the **Modify** tab, and then select the sub-object level in the modifier stack. Next, select the sub-object in the viewport, choose the **Chamfer** button, and move the cursor over the selected sub-object; the chamfer cursor will be displayed, as shown in Figure 6-33. Next, press and hold the left mouse button, move the cursor up to chamfer, and release the left mouse button; the sub-object will be chamfered at an angle of 45-degree, as shown in Figures 6-34 and 6-35. As you move the cursor, the chamfer value will be displayed in the spinner on the right side of the **Chamfer** button. You can also enter the value directly in this spinner to chamfer the selected sub-object.

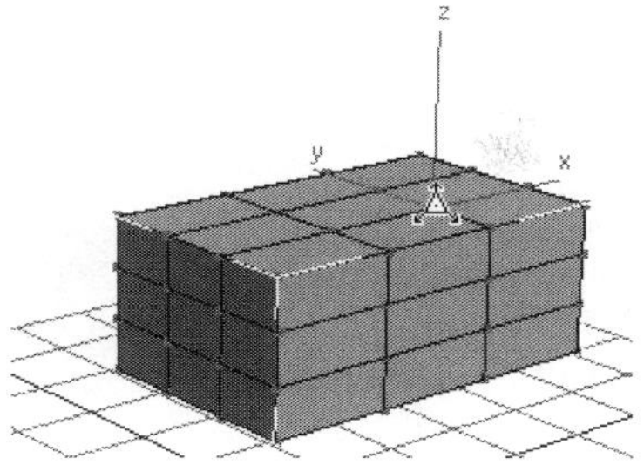

Figure 6-33 The chamfer cursor displayed over the selected vertex

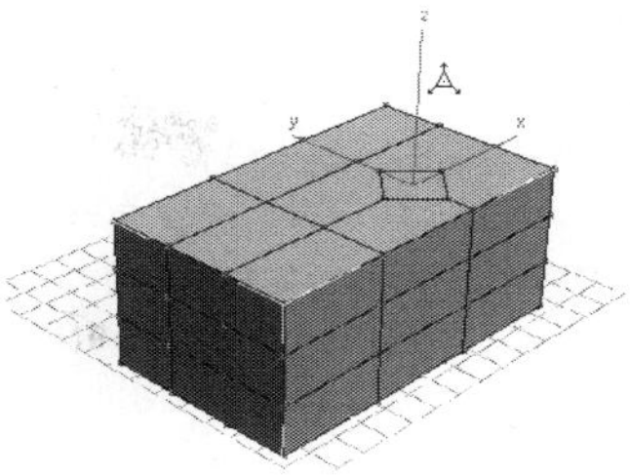

*Figure 6-34 The vertex sub-object chamfered using the **Chamfer** button*

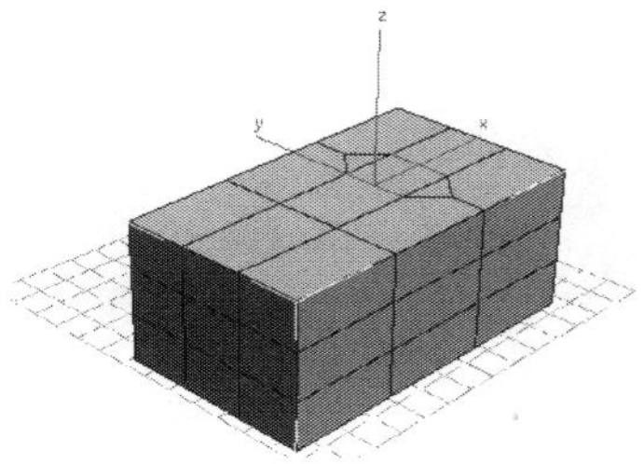

*Figure 6-35 The edge sub-object chamfered using the **Chamfer** button*

Slice Plane and Slice

The **Slice Plane** and **Slice** buttons are used to slice the sub-objects to create new vertices, faces, edges, polygons, and elements. To do so, select the editable mesh object in the viewport, choose the **Modify** tab, and then select the sub-object level in the modifier stack. Next, select one or more sub-objects in the viewport. Then, choose the **Slice Plane** button; a yellow colored slice plane gizmo will be displayed in the viewport, as shown in Figure 6-36. Set the position of the slice plane gizmo over the selected sub-objects by moving or rotating it at the position where you want to slice them. Then, choose the **Slice** button; the selected sub-objects will be divided to create new sub-objects, as shown in Figure 6-37. To view the sliced sub-objects in the viewport, press the F4 key.

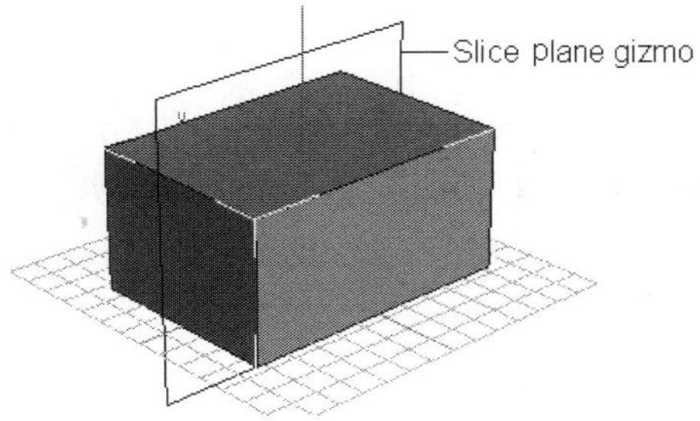

Figure 6-36 The slice plane gizmo displayed in the selected polygons

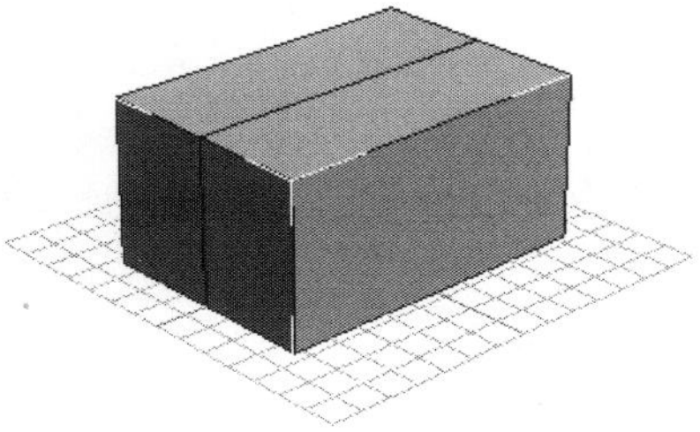

*Figure 6-37 The selected polygons sliced after using the **Slice** button*

Cut

The **Cut** button is available only for the **Edge**, **Face**, **Polygon**, and **Element** sub-object levels. It is used to cut the edge, face, polygon, or element of an object to create new vertices, edges, and faces. To do so, select the editable mesh object in the viewport, choose the **Modify** tab, and then select any sub-object level in the modifier stack, except **Vertex**. Next, choose the **Cut** button and move the cursor over the object; the cursor will change when it comes over any sub-object. Next, click on the sub-object to specify the first cut point and drag the mouse to specify the endpoint of the cut; a dotted line will be displayed, as shown in Figure 6-38. Now, click again to cut the sub-object and right-click to end the cut command; the object will be cut, as shown in Figure 6-39. You can also select the sub-object to be cut at a particular area, as shown in Figure 6-40.

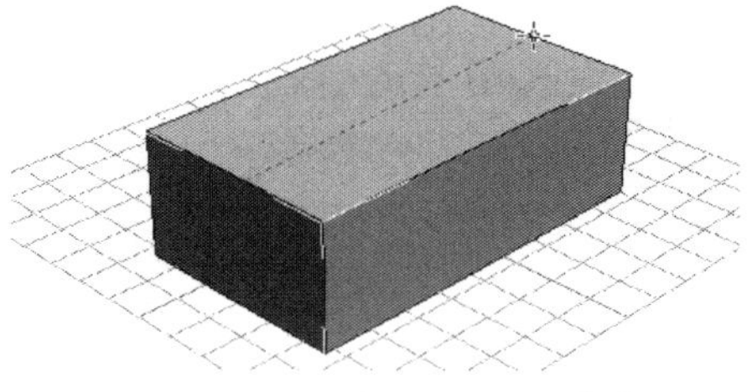

Figure 6-38 *The cursor with the dotted lines*

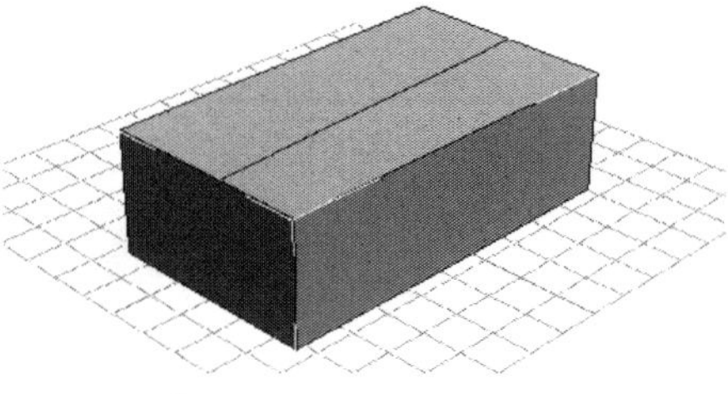

Figure 6-39 *The cut on the object after using the* ***Cut*** *button*

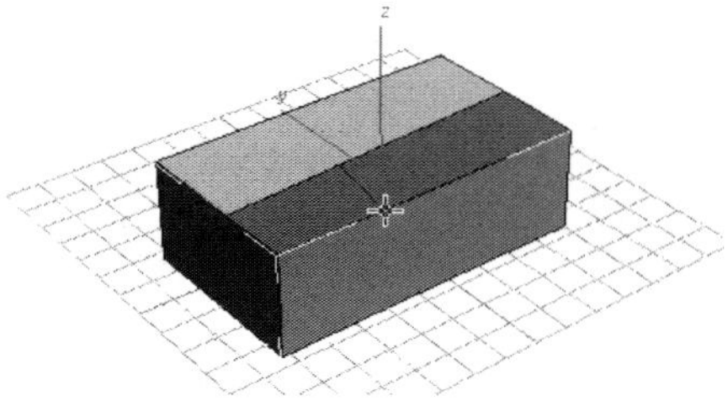

Figure 6-40 *The cut on the selected polygon sub-object*

Note

You need to press the F4 key to view all segments of the object.

While using the ***Cut*** *button, select the* ***Ignore Backfacing*** *check box to avoid the cut on the back face of the sub-object.*

Weld Area

The options in the **Weld** area are available only at the **Vertex** sub-object level. It is used to weld or join the vertices of the object. The **Selected** button in the **Weld** area is used to weld the selected vertices. To perform the weld command, select the editable mesh object in the viewport, choose the **Modify** tab, and then select the **Vertex** sub-object level in the modifier stack; all vertices of the object will be displayed in the viewport. Next, select the vertices of the object in the viewport that you need to weld together by dragging a selection box around them, as shown in Figure 6-41. Now, set the value in the spinner located on the right side of the **Selected** button to define the weld threshold area. All the vertices that you want to weld together must be inside this area. Choose the **Selected** button; the vertices will be welded together, as shown in Figure 6-42. If the vertices are not within the weld threshold area, whose value you have defined in the spinner, the **Weld** message box will be displayed, as shown in Figure 6-43, warning you that there is no vertex in the weld threshold area. Therefore, you need to increase the threshold area by modifying the value in the spinner, and then choose the **Selected** button again to weld the vertices.

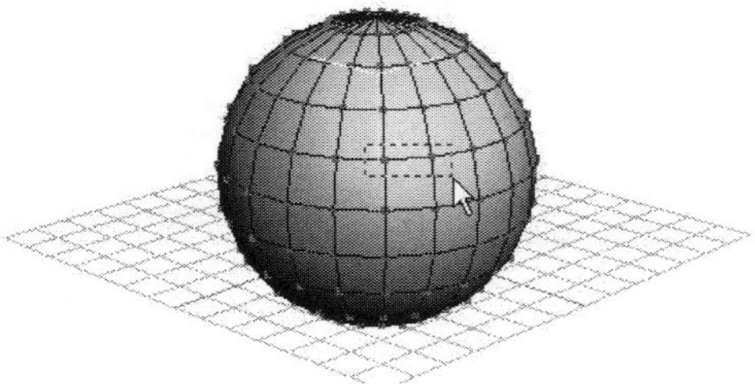

Figure 6-41 *The selection box around the vertices to be welded*

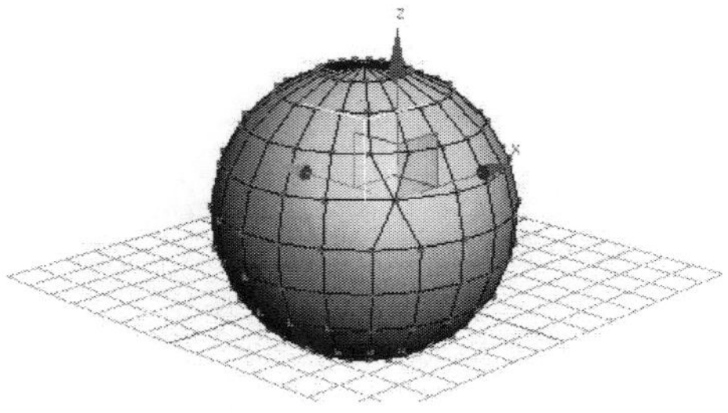

Figure 6-42 *The vertices welded together*

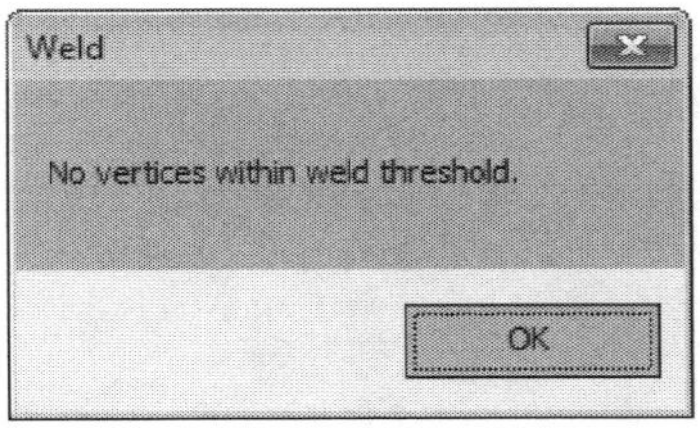

Figure 6-43 *The **Weld** message box*

The **Target** button in the **Weld** area is used to weld the selected vertices to the unselected target vertex. To do so, select the editable mesh object in the viewport and choose the **Modify** tab. Now, select the **Vertex** sub-object level in the modifier stack; all vertices of the object will be displayed in the viewport. Next, select the vertices of the object in the viewport by dragging a selection box around them, as shown in Figure 6-44. Then, choose the **Target** button and move the vertices toward the unselected target vertex to which you want to weld the selected vertices. As you bring the selected vertices over the unselected target vertex, the cursor will convert into a plus sign. Release the mouse button; the vertices will be joined to the target vertex, as shown in Figure 6-45.

Modifying Editable Mesh Objects Using Sub-object Levels

To get the advance level modeling of the objects, you need to convert the object into editable mesh object, which provides you the sub-object levels of an object as discussed earlier in this chapter. To view the sub-object levels, you need to click on the plus sign on the left side of the **Editable Mesh** in the modifier stack. By using these sub-object levels, you can select the sub-objects in the viewport and modify the object in different ways.

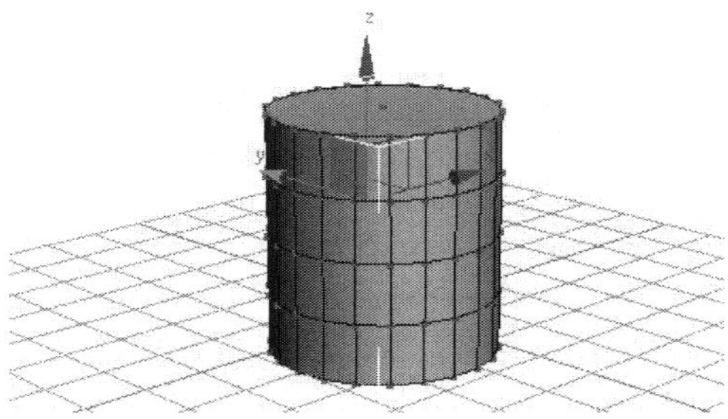

Figure 6-44 *The vertices selected for welding*

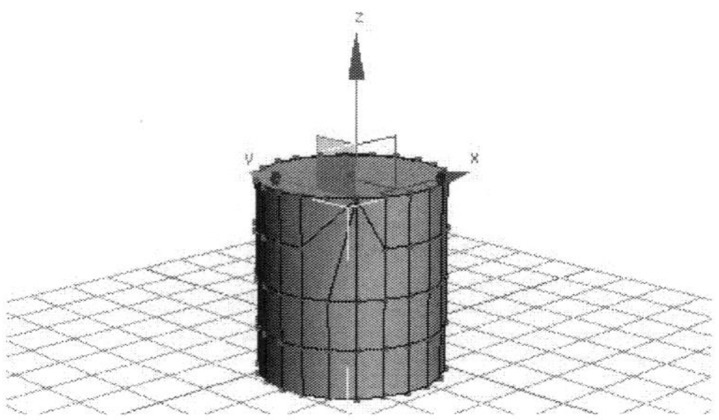

Figure 6-45 *The selected vertices welded to the target vertex*

When you select one of the sub-object levels in the modifier stack, it is activated and turns yellow. Also, you are prompted to select the corresponding sub-objects in the viewport to modify the shape of the object. You can select a sub-object by clicking on it in the viewport. To select more than one sub-object simultaneously, hold the CTRL key, and select them one by one. Alternatively, you can drag a selection box around the sub-objects to select them simultaneously; they will turn red. After selecting the sub-objects, you can modify them using the following options:

1. You can move, rotate, and scale the selected sub-objects using the **Select and Move**, **Select and Rotate**, and **Select and Scale** tools, respectively in the **Main Toolbar**.

2. You can use different options in the **Edit Geometry** rollout, as described earlier in this chapter.

3. You can use different modifiers from the **Modifier List** drop-down list. You will learn about it in the later chapters.

Converting Objects into Editable Poly

To modify an object with editable poly is similar to modifying an object with the editable mesh. The only difference is that editable poly works with the advance tools meant for polygonal mesh editing. To work with editable poly, you need to convert the object into editable poly. To do so, you need to use one of the following methods:

1. Create an object and select it in the viewport. Next, right-click on the object; a quad menu will be displayed. Choose the **Convert To:** option; a cascading menu will be displayed. Choose the **Convert to Editable Poly** option; the object will be converted into editable poly.

2. Create an object and select it in the viewport. Choose the **Modify** tab in the **Command Panel**; the modifier stack will be displayed in the modify panel. In the modifier stack, right-click on the name of the tool which you have used to create the object; a shortcut menu will be displayed. Choose the **Editable Poly** option; the object will be converted into editable poly.

3. Create an object and select it in the viewport. Next, move the cursor over the **Polygon Modeling** panel in the **Graphite Modeling Tools** tab; a flyout will be displayed, as shown in Figure 6-46. Choose the **Convert to Poly** option; the selected object will be converted into editable poly.

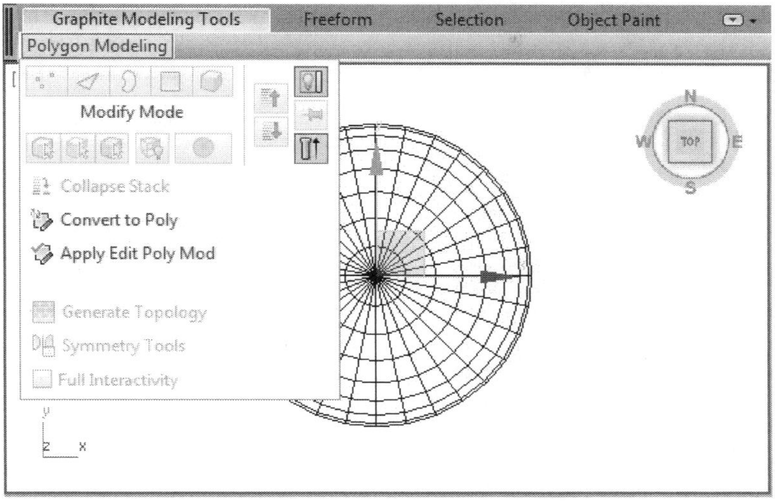

*Figure 6-46 A flyout displayed after moving the cursor over the **Polygon Modeling** panel*

Note

*When you convert an object into editable poly, various panels will be displayed in the **Graphite Modeling Tools** tab such as **Edit**, **Geometry (All)**, **Subdivision**, and so on. You will learn about these panels in the later chapters.*

Modifying Editable Poly Objects Using Sub-object Levels

When you convert an object into editable poly, the name of the tool in the modifier stack will be replaced with **Editable Poly**, which is known as object level. You can click on the plus sign on the left side of Editable Poly to view the sub-object levels such as **Vertex**, **Edge**, **Border**, **Polygon**, and **Element**, as shown in Figure 6-47. Various rollouts will also be displayed below the modifier stack such as **Selection**, **Soft Selection**, **Edit Geometry**, **Subdivision Surface**, **Subdivision Displacement**, and **Paint Deformation**. Other rollouts such as **Edit Vertices**, **Vertex Properties**, **Edit Edges**, **Edit Borders**, **Edit Polygons**, **Polygon: Material IDs**, **Polygon: Smoothing groups**, **Polygon: Vertex Colors**, and **Edit Elements** will also be displayed, depending on the selection of the sub-object level.

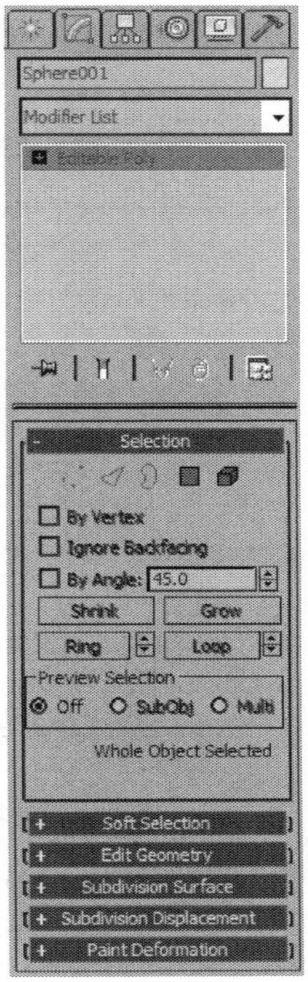

Figure 6-47 Partial view of various rollouts and the sub-object levels after converting the object into editable poly

Next, to modify the object using the sub-object levels, select one of the sub-object levels in the modifier stack; it is activated and turns yellow. Also, you will be prompted to select the corresponding sub-objects in the viewport. Now, select the sub-object by clicking on it in the viewport. To select more than one sub-object at a time, hold the CTRL key and select them one by one. Alternatively, you can drag a selection box around the sub-objects to select them simultaneously; they will turn red. After selecting the sub-objects, you can modify them using the following methods:

1. You can move, rotate, and scale the selected sub-objects using the **Select and Move**, **Select and Rotate**, and **Select and Scale** tools, respectively in the **Main Toolbar**.

2. You can use different modifiers from the **Modifier List** drop-down list, about which you will learn in the later chapters.

3. You can use various options available in different rollouts of the modify panel for a particular sub-object level.

4. You can use different tools available in the **Graphite Modeling Tools** tab. You will learn about it in the later chapters.

The sub-object levels and various rollouts in an editable poly object are discussed next.

Sub-object Levels

The editable poly objects have the **Vertex**, **Edge**, **Border**, **Polygon**, and **Element** sub-object levels. They do not have the **Face** sub-object level like the editable mesh. Therefore, you cannot select the triangular faces in the editable poly object. Additionally, the editable poly has the **Border** sub-object level. The **Vertex**, **Edge**, **Polygon**, and **Element** sub-objects are the same as discussed in the editable mesh object. The **Border** sub-object is discussed next.

Border

The border is a series of edges that forms a ring around a hole in the object, as shown in Figures 6-48 and 6-49.

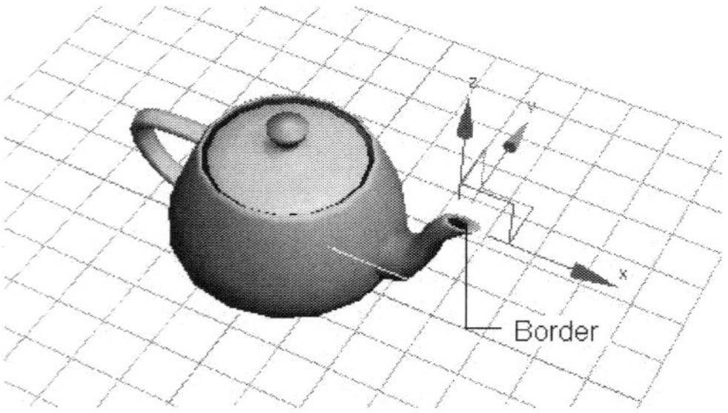

Figure 6-48 The border selected around the hole of the spout of a teapot

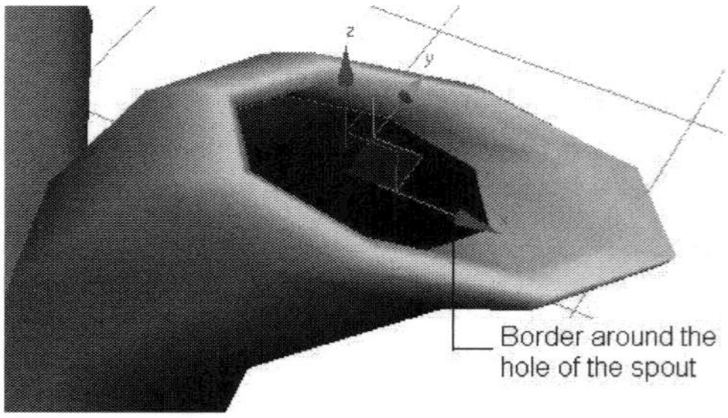

Figure 6-49 The maximized view of the border selected around the hole of the spout of a teapot

Rollouts

When you convert an object into editable poly, various rollouts will be displayed below the modifier stack. The number and name of the rollouts depend on the selection of the sub-object level. These rollouts are used to modify the objects at the sub-object levels and are discussed next.

Selection Rollout

At the top of the **Selection** rollout, there are five buttons, **Vertex**, **Edge**, **Border**, **Polygon**, and **Element**, as shown in Figure 6-50. These buttons are used to select the sub-objects of an object in the viewport and are the same as described earlier. Choose any button to make it active and it is similar to selecting the sub-object level in the modifier stack. The other options in this rollout are discussed next.

Shrink/Grow

The **Shrink** and **Grow** buttons are available for all the sub-object levels in this rollout. The **Shrink** button is used to reduce the selection area of the sub-objects in the viewport. The **Grow** button is used to increase the selection area of the sub-objects in the viewport. To use these buttons, select the editable poly object in the viewport, choose the **Modify** tab, and then select one of the sub-object levels in the modifier stack. Next, select the sub-objects in the viewport. Choose the **Shrink** or **Grow** button in the **Selection** rollout; the selection area will decrease or increase in the viewport, refer to Figures 6-51, 6-52, and 6-53.

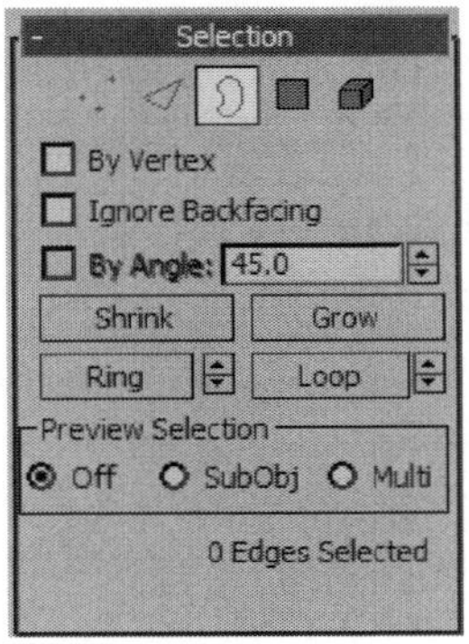

*Figure 6-50 The **Selection** rollout with the **Border** sub-object level selected*

Figure 6-51 The selection area in the teapot

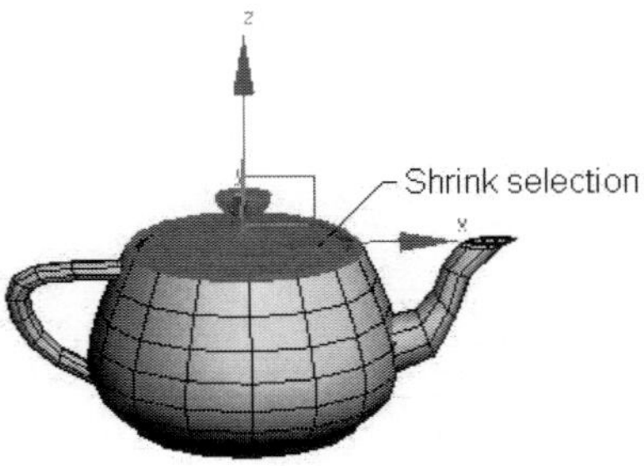

*Figure 6-52 The selection area in the teapot reduced after choosing the **Shrink** button*

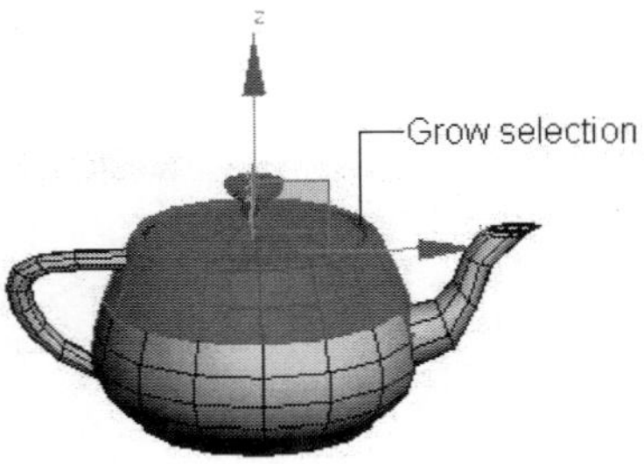

*Figure 6-53 The selection area in the teapot increased after choosing the **Grow** button*

Ring

The **Ring** button is available only for the **Edge** and **Border** sub-object levels. It is used to select all edges and borders of the object that are parallel to the selected edge. To do so, select an edge of the object in the viewport, as shown in Figure 6-54, and choose the **Ring** button; all edges parallel to the selected edge will be selected, as shown in Figure 6-55.

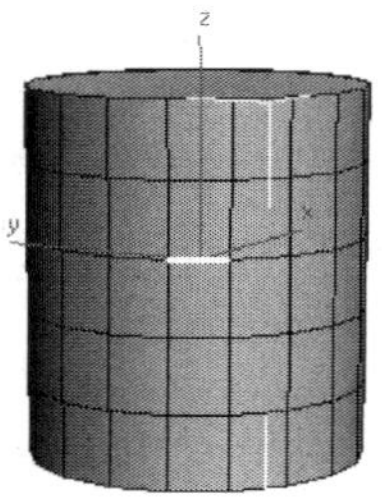

Figure 6-54 *An edge selected in a cylinder*

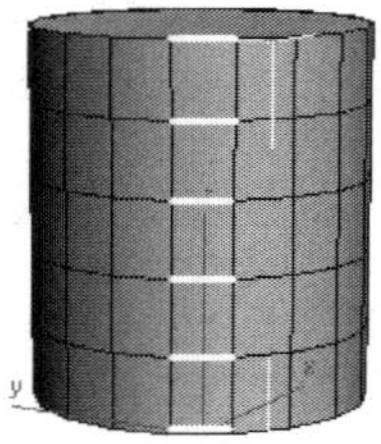

Figure 6-55 *The parallel edges selected after choosing the **Ring** button*

Loop

The **Loop** button is available only for the **Edge** and **Border** sub-object levels. It is used to select all the edges or borders of the object that are aligned with the selected edge or border. To use this button, select an edge or a border of the object in the viewport, as shown in Figure 6-56, and then choose the **Loop** button; all edges or borders that are aligned with the selected edge will be selected, as shown in Figure 6-57.

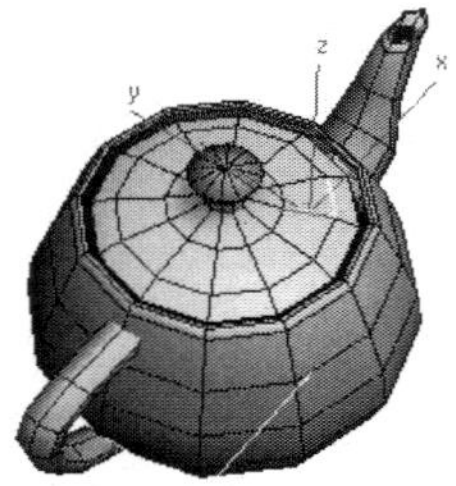

Figure 6-56 *The edge selected in a cylinder*

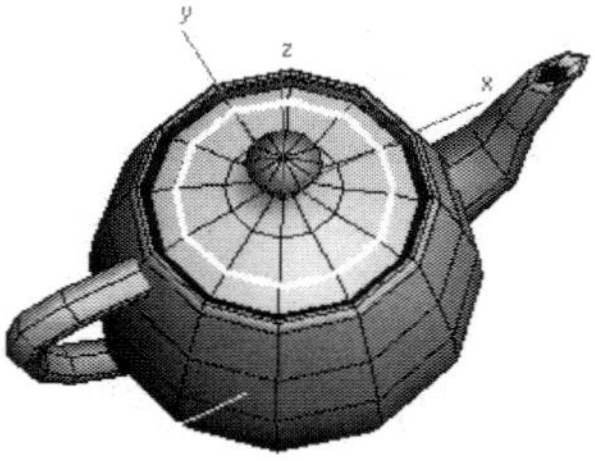

Figure 6-57 *The edges selected after choosing the **Loop** button*

Preview Selection Area

This area is used to preview the selection of sub-objects in the viewport before selecting them. To do so, you need to use the options in the **Preview Selection** area. The **Off** radio button is selected by default in this area therefore, the preview of the sub-objects selection will not be available in the viewport.

The **SubObj** radio button in this area enables you to preview the selection of the sub-objects at the current sub-object level only. To do so, select any sub-object level in the **Selection** rollout. Now, select the **SubObj** radio button in the **Preview Selection** area. Next, move the cursor over the object; the corresponding sub-object will be highlighted in yellow color in the viewport, as shown in Figure 6-58. Click on it; the sub-object will be selected. If you need to select multiple sub-objects at a time, move the cursor over the object and hold the CTRL key. Now, move the mouse over the sub-objects that you need to select; they will be highlighted, as shown in Figure 6-59. Click on them and release the CTRL key; the highlighted sub-objects will be selected. Similarly, to deselect a sub-object from the current selection, hold the ALT key, and move the cursor over the sub-object that you want to deselect; it will be highlighted. Now, click on it; the highlighted sub-object will be deselected. To deselect more than one sub-object, you need to hold the ALT+CTRL keys.

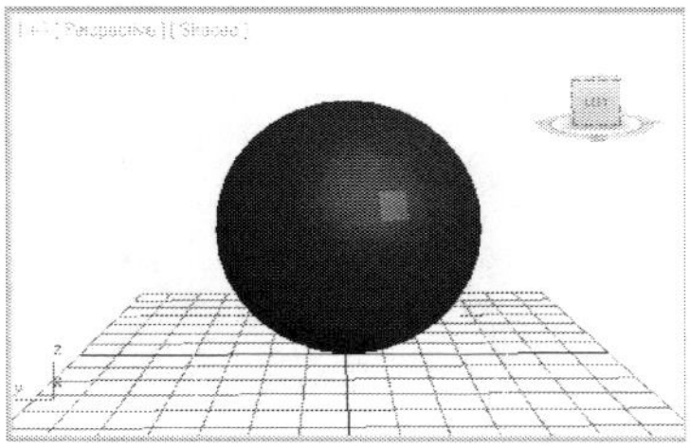

***Figure 6-58** The polygon highlighted*

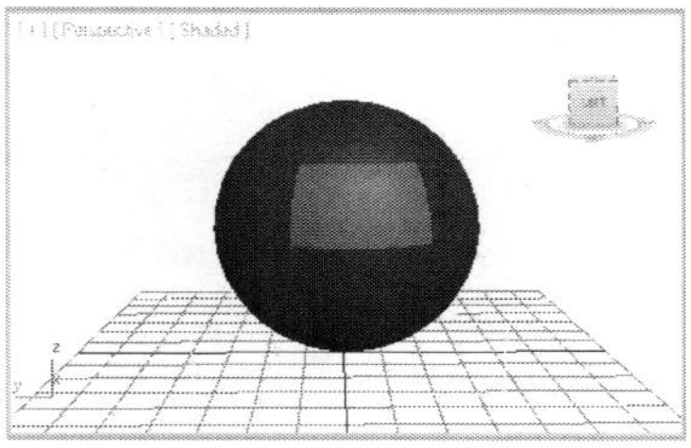

***Figure 6-59** More than one polygon highlighted*

The **Multi** radio button in the **Preview Selection** area works similar to the **SubObj** radio button. Additionally, the **Multi** radio button enables you to switch among the sub-object levels in the modify panel while selecting the sub-object in the viewport. For example, if you move the cursor over the **Polygon** sub-object in the viewport, then the polygon of the object will be highlighted. Click on it; the highlighted polygon will be selected. Also, the **Polygon** sub-object level will be activated in the modify panel. Similarly, if you select an edge, vertex, or element in the viewport, then the corresponding sub-object level will be activated in the modify panel. Therefore, you do not need to manually switch among the sub-object levels.

Just below the **Preview Selection** area, a text line is displayed which provides the information about the current selection. Also, when you move the cursor over the object to highlight the sub-objects in the viewport, another text line will be displayed that will provide the information about the number and name of the highlighted sub-objects.

Soft Selection Rollout

The options in this rollout are the same as described in the editable mesh.

Edit Geometry Rollout

The options in this rollout are used to edit the object at the object as well as the sub-object level. Some of the options in this rollout are discussed next.

Repeat Last

The **Repeat Last** button is used to repeat the recently used command. For example, if you have applied a command to a polygon of an object, and need to apply the same command upto the same level to other polygons, then select the other polygons in the viewport and choose the **Repeat Last** button; the same command will be applied to the selected polygons, refer to Figures 6-60 and 6-61.

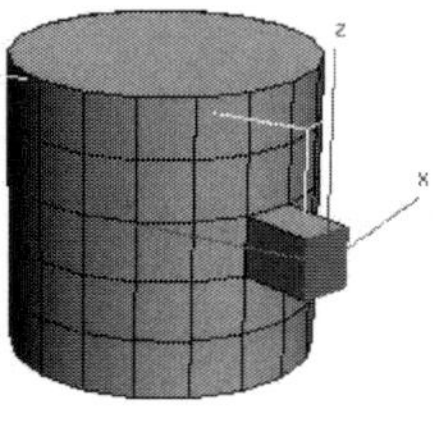

Figure 6-60 *The extruded polygon in a cylinder*

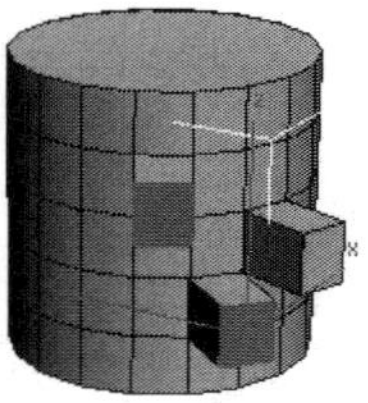

Figure 6-61 *The same extrusion on other polygons after choosing the **Repeat Last** button*

Attach

The **Attach** button is the same as discussed in the editable mesh object. Choose the **Attach List** button on the right side of the **Attach** button to display the **Attach List** dialog box. The options in this dialog box are the same as discussed in the editable mesh object.

The **Create**, **Detach**, **Slice Plane**, **Slice**, and **Cut** buttons are the same as discussed in the editable mesh object.

Reset Plane

The **Reset Plane** button is used to reset the default position of the slice plane. When you choose the **Slice Plane** button, the **Reset Plane** and **Slice** buttons get activated.

QuickSlice

The **QuickSlice** button is used to slice the object or the sub-objects very quickly and easily. To slice the object quickly, choose the **QuickSlice** button; a quick slice cursor will be displayed, as shown in Figure 6-62. Click on an object in the viewport to define the first point of the slice plane; a slice plane will be displayed, as shown in Figure 6-62. Move the cursor to define an angle for the slice and click again to specify the endpoint of the slice; the object will be sliced according to the slice plane, as shown in Figure 6-63. It affects the slice operation on the entire object. If you need to slice particular sub-objects, then you need to select them. Next, right-click to end the **QuickSlice** command.

Note

It is recommended to avoid performing the slice operation in the Perspective viewport.

MSmooth

The **MSmooth** button is used to smoothen an object or sub-objects. To smoothen the object, select it in the viewport, as shown in Figure 6-64, and choose the **MSmooth** button in the **Edit Geometry** rollout; the object will be smoothened, as shown in Figure 6-65. Choose the **Settings** button on the right of the **MSmooth** button; the **MeshSmooth Selection** caddy control will be displayed in the viewport, as shown in Figure 6-66. Set the value in the **Smoothness** spinner to define the smoothness of the object. The value in this spinner varies from 0.0 to 1.0.

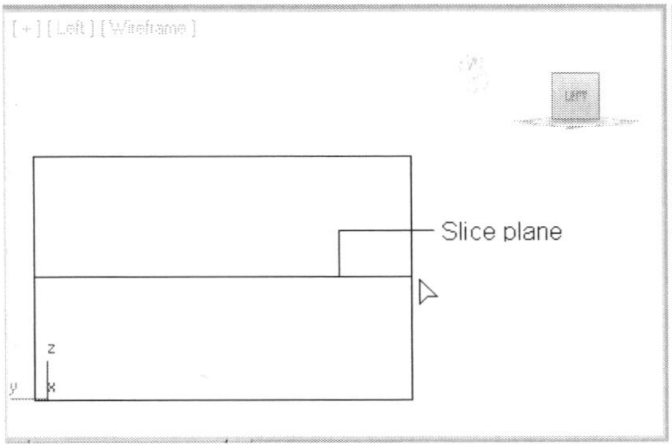

Figure 6-62 The quick slice cursor and slice plane displayed

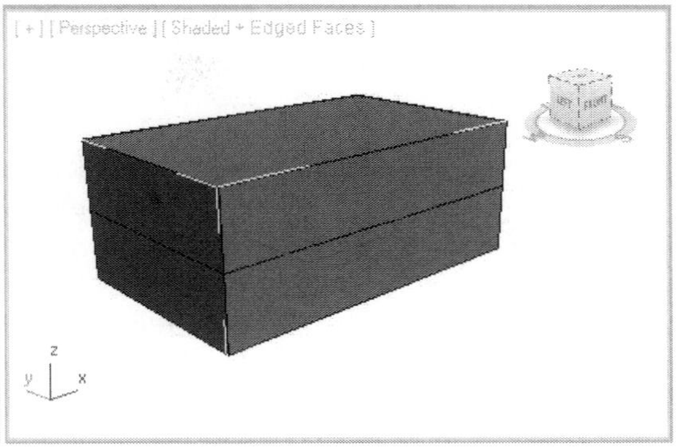

Figure 6-63 The box sliced in the Perspective viewport

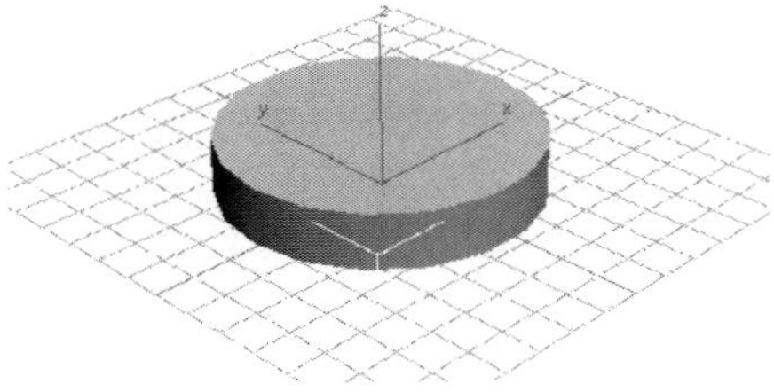

Figure 6-64 A cylinder

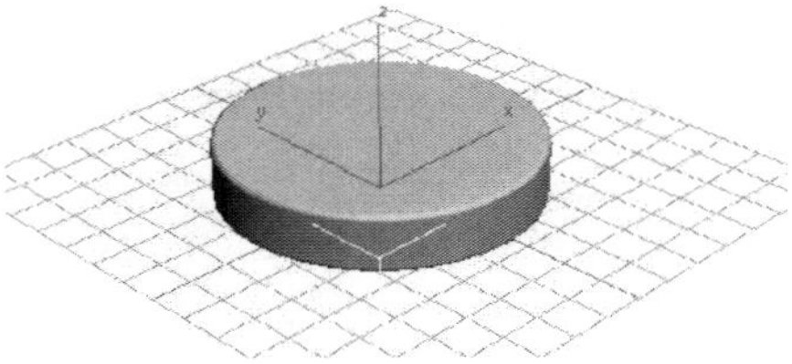

*Figure 6-65 The cylinder smoothened after choosing the **MSmooth** button*

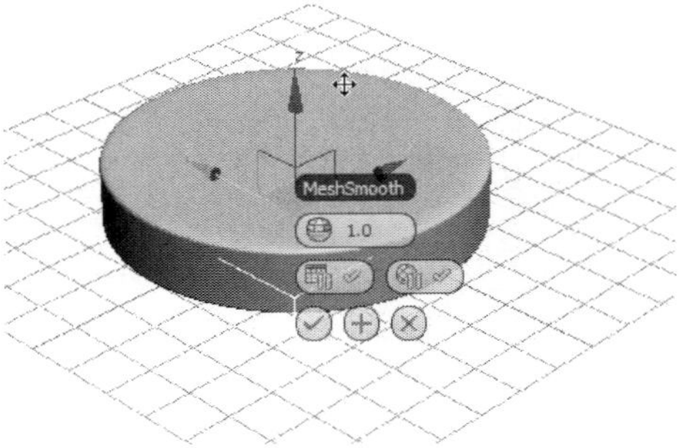

*Figure 6-66 The **MeshSmooth Selection** caddy control*

Note

*To view the **Smoothness** spinner, you need to move the cursor over the buttons in the **MeshSmooth Selection** caddy control; the corresponding name will be displayed at the place of the name of the caddy control.*

Tessellate

The **Tessellate** button is used to increase the number of edges or faces in an object and allows you to define how the smoothness will be applied. By default, when you choose the

Tessellate button, the number of edges of the object will increase. To change the settings, choose the **Settings** button on the right side of the **Tessellate** button; the **Tessellate Selection** caddy control will be displayed in the viewport, as shown in Figure 6-67. Next, click on the arrow placed on the **Edge** button; a drop-down list will be displayed to select the tessellation method, as shown in Figure 6-68. Select the **Edge** or the **Face** option and choose the **Apply and Continue** button; the number of edges or faces will be increased in the object, refer to Figures 6-69, 6-70, and 6-71. If you need to apply the same settings again, then choose the **Apply and Continue** button again. To end the command and close the caddy control, choose the **OK** button. In case you need to close the caddy control without applying the settings to the selection, choose the **Cancel** button.

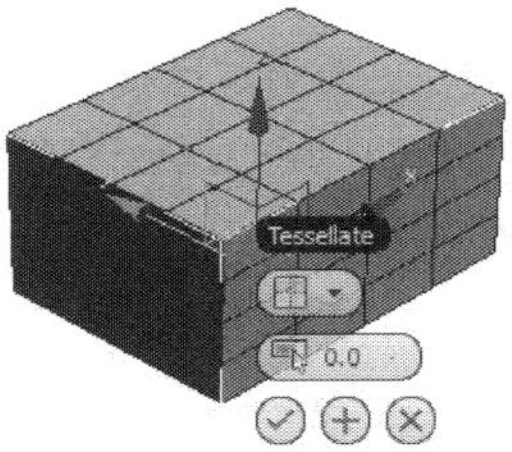

Figure 6-67 *The* ***Tessellate Selection*** *caddy control*

Figure 6-68 *A drop-down list displayed after clicking on the arrow*

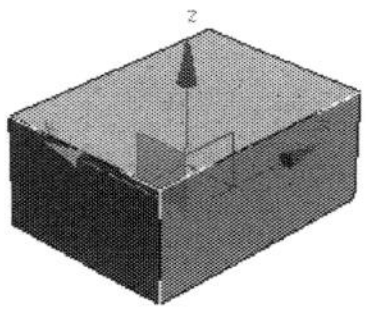

Figure 6-69 *A box*

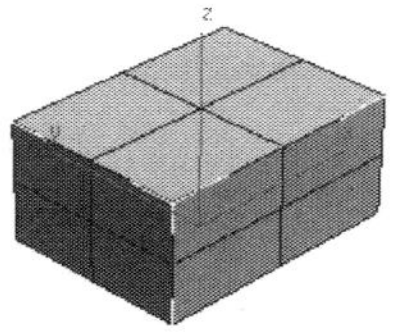

Figure 6-70 *The box after selecting the* ***Edge*** *radio button*

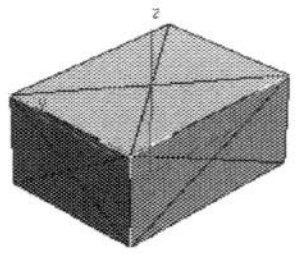

Figure 6-71 *The box after selecting the* ***Face*** *radio button*

Make Planar

Choose the **Make Planar** button to bring all vertices of the object in the same plane. However, if you select the sub-objects in the viewport, then it will enable you to bring all the selected sub-objects in the same plane. Choose the **X**, **Y**, and **Z** buttons to align the object according to the local coordinate system.

The **Hide Selected** button is available only for the **Vertex**, **Polygon**, and **Element** sub-object levels. It is used to hide the selected sub-objects in the viewport.

The **Unhide All** button is available for the **Vertex**, **Polygon**, and **Element** sub-object levels. It is used to unhide all the hidden sub-objects in the viewport.

The **Hide Unselected** button is available for the **Vertex**, **Polygon**, and **Element** sub-object levels. It is used to hide the unselected sub-objects in the viewport.

Subdivision Surface Rollout

The options in this rollout are used to apply the subdivision to the object to make it more effective and smoother. The different areas in this rollout are discussed next.

Display and Render Areas

The value in the **Iterations** spinner is used to specify the number of iterations that will smoothen the object in the viewport as well as at rendering. If you select the **Iterations** check box in the **Render** area, then the value in the **Iterations** spinner of the **Display** area will show its effect only in the viewport. Note that when you increase the number of iterations in the spinner, the number of segments also gets increased and it takes a long time to display its effect in the viewport as well as at rendering. Therefore, use the number of iterations as per your requirement. The value in the **Smoothness** spinner is used to add the new polygons at all vertices to make a smoother object in the viewport as well as at rendering. The value in this spinner varies from 0.0 to 1.0. If you select the **Smoothness** check box in the **Render** area, then the value in the **Smoothness** spinner of the **Display** area will show the effect only in the viewport.

The **Iterations** and **Smoothness** spinners in the **Render** area are used to smoothen the poly objects at rendering. Select the check boxes on the left side of the spinners to make them active.

Separate By Area

Select the **Smoothing Groups** check box in this area to stop the creation of new polygons at edges between faces that are not under the smoothing group. Select the **Materials** check box to stop the creation of new polygons at edges between the faces that do not share the material IDs.

Update Options Area

Select the **Always** radio button in this area to automatically view the output of the smoothness settings in the viewport as well as at rendering. Select the **When Rendering** radio button to view the output of the smoothness settings only at the time of rendering. Select the **Manually** radio button to view the output of the smoothness settings only when you choose the **Update** button below the **Manually** radio button. In this case, if you change the settings as per the requirement, then to update the settings you need to choose the **Update** button.

Paint Deformation Rollout

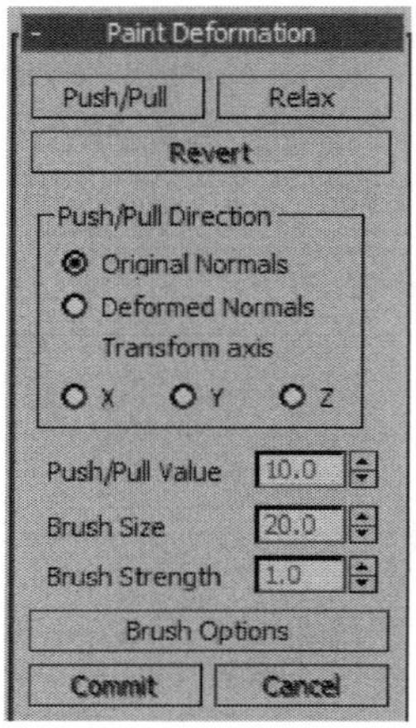

*Figure 6-72 The **Paint Deformation** rollout*

The options in this rollout are used to deform the surface of an object by pushing or pulling its vertices using the **Push/Pull** button, refer to Figure 6-72. At the object level, it affects the vertices of the entire object. While at the sub-object level, it affects only the vertices of the selected sub-object. This rollout has three buttons. The **Push/Pull** button is used to push or pull the vertices of the object. Choose the **Push/Pull** button to activate it and move the cursor over the object in the viewport; a light blue colored brush along with the cursor will be displayed in the viewport, as shown in Figure 6-73. Press the left mouse button; the brush will turn red. Drag the cursor to deform the surface of the object, as shown in Figure 6-74, and release the left mouse button; the object will be deformed. At the sub-object level, choose the **Push/Pull** button to activate it and move the cursor over the selected sub-objects; a light blue colored brush will be displayed in the viewport. Now, click on it to deform the surface and right-click to exit the command. While performing the push/pull command, the object will be pushed or pulled, depending on the value that you have entered in the **Push/Pull Value** spinner.

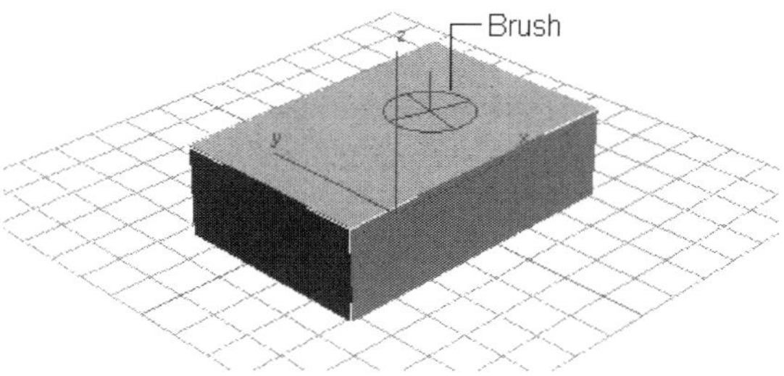

*Figure 6-73 The brush displayed on choosing the **Push/Pull** button*

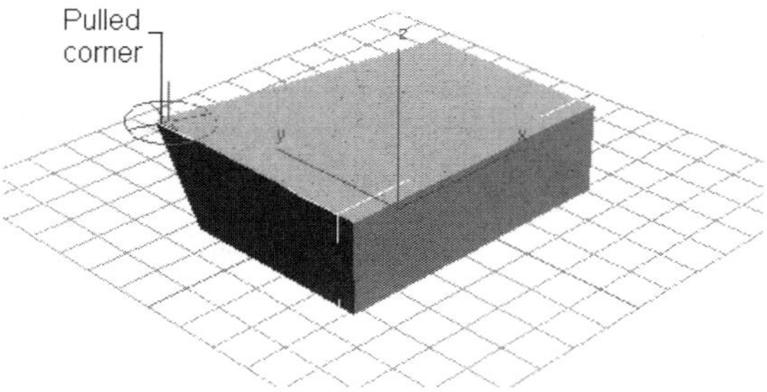

Figure 6-74 The object deformed at the corner vertex

The **Relax** button is used to maintain the distance between the vertices of the object. The **Revert** button is used to erase the effect of the **Push/Pull** button by clicking on the same vertices or object. To reverse the effect of the **Push/Pull** button simultaneously while using it, you need to hold the CTRL key and click on the same vertex.

Push/Pull Direction Area

The radio buttons in this area are used to specify the direction of the push or pull over the object. If you select the **Original Normals** radio button, then after pushing or pulling, the vertices of the object will move in the direction of its normal before deformation. If you select the **Deformed Normals Transform axis** radio button, then after pushing or pulling, the vertices of the object will move in the direction of its normal after deformation. Select the **X**, **Y**, or **Z** radio button to move the vertices along the direction of the selected radio button.

As mentioned earlier, the value in the **Push/Pull Value** spinner is used to specify the extent of pushing or pulling the vertices of the object. The positive value enables you to pull the vertices, and the negative value enables you to push the vertices. The **Brush Size** spinner is used to specify the size of the brush cursor in the viewport. The value in the **Brush Strength** spinner is used to specify the strength of the brush by which it applies the push or pull effect. It varies from 0.0 to 1.0. Choose the **Brush Options** button; the **Painter Options** dialog box will be displayed. You can set various parameters of the brush in this dialog box. Choose the **Commit** button to deform the object permanently. Note that you cannot use the **Revert** button after choosing the **Commit** button. Choose the **Cancel** button to erase all the changes that you made to deform the object. However, if you have already committed the effects, then you cannot use the **Cancel** button to erase the effects.

Edit Vertices Rollout

On selecting the **Vertex** sub-object level, the **Edit Vertices** rollout will be displayed in the modify panel, as shown in Figure 6-75. The options in this rollout are used to edit the vertices of an object. To delete the vertices of an object, select them in the viewport and choose the **Remove** button; the vertices will be deleted. Alternatively, you can press the DELETE key, but it will create a hole in the object. The **Connect** button is used to connect the two selected vertices by creating an edge between them, refer to Figures 6-76 and 6-77.

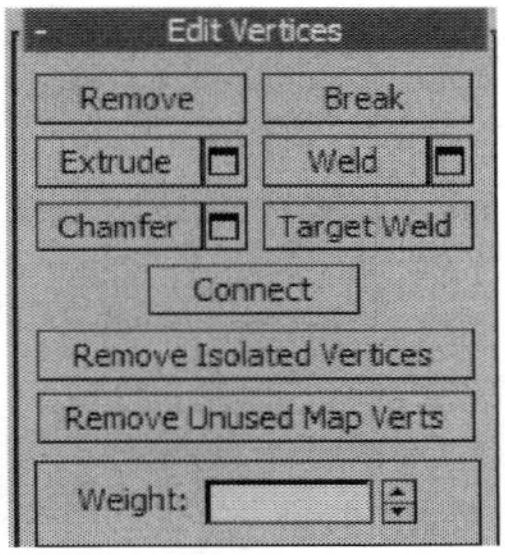

Figure 6-75 *The **Edit Vertices** rollout*

Choose the **Remove Isolated Vertices** button to remove the vertices that are not attached to any polygon in the object. Choose the **Remove Unused Map Verts** button to remove the vertices that cannot be used for mapping. The **Weight** spinner is used to set the weight of the vertex that specifies the smoothness toward the vertex in the output. The **Break**, **Extrude**, **Weld**, **Chamfer**, and **Target Weld** buttons are the same as discussed in the editable mesh. Also note that the **Extrude**, **Weld**, and **Chamfer** buttons have the **Settings** button on their right side to apply the selected command more accurately.

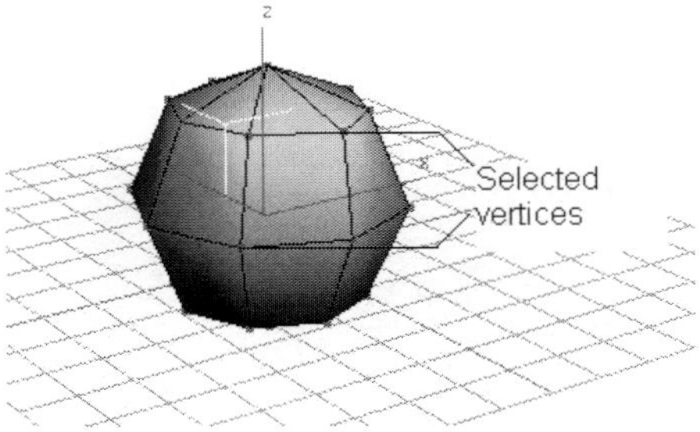

Figure 6-76 *The vertices selected in the object*

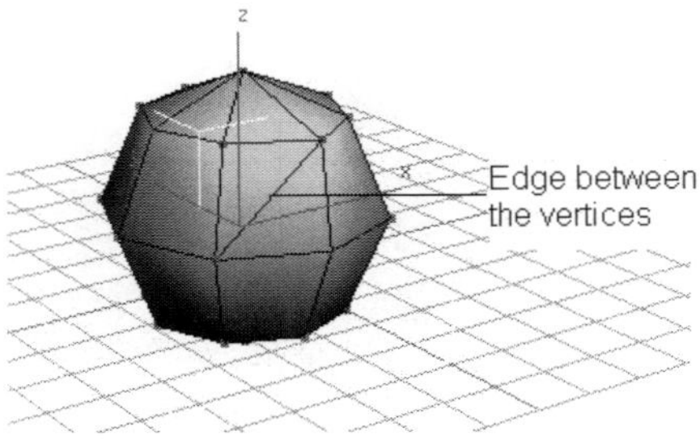

Figure 6-77 *The edge created between the vertices selected*

Edit Edges Rollout

On selecting the **Edge** sub-object level, the **Edit Edges** rollout will be displayed, as shown in Figure 6-78. The options in this rollout are used to edit the edges of an object. The **Insert Vertex** button is used to add a vertex on the edge. To do so, choose the **Insert Vertex** button; the vertices of the object will be displayed in the viewport. Now, click on an edge of the object; a new vertex will be created. Right-click to exit the command. To delete an edge of the object, select the edge in the viewport, and choose the **Remove** button; the selected edge will be deleted.

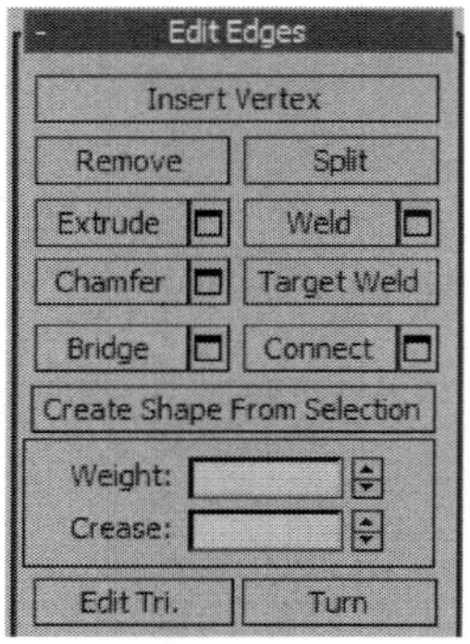

*Figure 6-78 The **Edit Edges** rollout*

Alternatively, you can press the DELETE key, but it will create a hole in the object. The **Connect** button is used to connect the two selected edges by creating a new edge between them. Choose the **Settings** button on the right side of the **Connect** button; the **Connect Edges** caddy control will be displayed in the viewport, as shown in Figure 6-79. It is used to set the parameters of the additional edge created using the **Connect** button. The value in the **Segments** spinner in this caddy control is used to specify the number of new edges in between the selected edges. The value in the **Pinch** spinner is used to set the distance between the new edges. The value in the **Slide** spinner specifies the position of the new edges. By default, the new edges are created at the center.

To set the number of segments per chamfer using the **Chamfer** button, select an edge of the object in the viewport. Now, choose the **Settings** button on the right side of the **Chamfer** button; the **Chamfer** caddy control will be displayed in the viewport, as shown in Figure 6-80. Set the value in the **Edge Chamfer Amount** spinner to specify the amount of chamfering for the selected edge, refer to Figures 6-81 and 6-82. Set the value in the **Connect Edge Segments** spinner to define the number of segments in the chamfer, refer to Figure 6-83. The more number of segments affect the roundness of the chamfer. On selecting the **Open Chamfer** check box, the chamfered area will be deleted and a hole will be created in its place, as shown in Figure 6-84. Note that you need to move the cursor over the buttons to know their respective names.

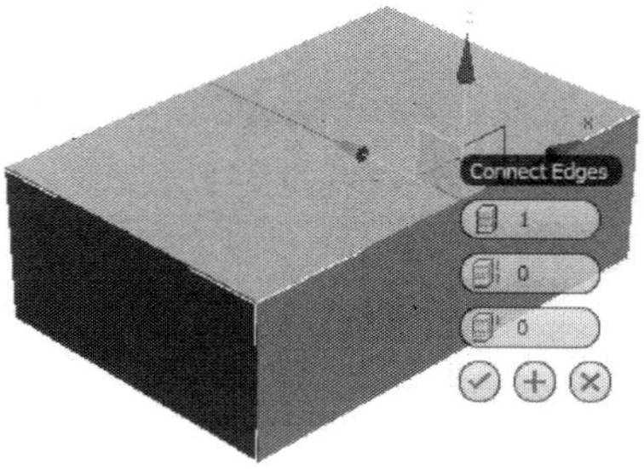

*Figure 6-79 The **Connect Edges** caddy control in the viewport*

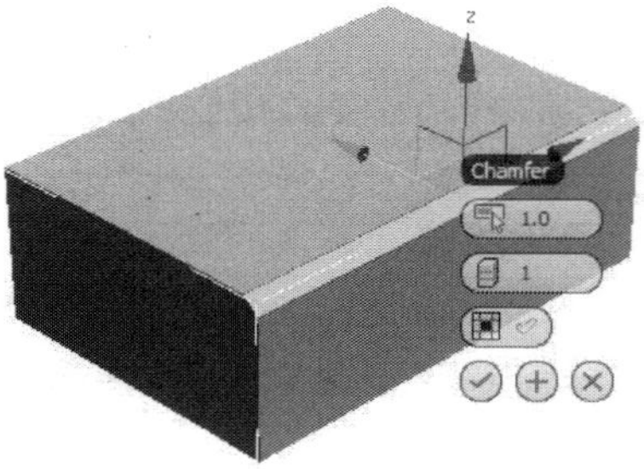

*Figure 6-80 The **Chamfer** caddy control*

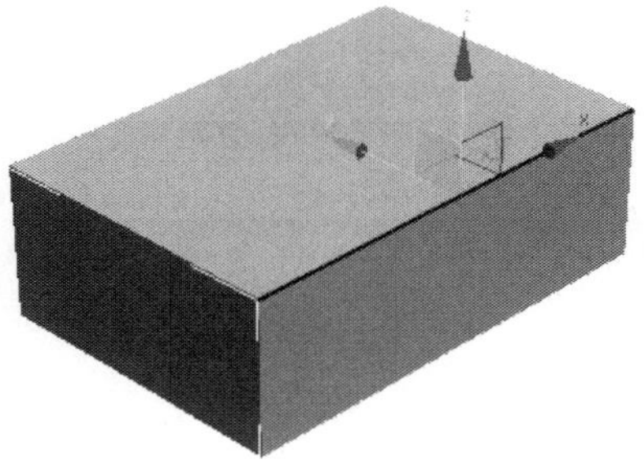

Figure 6-81 An edge selected to be chamfered

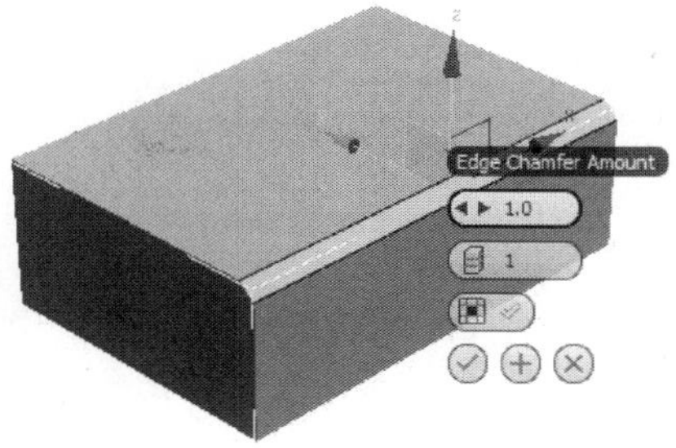

Figure 6-82 The edge after chamfering

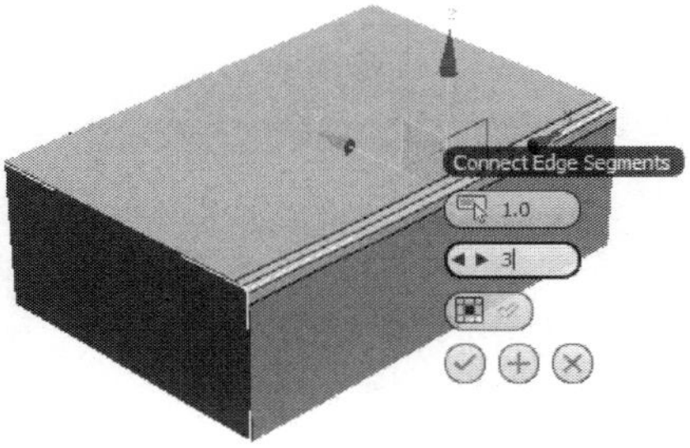

Figure 6-83 The number of segments increased in the chamfer

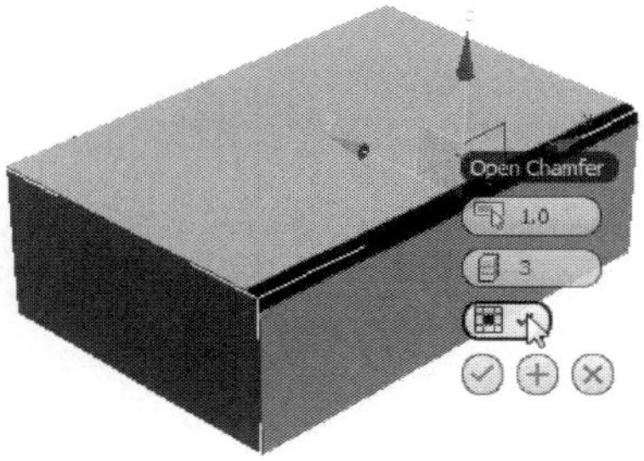

*Figure 6-84 A hole created on selecting the **Open** check box*

The **Create Shape From Selection** button in the **Edit Edges** rollout is used to create a spline shape from the selected edges. To do so, select the edges of an object in the viewport and then choose the **Create Shape From Selection** button; the **Create Shape** dialog box will be displayed, as shown in Figure 6-85. Enter a name in the **Curve Name** text box for the newly created shape. Select the **Smooth** or **Linear** radio button to create a smooth or a linear curve, respectively. Next, choose the **OK** button; a spline will be created along with the selected edges, as shown in Figures 6-86 and 6-87.

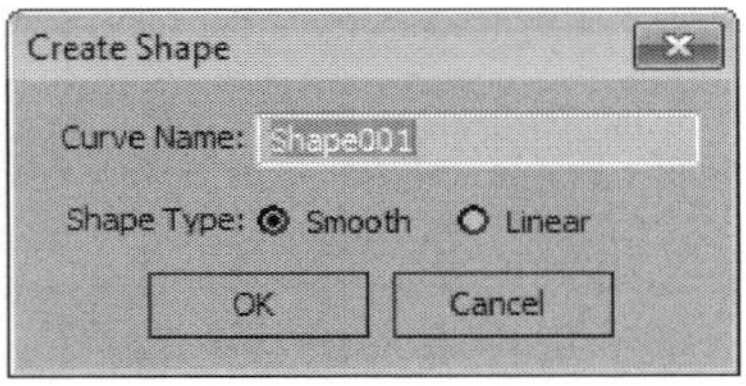

*Figure 6-85 The **Create Shape** dialog box*

Edit Borders Rollout

On selecting the **Border** sub-object level, the **Edit Borders** rollout will be displayed, as shown in Figure 6-88. The options in this rollout are used to edit the border of an object. The **Cap** button is used to create a polygon to cap the selected border of the object. To do so, select the border of the object in the viewport and then choose the **Cap** button; a polygon will be displayed to cap the border, as shown in Figures 6-89 and 6-90. The other options in this rollout are the same as described earlier in this chapter.

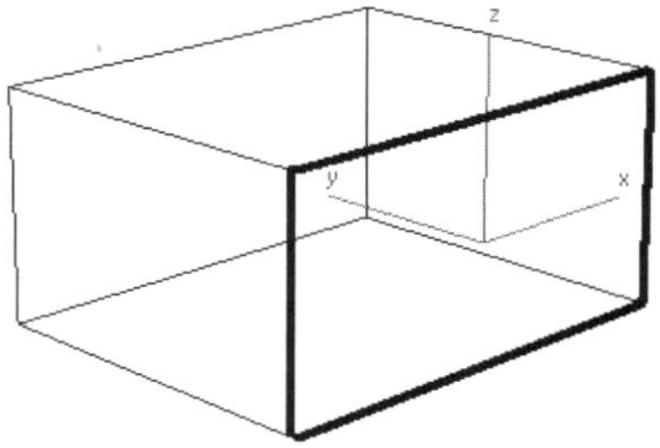

Figure 6-86 The edges selected in the box

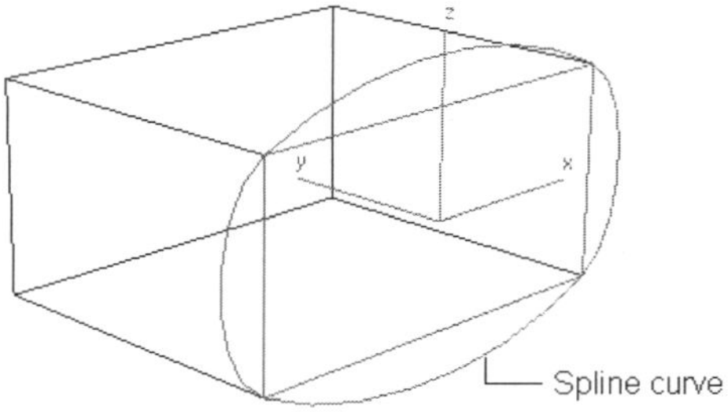

*Figure 6-87 The spline created after using the **Create Shape From Selection** button*

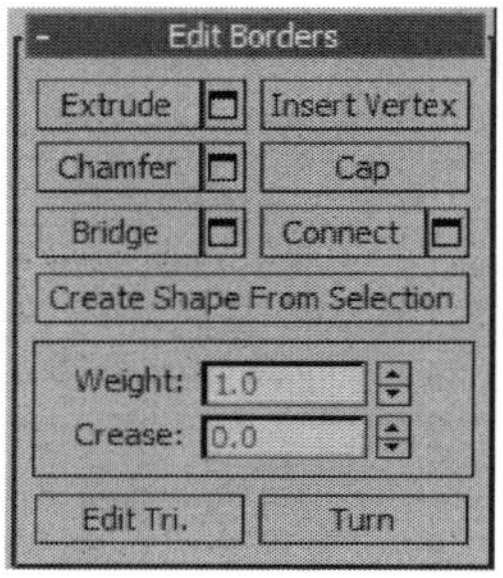

*Figure 6-88 The **Edit Borders** rollout*

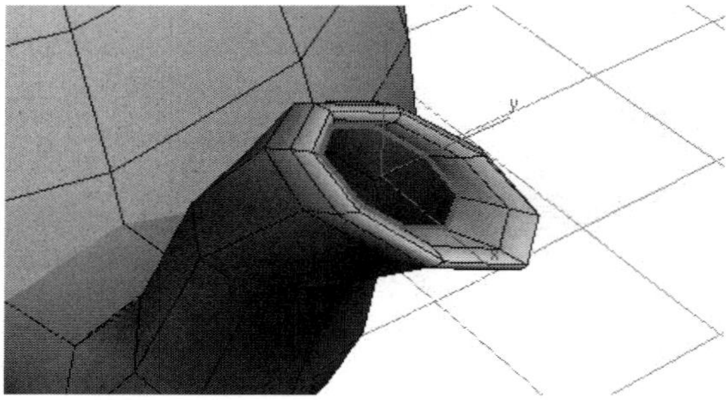

Figure 6-89 The border selected in the spout of a teapot

Edit Polygons Rollout

When you select the **Polygon** sub-object level, the **Edit Polygons** rollout will be displayed, as shown in Figure 6-91. The options in this rollout are used to edit the polygons of the object. The **Outline** button is used to increase or decrease the outside edges of the selected polygons, refer to Figures 6-92 and 6-93. Choose the **Settings** button on the right of the **Outline** button; the **Outline** caddy control will be displayed in the viewport, refer to Figure 6-93. Set the value in the **Amount** spinner to specify the increment or decrement of the outside edge of the selected polygon. Choose the **OK** button to apply the function and exit the **Outline** dialog box.

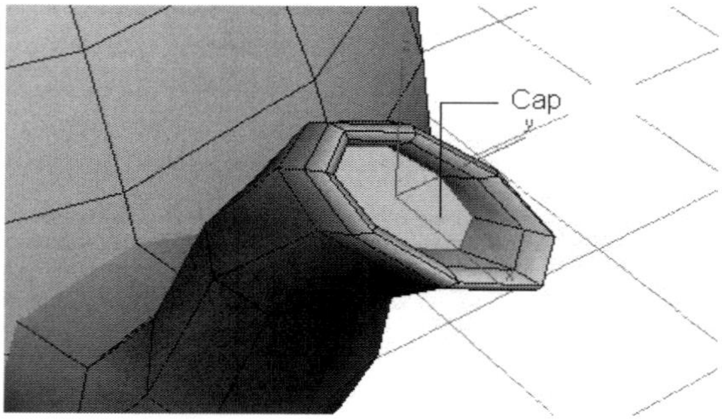

*Figure 6-90 The cap after choosing the **Cap** button*

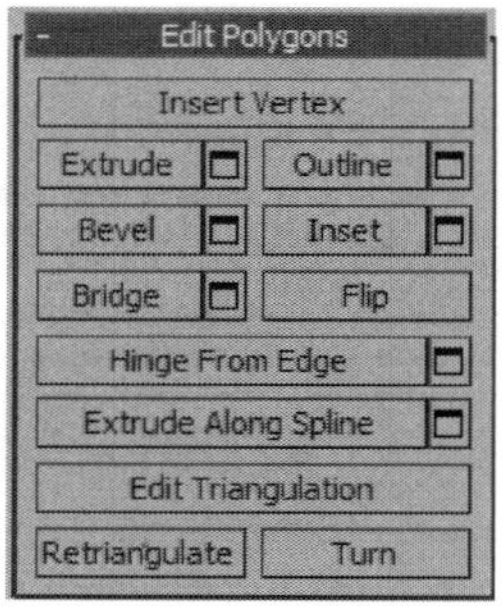

*Figure 6-91 The **Edit Polygons** rollout*

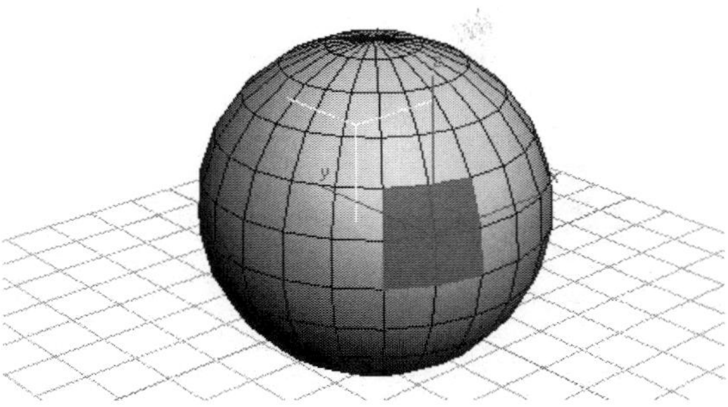

Figure 6-92 *The selected polygons in a sphere*

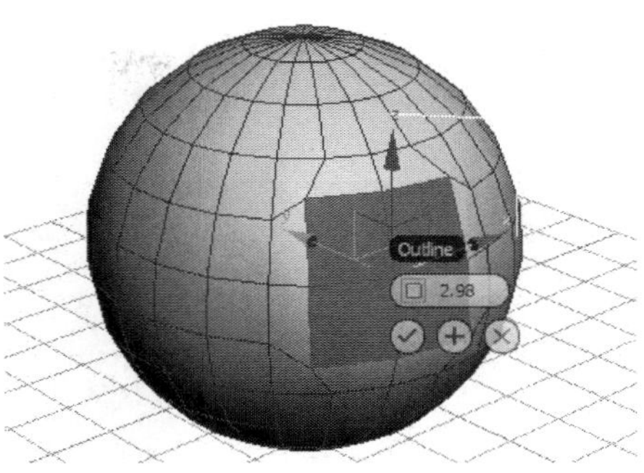

Figure 6-93 *The selected polygons after choosing the* ***Outline*** *button*

The **Inset** button in the **Edit Polygons** rollout is used to inset the outside edges of the selected polygons, as shown in Figures 6-94 and 6-95. Choose the **Settings** button on the right of the **Inset** button; the **Inset** caddy control will be displayed in the viewport, refer to Figure 6-95. Set the value in the **Amount** spinner to specify the amount of inset. Next, click on the arrow placed on the **Group** button; a drop-down list will be displayed, as shown in Figure 6-96. Select the **Group** option to inset the group of polygons. Select the **By Polygon** option to inset the polygons in the group individually. Choose the **OK** button to apply the function and exit the caddy control. The **Flip** button in the **Edit Polygons** rollout is used to flip the direction of the selected polygons.

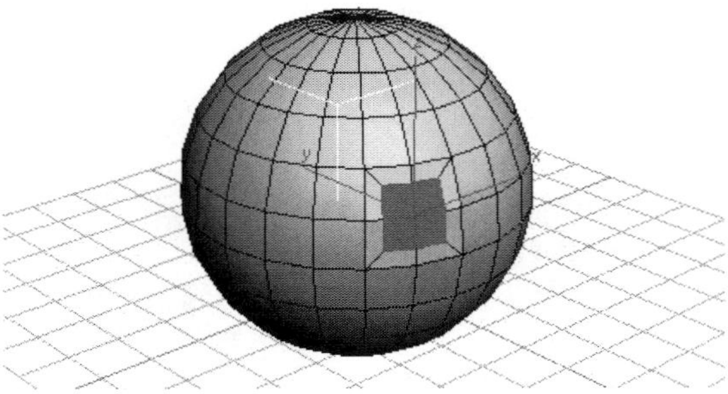

Figure 6-94 *Inset the group of polygons by selecting the* ***Group*** *option*

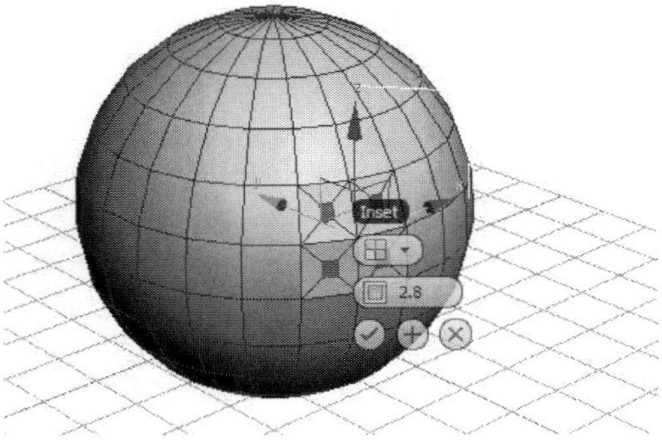

Figure 6-95 *Inset the polygons individually by selecting the* ***By Polygon*** *option*

The **Hinge From Edge** button is used to create a hinge on the selected polygon along with the edge. To do so, select a polygon of the object in the viewport and choose the **Hinge From Edge** button. Now, move the cursor on an edge of the selected polygon and drag the cursor in the vertical direction; the hinge will be created, refer to Figures 6-97 and 6-98. You can also create a hinge on the polygon using the **Settings** button on the right side of the **Hinge From Edge** button. To do so, select a polygon of the object in the viewport and choose the **Settings** button; the **Hinge From Edge** caddy control will be displayed in the viewport, as shown in Figure 6-99. The value in the **Angle** spinner is used to specify the angle of rotation. You can set a positive or a negative value in this spinner. The value in the **Segments** spinner specifies the number of segments in the selected polygon. Choose the **Pick Hinge** button to activate it and click on an edge of the selected polygon in the viewport; the hinge will be created. Choose the **OK** button to close the caddy control.

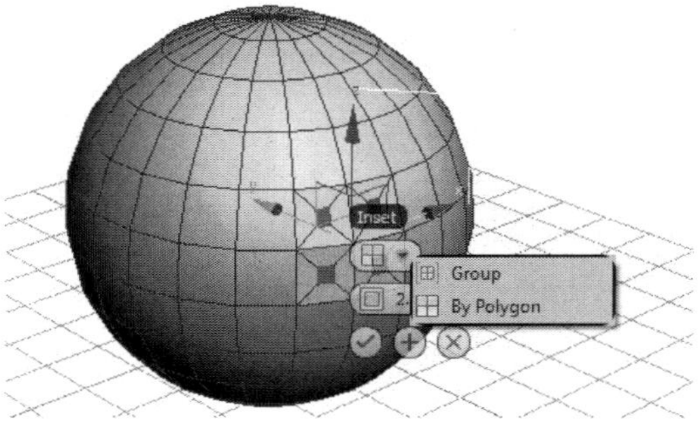

Figure 6-96 *A drop-down list displayed in the* ***Inset*** *caddy control in the viewport*

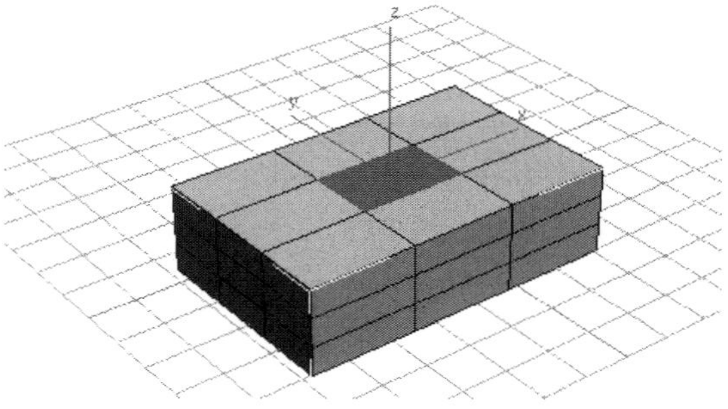

Figure 6-97 *The polygon selected in the box*

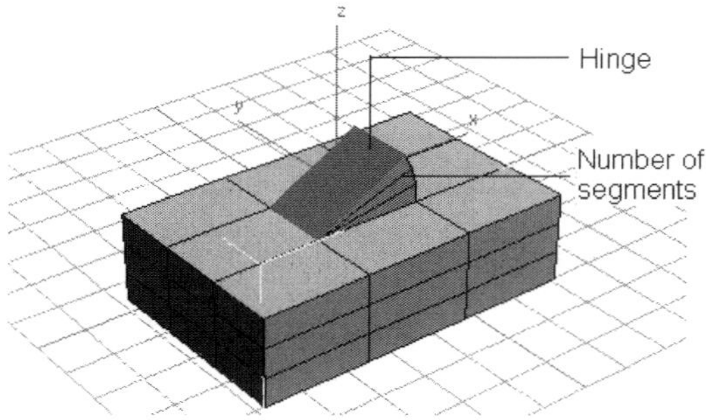

Figure 6-98 *The hinge created on choosing the* ***Hinge From Edge*** *button*

The **Extrude Along Spline** button in the **Edit polygons** rollout is used to extrude the polygons of an object along the spline in the viewport. To do so, select a polygon of the editable poly object in the viewport. Now, choose the **Settings** button on the right side of the **Extrude Along Spline** button; the **Extrude Along Spline** caddy control will be displayed in the viewport, as shown in Figure 6-100. Choose the **Pick Spline** button in the caddy control to activate it; you will be prompted to select the spline in the viewport. Select the spline in the viewport; the selected polygon will be extruded along the spline, refer to Figures 6-101 and 6-102. Set the parameters of the extruded spline using the options in the **Extrude Polygons Along Spline** caddy control.

Converting Objects into Editable Patch

You can also modify the 3D objects at a very high level by converting them into an editable patch. When you convert a mesh object into editable patch, it will get converted into bezier patches, which consist of bezier vertices, edges, and surfaces. You can also convert the patch grid objects into editable patch to modify them. You can create these patch grid objects by selecting the **Patch Grids** option from the drop-down list provided below the **Geometry** button in the **Command Panel** as discussed in Chapter 4. The editable patch provides you the sub-object levels of an object such as **Vertex**, **Edge**, **Patch**, **Element**, and **Handle**. You need to move, rotate, and scale these sub-objects to modify the shape of the object.

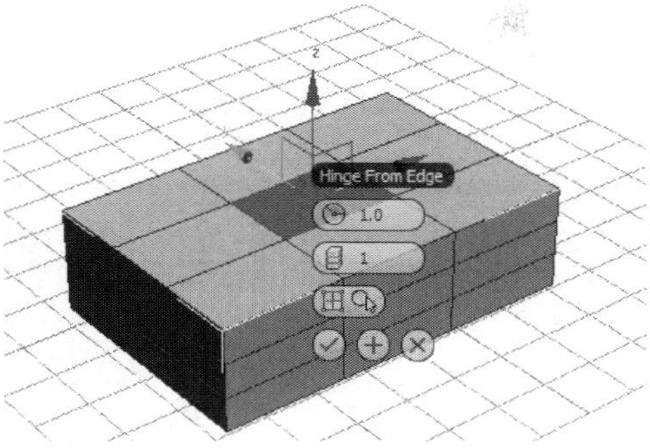

*Figure 6-99 The **Hinge From Edge** caddy control*

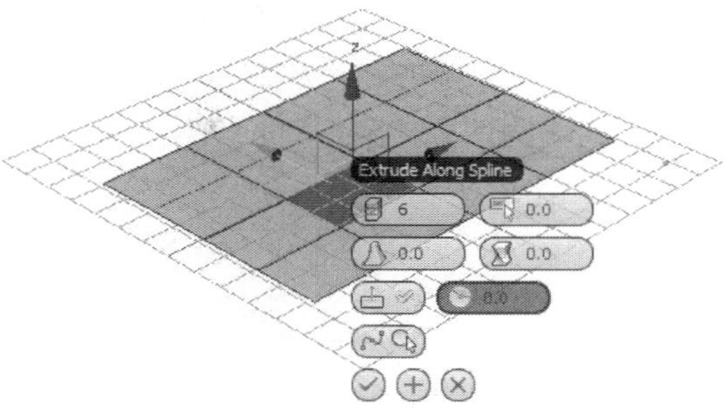

*Figure 6-100 The **Extrude Along Spline** caddy control*

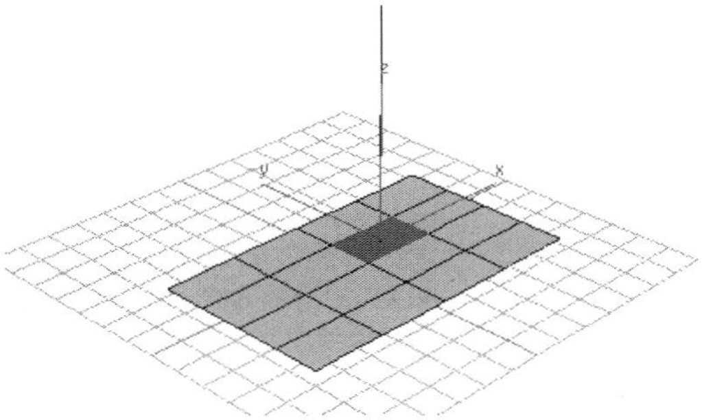

Figure 6-101 The polygon selected in the plane and the spline

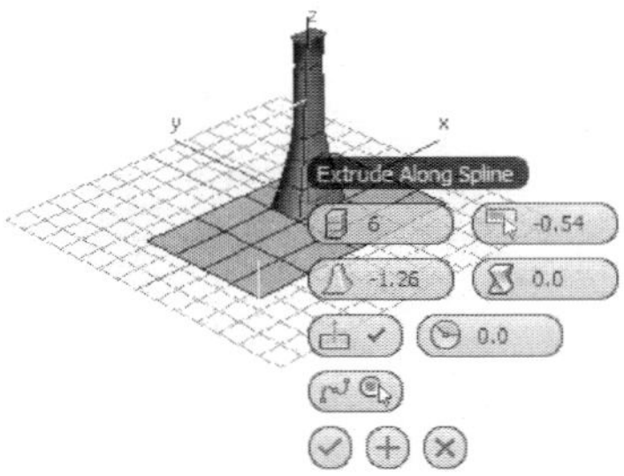

Figure 6-102 The selected polygon extruded along the spline

To work with the editable patch, first you need to convert an object into editable patch object. To do so, you need to follow one of the following methods:

1. Create an object and select it in the viewport. Next, right-click on the object; a quad menu will be displayed. Choose the **Convert To:** option; a cascading menu will be displayed. Choose **Convert to Editable Patch**; the object will be converted into editable patch.

2. Create an object and select it in the viewport. Choose the **Modify** tab in the **Command Panel**; the modify panel will be displayed. In the modifier stack, right-click on the name of the tool using which has been used to create the object; a shortcut menu will be displayed. Choose the **Editable Patch** option; the object will be converted into editable patch.

When you convert an object into editable patch; the name of the tool in the modifier stack will be replaced by Editable Patch, which is known as object level. By clicking on the plus sign at the left side of Editable Patch, you can view the sub-object levels such as **Vertex**, **Edge**, **Patch**, **Element**, and **Handle**. Various rollouts such as **Selection**, **Soft Selection**, **Geometry**, and **Surface Properties** will also be displayed in the modify panel. These rollouts and sub-object levels are discussed next.

Sub-object Levels

The editable patch provides you the sub-object levels of an object such as **Vertex**, **Edge**, **Patch**, **Element**, and **Handle**. To select the **Vertex**, **Edge**, **Patch**, **Element**, and **Handle** sub-object levels quickly, press the numeric keys 1, 2, 3, 4, and 5, respectively on the keyboard. You can modify an editable patch object by moving, rotating, and scaling the sub-objects in it. These sub-objects are discussed next.

Vertex

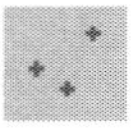

An editable patch object has the vertices with their vector handles. To modify the object through vertices, you need to select the **Vertex** sub-object level. On doing so, the vertices of the object will be displayed in the viewports. When you select the vertex of the object in the viewport, the vector handles will be displayed in green color, as shown in Figures 6-103 and 6-104. Some mesh objects also display the interior vertices in yellow colored squares, refer to Figure 6-103.

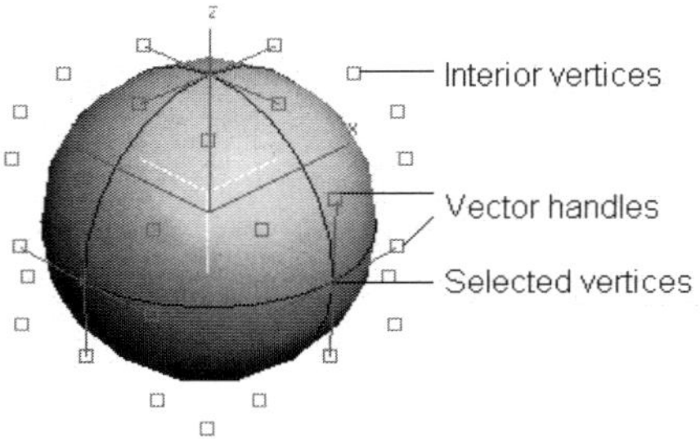

Figure 6-103 An editable patch sphere with vector handles and interior vertices

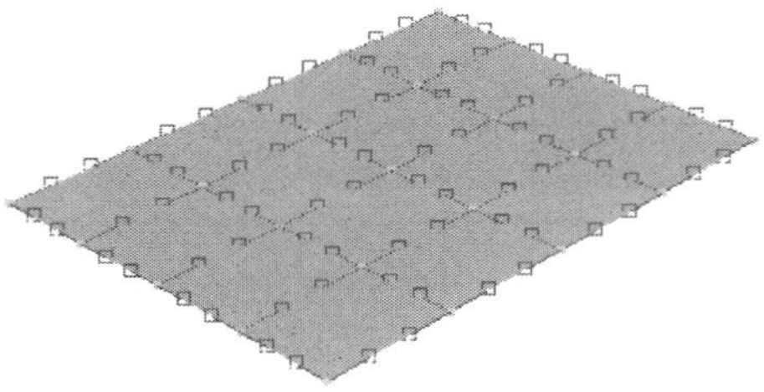

Figure 6-104 The vector handles in a plane

Handle

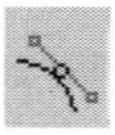

When you select the **Handle** sub-object level, the green colored vector handles of the object will be displayed in the viewports, refer to Figure 6-103. In some objects, yellow colored interior vertices will also be displayed. The numbers of vector handles are related with the numbers of vertices in the object. You can directly modify an object using the vector handles of the object, without using its vertices.

Edge

The **Edge** sub-object level is the same as described earlier.

Patch

The **Patch** sub-object level is used to select the patch in an object, as shown in Figure 6-105.

Element

To modify an object through elements, you need to select the **Element** sub-object level. On doing so, all the adjacent faces of the object will be selected, as shown in Figure 6-106.

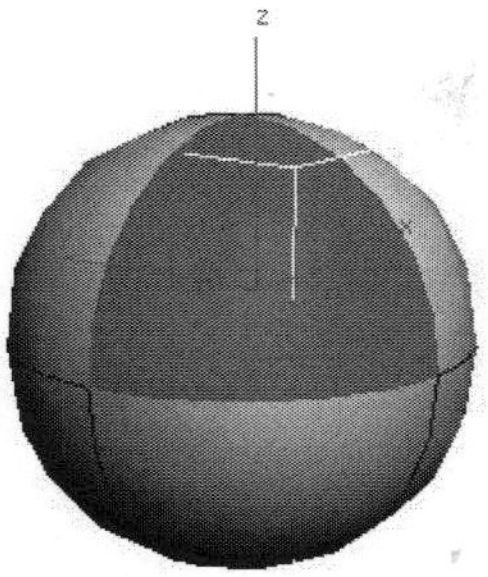

Figure 6-105 The patch sub-object selected in an editable patch sphere

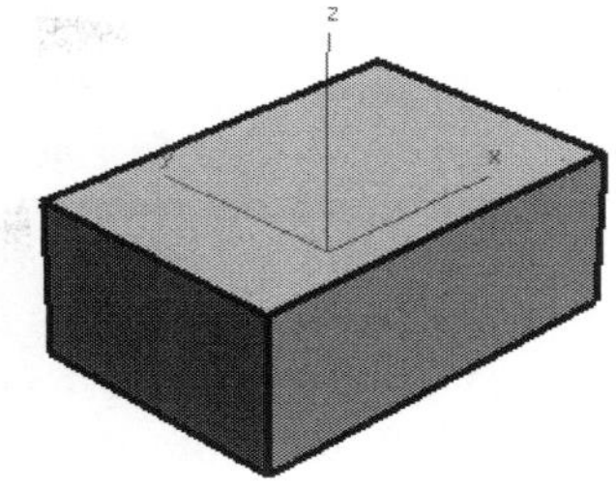

Figure 6-106 The element sub-object selected in an editable patch box

Rollouts

When you convert an object into editable patch, various rollouts will be displayed at the bottom of the modifier stack in the modify panel to modify the objects at sub-object levels. These rollouts are discussed next.

Selection Rollout

At the top of the **Selection** rollout, there are five buttons, **Vertex**, **Handle, Edge**, **Patch**, and **Element**, as shown in Figure 6-107. These buttons are used to select the sub-objects of the object in the viewport and are the same as described earlier. Choose one of the buttons to activate it and it is the same as selecting the sub-object level in the modifier stack.

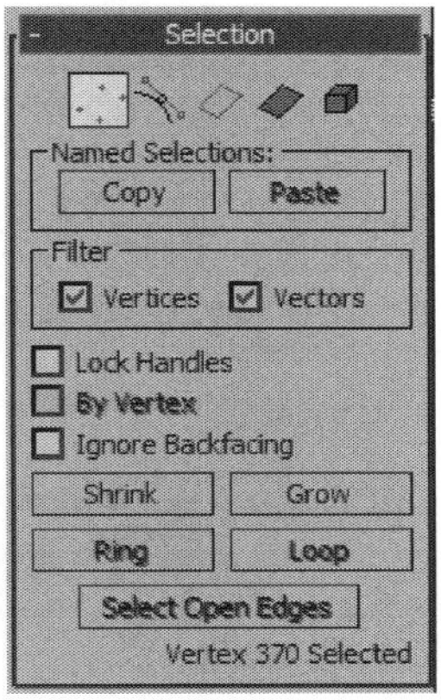

*Figure 6-107 The **Selection** rollout with the **Vertex** button chosen*

The options in the **Filter** area are available only at the **Vertex** sub-object level. The **Vertices** check box in the **Filter** area is used to select and move the vertices of the object. The **Vectors** check box is used to select and move the vector handles of the object. The **Lock Handles** check box is available only at the **Vertex** and **Handle** sub-object levels. Select the **Lock Handles** check box to move all the vector handles together. The other options are the same as described in the editable poly objects.

Soft Selection Rollout

The options in this rollout are the same as described in the editable mesh objects.

Geometry Rollout

The options in this rollout are used to edit the patch of an object, as shown in Figure 6-108. They vary according to the selection of the sub-object level in the modifier stack. The areas in this rollout are discussed next.

Subdivision Area

This area is available on the **Vertex**, **Edge**, **Patch**, and **Element** sub-object levels. The **Subdivide** button in this area is used to subdivide the selected sub-object. When you select the **Edge**, **Patch**, or **Element** sub-object level; the **Subdivide** button is activated. To subdivide a sub-object, select the corresponding sub-object of the editable patch object in the viewport, as shown in Figure 6-109. Next, choose the **Subdivide** button; the selected sub-object will be subdivided, as shown in Figure 6-110. To subdivide all sub-objects around the selected sub-object, you need to select the **Propagate** check box before choosing the **Subdivide** button, as shown in Figure 6-111.

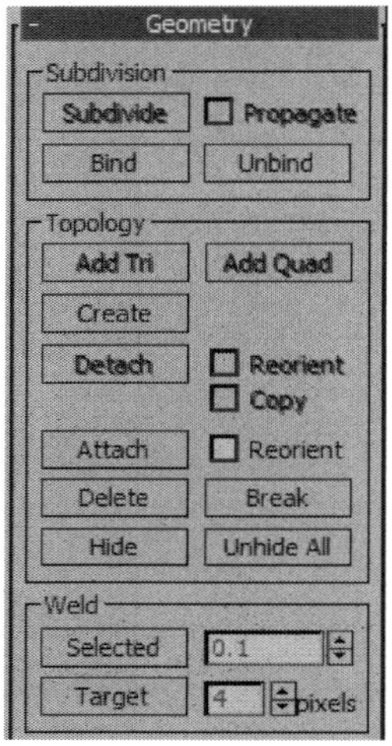

Figure 6-108 *Partial view of the* ***Geometry*** *rollout*

Figure 6-109 *The patch selected in an editable patch box*

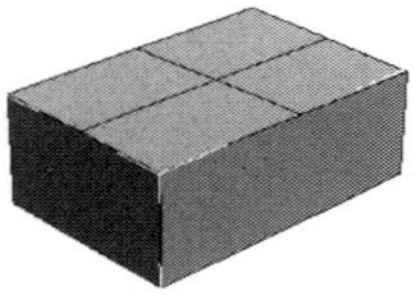

Figure 6-110 *The selected patch subdivided on choosing the* ***Subdivide*** *button*

The **Bind** and **Unbind** buttons are available only at the **Vertex** sub-object level. The **Bind** button is used to bind the two patch edges that have unequal number of vertices and belong to the same object. The **Unbind** button is used to unbind the vertices that are bound using the **Bind** button.

The **Add Tri** and **Add Quad** buttons in the **Topology** area are available only at the **Edge** sub-object level. These buttons are used to add a tri patch or a quad patch on the selected edge. To create an open edge, you need to delete a patch of an object in the viewport. Next, select the open edge, as shown in Figure 6-112, and then choose the **Add Tri** or **Add Quad** button to add a tri patch or a quad patch to the open edge, as shown in Figures 6-113 and 6-114.

The **Detach** button is available only at the **Patch** and **Element** sub-object levels. It is used to detach the selected patches or elements from the current object. To do so, select one or more patches or elements in the viewport. Next, choose the **Detach** button; the **Detach** dialog box will be displayed. Enter the name of the new detached element in the **Detach**

as text box and choose the **OK** button. The other options in this rollout are the same as described earlier in this chapter.

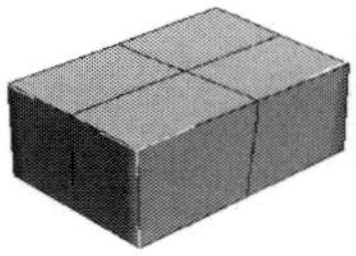

Figure 6-111 *The selected patch subdivided after selecting the* ***Propagate*** *check box*

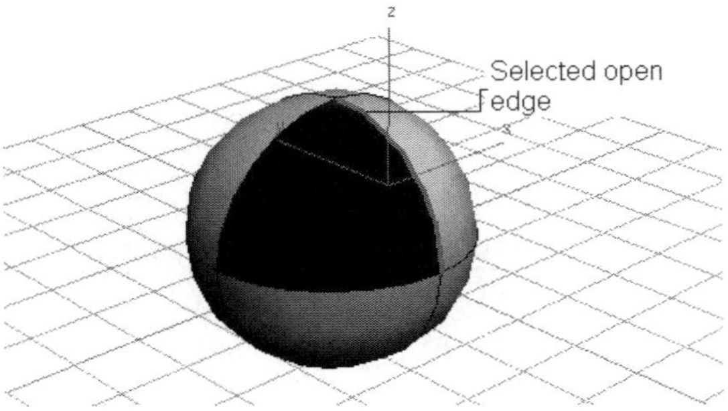

Figure 6-112 *The open edge selected in the editable patch sphere*

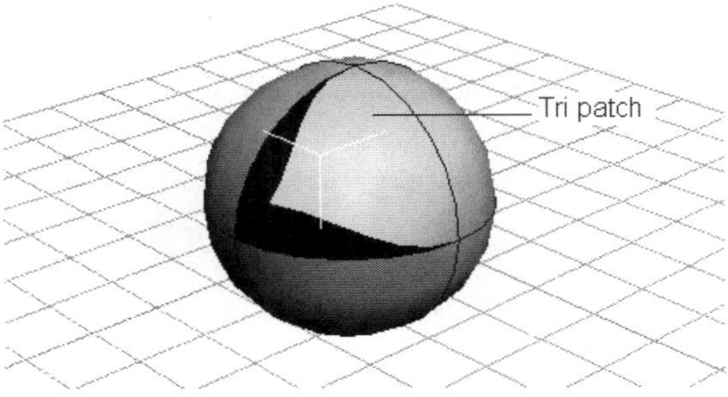

Figure 6-113 *The tri patch after choosing the* ***Tri Patch*** *button*

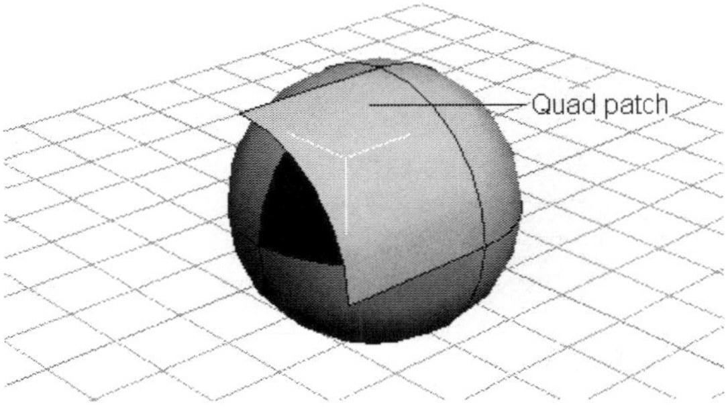

Figure 6-114 *The quad patch after choosing the* ***Quad Patch*** *button*

Tutorial 1

In this tutorial, you will create a golf ball, as shown in Figure 6-115, by modifying the standard primitives at advanced level. **(Expected time: 20 min)**

The following steps are required to complete this tutorial:

a. Set the project folder.
b. Create a geosphere from standard primitives.
c. Convert the geosphere into an editable mesh.

d. Modify the geosphere.
e. Render the scene for the final output.
f. Save the file.

Figure 6-115 *A golf ball model*

Setting the Project Folder

1. Set the project folder with the name *c06_tut1* in the *3dsmax* folder as discussed in earlier chapters.

Creating a Geosphere

First, reset Autodesk 3ds Max to start afresh and then create a geosphere using the **GeoSphere** tool.

1. Activate the Top viewport and choose **Create > Geometry** in the **Command Panel**; the **Standard Primitives** option is displayed by default in the drop-down list below the **Geometry** button. Now, invoke the **GeoSphere** tool from the **Object Type** rollout.

2. Expand the **Keyboard Entry** rollout and set **130.0** as the radius value in the **Radius** spinner. Next, choose the **Create** button; a geosphere is displayed in all viewports.

3. In the **Parameters** rollout, set the value **8** in the **Segments** spinner.

4. Invoke the **Zoom Extents All** tool to display the entire geosphere in all viewports, as shown in Figure 6-116.

5. In the **Name and Color** rollout, enter **golf ball** and press ENTER; the geosphere is named as *golf ball*.

6. Use the color swatch to change the color of the *golf ball* to white.

Next, you need to modify the *golf ball* at an advanced level by converting it into an editable mesh.

Converting the Golf Ball into Editable Mesh

1. Select the *golf ball* in any viewport and right-click on it; a quad menu is displayed. Choose the **Convert To:** option; a cascading menu is displayed. Choose **Convert to Editable Mesh**; the *golf ball* is converted into editable mesh.

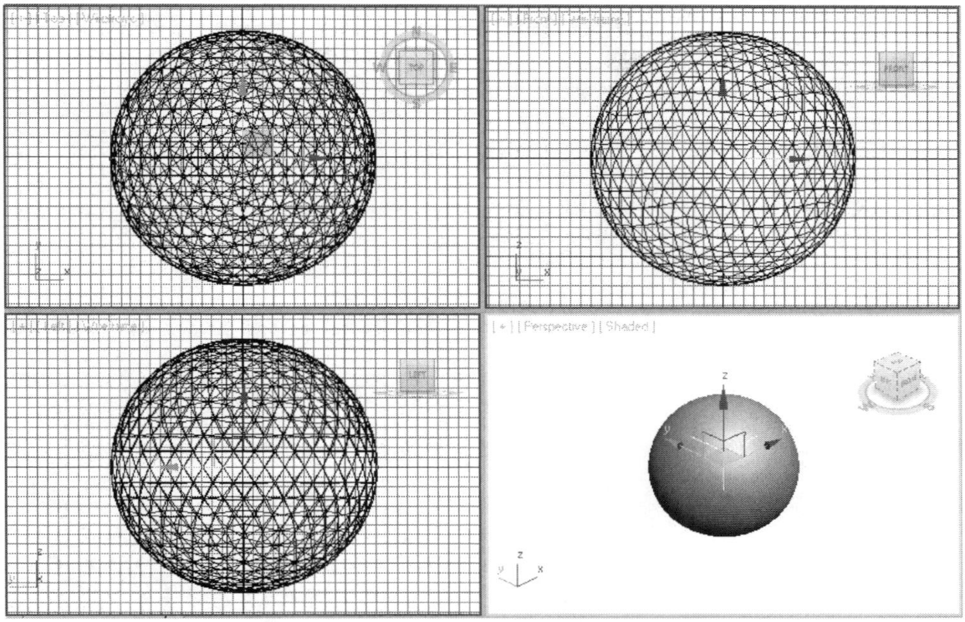

Figure 6-116 The geosphere displayed in all viewports

2. When you convert the *golf ball* into editable mesh, the **GeoSphere** text in the modifier stack gets replaced by the Editable Mesh.

   Next, you need to modify the *golf ball* using the sub-object levels in the modifier stack to give it a perfect shape.

Modifying the Golf Ball Using the Sub-object Levels

1. Activate the Perspective viewport. Press the F4 key to view all segments of the *golf ball*, as it helps you modify it precisely.

2. Next, invoke the **Zoom** tool and zoom in the Perspective viewport to view the *golf ball*, as shown in Figure 6-117.

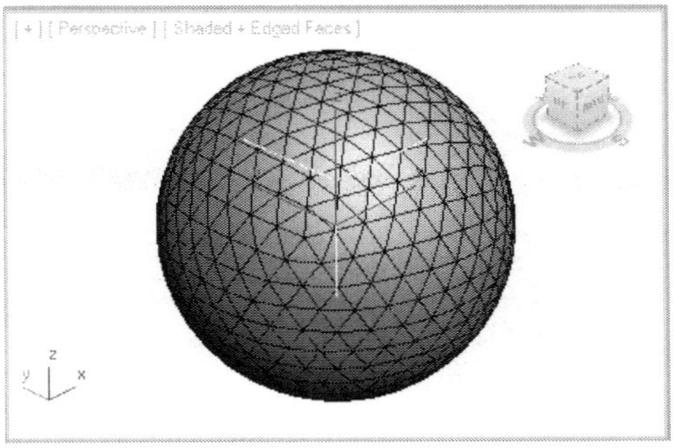

Figure 6-117 The golf ball with all segments zoomed in the Perspective viewport

3. Invoke the **Maximize Viewport Toggle** tool to maximize the Perspective viewport.

4. Make sure that the *golf ball* is selected in the Perspective viewport. In the modifier stack, click on the plus sign on the left of the Editable Mesh to view all sub-object levels.

5. Select the **Polygon** sub-object level; it turns yellow and gets activated. Also, you are prompted to select the polygons of the *golf ball* in the viewport.

Note

On selecting the ***Polygon*** *sub-object level in the modifier stack, the* ***Polygon*** *button will also be chosen in the* ***Selection*** *rollout.*

6. Select any polygon of the *golf ball* in the viewport, as shown in Figure 6-118.

7. Press the CTRL+A keys to select all polygons of the *golf ball*, as shown in Figure 6-119.

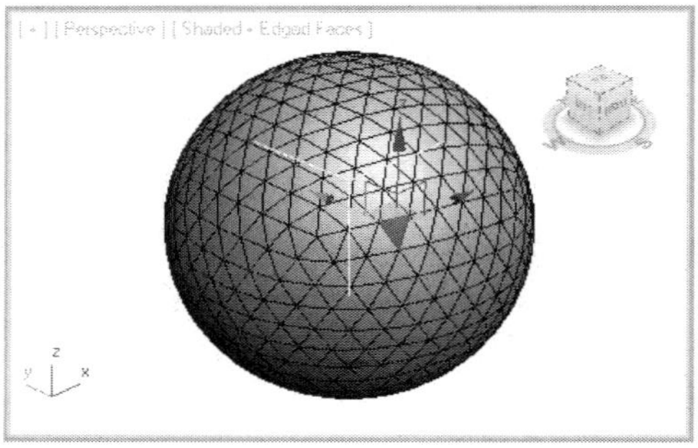

Figure 6-118 *The polygon selected on the golf ball*

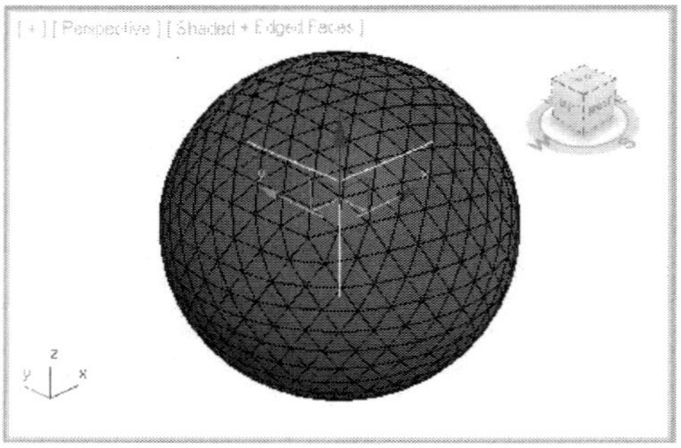

Figure 6-119 *All polygons selected on the golf ball*

8. Next, select the **Edge** sub-object level in the modifier stack to activate it; you are prompted to select an edge of the *golf ball* in the viewport.

9. Select an edge of the *golf ball* in the viewport, as shown in Figure 6-120.

10. Press the CTRL+A keys to select all the edges of the *golf ball*, as shown in Figure 6-121.

    Now, if you select the **Polygon** sub-object level in the modifier stack, all polygons of the *golf ball* are selected in the viewport. And, if you select the **Edge** sub-object level, then all the edges of the *golf ball* are selected in the viewport.

11. Select the **Edge** sub-object level, if it is not already selected; all edges of the *golf ball* are selected in the viewport.

12. In the **Edit Geometry** rollout, set **5** in the **Chamfer** spinner and press ENTER; all the selected edges of the *golf ball* are chamfered and hexagonal polygons are created, as shown in Figure 6-122.

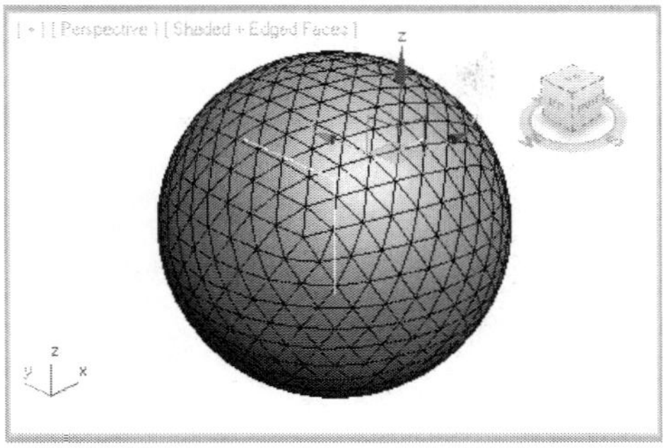

Figure 6-120 The edge selected in the golf ball

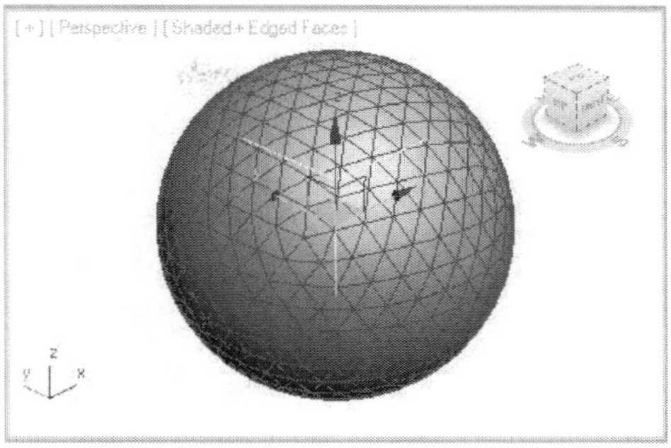

Figure 6-121 All edges of the golf ball selected

Note

*After entering a value in the **Chamfer** spinner and pressing the ENTER key, the value changes to 0 automatically.*

13. In the modifier stack, select the **Polygon** sub-object level; all polygons of the *golf ball* get selected, except the new hexagonal polygons, as shown in Figure 6-123. Next, you need to select all new hexagonal polygons in the *golf ball*.

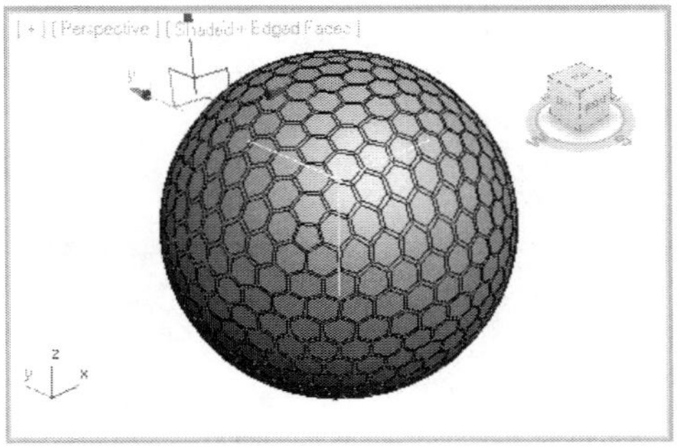

Figure 6-122 All selected edges of the golf ball chamfered

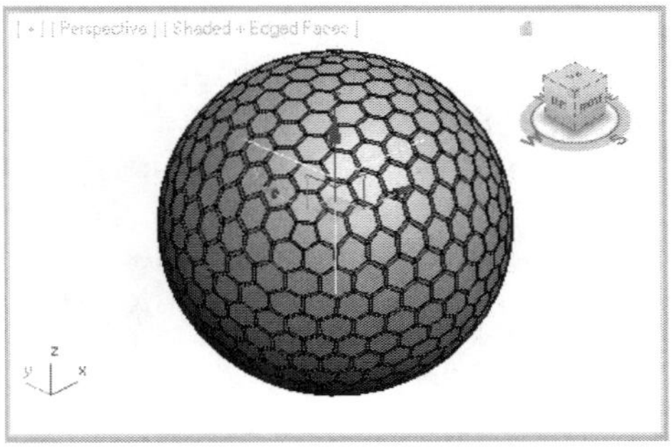

Figure 6-123 All polygons in the golf ball, except new hexagonal polygons selected

14. Choose the **Select Invert** option from the **Edit** menu bar; all new hexagonal polygons of the *golf ball* are selected in the viewport, as shown in Figure 6-124.

15. In the **Edit Geometry** rollout, set **-1** in the **Extrude** spinner for the negative extrusion of the selected hexagonal polygons and press ENTER, refer to Figure 6-125.

16. Next, enter the value **-4** in the **Bevel** spinner of the **Edit Geometry** rollout to bevel the selected hexagonal polygons and press ENTER.

    Now, you need to smoothen the selected polygons of the *golf ball*.

17. Select the **MeshSmooth** modifier from the **Modifier List** drop-down list at the top of the modifier stack in the modify panel. Use the default settings for the **MeshSmooth** modifier.

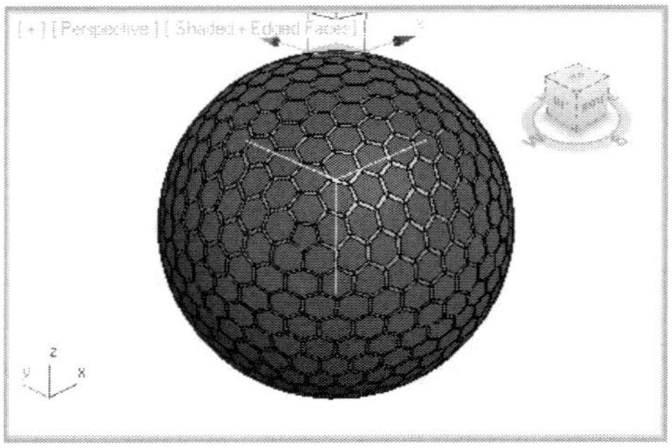

Figure 6-124 *All hexagonal polygons of the golf boll selected in the viewport*

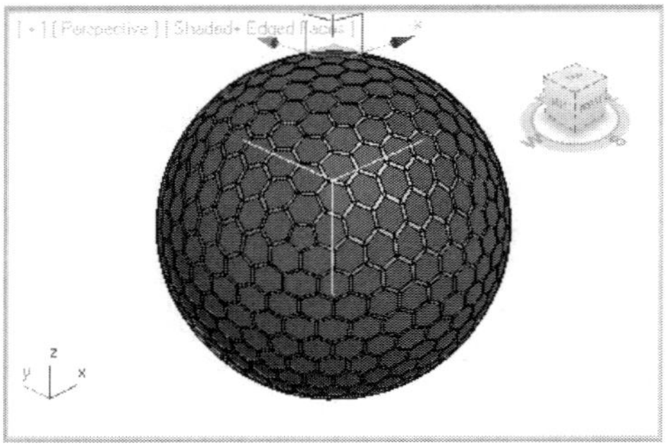

Figure 6-125 *Hexagonal polygons displayed after negative extrusion*

18. Click anywhere in any viewport to deselect the sub-objects. Press the F4 key; the *golf ball* is displayed in the viewport, as shown in Figure 6-126.

19. Now, invoke the **Maximize Viewport Toggle** tool to view the *golf ball* in all viewports.

Rendering the Scene for the Final Output

Before rendering the final output, you can change the background color as discussed earlier.

1. Activate the Perspective viewport.

2. Invoke the **Render Production** tool in the **Main Toolbar**; the **Perspective, frame 0, Display Gamma:2.2, RGBA Color 16 Bits/Channel (1:1)** dialog box is displayed. This dialog box shows the final output of the *golf ball* at one frame, as shown in Figure 6-127.

Figure 6-126 *The golf ball*

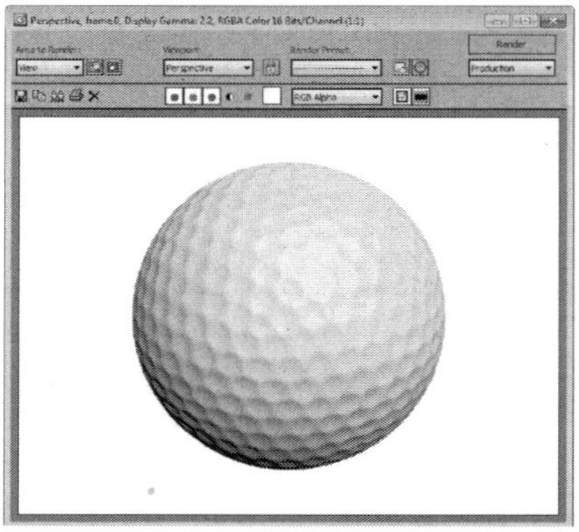

Figure 6-127 *The final output at rendering*

3. Close this dialog box.

You can view the final rendered image of this model by downloading the *c06_3dsmax_2012_render.zip* file from *http://www.cadcim.com*.

Saving the File

1. Save the file with the name *c06tut1.max* as discussed in earlier chapters. The location of this file is given below:

   \Documents\3dsmax\c06_tut1\scenes

Tutorial 2

In this tutorial, you will create the model of a LCD monitor by modifying 3D mesh objects at advanced level, as shown in Figures 6-128 and 6-129. **(Expected time: 30 min)**

Figure 6-128 *A LCD monitor model (view 1)*

Figure 6-129 *A LCD monitor model (view 2)*

The following steps are required to complete this tutorial:

a. Set the project folder.
b. Create the front portion of the LCD monitor.
c. Create the back portion of the LCD monitor.
d. Create speakers of the LCD monitor.
e. Create buttons of the LCD monitor.
f. Create the support of the LCD monitor.
g. Render the scene for the final output.
h. Save the file.

Setting the Project Folder

1. Set the project folder with the name *c06_tut2* in the *3dsmax* folder as discussed in earlier chapters.

Creating the Front Portion of the LCD Monitor

First, reset Autodesk 3ds Max to start afresh, as discussed earlier.

1. Activate the Front viewport and choose **Create > Geometry** in the **Command Panel**; the **Standard Primitives** option is displayed by default in the drop-down list below the **Geometry** button. Now, invoke the **Box** tool from the **Object Type** rollout.

2. Expand the **Keyboard Entry** rollout and set the values as given below:

   Length: **86** Width: **127.893** Height: **3.0**

3. Choose the **Create** button; a box is displayed in all viewports.

4. In the **Parameters** rollout, set the values as given below:

   Length Segs: **12** Width Segs: **15** Height Segs: **1**

5. Invoke the **Zoom Extents All** tool; a box is displayed in all viewports, as shown in Figure 6-130.

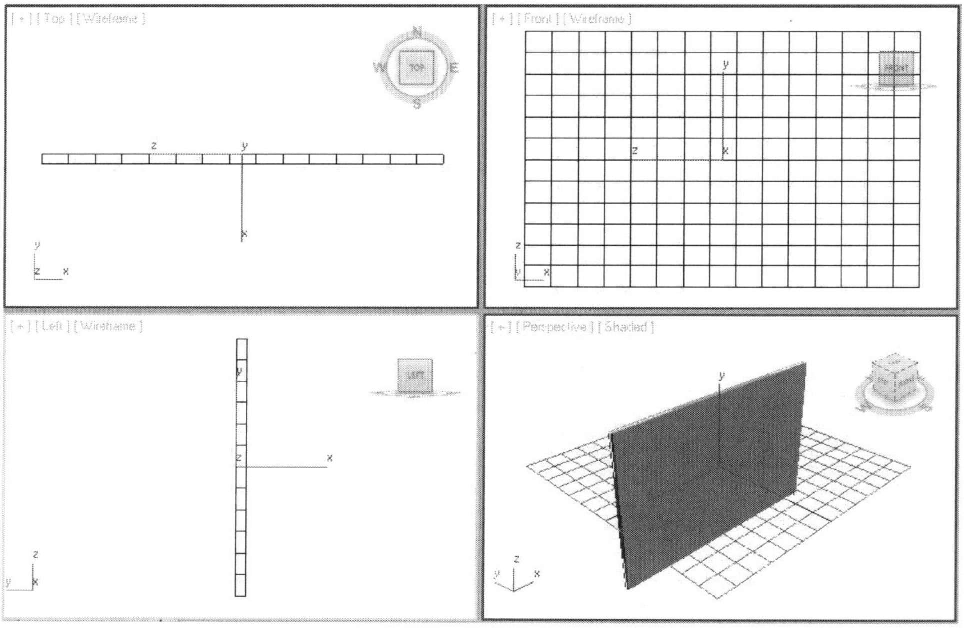

***Figure 6-130** The box for the front portion of the monitor displayed in all viewports*

6. In the **Name and Color** rollout, enter **front portion** and press ENTER; the box is named as *front portion*. Also, change the color of the *front portion* to white.

   Next, you need to convert the *front portion* into editable poly to modify it at an advanced level.

7. Select the *front portion* in any viewport and right-click on it; a quad menu is displayed. Choose the **Convert To** option; a cascading menu is displayed. Choose **Convert to Editable Poly**; the *front portion* is converted into editable poly.

8. When you convert the *front portion* into editable poly, the name of the **Box** tool in the modifier stack gets replaced with **Editable Poly**.

Next, you need to modify the *front portion* using sub-object levels in the modifier stack to give it a shape similar to the front portion of the monitor.

9. Activate the Front viewport and invoke the **Maximize Viewport Toggle** tool to maximize it.

10. Make sure that the *front portion* is selected in the viewport. In the modifier stack, click on the plus sign on the left of the Editable Poly to view all sub-object levels.

11. Select the **Polygon** sub-object level; it turns blue and gets activated. Also, you are prompted to select the polygons of the *front portion* in the viewport.

12. In the **Selection** rollout, select the **Ignore Backfacing** check box. Next, select a polygon of the *front portion* in the viewport, as shown in Figure 6-131.

13. In the Front viewport, hold the CTRL key and select all polygons of the *front portion*, except the outer rows, as shown in Figure 6-132.

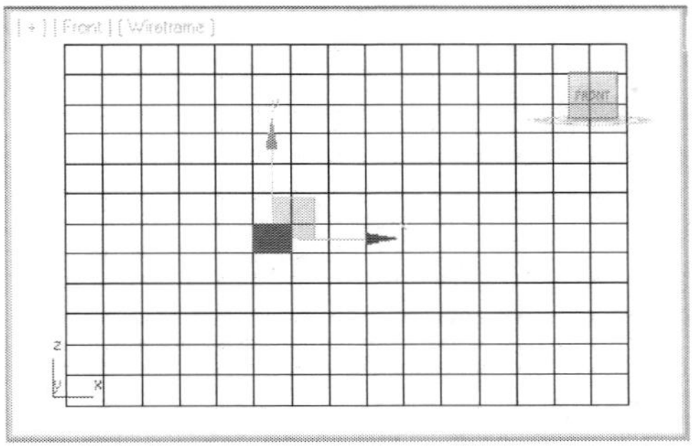

Figure 6-131 *A polygon selected in the Front viewport*

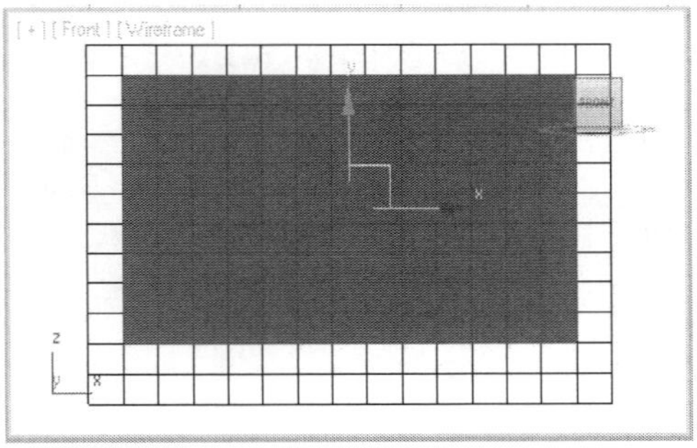

Figure 6-132 *All polygons selected in the Front viewport*

Note

*You can also use the **Grow** button in the **Selection** rollout to increase the selection area of polygons in the viewport.*

14. Next, in the **Edit Polygons** rollout, choose the **Settings** button on the right side of the **Extrude** button to extrude the selected polygons; the **Extrude Polygons** caddy control is displayed in the viewport, as shown in Figure 6-133. In the **Height** spinner, set the value **-3** for negative extrusion and choose **OK** to close the dialog box.

15. Now, click on the **Polygon** sub-object level in the modifier stack to deactivate it. Next, click anywhere in the viewport to deselect the *front portion*.

16. Invoke the **Maximize Viewport Toggle** tool to view all the four viewports simultaneously. The extrusion effect is displayed in the Perspective viewport is displayed, as shown in Figure 6-134.

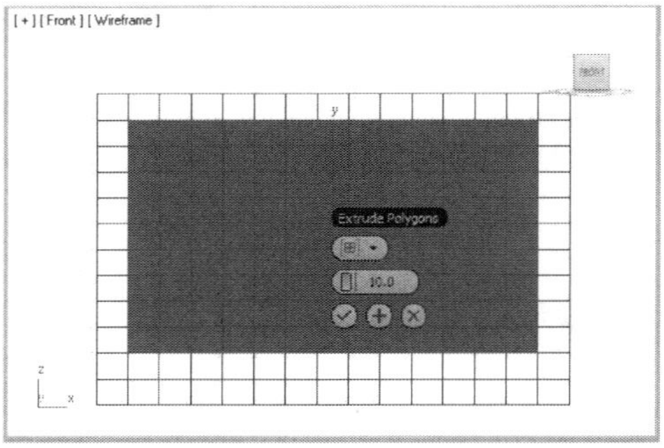

Figure 6-133 *The* ***Extrude Polygons*** *caddy control*

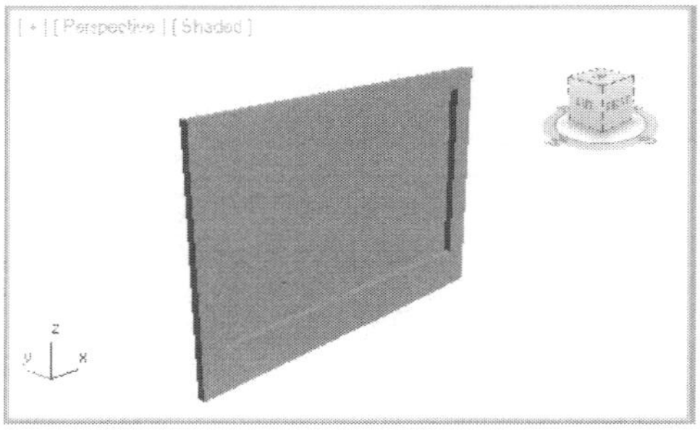

Figure 6-134 *The selected polygons extruded in the Perspective viewport*

Now, you need to create a box for the screen of the *front portion*.

17. Activate the Front viewport, choose **Create > Geometry** in the **Command Panel**; the **Standard Primitives** option is displayed by default in the drop-down list below the **Geometry** button. Now, invoke the **Box** tool from the **Object Type** rollout.

18. Expand the **Keyboard Entry** rollout and set the values as given below:

    Length: **64.756** Width: **110.532** Height: **0.5**

19. Choose the **Create** button; a box is displayed in all viewports.

20. In the **Parameters** rollout, set the values as given below:

    Length Segs: **5** Width Segs: **5** Height Segs: **5**

21. In the **Name and Color** rollout, enter **screen** and press ENTER; the box is named as *screen*. Change the color of the *screen* to black.

22. Activate the Left viewport and align the *screen* with the *front portion*, as shown in Figure 6-135.

23. In the Front viewport, align the *screen* with the *front portion*, as shown in Figure 6-136.

Note

You can assign a desktop picture to the screen to give it a realistic effect. You will learn more about assigning pictures in the later chapters.

24. Next, group the *screen* and the *front portion* as described earlier and name it as *front part*.

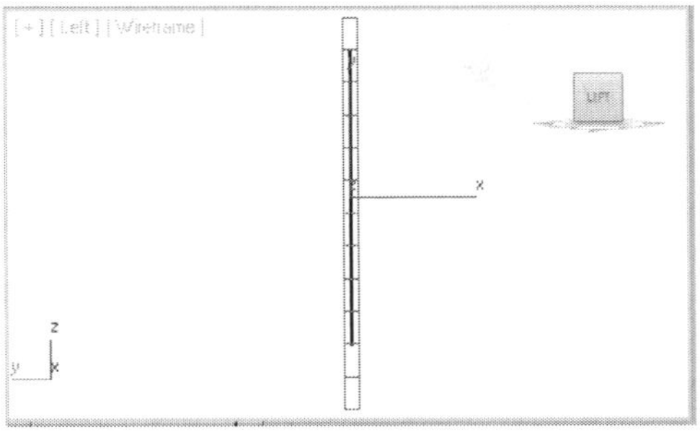

Figure 6-135 Alignment of the screen with the front portion in the Left viewport

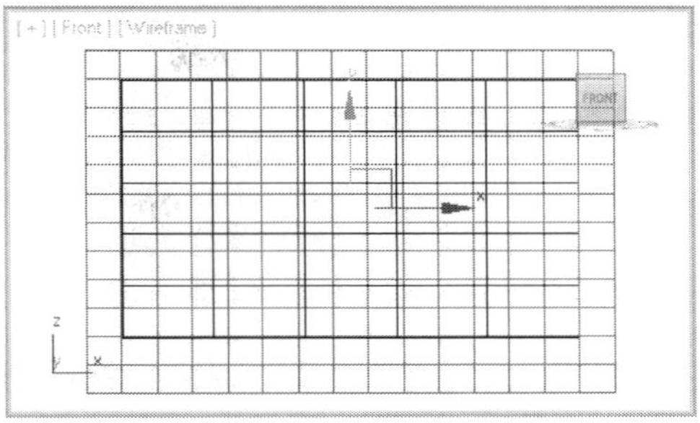

Figure 6-136 Alignment of the screen with the front portion in the Front viewport

Creating the Back Portion of the LCD Monitor

1. Activate the Front viewport, choose **Create > Geometry** in the **Command Panel**; the **Standard Primitives** option is displayed by default in the drop-down list below the **Geometry** button. Now, invoke the **Box** tool from the **Object Type** rollout.

2. Expand the **Keyboard Entry** rollout and set the values as given below:

   Length: **86** Width: **127.893** Height: **5.0**

3. Choose the **Create** button; a box is displayed in all viewports.

4. In the **Parameters** rollout, set the values as given below:

   Length Segs: **12** Width Segs: **15** Height Segs: **1**

5. In the **Name and Color** rollout, enter **back portion** and press ENTER; the box is named as *back portion*. Now, change the color of the *back portion* to black.

6. Activate the Left viewport and align the *back portion* with the back of the *front part*, as shown in Figure 6-137.

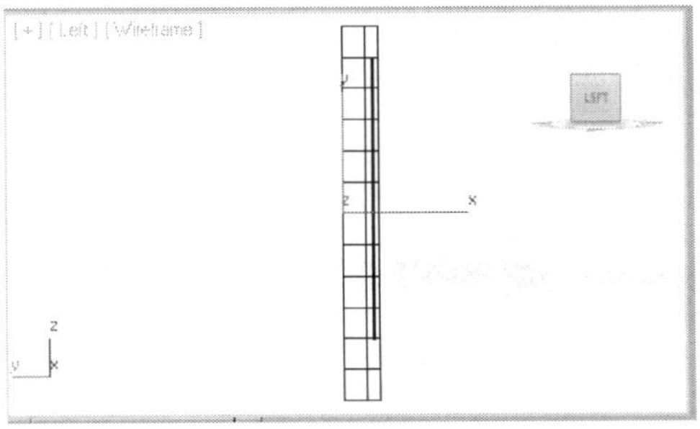

Figure 6-137 Alignment of the back portion with the front part in the Left viewport

7. Convert the *back portion* into editable poly to modify it at an advanced level.

8. Activate the Front viewport by right-clicking in it and make sure the *back portion* is selected. Now, right-click on the *back portion*; a quad menu is displayed. Choose the **Hide Unselected** option; the *front part* hides in the viewport and only the *back portion* is displayed in all viewports. This will help you to modify the *back portion* easily.

   Next, you need to modify the back side of the *back portion*. To do so, you need to change the Front viewport to the Back viewport so that you can view the back side of the object.

9. To display the Back viewport, click on the **Front** label in the Front viewport; a flyout is displayed that shows various options to display different views of the viewport, as shown in Figure 6-138. Choose the **Back** option; the Back viewport is displayed.

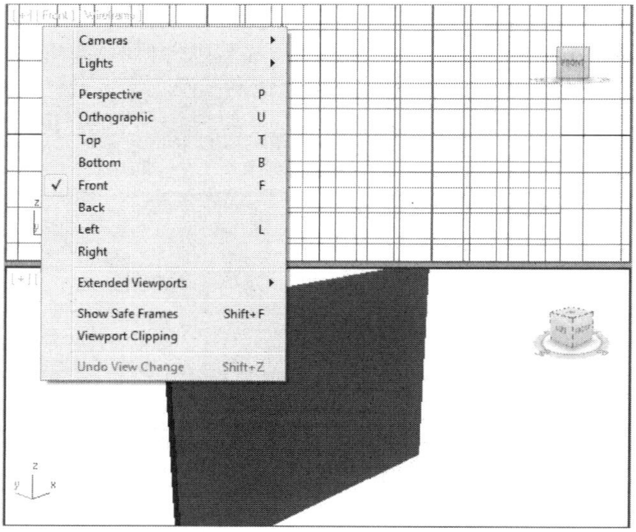

***Figure 6-138** A flyout displayed to change the viewport label*

10. Next, select the *back portion* in the Back viewport. In the modifier stack, click on the plus sign that is on the left of Editable Poly to view all sub-object levels.

> **Tip:** *To perform precise modeling at advanced level, you can invoke the* ***Maximize Viewport Toggle*** *tool.*

11. Select the **Polygon** sub-object level; it turns yellow and gets activated. Also, it prompts you to select the polygons of the *back portion* in the viewport.

12. In the Back viewport, hold the CTRL key and select the outer polygons of the *back portion*, as shown in Figure 6-139.

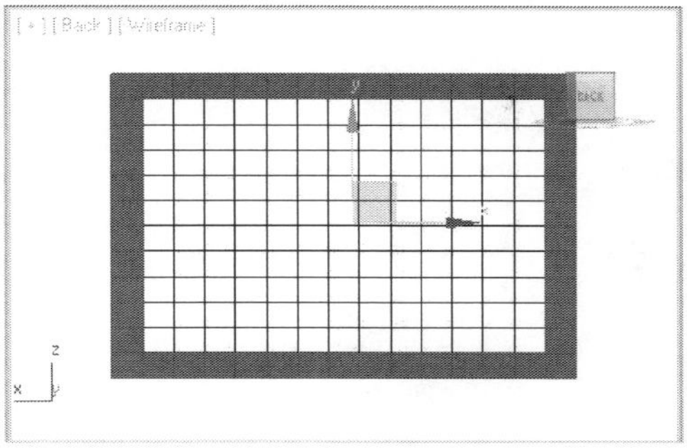

Figure 6-139 *The outer polygons selected in the back portion*

13. Next, right-click on the **Select and Uniform Scale** tool from the **Main Toolbar**; the **Scale Transform Type-In** dialog box is displayed. In the **Offset: Screen** area, set the value **90** in the **%** spinner and press ENTER; the selected polygons are uniformly scaled to 90 percent, as shown in Figure 6-140. Next, close this dialog box.

14. Click anywhere in the viewport to deselect polygons.

15. In the Back viewport, hold the CTRL key again and select the inner polygons of the *back portion*, as shown in Figure 6-141.

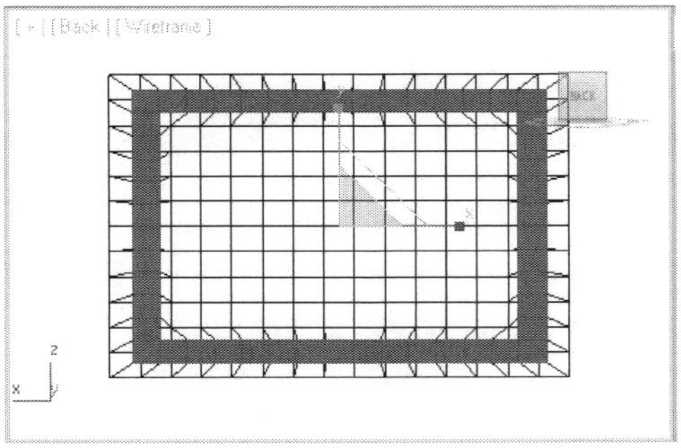

Figure 6-140 *The selected polygons uniformly scaled in the back portion*

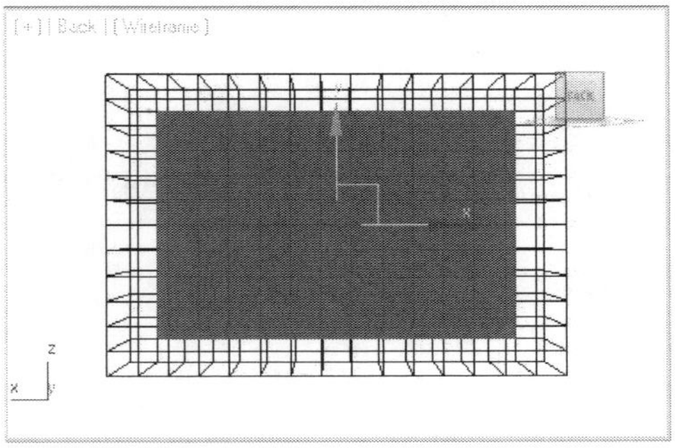

Figure 6-141 *The inner polygons selected in the back portion*

16. Right-click on the **Select and Uniform Scale** tool from the **Main Toolbar**; the **Scale Transform Type-In** dialog box is displayed. In the **Offset: Screen** area, set the value **90** in the **%** spinner and press ENTER; the selected polygons are uniformly scaled to 90 percent, as shown in Figure 6-142. Next, close this dialog box.

17. Activate the Left viewport by right-clicking in it and make sure that the polygons are still selected. Invoke the **Select and Move** tool and right-click on it; the **Move Transform Type-In** dialog box is displayed. In the **Offset: Screen** area, set the value **-7** in the **X**

spinner and press ENTER; the selected polygons move in the horizontal direction, as shown in Figure 6-143. Close this dialog box.

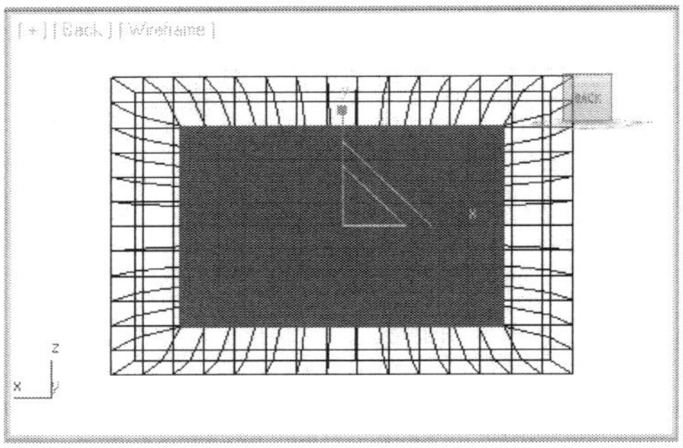

Figure 6-142 *The selected polygons uniformly scaled in the back portion*

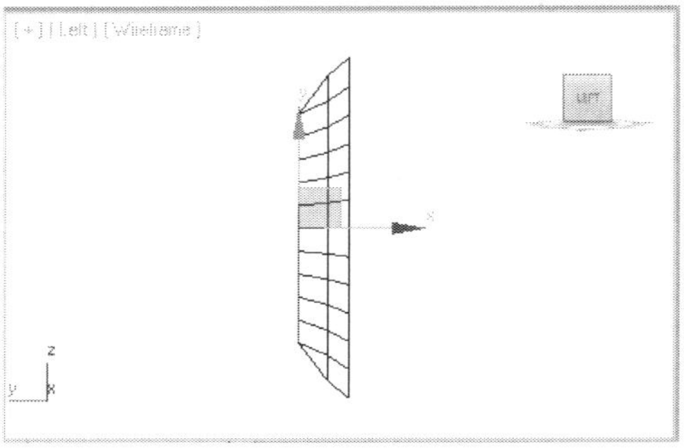

Figure 6-143 *Selected polygons dragged horizontally*

18. Select the **Polygon** sub-object level in the modifier stack to deactivate it. Next, click anywhere in the screen to deselect the object in the viewport.

Note
While working in the Back or Left viewport, you can view the output of the modification in the Perspective viewport using the ***Orbit*** *tool.*

19. Next, change the Back viewport to Front viewport as described earlier. Now, right-click in the viewport; a quad menu is displayed. Choose the **Unhide All** option; all objects are displayed in the viewports.

20. Select the *back portion* and the *front part* in any viewport simultaneously by dragging a selection box around them and group them as *monitor*.

Creating the Speaker of the LCD Monitor

1. Activate the Front viewport and choose **Create > Geometry** in the **Command Panel**. By default, the **Standard Primitives** option is displayed in the drop-down list below the **Geometry** button. Now, invoke the **Box** tool from the **Object Type** rollout.

2. Expand the **Keyboard Entry** rollout and set the values as given below:

   Length: **7.059** Width: **127.893** Height: **0.2**

3. Choose the **Create** button; a box is displayed in all viewports.

4. In the **Parameters** rollout, set the values as given below:

   Length Segs: **15** Width Segs: **15** Height Segs: **1**

5. In the **Name and Color** rollout, enter **speaker** and press ENTER; the box is named as *speaker*. Also, change the color of the *speaker* to black.

6. Align the *speaker* in all viewports with the *monitor*, as shown in Figure 6-144.

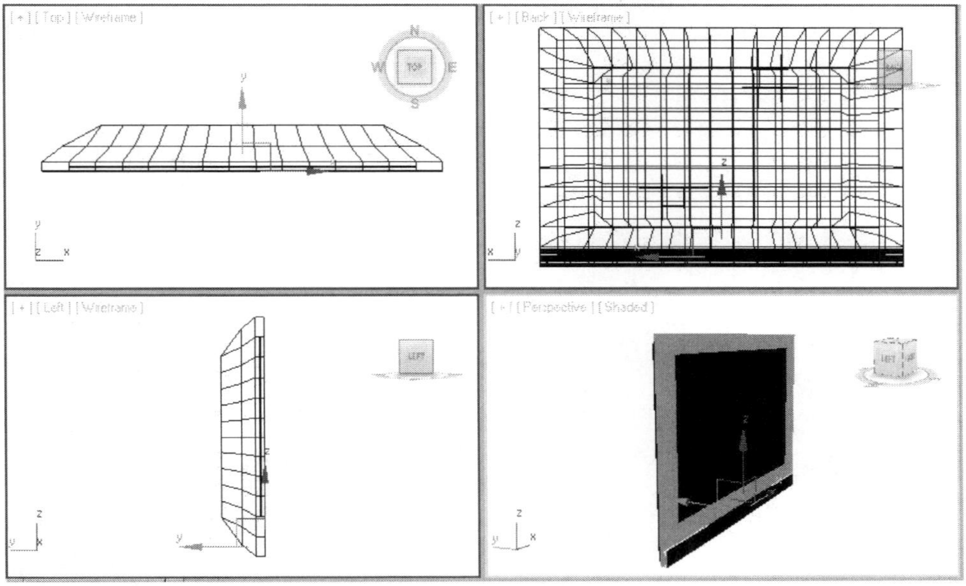

Figure 6-144 *Alignment of the speaker with the monitor in all viewports*

7. You need to apply the **Lattice** modifier to the *speaker* from the **Modifier List** drop-down list at the top of modifier stack. To do so, make sure that the *speaker* is selected in the viewport and choose the **Modify** tab in the **Command Panel**. Now, select the **Lattice** modifier from the **Modifier List** drop-down list; the **Lattice** modifier is displayed in the modifier stack. In the **Parameters** rollout of the **Lattice** modifier, select the **Struts Only from Edges** radio button. In the **Struts** area, enter the value **0.5** in the **Radius** spinner. Also, select the **Smooth** check box. Now, the *speaker* displays all its segments at rendering, which appear like a net on the *speaker*.

8. Click anywhere in the viewport to deselect the *speaker* and invoke the **Zoom Extents All** tool to view all objects in all viewports.

Creating Buttons of the LCD Monitor

In this step, you need to create a chamfer cylinder using the **ChamferCyl** tool to create the buttons of the monitor.

1. Activate the Front viewport and choose **Create > Geometry** in the **Command Panel**. Now, select **Extended Primitives** from the drop-down list below the **Geometry** button and invoke the **ChamferCyl** tool from the **Object Type** rollout.

2. Expand the **Keyboard Entry** rollout and set the values as given below:

Radius: **1.5** Height: **1.0** Fillet: **0.5**

3. Choose the **Create** button; a chamfer cylinder is displayed in all viewports.

4. In the **Name and Color** rollout, enter **b01** and press ENTER; the chamfer cylinder is named as *b01*. Also, change the color of the *b01* to white.

5. Align *b01* in all viewports with the *front portion*, as shown in Figure 6-145. You need to invoke the **Zoom** or **Zoom Region** tool to align it properly.

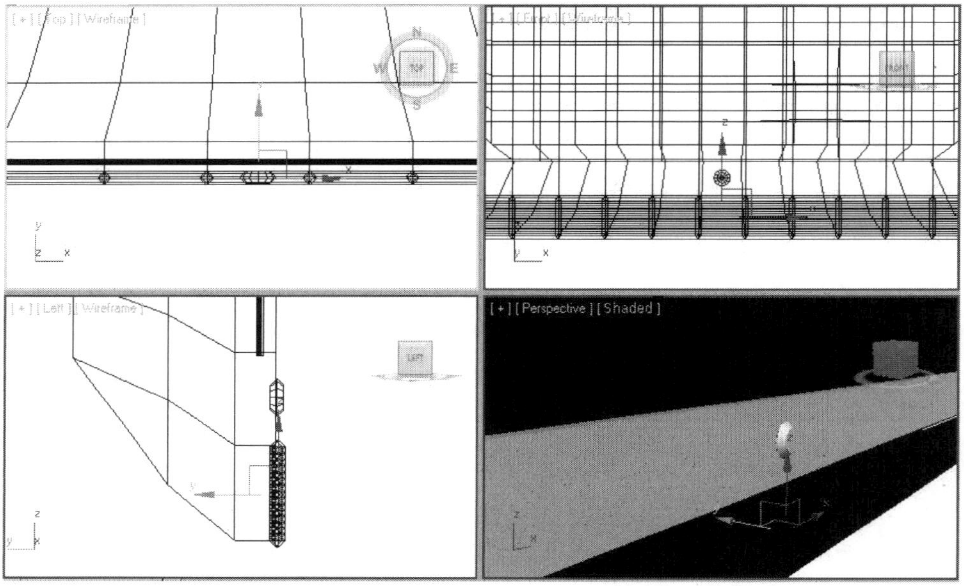

Figure 6-145 *Alignment of b01 with the front portion in all viewports*

6. In the Front viewport, create four copies of *b01*. They are automatically named as *b002*, *b003*, *b004*, and *b005*. Next, align them, as shown in Figure 6-146.

7. Select all objects in the viewport and group them as *LCD Monitor*.

8. Activate the Left viewport and select the *LCD Monitor*. Now, right-click on the **Select and Rotate** tool from the **Main Toolbar**; the **Rotate Transform Type-In** dialog box is displayed. In the **Offset: Screen** area, set the value **15** in the **Z** spinner and press the ENTER key. Next, close this dialog box; the *LCD Monitor* is displayed in the viewports, as shown in Figures 6-147 and 6-148.

Creating the Support for the LCD Monitor

In this step, you need to create a chamfer cylinder using the **ChamferCyl** tool to create the support of the monitor.

1. Activate the Top viewport and choose **Create > Geometry** in the **Command Panel**. Next, select **Extended Primitives** from the drop-down list below the **Geometry** button, and then invoke the **ChamferCyl** tool from the **Object Type** rollout.

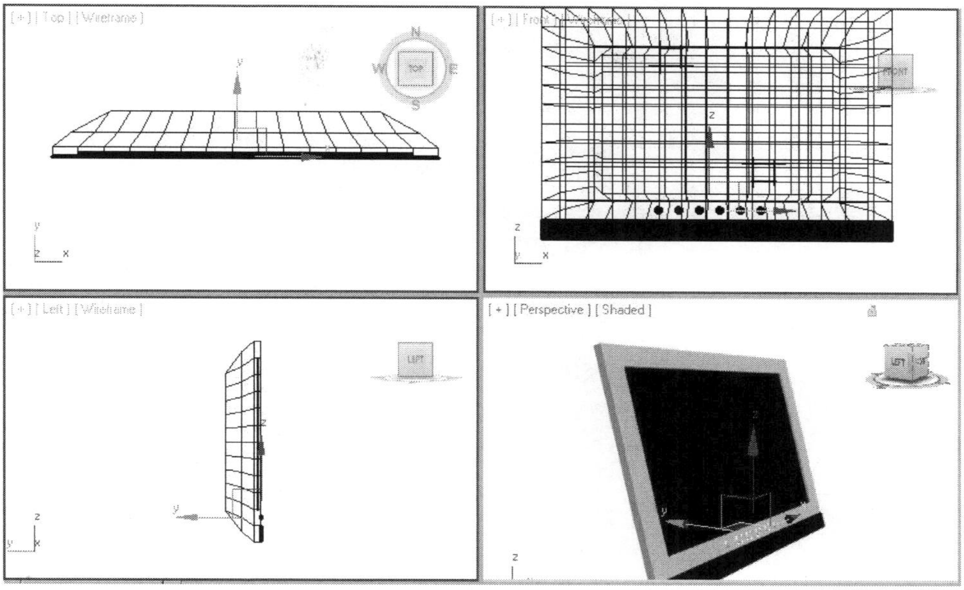

Figure 6-146 *Alignment of b002, b003, b004, and b005 in all viewports*

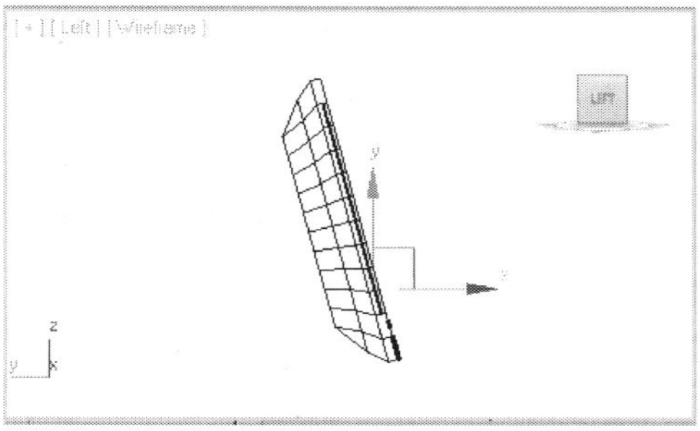

Figure 6-147 *The LCD monitor displayed after rotating it in the Left viewport*

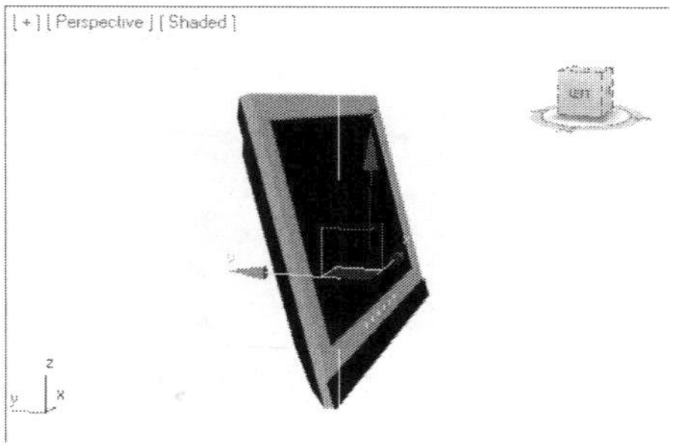

Figure 6-148 *The LCD monitor displayed after rotating it in the Perspective viewport*

2. Expand the **Keyboard Entry** rollout and set the values as given below:

   Radius: **23.698** Height: **6.091** Fillet: **2.284**

3. Choose the **Create** button from the **Command Panel**; a chamfer cylinder is displayed in all viewports.

4. In the **Parameters** rollout, set the values as given below:

   Fillet Segs: **5** Sides: **18** Cap Segs: **4**

5. In the **Name and Color** rollout, enter **support** and press ENTER; the chamfer cylinder is named as *support*. Also, use the color swatch to change the color of the *support* using the values given below:

   Red: **115** Green: **115** Blue: **115**

6. In the Left viewport, move the cursor over the vertical axis and move the *support* below the *LCD monitor*. Also, move the *support* in the horizontal direction, as shown in Figure 6-149.

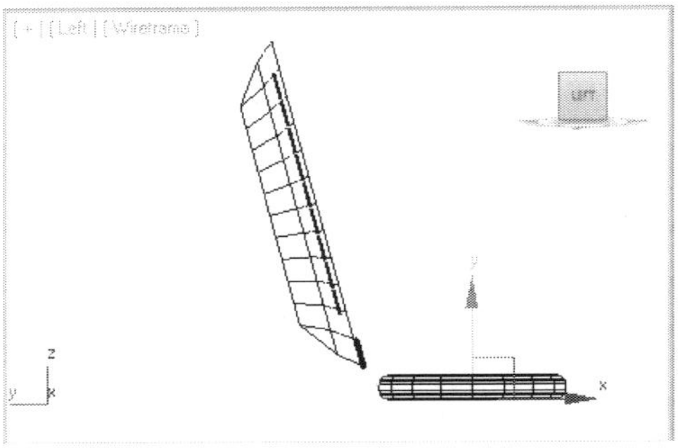

Figure 6-149 *The support moved in the Left viewport*

7. Make sure that the *support* is selected and invoke the **Zoom Extents All Selected** tool; the *support* is zoomed in all viewports, as shown in Figure 6-150.

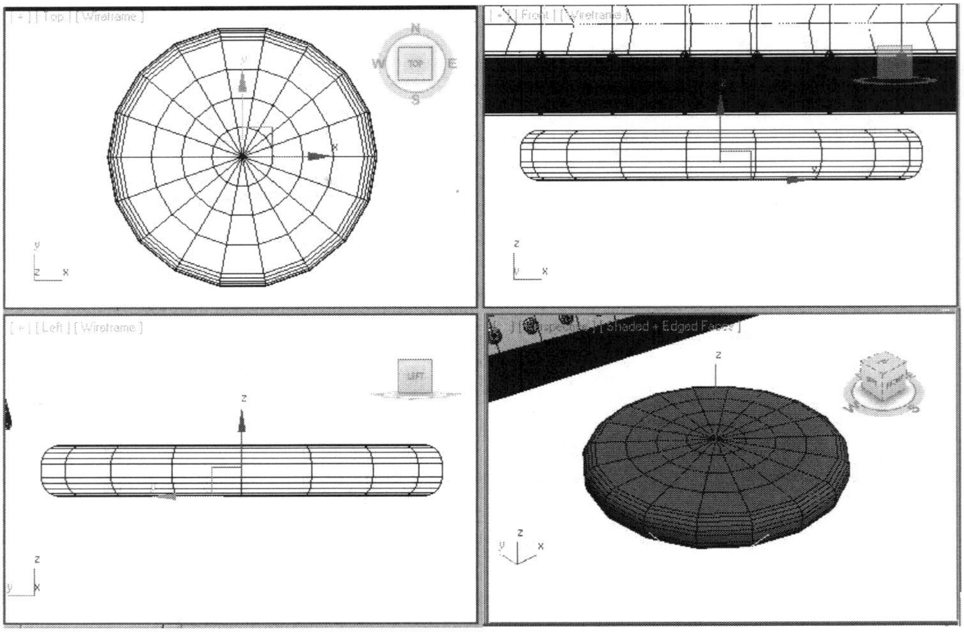

Figure 6-150 *The support zoomed in all viewports*

8. Convert the *support* into editable poly to modify it at an advanced level.

9. In the modifier stack, click on the plus sign on the left of Editable Poly to view all the sub-object levels.

10. Select the **Polygon** sub-object level; it turns yellow and gets activated. Also, you are prompted to select the polygons of the *support* in the viewport.

11. Now, hold the CTRL key and select the inner polygons of the *support* in the Top viewport, as shown in Figure 6-151.

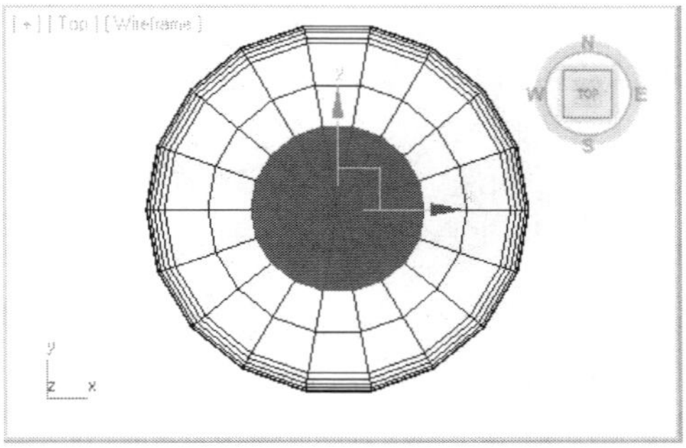

Figure 6-151 *The inner polygons of the support selected*

12. In the **Edit Polygons** rollout, choose the **Settings** button on the right of the **Extrude** button; the **Extrude Polygons** caddy control is displayed in the viewport. Set the value **2.0** in the **Height** spinner, refer to Figure 6-152, and choose the **OK** button to close this caddy control.

13. Now, choose the **Settings** button on the right of the **Bevel** button; the **Bevel** caddy control is displayed in the viewport. Set the value **1.0** in the **Height** spinner, refer to Figure 6-153, press ENTER, and choose the **OK** button to close this caddy control; the support is displayed in all viewports. Figures 6-154 and 6-155 show the support displayed in the Top and Perspective viewports, respectively.

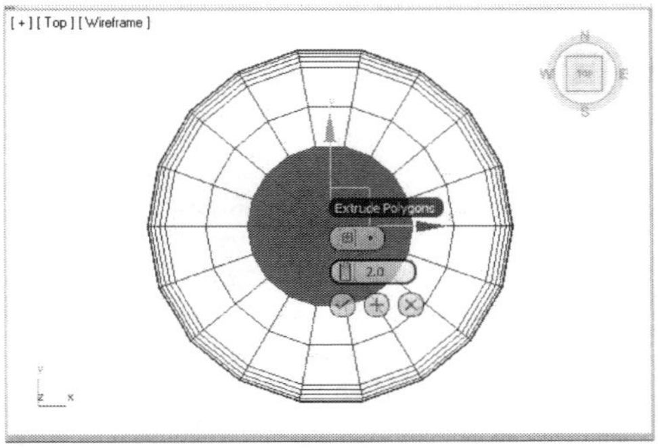

Figure 6-152 *The* ***Extrude Polygons*** *dialog box*

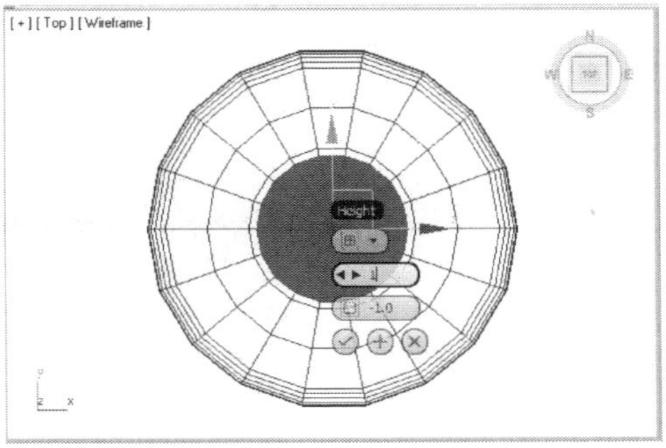

Figure 6-153 *The value set in the* ***Height*** *spinner of the* ***Bevel*** *dialog box*

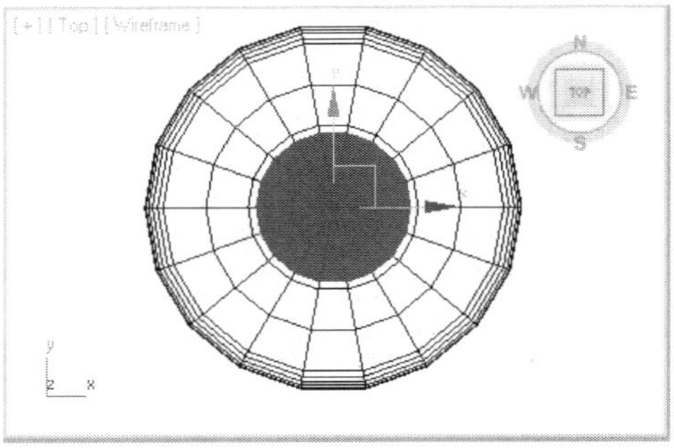

Figure 6-154 The selected polygons in the Top viewport after using the ***Extrude*** *and* ***Bevel*** *buttons*

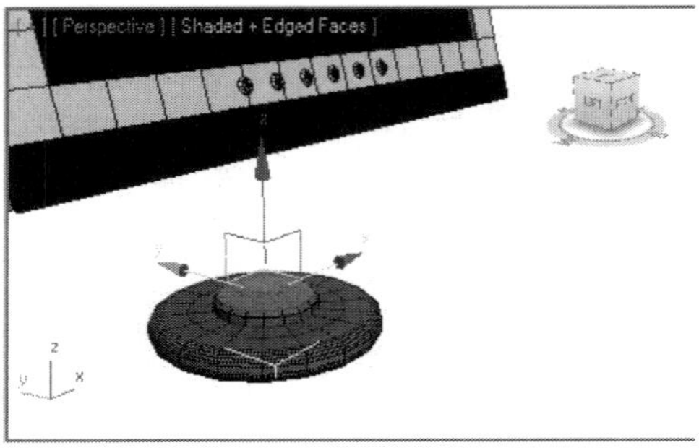

Figure 6-155 The selected polygons in the Perspective viewport after using the extrude and bevel functions

14. Select the **Polygon** sub-object level in the modifier stack to deselect it and then click anywhere in the viewport to deselect the object.

15. Invoke the **Zoom Extents All** tool and align the *support* in all viewports, as shown in Figure 6-156.

16. Select the *support* and invoke the **Zoom Extents All Selected** tool. Now, select the **Polygon** sub-object level in the modifier stack; all the selected polygons are displayed.

17. Activate the Perspective viewport by right-clicking on it and set the view using the **Zoom**, **Select and Move** and **Orbit** tools, as shown in Figure 6-157. Then, deselect the polygons, except the five polygons on the back, by holding the ALT key, refer to Figure 6-158.

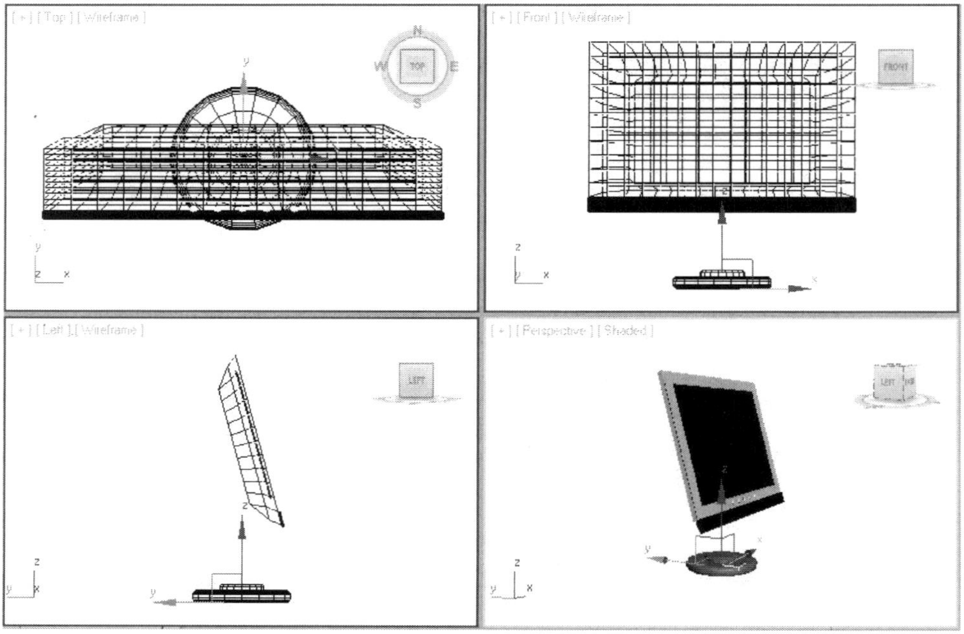

Figure 6-156 Alignment of the support in all viewports

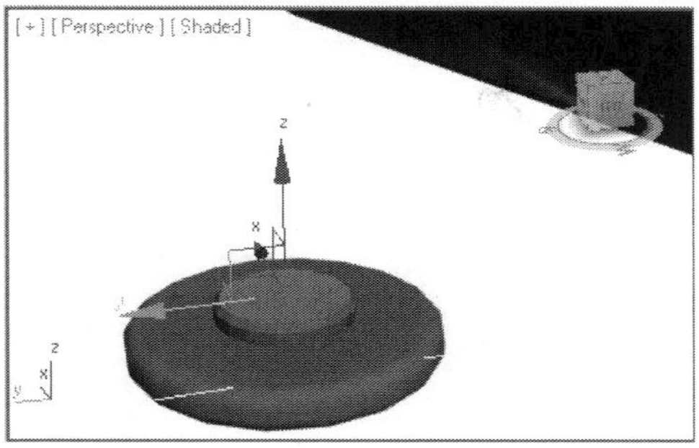

*Figure 6-157 The Perspective viewport after using the **Zoom** and **Orbit** tools*

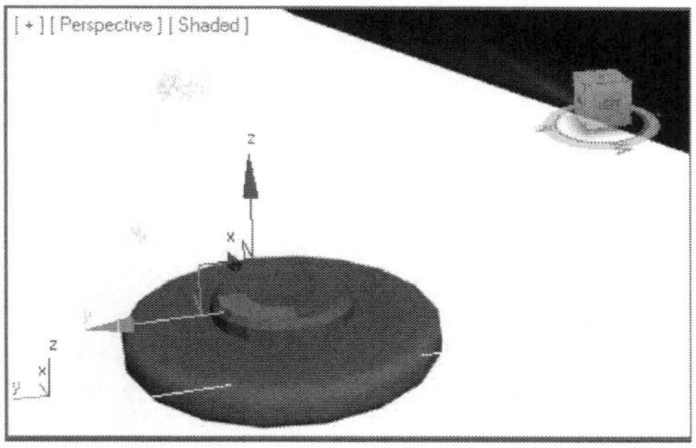

Figure 6-158 The polygons selected in the Perspective viewport

18. Next, select the **Polygon** sub-object level in the modifier stack to deactivate it and then click anywhere in the viewport to deselect the object.

19. Invoke the **Zoom Extents All** tool and set the view of the Perspective viewport to view the back side of the *LCD monitor*, as shown in Figure 6-159.

20. Activate the Left viewport and select the *support* from it. Then, select the **Polygon** sub-object level; all selected polygons are highlighted.

21. In the **Edit Polygons** rollout, choose the **Settings** button on the right side of the **Extrude** button; the **Extrude Polygons** caddy control is displayed. Set the value **29** in the **Height** spinner, press ENTER, and choose the **OK** button to close this caddy control; the selected polygons are extruded and displayed in the Left viewport, as shown in Figure 6-160.

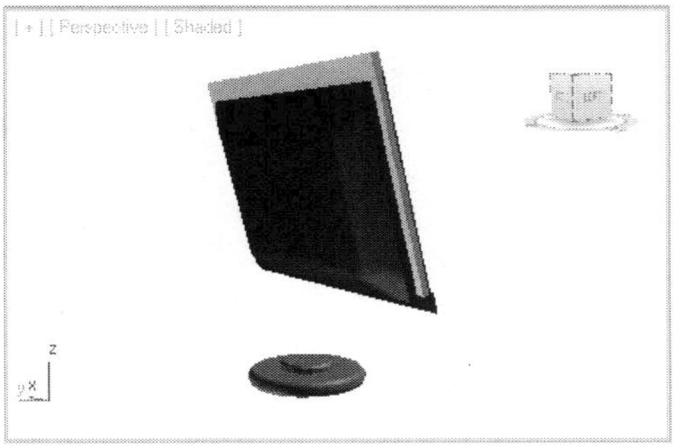

Figure 6-159 The back side of the LCD monitor in the Perspective viewport

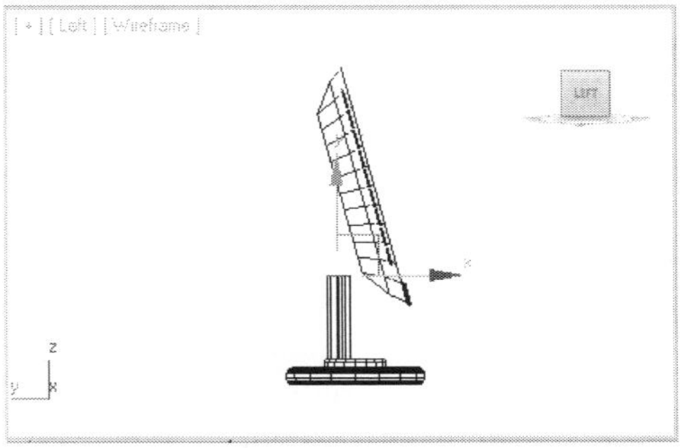

Figure 6-160 Extruding the selected polygons in the Left viewport

22. In the Left viewport, move the cursor over the horizontal axis and drag the selected polygons horizontally toward the right side until they touch the *LCD monitor*, as shown in Figure 6-161.

23. In the **Edit Polygons** rollout, again choose the **Settings** button on the right of the **Extrude** button; the **Extrude Polygons** caddy control is displayed. Set the value **19** in the **Height** spinner and press ENTER. Next, and choose the **OK** button to close this caddy control.

The extrusion of the *support* in the Left viewport is shown in Figure 6-162.

24. Now, in the Left viewport, move the cursor over the horizontal axis, and drag the selected polygons horizontally toward the left to align them with the *LCD monitor*, as shown in Figure 6-163.

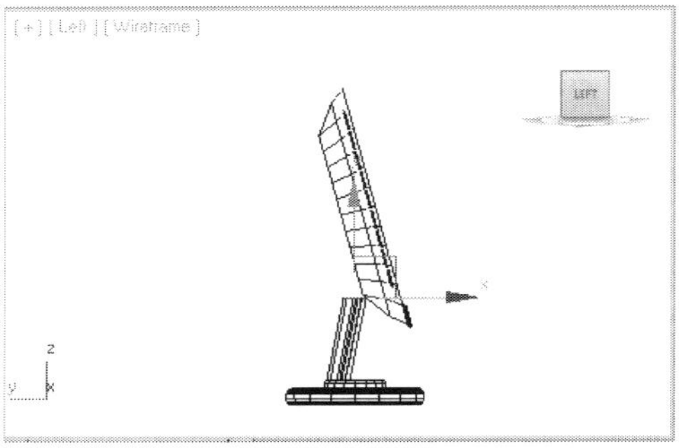

Figure 6-161 *The support in the Left viewport after moving it horizontally*

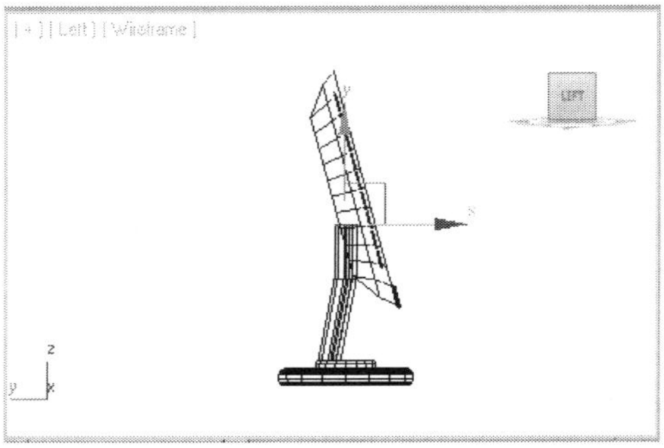

Figure 6-162 *The support in the Left viewport after extrusion*

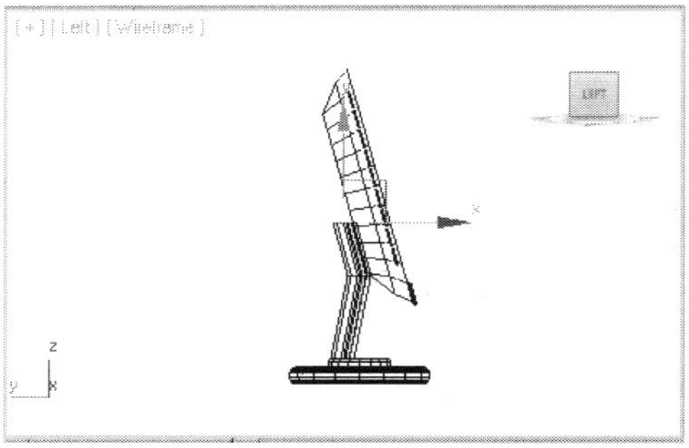

Figure 6-163 *The support in the Left viewport after moving the polygons in the horizontal axis*

25. Select the **Polygon** sub-object level in the modifier stack to deselect it.

26. Make sure that the *support* is selected. In the **Edit Geometry** rollout, choose the **Settings** button on the right of the **MSmooth** button; the **MeshSmooth** caddy control is displayed. In this caddy control, choose the **Apply and Continue** button to apply smoothness and then choose the **OK** button to close this caddy control.

Rendering the Scene for the Final Output

1. Activate the Perspective viewport and set the view using the **Orbit** tool. Now, render the scene as discussed in Tutorial 1.

You can view the final rendered image of this model by downloading the *c06_3dsmax_2012_render.zip* file from *http://www.cadcim.com*.

Saving the File

1. Save the file with the name *c06tut2.max* as discussed in earlier chapters. The location of this file is given below:

   \Documents\3dsmax\c06_tut2\scenes

Self-Evaluation Test

Answer the following questions and then compare them to those given at the end of this chapter:

1. Which of the following options is used to modify the 3D mesh object at an advanced level?

   (a) **Convert to Editable Mesh** (b) **Convert to Editable Poly**
   (c) **Convert to Editable Patch** (d) All of these

2. Which of the following sub-objects is not a part of the editable poly objects?

   (a) **Border** (b) **Face**
   (c) **Polygon** (d) **Element**

3. Which of the following rollouts does not belong to editable mesh objects?

   (a) **Subdivision Surface** (b) **Subdivision Displacement**
   (c) **Paint Deformation** (d) All of these

4. Which of the following buttons in the **Edit Geometry** rollout of editable mesh object is used to rotate the edge of an object?

   (a) **Extrude** (b) **Chamfer**
   (c) **Turn** (d) **Divide**

5. To change the shape of an extruded sub-object, you need to choose the __________ button in the **Edit Geometry** rollout.

6. To cut the corners of sub-objects, you need to choose the __________ button in the **Edit Geometry** rollout of editable mesh objects.

7. Select the __________ check box in the **Selection** rollout of editable poly objects to avoid selecting backfacing sub-objects.

8. In Autodesk 3ds Max 2012, you can set the number of segments per chamfer using the **Chamfer** button. (T/F)

9. You can view sub-objects such as vertex, polygons, and so on at rendering. (T/F)

10. The border sub-object in the editable poly objects is a series of edges that forms a ring around a hole in the mesh object. (T/F)

Review Questions

Answer the following questions:

1. Which of the following buttons in editable poly objects is used to define the selection area of sub-objects?

   (a) **Shrink** (b) **Grow**
   (c) **Ring** (d) All of these

2. Which of the following buttons in editable poly objects is used to repeat the recently used command?

   (a) **Collapse** (b) **Quick Slice**
   (c) **Repeat Last** (d) **Make Planar**

3. Which of the following sub-objects is not a part of the editable patch objects?

   (a) **Border** (b) **Vertex**
   (c) **Patch** (d) **Handle**

4. In editable patch objects, when you select the vertices of an object in the viewport, the vertices with vector handles are displayed. (T/F)

5. After converting an object into editable mesh, editable poly, or editable patch, the creation parameters of the object get collapsed. (T/F)

6. You can add a tri patch or a quad patch to any open edge of the objects. (T/F)

7. To attach a number of objects to the selected object simultaneously, you need to choose the **Attach** button in the modify panel. (T/F)

8. The **Break** button is available only for the __________ sub-object level.

9. The __________ button is used to divide a face into __________ smaller faces.

10. The __________button is used to extrude sub-objects.

Exercises

Exercise 1

Start Autodesk 3ds Max 2012 and then perform the following operations:

Create an object in the viewport and convert it into an editable mesh object and then try the following operations:

1. Select the **Vertex** sub-object level in the modifier stack. Then, choose the **Create** button in the **Edit Geometry** rollout and add new vertices in the viewport.

2. Select the **Edge** or **Polygon** sub-object level in the modifier stack and then select the respective sub-objects in the viewport. Next, choose the **Extrude** button in the **Edit Geometry** rollout. Now, increase the value in the **Extrude** spinner to view the extrusion effect on the selected sub-object. Try to use different buttons in the **Edit Geometry** rollout and notice the modification in the object.

Create an object in the viewport and convert it into an editable poly object. Then, perform the following operations:

3. In the modifier stack, click on the plus sign on the left side of the Editable Poly and compare its sub-object levels to the sub-object levels of the editable mesh objects.

4. Select the sub-objects levels in the modifier stack and notice the changes in the rollouts displayed. Try to create an object using different buttons available in various rollouts displayed after selecting any sub-object level.

Create an object in the viewport and convert it into editable patch. Now, perform the following operations:

5. Select the **Vertex** sub-object level in the modifier stack, select the vertices in the viewport; the vertices with the vector handles are displayed in the viewport. Try to modify the object by moving the vector handles.

6. Try to use different buttons in the **Selection** and **Edit Geometry** rollouts and notice the modification in the object.

Exercise 2

Create the model shown in Figure 6-164 using dimensions of your choice.

(Expected time: 30 min)

Figure 6-164 *Model for Exercise 2*

Answers to Self-Evaluation Test

1. d, **2.** b, **3.** d, **4.** c, **5. Chamfer**, **6. Cut**, **7. Ignore Backfacing**, **8.** T, **9.** F, **10.** T

7

Modifying Splines

Learning Objectives

After completing this chapter, you will be able to:

- *Adjust the pivot point of an object*
- *Use the Lathe modifier to modify objects*
- *Modify shapes*
- *Use editable spline objects*

INTRODUCTION

In the previous chapters, you have learned to modify different 3D mesh objects at advanced level by converting them into editable mesh, poly, or patch objects. In this chapter, you will learn to modify shapes such as splines and extended splines at advanced level. Also, you will learn about the pivot point and the **Lathe** modifier.

PIVOT POINT

The pivot point of an object represents the local center and its local coordinate system. When you rotate or scale an object, the pivot point behaves like a center for rotating or scaling the object. To adjust the pivot point of an object, select the object in the viewport and then choose the **Hierarchy** tab in the **Command Panel**. By default, the **Pivot** tab is chosen in the **Command Panel**, as shown in Figure 7-1. You can set the position of the pivot point of an object using the rollouts displayed in the **Pivot** tab. Some of the rollouts in the **Pivot** tab are discussed next.

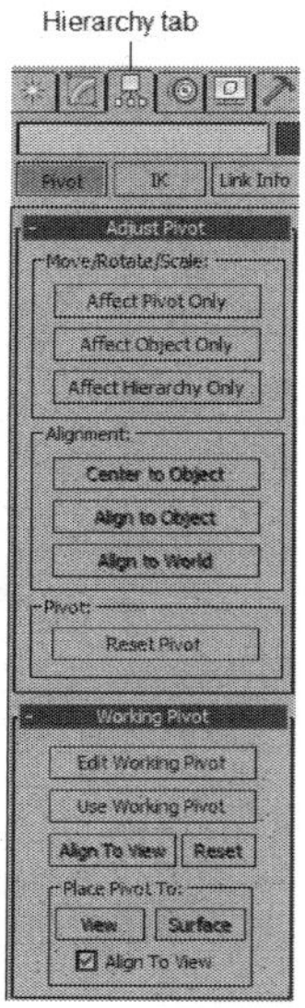

*Figure 7-1 The **Pivot** tab chosen in the **Command Panel***

Adjust Pivot Rollout

The options in this rollout are used to adjust the position and orientation of an object's pivot point. The areas in this rollout are discussed next.

Move/Rotate/Scale Area

There are three buttons in this area, **Affect Pivot Only**, **Affect Object Only**, and **Affect Hierarchy Only**. These buttons are used to specify the part of an object that will be affected while performing the functions such as rotation, movement, and so on. When you choose these buttons, they turn blue and get activated.

The **Affect Pivot Only** button affects the pivot point of the selected object. You can use this button to adjust the pivot point of the selected object. Choose the **Affect Pivot Only** button; the pivot point of the selected object will be displayed in the viewport, as shown in Figure 7-2. Now, you can adjust the position of the pivot point by moving or rotating it. Also, you can use the **Align** tool from the **Main Toolbar** to align the pivot point. You will learn more about the **Align** tool in the later chapters.

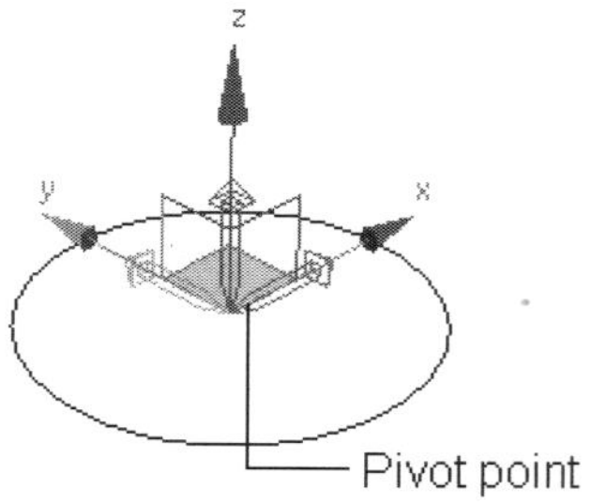

Figure 7-2 The pivot point of a circle

Note
Scaling has no effect on the pivot of an object.

The **Affect Object Only** button is used to affect only the selected object. It means that transforms are applied only to the selected object and do not affect the pivot point of the object.

On choosing the **Affect Object Only** button; the pivot point of the object will be displayed in the viewport. You can now adjust the position of the object according to the pivot point by moving, rotating, and aligning the object.

The **Affect Hierarchy Only** button affects only the hierarchy of the objects by rotating or scaling the position of the pivot point. But, the pivot point will not be affected. Select the object in the viewport, choose the **Affect Hierarchy Only** button, and then use the **Select and Scale** or the **Select and Rotate** tool to view the effects on the hierarchy of the objects. You will learn about creating the hierarchy in the later chapters.

Note
*When you choose the buttons in the **Move/Rotate/Scale** area of the **Adjust Pivot** rollout, it is recommended to exit the command after adjusting the position of the pivot point or the object. To exit the command, you need to choose the activated button again.*

Alignment Area
The options in this area depend on the selection of buttons in the **Move/Rotate/Scale** area.

If you choose the **Affect Pivot Only** button in the **Move/Rotate/Scale** area, then the **Center to Object**, **Align to Object**, and **Align to World** buttons will be displayed in the alignment area. Choose the **Center to Object** button to align the pivot point to the center of the object. Choose the **Align to Object** button to rotate the pivot to align with the object's transformation matrix axes. Choose the **Align to World** button to rotate the pivot to align it with the world coordinate axes.

If you choose the **Affect Object Only** button in the **Move/Rotate/Scale** area, then the **Center to Pivot**, **Align to Pivot**, and **Align to World** buttons will be displayed in the alignment area. Choose the **Center to Pivot** button to align the center of the object to its pivot point. Choose the **Align to Pivot** button to rotate the object to align its transformation matrix axes with the pivot point. Choose the **Align to World** button to rotate the object to align its transformation matrix axes with the world coordinate axes.

If you choose the **Affect Hierarchy Only** button in the **Move/Rotate/Scale** area, then the options in the **Alignment** area will be deactivated.

Pivot Area
The **Reset Pivot** button in this area is used to reset the original position of the pivot point of the object.

Working Pivot Rollout
You can use the working pivot to transform the objects without affecting their main pivot point at the object or the sub-object level. For example, you can rotate an object in a scene about an arbitrary point without affecting its own pivot point.

Note
A scene has only one working pivot along with the gizmo, which is independent of other objects in the scene, as shown in Figure 7-3.

You can also modify the position of the working pivot. To do so, choose the **Edit Working Pivot** button; by default, the working pivot will be displayed at the center of the scene, refer to Figure 7-3. Also, the EDIT WP text will be displayed below each viewport label. You can modify the position of the working pivot by moving or rotating it.

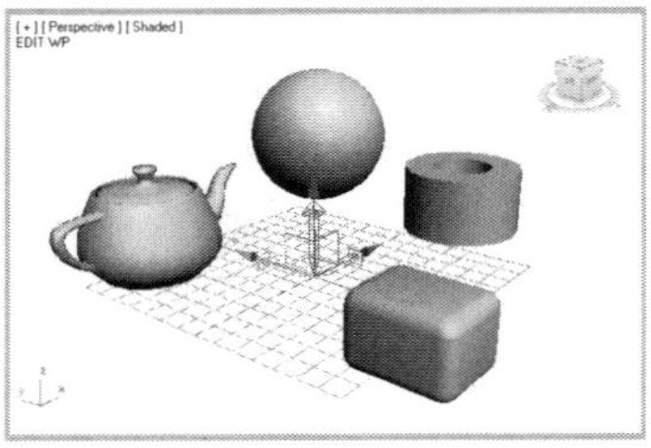

***Figure 7-3** The working pivot along with the gizmo in the scene*

If you choose the **Use Working Pivot** button and select any of the objects from the scene, then a transform gizmo will be displayed at the location of the working pivot, as shown in Figures 7-4 and 7-5. Also, the USE WP text will be displayed below each viewport label. Now, the objects or the sub-objects in the scene will be transformed according to the working pivot.

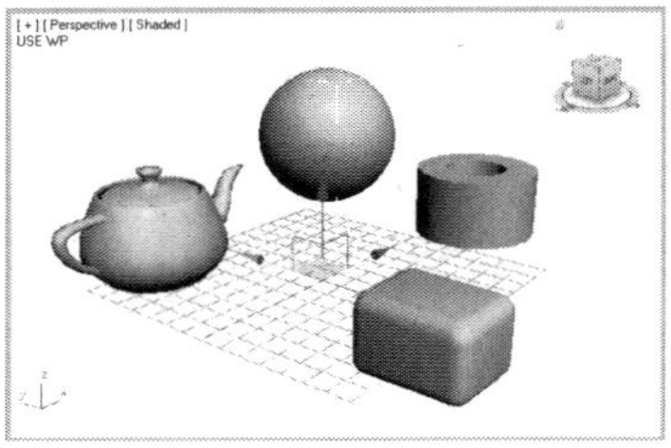

***Figure 7-4** The move transform gizmo displayed*

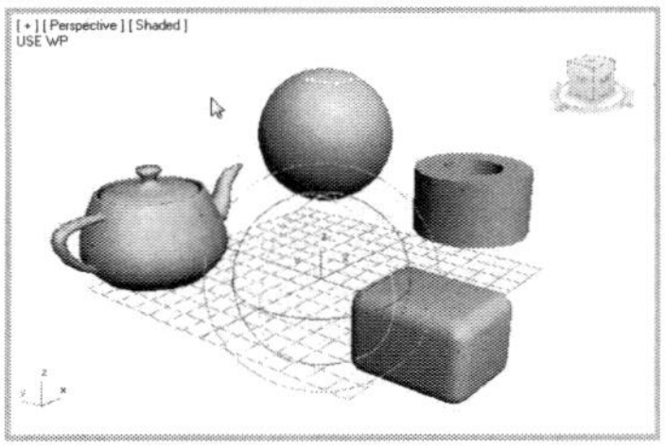

***Figure 7-5** The rotate transform gizmo displayed*

The **Reset** button in the **Working Pivot** rollout is used to move the working pivot to a location where the pivot of the selected object is placed. If there are more than one objects selected in the viewport, then the working pivot will move to the pivot position of the last selected object.

Place Pivot To Area

The options in this area are used to position the working pivot using the mouse. This enables you to set the working pivot quickly on the screen. To do so, choose the **View** button, move the cursor in the viewport, and click on any location; the working pivot will be placed accordingly. Next, right-click to exit the command. Alternatively, you can choose the **Surface** button and move the cursor in the viewport. Now, click on the surface of any of the objects in the scene to place the working pivot on the surface. You can also click on the active grid to place the working pivot on it.

LATHE MODIFIER

The **Lathe** modifier is a shape modifier and is used to create 3D objects by rotating shapes about their axis. The direction of the axis of revolution depends on the pivot point of the shape. To apply the **Lathe** modifier on a shape, create a shape in the Front viewport and select it. The shape will be displayed in the Perspective viewport, as shown in Figure 7-6. Choose the **Modify** tab in the **Command Panel** and then select **OBJECT-SPACE MODIFIERS > Lathe** from the **Modifier List** drop-down list; the 2D shape will be converted into a 3D object and it will be displayed in the Perspective viewport, as shown in Figure 7-7. When you apply the

Lathe modifier on a shape, it will be displayed in the modifier stack. Also, the **Parameters** rollout will be displayed below the modifier stack. You will learn more about this modifier in Chapter 10.

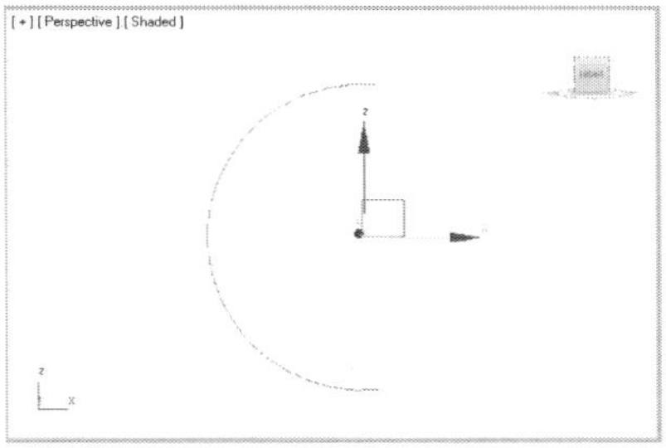

Figure 7-6 An arc displayed in the Perspective viewport

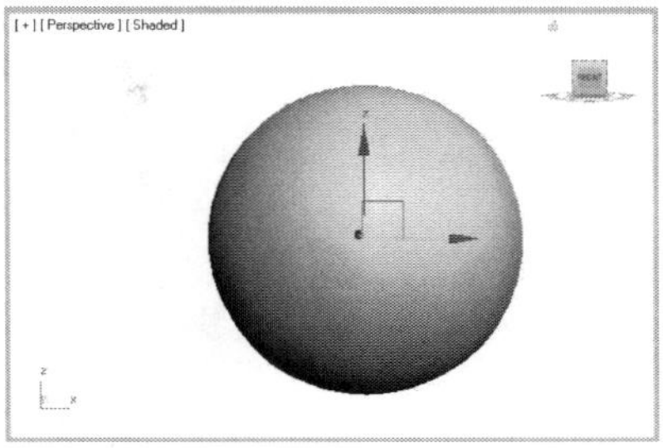

*Figure 7-7 The arc converted into a 3D object after applying the **Lathe** modifier*

MODIFYING THE SHAPES

To modify the shapes in Autodesk 3ds Max, first create a shape using the tools from **Create > Shapes > Splines/Extended Splines > Object Type** rollout in the **Command Panel** as discussed earlier. Next, select the shape in the viewport and choose the **Modify** tab in the **Command Panel**; the modify panel will be displayed with various rollouts. Now, you can modify the shapes using one of the following methods:

1. By entering new parameters in the rollouts displayed in the **Modify** panel. You have already learned about it in the previous chapters.
2. By applying a modifier from the **Modifier List** drop-down list. You will learn about applying modifiers in Chapter 10.
3. By converting the shapes into editable splines, which is discussed next.

Converting the Shapes into Editable Splines

You can modify all spline and extended spline shapes at advanced level by converting them into editable spline objects. The editable spline objects provide the sub-object levels of the shape. These sub-object levels help you to select the sub-objects of the shape in the viewport. You need to move, rotate, and scale these sub-objects to modify the shape of the splines. You can convert a shape into an editable spline using one of the following methods:

1. Create a shape and then select it in the viewport. Next, right-click on the shape; a quad menu will be displayed. Choose the **Convert To** option; a cascading menu will be displayed. Choose **Convert to Editable Spline**; the shape will be converted into editable spline.
2. Create a shape and then select it in the viewport. Choose the **Modify** tab in the **Command Panel**. In the modifier stack, right-click on the name of the tool; a shortcut menu will be displayed. Choose the **Editable Spline** option; the shape will be converted into editable spline.

Sub-object Levels in Editable Spline

When you convert a spline object into editable spline, the name of the tool in the modifier stack will be replaced by the **Editable Spline**. This level is known as the object level. By clicking on the plus sign on the left of the **Editable Spline**, you can view the sub-object levels such as **Vertex**, **Segment**, and **Spline**, as shown in Figure 7-8. On converting a spline object into editable spline, various rollouts such as **Rendering**, **Interpolation**, **Selection**, **Soft Selection**, and **Geometry** will also be displayed in the modify panel. These sub-object levels and rollouts are discussed next.

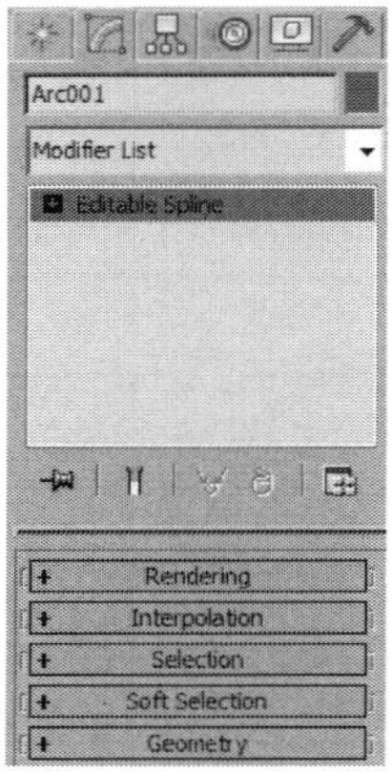

***Figure 7-8** The sub-object levels and rollouts displayed*

Sub-object Levels

The sub-object levels help you to modify the object by moving, rotating, and scaling the sub-objects. To do so, select one of the sub-object levels in the modifier stack; it will be activated and turn yellow. Also, it will prompt you to select the corresponding sub-objects in the viewport. You can select a sub-object in the viewport by clicking on it. If you want to add more sub-objects, then hold the CTRL key and click on the sub-objects that you want to add. You can also drag a selection box around the sub-objects to select them simultaneously. These sub-objects are discussed next.

Vertex

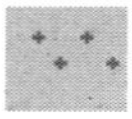

The vertex is a point on the spline. To modify an object using vertices, select the **Vertex** sub-object level; the white and yellow colored vertices of the spline will be displayed in the viewports, as shown in Figure 7-9. The yellow colored vertex is the first vertex or the starting point of the spline, refer to Figure 7-9.

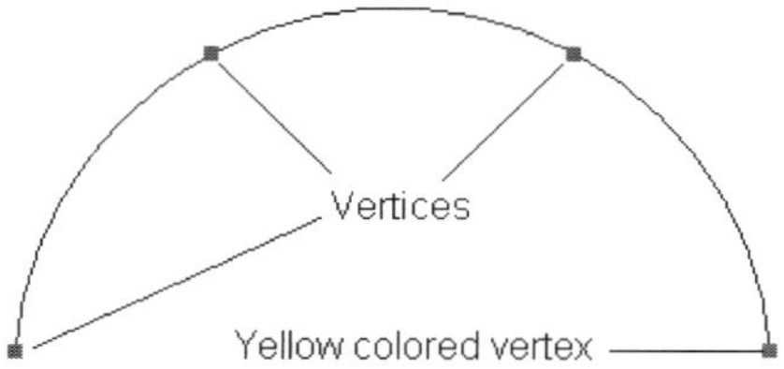

***Figure 7-9** The vertices of an arc spline displayed after selecting the **Vertex** sub-object level*

There are various types of vertices such as bezier, corner, smooth, and bezier corner vertices, which depend on the type of spline. You can convert a vertex into a bezier, corner, smooth, or bezier corner vertex. To do so, select a vertex in the viewport and right-click on it; a quad menu will be displayed, as shown in Figure 7-10. Choose the type of vertex from the quad menu, refer to Figure 7-10; the vertex will change based on the option chosen from the quad menu.

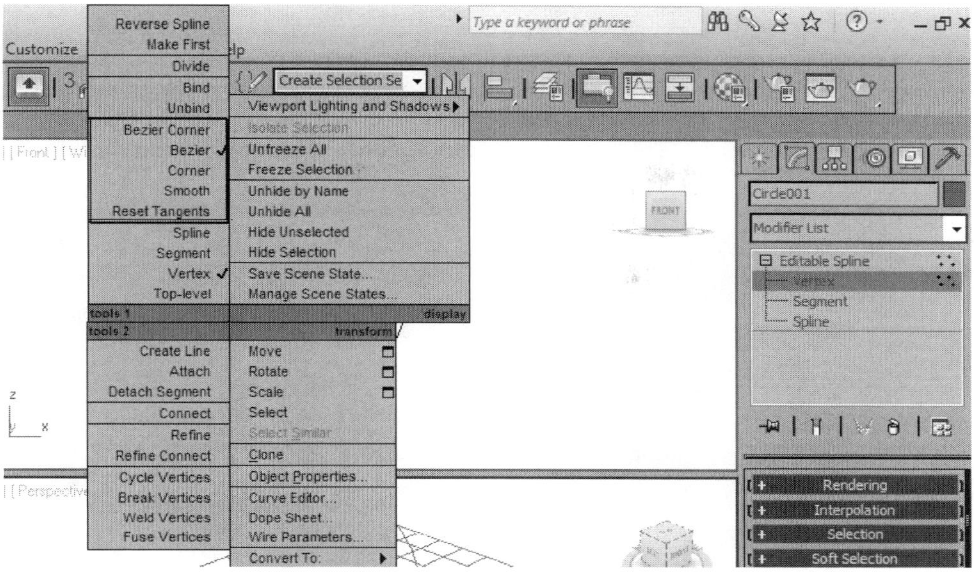

Figure 7-10 *Various types of vertices highlighted in a quad menu*

The bezier vertex has bezier handles to adjust the shape of the spline on both sides of the vertex. The smooth vertex is used to smoothen the curve of the spline. The corner vertex is used to make the corners of the spline. The bezier corner vertex also has bezier handles and is used to adjust the shape of the spline independently on both the sides, as shown in Figure 7-11.

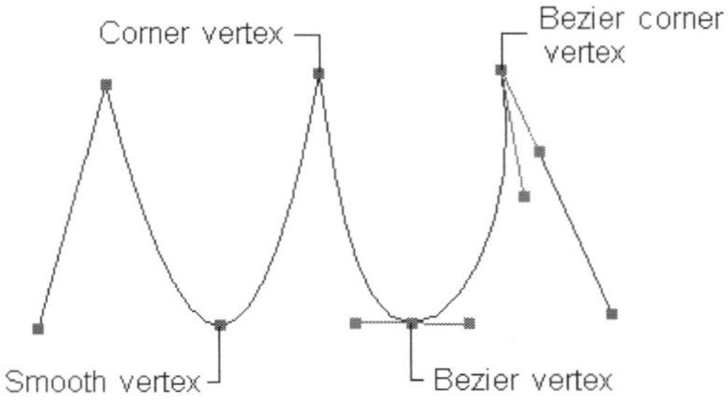

Figure 7-11 *Various types of vertices in a line spline*

Segment

The segment is a line or a curve between two vertices. To modify an object through segments, you need to select the **Segment** sub-object level. On doing so, you will be prompted to select the segments of the object, refer to Figures 7-12 and 7-13.

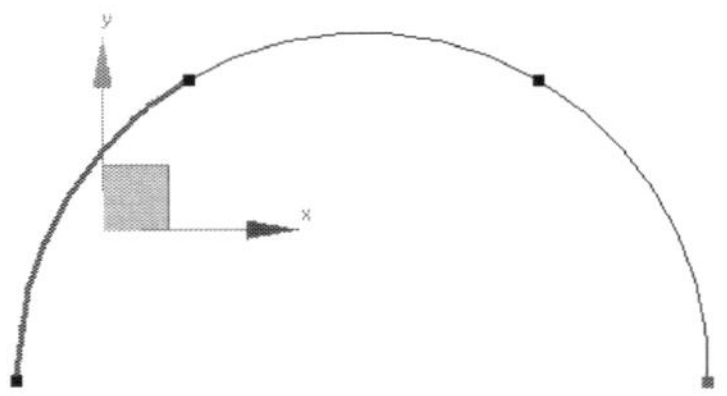

Figure 7-12 *The curved segment selected in an arc spline*

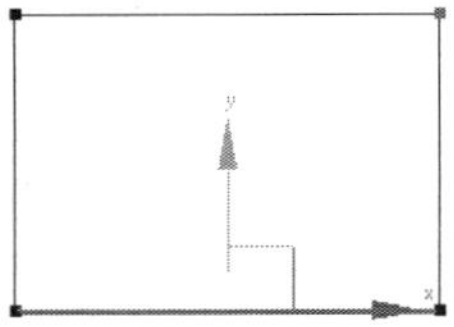

Figure 7-13 *The line segment selected in a rectangular spline*

Spline

A spline consists of all adjacent segments of an object. To modify an object using the spline, you need to select the **Spline** sub-object level. On doing so, you will be prompted to select all adjacent segments of the object, as shown in Figure 7-14.

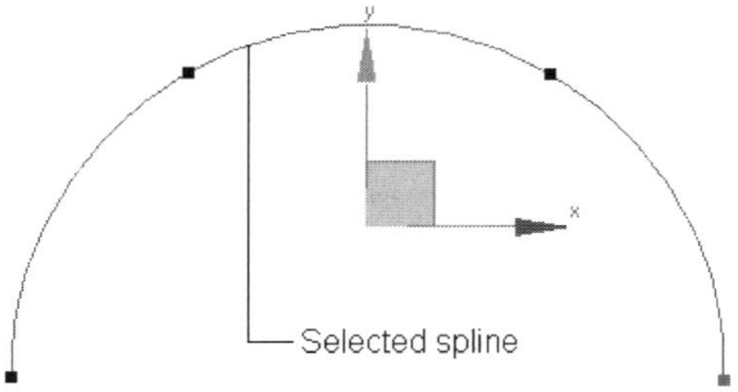

Figure 7-14 *The spline selected in an arc*

Rollouts

When you convert a spline object into an editable spline object, various rollouts will be displayed below the modifier stack in the modify panel. You can modify the spline objects at sub-object levels using these rollouts. These rollouts are discussed next.

Note

By default, the line spline has all the sub-object levels and rollouts. So, you do not need to convert it into editable spline.

*The options in the **Rendering** and **Interpolation** rollouts are the same as described in Chapter 5.*

*The **Surface Properties** rollout will not be displayed at the **Vertex** sub-object level.*

Selection Rollout

At the top of the **Selection** rollout, there are three buttons, **Vertex**, **Segment**, and **Spline**, refer to Figure 7-15. These buttons are used to select the sub-objects of a spline and have been discussed in the previous section. Choose one of the buttons to make it active and it is same as selecting the sub-object level in the modifier stack.

The check boxes in the **Display** area are used to display the vertex numbers in the viewport. When you select the **Show Vertex Numbers** check box, the vertex numbers will be displayed in the viewport, as shown in Figure 7-16. Select the **Selected Only** check box to display the vertex number only for the selected vertex.

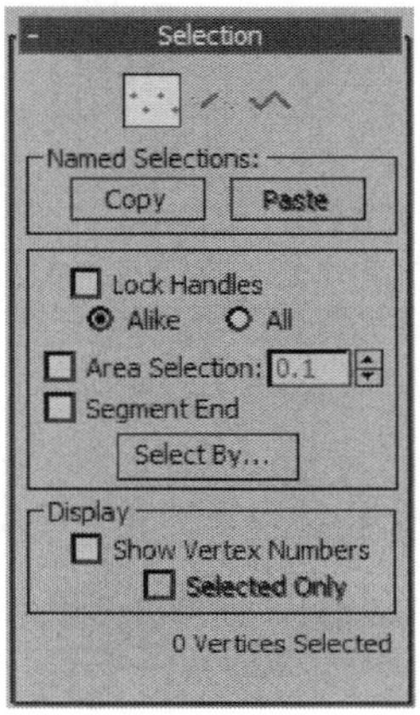

*Figure 7-15 The **Selection** rollout*

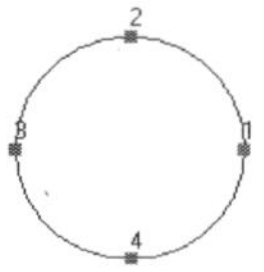

*Figure 7-16 The vertex numbers displayed after selecting the **Show Vertex Numbers** check box*

Soft Selection Rollout

The options in this rollout are the same as discussed earlier in Chapter 6.

Geometry Rollout

The options in this rollout are used to edit the spline at the object and sub-object levels, refer to Figure 7-17. These options are discussed next.

Create Line

The **Create Line** button is used to add a line spline to the selected spline. To do so, select the editable spline object in the viewport and choose the **Modify** tab; all rollouts will be displayed in the modify panel. Now, choose the **Create Line** button in the **Geometry** rollout; the button will be activated and turn yellow. Move the cursor in the viewport; its shape will change, as shown in Figure 7-18. Also, you will be prompted to create a new line in the viewport. Create a new line; it will automatically be attached to the selected spline. Next, right-click in the viewport or choose the **Create Line** button again to exit the command. The functions of the **Attach** and **Attach Mult.** buttons are the same as discussed earlier.

The **Reorient** check box, next to the **Attach** and **Attach Mult.** buttons is used to align the local coordinate system of the attached spline with the local coordinate system of the selected spline.

Insert

The **Insert** button is used to insert additional vertices in the splines to create new segments. To do so, select the editable spline object in the viewport and choose the **Modify** tab;

all rollouts will be displayed in the modify panel. Now, choose the **Insert** button in the **Geometry** rollout; it will turn yellow and get activated. Next, move the cursor over the spline; the shape of the cursor will change, as shown in Figure 7-19. Then, click to create a new vertex and move the cursor to place it. Again, move the cursor and click in the viewport to place the new vertices on the spline and right-click to exit the command.

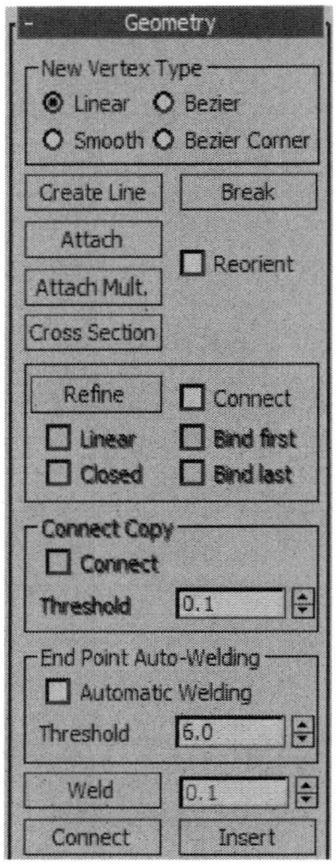

*Figure 7-17 Partial view of the **Geometry** rollout*

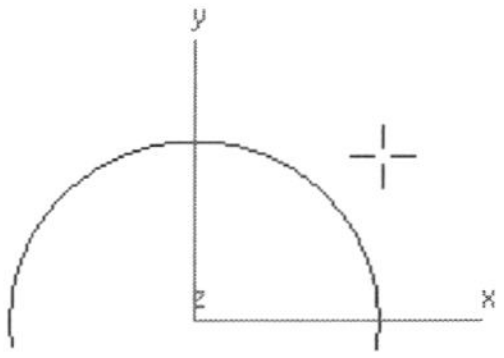

*Figure 7-18 The cursor displayed in the viewport on choosing the **Create Line** button*

*Figure 7-19 The cursor displayed after choosing the **Insert** button*

Break

The **Break** button is available for the **Vertex** and **Segment** sub-object levels. It is used to break a spline at the selected point. If you select the **Vertex** sub-object level, then select one or more vertices in the viewport to break the spline. Next, choose the **Break** button in the **Geometry** rollout; the spline will split at the selected point. Similarly, if you select the **Segment** sub-object level, then choose the **Break** button and click on a point on the selected spline to break it. To view the split splines, select the **Spline** sub-object level in the modifier stack.

Refine and Connect

The **Refine** button and the **Connect** check box are available for the **Vertex** and the **Segment** sub-object levels. The **Refine** button is used to add new vertices to the selected spline. To add new vertices, choose the **Refine** button and move the cursor over the selected spline; the cursor for refining the spline will be displayed. Then, click on a point to add a new vertex. You can repeatedly click on the spline to create more than one vertices. Next, right-click or choose the **Refine** button again to exit the command.

The **Connect** check box on the right of the **Refine** button is used to connect the new vertices by a segment. To do so, select the **Connect** check box, choose the **Refine** button, and then move the cursor over the selected spline; the cursor for refining will be displayed. Now, click on a point to add a new vertex and then click again to create another vertex. Next, right-click to exit the command; a segment will be created to join the two new vertices, as shown in Figure 7-20.

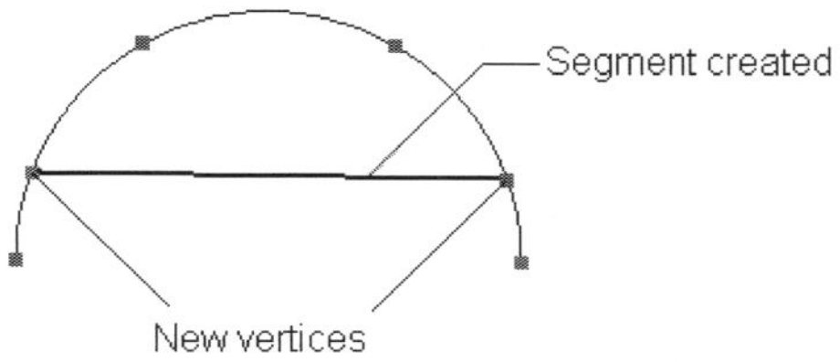

***Figure 7-20** The new vertices and the segment created using the **Refine** button and the **Connect** check box*

Note

*If you insert a vertex using the **Refine** button, then the curve shape of the selected spline will not be changed. But, if you insert the vertex using the **Insert** button, then the curve shape will be changed.*

Weld

The **Weld** button is available only for the **Vertex** sub-object level. It is used to join the selected vertices into a single vertex. To do so, select the editable spline object in the viewport and then select the **Vertex** sub-object level; the **Weld** button will be available in the **Geometry** rollout. Next, select the vertices that you want to join together in the viewport and choose the **Weld** button; the vertices will be joined together to create one vertex. The value in the spinner on the right side of the **Weld** button specifies the distance between the vertices that can be welded. If the value in the spinner is less than the distance between the vertices, then the vertices will not be welded.

Connect

The **Connect** button is available only for the **Vertex** sub-object level. It is used to connect two end vertices of a spline by creating a segment in between the vertices. To do so, select the editable spline object in the viewport, select the **Vertex** sub-object level in the modifier stack, and then choose the **Connect** button in the **Geometry** rollout. Next, move the cursor over one of the end vertices of the spline; the shape of the cursor will change, refer to Figures 7-21 and 7-22. Now, press and hold the left mouse button and drag it to move the cursor over another end vertex; the shape of the cursor will change again and a dotted line will be generated, as shown in Figure 7-23. Now, release the left mouse button; a segment will be created joining the end vertices, as shown in Figure 7-24.

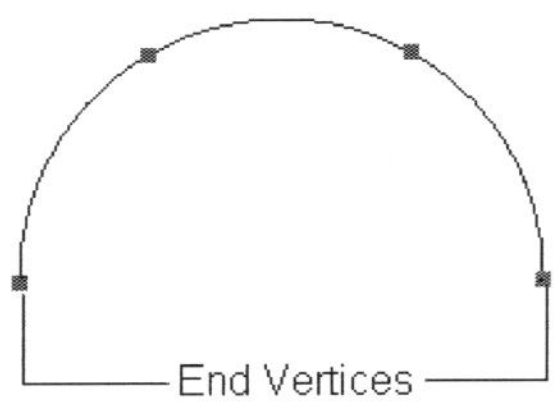

Figure 7-21 *The end vertices in an arc spline*

Figure 7-22 *The cursor over one of the end vertices*

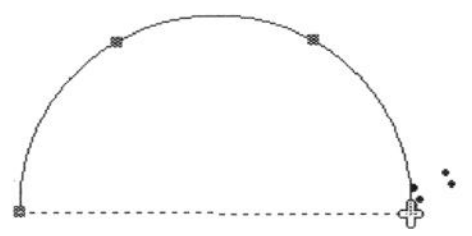

Figure 7-23 *The cursor over another end vertex and the dotted line displayed*

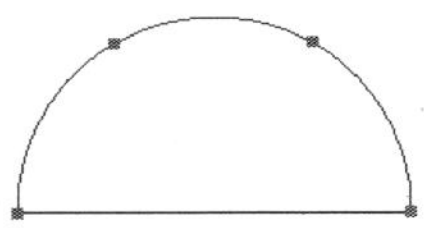

Figure 7-24 *The end vertices connected with a segment*

Make First

The **Make First** button is used to make any vertex of the spline as its first vertex or the starting point. To do so, select a vertex of the spline in the viewport and choose the **Make First** button in the **Geometry** rollout; the selected vertex will turn yellow and become the first vertex of the spline.

Note

In an open spline such as line, arc, and so on, only the end vertex can be the first vertex.

Fuse

The **Fuse** button is used to move all selected vertices of a spline to their average center. Select the vertices of a spline in the viewport, as shown in Figure 7-25, and then, choose the **Fuse** button in the **Geometry** rollout; the selected vertices will fuse together at their average center, as shown in Figure 7-26.

Fillet

The **Fillet** button is used to create round corners in a spline by creating two new vertices. To do so, select the corner vertex of an editable spline object in the viewport, as shown in Figure 7-27. Next, choose the **Fillet** button in the **Geometry** rollout and move the cursor over the selected vertex; the cursor will change into a different shape, as shown in Figure 7-28. Now, press the left mouse button and drag the cursor up; the new vertices with a round corner will be displayed, as shown in Figure 7-29. When you drag the cursor to fillet the selected vertex, the value of fillet will also be displayed in the spinner on the right side of the **Fillet** button. You can also perform this command by selecting a vertex and entering the value for the fillet in this spinner.

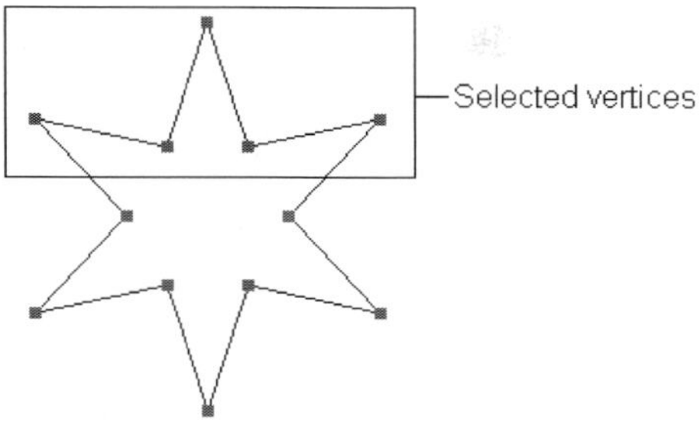

Figure 7-25 *The selected vertices inside the rectangular area*

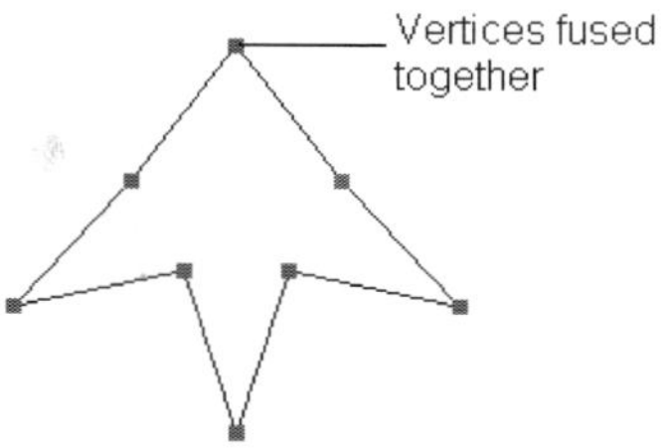

Figure 7-26 *The selected vertices fused at their average center*

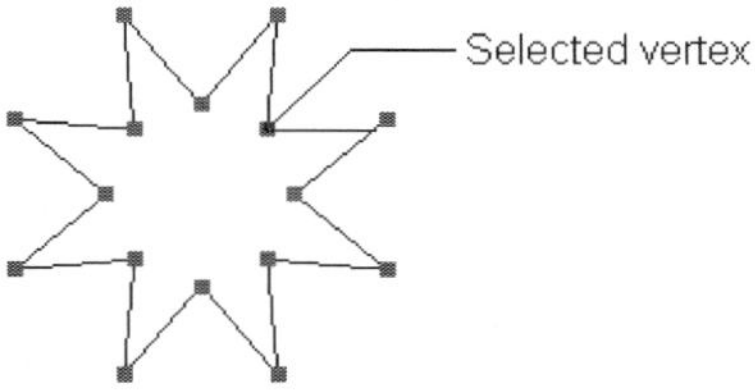

Figure 7-27 *The selected vertex in a star spline*

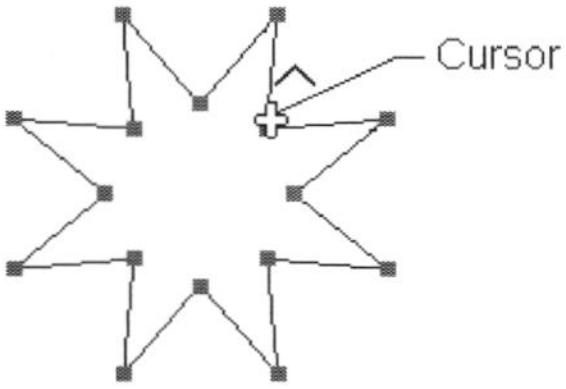

Figure 7-28 *The cursor displayed after moving the cursor over the selected vertex*

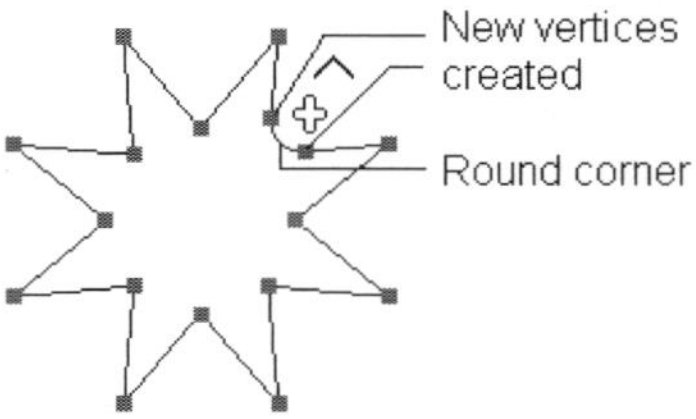

Figure 7-29 *The two new vertices and the round corner displayed*

Chamfer

The **Chamfer** button is used to create bevel corners in a spline by creating two new vertices. To do so, select the corner vertex of an editable spline object in the viewport. Next, choose the **Chamfer** button in the **Geometry** rollout and move the cursor over the selected vertex; the cursor will get changed. Now, press the left mouse button and drag the cursor up; the new vertices with a beveled corner will be displayed, as shown in Figure 7-30. Next, release the left mouse button. When you drag the cursor to chamfer the selected vertex, the value of chamfer will be displayed in the spinner on the right side of the **Chamfer** button. You can also chamfer by selecting a vertex and entering the value for the chamfer in this spinner.

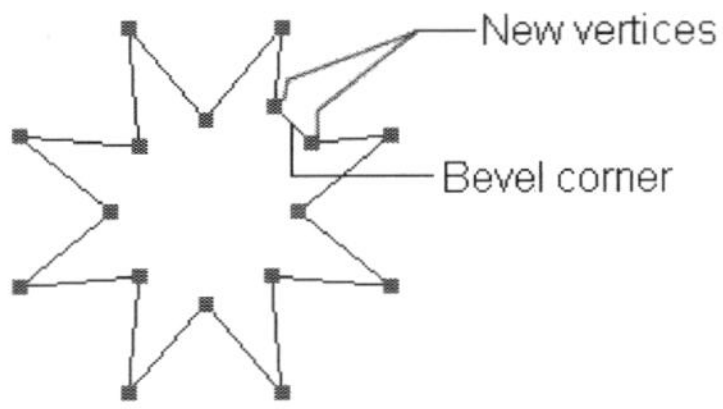

Figure 7-30 *The new vertices with a beveled corner*

Hide and Unhide All

The **Hide** and **Unhide All** buttons are available for all sub-object levels in the editable spline object. The **Hide** button is used to hide the selected sub-object in the viewport. The **Unhide All** button is used to show all hidden sub-objects in the viewport. To hide the sub-objects of the editable spline object, select them in the viewport and choose the **Hide** button in the **Geometry** rollout. Similarly, to unhide the hidden sub-objects, choose the **Unhide All** button in the **Geometry** rollout.

Delete

The **Delete** button is available at all sub-object levels and is used to delete the selected sub-objects in the viewport. To do so, select a sub-object in the viewport and choose the **Delete** button; the selected sub-object will be deleted.

Divide

The **Divide** button is available only for the **Segment** sub-object level. It is used to subdivide the selected segment by inserting a number of vertices on it. The number of vertices to be inserted can be set in the spinner on the right side of the **Divide** button. To subdivide a selected segment, select the **Segment** sub-object in the viewport, as shown in Figure 7-31. Then, choose the **Divide** button; the selected segment will be sub-divided, as shown in Figure 7-32.

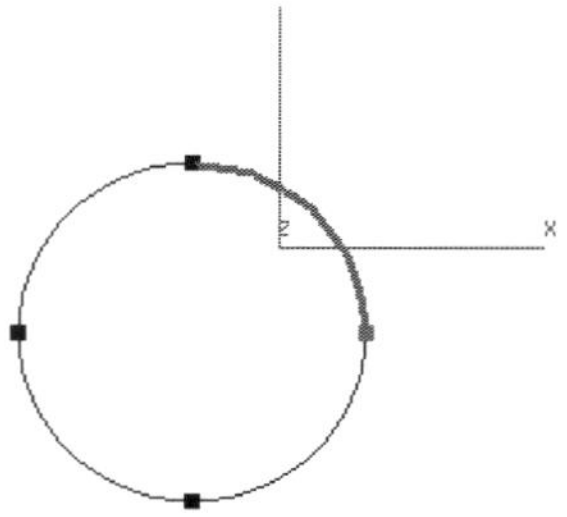

Figure 7-31 A segment selected in the circle spline

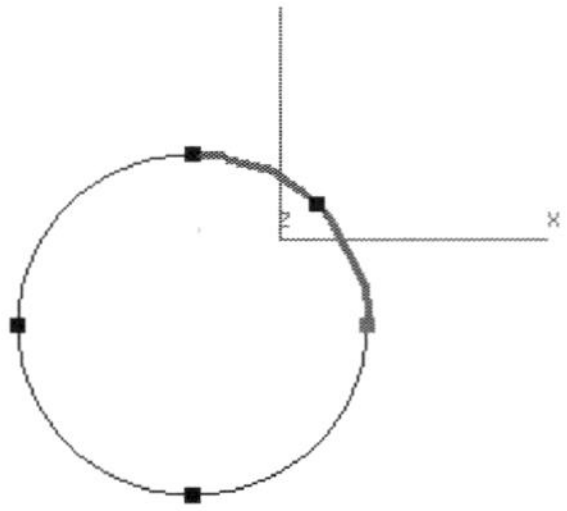

Figure 7-32 *The selected segment sub-divided after using the* ***Divide*** *button*

Detach

The **Detach** button is available at the **Segment** and **Spline** sub-object levels. It is used to detach the selected sub-objects from the original one and create a new shape. To do so, select one or more sub-objects of the editable spline object in the viewport, as shown in

Figure 7-33. Next, choose the **Detach** button in the **Geometry** rollout; the **Detach** dialog box will be displayed, as shown in Figure 7-34. By default, the name of the new shape will be displayed as Shape001 in the **Detach as** text box. Modify the name if you want and then choose the **OK** button; the detached sub-object will now behave like a new independent shape, refer to Figure 7-35.

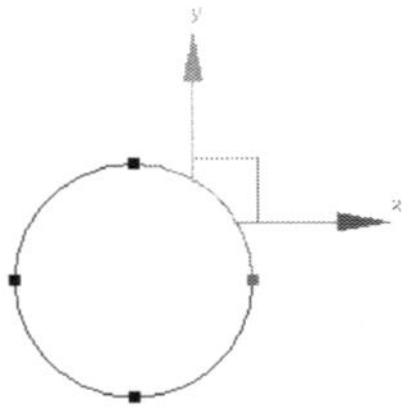

Figure 7-33 *A segment sub-object selected in the circle spline*

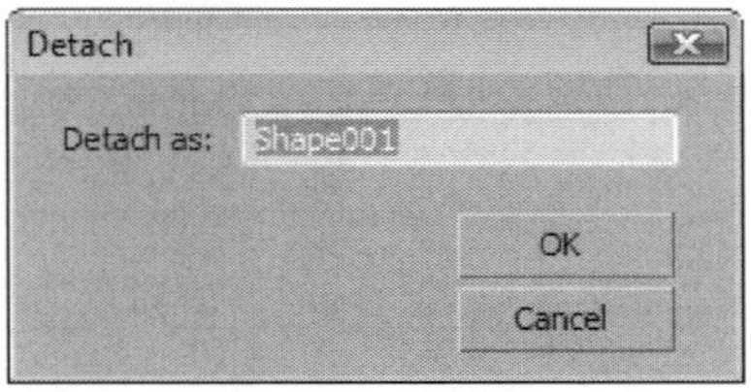

Figure 7-34 *The **Detach** dialog box*

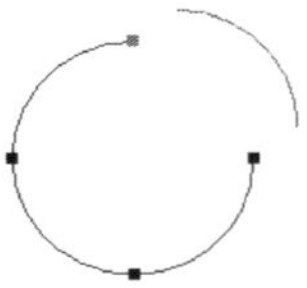

Figure 7-35 *The detached segment as a new independent shape*

Reverse

The **Reverse** button is available only at the **Spline** sub-object level. It is used to reverse the direction of the spline. To do so, select the editable spline object in the viewport, select the **Spline** sub-object level in the modifier stack, and then select the **Spline** sub-object in the viewport, as shown in Figure 7-36. Now, choose the **Reverse** button in the **Geometry** rollout; the direction of the selected spline will get reversed, as shown in Figure 7-37. To view the reversed direction, you need to select the **Show Vertex Numbers** check box in the **Display** area of the **Selection** rollout.

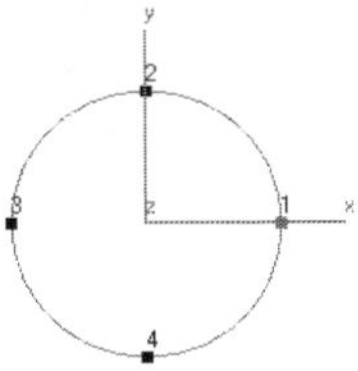

Figure 7-36 *The spline selected in a circle*

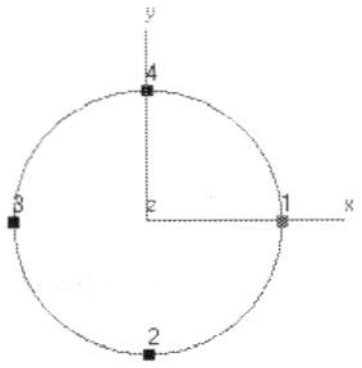

Figure 7-37 *The reversed direction of the selected spline after choosing the **Reverse** button*

Outline

The **Outline** button is available only at the **Spline** sub-object level. It is used to create a copy of the spline at a distance that you enter in the spinner on the right side of the **Outline** button. To do so, select the spline of the editable spline object in the viewport. Next, choose the **Outline** button; the button will be activated and turn yellow. Next, move the cursor over the selected spline; the cursor will be changed, as shown in Figure 7-38. Now, press and hold the left mouse button and move the cursor up or down over the selected spline to create a copy of the spline which behaves like its outline, as shown in Figure 7-39. Now, release the left mouse button. Also, right-click in the viewport or choose the **Outline** button again to exit the command.

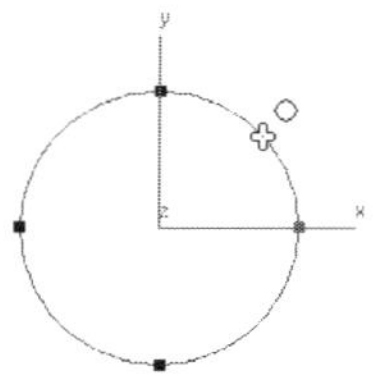

***Figure 7-38** The cursor changed after choosing the **Outline** button*

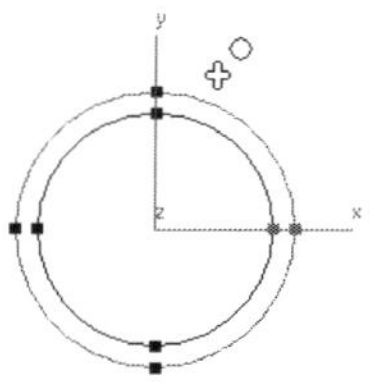

***Figure 7-39** A copy of the spline created as an outline of the selected spline*

Note

*If you use the **Outline** button for an open spline such as arc, line, and so on, then the copied spline will be attached to the selected spline. Also, the resultant spline will be a closed one, refer to Figures 7-40 and 7-41*

***Figure 7-40** An open arc spline*

***Figure 7-41** The closed spline after using the **Outline** button on the open spline*

Boolean

The **Boolean** button is available only at the **Spline** sub-object level. It is used to create complex shapes using two attached splines. These two splines must be closed, attached, and should intersect with each other. Also, they should be in the same plane. There are three buttons available on the right side of the **Boolean** button, **Union**, **Subtraction**, and **Intersection**.

The **Union** button is used to remove the overlapping portion of two splines and create a single spline by combining them, refer to Figures 7-42 and 7-43. The **Subtraction** button is used to subtract the overlapping portion of the second spline from the selected spline and remove the extra portion of the second spline, as shown in Figure 7-44. The **Intersection** button is used to remove the non-overlapping portion of the splines and retain the overlapping portion of the splines, as shown in Figure 7-45.

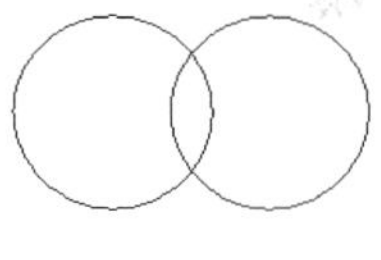

Figure 7-42 The two attached splines overlapping each other

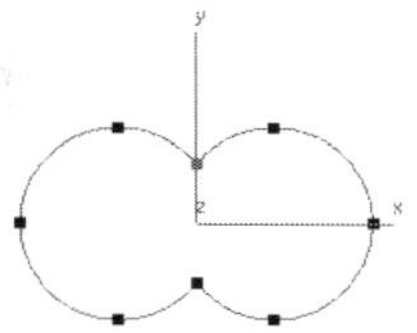

Figure 7-43 *The union boolean*

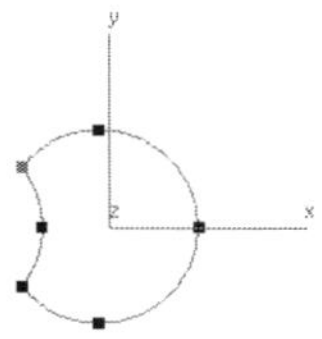

Figure 7-44 *The subtraction boolean*

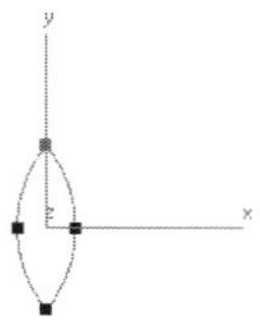

Figure 7-45 *The intersection boolean*

To perform the boolean operation, create two splines and convert them into editable splines. Then, attach them using the **Attach** button as discussed earlier. Next, select the **Spline** sub-object level in the modifier stack. Now, select the spline in the viewport and choose one of the boolean type buttons on the right side of the **Boolean** button in the **Geometry** rollout. Then, choose the **Boolean** button and move the cursor over the overlapping area of the two splines; the cursor will get changed. Click on the overlapping area; the splines will be converted into a complex spline according to the boolean type button chosen.

Mirror

The **Mirror** button is available only at the **Spline** sub-object level. It is used to move the selected spline in a particular direction. There are three buttons on the right side of the **Mirror** button, **Mirror Horizontally**, **Mirror Vertically**, and **Mirror Both**. These buttons are used to define the direction of movement of the spline. To mirror a spline, select the editable spline in the viewport and then select the **Spline** sub-object level in the modifier stack. Specify the direction of movement of the spline by choosing one of the buttons on the right side of the **Mirror** button. Next, choose the **Mirror** button; the spline will move in the specified direction, refer to Figures 7-46 through 7-48.

Select the **Copy** check box below the **Mirror** button to create a copy of the spline while mirroring, as shown in Figures 7-49 through 7-51. Select the **About Pivot** check box to mirror the spline according to the pivot point of the spline.

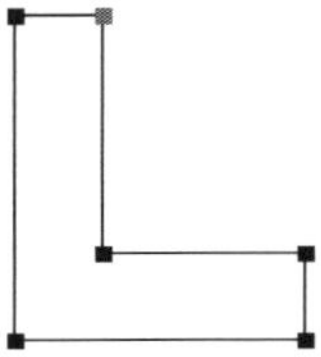

Figure 7-46 *The angle extended spline created to mirror*

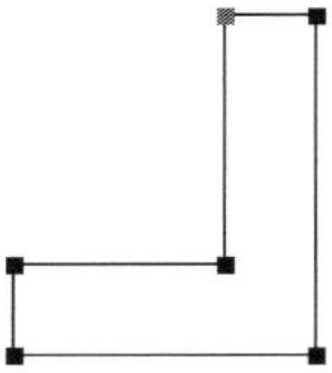

Figure 7-47 *The spline mirrored horizontally*

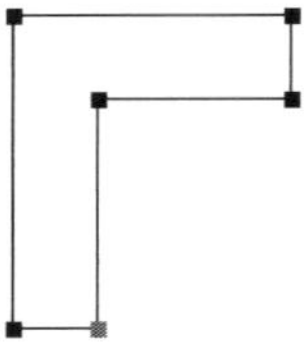

Figure 7-48 *The spline mirrored vertically*

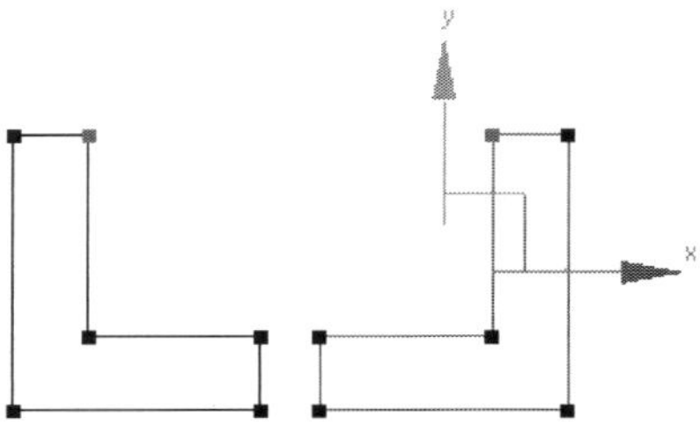

Figure 7-49 *The spline mirrored horizontally after selecting the* ***Copy*** *check box*

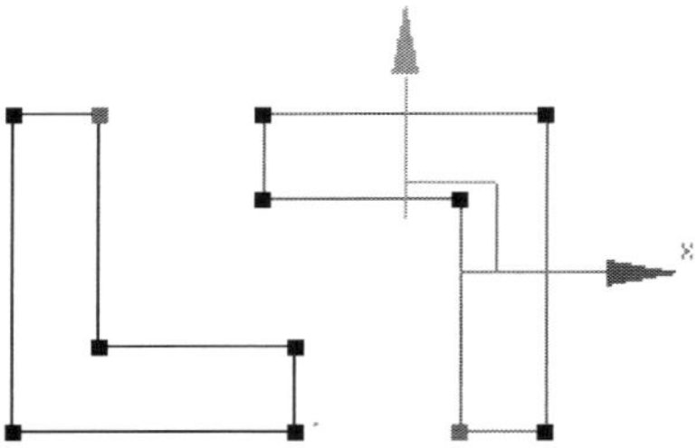

Figure 7-50 *The spline mirrored on both the sides after selecting the* ***Copy*** *check box*

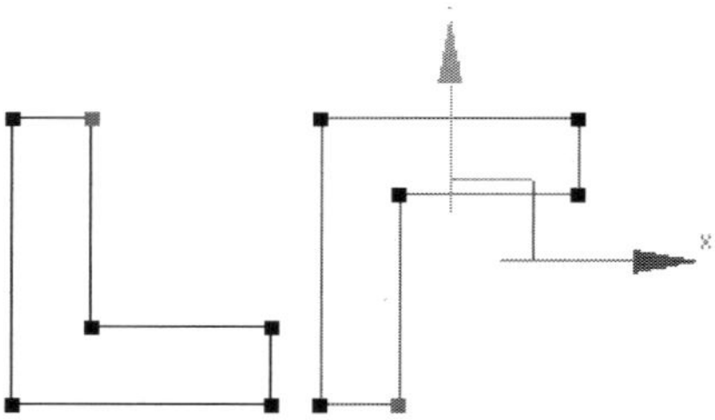

Figure 7-51 *The spline mirrored vertically after selecting the* ***Copy*** *check box*

Trim

The **Trim** button is available only at the **Spline** sub-object level. It is used to remove the overlapping segments of the two attached splines. To do so, create two splines, convert them into editable splines, and then attach them using the **Attach** button as described earlier, refer to Figure 7-52. Next, select the **Spline** sub-object level in the modifier stack. Choose the **Trim** button in the **Geometry** rollout and move the cursor over the overlapping segments of the two splines; the cursor will get changed, as shown in Figure 7-52. Now, click on the overlapping segments to remove them, refer to Figure 7-53.

Explode

The **Explode** button is available only at the **Spline** sub-object level. It is used to break a spline into a number of splines. The number of broken splines depends on the number of segments of the spline. To break a spline into a number of splines, select the editable spline in the viewport and select the **Spline** sub-object level in the modifier stack. Next, choose the **Explode** button; the spline will be broken into a number of splines, refer to Figures 7-54 and 7-55.

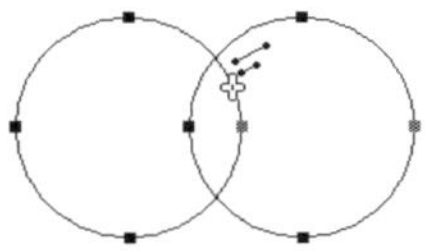

Figure 7-52 *The two attached splines and the cursor over the overlapping segments*

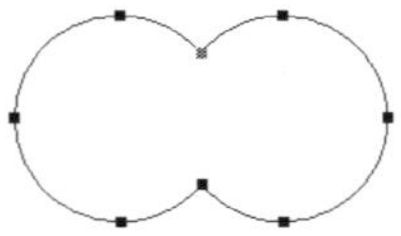

Figure 7-53 The splines after using the Trim button

Figure 7-54 *The rectangular spline for explosion*

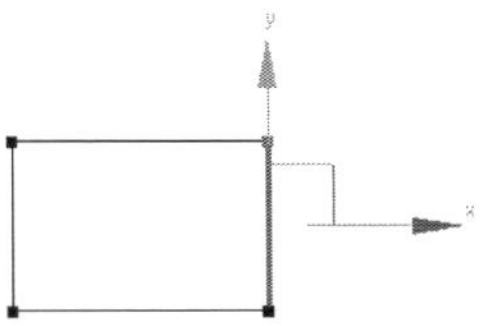

Figure 7-55 One of the broken splines selected after using the Explode button

There are two radio buttons in the **To** area below the **Explode** button, **Splines** and **Objects**. These buttons are used to select the type of explosion of the spline. By default, the **Splines** radio button is selected, which enables you to break the spline into a number of splines that will be attached together. On selecting the **Objects** radio button, the new splines will be created but they will behave as independent shapes.

Select the **Objects** radio button and then choose the **Explode** button to explode the spline; the **Explode** dialog box will be displayed, as shown in Figure 7-56. Enter a name in the **Object Name** text box and choose the **OK** button; all new shapes will be named according to the name entered in the **Object Name** text box.

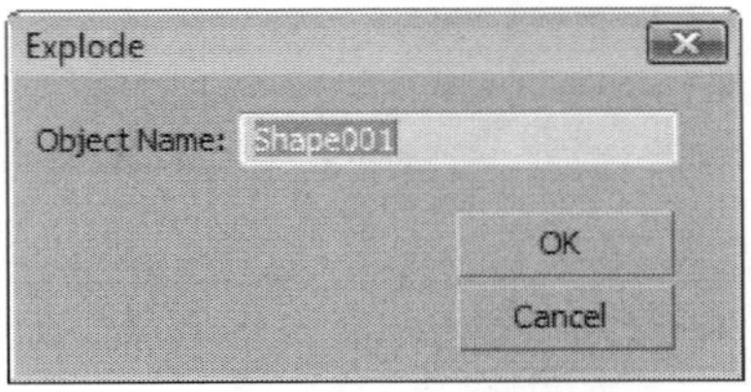

Figure 7-56 *The **Explode** dialog box*

Display Area

The **Display** area will be active in **Vertex** and **Segment** sub-object levels. In this area, the **Show selected segs** check box is cleared. As a result, the selected segments will be displayed in the **Segment** sub-object level only. But, if you select the **Show selected segs** check box, the selected segments will be displayed in red color at the **Vertex** sub-object level also.

Tutorial 1

In this tutorial, you will create a pair of cocktail glasses, as shown in Figure 7-57, by converting 2D splines into 3D mesh objects. **(Expected time: 15 min)**

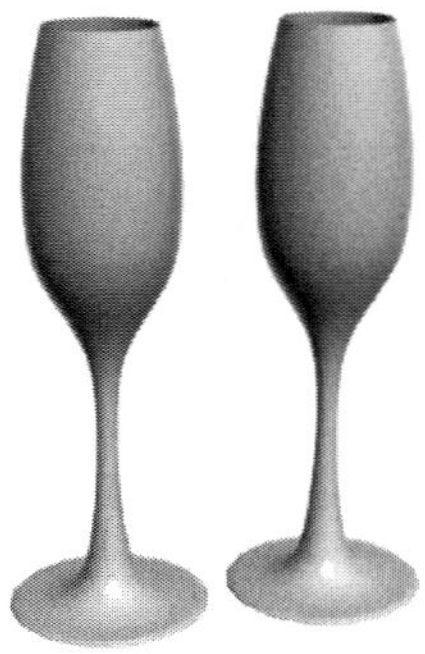

Figure 7-57 *A pair of cocktail glasses*

The following steps are required to complete this tutorial:

a. Set the project folder.
b. Create a line spline for glasses.
c. Apply the **Lathe** modifier.
d. Assign material to glasses.
e. Render the scene for the final output.
f. Save the file.

Setting the Project Folder

1. Set the project folder with the name *c07_tut1* in the *3dsmax* folder as discussed in earlier chapters.

Creating a Line Spline

First, reset Autodesk 3ds Max to start afresh. Now, in this section, you need to create a shape similar to the half portion of the cocktail glass using the **Line** tool.

1. Activate the Front viewport and choose **Create > Shapes** in the **Command Panel**. The **Splines** option is selected by default in the drop-down list below the **Shapes** button. Now, invoke the **Line** tool from the **Object Type** rollout.

2. In the **Creation Method** rollout, select the **Smooth** radio button in the **Initial Type** area and select the **Corner** radio button in the **Drag Type** area.

3. Click at the bottom middle point of the Front viewport to create the first vertex or the starting point of the line spline. Now, move the cursor around four grid points toward left to define the distance between the first and the second vertex, and then click on the screen to create the second vertex. Again, move the cursor and click to create additional vertices to get the required shape of the spline, as shown in Figure 7-58. After getting the required shape, right-click to end the creation of line spline.

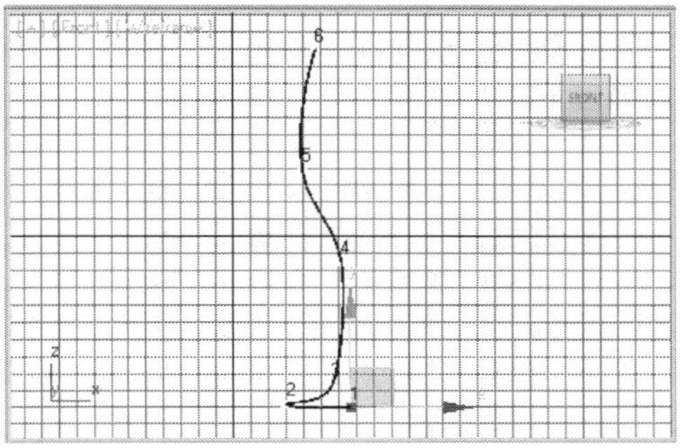

***Figure 7-58** The line spline created for the cocktail glass*

4. You can also modify the shape of the line spline after creating it. To do so, make sure that the line spline is selected in the viewport and choose the **Modify** tab in the **Command Panel**. Now, select the **Vertex** sub-object level in the modifier stack; all vertices of the line spline are displayed in the viewport. Next, select the vertices in the viewport one by one and modify the shape by moving them as per the requirement. After getting the required shape, select the **Vertex** sub-object level in the modifier stack again to deactivate it.

Next, you need to apply the **Lathe** modifier to convert the 2D spline into a 3D mesh object.

Applying the Lathe Modifier

First, you need to set the pivot point of the line spline because the **Lathe** modifier creates the 3D object by rotating a 2D shape about an axis. The direction of the axis of revolution depends on the pivot point of the shape.

1. To set the position of the pivot point, select the line spline in the viewport and choose the **Hierarchy** tab in the **Command Panel**. By default, the **Pivot** tab is chosen in the hierarchy panel. In the **Adjust Pivot** rollout of the **Pivot** tab, choose the **Affect Pivot Only** button; the pivot point of the line spline is displayed in the viewports, as shown in Figure 7-59.

2. In the Front viewport, adjust the pivot point on the first vertex of the line spline using the **Select and Move** tool, as shown in Figure 7-60. Now, choose the **Affect Pivot Only** button again to deactivate it; the pivot point disappears.

Note

*While applying the **Lathe** modifier, you can also select the first vertex of the line spline instead of adjusting its pivot point, as shown in Figure 7-61.*

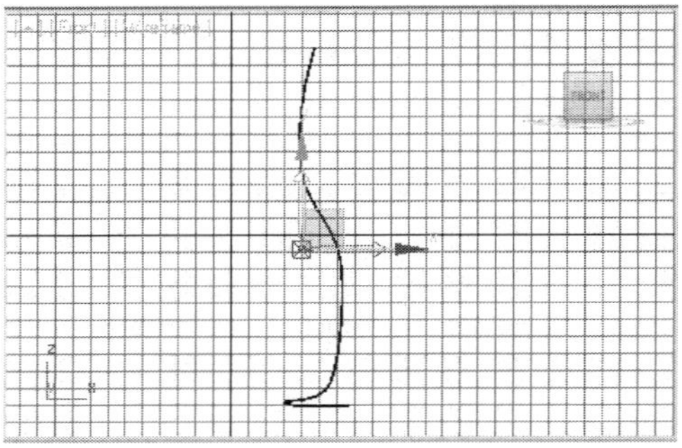

***Figure 7-59** The pivot point of the line spline at its original position*

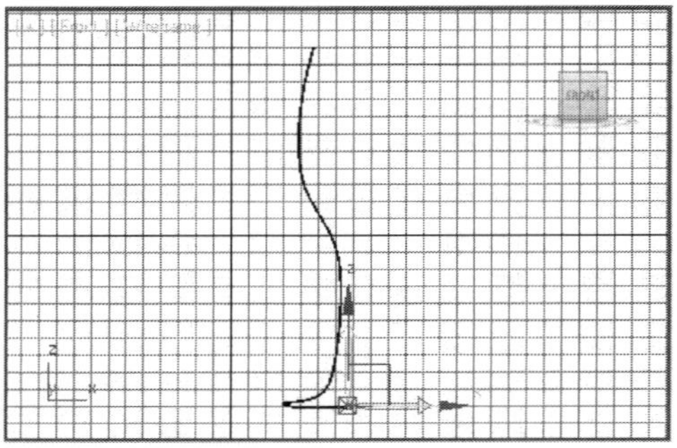

***Figure 7-60** The pivot point after adjusting its position in the Front viewport*

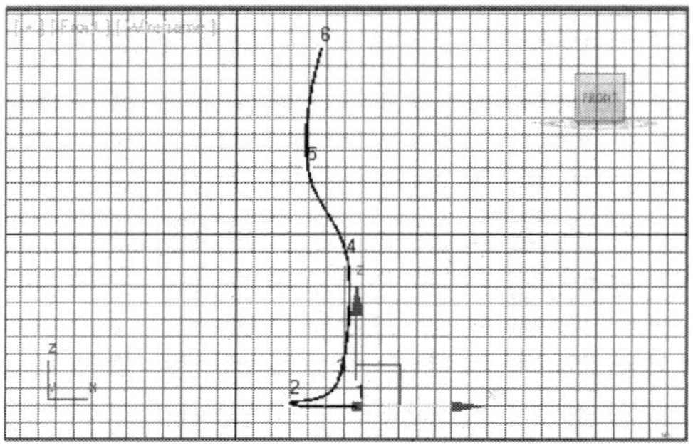

***Figure 7-61** The first vertex selected in the line spline*

3. Now, make sure that the line spline is selected in the viewport and choose **Modifiers > Patch/Spline Editing > Lathe** from the menu bar; the 2D line spline is converted into the 3D mesh object. Also, the **Parameters** rollout is displayed in the modify panel.

4. In the **Parameters** rollout, select the **Flip Normals** check box.

5. Name the new 3D object to *cocktail glass* and press ENTER. Next, click anywhere in the viewport to deselect the *cocktail glass*.

6. Invoke the **Zoom Extents All** tool; the *cocktail glass* is displayed in all viewports, as shown in Figure 7-62.

7. Create a copy of the *cocktail glass* in the Front viewport to make a pair and invoke the **Zoom Extents All** tool; a pair of cocktail glasses is displayed in all viewports, as shown in Figure 7-63.

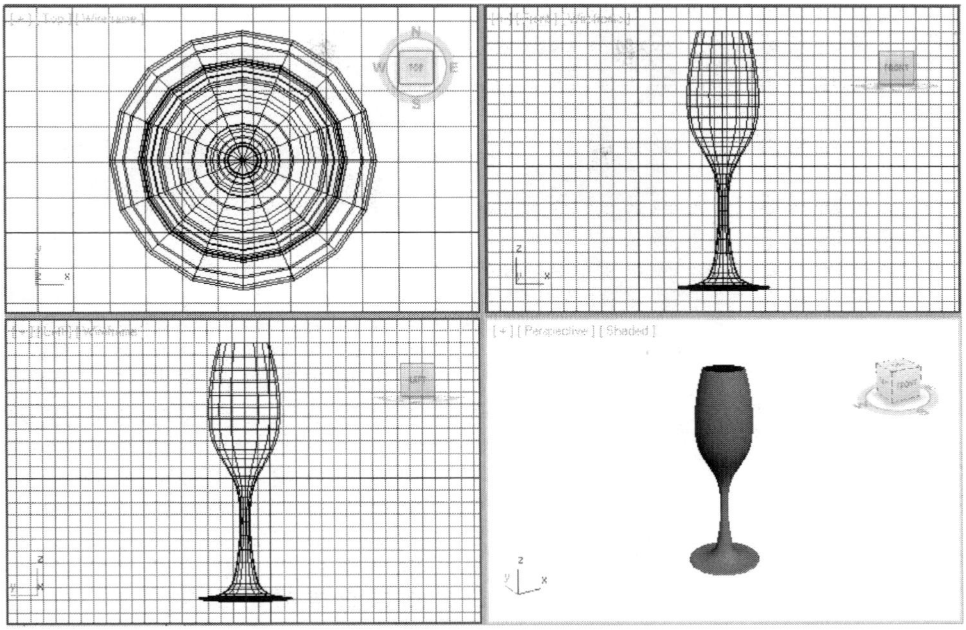

Figure 7-62 *The cocktail glass displayed in all viewports after applying the **Lathe** modifier*

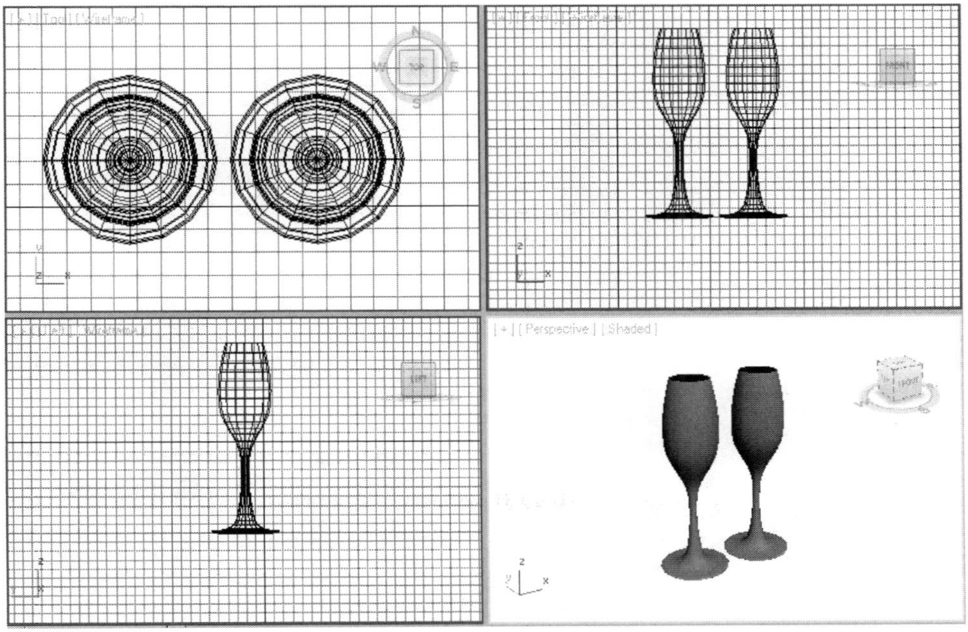

Figure 7-63 *A pair of cocktail glasses in all viewports*

Rendering the Scene

1. Activate the Perspective viewport and render it as discussed in the previous chapters. You will be able to view only one side of the cocktail glasses in the final output, as shown in Figure 7-64.

Figure 7-64 *The cocktail glasses in the final output at rendering*

To view both sides of the faces of the cocktail glasses, you need to apply material on them. The procedure to apply material is discussed in the next section. You will learn in detail about applying materials to objects in the later chapters.

Applying the Material

1. Invoke the **Material Editor** tool from the **Main Toolbar**; the **Material Editor** dialog box is displayed, as shown in Figure 7-65.

2. Select the **01 - Default** sample slot in the **Material Editor** dialog box, if it is not already selected. Now, in the **Shader Basic Parameters** rollout, select the **2-Sided** check box to apply the material on both sides of the faces, refer to Figure 7-65.

3. In the **Blinn Basic Parameters** rollout, choose the **Diffuse** color swatch; the **Color Selector: Diffuse Color** dialog box is displayed. Set the white color in it and choose the **OK** button; the white color is displayed in the **Diffuse** color swatch.

4. In the **Specular Highlights** area, set the value **123** in the **Specular Level** spinner and set the value **30** in the **Glossiness** spinner, refer to Figure 7-65.

5. Select the cocktail glasses in any of the viewports and make sure that the **01-Default** sample slot is selected in the **Material Editor** dialog box. Then, in the **Material Editor** dialog box, choose the **Assign Material to Selection** button; the material is assigned to the pair of cocktail glasses in the viewport. Next, choose the **Show Shaded Material in Viewport** button to view the material in the viewports and close the dialog box.

6. Now, render the Perspective viewport as discussed earlier. The final output at one frame is displayed, as shown in Figure 7-66.

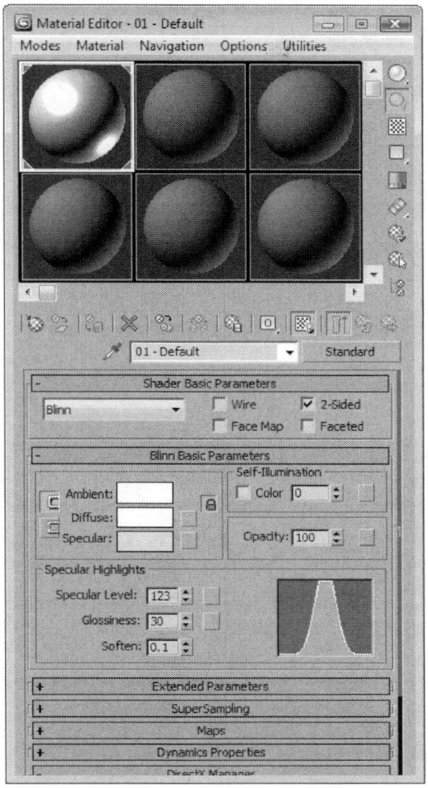

Figure 7-65 Partial view of the ***Material Editor*** *dialog box*

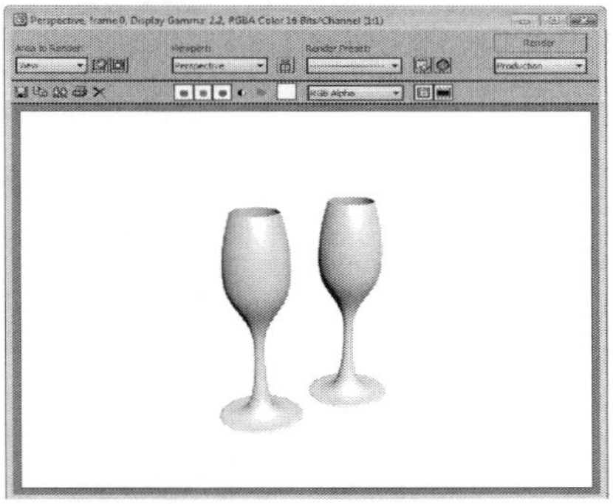

Figure 7-66 The final output after applying the material

You can view the final rendered image of this model by downloading the *c07_3dsmax_2012_render.zip* file from *http://www.cadcim.com*.

Saving the File

1. Save the file with the name *c07tut1.max* as discussed in earlier chapters. The location of this file is given below:

   \Documents\3dsmax\c07_tut1\scenes

Tutorial 2

In this tutorial, you will create a vase to hold plants, as shown in Figure 7-67, by converting 2D spline into 3D mesh object. **(Expected time: 15 min)**

Figure 7-67 *A vase model*

The following steps are required to complete this tutorial:

a. Set the project folder.
b. Create a line spline for the vase.
c. Apply the **Lathe** modifier.
d. Assign the material to the vase.
e. Create a stand for the vase.
f. Render the scene for the final output.
g. Save the file.

Setting the Project Folder

1. Set the project folder with the name *c07_tut2* in the *3dsmax* folder as discussed in earlier chapters.

Creating a Line Spline

First, reset Autodesk 3ds Max to start afresh. In this section, you need to create a shape similar to the half portion of the vase using the **Line** tool.

1. Activate the Front viewport and choose **Create > Shapes** in the **Command Panel**; the **Splines** option is selected by default in the drop-down list below the **Shapes** button. Now, invoke the **Line** tool from the **Object Type** rollout.

2. In the **Creation Method** rollout, select the **Corner** radio button in the **Initial Type** area and select the **Corner** radio button in the **Drag Type** area.

3. Next, create a line spline as discussed in Tutorial 1. This spline should be similar to the half portion of the vase, refer to Figure 7-68.

4. If you need to modify the shape of the line spline after it is created, choose the **Modify** tab and select the **Vertex** sub-object level in the modifier stack; all vertices of the line spline are displayed in the viewport. Next, select the vertices one by one in the viewport and modify the shape by moving them to get a perfect shape.

   Next, you need to apply the **Lathe** modifier to convert the 2D spline into the 3D mesh object.

5. Select the first vertex of the spline in the Front viewport, as shown in Figure 7-69.

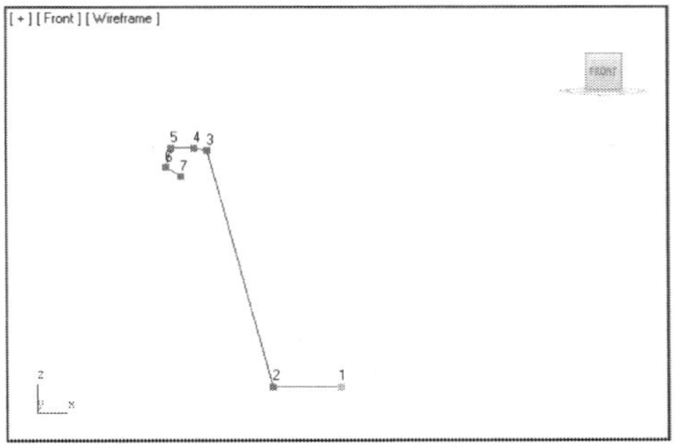

Figure 7-68 *A line spline created for the vase*

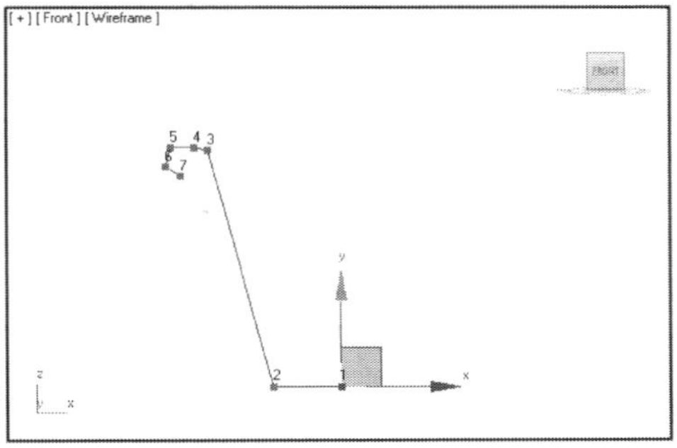

Figure 7-69 *The first vertex of the line spline selected in the Front viewport*

6. Now, choose **Modifiers > Patch/Spline Editing > Lathe** from the menu bar; the 2D line spline is converted into the 3D mesh object.

7. Name the new 3D mesh object as *vase*. Also, click anywhere in the viewport to deselect the *vase*.

8. Invoke the **Zoom Extents All** tool; the entire *vase* is displayed in all viewports, as shown in Figure 7-70.

9. Next, create the material for the *vase* using the **Material Editor** tool as discussed in Tutorial 1 of this chapter. Make sure that in the **Shader Basic Parameters** rollout of the **Material Editor** dialog box, the **2-Sided** check box is selected. This enables you to view both sides of the *vase* in the final output. Also, in the **Blinn Basic Parameters** rollout, choose the **Diffuse** color swatch; the **Color Selector: Diffuse Color** dialog box is displayed. Set the following values in the respective spinners:

   Red: **177** Green: **88** Blue: **27**

   Choose the **OK** button in the **Color Selector: Diffuse Color** dialog box; the selected color is displayed in the **Diffuse** color swatch.

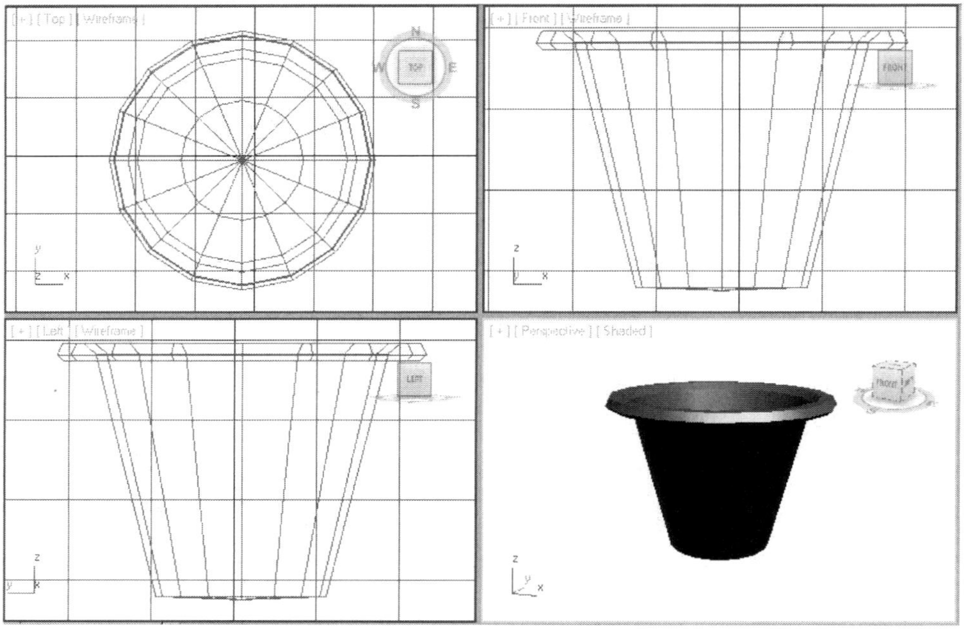

***Figure 7-70** The vase after applying the **Lathe** modifier*

10. Make sure that the *vase* is selected in the viewports and choose the **Assign Material to Selection** button in the **Material Editor** dialog box; the selected material is assigned to the *vase* in the viewport. Next, choose the **Show Shaded Material in Viewport** button in the same dialog box to view the material in viewports and close the **Material Editor** dialog box.

    Next, you need to use the **Foliage** tool to put a plant in the *vase*.

11. Activate the Top viewport. Choose **Create > Geometry** in the **Command Panel**; a drop-down list is displayed below the **Geometry** button. Select **AEC Extended** from the drop-down list and then invoke the **Foliage** tool from the **Object Type** rollout.

12. Now, in the **Favorite Plants** rollout, select and double-click on the **Society Garlic** foliage; it is displayed in all viewports.

13. In the **Name and Color** rollout, name the foliage to *plant* and press ENTER.

14. Make sure that the *plant* is still selected. Choose the **Modify** tab in the **Command Panel**; the **Parameters** rollout is displayed.

15. In the **Parameters** rollout, set a value in the **Height** spinner to adjust the height of the *plant* according to the *vase*.

16. Invoke the **Select and Move** tool and align the *plant* with the *vase* in all viewports, as shown in Figure 7-71.

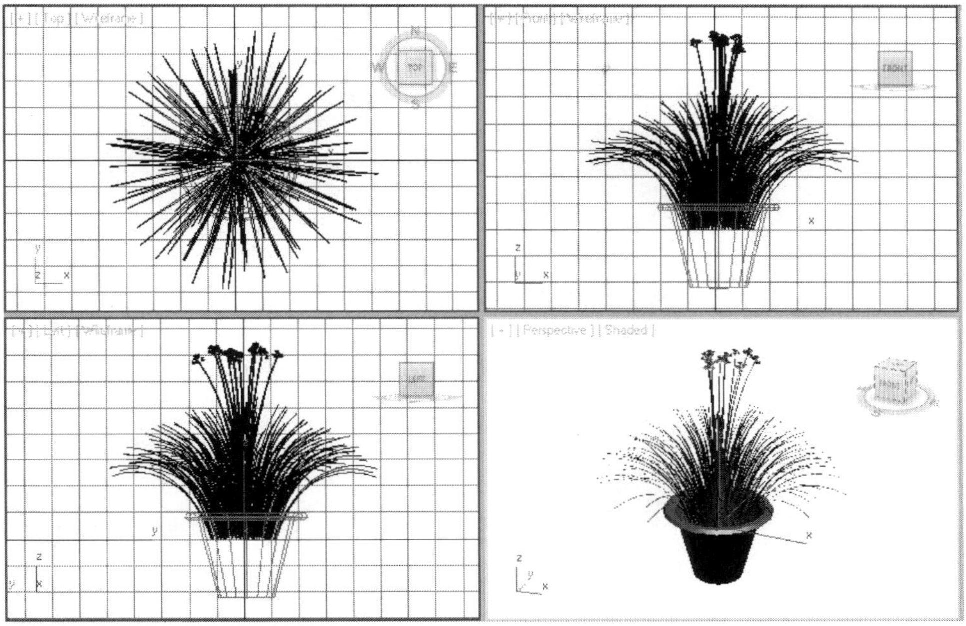

Figure 7-71 *Alignment of the plant with the vase in all viewports*

17. Select the *plant* and the *vase* in the viewports and group them as *flower vase*.

    Next, you need to create a stand for the *flower vase*.

Creating a Stand for the Flower Vase

First, select the *flower vase* and right-click on it; a quad menu is displayed. Choose the **Hide Selection** option from it; the *flower vase* disappears temporarily from the viewports and now you can work easily in the viewports.

1. Activate the Top viewport. Choose **Create > Shapes** in the **Command Panel**; the **Splines** option is selected by default in the drop-down list below the **Shapes** button. Now, invoke the **Circle** tool from the **Object Type** rollout and create a circular spline.

2. In the **Parameters** rollout, set the radius of the circle to **11.662** in the **Radius** spinner. You may need to modify the radius according to the scene in the later section.

3. In the **Rendering** rollout, set the parameters as given next:

    Select the **Enable In Renderer** and **Enable In Viewport** check boxes.

Select the **Radial** radio button, if it is not already selected. Also, set the following parameters:

Thickness: **2.0** Sides: **15** Angle: **0.99**

Make sure that the **Auto Smooth** check box is selected.

4. The circular spline is automatically named as *Circle001*. Now, change its color by entering the values as given below:

   Red: **193** Green: **193** Blue: **193**

5. Next, create another circle in the Top viewport; it is automatically named as *Circle002*.
6. In the **Parameters** rollout, set the radius value of *Circle002*, which should be just the double of radius value of *Circle001*.
7. Now, change the color of *Circle002* to black.
8. Invoke the **Zoom Extents All** tool and align both the circles using the **Select and Move** tool, as shown in Figure 7-72.

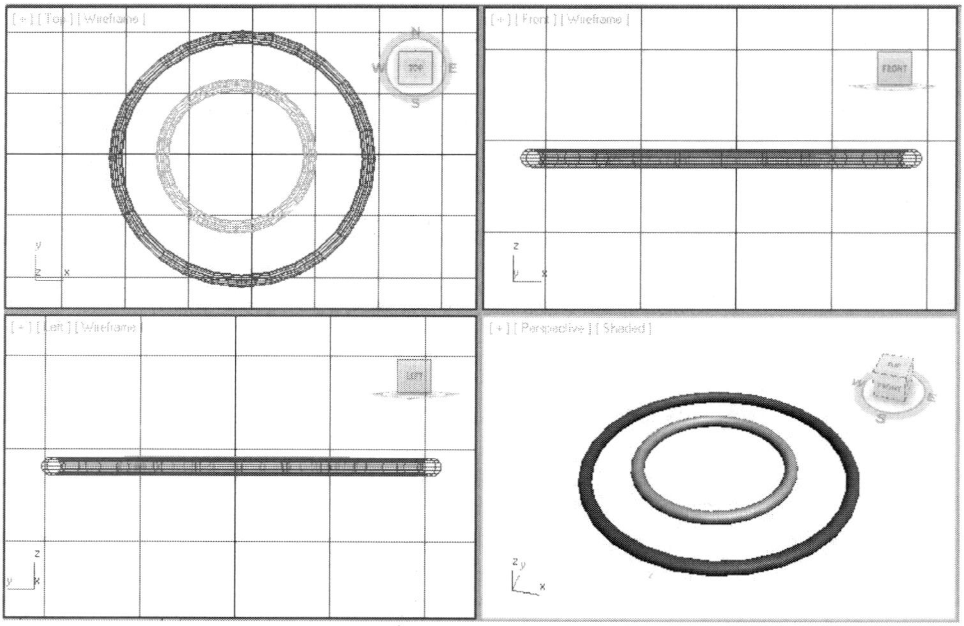

Figure 7-72 *Alignment of the circles in all viewports*

Note

When you set the parameters for a spline in the ***Rendering*** *rollout, they remain constant on creating another spline. Therefore, the new spline automatically takes the same parameters unless you change them.*

9. Invoke the **Line** tool from **Create > Shapes > Splines > Object Type** rollout.

10. In the **Creation Method** rollout, select the **Corner** radio button both in the **Initial Type** area and the **Drag Type** area.

11. Activate the Top viewport by right-clicking in it. Next, create four line splines to join both the circles, as shown in Figure 7-73.

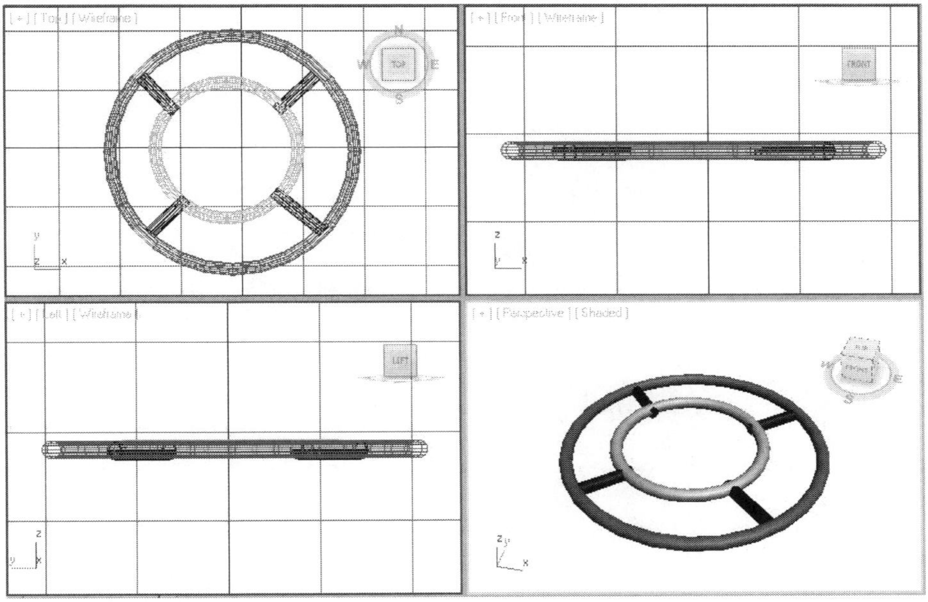

Figure 7-73 *The line splines created to join both the circles*

12. Assign the black color to all line splines.

13. Select the line splines and both the circles in any viewport by dragging a selection box around them, and then group them as *upper portion*.

14. Select the *upper portion* and hide it temporarily as described earlier. Then, invoke the **Zoom Extents All** tool.

    Next, you need to create the legs for the stand using the **Line** tool.

15. Activate the Front viewport. Next, invoke the **Line** tool from **Create > Shapes > Splines > Object Type** rollout.

16. In the **Creation Method** rollout, select the **Smooth** radio button both in the **Initial Type** area and the **Drag Type** area.

17. Next, create a line spline in the Front viewport, as shown in Figure 7-74. It takes the same parameters from the **Rendering** rollout that you had set earlier.

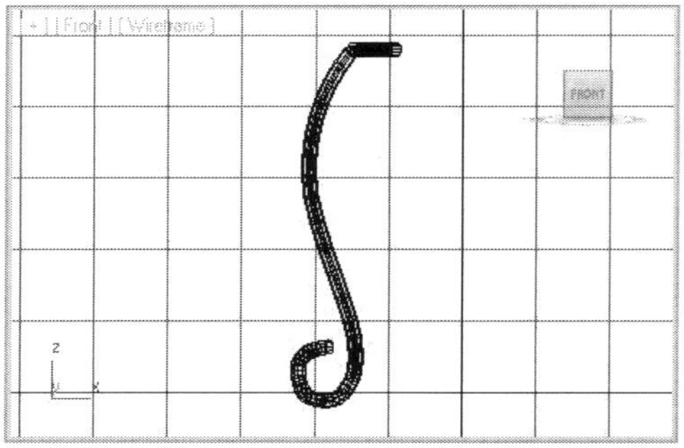

Figure 7-74 *The line spline for the leg of stand*

18. In the **Rendering** rollout, set the following parameters:

    Make sure that the **Enable In Renderer** and **Enable In Viewport** check boxes are selected.

    Select the **Rectangular** radio button and set the parameters as given below:

    Length: **2.0** Width: **1.5** Angle: **0.0**

    Also, make sure that the **Auto Smooth** check box is selected.

19. Name the line spline as *leg01* and change its color to black.

20. Next, right-click in any of the viewports; a quad menu is displayed. Choose the **Unhide by Name** option; the **Unhide Objects** dialog box is displayed. Select the *upper portion* from the list given in this dialog box and choose the **Unhide** button; the *upper portion* is now displayed in the viewport. Invoke the **Zoom Extents All** tool.

Note

You can resize the leg01 according to the size of the upper portion using the ***Select and Uniform Scale*** *tool.*

21. Now, align the *upper portion* and the *leg01* in all viewports, as shown in Figure 7-75.

    Next, you need to copy the *leg01* to create other legs.

22. Create three copies of the *leg01*; they are automatically named as *leg002, leg003,* and *leg004*.

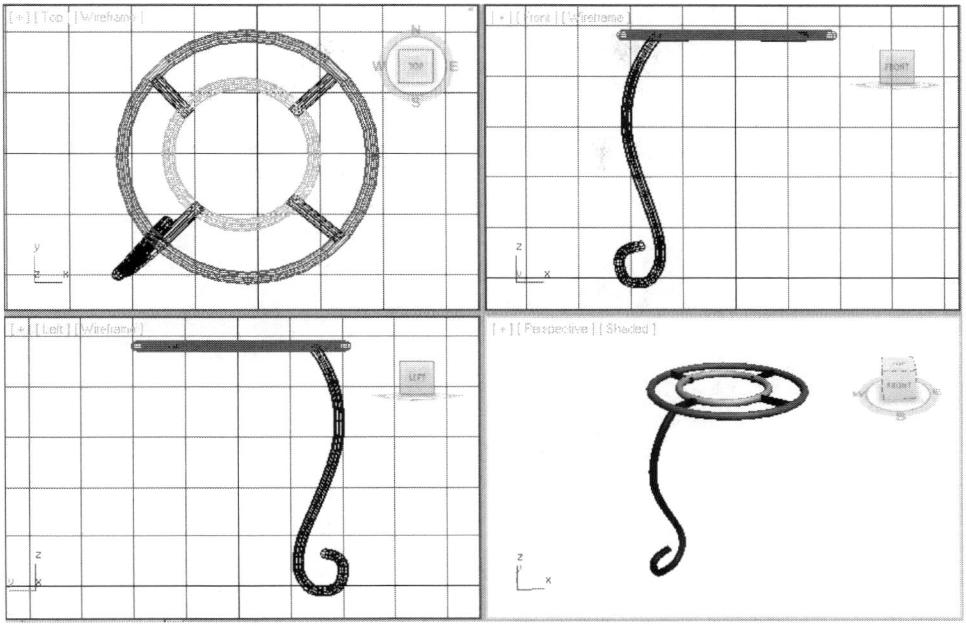

Figure 7-75 *Alignment of the upper portion and the leg01 in all viewports*

23. Align the *leg01*, *leg002*, *leg003*, and *leg004* using the **Select and Move** and **Select and Rotate** tools, as shown in Figure 7-76.

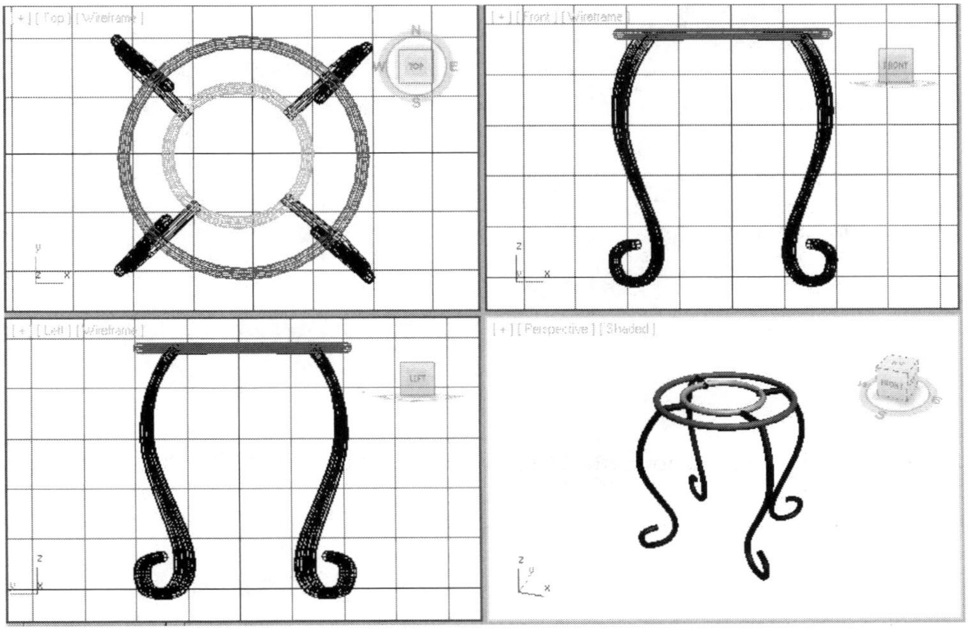

Figure 7-76 *Alignment of the leg01, leg02, leg03, and leg04 in all viewports*

24. Select all objects in the viewport and group them as *vase stand*.

25. Next, right-click in any viewport; a quad menu is displayed. Choose the **Unhide All** option; all the hidden objects are displayed in the viewports.

26. Align the *flower vase* and the *vase stand*, as shown in Figure 7-77.

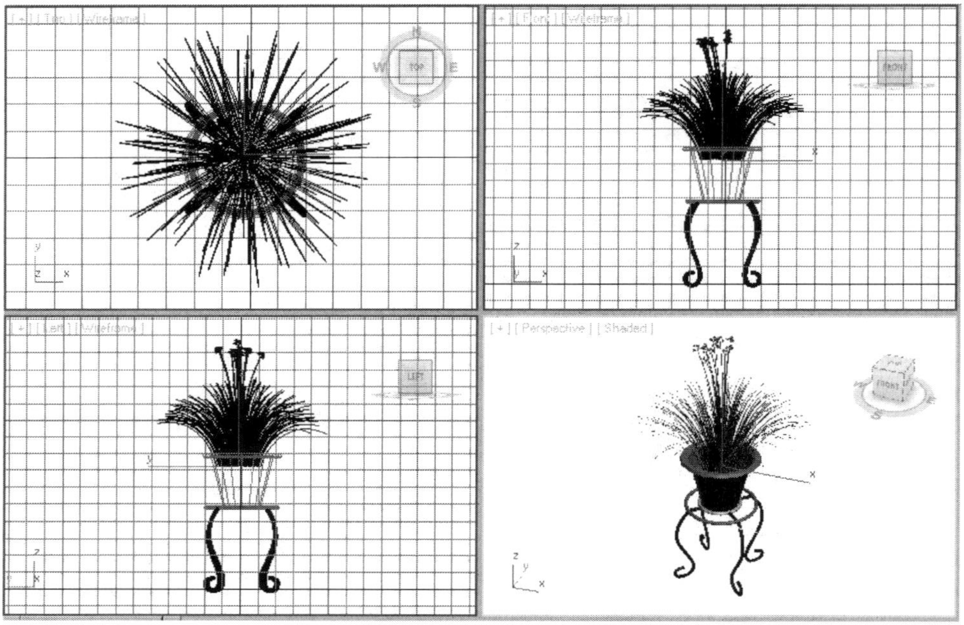

Figure 7-77 *Alignment of the flower vase and the vase stand in all viewports*

Note

You can adjust the size of the flower vase according to the size of the vase stand using the ***Select and Uniform Scale*** *tool.*

Rendering the Scene for the Final Output

1. Activate the Perspective viewport and render it as discussed in Tutorial 1.

   You can view the final rendered image of this model by downloading the *c07_3dsmax_2012_render.zip* file from *http://www.cadcim.com*.

Saving the File

1. Save the file with the name *c07tut2.max* as discussed in earlier chapters. The location of this file is given below:

   \Documents\3dsmax\c07_tut2\scenes

Self-Evaluation Test

Answer the following questions and then compare them to those given at the end of this chapter:

1. Which of the following modifiers is used to convert 2D splines into 3D mesh objects?

   (a) **Bend** (b) **Lathe**
   (c) **Taper** (d) All of these

2. Which of the following options is used to modify the 2D splines at advanced level?

   (a) **Convert to Editable Patch** (b) **Convert to Editable Spline**
   (c) **Convert to Editable Poly** (d) **Convert to Editable Mesh**

3. Which of the following sub-object levels is not a part of editable spline objects?

   (a) **Border** (b) **Segment**
   (c) **Vertex** (d) **Spline**

4. Which of the following tools is used to create a spline that has all sub-object levels by default and you do not need to convert it into the editable spline object?

   (a) **Circle** (b) **Line**
   (c) **Helix** (d) **Star**

5. Which of the following buttons in the **Geometry** rollout is used to create a new line that will be automatically attached to a selected spline?

   (a) **Attach** (b) **Attach Mult.**
   (c) **Refine** (d) **Create Line**

6. The __________ button in the **Geometry** rollout is used to add new vertices to a selected spline in the viewport.

7. The __________ button in the **Geometry** rollout is used to join multiple vertices into a single vertex.

8. The __________ button in the **Geometry** rollout is used to make any vertex of a spline as the first vertex.

9. The pivot point of an object represents its local center. (T/F)

10. The **Weld** button is used to move all selected vertices of a spline to their average center. (T/F)

Review Questions

Answer the following questions:

1. Which of the following buttons in the **Geometry** rollout of an editable spline object is used to create the round corners of a spline by creating two new vertices?

   (a) **Fillet** (b) **Fuse**
   (c) **Chamfer** (d) All of these

2. Which of the following buttons in the **Geometry** rollout of an editable spline object is used to sub-divide the selected segment by inserting a value for the number of vertices in the spinner on the right side of that button?

   (a) **Refine** (b) **Insert**
   (c) **Divide** (d) All of these

3. Which of the following buttons in the **Geometry** rollout of an editable spline object is used to separate the selected sub-objects from the original one and create a new shape?

   (a) **Attach** (b) **Delete**
   (c) **Detach** (d) **Divide**

4. The **Reverse** button is used to display the number of vertices in the viewport. (T/F)

5. To perform the boolean operation, the two splines must be closed, attached, and must intersect with each other. (T/F)

6. The **Mirror** button is used to create a copy of the spline. (T/F)

7. To attach a number of objects simultaneously to the selected object, you need to select the **Attach Mult.** button in the **Geometry** rollout. (T/F)

8. The **Weld** button is available only for the __________ sub-object level.

9. The __________ button is used to create the outline of an object.

10. The __________button is used to break up a spline into a number of splines.

Exercises

Exercise 1

Start Autodesk 3ds Max 2012 and perform the following operations:

1. Choose **Create > Shapes** in the **Command Panel**; the **Splines** option is selected by default in the drop-down list below the **Shapes** button. Now, invoke any of the tools from the **Object Type** rollout and create the corresponding spline in the viewport. Convert the spline into an editable spline object.

2. Select the **Vertex** sub-object level in the modifier stack, choose the **Create Line** button in the **Geometry** rollout, and add the new spline in the viewport.

3. Choose the **Refine** button in the **Geometry** rollout and insert a new vertex in the spline. Next, choose the **Insert** button in the **Geometry** rollout and insert a new vertex and notice the difference.

4. Select the sub-objects levels in the modifier stack one by one and notice the changes in the rollouts displayed. Also, try to create different objects using different buttons available in the rollouts that are displayed after selecting the sub-object level.

5. Create two closed, attached, and intersecting splines in the viewport and then convert them into editable splines. Next, select the **Spline** sub-object level in the modifier stack and try to perform different boolean operations using the **Union**, **Subtraction**, and **Intersection** buttons in the **Geometry** rollout. Notice the difference.

6. Try to use different buttons in the **Edit Geometry** rollout and notice the advance modifications in the splines.

Exercise 2

Create the model shown in Figure 7-78 using your own dimensions.

(Expected time: 15 min)

Figure 7-78 *Model for Exercise 2*

Exercise 3

Create the models shown in Figure 7-79 using your own dimensions.

(Expected time: 15 min)

Figure 7-79 *Models for Exercise 3*

Exercise 4

Create the model shown in Figure 7-80 using your own dimensions.

(Expected time: 15 min)

Figure 7-80 *Model for Exercise 4*

Exercise 5

Create the models shown in Figure 7-81 using your own dimensions.

(Expected time: 15 min)

Figure 7-81 *Models for Exercise 5*

You can view the final rendered image of these exercises by downloading them from *http://www.cadcim.com*.

Answers to Self-Evaluation Test

1. b, **2.** b, **3.** a, **4.** b, **5.** d, **6. Refine**, **7. Weld**, **8. Make First**, **9.** T, **10.** F

8

Materials and Maps

Learning Objectives

After completing this chapter, you will be able to:

- *Use the Material Editor tool*
- *Understand the types of materials and maps*
- *Create materials and maps*
- *Assign materials to objects*

INTRODUCTION

In this chapter, you will learn to assign various materials and maps to the objects in a scene to make it more realistic. To do so, you need to use the **Material Editor** tool from the **Main Toolbar**, which is discussed next.

MATERIAL EDITOR

Menu bar: Rendering > Material Editor > Compact/Slate Material Editor
Main Toolbar: Material Editor flyout > Compact/Slate Material Editor
Keyboard: M

In Autodesk 3ds Max, there are two types of material editors, Slate material editor and Compact material editor. You can use any of these material editors to create new materials and maps, modify the existing materials, apply these new materials and maps to the models in the scene, and create a new environment for the scene.

The Slate material editor is mostly used to design the materials of your choice. It uses nodes and wiring to graphically display the design of the materials created by you. The Compact material editor is more useful when you just need to apply the materials to the objects that have already been designed. In this chapter, you will learn about the Compact material editor.

To create a new material, press the M key; the **Slate Material Editor** dialog box will be displayed, as shown in Figure 8-1. Next, if you choose **Modes > Compact Material Editor** from the material editor menu bar; the **Material Editor** dialog box will be displayed, as shown in Figure 8-2. The title bar of the **Material Editor** dialog box displays the number and name of the current material, which gets changed depending on the material that you select. The **Material Editor** dialog box is divided into various parts, refer to Figure 8-2. These parts are discussed next.

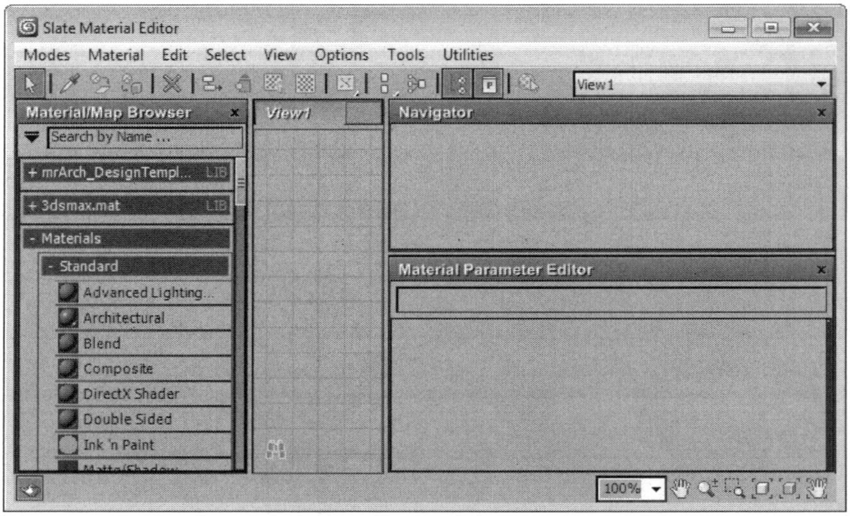

*Figure 8-1 The **Slate Material Editor** dialog box*

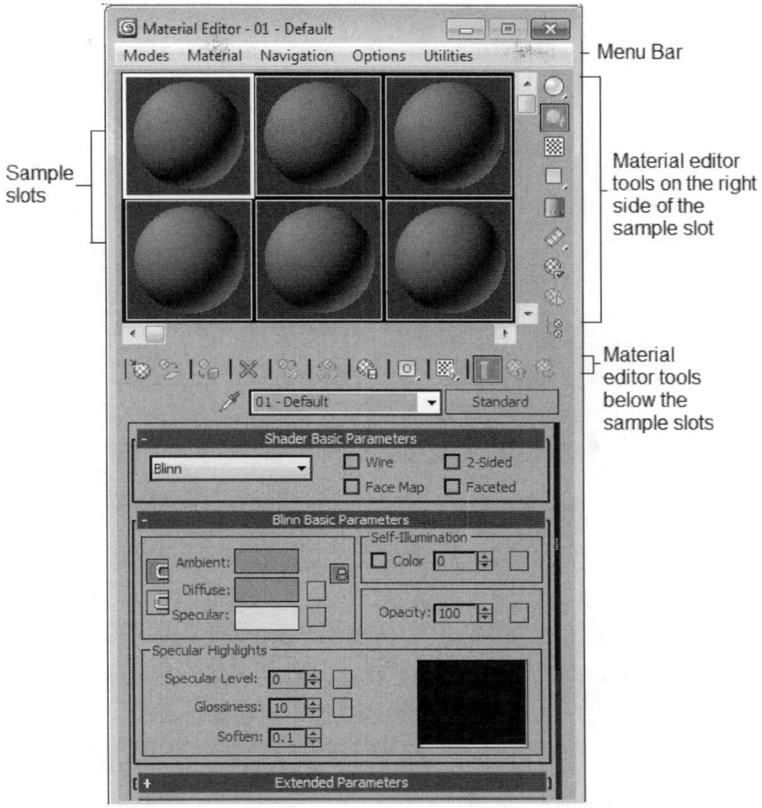

Figure 8-2 Partial view of the ***Material Editor*** *dialog box*

Note

When you press the M key, the material editor that you opened last in Autodesk 3ds Max will be displayed. However, if you press the M key for the first time in Autodesk 3ds Max, then the Slate material editor will be displayed.

Menu Bar

The menu bar is located at the top of the **Material Editor** dialog box. It consists of various pull-down menus such as **Material**, **Navigation**, and so on. The options in these pull-down menus are used to invoke various tools. These tools can also be invoked using the options available below as well as on the right side of the sample slots in the **Material Editor** dialog box, refer to Figure 8-2.

Sample Slots

The sample slots in the **Material Editor** dialog box are used to preview the material or the maps that you will assign to the objects in the viewport. By default, there are 24 sample slots and each sample slot represents a single material or map. You can view only six sample slots at a time. To view other sample slots, you need to scroll the scroll bar available on the right, and just below the sample slots. You can also increase the number of visible sample slots.

To do so, select one of the sample slots; it will be surrounded by a white colored boundary and will get activated. Next, right-click on the active sample slot; a shortcut menu will be displayed, as shown in Figure 8-3. By default, the **3x2 Sample Windows** option is chosen in the shortcut menu. Next, choose the required option; the number of visible sample slots will be increased accordingly, refer to Figures 8-4 and 8-5.

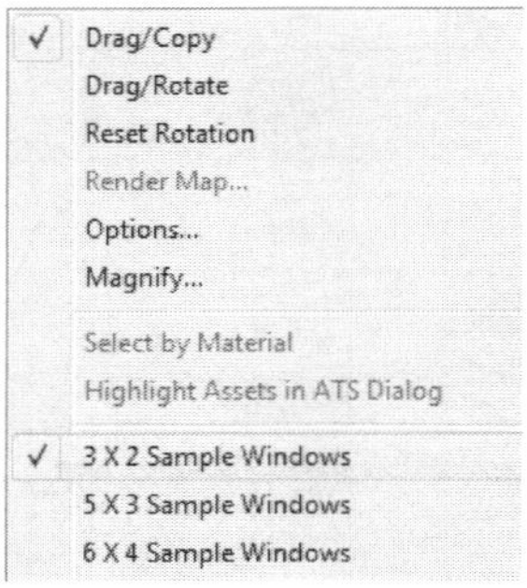

Figure 8-3 *The shortcut menu displayed*

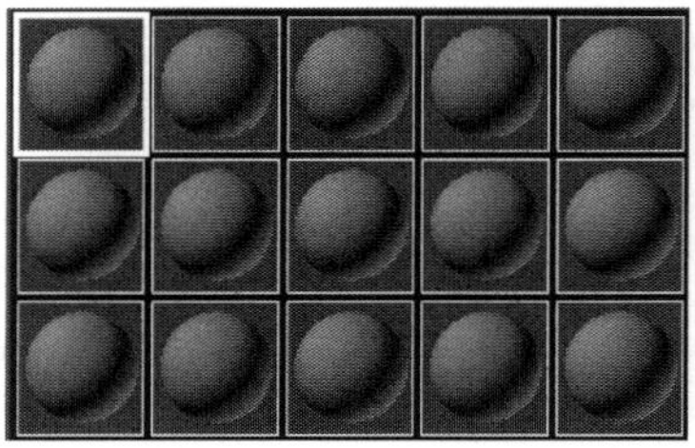

Figure 8-4 *The sample slots after choosing the **5x3 Sample Windows** option*

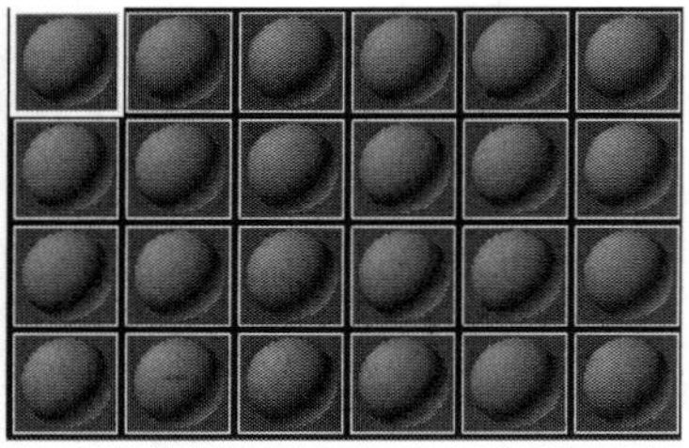

Figure 8-5 *The sample slots after choosing the **6x4 Sample Windows** option*

In the shortcut menu, the **Drag/Copy** option is also chosen by default. It is used to copy the material or the map from one sample slot to another. To do so, select the sample slot whose material or map you want to copy. Now, press and hold the left mouse button on it, drag it to another sample slot, and then release the left mouse button; the same material or the map will be copied to the other sample slot, as shown in Figures 8-6 and 8-7.

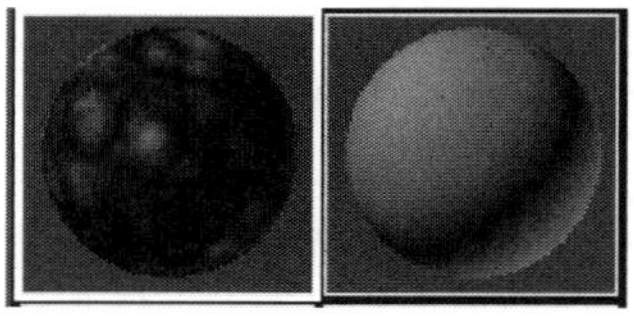

Figure 8-6 *Two sample slots in the **Material Editor** dialog box*

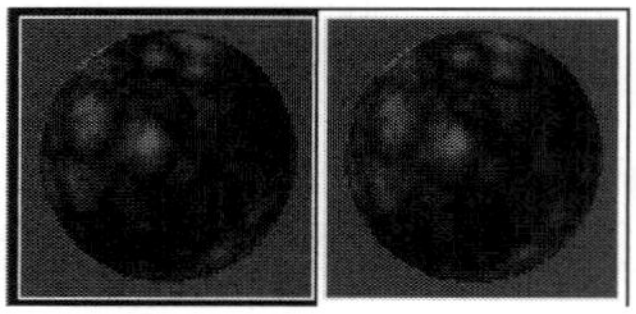

Figure 8-7 *The map/material of one sample slot copied to the other*

When you choose the **Drag/Rotate** option in the shortcut menu, the shape of the cursor is changed. Now, you can view the material map on the sample slot by rotating it. The **Reset Rotation** option in the shortcut menu is used to reset the sample slot to its default orientation. By default, the **Render Map** option in the shortcut menu is not activated. It will be activated, when you assign a map to the sample slot. This option is used to render the map in the selected sample slot by creating a bitmap or an *avi* file (if the map is animated). When you choose the **Options** option, the **Material Editor Options** dialog box is displayed. The options in this dialog box are used to modify the sample slots.

Choose the **Magnify** option; the selected sample slot will be displayed in a separate window, as shown in Figure 8-8. Alternatively, double-click on the selected sample slot to display it in a separate window. To resize the window, move the cursor at the bottom of the window; the cursor will change to an arrow, as shown in Figure 8-8. Now, drag the cursor to resize the window.

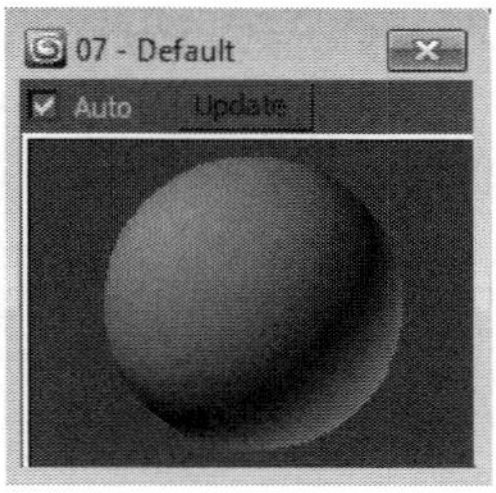

Figure 8-8 *The sample slot displayed in a separate window*

Material Editor Tools

The material editor tools are used to modify the default settings of the selected sample slot, and apply the materials or the maps to the objects. These tools are available below as well as on the right side of the sample slots in the **Material Editor** dialog box. The most commonly used tools are discussed next.

Get Material

Material Editor Menu:	Material > Get Material
Material Toolbar:	Get Material
Keyboard:	G

The **Get Material** tool is used to get a material or a map for the selected sample slot. Materials affect the color, opacity, glossiness, and other physical properties of objects.

To get a material, select one of the sample slots to activate it. Invoke the **Get Material** tool available below the sample slots; the **Material/Map Browser** dialog box with a list of materials and maps will be displayed, as shown in Figure 8-9. You can collapse and expand this list as per your requirement. Now, double-click on one of the materials or maps from the list; the default material will be replaced by the new material or map. Also, the new material will be displayed on the sample slot in the **Sample Slots** rollout of the **Material/Map Browser** dialog box. The **Material/Map Browser** dialog box is discussed next.

Note

*The shortcut key G mentioned above will work only if the **Keyboard Shortcut Override Toggle** tool in the **Main Toolbar** is activated and the **Material Editor** dialog box is displayed.*

Material/Map Browser

The **Material/Map Browser** dialog box is used to select different types of materials and maps from the lists displayed in it. Various options in this dialog box are discussed next.

Search by Name

The **Search by Name** text box is located on the top of this dialog box. It is used to search and select the name of the materials or the maps. For example, enter the alphabet **d** in this text box; a drop-down list of all the materials and maps starting with the alphabet d will be displayed, as shown in Figure 8-10. Next, double-click on the required material or map; it will be displayed on the selected sample slot. Now, choose the **Clear Results** button on the right side of the text box; the drop-down list will be cleared.

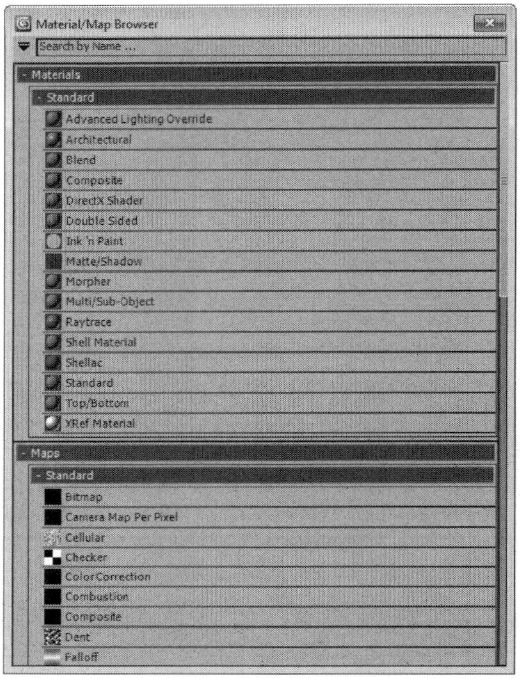

*Figure 8-9 Partial view of the rollouts in the **Material/Map Browser** dialog box*

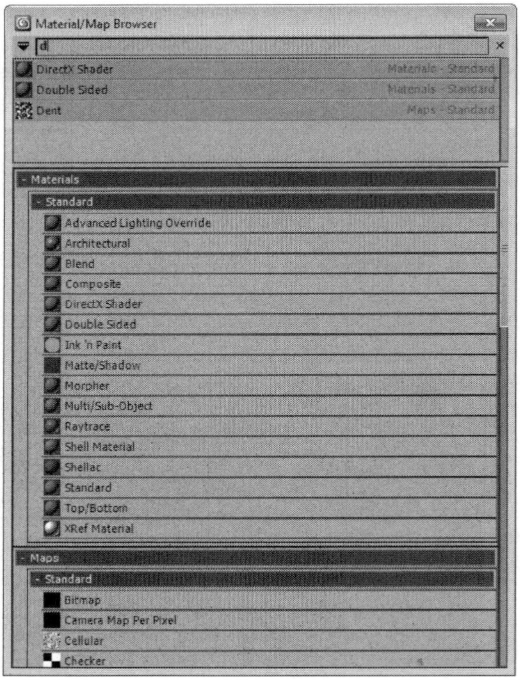

*Figure 8-10 The drop-down list displayed after entering the alphabet **d** in the text box*

Material/Map Browser Options

The **Material/Map Browser Options** button is located on the left of the **Search by Name** text box. Choose the **Material/Map Browser Options** button; a flyout with various options will be displayed, as shown in Figure 8-11. The options in the shortcut menu are used to manage the **Material/Map Browser** dialog box based on the requirement. Also, they will help to create new material library, manage Autodesk material library, and so on. These options are discussed next.

The **New Group** option is used to create a new group and add it to the **Material/Map Browser** dialog box. To do so, select the **New Group** option from the shortcut menu; the **Create New Group** dialog box will be displayed, as shown in Figure 8-12. Type a name of your choice in the text box and choose the **OK** button; a new group with the specified name will be displayed in the **Material/Map Browser** dialog box. You can expand and collapse the group based on your requirement.

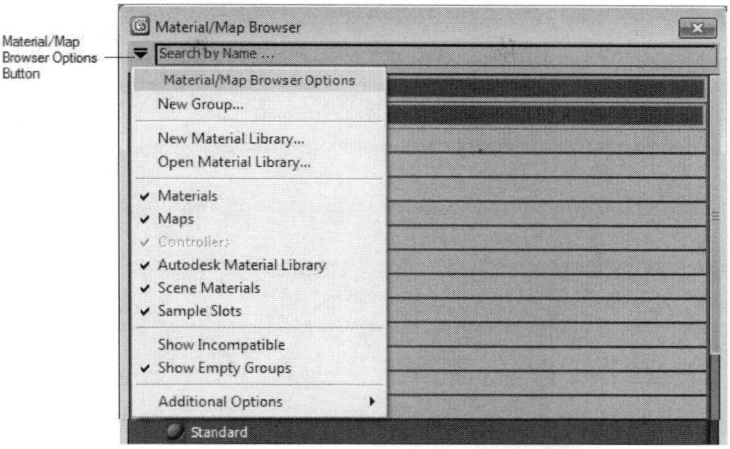

Figure 8-11 *The flyout displayed after choosing the* ***Material/Map Browser Options*** *button*

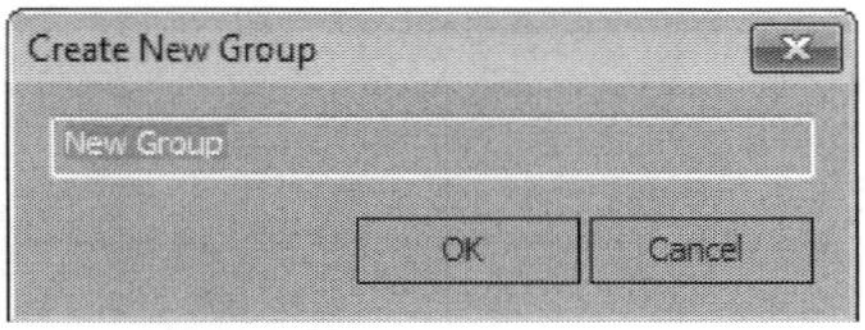

Figure 8-12 *The* ***Create New Group*** *dialog box*

When you install Autodesk 3ds Max, the material library will automatically get installed on your system in the **.mat* format. To select the material library of your choice, choose the **Open Material Library** option from the shortcut menu; the **Import Material Library** dialog box will be displayed. Navigate to the location *Program Files\Autodesk\3ds Max 2012\materiallibraries*; the material libraries will be displayed in the **Import Material Library** dialog box, as shown in Figure 8-13. Next, select the required material and choose the **Open** button; all materials of the selected material library will be displayed in the **Material/ Map Browser** dialog box in a group, as shown in Figure 8-14.

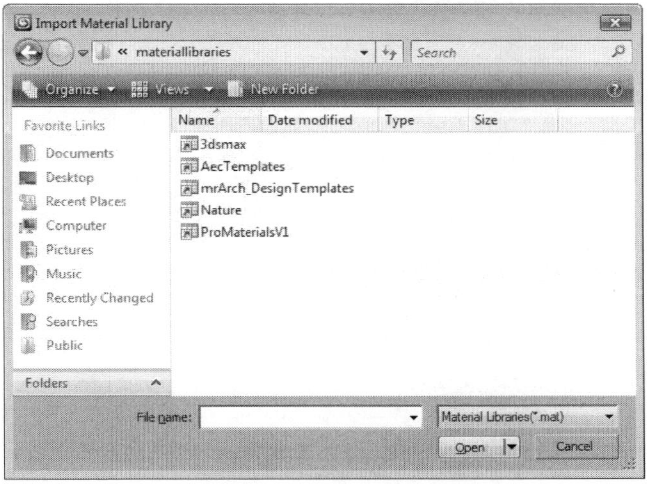

Figure 8-13 *The* ***Import Material Library*** *dialog box*

You can also create a new library to put all materials and maps defined in the sample slots of the current file. To create a new library, choose the **New Material Library** option from the shortcut menu; the **Create New Material Library** dialog box will be displayed, as shown in Figure 8-15. Type a name in the text box and choose the **OK** button; a new library with the specified name will be displayed in the **Material/Map Browser** dialog box. You can expand and collapse it based on your requirement. Next, you can put the materials defined in the sample slots to the new library using the **Put To Library** tool in the **Material Editor** dialog box, about which you will learn later in this chapter.

When you create a new library using the **New Material Library** option, the newly created library will have a default name and location assigned to it. To modify the name and location, right-click on the title bar of the new library in the **Material/Map Browser** dialog box; a shortcut menu will be displayed, as shown in Figure 8-16. Now, choose the **Save As** option from the shortcut menu; the **Export Material Library** dialog box will be displayed. Next, navigate to the location where you want to save the new library. Also, type a new name in the **File name** text box and make sure that the **Material Libraries (*.mat)** option is selected in the **Save as type** drop-down list. Now, choose the **Save** button; the new library will be saved at the specified location. You can use the newly created library in another scene.

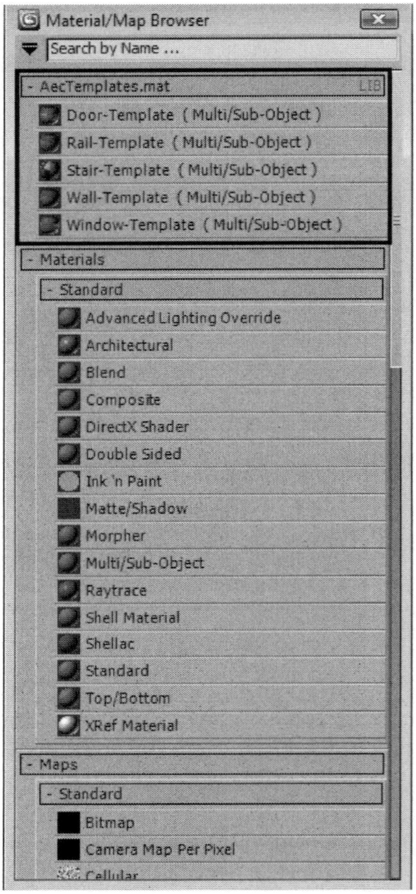

***Figure 8-14** The materials displayed in the **Material/Map Browser** dialog box*

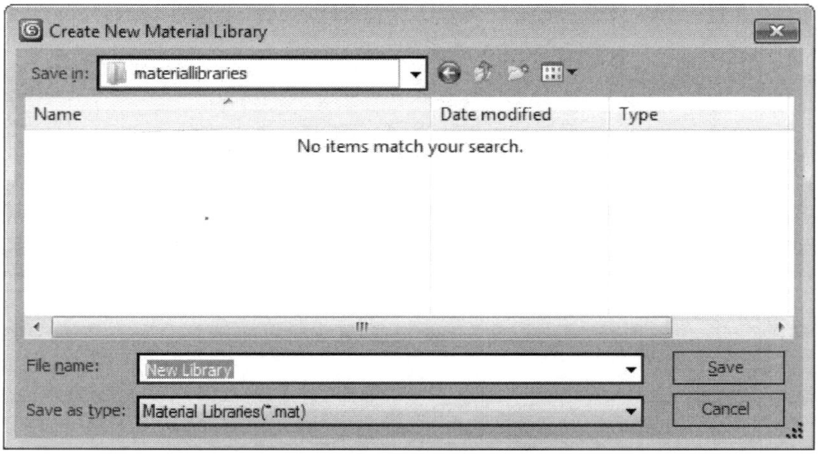

***Figure 8-15** The **Create New Material Library** dialog box*

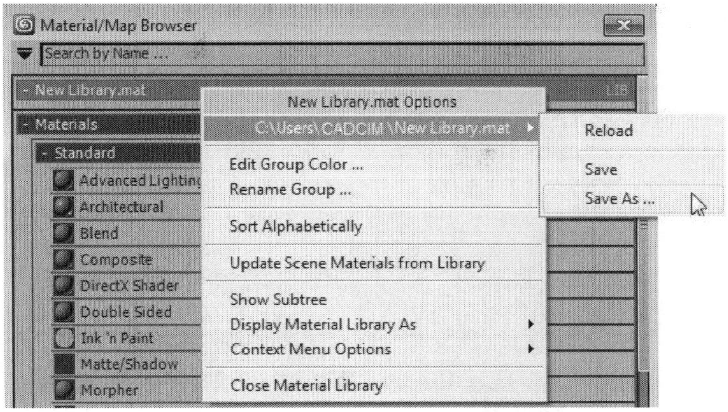

Figure 8-16 *The shortcut menu displayed*

There are various groups such as **Materials**, **Maps**, **Scene Materials**, and **Sample Slots** in the **Material/Map Browser** dialog box. You can toggle the display of these groups by choosing the respective option from the shortcut menu.

You can also reset the **Material/Map Browser** to its default appearance. To do so, choose the **Additional Options** option from the shortcut menu; a cascading menu will be displayed. Now, choose the **Reset Material/Map Browser** option; the **Reset Material/Map Browser** message box will be displayed. Choose the **Yes** button; the **Material/Map Browser** dialog box will be reset to its default appearance.

Assign Material to Selection

Material Editor Menu:	Material > Assign to Selection
Toolbar:	Assign Material to Selection

The **Assign Material to Selection** tool is used to assign the material or map of the active sample slot to the selected object in the viewport. When you invoke the **Assign Material to Selection** tool, the active sample slot will be surrounded by four triangular faces at corners, as shown in Figure 8-17.

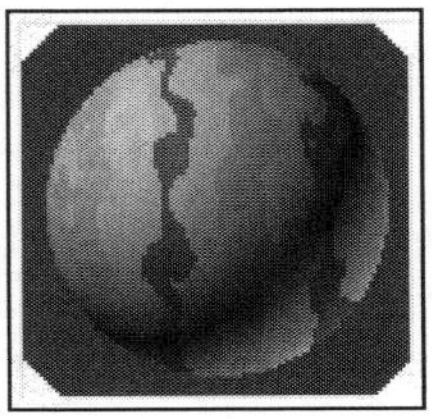

Figure 8-17 *The triangular faces in a sample slot*

To assign a material to the selected object in the viewport, select the sample slot to which you have already assigned the material or map. Next, select the object to which you need to assign the material in the viewport. You can also select more than one object to assign the same material to all of them. Then, choose the **Assign Material to Selection** button in the **Material Editor** dialog box. Alternatively, you can drag the material from the sample slot to the selected object in the viewport to assign it. Note that you need to choose the **Show Shaded Material in Viewport** tool in the **Material Editor** dialog box to view the assigned material in the viewport, if not already chosen. You will learn more about this tool later in the chapter.

Reset Map/Mtl to Default Settings

Toolbar: Reset Map/Mtl to Default Settings

The **Reset Map/Mtl to Default Settings** tool is used to reset the values that were assigned to the map or material in the active sample slot using various rollouts displayed in the **Material Editor** dialog box.

Put to Library

Material Editor Menu: Material > Put to Library
Toolbar: Put to Library

The **Put to Library** tool is used to add the selected material to the temporary library or the library created by you. To do so, select the sample slot that has the material that you want to add to the library. If you have not created a new library then on invoking the **Put to Library** tool, the **Material Editor** message box will be displayed, as shown in Figure 8-18. In this message box, you will be prompted to specify if you want to put the entire material/map tree to the library. Choose the required option from it; the **Put to Library** dialog box will be displayed. In the **Name** text box, enter a new name of the material and choose the **OK** button; the material will be saved in the temporary library. Also, the **Temporary Library** rollout will be displayed in the **Material/Map Browser** dialog box.

If you have already created a library, then on invoking the **Put to Library** tool, the **Material Editor** message box is displayed, refer to Figure 8-18. In this message box, you will be prompted to specify if you want to put the entire material/map tree to the library. Choose the required option from it; a shortcut menu will be displayed consisting of the name of the library and the temporary library. Next, choose the library in which you want to put the material; the **Put to Library** dialog box will be displayed. In the **Name** text box, enter a new name of the material and choose the **OK** button; the material will be saved in the newly created library you specified. Also, the newly created library rollout will be displayed in the **Material/Map Browser** dialog box.

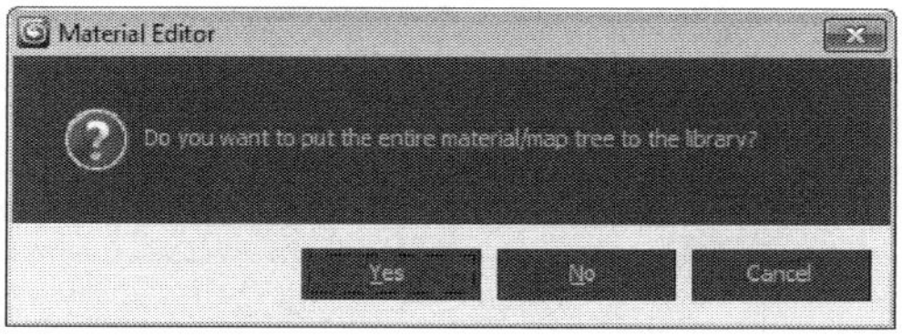

***Figure 8-18** The **Material Editor** message box*

Show Shaded Material in Viewport

Toolbar: Show Shaded Material in Viewport

The **Show Shaded Material in Viewport** tool is used to display the assigned material or map to the selected object in the viewport. To do so, select the object in the viewport and assign the material to it. Then, invoke the **Show Shaded Material in Viewport** tool; the material will be displayed in the selected object in the viewport.

Go to Parent

Material Editor Menu:	Navigation > Go to Parent
Toolbar:	Go to Parent
Keyboard:	Up Arrow key

The **Go to Parent** tool is used to go one level up in the current material.

Go Forward to Sibling

Material Editor Menu:	Navigation > Go Forward to Sibling
Toolbar:	Go Forward to Sibling
Keyboard:	Right Arrow key

The **Go Forward to Sibling** tool is used to go to the next map or material at the same level in the current material. This tool is active in compound materials such as **Composite** material, **Blend** material, and so on. These materials are discussed later in the chapter.

Sample Type

Toolbar:	Sample Type

The **Sample Type** flyout has three options: sphere, cylinder, and cube. These options are used to choose the geometry type to be displayed in the active sample slot. By default, the material will be displayed on a spherical sample slot. But, you can change the geometry to cylinder or cube.

Backlight

Material Editor Menu:	Options > Backlight
Toolbar:	Backlight
Keyboard:	L

The **Backlight** tool is invoked by default. It is used to insert the backside light into the active sample slot, refer to Figures 8-19 and 8-20.

Figure 8-19 *The effect of the* ***Backlight*** *tool in the sample slot*

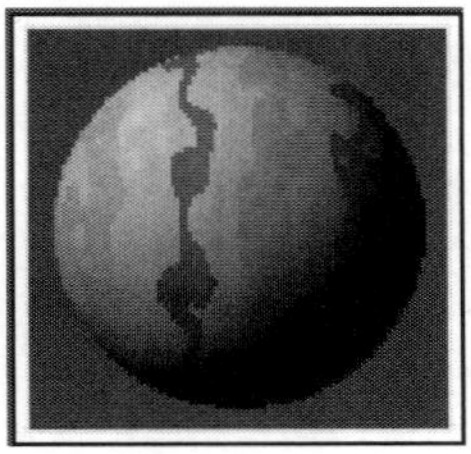

Figure 8-20 *The sample slot without the Backlight effect*

Background

Material Editor Menu:	Options > Background
Toolbar:	Background
Keyboard:	B

The **Background** tool is used to add a multicolored background in the active sample slot, refer to Figures 8-21 and 8-22.

Figure 8-21 *The **Background** tool invoked in the sample slot*

Figure 8-22 *The sample slot without invoking the **Background** tool*

Sample UV Tiling

Toolbar:	Sample UV Tiling

The buttons in the **Sample UV Tiling** flyout are used to set the number of times the map will be repeated on the active sample slot. To set the tiling pattern, this flyout has four buttons, 1x1, 2x2, 3x3, and 4x4. When you set the tiling pattern, it will not affect the object in the viewport. This pattern will be displayed only in the active sample slot, refer to Figures 8-23, 8-24, and 8-25.

Figure 8-23 *The 1x1 sample UV tiling in a cube sample slot*

Figure 8-24 *The 2x2 sample UV tiling in a cube sample slot*

Figure 8-25 *The 3x3 sample UV tiling in a cube sample slot*

Pick Material From Object

The **Pick Material From Object** tool is used to pick the material from the object in the viewport and apply it to the active sample slot. To do so, select the sample slot to activate it and invoke the **Pick Material From Object** tool; the shape of the cursor will be changed to an eye dropper. Now, move the cursor over the object in the viewport from which you want to pick the material and click on the object; the selected sample slot will display the same material.

You can change the name of a material of each sample slot by entering a new name in the **Material Name** text box on the right of the **Pick Material From Object** tool. The **Material Type** button on the right of the **Material Name** text box displays the name of the material that you get from the **Material/Map Browser** dialog box, refer to Figure 8-26.

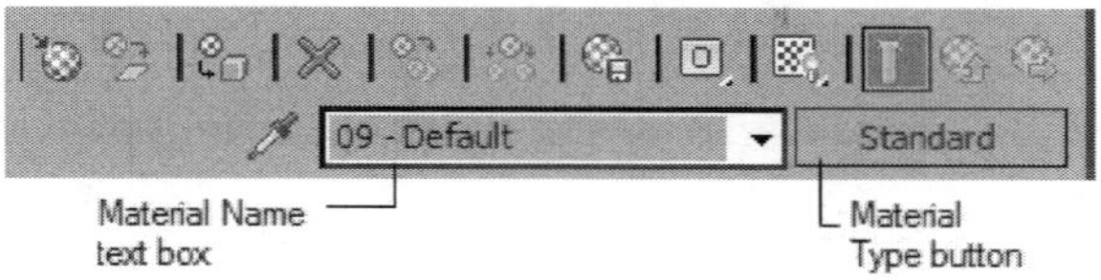

***Figure 8-26** The **Material Name** text box and the **Material Type** button*

MATERIALS

In this section, you will learn to create materials and assign them to the objects to make them more realistic using the **Material Editor** tool. The materials assigned to the objects give the best results with lights, about which you will learn in the later chapters. In Autodesk 3ds Max, you can create and assign various materials to the objects using the **Material Editor** tool from the **Main Toolbar**, which are discussed next.

TYPES OF MATERIALS

In Autodesk 3ds Max, invoke the **Material Editor** tool to select a material; the **Material Editor** dialog box will be displayed. Now, choose the **Material Type** button on the right side of the **Material Name** text box, refer to Figure 8-26; the **Material/Map Browser** dialog box will be displayed. Next, expand the **Materials > Standard** rollouts, if they are not already expanded; a list of 16 types of materials will be displayed. In this list, there are some materials that can combine other materials in them. These are known as Compound materials. These are **Blend**, **Composite**, **Double-Sided**, **Morpher**, **Multi/Sub-Object**, **Shellac**, and **Top/Bottom**. Select the material that you require from the list and choose the **OK** button; the name of the selected material will be displayed on the **Material Type** button in the **Material Editor** dialog box. Also, the rollouts related to that material will be displayed in the **Material Editor** dialog box. You can modify the material using the parameters available in these rollouts. The most commonly used materials are discussed next.

Note

*You can also get the default materials using the **Get Material** tool in the **Material Editor** dialog box as discussed earlier in this chapter.*

Standard Material

By default, the **Standard** material is selected in the **Material Editor** dialog box. Various rollouts are also displayed below the **Material Type** button to create new materials or modify the properties of the current materials. The most commonly used rollouts are discussed next.

Shader Basic Parameters Rollout

The options in this rollout are used to specify the shading types and other properties for the material, refer to Figure 8-27. Select the **Wire** check box in this rollout to render the material as wireframe, as shown in Figure 8-28. Select the **2-Sided** check box to apply the material to both sides of the selected faces at rendering. Select the **Face Map** check box to apply the maps or images to each face of the object, as shown in Figure 8-29. Select the **Faceted** check box to create a faceted object, as shown in Figure 8-30. In this case, each face of the surface will be rendered as flat face.

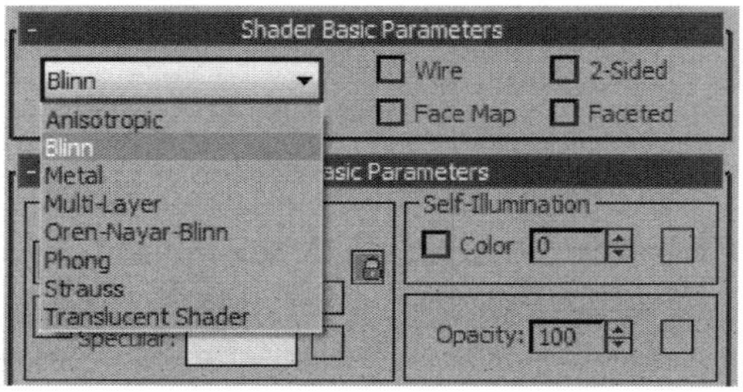

Figure 8-27 *The **Shader Basic Parameters** rollout with eight shaders displayed in the drop-down list*

Figure 8-28 *The sphere with the **Wire** check box selected*

Figure 8-29 *The sphere with the **Face Map** check box selected*

Figure 8-30 *The sphere with the **Faceted** check box selected*

Note

*1. To view the effect of the selection of the **Face Map** or **Faceted** check box on an object, you need to assign an image or a map to the object. You will learn more about assigning an image or a map to the object later in this chapter.*

*2. You can see the effect of the selection of the **Faceted** check box only in rendering.*

There are eight types of shaders in the drop-down list located on the top of this rollout, refer to Figure 8-26. These shaders provide different effects to the material at rendering. Various shaders and their rollouts are discussed next.

Anisotropic Shader

The **Anisotropic** shader is used to create elliptical highlights, as shown in Figure 8-31. This shader is suitable for creating glasses, brushed metals, grass, and so on. To assign this shader to the material, you need to select the **Anisotropic** option from the drop-down list in the **Shader Basic Parameters** rollout. On doing so, the **Anisotropic Basic Parameters** rollout will be displayed below the **Shader Basic Parameters** rollout, as shown in Figure 8-32. This rollout is discussed next.

Figure 8-31 *The sphere with* ***Anisotropic*** *shader*

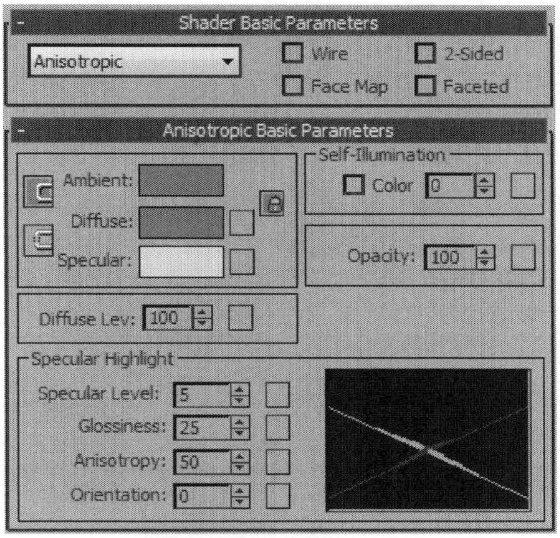

Figure 8-32 *The* ***Anisotropic Basic Parameters*** *rollout*

Note

To view the effects of shaders, you need to set the parameters in the ***Basic Parameters*** *rollout of the corresponding shader.*

Anisotropic Basic Parameters Rollout

The options in the **Anisotropic Basic Parameters** rollout are used to set the colors, transparency, shininess, and so on of the material.

The **Ambient**, **Diffuse**, and **Specular** color swatches are used to set the colors of the material. The **Ambient** color swatch is used to specify the color of an object in shadow. It is usually the darkest component of the material. The **Diffuse** color swatch is used to specify the color of an object in direct light. It is the main color of the material. The **Specular** color swatch is used to specify the color of the highlight or the shiny part of the material, refer to Figure 8-33.

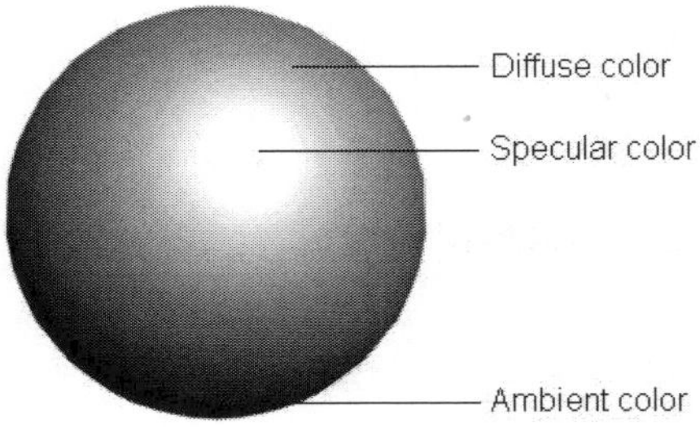

Figure 8-33 *The ambient, diffuse, and specular colors in a sphere*

To set the color of the material, select one of the color swatches; the **Color Selector** dialog box will be displayed along with the name of the color swatch that you have selected. Select a color and choose the **OK** button; the selected color will be displayed in the color swatch and the active sample slot.

Self-Illumination Area

The **Self-Illumination** area is used to replace the shadow on the surface of the material with the color used in the **Diffuse** color swatch. It creates an illusion of light being generated from the material. The value of the spinner in the **Self-Illumination** area specifies the percentage of shadow replaced with the color. To set the illumination of the object, select the **Color** check box in this area; the spinner on its right will be replaced by a color swatch. You can change the intensity as well as the color for the self-illumination using the color swatch. Choose the color swatch in the **Self-Illumination** area; the **Color Selector: Self Illum Color** dialog box will be displayed. As you increase the value in the **Value** spinner, the intensity of the material also increases, refer to Figures 8-34 and 8-35.

Figure 8-34 *A sphere without self-illumination*

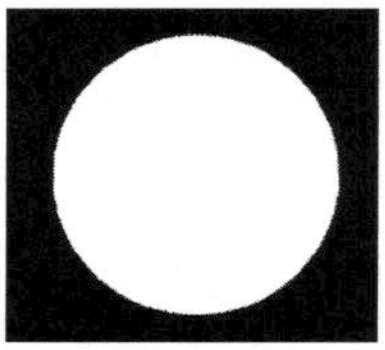

Figure 8-35 *A sphere with self-illumination*

The value in the **Opacity** spinner is used to control the transparency of the material. By default, the value in the spinner is 100, which makes a material opaque. As you decrease the value, the transparency will increase, refer to Figure 8-36.

Figure 8-36 *A teapot within a transparent box*

The value in the **Diffuse Lev** spinner is used to control the brightness of the diffuse color in the material, refer to Figures 8-37 and 8-38. By default, the value in this spinner is 100.

Specular Highlight Area

The options in the **Specular Highlight** area are used to set the shape, appearance, strength, and orientation of the specular highlight or the shiny part of the material.

Figure 8-37 *The torus knot with the default value in the **Diffuse Lev** spinner*

Figure 8-38 *The torus knot with the value **150** in the **Diffuse Lev** spinner*

The value in the **Specular Level** spinner is used to set the brightness or intensity of the specular highlight of the material. By default, the value in this spinner is 0. As you increase the value in the spinner, the brightness of the specular highlight will also increase, refer to Figures 8-39 and 8-40.

Figure 8-39 *The sphere with the value **0** in the **Specular Level** spinner*

Figure 8-40 *The sphere with the value **66** in the **Specular Level** spinner*

The value in the **Glossiness** spinner is used to set the size of the specular highlight of the material. By default, its value is 10. However, if you increase the value in the **Glossiness** spinner, the size of the specular highlight will decrease, refer to Figures 8-41 and 8-42.

Figure 8-41 *The sphere with less value in the **Glossiness** spinner*

Figure 8-42 *The sphere with more value in the **Glossiness** spinner*

The value in the **Anisotropy** spinner is used to set the shape of the specular highlight of the material. By default, its value is 50 and it ranges from 0 to 100. As you increase the value in the **Anisotropy** spinner, the shape of the specular highlight will reduce, refer to Figures 8-43 and 8-44.

The value in the **Orientation** spinner is used to change the orientation of the specular highlight of the material in degrees. By default, its value is 0. By changing the value in the **Orientation** spinner, you can change the orientation of the specular highlight of the material, as shown in Figures 8-45 and 8-46.

Figure 8-43 *The teapot with less value in the* ***Anisotropy*** *spinner*

Figure 8-44 *The teapot with more value in the* ***Anisotropy*** *spinner*

Figure 8-45 *The teapot with the value 0 in the* ***Orientation*** *spinner*

Figure 8-46 *The teapot with the value 45 in the* ***Orientation*** *spinner*

Note

In the ***Specular Highlight*** *area, there is a graph on the right side that displays the graphical representation of the changes in all spinners.*

Blinn Shader

The **Blinn** shader is used to create round and soft highlights, as shown in Figure 8-47. To assign this shader to the material, you need to select the **Blinn** option from the drop-down list available in the **Shader Basic Parameters** rollout; the **Blinn Basic Parameters** rollout will be displayed below the **Shader Basic Parameters** rollout. This rollout is discussed next.

Figure 8-47 *The sphere with the* ***Blinn*** *shader*

Blinn Basic Parameters Rollout

The **Ambient**, **Diffuse**, and **Specular** color swatches, the **Self-Illumination** area, and the **Opacity** spinner are the same as those discussed in the **Anisotropic Basic Parameters** rollout.

In the **Specular Highlights** area, the **Specular Level** and **Glossiness** spinners are the same as those discussed in the **Anisotropic Shader**. The value in the **Soften** spinner is used to soften the effect of the specular highlight. By default, its value is 0.1.

Metal Shader

The **Metal** shader is used to give a metallic effect to objects, as shown in Figure 8-48. To assign this shader to the material, you need to select the **Metal** shader from the drop-down list available in the **Shader Basic Parameters** rollout; the **Metal Basic Parameters** rollout will be displayed below the **Shader Basic Parameters** rollout. This rollout is discussed next.

Figure 8-48 *The teapot with the* ***Metal*** *shader*

Metal Basic Parameters Rollout

The options in this rollout are the same as discussed in the **Anisotropic Basic Parameters** rollout.

Multi-Layer Shader

The **Multi-Layer** shader is similar to the **Anisotropic** shader with the only difference that the **Multi-Layer** shader has two specular highlight controls. To assign this shader to the material, you need to select the **Multi-Layer** shader from the drop-down list available in the **Shader Basic Parameters** rollout; the **Multi-Layer Basic Parameters** rollout will be displayed. This rollout is discussed next.

Multi-Layer Basic Parameters Rollout

In the **Multi-Layer Basic Parameters** rollout, the **Ambient** and **Diffuse** color swatches are the same as those discussed in the **Anisotropic Basic Parameters** rollout. Also, the **Self-Illumination** area, the **Opacity** spinner, and the **Diffuse Level** spinner are the same as those discussed in the **Anisotropic Basic Parameters** rollout.

The **Roughness** spinner is used to set the transition from diffuse color to the ambient color. By default, its value is 0 and it ranges from 0 to 100. When you increase the value in the **Roughness** spinner, the material becomes less shiny, refer to Figures 8-49 and 8-50.

In the **Multi-Layer Basic Parameters** rollout, there are two specular highlight areas, **First Specular Layer** and **Second Specular Layer**. You can use both highlights independently to produce complex and blend shadings in the material. The options in the **First Specular Layer** and the **Second Specular Layer** areas are the same. However, you can use different settings to produce the blend shadings in the material, as shown in Figure 8-51. These options are discussed next.

Figure 8-49 *The teapot with less value in the* ***Roughness*** *spinner*

Figure 8-50 *The teapot with more value in the* ***Roughness*** *spinner*

Figure 8-51 *The teapot with the* ***Multi-Layer*** *shader*

Choose the **Color** color swatch to change the specular color of the first and the second highlights in the respective areas. The **Level** spinner is used to set the brightness or the intensity of the specular highlight of the material. By default, its value is 0. As you increase the value in the spinner, the brightness of the specular highlight will also increase. The **Glossiness**, **Anisotropy**, and **Orientation** options are the same as those discussed in the **Anisotropic** shader.

Oren-Nayar-Blinn Shader

The **Oren-Nayar-Blinn** shader is a variant of the **Blinn** shader and is used to create dull or matte highlights, as shown in Figure 8-52. This shader can be used for rubber, clay, clothes, and so on. To assign this shader to the material, you need to select the **Oren-Nayar-Blinn** shader from the drop-down list available in the **Shader Basic Parameters** rollout; the **Oren-Nayar-Blinn Basic Parameters** rollout will be displayed. This rollout is discussed next.

Figure 8-52 *The teapot with the* ***Oren-Nayer-Blinn*** *shader*

Oren-Nayar-Blinn Basic Parameters Rollout

The **Ambient**, **Diffuse**, and **Specular** color swatches, the **Self-Illumination** area, and the **Opacity** spinner are the same as discussed in the **Anisotropic Basic Parameters** rollout. In the **Advanced Diffuse** area, the **Diffuse Level** and **Roughness** spinners are the same as discussed in the **Multi-Layer** shader.

In the **Specular Highlights** area, the **Specular Level**, **Glossiness**, and **Soften** spinners are the same as discussed in the **Blinn** shader.

Phong Shader

The **Phong** shader is very similar to the **Blinn** shader. The only difference is that the highlights produced by the **Phong** shader are stronger than those produced by the **Blinn** shader, as shown in Figure 8-53. To assign this shader to the material, select the **Phong** shader from the drop-down list available in the **Shader Basic Parameters** rollout; the **Phong Basic Parameters** rollout will be displayed. This rollout is discussed next.

Figure 8-53 *The sphere with the* ***Phong*** *shader*

Phong Basic Parameters Rollout

The **Ambient**, **Diffuse**, and **Specular** color swatches, the **Self-Illumination** area, and the **Opacity** spinner are the same as described in the **Anisotropic Basic Parameters** rollout. In the **Specular Highlights** area, the **Specular Level**, **Glossiness**, and **Soften** spinners are the same as those discussed in the **Blinn** shader.

Strauss Shader

The **Strauss** shader is used to create the metallic and non-metallic surfaces, as shown in Figure 8-54. To assign this shader to the material, you need to select the **Strauss** shader from the drop-down list; the **Strauss Basic Parameters** rollout will be displayed. This rollout is discussed next.

Figure 8-54 *The teapot with the* ***Strauss*** *shader*

Strauss Basic Parameters Rollout

The **Strauss** shader does not have the **Ambient**, **Diffuse**, and **Specular** color swatches. Choose the **Color** swatch to change the color of the material. The value in the **Glossiness** spinner is used to set the size and the intensity of the specular highlight of the material. The value in the **Metalness** spinner is used to set the metallic effect in the material. The value in the **Opacity** spinner is used to set the transparency of the material.

Translucent Shader

The **Translucent** shader is used to create translucent materials. In such materials, the light gets scattered as it passes through them, as shown in Figure 8-55. It is very similar to the **Blinn** shader. Additionally, it defines the translucency of the material. To assign this shader to the material, you need to select the **Translucent Shader** from the drop-down list in the **Shader Basic Parameters** rollout; the **Translucent Basic Parameters** rollout will be displayed. This rollout is discussed next.

***Figure 8-55** The sphere with **Translucent** shader*

Translucent Basic Parameters Rollout

Most of the options in this rollout are the same as discussed earlier. Select the **Backside specular** check box in this rollout to get the specular highlight on both sides of the material.

Note

*Select the **Backside specular** check box in the **Specular Highlights** area in the **Translucent Basic Parameters** rollout to create materials such as plastic or smooth glass. Clear the **Backside specular** check box to create the frosted or rough material.*

In the **Translucency** area, the **Translucent Clr** swatch is used to define the color of the light that will be scattered inside the material. The **Filter Color** swatch is used to define the color of the light that will be transmitted by the material.

Architectural Material

The **Architectural** material is used to provide a highly realistic view of an object when rendered with photometric lights and radiosity, about which you will learn in the later chapters. To apply the **Architectural** material, choose the **Material Type** button on the right side of the **Material Name** text box; the **Material/Map Browser** dialog box will be displayed. Choose the **Architectural** material from the **Material/Map Browser** dialog box; the **Architectural** label will be displayed on the **Material Type** button. Also, various rollouts such as **Physical Qualities**, **Special Effects**, and so on will be displayed below the **Architectural** button. You can use these rollouts to create new materials and modify the physical properties of those materials. The most commonly used rollouts are discussed next.

Templates Rollout

The drop-down list in the **Templates** rollout consists of a number of preset materials such as **Water**, **Glass-Clear**, **Metal**, **Paper,** and so on, as shown in Figure 8-56. On selecting one of the preset materials from the drop-down list, you will get a template in the selected sample slot for the type of material you have selected. After selecting the material, you can set the parameters in other rollouts to get a realistic view of the material, as shown in Figure 8-57.

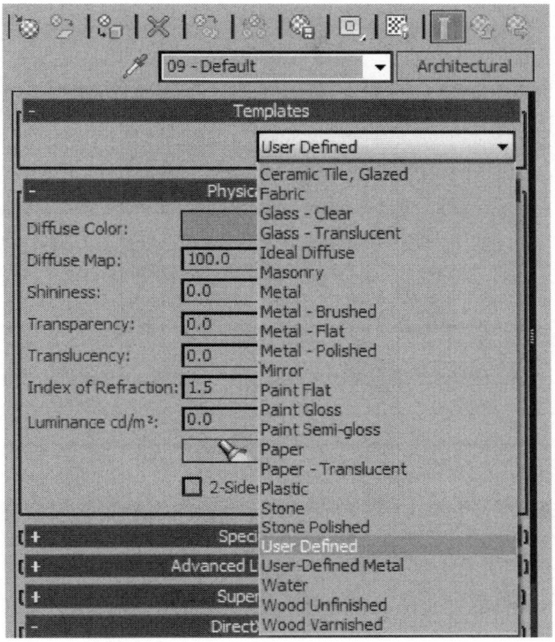

Figure 8-56 *The preset materials in the drop-down list in the **Templates** rollouts*

Figure 8-57 *The teapot with the **Architectural** material applied*

Physical Qualities Rollout

The **Diffuse Color** swatch is used to specify the color of an object in direct light. It is the main color of the material. Choose the **Diffuse Color** swatch to define the color of the material. The **Diffuse Map** option is used to assign a map or an image to the material. To do so, choose the **Diffuse Map** button labeled as **None** on the right side of the **Diffuse Map** spinner; the **Material/Map Browser** dialog box will be displayed. Select one of the maps from the **Maps > Standard** rollouts and double-click on it to assign it. The basic parameters rollouts of the selected map will be displayed. Set the parameters as per your requirement and then choose the **Go To Parent** button to go back to the previous level; the **None** label will be replaced by the name of the selected map. The spinner on the right side of the **Diffuse Map** option is used to set the amount of visibility of the map in the material in percentage. By default, its value is 100. On decreasing the value in this spinner, the visibility of the map in the material will be decreased. By default, the check box located in between the spinner and the button is selected, which is used to view the map in the material.

The **Set color to texture average** button will be available next to the **Diffuse Color** color swatch, only if you assign a diffuse map to the material using the **Diffuse Map** button. The **Set color to texture average** button is used to set the diffuse color according to the map that you have assigned to the material using the **Diffuse Map** button.

The **Shininess**, **Transparency**, and **Translucency** options in the **Physical Qualities** rollout are used to define the shininess, transparency, and the translucency of the material. Also, you can assign a map or an image to these options as you did for the **Diffuse Map** option. The

Index of Refraction spinner is used to set the amount of refraction of the light transmitted by the material. The **Luminance cd/m²** spinner is used to give the glow effect to the material. The luminance is measured in candelas per meter square. The **Set luminance from light** button uses the scene light to obtain the materials luminance. Select the **2-Sided** check box to assign the material on both sides of the selected faces.

Note
*The **Architectural** material gives a realistic result only with photometric lights.*

Raytrace Material

A raytrace material creates highly refractive and reflective surfaces. When this material is assigned to an object in the scene, the materials/maps of other objects in the scene get reflected on it, as shown in Figure 8-58. It is an advance material and is used to provide realistic raytraced images. It also creates raytraced reflections and refractions, and takes a longer time to render. On selecting the **Raytrace** material, various rollouts will also be displayed below the **Material Type** button to create new materials and modify the properties of those materials. The **Raytrace Basic Parameters** rollout is most commonly used and is discussed next.

Raytrace Basic Parameters Rollout

The basic parameters in this rollout are similar to those used in the **Standard** material but the color swatches in this rollout act differently, refer to Figure 8-59. These color controls are discussed next.

*Figure 8-58 The teapot with the **Raytrace** material*

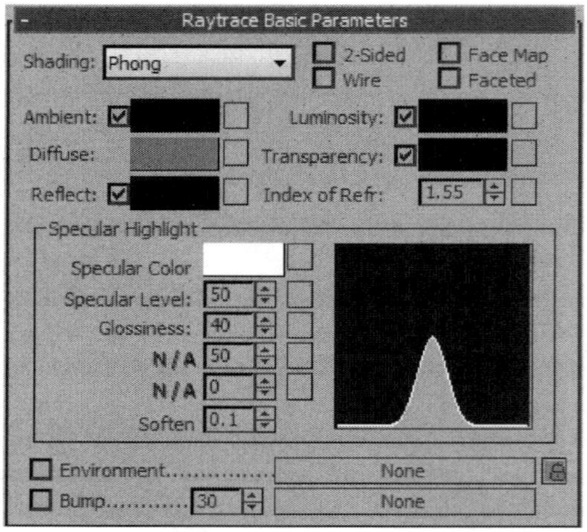

*Figure 8-59 The **Raytrace Basic Parameters** rollout*

By default, the check box on the left side of the **Ambient** color swatch is selected, which is used to specify the amount of absorption of the ambient light by the material. By default, the black color is selected in this color swatch and it specifies the maximum absorption of the ambient light by the material. On setting a lighter color in the **Ambient** color swatch, the ambient light will be reflected. If you clear the check box, the color swatch will be replaced by a spinner. The value in the spinner specifies the grayscale value.

The **Diffuse** color swatch specifies the color of the object without the specular highlight. The **Reflect** color swatch is used to specify the specular reflection color. By default, the color in this color swatch is black and the object does not reflect. If you change the color to white, then the object will reflect everything and will be visible. If you clear the check box, the color swatch will be replaced by a spinner. If you set the value in the **Reflect** spinner to 100, then the diffuse color will not be visible on the object. The value in the spinner specifies the grayscale value. If you select this check box again, the spinner will be replaced by the **Fresnel** option. This option adds the fresnel effect to the reflecting object resulting in a bit of extra reflection in the reflecting object.

The **Luminosity** color swatch is very similar to the **Self-Illumination** area in the **Standard** material. By default, the check box on the right side of the **Luminosity** option is selected. If you clear the check box, the **Luminosity** label will be replaced by **Self-Illum** and the color swatch will be replaced by a spinner. The value in the spinner specifies the grayscale value.

The **Transparency** color swatch is used to define the transparency of the object. By default, the check box on the right side of the **Transparency** option is selected. If you clear this check box, the **Transparency** color swatch is replaced by a spinner. The value in the spinner also defines the transparency of the object.

Blend Material

The **Blend** material is a compound material and is used to mix two different materials, as shown in Figure 8-60. You can assign this mixed or blend material as a single material. When you select the **Blend** material from the **Material/Map Browser** dialog box; the **Replace Material** dialog box will be displayed, as shown in Figure 8-61. Select the **Discard old material?** radio button to remove the current material of the selected sample slot. Select the **Keep old material as sub-material?** radio button to keep the material of the selected sample slot as a sub-material in the **Blend** material. Choose the **OK** button; the **Blend** material will be displayed in the **Material Type** button with a number of rollouts. The most commonly used rollout is discussed next.

Figure 8-60 *The sphere with the* ***Blend*** *material applied*

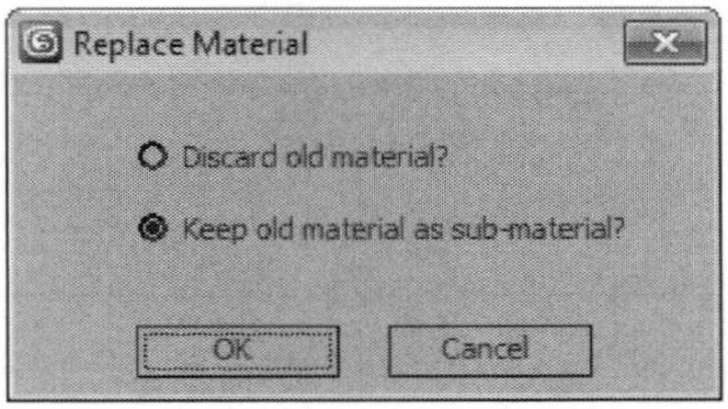

Figure 8-61 *The* ***Replace Material*** *dialog box*

Blend Basic Parameters Rollout

On the top of this rollout, there are two buttons, **Material 1** and **Material 2**, as shown in Figure 8-62. These buttons are labeled with the name of the default materials and are used to select two different materials to blend. By default, the **Standard** material is displayed as the sub-material. Choose these buttons to assign desired materials. Next, invoke the **Go To Parent** tool to go back to the **Blend** material.

The **Mask** button is used to insert an image or a map as a mask. The amount of blending of the two materials depends on the mask image. The lighter area of the mask image will show more of **Material 1** and the darker area of the mask image will show more of **Material 2**.

By default, the check boxes on the right side of the **Material 1**, **Material 2**, and **Mask** buttons are selected, which specify that the concerned material or the mask will be displayed on the object. If you clear any of the check boxes, the corresponding material or mask will not be displayed.

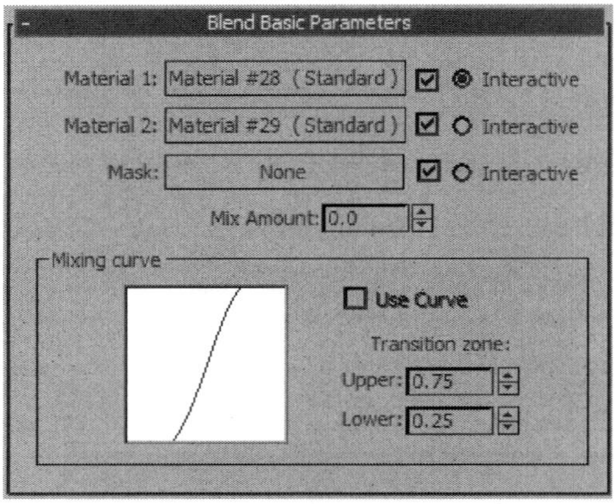

***Figure 8-62** The **Blend Basic Parameters** rollout*

Select the two **Interactive** radio buttons on the right side of the check boxes to specify the materials that will be displayed on the object in the shaded viewports. The value in the **Mix Amount** spinner is used to set the blending amount of the materials in percentage. When you insert a map using the **Mask** button; the **Mix Amount** spinner will become inactive.

The **Mixing Curve** area is used to define the transition between two colors being blended. It affects the transition only when the mask map is applied to the **Mask** button. Select the **Use Curve** check box to apply the curve settings to the blending. This check box will be available only if you have assigned the mask map. In the **Transition zone** group, the values in the **Upper** and **Lower** spinners set the transition of the materials. The values in these spinners vary from 0 to 1.0.

Note
The amount of blend can be animated over time.

Composite Material

The **Composite** material is similar to the **Blend** material and is used to mix ten different materials. You can assign this mixed material as a single material. To do so, choose the **Material Type** button; the **Material/Map Browser** dialog box will be displayed. Select the **Composite** material and choose the **OK** button; the **Replace Material** dialog box will be displayed. Select the **Discard old material?** radio button to remove the material of the selected sample slot. Else, select the **Keep old material as sub-material?** radio button to retain the material of the selected sample slot as a sub-material in the **Composite** material. Choose the **OK** button; the

Composite material will be displayed in the **Material Type** button with a number of rollouts. The most commonly used rollout is discussed next.

Composite Basic Parameters Rollout

On the top of this rollout, there is the **Base Material** button which is labeled with the name of the material on it, refer to Figure 8-63. It is used to define the base material of the object. By default, the **Standard** material is displayed on it. Choose this button and set the parameters for the base material as per your requirement. Then invoke the **Go to Parent** tool to go back to the parent level.

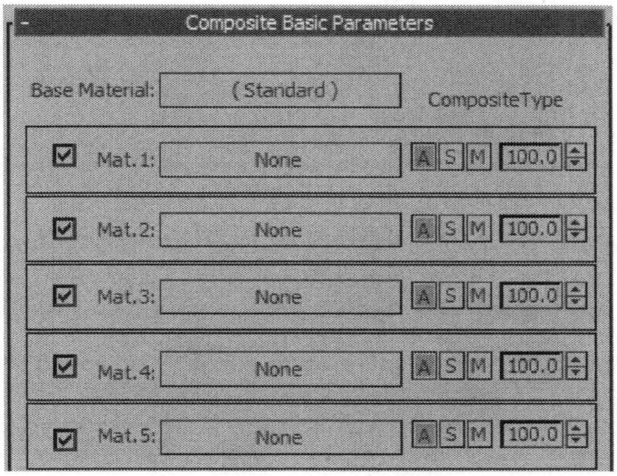

Figure 8-63 *The* ***Composite Basic Parameters*** *rollout*

There are nine buttons below the **Base Material** button, from **Mat.1** to **Mat.9**, labeled with **None**. These are used to composite nine materials. Choose these buttons one by one to assign different materials; the **None** labels will be replaced by the names of the materials that will be assigned to them. The check boxes on the left side of these buttons are selected to display the corresponding materials in the objects. If you do not want to display any of the materials, then clear the respective check boxes.

The **A**, **S**, and **M** buttons are used to specify the composition of the materials. Choose the **A** button to use the additive color to compose the materials. It specifies that the color of the base material will be added to the color of the composed material. Choose the **S** button to use the subtractive color to compose. It specifies that the color of the composed material will be subtracted from the color of the base material. Choose the **M** button to blend the materials as discussed in the Blend Material section with the only difference that the option for masking is not available in this case. For each material, the spinner on the right of the **A**, **S**, and **M** buttons determines the amount of mixing of the respective material with the **Base Material**. When the **A** and **S** buttons are active, the value in the spinner ranges from 0 to 200. Whereas, when the **M** button is active, the value in the spinner ranges from 0 to 100.

Double Sided Material

The **Double Sided** material is used to assign two different materials to the front and back faces of an object, refer to Figures 8-64 and 8-65. To do so, choose the **Double Sided** material from the **Material/Map Browser** dialog box; the **Double Sided** material will be displayed in the **Material Type** button with a number of rollouts. The **Double Sided Basic Parameters** rollout is discussed next.

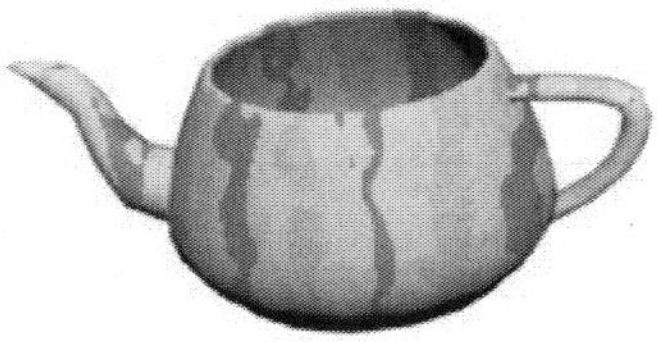

Figure 8-64 *The object with the* ***Standard*** *material*

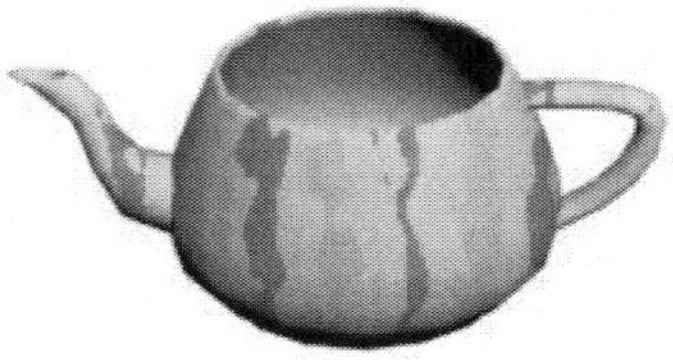

Figure 8-65 *The object with the* ***Double Sided*** *material*

Double Sided Basic Parameters Rollout

The **Translucency** spinner at the top of this rollout specifies the amount of blending of **Facing Material** and **Back Material**, refer to Figure 8-66. The value in this spinner varies from 0 to 100.0. If you set the value **100** in the **Translucency** spinner; the back material will completely cover the face material. Choose the **Facing Material** and **Back Material** buttons to select the material for the front and back sides of the object, respectively.

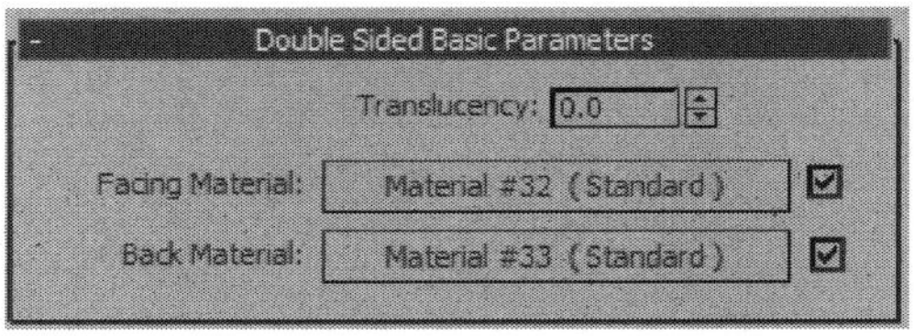

Figure 8-66 *The* ***Double Sided Basic Parameters*** *Rollout*

Note

If the double sided material is not displayed correctly in the viewport, then you need to change the settings as follows:

Choose ***Customize > Preferences*** *from the menu bar; the* ***Preference Settings*** *dialog box will be displayed. In this dialog box, choose the* ***Viewports*** *tab. Next, choose* ***Configure Driver*** *from the* ***Display Drivers*** *area; the* ***Configure Direct3D*** *dialog box will be displayed. In this dialog box, clear the* ***Use Cached D3DXMeshes*** *check box. Now, restart 3dsMax to view the double sided material correctly in the viewport.*

Multi/Sub-Object Material

The **Multi/Sub-Object** material is used to assign different materials to an object at the sub-object level, as shown in Figure 8-67. To do so, select the object to which the **Multi/Sub-Object** material is to be assigned. Convert the object to editable poly. Now, select the **Polygon** sub-object level and select the group of polygons in the viewport, refer to Figure 8-68. Next, expand the **Polygon Material IDs** rollout and enter the value **1** in the **Set ID** spinner and press ENTER. Then, invert the selection and enter the value **2** in the **Set ID** spinner and press ENTER, refer to Figure 8-69. Note that you can assign any number of IDs to an object depending on the number of materials to be assigned to it. Once you set IDs to different parts of the object, choose the **Multi/Sub-Object** material from the **Material/Map Browser** dialog box; the **Replace Material** message box will be displayed. Select the **Discard old material?** radio button from it and choose the **OK** button; the **Multi/Sub-object** material will be displayed in the **Material Type** button. Also, the **Multi/Sub-Object Basic Parameters** rollout will be displayed, refer to Figure 8-70. This rollout is discussed next.

Figure 8-67 *The object with the* ***Multi/Sub-Object*** *material*

Figure 8-68 *The object with group of polygons selected*

Figure 8-69 *The object with remaining polygons selected*

Multi/Sub-Object Basic Parameters Rollout

Choose the **Set Number** button in this rollout; the **Set Number of Materials** dialog box will be displayed. Enter **2** in the **Number of Materials** spinner and choose the **OK** button; the **Multi/Sub-Object Basic Parameters** rollout will display two entries instead of ten entries. Note that the value entered in the **Number of Materials** spinner should be equal to the number of IDs created for the object which in turn is equal to the entries in this rollout. Now, choose the **None** button for each of the IDs to assign the required sub-material. Also, you can enter the name of the sub-material in the **Name** text box. Next, assign the material to the object to see the effect of the **Multi-Sub-Object** material.

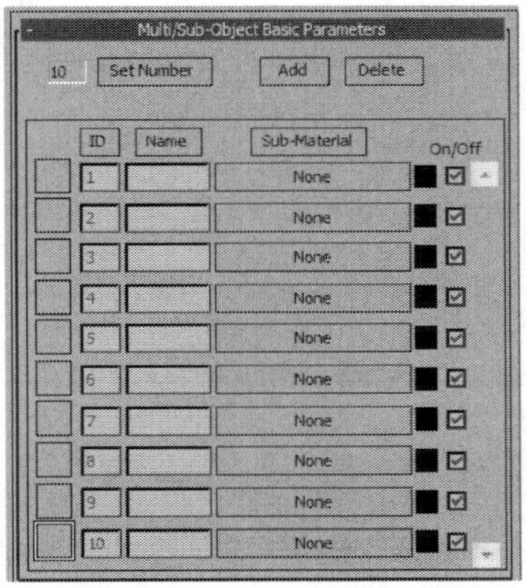

Figure 8-70 *The* ***Multi/Sub-Object Basic Parameters*** *Rollout*

Note

If you want to change only the color of the sub-material without assigning any map to it, then the color swatch next to it will be inactive. It will be activated only when you assign ***Standard*** *Material to it.*

Top/Bottom Material

The **Top/Bottom** material is used to assign two different materials on the top and bottom portions of the object, as shown in Figure 8-71. To do so, choose the **Top/Bottom** material from the **Material/Map Browser** dialog box; the **Top/Bottom** material will be displayed in the **Material Type** button with a number of rollouts. The **Top/Bottom Basic Parameters** rollout is discussed next.

Top/Bottom Basic Parameters Rollout

Choose the **Top Material** and **Bottom Material** buttons to select the material for the top and bottom portions of the object, respectively, refer to Figure 8-72. Choose the **Swap** button to exchange the material of the **Top Material** and **Bottom Material** buttons.

*Figure 8-71 The object with the **Top/Bottom** material applied*

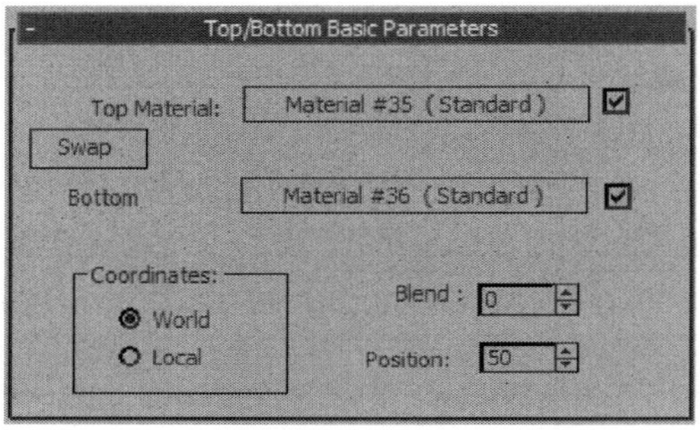

*Figure 8-72 The **Top/Bottom Basic Parameters** rollout*

The **Coordinates** area is used to set the boundary between the top and bottom of the object. By default, the **World** radio button is selected and the faces will point up or down according to the world coordinates of the scene. In this case, if you transform the object, then the boundary remains constant at its place. If you select the **Local** radio button, then the faces will point up or down according to the local coordinates of the object. In this case, if you transform the object, the material will also get transformed. The value in the **Blend** spinner is used to blend the edges of the top and bottom materials. The value in the **Position** spinner is used to specify the position of the top and bottom materials on the object. By default, the value in both the spinners ranges from 0 to 100.0.

MAPS

Enhanced

In Autodesk 3ds Max, maps are the default images assigned to a material. These are used to create texture for the objects to make them appear more realistic. In this section, you will learn about assigning the maps to the objects. When maps are applied to the objects, the objects demonstrate best effects on applying lights.

To assign a map to the material, press the M key; the **Slate Material Editor** dialog box will be displayed. Next, choose **Modes > Compact Material Editor** from the material editor menu bar; the **Material Editor** dialog box will be displayed. Select one of the sample slots in the **Material Editor** dialog box to activate it. Now, in the basic parameters rollout of the selected material, choose the small square buttons on the right of the parameters available, refer to

Figure 8-73; the **Material/Map Browser** dialog box will be displayed with a list of default maps available in Autodesk 3ds Max. Next, select the required map from the **Maps > Standard** rollouts and choose the **OK** button; the name of the selected map will be displayed on the **Material Type** button and the rollouts related to that map will also be displayed. Set the parameters for the map in various rollouts displayed. Next, choose the **Go to Parent** button to go back to the previous level; the small square button will be labeled as **M**. Also, when you move the cursor over the **M** button, it will display the name of the map that you assigned to it.

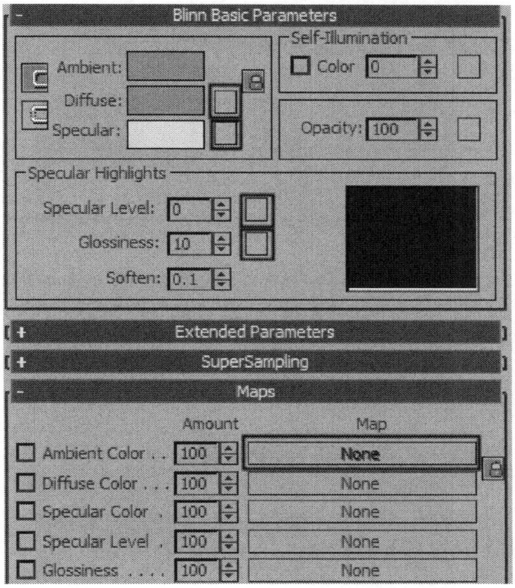

Figure 8-73 *The square buttons highlighted for inserting maps*

Various types of maps available in the **Material/Map Browser** dialog box are discussed next.

Note

You can also assign maps using different options such as ***Ambient Color****,* ***Diffuse Color****,* ***Specular Color****, and so on in a material using the* ***Maps*** *rollout in the* ***Material Editor*** *dialog box. To do so, you need to choose the buttons on the right side of these options that are labeled as* ***None****, refer to Figure 8-73.*

Types of Maps

In Autodesk 3ds Max, you can categorize the maps as the bitmaps and procedural maps. The bitmaps are 2D images and they get pixelised when you zoom in on them. The procedural maps are **Noise**, **Tiles**, **Marble**, **Gradient**, and so on and they do not get pixelised when you zoom in on them. There are various maps that can be categorized into 2D maps, 3D maps, Compositors, Color Mods, and Others. These maps are discussed next.

2D Maps

The 2D maps are two-dimensional images that can be assigned to geometric objects and are used to create an environment for the scene. The most commonly used two-dimensional maps such as **Bitmap**, **Checker**, **Combustion**, **Gradient**, **Gradient Ramp**, **Swirl**, and **Tiles** discussed next.

Bitmap

The bitmaps are the simplest 2D images. To apply this map on an object, select the **Bitmap** map in the **Material/Map Browser** dialog box; the **Select Bitmap Image File** dialog box will be displayed. In this dialog box, select the image that you want to insert and choose the **Open** button; the image will be displayed in the selected sample slot. Also, various rollouts to modify the image map will be displayed in the **Material Editor** dialog box. Now, when you assign the material to the object in the viewport, the object will be displayed with the assigned bitmap, as shown in Figure 8-74. You can select all the still or animated files that Autodesk 3ds Max supports.

Checker

The **Checker** map is a combination of two colors, as shown in Figure 8-75. You can change the colors or replace the colors with the images using the **Checker Parameters** rollout in the **Material Editor** dialog box.

Gradient

The **Gradient** map is used to create a ramp of three colors, as shown in Figure 8-76. You can modify or replace colors with images using the **Gradient Parameters** rollout of the **Material Editor** dialog box.

Figure 8-74 *A sphere with the* ***Bitmap*** *map applied*

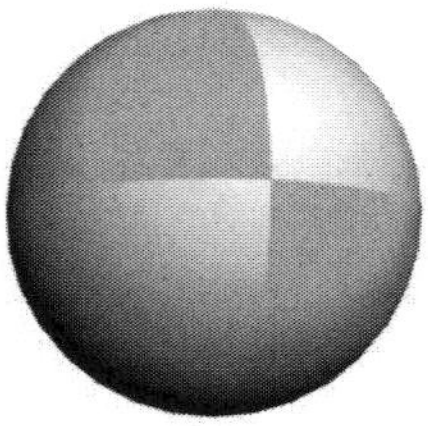

Figure 8-75 *A sphere with the* ***Checker*** *map applied*

Figure 8-76 *An object with the* ***Gradient*** *map applied*

Gradient Ramp

The **Gradient Ramp** map is an advanced map of the **Gradient** map and is shown in Figure 8-77. It is used to create the ramp using different colors and maps at advance level. You can get the best effect using the **Gradient Ramp Parameters** rollout in the **Material Editor** dialog box.

Swirl

The **Swirl** map is a procedural map and is used to produce whirl effect in materials, as shown in Figure 8-78. You can modify the colors or replace the colors with the images using the **Swirl Parameters** rollout in the **Material Editor** dialog box.

*Figure 8-77 A box with the **Gradient Ramp** map applied*

*Figure 8-78 A sphere with the **Swirl** map applied*

Tiles

The **Tiles** map is a procedural map and is used to create bricks or tiles effect using different colors and maps, as shown in Figure 8-79. You can get the best effect of this map using the different rollouts displayed in the **Material Editor** dialog box.

*Figure 8-79 A sphere with the **Tiles** map applied*

Substance Map and Map Output Selector Map

The **Substance** map is a collection of 2D textures. To use a texture from the **Substance** map, choose any of the desired map buttons from the **Material Editor** dialog box and select the **Map Output Selector** map from the **Maps** rollout in the **Material/Map Browser** dialog box. On doing so, the **Map Output Selector** map will be displayed in the **Material Type** button. Also, the **Parameters** rollout will be displayed, as shown in Figure 8-80. Next, choose the **None** button on the right of the **Source Map** parameter from the **Parameters** rollout and then select **Substance** from the **Material/Map Browser** dialog box; various rollouts such as **Global Substance Settings**, **Substance Package Browser**, **Coordinates**, and so on will be displayed in the **Material Editor** dialog box as shown in Figure 8-81.

Now, choose the **Load Substance** button from the **Substance Package Browser** rollout; the **Browse from Substances** dialog box will be displayed. In this dialog box, select the desired texture and choose the **Open** button; the **Load Substance** button will be replaced by the texture you have selected. Also rollout for the respective texture parameters will be added at the bottom in the **Material Editor** dialog box. In this rollout, you can change different parameters to get the desired result. You can choose the **Get Substance From Marketplace** button to buy textures online. Next, choose the **Go to Parent** button and select the desired channel name from the **Channel Name** drop-down list.

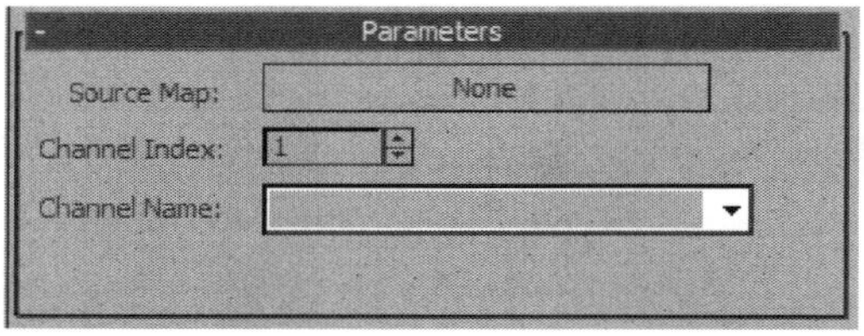

Figure 8-80 *The* ***Parameters*** *rollout of the* ***Map Output Selector*** *map*

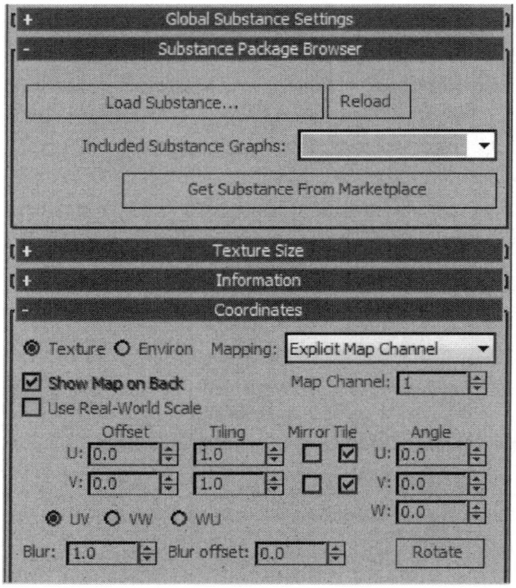

Figure 8-81 *The rollouts displayed on selecting the* ***Substance*** *map*

3D Maps

The 3D Maps are three-dimensional images that can be assigned to geometric objects. These are also known as procedural maps. The most commonly used three-dimensional maps such as **Cellular**, **Falloff**, **Noise**, and so on are discussed next.

Dent

The **Dent** map is used to produce material with 3D bumps on its surface. It is basically used as the **Bump** map using the **Maps** rollout, refer to Figure 8-82. You can modify the effect of this map at advanced level using the **Dent Parameters** rollout in the **Material Editor** dialog box.

Cellular

The **Cellular** map is a 3D procedural map. It is used to produce materials such as sand, pebbled surfaces, and so on, as shown in Figure 8-83. You can modify the effect of this map at advanced level using the **Cellular Parameters** rollout in the **Material Editor** dialog box.

Noise

The **Noise** map is used to create disturbance on the surface of an object by combining two colors or materials in different ways, as shown in Figure 8-84. You can modify the effect of this map at advanced level using the **Noise Parameters** rollout in the **Material Editor** dialog box.

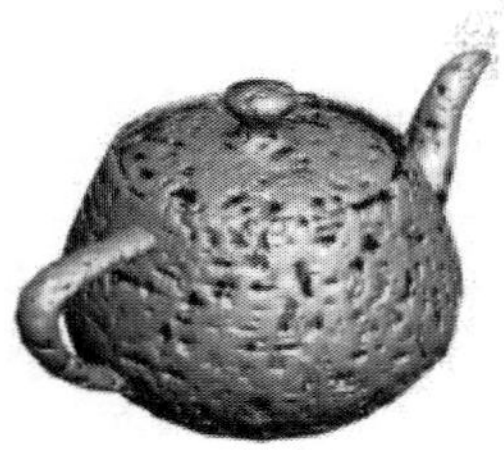

*Figure 8-82 A teapot with the **Dent** map applied*

*Figure 8-83 An object with the **Cellular** map*

*Figure 8-84 A sphere with the **Noise** map*

Smoke

The **Smoke** map is used to produce the texture such as smoke from the fire, cloudy effect, or the beam of lights on the surface of an object, as shown in Figure 8-85. You can modify the effect of this map at advanced level using the **Smoke Parameters** rollout of the **Material Editor** dialog box.

Speckle

The **Speckle** map is used to produce the texture of the patterned surfaces such as granite and so on, as shown in Figure 8-86. You can modify the effect of this map at advanced level using the **Speckle Parameters** rollout in the **Material Editor** dialog box.

Splat

The **Splat** map is used to produce texture such as splattered paint on the surface of an object, as shown in Figure 8-87. You can modify the effect of this map at advanced level using the **Splat Parameters** rollout of the **Material Editor** dialog box.

*Figure 8-85 A sphere with the **Smoke** map applied*

*Figure 8-86 A box with the **Speckle** map applied*

*Figure 8-87 A box with the **Splat** map applied*

Stucco

The **Stucco** map is used to produce the texture such as plaster or cement on the surface of an object, as shown in Figure 8-88. You need to assign a **Bump** map using the **Maps** rollout to get its best effect. You can modify the effect of this map at advanced level using the **Stucco Parameters** rollout in the **Material Editor** dialog box.

Waves

The **Waves** map is used to create wavy surface, as shown in Figure 8-89. You can modify the effect of this map at advanced level using the **Waves Parameters** rollout in the **Material Editor** dialog box.

Wood

The **Wood** map is used to create the 3D wood texture on the surface of the object, refer to Figure 8-90. You can modify the effect of this map at advanced level using the **Wood Parameters** rollout in the **Material Editor** dialog box.

Figure 8-88 *A wall with the* ***Stucco*** *map applied*

Figure 8-89 *A plane with the* ***Waves*** *map applied*

Figure 8-90 *A box with the* ***Wood*** *map applied*

Compositors Maps

The **Compositors** maps are used to combine the colors or the maps together. Various maps in this category are: **Composite**, **Mask**, **Mix**, and **RGB Multiply**.

Color Mods Maps

The **Color Mods** maps are used to modify or change the color of pixels in a material. Various maps in this category are: **Output**, **RGB Tint**, and **Vertex Color**.

Other Maps

There are some other types of maps such as **Raytrace**, **Flat Mirror**, and so on, which are used in a different way. These maps are discussed next.

Flat Mirror

The **Flat Mirror** map is used to create a material that generates reflection of other objects in the scene when assigned to the flat surfaces. You can get the best effect of this map using the **Flat Mirror Parameters** rollout in the **Material Editor** dialog box.

Raytrace

The **Raytrace** map is used to create the raytraced reflections and refractions on the surface of the objects. You can get the best effect of this map using the **Raytrace Parameters** rollout in the **Material Editor** dialog box.

Reflect/Refract

The **Reflect/Refract** map is used to produce the reflection and the refraction based on the objects in the scene. You can modify the effects using the **Reflect/Refract Parameters** rollout in the **Material Editor** dialog box.

Once you assign any of the above maps on the square button in the **Material Editor** dialog box; **M** will be displayed on it. If you right-click on this button; a shortcut menu will be displayed, as shown in Figure 8-91. Using the options in the shortcut menu, you can cut or copy the map and paste it at the desired place. You can also clear the unwanted map using the **Clear** option.

Figure 8-91 *The shortcut menu displayed on right-clicking on the **M** button*

Tutorial 1

In this tutorial, you will assign material to two cocktail glasses that were created in Tutorial 1 of Chapter 7, refer to Figure 8-92. **(Expected time: 15 min)**

Figure 8-92 *Model for Tutorial 1*

The following steps are required to complete this tutorial:

a. Set the project folder.
b. Download and open the file.
c. Create the floor.
d. Create material for the floor.
e. Create material for the cocktail glasses.
f. Render the scene for the final output.
g. Save the file.

Setting the Project Folder

1. Set the project folder with the name *c08_tut1* in the *3dsmax* folder as discussed in earlier chapters.

Downloading and Opening the File

1. Download the *c08_3dsmax_2012_tut.zip* file from *http://www.cadcim.com*. The path of the file is as follows:

   Textbooks > Animation and Visual Effects > 3ds Max > Autodesk 3ds Max 2012: A Comprehensive Guide

Extract the contents of the zipped file and save them in the *\Documents* folder.

2. Choose **Open** from the **Application menu**; the **Open File** dialog box is displayed. In this dialog box, browse to the location *\Documents\c08_3dsmax_2012_tut* and select the *c08_tut1_start.max* file in it. Choose the **Open** button to open the file, refer to Figure 8-93.

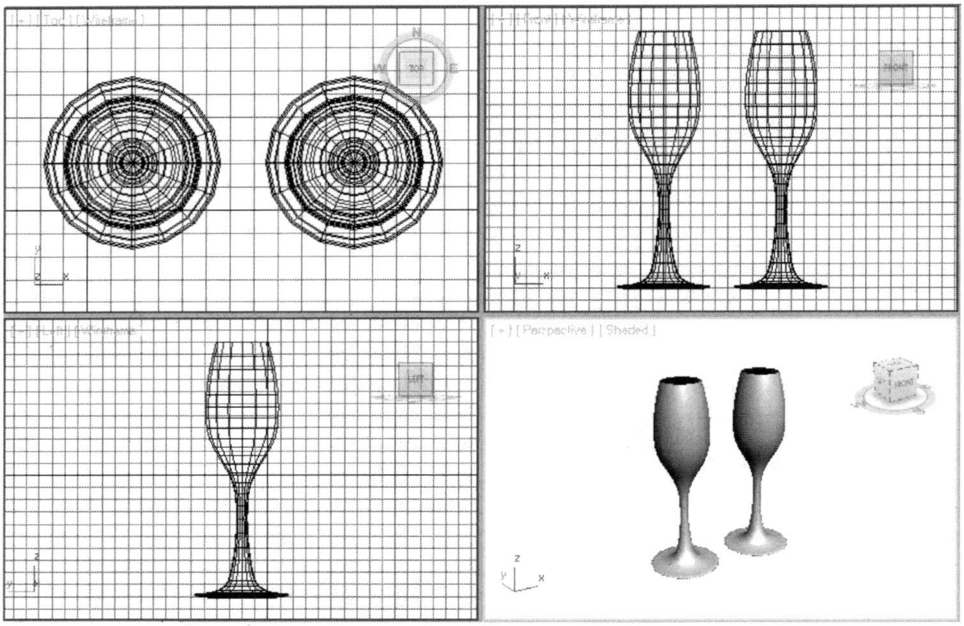

Figure 8-93 *The file with the cocktail glasses displayed*

Note

Instead of following steps 1 and 2, you can directly open the file that you created in Tutorial 1 of Chapter 7 and then follow step 3 given below to save it.

3. Now, choose **Save As** from the **Application menu**; the **Save File As** dialog box is displayed. Browse to the location *\Documents\3dsmax\c08_tut1\scenes*. Save the file with the name *c08tut1.max* at this location.

4. Browse to the *c08_3dsmax_2012_tut* folder and copy the *CHROMBLU.jpg* file from this folder to the location *\Documents\3dsmax\c08_tut1\sceneassets\images.*

Creating the Floor

1. Activate the Top viewport and choose **Create > Geometry** in the **Command Panel**; the **Standard Primitives** option is displayed in the drop-down list below the **Geometry** button. Invoke the **Box** tool from the **Object Type** rollout and create a box in the Top viewport.

2. Name the box as *floor*.

3. In the **Parameters** rollout, set the length and width parameters of the box according to your scene. Set the value in the **Height** spinner to **1.0**.

4. Align the *floor* with the cocktail glasses using the **Select and Move** tool, as shown in Figure 8-94. Invoke the **Zoom Extents All** tool.

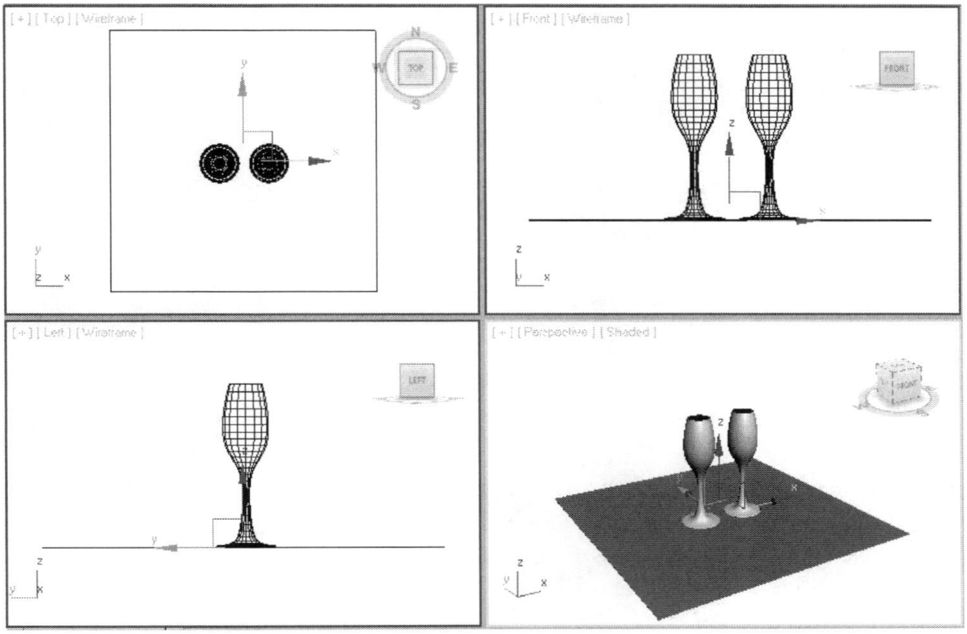

Figure 8-94 *Alignment of floor in all viewports*

Next, you need to create materials for objects in the scene.

Creating Material for the Floor

1. Select the *floor* in any viewport. Then, choose **Rendering > Material Editor > Compact Material Editor** from the menu bar; the **Material Editor** dialog box is displayed.

2. In the **Material Editor** dialog box, select the second sample slot to which no material is assigned; the selected sample slot is surrounded by a white square. In the **Material Name** drop-down list, enter **floor** and press the ENTER key.

   Next, you need to use the **Standard** material for the *floor*.

3. By default, the **Standard** material is selected in the **Material Type** button.

   Next, you need to set parameters for the **Standard** material.

4. In the **Shader Basic Parameters** rollout, make sure that the **Blinn** shader is selected in the drop-down list.

5. In the **Blinn Basic Parameters** rollout, choose the small square button on the right of the **Diffuse** color swatch, as shown in Figure 8-95; the **Material/Map Browser** dialog box is displayed.

6. Expand the **Maps > Standard** rollouts and select the **Checker** map from the list displayed in the **Material/Map Browser** dialog box. Choose the **OK** button; the **Checker** map is displayed in the selected sample slot, as shown in Figure 8-96. Also, the **Coordinates**, **Noise**, and **Checker Parameters** rollouts are displayed in the **Material Editor** dialog box, as shown in Figure 8-97.

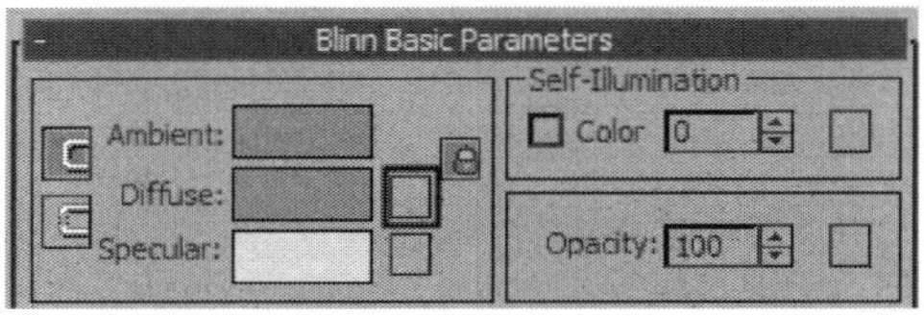

Figure 8-95 The highlighted square button to be chosen

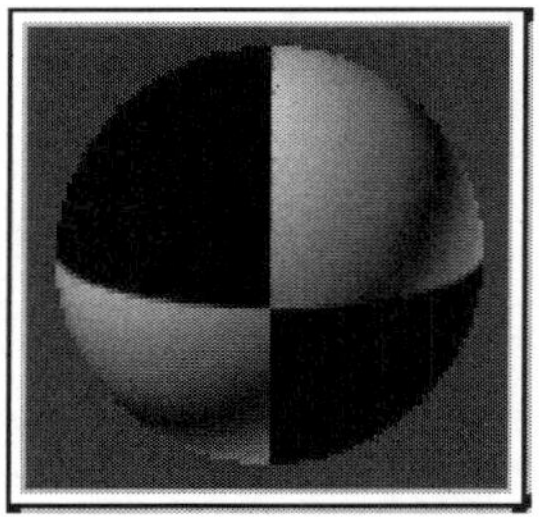

*Figure 8-96 The **Checker** map in the sample slot*

7. In the **Coordinates** rollout, set the value **3** in the **U Tiling** and **V Tiling** spinners to apply the **Checker** map thrice on the X and Y-axes. Note that the map is displayed in the selected sample slot, as shown in Figure 8-98. Use the default values for other options.

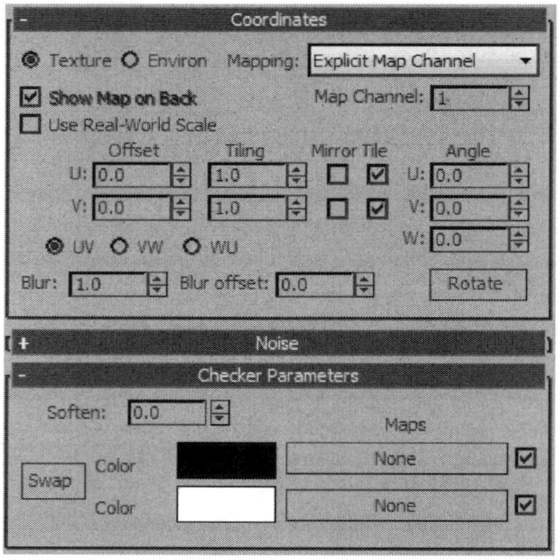

*Figure 8-97 The rollouts displayed on selecting the **Checker** map*

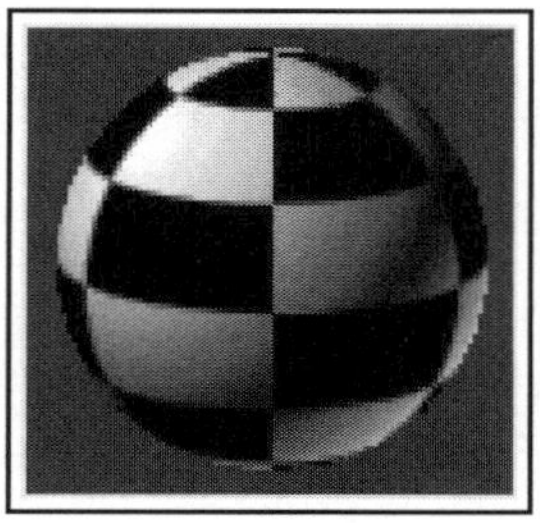

*Figure 8-98 The **Checker** map with 3x3 tiling*

8. In the **Checker Parameters** rollout, select the black color swatch; the **Color Selector: Color1** dialog box is displayed. Set the values as given below:

Red: **0** Green: **12** Blue: **104**

Now, choose the **OK** button to close this dialog box.

9. Make sure that the white color is selected in the other color swatch, refer to Figure 8-97.

10. Invoke the **Go to Parent** tool to go back to the **Standard** material.

    Next, you need to assign the **Raytrace** map to the material to give it a realistic effect.

Note

After assigning the map, the small square button on the right of the ***Diffuse*** *color swatch is labeled as* ***M****.*

11. Expand the **Maps** rollout; a list of maps is displayed, as shown in Figure 8-99.

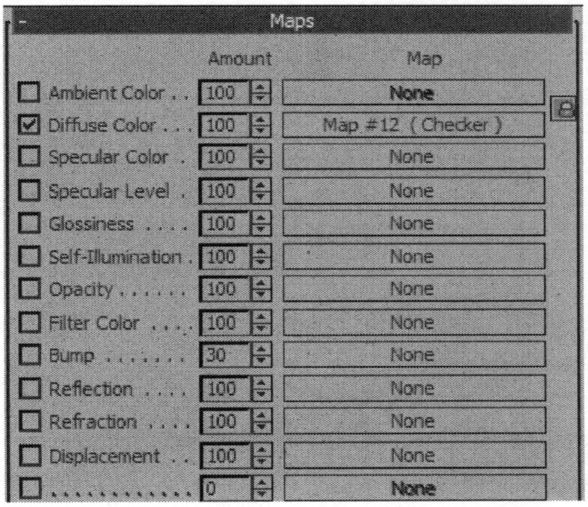

Figure 8-99 *The* ***Maps*** *rollout*

12. In this rollout, select the **Reflection** check box to make it active. Choose the **Reflection** map button on the right of the spinner that is labeled as **None**; the **Material/Map Browser** dialog box is displayed. Select the **Raytrace** map from the **Maps > Standard** rollouts and choose the **OK** button; the **Raytrace** map with various rollouts is displayed in the **Material Editor** dialog box. Use the default values for the **Raytrace** map.

13. Invoke the **Go to Parent** tool. Expand the **Maps** rollout and set the value **20** in the **Reflection** spinner.

    Now, you need to assign the **floor** material to the *floor*.

14. Make sure that the *floor* is selected in the viewport and the **floor** material is selected in the **Material Editor** dialog box.

15. Next, invoke the **Assign Material to Selection** tool from the **Material Editor** dialog box; the **floor** material is assigned to the *floor* in the viewport.

16. Now, invoke the **Show Shaded Material in Viewport** tool to display the **floor** material on the object in the viewport, as shown in Figure 8-100.

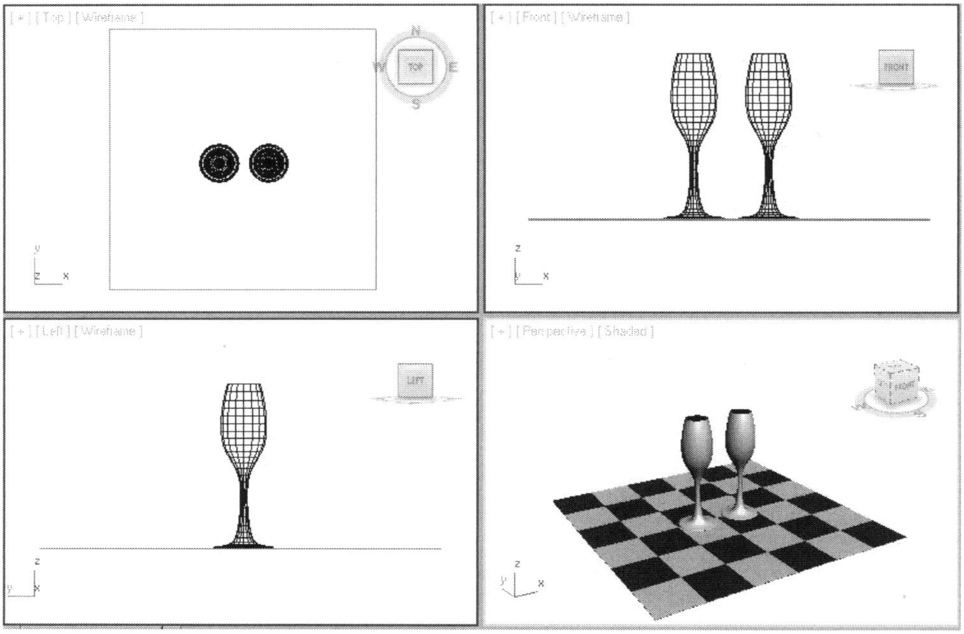

*Figure 8-100 The **floor** material displayed on the floor*

Creating Material for the Cocktail Glasses

The material has already been assigned to the cocktail glasses in Tutorial 1 of Chapter 7. But, in this section, you will assign another material to it.

1. Select the cocktail glasses in the viewport and then select another sample slot in the **Material Editor** dialog box. In the **Material Name** drop-down list, enter **glass** and press ENTER.

2. Use the **Standard** material for the cocktail glasses. By default, it is selected in the **Material Type** button.

   Next, you need to set parameters for the **Standard** material.

3. In the **Shader Basic Parameters** rollout, select the **Phong** shader; the **Phong Basic Parameters** rollout is displayed. Select the **2-Sided** check box.

4. In the **Phong Basic Parameters** rollout, choose the small square button on the right of the **Diffuse** color swatch; the **Material/Map Browser** dialog box is displayed.

5. Select the **Bitmap** map from the list displayed in the **Material/Map Browser** dialog box and double-click on it; the **Select Bitmap Image File** dialog box is displayed.

As the project folder is already set, the path *\Documents\3dsmax\c08_tut1\sceneassets\images* is displayed in **Look in** text box of this dialog box.

6. Select the file *CHROMBLU.jpg* from it and choose the **Open** button; the image is displayed in the selected sample slot, as shown in Figure 8-101.

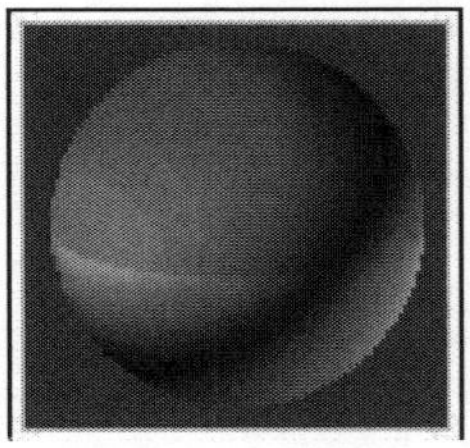

Figure 8-101 *The sample slot after assigning the* ***Bitmap*** *map*

7. Next, invoke the **Go to Parent** tool from the **Material Editor** dialog box to go back to the **Standard** material.

8. In the **Specular Highlights** area of the **Material Editor**, set the values as given below:

   Specular Level: **96** Glossiness: **18** Soften: **0.1**

9. In the **Opacity** spinner, set the value **30** to make the object transparent.

   Next, you need to assign the same image (*CHROMBLU.jpg*) to the **Opacity** map that you have assigned to the **Diffuse** map to get a realistic effect.

10. Move the cursor over the **Diffuse** map button that is labeled as **M**. Press and hold the left mouse button and then drag it to the **Opacity** map button on the right of the **Opacity** spinner. Next, release the left mouse button; the **Copy (Instance) Map** dialog box is displayed.

11. In this dialog box, select the **Copy** radio button and choose the **OK** button; the same image is assigned to the **Opacity** map. Also, the square button is labeled as **M**.

Note
You can also insert the ***Diffuse*** *and* ***Opacity*** *maps using the* ***Maps*** *rollout.*

Next, you need to apply the **glass** material to the cocktail glasses.

12. Make sure that the cocktail glasses are selected in the viewport. In the **Material Editor** dialog box, make sure that the **glass** material is selected.

13. Next, invoke the **Assign Material to Selection** tool; the **glass** material is assigned to the cocktail glasses in the viewport.

14. Now, invoke the **Show Shaded Material in Viewport** tool to display the **glass** material on the object in the viewport, as shown in Figure 8-102. Close the **Material Editor** dialog box.

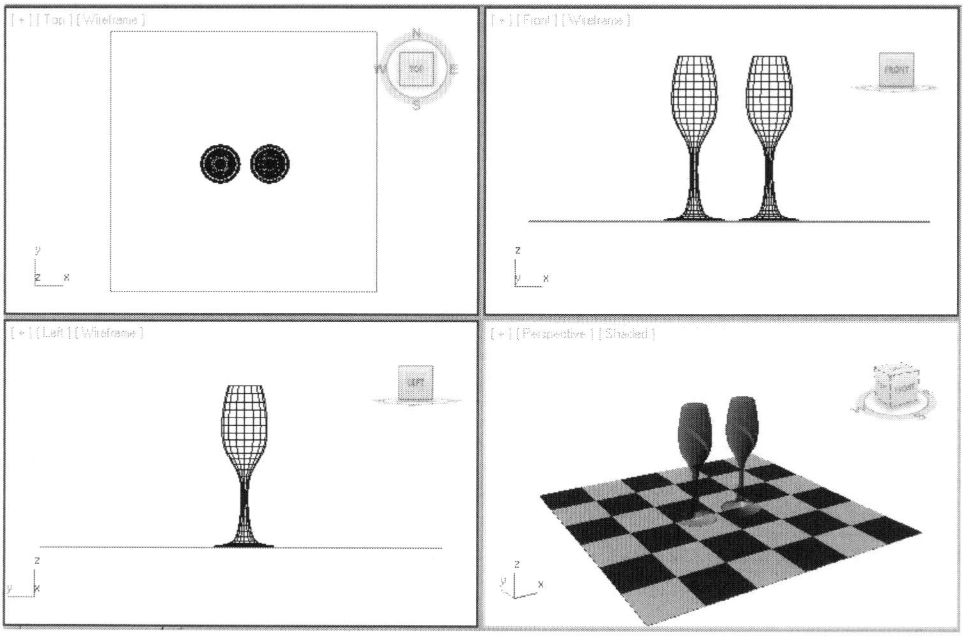

Figure 8-102 *The **glass** material displayed on the cocktail glasses*

Rendering the Scene for the Final Output

1. Activate the Perspective viewport. Render the view using the **Render Production** tool in the **Main Toolbar**; the final output of the scene is displayed, as shown in Figure 8-103.

   You can view the final rendered image of this model by downloading the file *c08_3dsmax_2012_render.zip* from *http://www.cadcim.com*.

Figure 8-103 *The final output of the scene*

Saving the File

1. Save the file with the name *c08tut1.max* as discussed in earlier chapters. The location of this file is given below:

   \Documents\3dsmax\c08_tut1\scenes

Tutorial 2

In this tutorial, you will assign a brass material to a flower pot, as shown in Figure 8-104.

(Expected time: 15 min)

Figure 8-104 *Model for Tutorial 2*

The following steps are required to complete this tutorial:

a. Set the project folder.
b. Download and open the file.
c. Create brass material for the flower pot.
d. Render the scene for the final output.
e. Save the file.

Setting the Project Folder

1. Set the project folder with the name *c08_tut2* in the *3dsmax* folder as discussed in earlier chapters.

Downloading and Opening the File

1. Before you start the tutorial, download the *c08_3dsmax_2012_tut.zip* file from *http://www.cadcim.com*. The path of the file is as follows:

   Textbooks > Animation and Visual Effects > 3ds Max > Autodesk 3ds Max 2012: A Comprehensive Guide

   Extract the contents of the zipped file and save them in the *\Documents* folder.

2. Choose **Open** from the **Application menu**; the **Open File** dialog box is displayed. In this dialog box, browse to the location *\Documents\c08_3dsmax_2012_tut* and select the *c08_tut2_start.max* file in it. Choose the **Open** button to open the file, refer to Figure 8-105.

Note

Instead of following steps 1 and 2, you can directly open the file that you created in Exercise 3 of Chapter 7 and follow step 3 given below to save it.

3. Now, choose **Save As** from the **Application menu**; the **Save File As** dialog box is displayed. Browse to the location *\Documents\3dsmax\c08_tut2\scenes*. Save the file with the name *c08tut2.max* at this location.

4. Browse to the *c08_3dsmax_2012_tut* folder and copy the *Lakerem2.jpg* file from this folder to the location *\Documents\3dsmax\c08_tut2\sceneassets\images.*

5. Delete two flowerpots from the scene; a single flowerpot remains in the viewport, as shown in Figure 8-105.

Figure 8-105 *The flower pot with a plant in all viewports*

Creating Brass Material for the Flower Pot

1. Select the *flower pot* in any viewport and invoke the **Compact Material Editor** tool from the **Main Toolbar**; the **Material Editor** dialog box is displayed.

2. Select one of the sample slots in the **Material Editor** dialog box. In the **Material Name** drop-down list of this dialog box, enter **brass** and then press the ENTER key.

3. By default, the **Standard** material is selected in the **Material Type** button and you need to use the same for creating the **brass** material.

   Next, you need to set parameters for the **Standard** material.

4. In the **Shader Basic Parameters** rollout, select the **Metal** shader option from the drop-down list; the **Metal Basic Parameters** rollout is displayed. Select the **2-Sided** check box.

5. In the **Metal Basic Parameters** rollout, use the **Diffuse** color swatch to change the color of the material; the **Color Selector** dialog box is displayed. Set the values as given below:

   Red: **253** Green: **159** Blue: **37**

   Now, choose the **OK** button to close this dialog box.

6. In the **Specular Highlights** area, set the values as given below:

   Specular Level: **80** Glossiness: **75**

   Next, you need to assign the **Reflection** map from the **Maps** rollout to get a realistic effect.

7. Expand the **Maps** rollout in the **Material Editor** dialog box; a list of maps is displayed.

8. Select the **Reflection** check box to make it active. Choose the **Reflection** map button that is labeled as **None** on the right of the **Reflection** spinner; the **Material/Map Browser** dialog box is displayed. Select the **Bitmap** map from the **Maps > Standard** rollouts and choose the **OK** button; the **Select Bitmap Image File** dialog box is displayed.

9. As the project folder is already set, the path *\Documents\3dsmax\c08_tut2\sceneassets\images* is displayed in the **Look in** text box of this dialog box. Select the file *Lakerem2.jpg* from it and choose the **Open** button; the image is displayed in the selected sample slot, as shown in Figure 8-106.

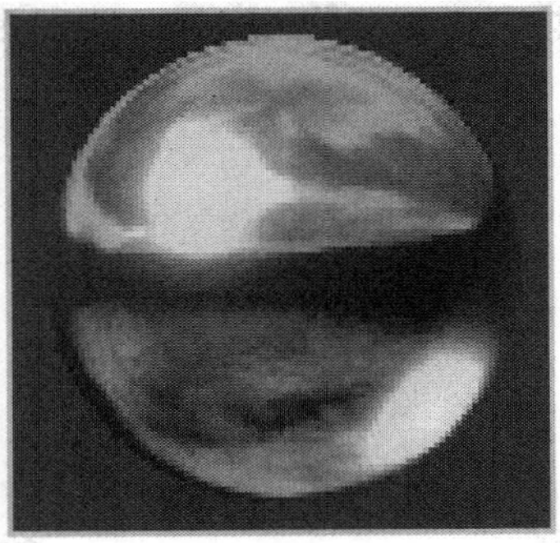

Figure 8-106 *The brass material displayed in the sample slot*

10. Invoke the **Go to Parent** tool from the **Material Editor** dialog box. In the **Maps** rollout, set the value **50** in the **Reflection** spinner.

    Next, you need to apply the **brass** material to the *flower pot*.

11. Make sure that the *flower pot* is selected in the viewport and the **brass** material is selected in the **Material Editor** dialog box.

12. Next, invoke the **Assign Material to Selection** tool; the **brass** material is assigned to the *flower pot*.

13. Now, invoke the **Show Shaded Material in Viewport** tool; the **brass** material is displayed on the *flower pot* in the Perspective viewport, as shown in Figure 8-107.

Rendering the Scene for the Final Output

1. Activate the Perspective viewport. Render the scene using the **Render Production** tool in the **Main Toolbar**; the final output is displayed, as shown in Figure 8-108.

*Figure 8-107 The **brass** material displayed in the flower pot*

Figure 8-108 The final output at rendering

You can view the final rendered image of this model by downloading the file *c08_3dsmax_2012_render.zip* from *http://www.cadcim.com*.

Saving the File

1. Save the file with the name *c08tut2.max* as discussed in earlier chapters. The location of this file is given below:

   \Documents\3dsmax\c08_tut2\scenes

Tutorial 3

In this tutorial, you will assign a map to the LCD computer, as shown in Figure 8-109, which you created in Tutorial 2 of Chapter 6. **(Expected time: 15 min)**

The following steps are required to complete this tutorial:

a. Set the project folder.
b. Download and open the file.
c. Assign the map to the LCD screen.
d. Render the scene for the final output.
e. Save the file.

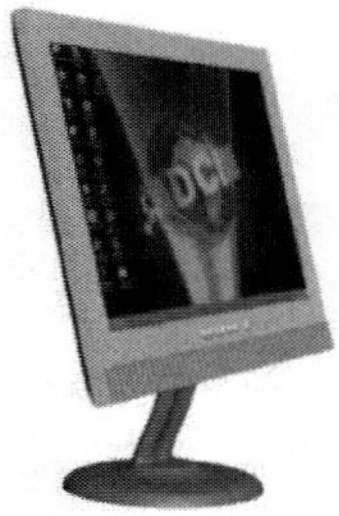

Figure 8-109 Model for Tutorial 3

Setting the Project Folder

1. Set the project folder with the name *c08_tut3* in the *3dsmax* folder as discussed in earlier chapters.

Downloading and Opening the file

1. Before you start the tutorial, download the *c08_3dsmax_2012_tut.zip* file from *http://www.cadcim.com*. The path of the file is as follows:

   Textbooks > Animation and Visual Effects > 3ds Max > Autodesk 3ds Max 2012: A Comprehensive Guide

   Extract the contents of the zipped file and save them in the *\Documents* folder.

2. Choose **Open** from the **Application menu**; the **Open File** dialog box is displayed. In this dialog box, browse to the location *\Documents\c08_3dsmax_2012_tut* and select the *c08_tut3_start.max* file in it. Choose the **Open** button to open the file, refer to Figure 8-110.

Note
Instead of following steps 1 and 2, you can directly open the file that you created in Tutorial 2 of Chapter 6 and follow step 3 given below to save it.

3. Now, choose **Save As** from the **Application menu**; the **Save File As** dialog box is displayed. Browse to the location *\Documents\3dsmax\c08_tut3\scenes*. Save the file with the name *c08tut3.max* at this location.

Assigning the Map to the LCD Screen

First, you need to create an image similar to the desktop of the computer for the screen.

1. To do so, display the image on your computer screen and press the Prt Scr key. Now, open a new file in the **Microsoft Paint** software. Press the CTRL+V keys to paste the image in

the file. Then, save the file with the name *desktop_screen* in the *jpg* format to the location *\Documents\3dsmax\c08_tut3\sceneassets\images*.

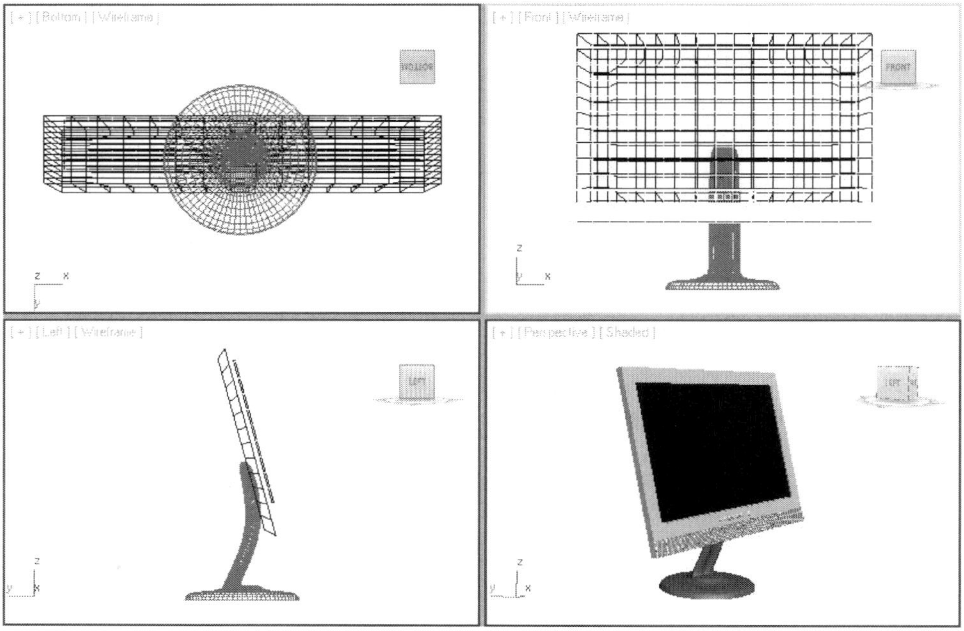

Figure 8-110 *The LCD computer in all viewports*

2. Select the *screen* of the LCD computer in any viewport and then invoke the **Compact Material Editor** tool from the **Main Toolbar**; the **Material Editor** dialog box is displayed.

3. Select one of the sample slots from the **Material Editor** dialog box. In the **Material Name** drop-down list, enter **screen** and press the ENTER key.

4. By default, the **Standard** material is selected in the **Material Type** button. You will use the same material for assigning the map.

   Next, you need to assign the *desktop_screen.jpg* image to the **Diffuse** map button.

5. Make sure that the **Blinn** shader is selected in the **Shader Basic Parameters** rollout.

6. In the **Blinn Basic Parameters** rollout, choose the **Diffuse** map button; the **Material/Map Browser** dialog box is displayed. Select the **Bitmap** map from the **Maps > Standard** rollouts and choose the **OK** button; the **Select Bitmap Image File** dialog box is displayed. As the project folder is already set, the path *\Documents\3dsmax\c08_tut3\sceneassets\images* is displayed in the **Look in** text box of this dialog box. Select the file *desktop_screen.jpg* and then choose the **Open** button; the image is displayed in the selected sample slot.

7. Invoke the **Go to Parent** tool.

8. In the **Specular Highlights** area, set the values as given below:

   Specular Level: **40** Glossiness: **16** Soften: **0.1**

   Next, you need to apply the map to the *screen*.

9. Make sure that the *screen* is selected in the viewport and the **screen** material is selected in the **Material Editor** dialog box.

10. Invoke the **Assign Material to Selection** tool; the **screen** material is assigned to the *screen* of the LCD computer in the viewport.

11. Now, invoke the **Show Shaded Material in Viewport** tool; the **screen** material is displayed on the *screen* in the Perspective viewport, as shown in Figure 8-111.

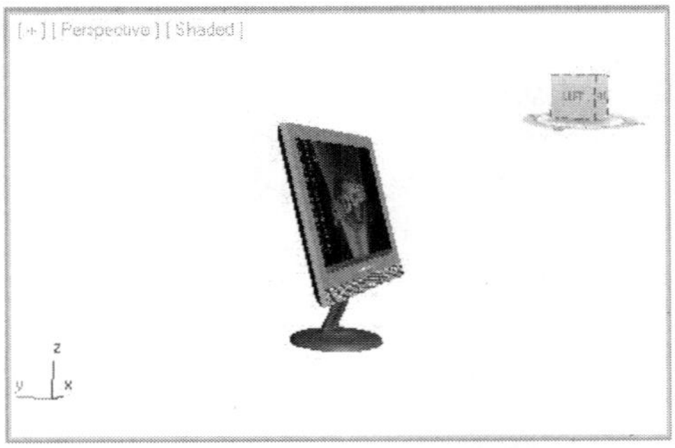

***Figure 8-111** The **screen** material assigned to the screen of the computer*

You can also assign other materials or maps to different parts of the computer to give it a realistic look.

Rendering the Scene for the Final Output

1. Activate the Perspective viewport. Render the scene using the **Render Production** tool in the **Main Toolbar**; the final output is displayed, as shown in Figures 8-112 and 8-113.

   You can view the final rendered image of this model by downloading the file *c08_3dsmax_2012_render.zip* from *http://www.cadcim.com*.

Saving the File

1. Save the file with the name *c08tut3.max* as discussed in earlier chapters. The location of this file is given below:

   \Documents\3dsmax\c08_tut3\scenes

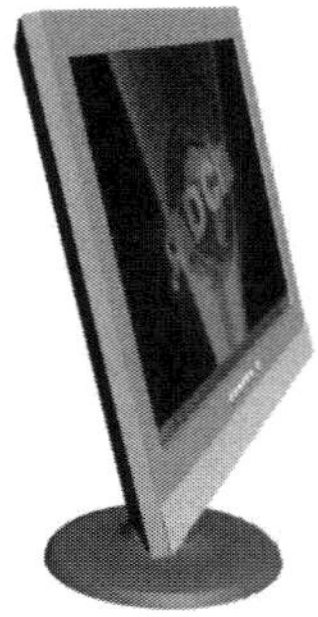

***Figure 8-112** The final output at rendering (view 1)*

***Figure 8-113** The final output at rendering (view 2)*

Self-Evaluation Test

Answer the following questions and then compare them to those given at the end of this chapter:

1. Which of the following key combination is used to invoke the **Slate Material Editor** dialog box?

    (a) ALT+M (b) CTRL+M
    (c) M (d) ALT+CTRL+M

2. Which of the following tools in the **Material Editor** dialog box is used to pick material from an object in the viewport to apply it to the active sample slot?

    (a) **Assign Material to Selection** (b) **Get Material**
    (c) **Pick Material From Object** (d) All of these

3. Which of the following materials is known as the **Compound** material?

    (a) **Blend** (b) **Composite**
    (c) **Double-Sided** (d) All of these

4. Which of the following materials has the **Templates** rollout to insert preset materials to the objects?

    (a) **Standard** (b) **Architectural**
    (c) **Raytrace** (d) **Composite**

5. Which of the following shaders in the **Standard** material is used to create elliptical highlights?

(a) **Anisotropic** (b) **Blinn**
(c) **Metal** (d) **Phong**

6. The __________ color swatch in the **Basic Parameters** rollout of shaders is used to specify the color of the objects in direct light.

7. The __________ shader in the **Standard** material is used to create dull or matte highlights.

8. The __________ material is used to provide highly realistic raytraced images.

9. The **Material Editor** tool is used to create new materials and maps for objects to make them look more realistic. (T/F)

10. The **Get Material** tool is used to select materials or maps for the selected sample slot. (T/F)

11. The **Phong** shader is very similar to the **Oren-Nayar-Blinn** shader. (T/F)

Review Questions

Answer the following questions:

1. Which of the following maps in the **Material/Map Browser** dialog box is a 2D map?

(a) **Checker** (b) **Bitmap**
(c) **Cellular** (d) **Wood**

2. Which of the following maps is used to select default images from the file to make the objects realistic?

(a) **Checker** (b) **Dent**
(c) **Bitmap** (d) All of these

3. Which of the following maps is used to produce textures such as plaster and cement?

(a) **Stucco** (b) **Speckle**
(c) **Splat** (d) **Smoke**

4. The **Compositor** maps are used to modify or change the color of pixels in a material. (T/F)

5. You can insert maps in different materials using the **Maps** rollout. (T/F)

6. The **Flat Mirror** map is used to generate reflections and refractions based on the objects in the scene. (T/F)

7. The **Anisotropic** shader in the **Standard** material has two specular highlight controls. (T/F)

8. The __________ spinner in the **Basic Parameters** rollout of the **Standard** material is used to control the transparency of material.

9. The __________ material is used to create the preset materials such as **Glass**, **Water**, **Paper**, and so on.

10. The **Ambient** color swatch in the __________ material is used to specify the amount of absorption of the ambient light by the material.

Exercises

Exercise 1

Start Autodesk 3ds Max 2012 and then perform the following operations:

Create an object in the viewport and invoke the **Compact Material Editor** tool; the **Material Editor** dialog box will be displayed. Then, try the following operations:

1. By default, the **Standard** material is selected. In the **Shader Basic Parameters** rollout, select the **Anisotropic** shader from the drop-down list. Modify the parameters of the **Anisotropic Basic Parameters** rollout and assign a material to the object in the viewport using the **Assign Material to Selection** tool. Then, render the Perspective viewport to notice the effects. Use different shaders in the drop-down list to notice the difference in the shaders.

2. Invoke the **Get Material** tool; the **Material/Map Browser** dialog box is displayed. Select the **Architectural** material from the material list in the dialog box. In the **Templates** rollout, select various preset materials from the drop-down list. Set the parameters for the selected materials using the **Physical Qualities** rollout. Then, assign a material to the object in the viewport using the **Assign Material to Selection** tool. Render the Perspective viewport to notice the effects in the output. Select different materials from the list displayed in the **Material/Map Browser** dialog box and assign them to the objects to view various realistic effects in the objects.

3. In the **Standard** material, select any shader from the drop-down list in the **Shader Basic Parameters** rollout. In the **Basic Parameters** rollout, select the **Diffuse** map button on the right of the **Diffuse** color swatch; the **Material/Map Browser** dialog box will be displayed. Select different maps from the maps list in the **Material/Map Browser** dialog box and

assign the maps to the objects in the viewports. Next, render the Perspective viewport to notice the effects in the final output.

4. In the **Standard** material, set the value below 100 in the **Opacity** spinner. Modify other parameters in the **Basic Parameters** rollout and assign the material to the objects in the viewport. Next, render the Perspective viewport to notice the effect of opacity in the final output.

5. Try to assign different maps and materials to all objects created in the previous chapters to make them more realistic.

Exercise 2

Create the model shown in Figure 8-114 using the **Line** tool and the **Lathe** modifier. To create the steel material, you need to use the **Oren-Nayar-Blinn** shader in the **Standard** material and the **Reflection** map in the **Maps** rollout. You can view the final rendered image of this model by downloading it from *http://www.cadcim.com*. **(Expected time: 15 min)**

Figure 8-114 *Model for Exercise 2*

Exercise 3

Download the file *c08_3dsmax_2012_exer.zip* from *http://www.cadcim.com*. Extract the contents of the zipped file and open *c08_exer3_start* from it. Next, assign different maps and materials to give it a realistic view, as shown in Figure 8-115. **(Expected time: 15 min)**

You can view the final rendered image of this scene by downloading it from the following website: *http://www.cadcim.com*.

Figure 8-115 *Scene for Exercise 3*

Exercise 4

Create an object in the viewport, as shown in Figure 8-116. Then, create a copper material using the **Phong** shader in the **Standard** material and assign this material to the object. You can view the final rendered image of this model by downloading it from *http://www.cadcim.com*.

(Expected time: 15 min)

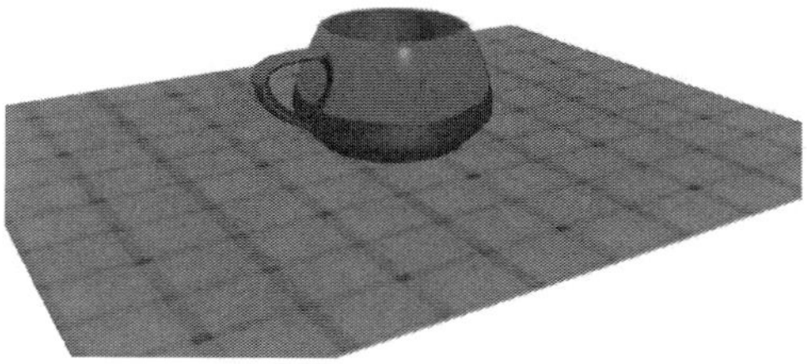

Figure 8-116 *Model for Exercise 4*

Answers to Self-Evaluation Test

1. c, **2.** c, **3.** d, **4.** b, **5.** a, **6. Diffuse**, **7. Oren-Nayar-Blinn**, **8. Raytrace**, **9.** T, **10.** T, **11.** F

9

Compound Objects

Learning Objectives

After completing this chapter, you will be able to:

- *Create compound objects*
- *Modify compound objects*

INTRODUCTION

This chapter will help you to create more complex models by combining two or more existing objects into a single object. The different techniques explained in this chapter will help you to combine different 2D and 3D shapes that would otherwise be difficult or impossible to do.

COMPOUND OBJECTS

In Autodesk 3ds Max, the compound objects are created by combining two or more objects. There are twelve methods to create various compound objects. To create these compound objects, you need to invoke their respective tools. To do so, choose **Create > Geometry** in the **Command Panel**; a drop-down list will be displayed below the **Geometry** button. Select the **Compound Objects** option from the drop-down list; the **Object Type** rollout will be displayed with all the tools to create compound objects, refer to Figure 9-1. In this chapter, you will learn to create simple compound objects.

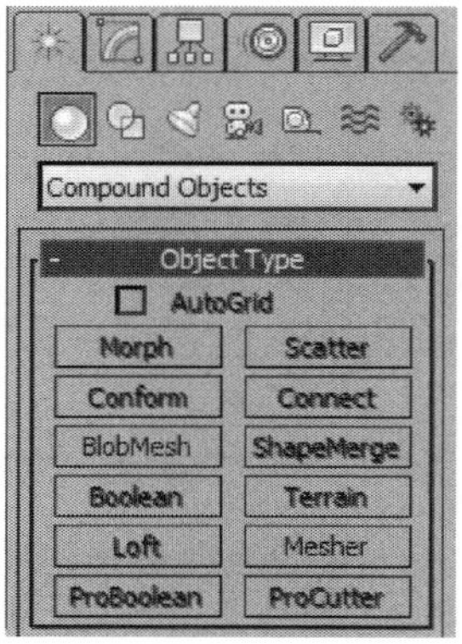

***Figure 9-1** The tools for creating compound objects displayed in the rollout*

Boolean

Menu bar:	Create > Compound > Boolean
Toolbar:	Create > Geometry > Compound Objects > Object Type rollout > Boolean

The boolean compound objects are created from two objects. These objects are known as operands. To create the boolean compound objects, you need to perform the boolean operation on these operands using the **Boolean** tool.

To create a boolean object, first create two overlapping objects in the viewport. Select one of the objects in the viewport. Choose **Create > Geometry** in the **Command Panel**; a drop-down list will be displayed. Select the **Compound Objects** option from the drop-down list and invoke the **Boolean** tool from the **Object Type** rollout; the **Name and Color**, **Pick Boolean**, **Parameters**, and **Display/Update** rollouts will be displayed, as shown in Figure 9-2. And, the selected object will become operand A. Next, choose the **Pick Operand B** button in the **Pick Boolean** rollout and move the cursor over the second object or operand B in the viewport; the cursor will get changed to the selection cursor. Now, select the second object to perform the boolean operation, refer to Figures 9-3 and 9-4. Right-click in the viewport to exit the boolean command. The most commonly used rollouts of this tool are discussed next.

Pick Boolean Rollout

The **Pick Operand B** button in this rollout is used to select the second object or operand B in the viewport to complete the boolean operation. There are four radio buttons to specify the type of operand B to be transferred to the boolean object. By default, the **Move** radio button is selected, which specifies that only the operand B will be used to create a boolean object. Select the **Reference** radio button to create a clone of operand B simultaneously that behaves like a reference object. Select the **Copy** radio button to create a copy of the operand B that you can use later in the scene. Select the **Instance** radio button to synchronize the animation of the Boolean object with animated changes to the original B object, and vice-versa.

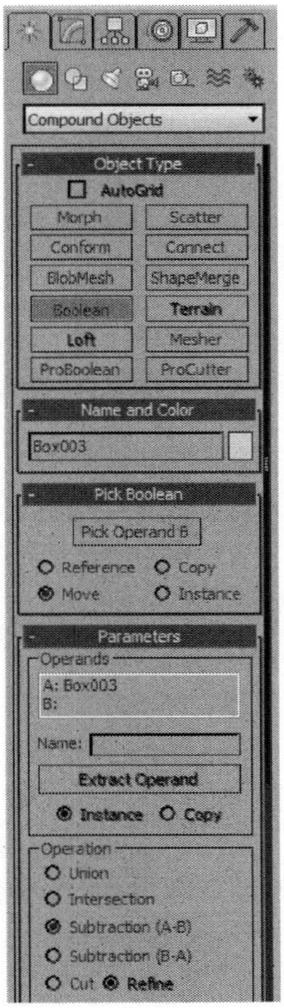

Figure 9-2 Partial view of the rollouts displayed after invoking the ***Boolean*** *tool*

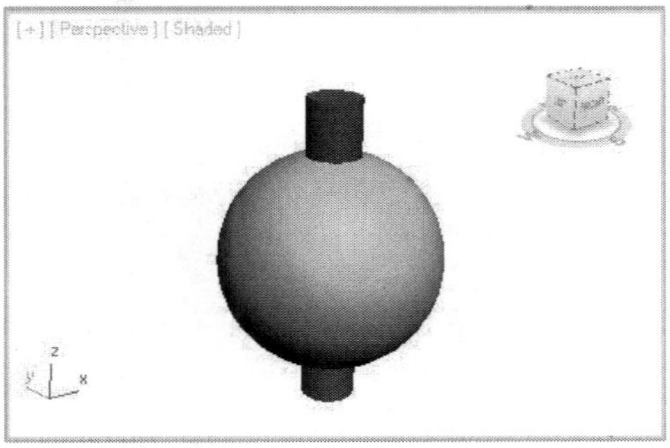

Figure 9-3 Two objects in the viewport

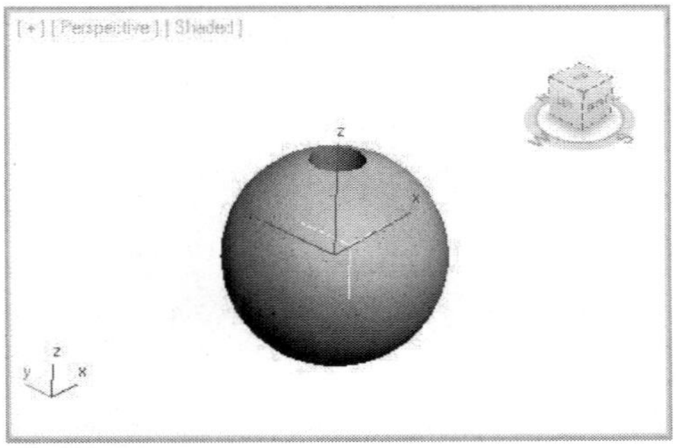

Figure 9-4 The object after performing the boolean operation

Parameters Rollout

The **Parameters** rollout is used to define the type of boolean commands. The two areas in this rollout are discussed next.

Operands Area

The list box at the top in this area displays the name of the current operands in the viewport. To change the name of the operands, make sure that the object is selected in the viewport. Now, select the operand in the list; the name of the selected operand will be displayed in the **Name** text box. You can modify its name in the **Name** text box.

The **Extract Operand** button will be available only after performing the boolean operation. It is used to extract a copy or an instance of the operands of the boolean object. To do so, select the boolean object in the viewport and choose the **Modify** tab in the **Command Panel**. Now, in the **Parameters** rollout, select the operand that you want to extract from the list box given in the **Operands** area; the **Extract Operand** button will be activated. Next, select the **Copy** radio button to extract a copy of the selected operand or select the **Instance** radio button to extract an instance of the selected operand. Choose the **Extract Operand** button; the instance or the copy of the selected operand will be displayed in the viewport.

Operation Area

The radio buttons in this area are used to specify the type of boolean operations to be performed on the operands. You need to select one of the radio buttons in this area before choosing the **Pick Operand B** button in the **Pick Boolean** rollout to perform various types of boolean operations.

Select the **Union** radio button to attach the two operands for creating one object. If the operands overlap, then the overlapping portion of the objects will be removed, refer to Figures 9-5, 9-6, and 9-7.

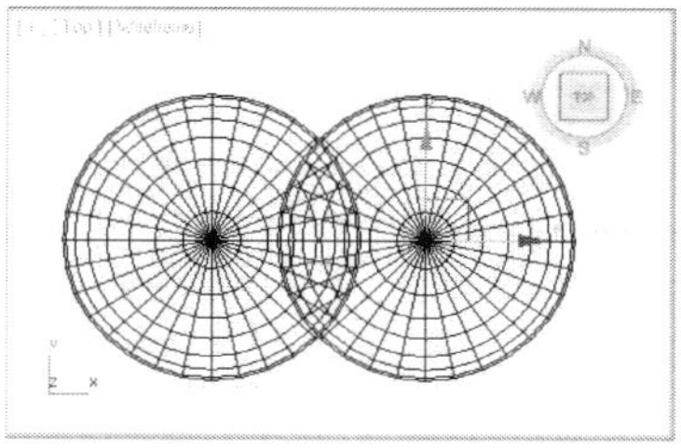

Figure 9-5 *Two spheres in the Top viewport before performing the* ***Union*** *boolean operation*

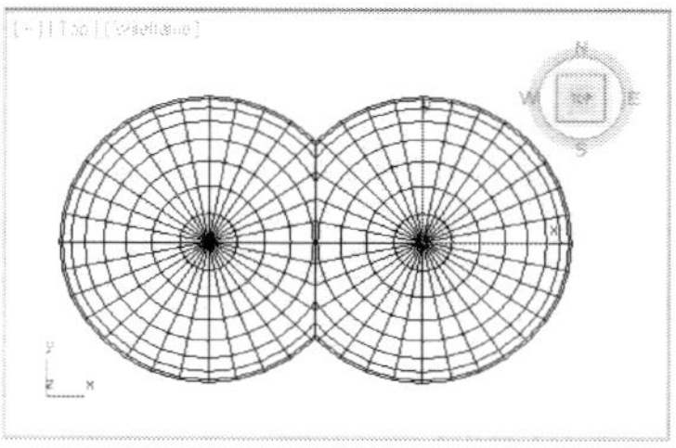

Figure 9-6 *Two spheres in the Top viewport after performing the* ***Union*** *boolean operation*

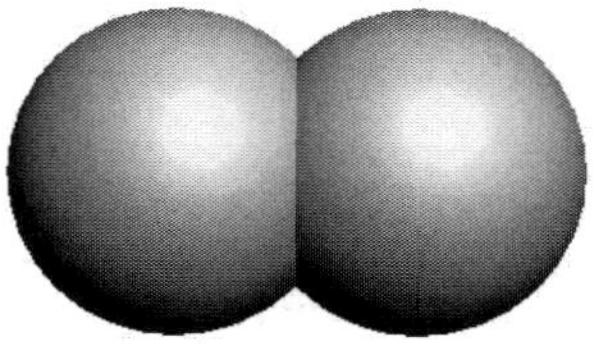

Figure 9-7 *Two spheres after performing the* ***Union*** *boolean operation in the final output*

Select the **Intersection** radio button to create a boolean object from the overlapping portion of the two operands. In this operation, the overlapping area will not be removed. Instead, the portions that are not overlapping will be removed, refer to Figures 9-8 and 9-9. Note that the operands must overlap to perform this operation.

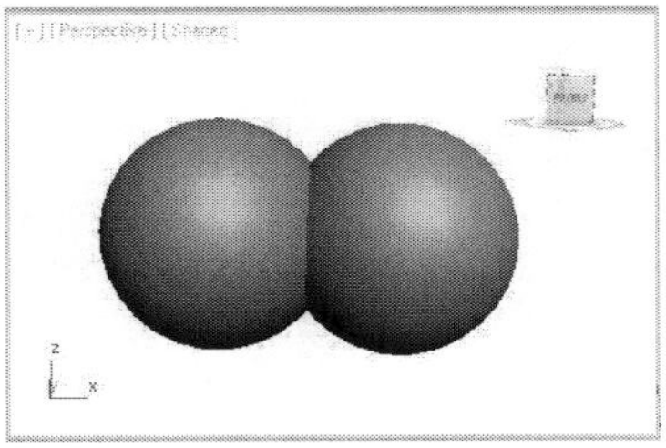

Figure 9-8 *Two spheres for the* ***Intersection*** *boolean operation*

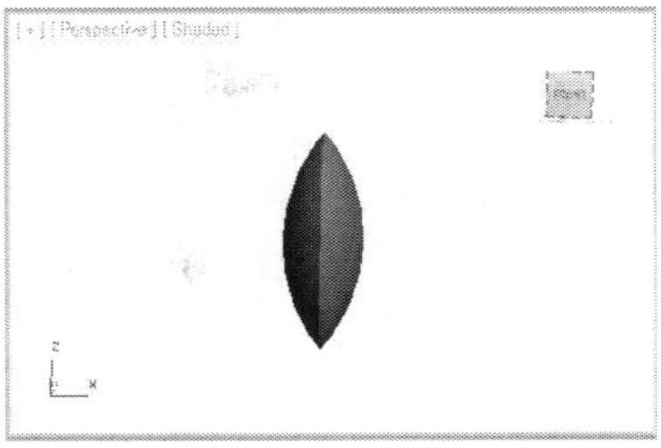

Figure 9-9 *Two spheres after performing the* ***Intersection*** *boolean operation*

By default, the **Subtraction(A-B)** radio button is selected. It is used to remove the overlapping portion of the operand B from operand A. Also, the boolean object will have the operand A with the intersection portion subtracted from it, refer to Figure 9-3 and 9-4. Note that the operands must overlap to perform this operation.

Select the **Subtraction(B-A)** radio button to remove the overlapping portion of operand A from operand B. Also, the boolean object will have the operand B with the intersection portion subtracted from it, refer to Figures 9-10 and 9-11. The operands must overlap to perform this operation.

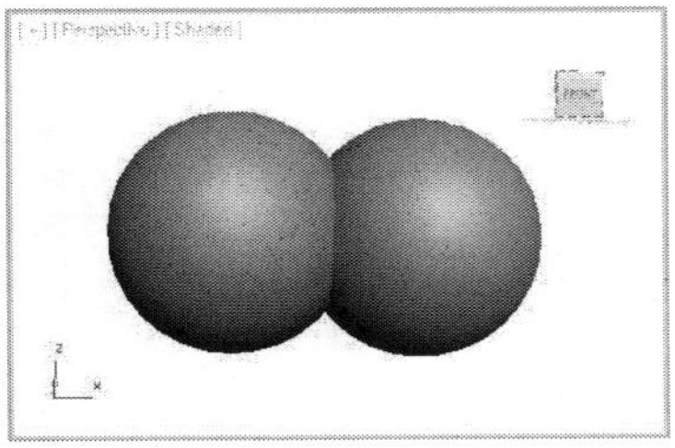

Figure 9-10 *The operand A selected to perform the* ***Subtraction(B-A)*** *boolean operation*

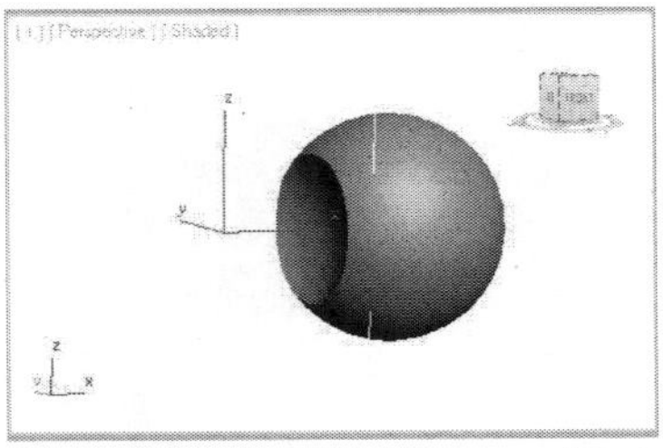

Figure 9-11 *The boolean object after performing the* ***Subtraction (B-A)*** *boolean operation*

Note

To view the effect of the **Cut** *radio button, you need to convert the operands into editable mesh objects.*

Select the **Cut** radio button; the four radio buttons, **Refine**, **Split**, **Remove Inside**, and **Remove Outside** will be activated. By default, the **Refine** radio button is selected, which is used to add new vertices, edges, and faces at the location where the operand B intersects the operand A. Select the **Split** radio button to add a double set of new vertices, edges, and faces where the operand B intersects the operand A. Select the **Remove Inside** radio button to remove all faces of operand A that are inside the operand B. Select the **Remove Outside** radio button to remove all faces of operand A that are outside the operand B.

Terrain

Menu bar: Create > Compound > Terrain
Toolbar: Create > Geometry > Compound Objects > Object Type rollout > Terrain

The terrain compound objects are created from splines. In this case, the splines represent the counter lines. The contour lines are the lines drawn on a map, which connect the points of equal height. Usually, the terrain objects are used to add buildings and roads on them to create virtual cities.

To create a terrain object, first create the contour lines in the Top viewport, as shown in Figure 9-12. Align these lines in the Front viewport, as shown in Figure 9-13. You can also import an AutoCAD drawing file to use as contour data. Next, select all the contour lines and invoke the **Terrain** tool from the **Object Type** rollout of the **Compound Objects**; a 3D terrain object will be created, as shown in Figure 9-14. The **Name and Color**, **Pick Operand**, **Parameters**, **Simplification**, and **Color by Elevation** rollouts will also be displayed to modify the terrain objects. The most commonly used rollouts are discussed next.

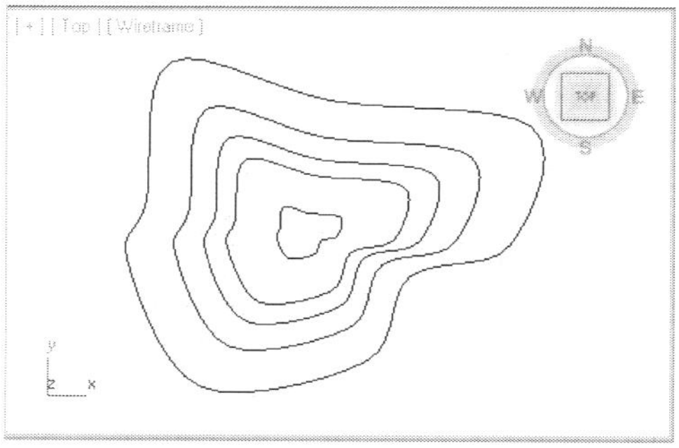

Figure 9-12 The contour lines created for the terrain object in the Top viewport

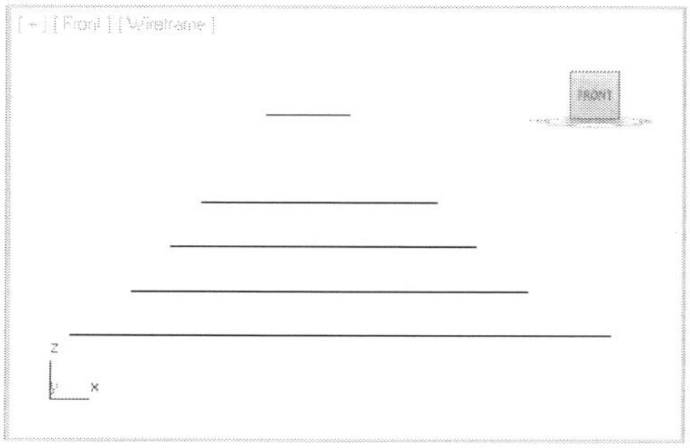

Figure 9-13 The contour lines aligned for the terrain object in the Front viewport

Pick Operand Rollout

The **Pick Operand** button in this rollout is used to add splines to the terrain object, refer to Figure 9-15. To do so, select the terrain object and choose the **Pick Operand** button. Now, move the cursor over the new spline in the viewport; the cursor will get changed to the selection cursor. Next, select the additional splines one by one to add them to the terrain object. In this rollout, the four radio buttons, **Reference**, **Copy**, **Move**, and **Instance** are used to specify the type of new contours to be added to the terrain object. The functions of these radio buttons are same as those discussed in the **Pick Boolean** rollout of the **Boolean** compound object earlier in the chapter.

Parameters Rollout

The areas in this rollout are discussed next.

Operands Area

The list box on the top of the **Operands** area displays the list of the current operands in the viewport, refer to Figure 9-16. The **Delete Operand** button is used to delete operand or contour lines from the terrain object. To do so, select the name of the operand from the list that you want to delete and choose the **Delete Operand** button.

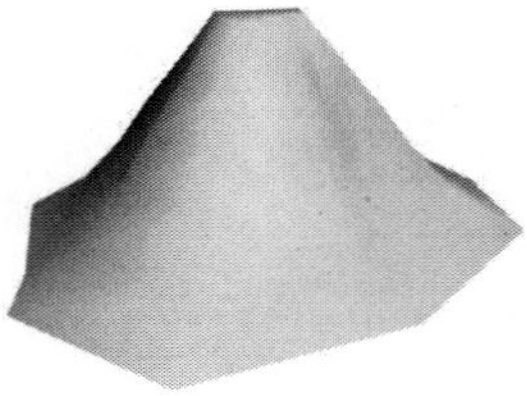

Figure 9-14 The terrain object created from the contour lines

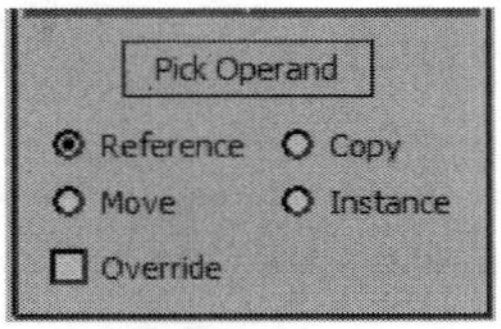

Figure 9-15 *The* ***Pick Operand*** *rollout*

Form Area

The radio buttons in this area are used to specify the type of terrain object to be created. By default, the **Graded Surface** radio button is selected to create an empty surface on the bottom of the terrain object. Select the **Graded Solid** radio button to create a solid bottom or edges on the terrain object. Select the **Layered Solid** radio button to create the layered terrain objects such as in case of cardboard architectural model, as shown in Figure 9-17. Select the **Stitch Border** check box to prevent the creation of new triangles at the edges of the terrain object when the splines are open. Select the **Retriangulate** check box to create more precise terrain objects by following the contour lines more closely.

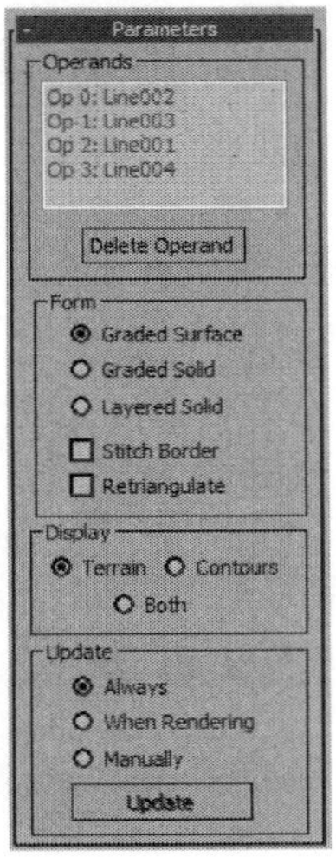

Figure 9-16 *Different areas in the* ***Parameters*** *rollout*

Figure 9-17 *The terrain object with the* ***Layered Solid*** *radio button selected*

Note

You can select the radio buttons and check boxes in the ***Form*** *area to view their effect on the terrain object in the viewport.*

Display Area

The options in the **Display** area are used to specify the type of terrain object to be displayed in the viewports. Select the **Terrain** radio button to display the triangulated mesh over the contour lines. Select the **Contours** radio button to display only the contour lines of the terrain object. Select the **Both** radio button to display the terrain as well as the contour lines in the viewport.

The options in the **Update** area are the same as those discussed in the previous chapters.

Simplification Rollout

The options in this rollout are used to set the complexity of the terrain object, refer to Figure 9-18. The areas in this rollout are discussed next.

Horizontal Area

The options in this area are used to set the number of vertices used in the terrain object. By default, the **No Simplification** radio button is selected and is used to include all vertices on the contour splines. Select the **Use 1/2 of Points** radio button to use half of the vertices of every contour line in the terrain object. Select the **Use 1/4 of Points** radio button to use one-fourth of the vertices of every contour line in the terrain object. Select the **Interpolate Points *2** radio button to double the vertices of every contour line in the terrain object. Select the **Interpolate Points *4** radio button to multiply the vertices of every contour line four times in the terrain object.

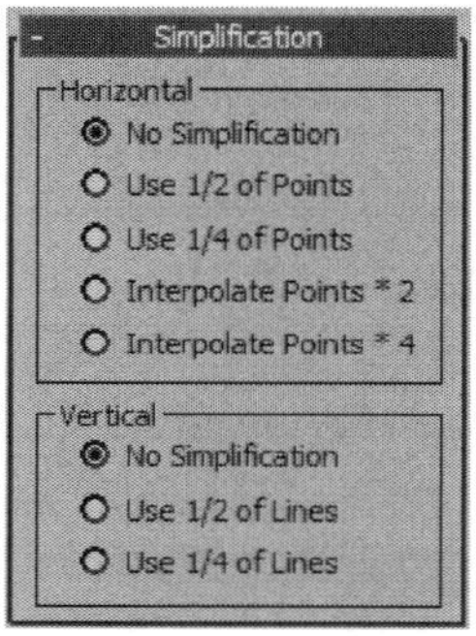

Figure 9-18 *Different areas in the* ***Simplification*** *rollout*

Vertical Area

The options in this area are used to set the number of contour lines used in the terrain object. By default, the **No Simplification** radio button is selected and is used to include all the selected contour lines in the terrain object. Select the **Use 1/2 of Lines** radio button to use half of the lines in the terrain object. Select the **Use 1/4 of Lines** radio button to use one-fourth of the contour lines in the terrain object.

Color by Elevation Rollout

The options in this rollout are used to set the color of the terrain object on the basis of the elevation of the terrain object.

Scatter

Menu bar:	Create > Compound > Scatter
Toolbar:	Create > Geometry > Compound Objects > Object Type rollout > Scatter

The **Scatter** tool is used to randomly distribute the source object as an array or over the surface of the distribution object. To create a scatter object, first create an object to be used as the source object and create another object to be used as the distribution object. Next, select the source object and invoke the **Scatter** tool from the **Object Type** rollout of the **Compound Objects**; the **Pick Distribution Object**, **Scatter Objects**, **Transforms**, **Display**, and **Load/Save Presets** rollouts will be displayed. Now, choose the **Pick Distribution Object** button in the **Pick Distribution Object** rollout and move the cursor over the distribution object; the cursor will get changed to the selection cursor. Select the distribution object in the viewport. Next, expand the **Scatters Objects** rollout. In the **Source Object Parameters** area, set the required value in the **Duplicate** spinner to create a number of duplicates of the source object, refer to Figures 9-19 and 9-20. The most commonly used rollouts of this tool are discussed next.

Pick Distribution Object Rollout

The **Pick Distribution Object** button in this rollout is used to select the distribution object in the viewport as discussed above. When you select the distribution object, the name of the selected object will be displayed next to the **Object** option at the top of the **Pick Distribution Object** rollout, refer to Figure 9-21. The four radio buttons, **Reference**, **Copy**, **Move**, and **Instance** in this rollout are used to specify the type of distribution object to be transferred to the scatter object.

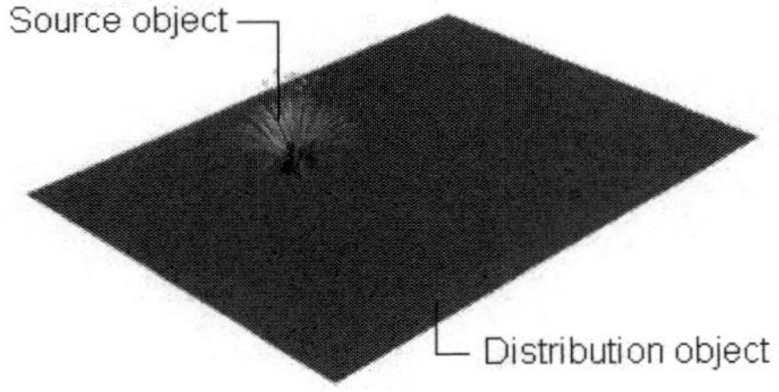

Figure 9-19 The distribution and source objects

Figure 9-20 The duplicates of the source objects distributed over the distribution object

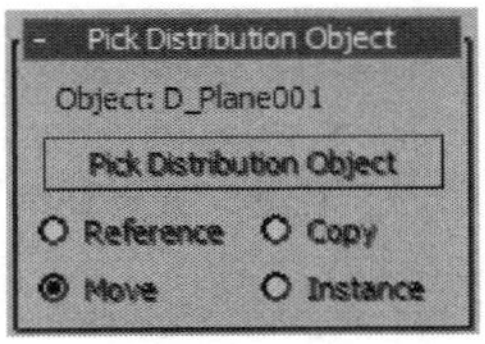

Figure 9-21 The ***Pick Distribution Object*** *rollout*

Scatter Objects Rollout

The areas in this rollout are discussed next.

Distribution Area

The two radio buttons in this area are used to specify the method of distribution of the source object. By default, the **Use Distribution Object** radio button is selected, which is used to scatter the source object according to the geometry of the distribution object. If you select the **Use Transforms Only** radio button to distribute the source object, then the distribution object is not needed. Instead, you need to use the **Transforms** rollout to position the duplicates of the source object.

To do so, select the source object and invoke the **Scatter** tool from the **Object Type** rollout in the **Compound Objects**. Make sure that the **Use Transforms Only** radio button is selected in the **Scatter Objects** rollout. Set the number of copies you want to scatter in the **Duplicate** spinner. Next, expand the **Transforms** rollout and set the transform parameters using various options in it.

Objects Area

The list box at the top of this area displays a list of source objects and the distribution objects, as shown in Figure 9-22. Select the objects in the list; their names will be displayed in the modifier stack. On selecting the name of an object in the modifier stack, the corresponding **Parameters** rollout will be displayed in the modify panel. You can modify the object using this rollout. The **Source Name** and **Distribution Name** text boxes display the names of the source object and the distribution objects, respectively. You can also modify their names by entering new names in the text box. The **Extract Operand** button is used to create an instance or a copy of the selected object in the viewport depending on the selection of the radio button below it.

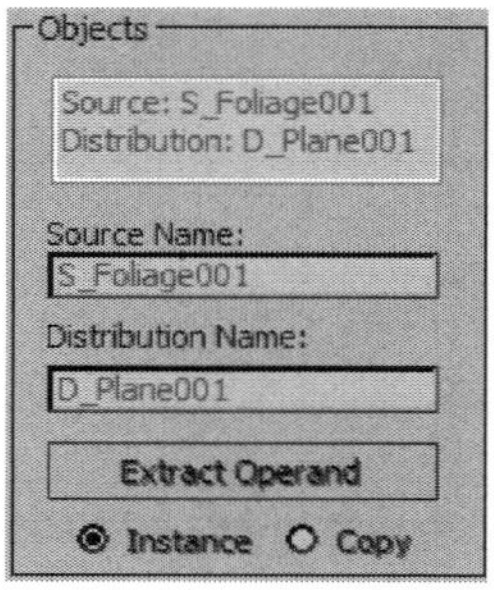

***Figure 9-22** The **Objects** area in the **Scatter Objects** area*

Source Object Parameters Area

Set the value in the **Duplicates** spinner to specify the number of source objects to be copied. Set the value in the **Base Scale** spinner to modify the scale of the source object, as shown in Figure 9-23. The value in the **Vertex Chaos** spinner is used to create a disturbance in the source object. The value in the **Animation Offset** spinner is used to create a wavy animation.

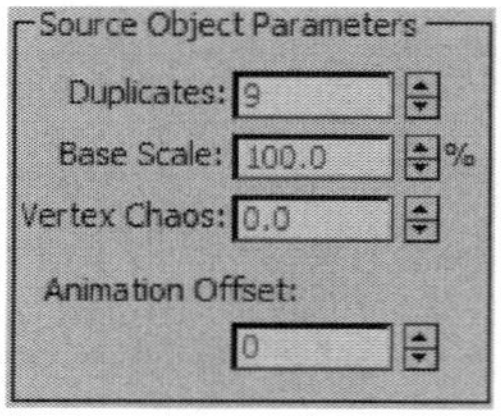

***Figure 9-23** The **Source Object Parameters** area*

Distribution Object Parameters Area

The options in this area are used to arrange the copied source object over the distribution object.

Display Area

In this area, select the **Result** radio button to display the final output after scattering or select the **Operands** radio button to display only the objects before scattering.

Transforms Rollout

Set the values in various spinners of this rollout to specify the random transform offsets for each copied source object.

Connect

Menu bar: Create > Compound > Connect
Toolbar: Create > Geometry > Compound Objects > Object Type rollout > Connect

The **Connect** tool is used to connect two or more objects at the holes on their surfaces. To connect the objects, create two objects and then convert them into editable mesh objects. Next, select the **Polygon** or **Face** sub-object level in the modifier stack. Now, select the sub-objects of the editable mesh objects in the viewport and then press the DELETE key to delete the selected sub-objects, as shown in Figure 9-24. Note that you need to position the objects in such a way that the holes should face each other. Next, select one of the objects and invoke the **Connect** tool from the **Object Type** rollout in the **Compound Objects**. Choose the **Pick Operand** button in the **Pick Operand** rollout and move the cursor over the second object in the viewport; the cursor will get changed to the selection cursor. Select another object; the new faces will be created to connect the holes of the objects, as shown in Figure 9-25. Next, right-click to end the connect command.

When you invoke the **Connect** tool, the **Name and Color**, **Pick Operand**, **Parameters**, and **Display/Update** rollouts will be displayed, as shown in Figure 9-26. The most commonly used rollouts are discussed next.

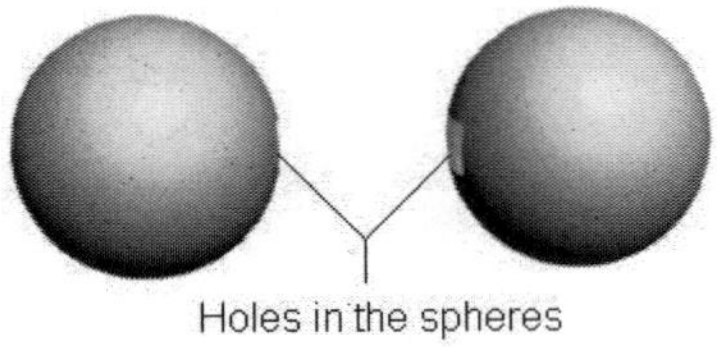

***Figure 9-24** Two spheres with holes on their surfaces*

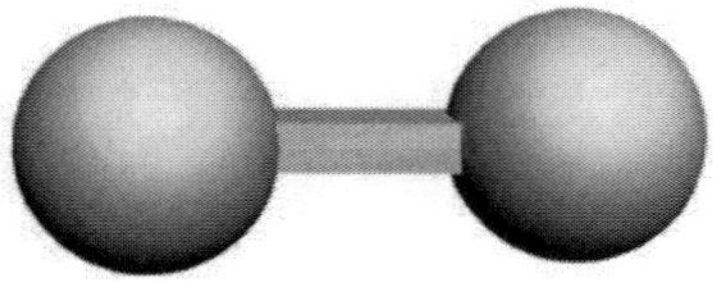

***Figure 9-25** The spheres after performing the **Connect** operation*

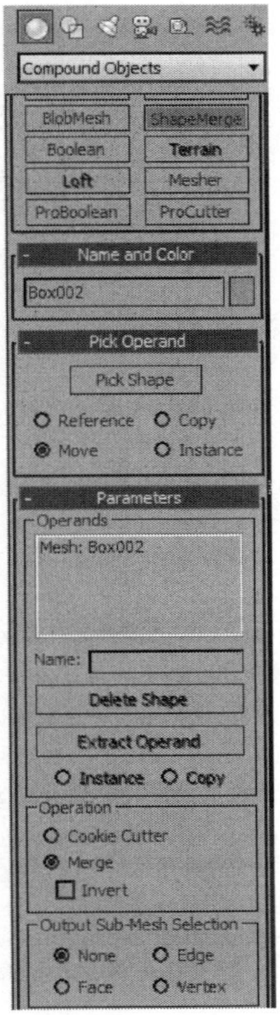

***Figure 9-26** Partial view of the rollouts displayed after invoking the **Connect** tool*

Pick Operand Rollout

As mentioned earlier, the **Pick Operand** rollout is used to select another object in the viewport. The **Pick Operand** button in this rollout has been discussed in the previous section.

Parameters Rollout

The areas in this rollout are discussed next.

Operands Area

The options in this area are the same as those discussed in the boolean compound objects.

Interpolation Area

Set the value in the **Segments** spinner to increase the number of segments in new faces, which connect the holes of the two objects. Set the value in the **Tension** spinner to create a curve in the connecting faces. To create a curve, the value in the **Segments** spinner should be high.

Smoothing Area

Select the **Bridge** check box to apply smoothness to the connecting faces of the object. Select the **Ends** check box to apply smoothness to the faces that are at the border of the old and new surfaces of the object.

Display/Update Area

The options in the **Display/Update** area are the same as those discussed in the **Boolean** tool.

Loft

Menu bar:	Create > Compound > Loft
Toolbar:	Create > Geometry > Compound Objects > Object Type rollout > Loft

The **Loft** tool is used to create 3D geometry or loft objects from the 2D shapes by lofting them along a spline path. For creating a loft object, you need to create a path and shape spline in the viewport.

To create a loft object, choose **Create > Shapes > Splines** in the **Command Panel**. Next, create a spline that you need to loft and create another spline to be used as a path. Select the spline in the viewport that you want to loft along the path. Invoke the **Loft** tool from the **Object Type** rollout in the **Compound Objects**; the **Name and Color**, **Creation Method**, **Surface Parameters**, **Path Parameters**, and **Skin Parameters** rollouts will be displayed, as shown in Figure 9-27. Now, choose the **Get Path** button in the **Creation Method** rollout and move the cursor over the path spline in the viewport; the cursor will get changed to the selection cursor. Select the path spline; the loft object will be created along the shape of the path spline, refer to Figures 9-28 and 9-29.

You can also create a loft object using the **Get Shape** button in the **Creation Method** rollout. To do so, first you need to select the path spline, and then invoke the **Loft** tool from the **Object**

Type rollout in the **Compound Objects**. Choose the **Get Shape** button in the **Creation Method** rollout; a selection cursor will be displayed in the viewport, which will prompt you to select the shape spline. Select the shape spline; the loft object will be created along the path. The most commonly used rollouts to modify the loft objects are discussed next.

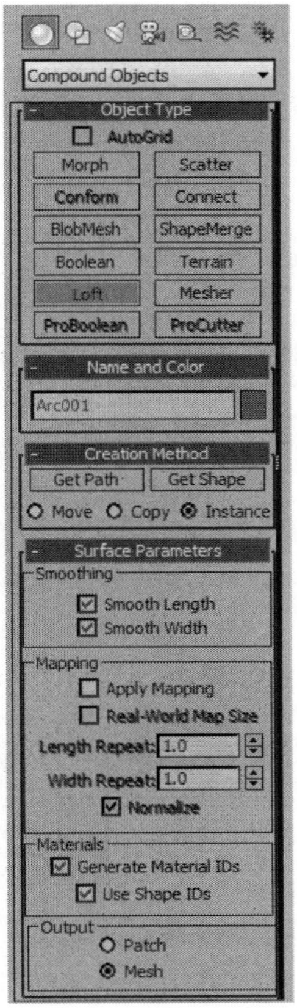

Figure 9-27 Partial view of the rollouts displayed after invoking the ***Loft*** *tool*

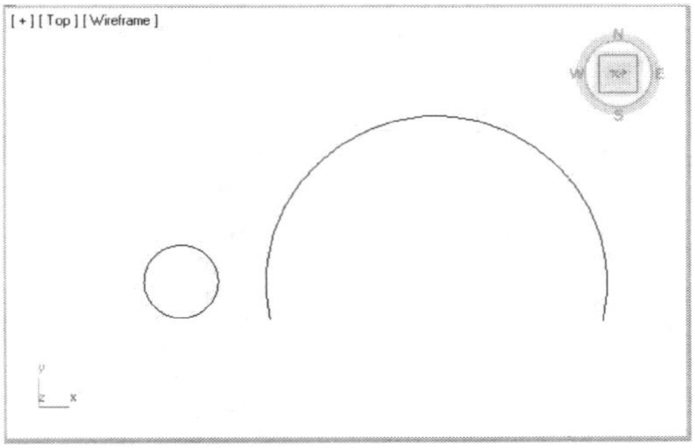

Figure 9-28 Two splines to create a loft object

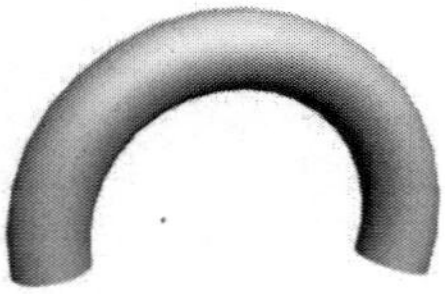

Figure 9-29 The loft object created

Creation Method Rollout

The options in the **Creation Method** rollout are used to select the path spline or the shape spline in the viewports to create a loft object. If you first select the shape spline in the viewport, then choose the **Get Path** button in the **Creation Method** rollout to select the path spline in the viewport, along which the shape will be extruded to create a loft object. If you first select the path spline in the viewport, then choose the **Get Shape** button in the **Creation Method** rollout to select the shape spline in the viewport to create a loft object along the path. Select the **Copy**, **Instance**, or **Move** radio button to specify the type of path or shape transferred to the loft object.

Surface Parameters Rollout

The options in the **Surface Parameters** rollout are used to specify the smoothness and the mapping coordinates of the lofting surface. The areas in this rollout are discussed next.

Smoothing Area

By default, the **Smooth Length** and **Smooth Width** check boxes are selected. The **Smooth Length** check box is used to provide the smoothness along the length of the path. The **Smooth Width** check box is used to provide smoothness around the circumference of the path.

Mapping Area

The **Apply Mapping** check box is used to apply the mapping coordinates to the loft object. Select this check box; the other options in this rollout will be activated. Set the value in the **Length Repeat** spinner to specify the number of times the map will be repeated along the length of the path. Set the value in the **Width Repeat** spinner to specify the number of times the map will be repeated around the circumference of the path.

Materials Area

By default, the **Generate Material IDs** and **Use Shape IDs** check boxes are selected in this area. The **Generate Material IDs** check box is used to provide the material IDs for the loft object. The **Use Shape IDs** check box is used to provide the spline material IDs to define the material IDs. The material ID is the identification number that determines which sub-material in the **Multi/Sub-Object** material is used to apply to the object in the viewport.

Output Area

The options in the **Output** area are used to define the type of the loft object to be displayed. By default, the **Mesh** radio button is selected that is used to produce a mesh loft object. Select the **Patch** radio button to produce a patch loft object.

Path Parameters Rollout

If you use more than one shape to create a complex loft object, then the options in this rollout will be used to specify the position of multiple shapes along the path of the loft object. Set the value in the **Path** spinner to define the distance between the multiple shapes along the path. Select the **On** check box; the **Snap** spinner will be activated. Set the value in the **Snap** spinner to define the snap increments while setting the value in the **Path** spinner. For example, if you set the value 10.0 in the **Snap** spinner, then on setting the value in the **Path** spinner, it will be increased in the multiples of 10.0.

By default, the **Percentage** radio button is selected. Therefore, the values in the **Path** and **Snap** spinners are defined as the percentage of the total path length. Select the **Distance** radio button to define the values in the **Path** and **Snap** spinners as the distance from the first vertex of the path. To place the shapes on the path steps and vertices, select the **Path Steps** radio button.

Skin Parameters Rollout

The options in this rollout are used to set the complexity of the mesh or patch loft object.

Deformations Rollout

This rollout will be available only when you choose the **Modify** tab in the **Command Panel**. The options in this rollout are used to modify the loft objects to get different shapes, refer to Figure 9-30. You can scale, twist, teeter, bevel, and fit the loft objects using the tools in this rollout. To modify a loft object, first select it in the viewport and then choose the **Modify** tab in the **Command Panel**. Now, expand the **Deformations** rollout and invoke one of the tools in this rollout to modify the selected loft object; the respective **Deformation** dialog box will be displayed. The **Scale Deformation(X)** dialog box is shown in Figure 9-31.

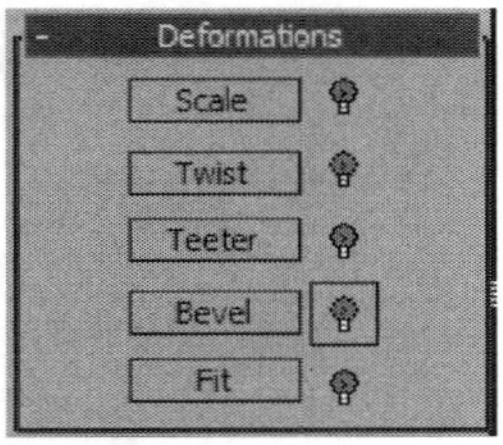

***Figure 9-30** The **Deformations** rollout*

By default, a horizontal red line is displayed in this dialog box that represents the path steps along the X-axis of the loft object. The left point on the line represents the first vertex of the path. The right point on the line represents the last vertex of the path. To modify the loft object along its X-axis, choose the **Move Control Point** button on the top of the dialog box, refer to Figure 9-31. Now, move the cursor over the first or the last vertex; the cursor gets changed. Press and hold the left mouse button on the vertex and move the cursor vertically to scale the shape of the loft object. You can also insert more vertices in between these two vertices. To do so, choose the **Insert Corner Point** button on the top of the dialog box and click on the path where you want to insert the vertices.

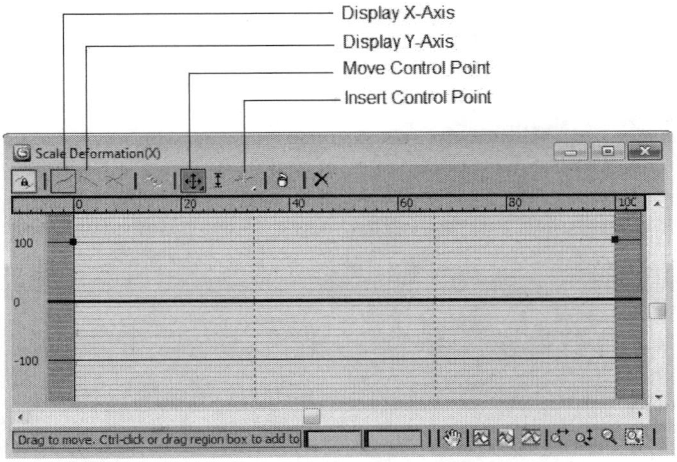

***Figure 9-31** The **Scale Deformation(X)** dialog box*

To modify the loft object along the Y-axis, choose the **Display Y-Axis** button on the top of the dialog box; the path for the Y-axis will be displayed in green color. Figures 9-32 through 9-36 show the loft objects modified using the **Scale**, **Twist**, **Fit**, **Bevel**, and **Teeter** tools.

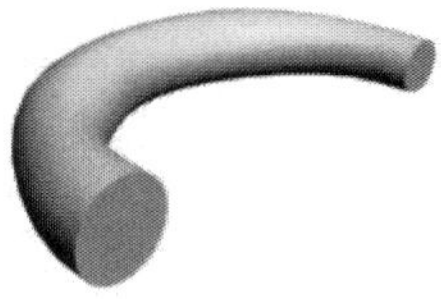

*Figure 9-32 The loft object modified using the **Scale** tool*

*Figure 9-33 The loft object modified using the **Twist** tool*

*Figure 9-34 The loft object modified using the **Fit** tool*

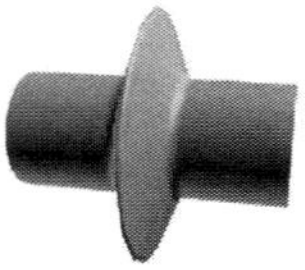

*Figure 9-35 The loft object modified using the **Bevel** tool*

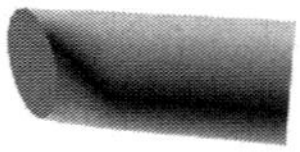

*Figure 9-36 The loft object modified using the **Teeter** tool*

ShapeMerge

Menu bar:	Create > Compound > ShapeMerge
Toolbar:	Create > Geometry > Compound Objects > Object Type rollout > ShapeMerge

In a shape merge object, the shape is either embedded in the mesh object or subtracted from it. To create a shape merge object, first you need to create a mesh object and a shape, and then align them, as shown in Figure 9-37. Next, select the mesh object and invoke the **ShapeMerge** tool from the **Object Type** rollout of the **Compound Objects**. Then, choose the **Pick Shape** button in the **Pick Operand** rollout; a selection cursor will be displayed that will prompt you to select the shape spline. Select the shape spline and right-click to exit the shape merge command.

To view the shape merge object with the embedded shape in it, select the shape merge object. Choose the **Modify** tab in the **Command Panel** and select the **Face Extrude** modifier from the **Modifier List** drop-down list. In the **Parameters** rollout of the **Face Extrude** modifier, set the value in the **Amount** spinner; the shape will be embedded in the mesh object, as shown in Figure 9-38.

To view the subtracted shape in the shape merge object, select the **ShapeMerge** object level in the modifier stack; various rollouts will be displayed. In the **Parameters** rollout, select the **Cookie Cutter** radio button in the **Operation** area; the shape will be subtracted from the mesh object, as shown in Figure 9-39.

Note
*The **Face Extrude** modifier is used to extrude the faces of the selected mesh object.*

When you invoke the **ShapeMerge** tool, the **Name and Color**, **Pick Operand**, **Parameters**, and **Display/Update** rollouts will be displayed, as shown in Figure 9-40. These rollouts are discussed next.

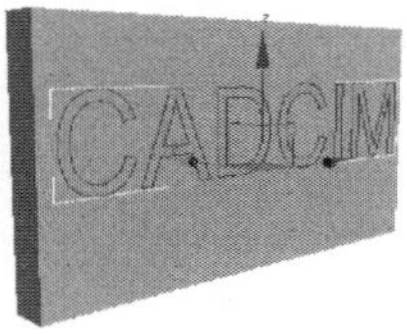

Figure 9-37 *Alignment of the shape with the mesh object*

Figure 9-38 *The shape embedded in the mesh object*

Figure 9-39 *The shape subtracted from the mesh object*

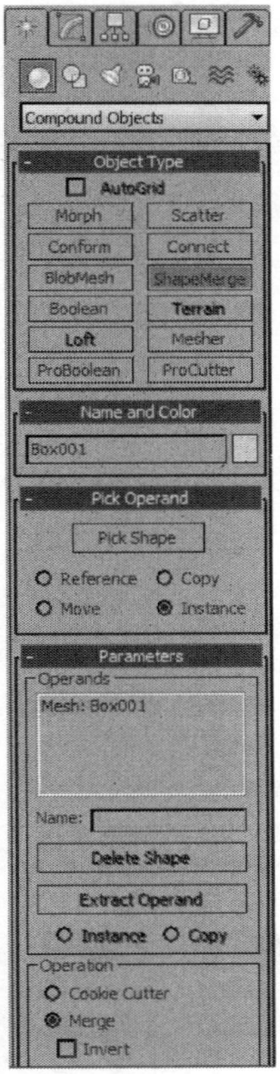

Figure 9-40 *Partial view of the rollouts displayed after invoking the **ShapeMerge** tool*

Pick Operand Rollout

The **Pick Shape** button in the **Pick Operand** rollout is used to select the shape in the viewport and to merge it in the mesh object. The other options are the same as discussed earlier.

Parameters Rollout

The areas in this rollout are discussed next.

Operands Area

The options in this area are the same as discussed earlier.

Operation Area

By default, the **Merge** radio button is selected, which is used to create an embedded shape merge object. Select the **Cookie Cutter** radio button to create the subtracted shape merge object. Select the **Invert** check box to invert the effects of the **Merge** or the **Cookie Cutter** radio button.

Display/Update Rollout

The options in this rollout are the same as discussed earlier.

Conform

Menu bar:	Create > Compound > Conform
Toolbar:	Create > Geometry > Compound Objects > Object Type rollout > Conform

The **Conform** tool is used to adjust the position of an object over another object such that the object completely fits on another object according to its shape, refer to Figure 9-41. The object that is to be positioned over another object is known as the Wrapper object, whereas the object on which the Wrapper object will be positioned is known as the Wrap-To object.

To create a conform object, create two objects. One of these objects will be used as the Wrapper object and another as the Wrap-To object. Position both the objects, refer to Figure 9-41. Select the Wrapper object and then invoke the **Conform** tool from the **Object Type** rollout in the **Compound Objects**. Choose the **Pick Wrap-To Object** button in the **Pick Wrap-To Object** rollout; a selection cursor will be displayed which will prompt you to select the Wrap-To object. Select the Wrap-To object; the Wrapper object will be positioned over the Wrap-To object in such a way that it fits according to the shape of the Wrap-To object, as shown in Figure 9-42. Next, you need to set the other parameters in the various rollouts displayed on invoking the **Conform** tool. These rollouts are discussed next.

Figure 9-41 *The road (Wrapper object) over a hilly area (Wrap-To object) before using the conform command*

Figure 9-42 *The road (Wrapper object) over a hilly area (Wrap-To object) after using the conform command*

Pick Wrap-To Object Rollout

The **Pick Wrap-To** button in this rollout is used to select the Wrap-To object in the viewport. The other options are the same as discussed earlier in this chapter.

Parameters Rollout

The areas in this rollout are discussed next.

Objects Area

The options in this area are the same as discussed earlier in this chapter.

Vertex Projection Direction Area

Select one of the radio buttons in this area to specify the projection of the vertices in the conform object.

Wrapper Parameters Area

Set the value in the **Default Projection Distance** spinner to adjust the distance of a vertex in the Wrapper object from its default position so that it intersects the Wrap-To object. Set the value in the **Standoff Distance** spinner to adjust the distance between a vertex of the Wrapper object and the surface of the Wrap-To object.

The **Update** and **Display** areas are the same as discussed earlier.

ProBoolean

Menu bar:	Create > Compound > ProBoolean
Toolbar:	Create > Geometry > Compound Objects > Object Type rollout > ProBoolean

The **ProBoolean** tool is used to perform some advance functions to boolean the objects such as selecting multiple objects to boolean at a time, changing the boolean operations, and reordering the operands. The objects that are used to create the proboolean object are called as operands. You need to perform the boolean operations on these operands using the **ProBoolean** tool.

To create a proboolean object, create two or more objects in the viewport and arrange them to perform the boolean operation. These objects should intersect each other, refer to Figure 9-43. Now, select the object from which you want to boolean the other objects. Invoke the **ProBoolean** tool from the **Object Type** rollout in the **Compound Objects**; the **Name and Color**, **Pick Boolean**, **Parameters**, and **Advanced Options** rollouts will be displayed. Next, choose the operation that you want to perform in the **Operations** area of the **Parameters** rollout. Then, choose the **Start Picking** button in the **Pick Boolean** rollout and move the cursor over another object; the boolean cursor will be displayed. Now, click on the object to perform the boolean operation. Note that the **Start Picking** button remains active and you can select more objects to boolean. Select other objects in the viewport one by one to perform the boolean operation. Then, choose the **Start Picking** button again to deactivate it, refer to Figures 9-44, 9-45, and 9-46.

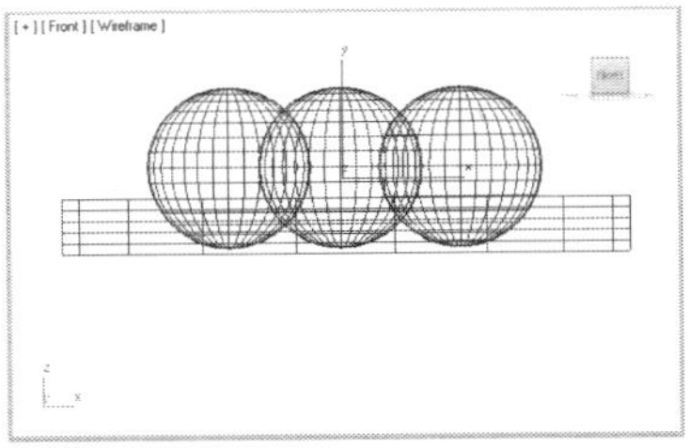

Figure 9-43 The objects to perform the proboolean operation in the Front viewport

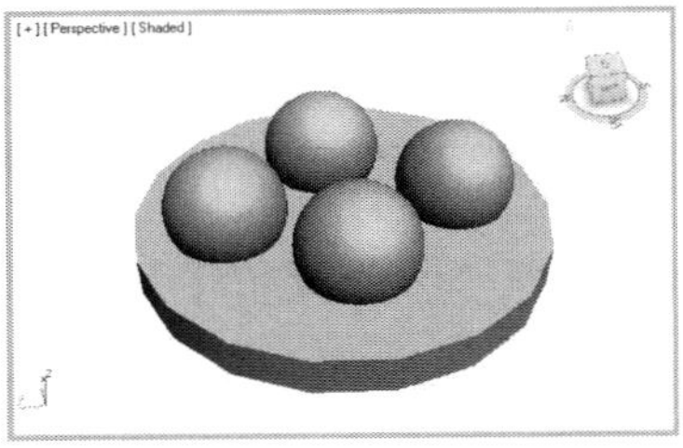

Figure 9-44 The objects to perform the proboolean operation in the Perspective viewport

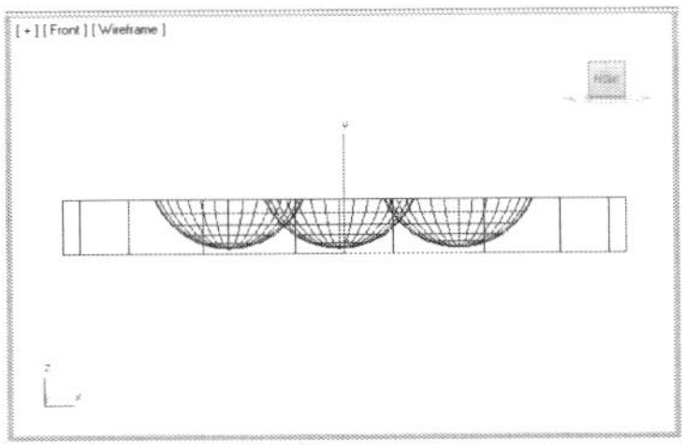

Figure 9-45 The objects after performing the proboolean operation in the Front viewport

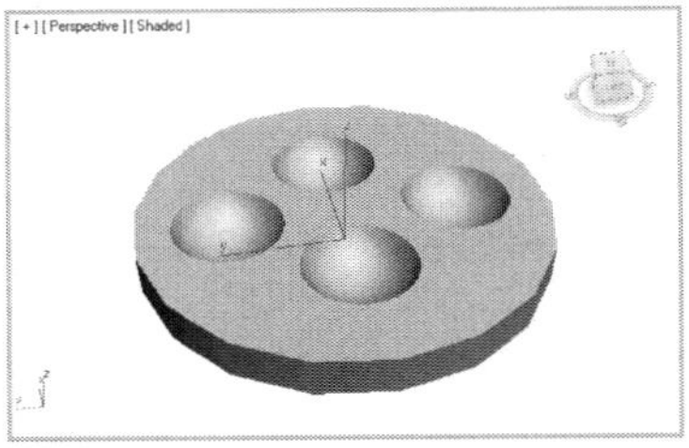

Figure 9-46 The objects after performing the proboolean operation in the Perspective viewport

The most commonly used rollouts are discussed next.

Note

*When you select the objects to boolean in the viewport, they will be displayed as operands in the text field of the **Sub-objects Operations** area in the **Parameters** rollout.*

Pick Boolean Rollout

The **Start Picking** button in this rollout is used to select the operands in the viewport to perform the proboolean operation. The other options in this rollout are the same as discussed earlier in this chapter.

Parameters Rollout

The **Parameters** rollout is used to define the type of the proboolean operation. The areas in this rollout are discussed next.

Operation Area

The options in the **Operation** area are used to specify the type of proboolean operations to be performed on the operands. You need to select one of the radio buttons in this area before choosing the **Start Picking** button in the **Pick Boolean** rollout to perform different boolean operations.

The **Union**, **Intersection**, and **Subtraction** radio buttons are the same as discussed earlier in this chapter. Select the **Merge** radio button to join the objects into a single object. You can also select one of the check boxes in this area to create more effects. Select the **Imprint** check box to print the outline of the intersecting edges of the object, refer to Figures 9-47, 9-48, and 9-49. Select the **Cookie** check box to delete the faces of the original object, as shown in Figure 9-50.

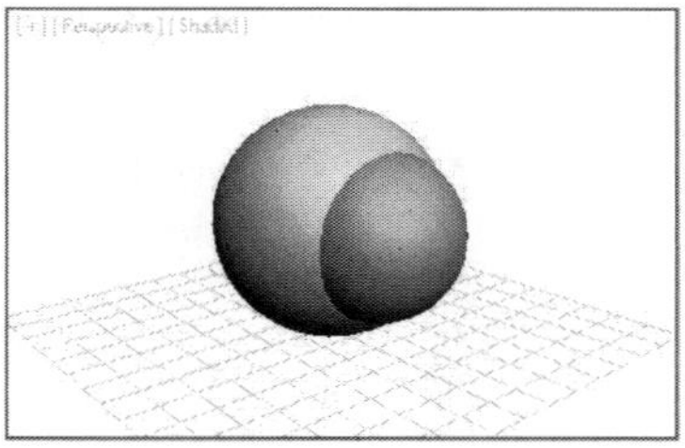

Figure 9-47 *The two spheres intersecting each other to perform the boolean operation*

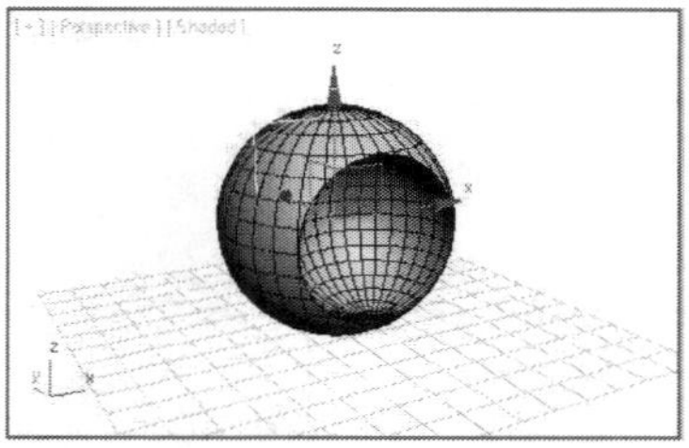

Figure 9-48 *The proboolean object after performing the boolean operation*

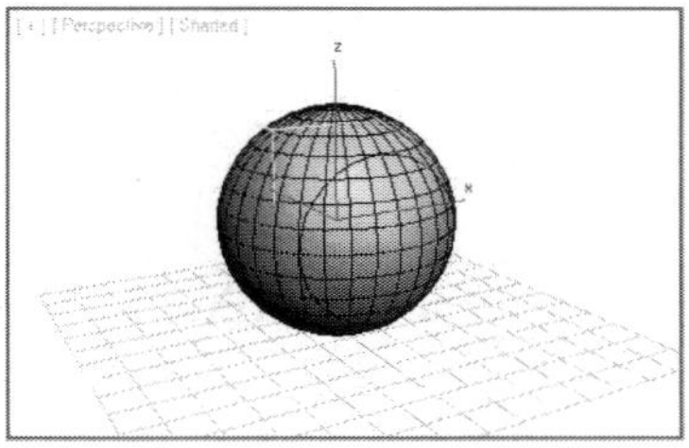

Figure 9-49 *The proboolean object after selecting the **Imprint** check box*

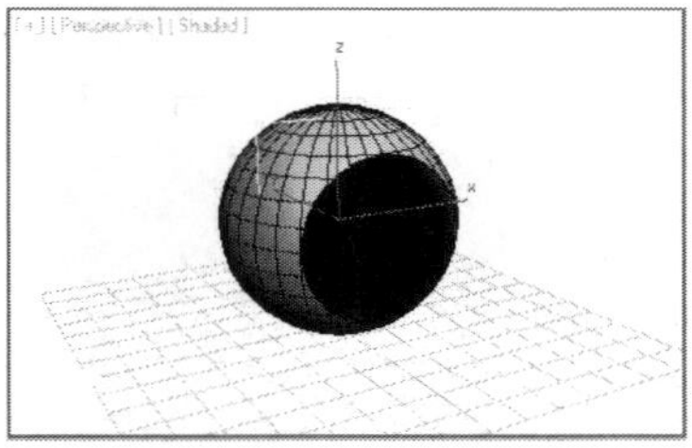

Figure 9-50 *The proboolean object after selecting the **Cookie** check box*

The options in the **Display** area are the same as discussed earlier.

Apply Material Area

Select the **Apply Operand Material** radio button in this area to apply the material of the operand to the new faces created by the proboolean operation. Select the **Retain Original Material** radio button to apply the material of the original object to the new faces created by using the proboolean operation, refer to Figures 9-51, 9-52, and 9-53.

Sub-object Operations Area

The options in this area are used on the operands created in the viewport. These operands are also highlighted in the list given at the bottom of the **Sub-object Operations** area. The **Extract Selected** button is used to extract a copy or an instance of the selected operand of the boolean object from the list. To do so, select the boolean object in the viewport, choose the **Modify** tab in the **Command Panel**, and then select the operand that you want to extract from the list in the **Parameters** rollout. Next, select the **Copy** radio button to create a copy of the selected operand. Select the **Remove** radio button to remove the selected operand from the list or select the **Inst** radio button to create an instance of the selected operand. Next, choose the **Extract Selected** button to extract the selected operand.

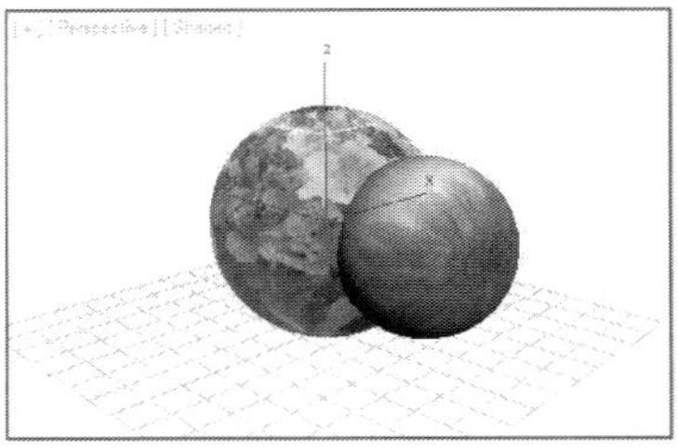

Figure 9-51 *The two spheres with materials applied on them*

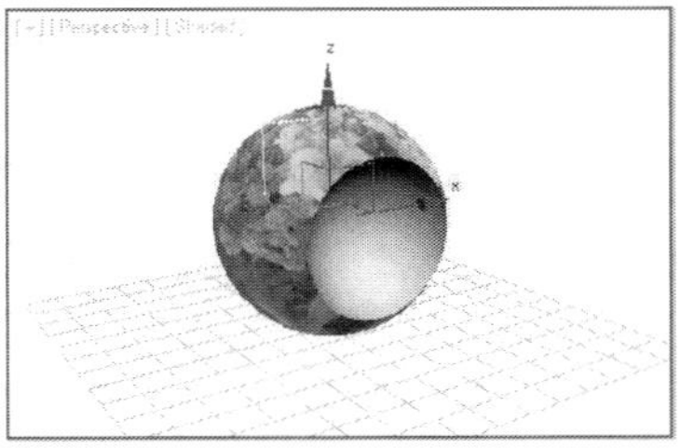

Figure 9-52 *The proboolean object after selecting the* ***Apply Operand Material*** *radio button*

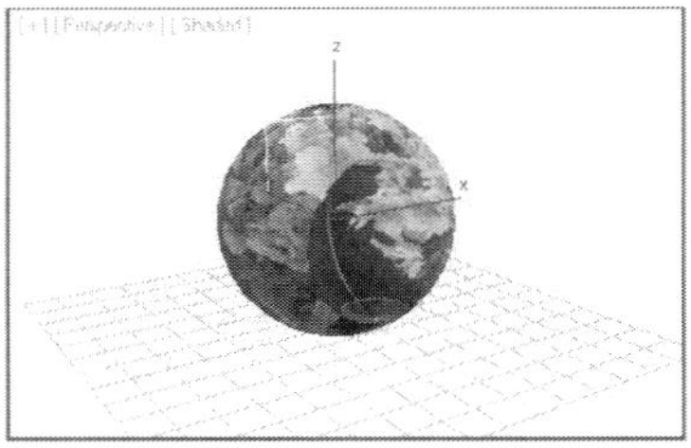

Figure 9-53 *The proboolean object after selecting the* ***Retain Original Material*** *radio button*

The **Reorder Ops** button is used to change the order of the boolean operations in the viewport. To do so, select an operand in the list, set the order in which you want the boolean operation to be performed by entering the corresponding number in the spinner on the right side of the **Reorder Ops** button. Next, choose the **Reorder Ops** button; the order of the boolean operations will be changed in the list as well as in the viewport.

The **Change Operation** button is used to change the type of operation for the selected operand. To do so, select the operand in the list and select the required operation by selecting the corresponding radio button in the **Operation** area. Next, choose the **Change Operation** button; the operand will show the changed boolean operation.

ProCutter

Menu bar:	Create > Compound > ProCutter
Toolbar:	Create > Geometry > Compound Objects > Object Type rollout > ProCutter

The **ProCutter** tool is used to break an object into separate objects with the help of the mesh objects. The mesh objects that are used to break the object are known as cutters and the object that is divided by cutters is known as the stock object.

To create a procutter object, first create an object to be broken into separate objects. Create one or more mesh objects to be used as cutters. Align both the objects, as shown in Figures 9-54 and 9-55. Select one of the cutter objects, invoke the **ProCutter** tool from the **Object Type** rollout in the **Compound Objects**; the **Name and Color**, **Cutter Picking Parameters**, **Cutter Parameters**, and **Advanced Options** rollouts will be displayed. In the **Cutter Picking Parameters** rollout, choose the **Pick Cutter Objects** button and select the additional cutters in the viewport. Next, choose the **Pick Stock Objects** button and select the object that you want to cut in the viewport; the object will be cut, as shown in Figure 9-56. Right-click to exit the command. The most commonly used rollouts are discussed next.

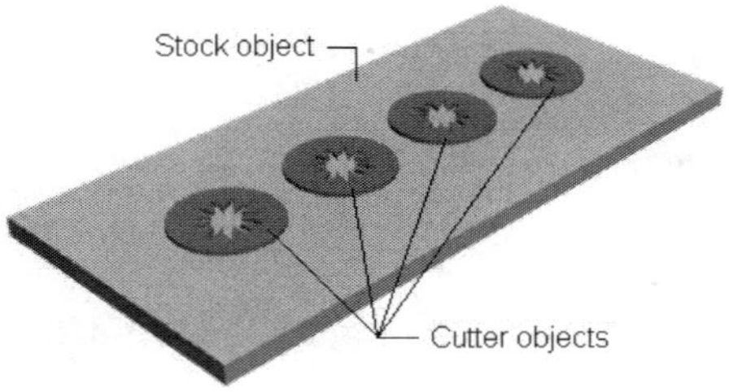

Figure 9-54 The cutter and stock objects aligned for the procutter operation

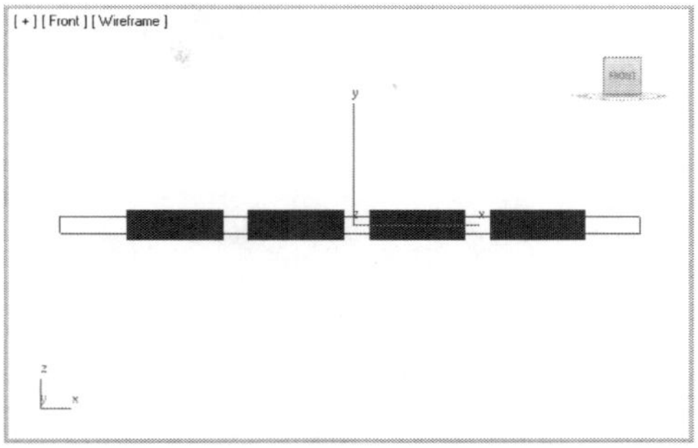

Figure 9-55 The cutter and stock objects before performing the procutter operation in the Front viewport

Figure 9-56 The cutter and stock objects after performing the procutter operation

Cutter Picking Parameters Rollout

The **Pick Cutter Objects** button in this rollout is used to select the objects or cutters in the viewport that are used to divide the object. The **Pick Stock Objects** button is used to select the object that will be separated by the cutters. The other options in this rollout are the same as discussed earlier.

Cutter Parameters Rollout

The **Cutter Parameters** rollout is used to define the type of procutter operations. The areas in this rollout are discussed next.

Cutting Options Area

The check boxes in this area are used to define the final output of the procutter operation. The **Stock Outside Cutter** check box is used to get the parts of the stock object that are outside the cutters, refer to Figure 9-56. Select the **Stock Inside Cutter** check box to get the parts of the stock object that are inside the cutters, refer to Figure 9-57. Select the **Cutter Outside Stock** check box to get the parts of the cutters that are outside the stock object, as shown in Figure 9-58.

*Figure 9-57 The cutter and stock objects after selecting the **Stock Inside Cutter** check box*

*Figure 9-58 The cutter and stock objects after selecting the **Cutter Outside Stock** check box*

The options in the **Display** and **Apply Material** areas are the same as discussed earlier.

Sub-object Operations Area

The options in this area are the same as discussed in the **ProBoolean** compound object.

Tutorial 1

In this tutorial, you will create a loft compound object (toothpaste tube), as shown in Figure 9-59, using the **Loft** and **Boolean** tools. **(Expected time: 30 min)**

Figure 9-59 The toothpaste model

The following steps are required to complete this tutorial:

a. Set the project folder.
b. Download the files.
c. Create the body of the toothpaste tube.
d. Create the cap of the toothpaste tube.
e. Assign the material and map to the tube.
f. Render the scene for the final output.
g. Save the file.

Setting the Project Folder

1. Set the project folder with the name *c09_tut1* in the *3dsmax* folder as discussed in earlier chapters.

Downloading the Files

Before starting the tutorial, you need to download the *c09_3dsmax_2012_tut.zip* file from *http://www.cadcim.com*. The path of the file is as follows:

Textbooks > Animation and Visual Effects > 3ds Max > Autodesk 3ds Max 2012: A Comprehensive Guide

Extract the contents of the zipped file and save the file *toothpaste_tube.jpg* at the location *\Documents\3dsmax\c09_tut1\sceneassets\images*.

Creating the Body of the Toothpaste Tube

To create the body of the toothpaste tube, you need to use the **Loft** tool. Now, create a spline path and a shape spline in the viewport.

1. Activate the Front viewport. Choose **Create > Shapes** from the **Command Panel**; the **Splines** option is displayed in the drop-down list in the command panel. Next, invoke the **Circle** tool from the **Object Type** rollout.

2. Create a circle in the viewport to use as a shape spline. It is automatically named as *Circle001*.

3. In the **Parameters** rollout, set the value **4.0** in the **Radius** spinner.

4. Create another circle in the Front viewport to use as a shape spline and set the value **16.0** in the **Radius** spinner. It is automatically named as *Circle002*.

5. Invoke the **Line** tool from **Create > Shapes > Splines > Object Type** rollout in the **Command Panel**.

6. Create a line in the Front viewport to use as a path spline. You can assume your own dimensions for the length of the line, refer to Figure 9-60. The line is automatically named as *Line001*.

7. Activate the Top viewport, and invoke the **Rectangle** tool from **Create > Shapes > Splines > Object Type** rollout in the **Command Panel**. Create a rectangle to use as a shape spline. The rectangle is automatically named as *Rectangle001*.

8. In the **Parameters** rollout of the *Rectangle001*, set the values as given below:

   Length: **55.033** Width: **5.76** Corner Radius: **1.0**

   The *Rectangle001* is displayed, as shown in Figure 9-61.

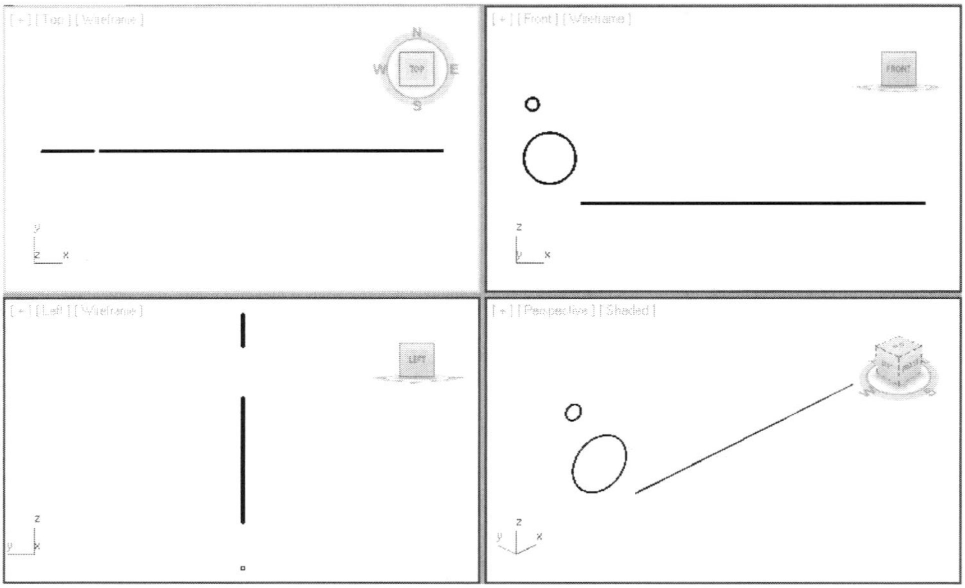

Figure 9-60 *The Circle001, Circle002, and Line001 in all viewports*

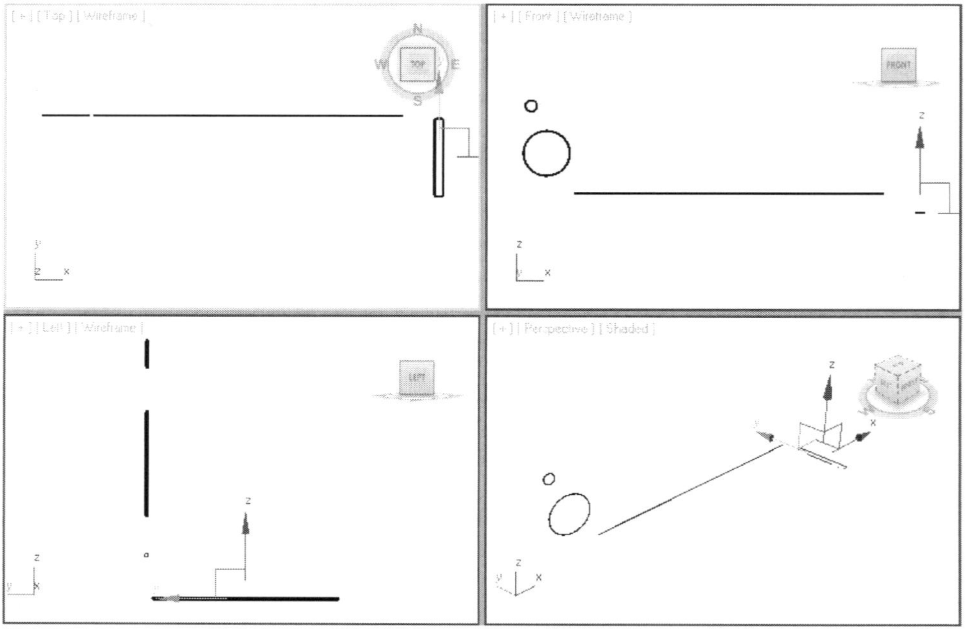

Figure 9-61 *The Rectangle001 in all viewports*

Next, you need to use the **Loft** tool to create the loft compound objects using the shape and path splines. You will use *Circle001*, *Circle002*, and *Rectangle001* as the shape splines and the *Line001* as the path spline.

9. Activate the Front viewport, select the *Line001* spline in the viewport along which the other splines will be lofted.

10. Now, choose **Create > Geometry** from the **Command Panel**; by default, the **Standard Primitives** option is displayed in the drop-down list in the **Command Panel**. Select **Compound Objects** from the drop-down list and then invoke the **Loft** tool from the **Object Type** rollout; various rollouts are displayed in the **Command Panel**.

11. In the **Creation Method** rollout, choose the **Get Shape** button and move the cursor over *Circle001* in the Front viewport; the cursor gets changed to the selection cursor. Now, select *Circle001*; a shape is created, as shown in Figure 9-62. The new shape is automatically named as *Loft001*.

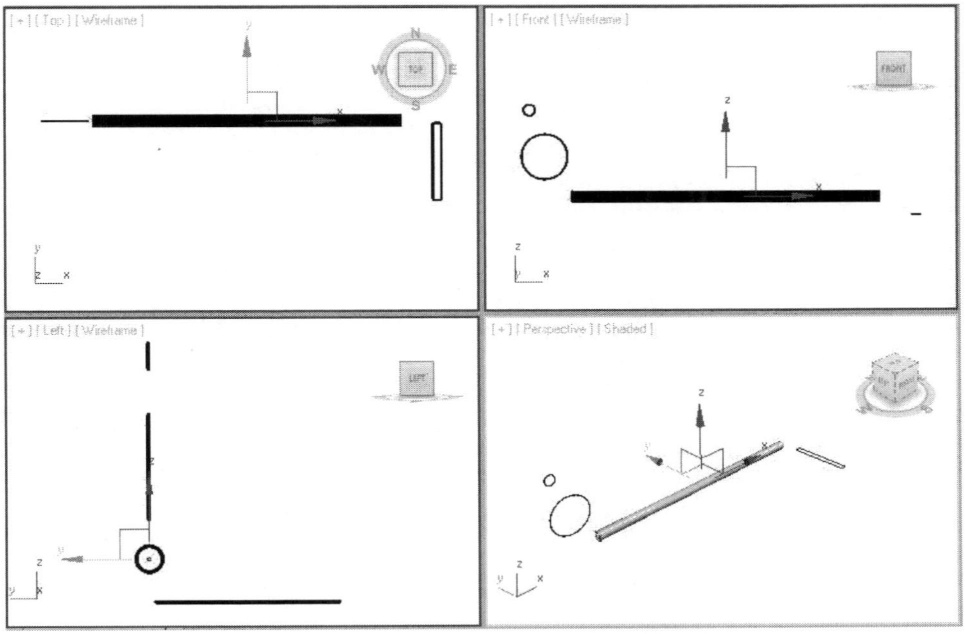

Figure 9-62 *A shape created along the path spline (Line001)*

12. Make sure that *Loft001* is selected in the viewport. In the **Path Parameters** rollout, set the value **12.0** in the **Path** spinner to define the distance between *Circle001* and *Circle002* along *Line001*.

13. In the **Creation Method** rollout, choose the **Get Shape** button and move the cursor over *Circle002* in the Front viewport; the cursor gets changed to the selection cursor. Select *Circle002*; the shape of the tube is created, as shown in Figure 9-63.

    Next, you need to create the shape of the lower portion of the tube. To do so, activate the Top viewport by right-clicking on it.

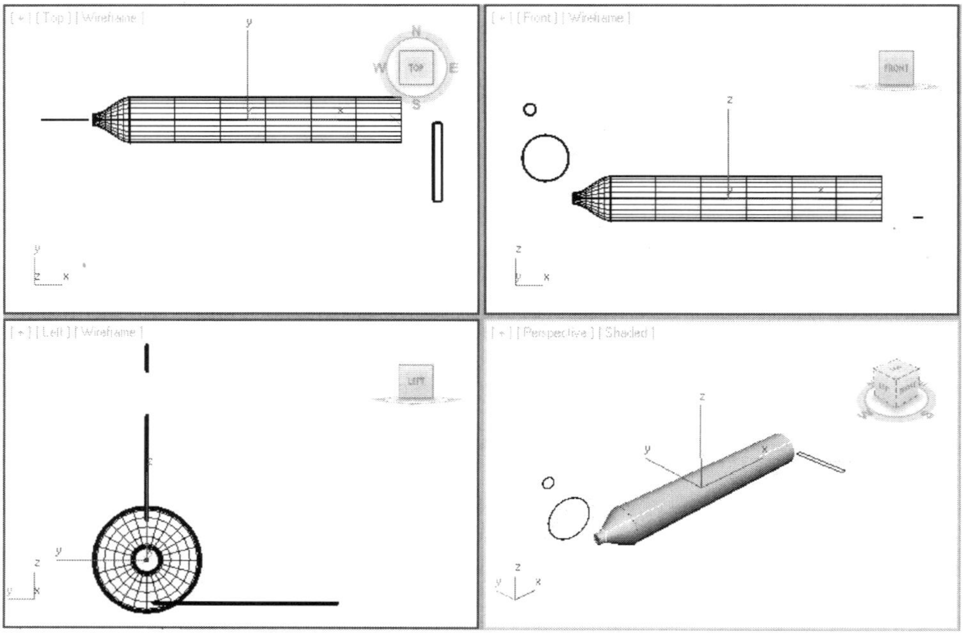

Figure 9-63 *The shape of the tube created along the path spline*

14. Make sure that *Loft001* is selected in the viewport. In the **Path Parameters** rollout, set the value **98.0** in the **Path** spinner.

15. In the **Creation Method** rollout, choose the **Get Shape** button and move the cursor over *Rectangle001* in the Top viewport; the cursor gets changed to the selection cursor. Select *Rectangle001*; a shape is created, as shown in Figure 9-64. Next, right-click in the viewport to exit the loft command.

16. Make sure that *Loft001* is selected. In the **Name and Color** rollout, replace *Loft001* with *toothpaste tube*.

Creating the Cap of the Toothpaste Tube

To create the cap of the toothpaste tube, you need to create a cone object.

1. Activate the Left viewport, choose **Create > Geometry** in the **Command Panel** and select the **Standard Primitives** option from the drop-down list. Now, invoke the **Cone** tool from the **Object Type** rollout and create a cone.

2. In the **Parameters** rollout, set the values as given below:

   Radius 1: **8.846** Radius 2: **4.0** Height: **19.99**

   Use the default values for other options.

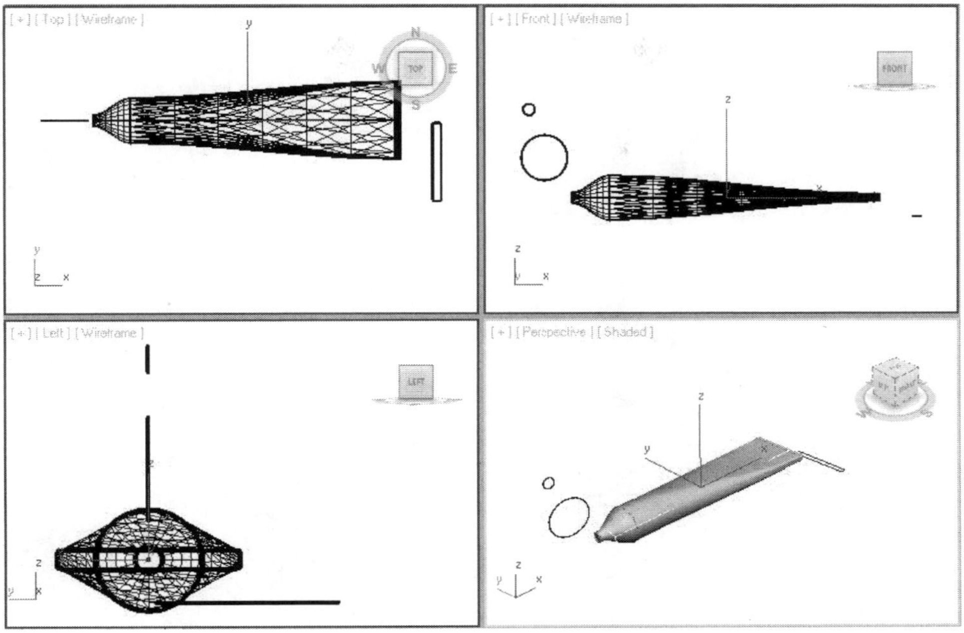

Figure 9-64 *The tube shape or the loft object created in all viewports*

3. In the **Name and Color** rollout, enter the name **cap01**.

4. Make sure that the *cap01* is selected. Next, right-click on it; a quad menu is displayed. Choose the **Hide Unselected** option to temporarily hide the other objects in the viewport.

5. Invoke the **Zoom Extents All Selected** tool, the *cap01* is zoomed in all viewports, as shown in Figure 9-65.

   Next, you need to create a hole in the *cap01* to create the space for inserting the top portion of the *toothpaste tube*. To do so, you need to use the **Boolean** tool in **Compound Objects**.

6. Activate the Top viewport and select the *cap01*.

7. Now, invoke the **Use Selection Center** tool from the **Main Toolbar**; the coordinate gizmo moves to the center of the *cap01*. Also, invoke the **Select and Uniform Scale** tool.

Note

*The **Use Selection Center** tool is available in the **Use Center** flyout. Tools in the **Use Center** flyout determine the geometric center for the scale and rotate operations.*

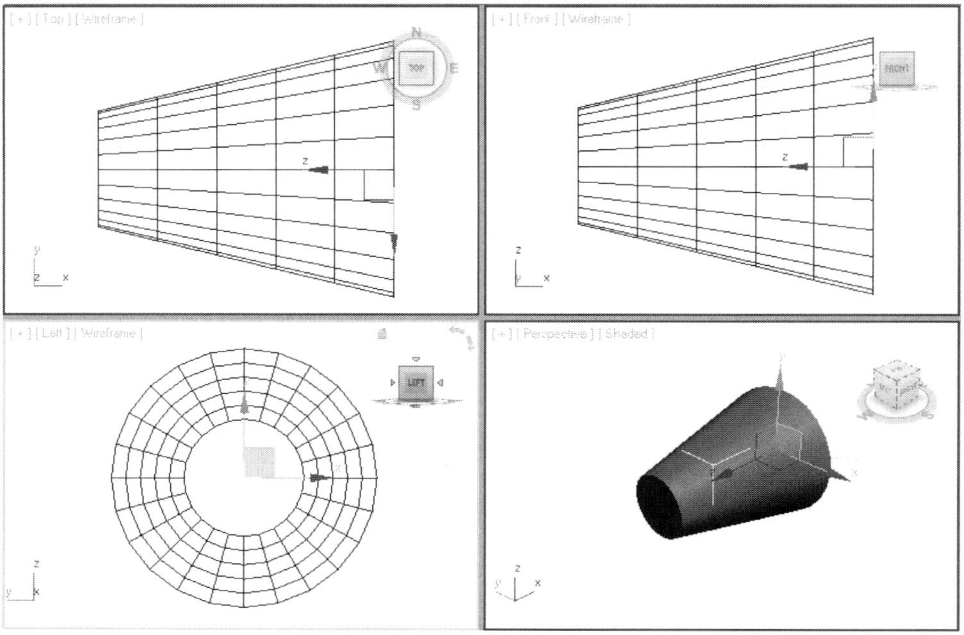

Figure 9-65 *The cap01 zoomed in all viewports*

8. Press and hold the SHIFT key and the left mouse button and move the cursor down until the value in the X, Y, and Z coordinates in the coordinate display becomes **90** and then release the left mouse button and the SHIFT key; the **Clone Options** dialog box is displayed. Make sure that the **Copy** radio button is selected. Set the value **1** in the **Number of Copies** spinner and choose the **OK** button; the *cap002* is displayed, as shown in Figure 9-66.

9. Invoke the **Select and Move** tool and align the *cap002* with the *cap01*, as shown in Figure 9-67.

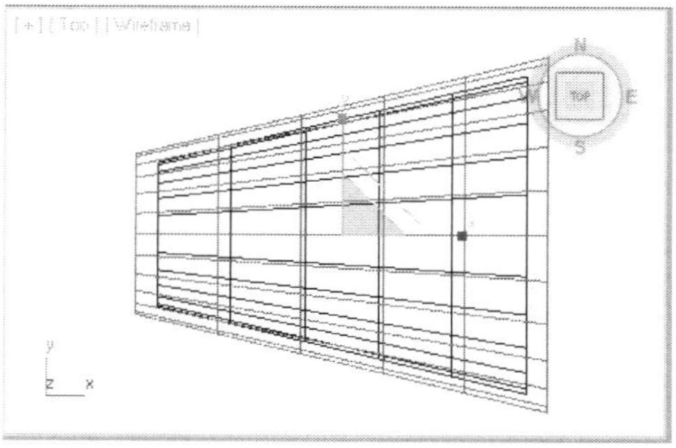

Figure 9-66 *The cap02 displayed*

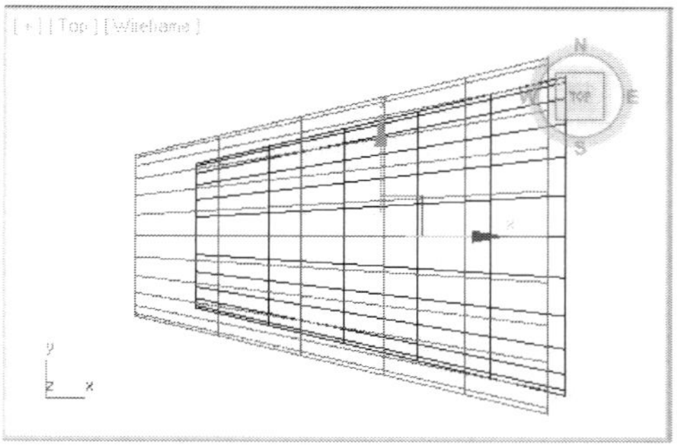

Figure 9-67 *The cap02 after the alignment*

10. Next, select the *cap01* in the Top viewport. Choose **Create > Geometry** in the **Command Panel**. Select the **Compound Objects** option from the drop-down list in the **Command Panel** and invoke the **Boolean** tool from the **Object Type** rollout.

11. Make sure that in the **Operation** area of the **Parameters** rollout, the **Subtraction(A-B)** radio button is selected.

12. In the **Pick Boolean** rollout, select the **Move** radio button if it is not already selected. Choose the **Pick Operand B** button and move the cursor over the *cap002*; the cursor gets changed to the selection cursor. Select the *cap002*; the overlapping portion of the *cap002* is removed from the *cap01*, as shown in Figure 9-68. Next, right-click to exit the boolean command.

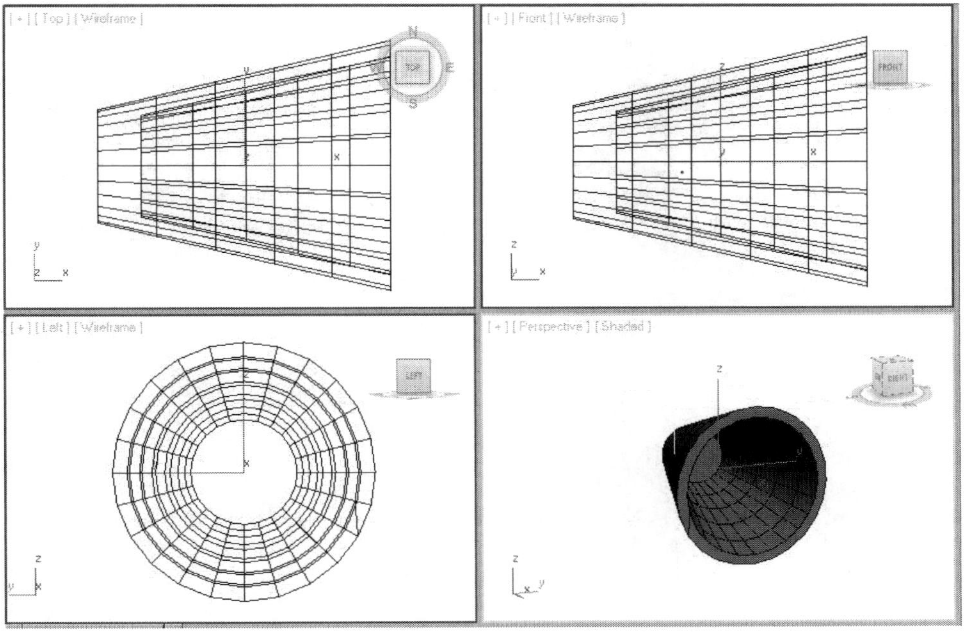

Figure 9-68 *The cap01 after performing the* ***Subtraction(A-B)*** *boolean operation in all viewports*

Note

To view the effect of the boolean operation in the Perspective viewport, you need to use the ***Orbit*** *tool.*

Next, you need to modify the cap using its sub-objects to make it realistic.

13. Convert the *cap01* into editable mesh object.

14. In the modifier stack, click on the plus (+) sign on the left side of **Editable Mesh**; all sub-object levels are displayed.

15. Select the **Polygon** sub-object level to make it active.

16. In the **Selection** rollout, select the **Ignore Backfacing** check box.

17. Now, activate the left viewport. Next, select the alternative row of polygons of the *cap01* by holding the CTRL key, as shown in Figure 9-69.

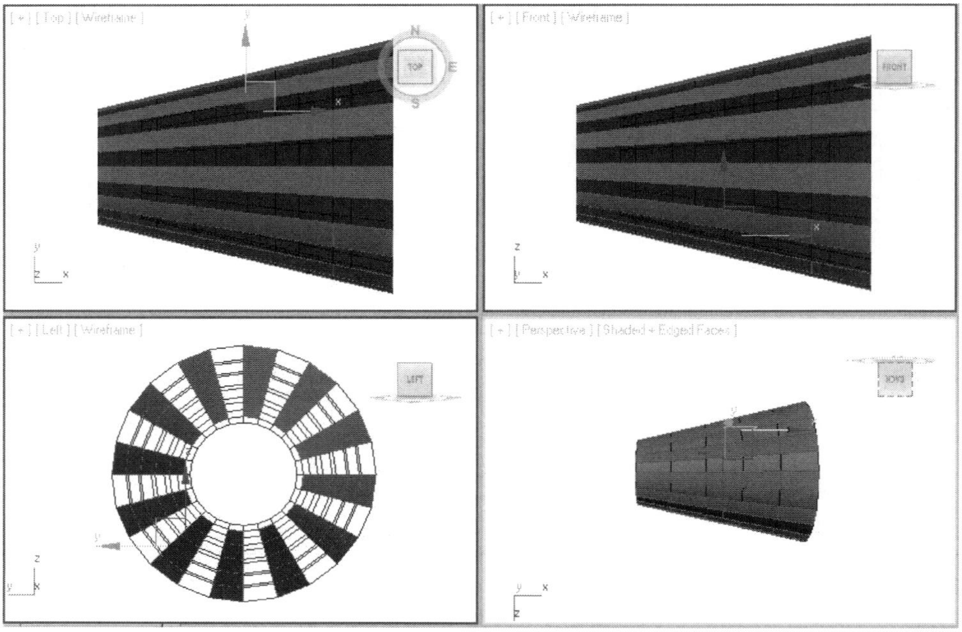

Figure 9-69 *The selected polygons of the cap01*

18. Create a selection set of the selected polygons. You can use this selection set of the selected objects or sub-objects later, if needed. To create a selection set, enter **selected polygons** in the **Named Selection Sets** drop-down list in the **Main Toolbar** and press ENTER, refer to Figure 9-70.

Figure 9-70 *The* ***Named Selection Sets*** *drop-down list*

19. Expand the **Edit Geometry** rollout, set the value **0.1** in the **Extrude** spinner, and then press the ENTER key; the selected polygons are extruded. In the modifier stack, select the Polygon sub-object level again to deactivate it. To view the extruded polygons in the Perspective viewport, press the F4 key again; the segments hide temporarily in the viewport and the extruded polygons are displayed, as shown in Figure 9-71.

20. Right-click in a viewport; a quad menu is displayed. Choose the **Unhide All** option; all objects and shapes are displayed in the viewport.

21. Invoke the **Zoom Extents All** tool; all objects are displayed, as shown in Figure 9-72.

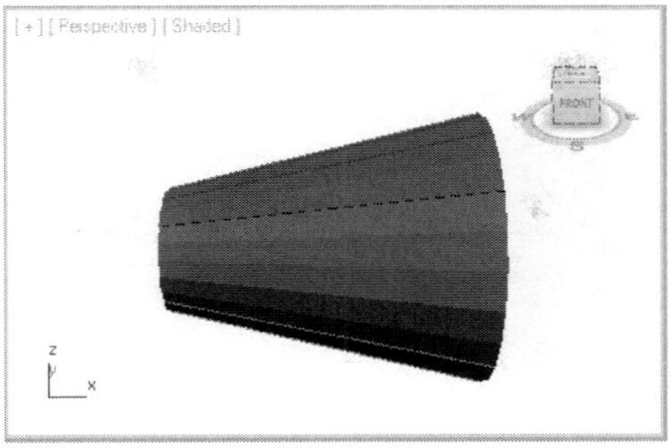

Figure 9-71 *The extruded polygons in the Perspective viewport*

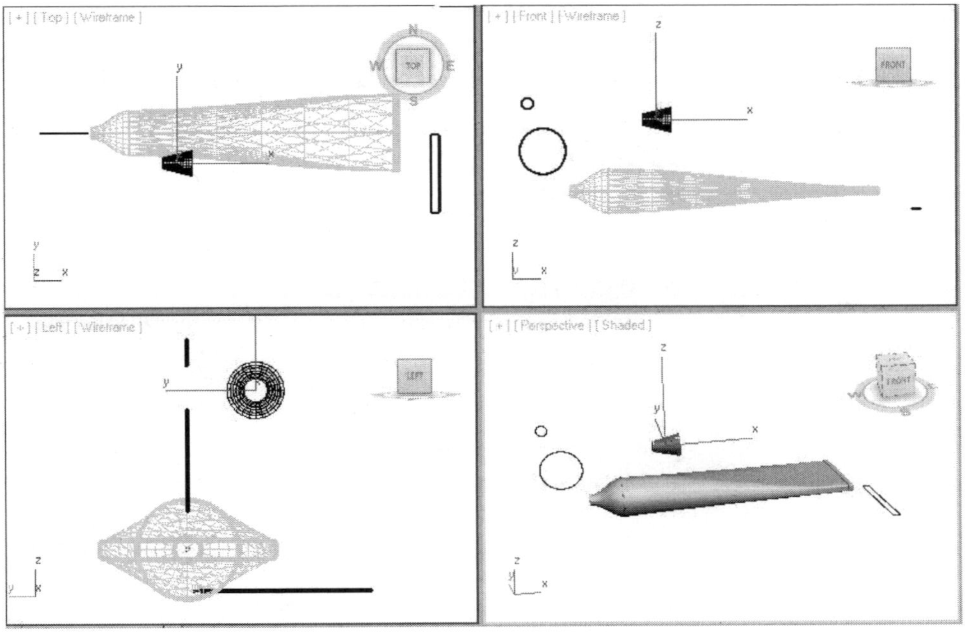

Figure 9-72 *The objects in all viewports*

22. Select *cap01* and invoke the **Use Pivot Point Center** tool from the **Main Toolbar**. Now, align *cap01* with the *toothpaste tube* using the **Select and Move** tool in all viewports, as shown in Figure 9-73.

23. Invoke the **Select by Name** tool from the **Main Toolbar**; the **Select From Scene** dialog box is displayed. Select the *Circle001*, *Circle002*, *Line001*, and *Rectangle001* shapes from the list given in the dialog box and choose the **OK** button. Next, press the DELETE key to delete all shapes from the scene.

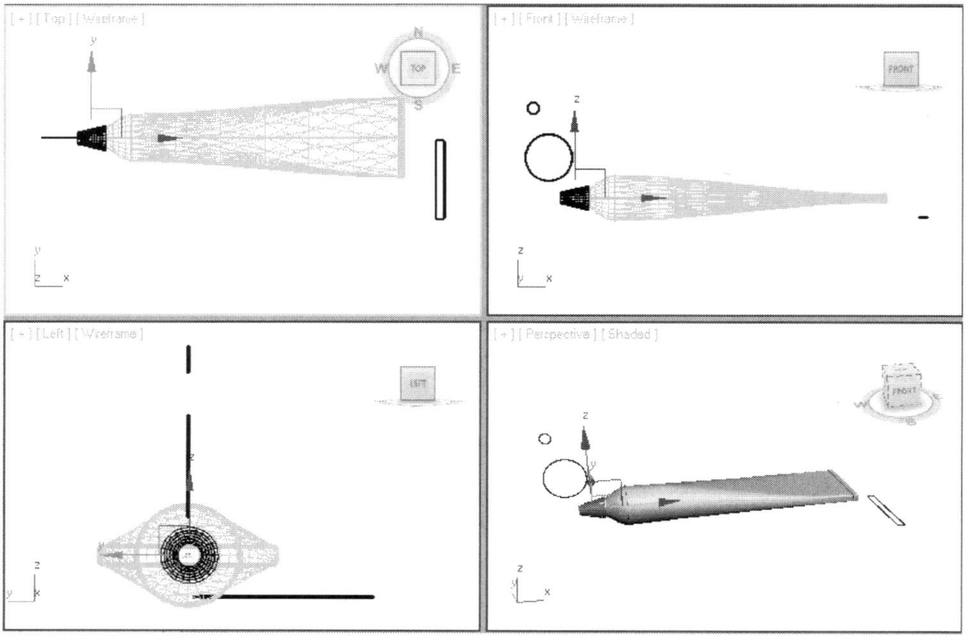

Figure 9-73 *The cap01 in all viewports after alignment with the toothpaste tube*

Assigning the Materials and the Maps

1. Select the *toothpaste tube* in any viewport. Next, choose **Rendering > Material Editor > Compact Material Editor** from the menu bar; the **Material Editor** dialog box is displayed.

2. Select the first sample slot in the **Material Editor** dialog box. By default, the **Standard** material is selected in it and you need to use the same for the *toothpaste tube*.

3. Make sure that the **Blinn** shader is selected in the **Shader Basic Parameters** rollout.

4. In the **Blinn Basic Parameters** rollout, choose the **Diffuse** map button on the right side of the **Diffuse** color swatch; the **Material/Map Browser** dialog box is displayed. Expand the **Maps > Standard** rollouts, select the **Bitmap** map, and choose the **OK** button; the **Select Bitmap Image File** dialog box is displayed. As the project folder is already set, the path *\Documents\3dsmax\c09_tut1\sceneassets\images* is displayed in the **Look in** text box of this dialog box. Select the file *toothpaste_tube.jpg* and choose the **Open** button; the image is displayed in the selected sample slot. Also, the rollouts to modify the bitmap are displayed in the **Material Editor** dialog box. Now, invoke the **Go to Parent** tool to go back to the parent level.

5. In the **Specular Highlights** area, set the values as given below:

   Specular Level: **56** Glossiness: **40**

6. Make sure that the *toothpaste tube* is selected in the viewport. Next, invoke the **Assign Material to Selection** tool in the **Material Editor** dialog box. Also, invoke the **Show Shaded Material in Viewport** tool to display the map in the viewport.

7. Notice that the map in the *toothpaste tube* is not aligned properly, refer to Figure 9-74. To align the map properly, you need to apply the **UVW Map** modifier.

8. Choose the **Modify** tab in the **Command Panel**. Select the **UVW Map** modifier from the **Modifier List** drop-down list; the **UVW Mapping** is displayed in the modifier stack. Also, the **Parameters** rollout is displayed in the modify panel.

9. In the **Parameters** rollout, select the **Box** radio button.

10. In the **Alignment** area of the **Parameters** rollout, select the **Y** radio button and set the values in the **Length**, **Width**, and **Height** spinners to align the map properly, refer to Figure 9-75.

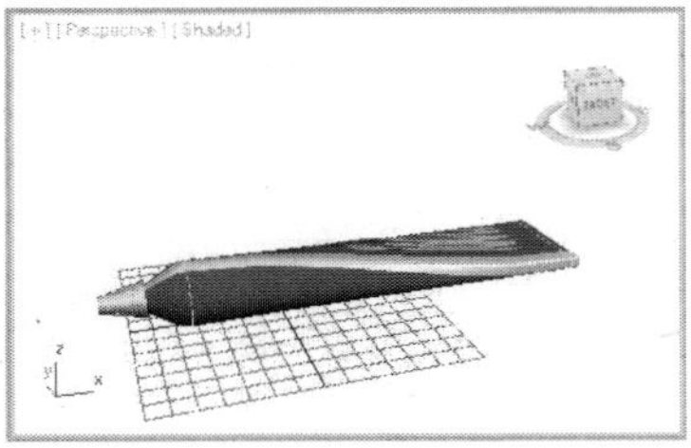

Figure 9-74 The map on the toothpaste tube

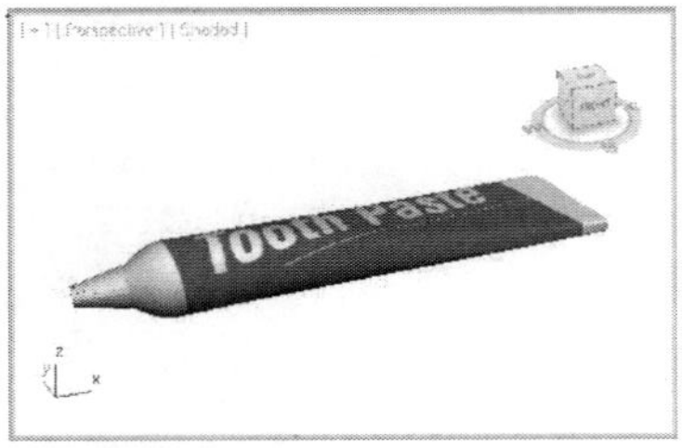

*Figure 9-75 The map on the toothpaste tube after applying the **UVW Map** modifier*

Next, you will create the material for the *cap01*.

11. Select *cap01* in the viewport and select another sample slot in the **Material Editor** dialog box.

12. By default, the **Standard** material is selected in it and you will use the same for *cap01*.

13. Make sure that the **Blinn** shader is selected in the **Shader Basic Parameters** rollout.

14. In the **Blinn Basic Parameters** rollout, choose the **Diffuse** color swatch; the **Color Selector: Diffuse Color** dialog box is displayed. Select the white color and choose the **OK** button to close the dialog box.

15. In the **Specular Highlights** area, set the values given below:

Specular Level: **44** Glossiness: **16**

16. Next, make sure that *cap01* is selected in the viewport. Next, invoke the **Assign Material to Selection** tool in the **Material Editor** dialog box. Also, invoke the **Show Shaded Material in Viewport** tool to display the map in the viewport.

17. The toothpaste tube is displayed, as shown in Figure 9-76. Close the **Material Editor** dialog box.

18. If you want to apply the twist deformation to the *toothpaste tube*, then select it in the viewport and choose the **Modify** tab in the **Command Panel**.

19. In the modifier stack, select the **Loft** option and expand the **Deformation** rollout in the modify panel. Now, in the **Deformation** rollout, choose the **Twist** button; the **Twist Deformation** dialog box is displayed, as shown in Figure 9-77.

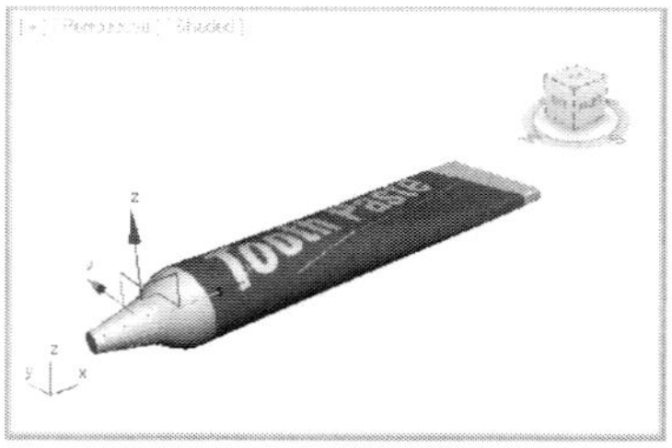

Figure 9-76 *The toothpaste tube after assigning the map*

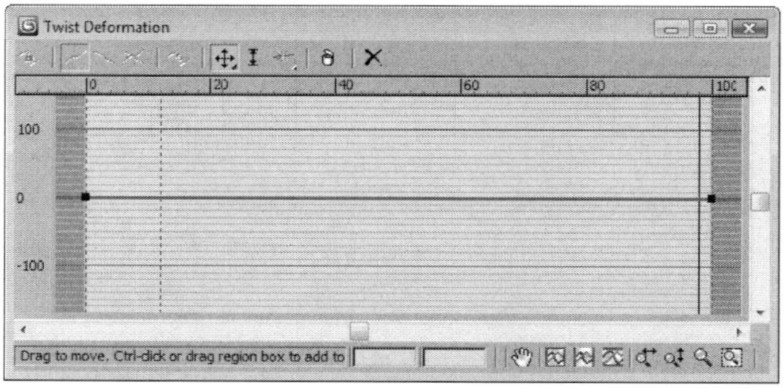

Figure 9-77 *The* ***Twist Deformation*** *dialog box*

20. In the **Twist Deformation** dialog box, invoke the **Move Control Point** tool and move the first vertex point (placed on the left side) vertically downward about **-65.0** points. You can also set the exact value in the text box given at the bottom of this dialog box, as shown in Figure 9-78. The toothpaste tube is twisted, as shown in Figure 9-79. Close the **Twist Deformation** dialog box.

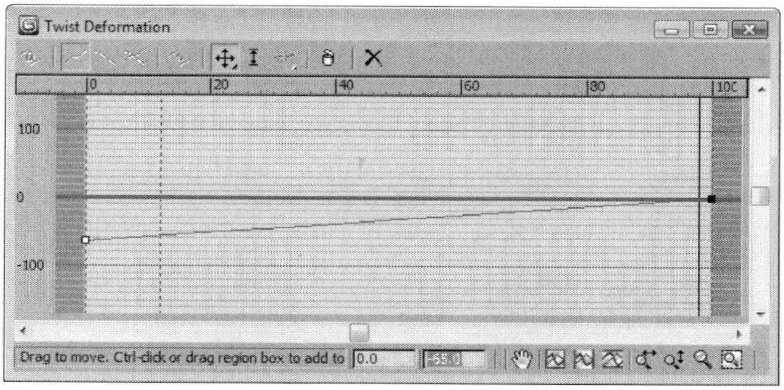

Figure 9-78 *The first vertex point moved in the* ***Twist Deformation*** *dialog box*

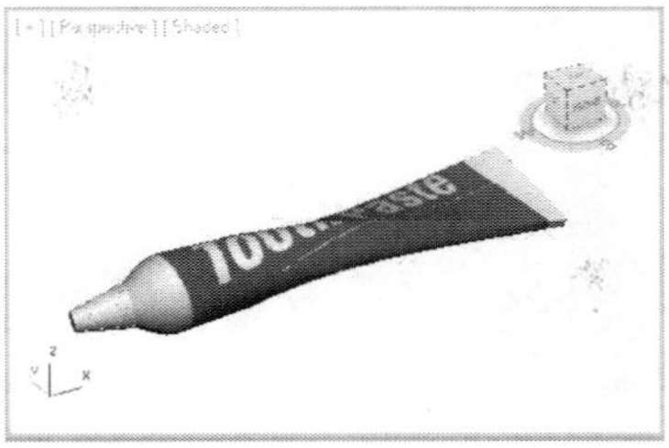

Figure 9-79 The twisted toothpaste tube

Rendering the Scene for the Final Output

1. Activate the Perspective viewport. Render the scene using the **Render Production** tool in the **Main Toolbar**; the final output at one frame is displayed in a separate window, as shown in Figures 9-80 and 9-81.

Figure 9-80 The final output at rendering (view 1)

Figure 9-81 The final output at rendering (view 2)

You can view the final rendered image of this model by downloading the *c09_3dsmax_2012_render.zip* file from *http://www.cadcim.com*.

Saving the File

1. Save the file with the name *c09tut1.max* as discussed in earlier chapters. The location of this file is given below:

\Documents\3dsmax\c09_tut1\scenes

Tutorial 2

In this tutorial, you will create a scene, as shown in Figure 9-82, using different compound objects. **(Expected time: 60 min)**

The following steps are required to complete this tutorial:

a. Set the project folder.
b. Create the ground.
c. Create hills using the **Terrain** tool.
d. Create plants.

e. Create road over the ground using the **Loft** tool.
f. Create the background for the final output.
g. Render the scene for the final output.
h. Save the file.

Figure 9-82 *Scene for Tutorial 2*

Setting the Project Folder

1. Set the project folder with the name *c09_tut2* in the *3dsmax* folder as discussed in earlier chapters.

Creating the Ground

Reset Autodesk 3ds Max to start afresh. To create a ground, first you need to create a plane.

1. Activate the Top viewport. Choose **Create > Geometry** in the **Command Panel**; the **Standard Primitives** option is displayed in the drop-down list. Invoke the **Plane** tool and create a plane.

2. In the **Parameters** rollout, set the values as given below:

   Length: **383.432** Width: **395.936**
   Length Segs: **20** Width Segs: **20**

   Next, you need to edit the plane using its sub-objects to make it look like a hilly surface.

3. Make sure that the plane is selected in the Top viewport and then convert it into editable poly object as discussed earlier.

4. In the modifier stack, expand **Editable Poly** by clicking on the plus sign on its left side. Select the **Vertex** sub-object level; all vertices of the plane are displayed in all viewports, as shown in Figure 9-83.

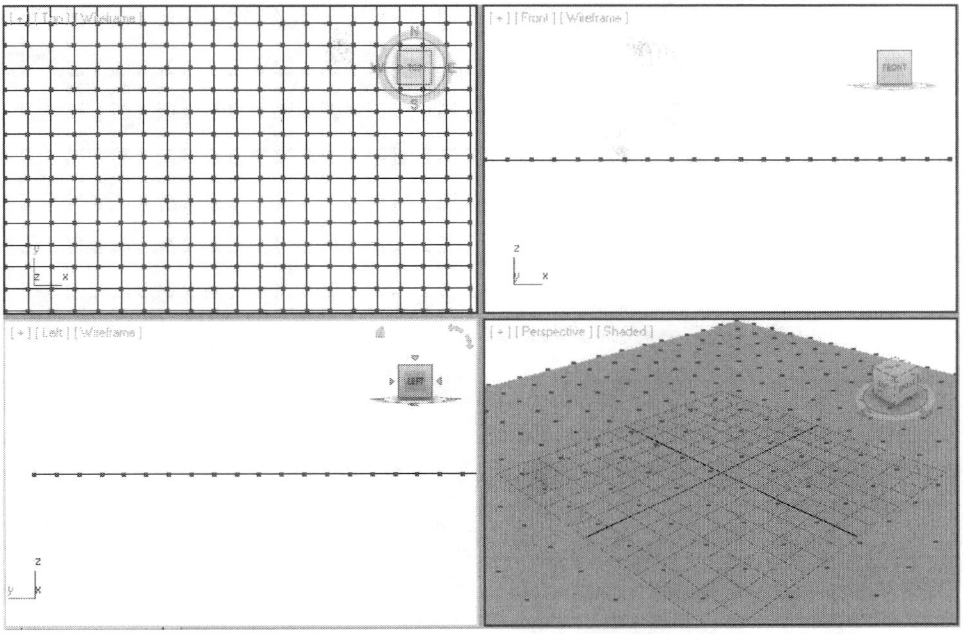

Figure 9-83 *All vertices displayed in the viewports*

5. In the Top viewport, select a vertex, as shown in Figure 9-84. Now, in the **Selection** rollout, choose the **Grow** button twice to select the vertices, as shown in Figure 9-85.

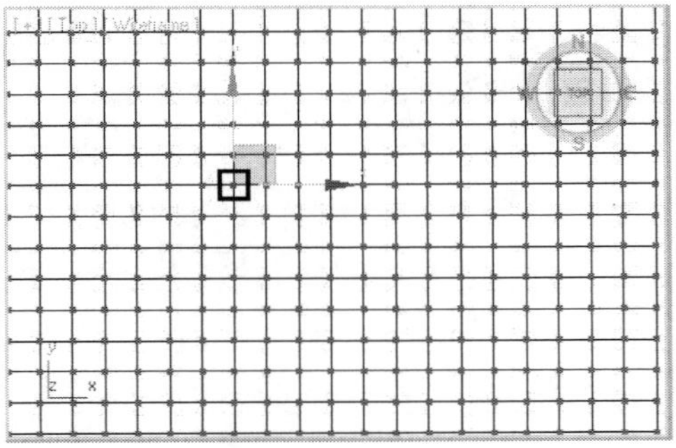

Figure 9-84 *A vertex selected in the Top viewport*

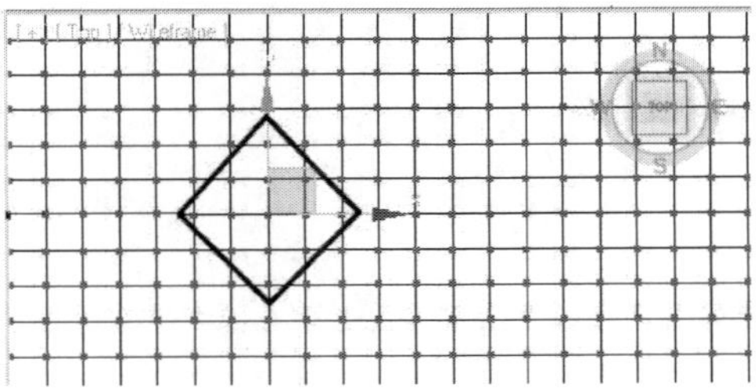

Figure 9-85 *The vertices selected after choosing the* ***Grow*** *button*

6. Activate the Front viewport by right-clicking in it. Move the cursor over the vertical axis and drag the selected vertices up by one grid point, refer to Figures 9-86 and 9-87.

7. Create the hilly surface by selecting the vertices at different places on the plane using the same method as discussed in steps 5 and 6, as shown in Figure 9-88.

8. Now, deselect the **Vertex** sub-object level in the modifier stack. Then, apply the **MeshSmooth** modifier from the **Modifier List** drop-down list, as discussed earlier, to make the surface smooth, as shown in Figure 9-89.

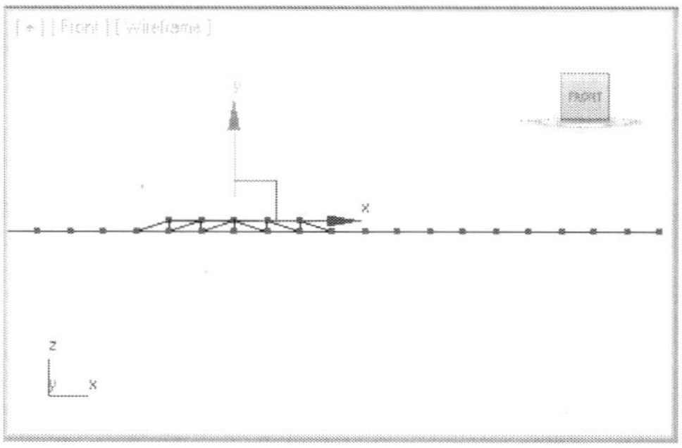

***Figure 9-86** The selected vertices dragged up in the Front viewport*

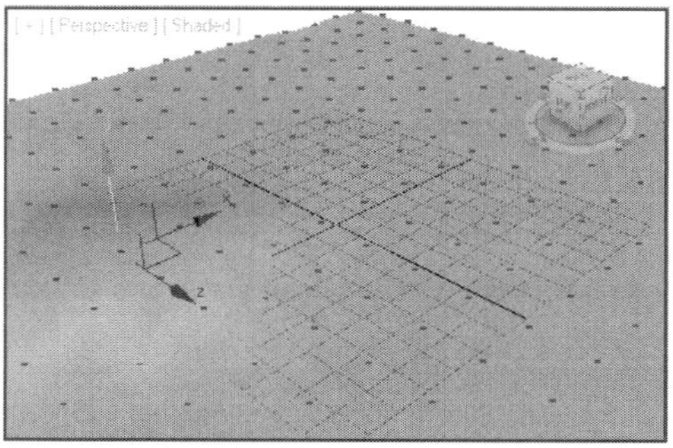

***Figure 9-87** The selected vertices dragged up in the Perspective viewport*

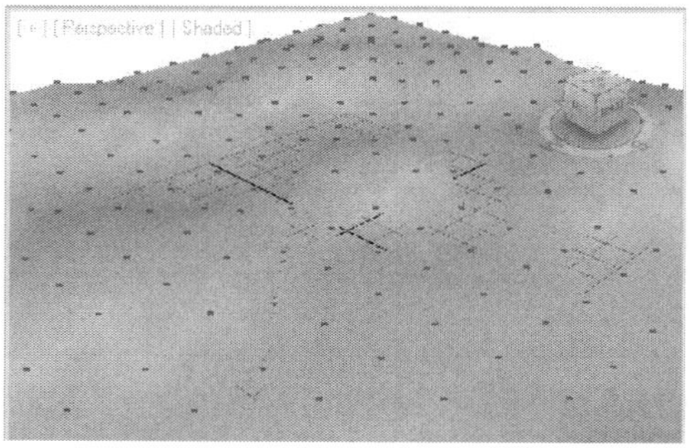

***Figure 9-88** The hilly surface created using the vertices of the plane*

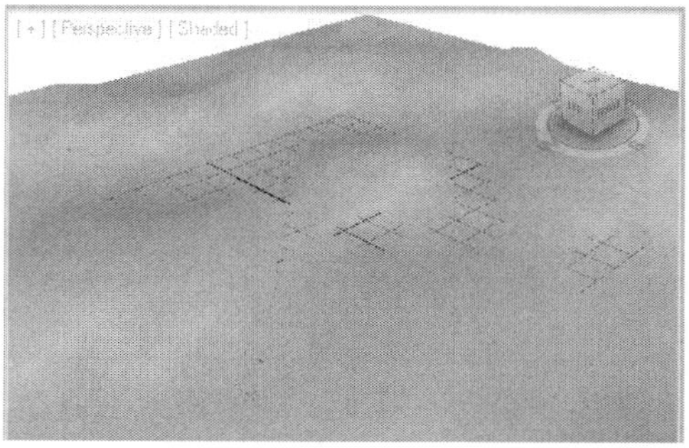

***Figure 9-89** The hilly surface after applying the **MeshSmooth** modifier*

Next, you need to assign a map to the plane to give it a realistic look.

9. Make sure that the plane is selected in the viewport. Next, choose **Rendering> Material Editor > Compact Material Editor** from the menu bar; the **Material Editor** dialog box is displayed.

10. Navigate to the *c09_3dsmax_2012_tut* folder that you have downloaded from the CADCIM website in Tutorial 1. Next, copy the *Grass.jpg, SANDSHOR.jpg*, and *Road.jpg* files at the location *\Documents\3dsmax\c09_tut2\Sceneassets\images.*

11. Select the **01-Default** sample slot in the **Material Editor** dialog box. Choose the **Diffuse** map button on the right side of the **Diffuse** color swatch; the **Material/Map Browser** dialog box is displayed. Select the **Bitmap** map from the **Maps > Standard** rollouts and choose the **OK** button; the **Select Bitmap Image File** dialog box is displayed. As the project folder is already set, the path *\Documents\3dsmax\c09_tut2\sceneassets\images* is displayed in the **Look in** text box of this dialog box. Select the file *Grass.jpg* and choose the **Open** button; the selected image is displayed in the selected sample slot.

12. In the **Coordinates** rollout of the **Material Editor** dialog box, set the values as given next:

    U-Tiling: **5** V-Tiling: **5**

13. Make sure that the plane is selected in the viewport. Next, invoke the **Assign Material to Selection** tool from the **Material Editor** dialog box. Now, invoke the **Show Shaded Material in Viewport** tool to display the map in the viewports.

14. The map is assigned to the plane, as shown in Figure 9-90. Now, close the **Material Editor** dialog box.

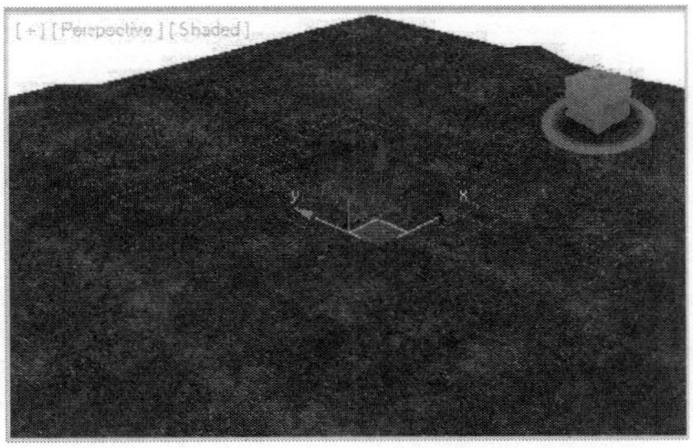

Figure 9-90 *The plane after assigning the map to it in the Perspective viewport*

15. Set the view of the plane in the Perspective viewport using the viewport navigation tools such as **Zoom**, **Orbit**, and so on, as shown in Figure 9-91.

16. Name the plane as *ground*.

Creating Hills

You will create hills using the **Terrain** tool in **Compound Objects**.

1. Activate the Top viewport, choose **Create > Shapes** in the **Command Panel**. Also, invoke the **Line** tool from the **Object Type** rollout.

2. In the **Creation Method** rollout, select the **Corner** radio button in the **Initial Type** area and select the **Smooth** radio button in the **Drag Type** area.

3. Create a close line spline, as shown in Figure 9-92.

4. Hide the *ground* temporarily, as discussed earlier, to get more room to create hills.

5. Activate the Front viewport by right-clicking in it and create four copies of the line spline, refer to Figure 9-93.

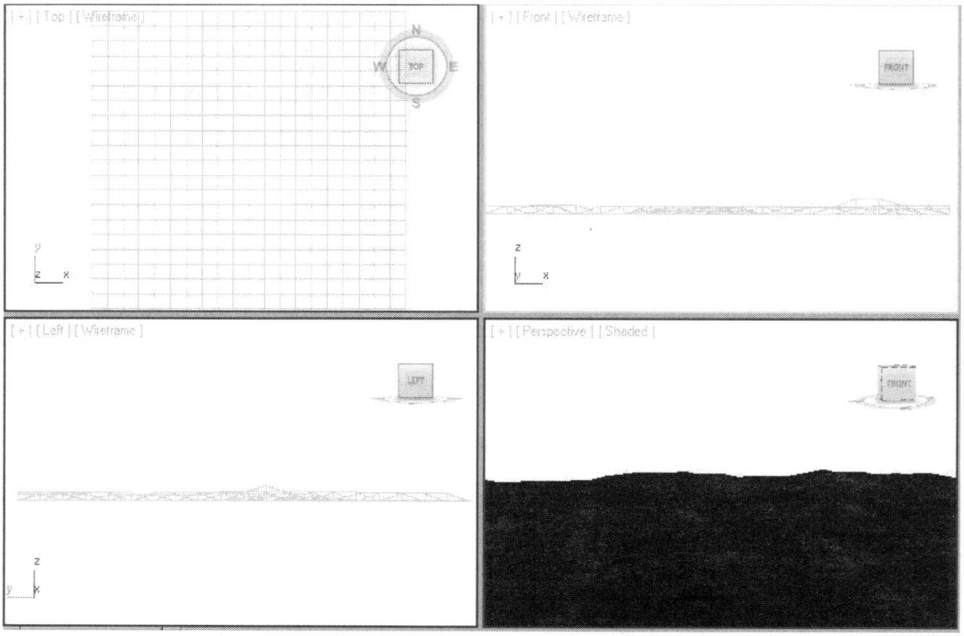

Figure 9-91 *The plane after using the viewport navigation tools*

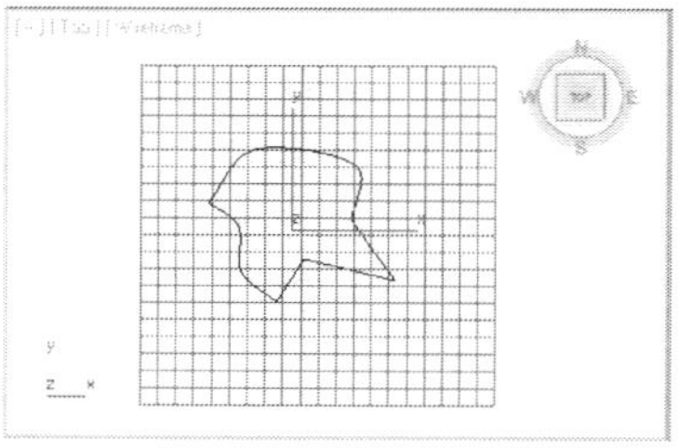

Figure 9-92 *A close line spline created in the Top viewport*

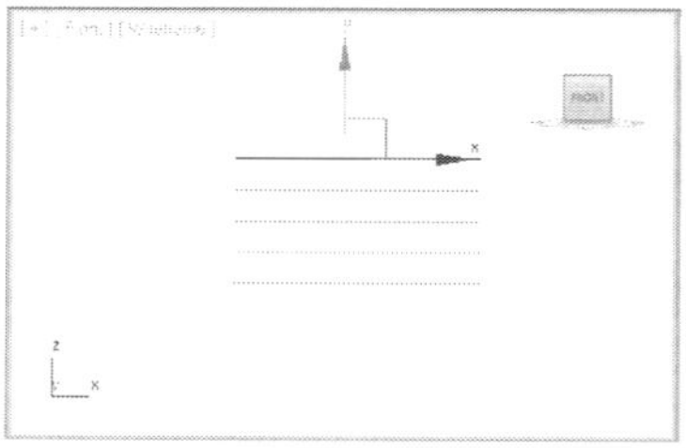

Figure 9-93 *Four copies of the line splines created in the Front viewport*

6. Invoke the **Select and Uniform Scale** tool in the Front viewport and scale the lines, as shown in Figure 9-94.

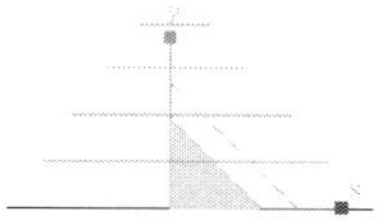

Figure 9-94 *The scaled lines after using the* ***Select and Uniform Scale*** *tool*

7. Invoke the **Select Object** tool and select all lines by dragging a selection box around them.

8. Now, choose **Create > Geometry** in the **Command Panel** and select **Compound Objects** from the drop-down list displayed below the **Geometry** button. Invoke the **Terrain** tool from the **Object Type** rollout; the terrain object is created, as shown in Figure 9-95.

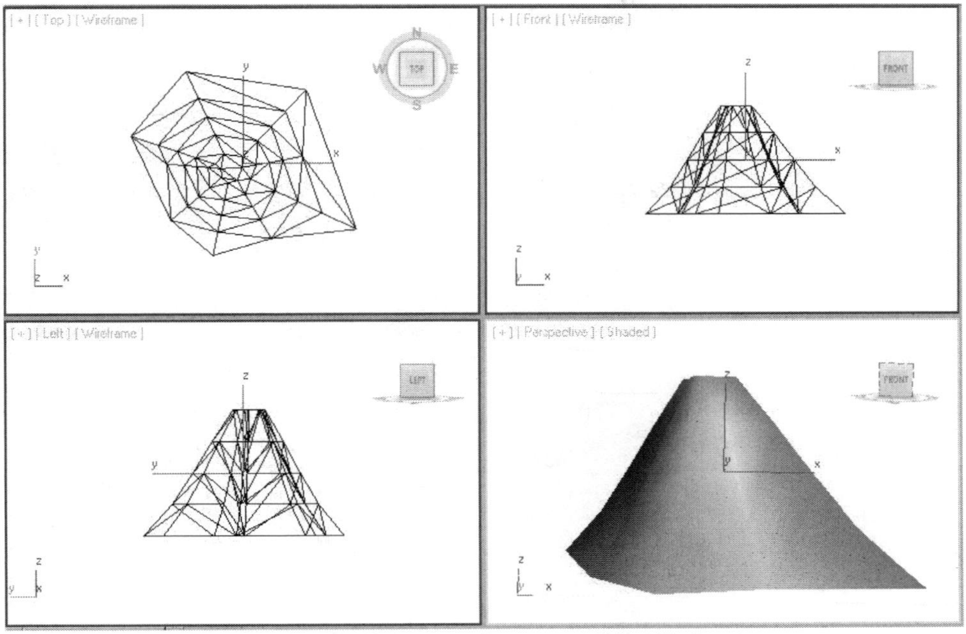

Figure 9-95 *The terrain object created in all viewports*

9. Modify the name of the terrain object as *hill01*.

   Next, you need to assign a map to *hill01*.

10. Make sure that *hill01* is selected in the viewport and press the M key to invoke the **Material Editor** dialog box.

Note

When you press the M key to invoke the ***Material Editor*** *tool, the material editor that you last opened in Autodesk 3ds Max will be displayed. However, if you press the M key for the first time in Autodesk 3ds Max, the* ***Slate Material Editor*** *dialog box will be displayed.*

11. Select the **02-Default** sample slot in the **Material Editor** dialog box. Select the **Diffuse** map button on the right of the **Diffuse** color swatch; the **Material/Map Browser** dialog box is displayed. Select the **Bitmap** map from the **Maps > Standard** rollouts and choose the **OK** button; the **Select Bitmap Image File** dialog box is displayed. As the project folder is already set, the path *\Documents\3dsmax\c09_tut2\sceneassets\images* is displayed in the **Look in** text box of this dialog box. Select the file *SANDSHOR.jpg* and choose the **Open** button; the image is displayed in the selected sample slot.

12. In the **Coordinates** rollout, select the **Planar from Object XYZ** option from the **Mapping** drop-down list and set the values as given below:

    U-Tiling: **3** V-Tiling: **3**

13. Make sure that *hill01* is selected in the viewport. Next, invoke the **Assign Material to Selection** tool in the **Material Editor** dialog box. Then, invoke the **Show Shaded Material in Viewport** tool to display the map in the viewport.

14. The map is assigned to *hill01*, as shown in Figure 9-96. Now, close the **Material Editor** dialog box.

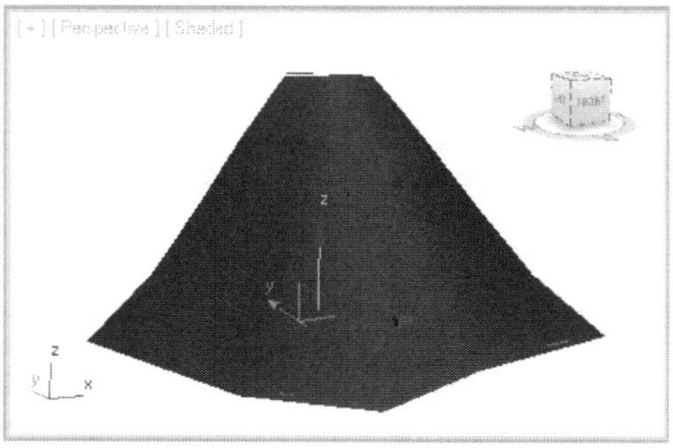

Figure 9-96 *The map assigned to hill01*

15. Next, unhide the *ground*. Also, scale and align the *hill01* with the *ground*, as shown in Figure 9-97.

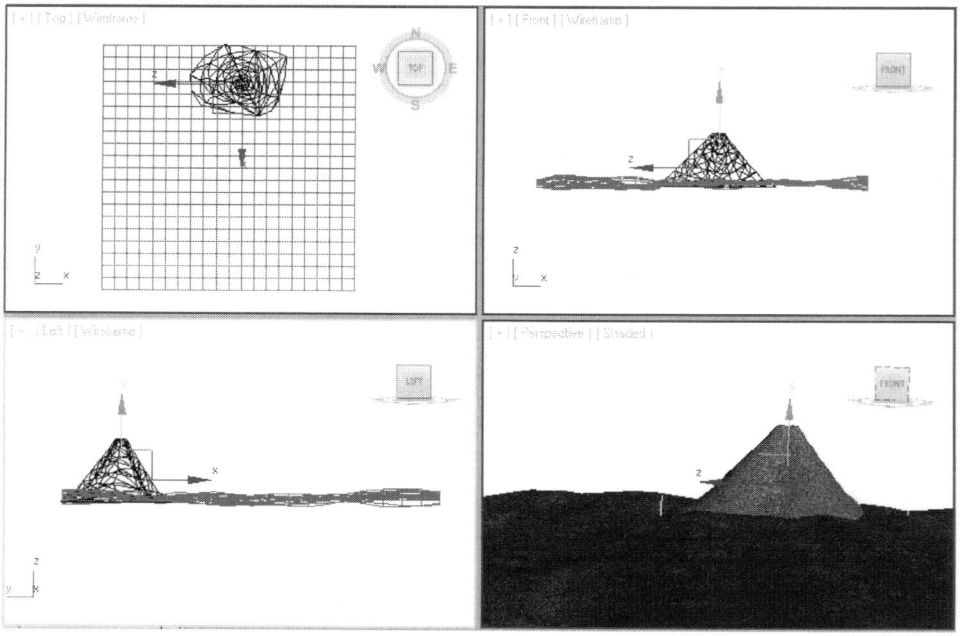

Figure 9-97 *The hill01 after scaling and aligning with the ground*

16. Create multiple copies of *hill01* as required. Now, scale, rotate, and align them, as shown in Figure 9-98.

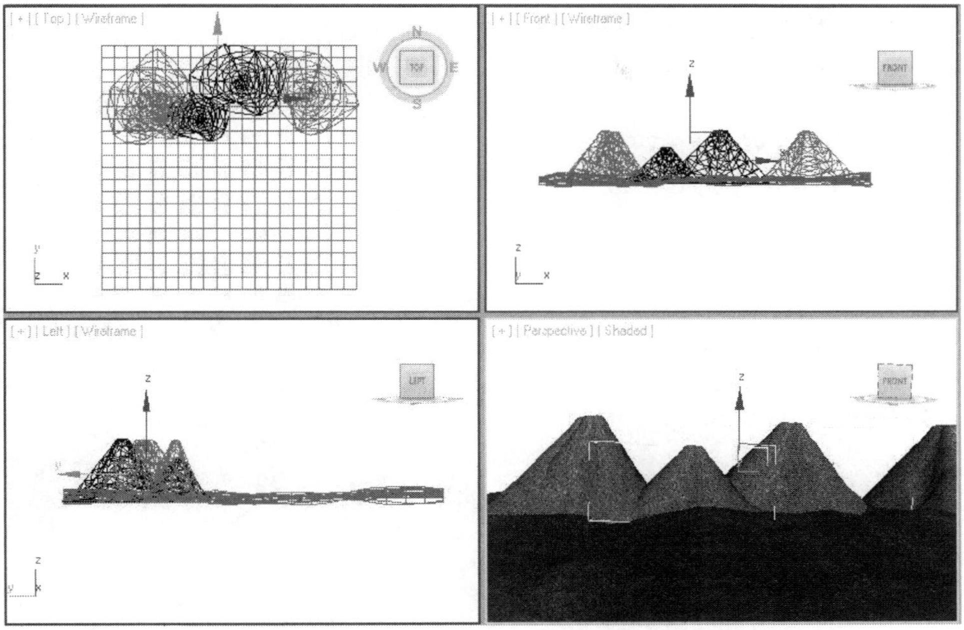

Figure 9-98 *The hills displayed after scaling and alignment*

17. Apply the **MeshSmooth** modifier to the hills as discussed earlier.

Creating the Plants

You will use the **Foliage** tool to create plants.

1. Activate the Top viewport. Choose **Create > Geometry** in the **Command Panel** and select **AEC Extended** from the drop-down list. Now, invoke the **Foliage** tool from the **Object Type** rollout; various rollouts are displayed in the modify panel.

2. In the **Favorite Plants** rollout, select and double-click on the **Banyan tree** option; the tree is displayed in all viewports.

3. Name the plant as *tree01*.

4. Make sure that *tree01* is still selected. Choose the **Modify** tab in the **Command Panel**; the **Parameters** rollouts is displayed.

5. In the **Parameters** rollout, set the value **45.0** in the **Height** spinner. Use default values for other options.

6. Invoke the **Select and Move** tool and align *tree01* in all viewports, as shown in Figure 9-99.

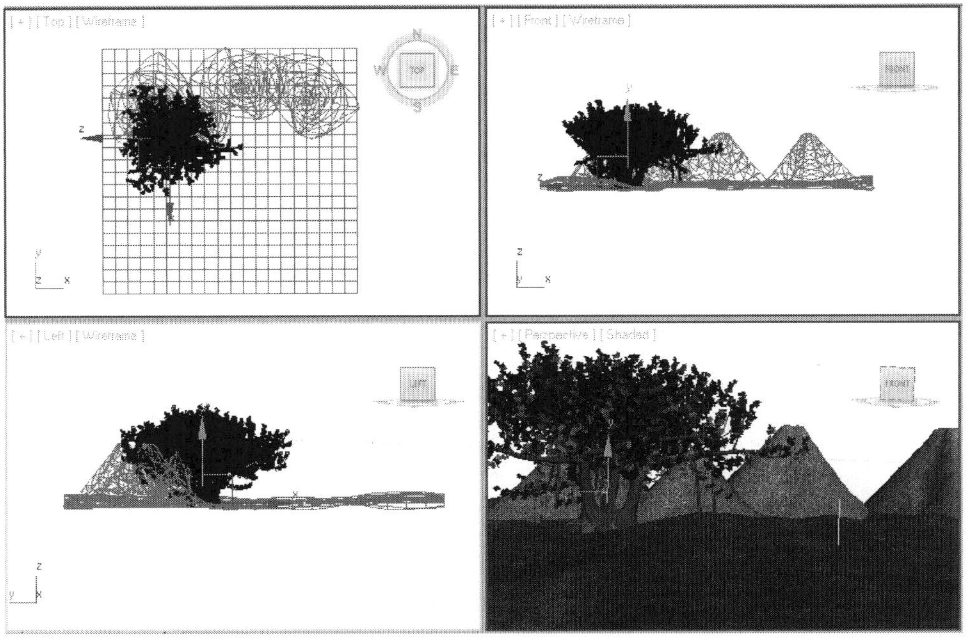

***Figure 9-99** Alignment of the tree01 in all viewports*

7. Activate the Top viewport. In the **Favorite Plants** rollout, select and double-click on the **Society Garlic** option; the tree is displayed in all viewports. In the **Parameters** rollout, set the value **18.0** in the **Height** spinner. Use default values for other options.

8. Modify the name of the plant as *tree02*.

9. Create multiple copies of the *tree02* and align them, as shown in Figure 9-100.

Creating the Road

First, you need to use the **Loft** tool for creating the road and then use the **Conform** tool to adjust the road according to the *ground*. To create the loft object, you need to create a path spline and a shape spline in the viewport.

1. Activate the Top viewport and choose **Create > Shapes** in the **Command Panel**; the **Splines** option is displayed in the drop-down list. Invoke the **Line** tool from the **Object Type** rollout and create a line, as shown in Figure 9-101, which will be used as a path spline.

2. Activate the Front viewport and create a rectangular spline using the **Rectangle** tool. It will be used as a shape spline. Set its parameters as given below:

   Length: **4.0**   Width: **30.702**

3. Make sure that the rectangle is selected in the viewport. Choose **Create > Geometry** in the **Command Panel**. Now, select the **Compound Objects** option from the drop-down list. Invoke the **Loft** tool from the **Object Type** rollout. Choose the **Get Path** button in the **Creation Method** rollout and move the cursor over the line that you have just created for the path spline in the Top viewport; the cursor gets changed to the selection cursor. Select the line; a shape is created.

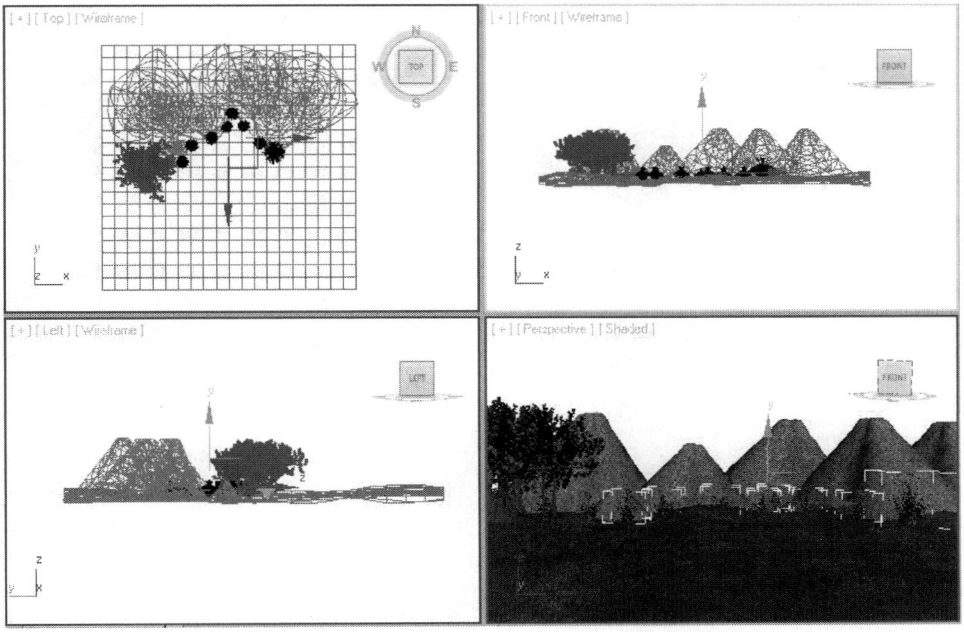

Figure 9-100 *Alignment of trees in all viewports*

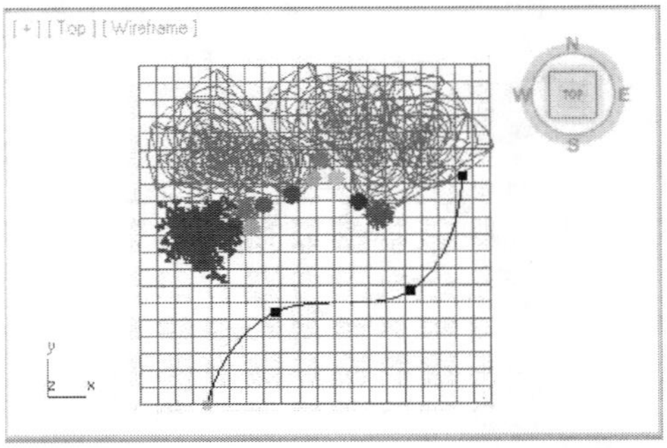

Figure 9-101 *The line to be used as a path spline*

4. The new shape is automatically named as *Loft001*. Replace its name to *road*.

5. Align the *road*, as shown in Figure 9-102.

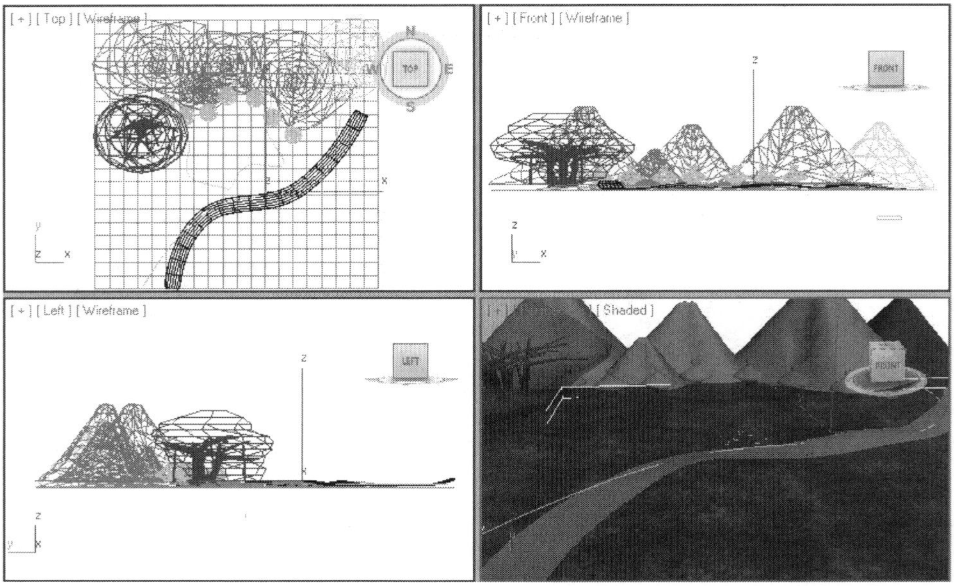

Figure 9-102 *The road aligned with the ground*

Now, assign a map to the *road*.

6. Make sure that the *road* is selected in the viewport. Next, press the M key to invoke the **Material Editor** dialog box.

7. Select the **03-Default** sample slot in the **Material Editor** dialog box. Choose the **Diffuse** map button on the right of the **Diffuse** color swatch; the **Material/Map Browser** dialog box is displayed. Select the **Bitmap** map from the **Maps > Standard** rollouts and choose the **OK** button; the **Select Bitmap Image File** dialog box is displayed. As the project folder is already set, the path *\Documents\3dsmax\c09_tut2\sceneassets\images* is displayed in the **Look in** text box of this dialog box. Select the file *Road.jpg* and choose the **Open** button; the image is displayed in the selected sample slot.

8. In the **Coordinates** rollout, set the values as given below:

   U-Tiling: **5** V-Tiling: **5**

9. Make sure that the *road* is selected in the viewport. Next, invoke the **Assign Material to Selection** tool from the **Material Editor** dialog box. Then, invoke the **Show Shaded Material in Viewport** tool to display the map in the viewport, as shown in Figure 9-103. Close the **Material Editor** dialog box.

   In Figure 9-103, you will notice that the *road* is not properly aligned with the *ground* because of its bumpy surface. To align the *road* properly with the *ground*, you need to use the **Conform** tool.

Figure 9-103 The road after assigning the map to it

The *road* will behave as a Wrapper object and the *ground* will behave as a Wrap-To object.

10. Select the *road* and invoke the **Conform** tool from **Compound Objects**. Choose the **Pick Wrap-To Object** button and move the cursor over the *ground*; the selection cursor is displayed. Select the *ground*; the *road* or the Wrapper object is positioned over the Wrap-To object to fit according to the shape of the *ground*.

11. In the **Wrapper Parameters** area of the **Parameters** rollout, set the value in the **Standoff Distance** spinner to adjust the distance between a vertex of the Wrapper object and the surface of the Wrap-To object. Also, apply the **MeshSmooth** modifier to the conform object.

12. In the **Update** area of the **Parameters** rollout, select the **Hide Wrap-To Object** check box; the scene is displayed, as shown in Figure 9-104.

Creating the Background in the Final Output

To make the scene more realistic, assign a map in the background.

1. Choose **Rendering > Environment** from the menu bar; the **Environment and Effects** dialog box is displayed.

2. In the **Common Parameters** rollout, choose the **Environment Map** button that is labeled as **None**; the **Material/Map Browser** dialog box is displayed. Select the **Bitmap** map from the **Maps > Standard** rollouts and choose the **OK** button; the **Select Bitmap Image File** dialog box is displayed. Navigate to the *Programs Files\3ds Max 2012\maps\Skies\sun cloud.jpg* file and choose the **Open** button; the image is displayed as the background at rendering. Close the **Environment and Effects** dialog box.

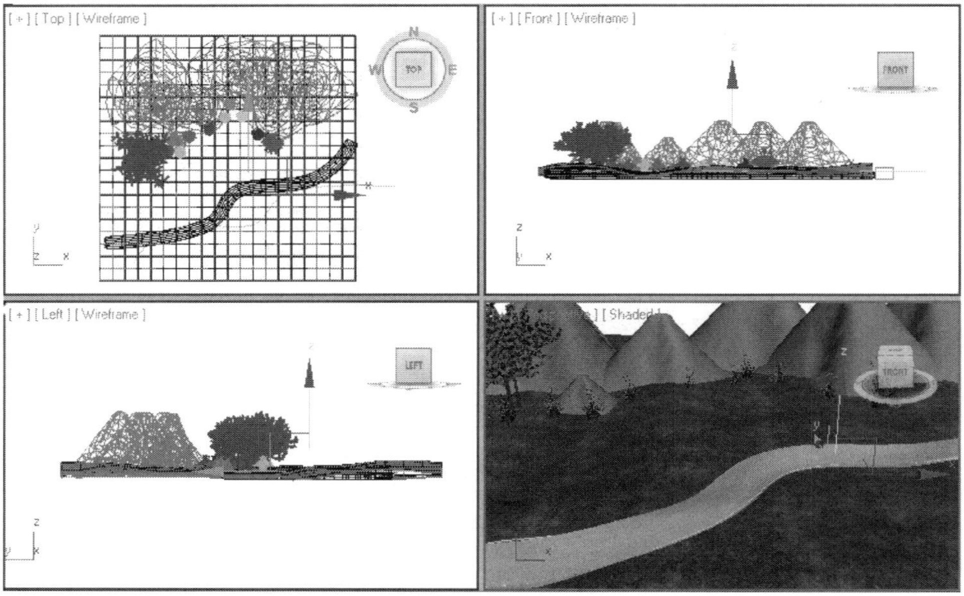

*Figure 9-104 The scene after using the **Conform** tool*

Rendering the Scene for the Final Output

1. Activate the Perspective viewport.

2. Invoke the **Render Production** tool in the **Main Toolbar**; the **Perspective, frame 0, Display Gamma:2.2, RGBA Color16Bits/ Channel (1:1)** dialog box is displayed with the final output of the scene at one frame, refer to Figure 9-105.

3. Close this dialog box.

   You can view the final rendered image of this model by downloading the *c09_3dsmax_2012_render.zip* file from *http://www.cadcim.com*.

Figure 9-105 The final output of the scene

Saving the File

1. Save the file with the name *c09tut2.max* as discussed in earlier chapters. The location of this file is given below:

   \Documents\3dsmax\c09_tut2\scenes

Self-Evaluation Test

Answer the following questions and then compare them to those given at the end of this chapter:

1. Which of the following options is not a type of boolean operation?

   (a) **Union** (b) **Cut**
   (c) **Subtraction(A-B)** (d) None of these

2. Which of the following tools in the **Compound Objects** is used to distribute the source object over the surface of the distribution object?

   (a) **Scatter** (b) **Loft**
   (c) **Conform** (d) **Terrain**

3. Which of the following tools is used to connect two or more objects at the holes on their surfaces?

   (a) **ShapeMerge** (b) **Conform**
   (c) **Connect** (d) All of these

4. Which of the following tools is used to create 3D objects using the 2D shapes by lofting them along a spline path?

   (a) **ProBoolean** (b) **ProCutter**
   (c) **Connect** (d) **Loft**

5. Which of the following tools is used to adjust the position of an object over the hilly surface exactly on the surface?

   (a) **Loft** (b) **Connect**
   (c) **Boolean** (d) **Conform**

6. In a terrain object, select the __________ radio button in the **Form** area of the **Parameters** rollout to create the layered objects such as the cardboard architectural models.

7. The __________ area in the **Surface Parameters** rollout of a loft object is used to smoothen the length and circumference of the path.

8. The ________ tool is used to select the multiple objects at a time to perform the boolean operation.

9. The terrain objects are created from the mesh objects. (T/F)

10. The **Reorder Ops** button in the **Parameters** rollout of a proboolean object is used to change the order of boolean operations in the viewport. (T/F)

Review Questions

Answer the following questions:

1. Which of the boolean operations is used to remove the non-overlapping area of two objects?

   (a) **Intersection** (b) **Union**
   (c) **Subtraction(B-A)** (d) **Subtraction(A-B)**

2. Which of the following tools is used to break an object into separate objects using the mesh objects as a cutter?

   (a) **ProBoolean** (b) **Conform**
   (c) **Scatter** (d) **ProCutter**

3. Which of the following tools is used to create the terrain objects?

   (a) **Scatter** (b) **Conform**
   (c) **ProBoolean** (d) **Terrain**

4. The **Change Operation** button in the **Parameters** rollout of the **ProBoolean** tool is used to change the type of boolean operation for the selected operand. (T/F)

5. The options in the **Color by Elevation** rollout of the **Terrain** tool are used to set its color on the basis of the elevation of the terrain object. (T/F)

6. The **Imprint** check box in the **Parameters** rollout of the **ProBoolean** tool is used to delete the faces of the original object. (T/F)

7. The boolean objects are created from two objects. These objects are known as operands. (T/F)

8. Select the __________ check box in the **Cutter Parameters** rollout of the **ProCutter** tool to get the parts of the stock object that are outside the cutters.

9. The options in the __________ rollout of the **Terrain** tool are used to set the complexity of the terrain object.

10. The __________ area in the **Scatters Object** rollout of the **Scatter** tool is used to arrange the copied source object over the distribution object.

Exercises

Exercise 1

Start Autodesk 3ds Max 2012 and then perform the following operations:

1. Create a line spline and a circle spline in the Top viewport. Select one of the splines and then invoke the **Loft** tool from **Create > Geometry > Compound Objects > Object Type** rollout. Next, choose the **Get Path** button in the **Creation Method** rollout and select another spline in the viewport and view the shape created. Perform the same function by choosing the **Get Shape** button and notice the difference in the output.

2. Create the contour lines in the Top viewport. Select all lines and then invoke the **Terrain** tool from the **Object Type** rollout of the **Compound Objects**; a terrain object will be created. Select the terrain object and choose the **Modify** tab in the **Command Panel**. In the **Parameters** rollout, select different radio buttons and check boxes in the **Form** area and notice the difference in the terrain object.

3. Create an object to break into separate objects. Create one or more mesh objects to be used as cutters. Align both the objects to create a procutter object. Select one of the cutter objects, invoke the **ProCutter** tool from the **Object Type** rollout in the **Compound Objects**. In the **Cutter Picking Parameters** rollout, choose the **Pick Cutter Objects** button; the selection cursor will be displayed. Select the additional cutters in the viewport. Next, choose the **Pick Stock Objects** button; the selection cursor will be displayed. Select the object that you want to cut in the viewport; the object will be cut. Then, in the **Cutter Parameters** rollout, select the different check boxes in the **Cutting Options** area and notice the difference.

4. Create different **Compound Objects** as discussed in this chapter and use various options in different rollouts to notice the difference.

Exercise 2

Create the model shown in Figure 9-106 using the **ShapeMerge** tool in the **Compound Objects**. You can view the final rendered image of this scene by downloading it from *http://www.cadcim.com*. **(Expected time: 15 min)**

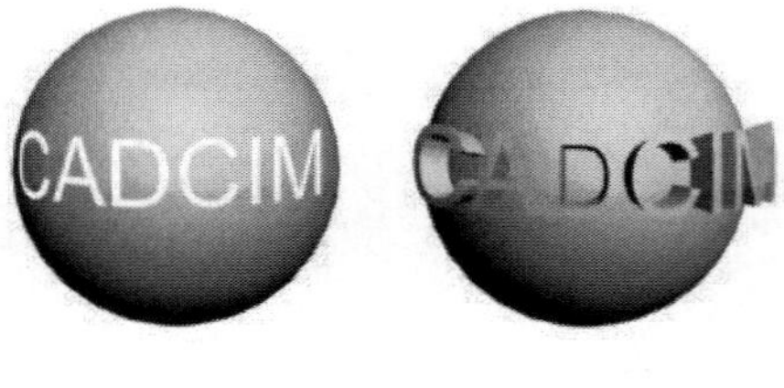

Figure 9-106 *Model for Exercise 2*

Exercise 3

Create the model shown in Figure 9-107 using the **Loft** tool in the **Compound Objects**. You can view the final rendered image of this scene by downloading it from *http://www.cadcim.com*.

(Expected time: 20 min)

Figure 9-107 *Model for Exercise 3*

Answers to Self-Evaluation Test

1. d, **2.** a, **3.** c, **4.** d, **5.** d, **6. Layered Solid**, **7. Smoothing**, **8. ProBoolean**, **9.** F, **10.** T

10

Modifiers

Learning Objectives

After completing this chapter, you will be able to:

- *Use modifiers and modifier stack*
- *Understand the uses of modifiers*
- *Create advance objects using modifiers*

INTRODUCTION

In this chapter, you will learn about modifiers. As the name indicates, modifiers are used to modify an object. Using modifiers, you can create various models that would otherwise be quite difficult to create. Apart from this, the chapter will help you modify the parameters of the objects created in the viewport.

MODIFIERS AND MODIFIER STACK

In Autodesk 3ds Max, the modifiers are used to modify or edit an object in an advance and realistic way. You can apply more than one modifier to an object. The modifiers can also be used to modify the object at sub-object levels.

To apply a modifier to an object, select the object in the viewport and then choose the **Modify** tab in the **Command Panel**; the **Modifier List** drop-down list will be displayed, as shown in Figure 10-1. To view the options in the drop-down list, click on the arrow on the right of **Modifier List**, as shown in Figure 10-2. There are different types of modifiers in this list. Select the modifier that you want to apply to the object; the selected modifier will be displayed in the modifier stack along with various rollouts in the modify panel to modify the object, refer to Figure 10-3.

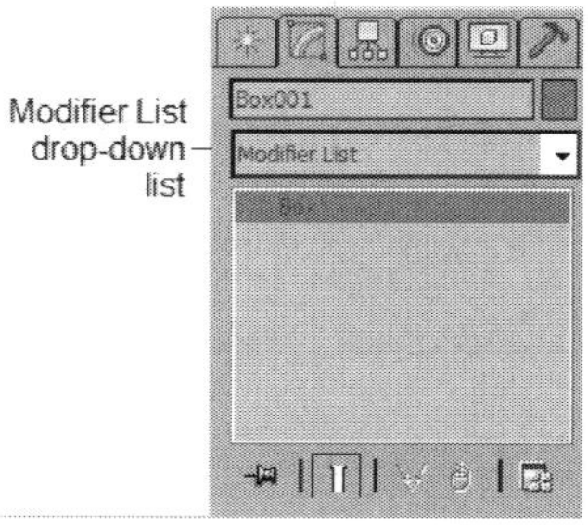

*Figure 10-1 The **Modifier List** drop-down list*

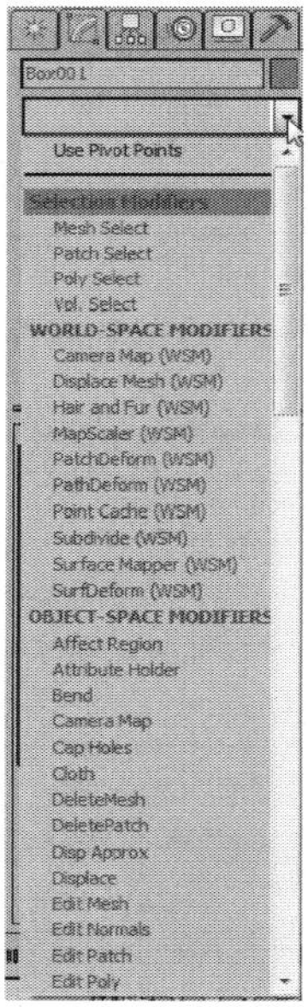

*Figure 10-2 Partial view of the **Modifier List** drop-down list*

Note

*The modifiers displayed in the **Modifier List** drop-down list depend on the selection of the object in the viewport.*

In the modifier stack, there is a bulb-like button, refer to Figure 10-3. It is used to show or hide the effects of the modifier in the viewport. By default, this button is active. Click on this button to make it inactive; the button will become dark and the effect of the modifier will not be displayed in the viewport. The buttons at the bottom of the modifier stack are used to control the modifier stack. These buttons are discussed next.

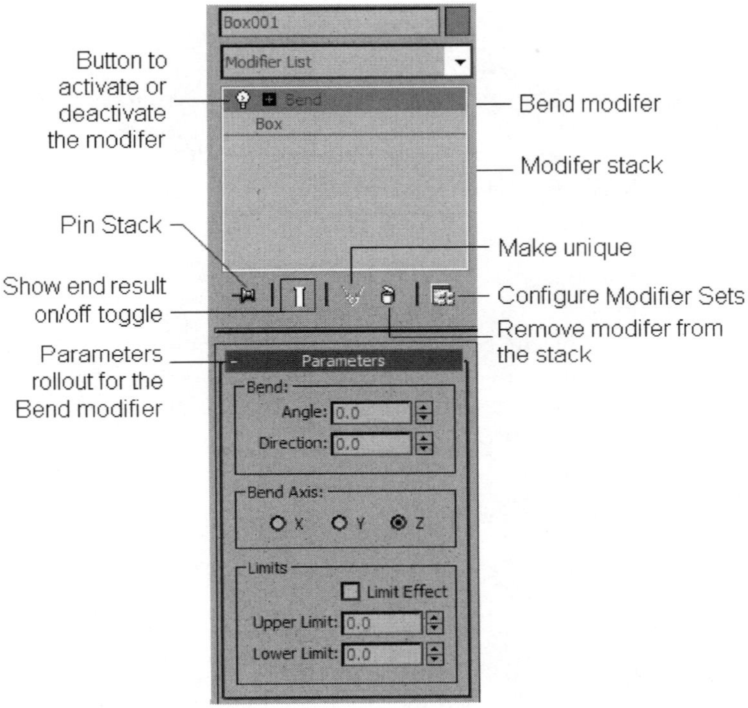

***Figure 10-3** The modifier displayed in the modifier stack after selecting it from the **Modifier List** drop-down list*

The **Pin Stack** button is used to lock the modifier stack for the selected object in the viewport. If you choose the **Pin Stack** button for the selected object in the viewport, and then select another object in the viewport, the **Modify** tab will display the modifier stack and the rollouts for the pinned object only.

By default, the **Show end result on/off toggle** button is chosen that displays the effect of all modifiers in the modifier stack on the selected object in the viewport. If you deselect the **Show end result on/off toggle** button, then the selected object in the viewport will display only the effect of the selected modifier in the modifier stack.

The **Make unique** button is used to convert an instanced object to unique copy. On making the instanced objects unique, they become independent and you can modify them independently without affecting the other objects in the viewport. By default, this button is inactive. When you create the instance of an object, this button will be activated. Select the instanced object in the viewport and choose the **Make unique** button in the modifier stack to make it unique.

The **Remove modifier from the stack** button is used to remove the selected modifier from the modifier stack.

When you choose the **Configure Modifier Sets** button, a shortcut menu will be displayed. The options in this menu are used to control the display of the modifiers in the modifier stack.

Note

1. If you change the order of the modifiers applied to an object in the modifier stack, the object will display different effects.

2. The object should have more number of segments to get the best effect of the applied modifier.

In the modifier stack, move the cursor over the modifier and right-click on it; a shortcut menu will be displayed, as shown in Figure 10-4. You can rename, delete, cut, copy, or paste the selected modifiers by choosing the corresponding option from the shortcut menu displayed. Choose the **Collapse All** option from the menu to collapse the entire stack; the **Warning: Collapse All** message box will be displayed. Choose the **Yes** button; all the parameters and modifiers will be replaced by Editable Mesh in the modifier stack. Choose the **Collapse To** option from the shortcut menu to collapse the selected modifier along with the modifiers and objects below it.

TYPES OF MODIFIERS

There are three categories of modifiers in the **Modifier List** drop-down list: **Selection Modifiers**, **WORLD-SPACE MODIFIERS**, and **OBJECT-SPACE MODIFIERS**. The **Bend** and **Taper** modifiers from the **OBJECT-SPACE MODIFIERS** category have already been discussed in Chapter 3. The most commonly used modifiers in these three categories are discussed in this chapter.

Mesh Select Modifier

The **Mesh Select** modifier is used to pass the sub-object selections of the selected object to the subsequent modifiers in the modifier stack. To do so, select the object in the viewport and choose the **Modify** tab in the **Command Panel**. In the modifier stack, click on the arrow on the right side of the **Modifier List** drop-down list and select the **Mesh Select** modifier from the **Selection Modifiers** category. Alternatively, choose **Modifiers > Selection > Mesh Select** from the menu bar; the **Mesh Select** modifier will be displayed in the modifier stack with various rollouts in the modify panel, as shown in Figure 10-5. Click on the plus sign (+) on the left of the **Mesh Select** modifier in the modifier stack; the sub-object levels will be displayed. Now, select any of the sub-object levels and then select the corresponding sub-objects of the object in the viewport. Next, apply another modifier; it will affect only the selected sub-objects in the viewport. The most commonly used rollout displayed in the modify panel is discussed next.

Mesh Select Parameters Rollout

On the top of this rollout, there are five buttons, **Vertex**, **Edge**, **Face**, **Polygon**, and **Element**. These buttons are used to select the sub-objects of the object and are the same as described earlier in Chapter 6. Choose any button to activate it and it is same as selecting the sub-object level in the modifier stack. When you choose any of the buttons; the transform tools such as **Select and Rotate**, **Select and Move**, and so on will be disabled in the **Main Toolbar**.

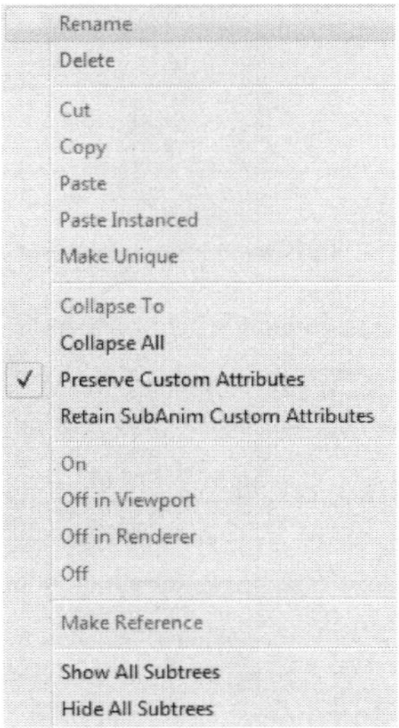

***Figure 10-4** The shortcut menu displayed after right-clicking on the modifier in the modifier stack*

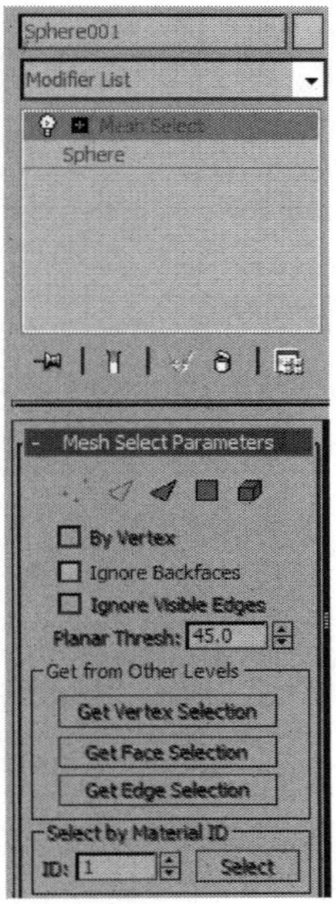

***Figure 10-5** Partial view of the rollouts displayed after selecting the **Mesh Select** modifier*

The options in the **Get from Other Levels** area are used to apply the selection of the sub-objects from one sub-object level to another. The **Get Vertex Selection** button is available for the **Face**, **Edge**, **Polygon**, and **Element** sub-object levels. Choose this button to select the faces of the object based on the last selection of the vertices. The **Get Face Selection** button is available only for the **Vertex** and **Edge** sub-object levels. Choose this button to select the vertices of the object based on the last selection of the faces, polygons, and elements. The **Get Edge Selection** button is available for the Vertex, Face, Polygon, and Element sub-object levels. Choose this button to select the faces based on the last selection of the edges.

Note

*The options in the **Patch Select** and **Poly Select** modifiers from the **Selection Modifiers** category are the same as discussed in the **Mesh Select** modifier. The only difference is in the sub-object levels that you have learned in Chapter 6.*

Displace Modifier

The **Displace** modifier is used to deform the shape of an object. You can distort the object either by using the gizmo of the modifier or by using the bitmap image. To apply the **Displace** modifier, select the object in the viewport and choose the **Modify** tab in the **Command**

Panel. Now, click on the **Modifier List** drop-down list and select the **Displace** modifier from the **OBJECT-SPACE MODIFIERS** category. Alternatively, choose **Modifiers > Parametric Deformers > Displace** from the menu bar; the **Displace** modifier will be displayed in the modifier stack and the **Parameters** rollout will be displayed in the modify panel. You need to use the options in this rollout to distort the surface of the object. These options are discussed next.

Parameters Rollout

The areas in this rollout are discussed next.

Displacement Area

The options in this area are used to specify the amount of displacement of an object from the position of its gizmo, refer to Figure 10-6. By default, the value in the **Strength** and **Decay** spinners is 0 which indicates that there will be no displacement. Set the value more than 0 in the **Strength** spinner to displace the object away from the gizmo. Set the value less than 0 in the **Strength** spinner to displace the object toward the gizmo. Set the value in the **Decay** spinner to decrease the strength of the displacement based on the distance of the object from the gizmo.

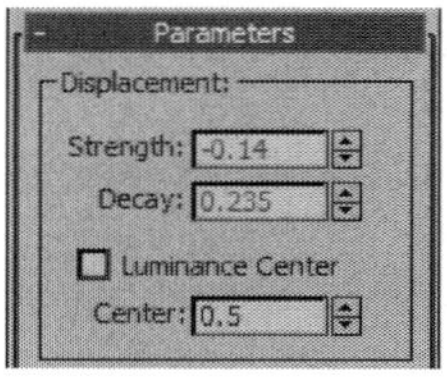

*Figure 10-6 The **Displacement** area in the **Parameters** rollout*

Image Area

The options in this area are used to choose a bitmap and map as the source for the displacement. The button labeled as **None** at the top of the **Bitmap** area is used to assign a bitmap image to the object for displacement. To do so, choose the button; the **Select Displacement Image** dialog box will be displayed. Select the image of your choice and choose the **Open** button; the name of the image will be displayed on the button. Next, set the values in the **Strength** and **Decay** spinners in the **Displacement** area to view the displacement, refer to Figures 10-7 and 10-8. Choose the **Remove Bitmap** button to remove the assigned bitmap image.

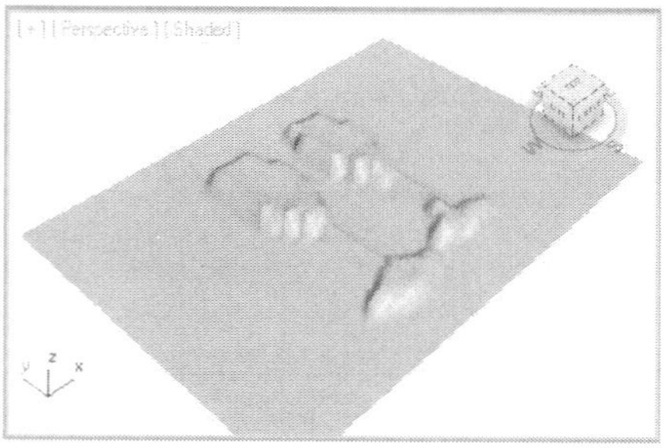

*Figure 10-7 The plane after using the bitmap image in the **Displace** modifier*

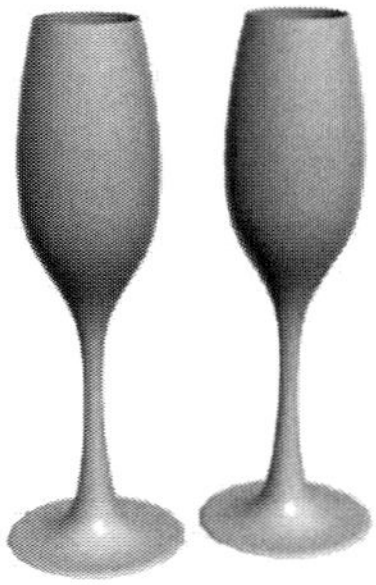

Figure 10-8 The bitmap image that has been used for displacement in Figure 10-7

The button, labeled as **None** at the top of the **Map** area, is used to assign a map to the object for displacement. To do so, choose the button; the **Material/Map Browser** dialog box will be displayed. Select the map of your choice from the **Maps > Standard** rollouts and choose the **OK** button; the name of the map will be displayed on the button. Next, set the values in the **Strength** and **Decay** spinners in the **Displacement** area to view the displacement, refer to Figures 10-9 and 10-10. Choose the **Remove Map** button to remove the assigned map. Set the value in the **Blur** spinner to soften the edges of the map or bitmap.

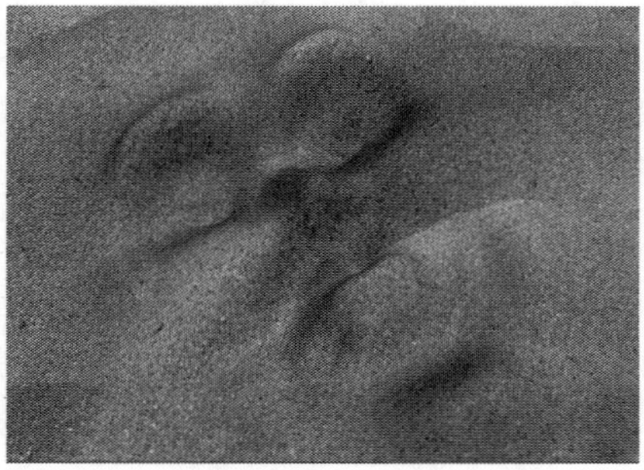

Figure 10-9 *The plane after using the map image in the* ***Displace*** *modifier*

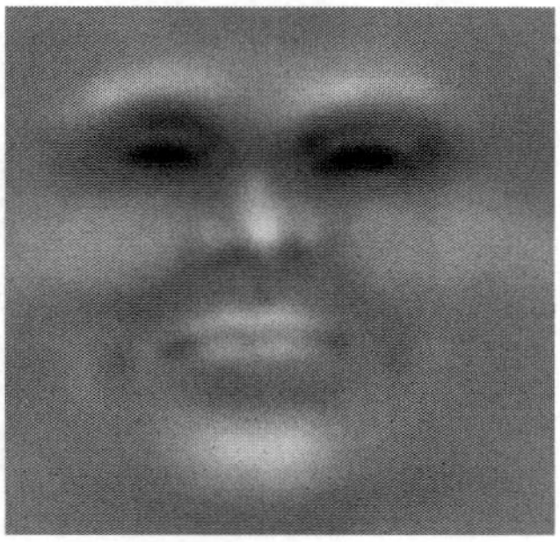

Figure 10-10 *The map image that has been used for displacement in Figure 10-9*

Note
You can apply the map and bitmap images simultaneously.

Set the parameters in the **Map**, **Channel**, and **Alignment** areas to define the placement or alignment of the map on the object.

Extrude Modifier

The **Extrude** modifier is used to convert a 2D spline into a 3D object. It provides thickness and depth to a spline. To apply the **Extrude** modifier, select the spline in the viewport and choose the **Modify** tab in the **Command Panel**. Now, select the **Extrude** modifier from the **OBJECT-SPACE MODIFIERS** category in the **Modifier List** drop-down list. Alternatively, choose **Modifiers > Mesh Editing > Extrude** from the menu bar; the modifier will be displayed in the modifier stack and the **Parameters** rollout will be displayed below the modifier stack in the modify panel, as shown in Figure 10-11. Next, you need to use the options in the **Parameters** rollout to view the effects of the **Extrude** modifier. These options are discussed next.

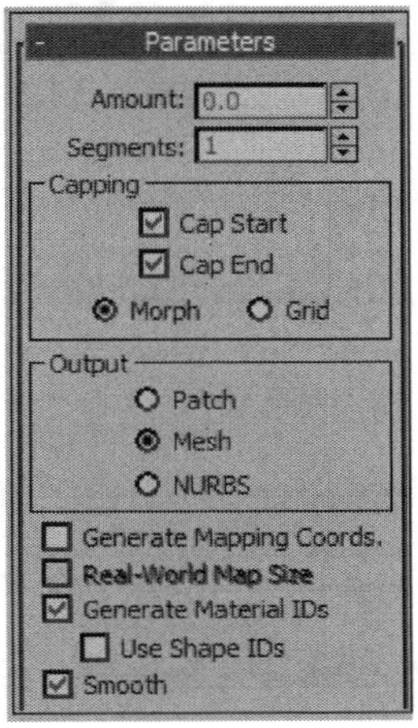

Figure 10-11 *The* ***Parameters*** *rollout*

Parameters Rollout

Set the value in the **Amount** spinner to specify the amount of extrusion of the spline, refer to Figures 10-12 and 10-13. Set the value in the **Segments** spinner to specify the number of segments in the extruded object. The areas in this rollout are discussed next.

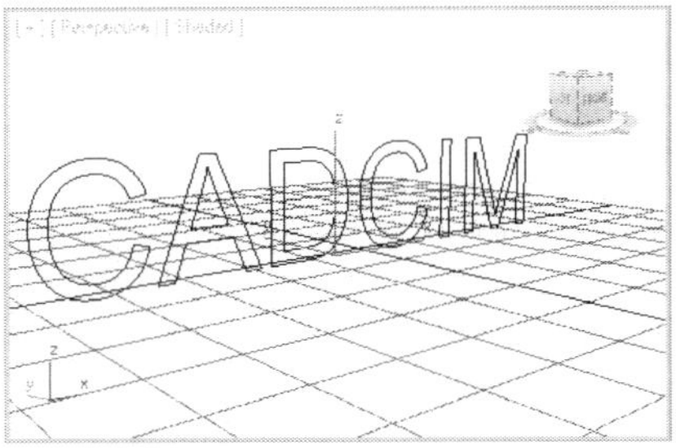

*Figure 10-12 The text spline before applying the **Extrude** modifier*

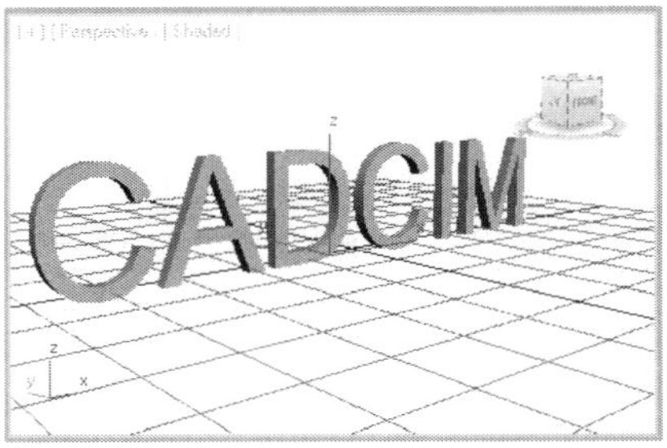

*Figure 10-13 The text spline after applying the **Extrude** modifier*

Capping Area

By default, the **Cap Start** and **Cap End** check boxes are selected. They are used to place a plane surface at the start and end of the extruded object. Clear the **Cap Start** check box to remove the surface at the start of the extruded object. Similarly, clear the **Cap End** check box to remove the surface at the end of the extruded object.

Output Area

The options in this area are used to specify the type of the object to be created by the **Extrude** modifier. By default, the **Mesh** radio button is selected that produces a mesh object. Select the **Patch** or the **NURBS** radio button to produce the patch or the nurbs object.

Face Extrude Modifier

This modifier is used to extrude the selected faces along their normals. A normal is an invisible line coming straight out of a face in a particular direction. To apply the **Face Extrude** modifier, first convert the object into editable poly object. Next, select the **Face** sub-object level and then select the faces of the object in the viewport. Now, select the **Face Extrude** modifier from the **OBJECT-SPACE MODIFIERS** category in the **Modifier List** drop-down list.

Alternatively, choose **Modifiers > Mesh Editing > Face Extrude** from the menu bar; the **Face Extrude** modifier will be displayed in the modifier stack and the **Parameters** rollout will also be displayed below the modifier stack in the modify panel. Now, you need to use the options in the **Parameters** rollout to view the effect of the **Face Extrude** modifier on the selected faces, refer to Figure 10-14. These options are discussed next.

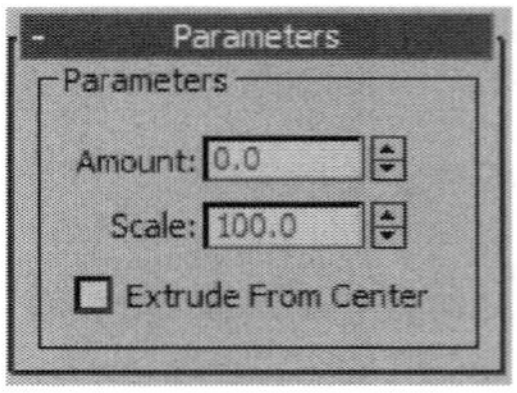

*Figure 10-14 The **Parameters** rollout*

Parameters Rollout

Set the value in the **Amount** spinner to specify the amount of extrusion of the selected faces, refer to Figures 10-15 and 10-16. Set the value in the **Scale** spinner to specify the percentage of the original face size used for the extruded face.

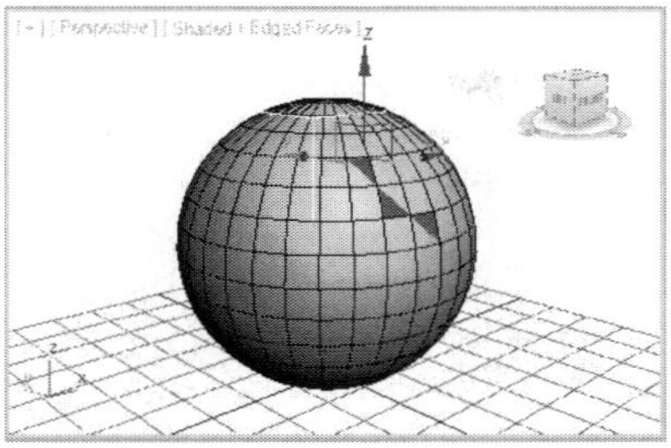

Figure 10-15 *The faces selected to be extruded in a sphere*

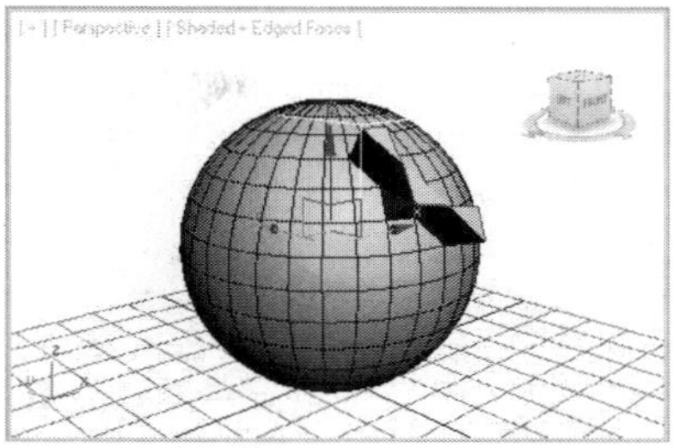

Figure 10-16 *The selected faces extruded*

Lattice Modifier

The **Lattice** modifier is used to convert the segments or edges of an object or shape into wireframes or cylindrical struts. To apply the **Lattice** modifier, select the object or shape in the viewport and choose the **Modify** tab in the **Command Panel**. Now, select the **Lattice** modifier from the **OBJECT-SPACE MODIFIERS** category in the **Modifier List** drop-down list. Alternatively, choose **Modifiers > Parametric Deformers > Lattice** from the menu bar; the modifier will be displayed in the modifier stack and its effect will be displayed on the object, as shown in Figure 10-17. The **Parameters** rollout will also be displayed below the modifier stack, as shown in Figure 10-18. Now, you need to use the options in the **Parameters** rollout to modify the effects of the **Lattice** modifier. These options are discussed next.

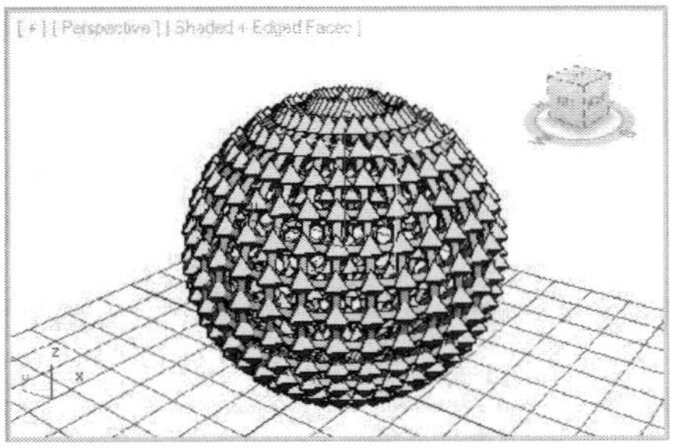

Figure 10-17 *The sphere after applying the **Lattice** modifier*

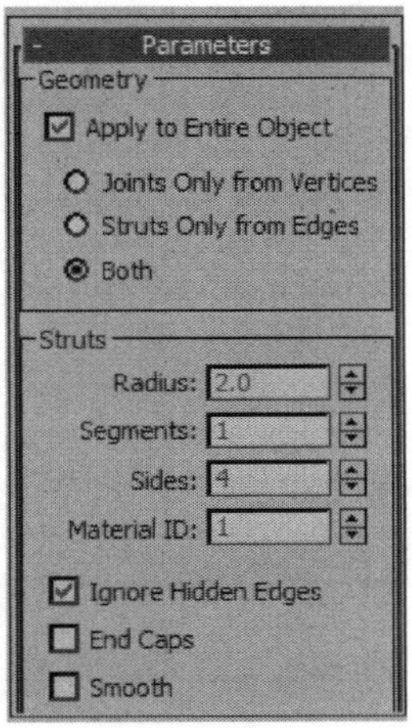

Figure 10-18 *Partial view of the **Parameters** rollout*

Parameters Rollout

The options in this rollout are used to specify whether the wireframes will be displayed on the joints, struts, or both of them. The areas in this rollout are discussed next.

Geometry Area

By default, the **Apply to Entire Object** check box is selected. As a result, wireframe is applied to all the segments or edges of the object. If you clear this check box, then the wireframes will be applied only to the selected segments or edges of the object.

By default, the **Both** radio button is selected to apply the wireframes both on the struts and joints, refer to Figure 10-17. Select the **Joints Only from Vertices** radio button to display the wireframes only on the joints generated from the vertices of the object, as shown in Figure 10-19. Select the **Struts Only from Edges** radio button to display the wireframes only on the struts generated from the edges of the object, as shown in Figure 10-20.

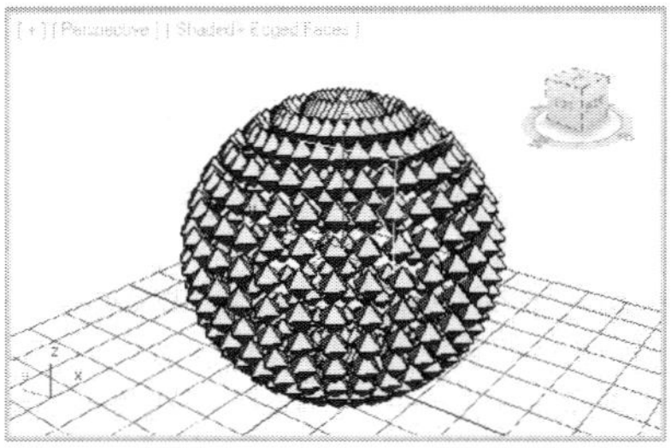

Figure 10-19 *The sphere after selecting the* ***Joints Only from Vertices*** *radio button*

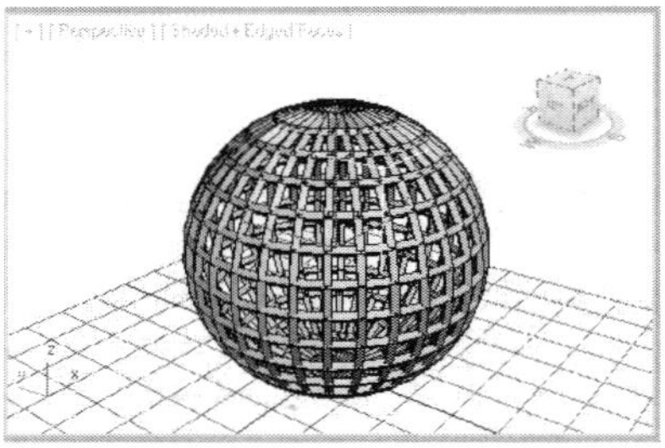

Figure 10-20 *The sphere after selecting the* ***Struts Only from Edges*** *radio button*

Struts Area

The options in this area are activated only if the **Struts Only from Edges** or **Both** radio button is selected in the **Geometry** area. Set the value in the **Radius** spinner to define the radius of the struts. Set the value in the **Segments** spinner to specify the number of segments along the struts. Set the value in the **Sides** spinner to specify the number of sides around the circumference of the struts. Set the value in the **Material ID** spinner to specify the material id for the struts to apply the material.

Joints Area

The options in this area are activated only if the **Joints Only from Vertices** or **Both** radio button is selected in the **Geometry** area. There are three radio buttons in the **Geodesic Base Type** group that specify the type of polyhedron to be used for the joints. By default, the **Octa** radio button is selected and is used to create the octahedron joints. Select the **Tetra** or the **Icosa** radio button to create the tetrahedron or icosahedron joints. The other options are the same as discussed in the **Struts** area.

Material Modifier

The **Material** modifier is used to assign the material ID to the object or the sub-objects. The material ID of an object is a value given to specify the sub-material that will be applied to it from the **Multi/Sub-Object** material. You can apply different materials to the selected sub-objects by assigning different material IDs. To do so, create an object in the Top viewport. Invoke the **Material Editor** tool from the **Main Toolbar** and apply the **Multi/Sub-Object** material to the object as described earlier in Chapter 8; the **Multi/Sub-Object Basic Parameters** rollout will be displayed in the **Material Editor** dialog box, as shown in Figure 10-21. In this rollout, assign two different colors to the first two sub-materials using the color swatches on the right side.

By default, the first two sub-materials have the material IDs, 1 and 2. Now, assign the **Multi/Sub-Object** material to the object in the viewport. Next, make sure that the object is selected and apply the **Mesh Select** modifier to it. Select the **Polygon** sub-object level and select the polygons of the object in the viewport. Now, make sure that the Polygon sub-object level is active and select the **Material** modifier from the **OBJECT-SPACE MODIFIERS** category in the **Modifier List** drop-down list. You can also choose **Modifiers > Surface > Material** from the menu bar; the **Material** modifier will be displayed in the modifier stack and the **Parameters** rollout will be displayed. Now, in the **Material ID** spinner of the **Parameters** rollout, set the value **1**; the selected polygons will display the color that you have assigned to the sub-material with the material ID 1. Select another set of polygons and set the value **2** in the **Material ID** spinner; the selected polygons will display the color that you have assigned to the sub-material with the material ID 2.

The options in the **Parameters** rollout are discussed next.

Parameters Rollout

The **Material ID** spinner in this rollout is used to change the material ID of the selected sub-object in the viewport. Set the value **1** or **2** in the **Material ID** spinner that you have assigned in the **Multi/Sub-Object Basic Parameters**; the selected sub-objects will display the color of the same material ID. For example, if you have assigned the blue color to the material ID 1 and red color to the material ID 2 in the **Multi/Sub-Object Basic Parameters**. Then, on entering the value **1** in the **Material ID** spinner; the selected sub-objects will appear blue color. And, if you enter the value **2** in the **Material ID** spinner; the selected sub-objects will appear red, refer to Figure 10-22.

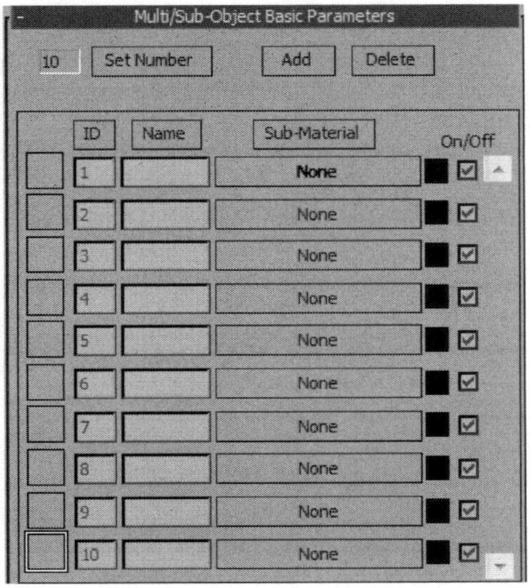

Figure 10-21 *Partial view of the* ***Multi/Sub-Object Basic Parameters*** *rollout in the* ***Material Editor*** *dialog box*

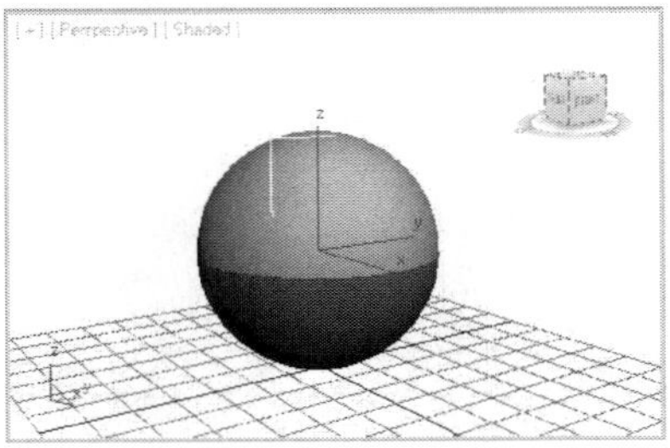

Figure 10-22 *The object in two different colors after applying the* ***Material*** *modifier*

Noise Modifier

The **Noise** modifier is used to generate the disturbances on the surface of an object to create irregular surfaces. It can also be used to animate the water or wavy surfaces.

To apply the **Noise** modifier, select the object in the viewport and choose the **Modify** tab in the **Command Panel**. Now, select the **Noise** modifier from the **OBJECT-SPACE MODIFIERS** category in the **Modifier List** drop-down list. You can also choose **Modifiers > Parametric Deformers > Noise** from the menu bar; the **Noise** modifier will be displayed in the modifier stack and the **Parameters** rollout will also be displayed in the modify panel. Next, you need to use the options in the **Parameters** rollout, refer to Figure 10-23, to apply the effects of the **Noise** modifier on the selected object. These options are discussed next.

Parameters Rollout

The options in this rollout are used to generate noise effects in an object, as shown in Figure 10-24. The areas in this rollout are discussed next.

Noise Area

The options in this area are used to define the appearance on the surface of the object on applying the **Noise** modifier. Set the value in the **Seed** spinner to specify the starting point for generating the noise randomly in the object. Set the value in the **Scale** spinner to specify the size of noise effects. By default, the value in the **Scale** spinner is 100. A higher value in this spinner produces smoother noise effects and a lower value produces scraggy noise effects. By default, the **Fractal** check box is cleared. Select the **Fractal** check box to produce the fractal-based noise effects, refer to Figure 10-25. When you select the **Fractal** check box, the **Roughness** and **Iterations** spinners get activated that are used to set the fractal effects in the noise. Set the lower value in the **Roughness** spinner to produce smooth fractal effects in noise. Set the higher value in the **Roughness** spinner to produce rough fractal effects in noise. The value in the **Roughness** spinner varies from 0 to 1.0. Set the value in the **Iterations** spinner to apply the fractal effects multiple times. By default, the value in the **Iterations** spinner is 1.0. It varies from 1.0 to 10.0.

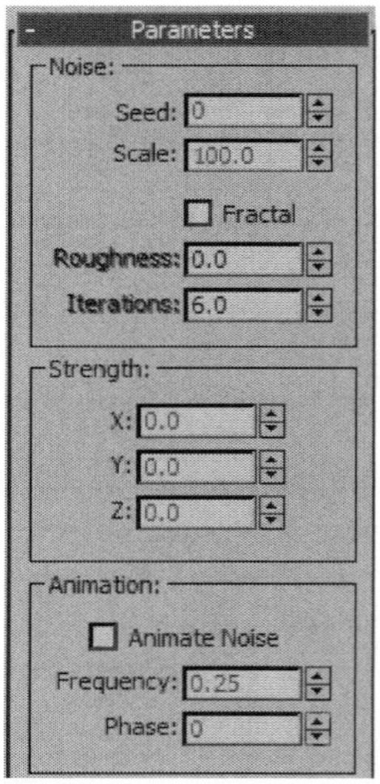

***Figure 10-23** The **Parameters** rollout*

Note

*1. The number of segments should be more in the object to generate a better effect of the **Noise** modifier.*

2. You can also create the terrain objects using this modifier.

Strength Area

The options in this area are used to specify the strength of the noise effects. By default, the value in the **X**, **Y**, and **Z** spinners is 0 that produces no noise effects in the object. Set the value in these spinners to generate the strength of the noise effects.

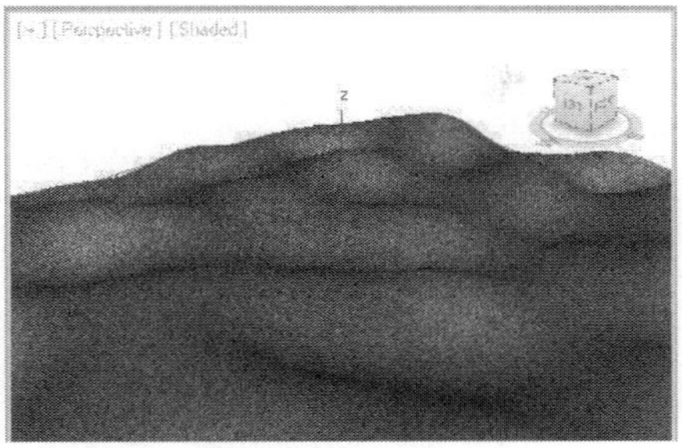

*Figure 10-24 The plane with the **Noise** modifier applied*

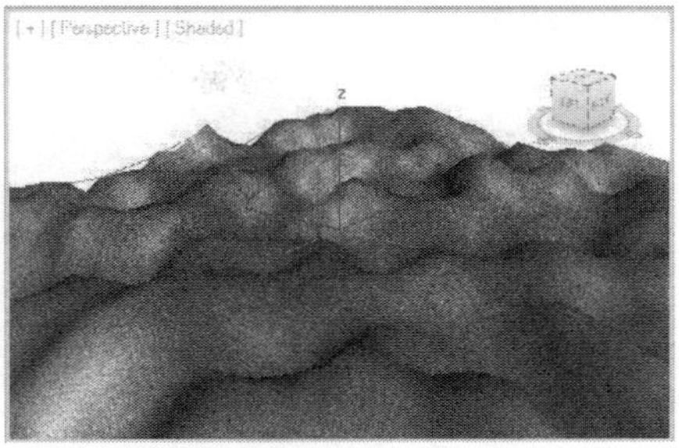

*Figure 10-25 The plane with the fractal value in the **Noise** modifier*

Animation Area

The options in this area are used to animate the noise effects of the object. To view the animation effects, you need to select the **Animate Noise** check box. Set the value in the **Frequency** spinner to specify the speed of the animation of noise waves. The lower value produces a slow animation and the higher value produces a fast animation. Set the value in the **Phase** spinner to set the start point and the end point of the wave animation along with the frames in the time slider.

Twist Modifier

The **Twist** modifier is used to produce the swirling effect on an object. To apply the **Twist** modifier, select an object in the viewport. Select the **Twist** modifier from the **OBJECT-SPACE MODIFIERS** category in the **Modifier List** drop-down list. Alternatively, choose the **Modifiers > Parametric Deformers > Twist** from the menu bar; the **Twist** modifier will be displayed in the modifier stack and the **Parameters** rollout will also be displayed in the modify panel. Next, you need to use the options in the **Parameters** rollout, refer to Figure 10-26, to apply the effects of the **Twist** modifier to the object. The **Parameters** rollout is discussed next.

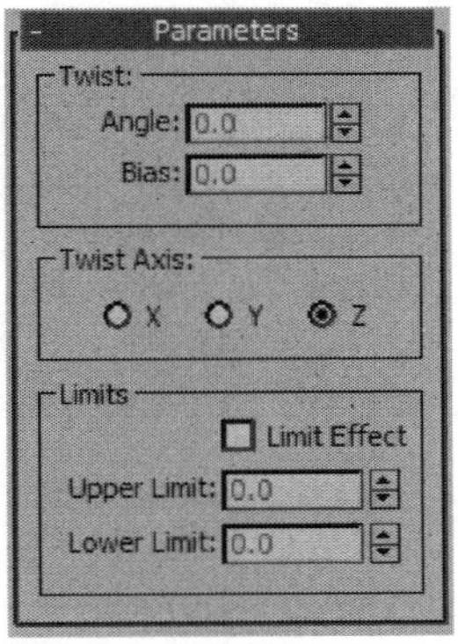

*Figure 10-26 The **Parameters** rollout*

Parameters Rollout

This rollout is used to set the parameters to generate the swirling effects on an object, as shown in Figure 10-27. The areas in this rollout are discussed next.

Twist Area

Set the value in the **Angle** spinner to specify the amount of twist in degrees along the selected axis in the **Twist Axis** area. Set the value in the **Bias** spinner to shift the twist at one of the ends of the object. By default, the value in this spinner is 0, which specifies that the twist is uniform along the length of the object. It varies from 100 to -100.

Twist Axis Area

By default, the **Z** radio button is selected. As a result, the object will twist along the **Z**-axis. Select the **X** or the **Y** radio button to twist the object along the **X**-axis or the **Y**-axis, respectively.

Limits Area

The options in this area are used to define the portion of an object to which the twist effects will be applied, refer to Figure 10-28. Select the **Limit Effect** check box to apply the limits to the twist effects of the object. Set the value in the **Upper Limit** spinner to specify the upper limit for the twist effect. Set the value in the **Lower Limit** spinner to specify the lower limit for the twist effect.

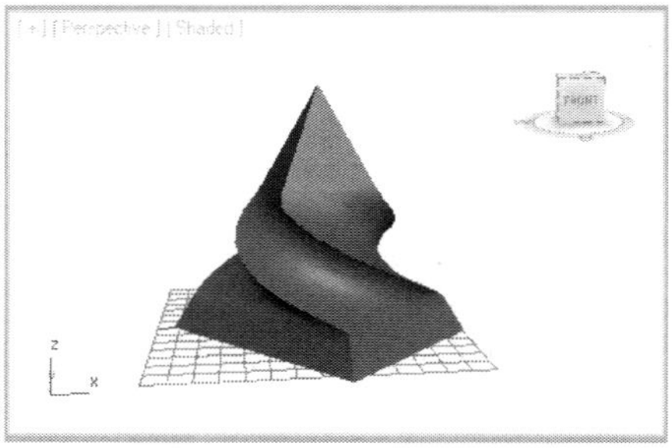

*Figure 10-27 The **Twist** modifier applied to the pyramid object*

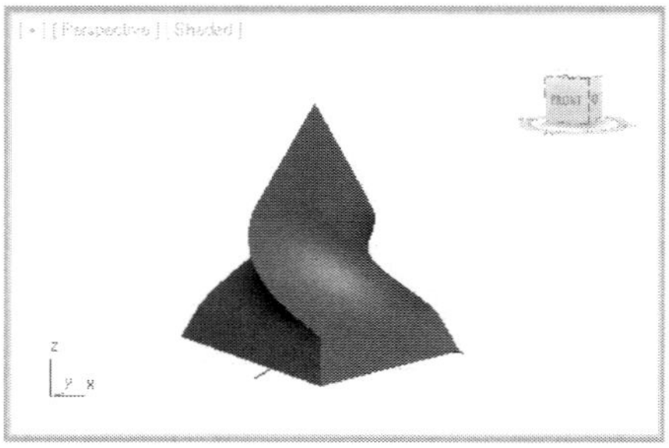

*Figure 10-28 The **Twist** modifier applied to a portion of the pyramid object using the options in the **Limits** area*

Lathe Modifier

The **Lathe** modifier is a shape modifier and is used to create a 3D object by rotating a shape about an axis. The direction of the axis of revolution depends on the pivot point of the shape. To apply the **Lathe** modifier on an object, create a shape in the Front viewport and choose the **Modify** tab in the **Command Panel**. Now, select the **Lathe** modifier from the **OBJECT-SPACE MODIFIERS** category in the **Modifier List** drop-down list. Alternatively, choose **Modifiers > Patch/Spline Editing > Lathe** from the menu bar; the 2D shape will be converted into a 3D object, as shown in Figures 10-29 and 10-30. And, the modifier will be displayed in the modifier stack. The **Parameters** rollout will also be displayed below the modifier stack, refer to Figure 10-31. This rollout is discussed next.

Parameters Rollout

Set the value in the **Degrees** spinner to specify the amount of rotation of the object in degrees around the axis specified in the **Direction** area. By default, the value in this spinner is 360.0, which indicates the complete rotation of the object around the axis. Set the value in **Segments** spinner to specify the number of segments around the axis of revolution. The areas in this rollout are discussed next.

Capping Area

The options in this area are the same as described in the **Extrude** modifier.

Direction Area

Choose the **X**, **Y**, or **Z** button to specify the axis around which the objects will rotate while applying the **Lathe** modifier.

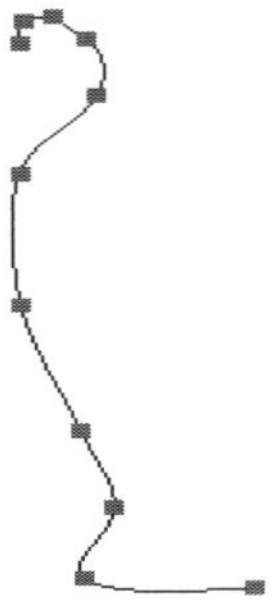

*Figure 10-29 The **Line** spline created to apply the **Lathe** modifier*

*Figure 10-30 The **Line** spline after applying the **Lathe** modifier*

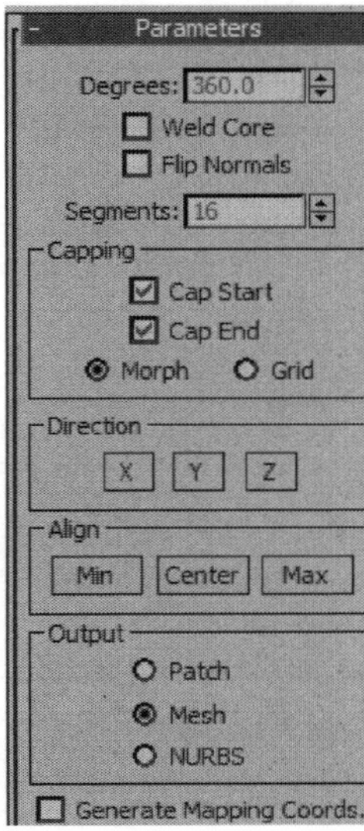

*Figure 10-31 Partial view of the **Parameters** rollout*

Align Area

Choose the **Min**, **Center**, or **Max** button to align the spline with the axis of revolution.

MeshSmooth Modifier

The **MeshSmooth** modifier is used to produce smoothness in 3D mesh objects. To apply the **MeshSmooth** modifier, select an object in the viewport. Select the **MeshSmooth** modifier from the **OBJECT-SPACE MODIFIERS** category in the **Modifier List** drop-down list; the edges of the object become smoother, as shown in Figures 10-32 and 10-33. Alternatively, you can choose **Modifiers > Subdivision Surfaces > MeshSmooth** from the menu bar; the **MeshSmooth** modifier will be displayed in the modifier stack and various rollouts will also be displayed below the modifier stack. The most commonly used rollout is discussed next.

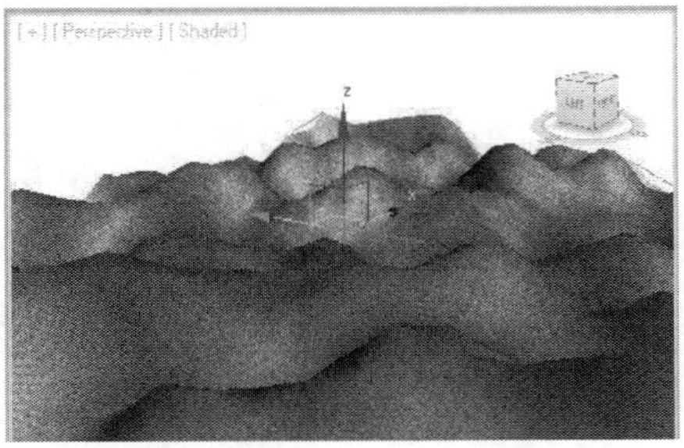

*Figure 10-32 The surface before applying the **MeshSmooth** modifier*

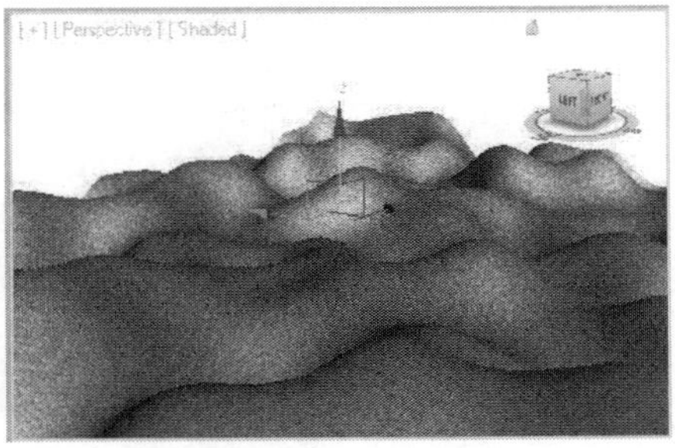

*Figure 10-33 The surface after applying the **MeshSmooth** modifier*

Subdivision Amount Rollout

Set the value in the **Iterations** spinner to specify the number of times you want to apply the **MeshSmooth** modifier, refer to Figure 10-34. Set the value in the **Smoothness** spinner to smoothen the edges of the object. The **Iterations** and **Smoothness** spinners in the **Render Values** area determine the effects of the **MeshSmooth** modifier at rendering. To activate these spinners, you need to select the check boxes on their left.

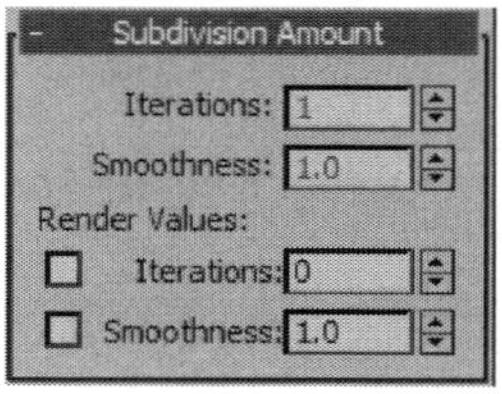

Figure 10-34 *The* ***Subdivision Amount*** *rollout*

Tessellate Modifier

The **Tessellate** modifier is used to subdivide the faces of an object. It provides smoothness at curved surfaces for rendering. To apply the **Tessellate** modifier on an object, create an object in the viewport and convert it into an editable mesh object. Select the sub-objects of the object in the viewport and select the **Tessellate** modifier from the **OBJECT-SPACE MODIFIERS** category in the **Modifier List** drop-down list. Alternatively, choose **Modifiers > Mesh Editing > Tessellate** from the menu bar; the selected sub-objects will be subdivided into faces, as shown in Figures 10-35 and 10-36. When you apply the **Tessellate** modifier on an object, the entire object is tessellated. The **Parameters** rollout of the **Tessellate** modifier is shown in Figure 10-37. This rollout is discussed next.

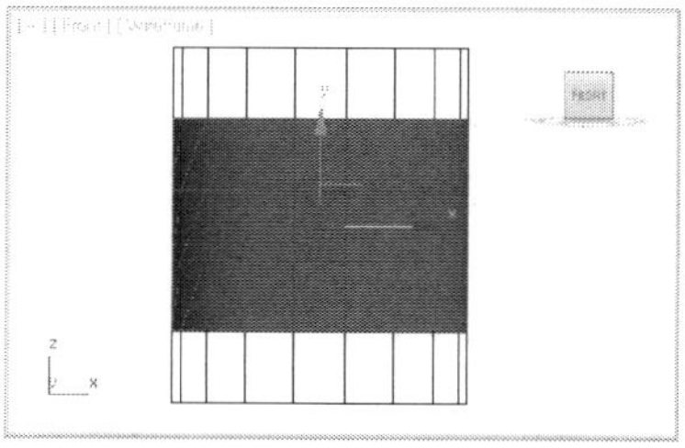

Figure 10-35 *The sub-objects selected in a cylinder to apply the* ***Tessellate*** *modifier*

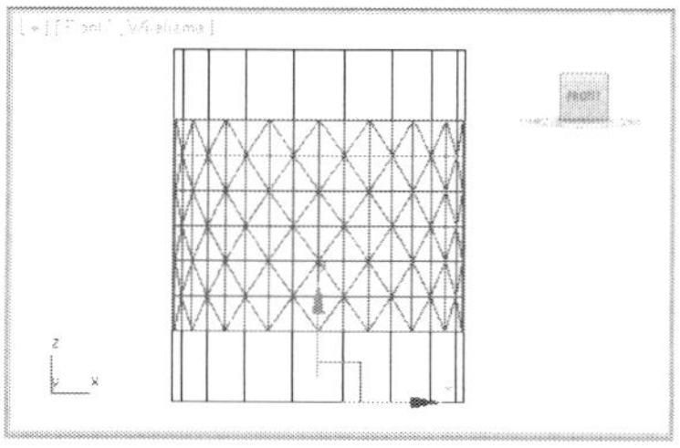

Figure 10-36 *The selected sub-objects converted into triangular faces after applying the* ***Tessellate*** *modifier*

Parameters Rollout

In the **Operate On** group, there are two buttons: **Faces** and **Polygons**. These buttons are used to define whether the modifier will be applied to the faces or the polygons of the object. The **Faces** button is chosen by default and it displays the selected sub-objects as triangular faces, refer to Figure 10-36. Choose the **Polygons** button to display the sub-objects as polygonal faces, as shown in Figure 10-38.

By default, the **Edge** radio button is selected and is used to subdivide the selection from the middle of each edge. Select the **Face-Center** radio button to subdivide the faces of the selection from the center to the vertex corners, as shown in Figure 10-39. The **Tension** spinner will be activated only if the **Edge** radio button is selected. The 0 value in the **Tension** spinner specifies that the new faces are flat. The positive value in this spinner specifies that the new faces are convex. The negative value in this spinner specifies that the new faces are concave. By default, the **1** radio button is selected in the **Iterations** area. Select the **2**, **3**, or **4** radio button to specify the number of times the modifier will be applied to the selection.

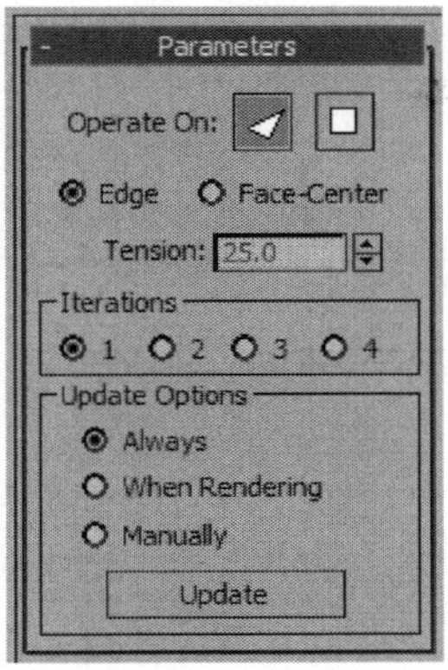

Figure 10-37 *The* ***Parameters*** *rollout*

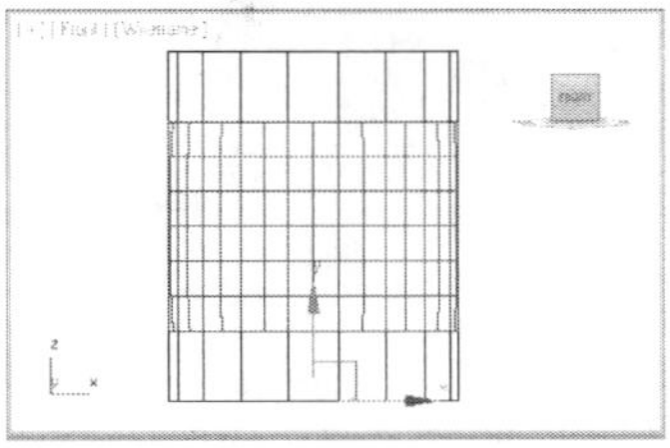

Figure 10-38 *The selected sub-objects converted into polygonal faces after choosing the* ***Polygons*** *button*

Push Modifier

The **Push** modifier is used to push an object inward or outward along the normals of its faces. A normal is an invisible line coming straight out of a face in a particular direction. To apply the **Push** modifier on an object, select the object or the sub-objects in the viewport and select the **Push** modifier from the **OBJECT-SPACE MODIFIERS** category in the **Modifier List** drop-down list. Alternatively, choose **Modifiers > Parametric Deformers > Push** from the menu bar; the **Push** modifier will be displayed in the modifier stack and the **Parameters** rollout will also be displayed in the modify panel, refer to Figure 10-40. To modify the effects of the **Push** modifier, you need to use the **Parameters** rollout, which is discussed next.

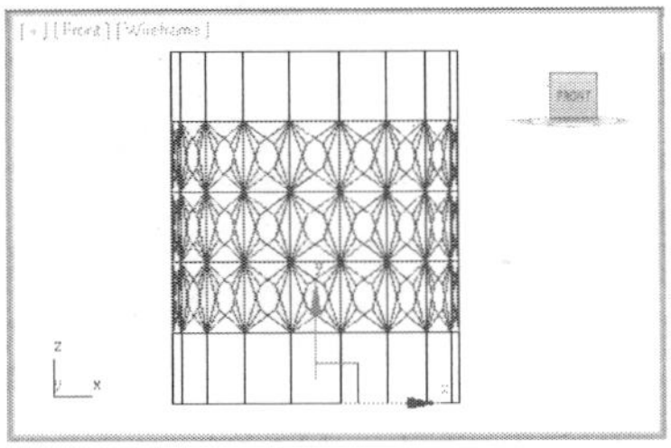

Figure 10-39 *The selected sub-objects converted into triangular faces after choosing the* ***Face-Center*** *radio button*

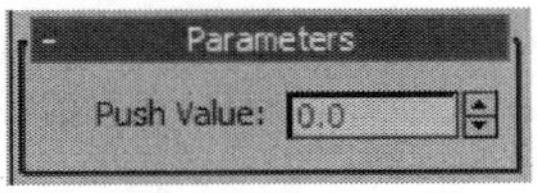

Figure 10-40 *The* ***Parameters*** *rollout*

Parameters Rollout

Set the value in the **Push Value** spinner to view the effects of the **Push** modifier, refer to Figures 10-41 and 10-42.

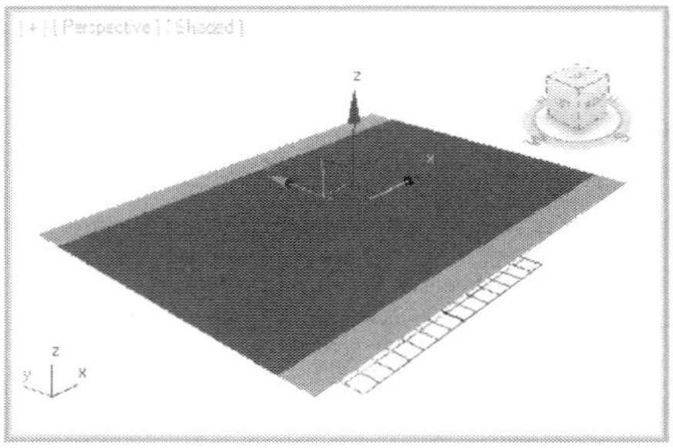

*Figure 10-41 The selected sub-objects of a plane to apply the **Push** modifier*

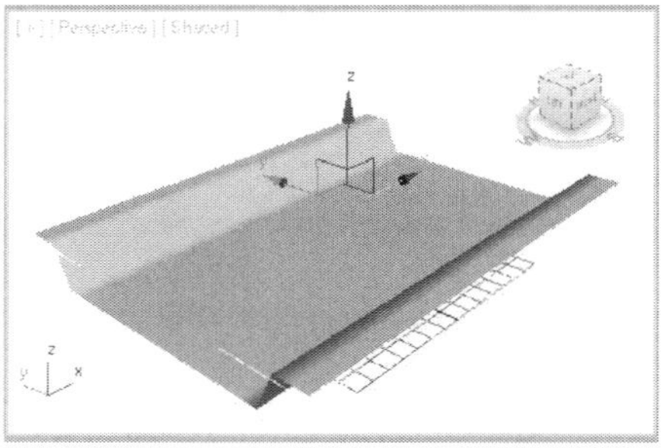

*Figure 10-42 The plane after applying the **Push** modifier*

Normal Modifier

The **Normal** modifier is used to flip the normals of an object without converting it into the editable mesh. To apply the **Normal** modifier to an object, select the object in the viewport and then select the **Normal** modifier from the **OBJECT-SPACE MODIFIERS** category in the **Modifier List** drop-down list. Alternatively, you can choose **Modifiers > Mesh Editing > Normal Modifier** from the menu bar; the normals of the object will be reversed, refer to Figures 10-43 and 10-44. Also, the **Parameters** rollout will be displayed in the modify panel, as shown in Figure 10-45. The **Parameters** rollout is discussed next.

Figure 10-43 The object with two different materials on the inner and outer sides

*Figure 10-44 The inner and outer materials interchanged after applying the **Normal** modifier*

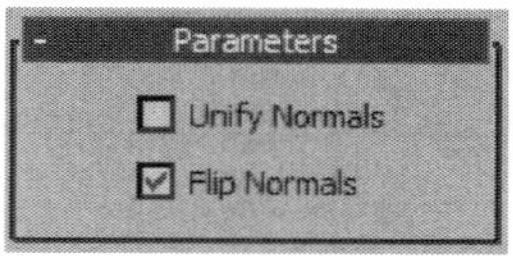

*Figure 10-45 The **Parameters** rollout*

Parameters Rollout

By default, the **Flip Normals** check box is selected. It is used to reverse the direction of the normals of all faces of the selected object. Select the **Unify Normals** check box to make all the normals of the object point toward the same direction.

Edit Mesh Modifier

Applying the **Edit Mesh** modifier to an object is the same as converting the object into editable mesh, as described in Chapter 6. The **Edit Mesh** modifier and the editable mesh object provide the same sub-object levels to modify the object at advanced level. The main difference is that you can retain the object creation parameters and then use them to edit the object, even after applying the **Edit Mesh** modifier. Note that you cannot animate the sub-objects of an object after applying the **Edit Mesh** modifier.

To apply the **Edit Mesh** modifier to an object, select the object in the viewport and choose the **Modify** tab in the **Command Panel**. Now, select the **Edit Mesh** modifier from the **OBJECT-SPACE MODIFIERS** category in the **Modifier List** drop-down list. Alternatively, choose **Modifiers > Mesh Editing > Edit Mesh** from the menu bar; the modifier will be displayed in the modifier stack and the rollouts will also be displayed below the modifier stack in the modify panel. Next, modify the object at sub-object levels as discussed in the previous chapters.

Applying **Edit Patch** and **Edit Poly** modifiers is same as converting the object into editable patch and editable poly respectively. The only difference is that the **Edit Patch** and **Edit Poly** modifiers retain the object creation parameters.

UVW Map Modifier

The **UVW Map** modifier is used to adjust the mapping coordinates on an object. Sometimes when you apply maps to the objects, they are not displayed properly on its surface. To apply the map properly, you need to adjust the mapping coordinates on the object. The UVW coordinate system is the same as the XYZ coordinate system. The U, V, and W axes of a map correspond to the X, Y, and Z axes, respectively.

To apply the **UVW Map** modifier, select the mapped object in the viewport and then select the **UVW Map** modifier from the **OBJECT-SPACE MODIFIERS** category in the **Modifier List** drop-down list. Alternatively, choose **Modifiers > UV Coordinates > UVW Map** from the menu bar; the **UVW Mapping** will be displayed in the modifier stack and the **Parameters** rollout will also be displayed below the modifier stack. The **Parameters** rollout is discussed next.

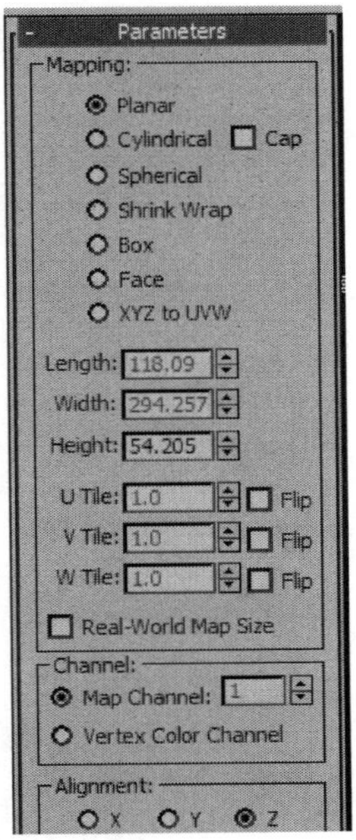

***Figure 10-46** Partial view of the **Parameters** rollout*

Parameters Rollout

The options in this rollout are used to set the mapping coordinates on an object, refer to Figure 10-46. These options are discussed next.

Mapping Area

The options in this area are used to adjust the type of mapping coordinates and the tiling used on an object. There are seven types of mapping coordinates such as **Planar**, **Cylindrical**, **Spherical**, and so on. These are discussed next.

By default, the **Planar** radio button is selected. As a result, the map is projected from a single flat plane to an object, as shown in Figure 10-47.

Select the **Cylindrical** radio button to project the map onto a cylinder, as shown in Figure 10-48. On selecting the **Cylindrical** radio button, the **Cap** check box will be activated. Select the **Cap** check box to apply mapping coordinates to the cap of the object, as shown in Figure 10-49.

Figure 10-47 *A box with the* ***Planar*** *mapping coordinate*

Figure 10-48 *A cylinder with the* ***Cylindrical*** *mapping coordinates*

Figure 10-49 *The* ***Cylindrical*** *mapping coordinates applied to a cylinder and its cap*

Select the **Spherical** radio button to project the map from a sphere, refer to Figure 10-50.

On selecting the **Shrink Wrap** radio button, the map will be projected onto a sphere. But in this case, the corners of the map will be truncated and they will join at a single pole, refer to Figure 10-51.

Figure 10-50 *The* ***Spherical*** *mapping coordinates applied to a sphere*

Figure 10-51 *The* ***Shrink Wrap*** *mapping coordinates applied to a sphere*

Select the **Box** radio button to project six planar maps from the six sides of a box, refer to Figure 10-52.

Select the **Face** radio button to project a copy of the map to every face of the object, refer to Figure 10-53.

Figure 10-52 *The **Box** mapping coordinates applied to a sphere*

Figure 10-53 *The **Face** mapping coordinates applied to a sphere*

Select the **XYZ to UVW** radio button to translate the XYZ coordinates of the procedural map into the UVW mapping coordinates. If you modify the object by changing its shape, the coordinates will adjust to match the new shape, as shown in Figure 10-54.

Figure 10-54 *Coordinates of the object adjusted to match the new shape*

Note

*The 3D maps such as **Cellular**, **Falloff**, **Noise** are known as procedural maps. These maps have already been discussed in Chapter 8.*

Set the value in the **Length**, **Width**, and **Height** spinners to define the length, width, and height of the modifier gizmo. Set the value in the **U Tile**, **V Tile**, and **W Tile** spinners to define the tiling for the map in the X, Y, and Z axes. The value 1 in these spinners indicates that the map has been applied only once. Select the **Flip** check box to reverse the direction of the map.

The **Real-World Map Size** check box is used to control the scaling of the textured mapped materials applied to the object. You can set these values using the **Use Real-World Scale** check box in the **Coordinates** rollout of the applied material in the **Material Editor** dialog box.

Channel Area

By default, the **Map Channel** radio button is selected. The value 1 in the **Map Channel** spinner is used to define that the object has 1 UVW mapping coordinate. Set the value in this spinner to assign more than one UVW mapping coordinates. An object can have up to 99 UVW mapping coordinates.

Alignment Area

The options in this area are used to define the alignment of the gizmo of the modifier with the object.

FFD (Free-Form Deformation) Modifiers

In Autodesk 3ds Max, the FFD modifiers are used to deform objects by creating a box around them. This box is made up of lattice and control points. You can deform an object using these control points and lattice. There are five different types of FFD modifiers: **FFD 2x2x2**, **FFD 3x3x3**, **FFD 4x4x4**, **FFD(box)**, and **FFD(cyl)**, refer to Figures 10-55 through 10-59.

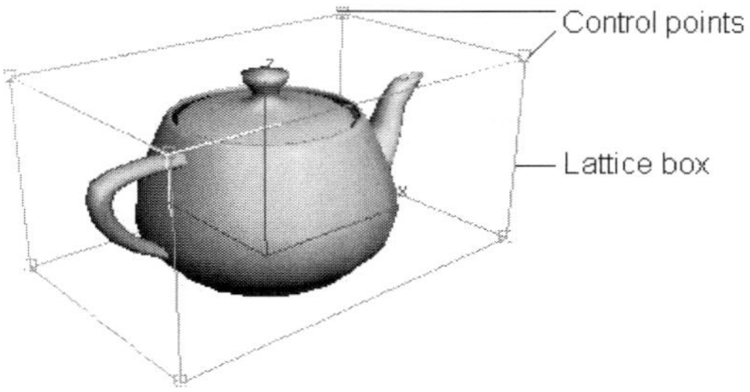

Figure 10-55 *The* ***FFD 2x2x2*** *modifier applied to the object*

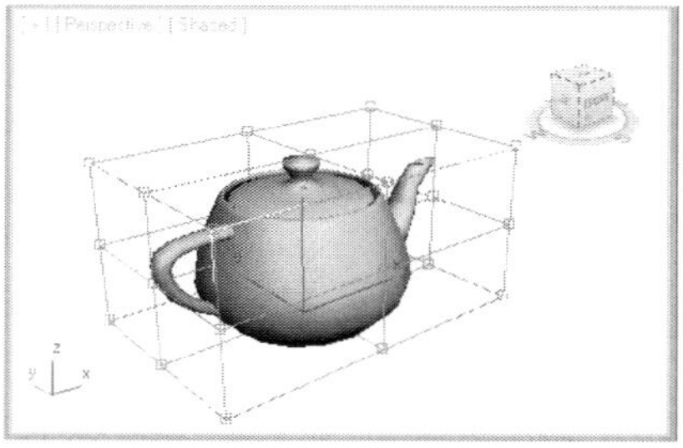

Figure 10-56 *The* ***FFD 3x3x3*** *modifier applied to the object*

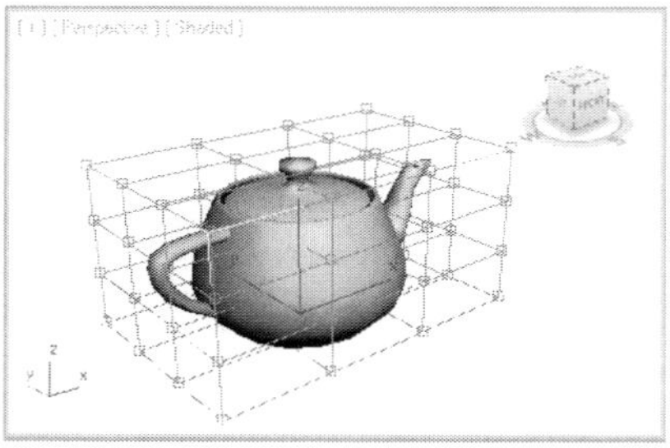

Figure 10-57 *The* ***FFD 4x4x4*** *modifier applied to the object*

Figure 10-58 *A box object with the* ***FFD(box)*** *modifier applied*

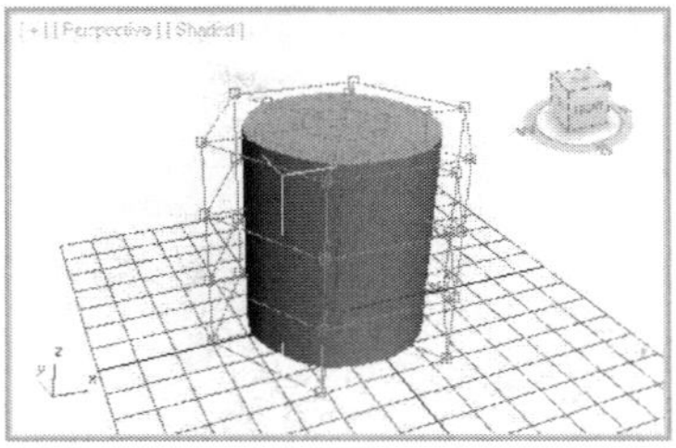

Figure 10-59 *A cylindrical object with the* ***FFD(cyl)*** *modifier applied*

The different types of FFD modifiers are based on the number of control points. The **FFD 2x2x2** modifier provides a lattice box with two control points on each of its edge. Similarly, **FFD 3x3x3** and **FFD 4x4x4** modifiers provide the lattice boxes with three and four control points on each of their edge, respectively.

The **FFD(box)** and **FFD(cyl)** modifiers are used with the box-shaped and cylinder-shaped objects. In these modifiers, you can adjust the number of control points in the lattice box in the **Parameters** rollout.

To apply the FFD modifiers, select an object in the viewport and then select one of the **FFD** modifiers from the **OBJECT-SPACE MODIFIERS** category in the **Modifier List** drop-down list. Alternatively, choose **Modifiers > Free Form Deformers** from the menu bar to select the FFD modifiers; the lattice box with the control points will be displayed around the selected object in the viewport. The selected FFD modifier will be displayed in the modifier stack. Also, the **FFD Parameters** rollout will be displayed below the modifier stack in the modify panel. To deform the object using the FFD modifiers, you need to use the sub-objects levels of the modifier in the modifier stack. The sub-object levels and **FFD Parameters** rollout are discussed next.

Sub-Object Levels

To view the sub-object levels of the selected modifier, you need to expand the modifier in the modifier stack by clicking on the plus sign on its left, as shown in Figure 10-60. There are three sub-object levels, Control Points, Lattice, and Set Volume. These are discussed next.

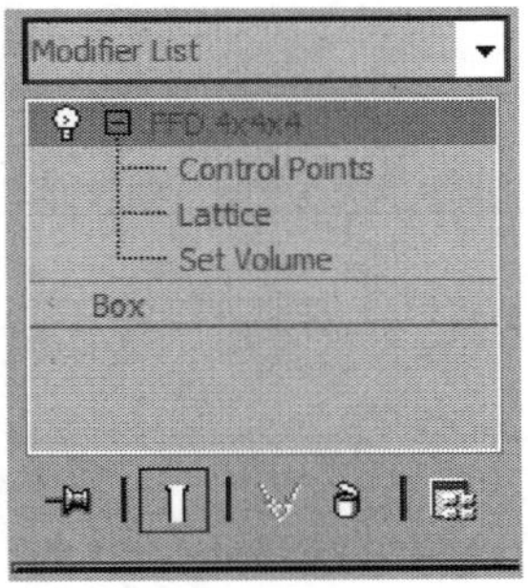

Figure 10-60 *The sub-object levels in the modifier stack*

Control Points

The control points are the vertices of the lattice box that surround the object after applying the FFD modifier. Select the **Control Points** sub-objects level; it will be activated and enable you to select the control points of the lattice in the viewport. Next, select the control points and manipulate them using the transforming tools such as **Select and Move**, **Select and Scale**, and so on. When you transform the control points, the shape of the lattice box will be modified. Also, the shape of the object will be modified accordingly, refer to Figures 10-61 and 10-62.

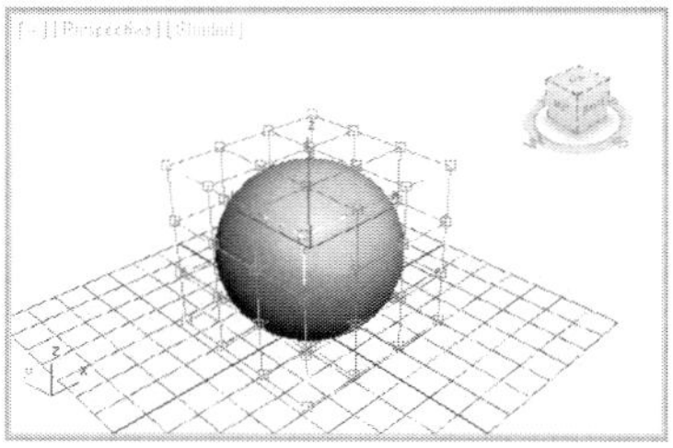

Figure 10-61 *The FFD modifier applied to the objects*

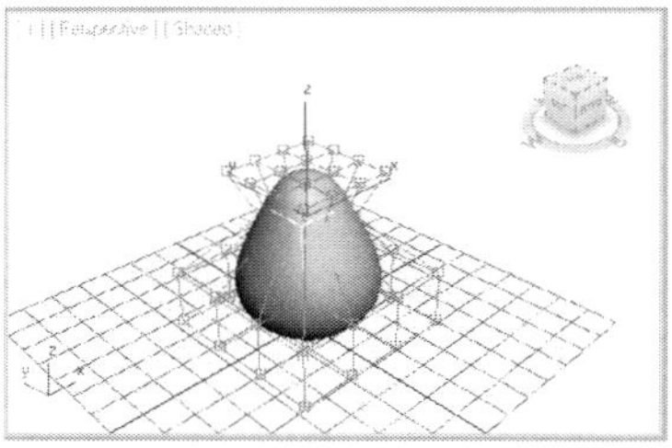

Figure 10-62 *The shape of the object modified after transforming the control points*

Lattice

Select the **Lattice** sub-object level; the lattice box will be highlighted in the viewport. Next, you can reshape the object by moving, rotating, or scaling the lattice box.

Set Volume

If you select this sub-object level, then the control points of the lattice box will turn green in color. You can select these green control points and move them to fit according to the shape of the object without affecting the object.

FFD Parameters Rollout

This rollout is displayed in the modify panel, as shown in Figure 10-63. The most commonly used areas in this rollout are discussed next.

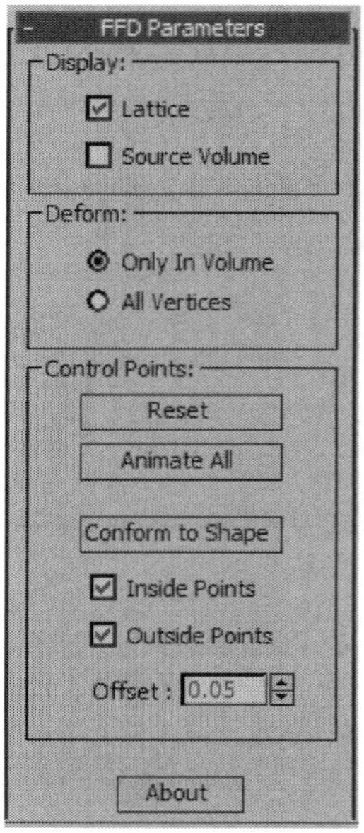

Figure 10-63 *Partial view of the* ***FFD Parameters*** *rollout*

Display Area

By default, the **Lattice** check box is selected. It is used to display the lines connecting the control points of the lattice box. On clearing the check box, only the control points of the lattice will be displayed in the viewport. Select the **Source Volume** check box to display the original shape of the lattice box. If you clear the check box, then the modified shape of the lattice box will be displayed in the viewport.

Deform Area

By default, the **Only In Volume** radio button is selected. It is used to deform the part of the object that is inside the lattice box. On selecting the **All Vertices** radio button, the entire object whether it is inside or outside the lattice box can be deformed.

Control Points Area

This area is used to modify the control points of the lattice box. Choose the **Reset** button to bring all control points to their original position. If you animate the control points, then a controller will be assigned to each control point. Choose the **Animate All** button to place the controllers in the track view for each control point. In the track view, you can view, edit, copy, or adjust the number of animation keys at the same time. You will learn more about adjusting the animation keys in the later chapters.

Choose the **Conform to Shape** button to bring the FFD control points to the intersection of the object with a straight line from the object's center to the original location of control points. The **Inside Points** and **Outside Points** check boxes are selected by default. If you clear the **Inside Points** check box, then the control points that are inside the lattice box will not be affected. If you clear the **Outside Points** check box; the control points that are outside the lattice box will not be affected. Set the value in the **Offset** spinner to specify the distance of the control points from the surface of the object.

Dimensions Area

This area is available only for the **FFD(box)** and **FFD(cyl)** modifiers and is used to define the number of control points in the lattice box. Choose the **Set Number of Points** button; the **Set FFD Dimensions** dialog box will be displayed, as shown in Figure 10-64. Set the value in the **Length**, **Width**, and **Height** spinners to specify the number of control points on each axis of the lattice box.

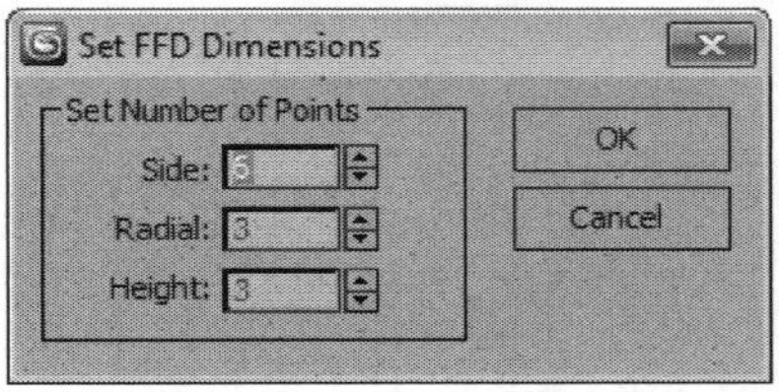

Figure 10-64 *The* ***Set FFD Dimensions*** *dialog box*

Tutorial 1

In this tutorial, you will create the 3D model of a tennis racket, as shown in Figure 10-65, using the **Lattice** modifier and shape splines. **(Expected time: 30 min)**

Figure 10-65 *A tennis racket model*

The following steps are required to complete this tutorial:

a. Set the project folder.
b. Create the head of the racket with the stringed area inside it.

c. Create the shaft of the racket.
d. Create the handle of the racket.
e. Render the scene for the final output.
f. Save the file.

Setting the Project Folder

1. Set the project folder with the name *c10_tut1* in the *3dsmax* folder as discussed in earlier chapters.

Creating the Head of the Racket

To create the head of the racket, you need to use the **Ellipse** tool.

1. Choose **Create > Shapes** in the **Command Panel**; the **Splines** option is displayed in the drop-down list. Invoke the **Ellipse** tool from the **Object Type** rollout.

2. Activate the Top viewport and create an ellipse as described in Chapter 5. Choose the **Modify** tab in the **Command Panel**. Expand the **Rendering** rollout and set the values as given below:

   Select the **Enable In Renderer** and **Enable In Viewport** check boxes.
   Select the **Rectangular** radio button and enter the values as given below:

   Length: **1.0** Width: **3.0**

   Make sure that the **Auto Smooth** check box is selected.

3. In the **Parameters** rollout, set the values as given below:

   Length: **145.894** Width: **93.72**

4. Modify the name of the ellipse to *head* and change its color to black.

   Next, you need to create the stringed area inside the *head*.

5. To do so, choose **Create > Geometry** in the **Command Panel**. Next, invoke the **Plane** tool from **Standard Primitives** and create a plane in the Top viewport, as shown in Figure 10-66. In the **Parameters** rollout, set the values as given below:

   Length: **148.314**
   Width: **131.401**
   Length Segs: **12**
   Width Segs: **12**

6. Modify the name of the plane to *stringed area* and change its color to black. Now, align the *stringed area* at the center of the *head*, as shown in Figure 10-66.

   Next, you need to modify the *stringed area*.

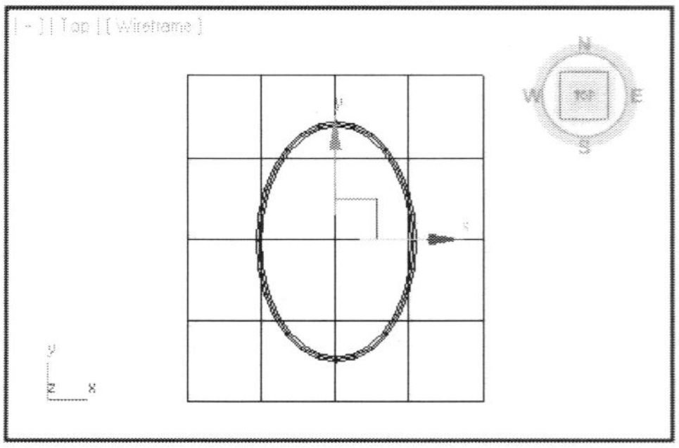

Figure 10-66 *The plane created in the Top viewport*

7. Invoke the **Maximize Viewport Toggle** tool to maximize the Top viewport.

8. Select the *stringed area* in the viewport and choose the **Modify** tab in the **Command Panel**. Next, select the **Edit Mesh** modifier from the **OBJECT-SPACE MODIFIERS** category in the **Modifier List** drop-down list; the **Edit Mesh** modifier is displayed in the modifier stack and rollouts are also displayed below the modifier stack.

Note

*By applying the **Edit Mesh** modifier, the name of the **Plane** tool will also be displayed in the modifier stack. To modify the creation parameters of the plane, you can select it in the modifier stack, and set new values in the rollouts displayed in the modify panel.*

9. In the **Selection** rollout, choose the **Vertex** button; all vertices of the *stringed area* are displayed in the viewport, as shown in Figure 10-67.

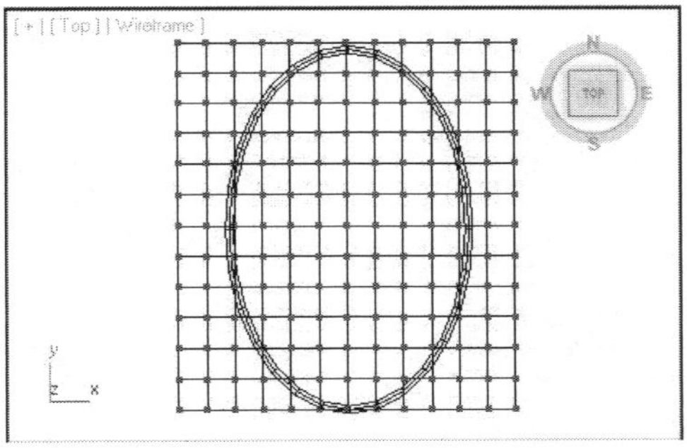

Figure 10-67 *The vertices of the stringed area displayed in the Top viewport*

10. Select the **Ignore Backfacing** check box in the **Selection** rollout.

    Next, you need to select and move the vertices of the *stringed area* one by one and then arrange them into the shape of the head.

11. To move vertices to the exact location, invoke the **Zoom Region** tool and drag a selection box around the vertices of the upper left portion of the *stringed area* to zoom in on them, refer to Figures 10-68 and 10-69.

12. Invoke the **Select and Move** tool to select the vertices one by one and arrange them into the shape of the *head*, as shown in Figure 10-70.

13. Invoke the **Zoom Extents** tool in the Top viewport; the *head* and the *stringed area* are displayed in the active viewport, refer to Figure 10-71.

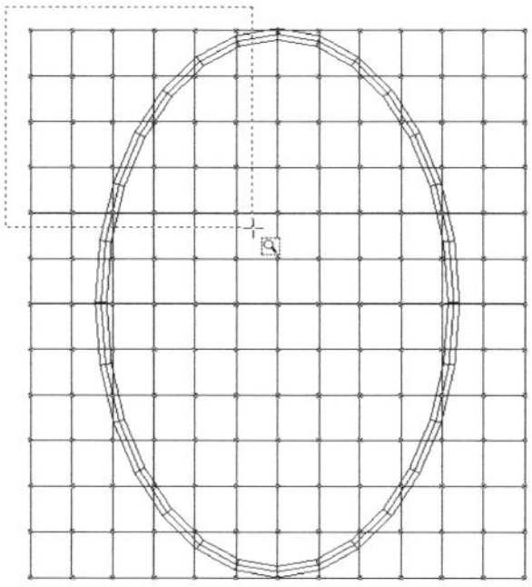

Figure 10-68 *A selection box dragged around the vertices using the **Zoom Region** tool*

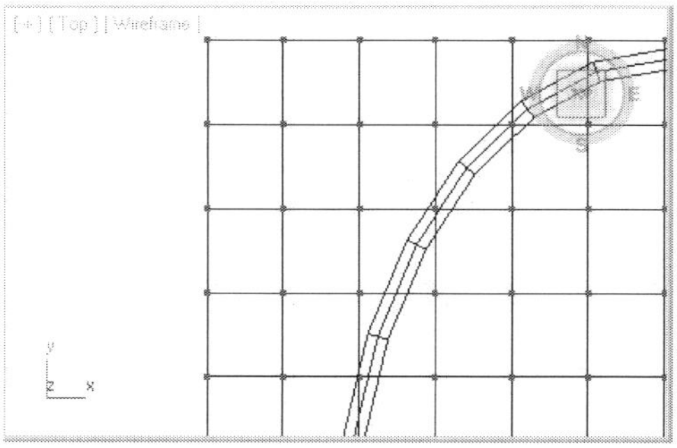

Figure 10-69 *The selected area zoomed in*

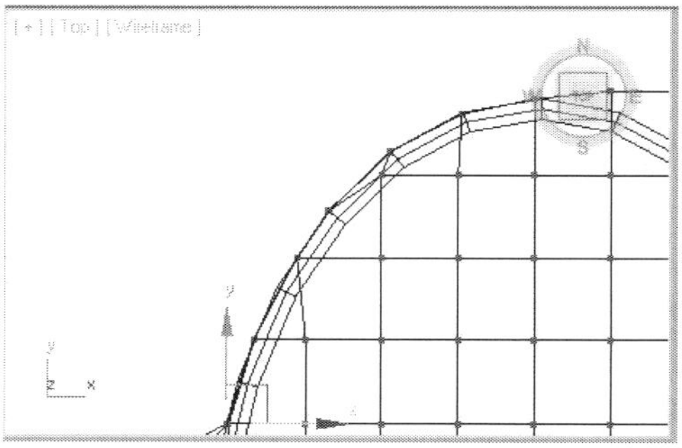

Figure 10-70 *The vertices arranged into the shape of the head*

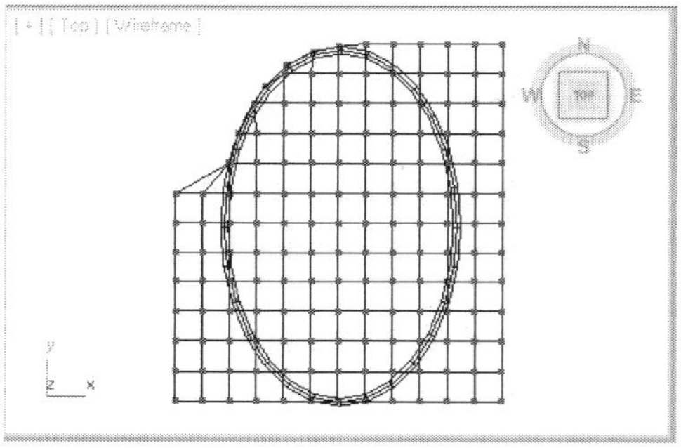

Figure 10-71 *The objects after invoking the **Zoom Extents** tool*

14. Now, follow the procedure discussed in steps 11 and 12 for the outer vertices and arrange them, as shown in Figure 10-72. Choose the **Vertex** button again in the **Selection** rollout to exit the sub-object level.

    Next, you need to apply the **Lattice** modifier to the *stringed area* of the *head*.

15. Make sure that the *stringed area* is selected in the viewport. Select the **Lattice** modifier from the **OBJECT-SPACE MODIFIERS** category in the **Modifier List** drop-down list; the **Lattice** modifier is displayed in the modifier stack and rollouts are also displayed below the modifier stack.

16. In the **Parameters** rollout, set the values as given next.

    Select the **Struts Only from Edges** radio button.

    Struts area
    Radius: **0.2**

    The *stringed area* is displayed, as shown in Figure 10-73.

17. Next, group the *stringed area* and *head* as *racket head*.

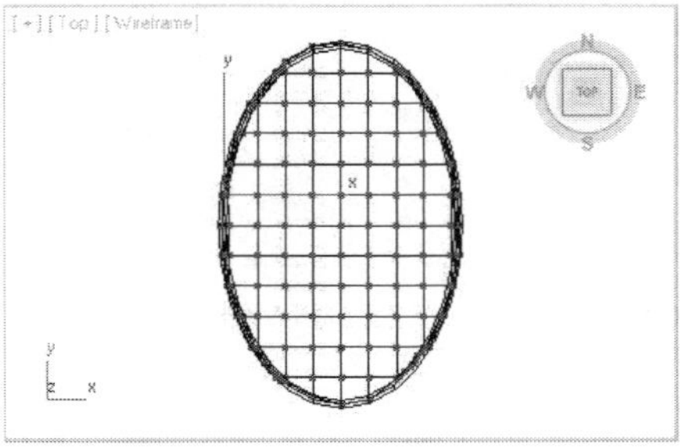

Figure 10-72 *All outer vertices aligned to the shape of the head*

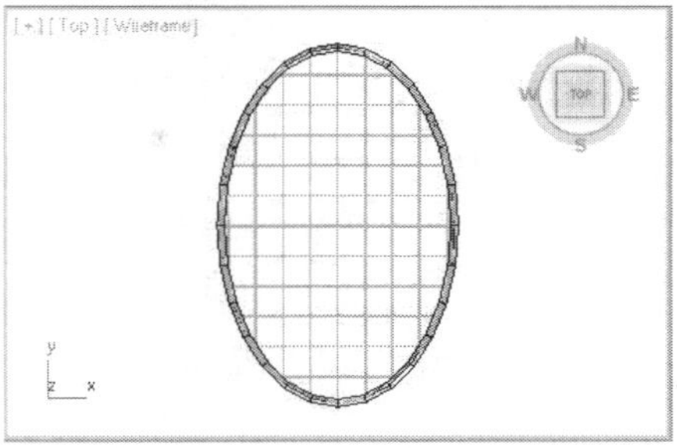

Figure 10-73 *The stringed area after applying the **Lattice** modifier*

Creating the Shaft of the Racket

Next, you need to create the shaft of the racket using the **Line** tool.

1. First, invoke the **Zoom** tool and zoom in the Top viewport to get sufficient room for creating the shaft of the racket, as shown in Figure 10-74.

2. Choose **Create > Shapes** in the **Command Panel**; the **Splines** option is displayed in the drop-down list. Invoke the **Line** tool from the **Object Type** rollout.

3. In the **Creation Method** rollout, select the **Smooth** radio button in the **Initial Type** area and then select the **Smooth** radio button in the **Drag Type** area.

4. In the Top viewport, click and drag the cursor to create a line around the *racket head*, as shown in Figure 10-75.

5. In the **Rendering** rollout, set the values as given below:

   Select the **Enable In Renderer** and **Enable In Viewport** check boxes.
   Make sure that the **Radial** radio button is selected and then enter the value as given below:

   Thickness: **3.0**

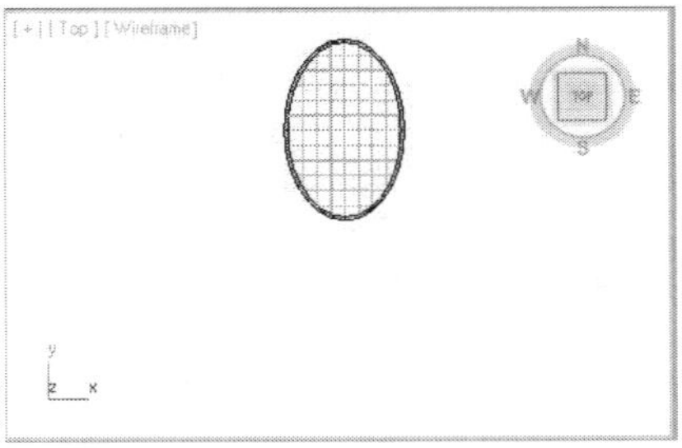

Figure 10-74 *The racket head in the Top viewport*

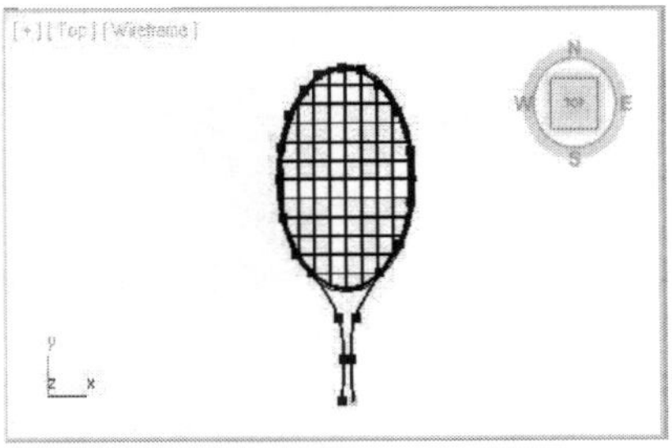

Figure 10-75 *A line created around the racket head*

6. Modify the name of the line to *shaft01* and then modify its color by entering the values as given below:

   Red: **8** Green: **8** Blue: **136**

7. Invoke the **Maximize Viewport Toggle** tool and activate the Front viewport. Now, align the *shaft01* at the bottom of the *racket head*, refer to Figure 10-76.

8. In the Front viewport, select the *shaft01* and create its copy in the vertical direction. It is automatically named as *shaft002*.

9. Align the *shaft002* at the top of the *racket head*, as shown in Figure 10-77.

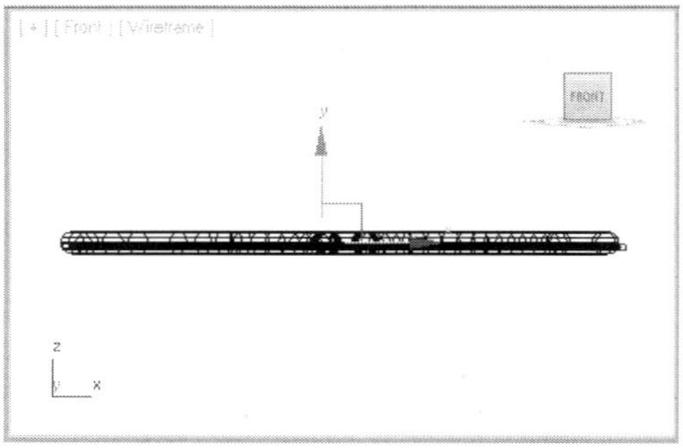

Figure 10-76 *Alignment of the shaft01 at the bottom of the racket head*

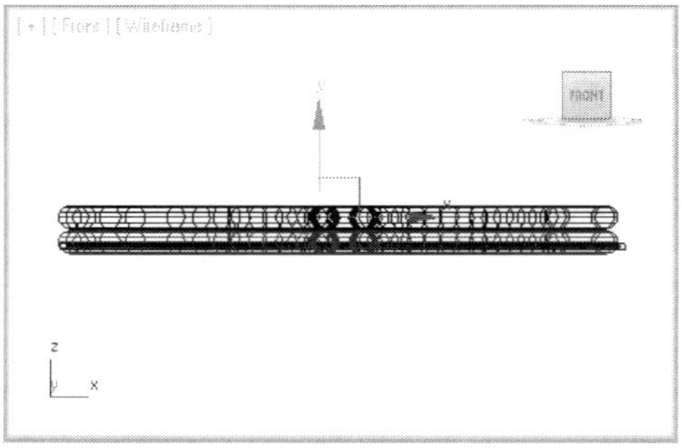

Figure 10-77 *Alignment of the shaft02 at the top of the racket head*

Creating the Handle of the Racket

Next, you need to invoke the **ChamferCyl** tool from **Extended Primitives** to create the handle of the racket.

1. First, invoke the **ChamferCyl** tool from **Extended Primitives** in the **Command Panel** and create a chamfer cylinder in the Front viewport.

2. In the **Parameters** rollout, set the values as given below:

   Radius: **7.0** Height: **74.477** Fillet: **2.816**

3. Modify the name of the cylinder to *handle* and change its color to black.

4. Next, align the *handle* with the *shaft01* and *shaft002* in all viewports, as shown in Figure 10-78.

Rendering the Scene for the Final Output

Change the background color for the final output as discussed earlier.

1. Activate the Perspective viewport.

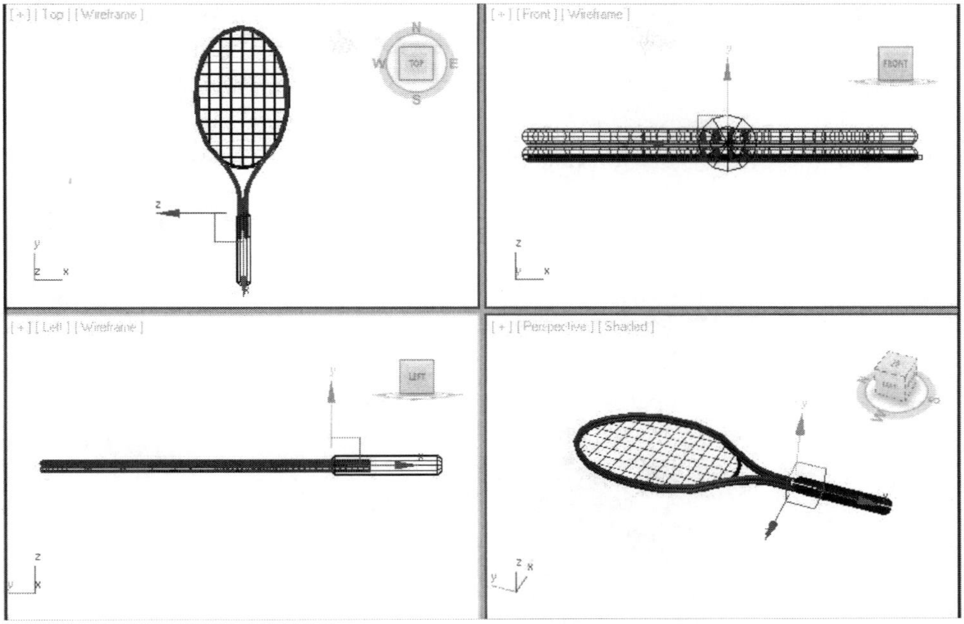

Figure 10-78 Alignment of handle in all viewports

2. Invoke the **Render Production** tool from the **Main Toolbar**; the **Perspective, frame 0, Display Gamma:2.2, RGBA Color16 Bits/Channel (1:1)** dialog box is displayed with the final output of the tennis racket at one frame, as shown in Figure 10-79.

3. Close this dialog box.

You can view the final rendered image of this model by downloading the *c10_3dsmax_2012_render.zip* file from *http://www.cadcim.com*.

Saving the File

Next, you need to save the file in the *.max* format.

1. Save the file with the name *c10tut1.max* as discussed in earlier chapters. The location of this file is given below:

\Documents\3dsmax\c10_tut1\scenes

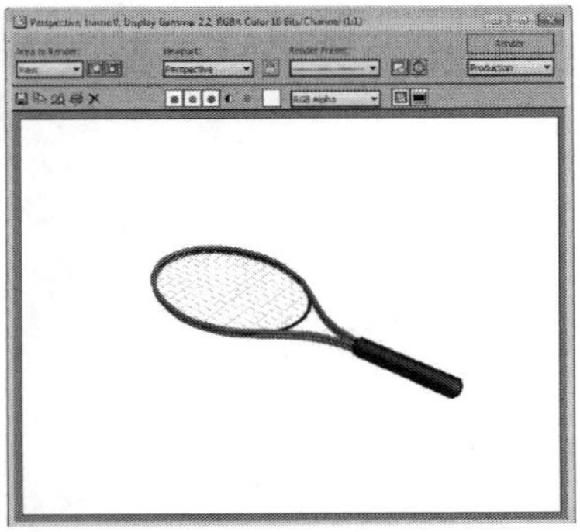

Figure 10-79 *The final output at rendering*

Tutorial 2

In this tutorial, you will create a water surface, as shown in Figure 10-80, using the **Noise** modifier. **(Expected time: 30 min)**

The following steps are required to complete this tutorial:

a. Set the project folder.
b. Create the water surface.
c. Create the environment.
d. Render the scene for the final output.
e. Save the scene.

Figure 10-80 *Model for Tutorial 2*

Setting the Project Folder

1. Set the project folder with the name *c10_tut2* in the *3dsmax* folder as discussed in earlier chapters.

Creating the Water Surface

First, you need to invoke the **Plane** tool to create a plane and then apply the **Noise** modifier to give it the wavy effect.

1. Choose **Create > Geometry** in the **Command Panel**; the **Standard Primitives** option is displayed in the drop-down list. Invoke the **Plane** tool from the **Object Type** rollout.

2. Activate the Top viewport and create a plane. In the **Parameters** rollout, set the values as given below:

   Length: **669.234** Width: **788.627**
   Length Segs: **10** Width Segs: **10**

3. Invoke the **Zoom Extents All** tool.

4. Modify the name of the plane to *water surface*.

5. Activate the Perspective viewport and set its view using the **Orbit** and **Zoom** tools, as shown in Figure 10-81.

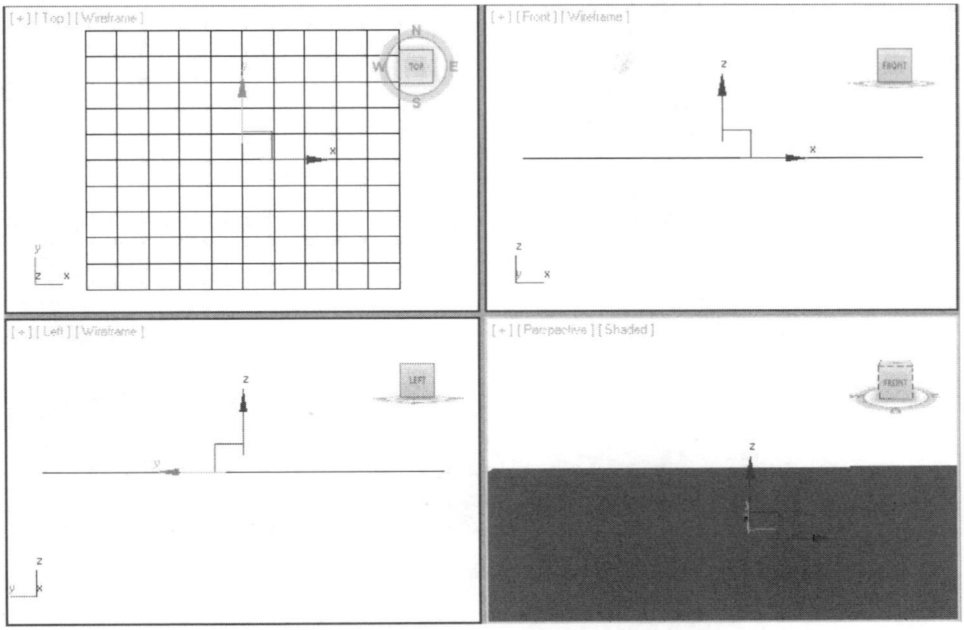

Figure 10-81 *The water surface in all viewports*

Next, you need to apply the **Noise** modifier to the *water surface*.

6. Make sure that the *water surface* is selected in the viewport. Choose the **Modify** tab in the **Command Panel**; the **Modifier List** drop-down list is displayed. Select the **Noise** modifier from the **OBJECT-SPACE MODIFIERS** category in the **Modifier List** drop-down list; the **Noise** modifier is displayed in the modifier stack and the **Parameters** rollout is displayed in the modify panel.

7. In the **Parameters** rollout, set the values as given below:

   Noise area
   Select the **Fractal** check box.
   Roughness: **0.5**   Iterations: **6.0**

   Strength area
   X: **120.0**   Y: **150.0**   Z: **5.0**

   After setting the values, the *water surface* is displayed, as shown in Figure 10-82. Next, you need to assign the material to the *water surface* to make it look realistic.

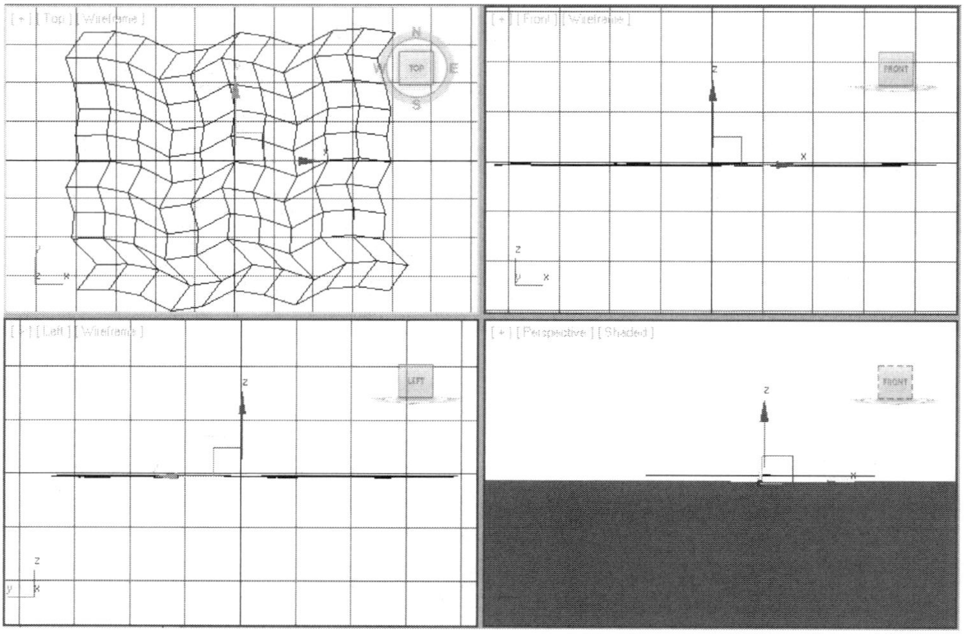

***Figure 10-82** The water surface displayed after entering the values in the **Parameters** rollout of the **Noise** modifier*

8. To do so, press the M key to invoke the **Material Editor** tool; the **Slate Material Editor** dialog box is displayed. Choose **Modes > Compact Material Editor** from the material editor menu bar; the **Material Editor** dialog box is displayed.

9. By default, the **01-Default** sample slot is selected in the **Material Editor** dialog box. Invoke the **Get Material** tool; the **Material/Map Browser** dialog box is displayed.

10. In the **Material/Map Browser** dialog box, choose the **Material/Map Browser Option** button; a drop-down list is displayed, as shown in Figure 10-83. Select the **Open Material Library** option from the drop-down list; the **Import Material Library** dialog box is displayed. Browse to the *Program Files\Autodesk\3ds Max 2012\materiallibraries\3dsmax.mat* file and choose the **Open** button; a list of 3ds max materials is displayed in the **Material/Map Browser** dialog box.

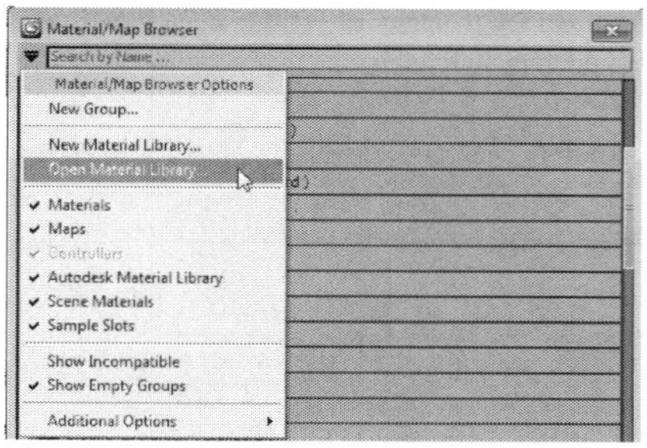

***Figure 10-83** The drop-down list displayed after choosing the **Material/Map Browser Option** button*

11. Select the **Ground_Water** material and double-click on it; the **Ground_Water** material is displayed in the sample slot. Also, the name of the sample slot is replaced with the **Ground_Water** in the **Material Name** text box.

12. Close the **Material/Map Browser** dialog box.

13. In the **Material Editor** dialog box, choose the **Diffuse** color swatch in the **Anisotropic Basic Parameters** rollout; the **Color Selector: Diffuse Color** dialog box is displayed. Set the values in the rollout as given below:

    Red: **164** Green: **214** Blue: **249**

14. Choose the **OK** button to close the **Color Selector: Diffuse Color** dialog box.

15. In the **Material Editor** dialog box, make sure that the **Ground_Water** material is selected. Also, select the *water surface* in the viewport. Next, invoke the **Assign Material to Selection** tool; the **Ground_Water** material is assigned to the *water surface*.

16. Invoke the **Show Shaded Material in Viewport** tool to view the material in the viewport. Close the **Material Editor** dialog box.

Note
You need to render the scene in the Perspective viewport to view the realistic effect of the ***Noise*** *modifier and the material.*

Creating the Environment of the Scene

To make the scene realistic at rendering, you need to apply the map in the environment.

1. Choose **Rendering > Environment** from the menu bar; the **Environment and Effects** dialog box is displayed.

2. By default, the **Environment** tab is chosen. You need to set the parameters in the **Common Parameters** rollout in this tab. In the **Background** area, choose the **Environment Map** button labeled as **None**; the **Material/Map Browser** dialog box is displayed.

3. In the **Material/Map Browser** dialog box, type **bitmap** in the **Search by Name** area; the **Bitmap** map is displayed in the drop-down list. Select the **Bitmap** map and choose the **OK** button; the **Select Bitmap Image File** dialog box is displayed. Select a sky image of your choice from the desired location. Next, choose the **Open** button; the name of the map is displayed on the **Environment Map** button. Close the **Environment and Effects** dialog box.

Note
To view the environment map in the scene, you need to render the Perspective viewport.

Rendering the Scene for the Final Output

1. Activate the Perspective viewport.

2. Invoke the **Render Production** tool from the **Main Toolbar**; the **Perspective, frame 0, Display Gamma: 2.2, RGBA Color16 Bits/Channel (1:1)** dialog box is displayed with the final output of the scene at one frame, refer to Figure 10-84.

3. Close this dialog box.

   You can view the final rendered image of this model by downloading the file *c10_3dsmax_2012_render.zip* from *http://www.cadcim.com.*

Figure 10-84 *The final output of the scene at rendering*

Saving the File

1. Save the file with the name *c10tut2.max* as discussed in earlier chapters. The location of this file is given below:

   \Documents\3dsmax\c10_tut2\scenes

Self-Evaluation Test

Answer the following questions and then compare them to those given at the end of this chapter:

1. Which one of the following tabs in the **Command Panel** is used to apply a modifier to an object?

   (a) **Create** (b) **Modify**
   (c) **Motion** (d) **Utilities**

2. Which of the following modifiers is used to deform the shape of an object using bitmap images?

   (a) **Mesh Select** (b) **Displace**
   (c) **Material** (d) **Edit Mesh**

3. Which of the following modifiers is used to produce smoothness in mesh objects?

   (a) **MeshSmooth** (b) **Normal**
   (c) **Edit Mesh** (d) **Lathe**

4. Which of the following modifiers is used to deform objects by creating a box around them?

   (a) **FFD 2x2x2** (b) **FFD 3x3x3**
   (c) **FFD 4x4x4** (d) All of these

5. The **Face Extrude** modifier is used to convert a 2D spline into a 3D object. (T/F)

6. You can apply different materials to the selected sub-objects using the **Material** modifier. (T/F)

7. On selecting the **Flip Normals** check box in the **Parameters** rollout of the **Normal** modifier, the direction of normals of all faces of the selected object is reversed. (T/F)

8. The __________ modifier is used to sub-divide the faces of an object which results in smoothness of the curved surfaces of the object.

9. The __________ modifier is used to adjust the mapping coordinates on an object.

10. An object can have up to __________ UVW mapping coordinates.

Review Questions

Answer the following questions:

1. Which of the following sub-object levels is a part of the FFD modifiers?

   (a) **Lattice** (b) **Control points**
   (c) **Set Volume** (d) All of these

2. Which of the following areas in the **Parameters** rollout of the **UVW Map** modifier is used to adjust the type of mapping coordinates?

   (a) **Channel** (b) **Alignment**
   (c) **Mapping** (d) None of these

3. Which of the following modifiers is used to push an object inward or outward along the normals of its faces?

   (a) **Twist** (b) **Normal**
   (c) **Push** (d) **Lattice**

4. The __________ modifier is a shape modifier and is used to create a 3D object by rotating a shape about an axis.

5. When you apply the FFD modifiers to an object, a box made up of lattice and control points is created around the object. (T/F)

6. The **Edit Mesh** modifier and the editable mesh object provide different sub-object levels to modify objects. (T/F)

7. The normal of a face is a line perpendicular to it. (T/F)

8. The **Iterations** area in the **Parameters** rollout of the **Tessellate** modifier is used to apply smoothness to the selected object. (T/F)

9. The __________ modifier is used to create disturbances on the surface of an object to produce irregular surface.

10. The __________ modifier is used to extrude the selected faces along their normals.

Exercises

Exercise 1

Start Autodesk 3ds Max 2012 and then perform the following operations:

1. Create an object using your own dimensions. Choose the **Modify** tab in the **Command Panel**. Click on the **Modifier List** drop-down list and then select the **Lattice** modifier from the **OBJECT-SPACE MODIFIERS** category. In the **Parameters** rollout, select the **Joints Only from Vertices**, **Struts Only from Edges**, and **Both** radio buttons one by one and notice the difference.

2. Create a cylinder using your own dimensions. Apply the **Tessellate** modifier to it. In the **Parameters** rollout, select different radio buttons in the **Iterations** area, and then notice the difference.

3. Create a plane using your own dimensions with the multiple numbers of segments. Apply the **Noise** modifier to it. In the **Parameters** rollout, select the **Fractal** check box. In the **Strength** area, set the value in the **Z** spinner to get the effect of the terrain object.

4. Create a cylinder and apply the **FFD(cyl)** modifier to it. In the **FFD Parameters** rollout, choose the **Conform to Shape** button. In the modifier stack, select the Control Points sub-object level, and modify the shape of the cylinder by selecting the control points in the viewport.

5. Create an object and apply the map or the material to it using the **Material Editor** tool. Next, apply the **UVW modifier** to it. In the **Mapping** area of the **Parameters** rollout, select different radio buttons to adjust the mapping coordinates on the object.

Exercise 2

Create the model shown in Figure 10-85 using the **Lattice** modifier. You can view the final rendered image of this model by downloading it from *http://www.cadcim.com*.

(Expected time: 15min)

Figure 10-85 *Model for Exercise 2*

Exercise 3

Create the model shown in Figures 10-86 using the **Bend** and **Taper** modifiers. You can view the final rendered image of this model by downloading it from *http://www.cadcim.com*.

(Expected time: 15 min)

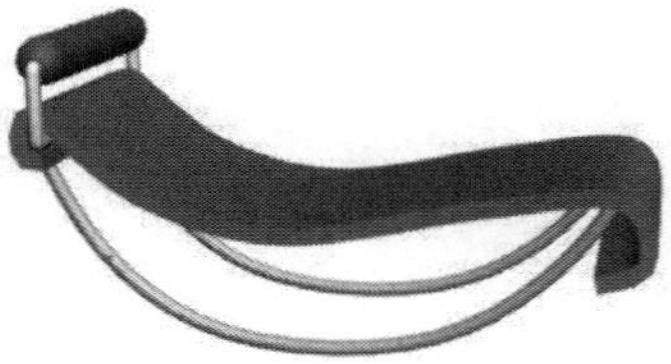

Figure 10-86 *Model for Exercise 3*

Exercise 4

Create the model shown in Figure 10-87 using the **Lathe** and **MeshSmooth** modifiers. You can view the final rendered image of this model by downloading it from the *http://www.cadcim.com*.

(Expected time: 15 min)

Figure 10-87 *Model for Exercise 4*

Answers to Self-Evaluation Test

1. b, **2**. b, **3**. a, **4**. d, **5**. F, **6**. T, **7**. T, **8**. **Tessellate**, **9**. **UVW**, **10**. 99

11

Lights and Cameras

Learning Objectives

After completing this chapter, you will be able to:

- *Understand standard lights*
- *Understand photometric lights*
- *Use the Place Highlight tool*
- *Understand cameras*
- *Understand camera viewport controls*
- *Work with the Align Camera tool*

INTRODUCTION TO LIGHTS

In Autodesk 3ds Max, lights are used to illuminate the scene and make it more realistic. They are also used to create the sources of illumination such as street lights, flashlights, and so on. In Autodesk 3ds Max, two main categories of lights are available: Standard and Photometric. In these categories, different types of lights are available. You need to select one or more lights based on the requirement of a scene. The Photometric lights provide more realistic lighting effects but they are more complex than the Standard lights. Also, they use the light energy values to create a realistic scene.

STANDARD LIGHTS

You can create eight types of standard lights in Autodesk 3ds Max. To create a light in a scene, choose **Create > Lights** in the **Command Panel**. By default, the **Photometric** option will be displayed in the drop-down list below the **Lights** button. Select the **Standard** option from the drop-down list. You can invoke one of the tools available in the **Object Type** rollout to create different types of lights in the viewport, as shown in Figure 11-1. You need to invoke one of the tools to create the light in the viewport. When you invoke a tool from the **Object Type** rollout, various rollouts will be displayed. These rollouts are used to modify the parameters of lights. The tools in the **Object Type** rollout are discussed next.

***Figure 11-1** The tools to create standard lights in the **Object Type** rollout*

Omni

Menu bar:	Create > Lights > Standard Lights > Omni
Command Panel:	Create > Lights > Standard > Object Type rollout > Omni

The **Omni** tool is used to create an omni light. An omni light is a single point in space that projects the rays uniformly in all directions. To create an omni light, invoke the **Omni** tool; the **Name and Color**, **General Parameters**, **Intensity/Color/Attenuation**, **Advanced Effects**, **Shadow Parameters**, and **Shadow Map Params** rollouts will be displayed in the modify panel. Move the cursor in the viewport; it will get changed. Click in the viewport to place the light. You can continue clicking in the viewport to add more than one light. Next, right-click in the viewport to exit the command. To modify the parameters of a light, select the light and choose the **Modify** tab in the **Command Panel**; various rollouts will be displayed. These rollouts are used to modify the parameters of the selected light. The most commonly used rollouts are discussed next.

Name and Color Rollout

You can modify the name of the selected light by entering the new name in the text box available in this rollout. You can also modify the color of the selected light using the color swatch. But, this will not affect the color of the light that will emit from it. On changing the color, only the color of the geometry of the light in the viewport will be changed.

General Parameters Rollout

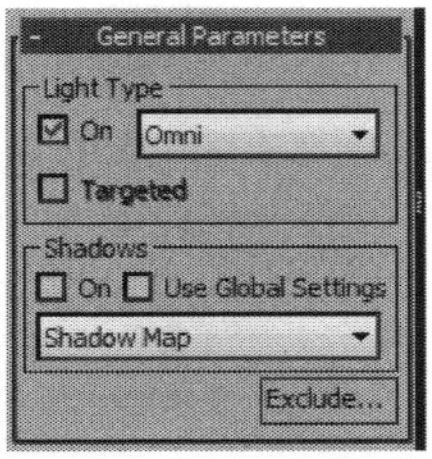

Figure 11-2 *The* ***General Parameters*** *rollout*

The options in this rollout are used to set the general parameters of the selected light, refer to Figure 11-2. In the **Light Type Parameters** area, the **On** check box is selected by default. As a result, the light is assigned to illuminate the scene, refer to Figures 11-3 and 11-4. If you clear the **On** check box, then the light will not be used in the scene. The drop-down list on the right side of the **On** check box is used to define the type of light. By default, the **Omni** option is selected in this drop-down list. You can also select the **Directional** or the **Spot** option to convert the omni light into directional or spot light. The **Targeted** check box is activated only if the **Directional** or **Spot Light** option is selected from the drop-down list. On selecting either of these options, a spinner is also displayed next to the **Targeted** check box. The value in the spinner is used to specify the distance of the target from the light. You will learn more about the spot and directional lights later in this chapter.

Figure 11-3 *The scene without any light*

Figure 11-4 *The scene with the omni lights applied*

In the **Shadows** area, select the **On** check box; the light will produce the shadow of the object at rendering. You can also preview the shadows of the object in the shaded viewports, which is discussed next.

Previewing the Shadows in the Viewport

To preview the shadows in the viewport, your system must have a graphics card that supports the Shader Model (SM) 2.0 or 3.0 standard. To ensure that your system supports interactive shadows, choose **Help > Diagnose Video Hardware** from the menu bar; the **MAXScript Listener** dialog box will be displayed, as shown in Figure 11-5. This dialog box will provide you the information about the graphic display configuration of your system.

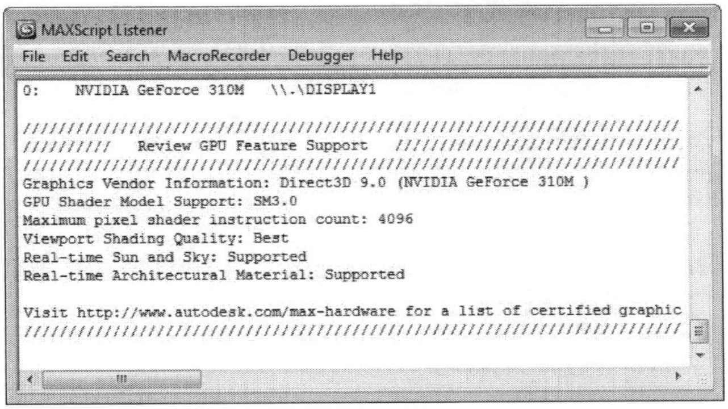

Figure 11-5 *The* ***MAXScript Listener*** *dialog box*

By default, the **Realistic** shading is displayed in the Perspective viewport. When you click on it; a flyout will be displayed. Choose the **Lighting and Shadows** option from the flyout; a cascading menu will be displayed, as shown in Figure 11-6. Note that in this menu the **Shadows** option is chosen by default. Next, when you place a light in the viewport, select it and right-click on it; a quad menu will be displayed, as shown in Figure 11-7. Choose the **Cast Shadows** option; the shadows of the object will be displayed in the viewport, as shown in Figure 11-8. To display the shadows for more than one lights in the scene, choose **Tools > Light Lister** from the menu bar; the **Light Lister** dialog box will be displayed, as shown in Figure 11-9. This dialog box will display the description of all lights used in the scene. Now, select the check box(es) in the **Shadows** column; the shadow of the light corresponding to the selected check box(es) will be displayed in the viewport, refer to Figure 11-9.

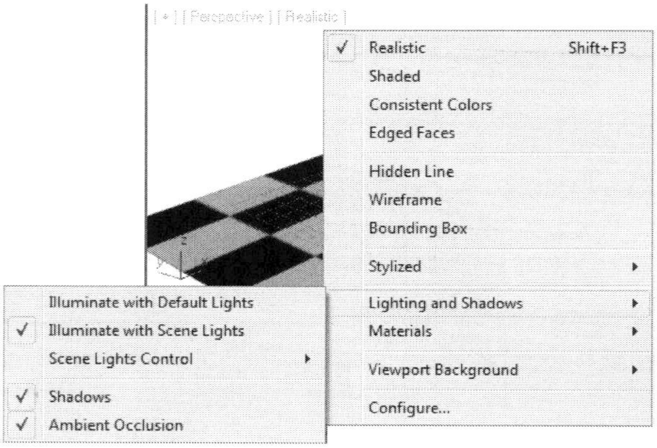

Figure 11-6 The cascading menu displayed in the viewport

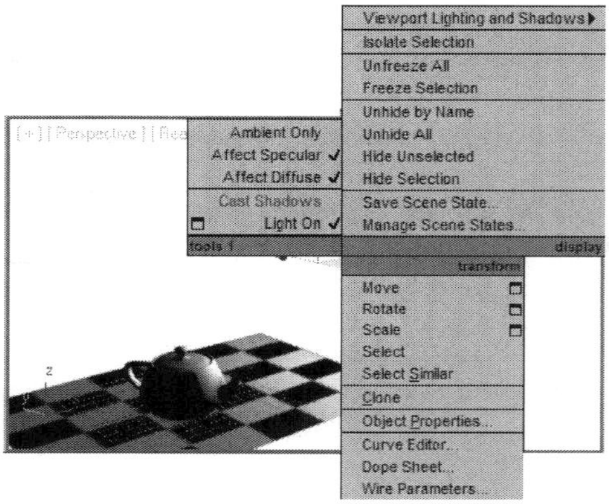

Figure 11-7 The quad menu displayed in the viewport

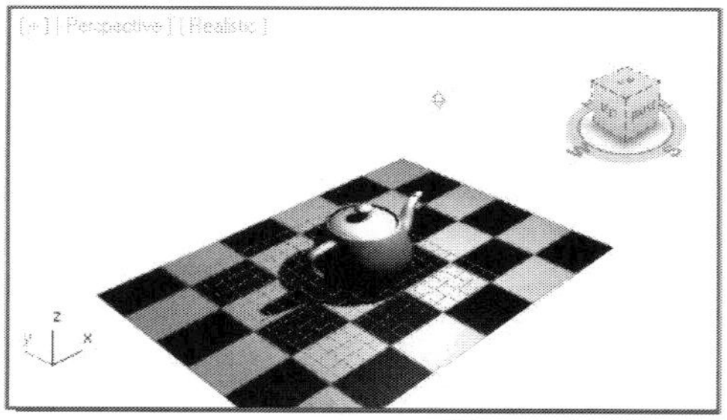

Figure 11-8 The shadow of the object displayed in the Perspective viewport

The drop-down list next to the **Shadows** check box in the **Light Lister** dialog box is used to select the types of shadow for the light. The **Exclude** button is used to define the number of objects in the scene that will not be affected by the light at rendering. By default, the light affects all objects in the scene.

To exclude or include an object from the effect of the light, choose the **Exclude** button; the **Exclude/Include** dialog box will be displayed, as shown in Figure 11-10. The **Scene Objects** area on the left side of this dialog box displays the list of all objects in the current scene. On the top right of this dialog box, there are two radio buttons, **Include** and **Exclude**. By default, the **Exclude** radio button is selected. As a result, the objects will be excluded from the effect of light. To do so, select the objects that you want to exclude from the list displayed in the **Scene Objects** area. Then, choose the right arrow button; the selected object will be excluded from the selected light. Also, they will be displayed in the area on the right side of this dialog box. Similarly, to include the excluded objects again, select the excluded objects from the area on the right side, and choose the left arrow button; the selected objects will be included. Next, choose the **OK** button.

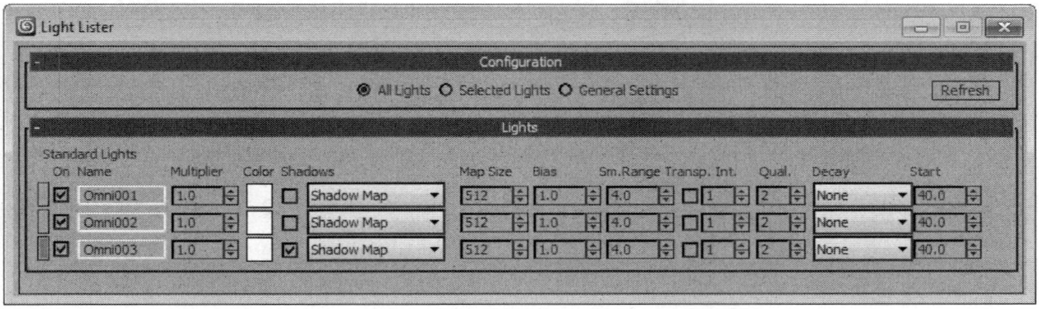

Figure 11-9 *The* ***Light Lister*** *dialog box*

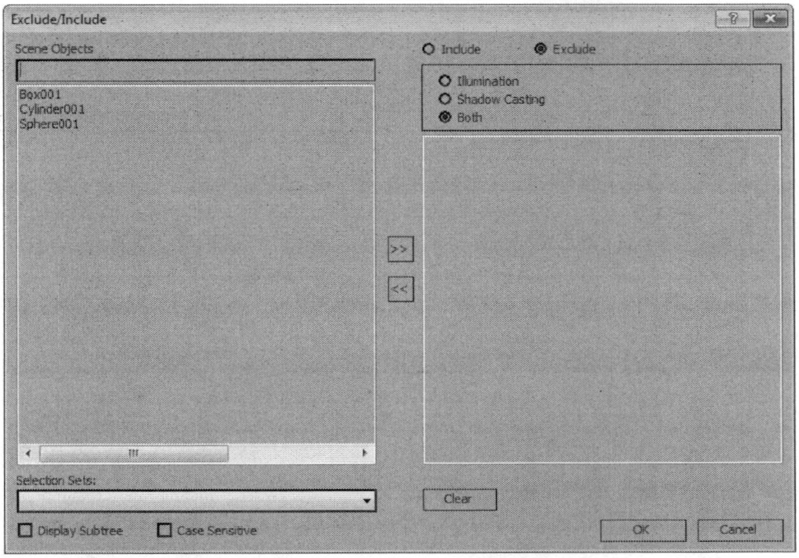

Figure 11-10 *The* ***Exclude/Include*** *dialog box*

Intensity/Color/Attenuation Rollout

The options in this rollout are used to set the color, intensity, and attenuation of the light, refer to Figure 11-11. The attenuation is the effect of light intensity that decreases with distance. Set the value in the **Multiplier** spinner to set the intensity of the light. By default, the value in this spinner is 1.0. You can decrease or increase the value to decrease or increase the brightness of the light. Choose the color swatch on the right side of the **Multiplier** spinner; the **Color Selector: Light Color** dialog box will be displayed. Select the color of the light and choose the **OK** button to assign a new color to the light. The areas in the **Intensity/Color/Attenuation** rollout are discussed next.

Note

If you increase the value in the ***Multiplier*** *spinner to a very high extent, the scene can be burned out. So, it is recommended that you increase the value gradually as required for the scene.*

Decay Area

The options in this area are used to reduce the intensity of the light over the distance. The **Type** drop-down list is used to define the type of decay that will be used for the selected light. By default, the **None** option is selected and therefore no decay is applied to the light, refer to Figure 11-12. In this case, if you use the options in the **Far Attenuation** area, then the decay will be applied to the light according to the values in the **Start** and **End** spinners. Select the **Inverse** option in the **Type** drop-down list to apply the inverse decay, as shown in Figure 11-13. Select the **Inverse Square** option to apply the inverse square decay, as shown in Figure 11-14. The **Inverse** and **Inverse Square** options use some mathematical equations to apply the decay effect on the light. When you select the **Inverse** or the **Inverse Square** option, the gizmo will be displayed in the viewport for the selected light to define the decay of the light. Set the value in the **Start** spinner of the **Decay** area to specify the distance of the decay from the light. On selecting the **Show** check box, a gizmo will be displayed even if the light is not selected.

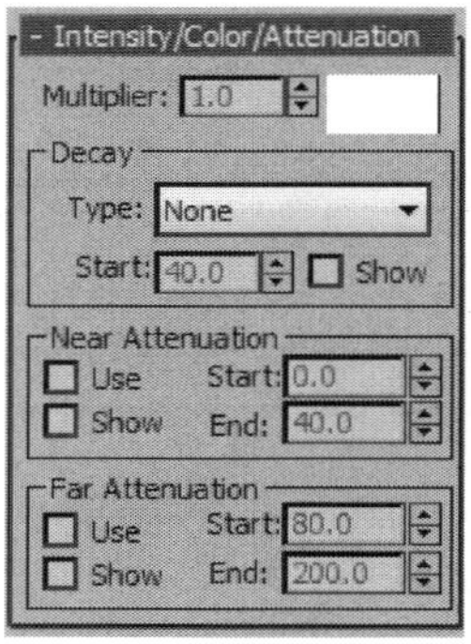

Figure 11-11 *The* ***Intensity/Color/Attenuation*** *rollout*

Figure 11-12 *The effect of light on selecting the* ***None*** *option*

Figure 11-13 *The effect of light on selecting the* ***Inverse*** *option*

Figure 11-14 *The effect of light on selecting the* ***Inverse Square*** *option*

Near Attenuation Area

The **Near Attenuation** area is used to set the distance at which the light begins to fade in. Select the **Use** check box to enable the near attenuation for the selected light; a gizmo will be displayed in the viewport to define the near attenuation. Select the **Show** check box to display the gizmo in the viewport even if the light is not selected. Set the value in the **Start** spinner to define the distance at which the light begins to fade in. Set the value in the **End** spinner to define the distance at which the light reaches its maximum value that is 100%.

Far Attenuation Area

The **Far Attenuation** area is used to set the distance at which the light begins to fade out. Select the **Use** check box to enable the far attenuation for the selected light; a gizmo will be displayed in the viewport to define the far attenuation. Select the **Show** check box to display the gizmo in the viewport even if the light is not selected. Set the value in the **Start** spinner to define the distance at which the light begins to fade out. Set the value in the **End** spinner to define the distance at which the light reaches its minimum value that is zero.

Advanced Effects Rollout

The options in this rollout are used to set the effects of the light on the surfaces, refer to Figure 11-15. This rollout is also used to provide settings for the projector lights. The areas in this rollout are discussed next.

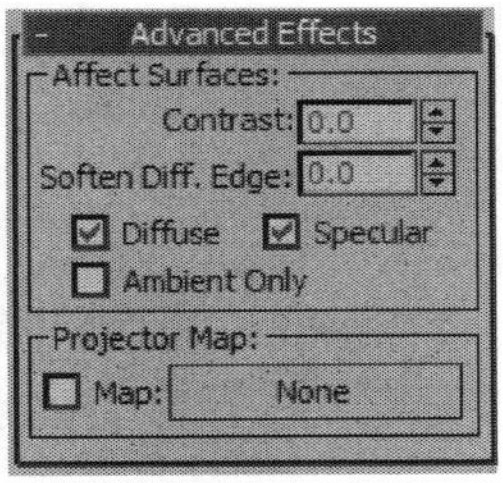

*Figure 11-15 The **Advanced Effects** rollout*

Affect Surfaces Area

Set the value in the **Contrast** spinner to adjust the contrast between different areas of the object that are affected by the diffuse and ambient lights. By default, the value in this spinner is 0 that provides the normal contrast. Set the value in the **Soften Diff. Edge** spinner to soften the transition between the ambient and the diffuse areas. The **Diffuse** and **Specular** check boxes are selected by default and are used to affect the diffuse and specular light areas, respectively. If you clear the **Diffuse** or the **Specular** check box, then the diffuse or specular light area will be excluded from the light effects. On selecting the **Ambient Only** check box, the light will affect only the ambient area of the illumination.

Note

To learn more about the ambient, specular, and diffuse areas, refer to Chapter 8.

Projector Map Area

This area is used to make a light to act as a projector. To do so, select the light in the viewport and choose the **Modify** tab in the **Command Panel**. Now, in the **Projector Map** area of the **Advanced Effects** rollout, select the **Map** check box to enable the projector effect. Choose **Rendering > Material Editor > Compact Material Editor** from the menu bar; the **Material Editor** dialog box will be displayed. Select a sample slot and assign a map to it as discussed earlier. Next, move the cursor over the map button (labeled as M) in the **Material Editor** dialog box and drag it to the map button that is labeled as **None** in the **Projector Map** area; the **Instance/Copy(Map)** dialog box will be displayed. Select the **Instance** radio button and then choose the **OK** button in this dialog box; the name of the map will be displayed on the map button. Also, the selected map will be projected on the object at rendering. Alternatively, choose the map button that is labeled as **None** in the **Projector Map** area; the **Material/Map Browser** dialog box will be displayed. Now, select the map that you want to project and choose the **OK** button; the selected map will be projected on the object at rendering.

Note
You can adjust the settings of the projector map in the ***Material Editor*** *dialog box.*

Shadow Parameters Rollout

The options in this rollout are used to control the properties of the shadow, as shown in Figure 11-16. Choose the color swatch to modify the color of the shadow. Set the value in the **Dens.** spinner to adjust the density of the shadow. By default, the value in this spinner is 1.0. On increasing the value, the shadow will become denser or darker. Select the **Map** check box to assign a map to the shadow, as shown in Figure 11-17. To do so, choose the map button labeled as **None** and assign a map as discussed earlier; the selected map will be displayed in the shadow. Select the **Light Affects Shadow Color** check box to blend the color of the light with the shadow.

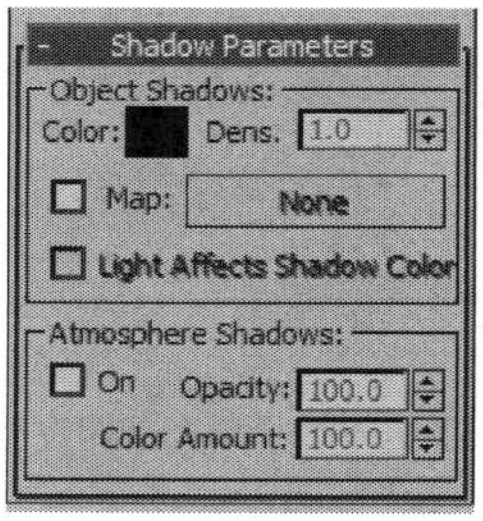

Figure 11-16 *The* ***Shadow Parameters*** *rollout*

Figure 11-17 *A dent map used as a shadow map*

Atmospheres & Effects Rollout

The options in this rollout are used to assign special effects such as fog, lighting effects, and so on to the environment at rendering, refer to Figures 11-18 and 11-19. To assign a new atmosphere to the scene, select the light in the viewport and expand the **Atmospheres & Effects** rollout. Now, choose the **Add** button; the **Add Atmosphere or Effect** dialog box will be displayed, as shown in Figure 11-20. Select the effect from this dialog box to add it to the light selected in the viewport and choose the **OK** button; the selected effect will be displayed in the **Atmospheres & Effects** rollout. Next, select the effect from the **Atmospheres & Effects** rollout and choose the **Setup** button; the **Environment and Effects** dialog box will be displayed, as shown in Figure 11-21. You can set the parameters of the selected effect using the corresponding rollout in this dialog box. If you want to delete an effect from the scene, select the effect in the **Atmospheres & Effects** rollout and choose the **Delete** button.

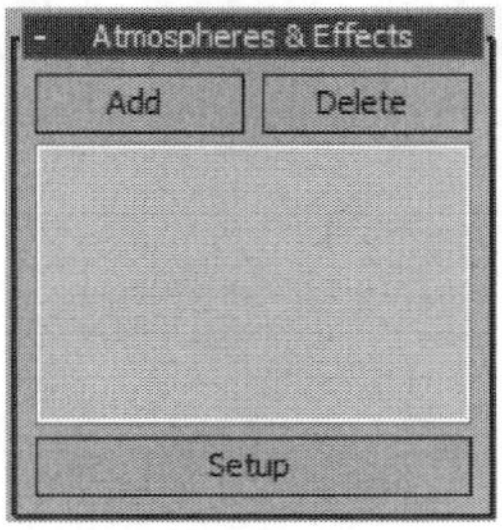

***Figure 11-18** The **Atmospheres & Effects** rollout*

***Figure 11-19** The lens effect applied to the omni light*

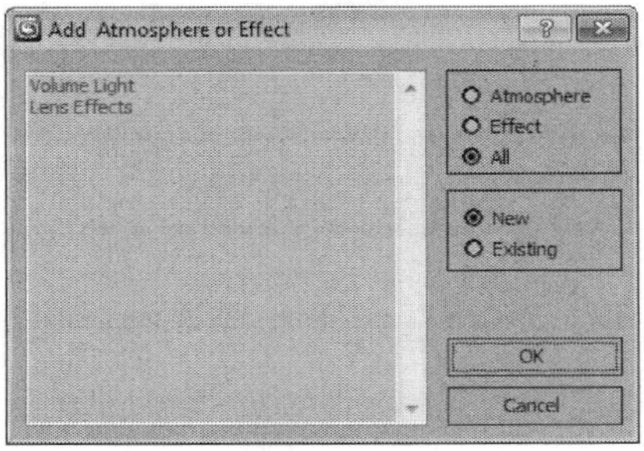

***Figure 11-20** The **Add Atmosphere or Effect** dialog box*

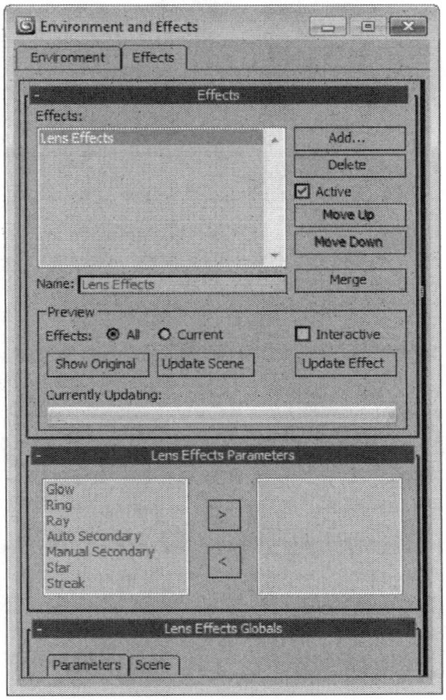

***Figure 11-21** The **Environment and Effects** dialog box*

Note

*To view the corresponding rollouts of the selected effect in the **Environment and Effects** dialog box, press and hold the left mouse button and drag the mouse inside the dialog box.*

Target Spot

Menu bar:	Create > Lights > Standard Lights > Target Spotlight
Command Panel:	Create > Lights > Standard > Object Type rollout > Target Spot

The **Target Spot** tool is used to create the spot lights. A spot light projects the rays in a particular direction from a source, as shown in Figure 11-22. The target spot light also has a target spot to locate the target, refer to Figure 11-23.

Figure 11-22 *The effect of the target spot light with the* ***Volume Light*** *effect*

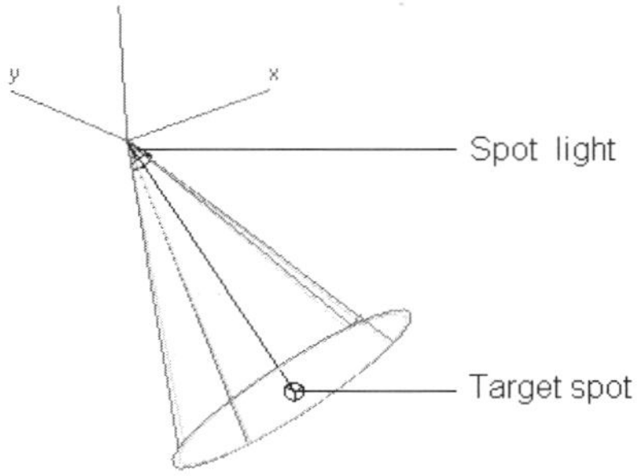

Figure 11-23 *The target spot light*

To create a target spot light, invoke the **Target Spot** tool; the **Name and Color**, **General Parameters**, **Intensity/Color/Attenuation**, **Spotlight Parameters**, **Advanced Effects**, **Shadow Parameters**, and **Shadow Map Params** rollouts will be displayed. Now, move the cursor over the viewport; the cursor will get changed. Press and hold the left mouse button to specify the starting point of the light and drag the cursor to locate the target of the light. Release the left mouse button; a target spot light will be created. Next, you can modify the parameters of the light using various rollouts displayed in the **Command Panel**. To exit the light command, right-click in the viewport. The most commonly used rollouts are discussed next.

Note

The ***Name and Color****,* ***General Parameters****,* ***Intensity/Color/Attenuation****,* ***Advanced Effects****,* ***Shadow Parameters****, and* ***Atmospheric Effects*** *rollouts are the same for all types of lights as discussed in the omni light.*

Spotlight Parameters Rollout

The options in the **Light Cone** area of this rollout are used to set the effects of the target spotlight, refer to Figure 11-24. Select the **Show Cone** check box to view the cone in the viewport even if the light is not selected. Select the **Overshoot** check box to project the light in all directions, but the shadows of the light will fall within the distance specified in the **Falloff/Field** spinner. When you select the **Overshoot** check box, the **Hotspot/Beam** spinner will be deactivated. The **Hotspot/Beam** spinner is used to set the angle of the cone of the target spot light in degrees. The hotspot is the part of the light cone that provides the most acute illumination. Set the value in the **Falloff/Field** spinner to adjust the angle of the falloff of the light. The falloff is the area at which the light intensity falls to zero.

By default, the **Circle** radio button is selected. It provides a circular shape of the hotspot and falloff areas. Select the **Rectangle** radio button to provide a rectangular shape of the hotspot and falloff areas. On selecting the **Rectangle** radio button, the **Aspect** spinner and **Bitmap Fit** button get activated. Set the value in the **Aspect** spinner to adjust the aspect ratio. The aspect ratio is the ratio of the width to the height. You need to set the aspect ratio to match a particular bitmap. Choose the **Bitmap Fit** button; the **Select Image File to Fit** dialog box will be displayed. Select the bitmap image and choose the **Open** button; the light will adjust the aspect ratio in the **Aspect** spinner according to the selected image.

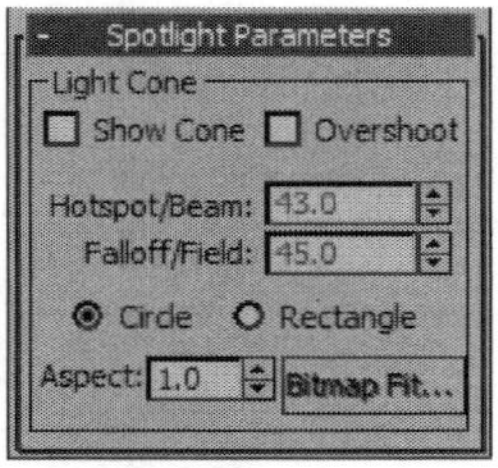

***Figure 11-24** The **Spotlight Parameters** rollout*

Free Spot

Menu bar:	Create > Lights > Standard Lights > Free Spotlight
Command Panel:	Create > Lights > Standard > Object Type rollout > Free Spot

The **Free Spot** tool is also used to create spot lights such as the target spot light. The only difference is that a free spot light does not have a target, refer to Figure 11-25. All the rollouts used to adjust the free spot light are the same as those discussed in the target spot light.

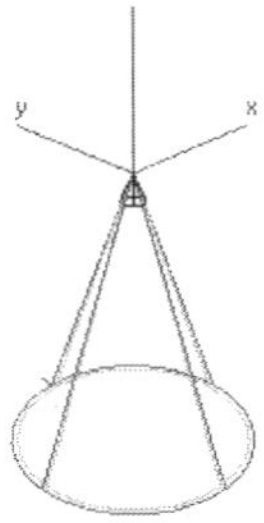

***Figure 11-25** The free spot light*

Target Direct

Menu bar:	Create > Lights > Standard Lights > Target Directional
Command Panel:	Create > Lights > Standard > Object Type rollout > Target Direct

The **Target Direct** tool is used to create direct lights. A direct light also projects the rays in a particular direction from a source. But it projects the parallel rays instead of a cone, refer to Figures 11-26 and 11-27. The target direct light simulates the sunlight.

To create a target direct light, invoke the **Target Direct** tool; the **Name and Color**, **General Parameters**, **Intensity/Color/Attenuation**, **Directional Parameters**, **Advanced Effects**, **Shadow Parameters**, and **Shadow Map Params** rollouts will be displayed. Move the cursor over the viewport; the cursor will get changed. Next, press and hold the left mouse button to specify the starting point of the light and drag the mouse to locate the target of the light. Release the left mouse button; the target direct light will be displayed in all viewports. Next, you can modify the parameters of the light using various rollouts in the **Command Panel**. Most of

Figure 11-26 The effect of the target direct light

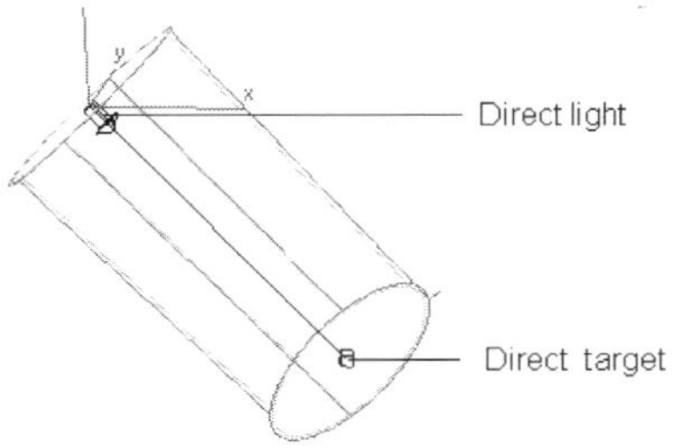

Figure 11-27 The target direct light

the rollouts are same as discussed earlier in this chapter, except the **Directional Parameters** rollout. The options in the **Directional Parameters** rollout are same as those discussed in the **Spotlight Parameters** rollout of the target spot light, refer to Figure 11-28.

Free Direct

Menu bar:	Create > Lights > Standard Lights > Directional
Command Panel:	Create > Lights > Standard > Object Type rollout > Free Direct

The **Free Direct** tool is also used to create the direct light such as the target direct light. The only difference is that the free direct light does not have a target, refer to Figure 11-29. All the rollouts to adjust the free direct light are same as those discussed in the target direct light.

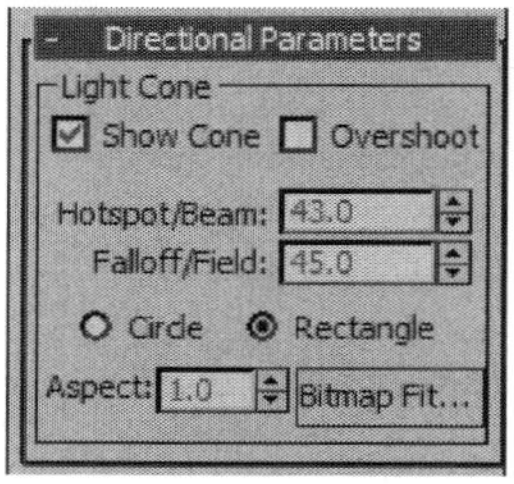

*Figure 11-28 The **Directional Parameters** rollout*

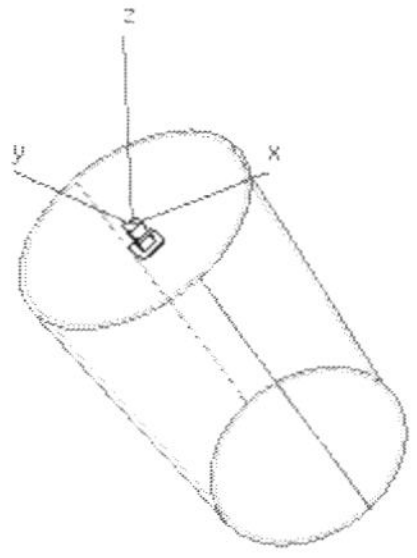

Figure 11-29 The free direct light

Skylight

Menu bar:	Create > Lights > Standard Lights > Skylight
Command Panel:	Create > Lights > Standard > Object Type rollout > Skylight

The **Skylight** tool is used to create the daylights. The best effect of the skylight comes when you use it with the **Light Tracer**.

To create a daylight, invoke the **Skylight** tool; the **Name and Color** and **Skylight Parameters** rollouts will be displayed. Now, move the cursor over the viewport; the cursor will get changed.

Click in the viewport; the light will be displayed in the viewports. Figure 11-30 shows the skylight displayed in the Perspective viewport. Now, choose **Rendering > Light Tracer** from the menu bar; the **Render Setup** dialog box will be displayed. The **Common** tab is chosen by default in this dialog box. Choose the **Advanced Lighting** tab and set the parameters in this tab and then choose the **Render** button; the effect of the light will be displayed, as shown in Figure 11-31. The **Skylight Parameters** rollout is discussed next.

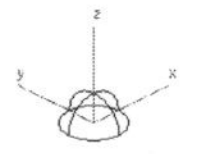

Figure 11-30 *The skylight*

Figure 11-31 *The effect of the skylight*

Skylight Parameters Rollout

The **On** check box is selected by default in this rollout, which enables the skylight to be used in the scene, as shown in Figure 11-32. Set the value in the **Multiplier** spinner to define the intensity of the light. The areas in this rollout are discussed next.

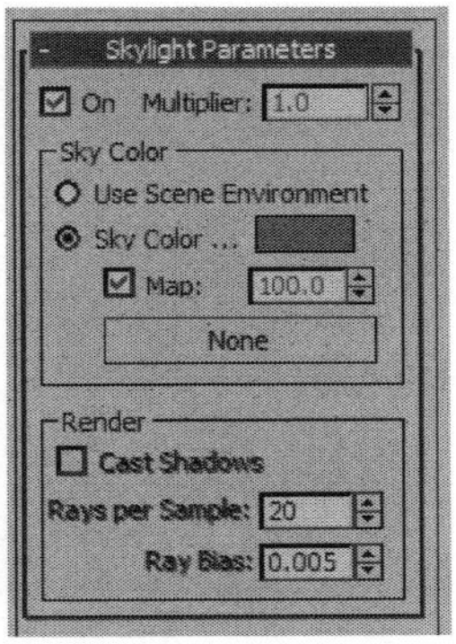

Figure 11-32 *The* ***Skylight Parameters*** *rollout*

Sky Color Area

By default, the **Sky Color** radio button is selected. Choose the color swatch on the right side of the **Sky Color** radio button to select the color for the skylight. The **Map** check box is selected by default. It is used to insert a map along with the light that affects the skylight. By default, the value in the spinner on the right side of the **Map** check box is 100.0. If you decrease the value, the color of the map will be mixed with the sky color. Choose the **Map** button labeled as **None**; the **Material/Map Browser** dialog box will be displayed. Select the desired map and choose the **OK** button to display the map along with the light.

Select the **Use Scene Environment** radio button to use the color that you have set in the **Environment and Effects** dialog box for the skylight.

Render Area

Select the **Cast Shadows** check box to project a shadow with the light. Set the value in the **Rays per Sample** spinner to define the number of rays in the skylight projecting in the scene. Set the value in the **Ray Bias** spinner to define the closest distance at which an object can project the shadows in the scene.

mr Area Omni

Menu bar:	Create > Lights > Standard Lights > mr Area Omni
Command Panel:	Create > Lights > Standard > Object Type rollout > mr Area Omni

The **mr Area Omni** light is used with the mental ray renderer. It is used to create an area omni light, refer to Figure 11-33. If you use the area omni light and render the scene using the default scanline renderer, then its effects will be similar to the standard omni light. To view the best effect of the mr area omni light, you need to change the renderer.

To render the scene with the mental ray renderer, invoke the **Render Setup** tool from the **Main Toolbar**; the **Render Setup** dialog box will be displayed. The **Common** tab is chosen by default in this dialog box. Now, scroll down in the dialog box and expand the **Assign Renderer** rollout. Choose the **Choose Renderer** button on the right side of the **Production** text box, as shown in Figure 11-34; the **Choose Renderer** dialog box will be displayed, as shown in Figure 11-35. Select the **mental ray Renderer** option and choose the **OK** button; the **Default Scanline Renderer** text will be replaced with the **mental ray Renderer** text in the **Production** text box. Choose the **Render** button and close the **Render Setup** dialog box. Now, the scene will be rendered using the mental ray renderer.

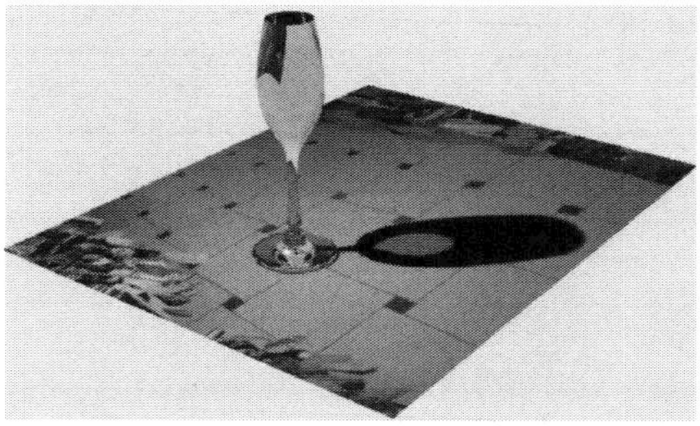

***Figure 11-33** The effect of the area omni light*

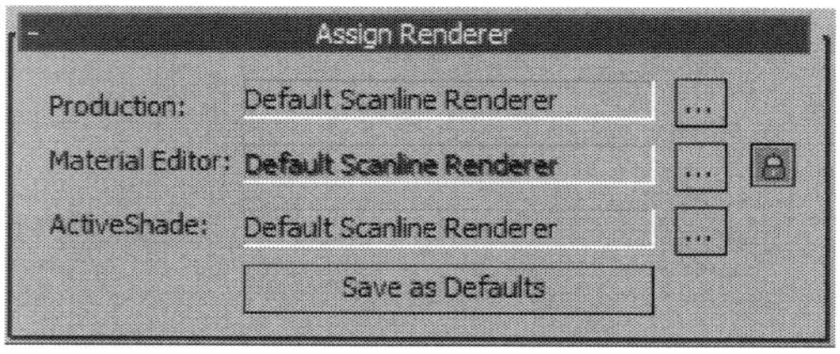

***Figure 11-34** The **Choose Renderer** button highlighted in the **Assign Renderer** rollout*

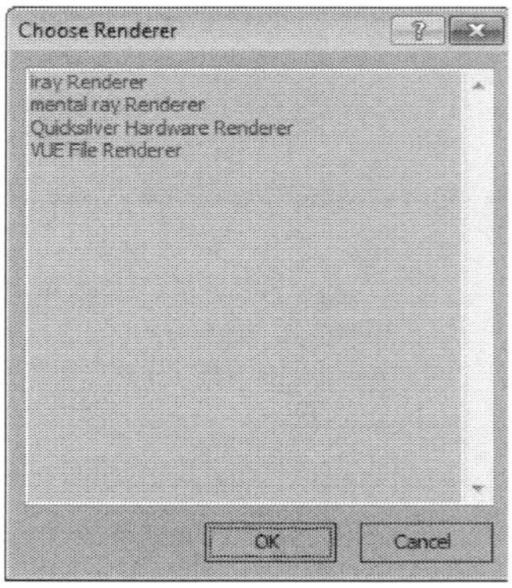

***Figure 11-35** The **Choose Renderer** dialog box*

Note

*To get the best results with the mental ray rendering, select the mr area omni light and choose the **Modify** tab in the **Command Panel**. Next, set the parameters in the **mental ray Indirect Illumination** and **mental ray Light Shader** rollouts.*

To create an area omni light, invoke the **mr Area Omni** tool; the **Name and Color**, **General Parameters**, **Intensity/Color/Attenuation**, **Advanced Effects**, **Shadow Parameters**, **Ray Traced Shadow Params**, and **Area Light Parameters** rollouts will be displayed in the modify panel. Now, move the cursor over the viewport; the cursor will get changed. Click in the viewport; the light will be displayed in the viewport. Next, you can modify the parameters of the light using various rollouts in the **Command Panel**. Most of the rollouts are same as discussed earlier in the omni light. The **Area Light Parameters** rollout is discussed next.

Area Light Parameters Rollout

In this rollout, the **On** check box is selected by default. This check box is used to display the light effects at rendering, refer to Figure 11-36. Select the **Show Icon in Renderer** check box to display a shape at the location of the area light at rendering. To view the shape at rendering, you need to render the scene using the **mental ray Renderer**. The **Type** drop-down list is used to select the type of shape for the area light. By default, the **Sphere** option is selected. Select the **Cylinder** option to display a cylindrical shape. Set the value in the **Radius** spinner to set the radius of the shape displayed. Note that when you select **Cylinder** in the **Type** drop-down list; the **Height** spinner is activated. Set the value in this spinner to define the height of the cylindrical shape displayed. **Samples** area is discussed next.

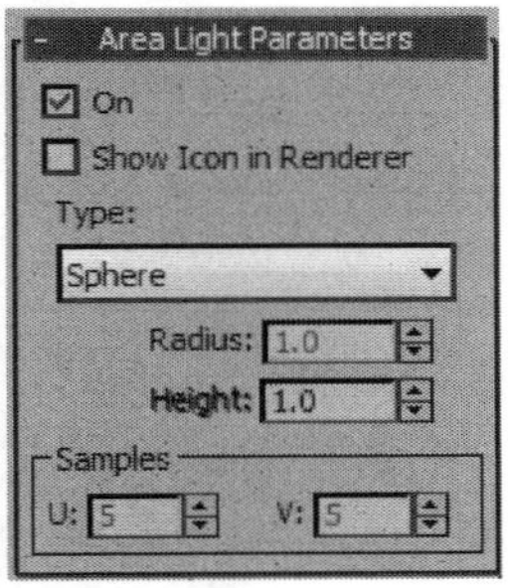

***Figure 11-36** The **Area Light Parameters** rollout*

Samples Area

The options in this area are used to set the quality of the shadow projected by the area omni light. Set the value in the **U** spinner to specify the number of subdivisions along the radius, or the height of the sphere or cylinder. Set the value in the **V** spinner to specify the number of angular subdivisions in the shape.

Note

*You need to use the **mental ray Renderer** to view the effects of the parameters set in the **Area Light Parameters** rollout.*

mr Area Spot

Menu bar:	Create > Lights > Standard Lights > mr Area Spot
Command Panel:	Create > Lights > Standard > Object Type rollout > mr Area Spot

The **mr Area Spot** tool is used to create an area spot light, as shown in Figure 11-37. It is same as the **mr Area Omni** light and is used with the **mental ray Renderer**. The only difference is that it projects the rays in a particular direction from the source.

To create an area spot light, invoke the **mr Area Spot** tool; the **Name and Color**, **General Parameters**, **Intensity/Color/Attenuation**, **Spotlight Parameters**, **Advanced Effects**, **Shadow Parameters**, **Ray Traced Shadow Params**, and **Area Light Parameters** rollouts will be displayed. Move the cursor over the viewport; the cursor will get changed. Now, press and hold the left mouse button to specify the location of the light, drag the mouse to locate the target of the light, and release the left mouse button; the light will be displayed in the viewports. You can modify the parameters of the light using various rollouts displayed in the **Command Panel**. Most of the rollouts have already been discussed. The **Area Light Parameters** rollout for the area spot light is discussed next.

Area Light Parameters Rollout

The options in this rollout are same as discussed in the area omni light tool, refer to Figure 11-38. In the **Type** drop-down list, the **Rectangle** shape is selected by default. It is used to display the area spot light in a rectangular shape. Specify the height and width in the **Height** and **Width** spinners, respectively. Select the **Disc** shape in the **Type** drop-down list to display the light in circular shape; the **Radius** spinner will get activated. Set the value in this spinner to specify the radius of the shape.

Figure 11-37 *The effect of the area spot light*

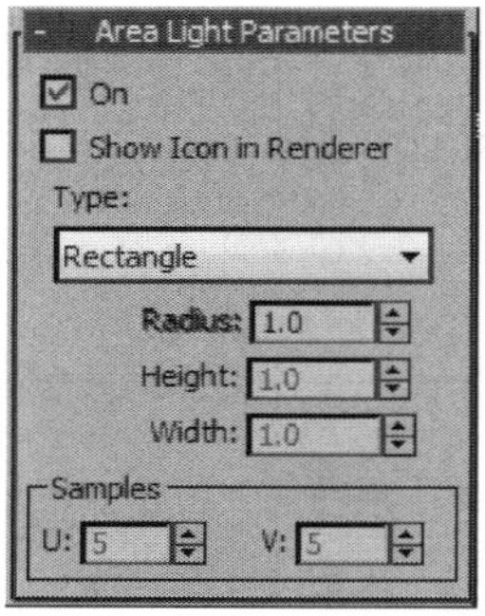

Figure 11-38 *The **Area Light Parameters** rollout*

PHOTOMETRIC LIGHTS

The photometric lights are used to add more realistic light effects to the scenes. The photometric lights use the light energy values to calculate the lights accurately as they are in the real world.

You can create three types of photometric lights in Autodesk 3ds Max. To create a photometric light in a scene, choose **Create > Lights** in the **Command Panel**; the **Photometric** light will be displayed by default in the drop-down list below the **Lights** button. Also, various tools to create photometric lights will be displayed in the **Object Type** rollout. These tools are **Target Light**, **Free Light**, and **mr Sky Portal**, refer to Figure 11-39. Invoke one of these tools and create the light in the viewport. If you invoke the **Target Light** or **Free Light** tool, the **Photometric Light Creation** dialog box will be displayed. Also, you will be prompted to use the Logarithmic Exposure Control. Choose the **Yes** button in this dialog box. When you invoke a tool from the **Object Type** rollout, various rollouts will be displayed to modify the parameters of the corresponding light.

The **Name and Color**, **General Parameters**, **Shadow Parameters**, **Advanced Effects**, and **Atmospheres & Effects** rollouts for photometric lights are same as discussed in the standard lights. The **Intensity/Color/Attenuation**, **Templates**, and **Shape/Area Shadows** rollouts for the target light and the free light are discussed next.

Intensity/Color/Attenuation Rollout

The options in this rollout are used to set the intensity, color, dimness, and attenuation of the light, refer to Figure 11-40. The areas in this rollout are discussed next.

Color Area

The drop-down list on the top of this area displays different common lamp specifications. By default, the **D65 Illuminant (Reference)** option is selected in the drop-down list. Select the other options; the color in the color swatch on the right side of the **Kelvin** radio button will get changed according to the selection in this drop-down list. Select the **Kelvin** radio button to specify the color of the light by setting the color temperature in the spinner on the right of this radio button. The value in this spinner is in kelvin unit. As you change the value (temperature) in this spinner, the color in the color swatch will change accordingly. Choose the **Filter Color** color swatch to specify the color of the color filter.

Figure 11-39 *Various tools to create* ***Photometric*** *lights*

Intensity Area

The options in this area specify the intensity of the light. By default, the **cd** radio button is selected that measures the intensity of the light in candela unit. Select the **lm** radio button to measure the intensity of the light in lumen unit. Select the **lx at** radio button to measure the intensity in lux unit. Set the values in the spinners below these radio buttons to specify the intensity of the light.

Dimming Area

The options in this area are used to set the intensity by dimming the light. The resulting intensity is set by the value in the **Resulting Intensity** spinner. By default. this spinner is not active. Select the **Resulting Intensity** check box. Then, enter the value in the spinner. A value of 100 indicates that the light will be displayed with its full intensity. Select the **Incandescent lamp color shift when dimming** check box to simulate an incandescent light as the light gets dimmed.

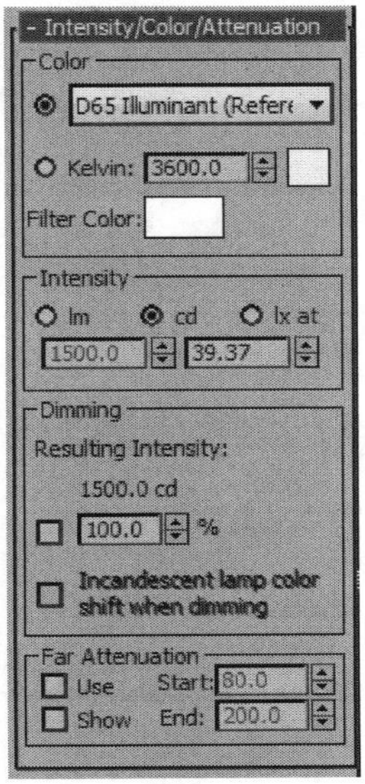

Figure 11-40 *The* ***Intensity/ Color/Attenuation*** *rollout*

Templates Rollout

The options in this rollout are used to specify preset light types such as 40W bulb, Street 400W Lamp, and so on, refer to Figure 11-41. To do so, select a light in the viewport and click on the down arrow at the bottom of the **Templates** rollout; a drop-down list will be displayed, as shown in Figure 11-42. Select the required light type from the drop-down list. You will notice a change in the light effect in the viewport. Also, the description of the selected light will be displayed in the text area just above the drop-down list.

Tip: *1. To get more familiar with the photometric lights, place them in the scenes and try out various options in the rollouts.*

*2. To get the best effect of the photometric lights, render the scene using **Light Tracer** or **Radiosity** from the **Advanced Lighting** tab in the **Render Setup** dialog box.*

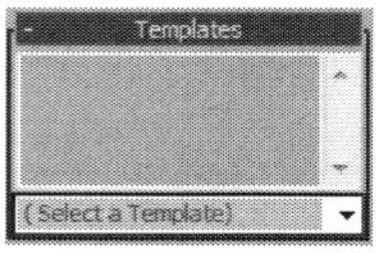

*Figure 11-41 The **Templates** rollout*

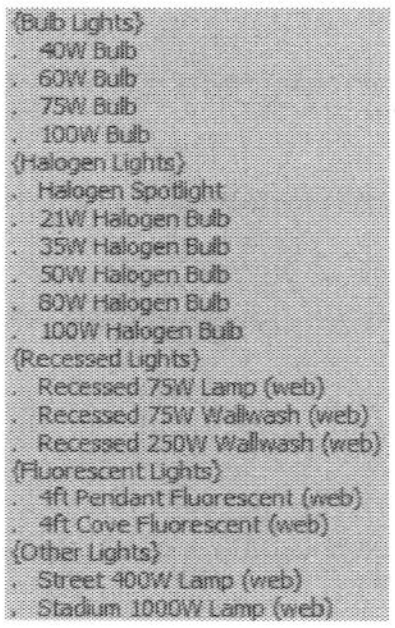

Figure 11-42 The drop-down list displayed to select the type of light

Shape/Area Shadows Rollout

The options in this rollout are used to specify a light shape that generate the shadows, refer to Figure 11-43. The controls in this rollout work with the mental ray renderer. To get a similar effect in the scanline renderer, you can select **Area Shadows** from the **General Parameters** rollout since photometric area shadows are not calculated in the scanline renderer. The areas in this rollout are discussed next.

Emit light from (Shape) Area

The drop-down list on the top in this area is used to select the shape for generating the shadows. On selecting an option from the drop-down list (except the **Point** option), the dimension controls related to the selected option will be displayed at the bottom of this area. You can set the dimensions in the respective spinners to modify the shape. Also, the **Shadows Samples** drop-down list will be displayed in the **Rendering** area.

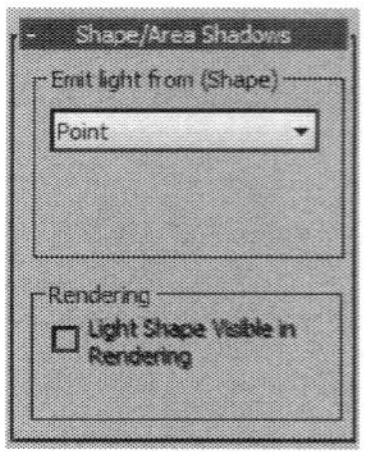

*Figure 11-43 The **Shape/Area Shadows** rollout*

Note

*If you choose the **Point** shape from the drop-down list in the **Emit light from (Shape)** area, then the **Shadows Samples** drop-down list will not be available in the **Rendering** area.*

Rendering Area

Select the **Light Shape Visible in Rendering** check box to view the light shape at rendering. The options in the **Shadows Samples** drop-down list are used to set the quality of the shadows of the light.

ADDING DEFAULT LIGHTS TO A SCENE

When you start 3ds Max, scene lights are used to light the scene, by default. You can also add default lights to the scene. To do so, click on **General viewport label** in any of the viewports; a shortcut menu will be displayed. Choose **Configure Viewports** from the shortcut menu; a **Viewport Configuration** dialog box will be displayed, as shown in Figure 11-44. By default, the **Visual Style and Appearance** tab is chosen in this dialog box. In this tab, the **Scene Lights** radio button is selected in the **Lighting and Shadows** area. As a result, only scene lights are used in the scene. If you want to add default lights to the scene, select the **Default Lights** radio button; the radio buttons located just below it will be activated. Now, choose the **OK** button to exit the dialog box. Next, choose **Create > Lights > Standard Lights > Add Default Lights to Scene** from the menu bar; the **Add Default Light to Scene** dialog box will be displayed, as shown in Figure 11-45. In this dialog box, the **Add Default Key Light** and **Add Default Fill Light** check boxes are selected, by default. Choose the **OK** button; default key light and fill light will be added to the scene. Both these lights will be omni lights. You can notice the difference between the scene lighting and default lighting by rendering the scene before and after adding default lighting.

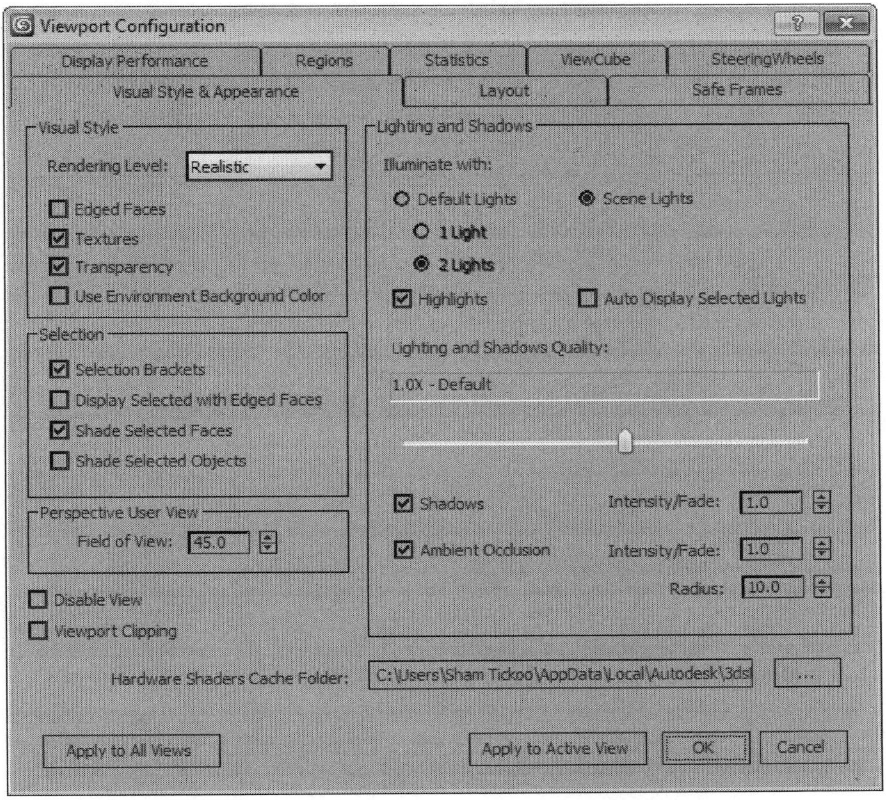

***Figure 11-44** The **Viewport Configuration** dialog box*

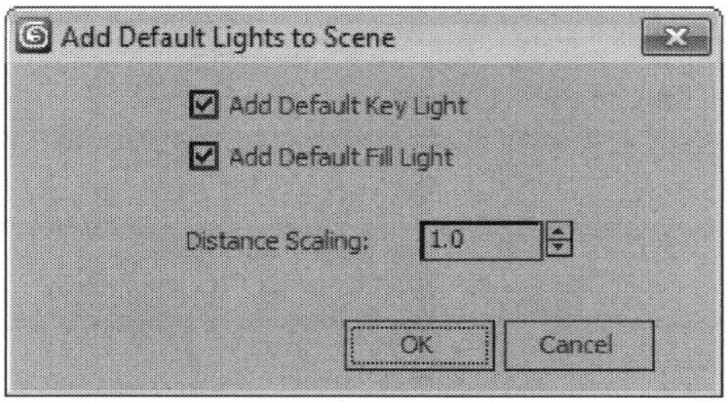

***Figure 11-45** The **Add Default Lights to Scene** dialog box*

PLACE HIGHLIGHT TOOL

Menu bar:	Tools > Align > Place Highlight
Main Toolbar:	Align flyout > Place Highlight
Keyboard:	CTRL + H

The **Place Highlight** tool is used to align a light to an object to position its reflection accurately. Before performing the alignment, make sure that the object that you want to highlight is visible in the viewport. Now, select the light in the viewport and invoke the **Place Highlight** tool; the cursor will get changed. Next, move the cursor over the face of the object that you want to highlight; a selection cursor will be displayed, as shown in Figure 11-46. Select the face; the light will be aligned accordingly, as shown in Figure 11-47.

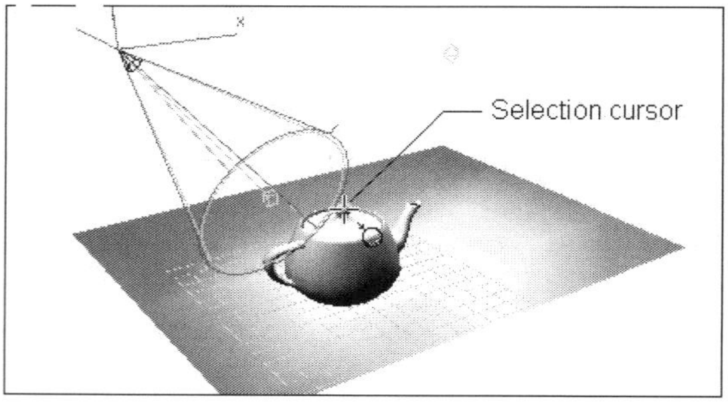

***Figure 11-46** The selection cursor displayed after invoking the **Place Highlight** tool*

***Figure 11-47** The light aligned as per the selection of the face of the object*

CAMERAS

In Autodesk 3ds Max, the cameras are used to adjust a particular view of a scene. These cameras act as the still-image or video cameras in the real world. There are two types of cameras in Autodesk 3ds Max, target and free.

The target camera has two parts, the target camera and a target object, as shown in Figure 11-48. It displays the view according to the position of the target object. You can move the target object and the target camera independently. The free camera does not have any target object, as shown in Figure 11-49. It displays the view in the direction of the camera. You can use the free camera to perform the walkthrough animation.

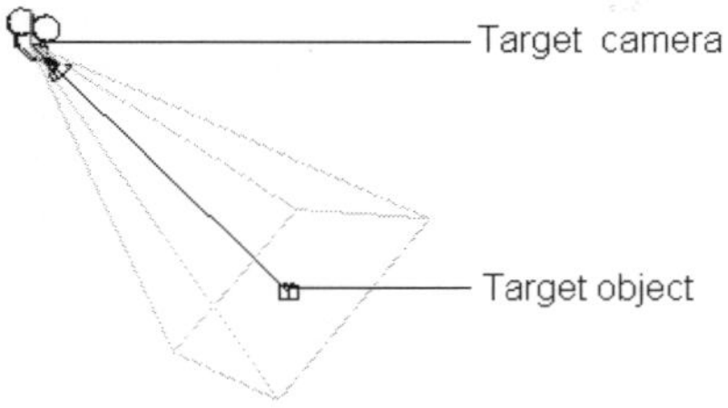

Figure 11-48 *The target camera*

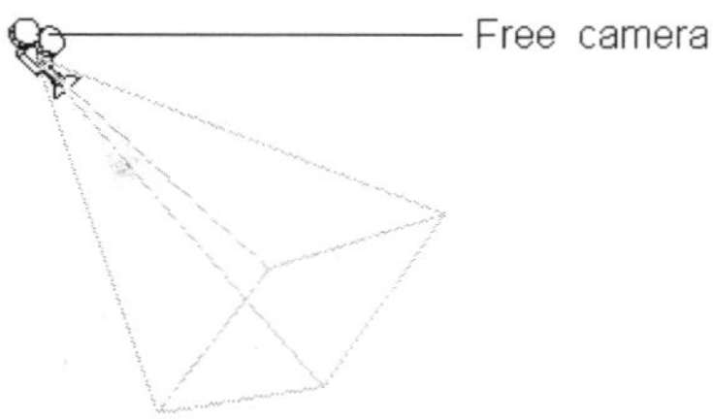

Figure 11-49 *The free camera*

Creating a Target Camera

Menu bar:	Create > Cameras > Target Camera
Command Panel:	Create > Cameras > Standard > Object Type rollout > Target

To create a target camera, choose **Create > Cameras** in the **Command Panel**; the **Standard** option will be displayed in the drop-down list below the **Cameras** button. You can use the tools in the **Object Type** rollout to create cameras, refer to Figure 11-50. Invoke the **Target** tool; the **Name and Color**, **Parameters**, and **Depth of Field Parameters** rollouts will be displayed in the **Command Panel**. Next, move the cursor over the viewport; the cursor will get changed. Press and hold the left mouse button to specify the location of the camera, drag the cursor to locate the target of the camera, and release the left mouse button; the target camera will be displayed in the viewports. You can modify the parameters of the camera using the rollouts displayed in the **Command Panel**. Next, right-click in the viewport to exit the command.

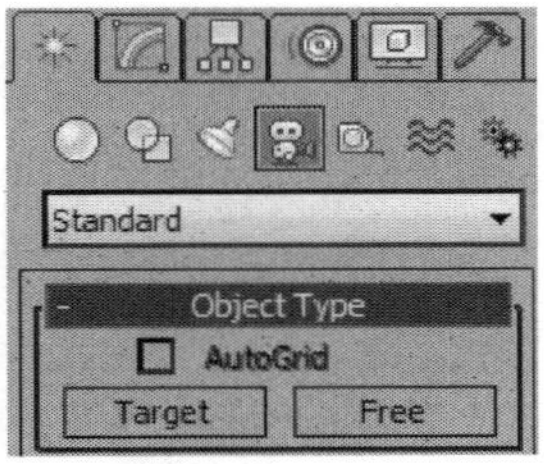

Figure 11-50 *The tools to create cameras in the* ***Object Type*** *rollout*

To display the camera view in the viewport, move the cursor over the POV viewport label and click on it; a flyout will be displayed. Choose the **Cameras** option; a cascading menu will be displayed, as shown in Figure 11-51. Choose the **Camera001** option; the current viewport label will be replaced by the Camera001 label. Alternatively, you can press the C key to display the camera view. The **Parameters** rollout is used to modify the parameters of the camera and is discussed next.

Parameters Rollout

To modify the parameters of the camera, make sure that the camera is selected in the viewport. Next, choose the **Modify** tab in the **Command Panel**; the **Parameters** rollout will be displayed, as shown in Figure 11-52.

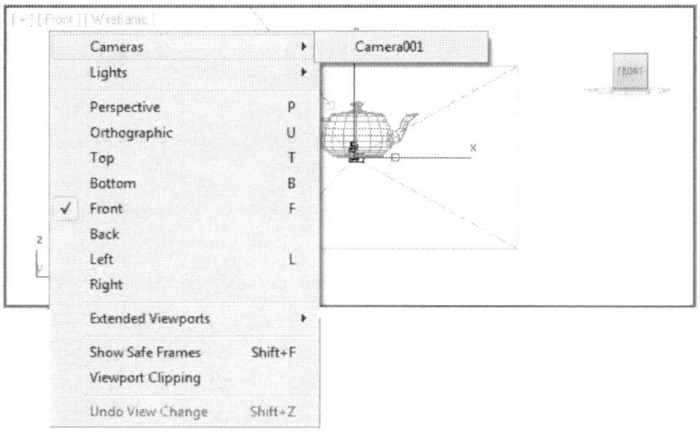

Figure 11-51 The cascading menu 3displayed to choose the camera view

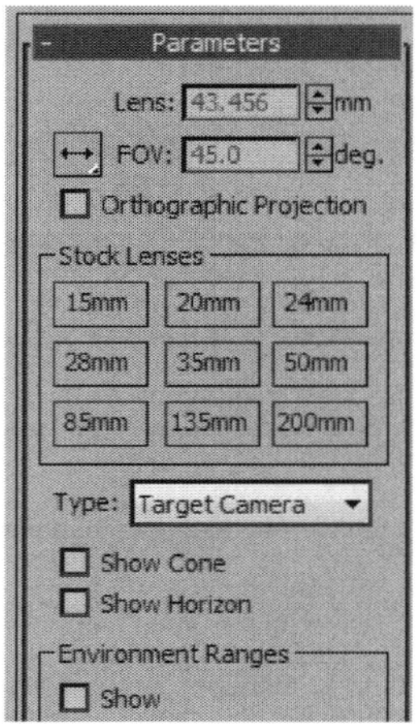

Figure 11-52 *Partial view of the* ***Parameters*** *rollout*

Set a value in the **Lens** spinner to specify the focal length of the camera in millimeters. The focal length is the distance between the camera lens and its focus. Set the value in the **FOV** spinner to specify the field of view of the camera in degrees. The field of view (FOV) determines the area that the camera can view in the viewport. The **Stock Lenses** area in this rollout is discussed next.

Stock Lenses Area

Choose one of the buttons in this area to set the focal length of the camera in millimeters. As you choose a button in this area, the value in the **Lens** and **FOV** spinners will also get changed automatically.

The **Type** drop-down list is used to set the type of camera in the viewport. The **Target Camera** is selected by default. Select the **Free Camera** option to use the free camera. Select the **Show Cone** check box to view the FOV cone in all viewports, even if the camera is not selected. Select the **Show Horizon** check box to view the horizon line displayed in dark gray color in the Camera viewport.

Creating a Free Camera

Menu bar:	Create > Cameras > Free Camera
Command Panel:	Create > Cameras > Standard > Object Type rollout > Free

To create a free camera, choose **Create > Cameras** in the **Command Panel**; the **Standard** option will be displayed in the drop-down list. Invoke the **Free** tool from the **Object Type** rollout; the **Name and Color**, **Parameters**, and **Depth of Field Parameters** rollouts will be displayed. Move the cursor over the viewport; the cursor will get changed. Now, click in the viewport; the camera will be displayed in the viewports. You can modify the parameters of the camera using the rollouts displayed in the **Command Panel**. The options in these rollouts are the same as those discussed in the target camera.

CAMERA VIEWPORT CONTROLS

When you change the viewport to display the camera view, the viewport navigation controls get changed to camera viewport controls. These tools are available on the lower right corner of the Autodesk 3ds Max screen and are used to adjust the view of the Camera viewport. These tools are discussed next.

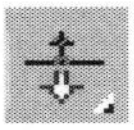

The **Dolly Camera** tool is used to move the camera or its target along its main axis. This increases or decreases the magnification of the view in the Camera viewport. You can zoom in on the view by pressing the left mouse button and then dragging the cursor down. Similarly, you can zoom out by pressing the left mouse button and then dragging the cursor up.

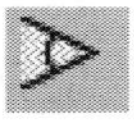

The **Field-of-View** tool is used to specify the area of the scene that will be visible in the Camera viewport. To do so, press the left mouse button and drag the cursor up or down to adjust the view.

The **Perspective** tool is used to perform the tasks of the **Dolly** and **Field-of-View** tools simultaneously.

The **Truck Camera** tool is used to pan the camera viewport without changing its magnification.

The **Walk Through** tool is used to do the walkthrough navigation in the camera active viewport. You can also use the arrow keys to do the navigation.

The **Roll Camera** tool is used to rotate the camera in the viewports. The free camera rotates along its local Z-axis. The target camera rotates around its line from target to camera.

The **Orbit Camera** tool is used to rotate the objects to view its 3D view in the Camera viewport. This enables you to view the objects from all sides.

ALIGN CAMERA TOOL

Menu bar:	Tools > Align > Align Camera
Main Toolbar:	Align flyout > Align Camera

The **Align Camera** tool is used to align a camera to a selected face normal. To do the alignment, select the camera in the viewport, invoke the **Align Camera** tool; the cursor will get changed. Next, move the cursor over the face of the object; a selection cursor will be displayed, as shown in Figure 11-53. Select the face; the camera will be aligned accordingly, refer to Figures 11-54, 11-55, and 11-56.

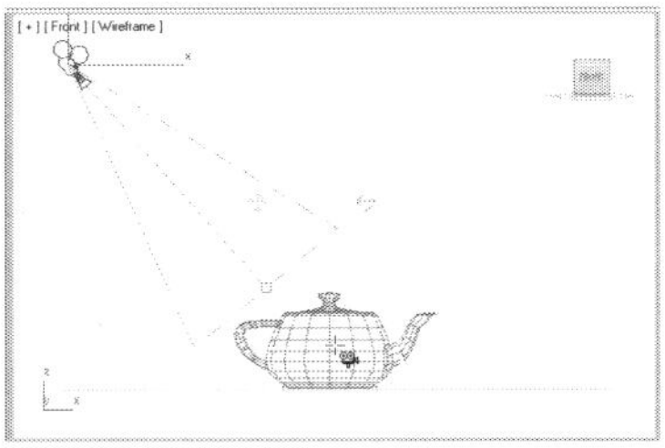

Figure 11-53 *The cursor displayed on the object to get the proper alignment*

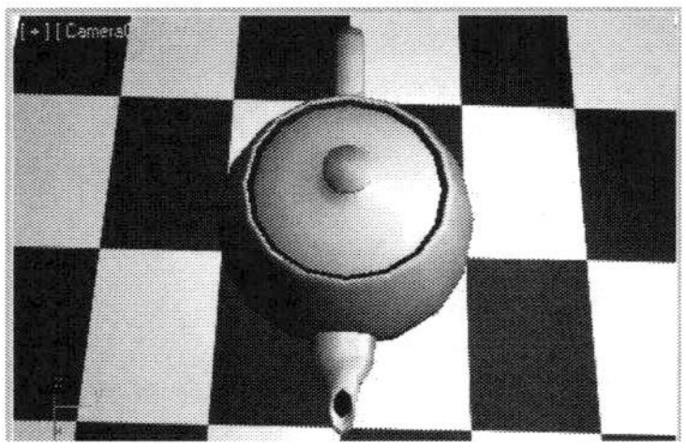

Figure 11-54 *The Camera viewport before alignment*

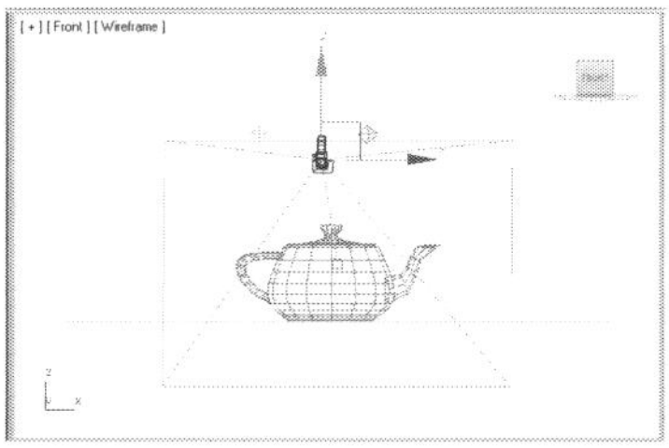

Figure 11-55 *The new position of the camera after using the **Align Camera** tool*

Figure 11-56 *The Camera viewport after using the **Align Camera** tool*

Tutorial 1

In this tutorial, you will create a nature scene using the lights and camera, as shown in Figure 11-57. **(Expected time: 30 min)**

Figure 11-57 *Nature Scene*

The following steps are required to complete this tutorial:

a. Set the project folder.
b. Download the file.
c. Create the water surface.

d. Assign the camera.
e. Create the background.
f. Assign the maps and materials.
g. Create the lights.
h. Render the scene for the final output.
i. Save the file.

Setting the Project Folder

1. Set the project folder with the name *c11_tut1* in the *3dsmax* folder as discussed in earlier chapters.

Downloading the File

Before starting the tutorial, you need to download the *c11_3dsmax_2012_tut.zip* file from *http://www.cadcim.com*. The path of the file is as follows:

Textbooks > Animation and Visual Effects > 3ds Max > Autodesk 3ds Max 2012: A Comprehensive Guide

Extract the contents of the zipped file and copy the file *sky_1.jpg* at the location *\Documents\3dsmax\c11_tut1\sceneassets\images*.

Creating the Water Surface

To create a water surface, you need to create a plane.

1. Activate the Top viewport and choose **Create > Geometry** in the **Command Panel**; the **Standard Primitives** option is displayed in the drop-down list below the **Geometry** button. Now, invoke the **Plane** tool from the **Object Type** rollout.

2. Create a plane in the Top viewport and set the values in the **Parameters** rollout as given below:

   Length: **273.604** Width: **297.462**

3. In the **Name and Color** rollout, rename the plane as *water surface*.

4. Invoke the **Zoom Extents All** tool to display the *water surface* in all viewports, as shown in Figure 11-58.

Assigning the Camera

You need to use the free camera to adjust the view.

1. Activate the Front viewport. Choose **Create > Cameras** in the **Command Panel**; the **Standard** option is displayed in the drop-down list.

2. Next, invoke the **Free** tool from the **Object Type** rollout to create a free camera for adjusting the view. In the Front viewport, click on the middle of the *water surface*; the free camera is displayed in all viewports. It is automatically named as *Camera001*.

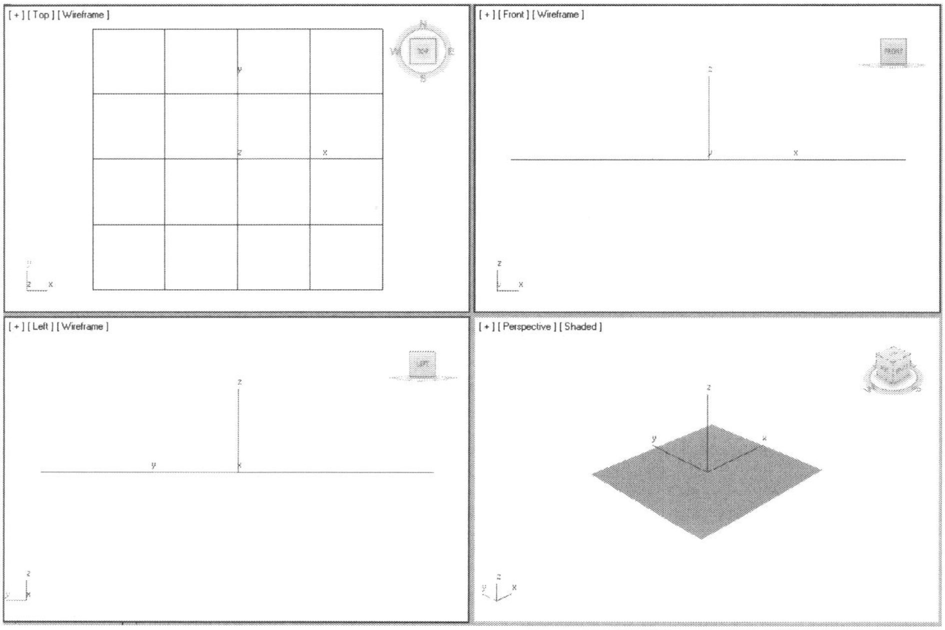

***Figure 11-58** A plane created for the water surface in all viewports*

Note

If you use more than one camera in a scene, then it is recommended that you modify the name of the cameras depending on the view you have adjusted.

3. Right-click anywhere in the viewport to exit the command.

4. Next, invoke the **Select and Move** and **Select and Rotate** tools and align the *Camera001* in all viewports. Also, activate the Perspective viewport and press the C key to view the Camera viewport; the Perspective label is replaced by the Camera001 label and the view is changed according to the position of the camera, refer to Figure 11-59.

Creating the Background

To create the background, you need to create a sphere.

1. Activate the Top viewport and choose **Create > Geometry** in the **Command Panel**; the **Standard Primitives** option is displayed in the drop-down list. Now, invoke the **Sphere** tool from the **Object Type** rollout.

2. Move the cursor at the center of the *water surface* and create a sphere in the Top viewport. Set the values in the **Parameters** rollout as given below:

Radius: **72.0** Hemisphere: **0.74**

3. In the **Name and Color** rollout, modify the name of the sphere as *background*.

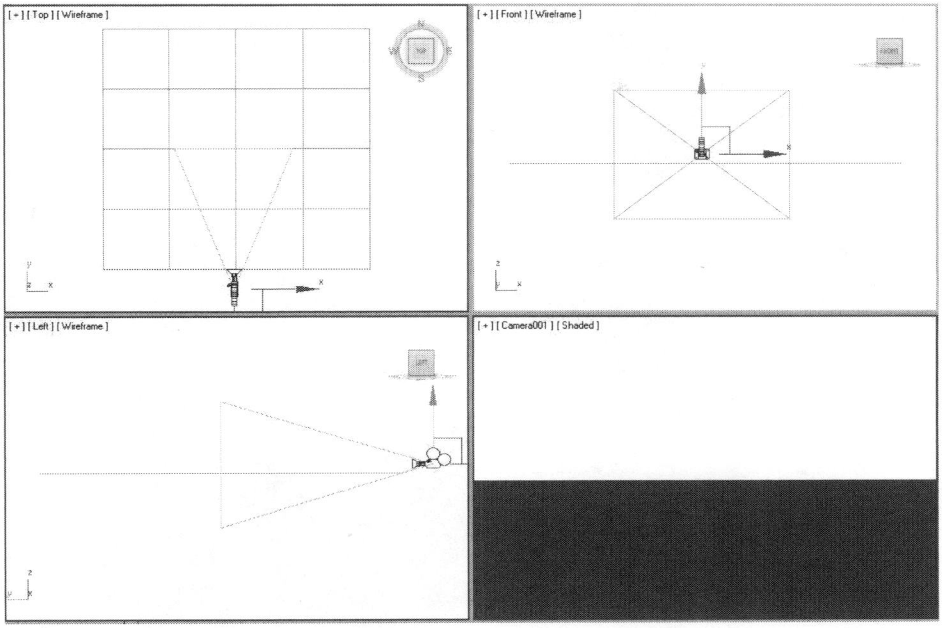

***Figure 11-59** Alignment of the Camera001 in all viewports*

4. Make sure that the *background* is selected in the Top viewport. Next, right-click on the **Select and Uniform Scale** tool; the **Scale Transform Type-In** dialog box is displayed. In the **Offset: Screen** area, set the value **260** in the **%** spinner; the *background* is scaled to touch the corners of the *water surface*, as shown in Figure 11-60. Close this dialog box.

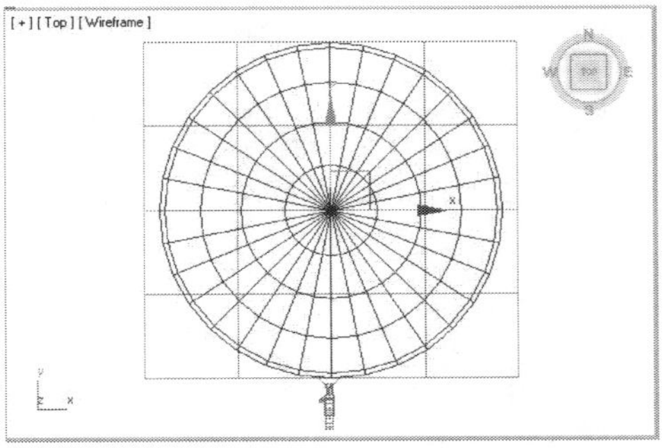

***Figure 11-60** The background after scaling*

5. Next, make sure that the *background* is selected and choose the **Modify** tab in the **Command Panel**. Select the **Normal** modifier from the **Modifier List** drop-down list; the rollouts are displayed in the modify panel.

6. In the **Parameters** rollout of the **Normal** modifier, make sure that the **Flip Normals** check box is selected.

7. Next, invoke the **Select and Move** tool and align the *background* and the *Camera001* in all viewports, as shown in Figure 11-61.

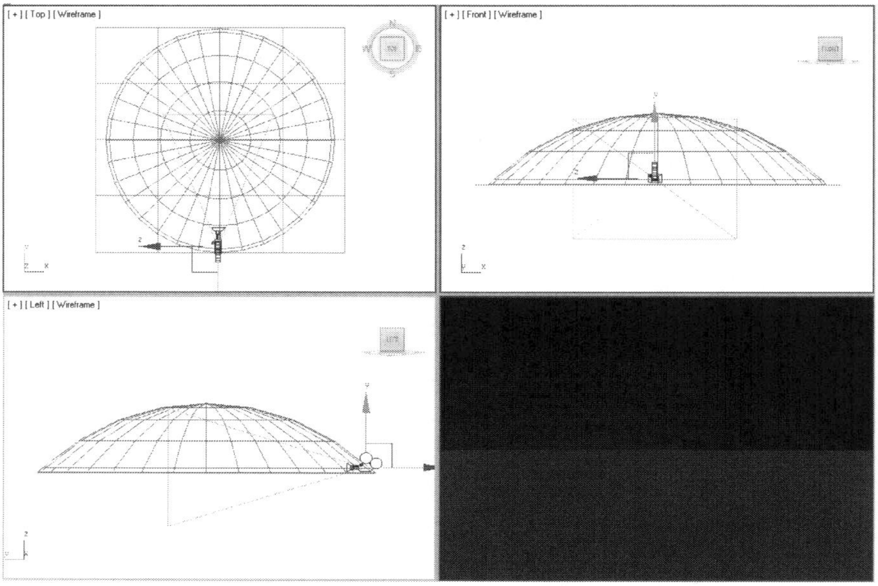

Figure 11-61 *Alignment of the Camera001 and background in all viewports*

Assigning Maps and Materials

Next, you need to assign the maps and materials to the *background* and the *water surface*.

1. Select the *water surface* in any viewport and invoke the **Compact Material Editor** tool; the **Material Editor** dialog box is displayed.

First, you will create the material for the *water surface* in the **Material Editor** dialog box.

2. Select the **01-Default** sample slot, if it is not already selected. Modify its name in the **Material Name** text box to **water surface material**.

3. Choose the **Material Type** button that is currently labeled as **Standard**; the **Material/Map Browser** dialog box is displayed. Select the **Raytrace** material from the **Materials > Standard** rollouts and choose the **OK** button; the **Standard** material is replaced by the **Raytrace** material.

4. In the **Raytrace Basic Parameters** rollout, make sure that the **Phong** shader is selected in the **Shading** drop-down list.

5. Choose the **Diffuse** color swatch; the **Color Selector: Diffuse** dialog box is displayed. Select the black color and choose the **OK** button to close the dialog box.

6. Choose the **Reflect** color swatch; the **Color Selector: Reflect** dialog box is displayed. Enter values in the **Red**, **Green**, and **Blue** spinners as given next.

   Red: **139** Green: **139** Blue: **139**

   Now, choose the **OK** button to close this dialog box.

7. In the **Raytrace Basic Parameters** rollout, select the **Bump** check box and choose the **Bump** button labeled as **None** to assign a map to it; the **Material/Map Browser** dialog box is displayed. Select the **Noise** map from the **Maps > Standard** rollouts and choose the **OK** button; the **Noise** map is displayed as the sub-material.

8. In the **Noise Parameters** rollout, set the values as given below:

   Select the **Fractal** radio button.
   Size: **5.0** High: **1.0** Low: **1.0**

9. Choose the **Go to Parent** button to go back to the parent level. Alternatively, you can select **water surface material** from the **Material Name** drop-down list.

10. Expand the **Maps** rollout and select the **Reflect** check box to make it available for the material. Choose the **Reflect** map button labeled as **None**; the **Material/Map Browser** dialog box is displayed. Select the **Falloff** map and choose the **OK** button; the **Falloff** map is displayed as the sub-material. Use the default settings and choose the **Go to Parent** button to go back to the parent level; the **None** label is replaced by **Map#1 (Falloff)**.

11. Make sure that the *water surface* is selected in the viewport and choose the **Assign Material to Selection** button; the **water surface material** is assigned to the *water surface* in the viewport.

   Next, you need to create the material for the *background*.

12. Select the **02-Default** sample slot and modify its name as **background material** in the **Material Name** text box.

13. In the **Shader Basic Parameters** rollout, make sure that the **Blinn** shader is selected in the drop-down list.

   Next, you need to assign a map to the selected sample slot.

14. In the **Blinn Basic Parameters** rollout, choose the **Diffuse** map button on the right side of the **Diffuse** color swatch; the **Material/Map Browser** dialog box is displayed. Select the **Bitmap** map from **Maps > Standard** rollouts and choose the **OK** button; the **Select Bitmap Image File** dialog box is displayed. As the project folder is already set, the

path *\Documents\3dsmax\c11_tut1\sceneassets\images* is displayed in the **Look in** text box of this dialog box. Select the file *sky_1.jpg* and choose the **Open** button; the selected image is displayed in the **background material** sample slot.

15. Make sure that the *background* is selected in the viewport and then choose the **Assign Material to Selection** button; the **background material** is assigned to the *background* in the viewport. Close the **Material Editor** dialog box.

    Next, you will apply the **UVW Map** modifier to the *background* to align the map properly.

16. Choose the **Modify** tab in the **Command Panel** and select the **UVW Map** modifier from the **Modifier List** drop-down list; the **UVW Mapping** is displayed in the modifier stack. The **Parameters** rollout is displayed below the modifier stack.

17. In the **Parameters** rollout, set the values as given below:

    Mapping area
    Select the **Box** radio button.
    Length: **-1.374** Width: **93.147**
    Height: **31.408**

    Alignment area
    Make sure that the **Z** radio button is selected.

18. Now, render the *Camera001* viewport using the **Render Production** tool; the scene is not visible properly, as shown in Figure 11-62. You need to create the lights to view the scene clearly.

Creating Lights

Figure 11-62 The scene after rendering

1. Activate the Top viewport. Choose **Create > Lights** in the **Command Panel**; the **Photometric** option is displayed in the drop-down list below the **Lights** button. Choose the **Standard** option from the drop-down list.

2. Invoke the **Omni** tool from the **Object Type** rollout in the **Command Panel** and click in the Top viewport; the omni light is displayed in the viewports. It is automatically named as *Omni001*.

3. Invoke the **Select and Move** tool and align the *Omni001* in all viewports, as shown in Figure 11-63.

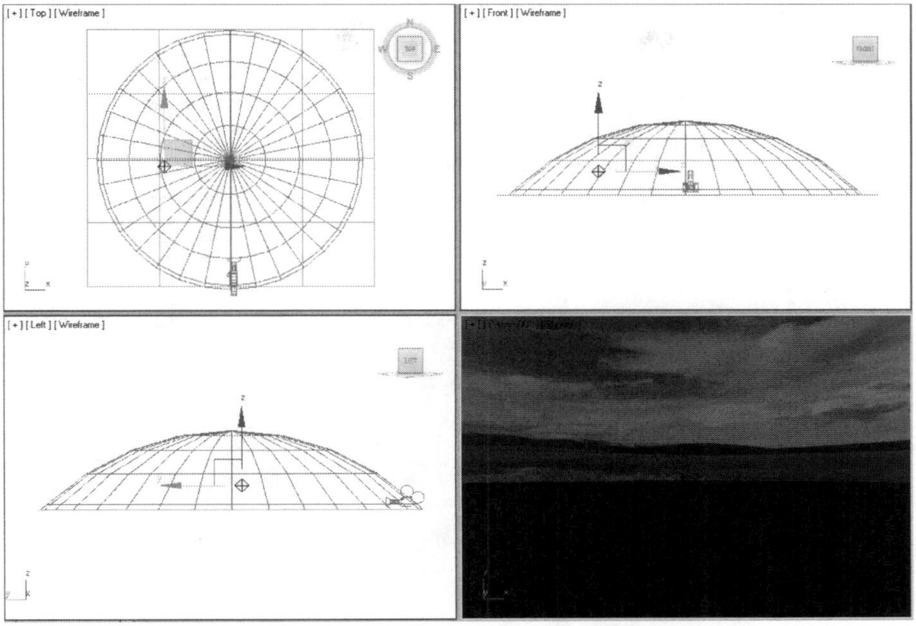

Figure 11-63 *Alignment of Omni001 in all viewports*

4. Next, create one more omni light at the center of the *background* in the Top viewport. It is automatically named as *Omni002*. Now, align *Omni002* in all viewports, as shown in Figure 11-64.

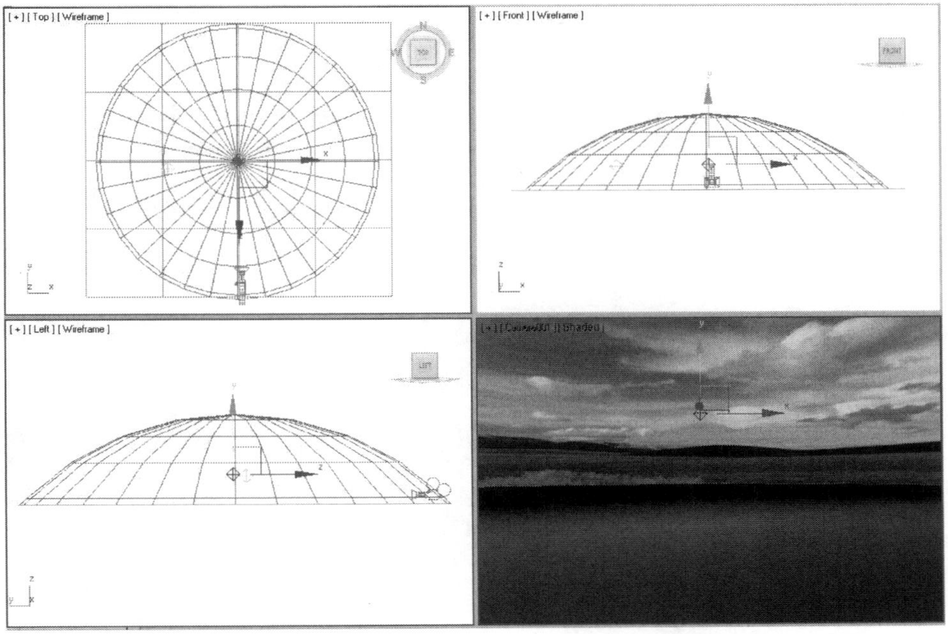

Figure 11-64 *Alignment of Omni002 in all viewports*

Next, you need to modify the *Omni002* light to create the sun effect.

5. Make sure that the *Omni002* light is selected and then choose the **Modify** tab in the **Command Panel**; the rollouts to modify the light are displayed in the modify panel.

6. Expand the **Atmospheres & Effects** rollout and choose the **Add** button; the **Add Atmosphere or Effect** dialog box is displayed. Select the **Lens Effects** option and choose the **OK** button; the **Lens Effects** option is displayed in the text area of the **Atmospheres & Effects** rollout.

Next, you need to modify the parameters of **Lens Effects**.

7. Select **Lens Effects** in the **Atmospheres & Effects** rollout and choose the **Setup** button; the **Environment and Effects** dialog box is displayed.

8. By default, the **Effects** tab is chosen in the **Environment and Effects** dialog box. In the **Effects** rollout, make sure that the **Lens Effects** option is selected in the **Effects** area.

9. In the **Lens Effects Parameters** rollout, select the **Glow** effect and choose the right arrow button; the **Glow** effect is displayed in the text area available on the right side, as shown in Figure 11-65. Also, the **Glow Element** rollout is displayed at the bottom of the **Environment and Effects** dialog box to modify the parameters of the **Glow** effect.

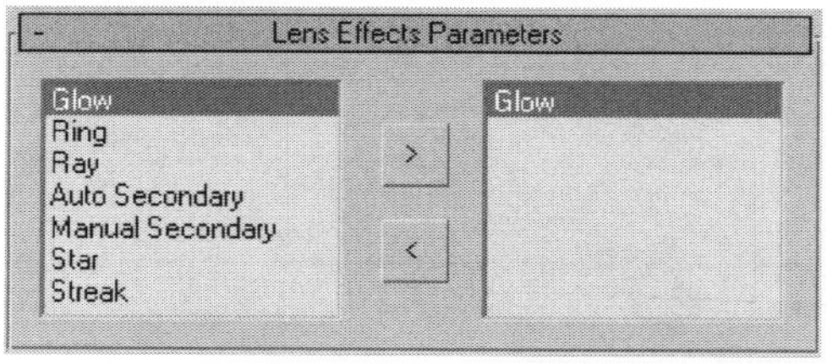

***Figure 11-65** The **Lens Effects Parameters** rollout*

Note

1. To view all rollouts, you need to scroll inside the dialog box.

*2. You can view the effects of the **Lens Effects** option only at rendering.*

10. In the **Glow Element** rollout, set the value **20.0** in the **Size** spinner. Use the default values for other options.

11. Next, in the **Lens Effects Parameters** rollout, select the **Ray** effect and choose the right arrow button; the **Ray** effect is displayed in the text area available on the right side. Also, the **Ray Element** rollout is displayed at the bottom of the **Environment and Effects** dialog box to modify the parameters of the **Ray** effect.

12. In the **Ray Element** rollout, set the values in the spinners as given below:

    Size: **50.0** Num: **20**
    Now, close the **Environment and Effects** dialog box.

Rendering the Scene for the Final Output

1. Activate the Camera001 viewport.

2. Invoke the **Render Production** tool in the **Main Toolbar**; the **Camera001, frame 0, Display Gamma 2.2, RGBA Color 16Bits/Channel (1:1)** dialog box is displayed showing the final output of the scene at one frame, as shown in Figure 11-66.

3. Close this dialog box.

   You can view the final rendered image of this model by downloading the *c11_3dsmax_2012_render.zip* file from *http://www.cadcim.com*.

Figure 11-66 *Final output at rendering*

Saving the File

1. Save the file with the name *c11tut1.max* as discussed in earlier chapters. The location of this file is given below:

   \Documents\3dsmax\c11_tut1\scenes\c11tut1.max

Tutorial 2

In this tutorial, you will create the lighting effect using the target direct light, as shown in Figure 11-67. **(Expected time: 30 min)**

Figure 11-67 *Model for Tutorial 2*

The following steps are required to complete this tutorial:

a. Set the project folder.
b. Create the floor of the room.
c. Create walls of the room.
d. Use the camera.
e. Create the roof of the room.
f. Create the window of the room.
g. Create the POP design of the room.
h. Apply maps and materials to objects.
i. Create lights.
j. Create the background.
k. Render the scene for the final output.
l. Save the file.

Setting the Project Folder

1. Set the project folder with the name *c11_tut1* in the *3dsmax* folder as discussed in earlier chapters.

Creating the Floor of the Room

To create the floor, first you need to create a plane.

1. Activate the Top viewport and choose **Create > Geometry** in the **Command Panel**; the **Standard Primitives** option is displayed in the drop-down list. Now, invoke the **Plane** tool from the **Object Type** rollout.

2. Create a plane in the Top viewport and set the values in the **Parameters** rollout as given below:

   Length: **867.0** Width: **600.0**

3. In the **Name and Color** rollout, modify the name of the plane to *floor*.

4. Invoke the **Zoom Extents All** tool to display the entire *floor* in all viewports.

Creating Walls of the Room

1. Activate the Top viewport. Choose **Create > Geometry** in the **Command Panel**; the **Standard Primitives** option is displayed by default in the drop-down list. Select the **AEC Extended** option from the list and invoke the **Wall** tool from the **Object Type** rollout.

2. In the **Parameters** rollout, set the values as given below:

   Width: **5.0** Height: **300.0**

3. In the Top viewport, create a closed wall as discussed earlier, as shown in Figure 11-68. It is automatically named as *wall001*. Invoke the **Zoom Extents All** tool.

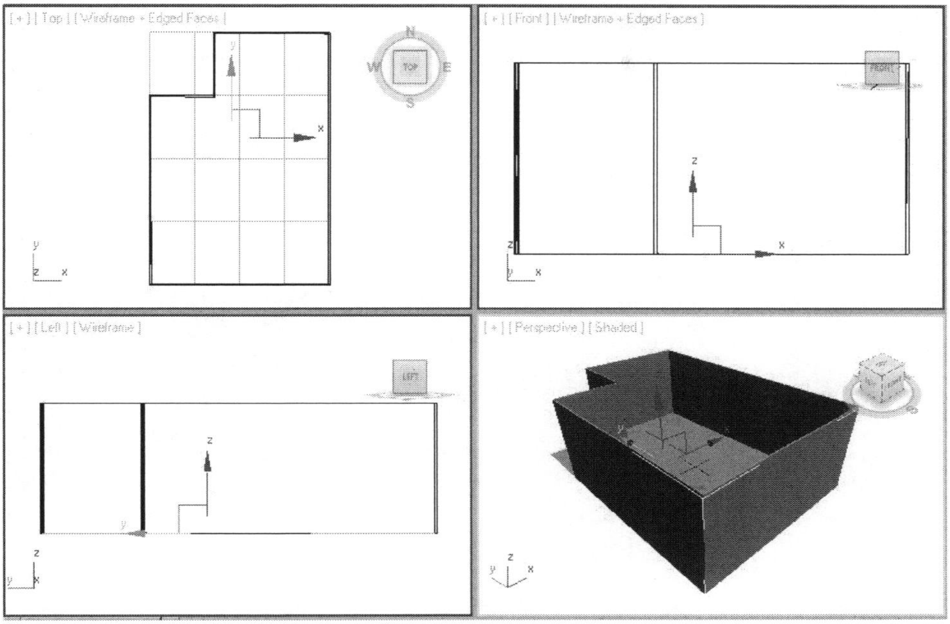

Figure 11-68 *The wall001 created in all viewports*

Using the Camera

You need to use the free camera to adjust the view.

1. Activate the Front viewport and choose **Create > Cameras** in the **Command Panel**; the **Standard** option is displayed in the drop-down list. Now, invoke the **Free** tool from the **Object Type** rollout.

2. Click at the middle point on the *wall001*; the free camera is displayed in all viewports. Now, right-click anywhere in the viewport to exit the command. The free camera is automatically named as *Camera001*.

3. Make sure that the *Camera001* is selected. Choose the **Modify** tab in the **Command Panel**. In the **Parameters** rollout, set the value **73.0** in the **FOV** spinner.

4. Next, activate the Perspective viewport and press the C key to view the Camera viewport; the Perspective label is replaced with the Camera001 label. Also, the view is changed based on the position of the camera. Invoke the **Select and Move** tool and align the *Camera001* in all viewports to display the proper view, refer to Figure 11-69.

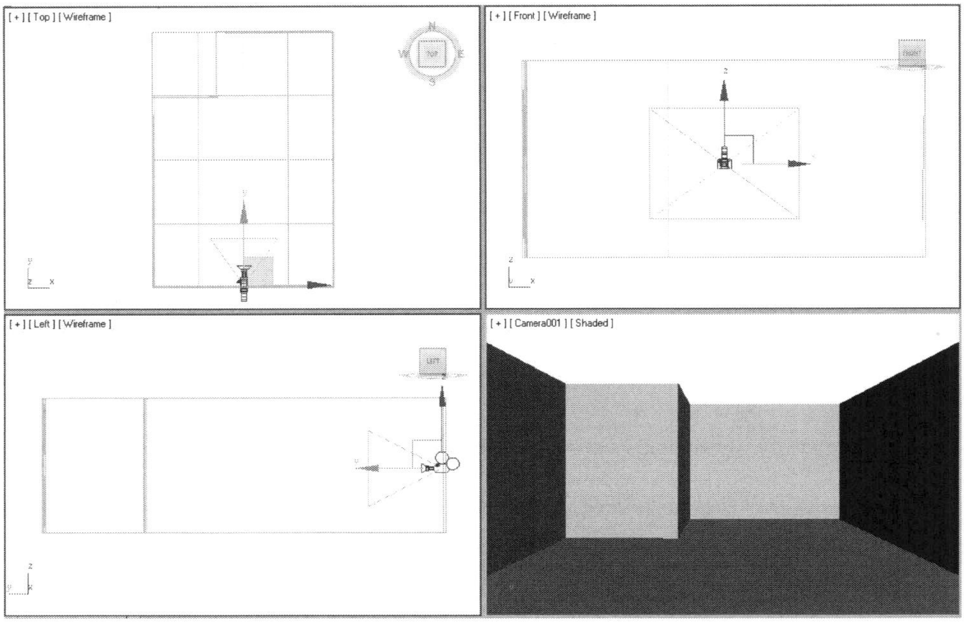

Figure 11-69 *Alignment of Camera001 in all viewports*

Creating the Roof of the Room

1. Activate the Top viewport and invoke the **Plane** tool from **Create > Geometry > Standard Primitives > Object Type** rollout.

2. Create a plane in the Top viewport and set the values in the **Parameters** rollout as given below:

   Length: **867.0** Width: **600.0**

3. In the **Name and Color** rollout, modify the name of the plane to *roof*.

4. Next, align the *roof* at the top of the *wall001* using the **Select and Move** tool, refer to Figure 11-70.

Creating the Window of the Room

First, you need to create a hole for the window in the *wall001*.

1. Create a box in the Top viewport and modify its dimensions in the **Parameters** rollout as given below:

   Length: **165.569** Width: **20.0** Height: **195.984**

2. Align the box with the *wall001* in all viewports, as shown in Figure 11-71.

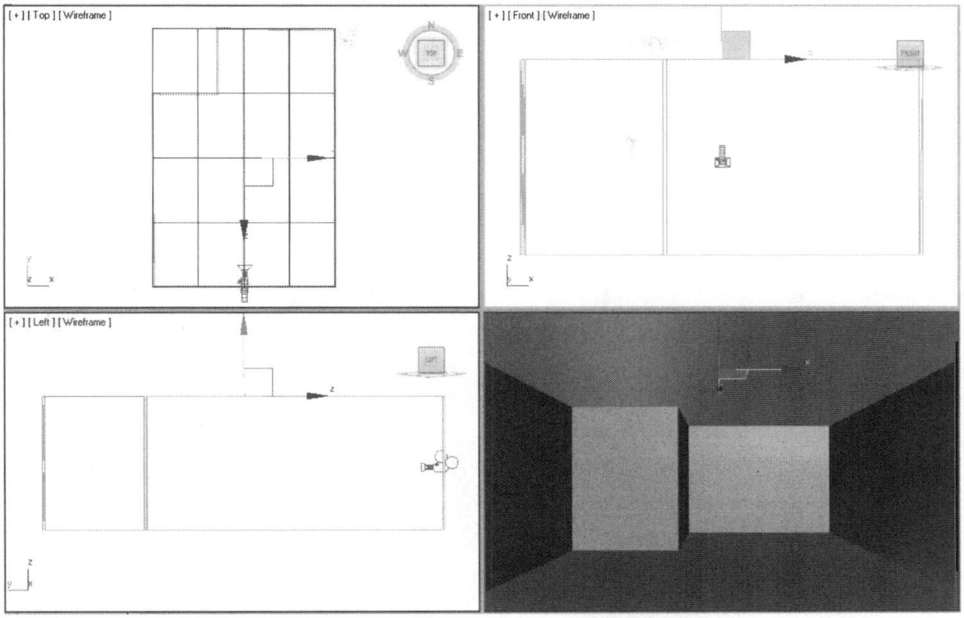

Figure 11-70 *The roof aligned at the top of the wall001 in all viewports*

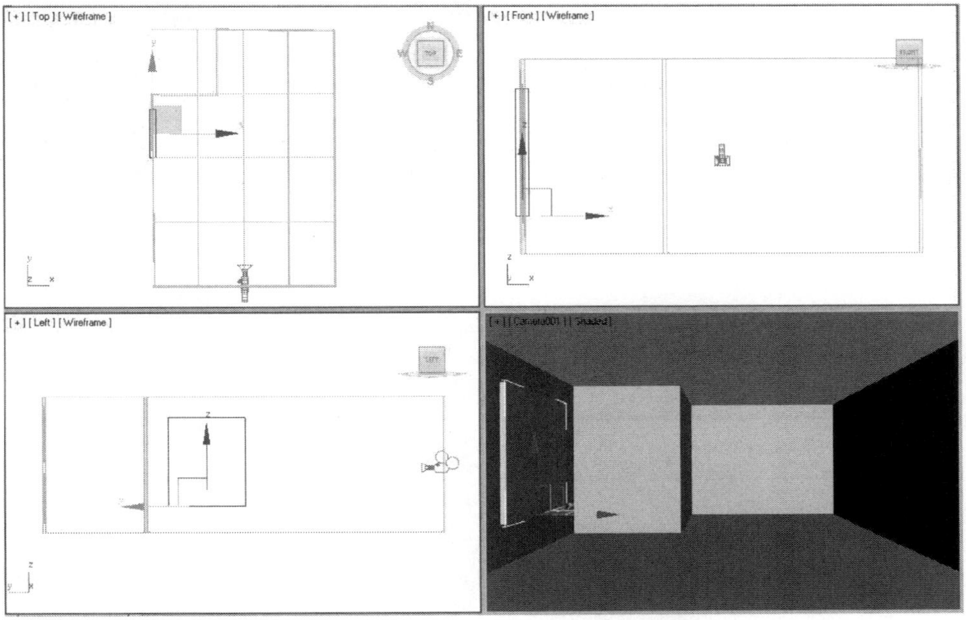

Figure 11-71 *Alignment of box in all viewports*

Next, you need to perform the boolean operation on the *wall001* to create a hole for the window.

3. Select the *wall001* in the Top viewport. Choose **Create > Geometry** in the **Command Panel**. Select the **Compound Objects** option from the drop-down list below the **Geometry** button. Now, invoke the **Boolean** tool from the **Object Type** rollout.

4. In the **Parameters** rollout, make sure that the **Subtraction(A-B)** radio button is selected in the **Operation** area.

5. Choose the **Pick Operand B** button in the **Pick Boolean** rollout, move the cursor over the box that you have created and then click on it; a hole is created in the *wall001*, as shown in Figure 11-72. Right-click in the viewport to exit the boolean command.

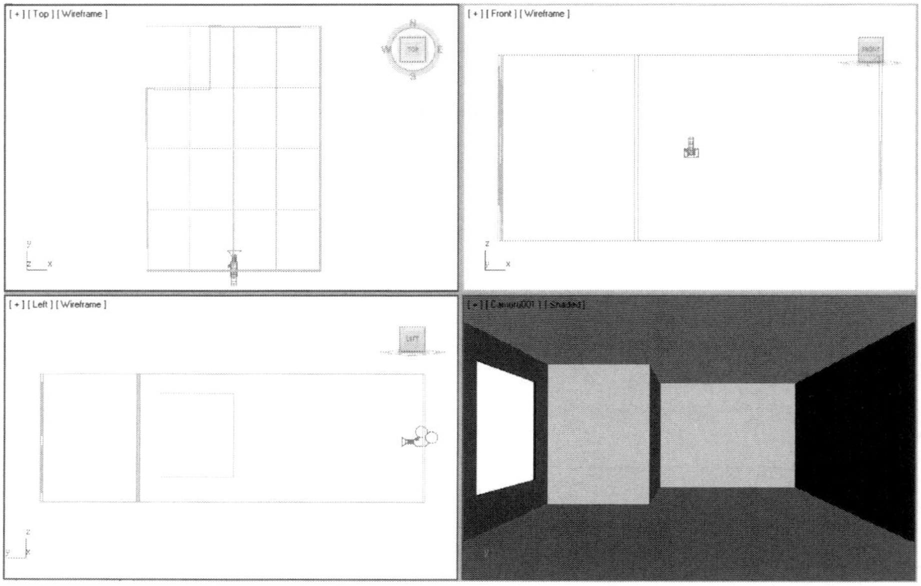

Figure 11-72 *A hole created in the wall001*

Next, you need to create another box to create a window.

6. Create another box in the Top viewport and modify its dimensions in the **Parameters** rollout as given next.

Length: **165.569**	Width: **2.0**	Height: **195.984**
Length Segs: **5**	Width Segs: **1**	Height Segs: **5**

7. Modify the name of the box to *window* and color to black. Also, align it in all viewports to cover the hole in the *wall001*, as shown in Figure 11-73.

Next, you need to apply the **Lattice** modifier to the *window*.

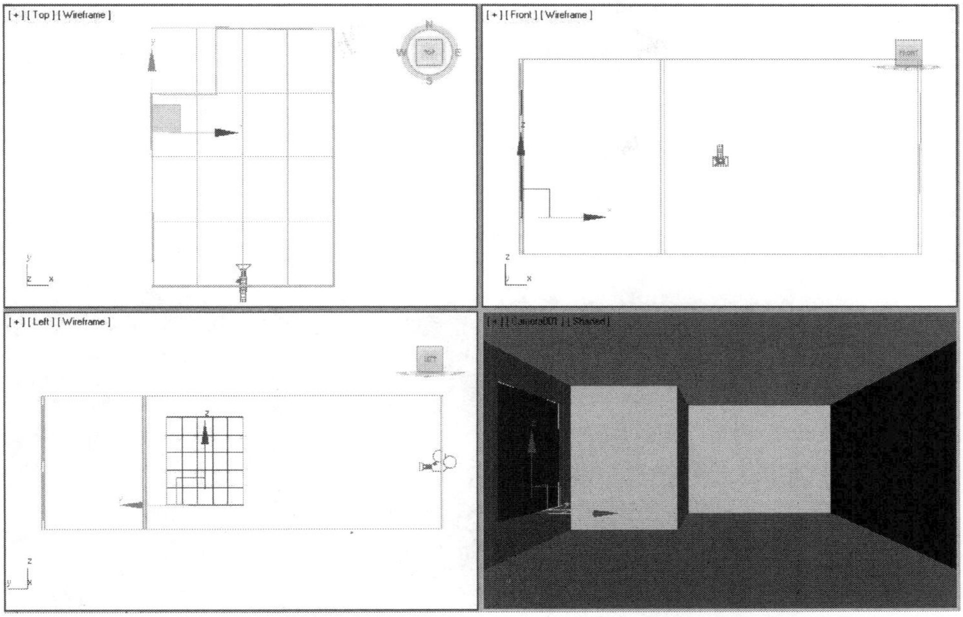

Figure 11-73 *Alignment of the window in all viewports*

8. Make sure that the *window* is selected and then choose the **Modify** tab in the **Command Panel**. Next, select the **Lattice** modifier from the **Modifier List** drop-down list; the segments and edges of the *window* are converted into wireframes.

9. In the **Parameters** rollout of the **Lattice** modifier, set the values as given below:

   Geometry area
   Select the **Struts Only from Edges** radio button.

   Struts area
   Radius: **1.0**
   Use the default values for other options.

   The *window* is displayed, as shown in Figure 11-74.

Creating the POP Design of the Room

1. Create a box in the Top viewport. In the **Parameters** rollout, set the values in the spinners as given below:

Length: **5.0**	Width: **210.581**	Height: **33.843**
Length Segs: **1**	Width Segs: **1**	Height Segs: **7**

2. Name the box as *design01*.

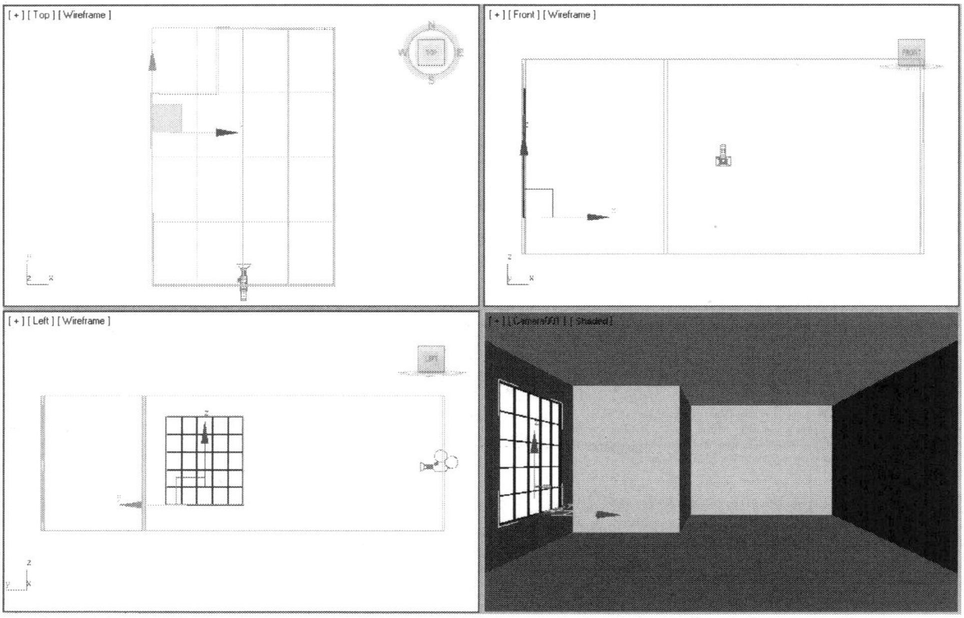

***Figure 11-74** The window after applying the **Lattice** modifier*

Next, you need to modify the *design01* at the sub-object level.

3. First, make sure that *design01* is selected and choose the **Display** tab in the **Command Panel**. In the **Hide** rollout, choose the **Hide Unselected** button; all unselected objects are hidden in the viewports.

4. Activate the Camera001 viewport and press the P key to display the Perspective viewport.

5. Next, invoke the **Zoom Extents All** tool to zoom in the *design01*.

6. Select the *design01* and convert it into an editable mesh object; the sub-object levels of the *design01* are displayed in the modifier stack.

7. In the Perspective viewport, press the F4 key to view the segments of the *design01*. Then, invoke the **Zoom** tool and zoom in the *design01* to its maximum extent, as shown in Figure 11-75.

8. Invoke the **Maximize Viewport Toggle** tool to maximize the Perspective viewport.

9. In the **Selection** rollout, choose the **Edge** button to activate the **Edge** sub-object level. Select the six inner edges of the *design01* by holding the CTRL key in the Perspective viewport, as shown in Figure 11-76.

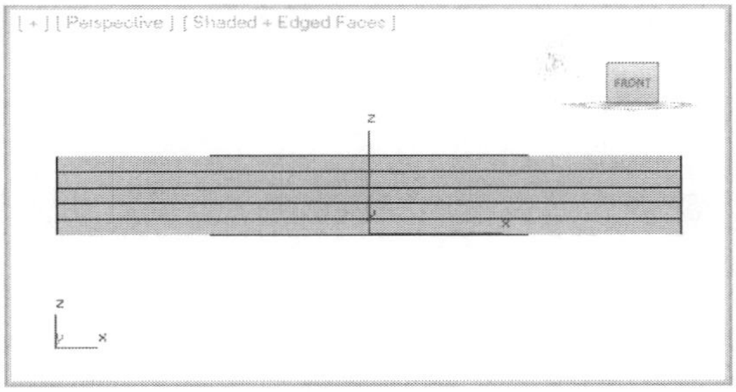

Figure 11-75 The design01 zoomed in to its extent in the Perspective viewport

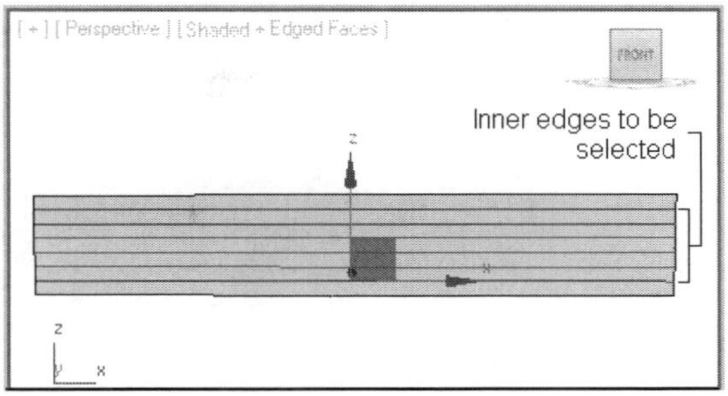

Figure 11-76 The inner edges selected in the design01

10. In the **Edit Geometry** rollout, enter the value **1** in the **Chamfer** spinner and press ENTER; the selected edges are chamfered, as shown in Figure 11-77.

11. In the **Selection** rollout, choose the **Polygon** button to activate the **Polygon** sub-object level. Select the polygon at the bottom of the *design01*, as shown in Figure 11-78. Then, in the **Edit Geometry** rollout, enter the value **2.0** in the **Extrude** spinner to extrude the selected polygon.

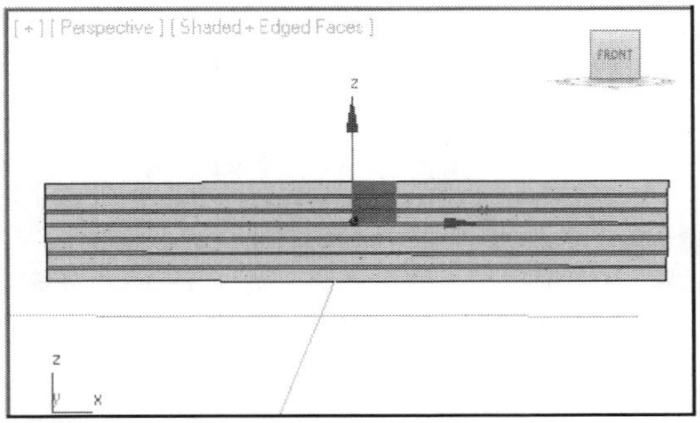

Figure 11-77 The selected edges after chamfering

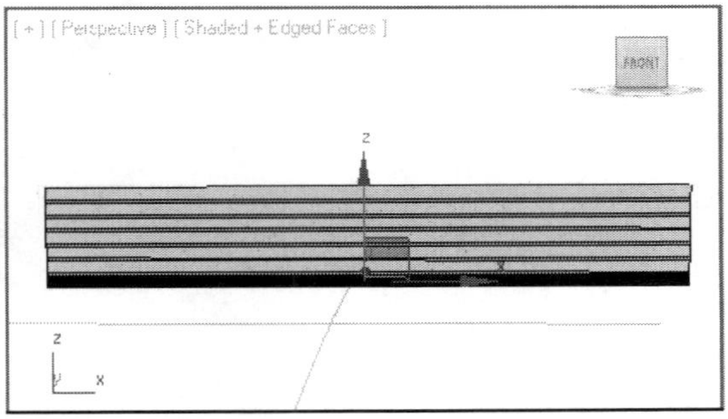

Figure 11-78 The polygon selected to be extruded

12. Select the alternate polygons one by one from the bottom and enter the values in multiples of 2 such as **4**, **6**, **8**, and so on in the respective **Extrude** spinners. Select the **Polygon** sub-object level in the **Selection** rollout to disable it.

13. Next, invoke the **Maximize Viewport Toggle** tool to view the four viewports; the *design01* is displayed in all viewports, as shown in Figure 11-79.

14. Choose the **Display** tab in the **Command Panel** and choose the **Unhide All** button in the **Hide** rollout; all objects are displayed in all viewports.

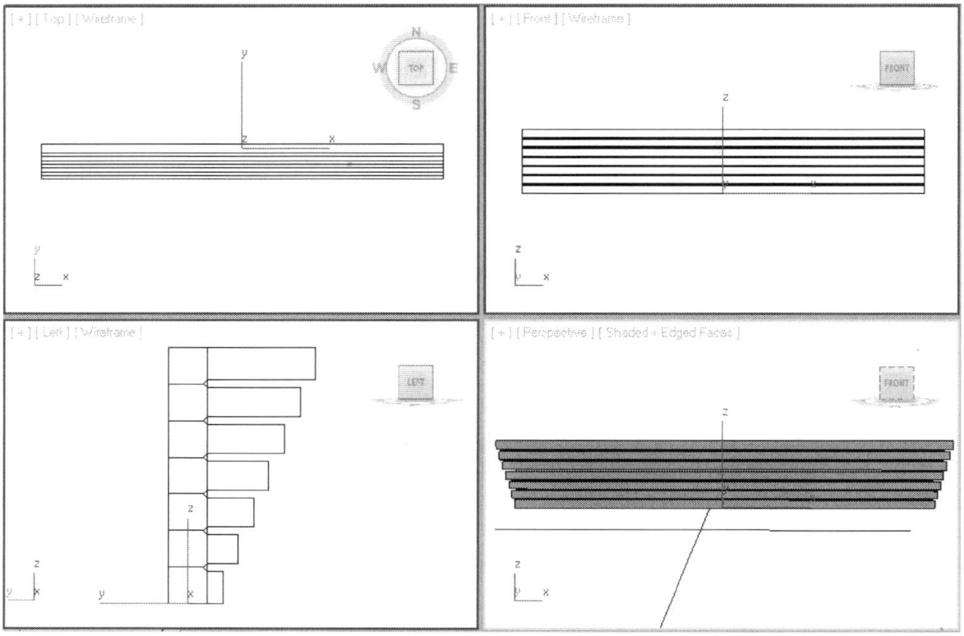

Figure 11-79 *The design01 displayed in all viewports after extruding the alternate polygons*

15. Activate the Perspective viewport and press the C key to view the Camera001 viewport. Also, press the F4 key. Now, invoke the **Zoom Extents All** tool to view all objects in all viewports.

16. Next, align *design01* to a portion of the *wall001* in all viewports, as shown in Figure 11-80. You can adjust the size of *design01* using the tools in the **Select and Scale** flyout in the **Main Toolbar**.

Note

To align the design01 properly, you can use the ***Zoom Extent All Selected*** *tool.*

17. Create five copies of *design01*; they are automatically named as *design002*, *design003*, *design004*, *design005*, and *design006*. Align all designs at the joining point of the *wall001* and *roof*, refer to Figure 11-78. You need to adjust the size of all designs using the **Select and Scale** tool accordingly. Also, you need to modify the corners at the **Vertex** sub-object level.

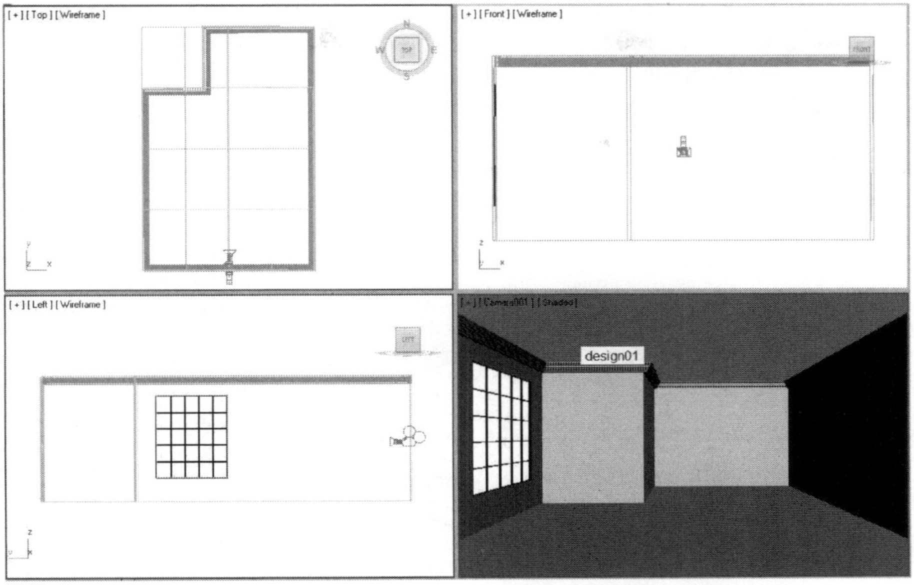

***Figure 11-80** Alignment of all designs in all viewports*

Applying Maps and Materials

You need to assign maps and materials to all objects.

1. Select the *wall001* in any viewport and press the M key to invoke the **Compact Material Editor** tool from the **Main Toolbar**; the **Material Editor** dialog box is displayed.

   Next, you need to create the material for the *wall001* in the **Material Editor** dialog box.

2. Select the **01-Default** sample slot, if it is not already selected, and then modify its name in the **Material Name** text box to **wall material**.

3. Choose the **Material Type** button that is currently labeled as **Standard**; the **Material/Map Browser** dialog box is displayed. Select the **Architectural** material from **Materials > Standard** rollouts and choose the **OK** button; the **Standard** material is replaced by the **Architectural** material now. Also, various rollouts are displayed in the **Material Editor** dialog box to modify the **Architectural** material.

4. In the **Templates** rollout, select the **Paint Semi-gloss** option from the drop-down list. In the **Physical Qualities** rollout, choose the **Diffuse Color** color swatch; the **Color Selector: Diffuse** dialog box is displayed. Set the values in the **Red**, **Green**, and **Blue** spinners as given below:

   Red: **251** Green: **239** Blue: **191**

   Now, choose the **OK** button.

5. Make sure that *wall001* is selected in the viewport and then choose the **Assign Material to Selection** button; the **wall material** is assigned to the *wall001*.

   Next, you need to create a material for the *floor*.

6. Select the **02-Default** sample slot and modify its name in the **Material Name** text box to **floor material**.

7. In the **Shader Basic Parameters** rollout, make sure that the **Blinn** shader is selected in the drop-down list.

   Next, you need to assign a map.

8. Navigate to the *c11_3dsmax_2012_tut* folder that you have downloaded from the CADCIM website in Tutorial 1. Next, copy the files *Concrete.jpg*, *Finishes.Masonry Flooring.jpg*, and *CLOUDS4.jpg* at the location *\Documents\3dsmax\c11_tut2\sceneassets\images*.

9. In the **Blinn Basic Parameters** rollout, choose the **Diffuse** map button on the right side of the **Diffuse** color swatch; the **Material/Map Browser** dialog box is displayed. Select the **Bitmap** map from **Maps > Standard** rollouts and choose the **OK** button; the **Select Bitmap Image File** dialog box is displayed. As the project folder is already set, the path *\Documents\3dsmax\c11_tut2\sceneassets\images* is displayed in the **Look in** text box of this dialog box. Select the file *Finishes.Masonry Flooring.jpg* and choose the **Open** button; the selected image is displayed in the selected sample slot. Also, the rollouts are displayed to modify the coordinates of the assigned map.

10. In the **Coordinates** rollout, set the value **4** in the **U Tiling** and **V Tiling** spinners. Next, choose the **Go to Parent** button to go back to the parent level.

11. Expand the **Maps** rollout and then select the **Reflection** check box to make it available for the material. Choose the **Reflection** map button labeled as **None**; the **Material/Map Browser** dialog box is displayed. Select the **Raytrace** map from the **Maps > Standard** rollouts and choose the **OK** button; the **Raytrace** map is displayed as the sub-material. Use the default settings for the options and choose the **Go to Parent** button to go back to the parent level; the **None** label is replaced by **Map#1 (Raytrace)**. Next, set the value **5** in the **Reflection** spinner.

12. Select the *floor* in the viewport and then choose the **Assign Material to Selection** button; the **floor material** is assigned to the *floor*. Choose the **Show Shaded Material in Viewport** button to display the **floor material** on the *floor* in the viewport.

    Next, you will assign a material to the *roof*.

13. Select the **03-Default** sample slot and modify its name in the **Material Name** text box as **roof material**.

14. In the **Shader Basic Parameters** rollout, select the **2-Sided** check box.

Next, you need to assign a map to the selected sample slot.

15. In the **Blinn Basic Parameters** rollout, choose the **Diffuse** map button on the right side of the **Diffuse** color swatch; the **Material/Map Browser** dialog box is displayed. Select the **Bitmap** map and choose the **OK** button; the **Select Bitmap Image File** dialog box is displayed. Select the file *Concrete.jpg* and choose the **Open** button; the selected image is displayed in the selected sample slot. Also, the rollouts are displayed to modify the coordinates of the assigned map.

16. In the **Coordinates** rollout, set the value **2** in the **U Tiling** and **V Tiling** spinners. Next, choose the **Go to Parent** button to go back to the parent level.

17. Make sure that the *roof* is selected in the viewport and then choose the **Assign Material to Selection** button; the **roof material** is assigned to the *roof* in the viewport. Choose the **Show Shaded Material in Viewport** button to display the **roof material** on the *roof* in the viewport.

Next, you will assign the material to the POP designs.

18. First, select all designs simultaneously in the viewport using the **Select by Name** tool, and then group them as *design*.

19. Select the **04-Default** sample slot in the **Material Editor** dialog box and modify its name in the **Material Name** text box to **design material**.

20. In the **Blinn Basic Parameters** rollout, choose the **Diffuse** color swatch; the **Color Selector: Diffuse Color** dialog box is displayed. Enter the values in the **Red**, **Green**, and **Blue** spinners as given below and then choose the **OK** button.

    Red: **146** Green: **68** Blue: **5**

21. Make sure that the group *design* is selected in the viewport and then choose the **Assign Material to Selection** button; the **design material** is assigned to the *design*. Also, choose the **Show Shaded Material in Viewport** button to display the **design material** on the *design* in the viewport.

22. Close the **Material Editor** dialog box.

To view all objects properly, you need to create lights in the viewport.

Creating Lights

1. Activate the Top viewport. Choose **Create > Lights** in the **Command Panel** and choose the **Standard** option from the drop-down list. Next, invoke the **Omni** tool from the **Object Type** rollout. Next, click in the Top viewport; the omni light is displayed in the viewport and it is automatically named as *Omni001*.

2. Align the *Omni001* in all viewports, as shown in Figure 11-81.

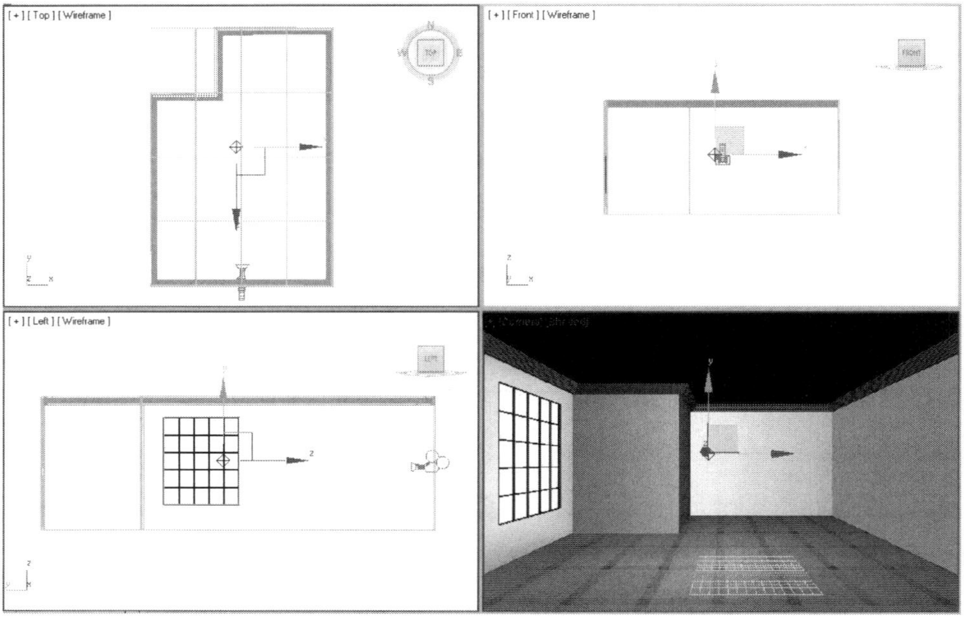

Figure 11-81 *The Omni001 light in all viewports*

Next, you need to create the target direct light in the scene to give the shadow effect.

3. Activate the Front viewport, invoke the **Zoom** tool, and zoom out until the objects are displayed about half of their original size.

4. Invoke the **Target Direct** tool from **Create > Lights > Standard > Object Type** rollout in the **Command Panel**. Move the cursor on the left side of the Front viewport; the cursor gets changed. Next, press and hold the left mouse button to specify the location of the light and drag the cursor near the front portion of the *wall001* to locate the target of the light. Release the left mouse button; the light is displayed in all viewports and it is automatically named as *Direct001*.

5. Choose the **Modify** tab in the **Command Panel**; various rollouts are displayed to modify the target direct light.

6. In the **General Parameters** rollout, select the **On** check box in the **Shadows** area.

7. In the **Directional Parameters** rollout, select the **Rectangle** radio button and set the values in the respective spinners as given below:

Hotspot/Beam: **84.0** Falloff/Field: **86.0**

8. In the **Atmospheres & Effects** rollout, choose the **Add** button; the **Add Atmosphere or Effect** dialog box is displayed. Select the **Volume Light** option and choose the **OK** button; the **Volume Light** option is displayed in the text area of the **Atmospheres & Effects** rollout.

   Next, you need to modify the parameters of the **Volume Light**.

9. Select the **Volume Light** option in the **Atmospheres & Effects** rollout and choose the **Setup** button; the **Environment and Effects** dialog box is displayed.

10. The **Environment** tab is chosen by default in the **Environment and Effects** dialog box. In the **Atmosphere** rollout, make sure that the **Volume Light** option is selected in the **Effects** area.

11. In the **Volume Light Parameters** rollout, set the value **1.5** in the **Density** spinner of the **Volume** area. Use the default values for other options and close the **Environment and Effects** dialog box.

Note

You can also use different settings in the ***Volume Light Parameters*** *rollout to give different effects in the scene.*

12. Align the *Direct001* light in all viewports to cover the window, as shown in Figure 11-82.

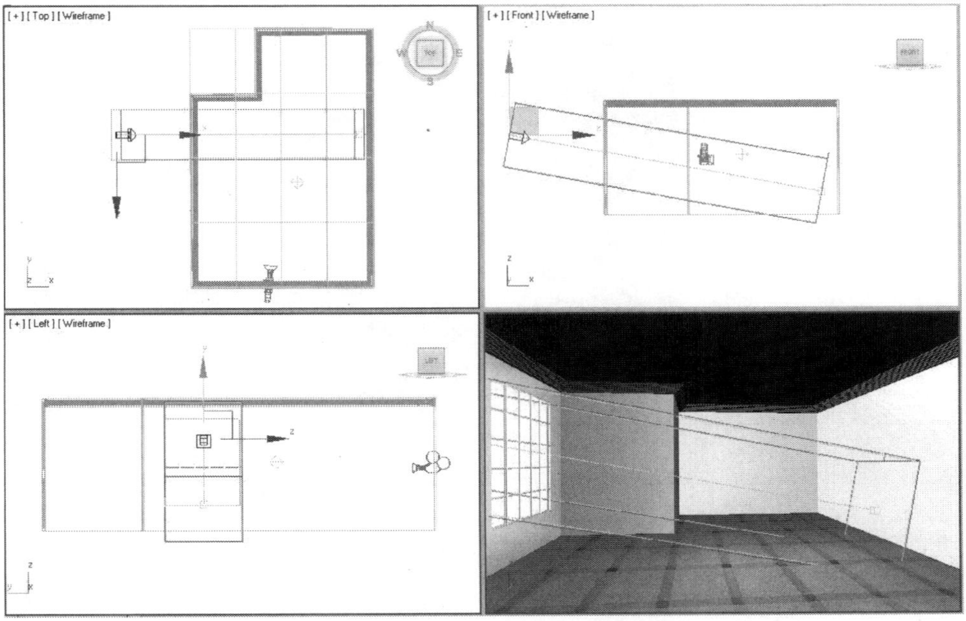

Figure 11-82 *Alignment of the Direct001 light in all viewports*

Note

You can adjust the position of the Camera001 to view the scene with desired light effects.

Creating the Background

1. To create the background, choose **Rendering > Environment** from the menu bar; the **Environment and Effects** dialog box is displayed.

2. The **Environment** tab is chosen by default in the **Environment and Effects** dialog box. In the **Background** area of the **Common Parameters** rollout, choose the **Environment Map** button that is currently labeled as **None**; the **Material/Map Browser** dialog box is displayed.

3. Select the **Bitmap** map and choose the **OK** button; the **Select Bitmap Image File** dialog box is displayed. As the project folder is already set, the path *\Documents\3dsmax\c11_tut2\sceneassets\images* is displayed in the **Look in** text box of this dialog box. Select the file *CLOUDS4.jpg* image and choose the **Open** button; the selected image is displayed in the background at rendering. Close the **Environment and Effects** dialog box.

Rendering the Scene for the Final Output

1. Activate the Camera001 viewport.

2. Invoke the **Render Production** tool in the **Main Toolbar**; the **Camera001, frame 0, Display Gamma 2.2, RGBA Color 16Bits/Channel (1:1)** dialog box is displayed, showing the final output of the scene at one frame, as shown in Figure 11-83.

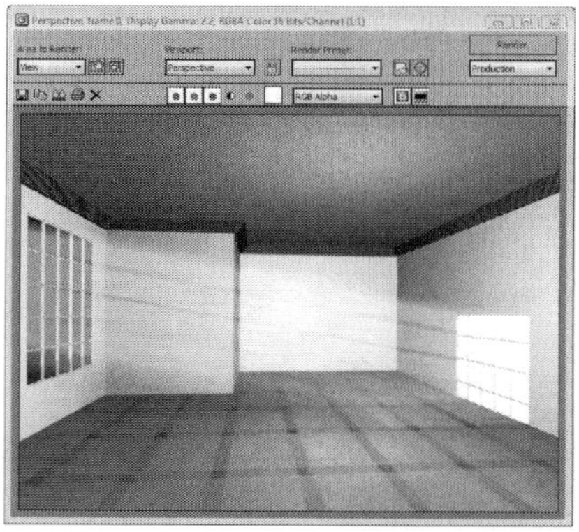

Figure 11-83 *The final output after rendering*

3. Close this dialog box.

You can view the final rendered image of this model by downloading the *c11_3dsmax_2012_render.zip* file from *http://www.cadcim.com*.

Saving the File

1. Save the file with the name *c11tut2.max* as discussed in earlier chapters. The location of this file is given below:

   \Documents\3dsmax\c11_tut2\scenes

Self-Evaluation Test

Answer the following questions and then compare them to those given at the end of this chapter:

1. Which of the following tools is used to create the photometric lights?

   (a) **Target Light** (b) **Free Light**
   (c) **mr Sky Portal** (d) All of these

2. Which of the following spinners is used to define the intensity of the light in the **Intensity/Color/Attenuation** rollout?

   (a) **Color Amount** (b) **Start**
   (c) **Multiplier** (d) None of these

3. Which of the following tools is used to create the area omni light?

   (a) **Target spot** (b) **mr Area Omni**
   (c) **Free Direct** (d) None of these

4. **Target Spot** is the only tool used to create a spot light. (T/F)

5. The standard lights use the light energy values to create the realistic scenes. (T/F)

6. The **Exclude** button is used to define a number of objects in the scene that will be affected by the light at rendering. (T/F)

7. Attenuation is the effect of the light intensity that decreases with the distance. (T/F)

8. To assign the special effects to the environment such as fog and glow at rendering, you need to use the __________ rollout in the **Modify** tab of the **Command Panel**.

9. To view the shadow of an object, you need to select the __________ check box in the __________ area of the **General Parameters** rollout.

10. The options in the __________ rollout are used to control the properties of the shadow.

Review Questions

Answer the following questions:

1. Which of the following tools is used to align the light to an object for positioning its reflection accurately?

   (a) **Place Highlight** (b) **Align**
   (c) **Align Camera** (d) None of these

2. Which of the following rollouts is not used with the photometric lights?

   (a) **Intensity/Color/Attenuation** (b) **Intensity/Color/Distribution**
   (c) **Shadow Parameters** (d) **Atmospheres & Effects**

3. Which of the following is a type of camera used in Autodesk 3ds Max?

   (a) Target camera (b) Free camera
   (c) Both of the above (d) None of the above

4. In the **Name and Color** rollout of the lights, you can use the color swatch to modify the color of the light that is emitted from it. (T/F)

5. The distance between the camera lens and its focus is called the focal length of the lens. (T/F)

6. You can view the special effects of the lights in the viewport as well as at rendering using the **Atmospheres & Effects** rollout . (T/F)

7. In the **Parameters** rollout of the target camera, set the value in the __________ spinner to specify the field of view for the camera in degrees.

8. To display the camera view in the viewport, you need to press the __________ key.

9. The __________ tool in the **Main Toolbar** is used to align a camera to a selected face normal of an object.

Exercises

Exercise 1

Start Autodesk 3ds Max 2012 and then perform the following operations:

Create a scene in the viewport, as shown in Figure 11-84. Choose **Create > Lights** in the **Command Panel**; the **Standard** option is displayed in the drop-down list. Now, invoke the **Omni** tool from the **Object Type** rollout. Click in the Top viewport; the **Omni** light is displayed. Align the omni light at the top in the Left viewport and then try the following operations:

Figure 11-84 *Model for Exercise 1*

1. Choose the **Modify** tab in the **Command Panel**. In the **General Parameters** rollout, select the **On** check box in the **Shadows** area and view the effect at rendering.

2. In the **Intensity/Color/Attenuation** rollout, set different values in the **Multiple** spinner, modify the color in the color swatch and notice the effect of light at rendering.

3. In the **Projector Map** area of the **Advance Effects** rollout, select the **Map** check box and assign a map by choosing the **Map** button. Then, notice the effect at rendering.

4. In the **Atmospheres & Effects** rollout, add the **Glow** effect by choosing the **Add** button, and notice the effect at rendering.

5. Delete the omni light and create a target spot light in the Front viewport by invoking the **Target Spot** tool and notice the difference.

6. Create different types of Standard and Photometric lights and notice the difference.

Exercise 2

Create a scene using the standard primitives and target spot lights, as shown in Figure 11-85. You can view the final rendered image of this model by downloading it from *http://www.cadcim.com*. **(Expected time: 15 min)**

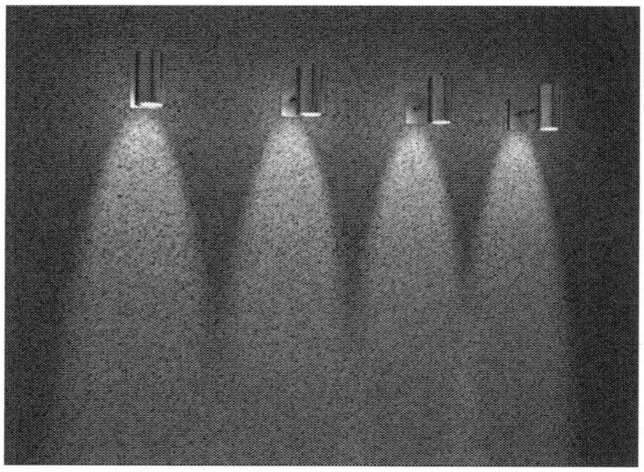

Figure 11-85 *Model for Exercise 2*

Exercise 3

Create a scene using the standard primitives and target spot lights, as shown in Figure 11-86. You can view the final rendered image of this model by downloading it from *http://www.cadcim.com*. **(Expected time: 30 min)**

Hints:

1. Create the hollow effect on the roof using the **ProBoolean** compound object and use the **Free Point** photometric light.

2. Create a **Target Spot** standard light for highlighting the object. You need to add the **Volume** effect using the **Atmospheres & Effects** rollout for the projector effect. Also, apply the projector map using the **Advanced Effects** rollout to get a realistic effect.

Figure 11-86 *Model for Exercise 3*

Exercise 4

Create a scene using the standard primitives and target spot lights, as shown in Figure 11-87. **(Expected time: 15 min)**

Hint:

1. Create three target spot lights and adjust their positions in all viewports. Choose separate colors for all three lights using the color swatch in the **Intensity/Color/Attenuation** rollout.

Figure 11-87 *Model for Exercise 4*

Answers to Self-Evaluation Test

1. d, **2.** c, **3.** b, **4.** F, **5.** F, **6.** T, **7.** T, **8. Atmospheres & Effects**, **9. On**, **Shadows**, **10. Shadow Parameters**

12

Animation Basics

Learning Objectives

After completing this chapter, you will be able to:

- *Use time slider*
- *Use animation playback controls*
- *Use animation and time controls*
- *Use Morph compound object*
- *Render and preview an animation*
- *Understand rendering effects*

INTRODUCTION TO ANIMATION

In Autodesk 3ds Max, you can create almost every type of animation. You can create character animation and animation based on different types of motions that you see in real life. You can also create special lighting effects in your scene by animating lights and cameras.

The basic concept of computer animation is to define different positions, rotations, and scale of an object at different key points in a sequence in the time slider. These defined points are known as keyframes. The interpolation between the keyframes consists of the information of the actions performed between those keyframes. When you play the animation, the computer plays a series of frames quickly and the object seems to be moving. In Autodesk 3ds Max, the standard frame rate is 30 frames per second. It means, if you want to create an animation for one minute, then you need to adjust about 1,800 frames. Therefore, before starting an animation, you need to calculate the frames according to the time limit.

TIME SLIDER AND ANIMATION PLAYBACK CONTROLS

Autodesk 3ds Max provides various options to animate the objects that you create in it. To do so, you need to be familiar with the animation playback controls and time slider. These controls enable you to play, pause, and stop an animation. They are available at the lower right corner of the Autodesk 3ds Max screen and are discussed briefly here.

Time Slider

The time slider displays the current frame and the total number of frames in the current time segment, refer to Figure 12-1. You can view the animation at each frame by dragging the time slider.

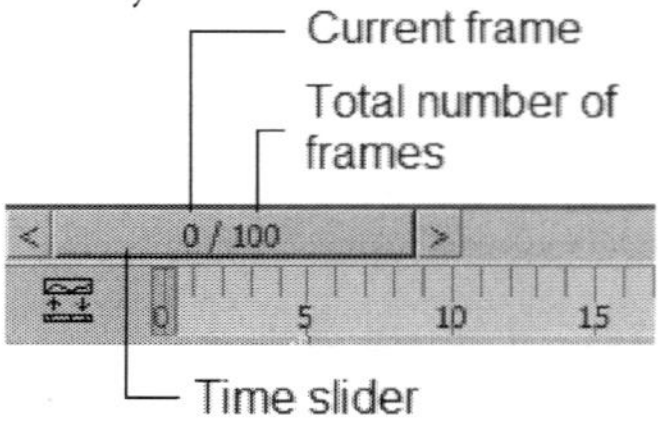

Figure 12-1 *The time slider*

Note

The time segment is the total range of frames that you can access using the time slider. By default, it ranges from 0 to 100. You can set the range using the ***Time Configuration*** *dialog box. You will learn about this dialog box in the later section.*

Animation Playback Controls

The animation playback controls are used to play and stop the animation in the active viewport. These controls are discussed next.

The **Play Animation** button is used to play or start the animation in the active viewport. When you click on the **Play Animation** button, it turns into a stop button.

The **Stop animation** button is used to stop the animation.

The **Go to Start** button is used to set the time slider at the first frame of the active time segment.

The **Go to End** button is used to set the time slider at the last frame of the active time segment.

The **Previous Frame** button is used to move the time slider one frame at a time in the reverse direction. You can view the current frame on the time slider when it moves from one frame to another.

The **Next Frame** button is used to move the time slider one frame at a time in the forward direction.

UNDERSTANDING ANIMATION AND TIME CONTROLS

In Autodesk 3ds Max, different types of tools are available at the bottom of the screen to control animation and its time settings, refer to Figure 12-2. You have already learned about the time slider and the animation playback controls in the previous section. The other controls are discussed next.

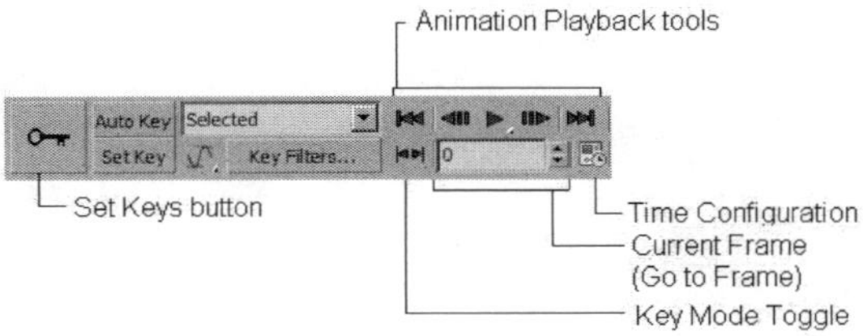

***Figure 12-2** The time control tools*

Toggle Auto Key Mode

The **Toggle Auto Key Mode** button that is labeled as **Auto Key** is chosen to turn on the auto key animation mode. When you choose the **Toggle Auto Key Mode** button, it turns red. Also, the background of the time slider and the border of the active viewport turn red, indicating that you are in the animation mode. Now, if you make any changes in the object, the changes will be keyframed in the time slider.

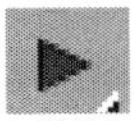

To perform an animation using the **Toggle Auto Key Mode** button, first you need to make sure that the object is selected in the viewport in which you want to create the animation. Choose the **Go to Start** button to set the time slider to the first frame. Next, choose the **Toggle Auto Key Mode** button to turn on the auto key animation mode; it will turn red. Now, drag the time slider to a frame other than 0 and animate the selected object by modifying its parameters or by transforming the object; a keyframe will be created on that frame and at frame 0 on the track bar below the time slider. Again, move the time slider to another frame and change the parameters. You can continue this process until you get all the keyframes in a sequential order for your animation. Next, choose the **Toggle Auto Key Mode** button again to turn it off. Choose the **Play Animation** button to view the animation of the selected object in the current viewport.

Toggle Set Key Mode

The **Toggle Set Key Mode** button that is labeled as **Set Key** is chosen to turn on the set key animation mode. In this mode, you need to set keys for the animation of the selected object by choosing the **Set Keys** button on the left side of the **Toggle Set Key Mode** button.

To perform the animation using the **Toggle Set Key Mode** button, select the object in the viewport in which you want to create the animation. Choose the **Go to Start** button to set the time slider to the first frame. Next, choose the **Toggle Set Key Mode** button to turn on the set key animation mode; the button will turn red. Choose the **Set Keys** button; it will flash in red color and a keyframe will be set for the current position of the selected object. Now, drag the time slider to set a frame other than 0 and animate the selected object. Again, choose the **Set Keys** button; it will flash in red color and another keyframe will be set on the track bar for the changed position. You can continue this process until you get all the keyframes in a sequential order for your animation. Then, choose the **Toggle Set Key Mode** button to turn it off. Also, choose the **Play Animation** button to view the animation of the selected object in the current viewport.

Note

If you transform an object when the ***Toggle Set Key Mode*** *button is chosen, then keyframe will be set only when you choose the* ***Set Keys*** *button.*

Current Frame (Go To Frame)

The value in this spinner shows the current frame number at which the time slider is positioned. While animating your scene, if you want to go to another frame, you can enter the frame number directly in the **Current Frame (Go To Frame)** spinner. As you drag the time slider, the value in the **Current Frame (Go To Frame)** spinner gets changed automatically according to its position.

Key Mode Toggle

By default, the **Key Mode Toggle** button is not activated. If activated, it allows you to jump between the keyframes directly. To understand the function of this button, you need to select the animated object in the viewport. Next, choose the **Key Mode Toggle** button; it will turn blue and the **Previous Frame** and **Next Frame** buttons in the animation playback controls will be replaced with the **Previous Key** and **Next Key** buttons, refer to Figures 12-3 and 12-4. Choose the **Previous Key** or **Next Key** button to move the time slider from one keyframe to the other.

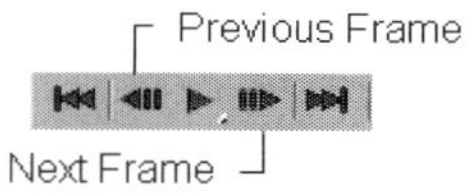

Figure 12-3 *Animation playback controls before choosing the* ***Key Mode Toggle*** *button*

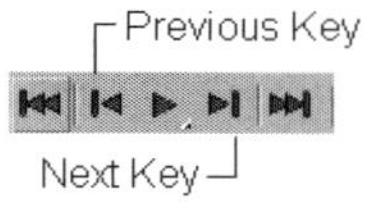

Figure 12-4 *Animation playback controls after choosing the* ***Key Mode Toggle*** *button*

Time Configuration

The **Time Configuration** button is used to set the length of an animation by defining the number of frames in the track bar. It is also used to set the frame rate, time display, and so on. To set these parameters, choose the **Time Configuration** button; the **Time Configuration** dialog box will be displayed, as shown in Figure 12-5. You need to use the options in this dialog box to set the animation length, frame rate, and time display. The options in this dialog box are discussed next.

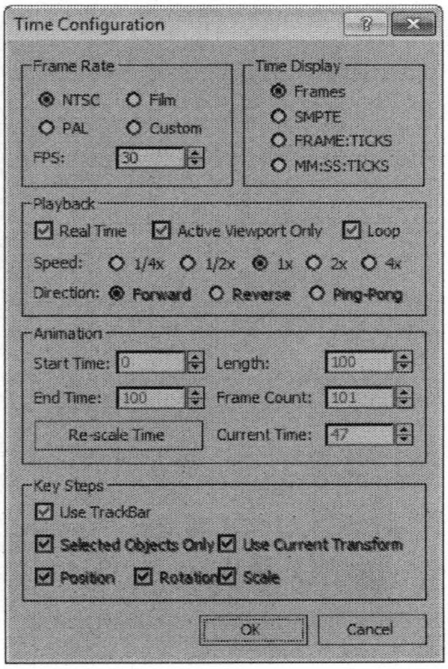

Figure 12-5 *The* ***Time Configuration*** *dialog box*

Frame Rate Area

The radio buttons in this area are used to define a particular frame rate for the animation in frames per second. By default, the **NTSC** radio button is selected.

Time Display Area

The radio buttons in this area are used to define the method of time displayed in the time slider.

Playback Area

By default, the **Real Time** check box is selected in this area. It is used to skip the frames so that the animation synchronizes with the current frame rate settings. You can select one of the radio buttons such as **1/4x**, **1/2x**, and so on in the **Speed** group to define the speed of the animation. If you clear the **Real Time** check box, then the **Speed** group will be deactivated and the **Direction** group will be activated. The radio buttons in the **Direction** group are used to define the direction of the animation. The **Active Viewport Only** check box is selected by default and is used to play the animation only in the active viewport. If you clear this check box, then the animation will be played in all viewports simultaneously. The **Loop** check box is also selected by default and is used to play the animation repeatedly.

Animation Area

The options in this area are used to set the length of animation. The default values in the spinners of this area specify the number of frames for the animation. Set the values in the **Start Time** and **End Time** spinners to specify the current time segment in the time slider. The current time segment is the total range of frames that you can access using the time slider. Set the value in the **Length** spinner to specify the total number of frames in the current time segment or the length of the animation. The value in the **Frame Count** spinner specifies the number of frames that will be rendered. The value in the **Current Time** spinner specifies the current frame number at which the time slider is positioned. Choose the **Re-scale Time** button; the **Re-scale Time** dialog box will be displayed. You can specify the options in this dialog box to change the existing time segment to a new time segment.

Track Bar

The track bar lies between the time slider and the status bar. It shows a timeline with the frame numbers in it, as shown in Figure 12-6.

Figure 12-6 *Partial view of the track bar*

Track View

Menu bar:	Graph Editors > Track View - Curve Editor Graph Editors > Track View - Dope Sheet
Main Toolbar:	Curve Editor (Open)

The track view is used to control the animation keys in the animation created by you. You can also insert sound in the scene and create notes about it. The track view uses two different modes, **Curve Editor** and **Dope Sheet**. In the **Curve Editor** mode, the animation is displayed as the function curves on a graph, as shown in Figure 12-7. In the **Dope Sheet** mode, the animation is displayed as a spreadsheet of keys, as shown in Figure 12-8.

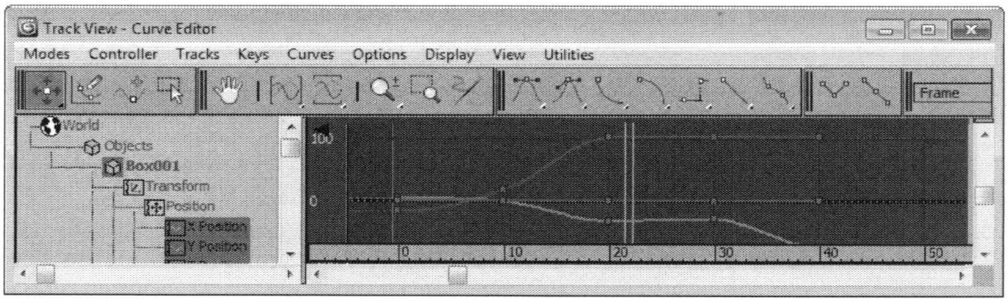

Figure 12-7 *The **Track View - Curve Editor** dialog box*

To edit the animation of an object using **Curve Editor**, select the animated object and invoke the **Curve Editor (Open)** tool from the **Main Toolbar**; the **Track View - Curve Editor** dialog box will be displayed, refer to Figure 12-7. The pull-down menus on the top of this dialog box are used to choose different options to edit the animation. The hierarchy on the left side of this dialog box is used to display all objects of the scene. To view the sub-options in this tree, you need to click on the plus sign (+). The edit window on the right of the hierarchy tree is used to edit the animation of the objects using the tangent handles available on the keys found on the curves.

Tip: *You can also invoke **Track View - Curve Editor** in place of the track bar. To do so, choose the **Open Mini Curve Editor** button on the left side of the track bar.*

To edit the animation of an object using **Dope Sheet**, select the animated object and choose **Graph Editors > Track View - Dope Sheet** from the menu bar; the **Track View - Dope Sheet** dialog box will be displayed, refer to Figure 12-8. In this dialog box, you can view all the keys in a spreadsheet format. You need to select the keys and edit them according to the animation.

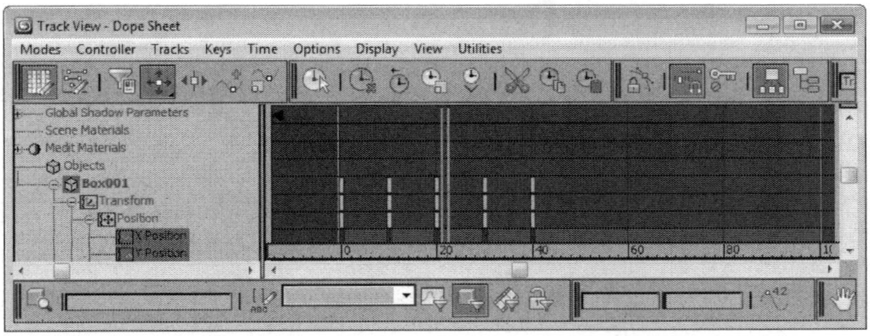

Figure 12-8 The **Track View - Dope Sheet** dialog box

MORPH COMPOUND OBJECT

Menu bar: Create > Compound > Morph
Main Toolbar: Create > Geometry > Compound Objects > Object Type rollout > Morph

The morph compound object is used to create morphing in the objects. The morphing is an animation technique, in which the morph object combines two or more objects by matching their vertices in a sequential form to produce the animation result. The original object is known as the base object and the other object into which the base object gets morphed is known as the target object. Note that to perform morphing, the base and target objects must be mesh, patch, or poly objects and they should have the same number of vertices.

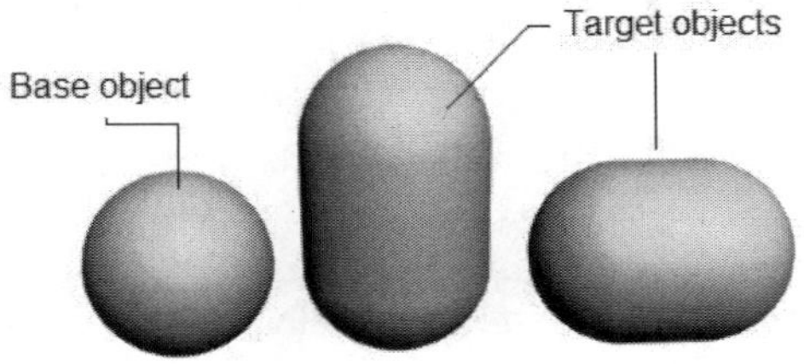

Figure 12-9 The base and target objects for morphing

To create a morph object, first create an object and convert it into an editable mesh object. This object will be the base object. Next, create two copies of the object and modify their shapes by selecting the **Vertex** sub-object level, as shown in Figure 12-9. You can also give the shape of your choice to the objects. These objects will be the target objects. Now, choose the **Toggle Auto Key Mode** button to turn it on and choose the **Go to Start** button to move the time slider to frame 0. Select the base object and choose **Create > Compound > Morph** from the menu bar; the **Pick Targets** and **Current Targets** rollouts will be displayed in the modify panel. Next, set the value **35** in the **Current Frame (Go To Frame)** spinner to move the time slider to frame 35. In the **Pick Targets** rollout, choose the **Pick Target** button and move the cursor over the first target object; a selection cursor will be displayed. Select the first target object in the viewport. Similarly, set the value **70** in the **Current Frame (Go To Frame)** spinner to move the time slider to frame 70 and select the second target object. When you select the target objects in the viewport, the names of the base and target objects get displayed in the **Morph Targets** area of the **Current Targets** rollout. Choose the **Toggle Auto Key Mode** button again to turn it off. Choose the **Play Animation** button to view the animation.

RENDERING AN ANIMATION

Menu bar:	Rendering > Render Setup
Main Toolbar:	Render Setup
Keyboard:	F10

Rendering is a process of generating a 2-dimensional image from a 3-dimensional scene. It shows the lighting effects, materials applied, background, and other settings that you set for the scene. In the earlier chapters, you have already learned about the basic rendering for the still images. The advanced rendering used for the animated scene is discussed next.

To render the final animation, invoke the **Render Setup** tool; the **Render Setup: Default Scanline Renderer** dialog box will be displayed, as shown in Figure 12-10. The **Common** tab is chosen by default in this dialog box. Set the parameters in different rollouts displayed in the **Common** tab. Make sure that the **Production** radio button is selected on the bottom of this dialog box. Also, in the **View** drop-down list, select the viewport that you want to render. Next, choose the **Render** button; the **Perspective, frame 0, Display Gamma:2.2, RGBA Color 16 Bits/Channel (1:1)** dialog box and the **Rendering** dialog box will be invoked, displaying the rendering process, refer to Figure 12-11. Various rollouts in the **Render Setup: Default Scanline Renderer** dialog box are discussed next.

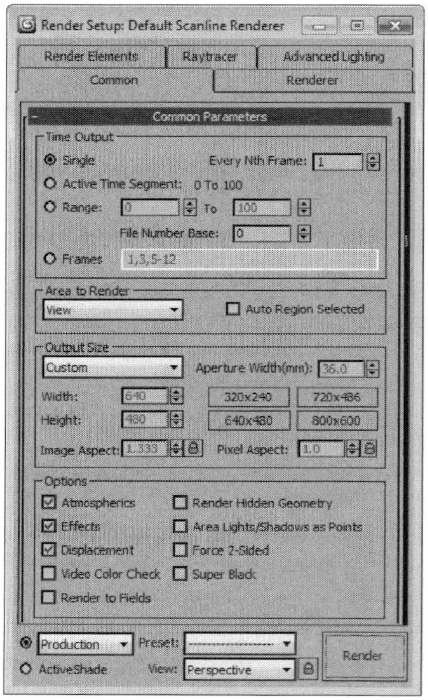

*Figure 12-10 The **Render Setup: Default Scanline Renderer** dialog box*

Common Parameters Rollout

There are different types of renderers to render the scene in Autodesk 3ds Max such as **mental ray Renderer**, **VUE File Renderer**, and so on. The options in this rollout are used to set the common parameters for all types of renderers. The commonly used areas in this rollout are discussed next.

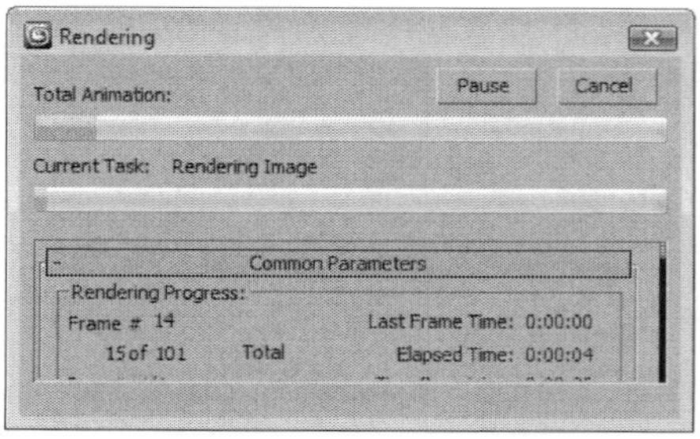

*Figure 12-11 The **Rendering** dialog box*

Time Output Area

This area is used to set the number of frames that you want to render. By default, the **Single** radio button is selected that enables you to render only a single frame. To render the animation, you need to select the **Active Time Segment** radio button. This radio button renders all the frames in the current time segment. Select the **Range** radio button to specify a range of frames for rendering by entering the start and end frame numbers in the spinners given on the right of this radio button. The **Frames** radio button allows you to render the frame numbers of your choice. To do so, select this radio button and enter the required frame number in the text box given on the right of this radio button.

Output Size Area

This area is used to define the size of the rendered image. Choose one of the default buttons, **320x240**, **640x480**, **720x486**, or **800x600** to define the size of the output window. When you choose any of these buttons, the corresponding values will be displayed in the **Width** and **Height** spinners. You can also set the values manually in the **Width** and **Height** spinners to define the size.

Options Area

The check boxes in this area are used to filter the options to render for the final output such as atmospheres, lighting effects, and so on.

Advanced Lighting Area

The check boxes in this area are used to select options for using advanced lighting or computing it on a per-frame basis when required.

Bitmap Performance and Memory Options Area

This area is used to decide whether Autodesk 3ds Max will use the full resolutions maps or the proxies of the maps at rendering. To assign the settings, you need to choose the **Setup** button in this area; the **Global Settings and Defaults for Bitmap Proxies** dialog box will be displayed. You can set the required parameters in this dialog box.

Render Output Area

This area is used to specify a file where the rendered animation can be saved. To do so, choose the **Files** button; the **Render Output File** dialog box will be displayed. Enter the name of the file in the **File name** text box and then select the type of file from the **Save as type** drop-down list. Next, choose the **Save** button; the **AVI File Compression Setup** dialog box will be displayed. Use the default settings and choose the **OK** button; the **Save File** check box will get selected and the path of the file will be displayed just below the Files button in the **Render Output** area.

Assign Renderer Rollout

This rollout is used to set renderer for the scene. The **Production** option is used to assign a renderer for the graphics. The **Material Editor** option is used to assign a renderer for the sample slots in the **Material Editor** dialog box. The **ActiveShade** option is used to assign a renderer for the lighting effects in the scene, refer to Figure 12-12.

To assign the renderer, choose the **Choose Renderer** button on the right of the options given in this rollout; the **Choose Renderer** dialog box will be displayed, as shown in Figure 12-13. Select the renderer and choose the **OK** button; the name of the selected renderer will be displayed in the text box on the right side of the selected option. Choose the **Save as Defaults** button in the **Assign Renderer** rollout to save the settings as default for further use.

Note

*If you install any additional renderer plug-ins in Autodesk 3ds Max, the renderer types will be added in the **Choose Renderer** list.*

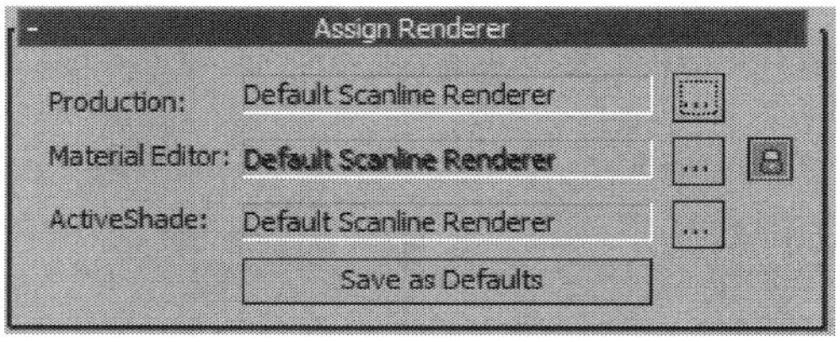

***Figure 12-12** The **Assign Renderer** rollout*

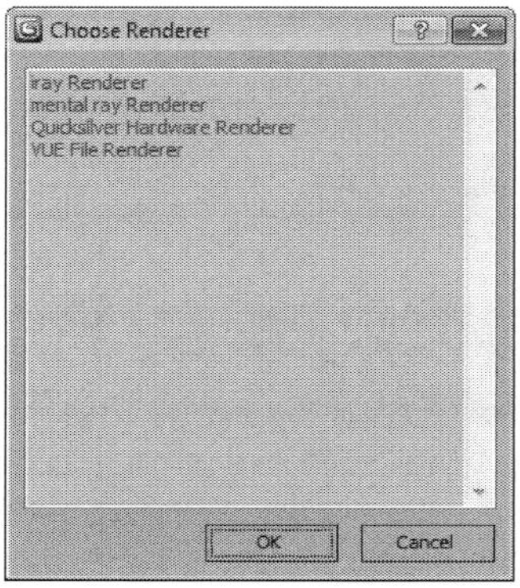

***Figure 12-13** The **Choose Renderer** dialog box*

PREVIEWING AN ANIMATION

If a scene has a large number of objects, lights, and special effects, it may take a longer time to render the final animation. To check the correctness of animation, Autodesk 3ds Max allows you to preview the animation in low resolution. Note that in the preview rendering, only the diffuse color maps are displayed. Therefore, it takes lesser time to render. You can have a look at your animation before the final rendering.

To create a preview animation, choose **Tools > Views - Grab Viewport > Create Animated Sequence File** from the menu bar; the **Make Preview** dialog box will be displayed, as shown in Figure 12-14. Alternatively, choose **Create Preview > Create Animated Sequence File** from the General viewport label to invoke the **Make Preview** dialog box, refer to Figure 12-15. Set the parameters for different options in this dialog box and select the viewport that you want to render from the **Render Viewport** drop-down list which is located at the bottom of the dialog box. Next, choose the **Create** button; the **Video Compression** dialog box will be displayed. Use the default settings and choose the **OK** button; the rendering of the preview will start. Once the preview has been created, it will automatically start in the Windows Media Player.

To view the last preview animation, choose **Tools > Views - Grab Viewport > View Animated Sequence File** from the menu bar; the animation will start playing in the Windows Media Player. Alternatively, choose **Create Preview > View Animated Sequence File** from the General viewport label, refer to Figure 12-15.

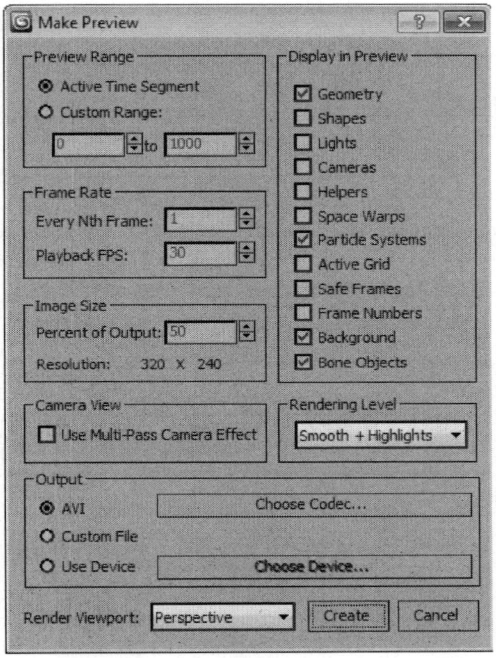

Figure 12-14 *The* ***Make Preview*** *dialog box*

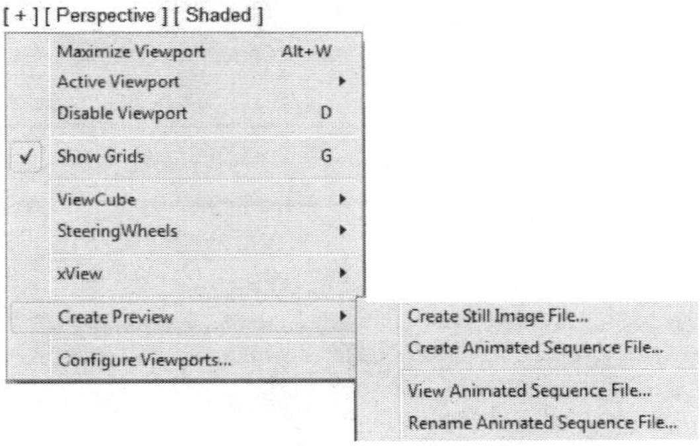

Figure 12-15 *The flyout and the cascading menu of the General viewport label*

RENDERING EFFECTS

The Rendering effects are the special effects assigned to a scene. These effects are visible only at rendering. To assign a rendering effect to a scene, choose **Rendering > Effects** from the menu bar; the **Environment and Effects** dialog box will be displayed, as shown in Figure 12-16. The **Effects** tab is chosen by default. In the **Effects** rollout of this tab, choose the **Add** button; the **Add Effect** dialog box will be displayed, as shown in Figure 12-17. Select the rendering effect from the list given in this dialog box and choose the **OK** button; the selected rendering effect will be displayed in the **Effects** text area of the **Effects** rollout. Also, the rollouts related to the selected effect will be displayed in the **Environment and Effects** dialog box. Next, set the parameters for the selected rendering effect in these rollouts and close the dialog box. Now, render the final scene; the rendering effects will be displayed in the final rendered image.

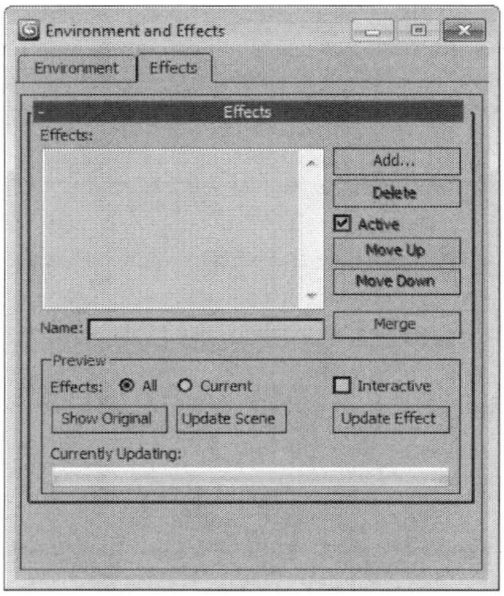

*Figure 12-16 The **Environment and Effects** dialog box*

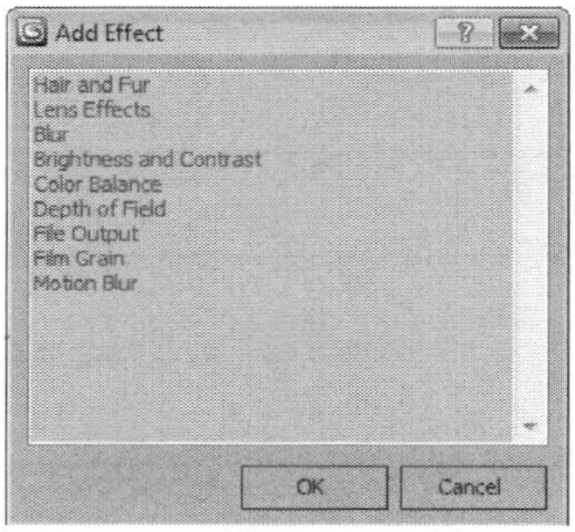

*Figure 12-17 The **Add Effect** dialog box*

Tutorial 1

In this tutorial, you will create a walkthrough animation in a water cave, refer to Figures 12-18 and 12-19. **(Expected time: 45 min)**

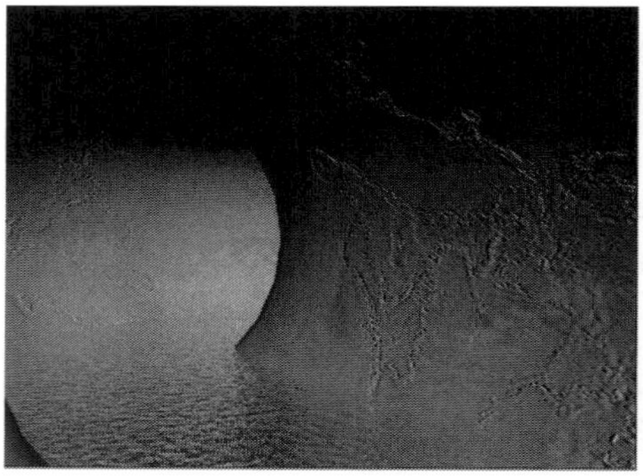

Figure 12-18 Animated scene for cave at one frame

Figure 12-19 Animated scene for cave at another frame

The following steps are required to complete this tutorial:

a. Set the project folder.
b. Download the files.
c. Create a cave.
d. Create a camera.
e. Create the water surface.
f. Create and assign materials to water surface.
g. Create the walkthrough animation.

h. Rescale the active time segment.
i. Create animation in water.
j. Assign environment to the scene.
k. Render and save the final output of the animation.
l. Save the file.

Setting the Project Folder

1. Set the project folder with the name *c12_tut1* in the *3dsmax* folder as discussed in earlier chapters.

Downloading the Files

Before starting the tutorial, you need to download the *c12_3dsmax_2012_tut.zip* file from *http://www.cadcim.com*. The path of the file is as follows:

Textbooks > Animation and Visual Effects > 3ds Max > Autodesk 3ds Max 2012: A Comprehensive Guide

Extract the contents of the zipped file and copy the files *cave_material.jpg* and *ice_environment.jpg* at the location *\Documents\3dsmax\c12_tut1\sceneassets\images*.

Creating a Cave

To create a cave, you need to use various splines and the **Loft** tool from **Compound Objects**.

1. Activate the Front viewport. Choose **Create > Shapes** in the **Command Panel**; the **Splines** option is displayed by default in the drop-down list below the **Shapes** button. Invoke the **Donut** tool from the **Object Type** rollout.

2. Create a donut in the Front viewport. It is automatically named as *Donut001*. Now, set its parameters in the **Parameters** rollout as given below:

   Radius 1: **720.539** Radius 2: **848.293**

3. In the **Interpolation** rollout, set the value **20** in the **Steps** spinner.

4. Invoke the **Zoom Extents All** tool to view the *Donut001* in all viewports properly.

5. Activate the Top viewport. Invoke the **Zoom** tool and zoom out the viewport so that the *Donut001* is visible only half of its original size.

6. Activate the Top viewport. Invoke the **Line** tool from **Create > Shapes > Splines > Object Type** rollout from the **Command Panel**. In the **Creation Method** rollout, select the **Smooth** radio button in the **Initial Type** area and the **Corner** radio button in the **Drag Type** area.

7. Create a line in the Top viewport, as shown in Figure 12-20. It is automatically named as *Line001*.

   Next, you need to create a loft compound object.

8. Make sure that the *Line001* is selected in the Top viewport. Choose **Create > Geometry** in the **Command Panel**; the **Standard Primitives** option is displayed by default in the drop-down list below the **Geometry** button. Select the **Compound Objects** option from the drop-down list and invoke the **Loft** tool from the **Object Type** rollout.

9. In the **Creation Method** rollout of the **Loft** tool, choose the **Get Shape** button and move the cursor over the *Donut001* in the Front viewport; the cursor is changed, as shown in Figure 12-21. Click on the *Donut001*; the shape of a cave is created in all viewports. Right-click to exit the loft command. Invoke the **Zoom Extents All** tool to view the entire shape in the viewports, as shown in Figure 12-22.

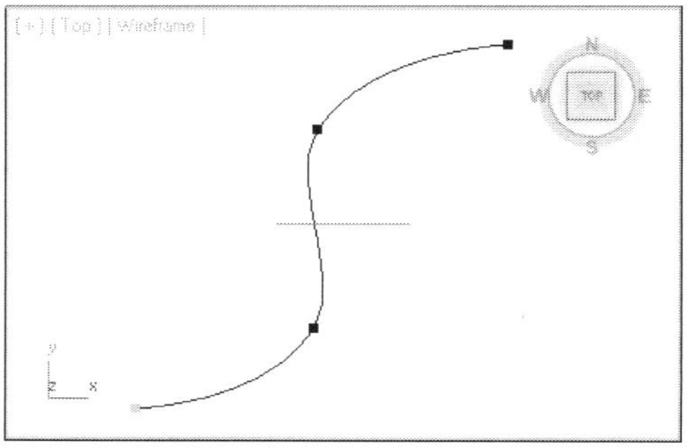

Figure 12-20 *A line created for the cave*

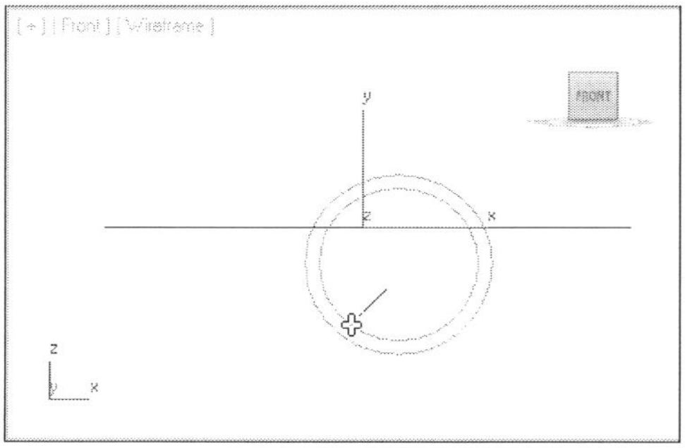

Figure 12-21 *The cursor displayed after moving it over the Donut001*

Note

If the shape displayed after performing the loft command is not similar to the cave, you need to modify the placement of vertices of the Line001 spline at the ***Vertex*** *sub-object level.*

10. The lofted object is automatically named as *Loft001*. Modify its name to *water cave*. Next, you need to use the target camera to create a walkthrough animation inside the *water cave*.

Creating a Camera

1. Activate the Front viewport. Choose **Create > Cameras** in the **Command Panel** and then invoke the **Target** tool from the **Object Type** rollout.

2. In the Front viewport, create a target camera and align it in all viewports using the **Select and Move** and **Select and Rotate** tools, as shown in Figure 12-23. It is automatically named as *Camera001*.

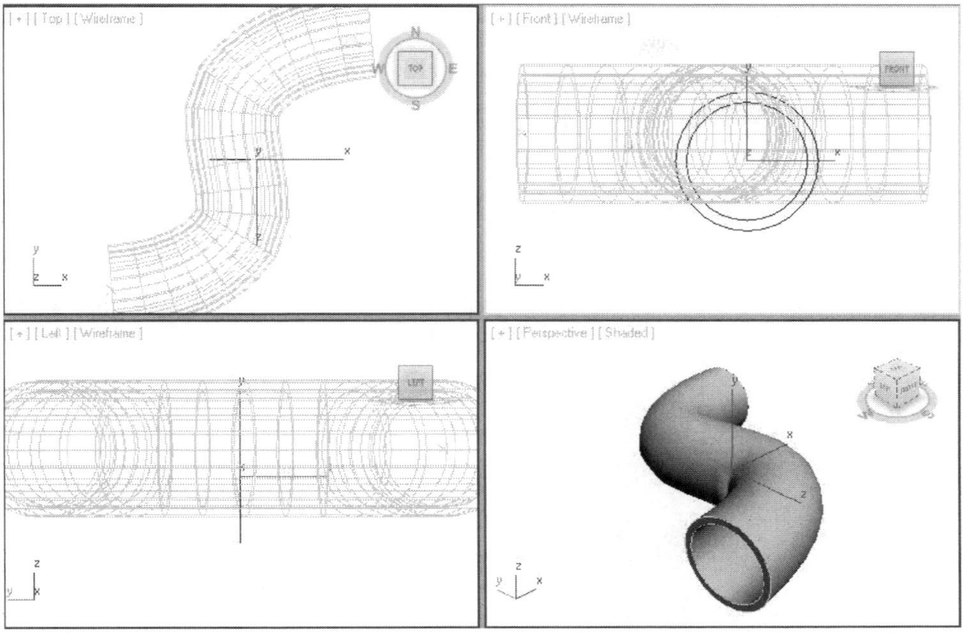

Figure 12-22 *The shape of a cave created in all viewports using the* ***Loft*** *tool*

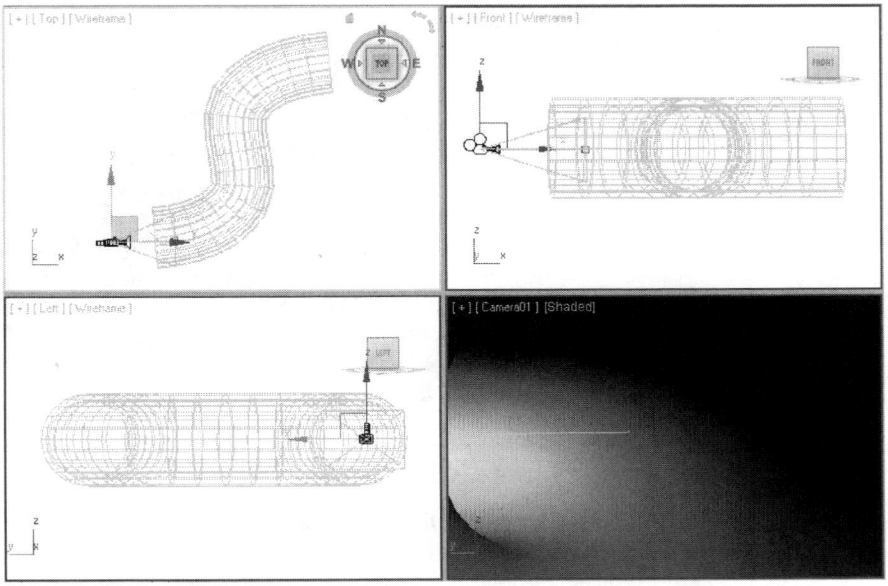

Figure 12-23 *Alignment of Camera001 in all viewports*

Note

While aligning the target camera, make sure that the target of the camera is also selected along with the Camera001.

3. Activate the Perspective viewport and press the C key to switch to the Camera001 viewport; the camera view is displayed, refer to Figure 12-23.

Creating the Water Surface

You need to create a plane to create the water surface.

1. Invoke the **Plane** tool from **Standard Primitives** in the **Command Panel**. Create a plane in the Top viewport.

2. In the **Parameters** rollout, set the values in the **Length** and **Width** spinners so that the plane covers the area around the cave, as shown in Figure 12-24. Also, set the values in the **Length Segs** and **Width Segs** spinners to **30**.

3. Name the plane in the **Name and Color** rollout as *water surface* and align it in all viewports, refer to Figure 12-24.

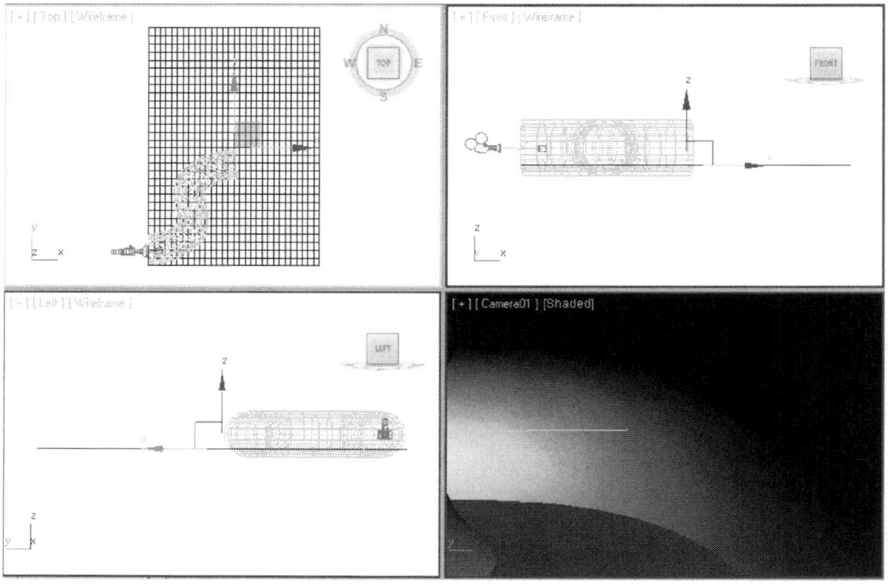

Figure 12-24 *The water surface created and aligned in all viewports*

Next, you need to create and assign materials to the *water cave* and the *water surface*.

Creating and Assigning Materials to the Water Surface

In this section, you will create the materials for the *water surface*.

1. Select the *water surface* in any viewport and press the M key; the **Material Editor** dialog box is displayed.

2. Select the **01-Default** sample slot, if it has not already been selected, and then modify its name in the **Material Name** text box to **water surface material**.

3. Choose the **Material Type** button that is currently labeled as **Standard**; the **Material/ Map Browser** dialog box is displayed. Select the **Raytrace** material from the **Materials > Standard** rollouts and choose the **OK** button; the **Standard** material is replaced by the **Raytrace** material.

4. In the **Raytrace Basic Parameters** rollout, make sure that the **Phong** shader is selected in the **Shading** drop-down list.

5. Choose the **Diffuse** color swatch; the **Color Selector: Diffuse** dialog box is displayed. Set the following values and then choose the **OK** button.

   Red: **136**   Green: **210**   Blue: **213**

6. Choose the **Reflect** color swatch; the **Color Selector: Reflect** dialog box is displayed. Set the following values and then choose the **OK** button.

   Red: **240**   Green: **240**   Blue: **240**

7. Choose the **Reflect** map button on the right of the **Reflect** color swatch; the **Material/ Map Browser** dialog box is displayed. Select the **Falloff** map from the **Maps > Standard** rollouts and choose the **OK** button; the **Falloff** map is displayed as sub-material. Use the default settings and choose the **Go to Parent** button to go back to the parent level.

Note

Assigning the map using the ***Reflect*** *map button in the* ***Raytrace Basic Parameters*** *rollout is same as assigning the map using the* ***Reflect*** *map button in the* ***Maps*** *rollout.*

8. Select the **Bump** check box in the **Raytrace Basic Parameters** rollout. Then, choose the button on the right of the **Bump** spinner that is labeled as **None**; the **Material/Map Browser** dialog box is displayed. Select the **Noise** map and choose the **OK** button; the **Noise** map is displayed as sub-material.

9. In the **Noise Parameters** rollout, select the **Fractal** radio button and set the following parameters:

   Size: **30.0**   High: **1.0**   Low: **1.0**

10. Choose the **Go to Parent** button to go back to the parent level. Alternatively, you can select the **water surface material** option from the **Material Name** drop-down list.

11. Make sure that the *water surface* is selected in the viewport, and then choose the **Assign Material to Selection** button; the **water surface material** is assigned to the *water surface* in the viewport.

    Next, you need to create material for the *water cave* to make it look more realistic.

12. Select the **02-Default** sample slot and modify its name in the **Material Name** text box to **water cave material**.

13. In the **Shader Basic Parameters** rollout, make sure that the **Blinn** shader is selected in the drop-down list.

    Next, you need to assign a map to the selected sample slot.

14. In the **Blinn Basic Parameters** rollout, choose the **Diffuse** map button on the right of the **Diffuse** color swatch; the **Material/Map Browser** dialog box is displayed. Select the **Bitmap** map and choose the **OK** button; the **Select Bitmap Image File** dialog box is displayed. As the project folder is already set, the path *\Documents\3dsmax\c12_tut1\sceneassets\images* is displayed in the **Look in** text box of this dialog box. Select the file *cave_material.jpg* and choose the **Open** button; the selected image is displayed in the sample slot.

15. Choose the **Go to Parent** button. Expand the **Maps** rollout and then select the **Bump** check box to make it available for material. Choose the **Bump** map button that is labeled as **None**; the **Material/Map Browser** dialog box is displayed. Select the **Bitmap** map and choose the **OK** button; the **Select Bitmap Image File** dialog box is displayed. Browse to the same image *(cave_material.jpg)* that you used for the **Diffuse** map and choose the **Open** button; various rollouts are displayed to modify the coordinates of the map.

16. In the **Coordinates** rollout, set the value **4** in the **U Tiling** and **V Tiling** spinners. Next, choose the **Go to Parent** button to go back to the parent level; the name of the selected image is displayed over the **Bump** map button.

17. In the **Bump** spinner, set the value **100**.

18. Make sure that the *water cave* is selected in the viewport, and then choose the **Assign Material to Selection** button; the **water cave material** is assigned to the *water cave* in the viewport.

19. Close the **Material Editor** dialog box.

20. Activate the Camera001 viewport and invoke the **Render Production** tool to view the maps and materials assigned to the objects. The scene is displayed, as shown in Figure 12-25.

Creating the Walkthrough Animation

To create the walkthrough animation, first you need to create a path inside the *water cave* in the Top viewport.

1. Activate the Top viewport and invoke the **Maximize Viewport Toggle** tool to maximize it.

2. Create a line from the lower left side to the upper right side of the viewport according to the shape of the *water cave*, as shown in Figure 12-26. Alternatively, you can also use the Line001 spline created earlier to loft the cave.

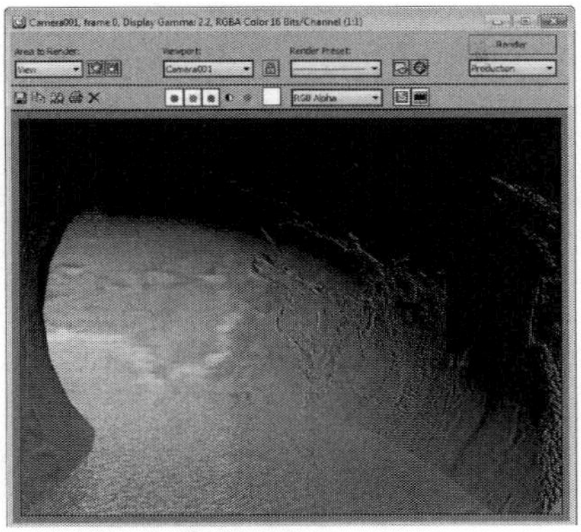

Figure 12-25 The scene after assigning the materials

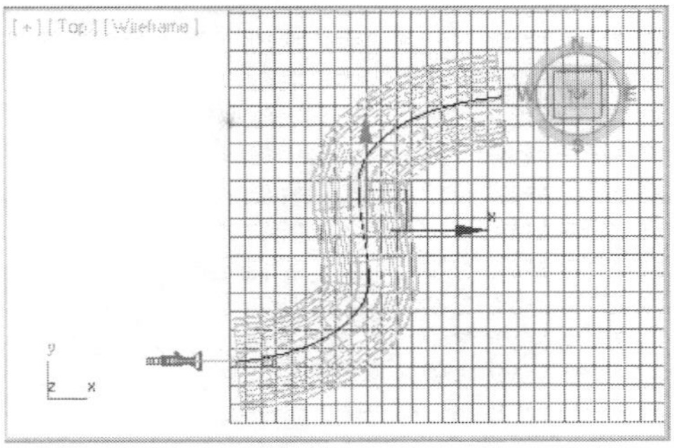

Figure 12-26 A line created for the path

3. Modify the name of the line as *path* and align it in all viewports, as shown in Figure 12-27.

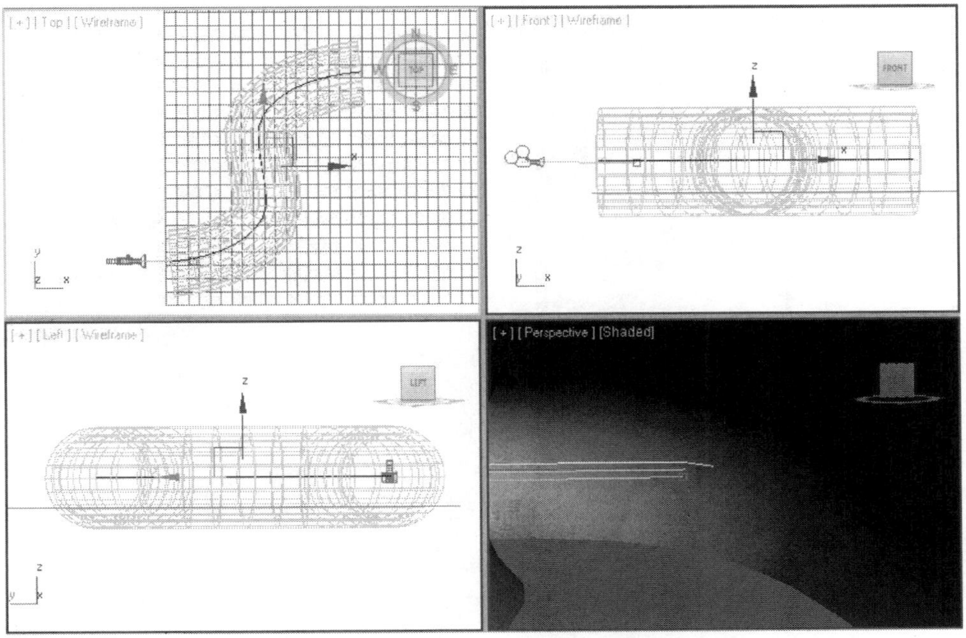

Figure 12-27 The path aligned in all viewports

Next, you need to increase the number of frames in the track bar to create a smooth animation.

4. Choose the **Time Configuration** button on the bottom of the screen; the **Time Configuration** dialog box is displayed. In the **Animation** area of this dialog box,

set the value **1000** in the **End Time** spinner and press the ENTER key; the number of frames increases in the track bar. Choose the **OK** button to exit the dialog box.

Next, you need to move the *Camera001* along with the *path*.

5. Select the *Camera001* in any viewport and choose the **Motion** tab in the **Command Panel**. By default, the **Parameters** tab is chosen.

6. Expand the **Assign Controller** rollout in the **Parameters** tab and then choose the **Position : Position XYZ** option from it; the **Assign Controller** button is activated, as shown in Figure 12-28.

7. Choose the **Assign Controller** button; the **Assign Position Controller** dialog box is displayed. Choose the **Path Constraint** option and choose the **OK** button to exit the dialog box; various rollouts are displayed below the **Assign Controller** rollout.

8. In the **Path Parameters** rollout, choose the **Add Path** button and select the *path* in the viewport; the name of the *path* is displayed in the **Target Weight** area, as shown in Figure 12-29. Also, the *Camera001* is moved along with the *path* in the viewport. Right-click to exit the command.

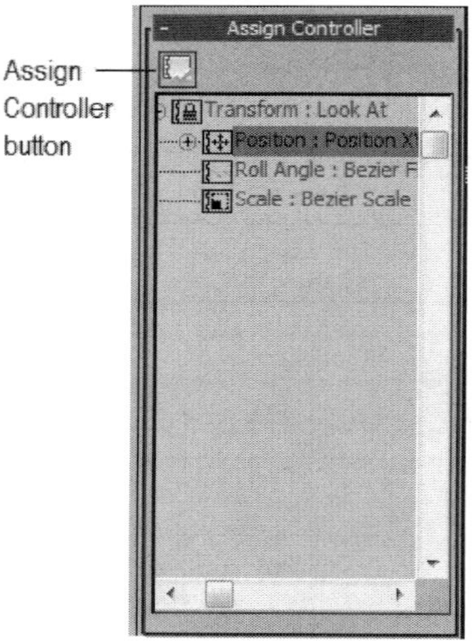

Figure 12-28 *The* ***Assign Controller*** *rollout*

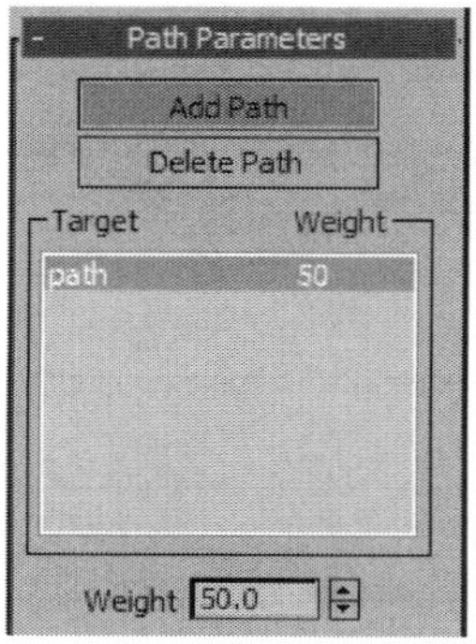

Figure 12-29 *Partial view of the* ***Path Parameters*** *rollout*

9. Activate the Top viewport and choose the **Play Animation** button from the time controls area; you will notice that the *Camera001* is moving along with the *path* but the movement is not proper. To create a proper movement, you need to adjust the target of the *Camera001* at different frames.

10. Choose the **Go to Start** button to drag the time slider to frame 0. Next, choose the **Toggle Auto Key Mode** button to turn on the animation mode.

11. Invoke the **Select by Name** tool; the **Select From Scene** dialog box is displayed. Select the *Camera001.Target* and choose the **OK** button to exit the dialog box; the *Camera001.Target* is selected in the viewport.

12. In the Top viewport, position the *Camera001.Target* using the **Select and Move** tool, as shown in Figure 12-30.

Note
While aligning the Camera001.Target, you need to view the Camera001 viewport simultaneously to make sure that the animation is proper.

13. Drag the time slider to frame 153 and move the *Camera001.Target* along the path, as shown in Figure 12-31. To move the time slider to a particular frame, you can also enter the frame number in the Current Frame (Go to frame) spinner.

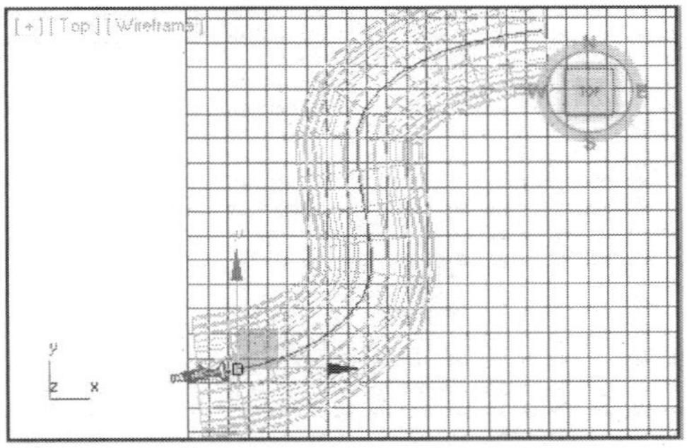

Figure 12-30 *The position of the Camera001.Target at frame 0*

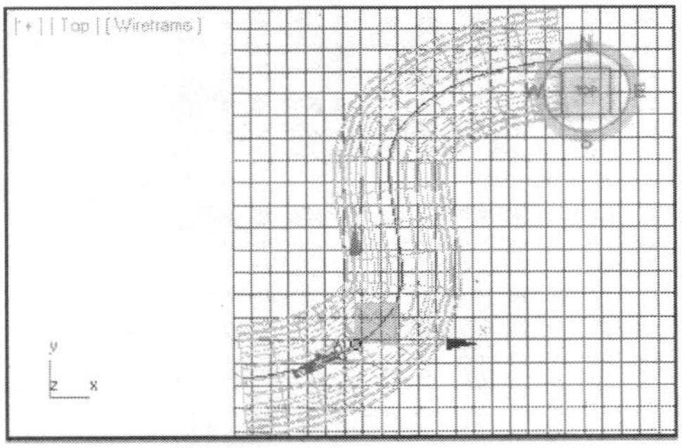

Figure 12-31 *The position of the Camera001.Target at frame 153*

14. Move the time slider to frame 300 by entering the frame number in the **Current Frame (Go to frame)** spinner. Then, align the *Camera001.Target*, as shown in Figure 12-32.

15. Move the time slider to frame 429 by entering the frame number in the **Current Frame (Go to frame)** spinner. Now, align the *Camera001.Target* with the *path*, as shown in Figure 12-33.

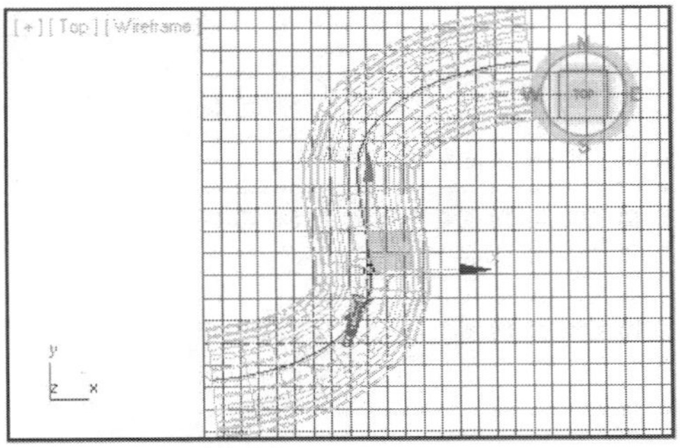

Figure 12-32 *The position of the Camera001.Target at frame 300*

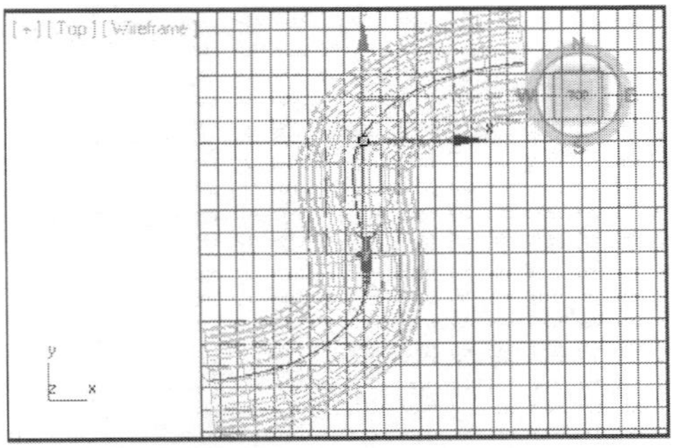

Figure 12-33 *The position of the Camera001.Target at frame 429*

16. Move the time slider to frame 581 and align the *Camera001.Target*, as shown in Figure 12-34.

17. Move the time slider to frame 700 and align the *Camera001.Target*, as shown in Figure 12-35.

18. Move the time slider to frame 801 and align the *Camera001.Target*, as shown in Figure 12-36.

19. Move the time slider to frame 935 and align the *Camera001.Target*, as shown in Figure 12-37.

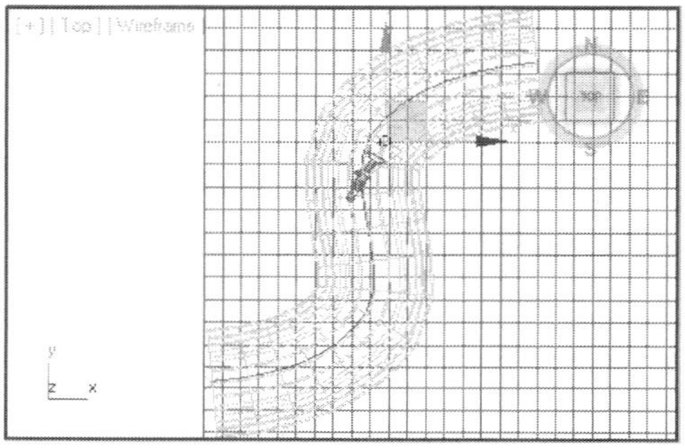

Figure 12-34 *The position of the Camera001.Target at frame 581*

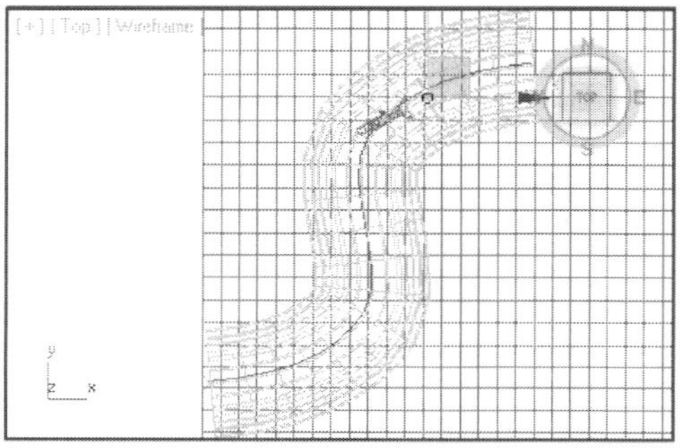

Figure 12-35 *The position of the Camera001.Target at frame 700*

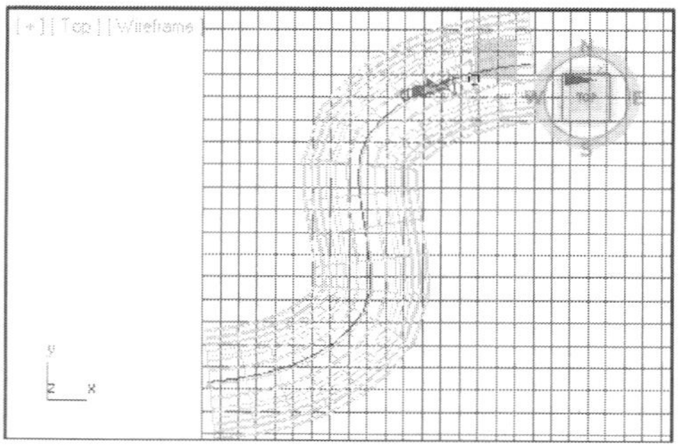

Figure 12-36 *The position of the Camera001.Target at frame 801*

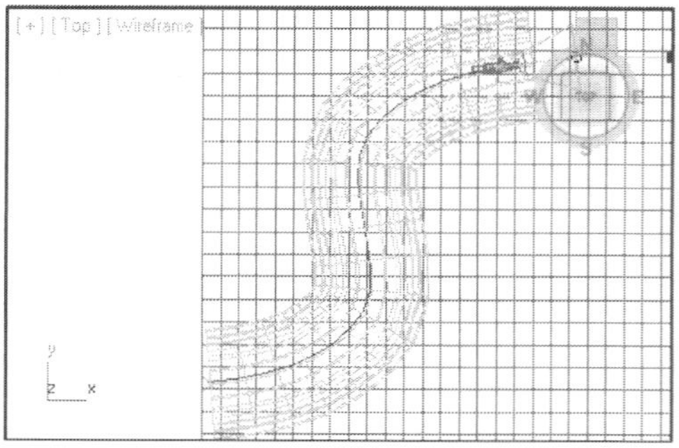

Figure 12-37 *The position of the Camera001.Target at frame 935*

20. Move the time slider to frame 1000 and align the *Camera001.Target*, as shown in Figure 12-38.

21. After creating the frame-by-frame animation, the frames are displayed in the track bar, as shown in Figure 12-39.

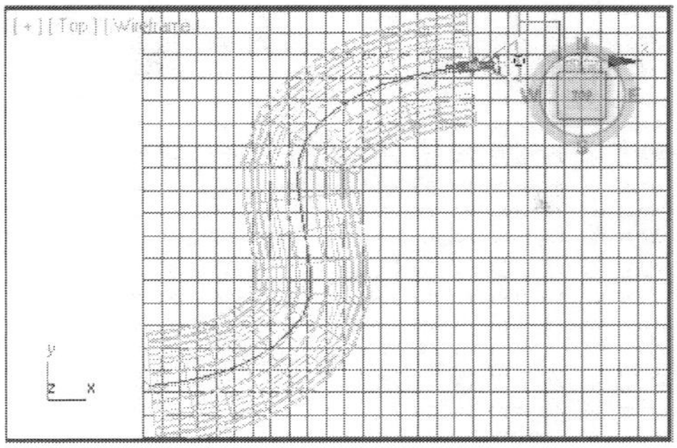

Figure 12-38 The position of the Camera001.Target at frame 1000

Figure 12-39 The track bar after creating the animation

22. Choose the **Toggle Auto Key Mode** button to turn off the animation mode and activate the Camera001 viewport. Next, choose the **Play Animation** button; the *Camera001* starts moving along the *path* inside the cave.

Note
You can also use your own dimensions to align the Camera001.Target at different frames.

Rescaling the Active Time Segment

While playing animation, if you feel that the pace of animation is very fast, you can increase the number of frames in the active time segment to make it slow and smooth. Also, your animation keys will get adjusted according to the new active time segment.

1. Choose the **Time Configuration** button at the bottom of the 3ds Max screen; the **Time Configuration** dialog box is displayed. In the **Animation** area of this dialog box, choose the **Re-scale Time** button; the **Re-scale Time** dialog box is displayed.

2. In the **New** area, set a new value in the **End Time** spinner and choose the **OK** button to exit the dialog box; the active time segment and animation keys are adjusted accordingly. Choose the **OK** button in the **Time Configuration** dialog box to close it.

Creating Animation in Water

1. To create animated waves of water inside the *water cave*, invoke the **Compact Material Editor** tool from the **Main Toolbar**; the **Material Editor** dialog box is displayed.

2. Select the **water surface material** sample slot. Now, in the **Raytrace Basic Parameters** rollout, choose the **Bump** map button that is labeled as **Map#2 (Noise)**; various rollouts are displayed for the **Noise** modifier.

Next, you need to animate the parameters of the **Noise** modifier to animate the *water surface*.

3. Choose the **Go to Start** button to drag the time slider to frame 0. Next, choose the **Toggle Auto Key Mode** button to turn on the animation mode; the selected sample slot is surrounded by a red border, which indicates that you are in the animation mode.

4. In the **Noise Parameters** rollout, make sure that the value in the **Phase** spinner is 0.0 at frame 0. Next, choose the **Go to End** button to move the time slider to the end frame, and then set the value **7.0** in the **Phase** spinner; the arrows of the spinner turn red.

5. Choose the **Toggle Auto Key Mode** button to turn off the animation mode and close the **Material Editor** dialog box.

Assigning Environment to the Scene

1. Choose **Rendering > Environment** from the menu bar; the **Environment and Effects** dialog box is displayed.

2. The **Environment** tab is chosen by default. In the **Background** area of the **Common Parameters** rollout, choose the **Environment Map** button that is labeled as **None**; the **Material/Map Browser** dialog box is displayed.

3. Select the **Bitmap** map and choose the **OK** button; the **Select Bitmap Image File** dialog box is displayed. Select the *ice_environment.jpg* image and choose the **Open** button; the selected image is displayed as background at rendering. Close the **Environment and Effects** dialog box.

   Note that when the *Camera001* moves toward the end frames, then only the background of the scene is displayed in the animation.

Rendering and Saving the Final Output of the Animation

Next, you need to render the scene to view the final output that contains all movements, textures, and animations.

1. Invoke the **Render Setup** tool from the **Main Toolbar**; the **Render Setup: Default Scanline Renderer** dialog box is displayed. In this dialog box, the **Common** tab is chosen by default. Also, various rollouts are displayed in the **Common** tab.

2. In the **Common Parameters** rollout, select the **Active Time Segment** radio button in the **Time Output** area.

3. In the **Output Size** area, choose the **640x480** button.

4. In the **Render Output** area, choose the **Files** button; the **Render Output File** dialog box is displayed. Enter a name for the file in the **File name** text box and then select the **AVI File**

(*.avi) file type from the **Save as type** drop-down list and specify the desired location of the file in the **Save in** text box. Next, choose the **Save** button; the **AVI File Compression Setup** dialog box is displayed. Use the default settings and choose the **OK** button to exit the dialog box.

5. Make sure that the **Camera001** option is selected in the **View** drop-down list at the bottom of the **Render Setup: Default Scanline Renderer** dialog box. Then, choose the **Render** button; both the **Camera001, frame** dialog box and the **Rendering** dialog box are displayed showing the rendering process.

   After the completion of the rendering process, the final output of the animation is saved at the specified location in the **.avi* format. You can view the final output of the animation by opening the corresponding **.avi* file.

   You can view the final rendered sequence by downloading the *c12_3dsmax_2012_render.zip* file from *http://www.cadcim.com.*

Saving the File

1. Save the file with the name *c12tut1.max* as discussed in earlier chapters. The location of this file is given below:

   \Documents\3dsmax\c12_tut1\scenes

Tutorial 2

In this tutorial, you will create an animated scene that contains light effects and animation of lights and objects, as shown in Figure 12-40. **(Expected time: 45 min)**

Figure 12-40 *The animated scene*

The following steps are required to complete this tutorial:

a. Set the project folder.
b. Create the wireframe earth sphere.
c. Create the text.
d. Assign the camera.
e. Create the animated space background.
f. Create and animate lights.
g. Animate the wireframe earth sphere and the text.
h. Render and save the final output.

Setting the Project Folder

1. Set the project folder with the name *c12_tut2* in the *3dsmax* folder as discussed in earlier chapters.

Creating the Wireframe Earth Sphere

In this section, you will create two spheres to create a wireframe earth sphere.

1. Invoke the **Sphere** tool from **Standard Primitives** in the **Command Panel** and create a sphere in the Top viewport.

2. Modify the name of the sphere to *earth sphere*. In the **Parameters** rollout, set the value **58.42** in the **Radius** spinner.

3. Invoke the **Select and Move** tool and create a copy of the *earth sphere* in the Top viewport and modify its name to *wireframe sphere*. In the **Parameters** rollout, set the radius of the *wireframe sphere* in the **Radius** spinner to **58.0**.

   Next, you need to apply maps and material to the *earth sphere* and the *wireframe sphere*.

4. Navigate to the *c12_3dsmax_2012_tut* folder that you have downloaded from the CADCIM website in Tutorial 1. Next, copy *EarthMap_colored.jpg* and *EarthMap_b&w.jpg* at the location *\Documents\3dsmax\c12_tut2\Sceneassets\images*.

5. Select the *earth sphere* in any viewport and invoke the **Compact Material Editor** tool; the **Material Editor** dialog box is displayed.

6. Select the **01-Default** sample slot, if it is not already selected, and then modify its name in the **Material Name** text box to **earth map**.

7. In the **Shader Basic Parameters** rollout, make sure that the **Blinn** shader is selected in the drop-down list, and then select the **2-Sided** check box.

   Next, you need to assign a map to the shader.

8. In the **Blinn Basic Parameters** rollout, choose the **Diffuse** map button on the right side of the **Diffuse** color swatch; the **Material/Map Browser** dialog box is displayed. Select the **Bitmap** map and choose the **OK** button; the **Select Bitmap Image File** dialog box is displayed. As the project folder is already set, the path *\Documents\3dsmax\c12_tut2\sceneassets\images* is displayed in the **Look in** text box of this dialog box. Select the file *EarthMap_colored.jpg* and choose the **Open** button; the selected image is displayed in the sample slot. Also, various rollouts are displayed to modify the coordinates of the map.

9. Choose the **Go to Parent** button to go back to the parent level and then choose the **Opacity** map button in the **Blinn Basic Parameters** rollout; the **Material/Map Browser** dialog box is displayed. Select the **Bitmap** map and choose the **OK** button; the **Select Bitmap Image File** dialog box is displayed. Select the *EarthMap_b&w.jpg* image and choose the **Open** button; the selected image is displayed in the sample slot, as shown in Figure 12-41.

10. Choose the **Go to Parent** button again and make sure that the *earth sphere* is selected in the viewport. Next, choose the **Assign Material to Selection** button; the **earth map** is assigned to the *earth sphere* in the viewport.

11. Choose the **Show Shaded Material in Viewport** button to view the assigned map in the viewport.

12. Render the Perspective viewport to view the map applied using the **Render Production** tool, as shown in Figure 12-42.

    Next, you need to create material for the *wireframe sphere*.

13. Select the **02-Default** sample slot and modify its name in the **Material Name** text box to **wireframe map**.

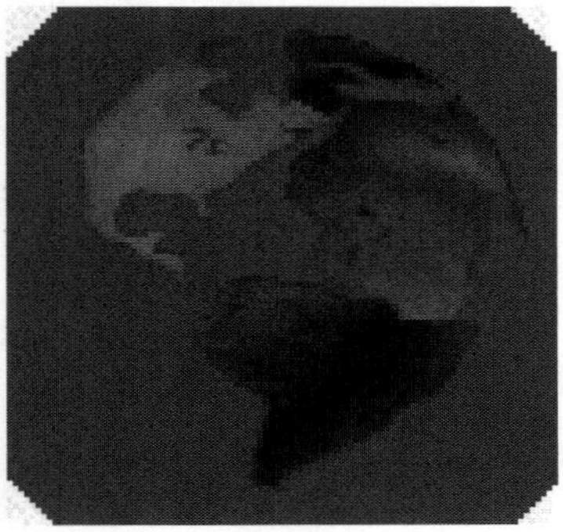

Figure 12-41 *The earth map in the sample slot*

14. In the **Shader Basic Parameters** rollout, make sure that the **Blinn** shader is selected in the drop-down list and then select the **Wire** check box; wireframes are displayed in the sample slot, as shown in Figure 12-43.

15. In the **Blinn Basic Parameters** rollout, choose the **Diffuse** color swatch; the **Color Selector: Diffuse Color** dialog box is displayed. Set the values in the **Red**, **Green**, and **Blue** spinners as given below and choose the **OK** button to exit the dialog box.

    Red: **239** Green: **106** Blue: **18**

16. In the **Specular Highlights** area, set the value **53** in the **Specular Level** spinner.

17. Next, select the *wireframe sphere* in the viewport and then choose the **Assign Material to Selection** button; the **wireframe map** is assigned to the *wireframe sphere* in the viewport.

Figure 12-42 The earth map applied to the earth sphere after rendering

Figure 12-43 Wireframes displayed in the sample slot

18. Choose the **Show Shaded Material in Viewport** button to view the assigned map in the viewport. Close the **Material Editor** dialog box.

19. Invoke the **Zoom Extents All** tool to view both the spheres in all viewports.

    Next, you need to align the *wireframe sphere* with the *earth sphere*.

20. To do so, select the *wireframe sphere* in the viewport and invoke the **Align** tool from the **Main Toolbar**; the shape of the cursor is changed and you are prompted to select the object to align in the viewport. Select the *earth sphere* in the viewport; the **Align Selection (earth sphere)** dialog box is displayed.

21. In the **Align Position (World)** area, select the **X Position**, **Y Position**, and **Z Position** check boxes. Next, select the **Pivot Point** radio button both in the **Current Object** and **Target Object** areas. Then, choose the **OK** button to close the dialog box.

22. Invoke the **Zoom Extents All** tool; the *wireframe sphere* is aligned with the *earth sphere*, as shown in Figure 12-44.

23. Activate the Perspective viewport and invoke the **Render Production** tool in the **Main Toolbar**; the rendered sphere is displayed, as shown in Figure 12-45.

24. Next, select the *wireframe sphere* and the *earth sphere* in the viewport simultaneously and then group them as *wireframe earth sphere*.

    Next, you need to create text around the *wireframe earth sphere*.

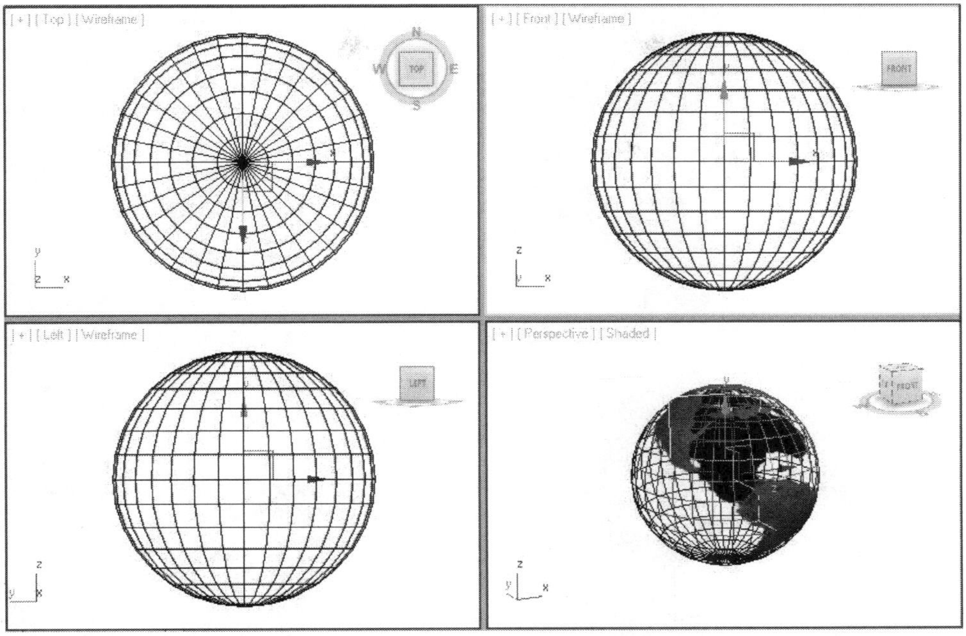

Figure 12-44 Alignment of the wireframe and the earth sphere in all viewports

Figure 12-45 The sphere at rendering

Creating the Text

1. Invoke the **Text** tool from **Create > Shapes > Splines > Object Type** rollout in the **Command Panel**. In the **Parameters** rollout, set the values as given below:

   Select the **Arial Italic** font type from the drop-down list located on the top of the rollout.
   Make sure that the left alignment button is chosen.
   Size: **30.0**

   Text area
   Enter **CADCIM Technologies**.

2. Click in the Front viewport; the **CADCIM Technologies** text is displayed in all viewports. It is automatically named as *Text001*.

3. Invoke the **Zoom Extents All** tool and align the *Text001* in all viewports, as shown in Figure 12-46.

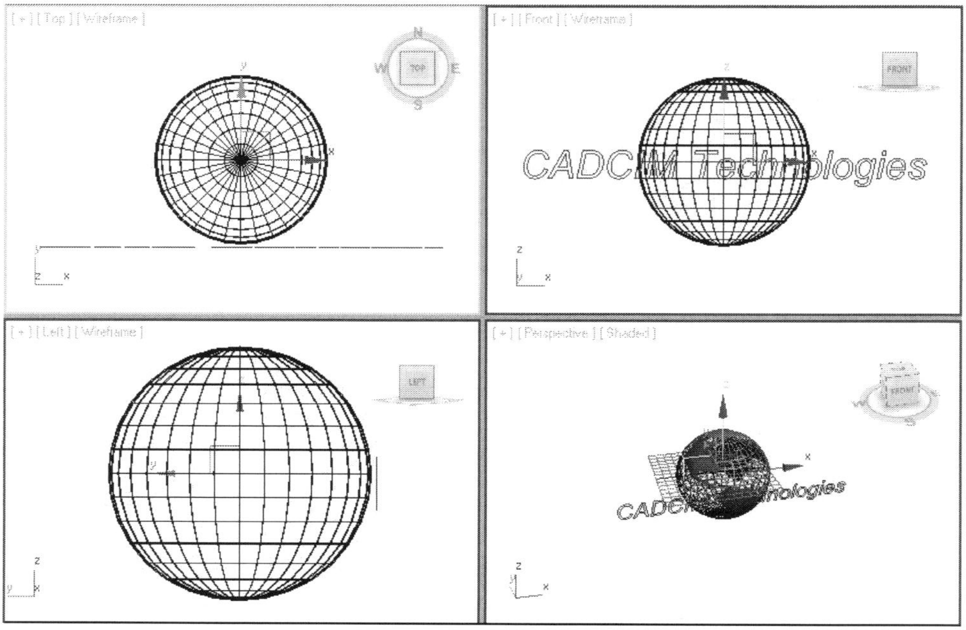

Figure 12-46 *Alignment of Text001 in all viewports*

Now, you need to apply the **Extrude** modifier to add depth to the text.

4. Make sure that the *Text001* is selected in the viewport. Choose the **Modify** tab in the **Command Panel**. Next, select the **Extrude** modifier from the **Modifier List** drop-down list; the **Extrude** modifier is displayed in the modifier stack.

5. In the **Parameters** rollout of the **Extrude** modifier, set the value **3.0** in the **Amount** spinner.

Next, you need to apply material to the *Text001*.

6. Invoke the **Material Editor** tool; the **Material Editor** dialog box is displayed. Select the **03-Default** sample slot and modify its name in the **Material Name** text box to **text material**.

7. In the **Blinn Basic Parameters** rollout, choose the **Diffuse** color swatch; the **Color Selector: Diffuse Color** dialog box is displayed. Set the following values in the **Red**, **Green**, and **Blue** spinners and then choose the **OK** button to exit the dialog box.

Red: **253** Green: **185** Blue: **2**

8. Make sure that the *Text001* is selected in the viewport and then choose the **Assign Material to Selection** button; the **text material** is assigned to the *Text001* in the viewport. Close the **Material Editor** dialog box.

   Next, you need to apply the **Bend** modifier to the *Text001* to bend it around the *wireframe earth sphere*.

9. Select *Text001* in the viewport and then choose the **Modify** tab in the **Command Panel**. Next, select the **Bend** modifier from the **Modifier List** drop-down list; the **Bend** modifier is displayed in the modifier stack.

10. In the **Parameters** rollout of the **Bend** modifier, set the values as given below:

    Bend area
    Angle: **237.5**
    Bend Axis area
    Select the **X** radio button.

11. Next, align the *Text001* in all viewports, as shown in Figure 12-47.

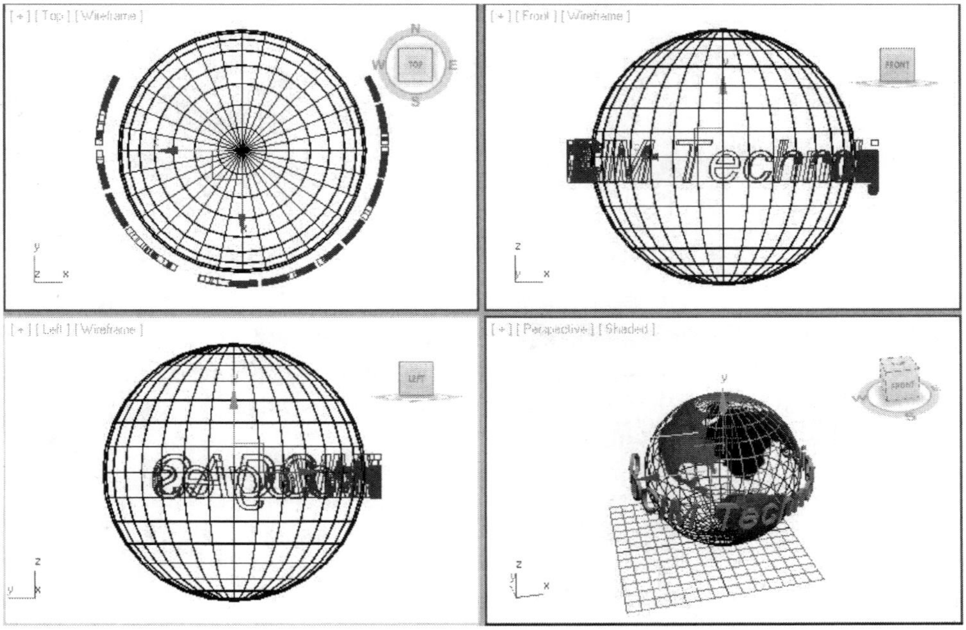

Figure 12-47 *The Text001 aligned in all viewports after applying the **Extrude** and **Bend** modifiers*

Assigning the Camera in the Scene

1. Invoke the **Zoom All** tool and zoom out in all viewports simultaneously to make a proper room around the *wireframe earth sphere*.

2. Invoke the **Free** tool from **Create > Cameras** in the **Command Panel** and click in the Front viewport; a free camera is displayed in all viewports and is automatically named as *Camera001*.

3. Next, align the *Camera001* in all viewports to view the front side of the scene and then press the C key in the Perspective viewport to activate the Camera001 viewport, as shown in Figure 12-48.

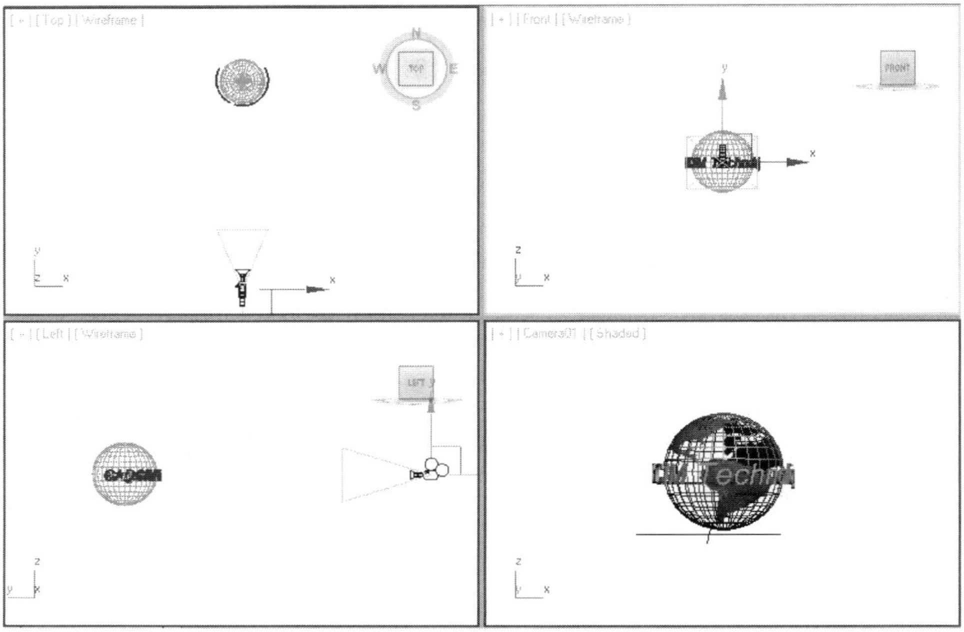

Figure 12-48 *The Camera001 aligned in all viewports*

Creating the Animated Space Background

1. Choose **Rendering > Environment** from the menu bar; the **Environment and Effects** dialog box is displayed with the **Environment** tab chosen by default. Also, various rollouts are displayed in the **Environment** tab.

2. In the **Common Parameters** rollout, choose the **Environment Map** button in the **Background** area; the **Material/Map Browser** dialog box is displayed. Select the **Noise** map from the **Maps > Standard** rollouts and choose the **OK** button; the **Noise** map is displayed on the **Environment Map** button and applied as the background.

   Next, you need to set the parameters of the **Noise** map.

3. Press the M key to invoke the **Material Editor** dialog box. Select the **04-Default** sample slot and modify its name in the **Material Name** text box to **space material**.

4. In the **Environment and Effects** dialog box, move the cursor over the **Environment Map** button, press and hold the left mouse button, drag it to the **04-Default** sample slot in the **Material Editor** dialog box, and release the left mouse button; the **Instance (Copy) Map** dialog box is displayed. Select the **Instance** radio button and choose the **OK** button; the **04-Default** sample slot is displayed, as shown in Figure 12-49. Also, various rollouts to modify the **Noise** map are displayed.

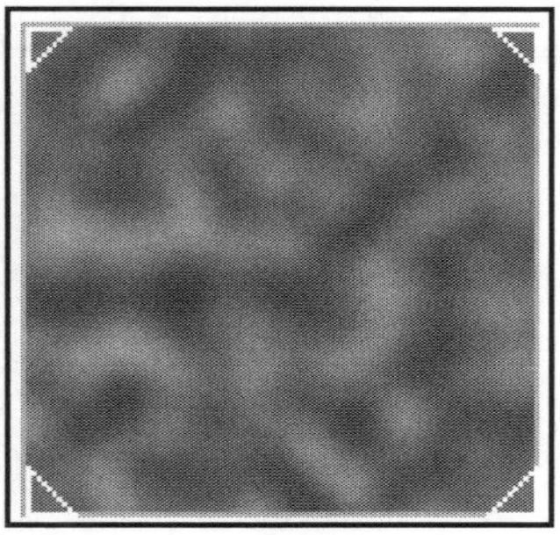

Figure 12-49 *The sample slot with the **Noise** environment*

5. Modify the name of the sample slot in the **Material Name** text box to **space environment map**.

   Next, you need to modify the parameters of the **Noise** map.

6. In the **Noise Parameters** rollout, set the values as given below:

   Select the **Fractal** radio button in the **Noise Type** area.
   Size: **0.2** High: **0.8**
   Low: **0.7** Levels: **3.0**

7. Render the Camera001 viewport; the scene is displayed with the **space environment map**.

   This scene displays stars in the space, as shown in Figure 12-50.

   Next, you need to animate the stars in the **space environment map**.

8. Choose the **Time Configuration** button; the **Time Configuration** dialog box is displayed. In the **Animation** area of this dialog box, set the value **1000** in the **End Time** spinner and press the ENTER key; the number of frames in the active time segment increases to 1000. Choose the **OK** button to exit the dialog box.

9. Choose the **Toggle Auto Key Mode** button to turn on the animation mode and then choose the **Go to Start** button to move the time slider to frame 0. In the **Noise Parameters** rollout of the **Material Editor** dialog box, make sure that the value in the **Phase** spinner is 0.0 at frame 0.

10. Choose the **Go to End** button to move the time slider to frame 1000. In the **Noise Parameters** rollout, set the value **7.0** in the **Phase** spinner. The stars in the **space environment map** appear to be blinking in the final output at rendering.

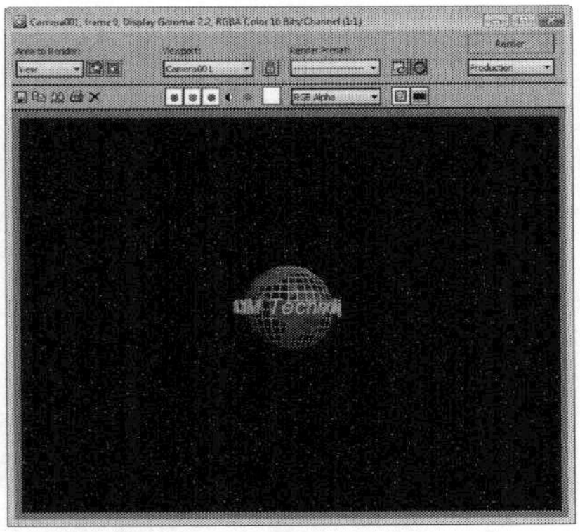

Figure 12-50 *The scene with the* ***space environment map***

11. Choose the **Toggle Auto Key Mode** button to turn off the animation mode and then close the **Material Editor** dialog box. Also, close the **Environment and Effects** dialog box.

Creating and Animating Lights in the Scene

To create light in the scene, you need to create omni and spot lights in the scene.

1. Invoke the **Zoom** tool and zoom out the Top, Front, and Left viewports to create proper room around the *wireframe earth sphere*, refer to Figure 12-51.

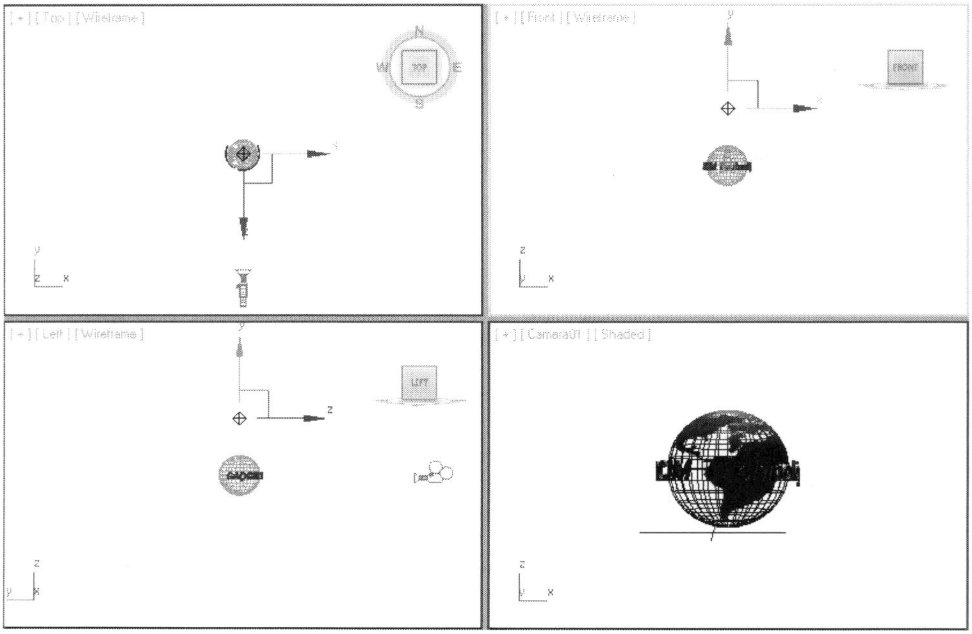

Figure 12-51 *The Omni01 light aligned in all viewports*

2. Activate the Top viewport and invoke the **Omni** tool from **Create > Lights > Standard > Object Type** rollout in the **Command Panel**. In the Top viewport, click at the center of the *wireframe earth sphere*; an omni light is displayed in all viewports. It is automatically named as *Omni001*. Right-click to exit the command.

3. Align the *Omni001* light in all viewports, refer to Figure 12-52.

4. Create four copies of the *Omni001* light and align all lights, as shown in Figure 12-52.

Note

If your scene is burning or has more lighting effects, then choose the ***Modify*** *tab in the* ***Command Panel*** *and set the intensity of omni lights. To do so, you need to modify the value in the* ***Multiplier*** *spinner of the* ***Intensity/Color/Attenuation*** *rollout.*

Next, you need to add advance effects to omni lights.

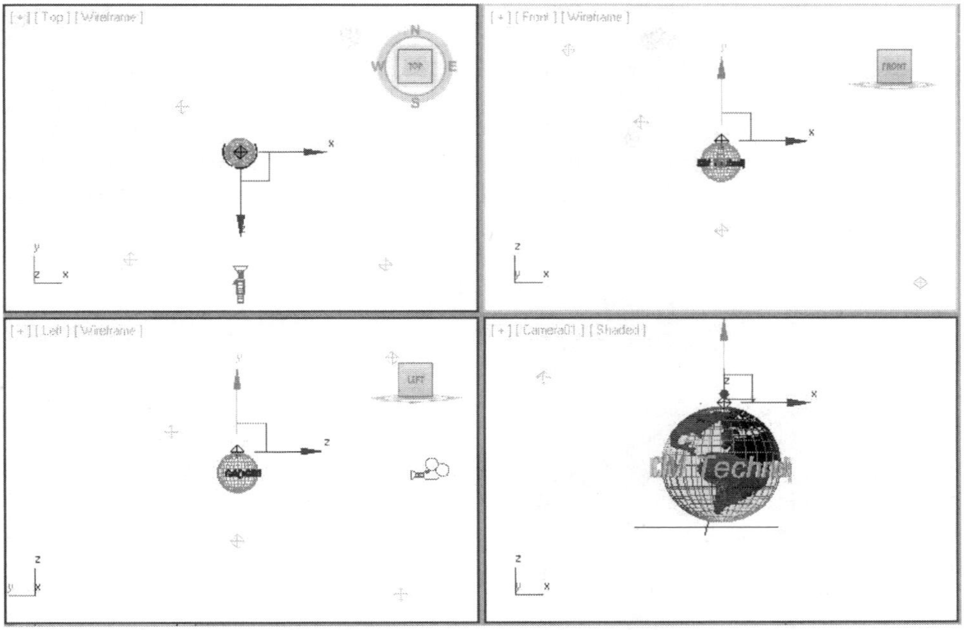

***Figure 12-52** Omni lights aligned in all viewports*

5. In the Front viewport, select the omni light that is placed on the left side of the *wireframe earth sphere*, as shown in Figure 12-53.

6. Choose the **Modify** tab in the **Command Panel** and expand the **Atmospheres & Effects** rollout. Choose the **Add** button; the **Add Atmospheres or Effect** dialog box is displayed. Select the **Lens Effects** option and choose the **OK** button to exit the dialog box; the **Lens Effects** option is displayed in the **Atmospheres & Effects** rollout.

   Next, you need to set the parameters for the **Lens Effects**.

7. Select the **Lens Effects** option in the **Atmospheres & Effects** rollout and choose the **Setup** button; the **Environment and Effects** dialog box is displayed with the **Effects** tab chosen. Also, various rollouts are displayed in this tab.

8. In the **Lens Effects Parameters** rollout, select the **Glow** option and choose the arrow that is pointing toward the right; the **Glow** effect is now available for the omni light at rendering. Also, the **Glow Element** rollout is displayed in the **Environment and Effects** dialog box to modify the parameters of the **Glow** effect.

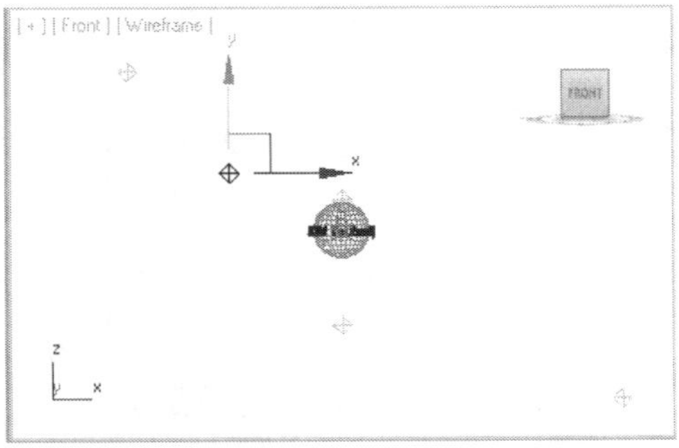

***Figure 12-53** Omni light selected to add the advance effects*

9. In the **Glow Element** rollout, set the values as given below:

   Size: **10.0** Intensity: **150.0**

10. In the **Lens Effects Parameters** rollout, select **Ray** and then choose the arrow that is pointing toward the right; the **Ray** effect is now available for the omni light at rendering. Also, the **Ray Element** rollout is displayed in the **Environment and Effects** dialog box to modify the parameters of the **Ray** effect.

11. In the **Ray Element** rollout, set the values as given below:

    Size: **50.0** Intensity: **10.0** Num: **50**

    Use the default values for other options.

12. To animate rays in the scene, choose the **Toggle Auto Key Mode** button to turn on the animation mode. Next, choose the **Go to Start** button to move the time slider to frame 0. In the **Ray Element** rollout, make sure that the value in the **Angle** spinner is 0.0 at frame 0.

13. Choose the **Go to End** button to move the time slider to frame 1000, and set the value in the **Angle** spinner to **180.0**. The rays appear to be rotating in the final output at rendering.

14. Choose the **Toggle Auto Key Mode** button to turn off the animation mode.

15. In the **Lens Effects Parameters** rollout, select the **Ring** option and then choose the arrow that is pointing toward the right side; the **Ring** effect becomes available for the omni light at rendering. Also, the **Ring Element** rollout is displayed in the **Environment and Effects** dialog box to modify the parameters of the **Ring** effect.

16. In the **Ring Element** rollout, set the values as given below:

    Size: **3.0** Intensity: **15.0**

    Use the default values for other options.

17. Close the **Environment and Effects** dialog box and render the Camera001 viewport; the omni light is displayed, as shown in Figure 12-54.

18. In the Front viewport, select the omni light that is placed just above the *wireframe earth sphere*. Align it at the top of the *wireframe earth sphere*, as shown in Figure 12-55. Then, add the **Lens Effects** as described above and set the parameters of different effects in the **Environment and Effects** dialog box as given next:

    Glow effect
    Size: **3.0** Intensity: **150.0**

Ray effect
Size: **10.0** Intensity: **30.0** Num: **10**

Star effect
Size: **10.0** Intensity: **50.0** Width: **1.0**

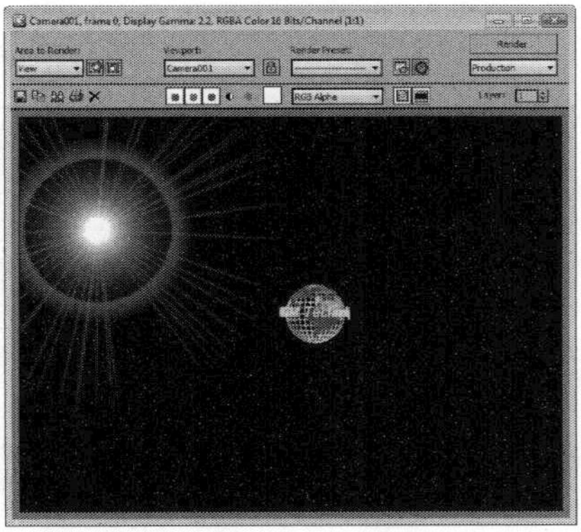

Figure 12-54 *The effect of the omni light displayed at rendering*

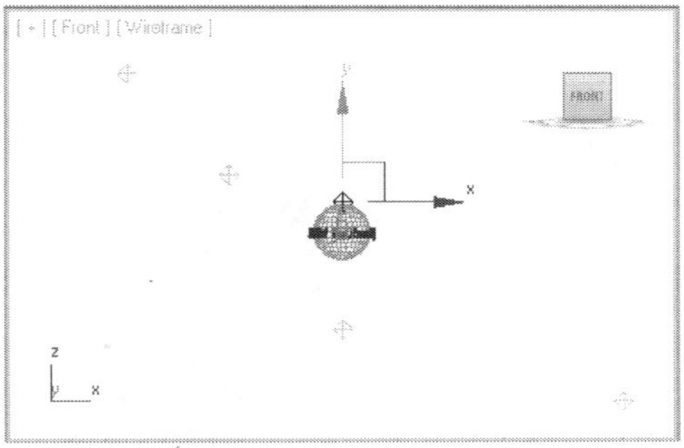

Figure 12-55 *The omni light aligned just above the wireframe earth sphere*

19. To animate the effects of this omni light in the scene, choose the **Toggle Auto Key Mode** button to turn on the animation mode. Now, choose the **Go to Start** button to move the time slider to frame 0. Also, in the **Star Element** rollout, make sure that the value in the **Angle** spinner is 0.0 at frame 0.

20. Choose the **Go to End** button to move the time slider to frame 1000 and set the value in the **Angle** spinner to **90.0**. The stars appear to be rotating in the final output at rendering.

21. Choose the **Toggle Auto Key Mode** button to turn off the animation mode.

After applying the effects, the omni light is displayed at rendering, as shown in Figure 12-56.

Next, you need to add spot lights to the scene.

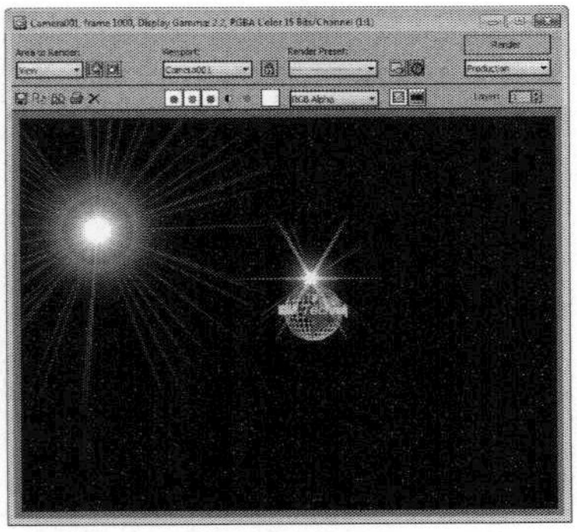

Figure 12-56 *The omni light with the lens effect at rendering*

22. Invoke the **Target Spot** tool from **Create > Lights > Standard > Object Type** rollout in the **Command Panel** and then create a spot light in the Front viewport, as shown in Figure 12-57. Also, create another spot light in the Top viewport, as shown in Figure 12-58.

The spotlights are automatically named as *Spot001* and *Spot002*.

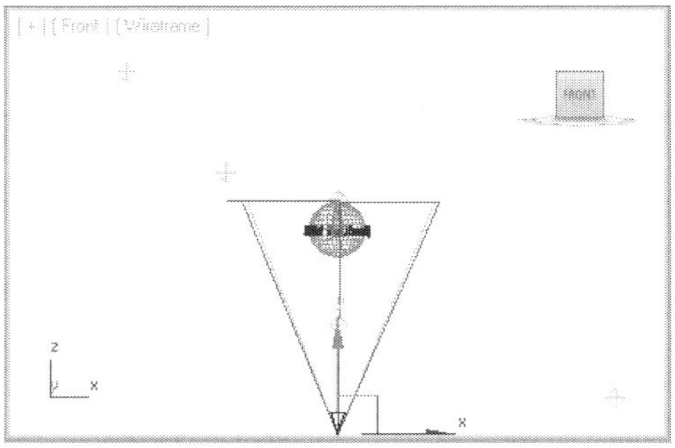

Figure 12-57 Spot light created in the Front viewport

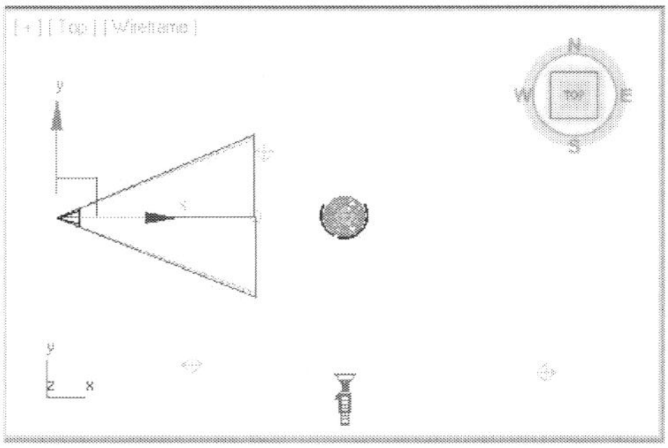

Figure 12-58 Spot light created in the Top viewport

Now, you need to modify the parameters of the spot lights.

23. Select the *Spot001* light that you created in the Front viewport and choose the **Modify** tab in the **Command Panel**; various rollouts are displayed to modify the parameters of the spotlight.

24. In the **Spotlight Parameters** rollout, set the values as given below:

    Hotspot/Beam: **25.3** Falloff/Field: **30.0**

25. In the **Atmospheres & Effects** rollout, add the **Volume Light** effect, select the **Volume Light** option in the rollout, and choose the **Setup** button; the **Environment and Effects** dialog box is displayed. In the **Volume** area of the **Volume Light Parameters** rollout, set the value in the **Density** spinner to **1.5**. Close the **Environment and Effects** dialog box.

26. Next, render the Camera001 viewport; the scene is displayed, as shown in Figure 12-59.

27. In the **Advance Effects** rollout of the modify panel, select the **Map** check box in the **Projector Map** area. Then, choose the **Projector Map** button labeled as **None** and assign a bitmap image of your choice to this map to give a more realistic effect to the **Volume Light** at rendering, refer to Figure 12-60.

28. At rendering, you will notice that the **Volume Light** is visible up to the infinite distance. To control the distance of the **Volume Light**, set the parameters in the **Far Attenuation** area in the **Intensity/Color/Attenuation** rollout as given below:

    Select the **Use** and **Show** check boxes.
    Start: **10** End: **850**

Note

You may need to adjust the values in the Start and End spinners as the values may differ depending on the placement of the light in the scene.

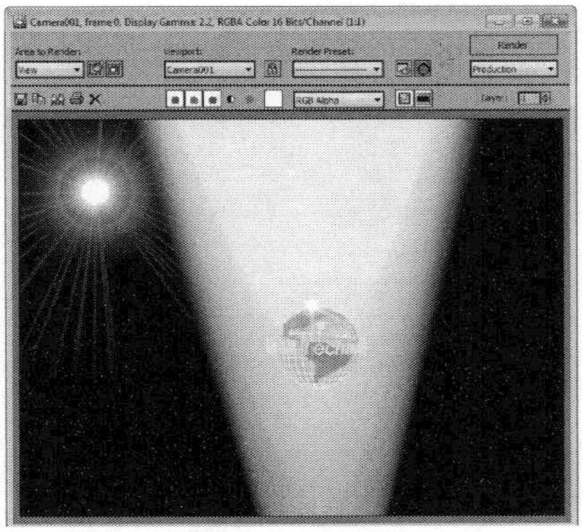

Figure 12-59 *The scene at rendering after applying the* ***Volume Light*** *effect in the Spot001 light*

Figure 12-60 *The scene at rendering after assigning a map to* ***Projector Map***

29. Render the Camera001 viewport; the scene is displayed, as shown in Figure 12-61.

30. Select the *Spot002* light in the viewport and choose the **Modify** tab in the **Command Panel**; all rollouts are displayed to modify the parameters of the selected light.

31. In the **Spotlight Parameters** rollout, set the values as given below:

    Hotspot/Beam: **5.0** Falloff/Field: **7.0**

32. Invoke the **Zoom Extents All** tool and align the *Spot002* light in all viewports, as shown in Figure 12-62.

Figure 12-61 *The scene displayed at rendering after setting the parameters in the* ***Far Attenuation*** *area*

Next, you need to animate the *Spot001* light.

33. Invoke the **Select by Name** tool and select *Spot001* and *Spot001.Target* in the Top viewport. Next, invoke the **Zoom Extents All Selected** tool to view the selected light properly.

34. Choose the **Toggle Auto Key Mode** button to turn on the animation mode and then choose the **Go to Start** button to move the time slider to frame 0.

35. Choose the **Go to End** button to move the time slider to frame 1000 and invoke the **Select and Rotate** tool. Next, in the Top viewport, move the cursor over the X-axis and rotate the *Spot001* and *Spot001.Target* in the clockwise direction until the value in the **Z** spinner becomes **-360** in the coordinate display.

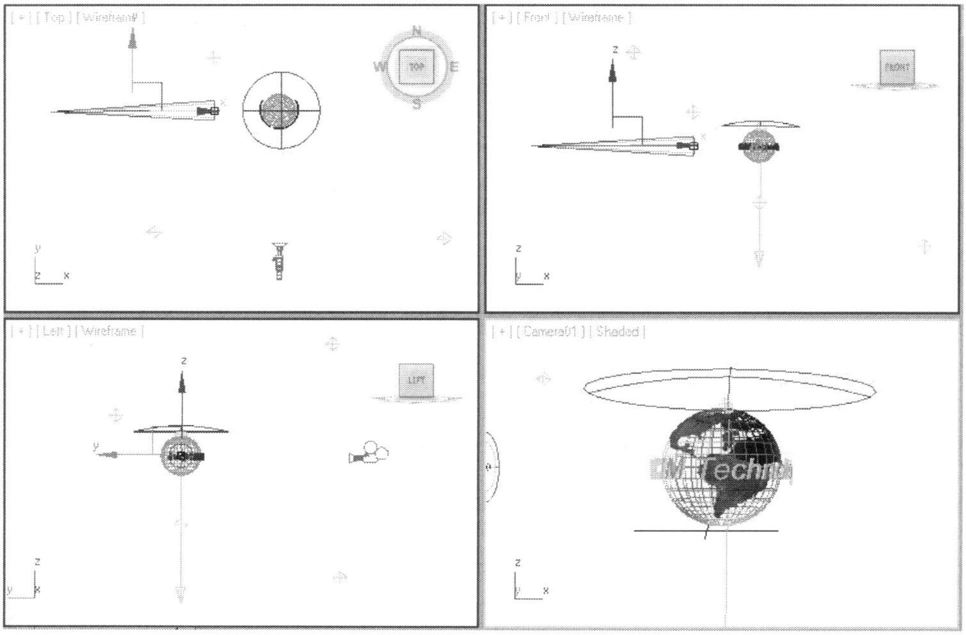

Figure 12-62 *The Spot002 light aligned in all viewports*

36. Choose the **Toggle Auto Key Mode** button to turn off the animation mode.

    Next, you need to animate the *wireframe earth sphere* and the *Text001* in the opposite directions.

Animating the Wireframe Earth Sphere and the Text

1. Activate the Top viewport and select the *wireframe earth sphere*. Then, invoke the **Zoom Extents All Selected** tool; the *wireframe earth sphere* is zoomed in all viewports, as shown in Figure 12-63.

Note

When you invoke a tool from the viewport navigation controls, it does not affect the Camera001 viewport.

2. Choose the **Toggle Auto Key Mode** button to turn on the animation mode and choose the **Go to Start** button to move the time slider to frame 0.

3. Next, choose the **Go to End** button to move the time slider to frame 1000 and then invoke the **Select and Rotate** tool. In the Top viewport, move the cursor over the X-axis and rotate the *wireframe earth sphere* in the counterclockwise direction until the value in the **Z** spinner becomes **360** in the coordinate display.

4. Choose the **Toggle Auto Key Mode** button to turn off the animation mode.

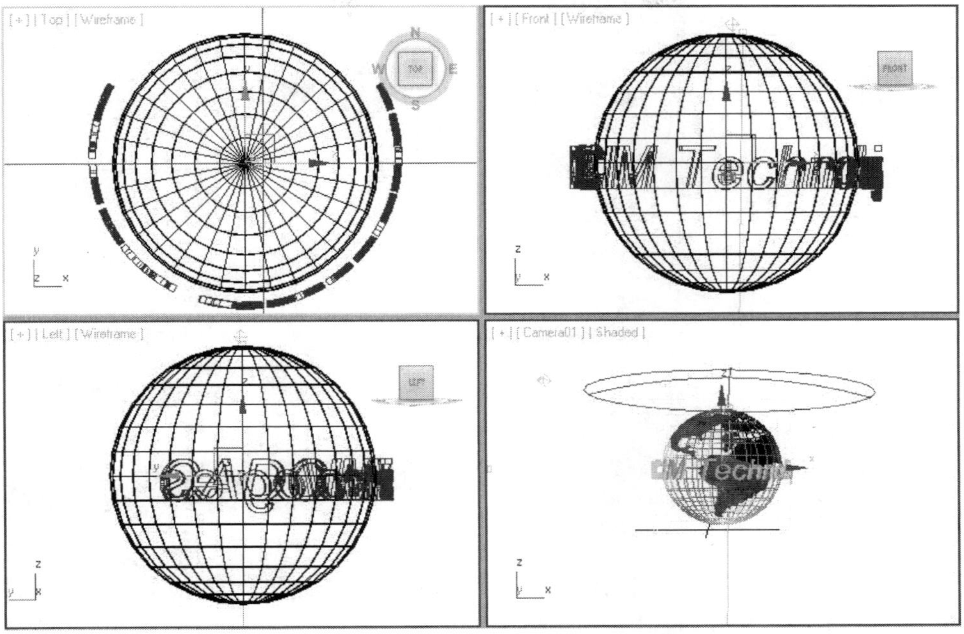

Figure 12-63 *The wireframe earth sphere zoomed in all viewports*

Next, you need to animate the *Text001* around the *wireframe earth sphere*.

5. Select the *Text001* in the Top viewport and choose the **Hierarchy** tab in the **Command Panel**. In the **Adjust Pivot** rollout, choose the **Affect Pivot Only** button; the pivot point of the *Text001* is displayed in the viewport, as shown in Figure 12-64.

6. Align the pivot point of the *Text001* at the center of the *wireframe earth sphere*, refer to Figure 12-65. Then, choose the **Affect Pivot Only** button again to deactivate it.

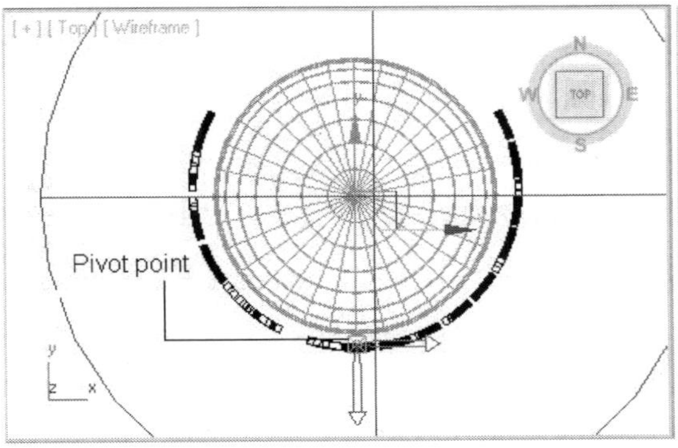

Figure 12-64 *The pivot point of the Text001 displayed in the Top viewport*

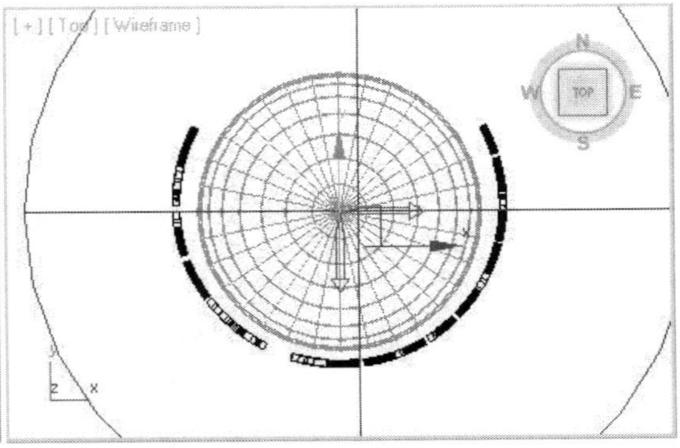

Figure 12-65 *The pivot point of the Text001 aligned in the Top viewport*

7. Invoke the **Select and Rotate** tool and rotate the *Text001* in the Top viewport along the Z-axis until the value in the **Z** spinner becomes **-180** in the coordinate display, as shown in Figure 12-66.

8. Similarly, rotate the *Text001* in the Front viewport along the Z-axis until the value in the **Z** spinner becomes **10** in the coordinate display, refer to Figure 12-67.

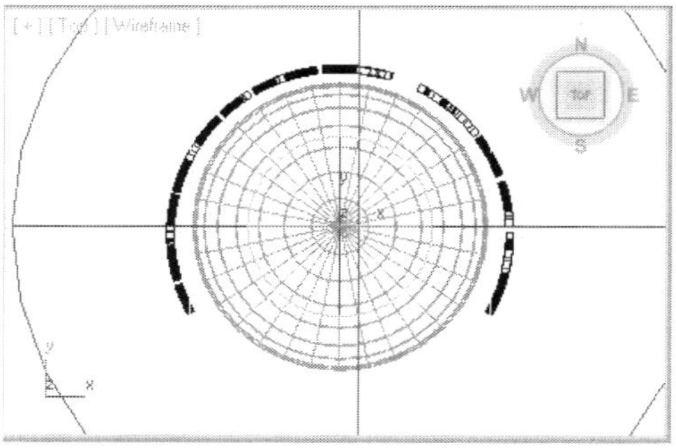

Figure 12-66 *The Text001 rotated in the Top viewport*

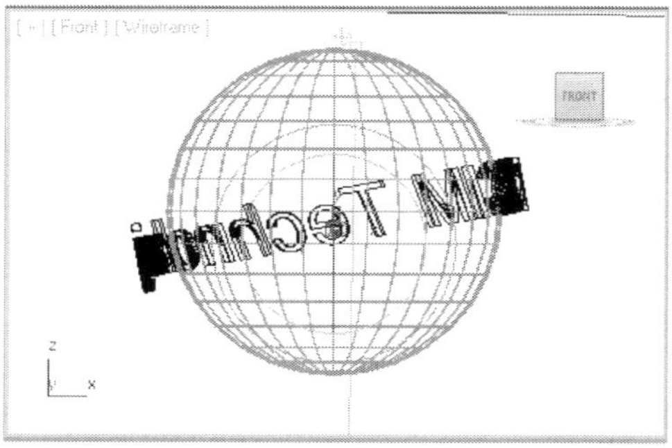

Figure 12-67 *The Text001 rotated in the Front viewport*

9. Choose the **Toggle Auto Key Mode** button to turn on the animation mode. Choose the **Go to End** button to move the time slider to frame 1000 and make sure that the *Text001* is selected. Invoke the **Select and Rotate** tool in the Top viewport, move the cursor over the X-axis, and rotate the *Text001* in the clockwise direction until the Z coordinate, just below the track bar, displays -360.

10. Choose the **Toggle Auto Key Mode** button to turn off the animation mode and choose the **Play Animation** button to view the animation.

Rendering and Saving the Final Output of the Animation

To view the final output of the scene that contains all movements, textures, lights, and animations, you need to render the scene. To do so, follow the procedure described in Tutorial 1 of this chapter.

You can view the final rendered sequence by downloading the *c12_3dsmax_2012_render.zip* file from *http://www.cadcim.com.*

Saving the File

1. Save the file with the name *c12tut2.max* as discussed in earlier chapters. The location of this file is given below:

   \Documents\3dsmax\c12_tut2\scene

Self-Evaluation Test

Answer the following questions and then compare them to those given at the end of this chapter:

1. Which of the following buttons is used to turn on the animation mode?

   (a) **Toggle Auto Key Mode** (b) **Toggle Set Key Mode**
   (c) **Set Keys** (d) None of these

2. Which of the following tools is used to control the animation keys in an animation?

   (a) **Track View** (b) **Key Mode Toggle**
   (c) **Play Animation** (d) **Time Configuration**

3. Which of the following modifiers is used to create morphing in objects?

   (a) **Morph** (b) **Scatter**
   (c) **Mesher** (d) **Terrain**

4. Which of the following options is used to add special effects at rendering in the **Rendering** pull-down menu?

   (a) **Render** (b) **Material Editor**
   (c) **Effects** (d) None of these

5. In the set key animation mode, you need to set the keys for the animation of the selected object by choosing the **Set Keys** button. (T/F)

6. To move the time slider to another frame, you can enter the frame number directly in the Current Frame (Go to frame) spinner. (T/F)

7. The **Time Configuration** button is used to set the animation length by defining the number of frames in the track bar. (T/F)

8. The __________ button is used to jump between the keyframes directly.

9. The __________ displays the timeline with the frame numbers in it.

10. To render the final animation, you need to invoke the __________ tool in the **Main Toolbar**.

Review Questions

Answer the following questions:

1. Which of the following effects can be assigned to the rendered scene from **Rendering > Effects** in the menu bar?

   (a) **Blur** (b) **Lens Effects**
   (c) **Motion Blur** (d) All of these

2. Which of the following options in the **Animation** pull-down menu is used to create a preview animation?

   (a) **View Preview** (b) **Make Preview**
   (c) **Rename Preview** (d) None of these

3. Which of the following areas in the **Render Setup** dialog box is used to decide whether Autodesk 3ds Max will use the full resolution maps or the proxies of maps at rendering ?

   (a) **Render Output**
   (b) **Bitmap Performance and Memory Options**
   (c) **Advanced Lighting**
   (d) None of these

4. In the **Curve Editor** mode of the track view, the animation is displayed as a spreadsheet of keys. (T/F)

5. The options in the **Frame Rate** area of the **Time Configuration** dialog box are used to define a particular frame rate for animation in frames per second. (T/F)

6. The **Playback** area in the **Time Configuration** dialog box is used to slow down the speed of the animation. (T/F)

7. To assign the **mental ray Renderer** for rendering the animation, you need to invoke the **Quick Render (Production)** tool in the **Main Toolbar**. (T/F)

8. To create the preview of an animation, select the __________ option from the __________ pull-down menu.

9. To save the rendered animation, you need to define a file with the __________ extension in the __________ area of the **Render Setup** dialog box.

10. The __________ button is used to play the animation of an object in the viewport.

Exercises

Exercise 1

Start Autodesk 3ds Max 2012 and then perform the following operations:

Create different primitives at some distance in the Top viewport and try the following steps:

1. Create a free camera in the viewport. Next, create an animation of the camera using the auto key animation mode such that it touches the top of all primitives one by one. Also, create the same animation using the set key animation mode and notice the difference.

2. Create an omni light in the scene, choose the **Modify** tab, and expand the **Atmospheres & Effects** rollout. Then, add atmospheric effects to the light to view special effects at rendering.

3. Select the free camera in the viewport and invoke the **Curve Editor** tool in the **Main Toolbar**; the **Track View - Curve Editor** dialog box is displayed. Next, edit the keys in the edit window and notice the effect in your animation.

4. Invoke the **Render Scene Dialog** tool; the **Render Scene** dialog box is displayed. In the **Assign Renderer** rollout, set the **mental ray Renderer** to render the Camera001 viewport and view the difference in the final output.

5. Select the **Make Preview** option from the **Animation** pull-down menu; the **Make Preview** dialog box is displayed. Set the parameters for different options and choose the **Create** button to create the preview of the animation.

6. Choose **Rendering > Effects** from the menu bar and add special effects to the scene.

Exercise 2

Create the early morning scene and animate the sea water, refer to Figure 12-68. You can view the final rendered image of this model by downloading it from *http://www.cadcim.com*.

(Expected time: 30 min)

Hints:
1. Create an omni light for the sun effect and use the **Lens** effects in it.
2. Create water as discussed in Tutorial 1 of this chapter.

Figure 12-68 *The scene for Exercise 2*

Exercise 3

Create the solar system using the standard primitives and lights, as shown in Figure 12-69. You can view the final rendered image of this model by downloading it from *http://www.cadcim.com*.

(Expected time: 45 min)

Figure 12-69 *An animated scene for Exercise 3*

Answers to Self-Evaluation Test

1. c, **2.** a, **3.** a, **4.** c, **5.** T, **6.** T, **7.** T, **8. Key Mode Toggle**, **9.** track bar, **10. Render Production**

13

Particle Systems and Space Warps-I

Learning Objectives

After completing this chapter, you will be able to:
* *Understand particle systems*
* *Understand space warps*
* *Understand mesher compound object*
* *Understand blobmesh compound object*

INTRODUCTION TO PARTICLE SYSTEMS

In Autodesk 3ds Max, the particle systems are used to create an object that generates other objects known as particles. These particles are used to simulate snow, dust, rain, and so on. You can also animate the particles in a particle system. To create a particle system, choose **Create > Geometry** in the **Command Panel**; a drop-down list will be displayed below the **Geometry** button. Select **Particle Systems** from the drop-down list; the **Object Type** rollout containing all tools to create the particle system will be displayed, as shown in Figure 13-1. In this chapter, you will learn to create and modify different types of particle systems using these tools.

Spray Particle System

Menu bar:	Create > Particles > Spray
Command Panel:	Create > Geometry > Particle Systems > Object Type rollout > Spray

The spray particle system is used to generate the particles that are similar to the water drops or spray, as shown in Figure 13-2. To create the spray particle system, invoke the **Spray** tool from **Create > Geometry > Particle Systems > Object Type** rollout in the **Command Panel**; the **Name and Color** and **Parameters** rollouts will be displayed. In the Top viewport, press and hold the left mouse button, and then drag the cursor from one point to another; a rectangular shape will be created that is known as emitter. You cannot view the emitter at rendering. Choose the **Play Animation** button from the animation playback controls; the particles will start emitting from the emitter, as shown in Figure 13-3. The straight line passing through the center of the emitter specifies the direction of the particles. If you create the emitter in the Front or the Left viewport, then the direction of the particles will be different. After creating the emitter, you need to set the size, shape, number, and other properties of the particles in the **Parameters** rollout, which is discussed next.

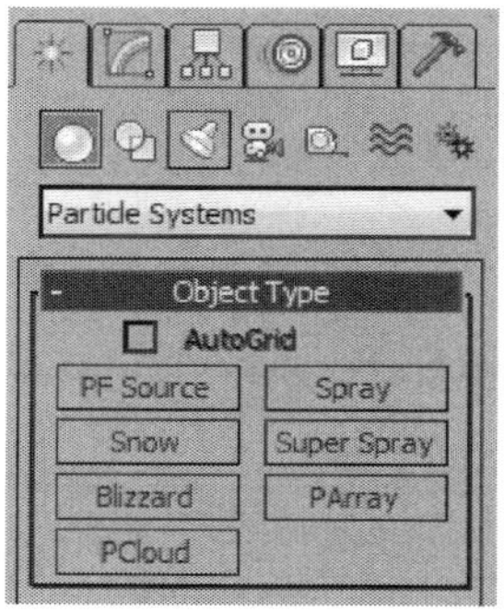

Figure 13-1 *Various tools displayed to create particle systems*

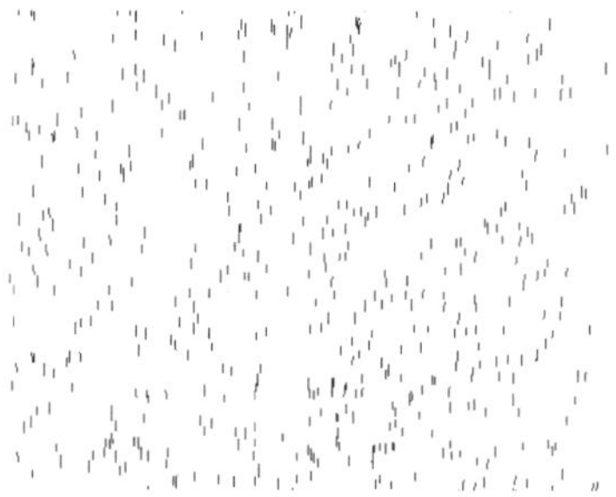

Figure 13-2 *The spray particle system*

Parameters Rollout

This rollout is used to modify the size, shape, number, and other properties of the spray particles. To invoke this rollout, select the emitter in the viewport and choose the **Modify** tab in the **Command Panel**; the **Parameters** rollout will be displayed. The different areas of this rollout that are used to modify the properties of the particles are discussed next.

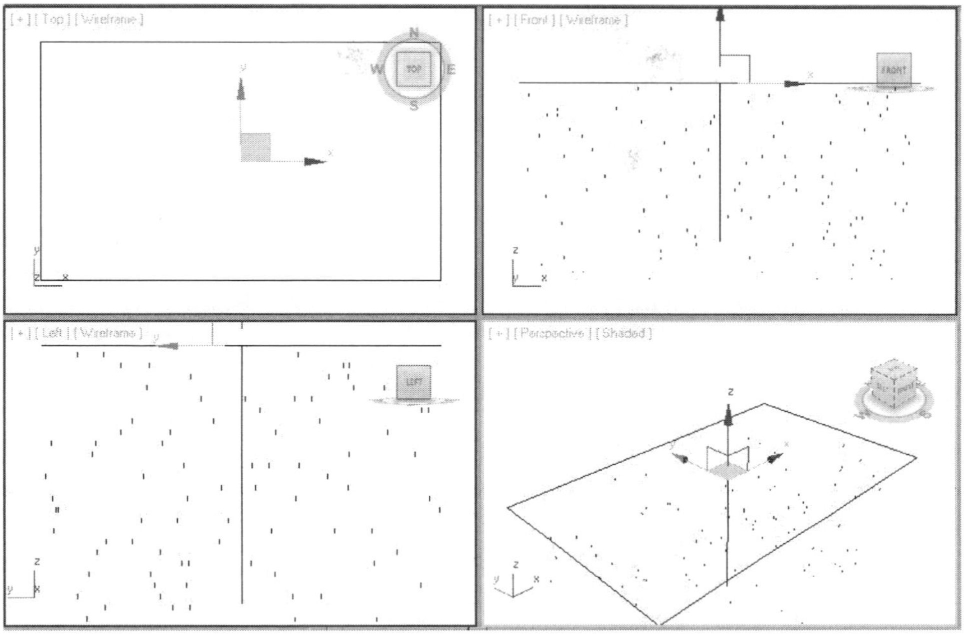

Figure 13-3 The emitter displayed in all viewports for the spray particle system

Particles Area

The options in this area are used to define how the particles will be generated, refer to Figure 13-4. Set the value in the **Viewport Count** spinner to define the number of particles displayed in the viewport at a frame. Set the value in the **Render Count** spinner to define the number of particles displayed at rendering at a frame. Set the value in the **Drop Size** spinner to modify the size of the particles. Set the value in the **Speed** spinner to define the initial velocity of the particles when they leave the emitter. The velocity is known as the distance traveled per unit time.

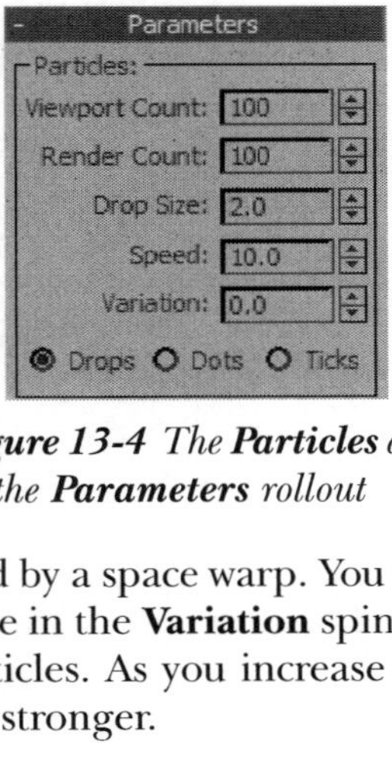

*Figure 13-4 The **Particles** area in the **Parameters** rollout*

The particles remain at the same speed unless they are affected by a space warp. You will learn more about space warps later in this chapter. Set the value in the **Variation** spinner to define the variation in the speed and direction of the particles. As you increase the value in the **Variation** spinner, the particles will get wider and stronger.

By default, the **Drops** radio button is selected in this area. As a result, the particles are displayed in the shape of drops in the viewports. Select the **Dots** or the **Ticks** radio button to display the particles in the shape of dots or ticks. These radio buttons do not affect the shape of the particles at rendering.

Render Area

This area is used to define the shape of the particles at rendering, refer to Figure 13-5. By default, the **Tetrahedron** radio button is selected in this area. As a result, the particles are displayed as tetrahedrons. Select the **Facing** radio button to display the particles as square faces.

Timing Area

The options in this area are used to define the lifetime of the particles, refer to Figure 13-6. The value in the **Start** spinner specifies the frame number at which the emitter will start generating the particles. The value in the **Life** spinner shows the life span of the particles in terms of the number of frames. The value in the **Birth Rate** spinner shows the number of new particles generated at each frame. By default, this spinner is not activated. To activate this spinner, you need to clear the **Constant** check box.

Emitter Area

This area is used to define the dimensions of the emitter, refer to Figure 13-7. Set the value in the **Width** and **Length** spinners to define the width and length of the emitter, respectively. Select the **Hide** check box to hide the emitter in the viewports.

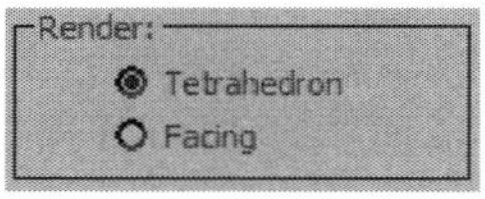

*Figure 13-5 The **Render** area*

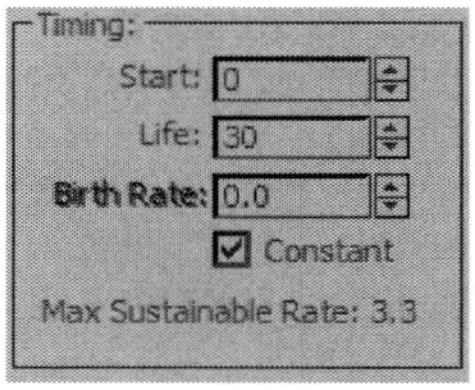

*Figure 13-6 The **Timing** area*

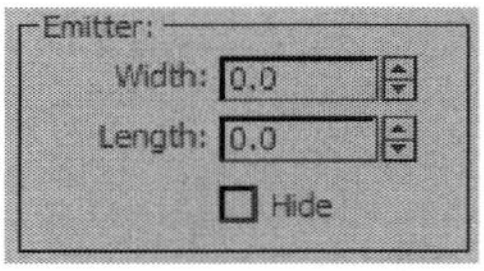

*Figure 13-7 The **Emitter** area*

Snow Particle System

Menu bar:	Create > Particles > Snow
Command Panel:	Create > Geometry > Particle Systems > Object Type rollout > Snow

The snow particle system is used to generate the particles that are similar to snow flakes, as shown in Figure 13-8. To create the snow particle system, invoke the **Snow** tool from **Create > Geometry > Particle Systems > Object Type** rollout in the **Command Panel**; the **Name and Color** and **Parameters** rollouts will be displayed. In the Top viewport, press and hold the left mouse button, and then drag the cursor from one point to another; the emitter will be created. Choose the **Play Animation** button; the particles will start emitting from the emitter, as shown in Figure 13-9. After creating the emitter, you need to set the size, shape, number, and other properties of the particles in the **Parameters** rollout, which is discussed next.

Figure 13-8 The snow particles at rendering

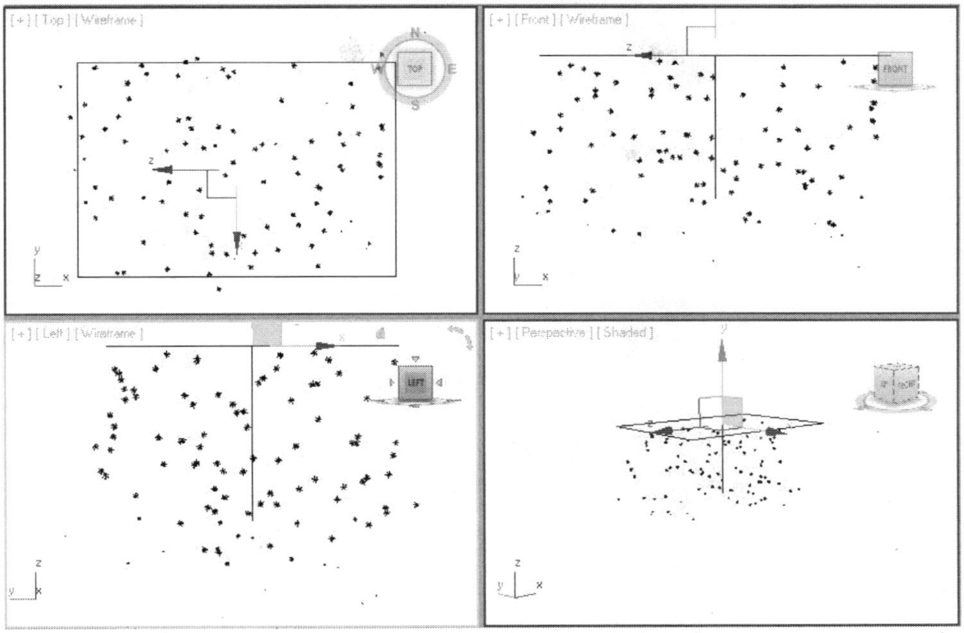

Figure 13-9 The particles displayed in all viewports for the snow particle system

Parameters Rollout

This rollout is used to modify the size, shape, number, and other properties of the snow particles. To invoke this rollout, select the emitter in the viewport and choose the **Modify** tab in the **Command Panel**; the **Parameters** rollout will be displayed. In the **Parameters** rollout, most of the options are the same as discussed in the spray particle system. The remaining options are discussed next.

Particles Area

Set the value in the **Flake Size** spinner to specify the size of the particles. The value in the **Tumble** spinner is used to specify the amount of random rotation of the snow particles. The value in the **Tumble Rate** spinner is used to specify the speed of rotation of the snow particles. As you increase the value in the **Tumble Rate** spinner, the speed of rotation will also increase.

Render Area

By default, the **Six Point** radio button is selected in this area. As a result, the particles are displayed as six point shape at rendering, refer to Figure 13-8. Select the **Triangle** or **Facing** radio button to display the triangular or facing particles at rendering, as shown in Figures 13-10 and 13-11.

***Figure 13-10** The triangular snow particles*

***Figure 13-11** The facing snow particles*

Super Spray Particle System

Menu bar:	Create > Particles > Super Spray
Command Panel:	Create > Geometry > Particle Systems > Object Type rollout > Super Spray

The super spray particle system is the advanced version of the spray particle system. To create the super spray particle system, you need to invoke the **Super Spray** tool from **Create > Geometry > Particle Systems > Object Type** rollout in the **Command Panel**; the **Name and Color**, **Basic Parameters**, **Particle Generation**, **Particle Type**, **Rotation and Collision**, **Object Motion Inheritance**, **Bubble Motion**, **Particle Spawn**, and **Load/Save Presets** rollouts will be displayed. In the Top viewport, press and hold the left mouse button, and then drag the cursor from one point to another; the emitter will be created. Choose the **Play Animation** button; the particles will start emitting from the emitter, as shown in Figure 13-12.

After creating the emitter, you need to set the size, shape, number, and other properties of the particles in various rollouts. The most commonly used rollouts are discussed next.

Basic Parameters Rollout

The options in this rollout are used to define the direction, spread, and other properties of the particles, refer to Figure 13-13. The areas in this rollout are discussed next.

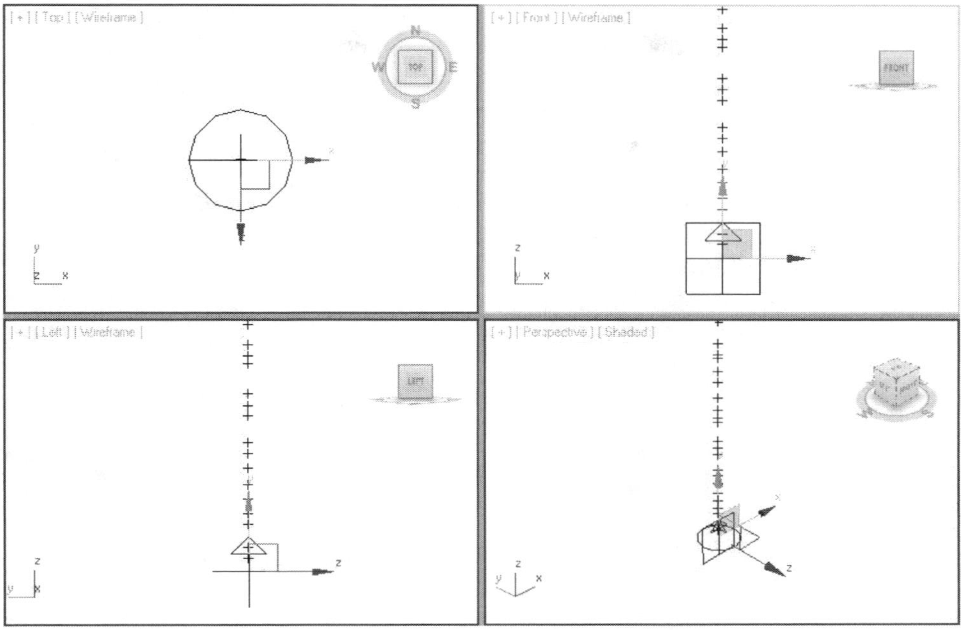

***Figure 13-12** The particles generated for the super spray particle system*

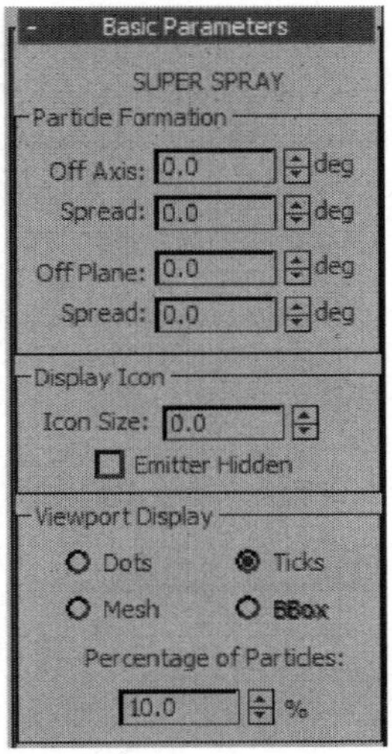

***Figure 13-13** The **Basic Parameters** rollout*

Particle Formation Area

Set the value in the **Off Axis** spinner to offset the angle of the particles in the Z-axis, along the plane of the X-axis. Set the value in the **Spread** spinner to spread the particles away from the emitter. Set the value in the **Off Plane** spinner to offset the direction of particles in the horizontal plane. The value in the **Spread** spinner is used to spread the particles around the off plane axis.

> **Note**
>
> *If you set the value **0** in the **Off Axis** spinner, then the value in the **Off Plane** spinner will not affect the particles.*

Display Icon Area

Set the value in the **Icon Size** spinner to define the size of the emitter icon in the viewport. Select the **Emitter Hidden** check box to hide the emitter icon in the viewport.

Viewport Display Area

The radio buttons in this area are used to define the shape of the particles in the viewport. Set the value in the **Percentage of Particles** spinner to define the percentage of the number of particles to be displayed in the viewport.

Particle Generation Rollout

The options in this rollout are used to define the motion, quantity, size, and other properties of the particles, refer to Figure 13-14. The areas in this rollout are discussed next.

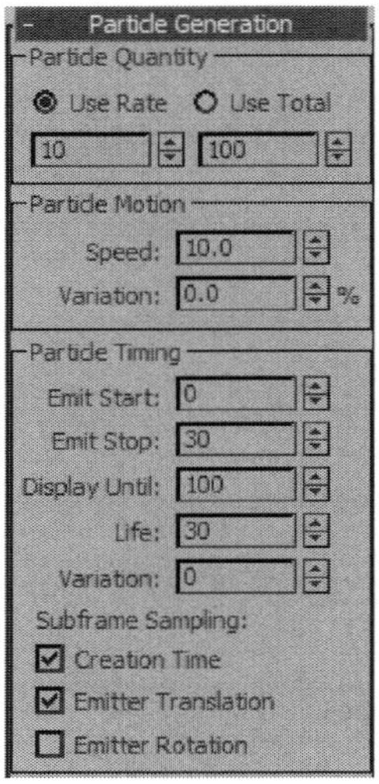

***Figure 13-14** Partial view of the **Particle Generation** rollout*

Particle Quantity Area

The radio buttons in this area are used to define how the particles will be generated over the time. By default, the **Use Rate** radio button is selected. It is used to define the number of particles generated at each frame. The spinner below this radio button defines the number of particles created per frame. Select the **Use Total** radio button to define the total number of particles generated over the life span of the system. Set the value in the spinner below this radio button to define the total number of particles created over the life span of the system.

Particle Motion Area

The options in this area are used to define the speed of the particles. Set the value in the **Speed** spinner to specify the initial velocity of the particles when they leave the emitter. Set the value in the **Variation** spinner to specify the variation in the speed and the direction of the particles.

Particle Timing Area

In the **Emit Start** and **Emit Stop** spinners, set the frame number at which the particles will begin and stop the emission. Set the value in the **Display Until** spinner to define the frame number at which all particles will disappear from the scene. The value in the **Life** spinner specifies the life span of the particles in terms of the number of frames. The value in the **Variation** spinner is used to define the number of frames by which the life of the particles can vary randomly.

Particle Size Area

The options in this area are used to define the size of the particles. Set the value in the **Size** spinner to specify the size of the particles. The value in the **Variation** spinner is used to define the variation in the size of the particles. The value in the **Grow For** spinner is used to define the number of frames in which the particles will grow from their original size to the size specified in the **Size** spinner. The value in the **Fade For** spinner is used to define the number of frames in which the particles will shrink to 1/10th of their size before their death.

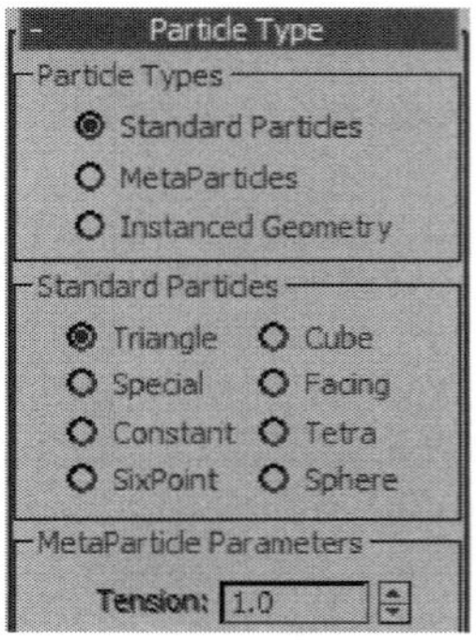

***Figure 13-15** Partial view of the **Particle Type** rollout*

Particle Type Rollout

The options in this rollout are used to define the type of particles used in the scene, refer to Figure 13-15. The areas in this rollout are discussed next.

Particle Types Area

The radio buttons in this rollout are used to define the type of geometry of the particles at rendering. When you select a radio button in the **Particle Types** area, its corresponding area will get activated in the rollout where you can modify the parameters as per your requirement. By default, the **Standard Particles** radio button is selected, and therefore, the **Standard Particles** area is activated. There are eight types of radio buttons such as **Cube**, **Tetra**, **Facing**, and so on in this area to define the geometry of the particles. Select the corresponding radio button to change the geometry of the particles at rendering.

Note

You cannot view the change in the geometry of the particles in the viewport. It will be displayed only at rendering.

Select the **MetaParticles** radio button in the **Particle Types** area; the **MetaParticle Parameters** area will be activated. It is used to create the particles in the form of metaballs. The metaball particles can join together to form a blob or a stream of particles. The blob is an indistinct form of particles, as shown in Figure 13-16. You can modify the parameters of the meta particles in the **MetaParticle Parameters** area.

Select the **Instanced Geometry** radio button in the **Particle Types** area; the **Instancing Parameters** area will be activated. This area is used to select an object in the viewport to be used as particles in a particle system. These particles will be the instance of the object. To create an instance of the object, choose the **Pick Object** button in the **Instancing Parameters** area; it will prompt you to select the object in the viewport. Select the object in the viewport; the particles will take the geometry of the selected object and they will be displayed at rendering, refer to Figure 13-17.

Figure 13-16 *The meta particles*

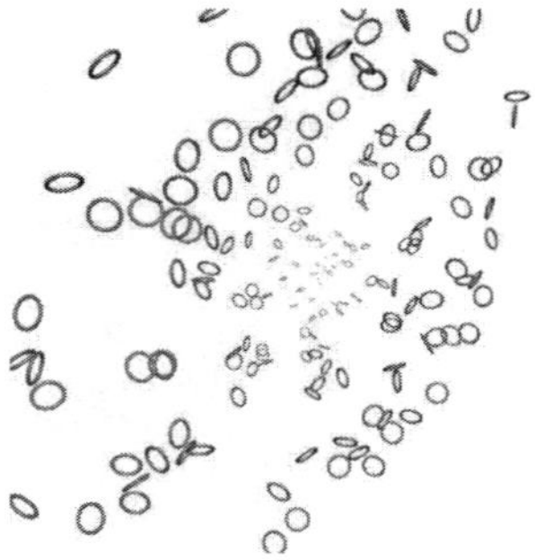

Figure 13-17 *The torus object selected to create the instance particles*

Mat'l Mapping and Source Area

The options in this area are used to define the material and the mapping for the particles.

Rotation and Collision Rollout

The options in this rollout are used to rotate the particles and add motion blur to them, refer to Figure 13-18. The motion blur is used to provide the blur effect to the fast moving animated objects to make them look more realistic. The areas in this rollout are discussed next.

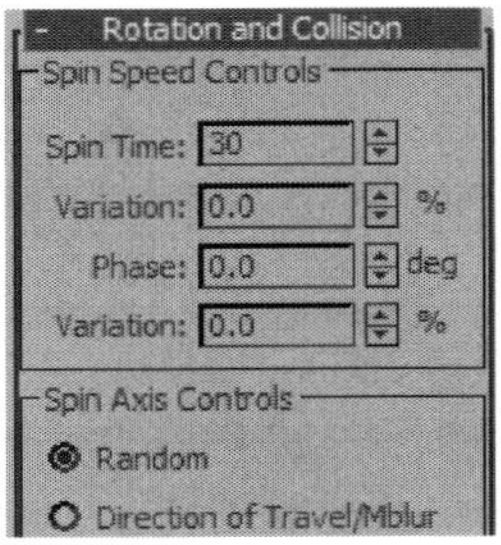

Figure 13-18 Partial view of the ***Rotation and Collision*** *rollout*

Spin Speed Controls Area

The value in the **Spin Time** spinner specifies the total number of frames that the particles will take to complete one rotation. Set the value in the **Variation** spinner to set the percentage of variation of the spin time. The value in the **Phase** spinner is used to define the initial rotation of the particles at birth. Set the value in the **Variation** spinner below the **Phase** spinner to specify the percentage of variation of phase.

Spin Axis Controls Area

The options in this area are used to set the axis of rotation for the particles. By default, the **Random** radio button is selected that is used to define the axis of rotation for each particle randomly. On selecting the **Direction of Travel/Mblur** radio button, the particles will rotate about a vector formed in the direction of the movement of the particles. In the **Stretch** spinner, set the value in percentage to stretch each particle. The **Direction of Travel/Mblur** radio button is also used to apply the motion blur to the object. Select the **User Defined** radio button to use a vector for the rotation that is defined in the **X Axis**, **Y Axis**, and **Z Axis** spinners.

Interparticle Collisions Area

This area is used to control the collisions between the particles.

Bubble Motion Rollout

The options in this rollout are used to provide a waveform motion path for the particles, refer to Figure 13-19. This rollout is also used to produce a wobbling effect in the particles. Set the value in the **Amplitude** spinner to specify the height of each wave. The value in the **Period** spinner is used to define the number of frames it takes to complete one cycle of the wave. The value in the **Phase** spinner specifies the initial position of a particle along the wave. Set the values in different **Variation** spinners to produce variations in the corresponding parameters.

Particle Spawn Rollout

The options in this rollout are used to specify the reaction of the particles when they die or collide with a particle deflector, refer to Figure 13-20. A deflector is a space warp about which you will learn later in this chapter. The most commonly used areas of this rollout are discussed next.

Particle Spawning Effects Area

By default, the **None** radio button is selected and therefore particles are not spawn. The properties of the deflector objects set the nature of particles at collision. On selecting the **Die After Collision** radio button, the particles disappear after colliding with the deflector object. Also, the **Persist** and **Variation** spinners get activated. Set the value in the **Persist** spinner to specify the number of frames, in which the particles remain alive after the collision.

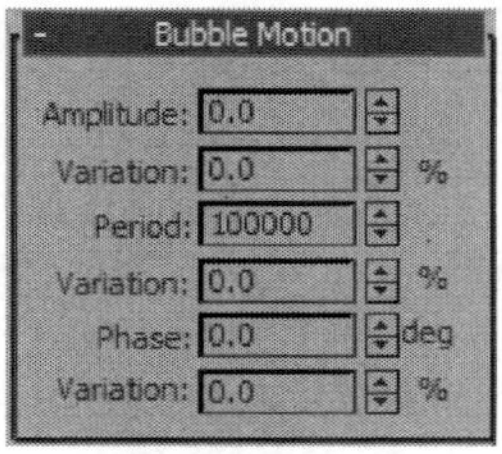

Figure 13-19 *The* ***Bubble Motion*** *rollout*

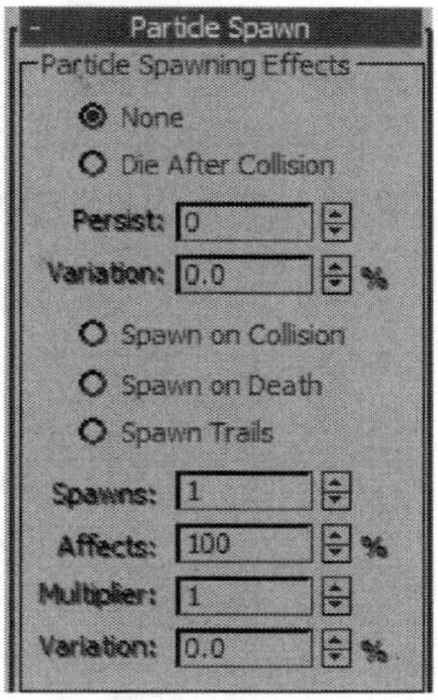

Figure 13-20 *The* ***Particle Spawn*** *rollout*

If you select the **Spawn on Collision** radio button, the particles will be generated after the collision. Whereas, on selecting the **Spawn on Death** radio button, the particles will be spawned at the end of their life span. On selecting the **Spawn Trails** radio button, the particles will be spawned from each existing particle at each frame of the particles life. Set the values in the **Spawns**, **Affects**, **Multiplier**, and **Variation** spinners to modify the spawn of the particles.

Direction Chaos Area

Set the value in the **Chaos** spinner to vary the direction of the spawned particles.

Speed Chaos Area

Set the values in different options of this area to vary the speed of the spawned particles.

Scale Chaos Area

Set the values in different options of this area to scale the spawned particles.

Load/Save Presets Rollout

The options in this rollout are used to load the predefined settings of the particle system, refer to Figure 13-21. You can save these settings to use in other particle systems. On the top of this rollout, enter a name for the settings in the **Preset Name** text box and choose the **Save** button; the name of the settings will be displayed in the list box given in the **Saved Presets** area. If you need to use the same settings for another particle system, then select the new particle system in the viewport and select the name of the settings from the list box in the **Saved Presets** area. Now, choose the **Load** button; the same settings will be applied to the new particle system.

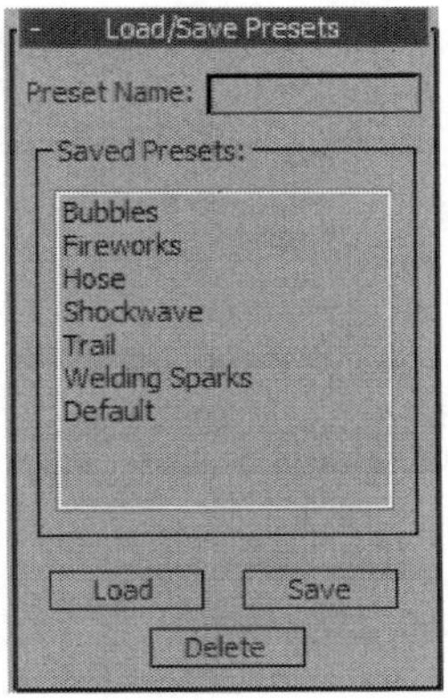

Figure 13-21 *The* ***Load/ Save Presets*** *rollout*

To delete the settings, select the name of the settings in the **Saved Presets** area, and then choose the **Delete** button. You can also use the default settings available in the list box such as **Bubbles**, **Fireworks**, and so on in the **Saved Presets** area.

Blizzard Particle System

Menu bar:	Create > Particles > Blizzard
Command Panel:	Create > Geometry > Particle Systems > Object Type rollout > Blizzard

The blizzard particle system is the advanced version of the snow particle system. To create the blizzard particle system, invoke the **Blizzard** tool from **Create > Geometry > Particle Systems > Object Type** rollout in the **Command Panel**; the **Name and Color**, **Basic Parameters**, **Particle Generation**, **Particle Type**, **Rotation and Collision**, **Object Motion Inheritance**, **Particle Spawn**, and **Load/Save Presets** rollouts will be displayed. In the Top viewport, press and hold the left mouse button, and then drag the cursor from one point to another; the emitter will be created. Choose the **Play Animation** button; the particles will emit from the emitter, as shown in Figure 13-22. After creating the emitter, you need to set the properties of the particles in various rollouts. The options in the rollouts are the same as discussed in the super spray particle system. However, the main difference is that in the **Basic Parameters** rollout of the blizzard particle system, you need to set the width and length of the emitter icon in their respective spinners in the **Display Icon** area.

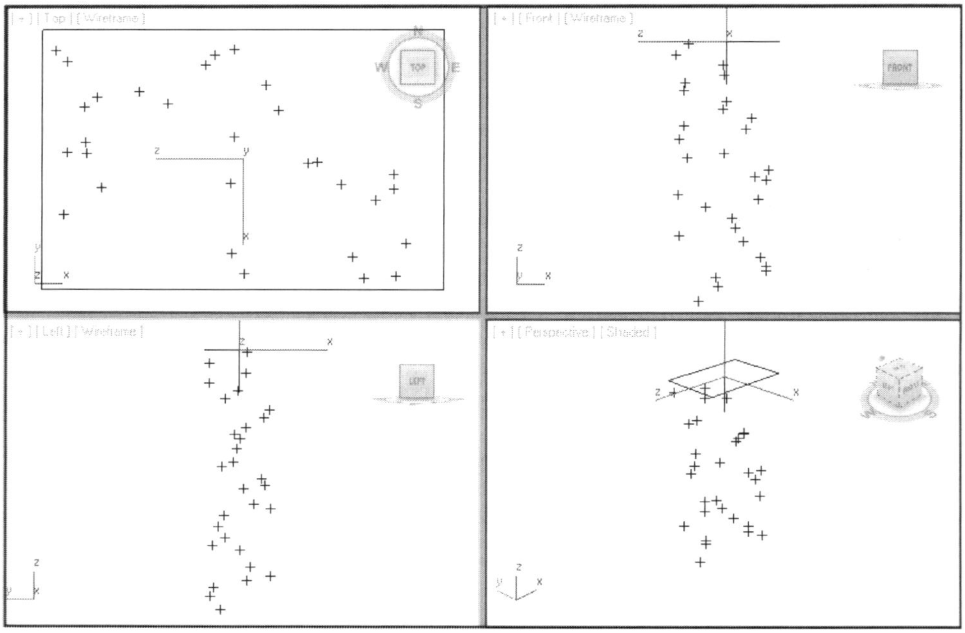

Figure 13-22 *The particles generated for the blizzard particle system*

PArray Particle System

Menu bar:	Create > Particles > PArray
Command Panel:	Create > Geometry > Particle Systems > Object Type rollout > PArray

The PArray particle system is used to generate particles from the selected geometry. Moreover, it is used to create an explosion of the objects. In the PArray particle system, the geometry that you use to emit the particles becomes the emitter and is referred to as the distribution object. To create the PArray particle system, first you need to create a geometry in the viewport and then invoke the **PArray** tool from **Create > Geometry > Particle Systems > Object Type** rollout in the **Command Panel**; the **Name and Color**, **Basic Parameters**, **Particle Generation**, **Particle Type**, **Rotation and Collision**, **Object Motion Inheritance**, **Particle Spawn**, **Bubble Motion**, and **Load/Save Presets** rollouts will be displayed. In the Top viewport, press and hold the left mouse button, and then drag the cursor to create the PArray particle system. Next, in the **Basic Parameters** rollout, choose the **Pick Object** button, move the cursor over the geometry that you want to use as the distribution object or the emitter, and then select the geometry; the selected geometry will act as the distribution object. Now, choose the **Play Animation** button, the particles will emit from the selected geometry, as shown in Figure 13-23. Now, you need to set the properties of the particles in various rollouts. Most of the options in the rollouts displayed are same as those discussed in the super spray particle system. The remaining ones are discussed next.

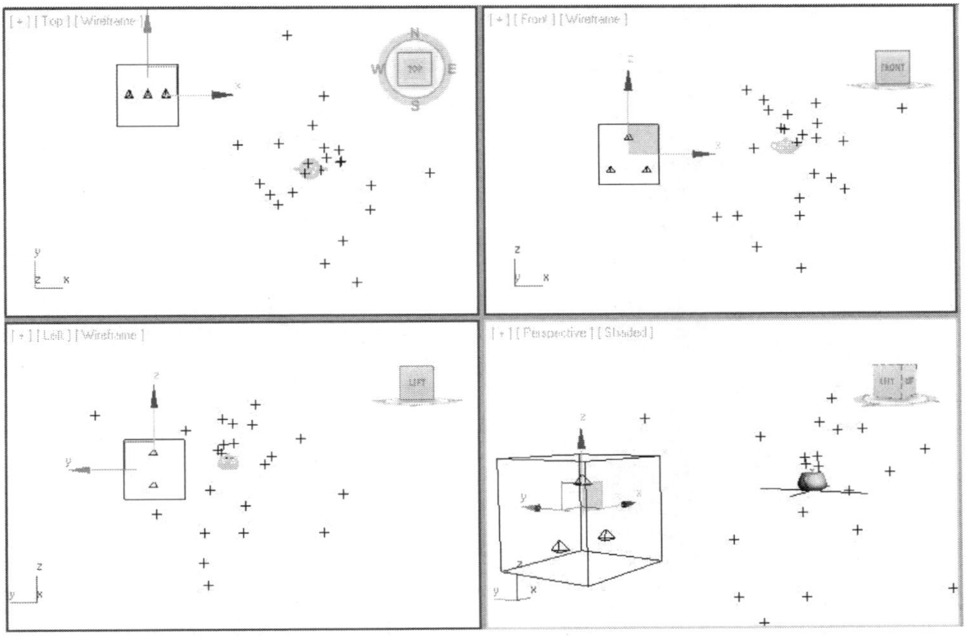

***Figure 13-23** The particles generated from the distribution object (teapot) in all viewports*

Basic Parameters Rollout

The options in this rollout are used to define the distribution object and set the properties of the PArray particle system, refer to Figure 13-24. The **Pick Object** button in the **Object-Based Emitter** area is used to select a geometry in the viewport to use it as the distribution object.

The **Particle Formation** area is discussed next.

Particle Formation Area

The options in this area are used to define how the particles will be distributed over the surface of the distribution object. By default, the **Over Entire Surface** radio button is selected that is used to emit the particles over the entire surface of the distribution object. Select the **Along Visible Edges** radio button to emit the particles randomly from the visible edges of the distribution object. Select the **At All Vertices** radio button to emit the particles from the vertices of the distribution object. On selecting the **At Distinct Points** radio button, the **Total** spinner will get activated. Set the value in this spinner to specify the number of points over the surface of the distribution object, from which the particles will be emitted. Select the **At Face Centers** radio button to emit the particles from the center of each triangular face. Select the **Use selected SubObjects** check box to emit the particles from the selected sub-object of the distribution object.

Particle Generation Rollout

The options in this rollout are the same as those discussed in the super spray particle system. In the **Particle Motion** area, set the value in the **Divergence** spinner to vary the direction of the particles in degrees.

Particle Type Rollout

On selecting the **Object Fragments** radio button in the **Particle Types** area of this rollout, the **Object Fragment Controls** area will get activated. This area is used to generate the particles from the fragments of the distribution object, as shown in Figure 13-25. Also, you can use this option to create an explosion of an object. Set the value in the **Thickness** spinner in the **Object Fragment Controls** area to specify the thickness of the fragments. By default, the **All Faces** radio button is selected, therefore, all faces of the selected object turn into fragments. Select the **Number of Chunks** radio button to break the object into irregular fragments. Set the value in the **Minimum** spinner to specify the minimum number of fragments that will be generated. Select the **Smoothing Angle** radio button to break the object based on the angle between the face normals.

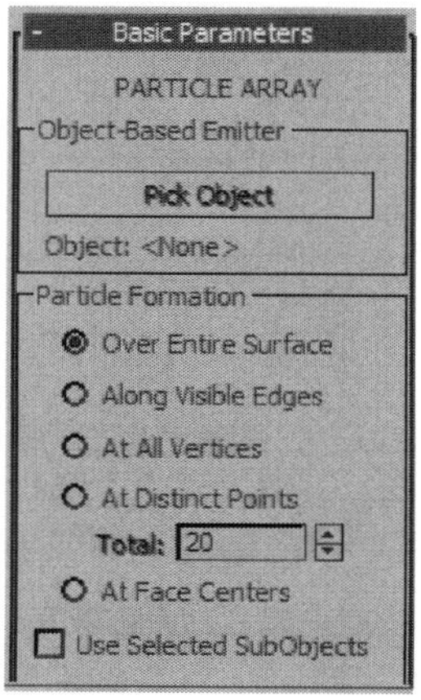

***Figure 13-24** Partial view of the **Basic Parameters** rollout*

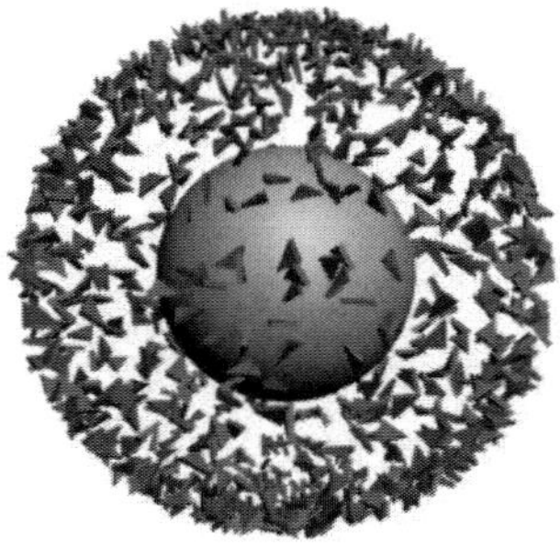

***Figure 13-25** The PArray particle system with the **Object Fragments** particle type*

PCloud Particle System

Menu bar:	Create > Particles > PCloud
Command Panel:	Create > Geometry > Particle Systems > Object Type > PCloud

The PCloud particle system is used to create the particles that will be enclosed in a specific volume. To create the PCloud particle system, invoke the **PCloud** tool from **Create > Geometry > Particle Systems > Object Type** rollout in the **Command Panel**; the **Name and Color**, **Basic Parameters**, **Particle Generation**, **Particle Type**, **Rotation and Collision**, **Object Motion Inheritance**, **Particle Spawn**, **Bubble Motion**, and **Load/Save Presets** rollouts will be displayed. In the Top viewport, press and hold the left mouse button, drag the cursor from one point to another, and then release the left mouse button. Move the cursor up or down to specify the height of the emitter and then click on the screen; an emitter will be created, as shown in Figure 13-26. Next, you need to set the properties of the particles in various rollouts. Most of the options in the rollouts are the same as discussed in the super spray particle system. The others are discussed next.

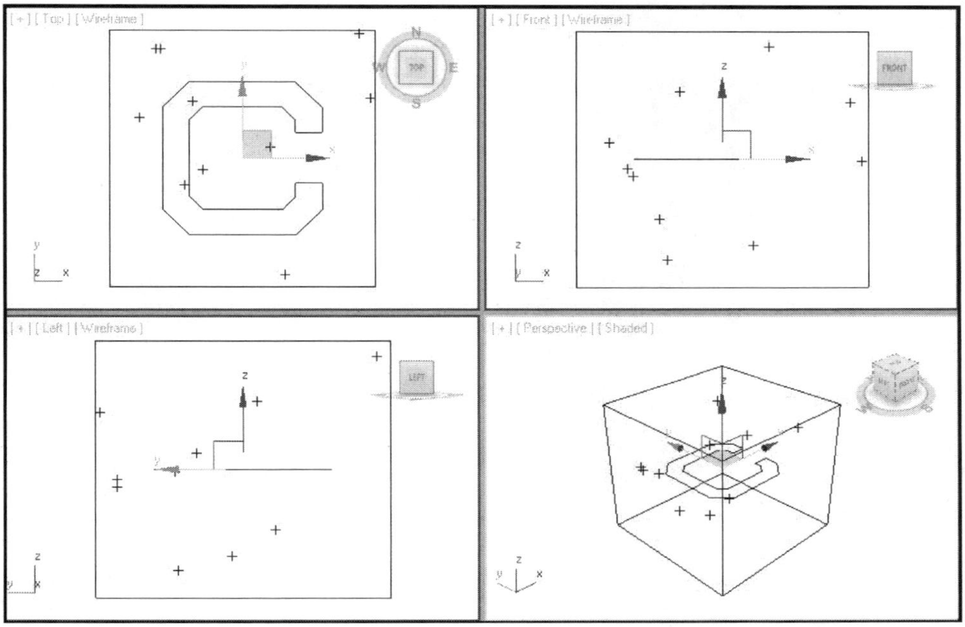

Figure 13-26 *The emitter created for the PCloud particle system*

Basic Parameters Rollout

The radio buttons in the **Particle Formation** area of this rollout are used to define the shape of the emitter icon, refer to Figure 13-27. By default, the **Box Emitter** radio button is selected and it is used to display a box shape emitter. Select the **Sphere** or the **Cylinder Emitter** radio button to display a spherical or a cylindrical shape emitter. If you use the geometry in the viewport as the distribution object, then the **Object-based Emitter** radio button will automatically get selected.

Particle Generation Rollout

In the **Particle Motion** area, there are some additional options to define the path of the particles, refer to Figure 13-28. By default, the **Random Direction** radio button is selected. It is used to emit the particles from the emitter in random directions. Select the **Direction Vector** radio button; the **X**, **Y**, and **Z** spinners will get activated. Set the value in these spinners to specify the direction of the particles along a vector. Select the **Reference Object** radio button to emit the particles along a vector defined by the local Z-axis of the selected object. Choose the **Pick Object** button to select an object. Set the value in the **Variation** spinner to vary the direction of the particles in percentage.

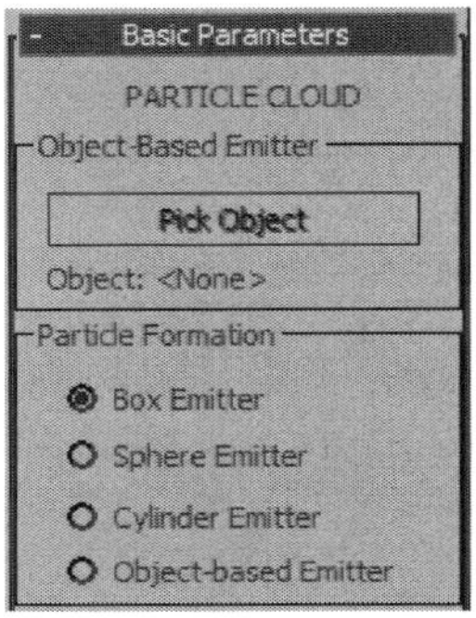

*Figure 13-27 The **Particle Formation** area in the **Basic Parameters** rollout*

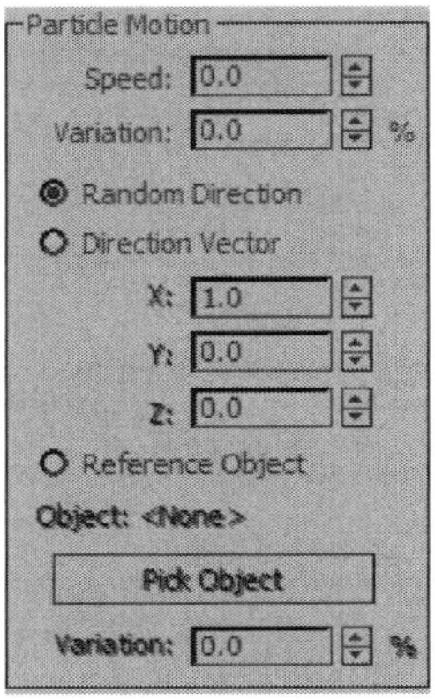

*Figure 13-28 The **Particle Motion** area in the **Particle Generation** rollout*

In the next section, you will learn to create the blobmesh and mesher compound objects with the help of various particle systems.

BLOBMESH

Menu bar:	Create > Compound > BlobMesh
Command Panel:	Create > Geometry > Compound Objects > Object Type rollout > BlobMesh

The **BlobMesh** tool is used to create metaballs based on the object selected in the viewport. These metaballs create the blobmesh objects that can flow, such as the thick liquids and the soft objects. A metaball is a type of sphere that connects itself to another object within a particular distance using a connecting surface. Therefore, a blobmesh compound object will generate the metaballs and then connect the spheres together to create the effect of thick liquid and so on. If the particles are in a certain range, they will connect together to give the effect of liquid. On moving the particles apart, they will unite again to take the spherical shape.

You can create a blobmesh compound object from any geometry or particle system. To create the blobmesh object using the particle system, first create a particle system as discussed earlier in this chapter, and set its parameters in the rollouts available in the modify panel. Next, choose **Create > Geometry** in the **Command Panel**; a drop-down list will be displayed below the **Geometry** button. Select the **Compound Objects** option from the list; the **Object Type** rollout will be displayed. Invoke the **BlobMesh** tool and click anywhere on the screen; a metaball will be created. Next, choose the **Modify** tab in the **Command Panel**; the **Parameters** rollout will be displayed, where you can specify the parameters to modify the metaball, refer to Figure 13-29. In the **Blob Objects** area of the **Parameters** rollout, choose the **Add** button; the **Add Blobs** dialog box will be displayed. Select the particle system from the list displayed in this dialog box and choose the **Add Blobs** button; the metaball will be displayed at each particle of the particle system. You can apply material to the blob mesh object to get the realistic effect, as shown in Figure 13-30. Also, you need to set the values in the **Parameters** rollout to get the desired effect.

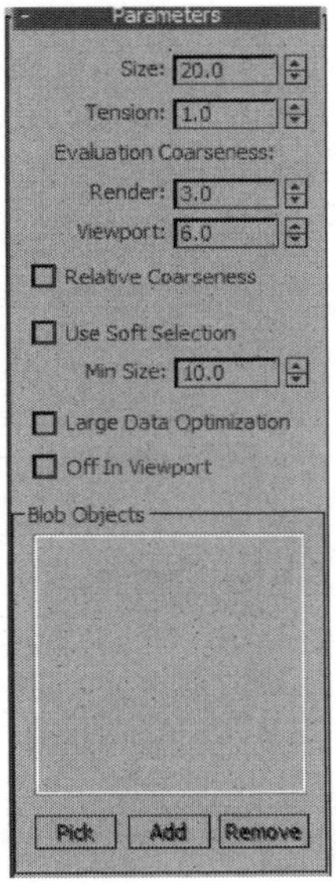

*Figure 13-29 The **Parameters** rollout*

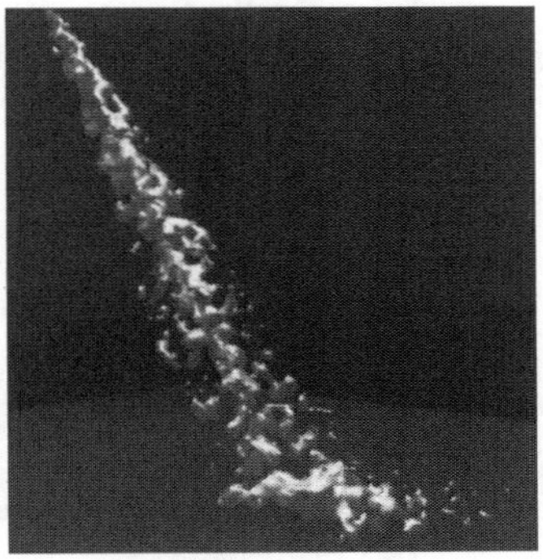

Figure 13-30 The blob mesh object created from the blob mesh compound object

MESHER

Menu bar:	Create > Compound > Mesher
Command Panel:	Create > Geometry > Compound Objects > Object Type rollout > Mesher

The **Mesher** tool is used to create instances of the animated objects. This tool has been mainly designed to be used with the particle systems. Moreover, you can use it with any object. You can also apply the modifiers to a particle system using the mesher compound object.

To create a mesher object, first create a particle system and then set its parameters as per your need. Next, choose **Create > Geometry** in the **Command Panel**; a drop-down list will be displayed below the **Geometry** button. Select the **Compound Objects** from the list; the **Object Type** rollout will be displayed. Invoke the **Mesher** tool in this rollout and drag the cursor from one place to another in the Top viewport; a pyramid shape will be created, as shown in Figure 13-31. Next, choose the **Modify** tab in the **Command Panel**; the **Parameters** rollout will be displayed, as shown in Figure 13-32. In the **Parameters** rollout, choose the **Pick Object** button labeled as **None**, and then select the particle system in the viewport; an instance of the particle system will be displayed once you play the animation, as shown in Figure 13-33. Also, the pyramid shape will disappear. When you play the animation, the instance particle system will behave exactly like the original one. You can also assign a modifier to the instanced particle system, as shown in Figure 13-34.

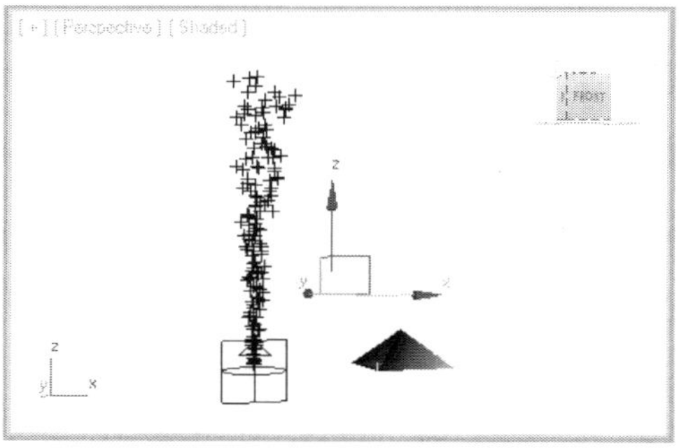

Figure 13-31 The mesher object in the Perspective viewport

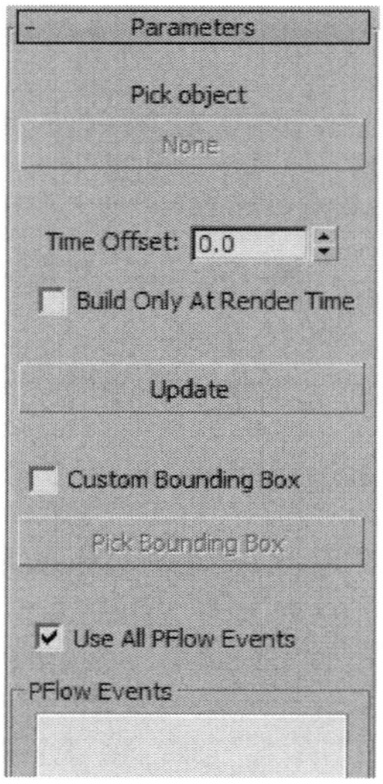

*Figure 13-32 The **Parameters** rollout*

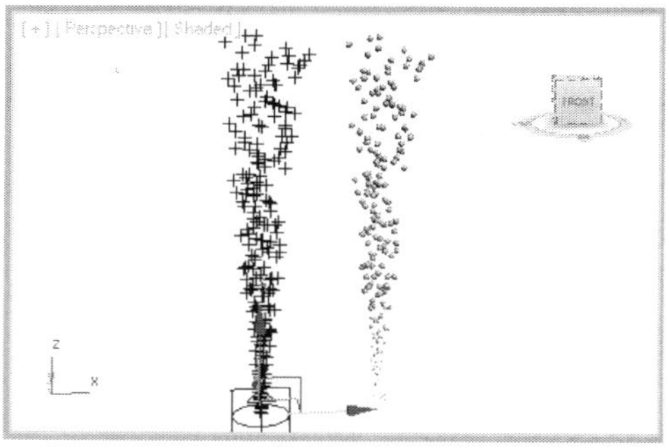

Figure 13-33 The instance of the particle system displayed

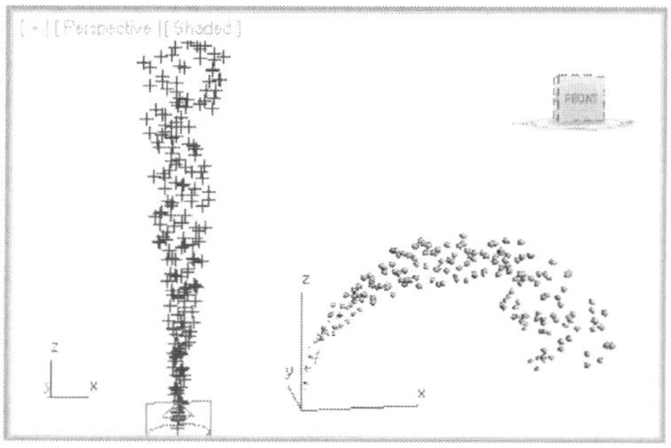

*Figure 13-34 The **Bend** modifier assigned to the instanced particle system*

Note

The size of the mesher object does not affect the particle system.

INTRODUCTION TO SPACE WARPS

In Autodesk 3ds Max, the space warps objects cannot be rendered and are used to affect the motion and appearance of the other objects. They can generate special effects such as blowing wind, flowing waves, and so on in the animation. There are five categories of space warps, **Forces**, **Deflectors**, **Geometric/Deformable**, **Modifier-Based**, and **Particles & Dynamics**.

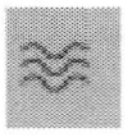

To create a space warp, choose **Create > Space Warps** in the **Command Panel**; the **Forces** category will be displayed by default in the drop-down list below the **Space Warp** button. Select another category from the drop-down list, if required; the **Object Type** rollout showing all tools related to the selected category will be displayed, as shown in Figure 13-35. Next, invoke the required space warp tool and drag the cursor in the viewport to create the space warp.

To view the effect of the space warp on the object, you need to bind the object with the space warp. To do so, select the object that you want to be affected by the space warp in the viewport. Next, invoke the **Bind to Space Warp** tool from the **Main Toolbar** and move the cursor over the selected object in the viewport; the cursor will be displayed, as shown in Figure 13-36. Now, click on the object and drag the cursor to the space warp object; a dotted line will be displayed from the selected object to the space warp object, as shown in Figure 13-37. Release the mouse button; the object will be bound to the space warp object. Also, the name of the space warp object will be displayed in the **Command Panel** to indicate that the object is linked to the space warp object, as shown in Figure 13-38.

*Figure 13-35 The **Forces** category selected in the drop-down list*

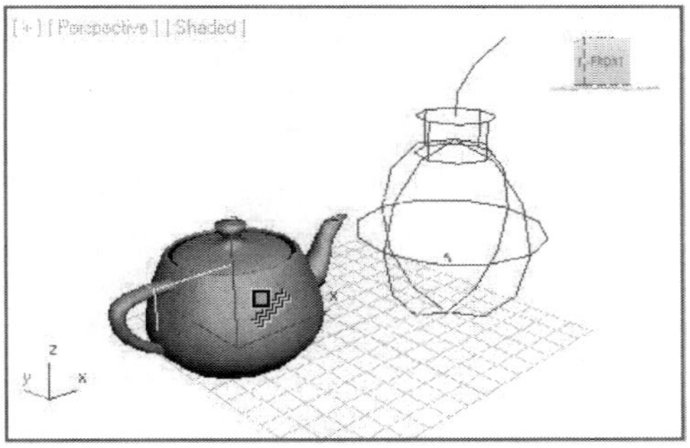

*Figure 13-36 The cursor displayed on invoking the **Bind to Space Warp** tool*

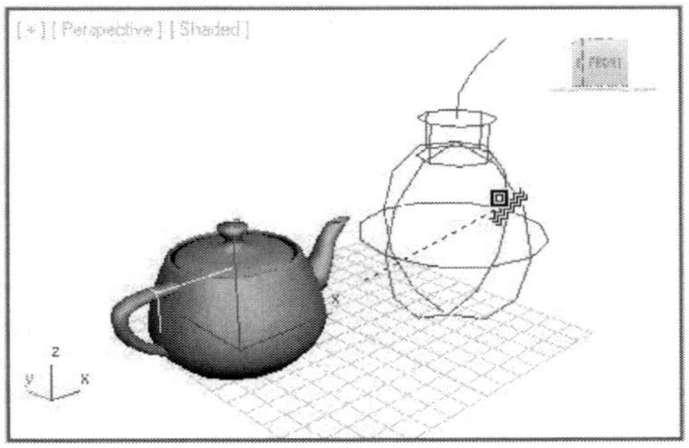

Figure 13-37 A dotted line displayed from the selected object to the space warp object

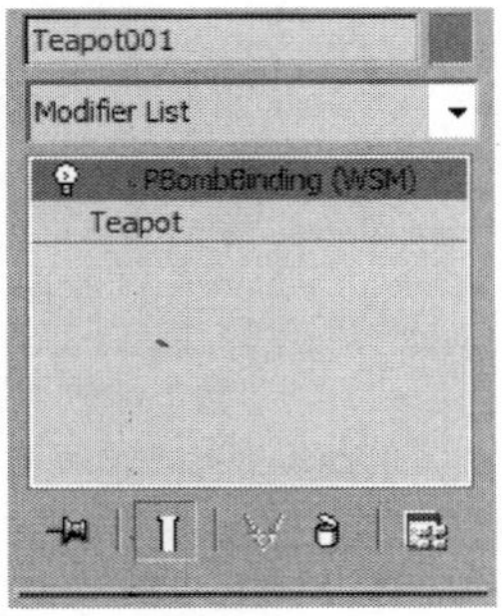

*Figure 13-38 The space warp object displayed in the **Command Panel***

Next, select the space warp object in the viewport and choose the **Modify** tab in the **Command Panel**; various rollouts will be displayed to modify the parameters of the space warp object. Modify the parameters to create special effects in the object. You can also transform the space warp object using the **Select and Move**, **Select and Rotate**, and other transforming tools. In the **Modify** tab of each space warp, there is a rollout named as **Supports Objects of Type**. This rollout displays a list of types of objects that you can bind with the selected space warp.

Note

You can bind multiple objects to a single space warp. In this case, all objects will be equally affected by the space warp. Also, you can apply multiple space warps to a single object.

CATEGORIES OF SPACE WARPS

There are five categories of space warps. You can select the required category from the drop-down list displayed on choosing **Create > Space Warps** in the **Command Panel**. You can use various tools in each category to create different space warps that generate special effects in the object. These categories are discussed next.

Forces

Menu bar:	Create > SpaceWarps > Forces > Push
Command Panel:	Create > Space Warps > Forces > Object Type rollout > Push

The tools in the **Forces** category are used to create the space warps that generate the effect of natural forces on the objects such as push, wind, gravity, and so on. Some of the space warps in this category are discussed next.

Push Space Warp

The push space warp is used to generate a force in the particle system in a single uniform direction, as shown in Figure 13-39. It can be used to create effects such as of blowing wind, cigarette smoke and so on.

*Figure 13-39 The effect of **Push** space warp on the particle system*

To create a push space warp in the viewport, invoke the **Push** tool; the **Name and Color**, **Supports Objects of Type**, and **Parameters** rollouts will be displayed. Next, activate the suitable viewport, press and hold the left mouse button, and drag the cursor to create the push space warp; the push space warp icon will be displayed in all viewports. Figure 13-40 displays the push space warp icon in the Perspective viewport. Next, you need to bind the push space warp with the particle system using the **Bind to Space Warp** tool. Also, you need to set the parameters in the **Parameters** rollout of push space warp to generate the effect. The **Parameters** rollout and its options are discussed next.

Note

The size of a space warp icon does not affect the particle system.

Parameters Rollout

The options in this rollout are used to set the effect of the push space warp on the particle system, refer to Figure 13-41. The different areas in this rollout are discussed next.

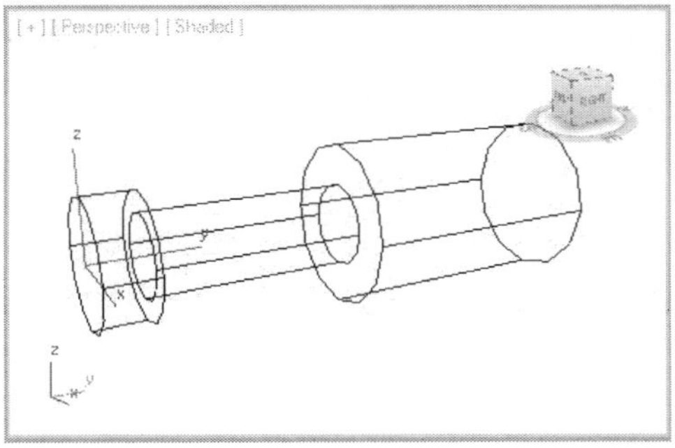

Figure 13-40 *The push space warp icon*

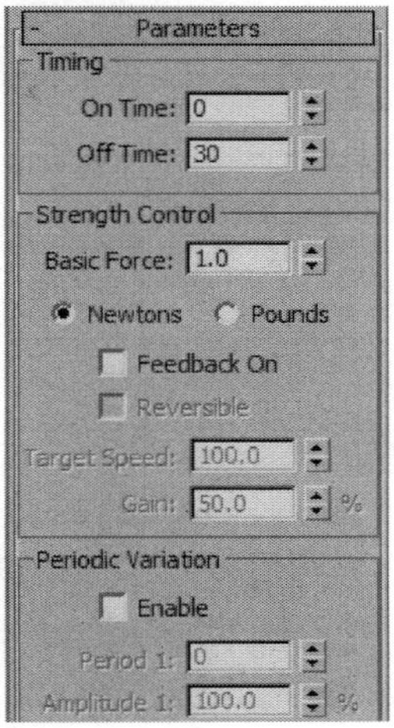

Figure 13-41 *Partial view of the **Parameters** rollout for the push space warp*

Timing Area

The options in this area are used to define the number of frames in which the push space warp will start and end the effect. Set the values in the **On Time** and **Off Time** spinners to set the frame number at which the push space warp will start and end the effect, respectively.

Strength Control Area

Set the value in the **Basic Force** spinner to specify the strength of the force by the push space warp. Select the **Newtons** or the **Pounds** radio button to define the units of the force. Select the **Feedback On** check box; the **Reversible** check box, the **Target Speed** spinner, and the **Gain** spinner will get activated. The **Feedback On** check box is used to vary the force that depends on the speed of the bounded particles relative to the speed in the **Target Speed** spinner. If the **Feedback On** check box is cleared, the force remains constant. On selecting the **Reversible** check box, the force is reversed if the speed of the particles exceeds the speed in the **Target Speed** spinner.

Periodic Variation Area

The options in this area are used to generate variations in the strength of the force applied by push space warp. Select the **Enable** check box to activate the options in this area. Set the values in the **Period 1** and **Period 2** spinners to set the number of frames it takes to complete one cycle of variation in strength of the push space warp. Set the values in the **Amplitude 1** and **Amplitude 2** spinners to define the strength of variation in percentage. Set the values in the **Phase 1** and **Phase 2** spinners to offset the variation pattern.

Particle Effect Range Area

Select the **Enable** check box in this area; a spherical shape will be displayed in the viewport, as shown in Figure 13-42. Set the value in the **Range** spinner to limit the range of the effect of the push space warp.

Display Icon Area

Set the value in the **Icon Size** spinner to specify the size of the push space warp icon.

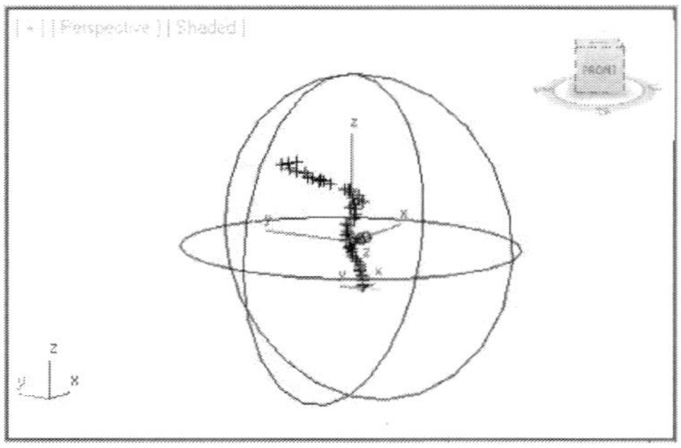

***Figure 13-42** The spherical shape of the push space warp*

Gravity Space Warp

Menu bar:	Create > SpaceWarps > Forces > Gravity
Command Panel:	Create > Space Warps > Forces > Object Type rollout > Gravity

The gravity space warp is used to generate a gravitational force in a particle system toward a particular direction. The particles affected by the gravity space warp will be accelerated in the direction of gravity arrow, as shown in Figure 13-43.

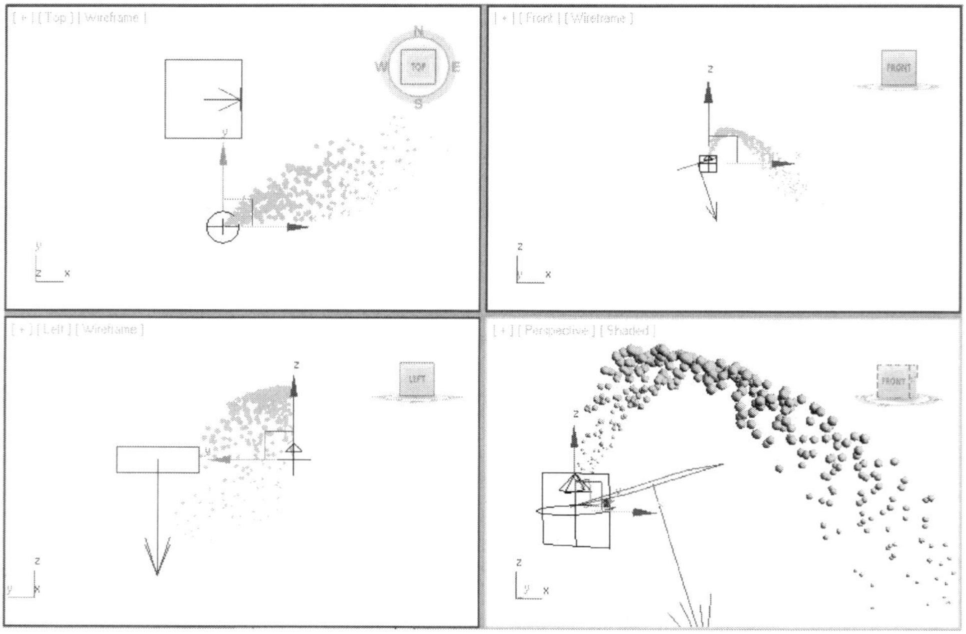

***Figure 13-43** The particle system with the gravity space warp*

To create a gravity space warp, invoke the **Gravity** tool; the **Name and Color**, **Supports Objects of Type**, and **Parameters** rollouts will be displayed. Next, activate the suitable viewport, press and hold the left mouse button, and drag the cursor to create the gravity space warp; the gravity space warp icon will be displayed in all viewports, refer to Figure 13-43.

Next, bind the gravity space warp with the particle system and set the parameters in the **Parameters** rollout to generate the desired effect. This rollout is discussed next.

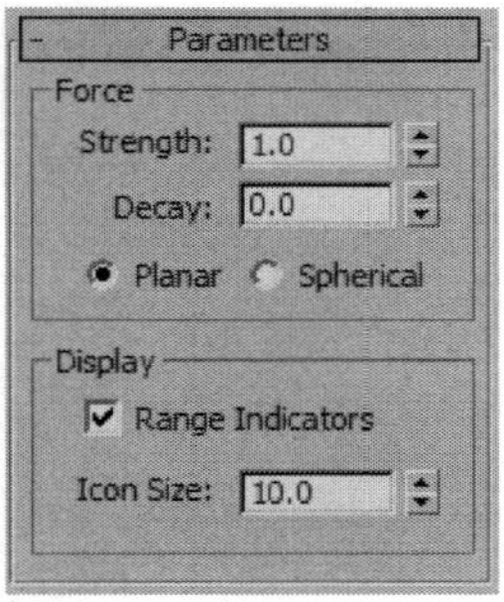

***Figure 13-44** The **Parameters** rollout for the gravity space warp*

Parameters Rollout

The options in this rollout are used to set the effect of the gravity space warp on the particle system, refer to Figure 13-44. The **Force** area in this rollout is discussed next.

Force Area

Set the value in the **Strength** spinner to set the effect of the gravity force on the particle system. As you increase the value in the **Strength** spinner, the effect of the gravity force will also be increased. If you set the negative value in the **Strength** spinner, then the particles will be affected by the negative gravitational force and therefore, they will be repelled from the gravity icon. The value in the **Decay** spinner affects the strength of the gravity force. If you increase the value in the **Decay** spinner, then the effect of the gravity force will be decreased. By default, the **Planar** radio button is selected in this area. As a result, the gravitational force will be applied on the particles in a direction that is perpendicular to the plane of the gravity space warp, refer to Figure 13-43. Select the **Spherical** radio button to apply the gravitational force on the particles toward the center of the sphere, as shown in Figure 13-45.

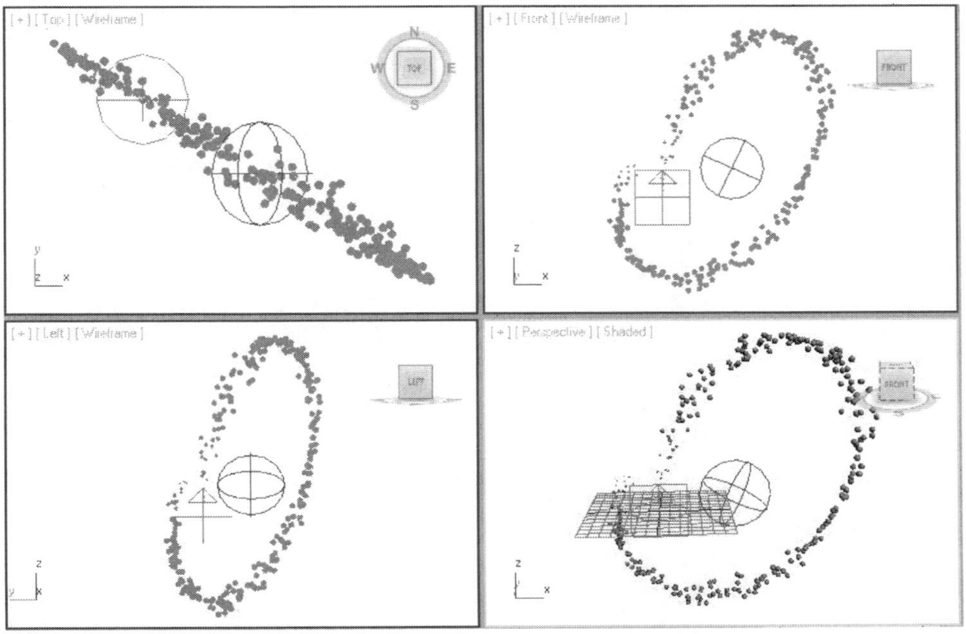

***Figure 13-45** The particle system with the spherical gravity space warp*

Path Follow Space Warp

Menu bar:	Create > SpaceWarps > Forces > Path Follow
Command Panel:	Create > Space Warps > Forces > Object Type rollout > Path Follow

The path follow space warp is used to select a spline in the viewport that will be used as a path for the particles, refer to Figure 13-46.

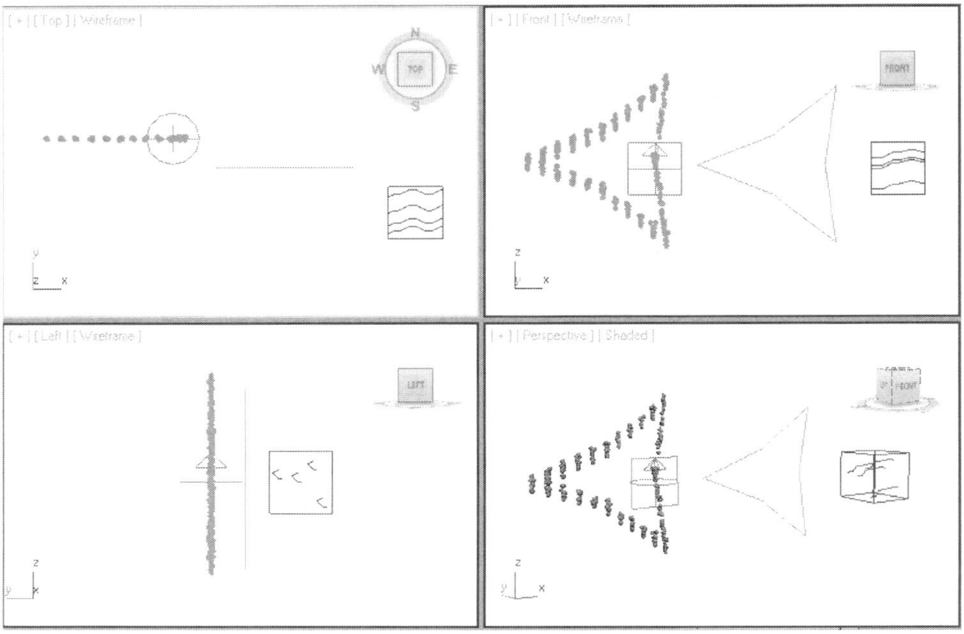

Figure 13-46 *The particle system with the path follow space warp*

To create a path follow space warp, first create a particle system and a spline. Next, invoke the **Path Follow** tool; the **Name and Color**, **Supports Objects of Type**, and **Basic Parameters** rollouts will be displayed. Next, activate the suitable viewport, press and hold the left mouse button, and drag the cursor to create the path follow space warp; the path follow space warp icon will be displayed in all viewports, refer to Figure 13-46. Now, bind the path follow space warp with the particle system. In the **Basic Parameters** rollout of the path follow space warp, choose the **Pick Shape Object** button and select the spline in the viewport. Next, you need to set the other parameters of the path follow space warp in the **Basic Parameters** rollout. This rollout and its options are discussed next.

Basic Parameters Rollout

The options in this rollout are used to set the parameters of the path follow space warp to affect the particles in a desired way, refer to Figure 13-47. The areas in this rollout are discussed next.

Current Path Area

The options in this area are used to select the spline path and limit the range of effect of the space warp. Choose the **Pick Shape Object** button to select the spline in the viewport.

Motion Timing Area

Specify the frame numbers at which the path follow space warp will start and stop affecting the particles in the **Start Frame** and **Last Frame** spinners, respectively. Set the value in the **Travel Time** spinner to specify the number of frames in which the particles will cross the entire path.

Particle Motion Area

The options in this area are used to control the motion of the particles along the path. The **Along Parallel Splines** radio button is selected by default. As a result, the path followed by the particles will be exactly the same as that of the selected spline. On selecting the **Along Offset Splines** radio button, the motion of the particles will be affected by the distance between the particle system and the spline path. The **Constant Speed** check box is used to generate the constant speed for the particles. Set the value in the **Stream Taper** spinner to specify the amount of the stream of the particles that will be tapered along the path, as shown in Figure 13-48. Set the value in the **Variation** spinner to specify the amount of deviation of the particles from the taper value. Set the value in the **Stream Swirl** spinner to specify the number of turns that the particles will take around the path, as shown in Figure 13-49. Set the value in the **Variation** spinner to specify the deviation of the particles from the swirl value.

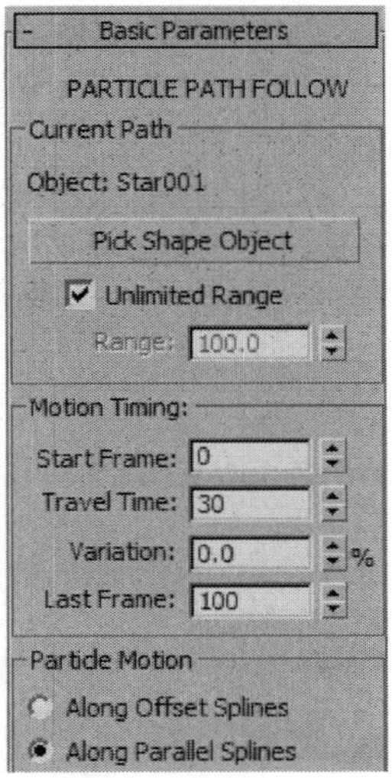

***Figure 13-47** Partial view of the **Basic Parameters** rollout*

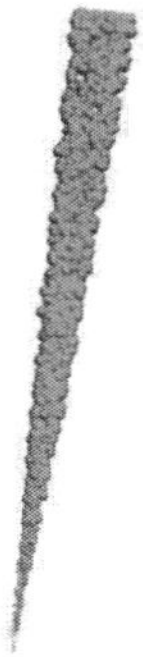

***Figure 13-48** The particles with the stream taper effect*

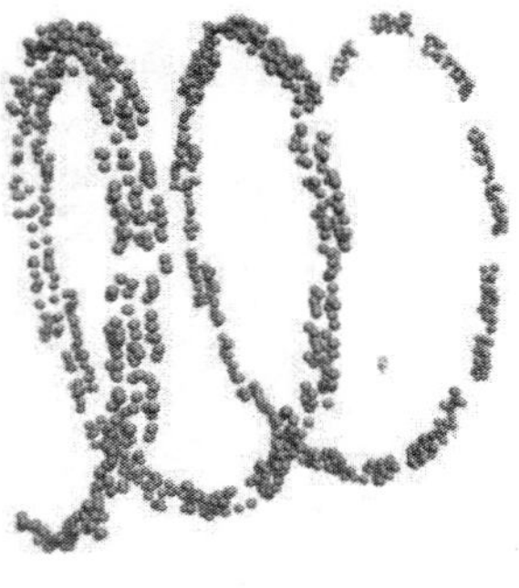

***Figure 13-49** The particles with the stream swirl effect*

Wind Space Warp

Menu bar:	Create > SpaceWarps > Forces > Wind
Command Panel:	Create > Space Warps > Forces > Object Type rollout > Wind

The wind space warp is used to generate the blowing wind affect in a particle system, refer to Figure 13-50. The wind space warp is very similar to the gravity space warp. The only difference is that the wind space warp has the additional turbulence effect, which gives a realistic view to the particle system.

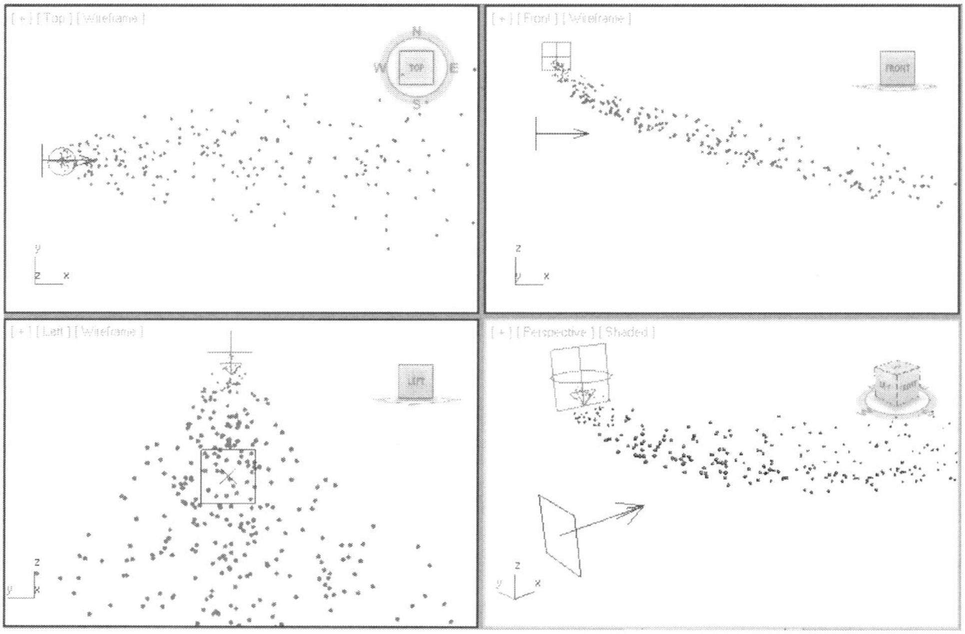

Figure 13-50 The effect of the wind space warp on the particle system

To create a wind space warp, invoke the **Wind** tool; the **Name and Color**, **Supports Objects of Type**, and **Parameters** rollouts will be displayed. Next, activate the suitable viewport, press and hold the left mouse button, and drag the cursor to create the wind space warp; the wind space warp icon will be displayed in all viewports, refer to Figure 13-50. Next, bind the wind space warp with the particle system and set the parameters in the **Parameters** rollout to generate a realistic effect. This rollout is discussed next.

Parameters Rollout

The options in the **Force** and **Display** areas are the same as those discussed in the gravity space warp. The **Wind** area, as shown in Figure 13-51, is discussed next.

Wind Area

Set the value in the **Turbulence** spinner to create random variations in the flow of particles when the wind space warp blows them. The value in the **Frequency** spinner is used to define how the turbulence will vary over the time. Set the value in the **Scale** spinner to scale the turbulence effect.

PBomb Space Warp

Menu bar:	Create > SpaceWarps > Forces > PBomb
Command Panel:	Create > Space Warps > Forces > Object Type rollout > PBomb

The PBomb space warp is used to explode a particle system, refer to Figure 13-52. The PBomb space warp is mostly used with the PArray particle system.

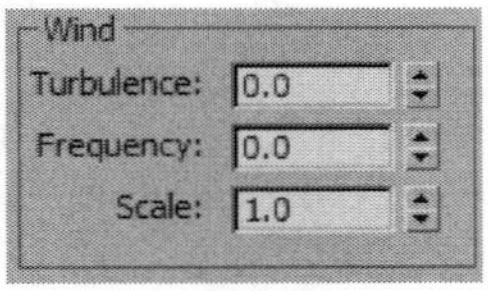

***Figure 13-51** The **Wind** area in the **Parameters** rollout*

***Figure 13-52** The effect of the PBomb space warp on a sphere at a single frame at rendering*

To use the PBomb space warp, first create an object that you want to explode. To do so, invoke the **PArray** tool from **Create > Geometry > Particle Systems > Object Type** rollout and then create a PArray particle system in the viewport. Next, choose the **Pick Object** button in the **Basic Parameters** rollout of the PArray particle system and select the object that you have created. In the **Particle Type** rollout of this particle system, select the **Object Fragments** radio button and set the other parameters. Next, invoke the **PBomb** tool from **Create > Space Warps > Forces > Object Type** rollout in the **Command Panel**; the **Name and Color**, **Supports Objects of Type**, and **Basic Parameters** rollouts will be displayed. Press and hold the left mouse button and drag the cursor in the viewport to create the PBomb space warp; the PBomb space warp icon will be displayed in all viewports, as shown in Figure 13-53. Next, bind the PBomb space warp with the PArray icon and set the parameters in the **Basic Parameters** rollout to generate a realistic effect. The **Basic Parameters** rollout is discussed next.

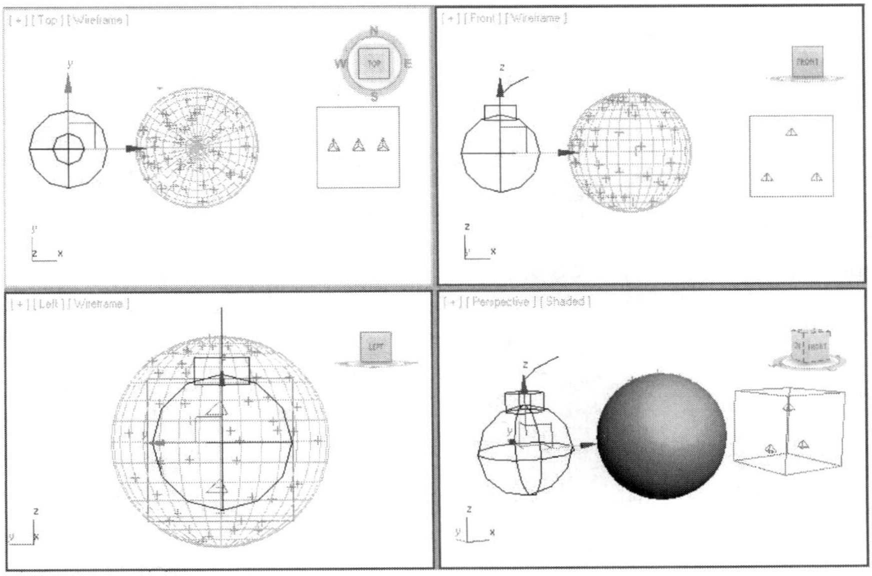

***Figure 13-53** The PBomb space warp icon in the viewport*

Basic Parameters Rollout

The options in this rollout are used to modify the parameters of the PBomb space warp, refer to Figure 13-54. The areas in this rollout are discussed next.

Blast Symmetry Area

By default, the **Spherical** radio button is selected. As a result, the force is applied outward from the PBomb icon in all directions, refer to Figure 13-52. Select the **Cylindrical** radio button; the PBomb icon will change to a cylindrical shape, refer to Figure 13-55. The **Cylindrical** radio button is used to apply the force outward in a cylindrical form from the PBomb icon, as shown in Figure 13-56. Select the **Planar** radio button; the PBomb icon will change to a plane with arrows in it, as shown in Figure 13-57. The **Planar** radio button is used to apply the force outward from the PBomb icon, perpendicular to the plane, as shown in Figure 13-58.

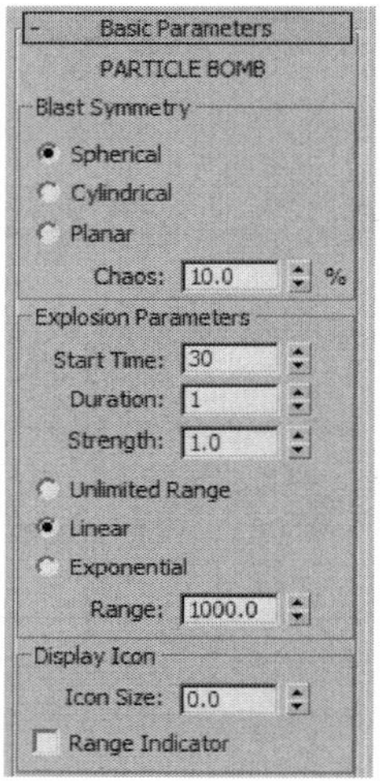

Figure 13-54 *The* ***Basic Parameters*** *rollout for the PBomb space warp*

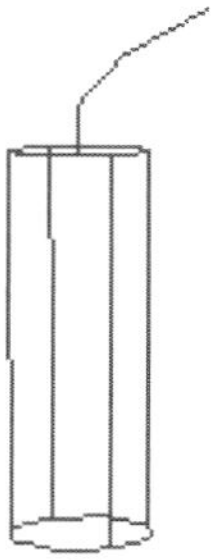

Figure 13-55 *The PBomb icon after selecting the* ***Cylindrical*** *radio button*

Figure 13-56 *The effect of the PBomb space warp on a sphere after selecting the* ***Cylindrical*** *radio button at rendering*

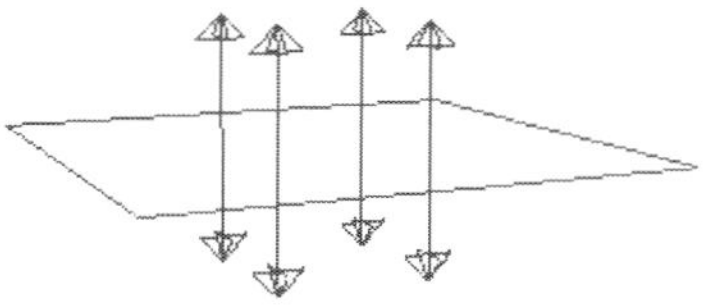

Figure 13-57 *The PBomb icon after selecting the* ***Planar*** *radio button*

Explosion Parameters Area

Set the value in the **Start Time** spinner to specify the frame number at which the explosion will start. Set the value in the **Duration** spinner to specify the number of frames over which the forces will be assigned. Set the value in the **Strength** spinner to specify the strength of the force.

Figure 13-58 *The effect of the PBomb space warp on a sphere at rendering after selecting the* ***Planar*** *radio button*

Self-Evaluation Test

Answer the following questions and then compare them to those given at the end of this chapter:

1. Which of the following tools is used create the particle system that generates particles similar to the water drops or spray?

   (a) **Spray** (b) **Blizzard**
   (c) **Snow** (d) **PCloud**

2. Which of the following is a category of the space warps?

   (a) **Forces** (b) **Geometric/Deformable**
   (c) **Deflectors** (d) All of these

3. Which of the following rollouts in the super spray particle system is used to load the settings that you can use further in other particle systems?

   (a) **Particle Spawn** (b) **Bubble Motion**
   (c) **Load/Save Presets** (d) **Particle Type**

4. Which of the following tools is used to create the space warps that generate the effect of natural forces on objects?

   (a) **Push** (b) **Gravity**
   (c) **Path Follow** (d) All of these

5. You can view the emitter of any particle system at rendering. (T/F)

6. The options in the **Particle Motion** area of the super spray particle system are used to define the speed of the particles. (T/F)

7. The space warp objects are used to affect the motion and appearance of other objects. (T/F)

8. A __________ is a type of sphere that connects itself to another object within a particular distance using a connecting surface.

9. The __________ tool is used to bind the object with the space warp object.

10. The __________ particle system is used to create a fountain.

Review Questions

Answer the following questions:

1. Which of the following space warps is used to generate a gravitational force in a particle system in a particular direction?

   (a) Push (b) Path Follow
   (c) Gravity (d) Wind

2. Which of the following space warps is used to explode a particle system?

   (a) Gravity (b) Wind
   (c) Push (d) PBomb

3. Which of the following space warps is used to select a spline in the viewport to use as a path for the particles?

   (a) Wind (b) Displace
   (c) Path Follow (d) PBomb

4. Which of the following options in the **Basic Parameters** rollout of the PBomb space warp is used to specify the number of frame at which the explosion will start?

   (a) **Start Time** (b) **Range**
   (c) **Duration** (d) **Strength**

5. The wind space warp is used to explode a particle system. (T/F)

6. The mesher compound object is used to create instances of the animated objects. (T/F)

7. The PCloud particle system is used to create the particles that will be enclosed within a specific volume. (T/F)

8. The __________ particle system is the advanced version of the snow particle system.

9. The __________ particle system is used to generate the particles from the selected geometry.

10. The __________space warp is used to generate the effect of blowing wind on a particle system.

Answers to Self-Evaluation Test

1. a, **2.** d, **3.** c, **4.** d, **5.** F, **6.** T, **7.** T, **8.** metaball, **9. Bind to Space Warp**, **10.** super spray

14

Particle Systems and Space Warps-II

Learning Objectives

After completing this chapter, you will be able to:

- *Use Deflector space warps*
- *Use Geometric/Deformable space warps*
- *Use Modifier-Based space warps*

INTRODUCTION

In continuation with the last chapter, in this chapter also you will learn about different space warps. Besides, you will learn about different parameters of the particle systems and its usage.

CATEGORIES OF SPACE WARPS

There are five categories of space warps, **Forces**, **Deflectors**, **Geometric/Deformable**, **Modifier-Based**, and **Particles & Dynamics**. You have learned about the **Forces** category in Chapter 13. The most commonly used categories of space warps are discussed next.

Deflectors

The tools in the **Deflectors** category are used to create the space warps that reflect or refract the particles colliding with them. Some of the space warps in this category are discussed next.

Deflector Space Warp

Menu bar:	Create > SpaceWarps > Deflectors > Deflector
Command Panel:	Create > Space Warps > Deflectors > Object Type rollout > Deflector

The deflector space warp is planar in shape and it is used to deflect the particles generated by the particle system that collide with it, as shown in Figure 14-1.

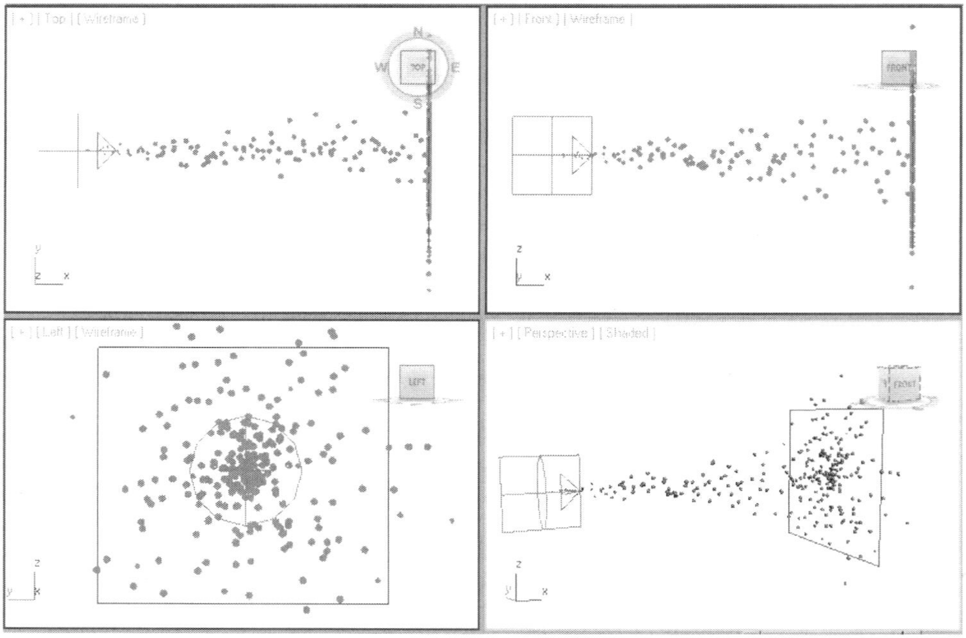

Figure 14-1 *The particles affected by the Deflector space warp*

To create a deflector space warp, invoke the **Deflector** tool from **Create > Space Warps > Deflectors > Object Type** rollout in the **Command Panel**; the **Name and Color**, **Supports Objects**

of Type, and **Parameters** rollouts will be displayed. Activate the suitable viewport. Now, press and hold the left mouse button and drag the cursor to create the deflector space warp; the deflector space warp icon will be displayed in all viewports, refer to Figure 14-1. Next, bind the deflector space warp icon with the particle system using the **Bind to Space Warp** tool in the viewport. Also, set the parameters in the **Parameters** rollout to generate the desired effect. The **Parameters** rollout is discussed next.

Note

1. The size and position of the deflector icon affect the particles of a particle system.

*2. The **Supports Objects of Type** rollout is the same for all space warps as discussed in Chapter 13.*

Parameters Rollout

The options in this rollout are used to set the effect of the deflector space warp on the particle system, refer to Figure 14-2. Make sure that the deflector space warp is selected in the viewport. Choose the **Modify** tab in the **Command Panel**; the **Supports Objects of Type** and **Parameters** rollouts will be displayed.

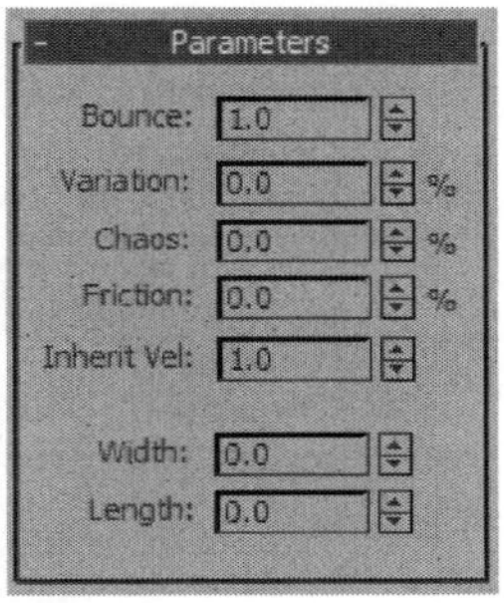

***Figure 14-2** The **Parameters** rollout for the deflector space warp*

In the **Parameters** rollout, set the value in the **Bounce** spinner to control the speed at which the particles bounce off the deflector space warp. By default, the value in the **Bounce** spinner is 1.0 and the particles bounce off the deflector with the same speed at which they strike. As you decrease the value in this spinner, the speed of the particles at which they bounce off the deflector gets reduced. Set the value in the **Variation** spinner to vary the particle bounce specified in the **Bounce** spinner. Set the value in the **Chaos** spinner to create variation in the angle of reflection of the particles. Set the value in the **Friction** spinner to specify the amount in percentage by which the speed of the particles slows down when they move across the deflector surface. On setting a value more than 0 in the **Inherit Vel** spinner, the motion of the deflector affects the particles. Set the value in the **Width** and **Length** spinners to specify the width and length of the deflector icon in the viewport.

Tip: *To get an effect similar to the particles reflected from an irregular surface, you need to set a higher value in the **Chaos** spinner.*

SDeflector Space Warp

Menu bar:	Create > SpaceWarps > Deflectors > SDeflector
Command Panel:	Create > Space Warps > Deflectors > Object Type rollout > SDeflector

The SDeflector space warp is similar to the deflector space warp. The only difference is that the SDeflector space warp is spherical in shape, as shown in Figure 14-3. It is used to deflect the particles that are generated by the particle system and collide with it.

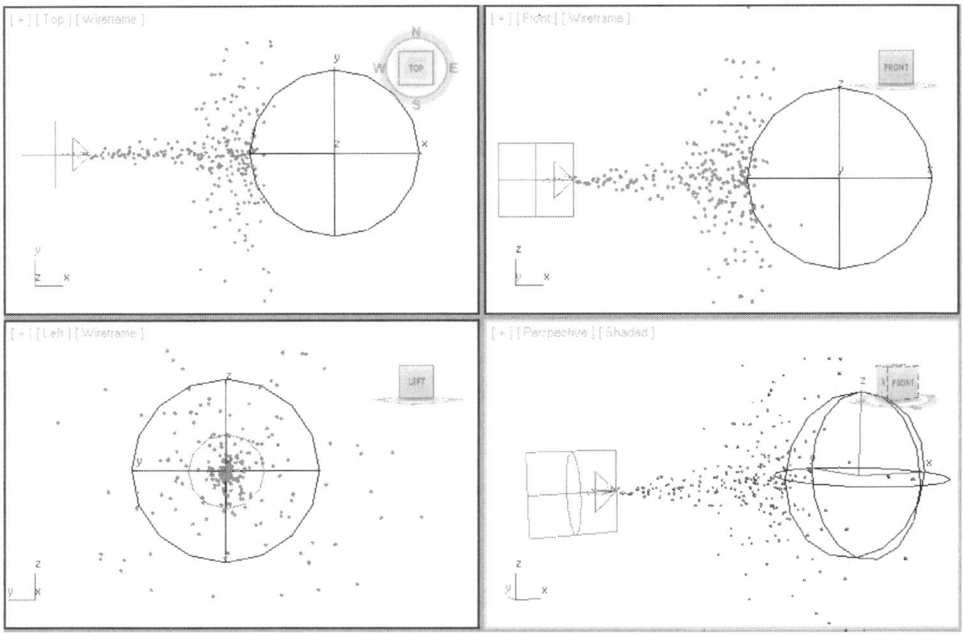

***Figure 14-3** The particles affected by the SDeflector space warp*

To create SDeflector space warp in a scene, you need to invoke the **SDeflector** tool from **Create > Space Warps > Deflectors > Object Type** rollout in the **Command Panel**; the **Name and Color**, **Supports Objects of Type**, and **Basic Parameters** rollouts will be displayed. The method of creating the SDeflector space warp and the options in the rollouts are the same as those discussed in the deflector space warp.

UDeflector Space Warp

Menu bar:	Create > SpaceWarps > Deflectors > UDeflector
Command Panel:	Create > Space Warps > Deflectors > Object Type rollout > UDeflector

The UDeflector space warp is known as the universal deflector. You can use any object in the scene as a deflector using this type of space warp, refer to Figure 14-4.

To create the UDeflector space warp, invoke the **UDeflector** tool from **Create > Space Warps > Deflectors > Object Type** rollout in the **Command Panel**; the **Name and Color**, **Supports Objects of Type**, and **Basic Parameters** rollouts will be displayed. Activate the suitable viewport. Now, press and hold the left mouse button and drag the cursor to create the UDeflector space warp; the UDeflector space warp icon will be displayed in all viewports, as shown in Figure 14-4. Next, bind the UDeflector space warp with the particle system in the viewport using the **Bind to Space Warp** tool. In the **Basic Parameters** rollout of the UDeflector space warp, choose the **Pick Object** button and select the object in the viewport that you want to create as a deflector object. Note that the object should be in front of the particle system. Also, set the parameters in the **Particle Bounce** area of the **Basic Parameters** rollout to generate the desired effect. The options in the **Particle Bounce** area of the **Basic Parameters** rollout are the same as discussed in the **Parameters** rollout of the deflector space warp, refer to Figure 14-5.

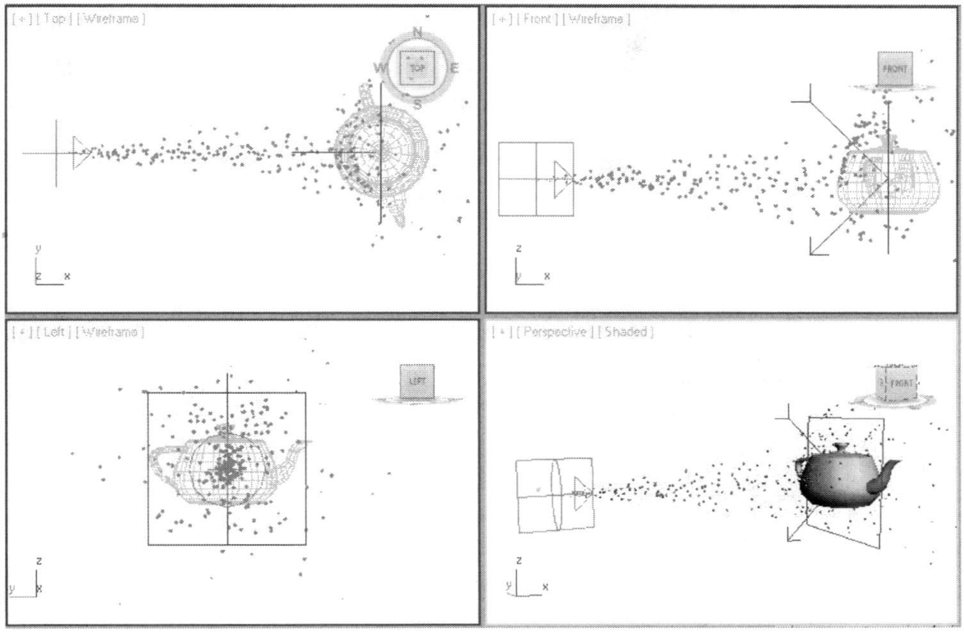

Figure 14-4 *The particles affected by the UDeflector space warp*

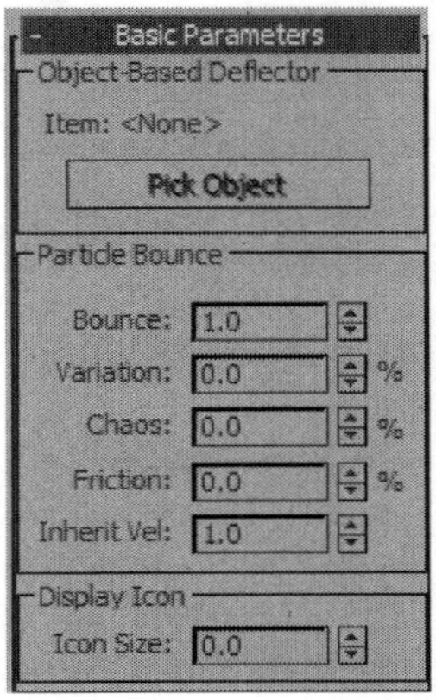

Figure 14-5 *The* ***Basic Parameters*** *rollout of the UDeflector space warp*

POmniFlect Space Warp

Menu bar:	Create > SpaceWarps > Deflectors > POmniFlect
Command Panel:	Create > Space Warps > Deflectors > Object Type rollout > POmniFlect

The POmniFlect space warp is very much similar to the deflector space warp. However, it consists of additional options such as spawning, refraction, and so on.

To create the POmniFlect space warp, invoke the **POmniFlect** tool from **Create > Space Warps > Deflectors > Object Type** rollout in the **Command Panel**; the **Name and Color**, **Supports Objects of Type**, and **Parameters** rollouts will be displayed. Activate the suitable viewport. Now, press and hold the left mouse button and drag the cursor to create the POmniFlect space warp; the POmniFlect space warp icon will be displayed in all viewports, as shown in Figure 14-6. Next, bind the POmniFlect space warp with the particle system using the **Bind to Space Warp** tool. Also, set the parameters in the **Parameters** rollout to generate the desired effect. The **Parameters** rollout is discussed next.

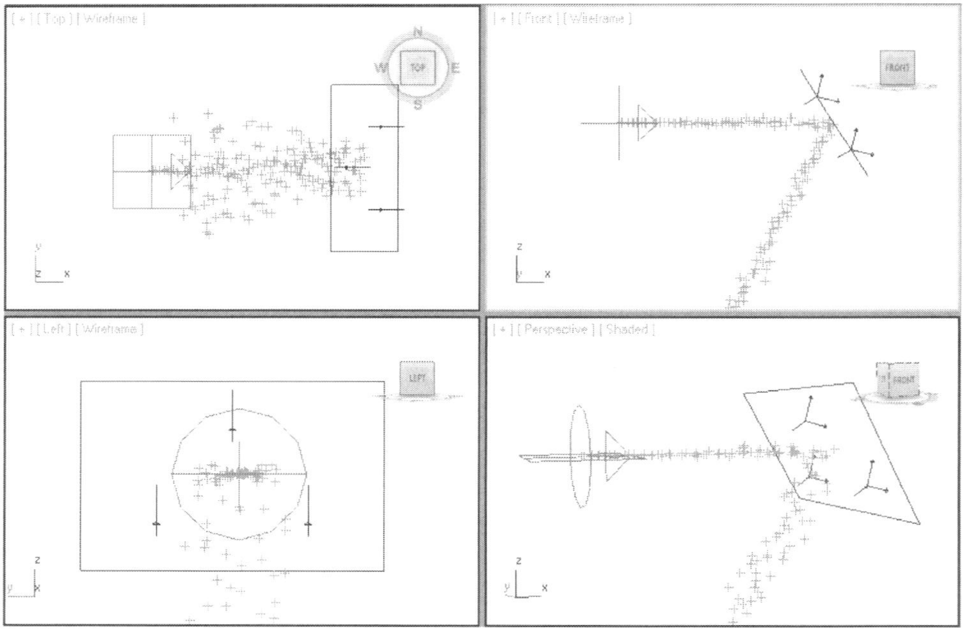

Figure 14-6 *The particles affected by the POmniFlect space warp*

Parameters Rollout

The options in this rollout are used to set the effect of the POmniFlect space warp on the particle system, refer to Figure 14-7. The areas in this rollout are discussed next.

Timing Area

The options in this area are used to specify the frame at which the deflector will start and end affecting the particles. Set the values in the **Time On** and **Time Off** spinners to specify the start and end frame number of the deflection effect, respectively.

Reflection Area

Set the value in the **Reflects** spinner to specify the number of particles affected by the space warp in terms of percentage, as shown in Figure 14-8. The other options in this area are the same as those discussed earlier in the deflector space warp.

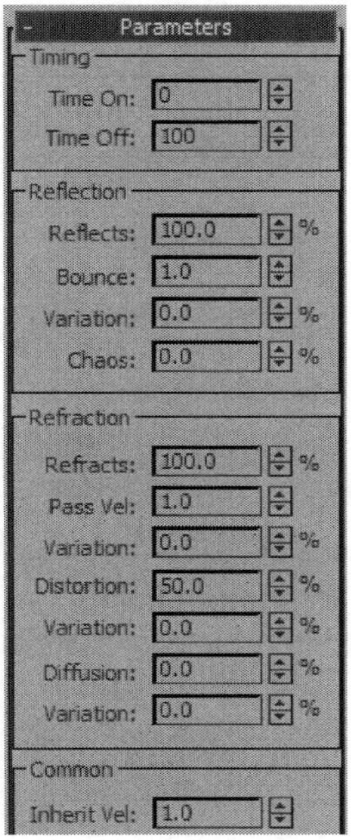

***Figure 14-7** Partial view of the **Parameters** rollout*

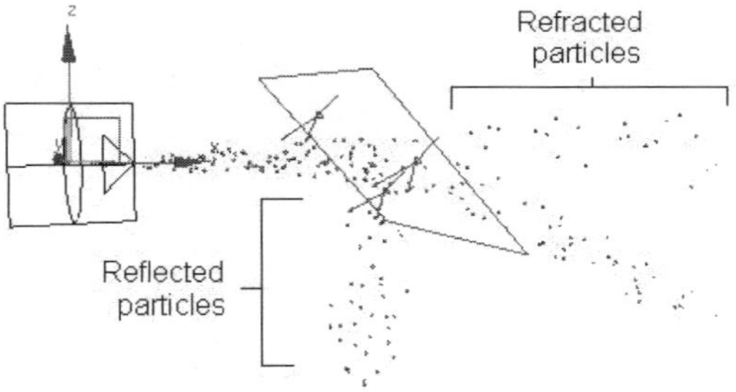

***Figure 14-8** The particles refracted and reflected by the space warp*

Refraction Area

The options in this area are used to specify the number of particles in percentage that will be refracted when they pass through the deflector, as shown in Figure 14-8. Set the value in the **Pass Vel** spinner to specify the speed of the particles refracted by the space warp. Set the value in the **Variation** spinner to vary the speed of particles in percentage. Set the value in the **Distortion** spinner to control the angle of refraction. Set the value in the **Diffusion** spinner to specify the angle at which all refracted particles will be scattered.

Common Area

The options in this area are the same as those discussed earlier in the **Parameters** rollout of the deflector space warp.

Spawn Effects Only Area

The options in this area are used to affect the particles that are set to spawn on collision. Also, these options affect the particles that are neither reflected nor refracted by the space warp. Set the value in the **Spawns** spinner to specify the percentage of particles that will be affected by the spawn effects. The other options in this area are the same as those discussed earlier.

Display Icon Area

Set the value in the **Width** and **Height** spinners in this area to define the width and height of the POmniFlect icon in the viewport.

Note

The SOmniFlect and UOmniFlect space warps are similar to the POmniFlect space warp. The only difference is that the SOmniFlect space warp is spherical in shape and the UOmniFlect space warp can make any object in the viewport as a space warp object.

Geometric/Deformable Space Warps

The tools in the **Geometric/Deformable** category are used to create the space warps that deform the mesh objects. Some of the space warps in this category are discussed next.

FFD(Box) Space Warp

Menu bar:	Create > SpaceWarps > Geometric/Deformable > FFD(Box)
Command Panel:	Create > Space Warps > Geometric/Deformable > Object Type rollout > FFD(Box)

The FFD(Box) space warp is used to deform an object by adjusting the control points of a lattice box. It is similar to the FFD modifier that has already been discussed in Chapter 10.

To create the FFD(Box) space warp, invoke the **FFD(Box)** tool from **Create > Space Warps > Geometric/Deformable > Object Type** rollout in the **Command Panel**; the **Name and Color**, **Supports Objects of Type**, and **FFD Parameters** rollouts will be displayed. Activate the suitable viewport. Now, press and hold the left mouse button and drag the cursor in the same way as you create a box from standard primitives; a box-shaped lattice with control points or FFD(Box) will be displayed, refer to Figure 14-9. Next, bind the FFD(Box) space warp with the object in the viewport that you want to modify using the **Bind to Space Warp** tool and set the position of the lattice box accordingly. Then, choose the **Modify** tab in the **Command Panel** and select the Control Points sub-object level in the modifier stack; the control points of the lattice will be displayed in the viewport. Now, adjust the position of the control points to modify the bound object, refer to Figure 14-10. Also, you need to modify the options in the **FFD Parameters** rollout. The options in the **FFD Parameters** rollout are the same as discussed in the **FFD Parameters** rollout of the **FFD Modifiers** in Chapter 10.

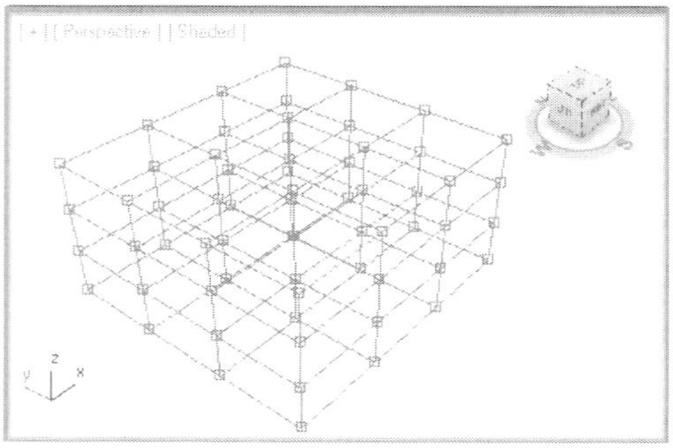

Figure 14-9 *The FFD(Box)*

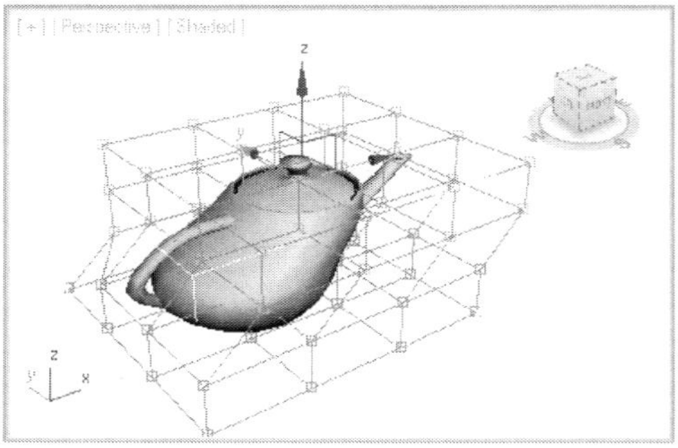

Figure 14-10 *The control points moved to modify the shape of the bound object*

Note
The FFD(Cyl) space warp is similar to the FFD(Box) space warp with the only difference that the FFD(Cyl) is cylindrical in shape.

Wave Space Warp

Menu bar:	Create > SpaceWarps > Geometric/Deformable > Wave
Command Panel:	Create > Space Warps > Geometric/Deformable > Object Type rollout > Wave

The wave space warp is used to create a linear wave in space and affects the objects that are bound to it. It is also used to create the wavy effect in the objects.

To create a wave space warp, invoke the **Wave** tool from **Create > Space Warps > Geometric/ Deformable > Object Type** rollout in the **Command Panel**; the **Name and Color**, **Supports Objects of Type**, and **Parameters** rollouts will be displayed. Activate the suitable viewport. Now, press and hold the left mouse button and drag the cursor to define the wavelength, and release the mouse button. Then, move the cursor up or down to define the amplitude of the waves; the wave space warp icon will be displayed, as shown in Figure 14-11. Next, bind the wave space warp icon with the object to which you want to apply the wave effect; the object will display the wave effect, as shown in Figure 14-12. Now, set the parameters in the **Parameters** rollout, which is discussed next.

Note
The number of segments on the object must be high to get the best effect of the wave space warp.

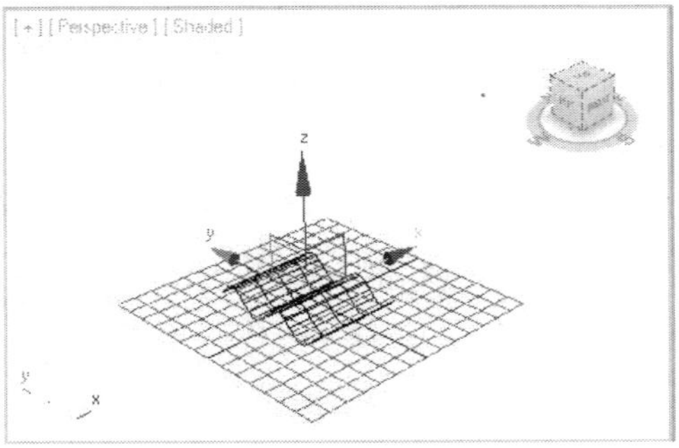

Figure 14-11 *The space warp icon for the wave space warp*

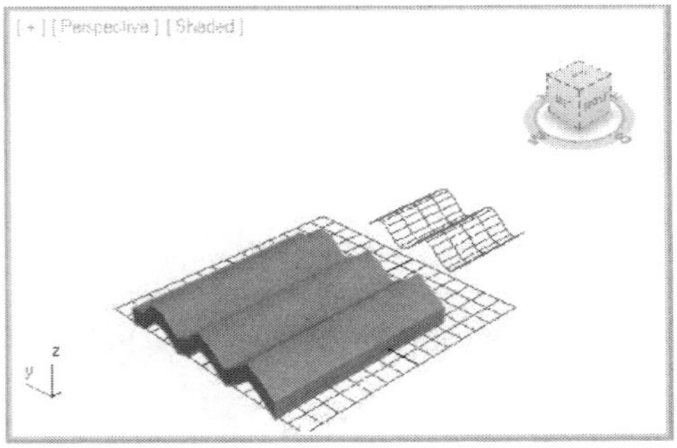

Figure 14-12 *The effect of the wave space warp*

Parameters Rollout

The options in this rollout are used to modify the wave effects, refer to Figure 14-13. The areas in this rollout are discussed next.

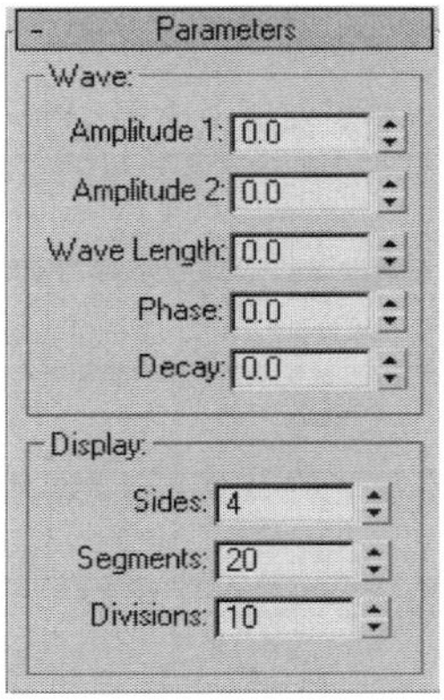

***Figure 14-13** The **Parameters** rollout*

Wave Area

Set the values in the **Amplitude 1** and **Amplitude 2** spinners to specify the wave amplitude along the X and Y axes of the wave space warp object, respectively. Set the value in the **Wave Length** spinner to define the distance between the crests of the waves. Set the value in the **Phase** spinner to offset the phase of the wave from its origin. The value in the **Decay** spinner is used to decrease the amplitude of the waves as its distance increases from the center of the wave space warp.

Display Area

Set the value in the **Sides** spinner to specify the number of segments across the width of the wave. Set the value in the **Segments** spinner to specify the number of segments across the length of the wave. Set the value in the **Divisions** spinner to specify the size of the wave icon without affecting the wave effect.

Select the object that is affected by the wave space warp and choose the **Modify** tab; the **Flexibility** spinner will be displayed in the **Parameters** rollout. Set the value in this spinner to specify how much the object will be affected by the wave space warp.

Ripple Space Warp

Menu bar:	Create > SpaceWarps > Geometric/Deformable > Ripple
Command Panel:	Create > Space Warps > Geometric/Deformable > Object Type rollout > Ripple

The ripple space warp is similar to the wave space warp. The main difference is that the ripple space warp is used to create circular and concentric waves, as shown in Figure 14-14.

To create a ripple space warp, invoke the **Ripple** tool from **Create > Space Warps > Geometric/Deformable > Object Type** rollout in the **Command Panel**; the **Name and Color**, **Supports Objects of Type**, and **Parameters** rollouts will be displayed. Activate the suitable viewport, press and hold the left mouse button, drag the cursor to define the wavelength, and release the mouse button. Now, move the cursor up or down to define the amplitude of the waves; the ripple space warp icon will be displayed. Next, bind the ripple space warp icon with the object in which you want to apply the ripple effect; the object will display the ripple effect, as shown in Figure 14-14.

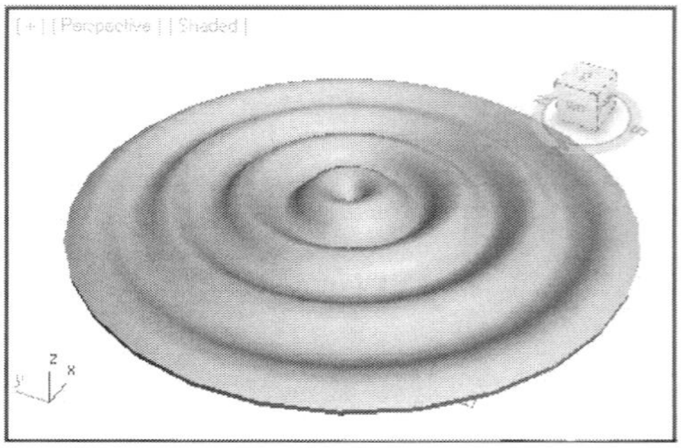

***Figure 14-14** The effect of the ripple space warp*

Now, set the parameters in the **Parameters** rollout. These parameters are the same as discussed in the wave space warp.

Note

*There are some other space warps in this category like displace and conform space warps. The effect of the displace space warp is similar to the **Displace** modifier discussed in Chapter 10. The effect of the conform space warp is similar to the **Conform** compound object.*

Bomb Space Warp

Menu bar:	Create > SpaceWarps > Geometric/Deformable > Bomb
Command Panel:	Create > Space Warps > Geometric/Deformable > Object Type rollout > Bomb

The bomb space warp is used to explode the objects into their individual faces, as shown in Figure 14-15.

To create a bomb space warp, first create an object that you want to explode. Next, invoke the **Bomb** tool from **Create > Space Warps > Geometric/Deformable > Object Type** rollout in the **Command Panel**; the **Name and Color**, **Supports Objects of Type**, and **Bomb Parameters** rollouts will be displayed. Next, click in the viewport to create the bomb space warp; the bomb space warp icon will be displayed, as shown in Figure 14-16. Now, bind the bomb space warp with the object to be exploded, and then set the parameters in the **Bomb Parameters** rollout to generate a realistic effect. You need to drag the time slider to view the effect of the bomb space warp. The **Bomb Parameters** rollout is discussed next.

Bomb Parameters Rollout

The options in this rollout are used to modify the bomb effect on the object, refer to Figure 14-17. The areas in this rollout are discussed next.

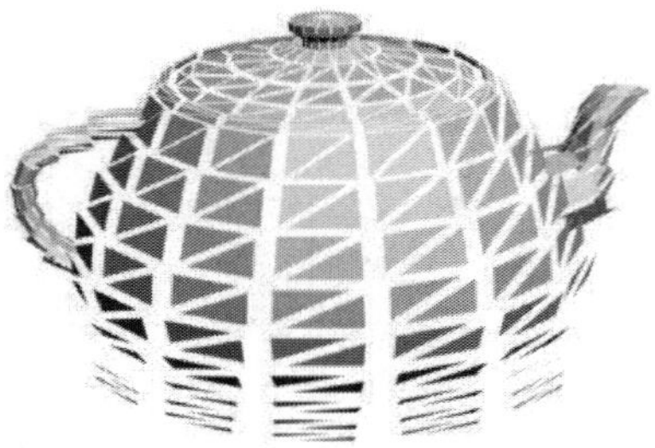

Figure 14-15 *The effect of the bomb space warp at one frame*

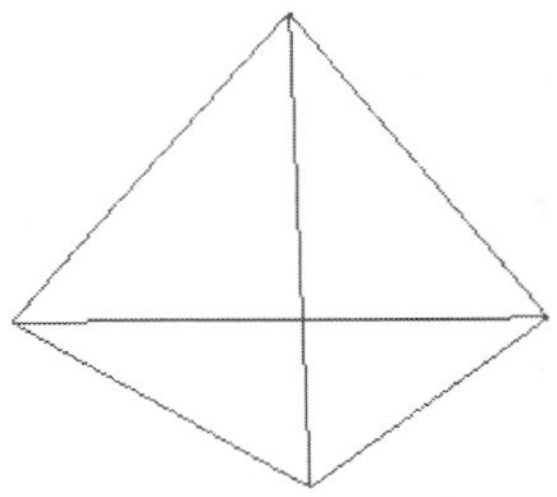

Figure 14-16 *The icon of the bomb space warp icon*

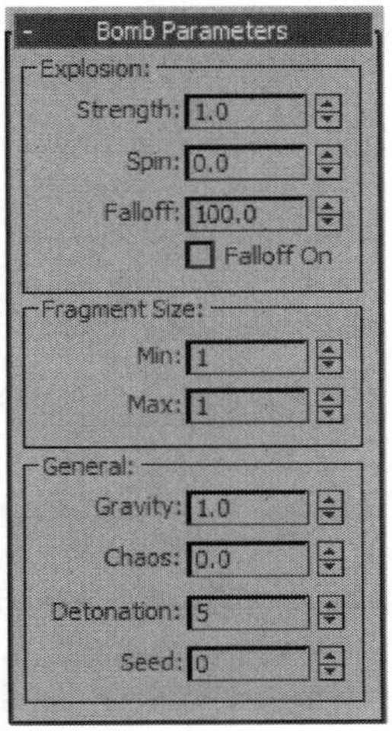

Figure 14-17 *The **Bomb Parameters** rollout*

Explosion Area

Set the value in the **Strength** spinner to specify the strength of the force to explode the object. Set the value in the **Spin** spinner to specify the rate of rotation of the fragments in revolutions per second. Select the **Falloff On** check box; the **Falloff** spinner will get activated. Also, a yellow gizmo will be displayed in the viewport. The value in the **Falloff** spinner is used to define the extents of the effect of the bomb space warp. The fragments that will be outside the yellow gizmo are affected by the gravity settings of the space warp.

Fragment Size Area

The options in this area are used to define the size of the fragments in the bomb space warp. Set the value in the **Min** spinner to specify the minimum number of faces per fragment that will be generated by explosion. Set the value in the **Max** spinner to specify the maximum number of faces per segment that will be generated by explosion.

General Area

Set the value in the **Gravity** spinner to specify the acceleration in the fragments due to gravity along the world Z-axis. Set the value in the **Chaos** spinner to bring random variation in the explosion. The value in the **Detonation** spinner is used to define the frame at which the explosion effect will start. Set the value in the **Seed** spinner to specify the random numbers generated for explosion.

Modifier-Based Space Warps

The tools in the **Modifier-Based** category are used to create the space warps that generate the effects similar to the object modifiers. However, the modifier-based space warps do not have the sub-object levels. The **Modifier-Based** space warps are used when you want to assign the effects to a group of objects. Some of the space warps in this category are discussed next.

Skew Space Warp

Menu bar:	Create > SpaceWarps > Modifier-Based > Skew
Command Panel:	Create > Space Warps > Modifier-Based > Object Type rollout > Skew

The effect of the skew space warp is similar to the skew modifier. It is used to offset the geometry of an object uniformly in any of the three axes.

To create a skew space warp, invoke the **Skew** tool from **Create > Space Warps > Modifier-Based > Object Type** rollout in the **Command Panel**; the **Name and Color**, **Gizmo Parameters**, and **Parameters** rollouts will be displayed. Activate the suitable viewport and create the space warp in the viewport as you create a box primitive; a gizmo will be displayed, as shown in Figure 14-18. Next, bind the space warp gizmo with the object in the viewport that you want to skew, and then set the parameters in the **Parameters** rollout to get the desired skew effect, refer to Figure 14-19. The **Gizmo Parameters** and **Parameters** rollouts are discussed next.

Note

*The space warp icon for the **Modifier-Based** space warps such as **Twist**, **Bend**, and so on is the same for all space warps.*

Gizmo Parameters Rollout

The options in this rollout are used to modify the dimensions of the space warp icon in the viewport, refer to Figure 14-20. Set the values in the **Length**, **Width**, and **Height** spinners in the **Gizmo Size** area to specify the length, width, and height of the space warp icon, respectively. Set the value in the **Decay** spinner in the **Deformation** area to decay the effect of the space warp on the bound object gradually.

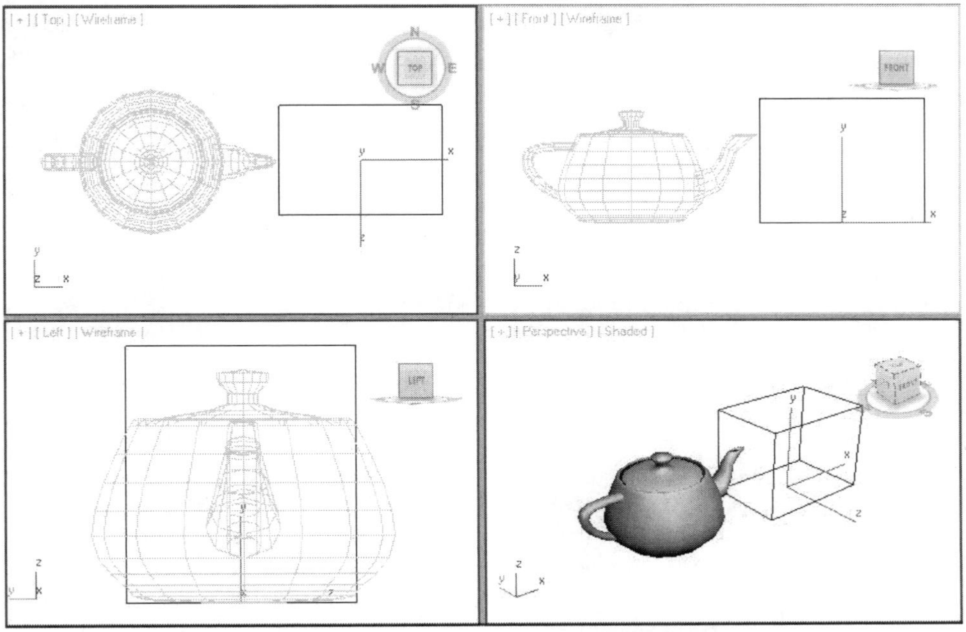

Figure 14-18 *The box shaped space warp gizmo displayed in all viewports*

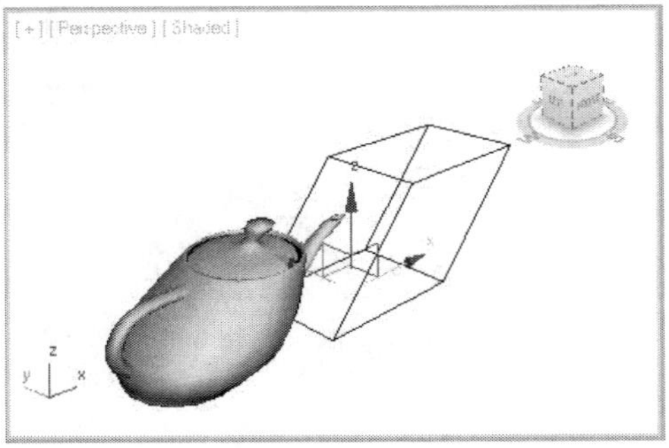

Figure 14-19 *The effect of the skew space warp*

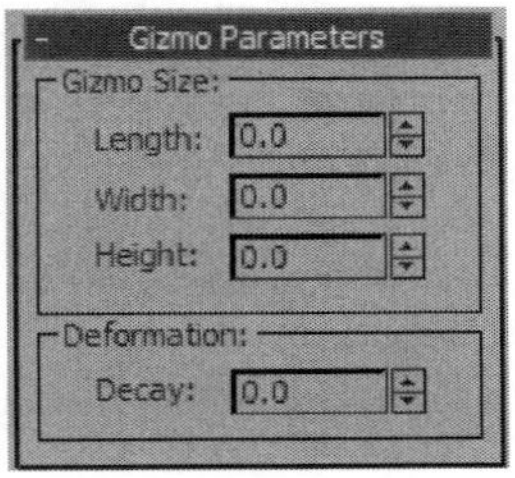

Figure 14-20 *The **Gizmo Parameters** rollout*

Note

*The options in the **Gizmo Parameters** rollout are the same for all the modifier-based space warps.*

Parameters Rollout

The options in this rollout are used to modify the skew effect, refer to Figure 14-21. The areas in this rollout are discussed next.

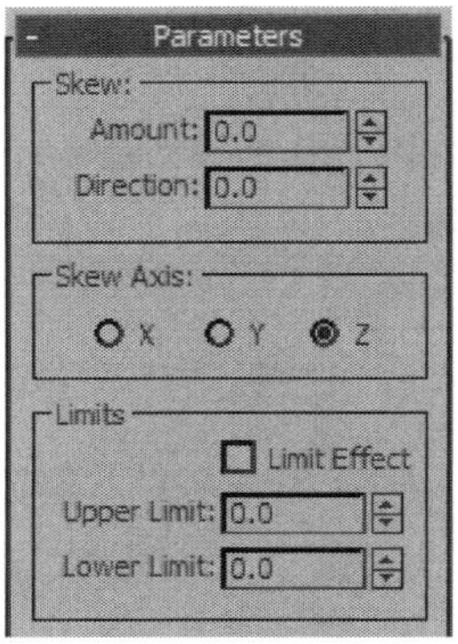

***Figure 14-21** The **Parameters** rollout*

Skew Area

The value in the **Amount** spinner is used to define an angle to skew the object from its vertical plane. Set the value in the **Direction** spinner to specify the direction of the skew.

Skew Axis Area

Select the **X**, **Y**, or **Z** radio button to specify the axis to be skewed.

Stretch Space Warp

Menu bar:	Create > SpaceWarps > Modifier-Based > Stretch
Command Panel:	Create > Space Warps > Modifier-Based > Object Type rollout > Stretch

The effect of the stretch space warp is similar to the stretch modifier. It is used to stretch the geometry of an object along the specified axis.

To create a stretch space warp, invoke the **Stretch** tool from **Create > Space Warps > Modifier-Based > Object Type** rollout in the **Command Panel**; the **Name and Color**, **Gizmo Parameters**, and **Parameters** rollouts will be displayed. Activate the suitable viewport and create the space warp in the viewport as you create a box primitive; a box gizmo will be displayed. Next, bind the space warp gizmo with the object in the viewport that you want to stretch, and then set the parameters in the **Parameters** rollout to get the desired stretch effect, refer to Figure 14-22. The **Parameters** rollout is discussed next.

Parameters Rollout

The options in this rollout are used to modify the stretch effect, refer to Figure 14-23. The areas in this rollout are discussed next.

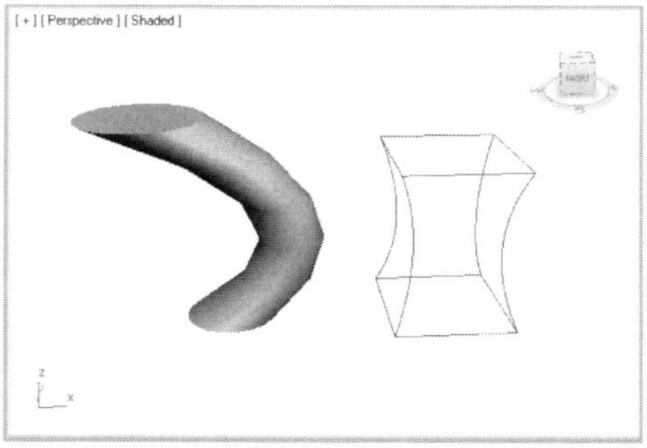

***Figure 14-22** The effect of the stretch space warp*

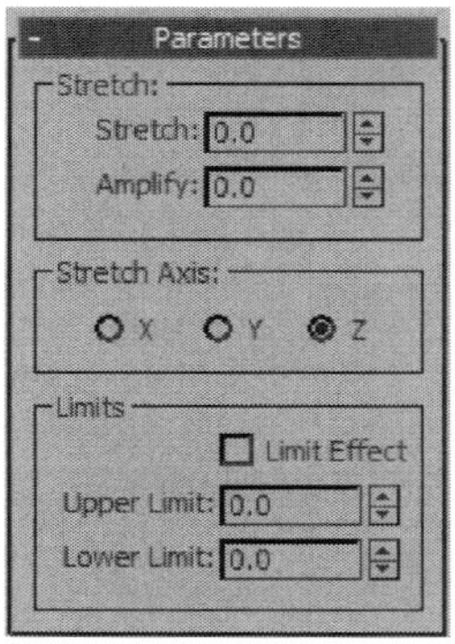

***Figure 14-23** The **Parameters** rollout*

Stretch Area
Set the value in the **Stretch** spinner to specify the amount of stretch on the object. Set the value in the **Amplify** spinners to adjust the stretch effect on the object.

Stretch Axis Area
Select the **X**, **Y**, or **Z** radio button to specify the axis in which the bound object will be stretched.

Tutorial 1

In this tutorial, you will create a scene with the animated fountains, as shown in Figure 14-24. **(Expected time: 60 min)**

Figure 14-24 *Model for Tutorial 1*

The following steps are required to complete this tutorial:

a. Set the project folder.
b. Download the files.
c. Create the ground.
d. Assign the camera.
e. Create the fountain wall.
f. Create the water surface.
g. Assign materials.
h. Create fountains.
i. Create plants, park benches, and railings.
j. Create lights.
k. Create the environment of the scene.
l. Render the scene for the final output.
m. Save the file.

Setting the Project Folder

1. Set the project folder with the name *c14_tut1* in the *3dsmax* folder as discussed in earlier chapters.

Downloading the Files

Before starting the tutorial, you need to download the *c14_3dsmax_2012_tut.zip* file from *http://www.cadcim.com*. The path of the file is as follows:

Textbooks > Animation and Visual Effects > 3ds Max > Autodesk 3ds Max 2012: A Comprehensive Guide

Extract the contents of the zipped file and copy the files *Grass.jpg*, *bricks.jpg*, and *water.jpg* at the location *\Documents\3dsmax\c14_tut1\sceneassets\images*.

Creating the Ground

To create the ground, you first need to create a plane:

1. Activate the Top viewport. Choose **Create > Geometry** in the **Command Panel**; the **Standard Primitives** option is displayed in the drop-down list below the **Geometry** button. Invoke the **Plane** tool from the **Object Type** rollout; various rollouts are displayed in the modify panel.

2. Expand the **Keyboard Entry** rollout and set the parameters as given below:

   Length: **3000.0** Width: **3000.0**

3. Choose the **Create** button; a plane is created in all viewports. Invoke the **Zoom Extents All** tool; the plane is zoomed and displayed in all viewports properly.

4. Modify the name of the plane to *ground*.

Assigning the Camera

1. Activate the Front viewport. Choose **Create > Cameras** in the **Command Panel**; the **Standard** option is displayed in the drop-down list. Invoke the **Free** tool from the **Object Type** rollout.

2. Click on the middle point of the *ground* in the Front viewport; a free camera is displayed in all viewports. It is automatically named as *Camera001*.

3. Align the *Camera001* in all viewports, as shown in Figure 14-25, and press the C key in the Perspective viewport to view the camera view.

Creating the Fountain Wall

To create the fountain wall, you need to create a tube.

1. Activate the Top viewport. Choose **Create > Geometry** in the **Command Panel**; the **Standard Primitives** option is displayed in the drop-down list. Invoke the **Tube** tool from the **Object Type** rollout; various rollouts are displayed in the modify panel.

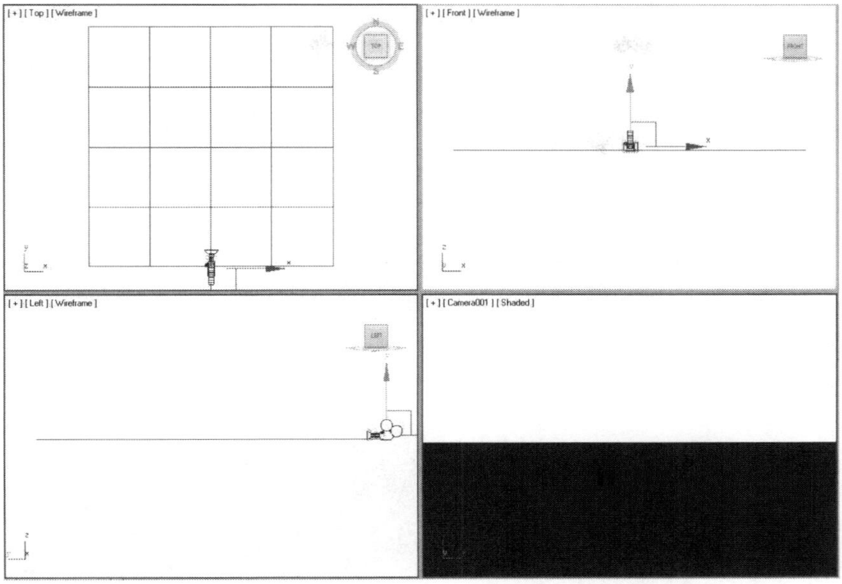

Figure 14-25 The Camera001 aligned in all viewports

2. Expand the **Keyboard Entry** rollout and set the parameters as given below:

   Inner Radius: **379.328** Outer Radius: **313.33** Height: **100.424**

3. Choose the **Create** button; a tube is created in all viewports.

4. In the **Parameters** rollout, set the values as given below:

   Height Segments: **10** Sides: **32**

5. Modify the name of the tube to *fountain wall.*

6. Position the *Camera001* in the Left viewport using the **Select and Move** and **Select and Rotate** tools to view the scene in the Camera001 viewport, as shown in Figure 14-26.

Creating the Water Surface

Now, you need to create a cylinder to create the water surface.

1. Activate the Top viewport. Invoke the **Cylinder** tool from **Standard Primitives**; various rollouts are displayed in the modify panel.

2. Expand the **Keyboard Entry** rollout and set the parameters as given below:

   Radius: **306.624** Height: **93.0**

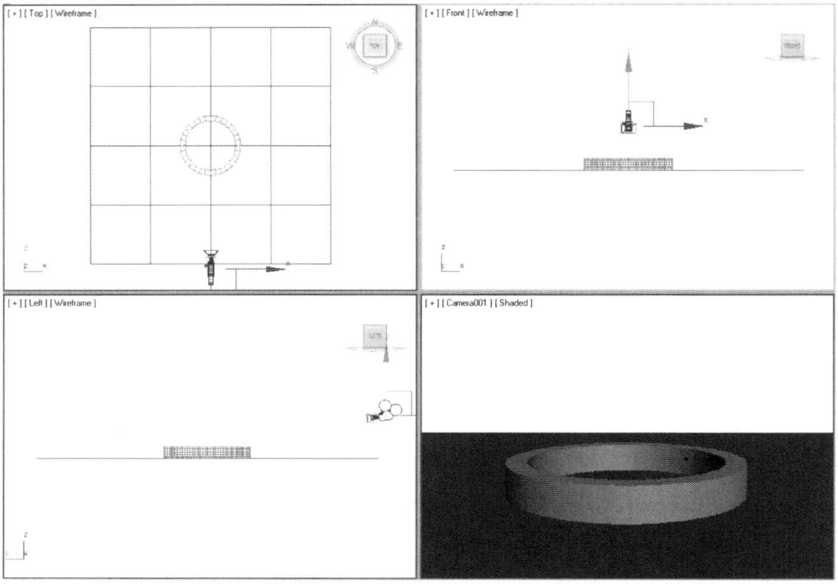

Figure 14-26 *The scene after aligning the Camera001 in all viewports*

3. Choose the **Create** button; a cylinder is created in all viewports, as shown in Figure 14-27.

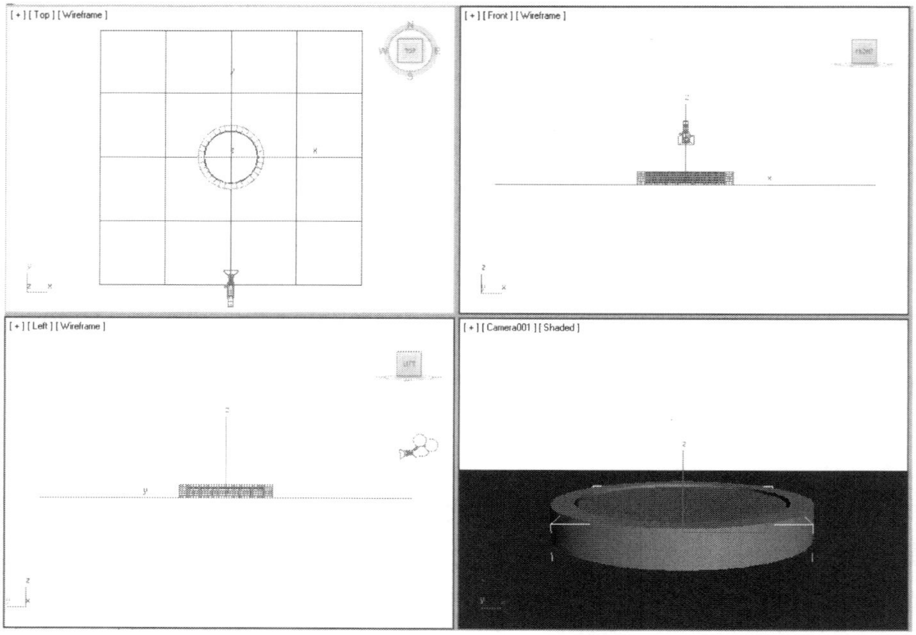

Figure 14-27 *The cylinder for creating the water surface*

4. Modify the name of the cylinder to *water01* and right-click in the viewport to exit the current command.

Next, you need to apply the materials to the objects to make them look realistic.

Assigning the Materials

1. First, select the *ground* in the viewport and invoke the **Compact Material Editor** tool; the **Material Editor** dialog box is displayed.

2. Select the **01-Default** sample slot and modify its name in the **Material Name** text box to **ground material**.

   Next, you need to assign a map to the selected sample slot.

3. In the **Blinn Basic Parameters** rollout, choose the **Diffuse** map button on the right side of the **Diffuse** color swatch; the **Material/Map Browser** dialog box is displayed. Select the **Bitmap** map from the **Maps > Standard** rollouts and choose the **OK** button; the **Select Bitmap Image File** dialog box is displayed. Select the *Grass.jpg* image and choose the **Open** button; the selected image is displayed in the selected sample slot. Also, various rollouts are displayed to modify the coordinates of the map.

4. In the **Coordinates** rollout, set the value **5** in the **U Tiling** and **V Tiling** spinners.

5. Make sure that the *ground* is selected in the viewport and then choose the **Assign Material to Selection** button; the **ground material** is assigned to the *ground* in the viewport. Also, choose the **Show Shaded Material in Viewport** button to display the assigned material in the viewport.

   Next, you will assign a material to the *fountain wall*.

6. Select the **02-Default** sample slot in the **Material Editor** dialog box. Modify its name in the **Material Name** text box to **fountain wall material**.

7. In the **Blinn Basic Parameters** rollout, choose the **Diffuse** map button on the right side of the **Diffuse** color swatch; the **Material/Map Browser** dialog box is displayed. Select the **Bitmap** map from the **Maps > Standard** rollouts and choose the **OK** button; the **Select Bitmap Image File** dialog box is displayed. Select the *bricks.jpg* image and choose the **Open** button; the selected image is displayed in the sample slot. Also, various rollouts are displayed to modify the coordinates of the map.

8. In the **Coordinates** rollout, set the value **10** in the **U Tiling** and **V Tiling** spinners. Next, choose the **Go to Parent** button to go back to the parent level.

9. Expand the **Maps** rollout and select the **Bump** check box to make it available for the material. Choose the **Bump** map button that is labeled as **None**; the **Material/Map Browser** dialog box is displayed. Select the **Bitmap** map from the **Maps > Standard** rollouts and choose the **OK** button; the **Select Bitmap Image File** dialog box is displayed. Browse to the same image (*bricks.jpg*) that you have used for the **Diffuse** map and choose the **Open** button.

10. In the **Coordinates** rollout, set the value **10** in both the **U Tiling** and **V Tiling** spinners. Next, choose the **Go to Parent** button to go back to the parent level; the name of the selected image is displayed over the **Bump** map button.

11. In the **Bump** spinner, set the value **100**.

12. Make sure that the *fountain wall* is selected in the viewport. Choose the **Assign Material to Selection** button; the **fountain wall material** is assigned to the *fountain wall* in the viewport. Also, choose the **Show Shaded Material in Viewport** button to display the assigned material in the viewport.

    Next, you need to apply the **UVW Map** modifier to the *fountain wall* to display the map properly.

13. Select the *fountain wall* in the viewport. Choose the **Modify** tab in the **Command Panel**. In the **Modifier List** drop-down list, select the **UVW Map** modifier; the **UVW Mapping** is displayed in the modifier stack. Also, the **Parameters** rollout is displayed to modify the parameters of the modifier.

14. In the **Parameters** rollout, set the values as given below:

    Mapping Area
    Select the **Spherical** radio button.
    Length: **456.88** Width: **456.88** Height: **456.88**

    Next, you need to assign a material to *water01*.

15. Select the **03-Default** sample slot in the **Material Editor** dialog box. Modify its name in the **Material Name** text box to **water01 material**.

16. Choose the **Material Type** button that is currently labeled as **Standard**; the **Material/Map Browser** dialog box is displayed. Select the **Architectural** material from the **Materials > Standard** rollouts and choose the **OK** button; the **Standard** material is replaced by the **Architectural** material now. Also, various rollouts are displayed to modify the **Architectural** material.

17. In the **Templates** rollout, select the **Water** option from the drop-down list.

18. In the **Physical Qualities** rollout, choose the **Diffuse Color** color swatch and enter the following values in the **Color Selector: Diffuse** dialog box:

    Red: **195** Green: **242** Blue: **246**

19. Choose the **Diffuse Map** button that is labeled as **None**; the **Material/Map Browser** dialog box is displayed. Select the **Bitmap** map from the **Maps > Standard** rollouts and choose

the **OK** button; the **Select Bitmap Image File** dialog box is displayed. Select the *water.jpg* image and choose the **Open** button; the selected image is displayed in the sample slot.

20. Choose the **Go to Parent** button to go back to the previous level. In the **Physical Qualities** rollout, set the value in the **Shininess** spinner to **85.0**.

21. Select *water01* in the viewport and choose the **Assign Material to Selection** button in the **Material Editor** dialog box; the **water01 material** is assigned to the *water01* in the viewport. Also, choose the **Show Shaded Material in Viewport** button to display the assigned material in the viewport.

22. Next, activate the Camera001 viewport and invoke the **Render Production** tool to view the maps and materials assigned to the objects. The *water01* displays the reflection of the **ground material**, as shown in Figure 14-28. Therefore, you need to create another water surface.

23. Activate the Front viewport and select *water01*. Choose **Edit > Clone** from the menu bar; the **Clone Options** dialog box is displayed. Select the **Copy** radio button in the **Object** area and make sure that *water002* is displayed in the **Name** text box. Choose the **OK** button; the *water002* is displayed at the same location as *water01*.

24. Choose the **Modify** tab in the **Command Panel** and set the values in the **Parameters** rollout as given below:

    Radius: **306.624**   Height: **11.0**

    The *water002* is displayed at the bottom of the *fountain wall*. Next, you need to assign a material to it.

25. Select the **04-Default** sample slot in the **Material Editor** dialog box. Modify its name in the **Material Name** text box to **water002 material**.

26. In the **Blinn Basic Parameters** rollout, choose the **Diffuse** color swatch and modify the color by entering the values as given below:

    Red: **195**   Green: **242**   Blue: **246**

27. Make sure that *water002* is selected in the viewport and choose the **Assign Material to Selection** button; the material is assigned to *water002*. Also, choose the **Show Shaded Material in Viewport** button to display the assigned material in the viewport. Close the **Material Editor** dialog box.

28. Next, activate the Camera001 viewport and invoke the **Render Production** tool; the objects are displayed, as shown in Figure 14-29.

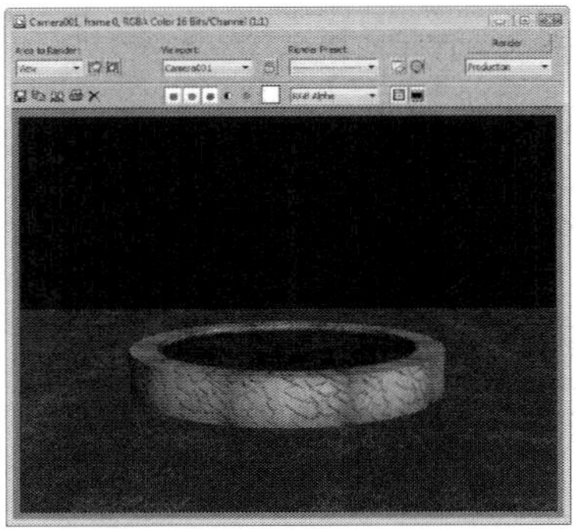

Figure 14-28 *The objects displayed at rendering after assigning the materials*

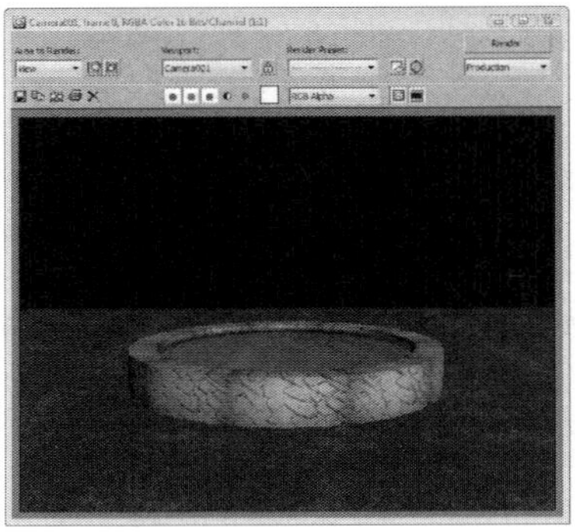

Figure 14-29 *The objects displayed at rendering after creating the water002 surface*

Creating Fountains

To create the fountains, you need to create the super spray particle system.

1. Activate the Top viewport and choose **Create > Geometry** from the **Command Panel**; the **Standard Primitives** option is displayed by default in the drop-down list. Select the **Particle Systems** option in the drop-down list and then invoke the **Super Spray** tool from the **Object Type** rollout.

2. In the Top viewport, press and hold the left mouse button, drag the cursor from one point to another, and release the left mouse button; the emitter is created for the super spray particle system. Align the emitter at the middle of the *water01* in all viewports, as shown in Figure 14-30.

3. Modify the name of the particle system to *fountain01*. Also, modify the color by entering the values as given below:

   Red: **154** Green: **215** Blue: **229**

   Next, you need to set the parameters in different rollouts.

4. Choose the **Modify** tab in the **Command Panel**; various rollouts are displayed. In the **Basic Parameters** rollout, set the values as given below:

   Particle Formation Area
   Off Axis: **0.0** Spread: **7.0**
   Off Plane: **0.0** Spread: **90.0**

   Display Icon Area
   Icon Size: **50.0**

   Viewport Display Area
   Make sure that the **Ticks** radio button is selected.

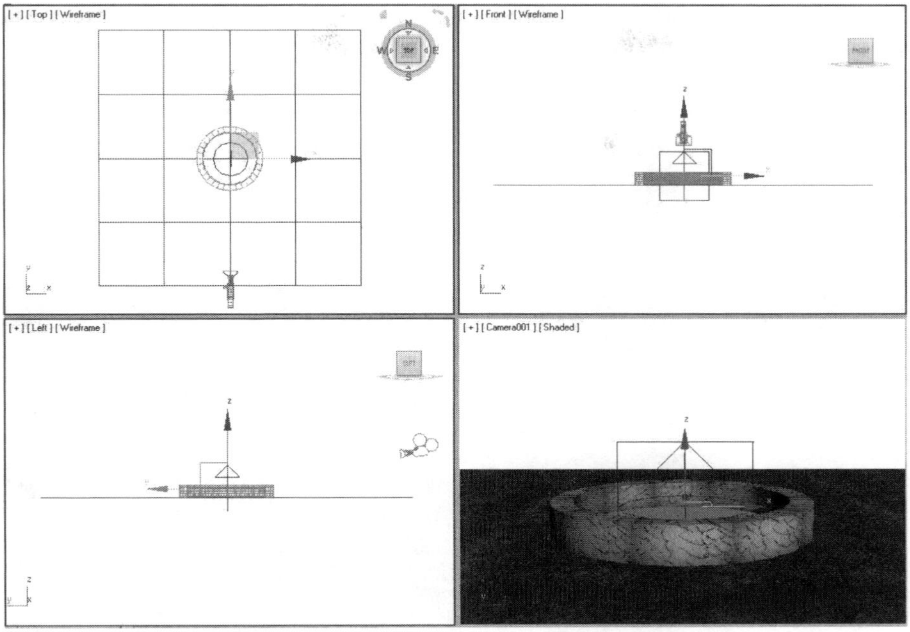

Figure 14-30 *The emitter aligned in all viewports*

Note

The icon size of the particle system does not affect the particles. However, the small size provides more room to work in the viewport.

5. In the **Particle Generation** rollout, set the values as given below:

   Particle Quantity area
   Make sure that the **Use Rate** radio button is selected and set the value **80** in the spinner below this radio button.

   Particle Motion Area
   Speed: **12.0**

   Particle Timing Area
   Emit Start: **10** Emit Stop: **100**
   Display Until: **100** Life: **75**

   Particle Size Area
   Size: **5.0**
   Use the default values for other options.

6. In the **Particle Type** rollout, set the values as given below:

   Particle Type area
   Make sure that the **Standard Particles** radio button is selected.

Standard Particles area
Select the **Tetra** radio button.

7. Activate the Camera001 viewport and choose the **Play Animation** button; the particles start moving towards the vertical axis.

   Next, you need to increase the number of frames for the animation.

8. Choose the **Time Configuration** button at the bottom of the 3ds Max screen; the **Time Configuration** dialog box is displayed.

9. In the **Animation** area, choose the **Re-scale Time** button; the **Re-scale Time** dialog box is displayed. In the **New** area, set the value **500** in the **Length** spinner and choose the **OK** button. Next, choose the **OK** button in the **Time Configuration** dialog box to close it.

10. Activate the Camera001 viewport and choose the **Play Animation** button; the particles start moving towards the vertical axis, as shown in Figure 14-31. Also, align the Camera001 in the viewports, as shown in Figure 14-31.

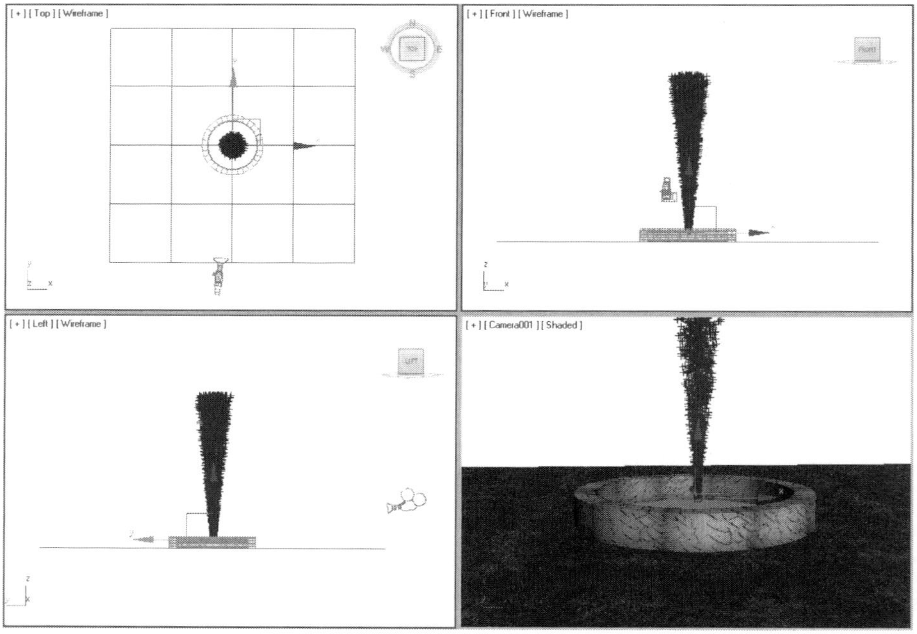

***Figure 14-31** The particles at a frame after choosing the **Play Animation** button*

Note
*When you change the values in the **Re-scale Time** dialog box, the values in the **Particle Timing** area of the **Particle Generation** rollout also get changed.*

Notice that the particles are moving in the upward direction. To bring them downward, you need to apply the gravity space warp to the particle system.

11. Activate the Top viewport. Choose **Create > Space Warps** in the **Command Panel**; the **Forces** category is displayed in the drop-down list. Invoke the **Gravity** tool from the **Object Type** rollout.

12. Press and hold the left mouse button, drag the cursor in the Top viewport, and then release the left mouse button; the gravity space warp icon is displayed in all viewports.

13. Next, choose the **Modify** tab in the **Command Panel** and set the values in the **Parameters** rollout as given below:

    Force Area
    Strength: **0.13**

    Use the default values for other options.

14. Select *fountain01* in any viewport and invoke the **Bind to Space Warp** tool from the **Main Toolbar**. Now, bind the *fountain01* with the gravity space warp icon; the direction of particles is changed, as shown in Figure 14-32. Invoke the **Select Object** tool to exit the **Bind to Space Warp** command.

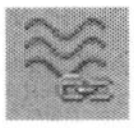

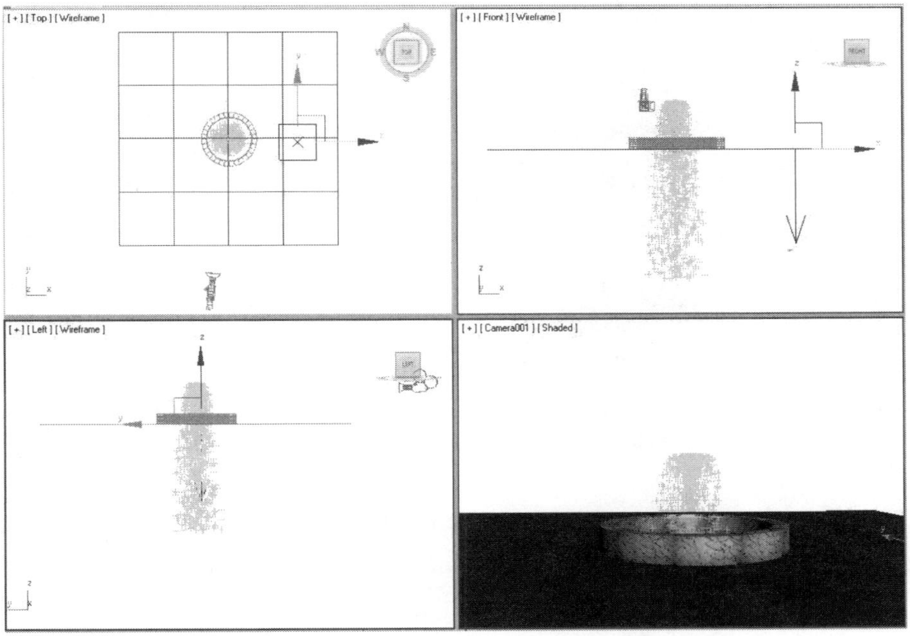

Figure 14-32 *The particles after applying the gravity space warp*

Note
You can vary the size and position of the gravity space warp icon as it does not affect the particles of the particle system.

After applying the gravity space warp, the particles start moving downward but they go under the *ground*, refer to Figure 14-33. To avoid this, you need to apply a deflector space warp to the particle system.

15. Activate the Top viewport. Make sure that **Create > Space Warps** is selected in the **Command Panel**. Select the **Deflectors** category in the drop-down list below the **Space Warps** button. Invoke the **Deflector** tool from the **Object Type** rollout.

16. In the Top viewport, press and hold the left mouse button, drag the cursor from one point to another, and then release the left mouse button; the deflector space warp icon is displayed in all viewports.

17. Select *fountain01* in any viewport and invoke the **Bind to Space Warp** tool from the **Main Toolbar**. Now, bind the *fountain01* with the deflector space warp icon.

18. Invoke the **Select and Move** tool and select the deflector space warp icon.

19. Choose the **Modify** tab in the **Command Panel** and set the values in the **Parameters** rollout as given below:

    Bounce: **0.2** Friction: **1.0**
    Width: **2500** Length: **2500**

    Use the default values for other options.

20. Align the deflector space warp icon in the Top viewport, as shown in Figure 14-33. As you align the deflector space warp icon, the position of the particles also changes.

    After colliding with the deflector space warp, some of the particles of the *fountain01* start moving outward, as shown in Figure 14-33. Therefore, you need to modify the settings of the *fountain01*.

21. Select the *fountain01* in the viewport and choose the **Modify** tab in the **Command Panel**. In the modifier stack, select the **Super Spray** option; various rollouts are displayed in the modify panel.

22. Expand the **Particle Spawn** rollout and select the **Die After Collision** radio button in it. As a result, the particles will die after colliding with the deflector space warp icon, as shown in Figure 14-34.

23. Activate the Camera001 viewport and invoke the **Render Production** tool; the scene is displayed at rendering, as shown in Figure 14-35.

    Next, to make the *fountain01* realistic, you need to apply the **Motion Blur** rendering effect to it.

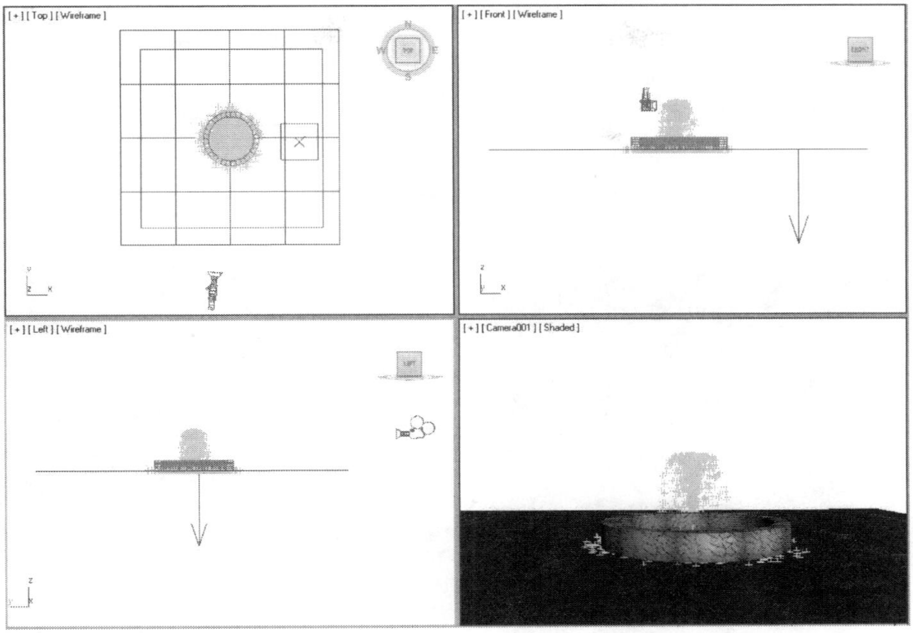

***Figure 14-33** The particles after applying the deflector space warp*

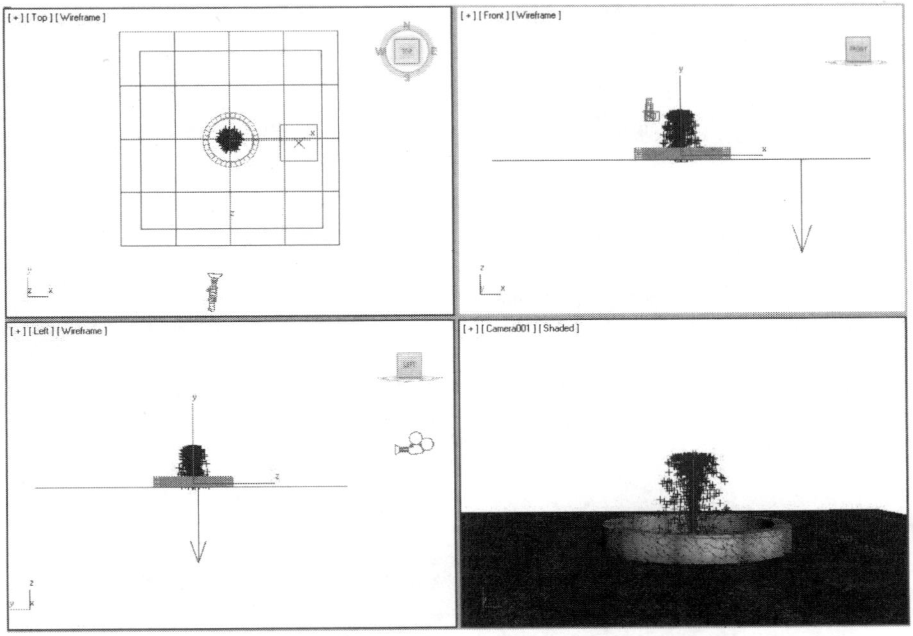

***Figure 14-34** The particles after modifying the settings*

24. Select the *fountain01* in any viewport and right-click on it; a quad menu is displayed. Choose the **Object Properties** option; the **Object Properties** dialog box is displayed. Next, select the **Image** radio button in the **Motion Blur** area; the **Multiplier** spinner is activated in this area. Set the value **8.0** in this spinner and choose the **OK** button to exit the dialog box.

25. Activate the Camera001 viewport and invoke the **Render Production** tool; the scene is displayed, as shown in Figure 14-36.

Figure 14-35 *The scene at rendering*

Figure 14-36 *The scene at rendering after applying the motion blur effect*

Next, you need to create other fountains.

26. Select the *fountain wall* and invoke the **Zoom Extents All Selected** tool.

27. Select the *fountain01* in the Top viewport and create its four copies. They are automatically named as *fountain002*, *fountain003*, *fountain004*, and *fountain005*. Next, align them in the Top viewport, as shown in Figure 14-37.

Note
All copied fountains are bound to the gravity and deflector space warps.

Next, to generate some variations in *fountain002*, *fountain003*, *fountain004*, and *fountain005*, you need to create another gravity space warp.

28. First, select the *fountain002* in any viewport. In the modifier stack, select the **Gravity Binding (WSM)** option and choose the **Remove modifier from the stack** button; the **Gravity Binding (WSM)** option is deleted.

29. Repeat the above step (step 28) for *fountain003*, *fountain004*, and *fountain005*.

30. Now, in the Top viewport, create a gravity space warp icon using the **Gravity** tool from the **Forces** category. It is automatically named as *Gravity002*. Bind it with the *fountain002*, *fountain003*, *fountain004*, and *fountain005* using the **Bind to Space Warp** tool.

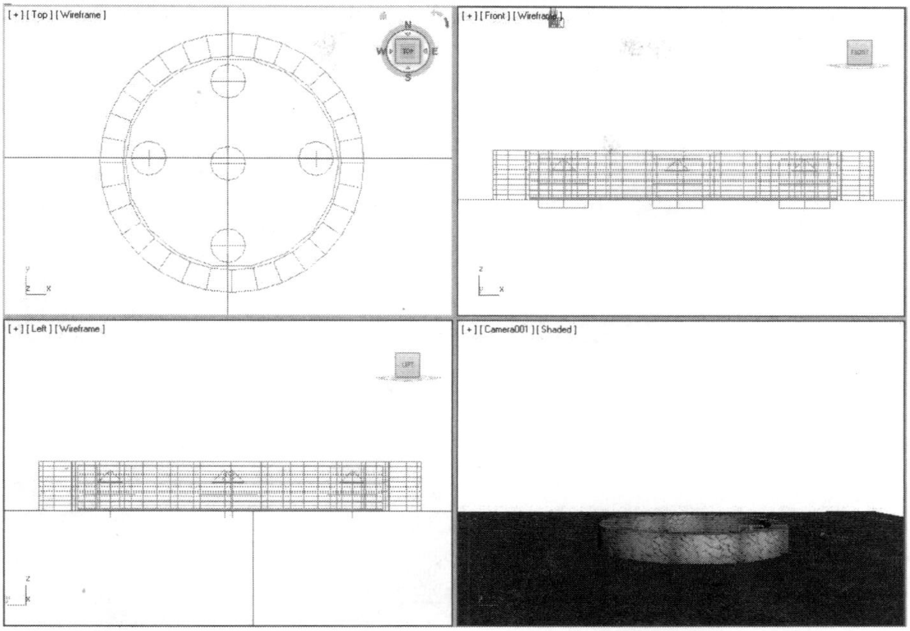

Figure 14-37 *The four copies of the fountain01 after alignment*

Tip: *Before binding the Gravity002 space warp with the fountain002, fountain003, fountain004, and fountain005, move the time slider to frame 0. It will help you to bind the fountains easily.*

31. Invoke the **Select and Move** tool, select the *Gravity002* space warp, and choose the **Modify** tab in the **Command Panel**. In the **Parameters** rollout, set the value **0.3** in the **Strength** spinner.

32. Choose the **Go to End** button in the animation playback controls and render the Camera001 viewport; the scene is displayed, as shown in Figure 14-38.

Figure 14-38 *The scene at rendering*

Creating Plants, Park Benches, and Railings

1. Create the plants of your choice by invoking the **Foliage** tool from **Create > Geometry > AEC Extended > Object Type** rollout.

2. Create railings all around the ground by invoking the **Railing** tool from **Create > Geometry > AEC Extended > Object Type** rollout.

3. Create the park benches as discussed in Tutorial 2 of Chapter 2 and align them, as shown in Figure 14-39.

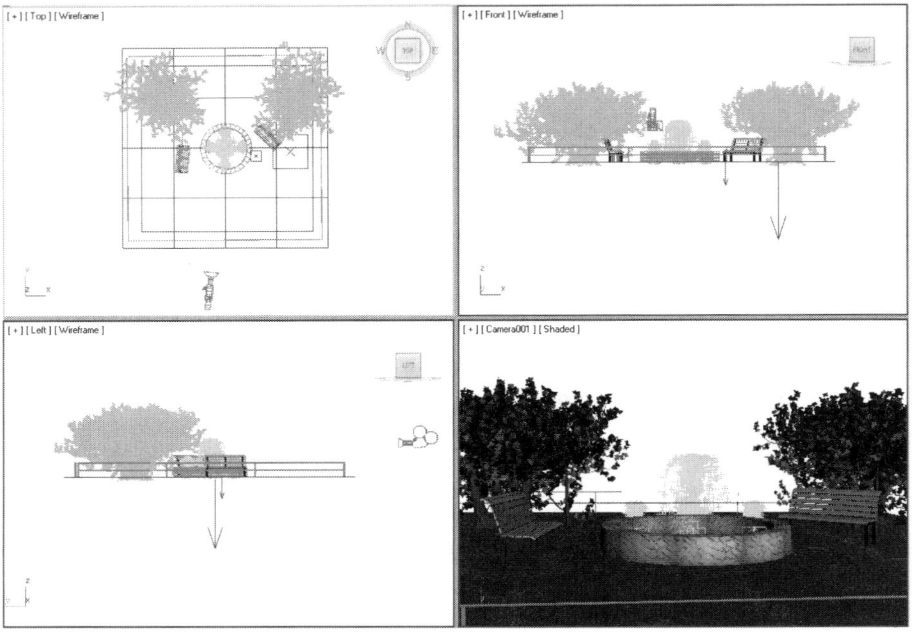

Figure 14-39 *The plants, railings, and park benches in the scene after the alignment*

Next, you need to assign lights to the scene.

Creating Lights

First, you need to create lights for the fountains in the scene.

1. Select the *fountain wall* in a viewport and invoke the **Zoom Extents All Selected** tool.

2. Activate the Top viewport and invoke the **Omni** tool from **Create > Lights > Standard > Object Type** rollout. Click in the Top viewport to create the omni light and align it in all viewports, as shown in Figure 14-40. It is automatically named as *Omni01*.

3. Next, make sure that the *Omni01* is selected and choose the **Modify** tab in the **Command Panel**.

4. Expand the **Intensity/Color/Attenuation** rollout and choose the color swatch at the extreme right of the **Multiplier** spinner; the **Color Selector: Light Color** dialog box is displayed. Enter the values given next to modify the color of the light.

   Red: **196** Green: **241** Blue: **243**

   Choose the **OK** button to close the dialog box.

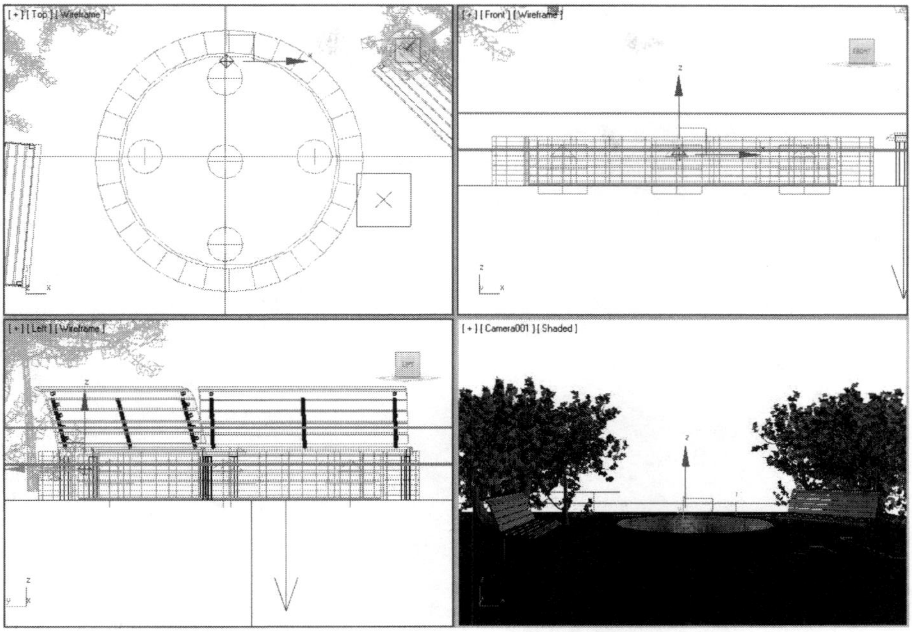

Figure 14-40 *The Omni01 light in all viewports after the alignment*

5. In the **General Parameters** rollout, choose the **Exclude** button; the **Exclude/Include** dialog box is displayed. Exclude the park benches and plants from the light effect.

6. Next, create three copies of the *Omni01* light in the Top viewport and align them, as shown in Figure 14-41. Also, make sure that the park benches and plants are excluded from the effect of the copied lights.

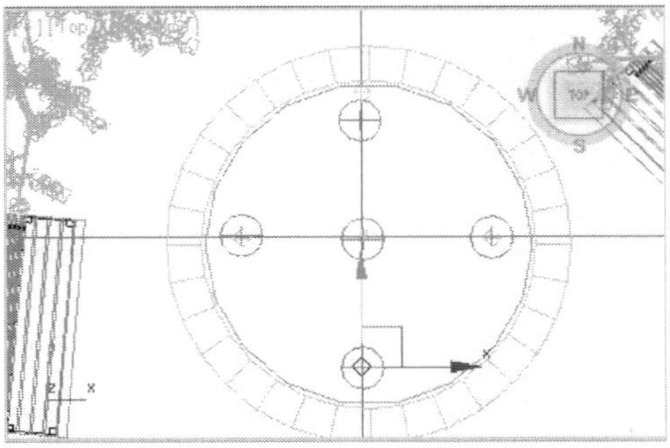

Figure 14-41 *All omni lights aligned in the Top viewport*

Note

You can exclude or include objects from the light effect depending on the effects to be generated in the scene.

Next, create the lights for the entire scene.

7. Invoke the **Zoom Extents All** tool and activate the Top viewport.

8. Invoke the **Zoom All** tool and zoom out in any viewport, except the Camera001 viewport, till all objects are displayed to half of their size, refer to Figure 14-42.

9. Invoke the **Omni** tool. In the Top viewport, click at the upper-right and lower-left corners to create two more omni lights. Align them in all viewports, as shown in Figure 14-42.

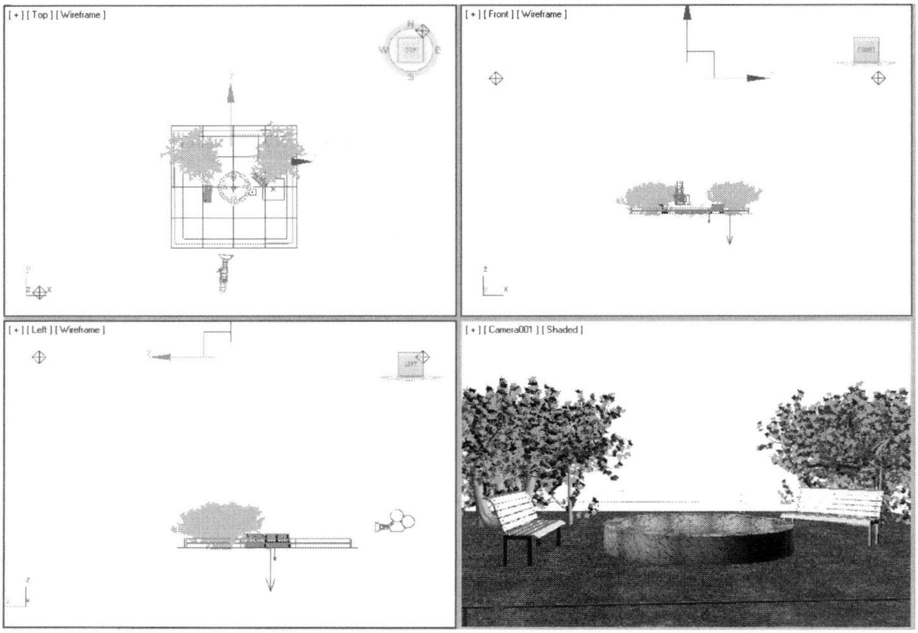

***Figure 14-42** The omni lights in all viewports after the alignment*

You can also create more lights depending on the scene's requirement.

10. Choose the **Go to End** button in the animation playback controls and render the Camera001 viewport; the scene is displayed, as shown in Figure 14-43.

Creating the Environment for the Scene

1. Create the environment for the scene as discussed in Tutorial 2 of Chapter 12.

2. Choose the **Go to End** button in the animation playback controls. Render the Camera001 viewport; the scene is displayed with the stars in the sky, as shown in Figure 14-44.

Rendering the Scene for the Final Output

To view the final output of the scene including the animation of fountains, you need to render the scene.

Figure 14-43 *The scene at rendering after assigning the lights*

Figure 14-44 *The scene with the environment at rendering*

1. Invoke the **Render Setup** tool from the **Main Toolbar**; the **Render Setup: Default Scanline Renderer** dialog box is displayed. The **Common** tab is chosen by default.

2. Set the values in the **Render Setup: Default Scanline Renderer** dialog box as discussed in Tutorial 1 of Chapter 12 and choose the **Render** button; the **Camera001, frame** and the **Rendering** dialog boxes are invoked, and they display the rendering process.

3. After the completion of rendering, the final output of the animation is saved in the **.avi* format at a location specified by you. You can view the final output of the animation by opening the corresponding *avi* file.

   You can view the final rendered sequence by downloading the *c14_3dsmax_2012_render.zip* file from *http://www.cadcim.com.*

Saving the File

1. Save the file with the name *c14tut1.max* as discussed in earlier chapters. The location of this file is given below:

   \Documents\3dsmax\c14_tut1\scenes

Tutorial 2

In this tutorial, you will create a scene displaying smoke rising from an incense stick, as shown in Figure 14-45. **(Expected time: 45 min)**

The following steps are required to complete this tutorial:

a. Set the project folder.
b. Create the scene.
c. Create smoke.
d. Assign the material to the smoke.
e. Create lights.

f. Create the environment.
g. Render the scene for the final output.
h. Save the file.

Figure 14-45 *Model for Tutorial 2*

Setting the Project Folder

1. Set the project folder with the name *c14_tut2* in the *3dsmax* folder as discussed in earlier chapters.

Creating the Scene

In this section, first you need to create a floor and then assign material to it.

1. Invoke the **Plane** tool from **Standard Primitives** in the **Command Panel** and create a plane in the Top viewport. Set the values in the **Parameters** rollout as given below:

   Length: **1239.908** Width: **1957.291**

2. Modify the name of the plane to *floor*.

3. Now, press the M key; the **Material Editor** dialog box is displayed.

4. Select the **01-Default** sample slot and modify its name in the **Material Name** text box to **floor material**.

   Next, you need to assign a map.

5. In the **Blinn Basic Parameters** rollout, choose the **Diffuse** map button on the right side of the **Diffuse** color swatch; the **Material/Map Browser** dialog box is displayed. Select the **Checker** map from the **Maps > Standard** rollouts and choose the **OK** button; the selected map is displayed in the sample slot. Also, the rollouts are displayed to modify the coordinates of the map.

6. In the **Coordinates** rollout, set the value **5** in both the **U Tiling** and **V Tiling** spinners.

7. Make sure that the *floor* is selected in the viewport and then choose the **Assign Material to Selection** button; the **floor material** is assigned to the *floor* in the viewport. Also, choose the **Show Shaded Material in Viewport** button to display the assigned material in the viewport. Close the **Material Editor** dialog box.

   Next, you need to create a stand for the incense stick.

8. Invoke the **Line** tool from **Create > Shapes > Splines > Object Type** rollout in the **Command Panel**. Create a line in the Front viewport, as shown in Figure 14-46.

9. Create an *incense stick stand* by applying the **Lathe** modifier to the line as discussed earlier in Tutorial 1 of Chapter 7. Note that before applying the **Lathe** modifier, you need to adjust the pivot point according to the shape you want to create. Now, assign a material of your choice to the *incense stick stand*.

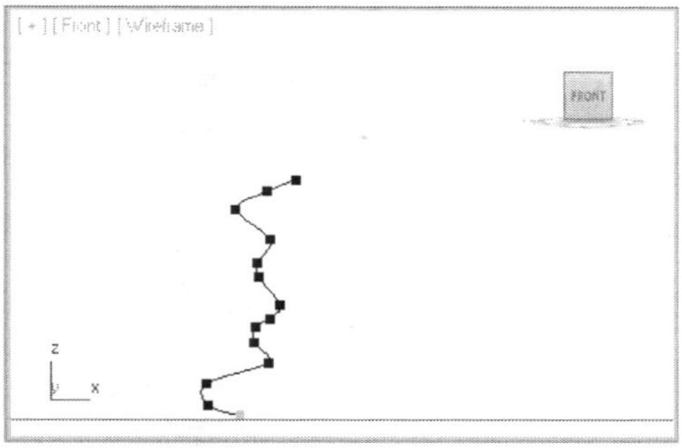

Figure 14-46 *A line for creating the incense stick stand*

10. Create a free camera in the Front viewport.

11. Now, create an *incense stick* using the **Capsule** tool from **Extended Primitives** in the **Command Panel**. Set its parameters according to scene's requirement. Align it in all viewports with the *incense stick stand*, as shown in Figure 14-47. Also, align the free camera in all viewports, as shown in Figure 14-47. Then, press the C key in the Perspective viewport to view the camera view.

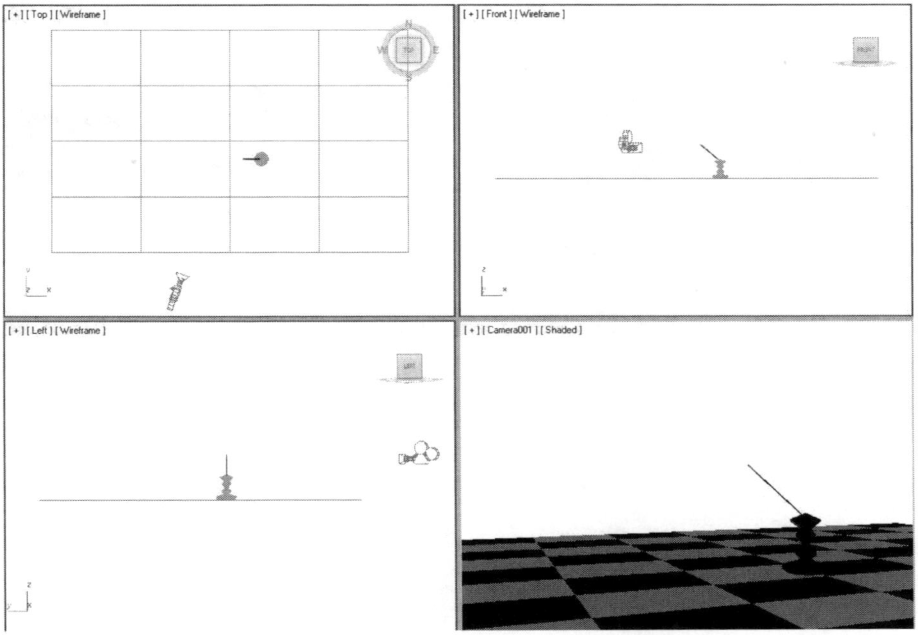

Figure 14-47 *The incense stick stand and the free camera aligned in all viewports*

Creating Smoke

To create the smoke, you need to create the super spray particle system.

1. Select the *incense stick stand* and invoke the **Zoom Extents All Selected** tool.

2. Activate the Top viewport and invoke the **Super Spray** tool from **Create > Geometry > Particle Systems > Object Type** rollout in the **Command Panel**.

3. In the Top viewport, press and hold the left mouse button, drag the cursor from one point to another, and release the left mouse button; an emitter is created. Now, align the emitter in all viewports using the **Select and Move** and **Select and Rotate** tools, as shown in Figure 14-48.

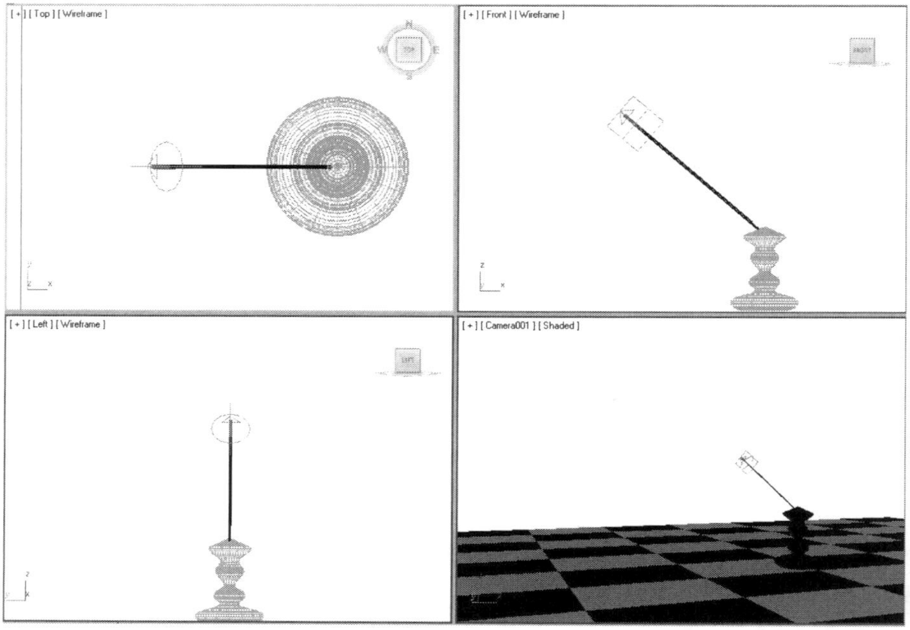

Figure 14-48 *The emitter for super spray particle system aligned in all viewports*

4. Modify the name of the particle system to *smoke*.

5. Increase the number of frames in the track bar to 300 as discussed in Tutorial 1 of this chapter.

   Next, you need to set the parameters of the *smoke* by using different rollouts.

6. Make sure that the *smoke* is selected in the **Modify** tab in the **Command Panel**; various rollouts are displayed.

7. In the **Basic Parameters** rollout, set the values as given next.

   Particle Formation Area
   Off Axis: **0.0** Spread: **4.0**

   Viewport Display Area
   Select the **Dots** radio button.

8. In the **Particle Generation** rollout, set the values as given below:

   Particle Quantity Area
   Make sure that the **Use Rate** radio button is selected. Next, set the value **30** in the spinner located below this radio button.

   Particle Motion Area
   Speed: **1.5**

   Particle Timing Area
   Emit Start: **30** Emit Stop: **300**
   Display Until: **300** Life: **225**

   Particle Size Area
   Size: **2.5** Variation: **30**
   Grow For: **90** Fade For: **30**

9. In the **Particle Type** rollout, set the values as given below:

   In the **Particle Types** area, make sure that the **Standard Particles** radio button is selected.

   Standard Particles Area
   Select the **Facing** radio button.

10. In the **Rotation and Collision** rollout, set the values as given below:

    Spin Time: **60** Variation: **20.0**

11. Activate the Camera001 viewport and choose the **Play Animation** button; the particles start moving in a single direction, as shown in Figure 14-49.

    Next, you need to create the wind space warp to generate variation in the motion of particles.

12. Activate the Left viewport and invoke the **Wind** tool from **Create > Space Warps > Forces > Object Type** rollout in the **Command Panel**.

13. Press and hold the left mouse button and drag the cursor in the Left viewport; the wind space warp icon is displayed.

14. Align the wind space warp icon in all viewports using the **Zoom All** and **Pan View** tools, refer to Figure 14-50.

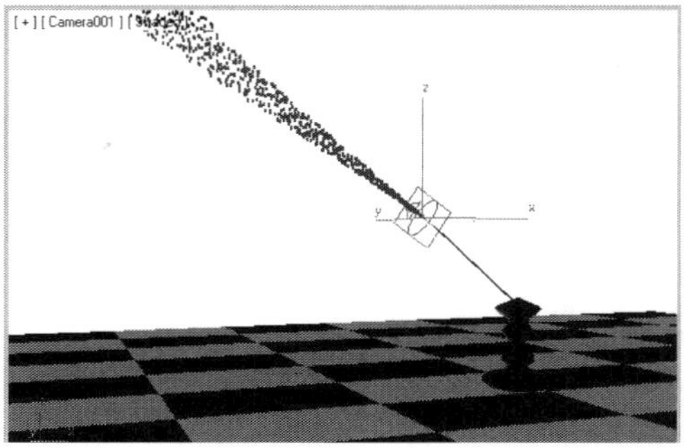

Figure 14-49 The particles in the Camera001 viewport at one frame

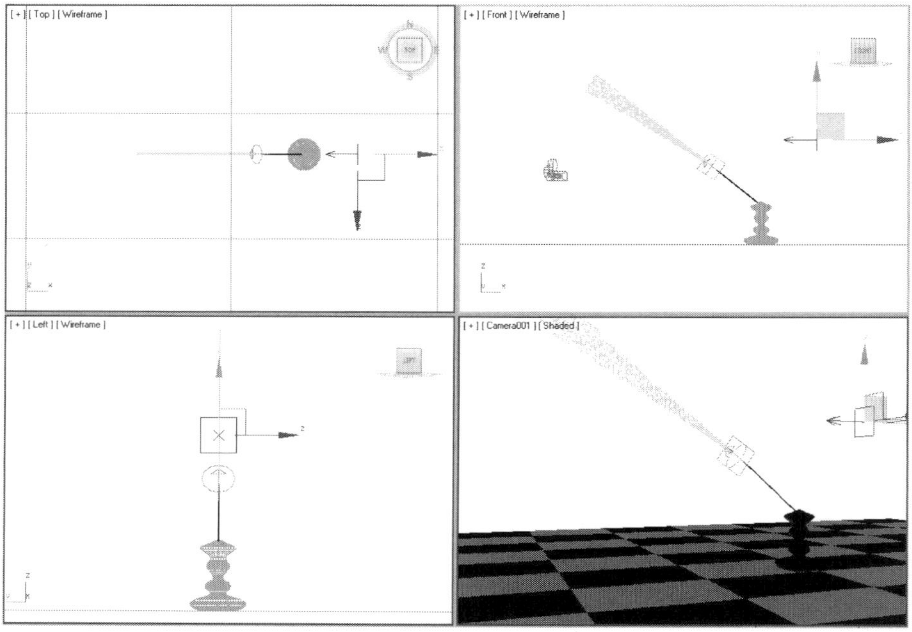

Figure 14-50 *The wind space warp icon aligned in all viewports*

15. Choose the **Modify** tab in the **Command Panel** and set the values in the **Parameters** rollout of the wind space warp as given below:

Force Area
Strength: **0.03**

Wind Area
Turbulence: **0.03** Frequency: **0.1** Scale: **0.2**

Use the default values for other options.

16. Select *smoke* in any viewport, invoke the **Bind to Space Warp** tool from the **Main Toolbar**, and then bind the *smoke* with the wind space warp icon; the direction of the particles is changed, as shown in Figure 14-51. Invoke the **Select Object** tool to exit the command.

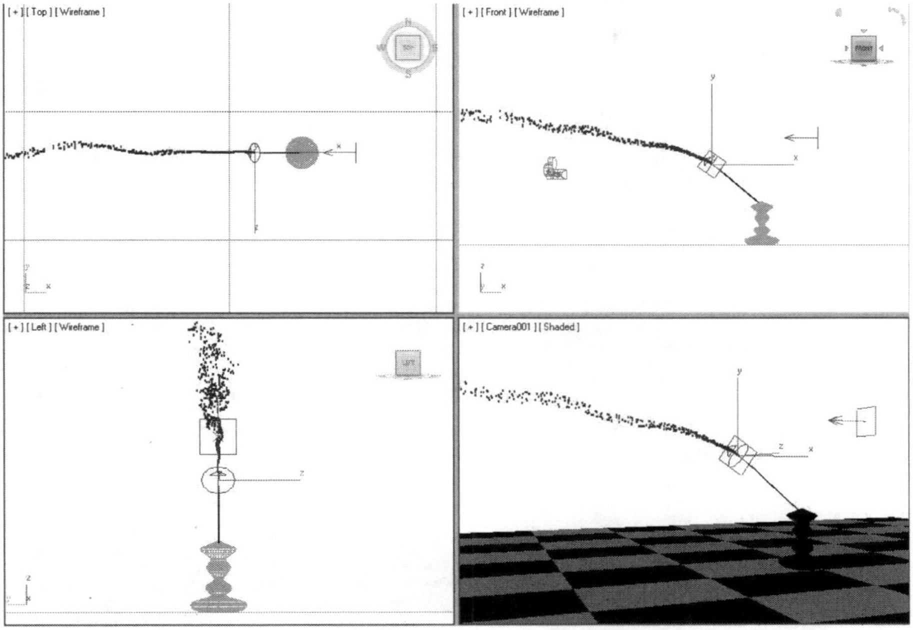

Figure 14-51 *The smoke after binding with the wind space warp in all viewports*

Next, you need to create the drag space warp to adjust the velocity of the *smoke* particles.

17. Activate the Top viewport and invoke the **Drag** tool from **Create > Space Warps > Forces > Object Type** rollout in the **Command Panel**.

18. Press and hold the left mouse button and drag the cursor in the Top viewport; the drag space warp icon is displayed.

19. Align the drag space warp icon in all viewports using the **Zoom All** and **Pan View** tools, refer to Figure 14-52.

20. Choose the **Modify** tab in the **Command Panel** and set the values in the **Parameters** rollout of the drag space warp as given below:

Timing Area
Time On: **0** Time Off: **300**

Damping Characteristics Area
Select the **Cylindrical Damping** radio button and set the values as given below:

Radial: **3.0** Tangential: **1.0** Axial: **2.0**

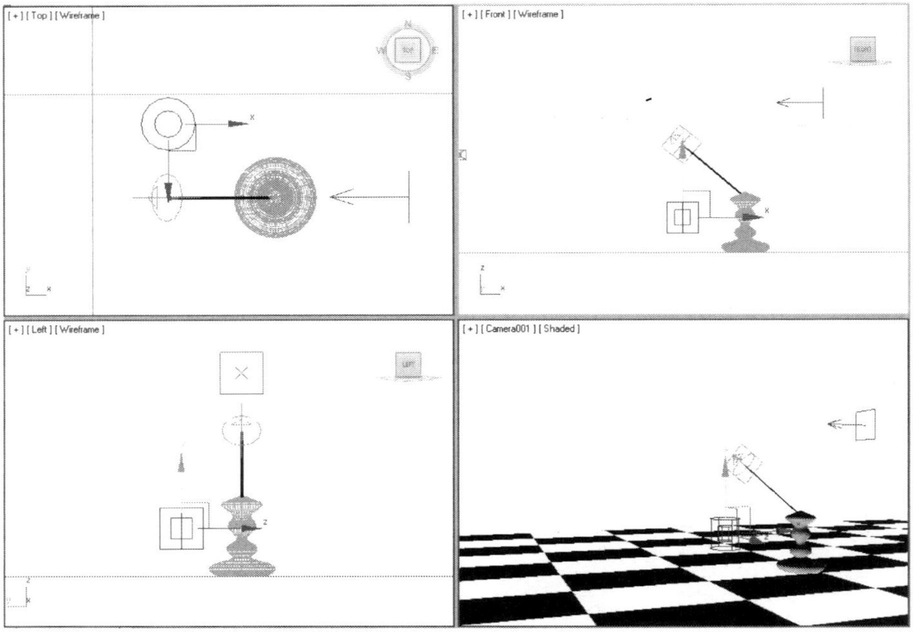

Figure 14-52 *The drag space warp icon aligned in all viewports*

21. Select *smoke* in any viewport, invoke the **Bind to Space Warp** tool from the **Main Toolbar**, and then bind the it with the drag space warp icon; the velocity of particles is changed, as shown in Figure 14-53.

Assigning the Material to the Smoke

1. First, select *smoke* in any viewport and press the M key; the **Material Editor** dialog box is displayed.

2. Select a sample slot to which no material has been assigned and modify its name in the **Material Name** text box to **smoke material**.

3. In the **Shader Basic Parameters** rollout, make sure that the **Blinn** option is selected in the drop-down list. Select the **Face Map** check box.

4. In the **Blinn Basic Parameters** rollout, choose the **Diffuse** color swatch and set the white color.

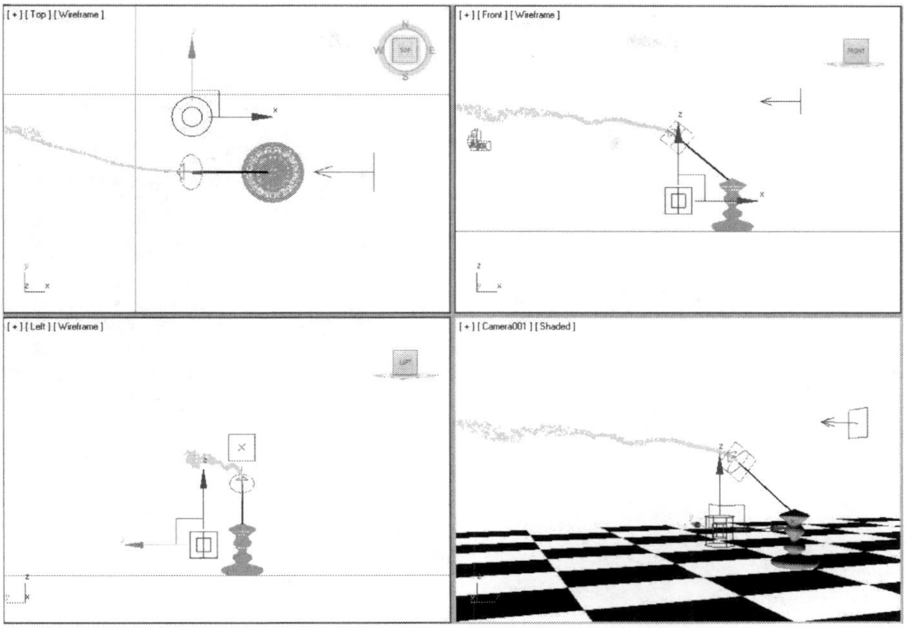

Figure 14-53 *The smoke after binding with the drag space warp icon in all viewports*

5. In the **Self-Illumination** area of the **Blinn Basic Parameters** rollout, select the **Color** check box; the spinner on its right side is replaced with a color swatch. Modify the color using the color swatch by entering the values as given below:

   Red: **215** Green: **197** Blue: **174**

6. Set the value **0** in the **Opacity** spinner. Choose the button on the right of the **Opacity** spinner; the **Material/Map Browser** dialog box is displayed. Select the **Gradient** map from the **Maps > Standard** rollouts and choose the **OK** button; various rollouts are displayed to modify the **Gradient** map.

7. In the **Gradient Parameters** rollout, set the value **1.0** in the **Color 2 Position** spinner. In the **Gradient Type** group, select the **Radial** radio button.

8. Choose the **Go to Parent** button to go back to the parent level.

9. Expand the **Maps** rollout and set the value **3** in the **Opacity** spinner.

10. Make sure that *smoke* is selected in the viewport and choose the **Assign Material to Selection** button; the **smoke material** is assigned to the *smoke* in the viewport. Close the **Material Editor** dialog box.

11. Choose the **Go to End** button from the animation playback controls and render the Camera001 viewport; the scene is displayed, as shown in Figure 14-54.

Next, you need to create the lights for the scene.

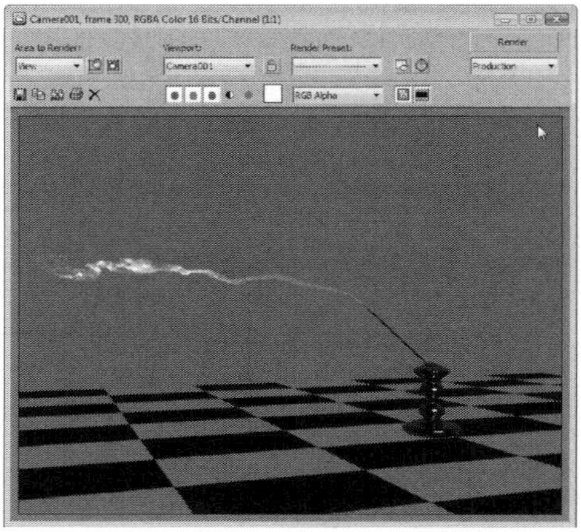

Figure 14-54 *The scene at rendering*

Creating Lights

1. Invoke the **Zoom Extents All** tool.

2. Activate the Top viewport and invoke the **Omni** tool from **Create > Lights > Standard > Object Type** rollout. Click on the lower left and upper right corners to create two omni lights.

3. Next, align the omni lights in all viewports, as shown in Figure 14-55.

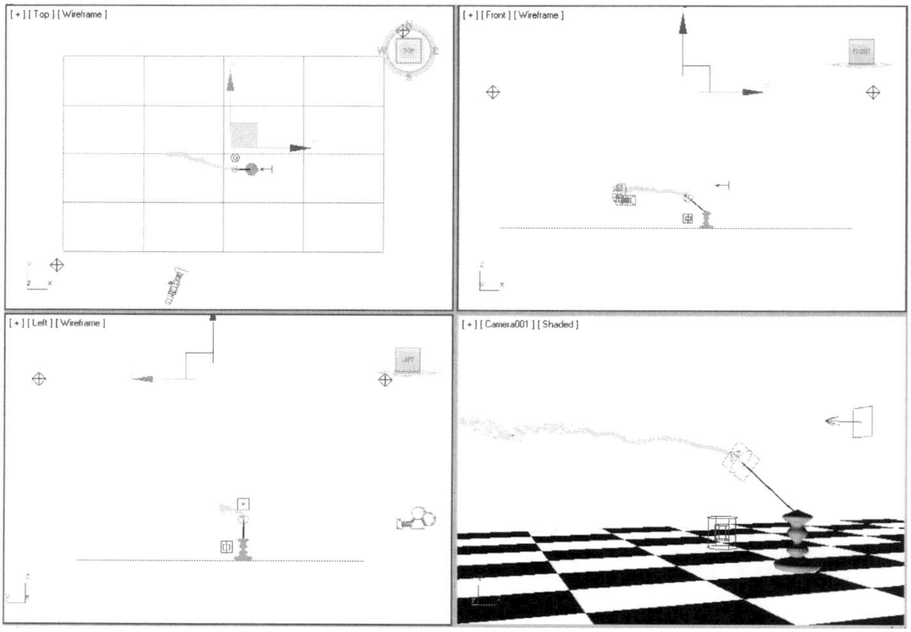

Figure 14-55 *The omni lights aligned in all viewports*

Creating the Environment

1. Modify the color of the environment as discussed earlier by entering the values as given below:

   Red: **102** Green: **102**
   Blue: **102**

2. Choose the **Go to End** button in the animation playback controls and render the Camera001 viewport. The scene is displayed with the modified color in the environment, as shown in Figure 14-56.

Figure 14-56 The scene at rendering after modifying the color of the environment

Rendering the Scene for the Final Output

1. To view the final output of the scene including the animation of smoke, render the scene as discussed in Tutorial 1 of Chapter 12.
2. After the completion of rendering, the final output of the animation is saved in the **.avi* format at a location specified by you. You can view the final output of the animation by opening the corresponding *avi* file.

   You can view the final rendered sequence by downloading the *c14_3dsmax_2012_render.zip* file from *http://www.cadcim.com.*

Saving the File

1. Save the file with the name *c14tut2.max* as discussed in earlier chapters. The location of this file is given below:

   \Documents\3dsmax\c14_tut2\scenes

Self-Evaluation Test

Answer the following questions and then compare them to those given at the end of this chapter:

1. Which of the following is a category of space warps in Autodesk 3ds Max?

   (a) **Forces** (b) **Deflectors**
   (c) **Modifier-Based** (d) All of these

2. Which of the following tools is used to create a space warp under the **Forces** category?

   (a) **Path Follow** (b) **Gravity**
   (c) Both of the above (d) None of the above

3. Which of the following space warps is used to twist the object?

   (a) Bend (b) Taper
   (c) Twist (d) Skew

4. Which of the following categories of space warps is used to deform the mesh objects?

   (a) **Forces** (b) **Deflectors**
   (c) **Geometric/Deformable** (d) All of these

5. The tools in the **Deflectors** category are used to create the space warps that reflect or refract the particles colliding with them. (T/F)

6. The tools in the **Modifier-Based** category are used to create the space warps that generate the effects similar to the object modifiers. (T/F)

7. The size and position of the deflector icon does not affect the particles of a particle system. (T/F)

8. You can use any object in the scene as a deflector using the __________ space warp.

9. The __________ space warp is used to stretch the geometry of an object along the specified axis.

10. The __________ space warp is used to offset the geometry of an object uniformly in any of the three axes.

Review Questions

Answer the following questions:

1. Which of the following space warps is used to deform an object by adjusting the control points of a lattice box?

   (a) FFD(Box) (b) FFD(Cyl)
   (c) Both of the above (d) None of the above

2. Which of the following space warps is used to explode an object into fragments?

   (a) Bomb (b) Wave
   (c) Ripple (d) PBomb

3. Which of the following space warps is used to create the wavy effect in the objects?

   (a) Wave (b) Displace
   (c) Ripple (d) Bomb

4. Which of the following tools in the **Deflector** category is used to create the spherical space warp icon?

   (a) **Deflector** (b) **SDeflector**
   (c) **POmniFlect** (d) **UDeflector**

5. The ripple space warp is similar to the wave space warp. (T/F)

6. The FFD(Cyl) space warp is similar to the FFD(Box) space warp with the only difference that the FFD(Cyl) space warp is cylindrical in shape. (T/F)

7. The bomb space warp is used to explode a particle system. (T/F)

8. The __________ space warp is used to create the wavy effects in the objects that are bound to it.

9. The __________ space warp is used to create the circular and concentric waves in the objects.

10. The __________ space warp is used to explode the objects into their individual faces.

Exercises

Exercise 1

Start Autodesk 3ds Max 2012 and then perform the following operations:

1. Invoke the **Super Spray** tool from **Create > Geometry > Particle Systems > Object Type** rollout and create a super spray particle system icon in the Top viewport. Adjust the view in the Perspective viewport. Set the values in the **Off Axis Spread** and **Off Plane Spread** spinners in the **Basic Parameters** rollout. Also, set the values in the **Particle Timings** area of the **Particle Generation** rollout. Modify the size of the particles in the **Size** spinner. In the **Particle Type** rollout, select the **MetaParticles** radio button and render the Perspective viewport. Next, select the **Standard** radio button and render the Perspective viewport. Now, notice the difference.

2. In the **Load/Save Presets** rollout, select an option from the **Saved Presets** area and choose the **Load** button. Now, render the Perspective viewport and notice the difference in the type of particles displayed.

3. Invoke the **Push** tool from **Create > Space Warps > Forces > Object Type** rollout. Create the push space warp icon in the Top viewport. Next, bind the push space warp with the particle system. Modify the parameters of the push space warp and notice the difference.

4. Create a sphere in the Top viewport. Next, invoke the **Bomb** tool from **Create > Space Warps > Geometric/Deformable > Object Type** rollout and create a bomb space warp icon in the Top viewport. Now, bind the bomb space warp icon to the sphere and notice the effect. Next, change the position of the bomb space warp icon in any viewport and notice the difference.

5. Create a plane in the Top viewport and increase the number of segments in it. Next, invoke the **Ripple** tool from **Create > Space Warps > Geometric/Deformable > Object Type** rollout and create a ripple space warp icon in the Top viewport. Now, bind the ripple space warp icon to the plane and notice the effect. Next, modify the parameters of the ripple space warp in the **Parameters** rollout and notice the difference.

Exercise 2

Create an animated scene in which an object falls into the sea and floats on it, thus creating wavy effect in the water, as shown in Figure 14-57. You can view the final rendered image of this scene by downloading it from *http://www.cadcim.com.* **(Expected time: 15 min)**

Hint:

1. Use the **Ripple** tool in the **Geometric/Deformable** category of space warps.

Exercise 3

Create an animated scene displaying the rainy effect, as shown in Figure 14-58. You can view the final rendered image of this scene by downloading it from *http://www.cadcim.com.*
(Expected time: 15 min)

Hint:

1. Use the spray particle system to create the rain effect.

Figure 14-57 *Model for Exercise 2*

Figure 14-58 *Model for Exercise 3*

Answers to Self-Evaluation Test

1. d, **2.** c, **3.** c, **4.** c, **5.** T, **6.** T, **7.** F, **8.** UDeflector, **9.** stretch, **10.** skew

15

Systems, Hierarchy, and Kinematics

Learning Objectives

After completing this chapter, you will be able to:

- *Create a ring array system*
- *Create a sunlight system*
- *Create a daylight system*
- *Understand hierarchy and kinematics*
- *Create a hierarchy*
- *Understand hierarchy tab*
- *Create a bone system*
- *Understand IK solver, interactive IK, and applied IK*
- *Create a biped system*

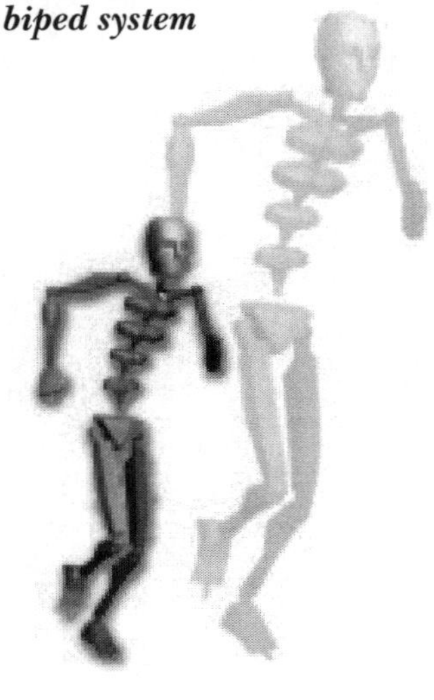

INTRODUCTION TO SYSTEMS

In Autodesk 3ds Max, a system is an object set that consists of objects, linkages, and controllers. These systems help you to simplify the complex animations. There are five types of systems: **Bones**, **Ring array**, **Sunlight**, **Daylight**, and **Biped**, refer to Figure 15-1.

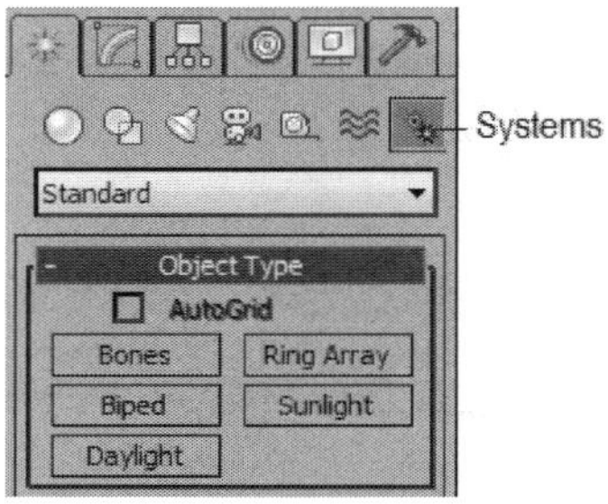

Figure 15-1** The **Systems** in the **Command Panel

To create a system, choose **Create > Systems** in the **Command Panel**; the **Standard** option will be displayed in the drop-down list. Also, the **Object Type** rollout will be displayed, as shown in Figure 15-1. There are various tools in the **Object Type** rollout to create systems. In this chapter, you will learn to create and modify different types of systems using these tools.

Creating a Ring Array System

Command Panel: Create > Systems > Standard > Object Type rollout > Ring Array

A ring array system consists of a number of boxes in a circular pattern with a dummy object placed at its center, as shown in Figure 15-2.

The dummy object is a wireframe box with a pivot point at its center. The pivot point is used as a center for transformations such as rotation and movement. Note that the dummy object cannot be rendered. You will learn more about the dummy objects in the later chapters.

To create a ring array system, invoke the **Ring Array** tool from **Create > Systems > Standard > Object Type** rollout in the **Command Panel**; the **Name and Color** and **Parameters** rollouts will be displayed. Next, in the Top viewport, press and hold the left mouse button to specify the center of the ring array system and then drag the cursor to define the radius of the array. Next, release the left mouse button; a dummy object will be created at the center. Also, four boxes will be created in a circular pattern around it, as shown in Figure 15-2. To modify the parameters of the ring array system, you need to use the options in the **Parameters** rollout. This rollout is discussed next.

Parameters Rollout

To modify the parameters of a ring array system, select one of the boxes in the viewport and choose the **Motion** tab in the **Command Panel**; the **Parameters** rollout will be displayed, as shown in Figure 15-3. Set the value in the **Radius** spinner to specify the radius of the ring array system. Set the value in the **Amplitude** spinner to specify the amplitude of ring's sine curve. It is a height offset from the local origin of a dummy object located at the center. Set the value in the **Cycles** spinner to specify the number of peaks in the ring's curve of the ring array system. Set the value in the **Phase** spinner to offset the phase of the wave. If you set the whole numbers in this spinner, then the ring array system will not be affected. Only the decimal values will affect the ring array system. Set the value in the **Number** spinner to specify the number of boxes in the ring array system.

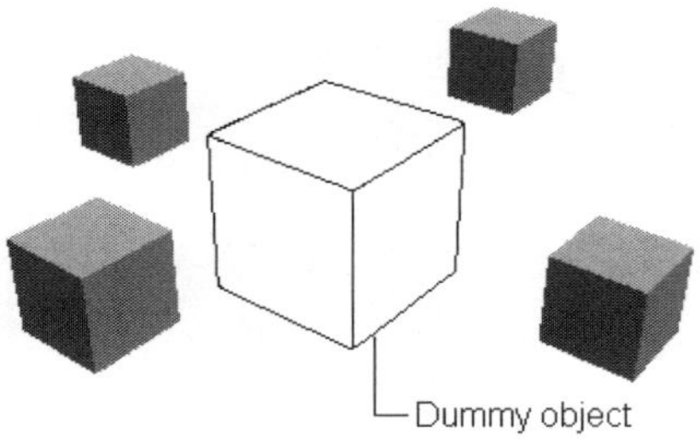

Figure 15-2 *The ring array system*

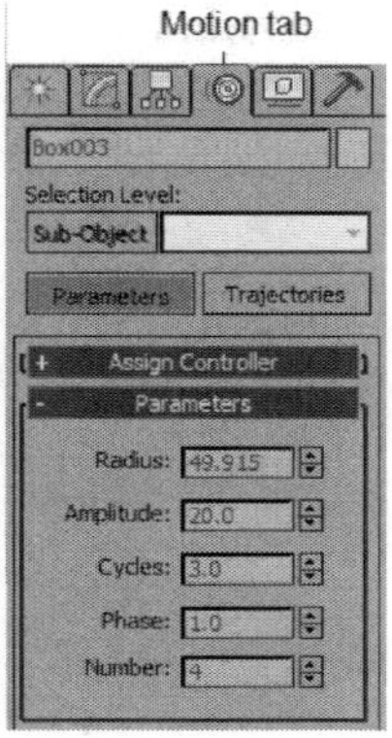

Figure 15-3 *The* ***Parameters*** *rollout in the* ***Motion*** *tab*

Note

To modify the parameters of the ring array system, you need to choose the ***Motion*** *tab in the* ***Command Panel****. However, if you need to modify the parameters of the boxes in the ring array system, then choose the* ***Modify*** *tab in the* ***Command Panel****.*

Using Different Objects in a Ring Array System

You can replace the boxes in a ring array system with other objects. To do so, create an object in the viewport with which you want to replace the boxes in the ring array system. Make sure that the object and the ring array system are selected in the viewport. Next, invoke the **Curve Editor (Open)** tool from the **Main Toolbar**; the **Track View - Curve Editor** dialog box will be displayed. The hierarchy tree on the left of this dialog box controls the objects in the viewport. In the hierarchy tree, select the name of the object that will replace the boxes of the ring array system, as shown in Figure 15-4, and then right-click on it; a quad menu will be displayed. Choose the **Copy** option from the quad menu. Next, select one of the boxes in the hierarchy tree, as shown in Figure 15-5. Right-click on it and choose the **Paste** option from the quad menu; the **Paste** dialog box will be displayed, as shown in Figure 15-6. Select the **Copy** or **Instance** radio button in the **Paste as** area. Also, select the **Replace all instances** check box in the **Paste Target** area to replace all boxes of the ring array system with the same object. Then, choose the **OK** button; the boxes in the ring array system will be replaced with the object created in the viewport, as shown in Figure 15-7.

Animating a Ring Array System

You can animate the radius, amplitude, cycles, and phase of a ring array system. To do so, choose the **Toggle Auto Key Mode** button from animation playback controls, move the time slider to a frame, and then modify the parameters in the **Parameters** rollout according to the animation. Repeat the same method at other frames till you want to animate it. Choose the **Toggle Auto Key Mode** button again to exit the animation mode.

To apply any transformation such as rotate, move, or scale to the ring array system, you need to select the dummy object. Also, you can apply the modifiers to the boxes of the ring array system. The modifier that you apply to any one of the boxes, will be applied automatically to the other boxes of the ring array system.

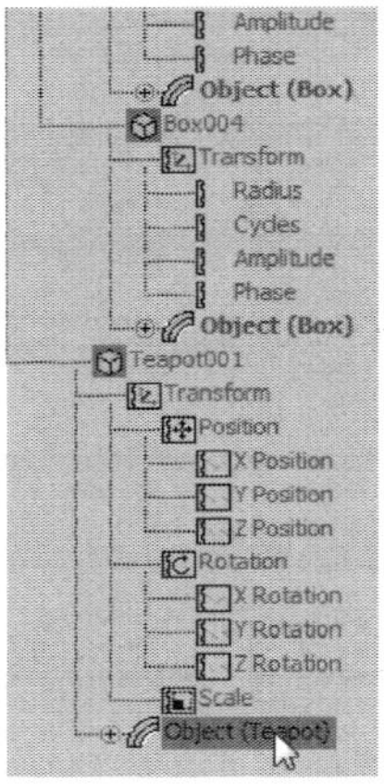

Figure 15-4 *The object selected in the hierarchy tree to replace the boxes of the ring array system*

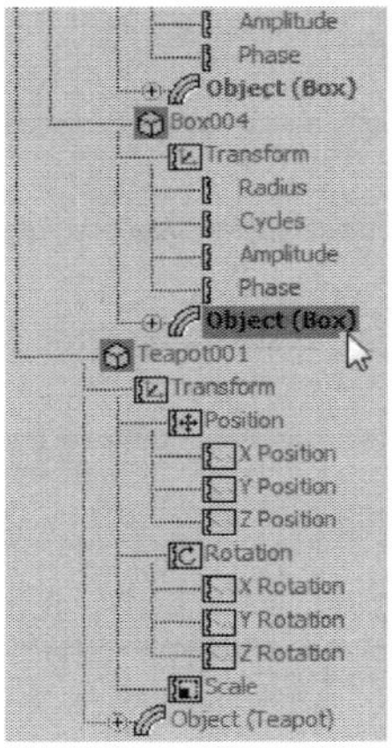

Figure 15-5 *The box selected in the hierarchy tree to be replaced with the object*

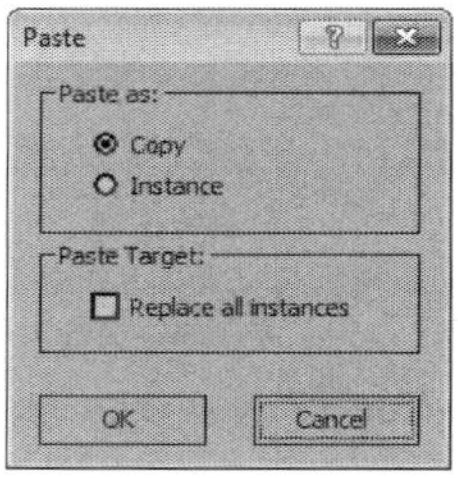

Figure 15-6 *The* ***Paste*** *dialog box*

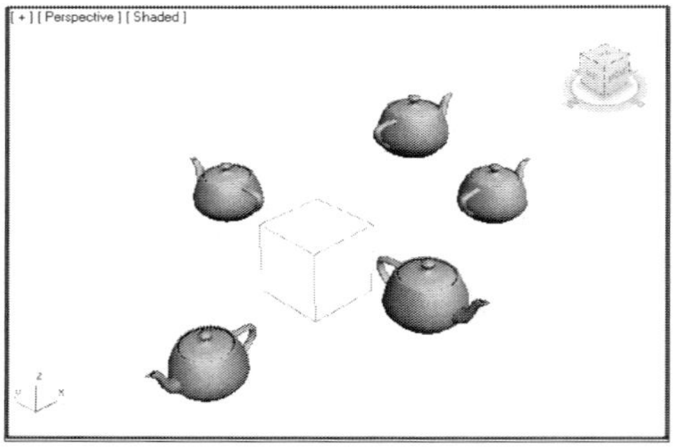

Figure 15-7 *The boxes of the ring array system replaced with the object (teapot)*

Creating a Sunlight System

Command Panel:	Create > Systems > Standard > Object Type rollout > Sunlight

The sunlight system is used to produce the light effects similar to the geographically accurate effects of the sun over the earth at a particular location, date, time, and so on, refer to Figures 15-8 and 15-9. Moreover, you can animate the position of the sun to get a better idea of the shadows cast by sun at different positions. The sunlight system uses a directional light.

To create a sunlight system, invoke the **Sunlight** tool from **Create > Systems > Standard > Object Type** rollout in the **Command Panel**; the **Name and Color** and **Control Parameters** rollouts will be displayed. Next, in the Top viewport, press and hold the left mouse button at the center of the scene to specify the center of the sunlight system and then drag the cursor to define the radius of the system. Release the left mouse button; a compass rose will be created, refer to Figure 15-10. Now, drag the cursor up or down to specify the distance of the directional light from the compass rose and then click on the screen to set the distance; the compass rose and the directional light will be created in the viewports, refer to Figure 15-10. Next, right-click in any viewport to exit the sunlight command.

Figure 15-8 *The scene after creating the sunlight system*

Figure 15-9 *The scene after changing the position of the sun*

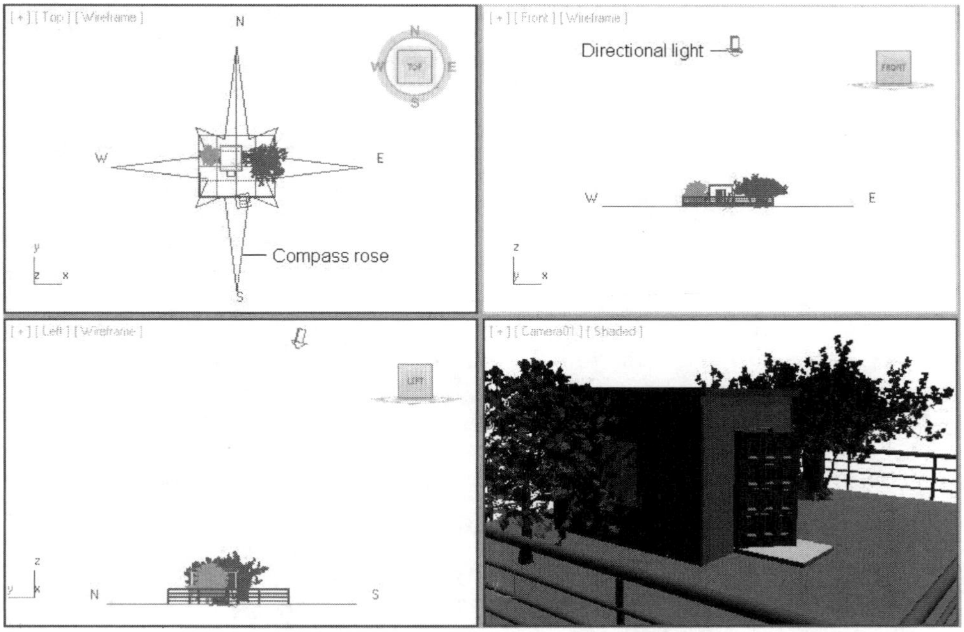

Figure 15-10 *The sunlight system in all viewports*

By default, the name of the light and the compass rose will be *Sun001* and *Compass001*, respectively. To modify the parameters of the sunlight system, you need to use the options in the **Control Parameters** rollout. This rollout is discussed next.

Control Parameters Rollout

To modify the parameters of the sunlight system, select *Sun001* in the viewport and choose the **Motion** tab in the **Command Panel**; the **Control Parameters** rollout will be displayed. The options in this rollout are discussed next.

Note

After selecting Sun001 in the viewport, if you choose the ***Modify*** *tab instead of the* ***Motion*** *tab in the* ***Command Panel****, then the rollouts of the directional light will be displayed.*

On selecting the **Motion** tab, the settings of the sun are displayed, as shown in Figure 15-11. On the top of this rollout, there are **Azimuth** and **Altitude** text boxes, which display the settings of the sun selected in the viewport. The values in these text boxes depend on the other settings in the **Control Parameters** rollout. The different areas in this rollout are discussed next.

Time Area

The options in this area are used to set the time, date, and time zone. Set the values in the **Hours**, **Mins.**, and **Secs.** spinners to specify the time of the day. Set the values in the **Month**, **Day**, and **Year** spinners to define the date. Set the value in the **Time Zone** spinner to specify the time zone. The value in this spinner ranges from -12 to 12.

Location Area

The options in this area are used to set the geographical location of the scene. Choose the **Get Location** button; the **Geographic Location** dialog box will be displayed, as shown in Figure 15-12. You can select the continent of the world from the **Map** drop-down list in this dialog box; the respective map will be displayed. Now, select the location or the city for the scene from the **City** area on the left side of this dialog box and then choose the **OK** button; the selected location will be displayed in the text box below the **Get Location** button in the **Control Parameters** rollout. Also, the position of *Sun001* will be changed in the viewport. If you change the location, then the values in the **Latitude** and **Longitude** spinners will also be changed.

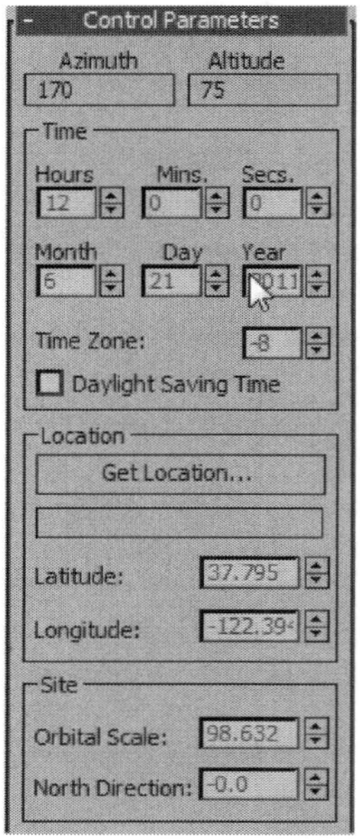

Figure 15-11 *The* ***Control Parameters*** *rollout*

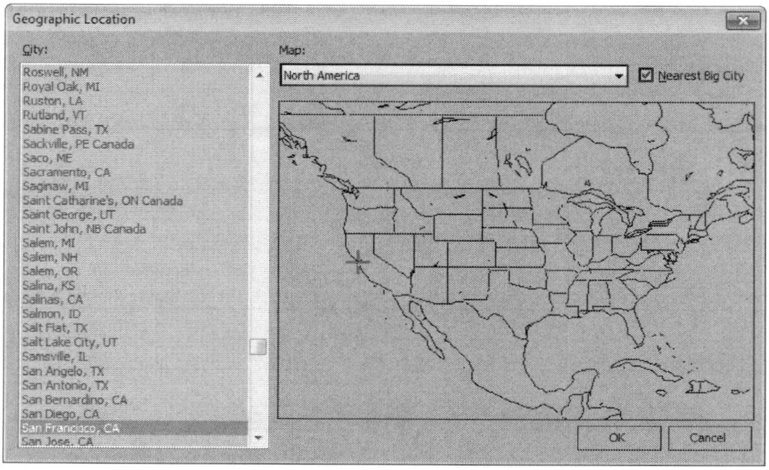

Figure 15-12 *The* ***Geographic Location*** *dialog box*

Site Area

The options in this area are used to set the direction of compass rose. Set the value in the **Orbital Scale** spinner to define the distance between the *Sun001* and *Compass001*. Set the value in the **North Direction** spinner to define the rotational direction of the compass rose in the scene.

To modify the radius of the compass rose, select the *Compass001* in the viewport, and then choose the **Modify** tab; the **Parameters** rollout will be displayed, as shown in Figure 15-13. Next, set the value in the **Radius** spinner; the radius of the compass rose will be changed.

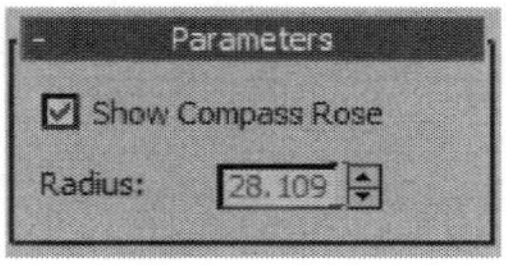

Figure 15-13 *The* ***Parameters*** *rollout*

Creating a Daylight System

Menu bar:	Create > Systems > Daylight System
Command Panel:	Create > Systems > Standard > Object Type rollout > Daylight

The daylight system is very similar to the sunlight system. The only difference is that the daylight system uses a combination of two lights, sunlight and skylight. You can use the IES sun light, mr sun light, or target direct light (standard light) as the sunlight in the daylight system. The IES sky light, mr sky light, or skylight (standard light) can be used as the skylight in the daylight system. The effect of the daylight system is shown in Figure 15-14.

Figure 15-14 *The daylight system in a scene at rendering*

To create a daylight system, invoke the **Daylight** tool from **Create > Systems > Standard > Object Type** rollout in the **Command Panel**; the **Daylight System Creation** dialog box will be displayed that will prompt you to use the Logarithmic Exposure Control. Choose the **Yes** button. Also, the **Name and Color** and **Control Parameters** rollouts will be displayed in the **Command Panel**. Next, create the daylight system using the same method as discussed for the sunlight system; a compass rose and the combination of the sunlight and skylight will be displayed in the viewports, as shown in Figure 15-15. By default, the name of the light and the compass rose will be *Daylight001* and *Compass001*, respectively. The *Daylight001* light consists of two lights, sunlight and skylight. To modify the parameters of the daylight system, you need to use the options in the **Control Parameters** rollout. This rollout is discussed next.

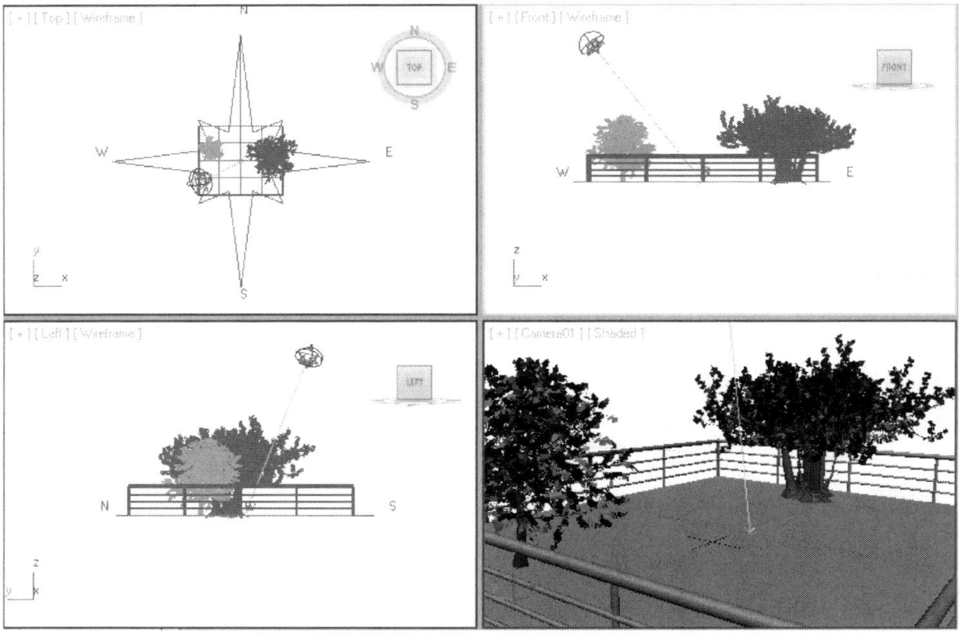

Figure 15-15 The daylight system in all viewports

Control Parameters Rollout

To modify the parameters of the daylight system, select the *Daylight001* in the viewport and choose the **Motion** tab in the **Command Panel**; the **Control Parameters** rollout will be displayed. Most of the options in this rollout are the same as those discussed for the sunlight system. Additionally, there is a **Manual** radio button on the top of this rollout. By default, this radio button is cleared and therefore, you can modify the parameters using the options displayed in the **Control Parameters** rollout. On selecting the **Manual** radio button, you can manually set the position of the light in the viewport. Also, you can manually set the intensity of the light by setting the value in the **Multiplier** spinner in the **Intensity/Color/Attenuation** rollout. To do so, select the *Daylight001* in the viewport. Choose the **Modify** tab in the **Command Panel**; various rollouts will be displayed in the modify panel. Most of the rollouts are the same as those discussed in Chapter 11. The **Daylight Parameters** rollout is discussed next.

Daylight Parameters Rollout

The options in this rollout are used to select the type of sunlight and the skylight used in the daylight system, refer to Figure 15-16. The **Active** check box on the right of the **Sunlight** label is selected by default. It is used to turn on the sunlight in the viewport. Just below the **Sunlight** label, there is a drop-down list. You can select the light to be used as the sunlight from this drop-down list.

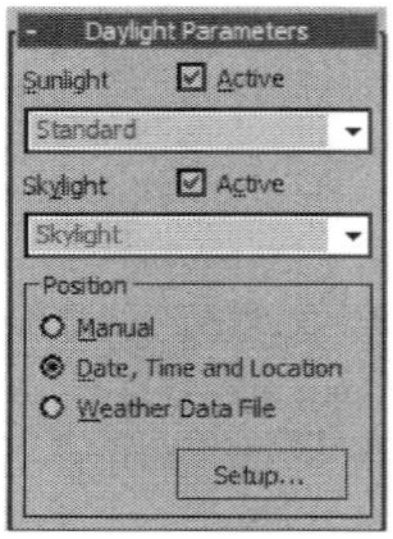

*Figure 15-16 The **Daylight Parameters** rollout*

The **Active** check box on the right of the **Skylight** label is selected by default. It is used to turn on the skylight in the viewport. Just below the **Skylight** label, there is a drop-down list. Select the option to be used as skylight from this drop-down list.

In the **Position** area, the **Date**, **Time and Location** radio button is selected by default. It is used to set the time, date, and location of the daylight system. Choose the **Setup** button; the **Control Parameters** rollout will be displayed in the **Motion** tab, where you can set the time, location, and other parameters of the daylight system in this rollout. Select the **Manual** radio button in the **Position** area to manually set the position and intensity of the *Daylight001* in the viewport. Select the **Weather Data File** radio button to derive the angle and intensity of the sun from a weather data (EPW) file.

Note

When you select the required sunlight or skylight option from the drop-down list, the corresponding rollouts will also be displayed to modify the selected light.

HIERARCHY AND KINEMATICS

The ability to link objects together to create a chain is known as hierarchy. When you create a complex computer animation, then the hierarchy is the most important tool to simplify the animation process. In a hierarchy, the movement, rotation, or scaling of an object is controlled by another object. It creates a parent-child relationship that is very similar to a family tree. The object that is being controlled is known as the child object and the object that controls another object is known as the parent object. The parent object is controlled by a superior parent object, known as the ancestor object of the first child object. The child object that does not have any child is known as the leaf object. The parent object that is superior to all objects in a hierarchy is known as the root object.

When you create an animation by moving, rotating, or scaling the parent object, the transformations will automatically be transferred to its child objects. In this case, there is no need to create separate animation for the child objects. For example, if you have created a car model in which main body of the car is parent object while all other parts of the car are child objects, then transformation applied to main body of the car will automatically be transferred to all other parts of the body.

A hierarchy is basically used to simplify a complex animation. You can link a number of objects to a single object and transfer its animation to the linked objects. It is also very useful for creating the character animation.

In Autodesk 3ds Max, there are two methods used for animating the hierarchies, forward kinematics (FK) and inverse kinematics (IK). These hierarchies are created by linking the objects. The inverse kinematics is more advanced than the forward kinematics. These kinematics are discussed next.

Forward and Inverse Kinematics

In forward kinematics, the child objects are animated based on the transformations in the parent object. It is a one-way system, in which, if a parent object moves, then the child objects will also move. But, if the child objects move, then the parent object will not be affected. In other words, you can control the top object of the hierarchy to animate the entire chain. While creating a hierarchy, the forward kinematics is created by default.

The inverse kinematics (IK) is just the opposite of the forward kinematics. In inverse kinematics, you can animate the object at the bottom of the hierarchy to control the entire chain. In this kinematics, if you move a child object, then the movement will be transferred to each ancestor in the hierarchy.

Creating a Hierarchy

To create a hierarchy, you need to link the objects that will generate a chain. First, create the objects in the viewport that you need to link together. Then, decide which one of them will be the parent object and which one will be the child object. Next, select one of the child objects in the viewport and then invoke the **Select and Link** tool from the **Main Toolbar**. Now, move the cursor over the child object; the cursor will get changed, as shown in Figure 15-17. Then, press and hold the left mouse button on the child object and drag the cursor to the parent object; a dotted line will be displayed between the child and parent objects, as shown in Figure 15-17. Next, release the left mouse button over the parent object; the parent object will blink for a second and will be linked to the child object. Next, invoke the **Select Object** tool to exit the command. You can link more than one child objects to the parent object using the same procedure.

To unlink the child object, select the child object in the viewport and then invoke the **Unlink Selection** tool from the **Main Toolbar**.

Hierarchy Tab

The **Hierarchy** tab is used to modify hierarchical linkage between the objects. To do so, select a linkage from the hierarchical linkage in the viewport and choose the **Hierarchy** tab in the **Command Panel**. The **Pivot** button is chosen by default in the **Hierarchy** tab. As discussed in the earlier chapters, the options displayed on choosing the **Pivot** button are used to adjust the pivot point of the object. Choose the **Link Info** button in the **Hierarchy** tab; the **Locks** and **Inherit** rollouts will be displayed, as shown in Figure 15-18.

The options in the **Locks** rollout are used to lock the transforms on an object about any of its local axes. In the **Locks** rollout, there are three areas, **Move**, **Rotate**, and **Scale**. Each area has **X**, **Y**, and **Z** check boxes. To lock a transform, select the corresponding check boxes in these areas.

The options in the **Inherit** rollout are used to control the transforms that the child objects inherit from the parent object. In this rollout, there are three areas, **Move**, **Rotate**, and **Scale**. Each area has **X**, **Y**, and **Z** check boxes. By default, all check boxes in each area are selected that means the child object inherits all transforms on all axes. To control the inheritance, select the corresponding check box from the respective area.

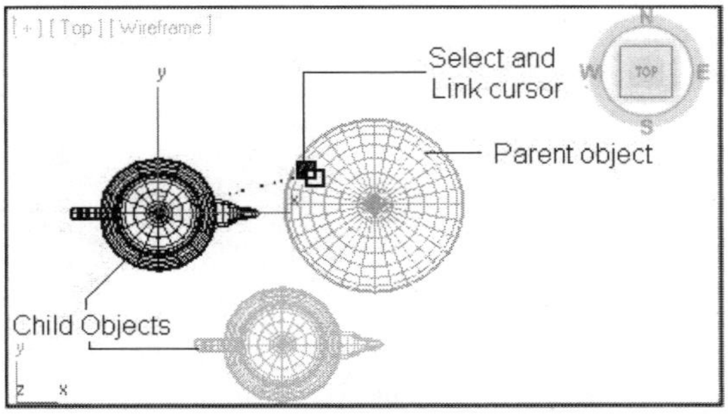

*Figure 15-17 The child object linked to the parent object using the **Select and Link** tool*

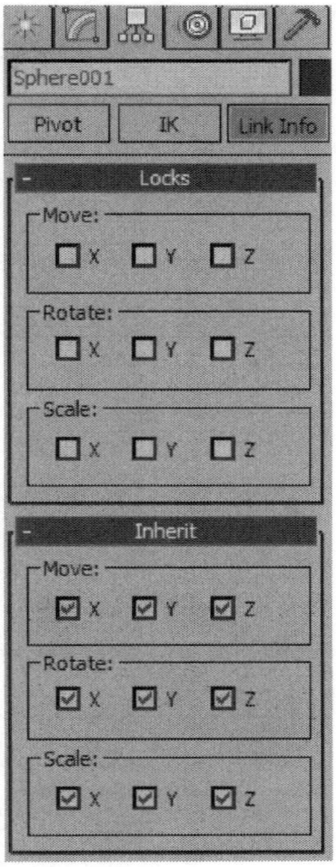

*Figure 15-18 The **Link Info** button chosen in the **Hierarchy** tab*

Creating a Bones System

Command Panel: Create > Systems > Standard > Object Type rollout > Bones

The bones system is created by linking the bones and joints in a hierarchy. You can animate and transform this hierarchy either using the forward kinematics or the inverse kinematics. However, animating the bones system using the inverse kinematics is easier. You can animate any type of characters as well as machineries using the bones system.

To create a bones system, invoke the **Bones** tool from **Create > Systems > Standard > Object Type** rollout in the **Command Panel**; the **Name and Color**, **IK Chain Assignment**, and **Bone Parameters** rollouts will be displayed. Next, click in the viewport to create the base of the hierarchy. Now, move the cursor up or down to define the length of the bone and click in the viewport again to end the creation of the first bone. Simultaneously, start creating the second bone. Repeat the same process to continue the creation of hierarchy. Next, right-click in the viewport to exit the command; a hierarchy of bones will be created, as shown in Figure 15-19. When you right-click to exit the command, a small bone will be created at the end of the hierarchy. This small bone is used at the time of assigning an IK about which you will learn in the later section.

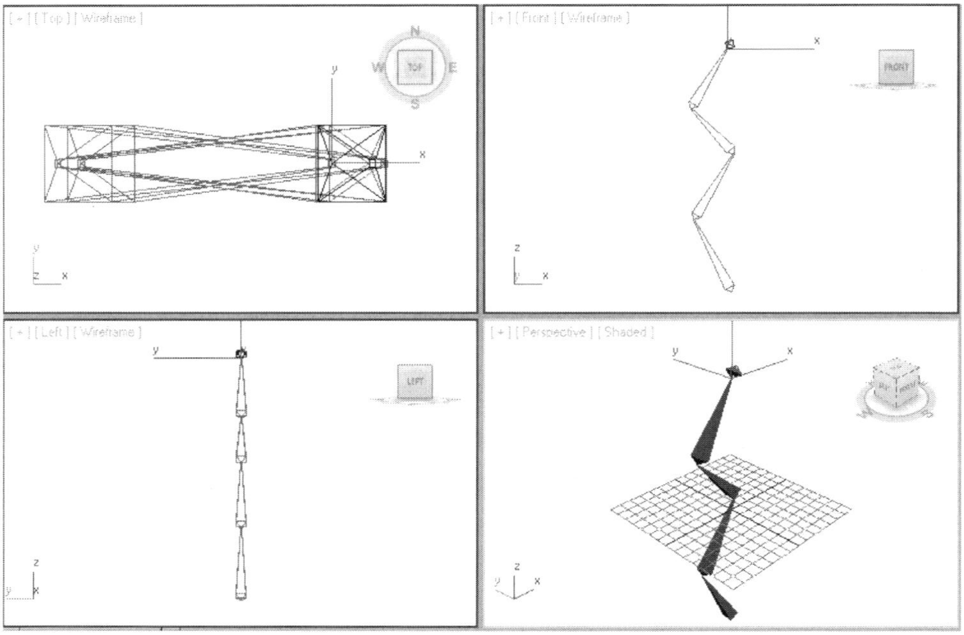

Figure 15-19 The hierarchy of bones displayed in all viewports

Note

When you create the bones in the viewport, the first bone will be the parent bone and the other will be the child bones of the first bone. The bones created in continuation form a hierarchy of bones. Also, the bone created first will be at the top of the hierarchy and the bone created last will be at the bottom of the hierarchy.

To modify the appearance of bones in the viewport, select the bones in the viewport and then choose the **Modify** tab in the **Command Panel**; the **Bones Parameters** rollout will be displayed. This rollout is discussed next.

Bones Parameters Rollout

There are two areas in this rollout to modify the appearance of bones, refer to Figure 15-20. These areas are discussed next.

Bone Object Area

Set the values in the **Width** and **Height** spinners to specify the width and height of the selected bone. Set the value in the **Taper** spinner to specify the taper amount of the bone in percentage.

Bone Fins Area

The options in this area are used to add fins in the bones to increase their thickness, refer to Figure 15-21. The fins help in improving the animation of bulky characters. Select the **Side Fins**, **Front Fin**, and **Back Fin** check boxes to add the fins on the sides, front, and back of the bones, respectively. Set the values in the **Size**, **Start Taper**, and **End Taper** spinners to specify the size, start taper, and end taper values of the fins.

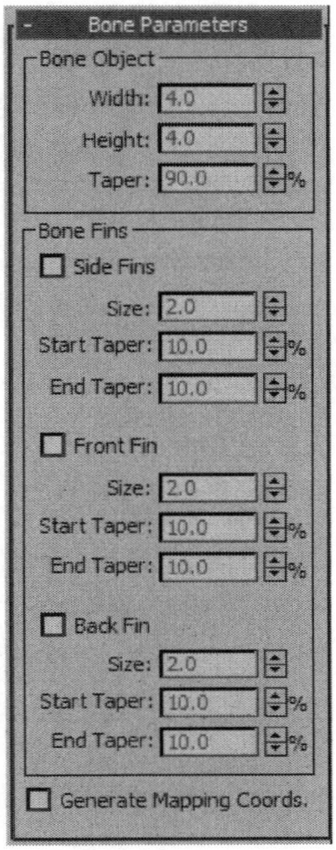

***Figure 15-20** The **Bones Parameters** rollout*

Making the Bones Visible at Rendering

By default, the bones created in the viewport will not be visible at rendering. To make them visible, select the bones in the viewport and right-click on them; a quad menu will be displayed. Choose the **Object Properties** option; the **Object Properties** dialog box will be displayed. By default, the **General** tab is chosen in this dialog box. In the **Rendering Control** area, select the **Renderable** check box and then choose the **OK** button to exit the **Object Properties** dialog box; the bones will be visible at rendering.

Modifying the Bones

Generally, the length of the bones is set while creating them in the viewport. After creating them, if you need to edit the length and other properties of the bones, then select the bone in the viewport. Choose **Animation > Bone Tools** from the menu bar; the **Bone Tools** dialog box will be displayed, as shown in Figure 15-22. The rollouts in this dialog box are discussed next.

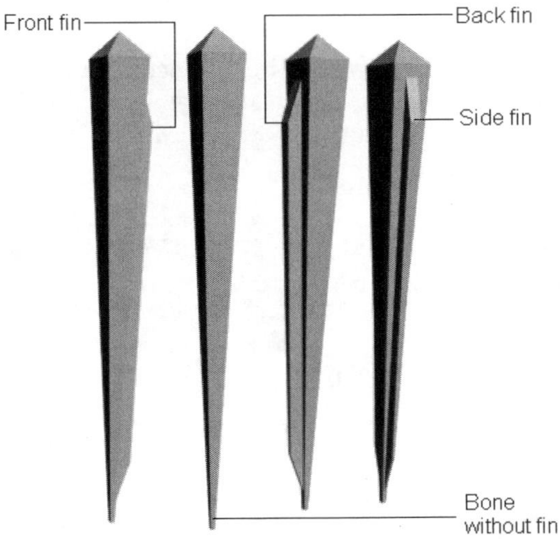

***Figure 15-21** The bones with the fins added to them*

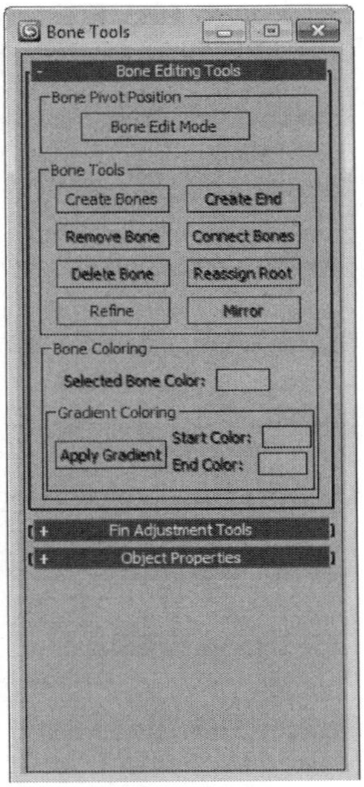

***Figure 15-22** Partial view of the **Bone Tools** dialog box*

Bone Editing Tools Rollout

The areas in this rollout are used to set the geometry and color of the selected bones. These areas are discussed next.

Bone Pivot Position Area

The **Bone Edit Mode** button in this area is used to edit the length and position of the bone in the viewport. To do so, choose the **Bone Edit Mode** button and move the bone along any axes in the viewport.

Bone Tools Area

Choose the **Create Bones** button; the **Bones** tool in the **Command Panel** will be activated, which can be used to create a bone in the viewport. Choose the **Create End** button; a small bone will be created at the end of the bone system. Choose the **Remove Bone** button to remove the selected bone. When you remove a bone, its parent bone stretches to cover the pivot point of the removed bone. Choose the **Connect Bones** button to connect the selected bone to another bone in the viewport. Choose the **Delete Bone** button to delete the selected bone and also to remove its parent-child relationship. Choose the **Reassign Root** button; the selected bone will become the parent bone of the hierarchy. To split the selected bone, choose the **Refine** button and then select a bone in the viewport; the bone will be split. Choose the **Mirror** button; the **Bone Mirror** dialog box will be displayed. Set the parameters in this dialog box and choose the **OK** button; the selected bone will be mirrored in the viewport.

Bone Coloring Area

The options in this area are used to modify the color of the bone.

Fin Adjustment Tools Rollout

The options in the **Fin Adjustment Tools** rollout are used to set the fins of the selected bones in the viewport.

Object Properties Rollout

You can specify the parameters in this rollout to set the other objects in the viewport to be used as bones. First, select the hierarchy in the viewport and then expand the **Object Properties** rollout in the **Bone Tools** dialog box. Now, select the **Bone On** check box; the selected objects in the hierarchy will behave as bones.

Understanding IK Solver, Interactive IK, and Applied IK

An IK Solver creates an inverse kinematic solution to rotate and position the links in a hierarchy. It applies an IK controller to each bone for controlling the motion of the child objects in a linkage. The hierarchy to which an IK solver is applied will be animated interactively. The behavior and controls on the linkage depend on the type of IK solver that you have selected.

In Interactive IK, the IK solution will be applied only to the specified keyframes. To apply the Interactive IK, select the end of the hierarchy in the viewport and then choose the **Hierarchy** tab in the **Command Panel**. Next, choose the **IK** button in the **Hierarchy** tab and then choose the **Interactive IK** button in the **Inverse Kinematics** rollout. Next, apply the transforms to the bones in the system.

The Applied IK is used to create the accurate motion in the hierarchy of linked objects. In this case, you need to bind the end of a hierarchy to the animated follow objects. After binding, select any object in your kinematic chain and choose the **Apply IK** button in the **Inverse Kinematics** rollout of the **Hierarchy** tab in the **Command Panel**; the IK solution will be calculated for each frame in the animation and it will create transform keys for every object in the IK chain.

Creating a Bone Hierarchy with an IK Solver

To create a bone system with an IK solver, invoke the **Bones** tool from **Create > Systems > Standard > Object Type** rollout in the **Command Panel**; the **Name and Color**, **IK Chain Assignment**, and **Bone Parameters** rollouts will be displayed. In the **IK Chain Assignment** rollout, select the required IK solver from the **IK Solver** drop-down list. Then, select the **Assign To Children** check box, refer to Figure 15-23. Next, create the bones in the viewport as discussed earlier; the selected IK solver will automatically be applied to them.

You can also apply the IK solvers after creating the hierarchy of the bones. To do so, select the bone in the hierarchy and then choose **Animation > IK Solvers** from the menu bar; a cascading menu will be displayed. Now, choose the required IK solver from the cascading menu and then select another bone in the hierarchy in the viewport to define the IK chain.

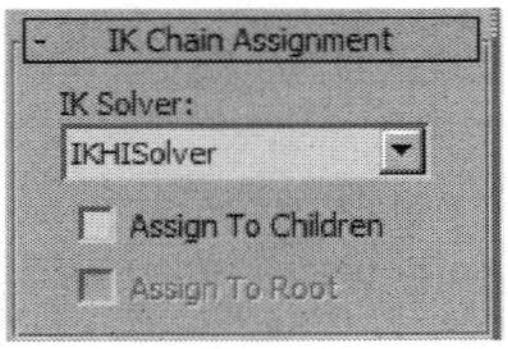

***Figure 15-23** The IK Chain Assignment rollout*

Creating a Biped System

Command Panel: Create > Systems > Standard > Object Type rollout > Biped

The biped system is used to create a biped model that has a two-legged figure. It is used to animate the characters such as humans and animals. To create a biped system, invoke the **Biped** tool from **Create > Systems > Standard > Object Type** rollout in the **Command Panel**; the **Name and Color** and **Create Biped** rollouts will be displayed. In the Top viewport, press and hold the left mouse button, and then drag the cursor to define the height of the biped model. Release the left mouse button; the biped model will be displayed in all viewports, as shown in Figure 15-24.

Invoke the **Select by Name** tool to view the names of all bones in a biped system. Make sure that the **Display Bones** button is chosen in the dialog box to display the names of the biped bones. Among all the bones in a biped system, the *Bip001* bone is the root bone.

You can modify the biped parameters before creating the biped model using the **Create Biped** rollout displayed on invoking the **Biped** tool. However, to modify the biped model after creating it, select the *Bip001* bone in the biped model. Choose the **Motion** tab in the **Command Panel**; various rollouts will be displayed. In the **Biped** rollout, choose the **Figure Mode** button; the **Structure** rollout will be displayed. Now, expand the **Structure** rollout to modify the parameters of the biped model. Most of the options in the **Structure**

rollout are the same as in the **Create Biped** rollout. The **Create Biped** rollout is discussed next.

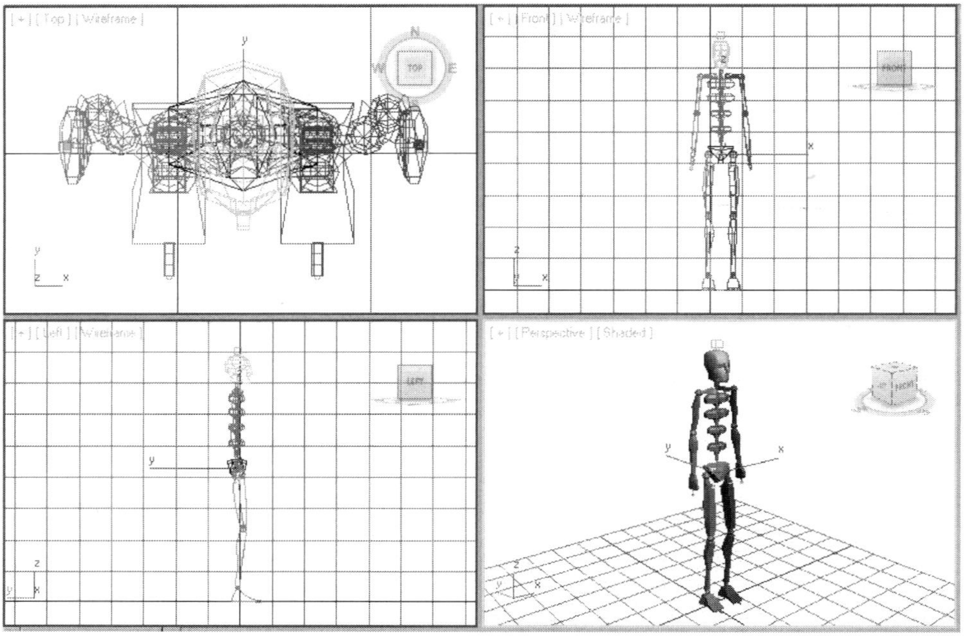

Figure 15-24 *The biped model displayed in all viewports*

Note

Before creating a biped model, you need to create a character mesh. Next, you need to put the biped model in it to animate the created character mesh.

Create Biped Rollout

The options in this rollout are used to define the method of creation of a biped system. You can also modify the number of bones in different parts of the body using this rollout. The areas in this rollout are discussed next.

Creation Method Area

The radio buttons in this area are used to define the method of creation of the biped system. The **Drag Height** radio button is selected by default. It is used to create the biped system as discussed earlier. If you select the **Drag Position** radio button, then to create a biped system, you need to press and hold the left mouse button and move the mouse in the viewport to set the position of the biped model, and then release the left mouse button.

The text box in the **Root Name** area displays the name of the root bone that is superior to all parent bones.

Body Type Area

The drop-down list in this area is used to select the type of body of the biped model. By default, the **Skeleton** option is selected in this drop-down list and it is used to create a skeleton in the viewport. Select the **Male**, **Female**, or **Classic** option from the drop-down list to create a biped model based on the character in the scene; the biped model will be created, as shown in Figure 15-25. Set the values in the **Neck Links**, **Spine Links**, and other spinners to set the number of bones in the biped model.

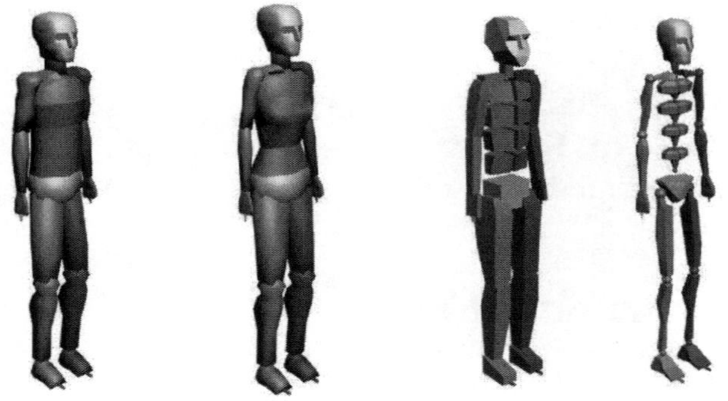

Figure 15-25 *The male, female, classic, and skeleton type biped models*

Note

Biped body parts cannot be removed. But, you can hide unwanted parts of the biped.

Tutorial 1

In this tutorial, you will create an animated scene to study the shadow pattern according to the position of the sun over the earth at a particular location, date, and time. The shadow at one of the frames is shown in Figure 15-26. **(Expected time: 30 min)**

Figure 15-26 *Model for Tutorial 1*

The following steps are required to complete this tutorial:

a. Set the project folder.
b. Create a ground and a tree.
c. Assign the camera.
d. Create the sunlight system.
e. Preview the shadow in the Camera001 viewport.
f. Animate the sunlight system.
g. Render the animation for the final output.
h. Save the file.

Setting the Project Folder

1. Set the project folder with the name *c15_tut1* in the *3dsmax* folder as discussed in earlier chapters.

Creating a Ground and a Tree

To create the ground, you need to create a plane.

1. Invoke the **Plane** tool from **Standard Primitives** and create a plane in the Top viewport as discussed earlier.

2. Modify the name of the plane to *ground*. Also, assign the grass material to it, as discussed in earlier chapters.

3. Invoke the **Foliage** tool from **Create > Geometry > AEC Extended** in the **Command Panel** and create a tree in the Top viewport as discussed earlier. Set the height of the tree according to the *ground*. Align the tree at the center of the ground in all viewports.

4. Next, modify the background color as per your choice.

Assigning the Camera

1. Invoke the **Free** tool from **Create > Cameras > Standard > Object Type** rollout in the **Command Panel** to create a free camera in the viewport.

2. Create a free camera in the Front viewport; it is automatically named as *Camera001*. Align the *Camera001* in all viewports, as shown in Figure 15-27.

   You need to press the C key in the Perspective viewport to display the camera view, as shown in Figure 15-28.

Creating the Sunlight System

To create the sunlight system, you need to invoke the **Sunlight** tool.

1. Invoke the **Zoom** tool and zoom out in the Top viewport to make room for creating the sunlight system.

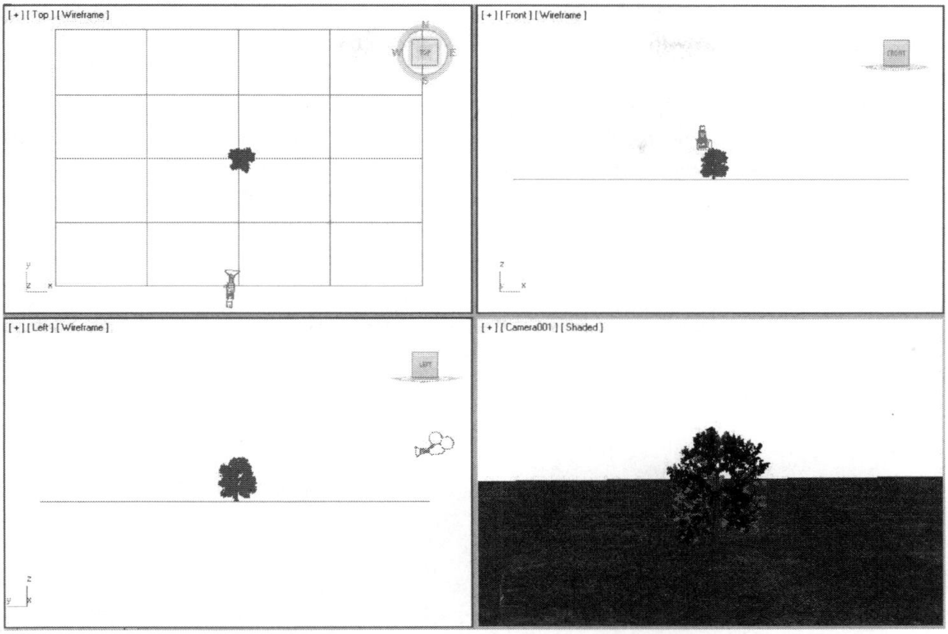

Figure 15-27 *Alignment of the Camera001 in all viewports*

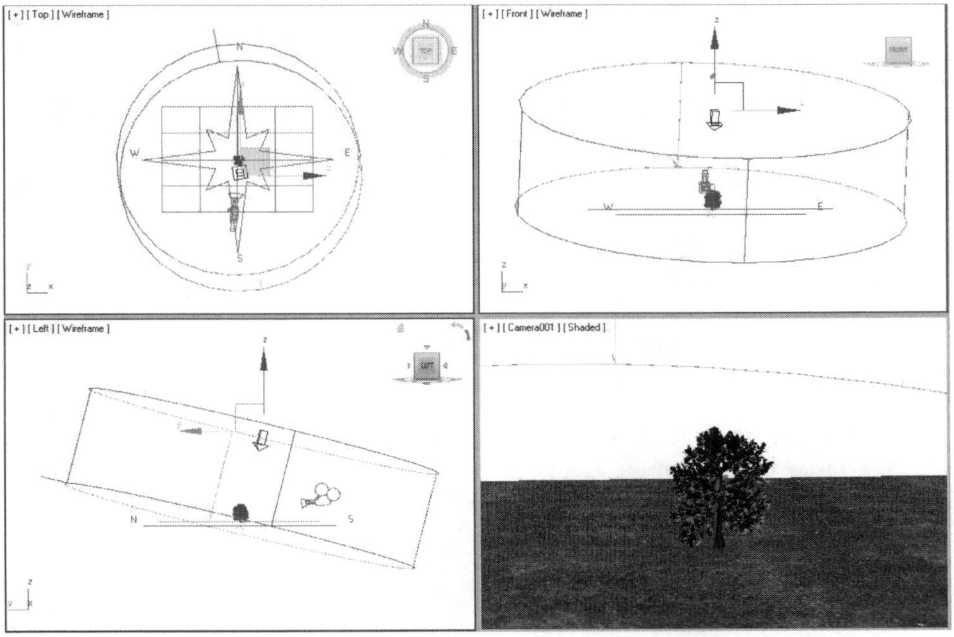

Figure 15-28 *The sunlight system created in all viewports*

2. Choose **Create > Systems** in the **Command Panel**; various tools are displayed in the **Object Type** rollout. Invoke the **Sunlight** tool from the **Object Type** rollout.

3. In the Top viewport, press and hold the left mouse button at the center of the scene to specify the center of the sunlight system and then drag the cursor to define the radius of the system. Now, release the left mouse button; a compass rose is created. Now, drag the cursor again and click in the viewport to set the distance of the light from the compass rose, as shown in Figure 15-28; the compass rose and the directional light are created in the viewports. Next, right-click in the viewport to exit the command.

4. The compass rose and the directional light are automatically named as *Compass001* and *Sun001*, respectively. Next, invoke the **Zoom Extents All** tool to see the objects in every viewport.

Animating the Sunlight System

To study the shadow pattern, you need to change the position of *Sun001* at different frames in the time slider.

1. Choose the **Time Configuration** button; the **Time Configuration** dialog box is displayed. In the **End Time** spinner of the **Animation** area, set the value to **500**. Now, choose the **OK** button; the total number of frames in the track bar increases.

2. Select *Sun001* in any viewport and choose the **Motion** tab in the **Command Panel**; the **Control Parameters** rollout is displayed.

3. By default, the sunlight system is placed at the latitude of San Francisco, CA. Also, the sun is set at 12 hours. You can modify the location of the sun in the **Location** area by choosing the **Get Location** button.

   Next, you need to change the position of the *Sun001* by modifying the time given in the **Time** area of the **Control Parameters** rollout.

4. Drag the time slider to frame 0. In the **Time** area of the **Control Parameters** rollout, set the value in the **Hours** spinner to **7** and press ENTER.

5. Make sure that the *Sun001* is selected in the viewport. Choose the **Toggle Auto Key Mode** button to enter the animation mode; the track bar, the **Toggle Auto Key Mode** button, and the active viewport turn red.

6. Drag the time slider to frame 40, as shown in Figure 15-29. In the **Time** area of the **Control Parameters** rollout, set the value in the **Hours** spinner to **8**; the arrows of the **Hours**, **Mins.**, and **Secs.** spinners turn red.

7. Drag the time slider to frame 80. In the **Time** area of the **Control Parameters** rollout, set the value in the **Hours** spinner to **9**.

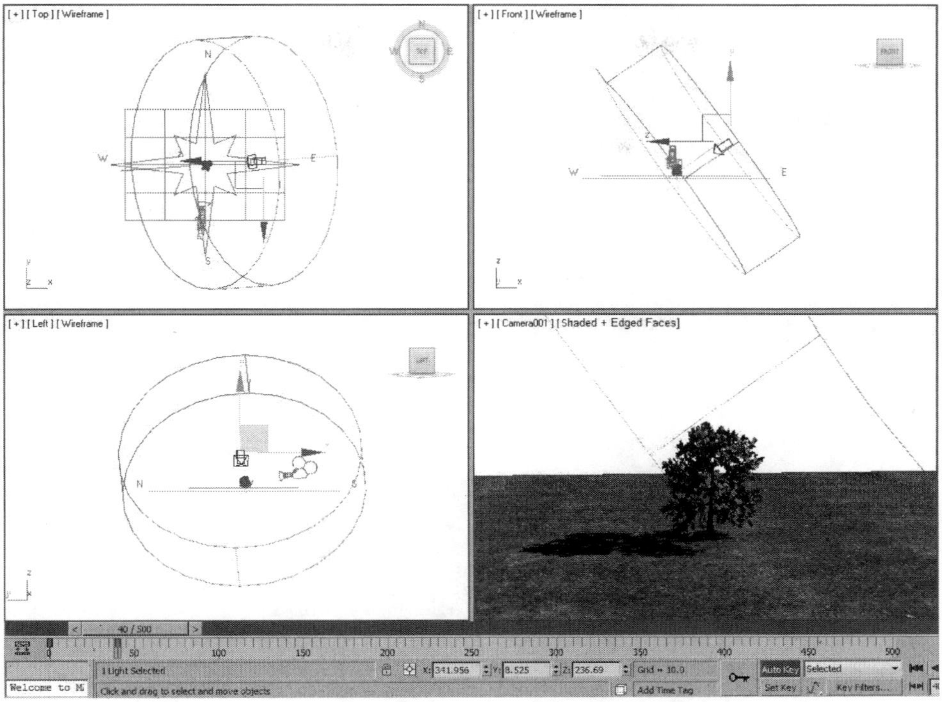

***Figure 15-29** The time slider at frame 40*

8. Drag the time slider to 40-frames increments and increase the time in the **Hours** spinner by one hour at each increment. You need to continue this process until the value in the **Hours** spinner is set to **18**. Also, by this time, the last frame number should be 440.

9. Choose the **Toggle Auto Key Mode** button again to turn off the animation mode.

10. Now, choose the **Play Animation** button to view the effect of the sunlight system in the Camera001 viewport.

Rendering the Animation

1. Invoke the **Render Setup** tool from the **Main Toolbar**; the **Render Setup: Default Scanline Renderer** dialog box is displayed. In this dialog box, the **Common** tab is chosen by default.

2. Set the values in the dialog box as discussed in Tutorial 1 of Chapter 12 and choose the **Render** button; the **Camera001, frame0, RGBA, Display Gamma:2.2, Color16 Bits/ Channel (1:1)** dialog box and the **Rendering** dialog box are displayed, showing the rendering process.

3. After the completion of the rendering process, the final output of the animation is saved in the *.avi format at the specified location. You can view the final output of the animation by opening the corresponding *avi* file.

You can view the final rendered sequence by downloading the *c15_3dsmax_2012_render.zip* file from *http://www.cadcim.com*.

Saving the File

1. Save the file with the name *c15tut1.max* as discussed in earlier chapters. The location of this file is given below:

   \Documents\3dsmax\c15_tut1\scenes

Tutorial 2

In this tutorial, you will create the footsteps animation in a biped model. The footsteps animation of a biped model at two frames is shown in Figure 15-30.

(Expected time: 45 min)

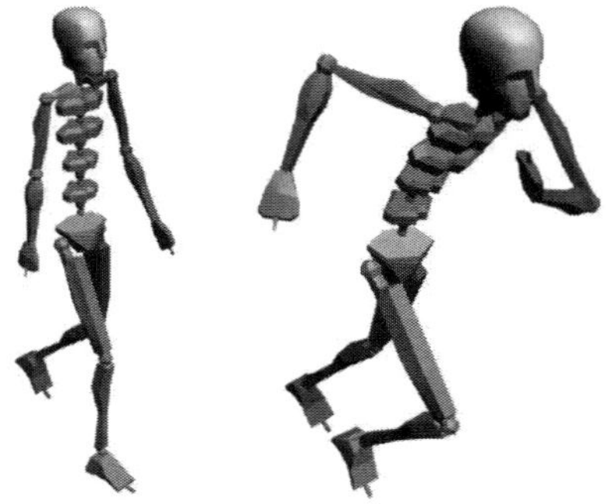

Figure 15-30 *Models for Tutorial 2*

The following steps are required to complete this tutorial:

a. Set the project folder.
b. Create a biped model.
c. Assign footsteps animation to the model.
d. Create multiple footsteps.
e. Save the biped animation in the BIP file.
f. Load the biped animation from the saved BIP file.
g. Save the file.

Setting the Project Folder

1. Set the project folder with the name *c15_tut2* in the *3dsmax* folder as discussed in earlier chapters.

Creating a Biped Model

1. To create a biped model, first activate the Top viewport. Then, invoke the **Biped** tool from **Create > Systems > Standard > Object Type** rollout in the **Command Panel**; various rollouts are displayed.

2. In the **Create Biped** rollout, select the **Drag Position** radio button in the **Creation Method** area and click at the center of the Top viewport; a biped model is displayed in all viewports.

   All bones in the biped model are named automatically. The *Bip001* bone is the root bone in the hierarchy and is selected by default after the creation of the model.

3. Invoke the **Zoom Extents All** tool; the biped model is displayed in all viewports, as shown in Figure 15-31.

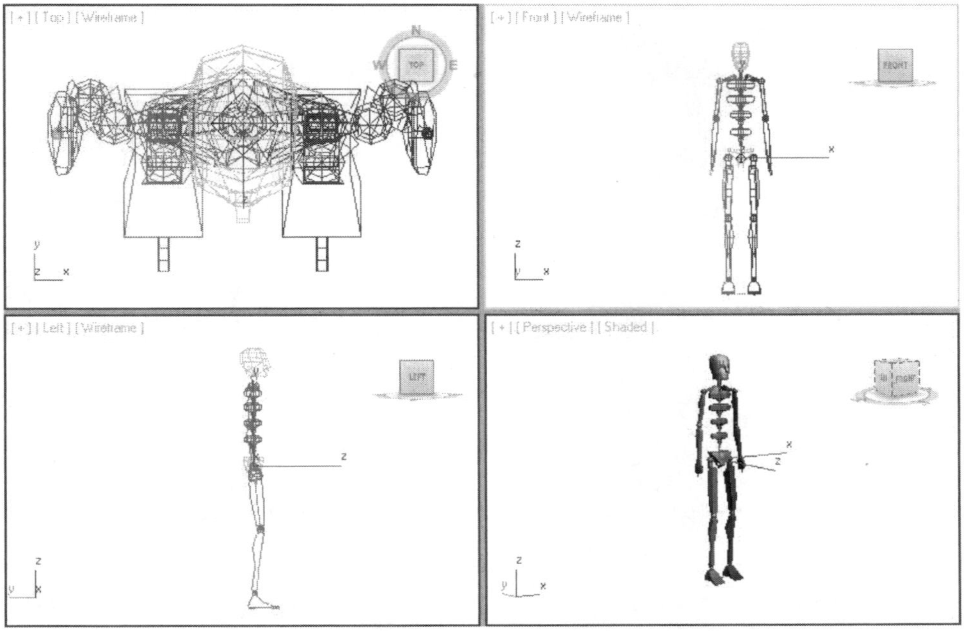

Figure 15-31 *The biped model displayed in all viewports*

Assigning the Footsteps Animation to the Model

1. Make sure that *Bip001* is selected in the viewport and choose the **Motion** tab in the **Command Panel**; various rollouts are displayed.

2. Expand the **Biped** rollout and then choose the **Footstep Mode** button from it; the **Footstep Creation**, **Footstep Operations**, and **Dynamics & Adaptation** rollouts are displayed, as shown in Figure 15-32.

3. Invoke the **Zoom** tool and zoom out in the Top viewport until one-fourth of the original biped model is visible. Also, set the view of the Top viewport using the **Pan** tool, as shown in Figure 15-33.

4. In the **Footstep Creation** rollout, make sure that the **Walk** button is chosen.

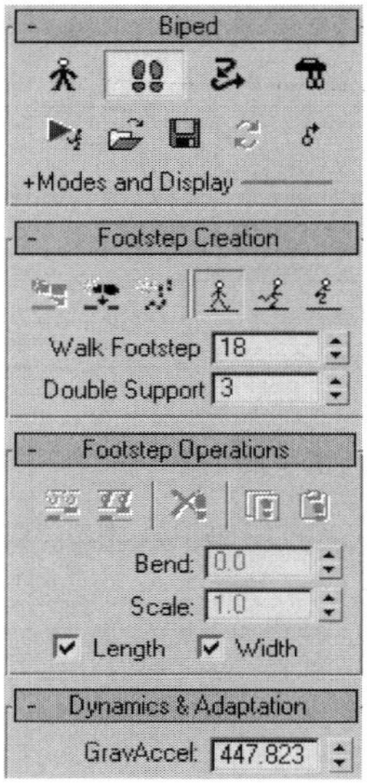

*Figure 15-32 The rollouts displayed after choosing the **Footstep Mode** button*

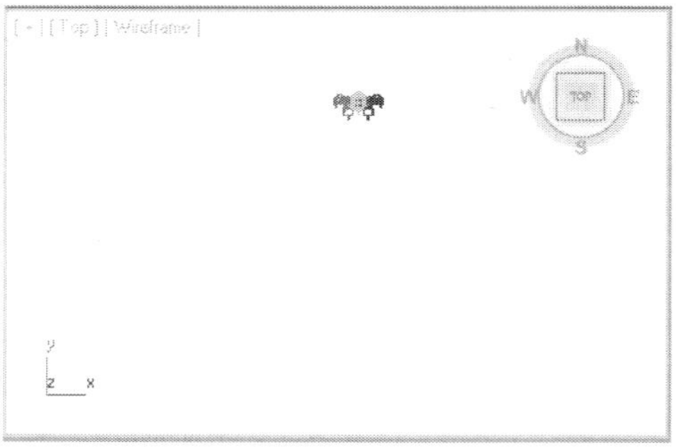

*Figure 15-33 The Top viewport after using the **Zoom** and **Pan** tools*

Note

*You can also choose the **Run** or **Jump** button.*

5. Choose the **Create Footsteps (at current frame)** button in the **Footstep Creation** rollout and then move the cursor over the Top viewport; the cursor gets changed. Now, click in the Top viewport to create the footsteps, as shown in Figure 15-34.

6. Invoke the **Select and Move** tool and align the footsteps in the Top viewport, as shown in Figure 15-35. Also, rotate some of the footsteps by 45-degree in the clockwise direction, as shown in Figure 15-36.

   Next, you need to create keys for the biped model.

7. In the **Footstep Operations** rollout, choose the **Create Keys for Inactive Footsteps** button; keys are created for the biped animation according to the footsteps.

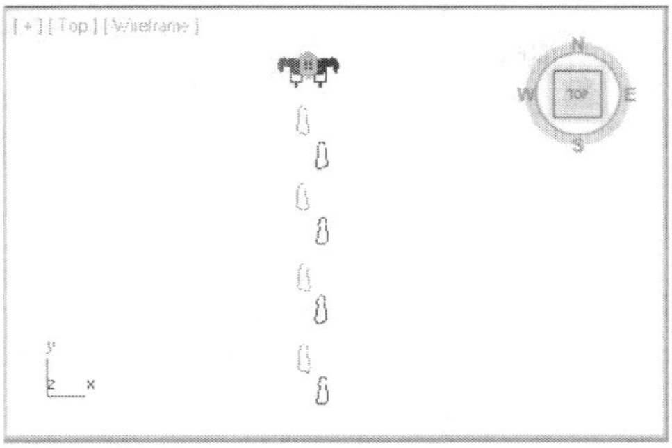

Figure 15-34 The footsteps created in the Top viewport

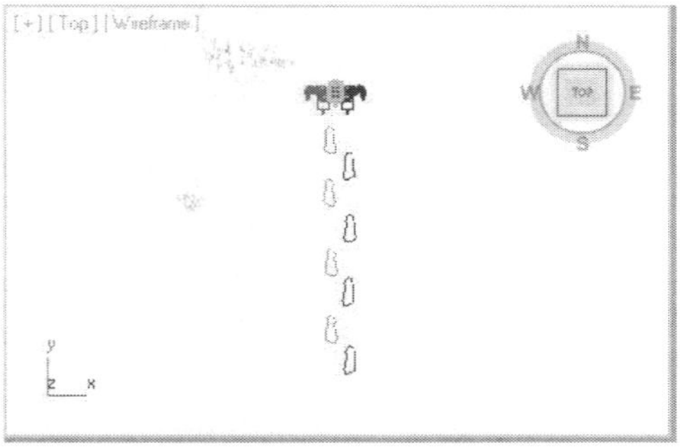

*Figure 15-35 The footsteps aligned using the **Select and Move** tool*

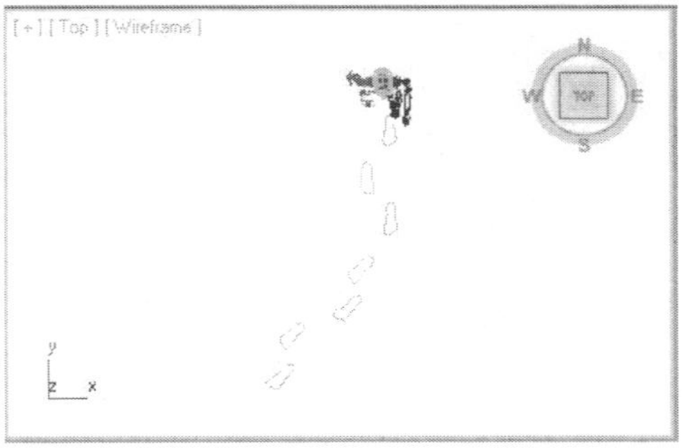

Figure 15-36 The footsteps after rotating them in the Top viewport

8. Invoke the **Select Object** tool and then invoke the **Zoom Extents All** tool.

9. Now, activate the Perspective viewport and choose the **Play Animation** button; the biped model starts moving according to the footsteps created, as shown in Figure 15-37.

10. If you want to add more footsteps in the viewport, then invoke the **Select by Name** tool; the **Select From Scene** dialog box is displayed. Now, select the *Bip001* bone and choose the **OK** button to close the dialog box.

11. Choose the **Motion** tab in the **Command Panel** and then choose the **Footstep Mode** button in the **Biped** rollout.

12. In the **Footstep Creation** rollout, choose the **Walk** button and then choose the **Create Footsteps (append)** button.

13. Move the cursor over the Top viewport; the cursor gets changed. Now, create additional footsteps in the Top viewport and align them based on your requirement, as shown in Figure 15-38.

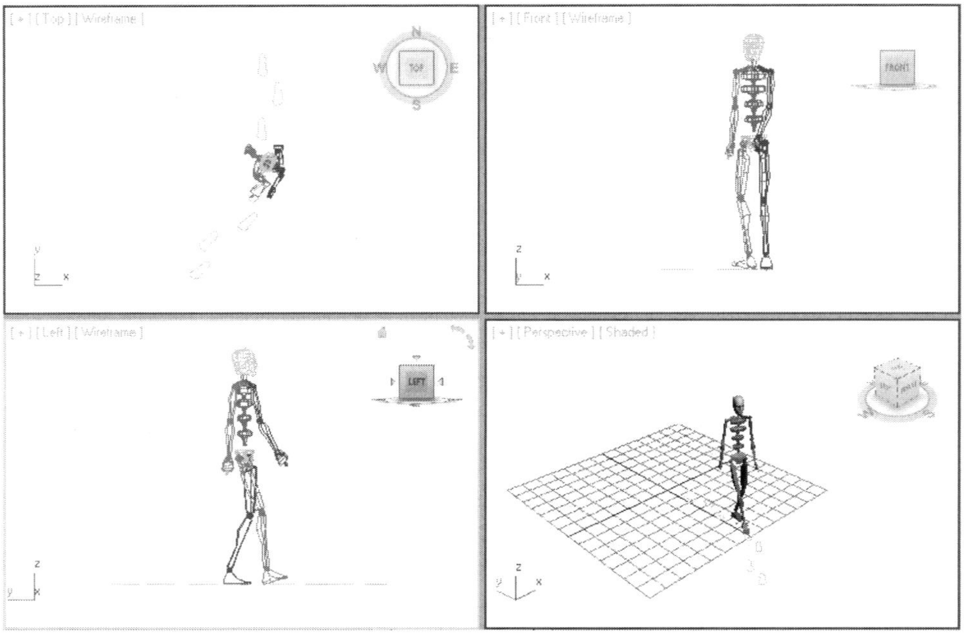

Figure 15-37 *The biped model moving after choosing the* ***Play Animation*** *button*

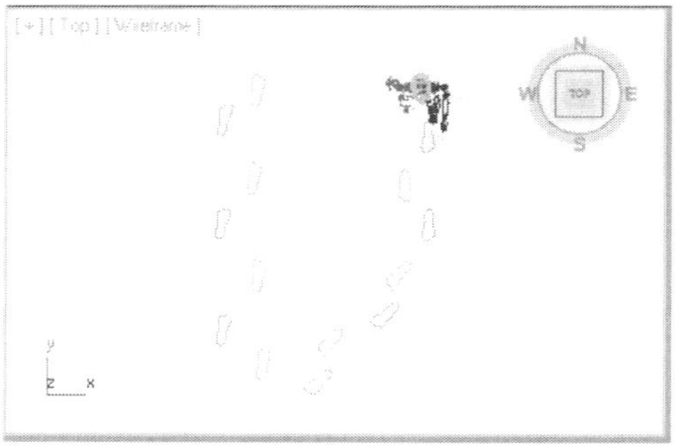

Figure 15-38 *New footsteps created in the Top viewport*

14. In the **Footstep Operations** rollout, choose the **Create Keys for Inactive Footsteps** button; keys are created for the biped animation according to the newly created footsteps.

15. Invoke the **Select Object** tool and then the **Zoom Extents All** tool.

16. Now, activate the Perspective viewport and choose the **Play Animation** button; the biped model starts moving according to the newly created footsteps, as shown in Figure 15-39.

    Next, you need to create multiple footsteps automatically.

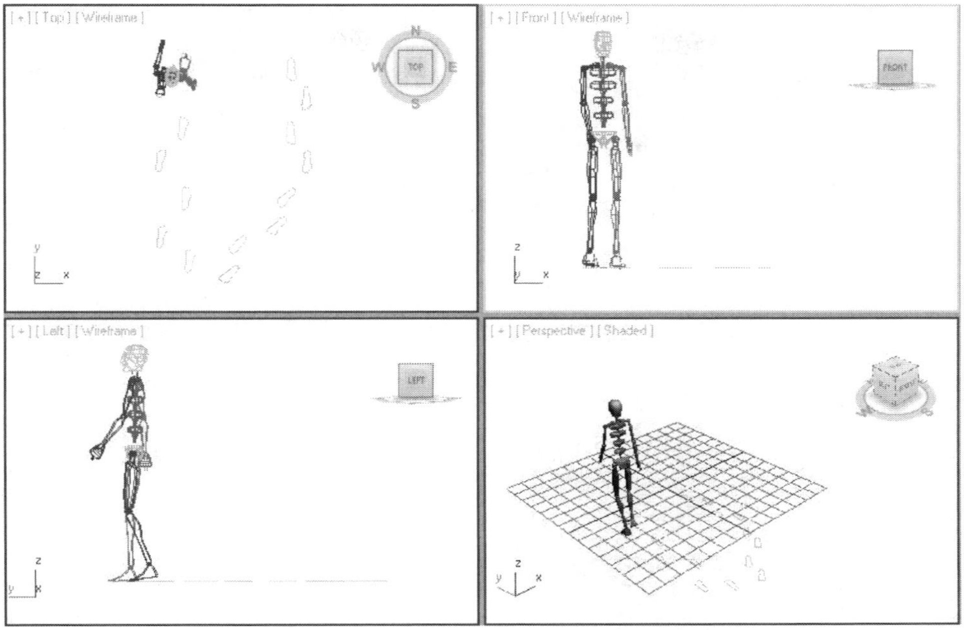

Figure 15-39 The biped model moving according to the newly created footsteps

Creating Multiple Footsteps

1. First, create another biped model in the viewport as discussed in the previous section and then invoke the **Zoom Extents All** tool to view it in all viewports.

2. Make sure that the *Bip002* bone of the biped model is selected in the viewport and then choose the **Motion** tab in the **Command Panel**; various rollouts are displayed.

3. Expand the **Biped** rollout. Choose the **Footstep Mode** button in this rollout.

4. In the **Footstep Creation** rollout, choose the **Run** button.

5. Choose the **Create Multiple Footsteps** button in this rollout; the **Create Multiple Footsteps: Run** dialog box is displayed.

6. In the **General** area of this dialog box, set the value **6** in the **Number of Footsteps** spinner to specify the number of footsteps and then choose the **OK** button. Based on your requirement, you can also set other parameters in the **Create Multiple Footsteps: Run** dialog box.

   Next, you need to create keys for the biped model.

7. In the **Footstep Operations** rollout, choose the **Create Keys for Inactive Footsteps** button; keys are created for the biped animation.

8. Invoke the **Select Object** tool and then the **Zoom Extents All** tool.

9. Now, activate the Perspective viewport and choose the **Play Animation** button; the biped model starts running, as shown in Figure 15-40.

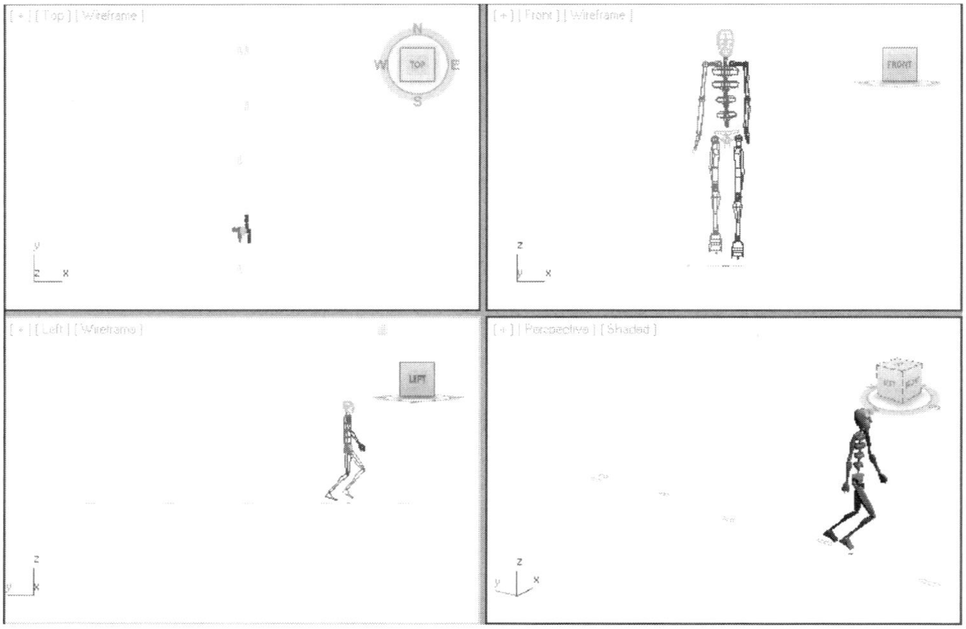

Figure 15-40 *The running biped model in all viewports*

10. When you create the keys for the biped model, various keys are created automatically for each bone in the biped model. Therefore, you can modify the keys created for arms, legs, spine, and head according to the animation you want to create for the biped model. To do so, select a bone in the viewport; the keys created for the selected bone are displayed in the track bar. Now, choose the **Toggle Auto Key Mode** button and modify the bone using the transforms such as move, rotate, and so on at the keys in the track bar.

Saving the Biped Animation in the BIP File

After creating the animation in the biped model, you need to save the animation in a BIP file for further use.

1. Make sure that the *Bip002* bone of the biped model is selected in the viewport and the **Motion** tab is chosen in the **Command Panel**.

2. Choose the **Save File** button in the **Biped** rollout; the **Save As** dialog box is displayed. Browse to the folder in which you want to save the file. Enter **Run** as the name of the animation file in the **File name** text box and make sure that the **(*.BIP)** option is selected in the **Save as type** drop-down list.

3. Choose the **Save** button; the animation of the biped model is saved with the name *Run.bip* at the specified location. Now, you can use the same biped animation for another scene.

Loading the Biped Animation from the Saved BIP File

1. Select the *Bip001* bone of the biped model, in which you want to load the animation of the BIP file.

2. Choose the **Motion** tab in the **Command Panel**. In the **Biped** rollout, choose the **Load File** button; the **Open** dialog box is displayed. Browse to the *Run.bip* file, select the file, and then choose the **Open** button; the same animation is loaded in the biped model.

3. Choose the **Play Animation** button; the biped model starts running, as shown in Figure 15-41.

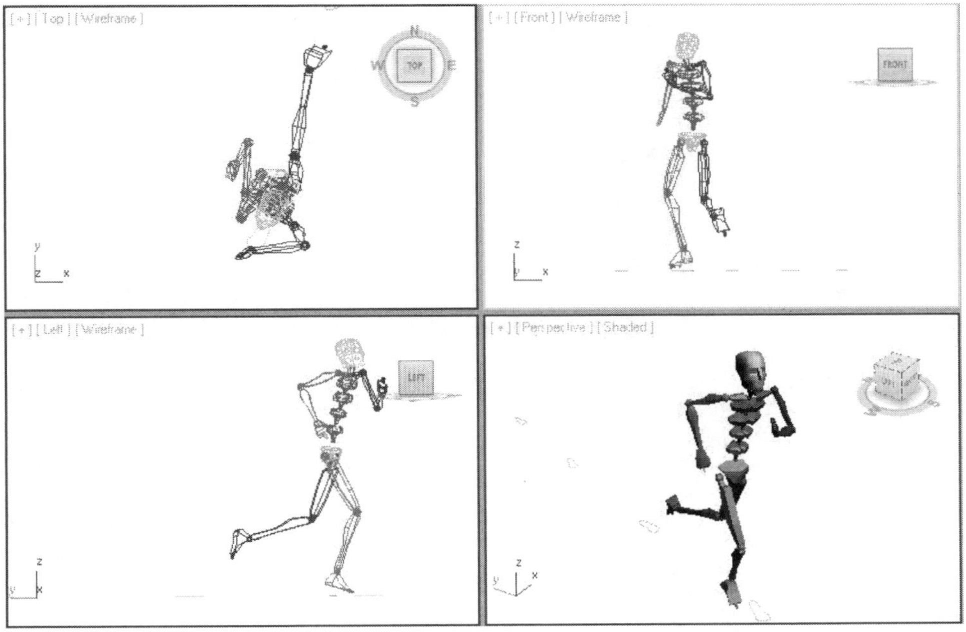

Figure 15-41 *The biped model in running position after loading the Run.bip file*

You can view the final rendered sequence by downloading the *c15_3dsmax_2012_render.zip* file from *http://www.cadcim.com.*

Saving the File

1. Save the file with the name *c15tut2.max* as discussed in earlier chapters. The location of this file is given below:

   \Documents\3dsmax\c15_tut2\scenes

Self-Evaluation Test

Answer the following questions and then compare them to those given at the end of this chapter:

1. Which of the following lights is used as the sunlight in the daylight system?

   (a) **IES Sun** (b) **Target Direct**
   (c) **mr Sun** (d) All of these

2. Which of the following lights is used as a skylight in the daylight system?

   (a) **IES Sky** (b) **Target Skylight**
   (c) **mr Skylight** (d) All of these

3. Which of the following tools is used to create a bone system in Autodesk 3ds Max?

   (a) **Bones** (b) **Biped**
   (c) **Point** (d) **Dummy**

4. Which of the following rollouts is used to modify the parameters of the daylight system?

   (a) **Control Parameters** (b) **IK Chain Assignment**
   (c) **Parameters** (d) All of these

5. The **Systems** are used to combine objects, linkages, and controllers to create an object set that will have all these features. (T/F)

6. A dummy object in the ring array system cannot be rendered. (T/F)

7. The ability to link objects together to create a chain is known as hierarchy. (T/F)

8. The daylight system uses a combination of two lights, __________ and __________.

9. In __________ kinematics, you can animate the object at the bottom of the hierarchy to control the entire chain.

10. To modify the parameters of the ring array system, you need to choose the __________ tab in the **Command Panel**.

Review Questions

Answer the following questions:

1. Which of the following options is used to create an inverse kinematic solution to rotate and position the links in a hierarchy?

   (a) **IK Solver** (b) **Interactive IK**
   (c) **Applied IK** (d) All of these

2. Which of the following options is used to create an inverse kinematic solution only for the specified keyframes?

   (a) **IK Solver** (b) **Interactive IK**
   (c) **Applied IK** (d) All of these

3. Which of the following options is used to create an accurate motion in the hierarchy of linked objects?

   (a) **IK Solver** (b) **Interactive IK**
   (c) **Applied IK** (d) All of these

4. Which of the following systems is used to create a hierarchical linkage of bones and joints?

   (a) Biped system (b) Ring array system
   (c) Sunlight system (d) Daylight system

5. You cannot replace the boxes in a ring array system with other objects. (T/F)

6. You can generate the light effect using a sunlight system according to the position of the sun over the earth at a particular location, date, and time. (T/F)

7. In forward kinematics, if a parent object moves, then the child objects will also move accordingly. (T/F)

8. The __________ tab is used to modify the hierarchical linkage between the objects.

9. You can animate and transform the hierarchy of bones using the __________ as well as the __________.

10. The options in the __________ rollout are used to set the fins of the selected bones in the viewport.

Exercises

Exercise 1

Start Autodesk 3ds Max 2012 and then perform the following operations:

1. Create an object in the viewport using your own dimensions. Invoke the **Ring Array** tool from **Create > Systems > Standard > Object Type** rollout in the **Command Panel**. Now, create a ring array system in the Top viewport. Next, replace the boxes of the ring array system with the object created using the **Curve Editor (Open)** tool from the **Main Toolbar**. Then, animate the amplitude of the ring array system and render the scene to view the final output.

2. Create bones in the viewport using the **Bones** tool from **Create > Systems > Standard > Object Type** rollout in the **Command Panel**. Now, link the bones to create a hierarchy. Next, apply the transforms to the bones and notice the difference after linking the bones.

3. Create a biped system using the **Biped** tool from **Create > Systems > Standard > Object Type** rollout in the **Command Panel**. Next, create an animation to jump the biped model using the **Biped** rollout in the **Motion** tab of the **Command Panel**.

4. Create a scene in the viewport. Then, invoke the **Daylight** tool from **Create > Systems > Standard > Object Type** rollout in the **Command Panel**. Next, create a daylight system in the viewport. Then, choose the **Motion** tab in the **Command Panel**. In the **Location** area of the **Control Parameters** rollout, choose the **Get Location** button and change the location of the sun. Next, choose the **OK** button and notice the difference.

5. Create a scene in the viewport. Next, invoke the **Daylight** tool from **Create > Systems > Standard > Object Type** rollout in the **Command Panel** and choose the **Modify** tab. In the **Daylight Parameters** rollout, select the required light option for the sunlight and skylight and then notice the difference.

Exercise 2

Create an animated swing using the ring array system. The position of the swing at different frames is shown in Figures 15-42, 15-43, and 15-44. You can view the final rendered image of this model by downloading it from *http://www.cadcim.com*. **(Expected time: 15 min)**

Hints:

1. Create the swings using **Extended Primitives**.

2. Link the parts of the swing with the dummy objects of the ring array system.

3. Replace the boxes of the ring array system with the swing using the **Curve Editor (Open)** tool.

4. Animate the dummy object accordingly.

Figure 15-42 *Model for Exercise 2 (view 1)*

Figure 15-43 *Model for Exercise 2 (view 2)*

Figure 15-44 *Model for Exercise 2 (view 3)*

Answers to Self-Evaluation Test

1. d, **2.** d, **3.** a, **4.** a, **5.** T, **6.** T, **7.** T, **8.** sunlight, skylight, **9.** inverse, **10. Motion**

16

NURBS Modeling

Learning Objectives

After completing this chapter, you will be able to:

- *Understand NURBS curves*
- *Understand NURBS surfaces*
- *Convert splines into NURBS curves*
- *Convert splines and extended splines into NURBS surfaces*
- *Convert primitives into NURBS surfaces*
- *Create NURBS models*
- *Understand NURBS sub-objects*

INTRODUCTION TO NURBS

In Autodesk 3ds Max, the NURBS (Non-Uniform Rational Basis Splines) curves and surfaces are used to create complex 3D models. The NURBS objects use the mathematical calculations to create accurate complex 3D objects from 2D splines. In this chapter, you will learn to create smooth and easily editable 3D models using the NURBS curves and surfaces.

NURBS CURVES

The NURBS curves are similar to the shape objects and are used to create complex surfaces for creating 3D models. You can use the NURBS curves to create the 3D surfaces using the **Lathe** and **Extrude** modifiers. Also, you can loft the NURBS curves to create the loft objects. In Autodesk 3ds Max, there are two types of NURBS curves, point curve and CV curve. These curves are discussed next.

Point Curve

Menu bar:	Create > NURBS > Point Curve
Command Panel:	Create > Shapes > NURBS Curves > Object Type rollout > Point Curve

The point curves are the NURBS curves in which the points lie on the curve, refer to Figure 16-1. To create a point curve, choose **Create > Shapes** in the **Command Panel**; a drop-down list will be displayed below the **Shapes** button. Select the **NURBS Curves** option from the drop-down list; the tools to create the point curve and the CV curve will be displayed in the **Object Type** rollout, as shown in Figure 16-2. Activate the viewport in which you want to create the point curve. Now, invoke the **Point Curve** tool from the **Object Type** rollout; the **Name and Color**, **Rendering**, **Keyboard Entry**, and **Create Point Curve** rollouts will be displayed. Next, click in the viewport to create the first point and then click again to create the second point; the first segment is created. Then, continue clicking in the viewport to add more points in the curve. Now, right-click to end the creation; a point curve will be created in the viewport, refer to Figure 16-1. The **Create Point Curve** rollout that is displayed on invoking the **Point Curve** tool is discussed next.

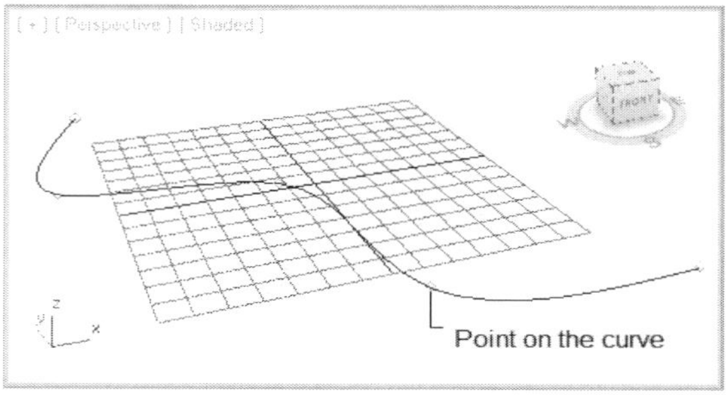

Figure 16-1 *A point curve*

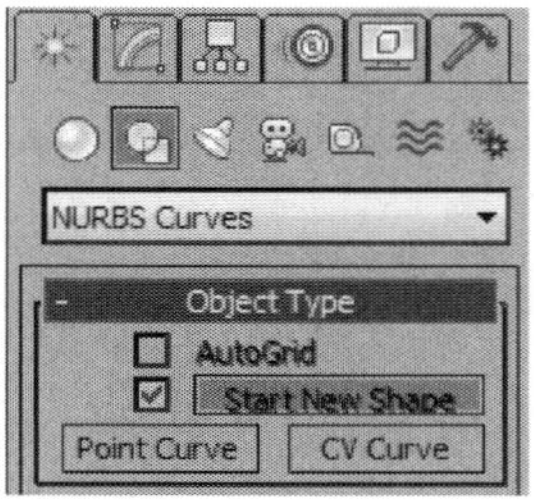

Figure 16-2 *The tools for creating NURBS curves*

Tip: *While creating a point curve, if you want to remove the last point that you have created, press the BACKSPACE key.*

Note

*The options in the **Rendering** and **Keyboard Entry** rollouts are the same as discussed in Chapter 5.*

Create Point Curve Rollout

The options in the **Interpolation** area of this rollout are the same as those discussed in Chapter 5. The **Draw In All Viewports** check box is selected by default in this rollout, as shown in Figure 16-3. It is used to create a 3D curve in all viewports simultaneously. For example, you can start by creating the first point in the Top viewport, continue creating the additional points in the Left viewport, and finish the creation of the point curve in the Front viewport.

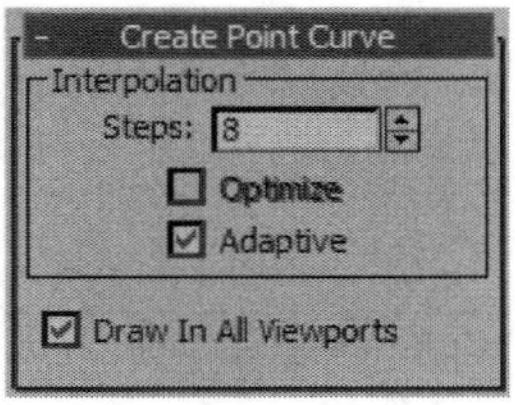

***Figure 16-3** The **Create Point Curve** rollout*

CV Curve

Menu bar:	Create > NURBS > CV Curve
Command Panel:	Create > Shapes > NURBS Curves > Object Type rollout > CV Curve

The CV curves are the NURBS curves that are controlled by the control vertices (CVs). The CVs are the points that lie outside the curve and control the shape of the CV curve. The CVs of a NURBS curve are connected with a lattice known as control lattice, which encloses the curve, refer to Figure 16-4. When you move the CVs in a CV curve, the control lattice gets changed, therefore, the shape of the CV curve also gets changed.

To create a CV curve, choose **Create > Shapes** in the **Command Panel**; a drop-down list will be displayed. Select the **NURBS Curves** option from this drop-down list and activate the viewport in which you want to create the CV curve. Now, invoke the **CV Curve** tool from the **Object Type** rollout; the **Name and Color**, **Rendering**, **Keyboard Entry**, and **Create CV Curve** rollouts will be displayed. Next, click and drag the cursor in the viewport to create the first point and the first segment. Then, continue clicking in the viewport to add more points in the curve; a CV curve will be created, as shown in Figure 16-4. Next, right-click in the viewport to end the creation.

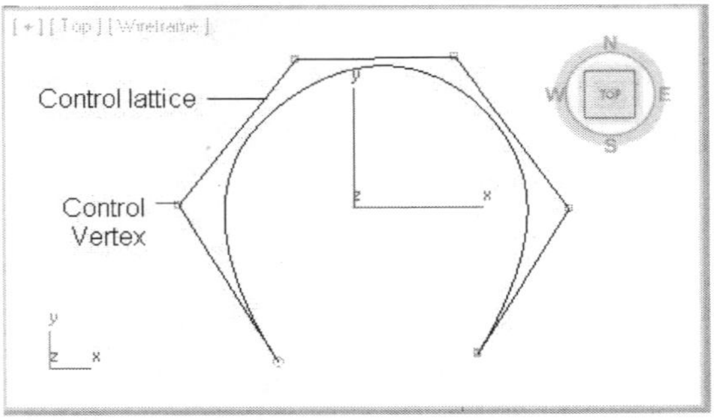

***Figure 16-4** A CV curve*

Note

*The rollouts that are displayed on invoking the **CV Curve** tool are the same as those discussed in the point curve.*

NURBS SURFACES

The NURBS surfaces are the base of the NURBS model. The NURBS models can be created by modifying these NURBS surfaces at advanced level. In Autodesk 3ds Max, there are two types of NURBS surfaces, point surface and CV surface. These are discussed next.

Point Surface

Menu bar:	Create > NURBS > Point Surface
Command Panel:	Create > Geometry > NURBS Surfaces > Object Type rollout > Point Surf

The point surfaces are the NURBS surfaces in which the points lie on the surface, refer to Figure 16-5. To create a point surface, choose **Create > Geometry** in the **Command Panel**; a drop-down list will be displayed below the **Geometry** button. Select the **NURBS Surfaces** option from this drop-down list; the tools to create the point surfaces will be displayed in the **Object Type** rollout, as shown in Figure 16-6. Activate the viewport in which you want to create the point surface. Now, invoke the **Point Surf** tool from the **Object Type** rollout; the **Name and Color**, **Keyboard Entry**, and **Create Parameters** rollouts will be displayed. Next, press and hold the left mouse button on the upper left corner of the viewport and drag the cursor toward the lower right corner of the viewport to specify the length and width of the point surface. Release the left mouse button; a point surface will be created in the viewport, as shown in Figure 16-5. The rollouts that are displayed on invoking the **Point Surf** tool are discussed next.

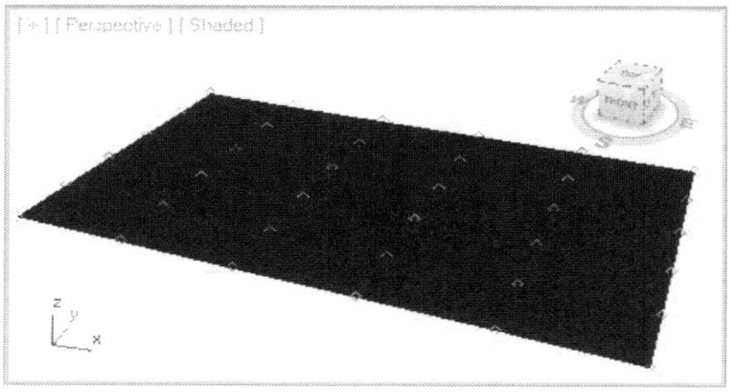

Figure 16-5 *A point surface*

Figure 16-6 *The tools displayed to create NURBS Surfaces*

Keyboard Entry Rollout

This rollout is used to create the point surface by entering the parameters using the keyboard. Set the values in the **Length** and **Width** spinners to specify the length and width of the point surface. Now, set the values in the **Length Points** and **Width Points** spinners to specify the number of points along the length and width of the point surface. Next, choose the **Create** button; a point surface will be created.

Create Parameters Rollout

The parameters in this rollout are used to modify the dimensions of the point surface, refer to Figure 16-7. Set the values in the **Length** and **Width** spinners to specify the length and width of the point surface. Set the values in the **Length Points** and **Width Points** spinners to specify the points along the length and width of the point surface. You can modify the geometry of the point surface by moving the points on it, as shown in Figure 16-8. To do so, select the point surface in the viewport and choose the **Modify** tab in the **Command Panel**. In the modifier stack, click on the plus sign on the left side of the **NURBS Surface**; the **Surface** and **Point** sub-object levels will be displayed. Select the **Point** sub-object level and then select the points in the viewport to modify them.

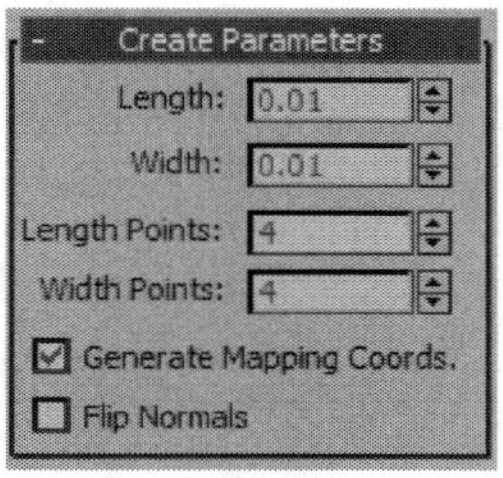

Figure 16-7 *The **Create Parameters** rollout*

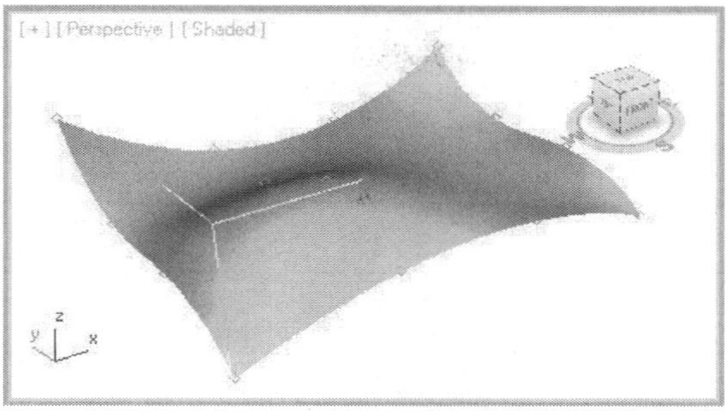

Figure 16-8 *The points moved on a point surface*

CV Surface

Menu bar:	Create > NURBS > CV Surface
Command Panel:	Create > Geometry > NURBS Surfaces > Object Type rollout > CV Surf

The CV surfaces are the NURBS surfaces that are controlled by control vertices (CVs). The CVs are the points that lie outside the surface and control the shape of the CV surface. The CVs of a NURBS surface are connected with a lattice known as control lattice that encloses the curve, refer to Figure 16-9. To create a CV surface, choose **Create > Geometry** in the **Command Panel**; a drop-down list will be displayed. Select the **NURBS Surfaces** option from the drop-down list; the tools to create CV surfaces will be displayed in the **Object Type** rollout. Activate the viewport in which you want to create the CV surface. Now, invoke the **CV Surf** tool from the **Object Type** rollout; the **Name and Color**, **Keyboard Entry**, and **Create Parameters** rollouts will be displayed. Next, click on the upper left corner of the viewport and move the cursor toward the lower right corner of the viewport to specify the length and width of the CV surface. Click again on the screen; a CV surface will be created in the viewport, as shown in Figure 16-9. The rollouts that are displayed on invoking the **CV Surf** tool are discussed next.

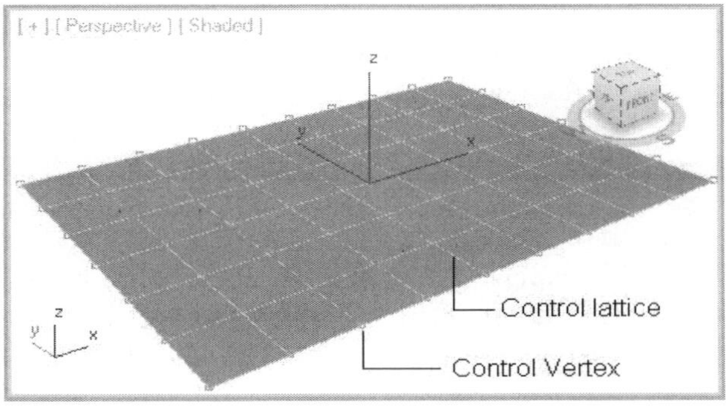

Figure 16-9 *A CV surface*

Keyboard Entry Rollout

You can also create a CV surface by entering the values in the spinners in this rollout. Set the values in the **Length** and **Width** spinners to specify the length and width of the CV surface. Now, set the values in the **Length CVs** and **Width CVs** spinners to specify the control vertices along the length and width of the CV surface. Next, choose the **Create** button; a CV surface will be created.

Create Parameters Rollout

The parameters in this rollout are used to modify the dimensions of the CV surface, refer to Figure 16-10. Set the values in the **Length** and **Width** spinners to specify the length and width of the CV surface. Set the values in the **Length CVs** and **Width CVs** spinners to specify the control vertices along the length and width of the CV surface, respectively.

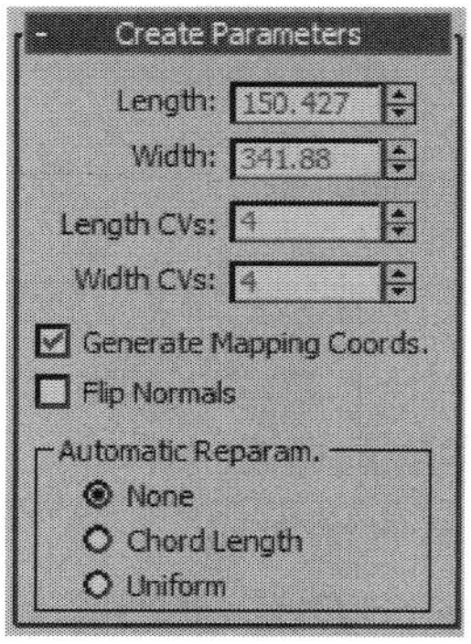

***Figure 16-10** The **Create Parameters** rollout*

Note

*If you deselect the NURBS surface objects in the viewport, then the **Create Parameters** rollout will not be displayed again. So, it is recommended to make all the changes before deselecting it.*

CONVERTING SPLINES AND EXTENDED SPLINES INTO NURBS SURFACES

To create a NURBS model, you can also use the splines or the extended splines shapes instead of using the point curve or the CV curve. To do so, you need to convert them into NURBS surfaces.

First, choose **Create > Shapes** in the **Command Panel**; a drop-down list will be displayed with the **Splines** option selected by default. Next, invoke one of the tools in the **Object Type** rollout and create a spline shape in the viewport. Now, you can convert the spline shape into NURBS surfaces using one of the following methods:

1. Select the spline shape in the viewport and right-click on it; a quad menu will be displayed. Choose the **Convert To:** option; a cascading menu will be displayed. Now, choose **Convert to NURBS**; the spline shape will be converted into NURBS surface.

2. Select the spline shape in the viewport and choose the **Modify** tab in the **Command Panel**; the modifier stack will be displayed. In the modifier stack, right-click on the name of the tool by which you have created the spline shape; a shortcut menu will be displayed. Now, choose the **NURBS** option; the spline shape will be converted into NURBS surface.

CONVERTING PRIMITIVES INTO NURBS SURFACES

To create a NURBS model, you can use the standard primitives as well as the objects created by standard primitives. To do so, you need to convert them into NURBS surfaces. First, create an object that you want to convert into NURBS surface. Then, select it in the viewport and follow one of the methods that has been discussed for converting a spline into NURBS surfaces.

Note

You cannot convert the extended primitives into NURBS surfaces. However, the torus knot and prism from extended primitives are exceptions.

CREATING NURBS MODELS USING THE MODIFY TAB

To create a NURBS model, you need to modify the NURBS objects (NURBS curves and NURBS surfaces). To modify the NURBS object, select the NURBS object in the viewport, and choose the **Modify** tab in the **Command Panel**; various rollouts will be displayed in the modify panel. The options in these rollouts are used to modify the NURBS objects. These rollouts are discussed next.

Note

1. Most of the rollouts are the same for the NURBS curves and surfaces.

*2. The options in the **Rendering** rollout are the same as discussed earlier.*

General Rollout

This rollout will be available for all NURBS objects. The buttons on top of the **General** rollout are used to add more objects to the selected NURBS object. The **Display** area is used to define the way in which the NURBS object will be displayed in the viewports, refer to Figure 16-11.

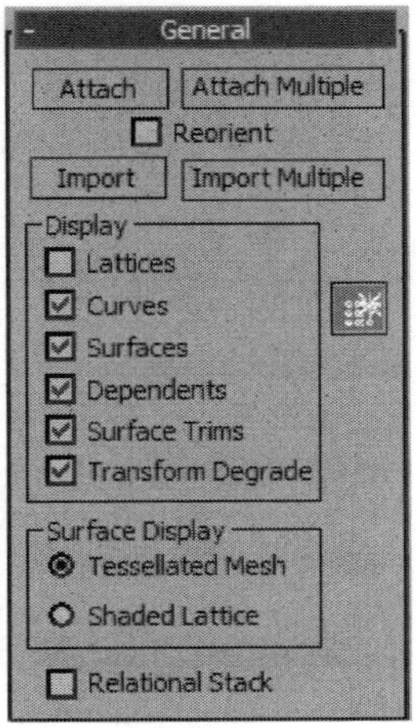

***Figure 16-11** The **General** rollout*

The **Attach** button is used to add other objects in the viewport to the selected NURBS object in the viewport. Once the objects in the viewport are added to the selected NURBS object, they will be converted into NURBS objects, and will become the sub-object of the NURBS object. Also, the original parameters of the additional objects will be lost. Choose the **Attach Multiple** button to add more than one object to the selected NURBS object at the same time.

The **Import** and **Import Multiple** buttons are also used to perform the same function as the **Attach** and **Attach Multiple** buttons. The only difference is that while using the **Import** and **Import Multiple** buttons, the original parameters of the objects are not lost.

Display Area

The check boxes in the **Display** area are used to define the way in which the NURBS object will be displayed in the viewports. In the NURBS curves objects, the **Lattices**, **Curves**, and **Dependents** check boxes are available in the **Display** area. But, in the NURBS surfaces objects, three additional check boxes are available. These are **Surfaces**, **Surface Trims**, and **Transform Degrade**. You need to select the required check box to make the corresponding option available in the viewport.

Surface Display Area

This area is available only for the NURBS surface objects. By default, the **Tessellated Mesh** radio button is selected in this area. As a result, the selected NURBS object will be displayed as iso lines or as mesh object in the viewport, depending on the settings made in the **Display Line Parameters** rollout, refer to Figures 16-12 and 16-13. Select the **Shaded Lattice** radio button to display the NURBS surface object as the shaded lattices in the shaded viewports, as shown in Figure 16-14.

NURBS Creation Toolbox

This button is available on the right of the **Display** area. When you choose this button, the **NURBS** toolbox will be displayed, as shown in Figure 16-15.

Note

The buttons in the ***NURBS*** *toolbox perform the same functions as the buttons in the* ***Create Points****,* ***Create Curves****, and* ***Create Surfaces*** *rollouts. These buttons will be discussed later in this chapter.*

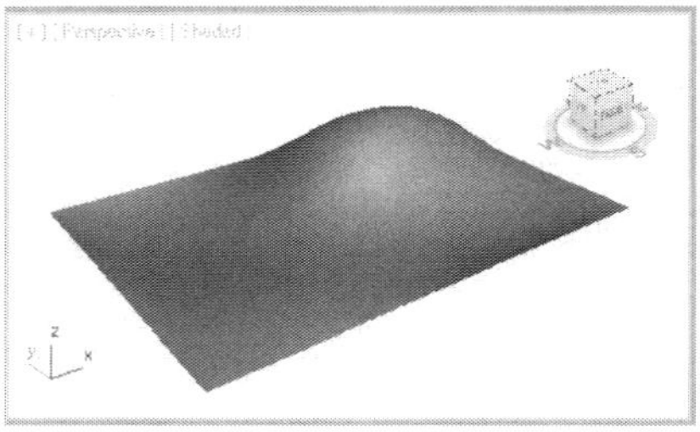

Figure 16-12 *The NURBS surface object displayed as a mesh object*

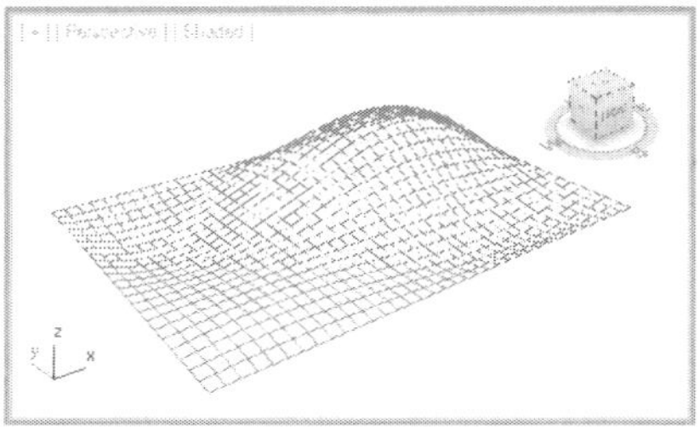

Figure 16-13 *The NURBS surface object displayed as iso lines*

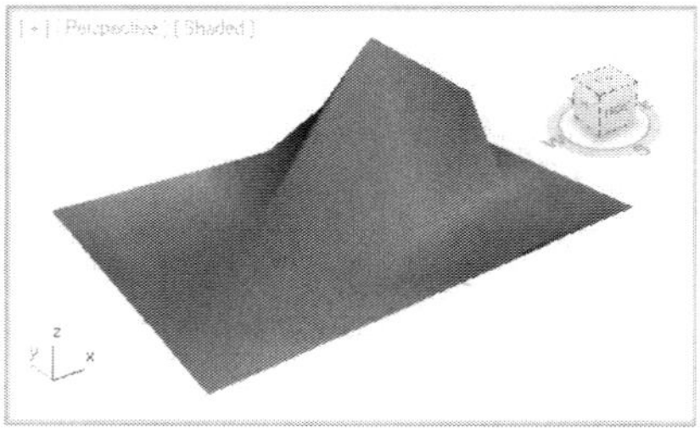

Figure 16-14 *The NURBS surface object displayed as shaded lattices*

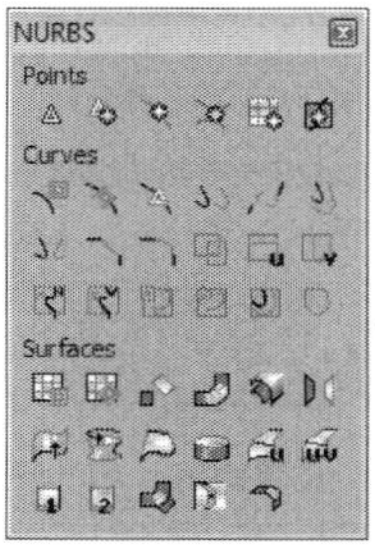

Figure 16-15 *The* ***NURBS*** *toolbox*

Display Line Parameters Rollout

This rollout is available only for the NURBS surface objects, refer to Figure 16-16. The values in the **U Lines** and **V Lines** spinners define the number of iso lines used to create the wireframe of the NURBS surface object in the viewport. Select the **Iso Only** radio button to display only the iso lines of the NURBS surface object in all viewports. The **Iso And Mesh** radio button is selected by default. It is used to display the iso lines of the NURBS object in those viewports that are set to display the wireframes. Also, the shaded viewports display the shaded surface of the NURBS object.

Select the **Mesh Only** radio button to display the NURBS object as a wire mesh in those viewports that are set to display the wireframes. Also, the shaded viewports display the shaded surface of the NURBS object.

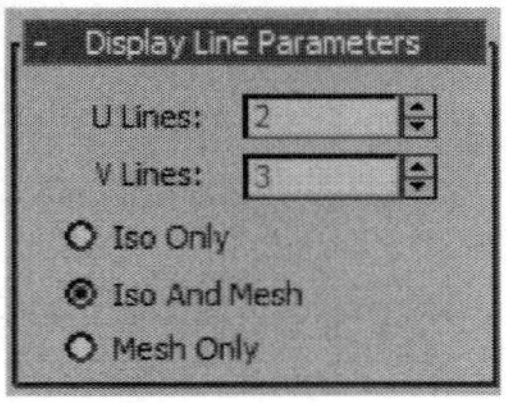

Figure 16-16 *The* ***Display Line Parameters*** *rollout*

Note
In the NURBS modeling, an iso line is known as a line of constant parameter value, similar to a contour line.

Tip: *To set a viewport to display the wireframes, click on the Shaded viewport label; a quad menu will be displayed. Now, choose the* ***Wireframe*** *option in it. Alternatively, you can press the F3 key.*

Before working with the other rollouts, you need to learn about the NURBS sub-objects. The buttons in the **Create Points**, **Create Curves**, and **Create Surfaces** rollouts are used to add the sub-objects in the NURBS curve and surface objects. These sub-objects can be dependent or independent. In other words, they can be child or parent sub-objects. For example, in the loft object shown in Figure 16-17, the surfaces are the dependent sub-objects as they are created from the curves. If you make any change in the curve, then the surface of the loft object will also be affected. But, the curves are the independent sub-objects because they are not created from any other object.

Create Points Rollout

The buttons in this rollout are used to add the point sub-objects to a NURBS object, refer to Figure 16-18. You can add the point sub-objects on the curve or surface as well as outside the curve or surface. These additional points help you to create fit curves or to trim the curves. To create different types of points, select the NURBS object in the viewport, choose the **Modify** tab, and then choose the corresponding button from the **Create Points** rollout. Alternatively, choose the **Nurbs Creation Toolbox** button from the **General** rollout; the **NURBS** toolbox will be displayed. Now, choose the corresponding button from the **Points** area in the **NURBS** toolbox. The point sub-objects are discussed next.

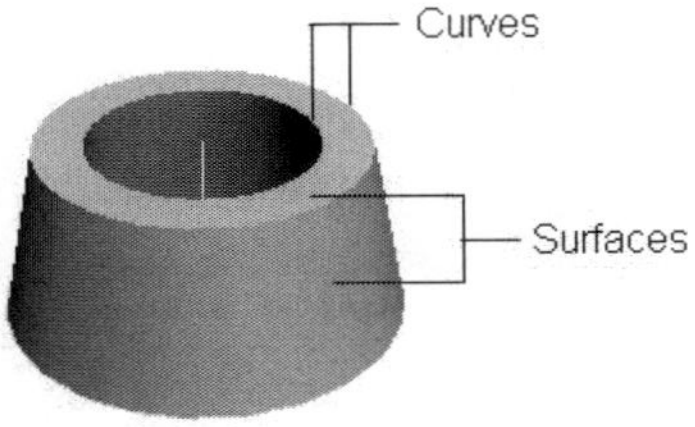

Figure 16-17 *The dependent and independent sub-objects in a loft object*

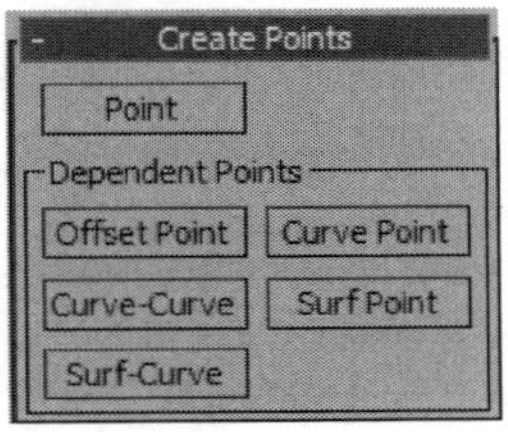

Figure 16-18 *The* ***Create Points*** *rollout*

Point

If you want to add an independent point, then select the NURBS object in the viewport. Next, choose the **Point** button in the **Create Points** rollout. Now, when you move the cursor in the viewport, the cursor will get changed, as shown in Figure 16-19. Now, click in the viewport to create a point and continue clicking to add more points. Next, right-click to exit the command. These points will be displayed as triangles in the viewport, as shown in Figure 16-20.

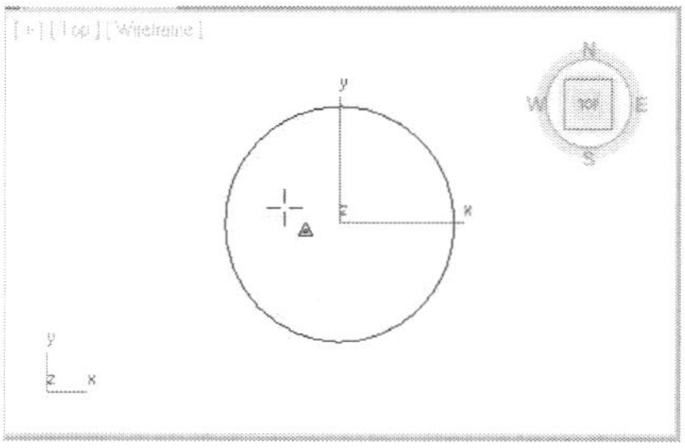

Figure 16-19 The cursor displayed to create independent points

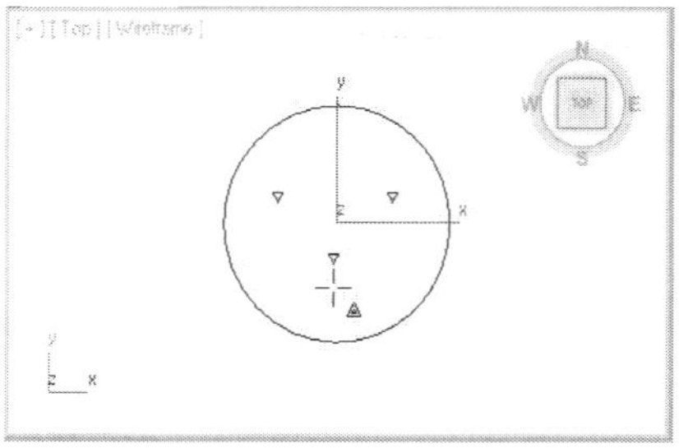

Figure 16-20 The independent points created in the viewport

Offset Point

An offset point is a dependent sub-object and lies at a specified distance from the parent point. To create an offset point, select the NURBS object in the viewport. Then, choose the **Offset Point** button in the **Create Points** rollout; the **Offset Point** rollout will be displayed at the bottom in the modify panel, as shown in Figure 16-21. Now, move the cursor over the existing point in the viewport; the cursor will get changed. Click on the existing point; a dependent offset point will be created as green asterisk in the viewport, as shown in Figure 16-22. Next, in the modify panel, expand the **Offset Point** rollout and set the values in the **X**, **Y**, and **Z** spinners to offset the new point from the original position. As you set the new values in these spinners, the distance between the offset point and its parent will be displayed as red line, as shown in Figure 16-23. If you do not want to change the position of the offset point, then select the **At Point** radio button in the **Offset Point** rollout.

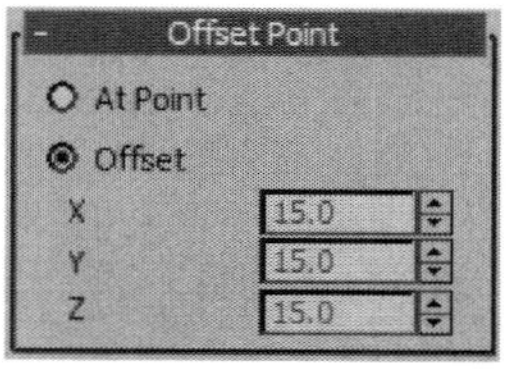

*Figure 16-21 The **Offset Point** rollout*

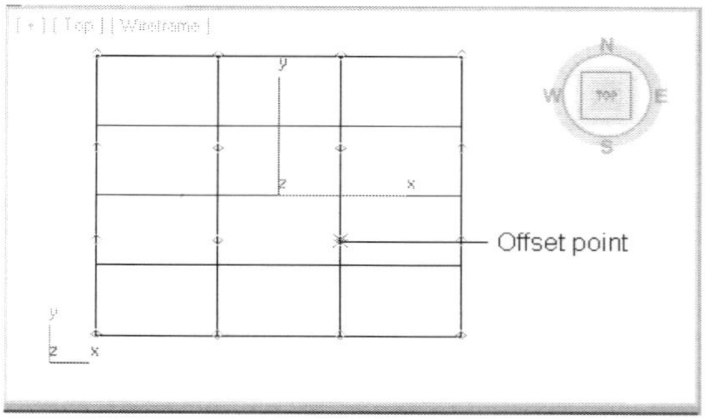

Figure 16-22 The offset point displayed

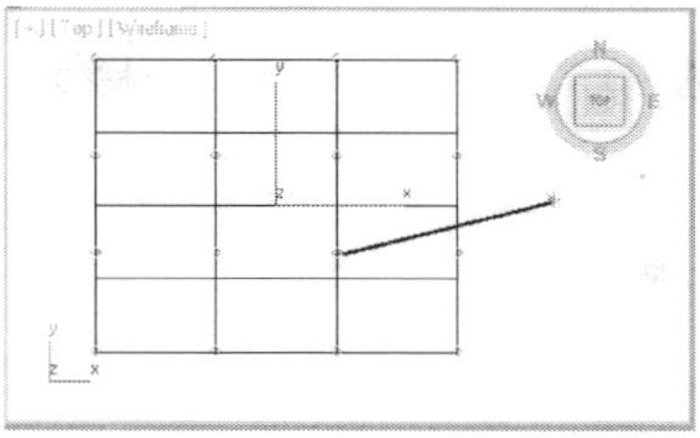

Figure 16-23 *The red line displayed between the parent point and the offset point*

Note

The independent point sub-objects will be displayed as black triangles in the viewports. And, the dependent point sub-objects will be displayed as green asterisks in the viewports.

Curve Point

A curve point is also a dependent sub-object and lies on a NURBS curve. To create a curve point, select the NURBS curve object in the viewport. Then, choose the **Curve Point** button in the **Create Points** rollout; the **Curve Point** rollout will be displayed in the modify panel, as shown in Figure 16-24. Alternatively, you can choose the **Create Curve Point** button from the **NURBS** toolbox in the **General** rollout. Now, move the cursor over the curve; the curve will turn blue. Also, a blue box along with the cursor will be displayed on the curve, as shown in Figure 16-25. Now, position the blue box on the curve at the location where you want to add a point and then click to add it. Next, you need to modify the parameters in the **Curve Point** rollout, which is discussed next.

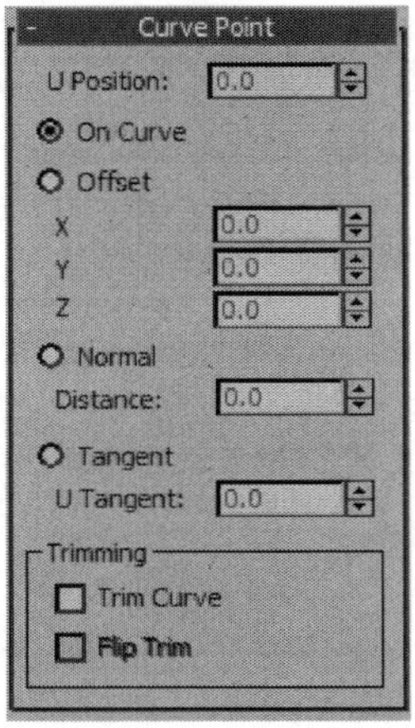

Figure 16-24 *The **Curve Point** rollout*

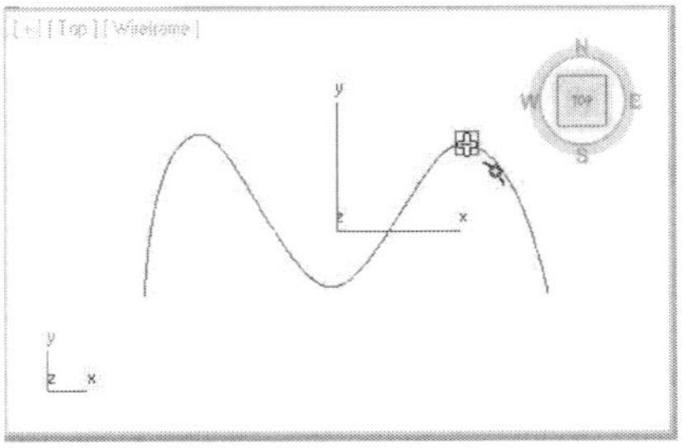

Figure 16-25 *A blue box displayed along with the cursor*

Curve Point Rollout

Set the value in the **U Position** spinner to define the position of the point on the curve. The **On Curve** radio button is selected by default and is used to position the point on the curve.

Select the **Offset** radio button to offset the points from the curve. Set the values in the **X**, **Y**, and **Z** spinners to define the location of the point in space.

Select the **Normal** radio button to offset the point along the curve's normal at the U position. Set the value in the **Distance** spinner to specify the distance of the point from the curve's normal.

Select the **Tangent** radio button to offset the point along the tangent at the U position. Set the value in the **U Tangent** spinner to specify the distance of the point from the curve along the tangent.

The options in the **Trimming** area are used to trim the curve. Select the **Trim Curve** check box to trim the curve according to the position of the curve point, refer to Figures 16-26 and 16-27. Select the **Flip Trim** check box to trim the curve in the opposite direction, refer to Figure 16-28.

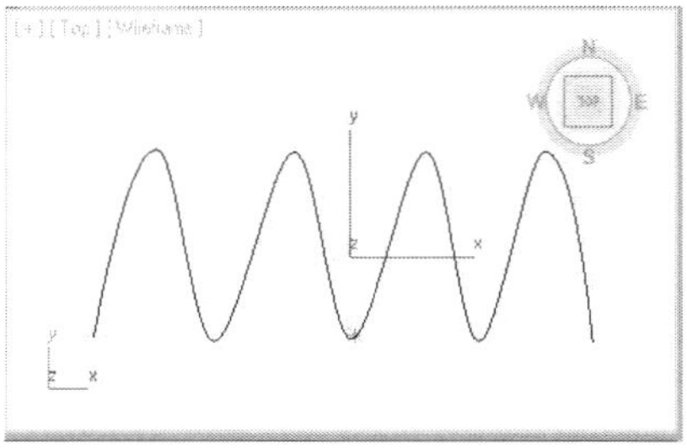

Figure 16-26 *A curve point placed on the curve*

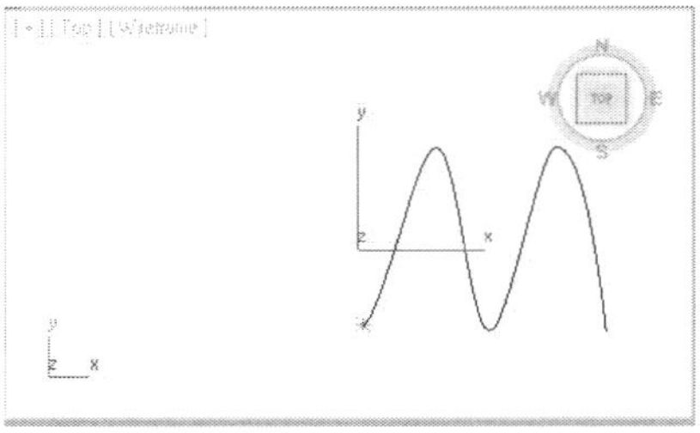

Figure 16-27 *The curve after selecting the **Trim Curve** check box*

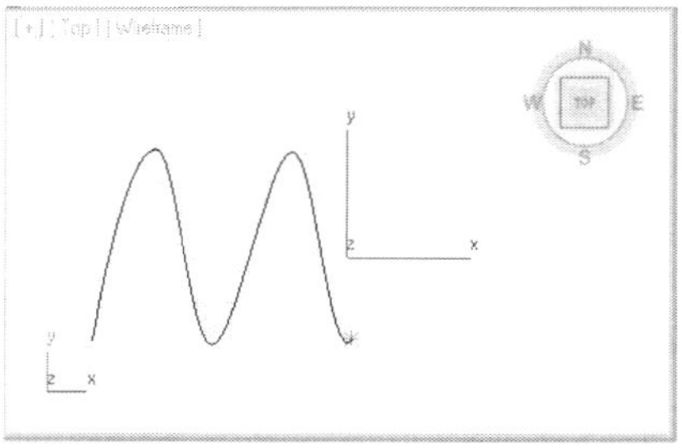

Figure 16-28 *The curve after selecting the **Flip Trim** check box*

Curve-Curve Intersection Point

The curve-curve intersection point is a dependent point sub-object created at the intersection of two NURBS curve objects, refer to Figure 16-29. Note that to create a curve-curve intersection point, the two selected NURBS curves should be attached to each other. To create this point, choose the **Curve-Curve** button in the **Create Points** rollout; the **Curve-Curve Intersection** rollout will be displayed in the modify panel. Now, move the cursor over one of the NURBS curves; a blue box will be displayed along with the cursor. Click on the curve to place the first seed and then click on another curve to place the second seed; an intersection point will be created at the nearest intersection between the curves and the point that is nearest to the seed points, refer to Figure 16-29. You can modify the curve-curve point by specifying the parameters in this rollout.

Surface Point

A surface point is also a dependent sub-object and lies on a NURBS surface. To create a surface point, select the NURBS surface object in the viewport. Now, choose the **Surf Point** button in the **Create Points** rollout; the **Surface Point** rollout will be displayed in the modify panel. Alternatively, you can choose the **Create Surf Point** button from the **NURBS** toolbox in the **General** rollout. Now, move the cursor over the NURBS surface; a pair of intersecting blue lines will be displayed along with the cursor, as shown in Figure 16-30. Click on the surface where you want to add a point and then modify its parameters in the **Surface Point** rollout in the modify panel. Next, right-click to exit the command. The options in the **Surface Point** rollout are the same as those discussed earlier in the **Curve Point** rollout.

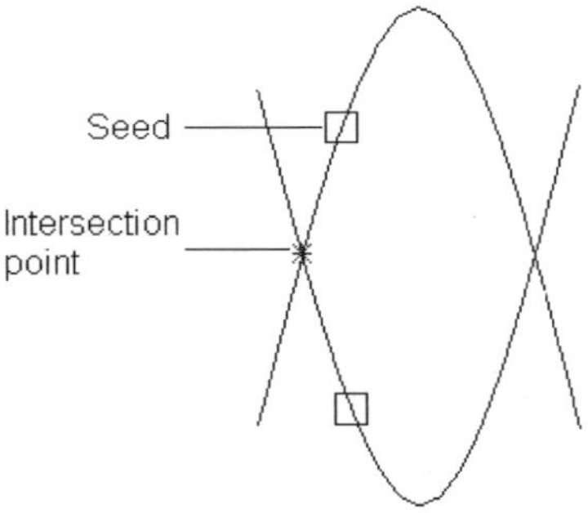

Figure 16-29 *The intersection point created*

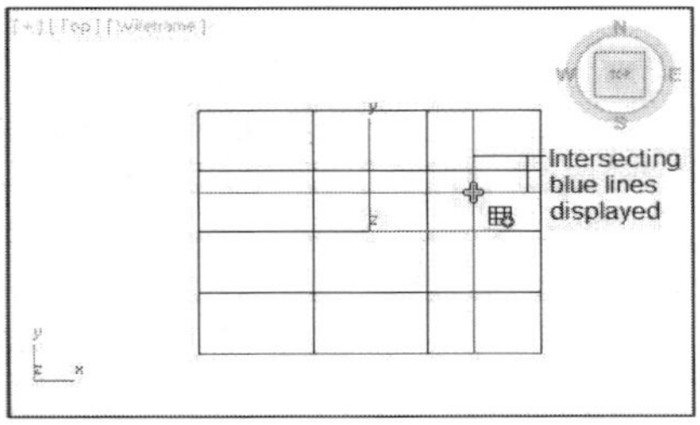

Figure 16-30 *The blue lines displayed*

Surface-Curve Intersection Point

The surface-curve intersection point is a dependent point sub-object created on the intersection of a NURBS curve and a NURBS surface object, refer to Figure 16-31. Note that to create a surface-curve intersection point, the NURBS curve and the NURBS surface should be attached to each other. To create this point, choose the **Surf-Curve** button in the **Create Points** rollout; the **Surface-Curve Intersection Point** rollout will be displayed in the modify panel. Now, move the cursor over the NURBS curve; a blue box will be displayed along with the cursor. Click on the curve to place the first seed. Then, move the cursor over the NURBS surface object; a blue box will be displayed along with the cursor. Click on it to place the second seed; an intersection point will be created at the nearest intersection between the curve and the surface that is nearest to the seed point, refer to Figures 16-31, 16-32, and 16-33. You can modify the surface-curve point by specifying the parameters in the **Surface-Curve Intersection Point** rollout.

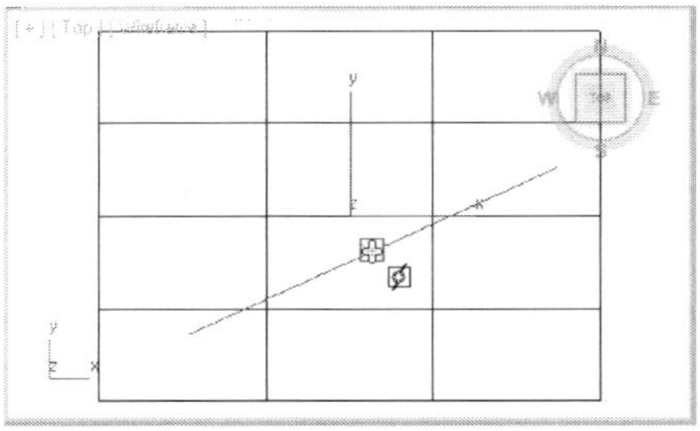

Figure 16-31 A seed created on the NURBS curve

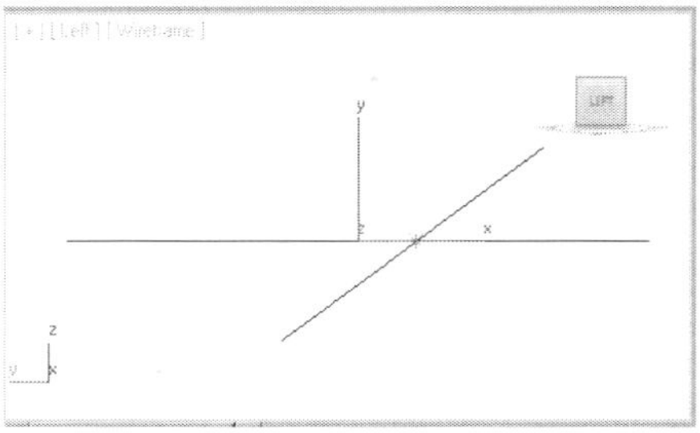

Figure 16-32 A surface curve intersection point created in the Left viewport

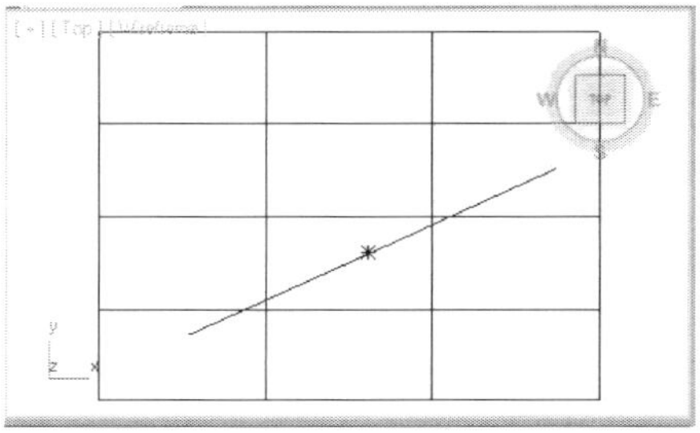

Figure 16-33 A surface curve intersection point created in the Top viewport

Create Curves Rollout

The buttons in this rollout are used to add the curve sub-objects to a NURBS object, refer to Figure 16-34. The curve sub-objects can be dependent or independent. The geometry of the dependent curves sub-objects depends on the curves, points, and surfaces of the NURBS object. The independent curve sub-objects can be added to an existing NURBS model. To create the curve sub-objects, select the NURBS object in the viewport, choose the **Modify** tab, and then choose the corresponding button from the **Create Curves** rollout. Some of the dependent and independent curves are discussed next.

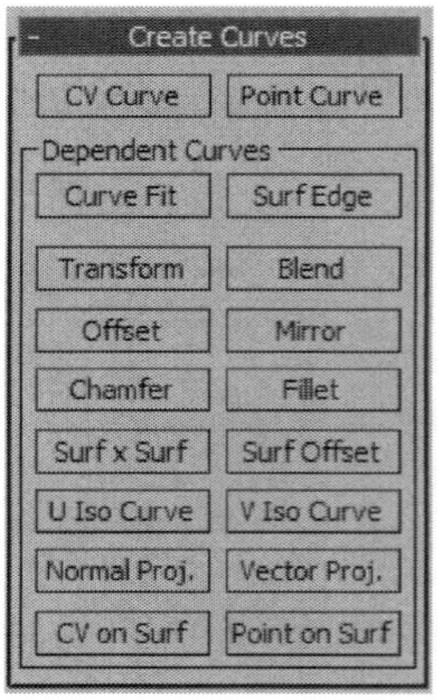

*Figure 16-34 The **Create Curves** rollout*

CV Curve

The CV curve sub-object is an independent curve sub-object. It is very much similar to the CV curve object. The only difference is that the CV curve sub-object cannot be provided the thickness at rendering. To create a CV curve sub-object, select the NURBS object in the viewport and then choose the **Modify** tab in the **Command Panel**. Now, choose the **CV Curve** button in the **Create Curves** rollout; the **CV Curve** rollout will be displayed in the modify panel. Also, the cursor will get changed, as shown in Figure 16-35. Now, create a CV curve in the viewport and then right-click to exit the command; the new CV curve will be added to the existing NURBS object, refer to Figures 16-36 and 16-37.

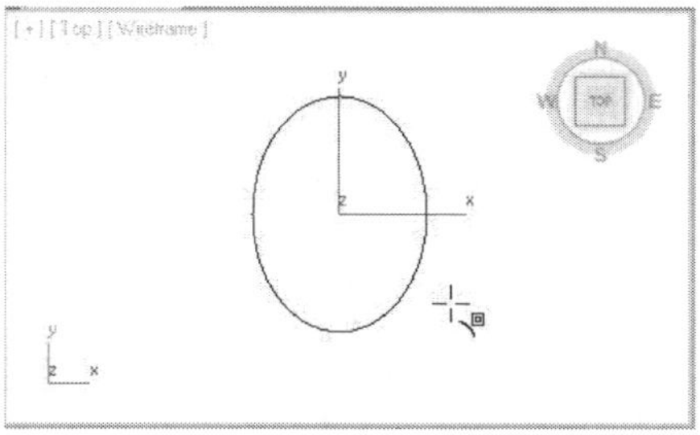

Figure 16-35 *The cursor changed after choosing the **CV Curve** button*

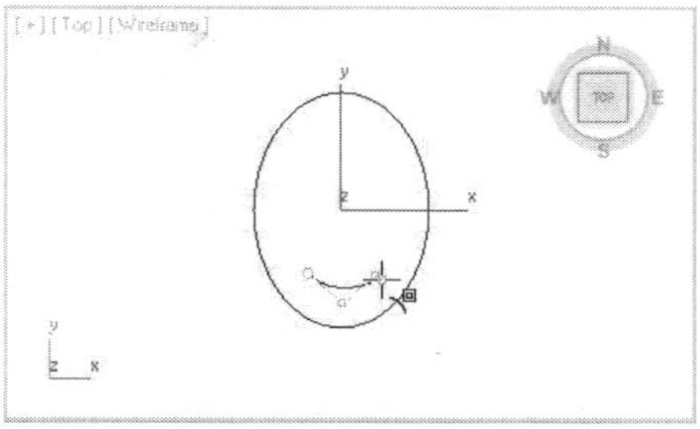

Figure 16-36 *The new CV curve created*

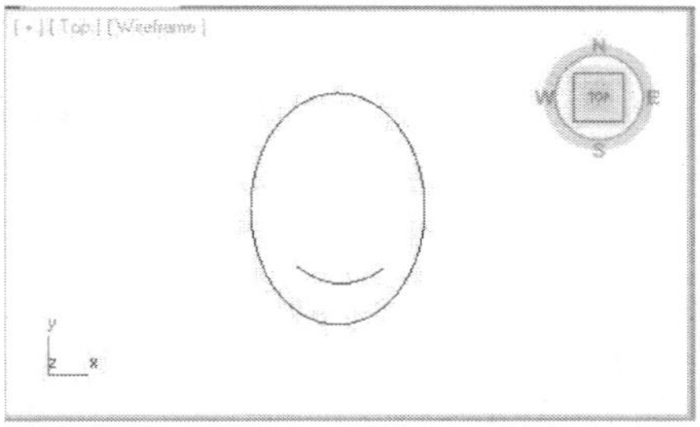

Figure 16-37 *The new CV curve attached to the NURBS object*

Point Curve

The point curve sub-object is also an independent curve sub-object and is very similar to the point curve object. The only difference is that the point curve sub-object cannot be provided the thickness at rendering. To create a point curve sub-object, select the NURBS object in the viewport. Now, choose the **Point Curve** button from the **Create Curves** rollout; the **Point Curve** rollout will be displayed in the modify panel. Now, create a point curve in the viewport and right-click to exit the command; the new point curve will be added to the existing NURBS object.

Fit Curve

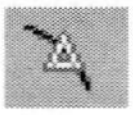

The fit curve is a dependent curve sub-object and is created between the existing points in a NURBS object. A fit curve can be created using any type of points such as curve points, surface points, independent points, and so on. To create a fit curve, select the NURBS object in the viewport and choose the **Modify** tab in the **Command Panel**. Next, in the **General** rollout, choose the **NURBS Creation Toolbox** button; the **NURBS** toolbox will be displayed. Next, choose the **Create Fit Curve** button in the **Curves** area; the cursor will get changed. Also, the **Point Curve** rollout will be displayed in the modify panel. Notice that there are no parameters in this rollout. Next, move the cursor over a point in the viewport and click to create the starting point of the fit curve. Now, drag the cursor to another point and click on it to continue the creation of the fit curve, refer to Figures 16-38 and 16-39. Next, right-click to exit the command.

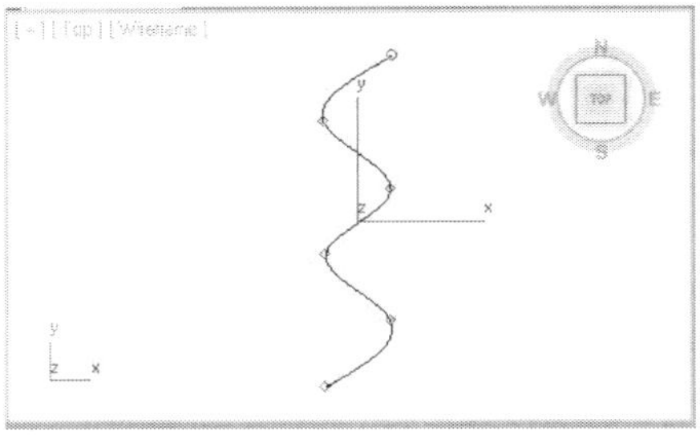

Figure 16-38 *A NURBS curve object*

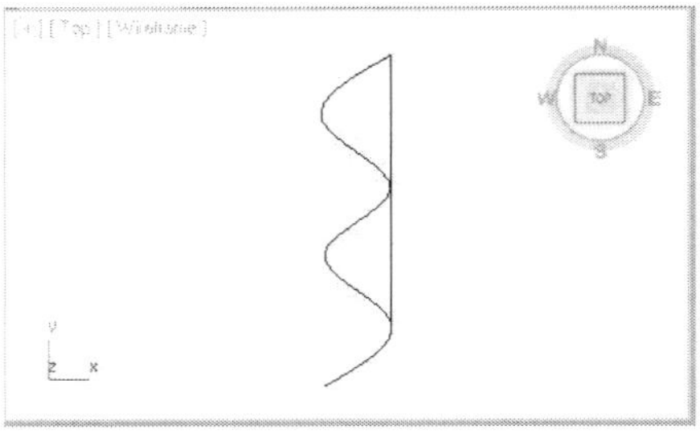

Figure 16-39 *A fit curve created between the points in a NURBS curve object*

Transform Curve

The transform curve is a dependent curve sub-object. It is a duplicate of the original curve and can be modified to a different position, rotation, or scale. To create a transform curve, select the NURBS curve in the viewport and choose the **Modify** tab in the **Command Panel**. Now, in the **General** rollout, choose the **NURBS Creation Toolbox** button; the **NURBS** toolbox will be displayed. Next, choose the **Create Transform Curve** button in the **Curves** area; the cursor will get changed. Then, move the cursor over the NURBS curve; it will turn blue. Now, press and hold the left mouse button on the curve, drag the cursor to create the duplicate of the selected curve, and then release the left mouse button; a transform curve will be created, refer to Figures 16-40 and 16-41.

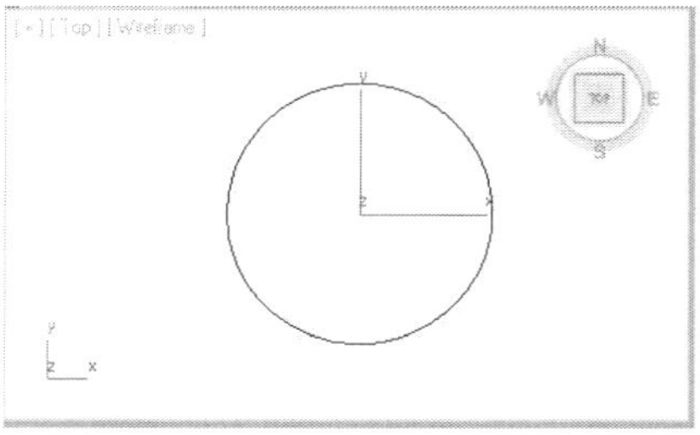

Figure 16-40 *A NURBS curve object*

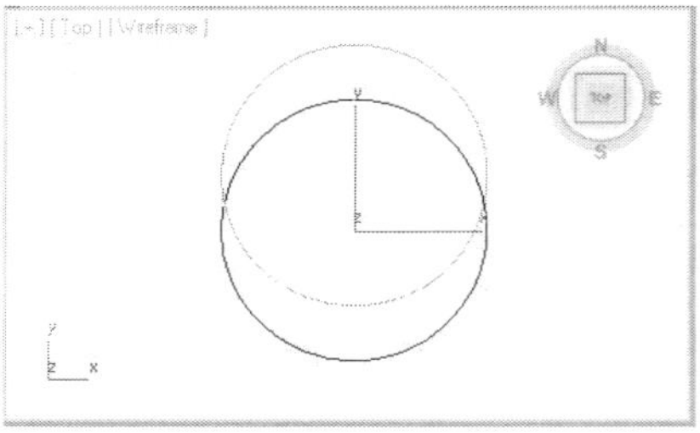

Figure 16-41 *A transform curve created*

To rotate or scale the duplicate curve, select the **Curve** sub-object level in the modifier stack, and then select the duplicate curve in the viewport. Next, rotate or scale the duplicate curve without affecting the original curve.

Chamfer Curve

The chamfer curve is a dependent curve sub-object. It is a straight line between two intersecting parent curve sub-objects. To create a chamfer curve, select the NURBS object that has the intersecting and attached curve sub-objects, as shown in Figure 16-42.

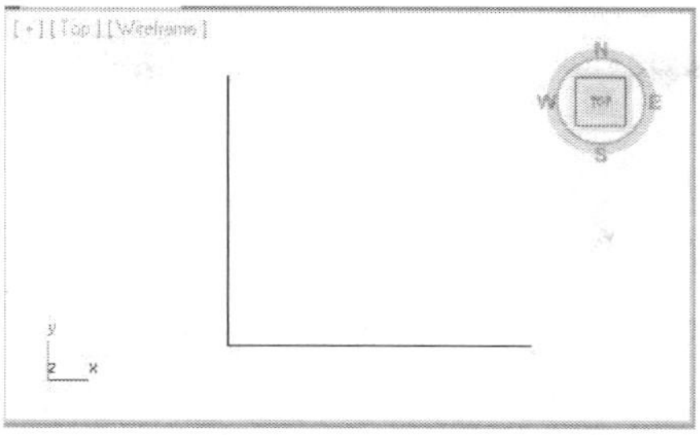

Figure 16-42 *A NURBS curve to create a chamfer curve*

Now, choose the **Modify** tab in the **Command Panel**. In the **General** rollout, choose the **NURBS Creation Toolbox** button; the **NURBS** toolbox will be displayed. Then, choose the **Create Chamfer Curve** button in the **Curves** area; the cursor will get changed. Also, the **Chamfer Curve** rollout will be displayed in the modify panel. Move the cursor over a curve in the NURBS object; the curve will turn blue. Also, a blue box will be displayed along with the cursor. Click on the curve to place the first seed to define the intersection to be chamfered. Then, move the cursor over another curve in the NURBS object and click to place another seed; a chamfer curve will be created, refer to Figures 16-43 and 16-44. You can modify the chamfer curve using the parameters in the **Chamfer Curve** rollout in the modify panel and then right-click to exit the command.

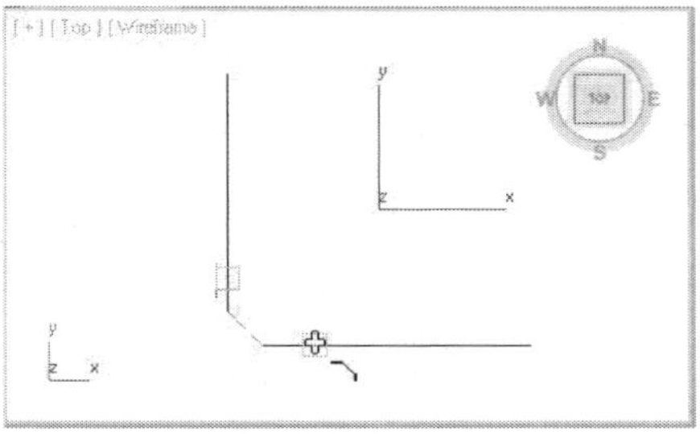

Figure 16-43 *The seeds placed on the curves*

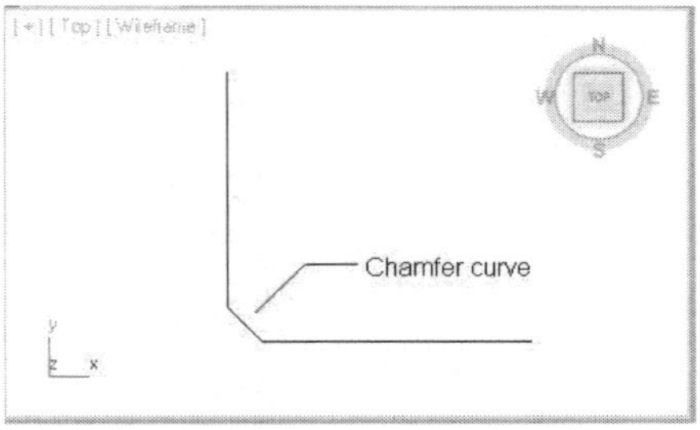

Figure 16-44 *A chamfer curve created*

Note

*While creating a chamfer curve, one or both the curves of the NURBS object get trimmed. To avoid the trimming of the curves, you can modify their parameters in the **Chamfer Curve** rollout.*

Surface Edge Curve

The surface edge curve is also a dependent curve and it lies on the boundary of the surface. The edge can be an outside edge or a trim edge. To create a surface edge curve, select the NURBS object that has a surface. Then, choose the **Modify** tab in the **Command Panel**. In the **General** rollout, choose the **NURBS Creation Toolbox** button; the **NURBS** toolbox will be displayed. Choose the **Create Surface Edge Curve** button in the **Curves** area; the cursor will get changed. Also, the **Surface Edge Curve** rollout will be displayed in the modify panel. Move the cursor over an edge in the NURBS object; the edge will be highlighted. Now, click on the edge; the surface edge will be created. Also, a seed will be displayed on the edge, as shown in Figure 16-45.

Create Surfaces Rollout

The buttons in this rollout are used to add surface sub-objects to a NURBS object, refer to Figure 16-46. The surface sub-objects can be dependent or independent. The geometry of the dependent surface sub-object depends on the curves and surfaces of another NURBS object. To create the surface sub-objects, select the NURBS object in the viewport, choose the **Modify** tab in the **Command Panel**, and then choose the corresponding button from the **Create Surfaces** rollout. Some of the dependent and independent surfaces are discussed next.

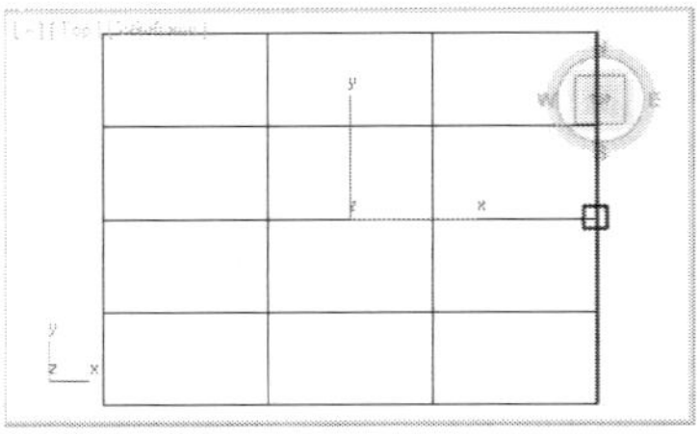

Figure 16-45 *A surface edge curve created*

Note

*The CV surface and point surface sub-objects are independent sub-objects. They can be added to the existing NURBS object using the **CV Surf** and **Point Surf** buttons in the **Create Surfaces** rollout.*

Blend Surface

A blend surface is a dependent surface sub-object that is used to connect two surfaces, two curves, or a curve to a surface. To create a blend surface, select the NURBS object in the viewport that contains two or more attached curves or surface sub-objects. Next, choose the **Modify** tab in the **Command Panel** and then choose the **Blend** button from the **Create Surfaces** rollout; the **Blend Surface** rollout will be displayed. Next, move the cursor over the edge that you want to connect; the edge will turn blue. Click on the edge and move the cursor over the edge of another NURBS object, as shown in Figure 16-47. Now, click on the edge of another NURBS object; a blend surface will be created between the two NURBS objects, as shown in Figure 16-48. You can modify the blend surface using the parameters in the **Blend Surface** rollout in the modify panel. Then, right-click to exit the command.

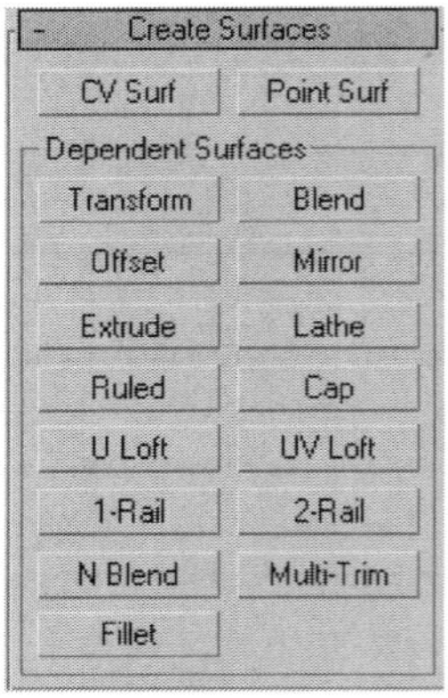

Figure 16-46 *The **Create Surfaces** rollout*

Ruled Surface

A ruled surface is a dependent sub-object. It can be created between two curve sub-objects. To create a ruled surface, select the NURBS object in the viewport that contains two or more curves. Next, choose the **Modify** tab in the **Command Panel** and then choose the **Ruled** button from the **Create Surfaces** rollout; the **Ruled Surf** rollout will be displayed. Next, move the cursor over the curve that you want to use to create the ruled surface; the curve will turn blue. Now, click on the curve and move the cursor over another curve, refer to Figure 16-49. Now, click on another curve; a ruled surface will be created between the two NURBS curves, as shown in Figure 16-50. You can modify the ruled surface using the parameters in the **Ruled Surf** rollout in the modify panel. Then, right-click to exit the command.

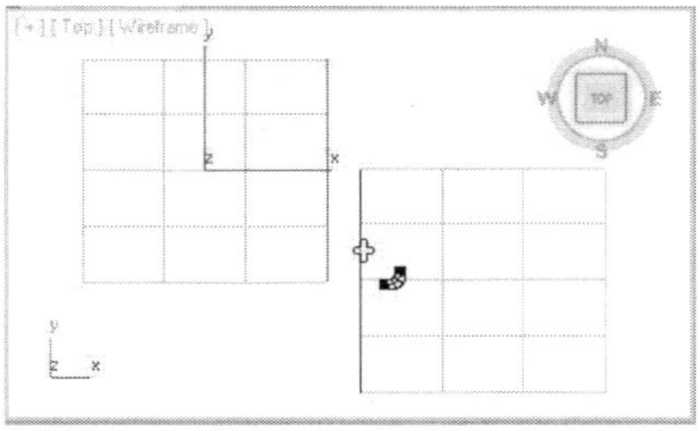

Figure 16-47 *The cursor placed over another edge*

Figure 16-48 *A blend surface created*

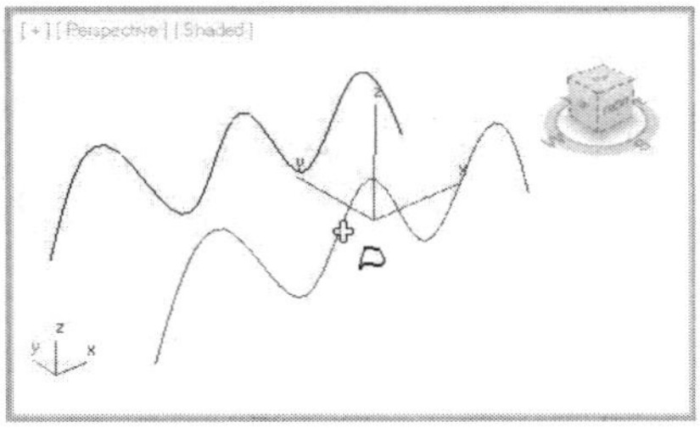

Figure 16-49 *The cursor displayed to create the ruled surface*

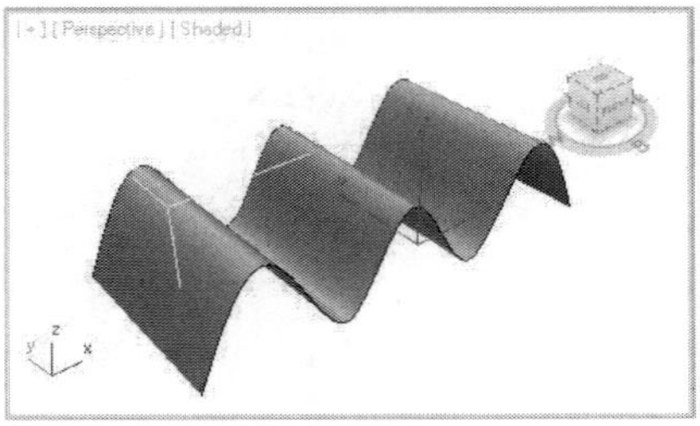

Figure 16-50 *A ruled surface created*

U Loft Surface

A U loft surface is a dependent surface sub-object and it is created across multiple curve sub-objects. To get the best effect, the curves that are to be used for U lofting should have the same number of CVs. To create a U loft surface, select one of the NURBS curves in the viewport. Choose the **Modify** tab in the **Command Panel** and then choose the **U Loft** button from the **Create Surfaces** rollout; the **U Loft Surface** rollout will be displayed. Next, move the cursor over the first curve that you want to use for creating the U loft surface; it will turn blue. Now, click on it and then click on all curves one-by-one to add them into the U loft surface. When you click on the curves, their names will be displayed in the **U Curves** area of the **U Loft Surface** rollout. Also, while adding the curves into the U loft surface, the green colored iso lines of the U loft surface will be displayed in the viewport, as shown in Figure 16-51. Next, right-click to end the command; a U loft surface will be created, as shown in Figure 16-52. Now, you can modify the U loft surface using the parameters in the **U Loft Surface** rollout. Next, right-click to exit the U loft command.

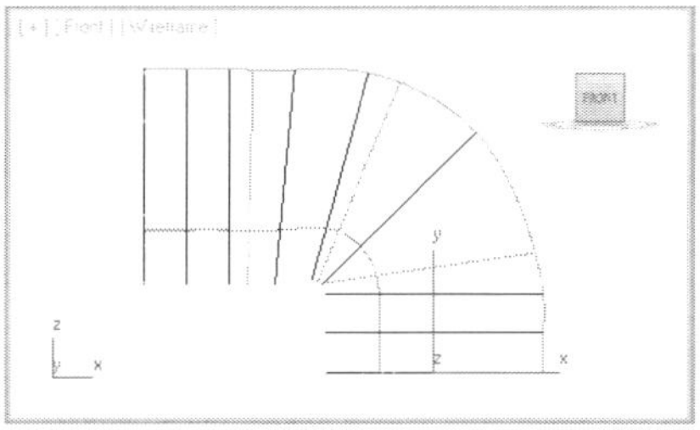

Figure 16-51 The green iso lines of the U loft surface displayed in the Front viewport

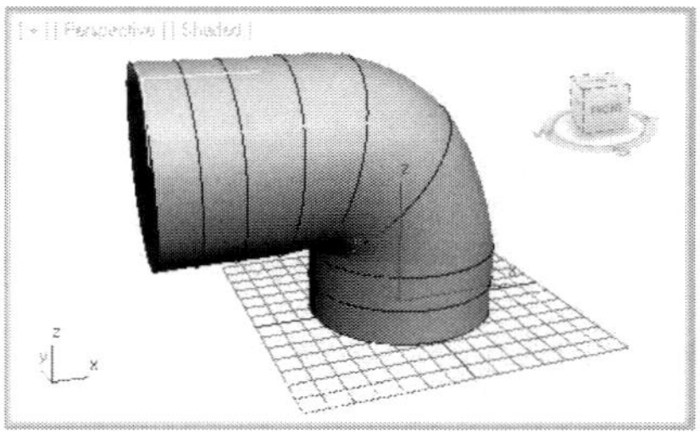

Figure 16-52 A U loft surface created

1-Rail Sweep Surface

The 1-rail sweep surface is a dependent sub-object. To create a 1-rail sweep surface, minimum two curves are required in the viewport. One curve is used to define the cross-section of the surface and another curve is used to define the edge of the surface, which is known as rail. Before creating a sweep surface, you need to make sure that the cross-section curve is intersecting the rail curve. The first cross-section curve should intersect the starting point of the rail and the last cross-section curve should intersect the end point of the rail. Also, the curves that you are using to create the cross-section of the surface should have the same direction.

Select the NURBS object that has the rail and cross-section curves, as shown in Figure 16-53. Choose the **Modify** tab in the **Command Panel** and then choose the **1-Rail** button from the **Create Surfaces** rollout; the **1-Rail Sweep Surface** rollout will be displayed. Next, move the cursor over the rail curve; the rail curve will turn blue. Click on it; the name of the rail curve will be displayed in the **Rail Curve** text box of the **1-Rail Sweep Surface** rollout. Select the first cross-section curve and add the other cross-section curves by selecting them one-by-one. When you click on the cross-section curves, their names will be displayed in the **Section Curves** area of the **1-Rail Sweep Surface** rollout. Next, right-click to end the command; a 1-rail surface will be created, as shown in Figure 16-54. You can modify the 1-rail surface using the parameters in the **1-Rail Sweep Surface** rollout. Now, right-click to exit the 1-rail command.

Cap Surface

The cap surface is a dependent sub-object and is created to cap a closed curve or an edge of a closed surface. To create a cap surface, select the NURBS object that has either a closed curve or an open-ended closed surface, as shown in Figure 16-55. Now, choose the **Modify** tab in the **Command Panel** and then choose the **Cap** button from the **Create Surfaces** rollout; the **Cap Surface** rollout will be displayed. Next, move the cursor over the closed curve or the closed surface; it will be highlighted. Now, click on it; a cap surface will be created, as shown in Figure 16-56. Right-click to exit the cap command.

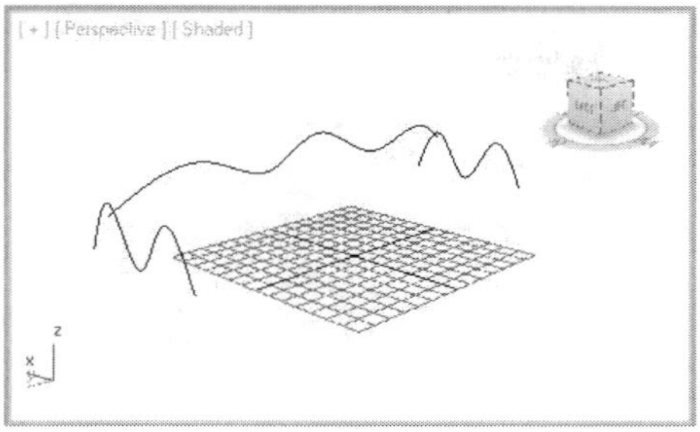

Figure 16-53 The curves to create 1-rail surface

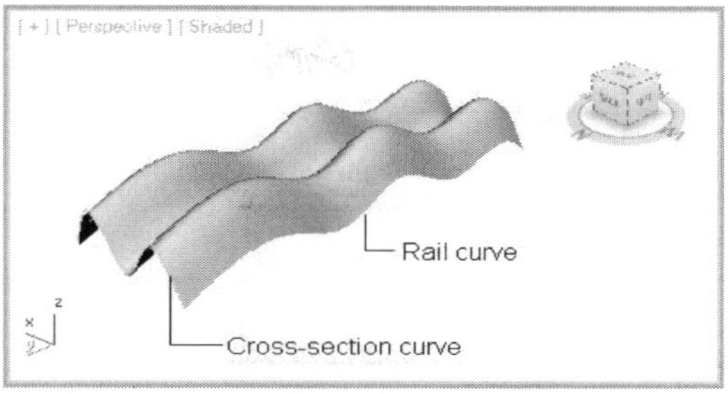

Figure 16-54 A 1-rail surface created

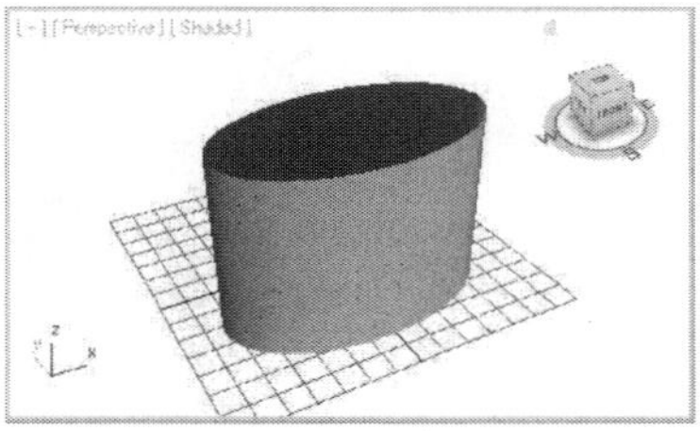

Figure 16-55 An open ended closed surface

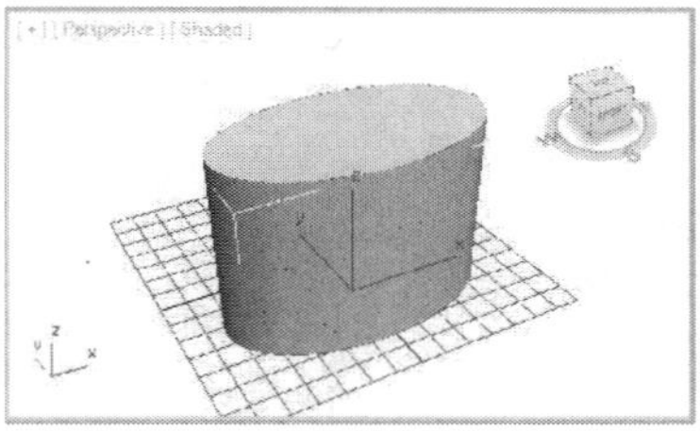

Figure 16-56 A cap created to cap the open end of the closed surface

EDITING NURBS SUB-OBJECTS

After creating a NURBS model or an object, you can edit it at the sub-object level. To do so, select the NURBS object in the viewport and choose the **Modify** tab in the **Command Panel**; the rollouts will be displayed in the modify panel to modify the NURBS object. You have already learned about modifying NURBS objects in the previous section. Now, to modify the NURBS object at the sub-object level, select the sub-object levels in the modifier stack.

First, click on the plus sign on the left side of **NURBS Surface** to display all the sub-object levels in the selected NURBS object, refer to Figure 16-57. Now, select a sub-object level in the modifier stack; it will turn yellow and get activated. Also, various rollouts related to the selected sub-object level will be displayed below the modifier stack.

Alternatively, right-click in the viewport; a quad menu will be displayed, as shown in Figure 16-58. Now, choose the sub-object level that you want to modify; it will also be activated in the modifier stack. Select the sub-object in the viewport and then modify it using the transforms or the rollouts displayed in the modify panel.

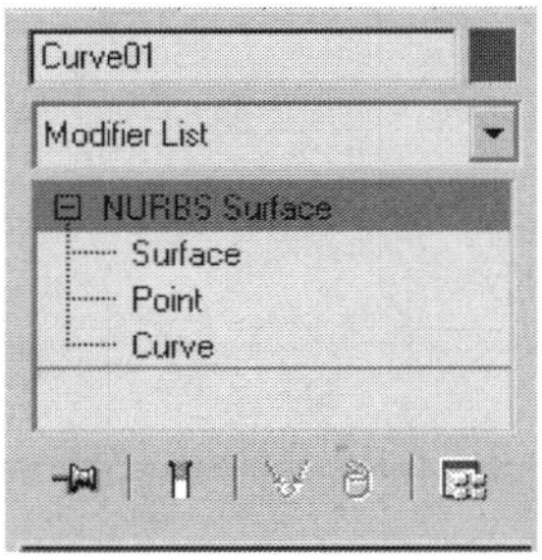

Figure 16-57 *The sub-object levels displayed in the modifier stack*

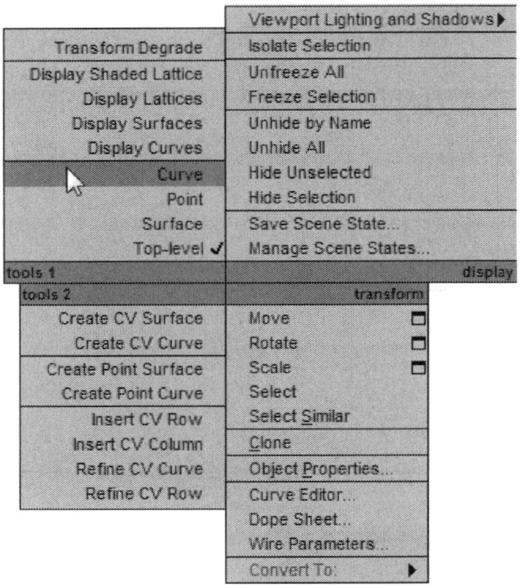

Figure 16-58 *The quad menu displayed to choose the sub-object level*

Tutorial 1

In this tutorial, you will create a washbasin, as shown in Figure 16-59, using the NURBS tools. **(Expected time: 60 min)**

Figure 16-59 *Model for Tutorial 1*

The following steps are required to complete this tutorial:

a. Set the project folder.
b. Create NURBS curves using splines.

c. Create washbasin and modify it using the NURBS curves.
d. Create washbasin, sieve, and duct.
e. Create washbasin slab.
f. Create washbasin taps.
g. Assign mental ray renderer and materials.
h. Render the scene for the final output.
i. Save the file.

Setting the Project Folder

1. Set the project folder with the name *c16_tut1* in the *3dsmax* folder as discussed in earlier chapters.

Creating NURBS Curves Using Splines

To create a washbasin, you need to create the elliptical NURBS curves.

1. Choose **Create > Shapes** in the **Command Panel** and then invoke the **Ellipse** tool from the **Object Type** rollout.

2. Create an ellipse in the Top viewport; it is automatically named as *Ellipse001*. Enter the values in the **Parameters** rollout as given below:

   Length: **111.739** Width: **202.96**

3. Invoke the **Zoom Extents All** tool.

   Next, you need to convert the *Ellipse001* to NURBS curve.

4. Select the *Ellipse001* in any viewport and right-click on it; a quad menu is displayed. Choose the **Convert To:** option in the quad menu; a cascading menu is displayed. Now, choose the **Convert to NURBS** option; the *Ellipse001* is converted into NURBS curve. Next, you need to create multiple copies of the *Ellipse001* to create the outer surface of the washbasin.

> **Tip**: *You can also create an elliptical curve using the* ***CV Curve*** *tool from* ***Create > Shapes > NURBS Curves > Object Type*** *rollout in the* ***Command Panel****. In this case, you do not need to convert it into NURBS curves.*

5. Select the *Ellipse001* in the Front viewport and move the cursor over its vertical axis. Press and hold the SHIFT key and the left mouse button and then move the *Ellipse001* in the upward direction by 16 points in the **Y** spinner of the coordinates display. Now, release the left mouse button and the SHIFT key; the **Clone Options** dialog box is displayed. Set the value **3** in the **Number of Copies** spinner and choose the **OK** button; the *Ellipse001*, *Ellipse002*, *Ellipse003*, and *Ellipse004* are displayed in all viewports, as shown in Figure 16-60.

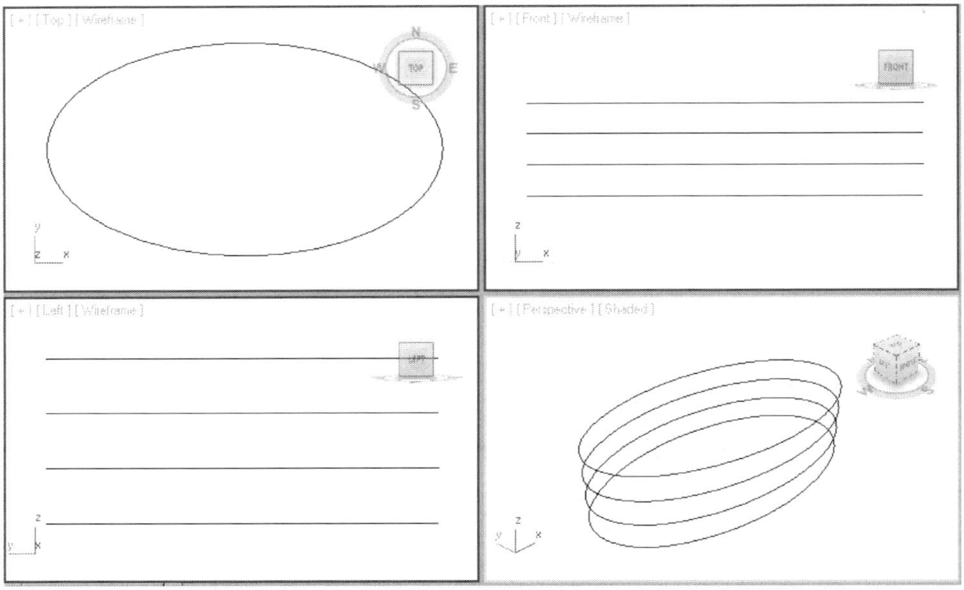

Figure 16-60 *All ellipses displayed in all viewports*

Next, you need to create the ellipses for the inner surface of the washbasin.

6. Select the *Ellipse004* (top ellipse spline) in the Front viewport. Now, move the cursor over the vertical axis of the *Ellipse004*. Press and hold the SHIFT key and the left mouse button and then move the *Ellipse004* in the downward direction until the value in the **Y** spinner in the coordinates display becomes about **-8**. Now, release the left mouse button and the SHIFT key; the **Clone Options** dialog box is displayed. Set the value **1** in the **Number of Copies** spinner and choose the **OK** button; the *Ellipse005* is displayed in all viewports.

7. Modify the color of the *Ellipse005* in such a way that you can differentiate between the curves for the inner and the outer surfaces.

8. Select the *Ellipse005* in the Front viewport and move the cursor over its vertical axis. Press and hold the SHIFT key and the left mouse button, and move the *Ellipse005* in the downward direction until the value in the **Y** spinner in the coordinates display becomes about **-16**. Now, release the left mouse button and the SHIFT key; the **Clone Options** dialog box is displayed. Set the value **3** in the **Number of Copies** spinner and choose the **OK** button; the *Ellipse006, Ellipse007*, and *Ellipse008* are created in all viewports. Now, there are total eight NURBS curves in the viewports.

Next, you need to scale the ellipses in the Front viewport.

9. Invoke the **Select and Uniform Scale** tool from the **Main Toolbar** and scale the NURBS curves uniformly in the Front viewport, as shown in Figure 16-61.

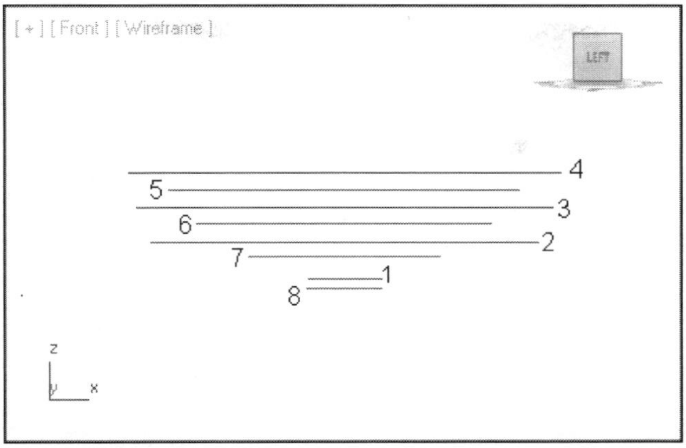

Figure 16-61 *All NURBS curves scaled in the Front viewport*

Creating Washbasin and Modifying it Using the NURBS Curves

Next, you need to create a surface between the NURBS curves in the viewport to give it a shape. To do so, you need to use the **U Loft** button.

1. Select the *Ellipse008* in the Front viewport and choose the **Modify** tab, if it is not already chosen. The **NURBS Surface** is displayed in the modifier stack and all rollouts to modify the NURBS object are displayed below the modifier stack.

2. Expand the **Create Surfaces** rollout and choose the **U Loft** button; the **U Loft Surface** rollout is displayed in the modify panel. Next, move the cursor over the *Ellipse008*; it turns blue. Now, click on the *Ellipse008* and then click one-by-one on the *Ellipse007, 006, 005, 004, 003, 002,* and *001* to add them into the U loft surface. Right-click to end the command. Then, in the **U Loft Surface** rollout, select the **Flip Normals** check box. Next, right-click to exit the U loft command; a NURBS surface is created in the viewports, as shown in Figure 16-62.

3. Modify the name of the surface to *washbasin*.

   Next, you need to modify it to give it a shape that should be exactly similar to a washbasin.

4. Select the *washbasin* in any viewport and click on the plus sign(+) on the left side of the **NURBS Surface** in the modifier stack; all the sub-object levels are displayed.

5. Select the **Curve** sub-object level and modify the NURBS object using the **Select and Move** and **Select and Uniform Scale** tools; you will get a perfect shape of washbasin, refer to Figure 16-63.

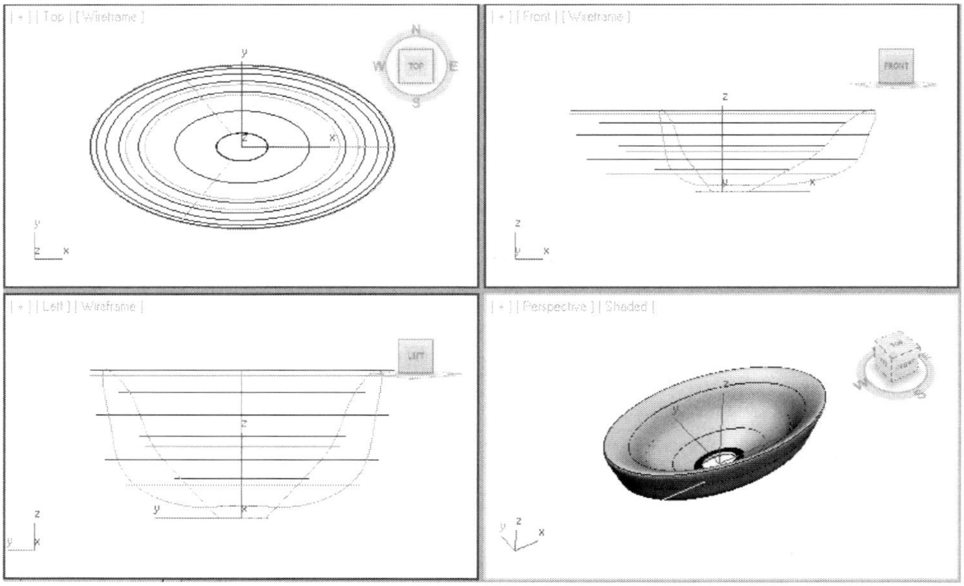

***Figure 16-62** A NURBS surface created in all viewports*

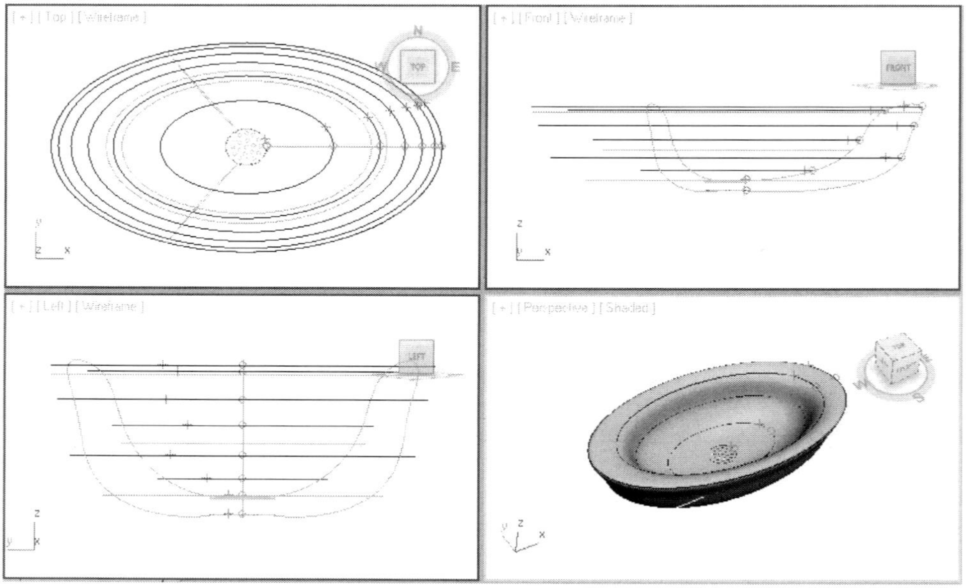

***Figure 16-63** The washbasin modified at the Curve sub-object level*

6. Again, select the **Curve** sub-object level in the modifier stack to exit the command.

Creating Washbasin Sieve and Duct

To create a washbasin sieve, first you need to create a cylinder and a capsule, and then you need to use the boolean command.

1. First, invoke the **Cylinder** tool from **Create > Geometry > Standard Primitives** in the **Command Panel**. Now, create a cylinder in the Top viewport at the center of the *washbasin*.

2. Modify the name of the cylinder to *sieve*. Next, in the **Parameters** rollout, modify the radius of *sieve* to the same value as that of *Ellipse008*. Also, change the values of the following parameters:

   Height: **1.0** Height Segments: **20** Sides: **30**

3. Invoke the **Capsule** tool from **Create > Geometry > Extended Primitives** in the **Command Panel**.

4. Create a capsule in the Top viewport at the center of the *sieve* and set its radius to **1.0**.

5. Next, hide the *washbasin* to get more space to perform the boolean command and invoke the **Zoom Extents All** tool.

6. Create multiple copies of the capsule according to the radius of the *sieve* and arrange them, as shown in Figure 16-64.

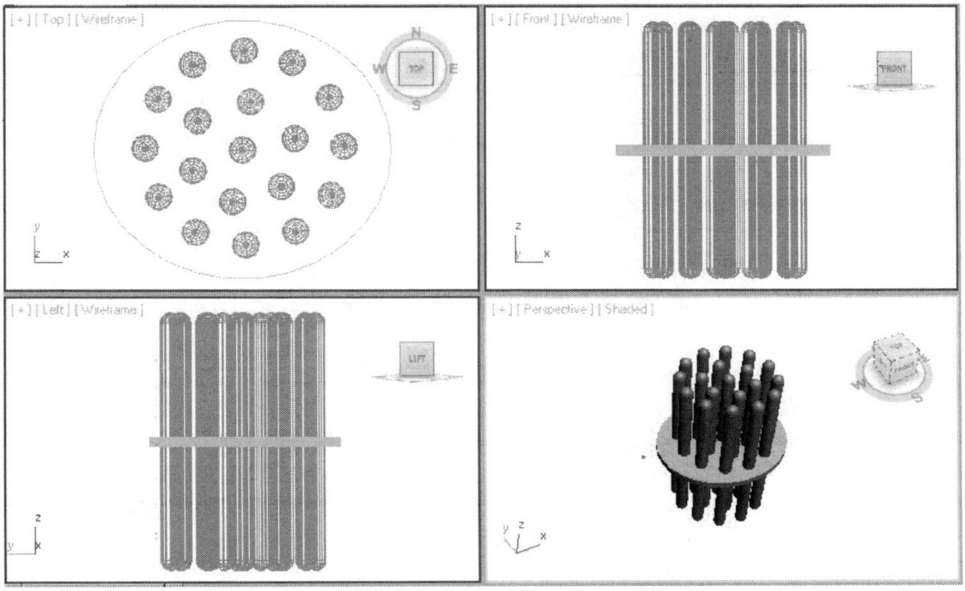

Figure 16-64 *A number of capsules created and aligned*

7. Select the *sieve* in the Top viewport and invoke the **ProBoolean** tool from **Create > Geometry > Compound Objects** in the **Command Panel**. In the **Pick Boolean** rollout, choose the **Start Picking** button and start clicking on the capsules in any viewport one-by-one. Next, right-click to exit the command; a *sieve* is created, as shown in Figure 16-65.

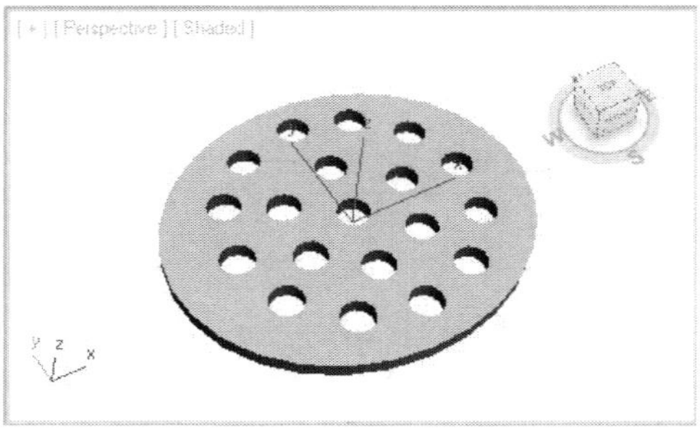

Figure 16-65 *A sieve created in the Perspective viewport*

8. Unhide washbasin in the viewports and align the *sieve* in all viewports, as shown in Figure 16-66.

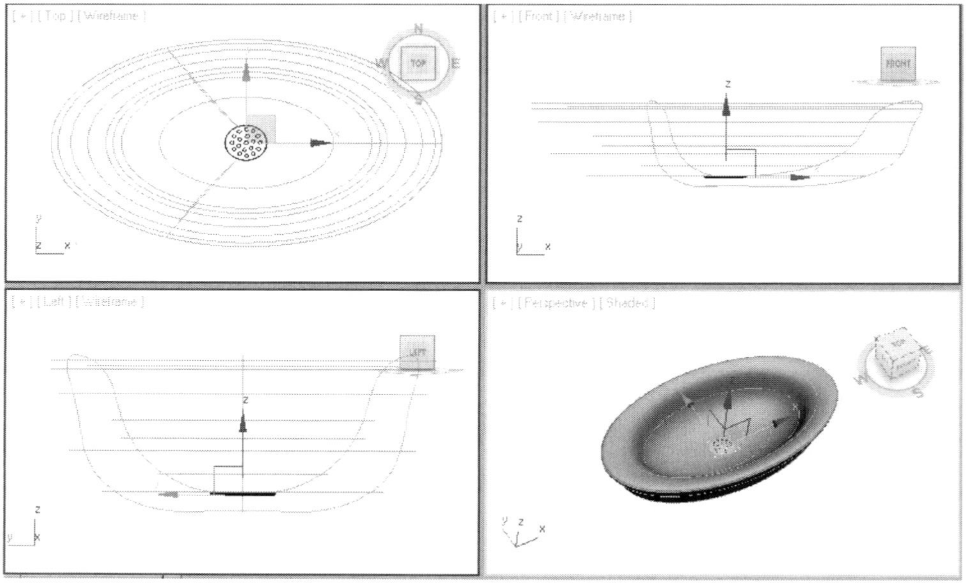

Figure 16-66 *A sieve created and aligned in all viewports*

To create a duct, you need to invoke the **Hose** tool from the **Extended Primitives**.

9. Create a hose in the Top viewport and set its height in the **Height** spinner in the **Free Hose Parameters** area according to the *washbasin* size. Also, set the parameters in the **Common Hose Parameters** rollout as given below:

   Segments: **80** Cycles: **15**
   Hose Shape Area

   Make sure that the **Round Hose** radio button is selected. Next, set the diameter in the **Diameter** spinner and sides in the **Sides** spinner according to the radius of the sieve.

10. Modify the name of the hose to *duct* and align it in all viewports, as shown in Figure 16-67.

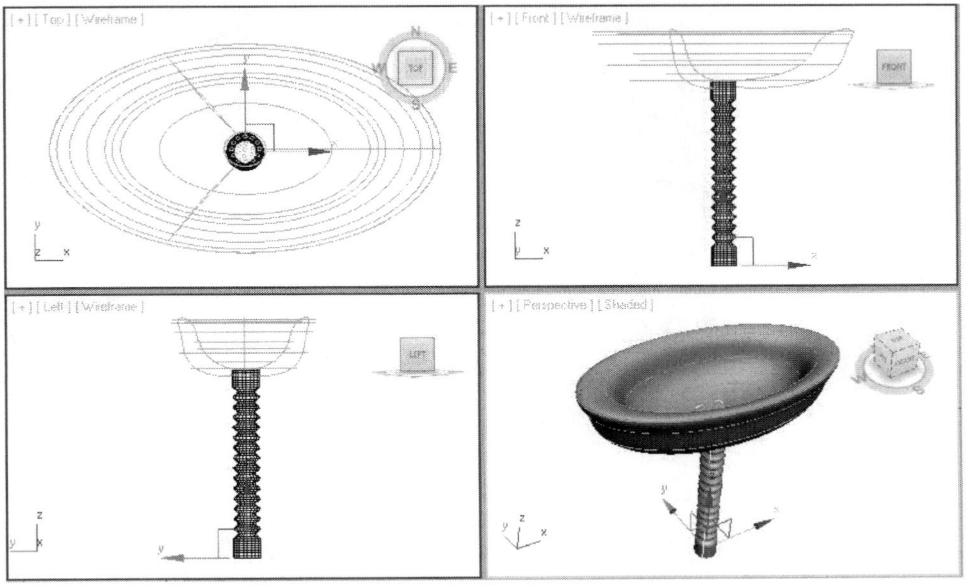

Figure 16-67 *A duct created and aligned in all viewports*

11. Next, apply the **Bend** modifier to the *duct* and set the values in the **Parameters** rollout as given below:

    Bend Area
    Angle: **40**

    Bend Axis Area
    Make sure that the **Z** radio button is selected.

12. Next, rotate the *duct* in the Top viewport and align it in all viewports, as shown in Figure 16-68.

13. Convert the *duct* into editable poly and at the **Vertex** sub-object level, move its vertices to align with the *washbasin* in the Left viewport, as shown in Figure 16-69.

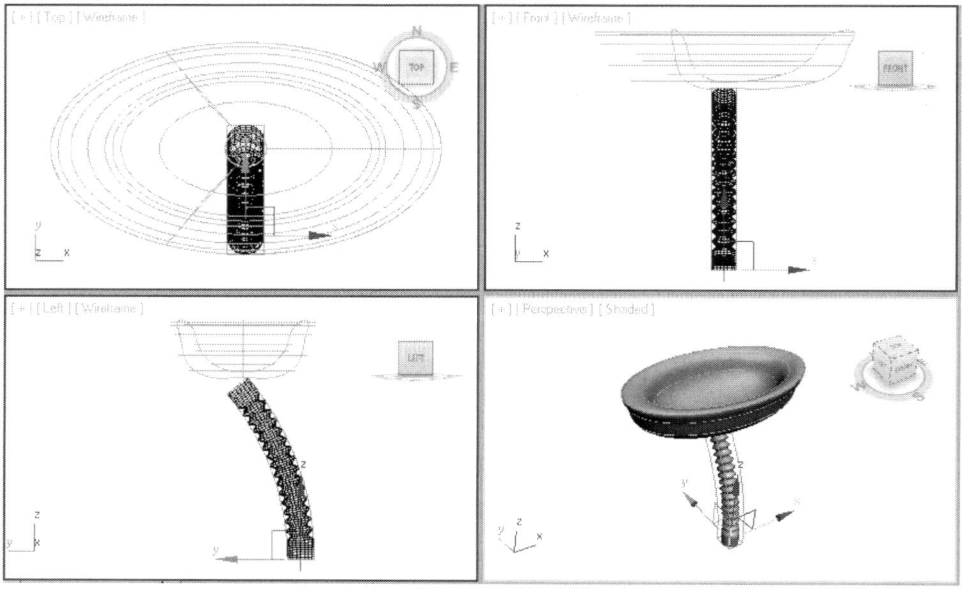

Figure 16-68 The duct rotated and aligned in all viewports

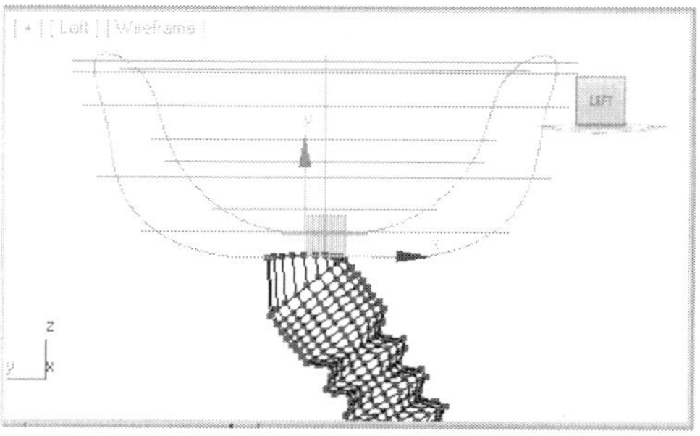

Figure 16-69 The vertices of the duct aligned in the Left viewport

Creating Washbasin Slab

To create a washbasin slab, you need to create a box in the Top viewport.

1. Create a box in the Top viewport and set its parameters in the **Parameters** rollout as given below:

   Length: **166.995** Width: **309.117** Height: **46.621**
   Length Segs: **15** Width Segs: **15**

2. Modify the name of the box to *washbasin slab* and align it, as shown in Figure 16-70.

3. Next, convert the *washbasin slab* into editable poly and select the **Polygon** sub-object level.

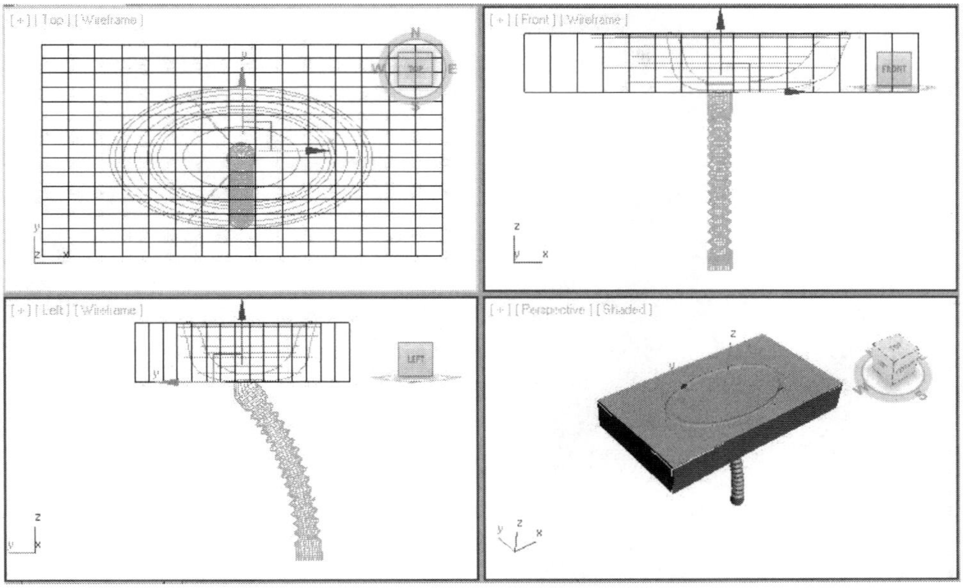

Figure 16-70 *The washbasin slab created and aligned in all viewports*

Now, select the inner polygons of the *washbasin slab* and delete them, refer to Figures 16-71 and 16-72.

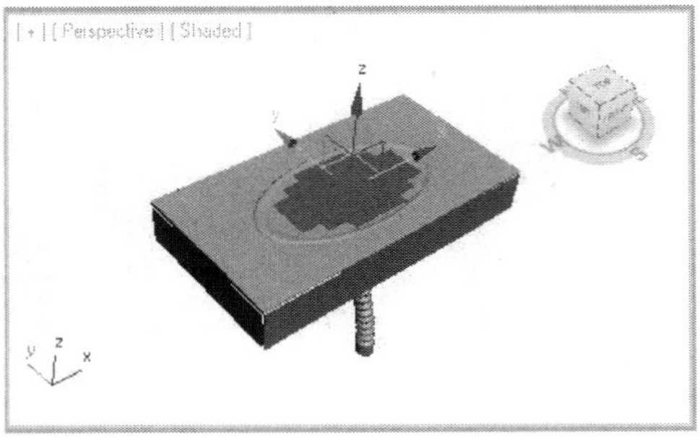

Figure 16-71 *The inner polygons selected to be deleted*

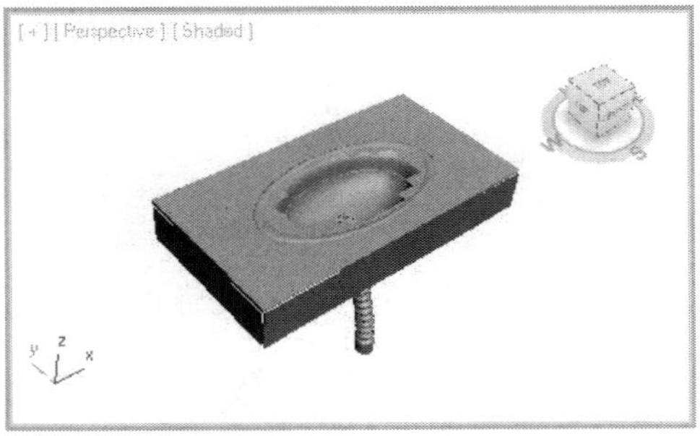

Figure 16-72 *The selected polygons deleted in the washbasin slab*

4. Now, select the **Vertex** sub-object level and modify the vertices of the *washbasin slab* to view the inner portion of the *washbasin* properly, as shown in Figure 16-73.

Creating Washbasin Taps

To create the washbasin taps, you need to invoke the **Cylinder** tool from the **Standard Primitives**.

1. Create a cylinder in the Top viewport and set its parameters in the **Parameters** rollout as given below:

   Radius: **12.0** Height: **3.0**

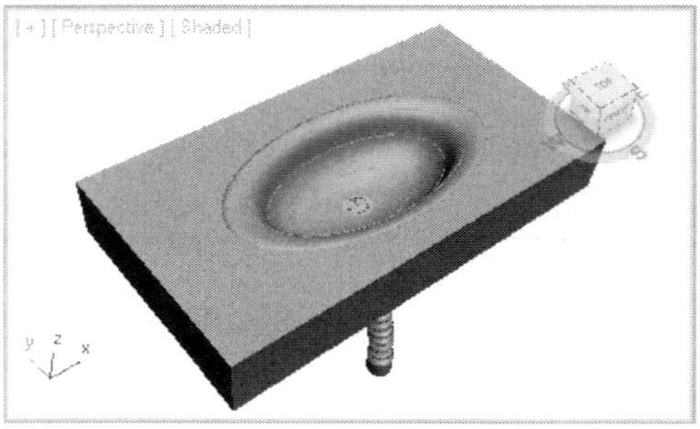

Figure 16-73 *The vertices moved to view the inner portion of the washbasin*

2. In the Front viewport, create four copies of the cylinder vertically in the downward direction. Now, set the radius of all five cylinders as **2.0**, **3.0**, **8.0**, **10.0**, and **12.0** from top to bottom. Now, select the cylinders, whose radii are **2.0** and **3.0**, and set their height to **20.0**.

3. Align the cylinders using the **Select and Move** and **Select and Rotate** tools, as shown in Figure 16-74. Also, group and name it as *tap01*.

4. Align the *tap01* on the left side of the *washbasin*. Also, create a copy of *tap01*, which is automatically named as *tap002*, and align it on the right side of the *washbasin*.

   Now, you need to create the main tap.

5. As discussed above, create the base of the main tap using three cylinders of radii **8.0**, **10.0**, and **12.0**, and group and name it as *base*. Now, invoke the **Line** tool and create a line spline in the Left viewport, as shown in Figure 16-75.

6. Now, create a cylinder in the Top viewport and set its parameters in the **Parameters** rollout as given below:

   Radius: **3.0** Height: **20.0** Height Segments: **30**

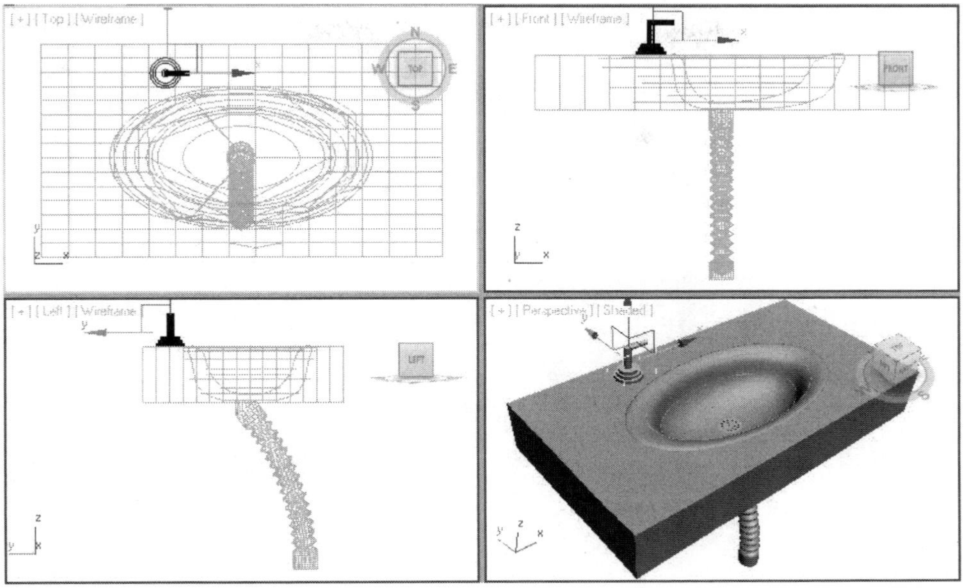

Figure 16-74 The tap01 created and aligned in all viewports

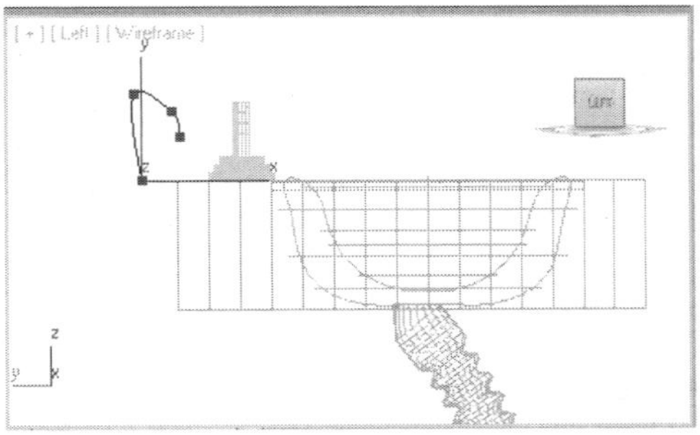

Figure 16-75 The line spline created in the Left viewport

7. Make sure that the cylinder is selected in the viewport and apply the **PathDeform** modifier to it; the **Parameters** rollout is displayed in the modify panel.

8. In the **Parameters** rollout of the **PathDeform** modifier, choose the **Pick Path** button and then select the line spline in the viewport. Now, choose the **Move to Path** button and Set the value in the **Stretch** spinner to get a shape similar to the tap.

Note

The number of segments in the object should be high to get the smoothness on applying the ***PathDeform*** *modifier.*

9. Group the line spline and the cylinder as *upper tap* and then align it with the *base* in all viewports using the **Select and Move** and **Select and Rotate** tools, as shown in Figure 16-76.

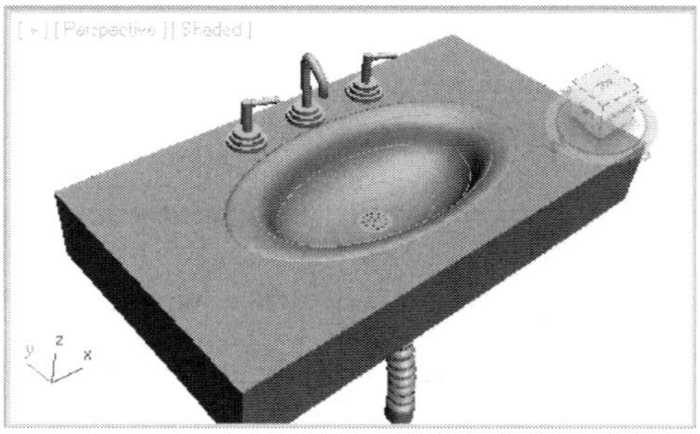

***Figure 16-76** Alignment of the upper tap and the base*

10. Next, group *base* and *upper tap* as *main tap* and then align it, as shown in Figure 16-77.

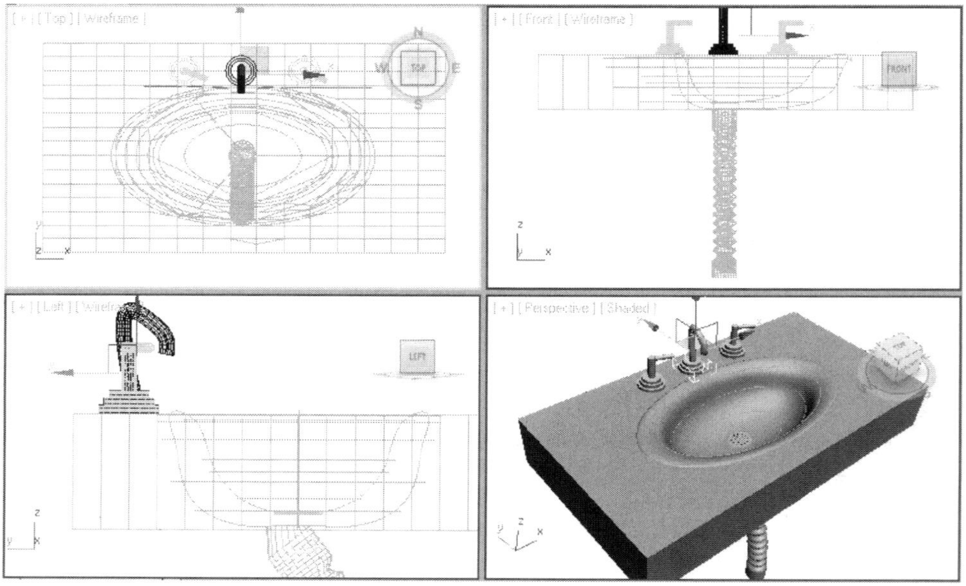

***Figure 16-77** Alignment of the main tap in all viewports*

Assigning the Mental Ray Renderer and Materials

1. To assign the **mental ray Renderer** to the scene, invoke the **Render Setup** tool; the **Render Setup** dialog box is displayed.

2. In the **Assign Renderer** rollout, choose the **Choose Renderer** button at the right side of the **Production** text box; the **Choose Renderer** dialog box is displayed. Select the **mental ray Renderer** option and choose the **OK** button. Notice that the **Production** text box displays the **mental ray Renderer** text.

3. Close the **Render Setup** dialog box.

Note

*When you assign the **mental ray Renderer**, the **mental ray** rollout will be displayed with some additional materials in the **Material/Map Browser** dialog box of the **Material Editor**.*

Next, you need to assign materials to the objects.

4. First, select the *washbasin* in the viewport and invoke the **Compact Material Editor** tool from the **Main Toolbar**; the **Material Editor** dialog box is displayed.

   By default, the **Standard** material is selected for the **01-Default** sample slot.

5. Select the **01-Default** sample slot and modify its name in the **Material Name** text box to **washbasin**.

6. Choose the **Material Type** button that is labeled as **Standard** in the **Material Editor**; the **Material/Map Browser** dialog box is displayed. Select the **Architectural** material from the **Materials > Standard** rollouts and choose the **OK** button. Notice that the **Material Type** button is labeled as **Architectural** now.

7. In the **Templates** rollout, select the **Ceramic Tile, Glazed** option from the drop-down list. Also, in the **Physical Qualities** rollout, choose the **Diffuse Color** color swatch and set the values in the **Color Selector: Diffuse** dialog box as given below:

   Red: **199** Green: **247** Blue: **251**

8. Make sure that the *washbasin* is selected in the viewport and choose the **Assign Material to Selection** button; the **washbasin** material is assigned to the *washbasin* in the viewport.

   Next, you need to assign the material to the *washbasin slab*.

9. Select the **02-Default** sample slot and modify its name in the **Material Name** text box to **washbasin slab**.

10. Next, assign the **Ceramic Tile, Glazed** architectural material to the selected sample slot as discussed above. In the **Physical Qualities** rollout, choose the **Diffuse Color** color swatch and assign black color to it. Also, assign the **washbasin slab** material to the *washbasin slab* in the viewport.

    Next, you need to assign the material to the taps.

11. Select the **03-Default** sample slot and modify its name in the **Material Name** text box to **tap**.

12. By default, the **Standard** material is selected. Choose the **Material Type** button that is labeled as **Standard** from the **Material Editor**; the **Material/Map Browser** dialog box is

displayed. Select the **Arch & Design** material from the **Materials > mental ray** rollouts and choose the **OK** button. Notice that the **Material Type** button is labeled as **Arch & Design** now.

13. In the **Templates** rollout, select the **Chrome** material in the drop-down list.

14. Make sure that the *main tap*, *tap01*, and *tap002* are selected in the viewport and then assign the **tap** material to them.

    Next, you need to assign the material to the duct and sieve.

15. Select the **04-Default** sample slot and modify its name in the **Material Name** text box to **duct and sieve**.

16. Now, select the **Chrome** material as discussed above. Then, in the **Main material parameters** rollout, choose the color swatch in the **Reflection** area and select the light gray color in it.

17. Select the *duct* and *sieve* in the viewport and then assign the **duct and sieve** material to them. Close the **Material Editor** dialog box.

Rendering the Scene for the Final Output

1. Activate the Perspective viewport.

2. Invoke the **Render Production** tool in the **Main Toolbar**; the **Perspective, frame 0, Display Gamma:2.2, RGBA Color 16 Bits/Channel (1:1)** dialog box is displayed, which shows the final output of the scene at one frame, refer to Figure 16-78.

3. Close this dialog box.

Note
You can also add the environment to the scene by creating the walls, roof, and floor in it, as shown in Figure 16-79.

Figure 16-78 *The final output at rendering*

Figure 16-79 *The scene after creating the environment*

You can view the final rendered image of this model by downloading the *c16_3dsmax_2012_render.zip* file from *http://www.cadcim.com*.

Saving the File

1. Save the file with the name *c16tut1.max* as discussed in earlier chapters. The location of this file is given below:

   \Documents\3dsmax\c16_tut1\scenes

Tutorial 2

In this tutorial, you will create a cap, as shown in Figures 16-80 and 16-81, using the NURBS curves. **(Expected time: 30 min)**

Figure 16-80 *Model for Tutorial 2 (view 1)*

Figure 16-81 *Model for Tutorial 2 (view 2)*

The following steps are required to complete this tutorial:

a. Set the project folder.
b. Download the files.
c. Create NURBS curves using splines.
d. Create cap and modify it using the NURBS curves.
e. Assign the material.
f. Render the scene for the final output.
g. Save the file.

Setting the Project Folder

1. Set the project folder with the name *c16_tut2* in the *3dsmax* folder as discussed in earlier chapters.

Downloading the Files

Before starting the tutorial, you need to download the *c16_3dsmax_2012_tut.zip* file from *http://www.cadcim.com*. The path of the file is as follows:

Textbooks > Animation and Visual Effects > 3ds Max > Autodesk 3ds Max 2012: A Comprehensive Guide

Extract the contents of the zipped file and copy the file *cloth.jpg* at the location *\Documents\3dsmax\c16_tut1\sceneassets\images.*

Creating NURBS Curves Using Splines

To create a cap, first you need to create the circular NURBS curves.

1. Choose **Create > Shapes** in the **Command Panel** and then invoke the **Circle** tool from **Object Type** rollout.

2. Create a circle in the Top viewport; it is automatically named as *Circle001*. Next, set its radius to **45** in the **Radius** spinner of the **Parameters** rollout.

3. Make sure that the *Circle001* is selected in the Top viewport. Invoke the **Select and Uniform Scale** tool from the **Main Toolbar** and right-click on it; the **Scale Transform Type-In** dialog box is displayed, as shown in Figure 16-82. Now, in the **Absolute:Local** area, set the value **111.0** in the **X** spinner; the *Circle001* is scaled in the X-axis, as shown in Figure 16-83. Now, close this dialog box.

4. Convert the *Circle001* into NURBS surface and invoke the **Zoom Extents All** tool.

   Next, you need to create multiple copies of the *Circle001* to create the surface.

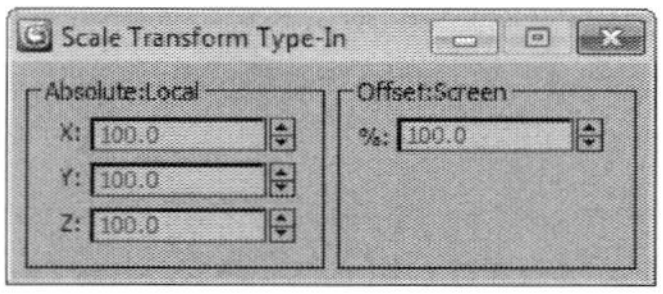

Figure 16-82 *The* ***Scale Transform Type-In*** *dialog box*

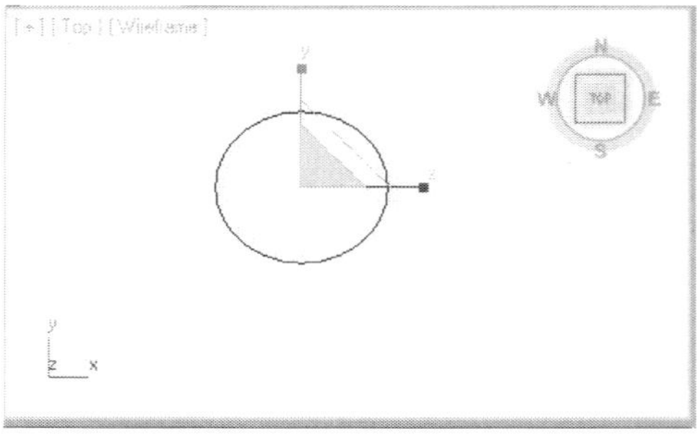

Figure 16-83 *The Circle001 scaled in the X-axis*

5. Select the *Circle001* in the Front viewport and move the cursor over its vertical axis. Press and hold the SHIFT key and the left mouse button, and then move the *Circle001* in the upward direction until the value in the **Y** spinner in the coordinates display becomes about **17**. Now, release the left mouse button and the SHIFT key; the **Clone Options** dialog box

is displayed. Set the value **4** in the **Number of Copies** spinner and choose the **OK** button; the *Circle002, Circle003*, *Circle004*, and *Circle005* are created in all viewports.

6. Invoke the **Zoom Extents All** tool; the circular NURBS curves are displayed in the viewports, as shown in Figure 16-84.

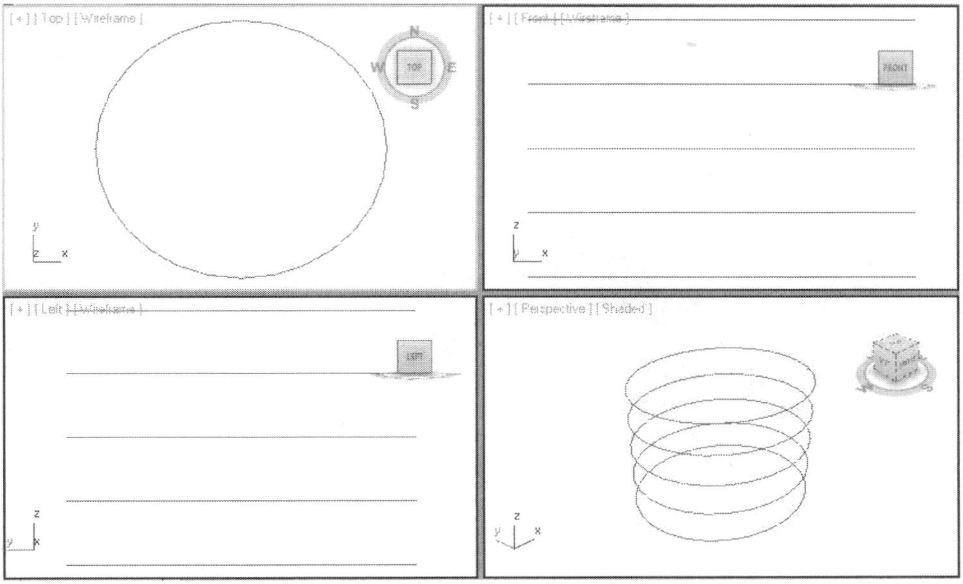

Figure 16-84 *The circular NURBS curves displayed in all viewports*

7. Select the *Circle001*, which is placed at the bottom in the viewport and right-click on the **Select and Move** tool; the **Move Transform Type-In** dialog box is displayed. In the **Offset:Screen** area, set the value **13** in the **Y** spinner and press the ENTER key; the *Circle001* moves in the vertical direction, as shown in Figure 16-85.

8. Close the **Move Transform Type-In** dialog box.

9. Select *Circle001* and then by pressing CTRL key, select *Circle002*. Next, right-click on the **Select and Uniform Scale** tool; the **Scale Transform Type-In** dialog box is displayed. In the **Offset:Screen** area, set the value **119** in the **%** spinner and press the ENTER key; the *Circle001* and *Circle002* are scaled, as shown in Figure 16-86.

10. Now, close the **Scale Transform Type-In** dialog box and invoke the **Zoom Extents All** tool.

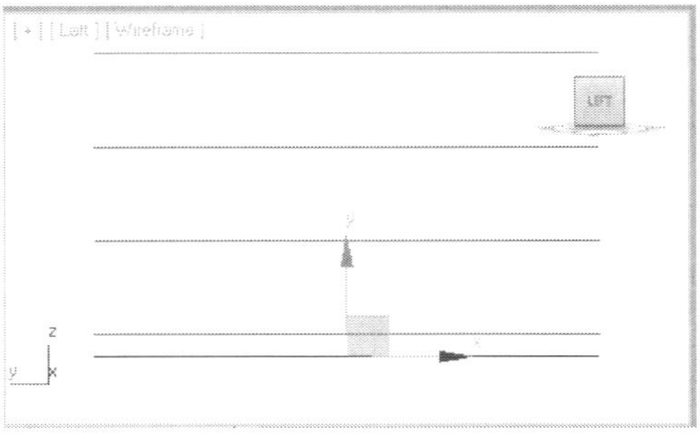

Figure 16-85 *The Circle001 moved in the vertical direction*

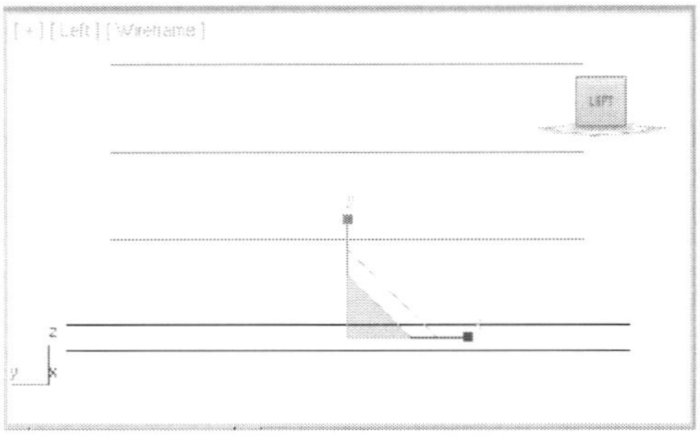

Figure 16-86 *The Circle001 and Circle002 scaled in the vertical direction*

Creating and Modifying the Cap

Next, you need to create a surface between the NURBS curves in the viewport to give it a shape. To do so, you need to use the **U Loft** button.

1. Select the *Circle001* in the Front viewport, which is placed at the bottom.

2. Choose the **Modify** tab, if it is not already chosen; the **NURBS Surface** is displayed in the modifier stack. All rollouts to modify the NURBS object are also displayed below the modifier stack.

3. Expand the **General** rollout and choose the **NURBS Creation Toolbox** button; the **NURBS** toolbox is displayed. Now, choose the **Create U Loft Surface** button from the **Surfaces** section; the **U Loft Surface** rollout is displayed in the modify panel. Next, move the cursor over the *Circle001*; it turns blue. Now, click on it and then click one-by-one on the *Circle002*, *003*, *004*, and *005* to add them into the U loft surface. Now, right-click to end the command and in the **U Loft Surface** rollout, select the **Flip Normals** check box. Next, right-click to exit the U loft command; a NURBS surface is created in the viewports, as shown in Figure 16-87.

4. Now, choose the **Create Cap Surface** button from the **Surfaces** section in the **NURBS** toolbox; the **Cap Surface** rollout is displayed in the modify panel. Now, move the cursor over the *Circle005*, which is placed at the top in the Front viewport, and then click on it. Also, in the **Cap Surface** rollout, select the **Flip Normals** check box. The open surface is now capped at one end, as shown in Figure 16-88.

5. Right-click to exit the command and modify the name of the surface to *cap* in the **Surface Common** *rollout*.

   Next, you need to modify the *cap* to give it a shape that is exactly similar to a cap.

6. Select the *cap* in any viewport and click on the plus sign on the left side of **NURBS Surface** in the modifier stack; all the sub-object levels are displayed.

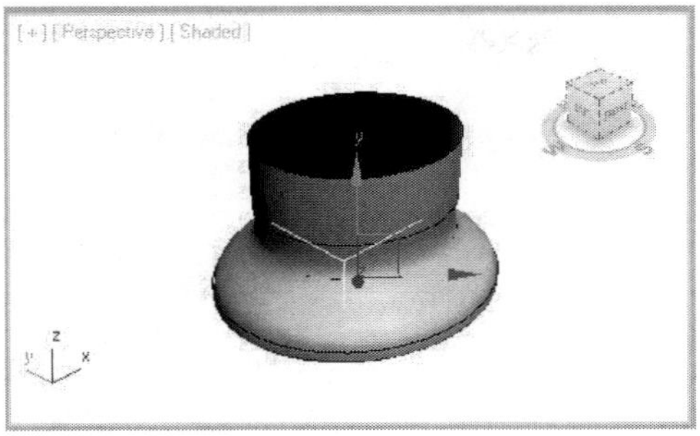

Figure 16-87 *A NURBS surface created*

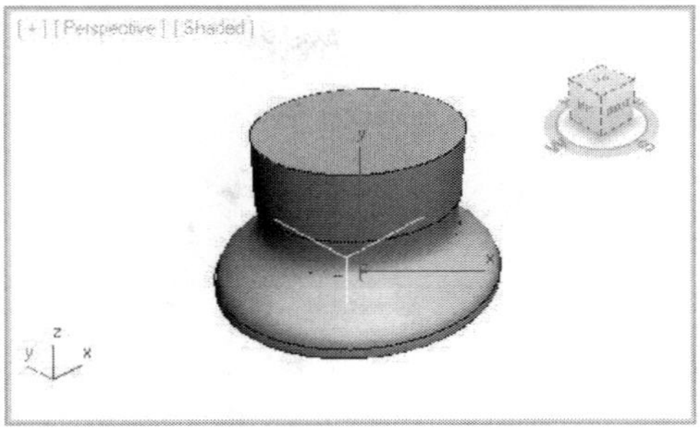

Figure 16-88 *The NURBS surface capped at one end*

7. Select the **Curve** sub-object level. In the Front viewport, modify the NURBS curves using the **Select and Move** and **Select and Uniform Scale** tool, as shown in Figure 16-89.

8. Again, select the **Curve** sub-object level in the modifier stack to exit the command.

9. Next, select the **Curve CV** sub-object level; all control vertices are displayed in the viewport. Now, select the outer control vertices of the bottom curves, refer to Figure 16-90. Then, move them until the value in the **Y** spinner in the coordinate display becomes about **15**, as shown in Figure 16-90.

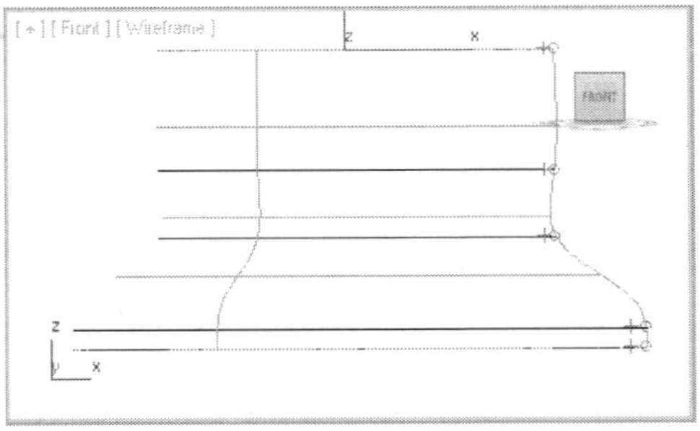

Figure 16-89 *The NURBS curves modified in the Front viewport*

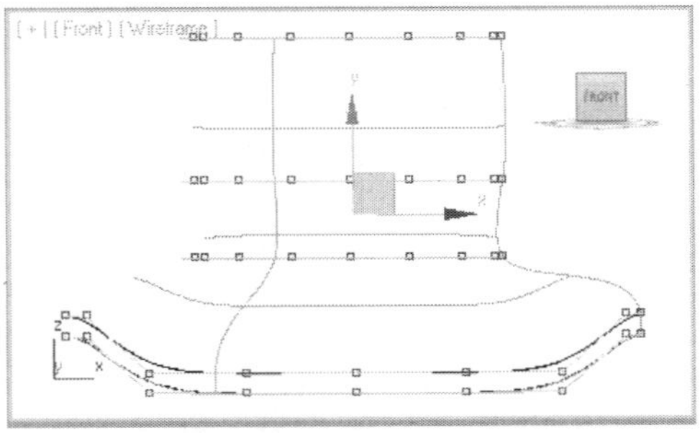

Figure 16-90 *The outer control vertices moved vertically*

10. Now, modify the surface using the control vertices and curves to get the required shape, as shown in Figure 16-91.

Assigning the Material

1. First, select the *cap* in the viewport and invoke the **Material Editor** tool from the **Main Toolbar**; the **Material Editor** dialog box is displayed.

2. By default, the **Standard** material is selected in the **Material Editor**. Select the **01-Default** sample slot and modify its name in the **Material Name** text box to **cap**.

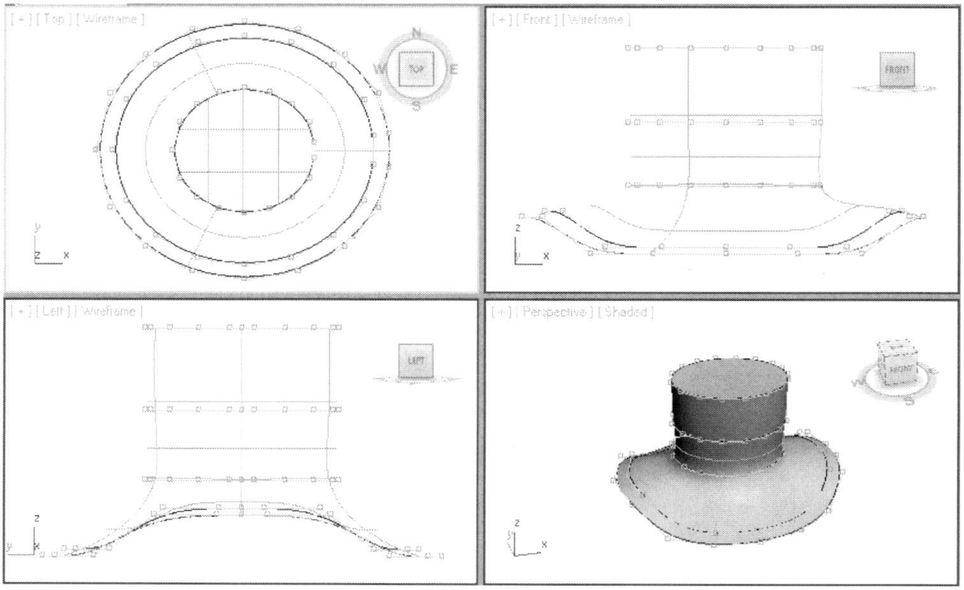

Figure 16-91 *The surface modified at the sub-object level*

3. Choose the **Material Type** button that is labeled as **Standard** from the **Material Editor**; the **Material/Map Browser** dialog box is displayed. Select the **Double Sided** material from the **Materials > Standard** rollouts and choose the **OK** button; the **Replace Material** dialog box is displayed. Select the **Discard old material** radio button and choose **OK**. Notice that the **Material Type** button is labeled as **Double Sided** now. Also, the rollouts to modify the material are displayed.

4. In the **Double Sided Basic Parameters** rollout, choose the **Facing Material** map button that is labeled as **Material#25 (Standard)**; the **Standard** material is displayed that is used to specify material for the outer surface of the *cap*.

5. Now, expand the **Maps** rollout, and choose the **Diffuse Color** map button that is labeled as **None**; the **Material/Map Browser** dialog box is displayed. Select the **Bitmap** map from the **Maps > Standard** rollouts and choose the **OK** button; the **Select Bitmap Image File** dialog box is displayed. Now, select the file *cloth.jpg* and choose the **Open** button; the selected image is displayed in the sample slot. Make sure that the **Use Real-World Scale** check box is cleared in the **Coordinates** rollout.

6. Choose the **Go to Parent** button twice to go back to the **Double Sided** material. Now, choose the **Back Material** button that is labeled as **Material#26 (Standard)**; the **Standard** material is displayed that is used to specify material for the inner surface of the *cap*.

7. Expand the **Maps** rollout, and choose the **Diffuse Color** map button that is labeled as **None**; the **Material/Map Browser** dialog box is displayed. Select the **Checker** map from the **Maps > Standard** rollouts and choose the **OK** button; the rollouts to modify the **Checker** map are displayed.

8. In the **Coordinates** rollout, set the value **25** in both the **U Tiling** and **V Tiling** spinners and assign the **cap** material to the *cap*.

9. Close the **Material Editor** dialog box.

Rendering the Scene for the Final Output

1. Activate the Perspective viewport and set the view using the **Orbit** tool to see the inner and outer surfaces of the *cap*.

2. Invoke the **Render Production** tool in the **Main Toolbar**; the **Perspective, frame 0, Display Gamma:2.2, RGBA Color 16 Bits/Channel (1:1)** dialog box is displayed, which shows the final output of the scene at one frame, refer to Figure 16-92.

3. Close this dialog box.

You can view the final rendered image of this model by downloading the *c16_3dsmax_2012_render.zip* file from *http://www.cadcim.com.*

Figure 16-92 *The final output at rendering*

Saving the File

1. Save the file with the name *c16tut2.max* as discussed in earlier chapters. The location of this file is given below:

   \Documents\3dsmax\c16_tut2\scenes

Self-Evaluation Test

Answer the following questions and then compare them to those given at the end of this chapter:

1. Which of the following buttons in the **General** rollout of the NURBS object is used to attach another object to the selected NURBS object in the viewport?

   (a) **Attach** (b) **Import**
   (c) **Offset** (d) **Loft**

2. Which of the following buttons in the **Create Points** rollout is used to add the independent point sub-object to a NURBS object?

   (a) **Point** (b) **Surf-Curve**
   (c) **Curve-Curve** (d) **Surf-Point**

3. Which of the following buttons in the **Create Surfaces** rollout is used to add the dependent surface sub-object to a NURBS object?

   (a) **Transform** (b) **Extrude**
   (c) **U Loft** (d) All of these

4. Which of the following buttons in the **Create Points** rollout is used to add the dependent point sub-object to a NURBS object?

   (a) **Offset Point** (b) **Curve Point**
   (c) **Curve-Curve** (d) All of these

5. The NURBS curves are the shape objects and are used to create complex surfaces to create the 3D models. (T/F)

6. The point curves are the NURBS curves in which the points lie outside the curve. (T/F)

7. In the NURBS modeling, an iso line is known as a line of constant parameter value similar to a contour line. (T/F)

8. The CV curves are the NURBS curves that are controlled by __________.

9. The CVs are the points that lie __________ the surface and control the __________ of the CV surface.

10. While creating a point curve, if you want to remove the last point that you have created, then press the __________ key.

Review Questions

Answer the following questions:

1. Which of the following buttons in the **Create Points** rollout is used to add the point sub-objects to a NURBS object?

   (a) **Point** (b) **Offset Point**
   (c) **Surf Point** (d) All of these

2. Which of the following buttons in the **Create Curves** rollout is used to add the dependent curve sub-object to a NURBS object?

   (a) **Transform** (b) **Blend**
   (c) **Chamfer** (d) All of these

3. Which of the following buttons in the **Create Surfaces** rollout is used to add the surface sub-object to a NURBS object?

   (a) **1-Rail** (b) **2-Rail**
   (c) **Offset** (d) All of these

4. Which of the following buttons in the **Create Curves** rollout is used to add the curve sub-object to a NURBS object?

   (a) **1-Rail** (b) **U Loft**
   (c) **Cap** (d) None of these

5. You cannot convert the torus knot and prism from extended primitives into NURBS surface. (T/F)

6. To create a NURBS model, you can also use the splines or extended splines shapes instead of using the point curve or the CV curve. (T/F)

7. The buttons in the **NURBS** toolbox perform the same functions as the buttons in the **Create Points**, **Create Curves**, and **Create Surfaces** rollouts. (T/F)

8. The __________ check box is used to create a 3D curve in all viewports simultaneously.

9. In the viewports, the dependent point sub-objects will be displayed as __________ and the independent point sub-objects will be displayed as __________.

10. The __________ button in the **Create Surfaces** rollout is used to create a surface sub-object between two curve sub-objects.

Exercise

Exercise 1

Start Autodesk 3ds Max 2012 and then perform the following operations:

1. Choose **Create > Shapes** in the **Command Panel**; a drop-down list will be displayed. Select the **NURBS Curves** option from the drop-down list. Now, activate the Top viewport and invoke the **Point Curve** tool from the **Object Type** rollout. Next, create two or more point curves in the viewport. Finally, invoke the **Modify** tab in the **Command Panel** and attach the NURBS curves in the viewport using the **Attach Multiple** tool.

2. Create a spline or a curve in the viewport from **Create > Shapes > Splines** in the **Command Panel**. Now, convert it into NURBS curve using the methods discussed in the chapter.

3. Create a NURBS object in the viewport that contains two or more curves or surface sub-objects. Choose the **Modify** tab in the **Command Panel** and then choose the **Blend** button from the **Create Surfaces** rollout. Next, move the cursor over the edge; it turns blue. Now, click on the edge and move the cursor over the edge of another NURBS object, and click on it; a blend surface will be created between the two NURBS objects. Next, modify the blend surface using the parameters in the **Blend Surface** rollout in the modify panel and right-click to exit the command.

4. Create a NURBS curve in the viewport, as shown in Figure 16-93. Next, create a NURBS model, as shown in Figure 16-94 using the **U Loft** tool. Also, apply a material to it.

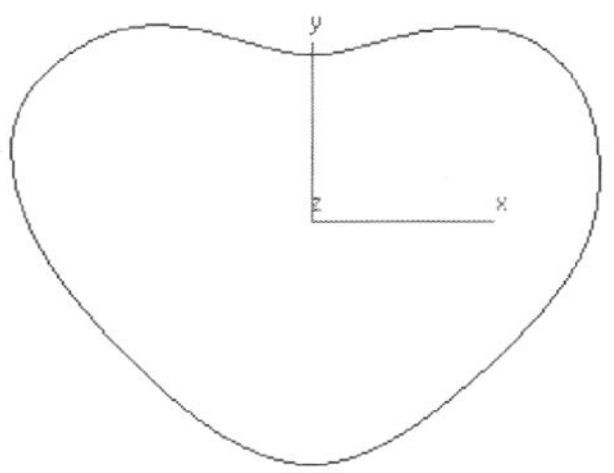

Figure 16-93 The NURBS curve to create the model for Exercise 1

Figure 16-94 Model for Exercise 1

Answers to Self-Evaluation Test

1. a, **2.** a, **3.** d, **4.** d, **5.** T, **6.** F, **7.** T, **8.** control vertices (CVs), **9.** outside; shape, **10.** BACKSPACE

17

Rigid Body Dynamics and Helpers

Learning Objectives

After completing this chapter, you will be able to:

- ***Understand static, dynamic, and kinematic rigid bodies***
- ***Understand the MassFX interface***
- ***Understand constraints***
- ***Understand simulation***
- ***Use standard helper objects***
- ***Use atmospheric apparatus helper objects***

INTRODUCTION

A rigid body is an object which does not deform when it collides with another object. You can convert an object into three types of rigid bodies using the **MassFX Toolbar**. This toolbar is a new feature added in 3ds Max 2012. It consists of options for converting an object into rigid bodies, various types of constraint helpers, and simulation controls. Conversion of an object into rigid bodies, constraint helpers, and simulation controls will be discussed in detail in this chapter. In addition, the helper objects which are used to support the animation and modeling in a scene will be discussed in this chapter.

TYPES OF RIGID BODIES

Rigid bodies can be classified into three types: Dynamic, Static, and Kinematic. These types are discussed next.

Dynamic Rigid Body

A dynamic rigid body represents an object in the real world. It means that it falls with gravity, can collide with other objects, and can also be pushed by other objects. The motion of the dynamic rigid body is completely controlled by simulation. It cannot be animated by using the standard animation methods.

Kinematic Rigid Body

Unlike a dynamic rigid body, a kinematic rigid body can be animated by using the standard animation methods. It does not fall with gravity and does not get affected by the dynamic rigid body. However, a dynamic rigid body will get affected by a kinematic rigid body. A kinematic rigid body can also act as a stationary object and can be converted into a dynamic rigid body at any point during simulation.

Static Rigid Body

A static rigid body is similar to a kinematic rigid body with the only difference that it cannot be animated. A dynamic rigid body can collide with it and may bounce off when collided with it, but the static rigid body will not be affected. A static rigid body is used to simulate walls, containers, and so on.

MassFX Toolbar

New

When you start 3ds Max 2012, the **MassFX Toolbar** is displayed in the floating state, as shown in Figure 17-1. If it is not displayed, right-click in the blank area on the **Main Toolbar**; a shortcut menu will be displayed. Choose **MassFX Toolbar** from it; the **MassFX Toolbar** is displayed in the floating state. If you double-click on it, it gets docked in the 3ds Max interface.

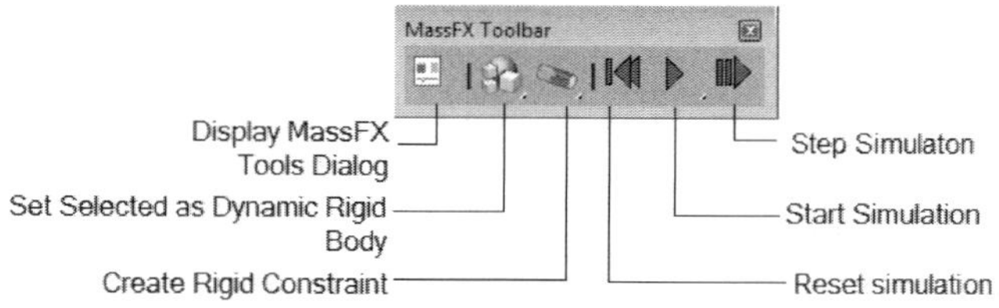

Figure 17-1** The **MassFX Toolbar

The **MassFX Toolbar** can be classified in four main categories: MassFX Tools Dialog, Rigid body flyout, Constraint flyout, and Simulation controls. The MassFX Tools Dialog category consists of the **Display MassFX Tools Dialog** button. If you choose this button, the **MassFX Tools** dialog box will be displayed. This dialog box is discussed later in the chapter in detail. The other categories of the **MassFX Toolbar** are discussed next.

Rigid Body Flyout

The Rigid body flyout consists of three tools: **Set Selected as Dynamic Rigid Body**, **Set Selected as Static Rigid Body**, and **Set Selected as Kinematic Rigid Body**, as shown in Figure 17-2. These tools are used to convert an object into dynamic, static, and kinematic rigid bodies, respectively. These tools are discussed next.

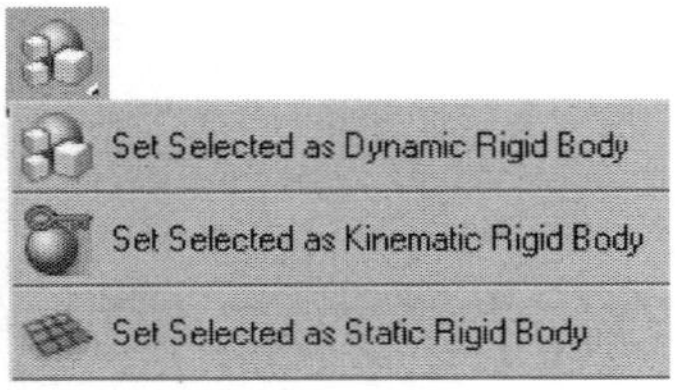

***Figure 17-2** Various options displayed in the flyout*

Set Selected as Dynamic Rigid Body

MassFX Toolbar:	Rigid Bodies > Set Selected as Dynamic Rigid Body
Menu bar:	Animation > Simulation - MassFX > Rigid Bodies > Set Selected as Dynamic Rigid Body

This tool is used to convert an object into a dynamic rigid body. To do so, select the object in the viewport. Now, click and hold on the **Set Selected as Dynamic Rigid Body** tool in the **MassFX Toolbar**; a flyout will be displayed, refer to Figure 17-2. Choose **Set Selected as Dynamic Rigid Body** from the flyout; the object will be converted into a dynamic rigid body and the **MassFX Rigid Body** modifier will be applied to the object in the modifier stack.

Set Selected as Static Rigid Body

MassFX Toolbar:	Rigid Bodies > Set Selected as Static Rigid Body
Menu bar:	Animation > Simulation - MassFX > Rigid Bodies > Set Selected as Static Rigid Body

This tool is used to convert an object into a static rigid body. To do so, select an object in the viewport. Next, click and hold on the **Set Selected as Dynamic Rigid Body** tool in the **MassFX Toolbar**; a flyout will be displayed, refer to Figure 17-2. Choose **Set Selected as Static Rigid Body** from the flyout; the object will be converted into a static rigid body and the **MassFX Rigid Body** modifier will be applied to the object in the modifier stack.

Set Selected as Kinematic Rigid Body

MassFX Toolbar:	Rigid Bodies > Set Selected as Kinematic Rigid Body
Menu bar:	Animation > Simulation - MassFX > Rigid Bodies > Set Selected as Kinematic Rigid Body

This tool is used to convert an object into a kinematic rigid body. To do so, select an object in the viewport. Now, click and hold on the **Set Selected as Dynamic Rigid Body**

tool in the **MassFX Toolbar**; a flyout will be displayed, refer to Figure 17-2. Choose **Set Selected as Kinematic Rigid Body** from the flyout; the object will be converted to a kinematic rigid body and the **MassFX Rigid Body** modifier will be applied to the object in the modifier stack. The **MassFX Rigid Body** modifier is discussed next.

MassFX Rigid Body Modifier

When you convert an object into a dynamic, static, or kinematic rigid body, the **MassFX Rigid Body** modifier is applied to the object, as discussed above. This modifier has different rollouts in the modify panel. These rollouts are discussed later. When you click on the + sign on the left of the **MassFX Rigid Body** modifier, the **Initial Velocity**, **Initial Spin**, **Center of Mass**, and **Mesh Transform** sub-object levels are displayed. These sub-object levels are discussed next.

Initial Velocity

This sub-object level gives a visual representation of the direction of the initial velocity of the rigid body, refer to Figure 17-3. You can change the direction of velocity by using the **Select and Rotate** tool.

Initial Spin

This sub-object level shows the axis and the direction of the initial spin of a rigid body, refer to Figure 17-4. You can change the axis by using the **Select and Rotate** tool.

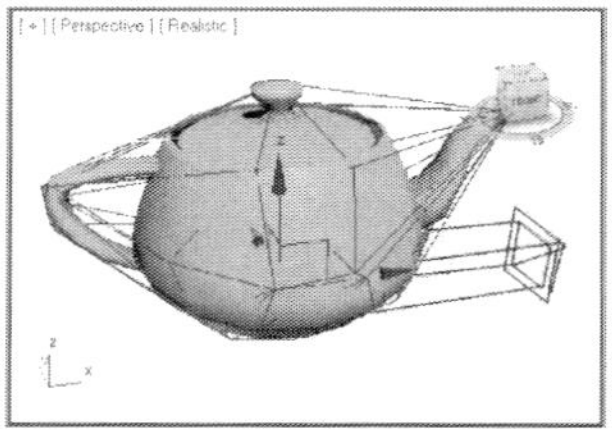

Figure 17-3 *The rigid body with the* ***Initial Velocity*** *sub-object level selected*

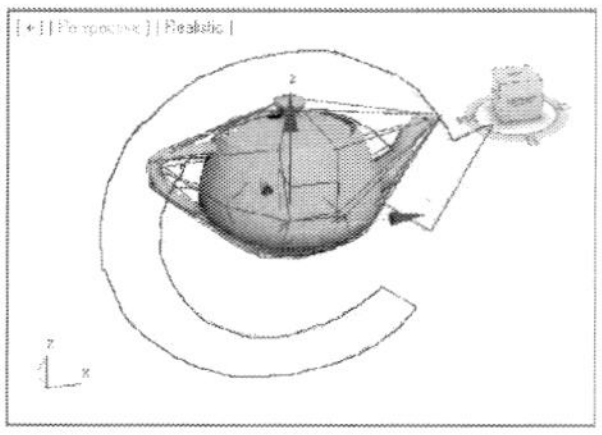

Figure 17-4 *The rigid body with the* ***Initial Spin*** *sub-object level selected*

Center of Mass

This sub-object level gives a visual representation of the location of the center of mass of a rigid body, refer to Figure 17-5. You can change the location of center of mass by using the **Select and Move** tool.

Mesh Transform

This sub-object level is used to adjust the position and rotation of the physical mesh of a rigid body. When you select this level, a physical mesh in the form of a wireframe will be displayed in the viewport, refer to Figure 17-6. You can adjust its placement with respect to the rigid body by using the **Select and Move** and **Select and Rotate** tools.

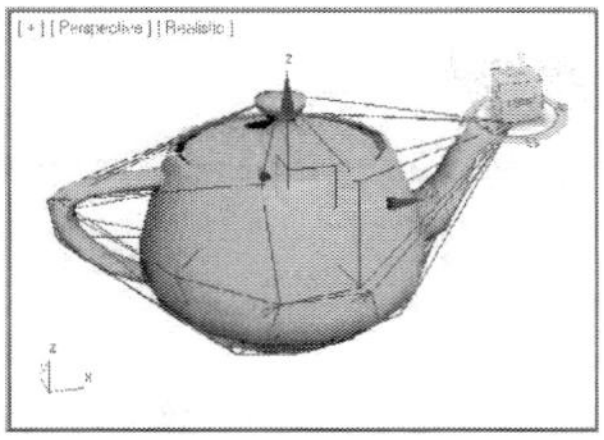

Figure 17-5 The rigid body with the ***Center of Mass*** *sub-object level selected*

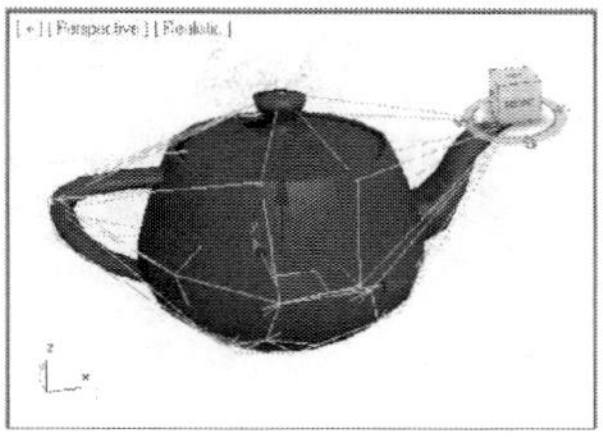

Figure 17-6 The rigid body with the ***Mesh Transform*** *sub-object level selected*

Next, you will learn about various rollouts displayed in the modify panel of the **MassFX Rigid Body** modifier such as **Rigid Body Properties**, **Physical Material**, **Physical Meshes**, and so on.

Rigid Body Properties Rollout

The parameters in the **Rigid Body Properties** rollout are discussed next, refer to Figure 17-7.

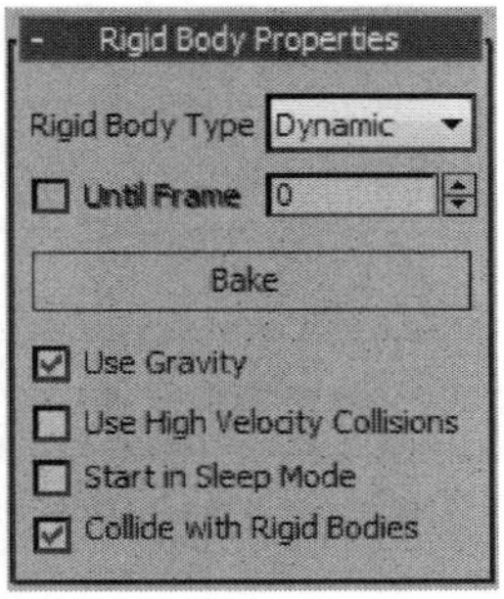

Figure 17-7 The ***Rigid Body Properties*** *rollout*

Rigid Body Type

The options in this drop-down list are used to specify the type of rigid body.

Until Frame

By default, this check box and the spinner next to it are inactive. These will be activated only when you select **Kinematic** from the **Rigid Body Type** drop-down list. If you select this check box, then the kinematic rigid body will be converted to a dynamic rigid body at the frame specified in the spinner next to it.

Bake/Unbake

This button gets activated only when the **Dynamic** option is selected in the **Rigid Body Type** drop-down list. When you choose this button, the simulated motion of the selected rigid body will be converted into standard animation keyframes for rendering. Once the selected rigid body is baked, this button will change into the **Unbake** button. Choose the **Unbake** button to remove the keyframes and restore to dynamic body.

Use Gravity

When this check box is selected, gravity is applied to the selected rigid body, provided the **Gravity Enabled** check box is selected in the **Scene Settings** rollout of the **World** tab in the **MassFX Tools** dialog box.

Use High Velocity Collisions

When this check box is selected, the high velocity collisions settings are applied to the selected rigid body, provided the **Use High Velocity Collisions** check box is selected in the **Scene Settings** rollout of the **World** tab in the **MassFX Tools** dialog box.

Start in Sleep Mode

If a rigid body in a simulation moves slower than a certain rate, it automatically goes in the sleep mode. It only wakes up when it is hit by a non-sleeping object. When you select the **Start in Sleep Mode** check box, the rigid body starts in sleep mode using the global sleep settings.

Collide with Rigid Bodies

This check box is selected by default. As a result, the selected rigid body will collide with other rigid bodies in the scene.

Physical Material Rollout

The parameters in the **Physical Material** rollout are used to control the way the rigid body interacts with the other elements in the scene, refer to Figure 17-8. These parameters are discussed next.

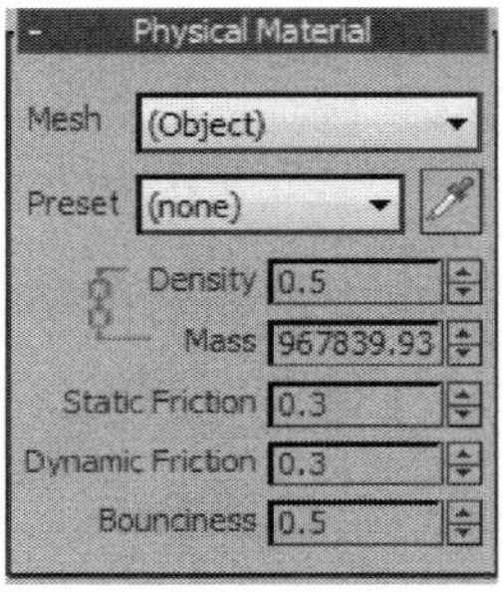

*Figure 17-8 The **Physical Material** rollout*

Mesh

This drop-down list is used to select the physical mesh of the rigid body for which you are changing the material parameters. By default, it has only one option, **Object**. However, if the **Override Physical Material** check box in the **Physical Meshes** rollout is selected, physical meshes will be displayed in the list.

Preset

This drop-down list consists of options for loading, saving, and creating a preset. Once you create a preset, it gets added in this drop-down list. You can select the preset from this drop-down list to specify physical material properties. It also consists of the **None** option. When **None** is selected, you can edit the values in the spinners below it. But when you select a preset from the list, you cannot edit these values.

Density

This spinner is used to specify the density of the selected rigid body measured in g/cm^3. It is linked with the **Mass** parameter which means that when you change the density, the mass of the rigid body will be calculated automatically.

Mass

This spinner is used to specify the mass of the selected rigid body measured in kg. If you change this value, density of the rigid body will be calculated automatically.

Static Friction

This spinner is used to specify the static friction value. If the value is 0, it indicates that there is no friction between two rigid bodies; if the value is 1, it indicates full friction.

Dynamic Friction

This spinner is used to specify the dynamic friction value. If the value is 0, it indicates that there is no friction between two rigid bodies; if the value is 1, it indicates full friction.

Bounciness

It specifies the effective bounciness between the two rigid bodies which is the product of their bounciness values. It determines how high any rigid body would bounce when it hits another rigid body.

***Figure 17-9** The **Physical Meshes** rollout*

Physical Meshes Rollout

The **Physical Meshes** rollout is used to edit the physical meshes assigned to an object in the simulation, refer to Figure 17-9. The parameters in this rollout are discussed next.

Select a Mesh to Modify

The list box in this area displays the physical meshes added to a selected rigid body. The **Add** button is used to add a mesh to the selected rigid body. Once you add a mesh, it will be displayed in the above mentioned list box. You can rename or delete mesh from this list by using the **Rename** or **Delete** button located below this list. Similarly, if you select a mesh and choose the **Copy Mesh** button, the selected mesh will get copied to the clipboard. Choose the **Paste Mesh** button to paste a mesh to another rigid body.

Mesh Type

This drop-down list is used to apply the physical mesh type to the selected physical mesh in the list box of the **Select a Mesh to Modify** area. If you change the mesh type, a new mesh will be generated which will fit around the graphical mesh.

Convert to Custom Mesh

When you choose this button, a new editable mesh object will be created from the highlighted physical mesh in the **Select a Mesh to Modify** list. You can edit this mesh using the standard mesh editing tools.

Override Physical Material

Some rigid bodies consist of many physical meshes. If you select the **Override Physical Material** check box, you can use different settings for certain physical meshes. By default, this check box is cleared, which means that all physical meshes of a rigid body use the settings specified in the **Physical Material** rollout.

Physical Mesh Parameters Rollout

The parameters in this rollout vary depending on the option selected in the **Mesh Type** drop-down list of the **Physical Meshes** rollout. Figure 17-10 shows the **Physical Mesh Parameters** rollout for the **Box** mesh type.

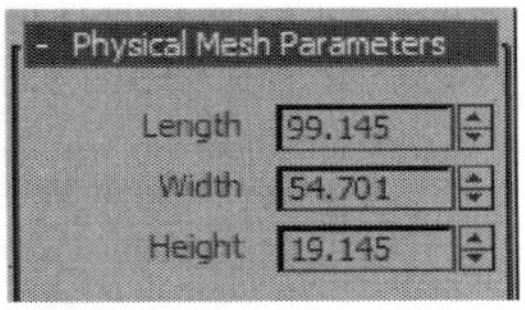

***Figure 17-10** The **Physical Mesh Parameters** rollout for the **Box** mesh type*

Advanced Rollout

The **Advanced** rollout contains **Simulation**, **Initial Motion**, **Center of Mass**, and **Damping** areas, as shown in Figure 17-11. The areas in this rollout are discussed next.

Simulation Area

The options in the **Simulation** area are discussed next.

Override Collision Overlap

The **Override Collision Overlap** check box is cleared by default. If you select this check box, the spinner below it will be activated and the value entered in this spinner will override the value in the **Collision Overlap** spinner in the **World** tab of the **MassFX Tools** dialog box for a selected rigid body.

Override Solver Iterations

By default, the **Override Solver Iterations** check box in the **Simulation** area is cleared. If you select this check box, the spinner below it will be activated and the value entered in the spinner will override the value specified in the **Solver Iter.** spinner in the **World** tab of the **MassFX Tools** dialog box for a selected rigid body.

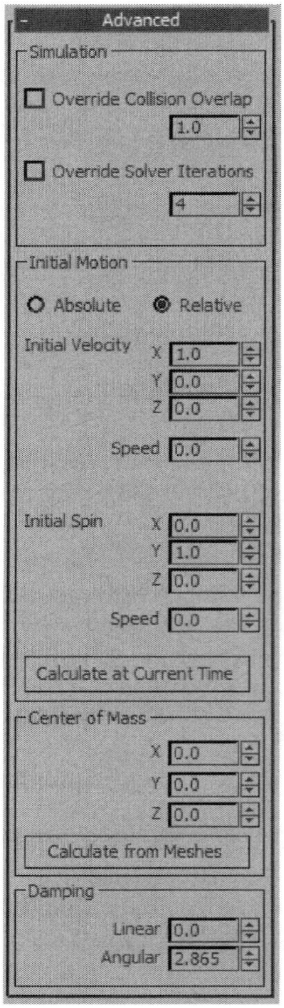

Figure 17-11 The ***Advanced*** *rollout*

Initial Motion Area

The options in the **Initial Motion** area are discussed next.

Absolute

When you select this radio button from the **Initial Motion** area, the values specified in the **Initial Velocity** and **Initial Spin** spinners in this area will be used instead of animation-based values. Note that these settings can be applied only to a rigid body which is kinematic at the start of the animation and then turns to a dynamic rigid body at the frame specified in the spinner in the **Rigid Body Properties** rollout.

Relative

By default, the **Relative** radio button is selected. As a result, the values specified in the **Initial Velocity** and **Initial Spin** spinners are added to the values calculated from the animation.

Initial Velocity

This option is used to specify the starting direction and speed for a kinematic rigid body when it is converted to a dynamic rigid body. You need to use the **Initial Velocity** sub-object level to see the initial velocity direction. You can use the **Select and Rotate** tool to change the direction of velocity.

Initial Spin

This option is used to specify the starting axis and the rotation speed of the kinematic rigid body when it is converted into a dynamic rigid body. You need to use the **Initial Spin** sub-object level to see the initial spin direction. You can use the **Select and Rotate** tool to change the direction of spin.

Calculate at Current Time

The **Calculate at Current Time** button is used to calculate the motion values of an animated kinematic rigid body at a frame other than the one at which it is converted into a dynamic rigid body and then sets the values in the **Initial Velocity** and **Initial Spin** spinners to those values.

Center of Mass Area

The center of mass of an object is a point around which the real physical object rotates unless it is constrained in some way. You need to select the **Center of Mass** sub-object level to visualize it. You can set the values in the **X**, **Y**, and **Z** spinners or use the **Select and Move** tool to adjust the center of mass.

Calculate from Meshes

The **Calculate from Meshes** button is used to automatically calculate the center of mass of a rigid body and set the values in the **X**, **Y**, and **Z** spinners accordingly.

Damping Area

The options in the **Damping** area are discussed next.

Linear

The value in the **Linear** spinner is the amount of force applied to reduce the velocity of a moving rigid body which in turn slows it down.

Angular

The value in the **Angular** spinner is the amount of force applied to reduce the rotational speed of a rotating rigid body.

Note

If you apply the ***MassFX Rigid Body*** *modifier to an object which is already a rigid body, then the existing rigid body will be replaced with the new one and the* ***MassFX Rigid Body*** *modifier will remain applied with the change in the rigid body type.*

CONSTRAINTS

Constraints are used to restrict the movement of rigid bodies in the simulation. Various types of constraints are available in the Constraint flyout, such as rigid constraint, slide constraint, hinge constraint, and so on. These constraints are used to make the two rigid bodies work together. A constraint links two rigid bodies together or links a single rigid body to a fixed point in global space. The constraints develop a hierarchical relationship in which the child object must be a dynamic rigid body, while the parent object can be a dynamic or a kinematic rigid body, or can be a point in the global space. The process of creating various constraints given in the **MassFX Toolbar** is discussed next.

Creating the Rigid Constraint

MassFX Toolbar:	Constraints > Create Rigid Constraint
Menu bar:	Animation > Simulation - MassFX > Constraints > Create Rigid Constraint

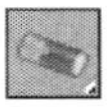

You can create a rigid constraint using the **Create Rigid Constraint** tool. To do so, select two objects in the viewport. The object selected first, will act as the parent object which means that it can either be a kinematic or a dynamic rigid body. The second object will act as a child object which means that it must be a dynamic rigid body. Next, choose the **Create Rigid Constraint** tool from the **MassFX Toolbar**; a transparent box will be displayed in the viewport. Move the cursor in the viewport and then click in the viewport when you get the required size of the constraint; a transparent white box representing the constraint will be displayed in the viewport. Also, the **Uconstraint** will be displayed in the modifier stack and various rollouts will be displayed in the modify panel, as shown in Figure 17-12. If the selected object is not a rigid body, the **MAXScript** message box will be displayed, as shown in Figure 17-13. Choose the **Yes** button in the message box and then create a rigid body constraint as discussed above. Note that here the **MassFX Rigid Body** modifier will be applied to the selected object and it will become a dynamic rigid body.

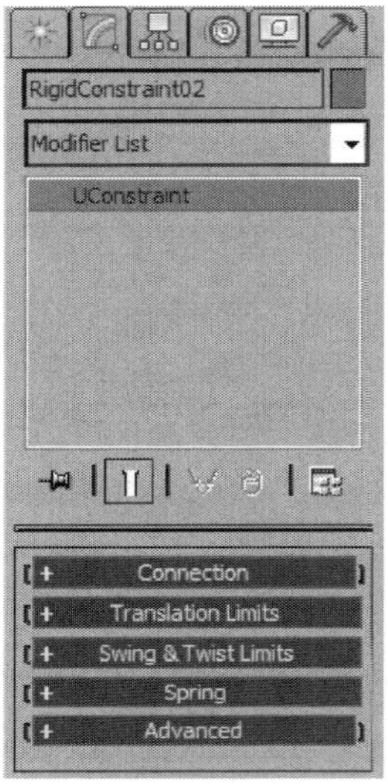

***Figure 17-12** The rollouts of rigid constraint in the modify panel*

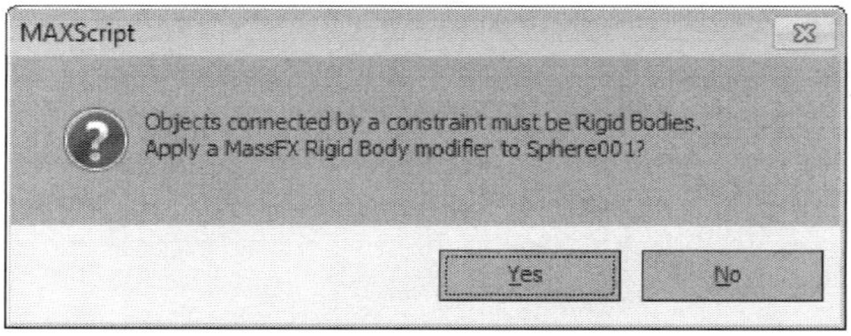

***Figure 17-13** The **MAXScript** message box*

Various rollouts of rigid constraint are discussed next.

Connection Rollout

The parameters in the **Connection** rollout are shown in Figure 17-14. These parameters are discussed next.

Parent

The button located next to **Parent** specifies a parent object in the constraint. To change the parent object, choose this button and select another object in the viewport; the parent object is replaced with the selected object. Note that the parent object can be a kinematic or dynamic rigid body. You can choose the **X** button located next to it to remove the parent object. On doing so, the button is replaced with the **None** label and the applied constraint is anchored to the global space.

Child

The button located next to **Child** specifies a child object in the constraint. To change the child object, choose this button and select another object in the viewport; the child object is replaced with the selected object. Note that the child object can only be a dynamic rigid body.

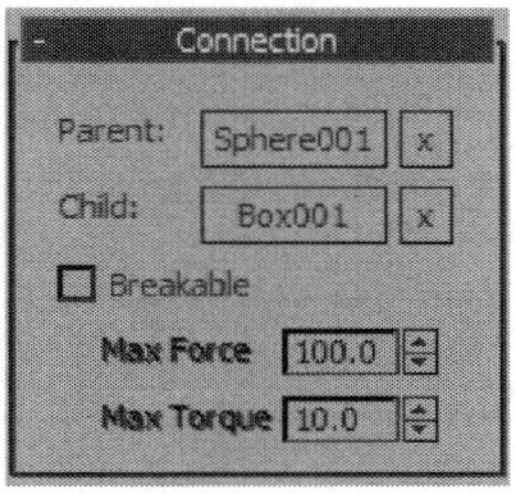

Figure 17-14 The ***Connection*** *rollout*

Breakable

By default, this check box is cleared. If you select it, the constraint will break at a certain linear force or at a certain twisting force during simulation. The linear force beyond which the constraint will break is specified in the **Max Force** spinner. The twisting force beyond which the constraint will break is specified in the **Max Torque** spinner.

Max Force

The **Max Force** spinner becomes active only when the **Breakable** check box is selected. As discussed above, you need to increase the **Max Force** spinner value to make the constraint more difficult to break.

Max Torque

The **Max Torque** spinner becomes active only when the **Breakable** check box is selected. As discussed above, you need to increase the **Max Torque** spinner value to make the constraint more difficult to break.

Translation Limits Rollout

The parameters in the **Translation Limits** rollout are shown in Figure 17-15. These parameters are discussed next.

Locked

If you select the **X**, **Y**, and **Z** radio buttons in the **Locked** column, then the rigid bodies will be prevented from sliding along the respective axes.

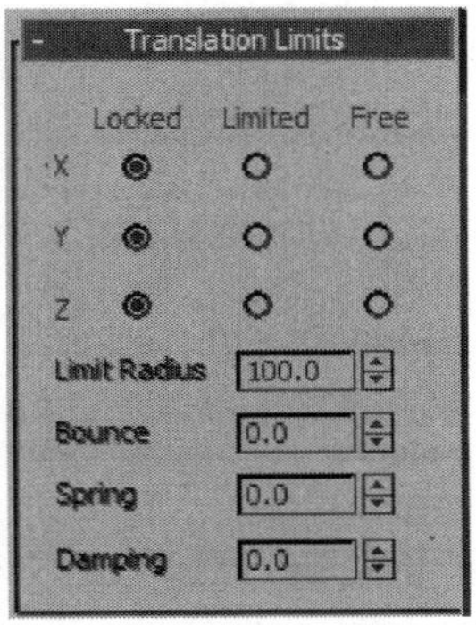

Figure 17-15 *The* ***Translation Limits*** *rollout*

Limited

If you select a radio button in the **Limited** column, then the rigid bodies will be able to move along the respective axis by an amount specified in the **Limit Radius** spinner. Note that on selecting a radio button from this column, the **Limit Radius**, **Bounce**, **Spring**, and **Damping** spinners will be activated. If you select more than one radio button in this column, then the motion will be limited radially.

Free
Select the radio buttons in the **Free** column to allow unrestricted motion of the rigid bodies along the axis corresponding to the selected radio button.

Limit Radius
The **Limit Radius** spinner is used to specify the distance that the rigid bodies can move along an axis or axes.

Bounce
The **Bounce** spinner is used to specify the amount by which the rigid bodies will rebound when hit.

Spring
The **Spring** spinner is used to specify the strength of the string which will pull back the rigid bodies to the limit if the limit is exceeded. The larger the values specified in the **Spring** spinner, the greater will be the force applied to the rigid bodies to pull them back to the limit and vice versa.

Damping
The **Damping** spinner is used to specify the amount by which the rigid bodies will move beyond the limit, if translation exceeds the limit. There will be no damping when the spinner value is 0.

Swing & Twist Limits Rollout
The parameters in the **Swing & Twist** rollout are shown in Figure 17-16. The parameters in the **Swing Y** and **Swing Z** areas are related to the rotation of rigid bodies around the local Z and Y axes whereas the parameters in the **Twist** area are related to the rotation of rigid bodies around the local X axis. Most of the parameters in these areas are similar to those discussed in the **Translation Limits** rollout.

Spring Rollout
The parameters in the **Spring** rollout are shown in Figure 17-17. The parameters in the **Spring to Resting Position** area of this rollout are discussed next.

Springiness
The value in the **Springiness** spinner indicates the amount of force which will pull the translation of the parent and child objects back to their initial offset positions.

Damping
The value in the **Damping** spinner indicates the amount of force that would restrict the spring force.

Advanced Rollout
The parameters in the **Advanced** rollout are shown in Figure 17-18. The most commonly used parameters are discussed next.

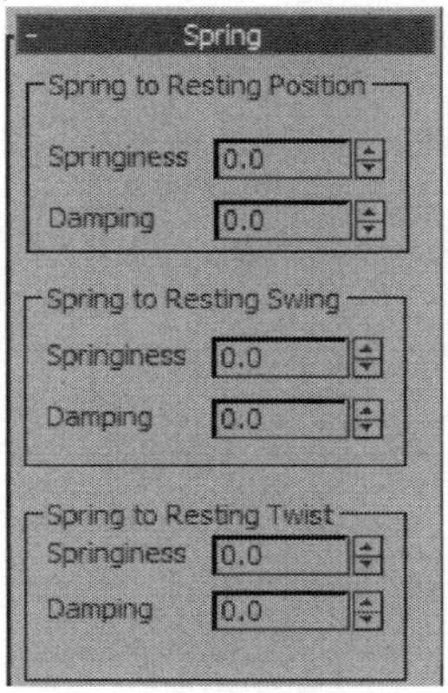

Figure 17-17 The ***Spring*** *rollout*

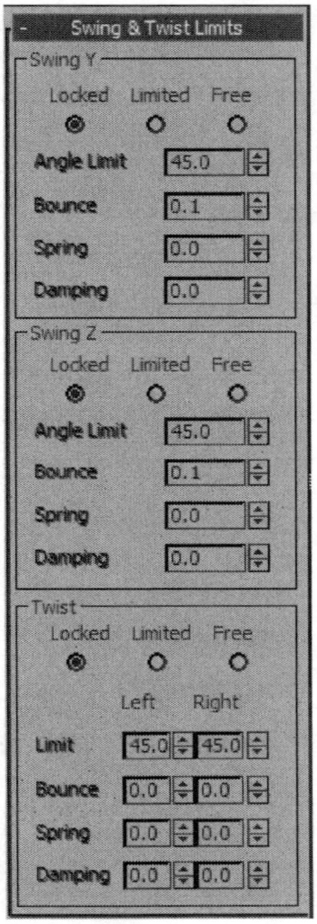

Figure 17-16 The ***Swing & Twist Limits*** *rollout*

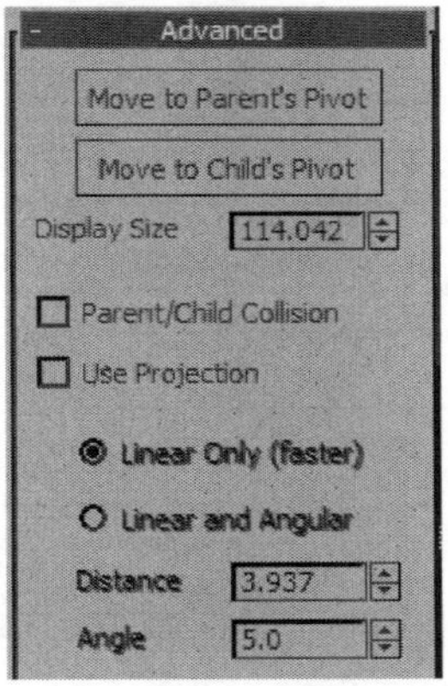

Figure 17-18 The ***Advanced*** *rollout*

Move To Parent's Pivot

This button is used to move the constraint to the pivot of the parent object. It is useful when you want to rotate the child object around the pivot of the parent object.

Move To Child's Pivot

This button is used to move the constraint to the pivot of the child object.

Display Size

The **Display Size** spinner is used to set the size of the constraint in the viewport.

Parent/Child Collision

By default, this check box is cleared. If you select this check box, the parent and child objects will be allowed to collide with each other.

Creating the Slide Constraint

MassFX Toolbar:	Constraints > Create Slide Constraint
Menu bar:	Animation > Simulation - MassFX > Constraints Create Slide Constraint

You can create the slide constraint by using the **Create Slide Constraint** tool. To do so, select two objects in the viewport as done in case of rigid constraint. Next, click and hold the cursor on the **Create Rigid Constraint** tool; a flyout will be displayed, as shown in Figure 17-19. Choose **Create Slide Constraint** from the flyout; a connecting line will be displayed in the viewport. Also, **Uconstraint** will be displayed in the modifier stack and various rollouts will be displayed in the modify panel. These rollouts have already been discussed in the **Create Rigid Constraint** section. The slide constraint is similar to the rigid constraint with the only difference that in the slide constraint, the translational motion along **Y** axis is set to **Limited** in the **Translation Limits** rollout by default.

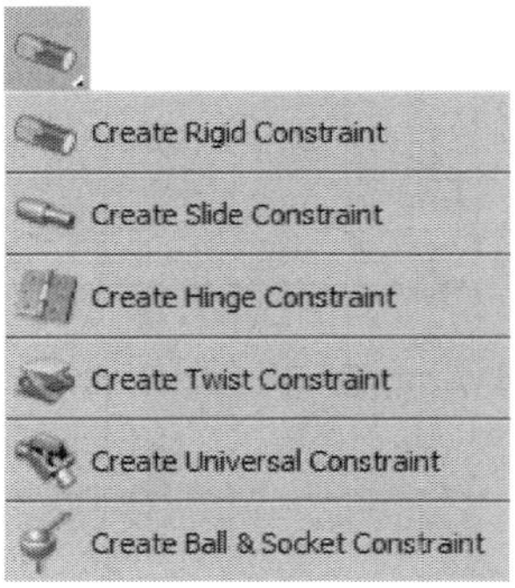

Figure 17-19 *Various options in the flyout*

Creating the Hinge Constraint

MassFX Toolbar:	Constraints > Create Hinge Constraint
Menu bar:	Animation > Simulation - MassFX > Constraints > Create Hinge Constraint

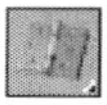

You can create the hinge constraint using the **Create Hinge Constraint** tool. To do so, select two objects in the viewport as done in case of rigid constraint. Next, click and hold the cursor on the **Create Rigid Constraint** tool; a flyout will be displayed, refer to Figure 17-19. Choose **Create Hinge Constraint** from the flyout; a hinge constraint will be displayed in the viewport. Also, **Uconstraint** will be displayed in the modifier stack and various rollouts will be displayed in the modify panel. These rollouts are same as those discussed in the **Create Rigid Constraint** section. The hinge constraint is similar to the rigid constraint with the only difference that in the hinge constraint, the **Angle** spinner in the **Swing Z** area is limited to **100** degrees in the **Swing & Twist Limits** rollouts.

Creating the Twist Constraint

MassFX Toolbar:	Constraints > Create Twist Constraint
Menu bar:	Animation > Simulation - MassFX > Constraints > Create Twist Constraint

You can create the twist constraint using the **Create Twist Constraint** tool. To do so, select two objects in the viewport as done in case of rigid constraint. Next, click and hold the cursor on the **Create Rigid Constraint** tool; a flyout will be displayed. Choose **Create Twist Constraint** from the flyout; a disc shaped constraint will be displayed in the viewport. Also, **Uconstraint** will be displayed in the modifier stack and various rollouts will be displayed in the modify panel. These rollouts are same as those discussed in the **Create Rigid Constraint** section. Twist constraint is similar to rigid constraint with the only difference that in the twist constraint the **Free** radio button is selected by default in the **Twist** area of the **Swing & Twist Limits** rollout.

Creating the Universal Constraint

MassFX Toolbar:	Constraints > Create Universal Constraint
Menu bar:	Animation > Simulation - MassFX > Constraints > Create Universal Constraint

You can create the universal constraint using the **Create Universal Constraint** tool. To do so, select two objects in the viewport as done in case of rigid constraint. Next, click and hold the cursor on the **Create Rigid Constraint** tool; a flyout will be displayed. Choose **Create Universal Constraint** from the flyout; a cone shaped constraint will be displayed in the viewport. Also, **Uconstraint** will be displayed in the modifier stack and various rollouts will be displayed in the modify panel. These rollouts are same as those discussed in the **Create Rigid Constraint** section. The universal constraint is similar to the rigid constraint with the only difference that in the universal constraint the **Angle** spinner in the **Swing Y** and **Swing Z** areas is limited to **45** degrees in the **Swing & Twist Limits** rollout.

Creating the Ball & Socket Constraint

MassFX Toolbar:	Constraints > Create Ball & Socket Constraint
Menu bar:	Animation > Simulation - MassFX > Constraints > Create Ball & Socket Constraint

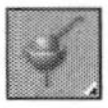

You can create the ball & socket constraint using the **Create Ball & Socket Constraint** tool. To do so, select two objects in the viewport as done in case of rigid constraint. Next, click and hold the cursor on the **Create Rigid Constraint** tool; a flyout will be displayed. Choose **Create Ball & Socket Constraint** from the flyout; a ball and socket constraint will be displayed in the viewport. Also, **Uconstraint** will be displayed in the modifier stack and various rollouts will be displayed in the modify panel. These rollouts are same as those discussed in the **Create Rigid Constraint** section. The ball & socket constraint is similar to the rigid constraint with the only difference that in the ball & socket constraint the **Angle** spinner in the **Swing Y** and **Swing Z** areas is set to **80** degrees and the **Free** radio button is selected by default in the **Twist** area of the **Swing & Twist Limits** rollout.

SIMULATION CONTROLS

Simulation controls are used to control the simulation of rigid bodies. These controls are located on the **MassFX Toolbar**. These controls are discussed next.

Reset Simulation

MassFX Toolbar:	Reset Simulation
Menu bar:	Animation > Simulation - MassFX > Simulation > Reset Simulation

The **Reset Simulation** button is used to halt the simulation and move the time slider to the first frame. It also resets the transform values of dynamic rigid bodies to their initial values.

Start Simulation

MassFX Toolbar:	Start Simulation
Menu bar:	Animation > Simulation - MassFX > Simulation > Start Simulation

The **Start Simulation** button is used to start the simulation from the current frame. You can choose the same button to pause the simulation if it is already running.

Start Simulation Without Animation

MassFX Toolbar:	Start Simulation Without Animation

This button is also used to start the simulation with the only difference that the time slider will not move as the simulation runs. It is useful when you want a dynamic rigid body to settle down to a position which can be used as initial transform.

Step Simulation

MassFX Toolbar:	Step Simulation
Menu bar:	Animation > Simulation - MassFX > Simulation > Step Simulation

This button is used to run the simulation for a single frame and move the time slider by a single frame.

Display MassFX Tools Dialog

MassFX Toolbar:	Display MassFX Tools Dialog
Menu bar:	Animation > Simulation - MassFX > Utilities > Show MassFX Tools

The **Display MassFX Tools Dialog** button is used to open the **MassFX Tools** dialog box, refer to Figure 17-20. If you choose this button again, this dialog box will close. This dialog box consists of four tabs: **World**, **Tools**, **Edit**, and **Display**. These tabs are discussed next.

World Tab

The **World** tab consists of different rollouts such as **Scene Settings**, **Advanced Settings**, **Simulation Settings**, and **Engine**. The parameters in these rollouts provide global settings and controls for creating physical simulations. Most commonly used rollouts in this tab are discussed next.

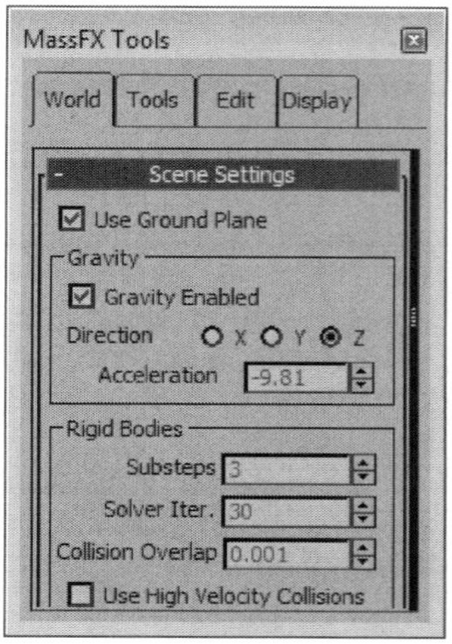

*Figure 17-20 The **MassFX Tools** dialog box*

Scene Settings Rollout

In this rollout, the **Use Ground Plane** check box is selected by default. It means that the MassFX interface uses an invisible static rigid body that is coplanar with the home grid. The **Gravity Enabled** check box is also selected by default. As a result, a rigid body is subjected to gravity, provided the **Use Gravity** check box in its **Rigid Body Properties** rollout is also selected. Select the **X**, **Y**, or **Z** radio button next to the **Direction** label to specify the global axis along which the gravity will be applied. The value in the **Acceleration** spinner is used to specify the force of gravity. A positive value in this spinner will pull the object in the upward direction, whereas a negative value will pull the object in the downward direction.

Simulation Settings Rollout

The options in this rollout are used to specify how the simulation will proceed at the last frame of the animation. For example, if the **Continue Selection** radio button is selected, the simulation will continue to run even after the time slider reaches the last frame.

Tools Tab

The **Tools** tab consists of two rollouts: **Simulation** and **Utilities**, as shown in Figure 17-21. These rollouts are discussed next.

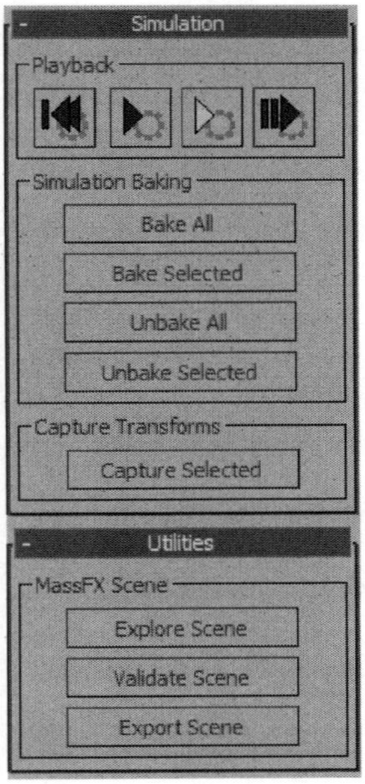

***Figure 17-21** The **Simulation** and **Utilities** rollouts in the **Tools** tab*

Simulation Rollout

The buttons in the **Simulation** rollout are used to control the simulation, baking dynamic transforms to keyframes, and specifying the starting transform for a dynamic rigid body. The buttons in the **Playback** area have already been discussed in the **Simulation Controls** section. You can choose a button in the **Simulation Baking** area depending on whether you need to bake the selected object, bake all objects, unbake selected object, or unbake all objects.

Utilities Rollout

The options in the **MassFX Scene** area of this rollout are discussed next.

Explore Scene

When you choose the **Explore Scene** button, the **Scene Explorer - MassFX Explorer** dialog box will be displayed, refer to Figure 17-22. In this dialog box, you can view and change the simulation properties of all rigid bodies and constraints in the scene. If you choose the **Display non-Dynamics Objects** button, all non-dynamic objects will also be displayed in this dialog box.

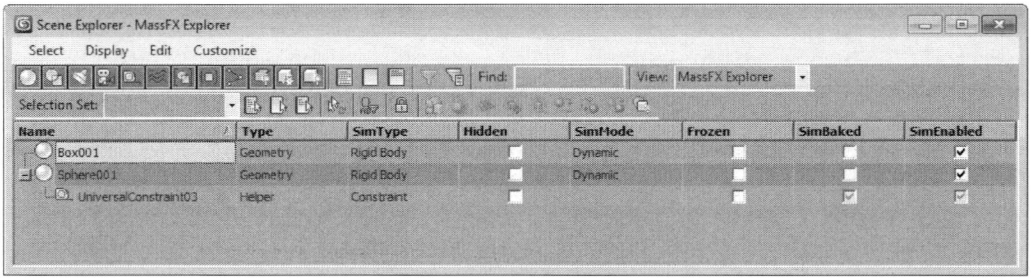

*Figure 17-22 The **Scene Explorer - MassFX Explorer** dialog box*

Validate Scene

When you choose the **Validate Scene** button, the **Validate PhysX Scene** dialog box will be displayed, as shown in Figure 17-23. The **Validate** button in this dialog box is used to check validation of the scene based on the check boxes selected in the dialog box. Green square at the right of the check box indicates that the result is 'valid', red square indicates that the result is 'Fail' and yellow square indicates that you need to take a note of the result.

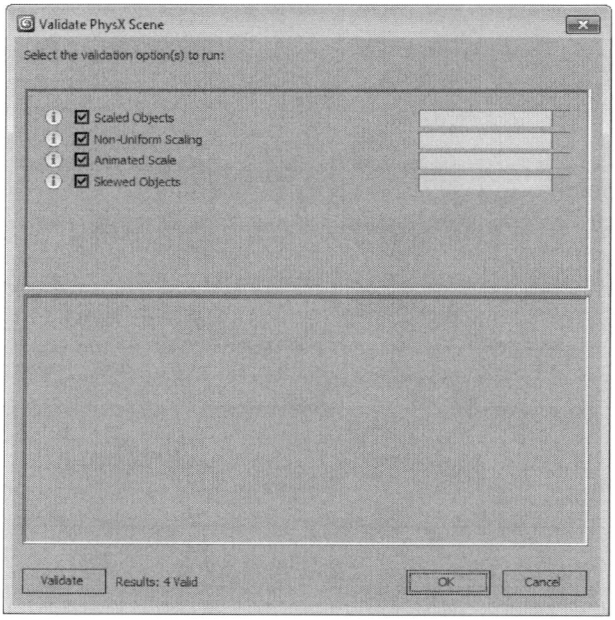

*Figure 17-23 The **Validate PhysX Scene** dialog box*

Export Scene

This button is used to export the MassFX information. On choosing the **Export Scene** button, the **MassFX Export** dialog box will be displayed. Select the **Validate scene before export** check box to check the validity of a scene. You need to choose the **Export to new file** button to save the file at the desired location. The drop-down list next to this button is used to specify the file types. You can choose the **Export to last file/type** button to save the file with the same file type as the last saved file.

Edit Tab

The rollouts in the **Edit** tab are the same as those in the modify panel of the **MassFX Rigid Body** modifier and have been discussed earlier. The differences between the settings in the **Edit** tab and those in the modify panel of the **MassFX Rigid Body** modifier are given in the Table 17-1:

Edit Tab	Modify Panel
Sets properties for all selected objects simultaneously	Sets properties for only one object at a time
Can create new physical material presets	Cannot create new physical material presets
Can edit the physical mesh property of rigid bodies having a single physical mesh	Can edit or create objects with multiple meshes using the parameters in the Physical Meshes rollout

Table 17-1 *Comparing the options in the* ***Edit*** *tab and the* ***MassFX Rigid Body*** *modifier*

Note

While using the ***Edit*** *tab to edit multiple selected objects that have different values for a given parameter in their respective modify panels, the spinner will remain blank or the check box will be filled with a color in this tab for that parameter. In such a case, you can enter a new value in the spinner or select the respective check box in this tab so that same settings can be applied to the selected objects.*

Display Tab

The two check boxes at the top of this tab are: **Display Physical Meshes** and **Selected Objects Only**. By default, these check boxes are selected and indicate that physical meshes will be displayed in the viewport for selected objects. The options in the **MassFX Visualizer** rollout are used to display various properties of rigid bodies when the simulation proceeds. These settings are used for debugging purposes and will be effective only when you select the **Enable Visualizer** check box in the **Options** area of the **MassFX Visualizer** rollout.

HELPERS

To create helper objects, choose **Create > Helpers** in the **Command Panel**; a drop-down list will be displayed with the **Standard** option selected by default, as shown in Figure 17-24. You can select any other option from this drop-down list. Depending on the option selected, different helpers will be displayed in the **Object Type** rollout. In this chapter, you will learn to use different types of helper objects.

Dummy Helper

Menu bar:	Create > Helpers > Dummy
Command Panel:	Create > Helpers > Standard > Object Type rollout > Dummy

The dummy helper object is a wireframe box, as shown in Figure 17-25. It has a pivot point at its geometric center.

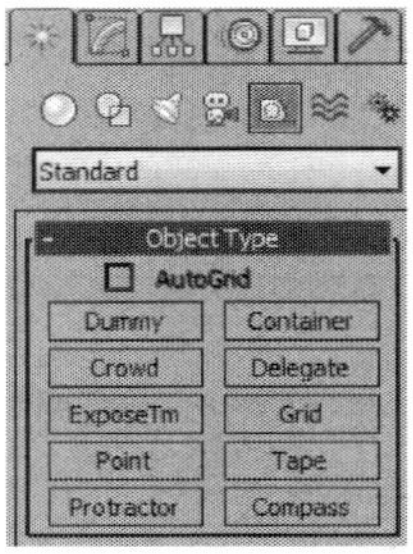

Figure 17-24** The **Helpers** button chosen in the **Command Panel

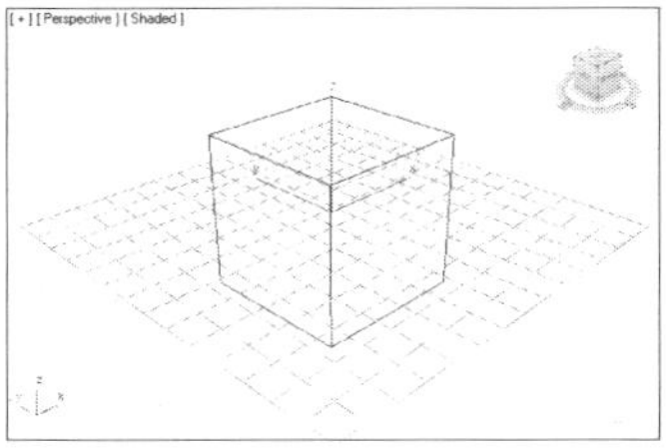

***Figure 17-25** A dummy helper object in the Perspective viewport*

A dummy object helps in animating the objects in a hierarchical linkage. For example, if you link a number of objects to a dummy object and then animate the dummy object, all the linked objects will follow the same animation. You can also use the dummy object to animate the target camera in your scene. To do so, you need to link the camera and its target to the dummy object. Now if you animate the dummy object, then the camera and its target will follow the same animation.

To create a dummy object, choose **Create > Helpers** in the **Command Panel**; the **Standard** option will be displayed in the drop-down list. Now, invoke the **Dummy** tool from the **Object Type** rollout and then drag the cursor in the viewport from one place to another; a dummy object will be created, refer to Figure 17-25. Note that you cannot modify the shape or size of the dummy object. You can scale it using the scaling tools in the **Main Toolbar**. However, it can create unexpected result if the dummy object is within a hierarchical linkage.

Point Helper

Menu bar:	Create > Helpers > Point
Command Panel:	Create > Helpers > Standard > Object Type rollout > Point

The point helper object is used to create a specific location in 3D space that can be used as a reference in a scene. To create a point object, choose **Create > Helpers** in the **Command Panel**; the **Standard** option will be displayed in the drop-down list. Invoke the **Point** tool from the **Object Type** rollout; the **Parameters** rollout will be displayed in the modify panel. Now, press and hold the left mouse button in the viewport and drag the cursor to specify the location of the point. Next, release the mouse button; a point helper object will be displayed, as shown in Figure 17-26. You can modify the shape and size of the point helper object by specifying the parameters in the **Parameters** rollout, refer to Figure 17-27. Select any of the check boxes in the **Display** area to modify the shape of the point helper object in the viewport. Set the value in the **Size** spinner to specify the size of the point helper object. Select the **Constant Screen Size** check box to keep the size of the point helper object constant while zooming the viewport. Select the **Draw On Top** check box to place the point object at the top of the objects in the viewport.

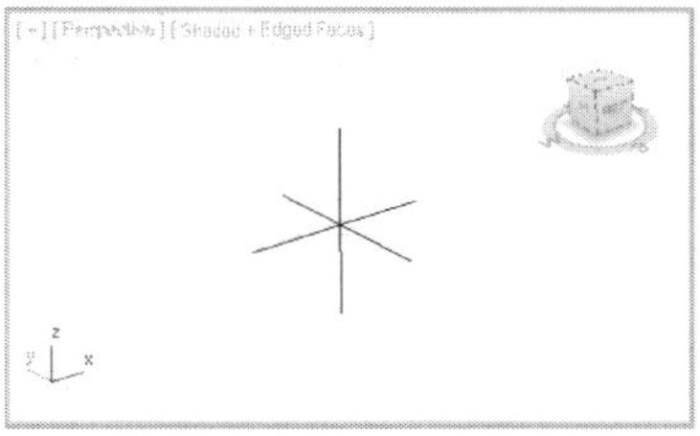

Figure 17-26 *A point helper object*

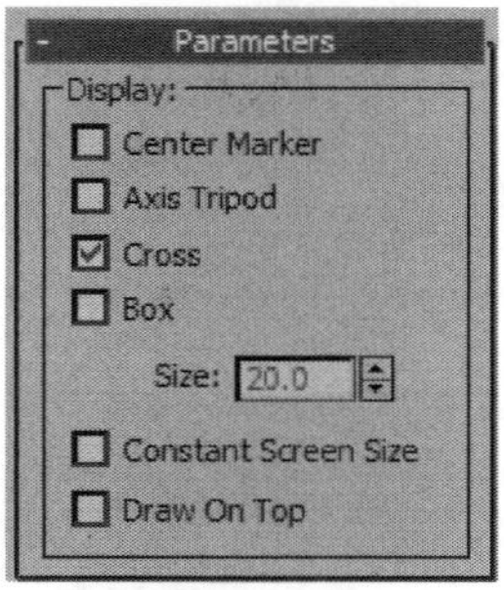

Figure 17-27 *The* ***Parameters*** *rollout*

Tape Helper

Menu bar:	Create > Helpers > Tape Measure
Command Panel:	Create > Helpers > Standard > Object Type rollout > Tape

The tape measure is used to create a virtual tape to measure and set on-screen distances. To create a tape measure object, choose **Create > Helpers** in the **Command Panel**; the **Standard** option will be displayed in the drop-down list. Invoke the **Tape** tool from the **Object Type** rollout; the **Parameters** rollout will be displayed in the modify panel. Now, press and hold the left mouse button in the viewport, drag the cursor from one point to another to place the target of the tape and then release the left mouse button; a tape measure will be created in the viewport, as shown in Figure 17-28. Also, the length of the tape measure object will be displayed in the **Length** spinner of the **Parameters** rollout, as shown in Figure 17-29. By default, the value in the **Length** spinner will be in gray and it cannot be modified.

To set specific on-screen distance, select the **Specify Length** check box in the **Parameters** rollout; the **Length** spinner will be activated. Set the value in the **Length** spinner; the length of the tape measure will be modified according to the value specified in the **Length** spinner. Moreover, you can set the position of the target by dragging the target.

Figure 17-28 *A tape measure created in a scene*

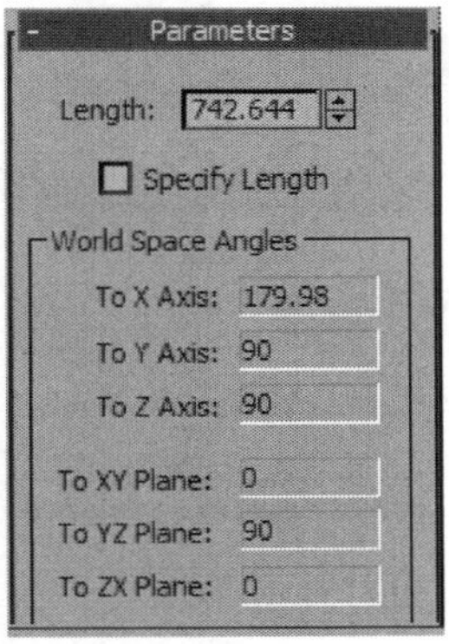

Figure 17-29 *The* ***Parameters*** *rollout*

Protractor Helper

Menu bar:	Create > Helpers > Protractor
Command Panel:	Create > Helpers > Standard > Object Type rollout > Protractor

The protractor helper is used to measure the angle between two objects in a scene. To create a protractor for measuring the angle between two objects, choose **Create > Helpers** in the **Command Panel**; the **Standard** option will be displayed in the drop-down list by default. Now, invoke the **Protractor** tool from the **Object Type** rollout; the **Parameters** rollout will be displayed in the modify panel. Click in the viewport to create the protractor helper, as shown in Figure 17-30. In the **Parameters** rollout, choose the **Pick Object 1** button and select an object in the viewport. Then, choose the **Pick Object 2** button and select another object in the viewport; the angle between the selected objects will be displayed in the **Angle** text box of the **Parameters** rollout, as shown in Figure 17-31. Also, the connecting lines will be displayed from the protractor object to the other objects in the viewport, refer to Figure 17-30.

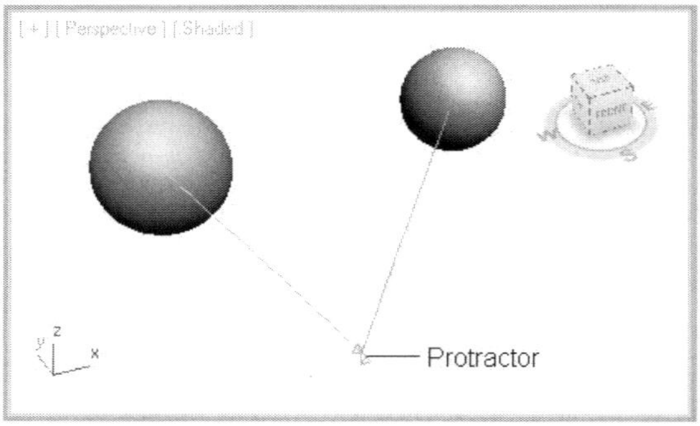

***Figure 17-30** A protractor helper object*

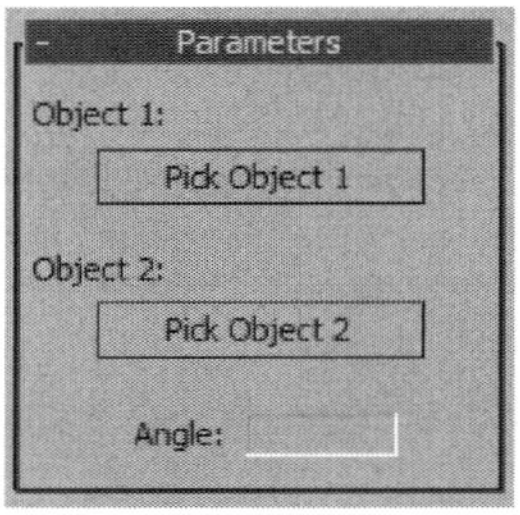

***Figure 17-31** The **Parameters** rollout*

Compass Helper

Menu bar:	Create > Helpers > Compass
Command Panel:	Create > Helpers > Standard > Object Type rollout > Compass

A compass is a part of the sunlight and daylight system and is automatically created with the system. The compass helper is used to create a compass rose in a scene, as shown in Figure 17-32. The compass rose is used to provide directional indicators in a scene. To create a compass rose, choose **Create > Helpers** in the **Command Panel**; the **Standard** option will be displayed in the drop-down list by default. Invoke the **Compass** tool from the **Object Type** rollout; the **Parameters** rollout will be displayed in the modify panel. Next, press and hold the left mouse button in the viewport and drag the cursor to specify the radius of the compass rose. Then, release the left mouse button; a compass rose will be created. You can also set the value in the **Radius** spinner of the **Parameters** rollout to modify its radius, as shown in Figure 17-33.

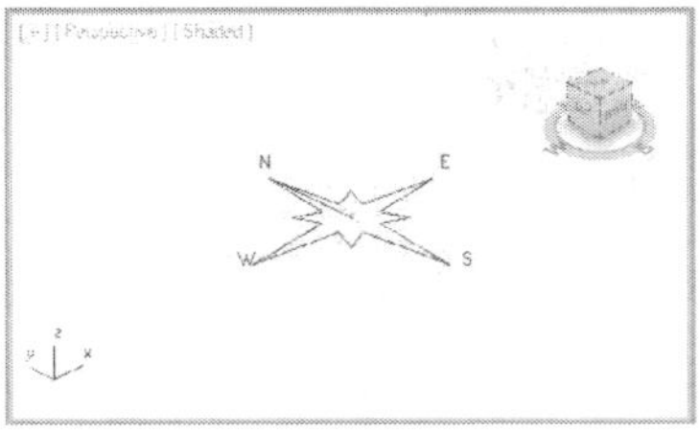

Figure 17-32 *A compass rose*

Figure 17-33 *The* ***Parameters*** *rollout*

Container Helper

Menu bar:	Create > Helpers > Container
Command Panel:	Create > Helpers > Standard > Object Type rollout > Container

A container is a helper object that is mainly used to organize scene components. On using this object, the scene components are organized in a logical group such that they can be handled as a single object. It also helps in reducing the scene complexity. To create a container helper, choose **Create > Helpers** in the **Command Panel**; the **Standard** option will be displayed in the drop-down list by default. Invoke the **Container** tool from the **Object Type** rollout and drag the cursor in the viewport; a container helper will be created, as shown in Figure 17-34. Next, choose the **Modify** tab; various rollouts to modify and set the parameters of the container will be displayed, as shown in Figure 17-35. To add scene components to the container, choose the **Add** button from the **Local Content** rollout; the **Add Container Node** dialog box will be displayed, as shown in Figure 17-36. Select the objects that you want to add to the container and choose the **Add** button in this dialog box; the selected objects will be added to the container. Now, if you transform the container helper by scaling, rotating, or moving, then the added objects will also get transformed in the same way.

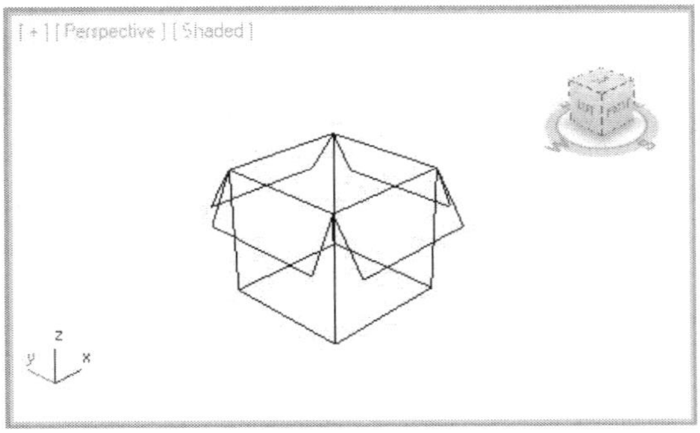

Figure 17-34 *A container helper*

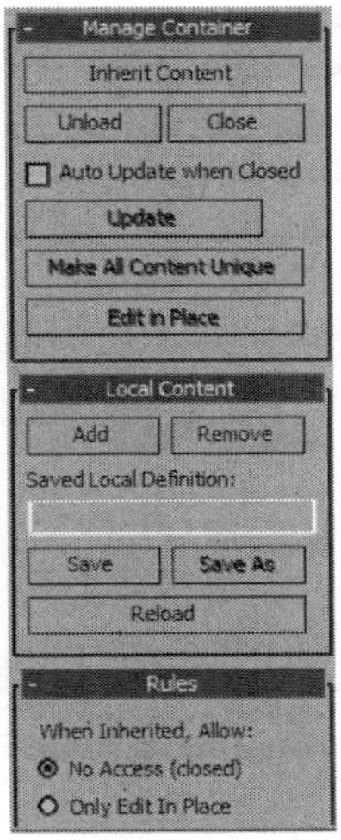

Figure 17-35 *Partial view of various rollouts displayed for the container helper*

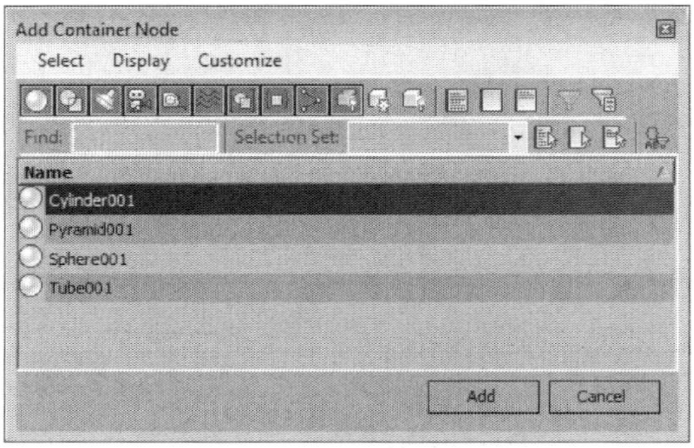

*Figure 17-36 The **Add Container Node** dialog box*

ATMOSPHERIC APPARATUS

In Autodesk 3ds Max, there are three types of gizmos that limit the fog or fire effects in a scene. You can create them by using the BoxGizmo, SphereGizmo, and CylGizmo helpers. These helpers are discussed next.

BoxGizmo Helper

Menu bar:	Create > Helpers > Atmospherics > Box Gizmo
Command Panel:	Create > Helpers > Atmospheric Apparatus > Object Type rollout > BoxGizmo

The BoxGizmo helper is used to create a box-shaped gizmo, as shown in Figure 17-37. To create a BoxGizmo helper object, choose **Create > Helpers** in the **Command Panel**; the **Standard** option will be displayed in the drop-down list by default. Select the **Atmospheric Apparatus** option from the drop-down list. Next, invoke the **BoxGizmo** tool from the **Object Type** rollout; the **Box Gizmo Parameters** rollout will be displayed in the modify panel. Create a gizmo in the viewport using the same method that was used to create a box. You can adjust the length, width, and height of the gizmo using the **Box Gizmo Parameters** rollout.

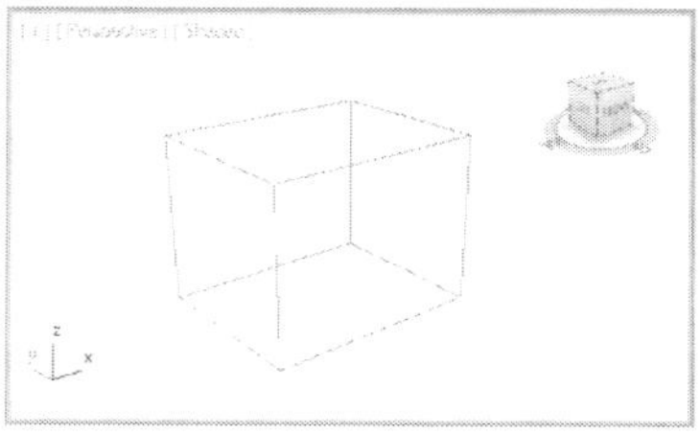

Figure 17-37 A BoxGizmo helper

To add an atmosphere to a scene, select the BoxGizmo in the viewport and then choose the **Modify** tab in the **Command Panel**; the **Box Gizmo Parameters** and **Atmospheres & Effects** rollouts will be displayed in the modify panel, as shown in Figure 17-38. Expand the **Atmospheres & Effects** rollout, if it is not already expanded. Choose the **Add** button; the

Add Atmosphere dialog box will be displayed, as shown in Figure 17-39. Select one of the effects from the text area of the **Add Atmosphere** dialog box and choose the **OK** button; the selected effect will be displayed in the text area of the **Atmospheres & Effects** rollout. Also, when you render the scene, the selected effect will be displayed. To set the parameters of the selected effect, select the name of the effect in the **Atmospheres & Effects** rollout and choose the **Setup** button; the **Environment and Effects** dialog box will be displayed. Set the parameters of the selected effect using the corresponding rollouts in the **Environment and Effects** dialog box.

Note

The SphereGizmo and CylGizmo helpers are the same as the BoxGizmo. The only difference is that the SphereGizmo is spherical and the CylGizmo is cylindrical in shape.

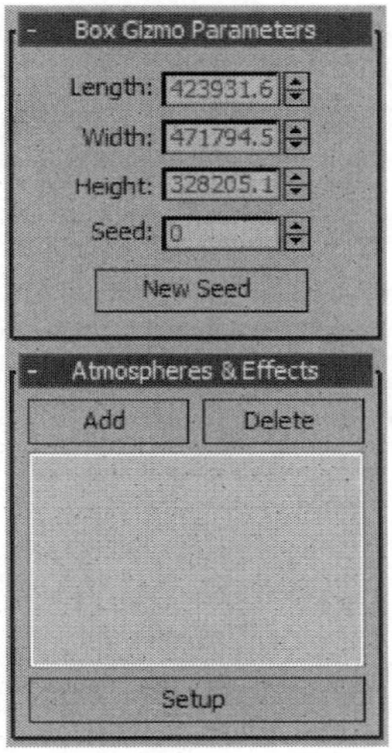

***Figure 17-38** The rollouts for modifying the BoxGizmo helper in the modify panel*

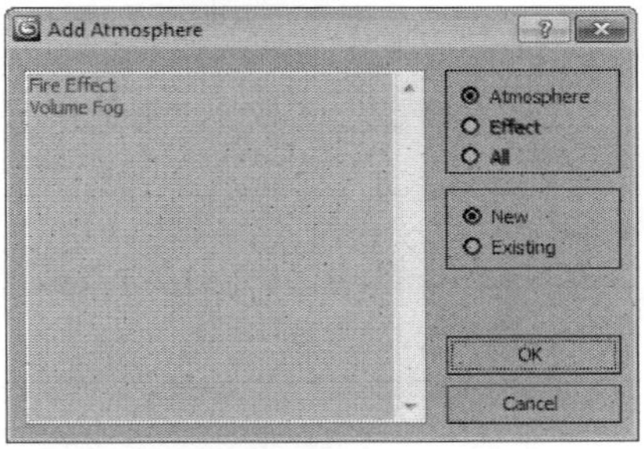

***Figure 17-39** The **Add Atmosphere** dialog box*

Tutorial 1

In this tutorial, you will simulate a falling ball using the MassFX interface, refer to Figure 17-40. **(Expected time: 30 min)**

The following steps are required to complete this tutorial:

a. Set the project folder.
b. Create the model and the ball.
c. Convert objects into rigid bodies.
d. Play the simulation.
e. Save the file.

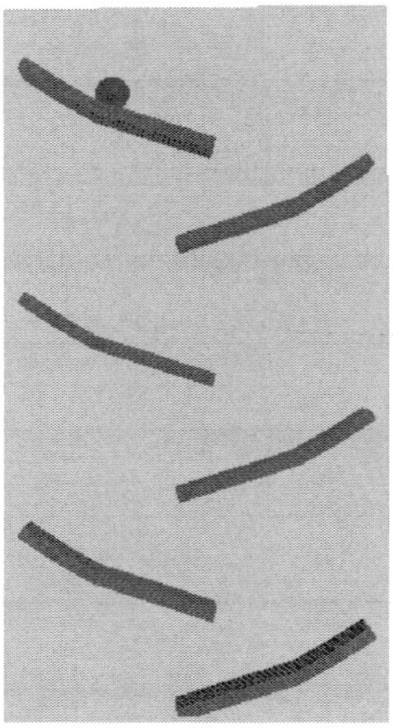

Figure 17-40 *The model for Tutorial 1*

Setting the Project Folder

1. Set the project folder with the name *c17_tut1* in the *3dsmax* folder as discussed in earlier chapters.

Creating the Model and the Ball

In this section, you need to create a ball and a model consisting of back support and six sliders.

1. Activate the Front viewport and choose **Create > Geometry** in the **Command Panel**; the **Standard Primitives** option is displayed in the drop-down list. Next, invoke the **Box** tool from the **Object Type** rollout.

2. Expand the **Keyboard Entry** rollout and set the values as given next:

   Length: **180** Width: **95** Height: **6**

3. Choose the **Create** button from the **Keyboard Entry** rollout; a box is created.

4. In the **Name and Color** rollout, enter **back support** as the name of the box and press ENTER.

5. Invoke the **Select and Move** tool and move the *back support* so that it is placed exactly on the grid in the Perspective viewport, as shown in Figure 17-41. This grid acts as a ground plane in the simulation.

Next, you need to create the sliders for the model.

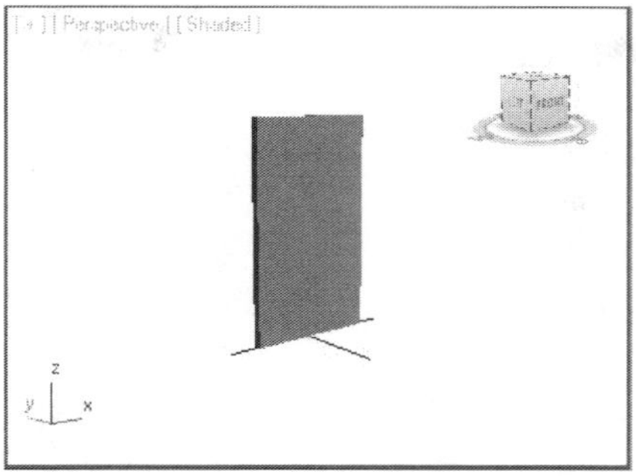

Figure 17-41 *Alignment of the back support with the grid*

6. Activate the Top viewport. Choose **Create > Geometry > Standard Primitives > Object Type** rollout **> Box** from the **Command panel**.

7. Expand the **Keyboard Entry** rollout and set the values as given next:

   Length: **15** Width: **50** Height: **3**

   Length Segs: **5** Width Segs: **5** Height Segs: **5**

8. Choose the **Create** button from the **Keyboard Entry** rollout; a box is created.

9. In the **Name and Color** rollout, enter **slider1** as the name of the box and then press ENTER.

10. Convert the *slider1* into editable poly to modify it at an advanced level.

11. Activate the Front viewport and select the **Polygon** sub-object level and align the left polygons using the **Select and Move** and **Select and Rotate** tools, as shown in Figure 17-42.

12. Select the **Polygon** sub-object level once again to deactivate it. Next, invoke the **Select and Move** tool and move the *slider1* at the top of the *back support* and rotate it using the **Select and Rotate** tool in the Front viewport, as shown in Figure 17-43.

    Next, you need to make copies of the *slider1*.

13. Make sure that *slider1* is selected and the Front viewport is activated. Press and hold the SHIFT key and drag the mouse downward using the left mouse button. Next, release the left mouse button and the SHIFT key approximately at a point above the middle of the *back support*; the **Clone Options** dialog box is displayed.

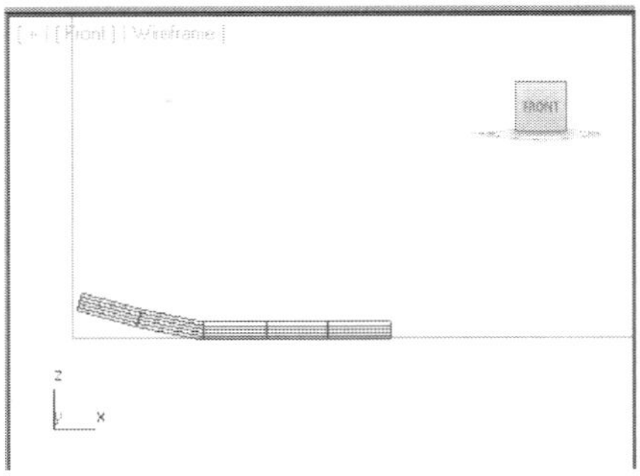

Figure 17-42 The slider1 after aligning the polygons

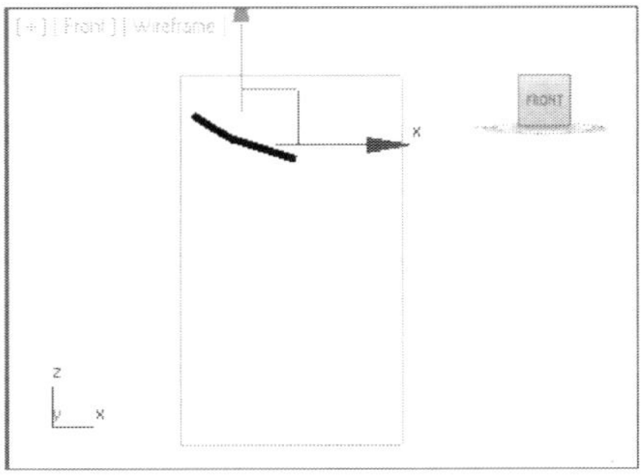

Figure 17-43 Alignment of the slider1 in the Front viewport

14. In the **Clone Options** dialog box, make sure that the **Copy** radio button is selected. In the **Number of Copies** spinner, set the value **2** and choose the **OK** button; two copies of the slider are formed and are automatically named as *slider002* and *slider003*.

15. Similarly, make three more copies of *slider1* and align them, as shown in Figure 17-44.

    Next, you need to create a ball.

16. Activate the Top viewport. Choose **Create > Geometry > Standard Primitives > Object Type** rollout **> Sphere** from the **Command panel**.

17. In the **Keyboard Entry** rollout, set the value of the **Radius** spinner to **4** and choose the **Create** button; a sphere is created.

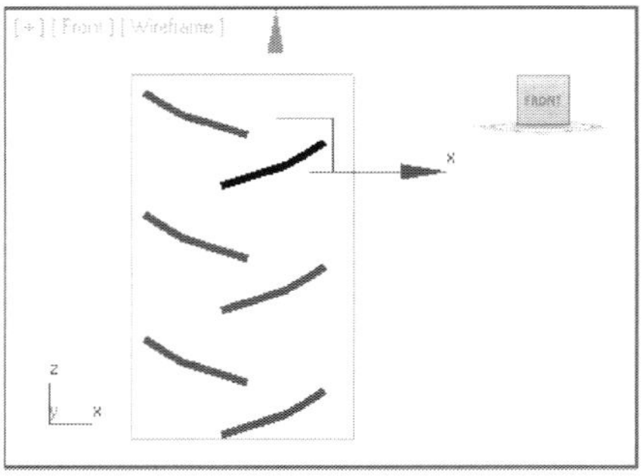

Figure 17-44 The sliders aligned in the Front viewport

18. Modify the name of the sphere to **ball**. Next, align the *ball* in all viewports so that it rests on the *slider1*, as shown in Figure 17-45.

Converting the Objects into Rigid Bodies

In this section, you need to convert the sliders, *ball*, and *back support* into suitable rigid bodies.

1. Select the *ball* in the viewport. Make sure that the **MassFX Toolbar** is displayed in the viewport. If not so, right click on the blank space on the **Main Toolbar**; a shortcut menu is displayed. Choose **MassFX Toolbar** from the shortcut menu; the **MassFX Toolbar** is displayed.

2. Choose the **Set Selected as Dynamic Rigid Body** tool; the *ball* is converted into a dynamic rigid body and the **MassFX Rigid Body** modifier is applied to it. 

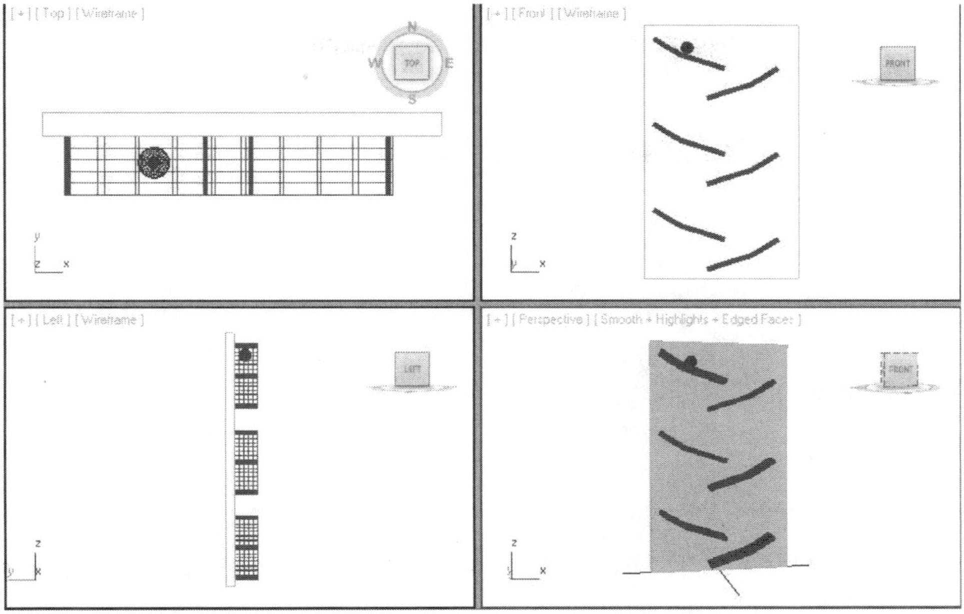

Figure 17-45 *Alignment of the ball in all viewports*

3. Select the *back support*. Click and hold on the **Set Selected as Dynamic Rigid Body** tool; a flyout is displayed. Choose the **Set Selected as Static Rigid Body** option from the flyout; *back support* is converted to a static rigid body and the **MassFX Rigid Body** modifier is applied to it. Retain the default settings of the modifier in the modify panel. 

4. Select the *slider1* in the viewport. Click and hold on the **Set Selected as Dynamic Rigid Body** tool; a flyout is displayed. Choose the **Set Selected as Kinematic Rigid Body** option from the flyout; the *slider1* is converted to a kinematic rigid body and the **MassFX Rigid Body** modifier is applied to it. 

5. Similarly, select other sliders and convert them into kinematic rigid bodies as discussed in step 3.

6. Choose the **Start Simulation** button from the Simulation flyout; simulation starts in all viewports. Maximize the Perspective viewport and observe the simulation carefully. 

7. Choose the **Reset Simulation** button to reset the simulation. 

Note

If the ball falls abruptly to the ground midway from any of the sliders, you may need to adjust the rotation angle or position of that slider.

You will observe that ball is sliding at a level slightly above the surface of sliders. Also, it is not sliding uniformly. To rectify these problems, you need to follow the steps given next.

8. Select the *slider1* in the viewport. Click on the plus sign on the left of the **MassFX Rigid Body** modifier to view all sub-object levels.

9. Select the **Mesh Transform** sub-object level; a convex physical mesh is displayed in the viewport around the *slider1*.

10. Expand the **Physical Meshes** rollout and click on the **Mesh Type** drop-down list; various options are displayed in the drop-down list. Select **Composite** from it.

11. In the **Physical Mesh Parameters** rollout, choose the **Generate** button; a composite mesh is formed around the *slider1*, as shown in Figure 17-46.

12. Repeat steps 8 to 11 for rest of the sliders.

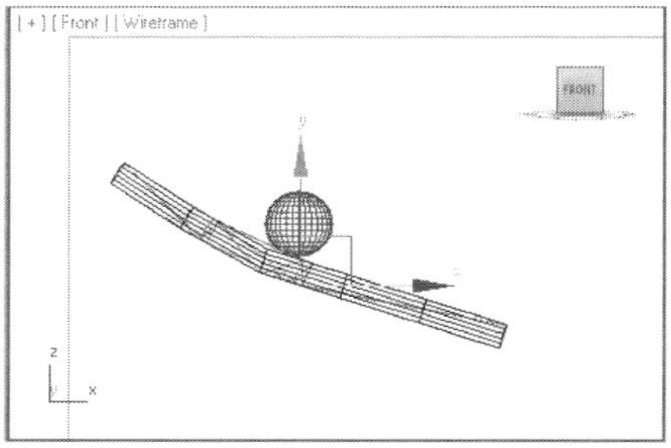

***Figure 17-46** Alignment of the physical mesh of the slider1*

13. Select the *ball1* in the viewport. Click on the plus sign on the left of the **MassFX Rigid Body** modifier to view all sub-object levels.

14. Select the **Mesh Transform** sub-object level; a convex physical mesh is displayed in the viewport around the *ball1*.

15. Expand the **Physical Meshes** rollout and click on the **Mesh Type** drop-down list; various options are displayed in the drop-down list. Select **Sphere** from it; the physical mesh around the *ball1* is changed to a sphere shape.

16. In the **Physical Material** rollout, set the value of the **Static Friction** spinner to **0**.

    You can also try changing other parameters of the *ball* to improve the result.

Playing the Simulation

1. Choose the **Start Simulation** button from the **MassFX Toolbar** to start the simulation.

   Notice that the *ball* now touches the surface of the sliders while sliding.

2. Choose the **Reset Simulation** button from the **MassFX Toolbar** to reset the simulation.

Saving the File

1. Save the file with the name *c17tut1.max* as discussed in earlier chapters. The location of this file is given below:

   \Documents\3dsmax\c17_tut1\scenes

Tutorial 2

In this tutorial, you will simulate the breaking of a brick wall by a metal ball using the tools in the MassFX interface, as shown in Figure 17-47. **(Expected time: 30 min)**

Figure 17-47 *The scene for Tutorial 2*

The following steps are required to complete this tutorial:

a. Set the project folder.
b. Download and open the file.
c. Convert the objects into rigid bodies.
d. Apply constraints on rigid bodies.
d. Play the simulation.
e. Save the file.

Setting the Project Folder

1. Set the project folder with the name *c17_tut2* in the *3dsmax* folder as discussed in earlier chapters.

Downloading and Opening the File

1. Before you start the tutorial, download the *c17_3dsmax_2012_tut.zip* file from *http://www.cadcim.com*. The path of the file is as follows:

   Textbooks > Animation and Visual Effects > 3ds Max > Autodesk 3ds Max 2012: A Comprehensive Guide

   Extract the contents of the zipped file and save them in the *\Documents* folder.

2. Choose **Open** from the **Application menu**; the **Open File** dialog box is displayed. In this dialog box, browse to the location *\Documents\c17_3dsmax_2012_tut* and select the *c17_tut2_start.max* file in it. Choose the **Open** button to open the file, refer to Figure 17-48.

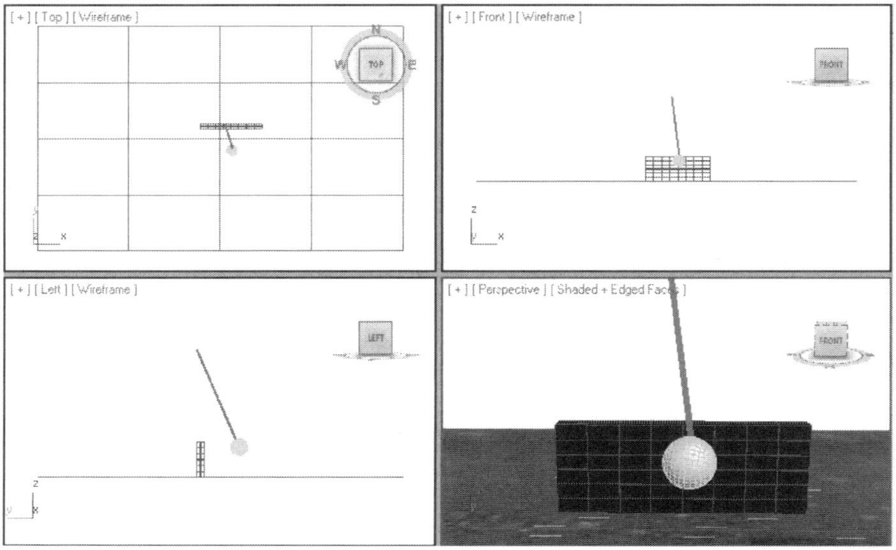

Figure 17-48 *The brick wall with a metal ball and metal rod in all viewports*

3. Now, choose **Save As** from the **Application menu**; the **Save File As** dialog box is displayed. Browse to the location *\Documents\3dsmax\c17_tut2\scenes*. Save the file with the name *c17tut2.max* at this location.

Converting the Objects into Rigid Bodies

In this section, you need to convert the bricks, metal ball, metal rod, and ground into suitable rigid bodies.

1. Select all bricks in the viewport. Click and hold on the **Set Selected as Dynamic Rigid Body** tool; a flyout is displayed. Choose **Set Selected as Dynamic Rigid Body** from the flyout; each brick is converted into a dynamic rigid body and the **MassFX Rigid Body** modifier is applied to it.

2. Similarly, convert the *metal ball* and *metal rod* into a dynamic rigid body as given in step 1.

3. Select the *ground* in the viewport. Click and hold on the **Set Selected as Dynamic Rigid Body** tool; a flyout is displayed. Choose **Set Selected as Static Rigid Body** from the flyout; the *ground* is converted into a static rigid body and the **MassFX Rigid Body** modifier is applied to it.

Applying Constraints on Rigid Bodies

In this section, you need to apply a universal constraint and a rigid body constraint to the rigid bodies.

1. Select *metal rod* and *metal ball* in any viewport. Click and hold on the **Create Rigid Constraint** tool from the **MassFX Toolbar**; a flyout is displayed. Choose **Create Rigid Constraint**

from the flyout; a rigid constraint is displayed in the viewport. Move the cursor and then click in the viewport to specify the size of the constraint.

2. Select *metal ball* in the viewport. Click and hold on the **Create Rigid Constraint** tool from the **MassFX Toolbar**; a flyout is displayed. Choose **Create Universal Constraint** from the flyout; a universal constraint is displayed in the viewport. Move the cursor and then click in the viewport to specify the size of the constraint.

3. Align the universal constraint in all viewports, as shown in Figure 17-49. Next, choose the **Start Simulation** button from the **MassFX Toolbar** to play the simulation.

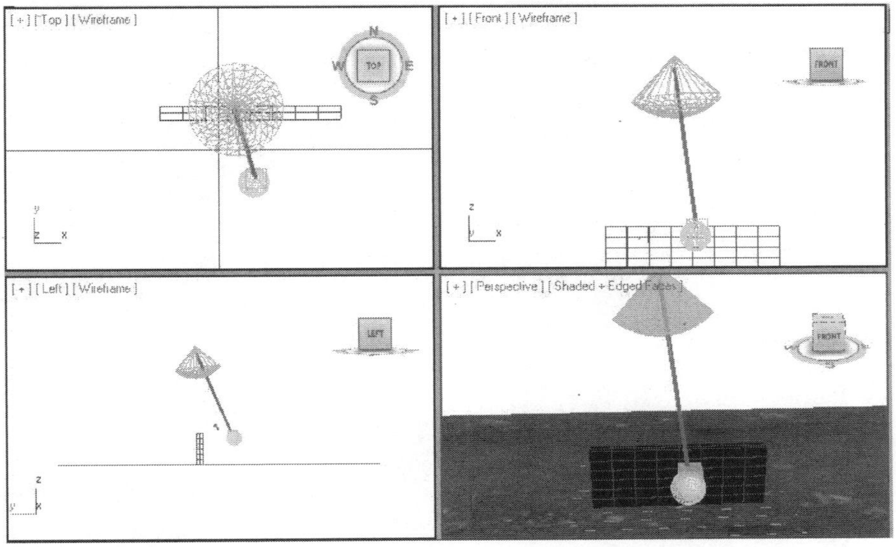

***Figure 17-49** Alignment of universal constraint in all viewports*

You will notice that as the simulation starts, first the bricks settle down and then the collision occurs. But, in actual practice, the bricks should remain settled till the collision occurs. To do so, you need to follow the steps given next:

4. Choose the **Reset Simulation** button to reset the simulation.

5. Select all the bricks in the viewport. Next, click on the **Step Simulation** button twice from the **MassFX Toolbar**; all bricks settle down in the viewport.

6. Choose the **Display MassFX Tools Dialog** button from the **MassFX Toolbar**; the **MassFX Tools** dialog box is displayed. Next, choose the **Tools** tab from this dialog box. Scroll down in it and choose the **Capture Selected** button from the **Capture Transforms** area and then close the **MassFX Tools** dialog box.

Playing the Simulation

1. Choose the **Reset Simulation** button. Now, choose the **Start Simulation** button again to play the simulation.

You will notice that the bricks are settled when you start the simulation.

Saving the File

1. Save the file with the name *c17tut2.max* as discussed in earlier chapters. The location of this file is given below:

   \Documents\3dsmax\c17_tut2\scenes

Self-Evaluation Test

Answer the following questions and then compare them to those given at the end of this chapter:

1. Which of the following tools is used to help the animation of objects in a hierarchical linkage?

   (a) **Dummy** (b) **CylGizmo**
   (c) **Compass** (d) **Tape**

2. Which of the following tools is used to measure the angle between two objects in a scene?

   (a) **Point** (b) **Dummy**
   (c) **Protractor** (d) **Compass**

3. Which of the following is a sub-object level of the **MassFX Rigid Body** modifier?

   (a) **Initial Spin** (b) **Center of Mass**
   (c) **Mesh Transform** (d) **Density**

4. A __________ rigid body represents an object in the real world.

5. A __________ is a helper object that is mainly used to organize scene components.

6. The tools of the __________ helpers are used to create the gizmos that limit the fog or fire effects in the scene.

7. __________ are used to restrict the movement of rigid bodies in simulation.

8. The MassFX interface uses an invisible static rigid body that is coplanar with the home grid. (T/F)

9. The helper objects are visible at rendering. (T/F)

10. You can change the type of a rigid body by using the options in the **Rigid Body Type** drop-down list of the **Rigid Body Properties** rollout. (T/F)

Review Questions

Answer the following questions:

1. Which of the following tools is used to create a specific location in the 3D space to be used as a reference in the specific scene?

   (a) **Point** (b) **Dummy**
   (c) **Protractor** (d) **Compass**

2. Which of the following tools is used to create a virtual tape to measure and set on-screen distances?

   (a) **Dummy** (b) **Point**
   (c) **Compass** (d) **Tape**

3. You can use the dummy object to animate the target camera in your scene. (T/F)

4. Static rigid body can be converted to a dynamic rigid body at a frame specified in the **Rigid Body Properties** rollout of the **MassFX Rigid Body** modifier. (T/F)

5. The position of constraints icons affects the behavior of objects in the scene. (T/F)

6. In the __________ dialog box, you can view and change the simulation properties of all rigid bodies and constraints in the scene.

7. The __________rollout in the **MassFX Rigid Body** modifier is used to edit the physical meshes assigned to an object in the simulation.

8. When you choose the __________ button, the simulated motion of the selected dynamic rigid body is converted into standard animation keyframes for rendering.

9. The __________ sub-object level displays the axis and the direction of the initial spin for a rigid body.

Exercises

Exercise 1

Create the scene shown in Figure 17-50 using the **SphereGizmo** tool in the **Atmospheric Apparatus** helper. Also, animate the fire effect in the scene. You can view the final rendered image of this scene from *http://www.cadcim.com.* **(Expected time: 15 min)**

Hint:
To animate the fire effect, set the values in the **Phase** and **Drift** spinners in the **Motion** area of the **Fire Effects Parameters** rollout in the **Environment and Effects** dialog box.

Figure 17-50 Scene for Exercise 1

Exercise 2

Create a scene as shown in Figure 17-51. Next, simulate the balls falling from a tray by using the MassFX interface, refer to Figure 17-51. **(Expected time: 20 min)**

Hint:
Convert the tray into kinematic rigid body and animate so that it tilts. Change the physical mesh of each ball to **Sphere**. Make sure that the physical mesh of the box is set to **Composite**.

Figure 17-51 Simulation of falling balls at different frames

Answers to Self-Evaluation Test

1. a, **2.** c, **3.** d, **4.** dynamic, **5.** container, **6. Atmospheric Apparatus**, **7.** Constraints, **8.** T, **9.** F, **10.** T

Index

Symbols

A

B

C

D

E

F

G

H

I

K

L

M

Q

R

S

Z

Other Publications by CADCIM Technologies

The following is the list of some of the publications by CADCIM Technologies. Please visit www.cadcim.com for the complete listing.

Autodesk 3ds Max Textbooks

- Autodesk 3ds Max 2011: A Comprehensive Guide
- Autodesk 3ds Max 2010: A Comprehensive Guide
- 3ds Max 2008: A Comprehensive Guide

Autodesk 3ds Max Design Textbooks

- Autodesk 3ds Max Design 2012: A Tutorial Approach
- Autodesk 3ds Max Design 2011: A Tutorial Approach
- Autodesk 3ds Max Design 2010: A Tutorial Approach
- 3ds Max Design 2009: A Tutorial Approach

Autodesk Maya Textbooks

- Autodesk Maya 2012: A Comprehensive Guide
- Autodesk Maya 2011: A Comprehensive Guide
- Autodesk Maya 2010: A Comprehensive Guide
- Character Animation: A Tutorial Approach

Autodesk Revit Textbooks

- Autodesk Revit Architecture 2012 for Architects and Designers
- Autodesk Revit Architecture 2011 for Architects & Designers
- Autodesk Revit Architecture 2010 for Architects & Designers
- Autodesk Revit Architecture 2009 for Architects & Designers
- Exploring Autodesk Revit Structure 2011

CATIA Textbooks

- CATIA V5R20 for Designers
- CATIA V5R19 for Designers
- CATIA V5R18 for Designers

Autodesk Inventor Textbooks

- Autodesk Inventor 2012 for Designers
- Autodesk Inventor 2011 for Designers
- Autodesk Inventor 2010 for Designers
- Autodesk Inventor 2009 for Designers
- Autodesk Inventor 2008 for Designers

ANSYS Textbook

- ANSYS 11.0 for Designers

Solid Edge Textbooks
- Solid Edge ST3 for Designers
- Solid Edge ST2 for Designers
- Solid Edge ST for Designers
- Solid Edge V20 for Designers

NX Textbooks
- NX 7 for Designers
- NX 6 for Designers
- NX 5 for Designers

Autodesk Alias Textbooks
- Learning Autodesk Alias Design 2010
- Autodesk AliasStudio 2009 for Designers

SolidWorks Textbooks
- SolidWorks 2011 for Designers
- SolidWorks 2010 for Designers
- SolidWorks 2009 for Designers

EdgeCAM Textbooks
- EdgeCAM 11.0 for Manufacturers
- EdgeCAM 10.0 for Manufacturers

Pro/ENGINEER Textbooks
- Pro/ENGINEER Wildfire 5.0 for Designers
- Pro/ENGINEER Wildfire 4.0 for Designers
- Pro/ENGINEER Wildfire 3.0 for Designers

AutoCAD Civil 3D Textbooks
- Exploring AutoCAD Civil 3D, 2012
- AutoCAD Civil 3D 2009 for Engineers

AutoCAD Map 3D Textbooks
- Exploring AutoCAD Map 3D, 2012
- Exploring AutoCAD Map 3D 2011

Coming Soon: New Textbooks from CADCIM Technologies
- Adobe Premiere Pro CS5: A Tutorial Approach
- Autodesk SoftImage 2012: A Tutorial Approach
- The Foundry NukeX: A Tutorial Approach
- Eyeon Fusion 6: A Tutorial Approach
- Adobe Flash Professional CS5: A Tutorial Approach
- ANSYS Workbench 13.0 for Designers
- Exploring Revit Structure 2012

Printed in Dunstable, United Kingdom

91342609R00464